Introduction

The task of courses in political thought sometimes called political theory or political philosophy is to help us explore the predicaments of human condition. The study of political thought will not give the right answer to moral and social questions. It is not that sort of discipline and they are not those sorts of questions. We will explore this a little further later in this chapter. It can, however, introduce to the complexities of the questions themselves and to the conceptual tools we can use to address them. When we do grapple with the big question of political life we are dealing with some profound issues. What is justice? What does it mean to say we know what is morally right or wrong? These are, for most people coming to the subject for the first time, new and unfamiliar sorts of questions. But they are questions that have been a constant feature of human society for millennia. It is certainly the case that the ways in which they have been posed and answered over the years vary across time and place. But in one form or another all human civilisation, from the ancient Greek city-states through the modern nation-states to the contemporary globalised world, ask challenging normative, moral and political questions.

This is an introduction to political thought. Our goal is to make the unfamiliar familiar and to give the readers a conceptual toolkit that will help them to understand and engage with political ideas. One of the principal driving forces of this book is the belief that there are two sets of tools that students of political thought need in order gain critical purchase on the subject. The first is a basic sense of the history and development of political thought; the second is a critical grasp of the theoretical or philosophical issues at the heart of politics. A sense of the historical context of political debates gives us a clearer grasp of the issues that confront us. For example, our contemporary understanding of the importance of human rights to justice has its own specific history. It is a product of the post-world war environment. It was not until we realized the danger that some sections of a society could face from their own government of the denial of a universal set of individual rights that were to be policed across sovereign borders. In the face of Hitler's genocide we decided that the suffering of citizens of other countries really was our business. A grasp of how the emphasis on human rights arose allows us to appreciate the role such rights have in our political context and thus to refine the instruments of their development and execution. An understanding of how other earlier attempts to claim universal rights for humankind arose, the issues they were addressing, their successes and failures, gives us further conceptual leverage when we are thinking about the issues at stake. Similarly a grasp of the historical development of concepts such as 'the state', 'sovereignty', 'citizenship' or 'justice' offers huge insights into the basic building blocks of politics. We still need, however, to supplement this historical understanding with a critical perception of the core theoretical issues at stake. Human rights are not just defended as measures designed to cope with a specific historical threat. They are also defended as morally correct. They are viewed as the most ethically important rights, which may not be violated for any other political, religious or cultural reason. How do we evaluate this sort of claim? Over the centuries there have been many arguments about who, or what, should be accorded moral standing. It has been variously claimed that only fellow citizens count, that the interests of the state are more vital than those of its individual citizens, that only white men count, that only law-abiding citizens count or that only adults count. On what grounds might we discriminate between these claims and the current thought that all persons, simply by virtue of their being human, have a certain moral standing that endows them with inalienable rights? In order to face this normative challenge we need to learn the language of moral and political argument.

In order to develop this conceptual toolbox we have split our table of contents into two parts. One table of contents is organized according to a chronological history of political thought, arranging chapters around particular thinkers and the development of political theory. The second table of contents is organized conceptually and highlights the theoretical questions and issues that each theorist is used to illustrate. Each chapter explicitly draws out important elements of both the historical and conceptual vocabularies. In doing so the reader is guided through the construction of their own critical glossary of important terms in political theory, thus furnishing them with a basic political vocabulary. This is intended to leave the reader with an historical and conceptual map to aid them in further study and a clear grasp of the basic vocabulary in which such study is undertaken. Most importantly it should give them the ability to add their voice to the debates. Beginning with the idea that laws and constitution are only good laws and constitutions in so far as they give effective expression to our considered moral and political beliefs, we invite the reader to explore the suggestion that moral and political ideas are the foundations of politics. Our aim is not only to highlight what in the history of political thought has counted as an adequate foundation, but to show the reader how such arguments work. In exploring these issues we guide the readers through a critical engagement with key arguments in the history of political thought and contemporary political theory.

Foundationlism

Philosophical discourse in the West depends on certain principles to prove the truth of its pronouncements. The law of identity (a = a; a thing is equal to itself) has arguably been the crucial principle involved. Without that it is difficult to see how anything at all could be proved or how we could ever have certain knowledge. In modern times, however, the law of identity has been called into question - for example, by developments in particle physics, where in some instances a particle appears not to be identical to itself and many philosophers have in consequence come to doubt the foundations of their subject. Such philosophers have been dubbed anti-foundationalists (poststructuralists and postmodernists being prominent among them), and they tend to argue that since we have no means of proving anything with certainly, truth is a relative concept. The ramifications of that debate extend well beyond the boundaries of philosophy.

Over the course of last century or so, various theories have been put forward to suggest that the self is far less of a unity than had traditionally been supposed. Freudian psychoanalysis, for example, saw us as being largely at the mercy of drives buried within our unconscious, and that notion of the individual subject not being in control of his or her own destiny has become deeply engrained within cultural theory. Poststructuralist theorists in general argue that the self is a very fluid entity and that unity is an illusion. There is no essence to the individual self: that is, something within us that remains constant over time, as western culture had generally maintained from about the Renaissance period onwards and with increasing emphasis from the Enlightenment. Our personal identity is instead in a continual state of flux-decentred, as it were. As was noted in anti-foundationalism recent science has provided a fruitful source of evidence for such views. To be decentred can be taken in a positive sense, to mean that we can escape from cultural conventions, such as those regarding gender identity. Feminist theorists in particular have pursued this line with some considerable enthusiasm. This is a movement deriving from the work of Jacques Derrida, one of the major figures in poststructuralist. Derrida argues that language is marked by instability and ambiguity, and that words never achieve full meaning at any one point.

This is the idea that philosophy, or science should be or is based on some set of privileged foundations, which are either better known, or more certain, or clearer, or temporally or logically prior to, the rest of philosophy, which is based on those foundations. Foundationalism comes in two varieties, justificatory and descriptive: the former claims that in order to be rigorous, philosophy must be based on such foundations; the latter claims that one can describe various different systems of philosophy solely by describing the foundations, and then deducing the other important features of the various systems from one's description of the foundations.

There has been a great deal of argument recently about justificatory foundationalism, and it is hard to find anyone in the contemporary philosophical scene who is a justificatory foundationalist. Things are quite otherwise with descriptive foundationalism: there arc many philosophers who take a strongly anti-foundationalist line as far as the justification of theories goes, but who are nevertheless foundationalist when they describe philosophical theories. Heidegger is such a philosopher; his arguments against justificatory foundationalism are well-known, but he has an explicitly foundationalist position when it comes to description, since he holds that what is fundamental for describing and analysing somebody's thought is their ontology. Similarly when Habermas describes Marxism as a variant of Hegel's philosophy of identity, he is using a descriptive terminology which dates back to the early nineteenth century which is used extensively for the description of philosophical positions, and which again is an instance of descriptive foundationalism. And, finally, Derrida's use of the term "logocentrism" is descriptively foundationalism; he is asserting that this is a basic feature of an enormous range of philosophies and also that it can be appropriately used to criticize those philosophies.

The principal writings of Derrida and Rorty are perhaps the most powerful statement of anti-foundationalism in its relation to social theory, and which offers a clear expression of how they see the immediate future of political thought. The opportunity to consider the anti-foundationalist approach to western political thought is, we believe, an essential part of any contemporary introduction to political thought. Whether we agree or disagree with their position one thing is certain; no one can engage fully with contemporary political thought without having confronted the anti-foundationalist challenge to its very basis. Rorty is only concerned to criticise systematic or foundational philosophy, that type of modernist or Enlightenment philosophy that searches for what is 'out there', the 'truth', 'knowledge' or moral certainty. Plato's view of a moralized universe and Aristotle's conception of human teleology rest on the 'truth'. Hobbes sought the 'truth' in his scientific method, Locke sought it in revelation and natural law; the list could go on and on. Rorty, on the other hand, allies his type of philosophy to the arts, to romantic poetry, to novelists and to the argument that philosophy like literature is a creative enterprise rather than a search for existing universal foundations. Philosophy, he insists, should not be tied to the truth. The first thing to note is Rorty 's claim about the desirability of a post-metaphysical and post-religious culture. We need to know why this is desirable and what it might entail. Second, there is a sense of genuine optimism about the prospect of a postmodern world emancipated from the shackles of foundationalism.

For the sake of clarity we can divide postmodernist critique of foundational philosophy into two distinct parts. The first set of argument claims that foundational philosophy is wrong because it is aiming at an impossible goal. The second set of arguments claims that foundational philosophy should be abandoned because it has such disastrous consequences for humanity. Taking the first set as our launching point we immediately gain a flurry of insights into the nature of anti-foundationalism. In most of its incarnations anti-foundationalism is made up of a series of sophisticated and critical arguments about the nature of truth. At least in part this is Rorty's initial point. Philosophy is aiming at the impossible because there is no truth 'out there' to find. On this reading the search for truth is very much like the search for the nature of God or the nature of man. On the basis of discoveries about such truths philosophers claim authority for their political prescriptions. Denying that there is a truth obviously makes this philosophical enterprise problematic. This is precisely what Rorty has in mind. Truth is not a property of the world. Rather it is a property of language.

Gender Bias

For most of Western history the expectations, sensibilities, and life activities of human beings have been divided into two, generally contraposed orders: male and female. While associated with the natural phenomenon of human physiological difference, this division has been a conventional, humanly-constructed one. Simply in view of the variety of its historical and cultural permutations, it cannot be called natural, inevitable, or biologically determined. Gender is a human affair, a protean arrangement of meanings, values, and activities born of human mind and endeavor, yet so thoroughly "naturalized" over time that the constructed character of the arrangement has been lost upon most of Western history's inhabitants.

With a few notable exceptions, the situation of women and the ideological antimony between female and male have been uninterrogated and unchallenged by even the most radical thinkers of any previous epoch. Yet, in a span of less than two decades, these matters have been the subject of one of the most remarkable revolutions in the history of human consciousness. At the level of ideas and attitudes as well as location and action in the world, " what a woman is" has been thrown into question.

Western political philosophy, as feminists have argued, has reinforced patriarchy, the systematic political, social and cultural subordination of woman to men, for thousands of years. Feminism is a body of thought that analyses the patriarchal nature of society, criticises the continued existence of patriarchy but, as a first step, draws our attention to it. In twenty first century western democracies we often pat ourselves on the back that we are equal societies, where women are liberated and one sex no longer dominates the other. However, brief reflection ought to lead us to reconsider this self-congratulation. Whilst positions of authority are no longer the sole province of men, men still hold an overwhelming majority of powerful posts. Likewise they seem to have the best jobs, with many women working in the most poorly paid and part-time jobs. Women often get paid less than men in similar jobs and usually get promoted more slowly. Finally, there is still all sorts of social pressure, exerted through families, the media and the state, on people to slot into a well-defined set of gender roles. Women usually stay at home and look after children whilst men usually bring home the bacon. Childless women and jobless men are not social outcasts, but are still often regarded as failures to be pitied. Women also still do the bulk of domestic work.

Inequality is a concern that political philosophy has sought to address but feminists argue this gender-based inequality seems to have been overlooked or ignored by political philosophers. Okin says that the great tradition of political philosophy consists of writings by men, for men, and about men. As such, it seems to have missed women out altogether, or treated them as something peripheral. This cannot continue, feminism argues, since we have a commitment to the democratic values of freedom and equality, whereby it is argued that people should not be constrained by social or innate differences from achieving success or well-being. Political theory, which until now has masked these inequalities, must now address them by adequately incorporating both sexes theoretically.

Feminists challenge the claims of political theory to have dealt with women adequately and challenge political theory's claim to be universal. How can it be universal if it can't properly account for half the human race? It judges political theory a failure, not because it actively discriminates, but at least partly as a result of its gender-blindness. This may be surprising, colour-blindness have often been taken to be virtues, but gender-blind thought has tended to take the traditional, patriarchal understandings of worker and citizen and simply treat them as if they now cover women as well as men. Instead, feminism argues that we need to rethink the way that our theories take gender into account. The two approaches we shall outline fall each side of what is called the 'equality-difference debate'. The 'equality' approach accepts that the universalism claims of political theory are appropriate but certainly misguided. Men and women are fundamentally the same but current gender roles mask this equality. What is needed is a rethink of the role of the family in political theory coupled with a recognition of the fact of interdependence, and then proper equality of opportunity and treatment can he realized. Rather than stress equality, the 'difference' approach focuses on important differences between men and women. 'Difference' feminists argue that political theory's universalism claims fail because they pay insufficient attention to these important differences. Moreover, once these differences are recognized, it will become apparent that our theory should be less universal anyway.

The idea that a discipline such as philosophy might be 'gendered' in some way is one that has been explored in a considerable amount of feminist writing; it is one, too, that is still often greeted with great skepticism. It is right to say that much of philosophy has been 'male' in some important senses, there are two things which establish the 'maleness' of philosophy in any really important sense. The first is that most of the practitioners of philosophy have been, and still are male. There may well be female philosophical work, which has been relegated to oblivion and not survived, and there have certainly been women who had an interest in philosophy but were prevented by institutional arrangements from making the most of that interest. Nevertheless, the dominance of males is clear. Second, there is no doubt about the way in which most male philosophers have devalued women, believed them to be inferior or held them in contempt. The history of the views of male philosophers about women is a dreary one of misogyny which is easy to document.

So what does one learn by discovering that for Hegel, women are subrational plants; for Rousseau, passive citadels of virtue; for Aristotle, deformed males; for Marx unproductive elements of the labor force; and for Jean-Paul Sartre, holes and slime that men are always wont to plug up or run from for fear of getting caught in a bog of unfreedom? One learns just that, how women were thought about or the permutations of women's oppression on an ideological level. Unless what these thinkers ascribed to women and decried in public life is considered in light of what is valued in men and the male world, this approach tends to leave one trapped in the blatantly anachronistic or flatly misogynist elements of a given theorist's work and to reduce feminist criticism to criticism of theorists' attitudes and statements about women. Aristotle has noted that between male and female, the former is by nature superior and ruler, the latter inferior. Schopenhauer argues that women are directly fitted for acting as the nurses and teachers of our early childhood by the fact that they are themselves childish, frivolous and short-sighted, in a word, they are big children all their life long.

Sentiments such as these, or similar, can be reduplicated from the work of many male philosophers. But again, this sort of misogyny is not in itself enough to establish the 'maleness' of philosophy in any philosophically important sense. The reason is this. Not all views that philosophers hold about anything are necessarily of relevance to interpreting or understanding their philosophical theories. Most commonly in philosophy, whatever has been seen as female has been devalued in one way or another. Characteristics or qualities deemed to be female have been regarded as inferior, or even if they have officially been regarded as 'equal but different' to male ones, they have in practice usually been regarded as of secondary importance, or as less worthy of being included in some ideal of human excellence. Even more importantly, however, those activities deemed to be especially female have, in varying ways, been seen as less important than those deemed to be male.

The distinction between men's and women's spheres has been marked in different ways. Thus in social and political philosophy one can find a series of distinctions between 'public' and 'private' life. The Greek attitude to marriage, as expressed at least in the philosophy of Plato and Aristotle was very pragmatic. The household was the realm of necessity, whose role was that of reproducing future citizens and providing the economic basis free men to associate with each other in the public life of the polis. Plato certainly did not see women as emotional companions for men; in his scheme of things, men's emotions were largely reserved for other men.

Now it would not be true to say that the sphere of life regarded as that of women has always been devalued or regarded as inferior in any simple or obvious sense. Sometimes it has been. But at other times, as in the work of Rousseau, it has been romanticised or idealised. And where it is idealised, it is not so much that it is regarded in an overt way as inferior; it is rather that, in a variety of ways, it is not regarded as so important. It may be charming, it may be necessary, it may be one's emotional stay, but she does not belong to public domain. But public domain belongs to man It is where one becomes fully human or achieves self-realization; it is where heroic exploits and daring deeds are done; it is where culture flourishes in the form of abstract ideas, intellectual achievements, or art; it is where Nature is mastered by science and technology, it is where males run kingdoms and empires, wage wars, conduct politics or manage businesses; it is where the lone soul faces the world in existentialist anguish. It is the realm of important things.

There are dangers, in an assertion of the value of what is feminine as against, what is masculine. The danger lies, in the fact that 'femininity', in its varying forms, has been largely constituted through a process of exclusion and polarisation. What is female has been defined as what is excluded from maleness, what is in opposition to it, what is complementary to it, what fills the gaps in male life or consciousness. And such definitions have usually existed in contexts where women were relatively powerless, dependent on and subordinate to men. A great deal of feminist argument has tried to show that the devaluation of the feminine has not only worked against women, although of course it has done that, but that it has led to a distortion of values, concerns and priorities that is of quite general human concern. The enterprise of considering the relationship between women and philosophy is not one that should just be the concern of women.

In a social system where mothers provide almost exclusive early care, children of both sexes have a primary relationship with the mother. It is in relation to her that an infant's sense of self will at first develop, and out of the initial sense of oneness with her that the processes of separation and individuation must begin. It has been argued that, given this initial relationship to the mother, and the father's absence from most primary care, boys tend to have a harder time establishing their identity as males. To achieve an identity as male is to be different from the mother, the person who is the ubiquitous presence in his early life and on whom he is at first totally emotionally and physically dependent. He has to define himself as like the 'absent' father, whose role in his life is so different, and who is 'out' and 'away' most of the time. Masculinity, membership of the community of men, is something over and against daily life, to be achieved in opposition to it, in escaping from the female world of the household. Given also the cultural stress on the importance and superiority of male pursuits and activities, the male develops a need to deny the power of women and to devalue women and to assert his autonomy and separateness, to repress the early infantile experience of near-symbiotic relatedness to a woman.

Western philosophy has asserted binany oppositions between mind and body, reason and passion, reason and sense. It has dealt with themes of mastery, domination and control of the body, the passions or the senses; and fears about loss of control. Feminists have argued that these sorts of themes can be found in the work of Plato, Machiavelli, Descartes, Hobbes, Locke and Rousseau. Plato is unusual among philosophers in that he allowed women a position of equality with men as guardians or rulers of his ideal state. The precise nature and implications of this apparent 'feminism' of Plato has been the subject of considerable debate.

Flax notes the themes of control of the passions and distrust of the senses, and the fear of disorder and chaos, which underlay the static unity of the ideal state that Plato presented in the *Republic.* She notes his ideal of love as uncorrupted by materiality or the body, and of knowledge as being of the unchanging world of Forms, free from the shifting illusions of the senses. She discusses the imagery of the cave in the *Republic:* the world of shadows, of the unconscious and of the womb, which the light of reason cannot penetrate or dispel, reveals the fear of regression to that pre-verbal state when feelings, the needs of the body and women rule. She reads many aspects of Plato's philosophy as a defence against infantile wishes, and against women and all that is associated with the mythical story about the origin of the two sexes; it is that there were originally three: male, female and hermaphrodite. Zeus decided that they were all troublesome creatures, so he cut them all in half, and this left each half yearning for its other half. But Aristophanes says, those who are the most virile and masculine are those who are slices of the original male sex. They take delight in the company of boys and they show the greatest manliness in public life, and they only marry as a duty to society in order to beget children. It is difficult to imagine a greater contrast than this to those modern conceptions of masculinity which stress an aggressive heterosexuality, lay stress on sexual prowess with women and regard a man's desire for women as one of the fundamental features of his masculinity.

It is from Plato's dialogue, the *Symposium* we learn that guests at a dinner party, including Socrates, are discussing the nature of love. It becomes clear form their discussion that the love of women is regarded as a second-rate thing. One of the guests, Pausanias, talks of the 'earthly Aphrodite' who governs the passions of the vulgar who are attracted by women as much as by boys. Sex itself is seen as a vulgar and dangerous distraction from the pursuit of heavenly love.

Descartes tell that philosophy can be read as a desperate attempt to escape from the body, sexuality and the wiles of the unconscious. Descartes' image of the self as created and maintained by thought and as not dependent on any material thing, replicates a typically male fear of regression to an infantile state and a loss of autonomy and independence.

As for Hobbes and Rousseau despite the differences between them, both deny in different ways the primary relatedness to and dependence on the female caretaker in infancy. Hobbes' human beings are rather like greedy infants locked into illusions of infantile omnipotence, and Hobbes' sovereign, the Leviathan, is rather like an externalized superego, whose task it is to restrain these infantile wishes. In Rousseau's philosophy, there is be believed intense dislike and fear of dependence of any form, which he thought necessarily led to servitude and inequality. Rousseau had his fear of the power of women and that this had at all costs to be restrained by patriarchal authority in the family. It is not really until the time of Rousseau that an interest in the idea of contrasting or complementary psychologies of masculinity and femininity begins to develop. This interest was related to the Romantic Movement in European thought. It was also related to changing conceptions of 'home' and 'family' and of the distinction and relationship between 'public' and 'private' life.

Locke assumes several things about women. He assumes a natural inequality of the sexes, and a natural authority of husband over wife. Natural is here opposed to that which is a result of specific social arrangements; thus, to talk of natural authority or inequality is to talk of that which is assumed to be given, a fact of nature, and not amenable to change. Locke sees the dependence of women on men, and the authority of men over women, as arising from the fact that women have the role of bearing children. He sees this role as necessarily generating female economic dependence on men and loss of autonomy with respect to the right to control property. When Locke discusses women, he in fact discusses married women; he assumes that women will marry and have children, and that their reproductive and marital role is the only important aspect of their lives. In his political philosophy in general, Locke aimed to establish the rights of citizens against the arbitrary powers of absolute monarchs or tyrants who thought they could dispose of the lives and property of their subjects at will. He was particularly concerned about the question of property. What gave a man a right to appropriation to property, was, Locke thought, the fact that he had contributed by his labour to the product. And Locke was concerned to defend the exclusive right of males to hold on to and dispose of their property as they wished normally to their legitimate heirs. The natural rights that he defended were those of life, liberty and properly; the property was to be under the individual control of male heads of families.

Unlike men, however, women did not in Locke's view have the right to dispose of the fruits of their productive labour and the theory that the contribution of labour generates a right to appropriation is forgotten in their case. The right to appropriation is only a male right. Women had, according to Locke, certain very limited rights over the property they might have brought into a marriage with them, but they were to have no legal say at all in the disposition of any of the products of their own or their husband's labour during the marriage. Equality in marriage, and the economic independence of women is not compatible with a system of property distribution based on an exclusive male right to dispose of family property. If women were to be independent, such a system would be bound to collapse. But since Locke's political philosophy proposes just such a system, it could not consistently recognize the equality of women. In other words, the inequality and dependence of women is a structural necessity of Locke's political theory, and of the objectives that this theory was intended to achieve. It is not an accidental or peripheral feature which can be easily removed, leaving the rest of the theory intact. It is not a question of mere prejudice against women, which can easily be discounted. And it is surprising how, in most of the standard commentaries on Locke, there is no discussion at all on this issue. It is common to find discussion of problems in Locke's theory of how we consent to government, in his view of property rights, in his theory of natural rights. But one of the most fundamental and integral features of his political philosophy, namely the exclusion of women, has apparently eluded the notice of most commentators.

It is a fact that most philosophers have been men and that many of them have expressed misogynistic views about women. And some of them wrote veritable diatribes on what they saw as distortions of femininity. The idea of woman as tender, receptive, emotional, as pleasing or delighting man by her feminine charms; of sexual relationships between men and women as providing some of the deepest human emotions and pleasures; of a polarity and complementarity between male and female qualities-these are historically relatively recent. There particularly vitriolic nature of some of the opinions about women expressed, by Schopenhauer and Nietzsche. If woman is believed potentially to be the source of some of man's most intense emotions and pleasures then what is seen as the undermining or corruption of those pleasures is so much the more horrendous, and the woman who oversteps her prescribed limits is so much more a monster. Nietzsche, for example, was most especially contemptuous of those women who became monstrosities if they forgot their natural tasks and graces.

Eurocertricism

Western political thought has been subjected to criticism for its Eurocentric bias and practice. Western prejudgments and prejudices about the 'Other' began with the giants of Western philosophy like Hume, Kant, Hegel and Marx, giants who have not yet been superseded and in whose praise and hair-splitting analyses oceans of ink are still flowing. Philosophers like Hume, Kant, Hegel and others who allegedly are at the vantage point of reason could not help in indulging in mere mythology in characterizing the Asian and African. In a time when the world was not as small as it is today but when the Europeans—particularly the Kants, and Hegels—had considerable information on Asia and Africa, they simply did not hesitate to give full reign to mythology, hatred, racism, imperialism and things of that nature.

The arrogance with which Hume and Kant treated the Africans ranges from such expressions as "Negroes are inferior to Whites" to "the blackness of the fellow from head to foot indicating his stupidity." These racial prejudices and judgments were based on colour and belonging to another geographical region. Indeed Marx himself whose philosophy was to spearhead the emancipation of humanity from all kinds of social evils and alienation was not able to overcome this very standard of European philosophy of history that places the European philosophy of history at the center of human history. Basing his understanding of history on the notion of the class struggle, as he knew it in Western Europe, Marx argued that Asians do not have history. That led him to declare that "Hindustan has no history", because they knew neither slavery in its Greek form nor capitalism in its European form. In capitalism's or more exactly colonialism's introduction into India, Marx saw a historic role for imperialism bringing India to the scene of history. He wrote: "England has a double mission in India: one destructive, the other regenerating—the annihilation of old Asiatic society, and the laying of the material foundations of Western society in India."

The whole point, however, is that Marx who declared war on previous philosophies as speculative and abstract is found to be using the very paradigm that he sharply criticized. The declaration of war on previous philosophies was perhaps nowhere so arrogantly expressed than in Marx's assertion of the inversion of Hegelian dialectic or turning it right upside down in order to discover the rational kernel within the mystical shell. In the light of his expressions on India, however, one can only wonder how far away Marx himself is from the mystical shell of Eurocentricism.

European history and values are the embodiments of universal human history and values. There is no nation that can escape this universal path of human history. It is from such an assumption that the ideas of the giants of European philosophy emanated. From the Greek historian Herodotus to Heidegger there persists a thinking which dichotomizes Asia and Europe far too heavily. Such a dichotomizing may take a conspiratorial form leading to some type of self-fulfilling prophecy. In his lecture entitled "Europe and the German Philosophy" which he gave in Rome in 1936, Heidegger speaks of the "protection of European peoples from all that is Asian." Heidegger also maintains that the phrase 'European philosophy' is a tautology because philosophy is just and can only be European. Karl Jaspers, the former friend and later opponent of Heidegger, warns us against hypostatising the Asian-European contrast. Karl Lowith has rightly taken Heidegger to task for the latter's conviction that the question of Being favours the Occidental mind. Heidegger goes even so far as to maintain that it is an inborn obligation to the Greek and European mind to philosophies. Philosophy is, for him, a European destiny. Such a judgement echoes the conviction of the colonialist, imperial and even missionary Europe under the dictum 'white man's burden.'

The established philosophical tradition has its declared intentions of universality, objectivity and placing man at the center of its undertakings. The declared intentions appear to be good in the sense that they appear to be speaking for humankind as such, objectivity as such and universality in general. But if one accepts these declared intentions as innocent and is convinced that they are meant to apply to humankind as such, one commits the dismal error of accepting European universality as applying to the whole of humanity. For what this framework stipulates is that the whole world give up other values, cultures, etc. and accept the European ones as the only truly universal human values. Behind such an understanding actually lurk also the true desires of a continent that has forced the whole of humanity to accept European values by renouncing the rest. This is done as we know by a self-declared civilizing mission which sees the rest of the world as half-devil and half-child.

European modernity began by projecting a picture of itself that makes Europe the true child of humanity whose achievements in philosophy, art, the sciences, religion and everything else have been unparalleled. In projecting itself with all possible positive attributes it could only see the 'Other' as the opposite of itself; barbarism and all that goes with that. It is also by virtue of this that Europe took upon itself the mission of civilizing others by forcing its particular beliefs, values and worldview on others. It is only the European's point of view and values that are correct since the barbarians are without values; they have to accept the values of the Europeans as the only universal human values. Such a self-understanding prepared then the basis to exploit, rule and subjugate the 'Other.' European colonial consciousness saw itself in the image of fulfilling both the demands of God and the requirements of civilized human existence. It was very forcefully argued that in colonising, the missionary Christian European was not violating or transgressing on non-European cultures. Rather he was realising divine providence, the mission bestowed on the twelve Apostles by Christ to spread the faith to the four corners of the globe.

The relationship between self and 'Other' has been a long-term concern of western philosophy, and how we view the Other, whether as friend or threat, depends largely on the concept of self we espouse. The more sharply defined our sense of self, the more we are likely to fear the encroachment of the Other-which in extreme cases would extend to the entire human race. In poststructuralist and postmodern debate, the 'Other' has come to take on the more specialized meaning of those excluded, exiled and marginalized by the dominant ideology. Thus in Michel Foucault, the Other becomes such groups as homosexuals, lesbians, the insane and the prisoners, all of whom have failed to conform to the norms laid down by the dominant section of the society and as a result find themselves marginalized. Jean-Francois Lyotard uses the term the Jews to refer to all those groups just the Jewish race itself who are demonized by western culture.

The deconstructionist Jacques Derrida argues that western philosophy has been infected with a inetaphysics of presence. He contends that western philosophy rests on the foundations of logocentrism, phonocentrism and phallocentrism. He further argues that all discourses in western culture is based on a belief that the meanings of words are fully 'present' to us in our minds, as we communicate them to others. For Derrida, on the other hand, the meanings have no stability, and that significant slippage ever occurs. On that basis, we can not communicate to each other with a confidence that the meaning of our phrases will be received as we intended them to be. He contends that this is an illusion, and that words and meaning are raven with instability instead. Meaning, as far as he is concerned, is always indeterminate.

Recent cultural theory regards the construction grand of narrative as a basic feature of western philosophy which is viewed as a series of narratives vying for our attention. According to thinkers such as Lyotard, ideolgy aspires to the condition of meta narrative or grand narrative whichis to say that given ideologies claim to be ultimate authorities, and seek to exclude all competitors. In the case of Marxism, this means that it regards its own narrative as the solution to all the world's socio-political problems, and treats all other ideologies as false. Lyotard, along with the postmodern movement in general, is suspicious of such claims to universal applicability, and champions the cause of 'little narratives' instead.

The central thesis we propose and defend here is the thesis of intercultural philosophy. There are different philosophical traditions of cultures, which can make substantial contributions to philosophy in general and to the various philosophical disciplines in particular. This they may accomplish by drawing our attention to the philosophical questions put and to the philosophical answers suggested. This is where an intercultural philosophical orientation begins, and it leads us to consider the philosophies of other cultures with a view to seeing their contributions to the general concept of philosophy which is always a response to a felt need in the face of the problems we are confronted within our attempt to understand and explain the world of things and beings.

That we are all human beings makes one thing abundantly clear: in spite of cultural differences, there are fundamental similarities between different philosophical traditions. Philosophy in world context today pleads for the thesis that the general applicability of the concept of philosophy remains unaffected by our recognition and acceptance of more than one genuine philosophical tradition. The naive dogmatism of identifying philosophy exclusively only with one particular philosophical convention and styles amounts to some sort of ethnocentrism, and such a move is always suspect. One particular contextual and relative perspective is thereby put in an absolute universal position. The Western philosophy, backed by so many extra-philosophical factors, e.g., social, economic, imperialist, colonialist and religious did universalise itself from the days of Diogenes up to say Husserl, Heidegger and even Gadamer and Rorty.

A cross-cultural consideration of philosophy allows for a common space in which intercultural philosophical discourses can take place. The recognition of cultural contingency does not destroy, but only decentralises philosophy. Philosophy as a common, rational human enterprise is, no doubt, culture-bound, but it is not hopelessly so. Intercultural philosophical orientation is guided by the firm conviction that the one *philosophia perennis* is not the exclusive possession of one particular philosophical tradition, whether Western or non-Western. Some of the most famous modern European philosophers, e.g., Husserl, Heidegger just to name a few, do claim that philosophy proper is Greek and Greek only. Husserl, rather onesidedly, defines Western philosophy by the theoretical attitude which he thinks is absent in non-European traditions. The Indian and Chinese philosophies, according to him, lack such a theoretical is attitude and are mainly religious and mythical. J.N. Mohanty rightly remarks that Husserl's judgement is the result of an inadequate factual knowledge, combined with a too hasty theoretical interpretation of the concept of 'theoria', and the all too-common romantic view of the oriental mode of thinking.

Intercultural philosophical discourse cannot take place if a particular philosophical tradition takes the undue liberty to universalise its own perspectival understanding of the general concept of philosophy. This is where absolutism and universalism endanger intercultural communication and dialogue. On the other hand, there are relativists who, no doubt, underline the relativistic origin of philosophy but absolutise this one particular philosophy. European philosophy, they say, is not only European, but the only philosophy as such. Relativism, thus understood, becomes universalism in disguise, and it takes a supremacist position in an intercultural discussion which really means an end of understanding before it begins. But relativism, which emphasises cultural differences may also lead to an open-mindedness, recognition, respect and acceptance between traditions. Relativism, thus, is not inherently bad. There is much discussion nowadays about the contextualism in relation to philosophy. Rorty represents such a position, but he seems to give a privileged treatment to the Western context and thereby becomes a relativist and universalist in disguise.

The dominant European philosophical tradition obviously has its locus, values, beliefs, and premises. These were the phenomena that were used in understanding others. From a preconceived position which from the very start is against the Other a programme is drafted for them in order to bring them into line with what is taken to be universal. But here the universal itself does not measure up to the standard of universality since it is the particular which is raised to the level of the universal incorrectly.

Without denying the achievements of Western philosophy one could say that in treating other cultures, civilisations and people, it could not go beyond a self-serving narrative that treats European history, civilisation and the white race as the nucleus of all human essence and endeavours. In the final analysis it turned out to be that you have to draw your legitimacy and *raison d'tat* from European philosophy. That this is inappropriate can be seen when we try to find out that particular values, a particular culture and minds representing these phenomena have wrongly transformed themselves into the universal culture of humanity. Why should an Asian philosopher who tries to understand the historical situation of his peoples' existence in the light of reason be judged by those who, only want to understand his culture, history, etc., as barbaric? Does a philosophy that does not talk to us to understand us but proceeds with its own prejudgments have the moral authority to claim to have treated us justly? Europe unjustly claimed the right to judge and evaluate the Other.

Decolonising the mind is important both to the colonised and the coloniser. The decolonisation of the mind frees the colonised from his chains and provides him with the opportunity to develop freely and unravel his potentials. It at the same time removes the veil from the coloniser, a veil that only reduced the Eurocentric thinkers to a self-eulogy, a self-eulogy which more often than not hindered them from understanding the others. Understanding the other means coming to communication with him/her and learning from them too instead of telling them the "absolute truth".

Intercultural philosophy is dealing with the question of whether it is possible and necessary to develop new ways of philosophising because of the present condition of humankind. We are living in a global world, while we are still thinking in frameworks conditioned by regionally bound cultural traditions. The answer to our question therefore demands of philosophy that can and ought to be made clear by way of interculturally orientated polylogues.

This book is a modest attempt to turn our attention to cross-cultural dialogues particularly encounters with non-Western perspectives and life-forms. Politically, one of the most dramatic developments of the past half century has been steady advance of globalisation fuelled by markets and information breakthroughs. In a new profound intellectual revolution, the Eurocentric worldview of the past with its corollaries of colonialism and orientalism—has been challenged by the rise of a global arena in which non-western cultures and societies are increasingly active participants in shaping the future of the world. Derrida is right in his remark that Europe is no longer the cultural and political capital of the world.

The human solidarity that we envisage is not a global uniformity but unity in diversity. We must learn to appreciate, tolerate and promote pluralities, multiplicities, cultural differences. Such unity in diversity has to be extended to the whole world to include Japan, China, India, Africa and also Muslim culture. Gadamer rightly insists that every culture, every people has something distinctive to offer for the solidarity and welfare of humanity. We can only hope that by struggling in our limited way against the 'clash of civilisations', the confluence of Western and Eastern philosophical initiatives and encounters open the path for a cross-cultural dialogue to a brighter and more peaceful future—to what Indian sages and seers have called 'lokasangraha' —world maintenance.

1

Study of Classics and the Problem of Interpretation

Western civilization is blessed with a long and rich tradition of political thought, constituted by a number of works written at a high level of comprehensiveness and logical coherence. These works are comprehensive in the sense that political problems are addressed in general terms, as contemporary manifestations of the difficulties to which all political communities are liable. Consequently, the most challenging and plausible of these works have been pondered by political actors and commentators centuries after they were written. The great books of Western political thought did not achieve their status as classics just because academicians considered them fine examples of scholarship and taught them to students. Instead, political actors and critics found in them useful or challenging arguments to justify or criticize existing political decisions, ideologies, or arrangements.

The classics of political thought are an indispensable component of a liberal arts education simply because their authors addressed themselves primarily to politically engaged intellectuals and intellectually sophisticated citizens. By understanding the reflections of each age's greatest sage, the serious student of political thought can gain a heightened appreciation of the possibilities and limits of political action. Because politics is a form of action and experience rather than the recurrent mechanical interplay of a set of mute forces, statesmanship depends much more on a sure sense of priorities and judicious habits than on technical proficiency. And even if statesmanship has become irrelevant to contemporary politics, understanding great works of political thought can at least be useful in clarifying the political values used to evaluate our condition.

As social scientists, political scientists have two distinguishing commitments that journalists, practical politicians, or governmental advisers will not necessarily share. The first of these commitments is perhaps obvious and has been the source of much skepticism among political scientists concerning the relevance of the classics of political thought. This is the commitment to empirical verification. To verify knowledge empirically requires that beliefs about reality by formulated into hypotheses that can be tested by observation. Now it is perfectly possible to find interesting hypotheses in the classics that could be tested in a contemporary context. For instance, Machiavelli asserts that a prince should take advice only after asking for it but should ask for it often. One wonders to what extent presidents and other political executives must establish such a relationship with their advisers in order both to remain on top and to stay informed.

But this may suggest that the classics are not likely to be a very fruitful source of such hypotheses. Most of the authors of these great works lived in societies far different from ours. There is some reason to doubt that fruitful hypotheses relevant to our society will easily be found in discussions of Greek or Italian city-states, early modern monarchies, or even the early stages of the industrial revolution. In what sense, then can the study of the classics of political thought be indispensable to the scientific study of politics? The answer is to be found in the second distinguishing commitment of social science, which is a concern for the systematic or interrelated processes that allow us to account for unforeseen and therefore unintended consequences. Scientists are not interested in simply accumulating a random assortment of confirmed hypotheses, and it is the very abstractness of the classics, their treatment of the political difficulties of their age as the result of the fundamental, inescapable nature of political association that renders them relevant to the systematic or theoretical concerns of social science.

Before discussing why this is so an example will help clarify the sense in which social scientists have theoretical interests not typically shared by other social observers. Every member of Congress and every journalist assigned to Capitol Hill knows that the committees of Congress exercise tremendous influence on the fate of proposed legislation falling within their respective policy jurisdictions. This decentralization of congressional power in turn creates a power vacuum that does much to explain the increased legislative influence of the president in the twentieth century. None of the great thinkers discussed in this book had much to say about Congress; indeed, only two of them lived after the United States was founded. Nonetheless, the classics of political thought are almost indispensable in helping political scientists to see this kind of systematic consequence, to see "the big picture." To appreciate why this is so, it must be understood that everyone is a political theorist in the sense that we all must make fundamental theoretical assumptions whenever we think about political affairs.

These basic theoretical assumptions make it possible for us to integrate our knowledge, to see information about election, legislatures, foreign policy, and the like, as details of a larger picture. Even though we all must make such assumptions, it is not really appropriate to say that we all have a political theory. What the classics of political thought offer to political science are conceptual options, alternatives to one another and to the unstated conventional wisdom of our cultural context. The latter is most important, for the only way to clarify and gain a critical perspective on our fundamental assumptions is to confront them with alternative viewpoints. We may, of course, reaffirm our faith in the intellectual foundations of our political culture. If so, our ability to analyze and relate aspects of our political experience in terms of these foundations will be greatly enhanced, and we will be doing it with our eyes open.

The question of how we can go about understanding the major classics inevitably gives rise to the question of why we should try to do so; and this is a part of the wider question of why we should study the history of political ideas. Again, there is a variety of possible responses, but again two basic approaches – the historical and the philosophical– may be discerned. The historical defense of the study of the classics might be based on the argument either that they illuminate most sharply the intellectual preconceptions and concerns of their time or that they have had an important casual influence on social and political and intellectual developments. Both arguments depend upon certain assumptions about the relationship between 'ideas' and 'actions' or 'reality'. If ideas are simply epiphenomenal, reflections of underlying economic or class tensions and antagonisms, or if theorizing is simply the construction of apologies for the pursuit of interests, the tribute the greed and the lust for power pay to moral and spiritual and intellectual virtue, the study of theory can reap little profit in terms of historical insight. If, on the other hand, understanding actions involves the reconstruction of their meaning and significance for the actors themselves, if ideas can inspire political action or even just shape how people behave whatever their motives, then an historical defence of the history of ideas may be mounted.

The argument that to understand the past we must try to enter past minds, to see the world as those past others saw it, is powerful and persuasive, but it may not provide strong support for concentration on the major political theorists. Certainly, if those theorists can themselves only be understood in terms of their ideological context, it becomes difficult then to use them as evidence of that context. What most marks out the major theorists is precisely their originality, the degree to which they questioned accepted ideas or altered the terms of political discourse. And this is as true of those who sought to justify established authorities, as did Hobbes and Hegel, and those who claimed simply to be articulating the concrete conception and aspirations of particular social groups, as did in their different ways Burke and Marx, as of those who took up a self-consciously innovatory intellectual stance. It might be argued that such challenges, whether overt or covert, to accepted ideas themselves illuminate those previously unquestioned common places. It seems, though, that a richer seam in which to mine for the generally accepted and untargeted assumptions of a period or plaçe or class might be found amongst the lesser writers and the more ephemeral literature.

Another possible historical defense of the study of the classics is forward rather than backward looking. On this view, it is the influence they have had, either in shaping subsequent widely held attitudes or in prompting political aspirations and movements that make them worthy of the historian's attention. All of the thinkers have been – and still are – appealed to as alleged progenitors of particular social and political positions or attacked in defense of allegedly opposed positions. They have all had an assured and persistent place not only in academic discussion but in the world of political controversy. Of course, they have been called in aid of many different and even opposing causes. Locke has been used in defense of eighteenth-century constitutionalism, nineteenth-century egalitarianism and twentieth-century libertarianism; Marx was invoked by both Mensheviks and Bolsheviks to justify quite different strategies and tactics for a social democratic movement in late Tsarist Russia. However various and even contradictory uses made of the classical theorists, it is still useful to return to them to assess how far their subsequent followers or opponents have actually stated their positions or in what ways the exemplars have been subsequently distorted or only partially represented.

One powerful motive for pursuing this search for influences might be to understand better the ideas current in our own time or even perhaps the genealogy of our own personal values and visions of the world. Such pursuits, origins, or roots have not on the whole been enthusiastically received by historians. Concentration on the explanation of present-day concerns and ideas may obviously undermine any endeavor to see the past in its own lights and can lead to the writing of 'Whig history', the recounting of the progress of modern conditions and ideas. Many modern histories of Marxism and of liberalism show that Whig history is by no means dead. However, whatever the professional dangers, the illumination of the present is a legitimate ground for interest in the past. We depend heavily, even entirely, in our personal memories to establish our personal identities; and one of the most important uses of history, our social memory is as an aid to communal identification. Of course, the study of political ideas is only part of this effort at identification, but to the degree that modern thought has stressed the centrality of political structure and political action, it is an important part. So the search for the roots of 'totalitarian' modes of thought, or the genealogy of 'liberal' ideas, or the origins of the modern 'state', although perhaps fraught with dangers from the pure historian's point of view, is a valuable and in any case inevitable project.

These are all, in one way or another, historical modes of justifying the study of the classical theorists. But we may believe instead that they can speak directly to our own present concerns and preoccupation. The past may be a foreign country, and they may do things differently there, but these foreigners face recognizably perennial human problems and predicament and travel may well broaden the mind. The reading of thinkers as historically distant as Plato and Aristotle can, mudatis mutandis, gives insight into modern problems, both intellectual and practical. This is even more the case with the post medieval thinkers. For they posed a range of questions which are clearly still present and pressing: the nature and actual functions of the modern state; what are, the desirable functions of the state; its relationship with other forms of human associations – the church, the family, the economy, civil society, the nation, the world of learning; the freedom or rights which the individual can properly claim against the state or other associations or individuals; the nature and value of personal freedom or rights which the individual can properly claim against the state or other associations or individuals; the degree to which political action – the human will – is bounded, or even determined, by a providential ordering of things, whether providence is envisaged as the agency of God or nature or the Absolute Spirit or the laws of history. To understand such questions, certainly to understand the complexity of the issues they raise, we must go back to those who have posed them most sharply and explored them most deeply. We must enter what has been called the 'conversation of mankind,' a conversion in which the first task, and in the light of the interpretative debate no easy one, is to gather what the subject of discussion is and what the others are saying. Conversation may of course lead to argument. In such confrontation we may clarify our own ideas, or extend them, or change them, or even just be confirmed in them.

Over and above any such particular contributions that the study of the classics might make to the informing and deepening of our present debates, there is value in trying to grasp the general vision of things they present. We might read Tolstoy to learn something about military campaigning or to gather some insights into the conditions of happy or unhappy families. But beyond that, we might wish to comprehend Tolstoy's particular conception of the human condition. The same is true of the reading of Hobbes or Marx or Gandhi. We may read the one to extend our understanding of the complex notion of sovereignty, or to deepen our understanding of the relationship between political and economic structures. At the most general level, the vision of thinkers such as Hobbes and Marx are as much mythological as they are analytic or empirical, and the attempt to understand them may broaden our own conception of how the human drama can be felt and understood, may help us reach that point at which the spiritual and moral and metaphysical and aesthetic and empirical worlds come together and can possibly cohere. For most persons at most times the central focus of such a comprehensive vision has been religious, the explorations of the intimations of divine ordination for our everyday practice life. Indeed, it would be difficult to comprehend the thinkers as primarily political in their vision without reference to other wider contexts. It would, for example, be difficult to grasp the real meaning of Hobbes or Locke or Rousseau or Gandhi without exploring the religious beliefs or bewilderments that underlie and haunt their political arguments. Nevertheless, for many thinkers in the modern world the secular has displaced the divine as the major point of focus and the prophets speak a terrestrial rather than a celestial language. Many might reject this as too narrow a range, too sparse a language. Nevertheless the emergence of specifically political visions, in which communal will and intelligence are the crux of human destiny, is a central feature of modern thought and these visions require and so that we might be converted to truths previously alien to us, but so that we may enlarge and deepen our own understanding of things.

The goods that may be gained from the study of the classics are then as various as the methods by which they can be studied. Like the methods, the goods are not strict alternatives amongst which we are forced to make a choice, so that we can only enhance the historian's insight at the expense of the philosopher's wisdom and vice versa. The assumption made here is that there are many ways in which classics can legitimately be approached and many values, which may be served by engagement in their study.

Approaches in the Study of Classics

There are many approaches in the study of classics. No single approach is sufficient and adequate. We have to use different approaches for the study of classics.

The Historical Approach

The historical or contextual approach believes in the sociology of knowledge. It holds that the text gets meaning from the context of its origin. The historical school is supported by persons like Dunning, Sabine, Gettle, Mcllwanin, Macpherson etc. Robert Blakey in his first study of the history of philosophy said that political truth like all other truths expands and develops itself as time rolls. The evolutionary perspective, therefore, requires a historical approach. He established the history of political thought as an independent discipline. According to him, the study of history of political theory shows the successive transformation through which the political consciousness has passed. He says that there is a clearly visible relationship between author's work and the current of institutional development.

During 1930s and 1940s, this approach becomes extremely popular. However, the school is best represented by G.H. Sabine. His book *A History of Political Theory* has exercised deeper influence than any other single book. In Sabine's opinion, theories of politics are structured in politics that they do not refer to an external reality but are produced as an integral part of the social reality. Political thought, according to Sabine, evolves with time along with the institutions, the agencies of government, and the moral and physical tensions through which the society passes. Consequently, political theory cannot step out of the relationship in which it stands to the problems, the habits or even the prejudices of its own time. He, therefore, cautions that the writer of history at least ought to be free from the arrogance that he is the heir of all the ages. Similarly, he should make no claims of impartiality beyond that of fidelity to be expected of every honest man. In any other sense, the claim of detachment is superficiality or a pretense. Sabine's own philosophical preferences are similar to those of Hume. He rejects the notion of historical necessity as well as the principle of rationally self-evident natural laws. He calls his position social relativism. He argues that in order to understand political theory it should be located in the wider social context as a reaction to which it had grown. He asserts that there is in every political theory a reference to a specific situation, which needs to be grasped in order to understand what the philosopher is thinking about.

C.B. Macpherson in his book *The Political Theory of Possessive Individualism* has tried to re-interpret the 17th century society in England as a market society to explain the paradox of Hobbes's individualism in the light of this possessive individualism of that market society. Macpherson is taking the help of the assumptions of possessive individualism, which are not very explicitly stated by the authors themselves. He is conscious of the general problem of interpretation, which it involves. He holds that the interpreter can supply the missing assumptions: (a) if it was common enough in those times so that the author could take it for granted, (b) if it fills a gap in his argument, (c) if the assumptions are mentioned in other context or are casually mentioned throughout the work, (d) the author may not be conscious of the assumptions he might unconsciously be carrying as a result of his life in his own society. Macpherson maintains that despite all this the task of interpreter in supplying the missing assumptions is a risky one; for there is no guarantee that he has the assumptions right. The underlying belief of Macpherson is that thinkers intended to be consistent within the limits of their vision. The task of the interpreter is not to resolve the inconsistencies but to make them obvious to show how the writer could have been unconscious of them.

The study of the history of political thought survived in 1950s and 1960s despite very severe attacks by positivist and behaviouralists because of the immense influence of Michael Oakeshott, Sheldon Wolin, and Eric Voegelin. They are philosophers in their own right. They not only saved the study of political philosophy from extinction but were also responsible for the resurrection of political philosophy itself which was declared dead in 1956.

Michael Oakeshott has given his view of politics and political activity which is reflected in the approach he adopts for interpreting past political philosophy. He writes: "In political activity, then, men sail a boundless and bottomless sea; there are neither harbour nor shelter nor floor for anchorage, neither starting-place nor appointed destination. The enterprise is to keep afloat on an even keel." In his attack on rationalism Oakeshott declares that political activity or political experience neither rests upon fundamentals nor culminates in an absolute. However, Oakeshott strongly believes that politics is a traditional activity to be understood in historical terms. Similarly he writes that because political philosophy is not what may be called a progressive science, accumulating solid results and reaching conclusions upon which further investigations may be based with confidence, its history is especially important. Indeed, in a sense, it has nothing but a history, which is more a history of the problems philosophers have detected and the manner of the solution they have proposed than history of doctrines and systems.

Sheldon Wolin is also of the view that the historical method represents the best method for understanding the presuppositions of political philosophy and its character as an intellectual enterprise. It is also his conviction that historical perspective is more effective than any other in exposing the nature of our present predicaments. Similarly for Eric Voegelin philosophy is bound by history.

The Textual Approach

The analytical approach, philosophical or the textual approach is another major approach for interpreting the classic texts. Its main exponents are John Plamenatz, Allan Bloom, Leo Strauss and Andrew Hacker. As opposed to the historians, they believe in the autonomy of the text. According to them, the classics contain timeless truths and so transcend history. Consequently they can be fully understood and interpreted by analyzing the perennial ideas they contain without any understanding of the socio-historical context of their origin. In the opinion of those writers, ideas are transhistorical.

Plamenatz argues that political theory is not a history of political thought by a critical examination of a number of political and social theories. He examines theories and the assumptions, ideas, attitudes and arguments involved in them on their own merit without a detailed investigation of their historical origins and effects. He accepts that every thinker, even the most abstract, is deeply influenced by the circumstances of his day. But this does not mean that whoever discusses their theories must also discuss those circumstances. Philosophical and historical understandings are different. This is not to belittle the latter, but as far as the former is concerned, we need understand only the sense in which the author is using words. That is in other words, to understand how Hobbes himself understood such words as 'law', 'right', 'liberty', 'covenant', 'obligation'. The meaning is to be obtained by a closer study of the arguments of Leviathan than by looking at the historical conditions of England or at political controversies of his day. The arguments Plamenatz advances for the textual as opposed to the historical approach are based upon the particularity and generality contained in the text. Regarding the particularities of the text he says that every writer is a child of his times but he is also idiosyncratic-that is, he has more to say that is unfamiliar. He uses the common language but uses it differently; "we need take less notice of the circumstances in which he wrote, this is because his style and method are different". Secondly, Plamenatz maintains that man and his situation do change from age to age but there is much that remains unchanged. Likewise, the philosophies contained in the classic texts do have a contextual element but they have a timeless element too, which is the major and the more important part of the texts. He explains that these theories are more than attempts to explain society and government, and more also than apologies for or attacks upon the established order. They are philosophies of life.

Allan Bloom also makes an appeal for the study of political thought through text alone. For Bloom, sociology of knowledge is a misnomer. The common view that economic or psychological or historical factors determine the thoughts of philosophers is wrong. The need is to understand the philosophers as they understood themselves, to try to determine their intention accepting the possibility that they may have fulfilled their intentions and attained the truth. Therefore, a line by line, word by word analysis must be undertaken. Every word must be understood. The argument or example that seems irrelevant, trivial or odd is to be taken more seriously because it is precisely the one most likely to be the sign of what is outside of one's own framework.

Leo Strauss is a political philosopher in his own right, besides being a historian of political philosophy. His comprehensive studies of the major political philosophers have won him recognition as our foremost historian of political philosophy. Strauss's understanding of political philosophy has influenced the interpretation of past political thought. According to him, political philosophy is a context-free enterprise. He defines political philosophy as the attempt truly to know both the nature of political things and the right or the good political order. It is a mix of fact and value, objectivism and subjectivism, ethics and politics. Political knowledge, according to Strauss, emerges only when history ceases to be the center of reference and assumptions about political life as such become the focus of critical enquiry.

Strauss is a trenchant critic of historicism and positivism. Positivism rejects the study of values because values are unverifiable. Historicism makes values relative to and determined by history. Thus, historicism ad positivism deny the very possibility of political philosophy because according to both we cannot gain knowledge of the good that holds true for all time and places. Strauss argues that what we know of history and specially of the history of political philosophy, fails to support the historicists' claim that we can have no insight into what is permanent or eternal. Strauss forcefully argues that history rather seems to prove that all-human thought is concerned with the same permanent problems or questions including the questions that are raised explicitly by political philosophy. Strauss strongly believes that there are eternal, universal and transhistorical problems and principles and that the classic texts should be interpreted with reference to them. Straus firmly believes that the question raised by the political philosophers of the past are alive in our own society.

Andrew Hacker is another defender of the textual approach. He supports the textual approach because according to him, the "Great Books" are timeless for both causal and ethical theory. First, they can go far toward explaining the political behaviour of today. They do this because of their universal application. Aristotle's comments on the role of the middle class, or on the causes of revolution, can tell us much about those phenomena in our own society. Rousseau's "general will" and Machiavelli's strictures on what rulers do are equally relevant today. Second, various classics prescribe norms which are as worthy of attention now as they never were. Mill's views on liberty, Plato's idea of justice, Rousseau's views on equality have enchanted the people in every age. Hacker strongly holds the view that there are many "timeless" questions and answers in those classics. He is highly critical of the excess historical, biographical and logical baggage which surrounds the "great books" and which, according to him, should be safely ignored.

The textualists highlight the eternal, universal issues and the timeless problems and solutions found in the classic texts. So the texts, according to them, can be and should be studied autonomously without referring to the socio-historical context of their origin. Plamenatz focuses on text, because in the classic texts the general problems of life of man are discussed in a style, which is particular to its author. The context will help neither in interpreting the general issues which are non-contextual nor the particular style which is idiosyncratic. Bloom focuses on text, because, political philosophy is a dialogue among philosophers. In order to understand a particular text, the dialogue should be heard and closely followed. For understanding Rousseau, Plato is to be referred and understood and not the historical context in which Rousseau had written. Leo Strauss emphatically writes that political philosophy is a non-historical endeavor. A study of its history sufficiently proves that there are eternal and universal principles, which are discussed in them. So, the classic texts should be interpreted in the light of these principles. Andrew Hacker focuses on the "Great Books" because the relevant parts of the timeless wisdom could be applied to solve the present day problems. However, all of them believe that the texts should be autonomously read.

The Linguistic Approach

The linguistic approach is provided as an alternative to these two approaches. It broadly maintains that in order to interpret a classic text, the interpreter has to recover the intention of the author which is expressed in language. This approach involves basically two principles—an emphasis on language and a theory of meaning. Interest in language is one of the predominant features of contemporary philosophy. What distinguishes our age is that a conceptual knowledge of language as such is held to be necessary preliminary to solving the fundamental problems of philosophy. The idea that theory of signs can and must be prior to a theory of things is characteristic of much of the philosophy of our time.

One particular tradition within the language philosophy is commonly called analytic. The postulate common to those approaches which assume this name is that philosophy consists in explaining and clarifying the conceptual systems elaborated in the field of science, art, ethics, religion, politics, etc., explaining and clarifying them in terms of that very language in which the conceptual knowledge is expressed. In this way the clarification of language becomes the main task of philosophy. All the important philosophical questions tend to be reduced to explaining and clarifying the grammar and syntax of the language. Within the linguistic movement there are the following three schools of thought: (a) logical positivism, (b) ordinary language philosophy, and (c) hermeneutics.

Both Logical Positivism and Ordinary Language Philosophy movements endow the task of clarification with a definitely therapeutic and preventive role with regard to metaphysical speculation. Sometimes such speculation arises due to the misuse of the natural languages through the uncritical and uncontrolled exercise of linguistic freedom. In order to eliminate the metaphysical nonsense, logical positivism makes an attempt to construct an artificial—ideal language and works out conventions for the formation of sentences and their semantic interpretation. The philosophies of ordinary language, on the other hand, remain within the confines of natural languages in order to bring into the open the rules, which govern the linguistic behaviour. It accepts the actual or natural languages as ideal.

The theory of meaning given by logical positivism and ordinary language philosophy is different. Logical positivism has propounded the verification theory of meaning. According to it, statement makes sense only to the extent of its empirical verification. The twin goals of empiricism or positivism are: (i) formulation of a logically transparent syntax, and (ii) an empirically grounded semantics. Bertrand Russell, Carnap, Schlick, and Ayer were among the more important persons who worked on positivistic theory of language and meaning. Wittgenstein in his early book *Tractatus* held the positivistic referential theory of meaning. In this book he gave his famous pictorial theory of meaning. As against the verification theory of meaning, the ordinary language philosophy gives the use theory of meaning. According it, a word or a sentence or an expression is meaningful when people can use it for certain purposes.

Hermeneutics

Hermeneutics has long been associated with the interpretation of the biblical texts. Today the label is more often attached to a philosophical search for meaning. Philosophers who engage in hermeneutics accept contingency and historicity. They seek meaning in both texts and life itself as it unfolds historically.

One can do hermeneutics from a variety of perspectives. For example, many critical theorists engage in hermeneutics; naturalistic philosophers like Dewey and Quine employ hermeneutic methods. Hermeneutics involves a careful search for meaning without an expectation that exactly one meaning will be found or that it will be anchored in an unassailable foundation.

Richard Rorty describes hermeneutics as an approach that sees the relations between various discourses as those of strands in a possible conversation, a conversation which presupposes no disciplinary matrix which unites the speakers, but where the hope of agreement is never lost as long as the conversation lasts. Hermeneutical work enlarges the scope of our vision, suggests new meanings and encourages further conversation. It pushes us into a holistic practice of sorts, one in which we can rarely attach separate meaning to the atomistic parts. Rorty reason that the holistic line of argument says that we shall never be able to avoid the "hermeneutic circle"—the fact we cannot understand the part of a strange culture, practice, theory, language, or whereas we cannot get a grasp on how the whole thing works until we have some understanding of its parts.

Hermeneutics has a practical bent. It tries to make sense out of history and contemporary contexts without trying either to rigid theoretical foundations. In telling the story of current philosophy's turn to narrative and conversation, Richard Bernstein points out the contrasts in Plato's work. One part represents the metaphysical Plato, a Plato who led western philosophy on its fruitless search for certainty; the other is the ever-questioning, conversational Plato. Dewey emphasizing this contrast argues that nothing would be more helpful to present philosophizing than a "Back to Plato" movement; but it would have to be back to the dramatic, restless, co-operatively inquiring Plato of the Dialogues, trying one mode of attack after another to see what it might yield; back to the Plato where the highest flight of metaphysics always terminated with a social and practical turn, and not to the artificial Plato constructed by unimaginative commentators who treat him as the original university professor.

In certain ways, Wittgenstein had earlier supported the positivist stand. However, later in *Philosophical Investigations* he gave up verifications and treated meaning not as the correlation between sentence and sense experience but as the use of words within the context of all those varied circumstances within which they are used. Thus later Wittgenstein emphasized the great variety of ways in which language may be employed in public conditions. This concern with what people actually do with language and language games came to replace the search for one strict theory of meaning derived from natural sciences, which positivists had given.

The linguistic approach thus emphasizes the actual uses of words, which are highly diverse. According to the linguistic approach, the meaning of a word is its use and language is taken as a practice or a custom. Consequently, linguistic philosophy makes usage and custom as the final authority. Whatever is in use is meaningful precisely because of being used. The goodness of a usage or custom is its continued use. It can be inferred but it cannot be rationally demonstrated. So there can be no external standards for judging the usages or the meanings. The task of the linguistic philosopher is to describe the immense variety of ways in which actual languages are played.

Hermeneutics deals with situations in which we encounter meanings which are not immediately understandable but require interpretive effort. Hermeneutics originated in the context of interpreting religious texts whose meanings were obscure. Hermeneutics developed in the Enlightenment after the historical consciousness arose and matured in the romantic period. Hermeneutical theory oriented itself to the task of interpreting expressions of life that were fixed in writing. Traditional hermeneutics as developed by Dilthey and Collingswood identified the meanings of a text with the subjective intention of its author. The task of understanding is then constructed as the recapturing or discovery of this original intention. Interpretation of a text thus required essentially a self-transposition or imaginative projection on the part of the interpreter. The interpreter by purging himself of his subjectivity overcomes the temporal distance that separates him from the author he is interpreting.

This theory of meanings has positivistic implications because according to it, author intended something specific, the interpretation that recovers and represents that original intention is the correct one and it banishes all competing interpretation as incorrect. Just as scientific experiments can be repeated exactly any number of times under the same conditions and mathematical problems have but one answer, so the author's intention constitutes a kind of fact, a "meaning in itself".

Traditional hermeneutics was critical of ontological hermeneutics. Most powerful representatives of the ontological hermeneutic tradition are Heidegger, Gadamer and Jurgen Habermas. According Gadamer understanding is not reconstruction but mediation. Understanding consists of an endless process in which the 'horizons' or 'the prejudices' of the author are not the sources of misunderstanding rather they form essential precondition of all understanding. The meaning of a text cannot be identified with the subjective intention of its author. The meaning of a text always surpasses its author.

Ontological hermeneutics unlike traditional hermeneutics emphasizes the centrality of language. Understanding and interpretation as a 'fusion of horizons' is essentially a linguistic process. It is in the medium of language that past and present interpenetrate. Heidegger asserts that language and understanding are inseparable structural aspects of human being in world. Our horizons are given to us pre-reflectively in our languages. Our prejudices are embedded and passed on in the language we use.

Contextualism

The ideas regarding language, meaning and interpretation are used by some historians of ideas to interpret the history of political thought. They accept the centrality of the language in the interpetration of a text. They believe in the original intention and the original meaning of the author but a public or a social act objectified in the language of his time. We can mention the efforts of the three historians—Quentin Skinner, J.A. Pocock and John Dunn. According to them, the history of past thought is the history of ideas or activity of thinking—which generates ideas. According to them, one can have expressed ideas only in and through the language. So thinking according to them, is a linguistic activity. Now we have seen that the ordinary language philosophy takes language as social custom or practice. It develops naturally. Its development is relative to the temporal and spatial setting in which it is used. So thinking according to the three historians is a social, historical and linguistic activity. Consequently, past thinking can be interpreted in terms of the language, which was available in a particular society at a particular time in which the past thoughts were expressed. Special emphasis is given to the analysis of the language and vocabulary used by the particular author. So, the language of the text is to be analyzed within the broader linguistic context.

Accordingly, the first task of the interpreter, while interpreting the text, is to delineate the prevailing linguistic context within which the author operated. Within this context, the language and the vocabulary used by the author needs a closer analysis. Therefore, an analysis of both the general linguistic context and the particular vocabulary used by the author is what is needed for interpreting the text.

We have seen that the writings of most of the scholars directly or indirectly advert to appropriate means of recovering what philosophers said and could be understood to mean. In the course of this it can be seen that textual and contextual approaches are sometimes treated as though perfectly and firmly distinguishable. It has to be observed, in a general way, that they are not always so. The context itself, for most purposes, either is or can be read as a text, with the same problems of reliability and consistency which all other texts present. Skinner, for example, where he seeks to reconstruct Hobbes's 'context', understood as the way in which Hobbes was received by his contemporaries, is doing no more than sieving other seventeenth-century documents, i.e., they are scrolling other 'text'.

If one must understand the context in order to grasp the text, and if the context is just one or a set of different texts, then before one can understand the context of the text, one must have a prior grasp of the context of the context. One must seize the context of the context of the context, and so on. There looms the risk of an infinite regress where we insist upon grasping contexts in advance of texts.

In as far as contexts and texts are substantively the same, then we may agree with Skinner that an exclusive reliance on textual analysis leads to a faulty understanding of these texts, courts the otiose. If texts have their own contexts, if a text of itself implies and adverts to a context, then there could not substantively be any such thing as 'exclusive reliance on textual analysis'. The text itself always falls short of being suigeneris. It in some measure refers and responds to external events. Texts minimally consist of language; language is social, hence there can be no text, which does not advert to and incorporate some social reality. Seen from the perspective of other events, the text itself becomes an external event. Texts may in this way be viewed as supplying the major content of what we call contexts. Assuming that contexts are largely constituted of texts and that a text at least in part generates its own context, no textual approach can consistently prove to be exclusively textual, nor any contextual approach to be exclusively contextual.

Contexts and texts are substantively the same. Yet there is good reason for insisting upon a difference. Where it is said that a context, at least in the history of ideas, is almost invariably some other sort of document or text, what is being signaled is a substantive identity. While we may accept that the substance of a context is essentially the same as the substance of a text, this need not stop us from distinguishing between context and text in relational terms. Though context and text are substantively the same, the context may be relationally viewed as some species of text which lies outside of or is external to another text; this 'other text', for whatever reason, is accorded greater importance or centrality: hence it is called the text.

Now on this relational understanding, though context and text are necessarily connected, they are not interchangeable. They are distinguished, by analogy, as is 'outside' from 'inside', or 'secondary' from 'primary', or 'last' from 'first'. On this relational understanding, it at least becomes conceivable that we might rather ambitiously study a context before its text, or more modestly seek to elicit the point of a text by reference to its context. We might compositely label these procedures 'methodological contextualism'. While the first approach (study the context before the text) becomes conceivable, it is not automatically made sensible. One can for example study the history of the English Civil War before one reads *Leviathan.* After all, though the history is a part of the book, the book is equally a part of the history. The 'history', the 'context', only consists of another book (such as Clarendon's book on the war), or of a series of books, of letters, of dispatches. *Leviathan* is itself, of course, but another page in the record, and though we most commonly view it as 'the text', there is nothing to stop us turning it round, perhaps to serve Clarendon as 'the context'. And this is the point.

Simply because we declare 'the context' to be Clarendon, there is no good reason to suppose that we absolutely ought not to read Hobbes before Clarendon. Either can be read before the other and most commonly one is read rather than the other, but there is no compelling reason for deferring the study of 'the text' just because we have chosen not to call it 'the context'. It is not persuasive to contend, simply because we light upon Hobbes's book as our 'text' that we ought in principle to read the text of someone else first, such as Clarendon or Ascham or Nedham.

At its most sensible and commonsensical level, methodological contextualism emits a modest and cogent claim. And this is a rule of thumb which enjoins that we seek to elicit the purpose of an author, in writing a text, by reference to the context in which that author was located at the time of writing, If there are significantly different interpretations of a text, it may be that a better understanding of the context will throw light upon the matter. Yet, it has to be confessed that we have no significant examples of this. There are no contextual discussions of Warrender, for example, which refute his claims about Hobbesian political obligation. And we have no contextual refutations of Macpherson's textual claims, since Macpherson's principal and distinctive claims are themselves contextual.

Methodological contextualism will have achieved much of its present vogue by virtue of its legitimate concern to avoid distorting the meaning of texts in the way that often results from taking them 'out of context'. It is an idiom of the language that to take any proposition 'out of context' involves some form of falsification. It is perfectly obvious as to the effect that leaving a word out here or there may have on the sense of a sentence. Judicious omission is a classic strategy for the tiring business of setting up and bowling out straw man. The shadowy atheist is widely reported to have admitted, there is a God; but when the record is inspected, what it reveals here to say is: 'I admit that most people believe there is a God'. Such distortion by omission can win virtually any debate and it is for this reason that we are to stand up 'for the whole truth', with each jot in its rightful place.

We should note, however, that this idiom, which enjoins us not to take matters out of context, is not altogether reliable. It tends to imply that to leave something out is itself to distort. And yet we know too well that any account must leave something out. The general problem of distortion and falsification is encountered, not simplistically where we leave something out, this being inescapable in supplying any account, but where we leave those things out, which being left out, effectively distort the account we give.

We may distort by cut-out as with President Nixon and the Watergate tapes, but equally by overload; it is for example information overload that is distinctive of new forms of censorship. Democratic politicians do not distort by refusing to answer, but by determinedly filling up the record with irrelevancies. Circumlocution is of course the classic stratagem deployed where the agent seeks to obscure or soften and thus distort his point by embalming it in a surfeit of date. The modern inflation of language in general is a part of this, as where we replace 'dustmen' with 'sanitary engineers'.

Shakespeare commits Antony to inflating the record to falsify intent. Antony's funeral speech is an exercise in irony, circumlocution and dissimulation, demonstrating as clearly as one might wish that subtracting from the record is far from being the only means of distorting it. What Antony intends is that Caesar was a great leader and patriot, that a pack of villains slew him, and that the murderers should be brought to book. But Antony dare not say what he means. He delays. He cries. He lies. There is a controlled padding out of the account: 'I come to bury Caesar, not to praise him'. 'Brutus is an honourable man.' 'So are they all honourable men.' 'I speak not to disprove what Brutus spoke.' Antony spins it all out, he adds and reiterates, all precisely with a view to concealing his purpose. Shakespeare knows all too well how to have him do this, to such a point that every school child knows the passage. So again, distortion is not only secured by deletion, but also by accretion, by putting in as by taking away an excess of context.

Skinner's account of Hobbes and the Royal Society, for example, depicts Hobbes as a genuinely autonomous intellect, a materially unencumbered mind, one perfectly free to comment upon the most serious and sensitive matters of the day. And yet Hobbes, even in his own words, must by implication be described as a servant, an attendant, a dependant, a traveling companion, tour guide, tutor, translator, hired man, and yet no relevant account whatsoever is taken of this servitude. There is legitimately more along these lines that Skinner could have done.

It appears sometimes to be supposed that contexts are more reliable than texts, or that they serve as a court of last resort, that they are more factual or more authoritative. This is sometimes reflected in the preference for history over philosophy, the concrete over the abstract and the empirical over the rational. The ideological concern with imposing an historical approach, the fear of being unhistorical, reflects in part this proclivity. Ashcraft's apparent inclination to banish or subordinate logic and scientific method seems consistent with this prejudice. In this connection, there are two points to be retained.

First, given that the context is usually reducible to some other sort of text, there is no authoritative reason for supposing that the one can be more reliable than the other. Second, given that every history, every era, every context, has or presupposes its own logic, reducing otherwise to sheer incoherence, there is no possible choice of history over logic. The history is subject to a firm logical structure or it is gibberish. It is more hysterical than historical. What we take to be history, what we construe as a context, is never self-evident or self-validating. The history, the context, these are themselves matters of logical construction and reconstruction.

Without in any way giving up on historical truth, reliability, testability and veracity, it remains that the products of any era or history or context can be packaged and repackaged in myriad ways. A context is a building that can be put up in as many different styles as there are many architects to design it. The factual array available to the historian is immense. The overall picture consists of an infinity of parts.

There can be no doubt that Hobbes himself was perfectly well aware of this interstitial logic. He knew well enough that history does not simply exist, that histories are inventions, that they are put together, that they have a point, that they tell a story, that they reflect choice, selection, order and judgment, that the good historian is both imaginative and accurate in adhering to the logic that enables and invites an audience to attend to what he or she has to say. This is surely Hobbes's point in commending Thucydides as he does: 'He filleth his narrations with that choice of matter, and ordered them with that judgment, and with such perspicuity and efficacy expressed himself that he maketh his auditor a spectator." In doing this, one must know not to say too little, but equally not to say too much.

The methodological problems of contextualism, demands that it is useful to distinguish between (1) text, (2) context, (3) history, (4) contextualism and (5) historicism. A text is by turn the outcome and object of all writing or research. A context is any perspective on a text, including the background data that one may append to it. History is a narrative, a story, which is focused upon a text or context – insofar as the two are the same, viewed as propositions. 'Contextualism' is a methodological claim that valid history is only secured or demonstrated via the reconstruction of the context, especially where the later is to do with a perspective on the background to a text.

Take the context to be a perspective on, including background to, a text. It is a matter of supplementary claims and arguments related and/or additional to a text. The context is just a subsequent set of such claims, which take the text as its object. Substantively, contexts and texts are identical. The text is a set of propositions, and so is the context a set of propositions. Contexts and texts are identical, taking account of their prepositional character.

Relationally, contexts and texts are different. The text comes first in time or emphasis, followed by the context. They constitute a sequential relationship featuring the context as subsequent, and the text as prior. We designate contexts as subsequent propositions, which are designated as texts. We can only distinguish between contexts and texts relationally or propositionally by holding constantly the identity between them as propositions. Substantively, the text is always privileged, since only it may be adjudged better/worse, true/false, and probable/improbable. Relationally, the context is always subordinate, since it can only serve as a context on the grounds that it is relevant to the text.

Plato's *Republic*, which advances one concept of justice, involves commentary upon and rejection of certain other concepts of justice, such as that justice is the same as 'giving everyman his due', or that it is the same as promoting the interests of the ruling powerful in society. The logic of the text, once we adjust to its focus, is not autonomous. It not merely relates to the world, it is a part of the world. It may be physically contained, like the pages between the covers of a book, but its claims cannot be similarly delimited. The text which we inspect, once entered into, can be seen itself to supply a perspective on and background to still earlier texts, related concerns and antecedent arguments.

Look at Pocock's book *The Machiavellian Moment*. We note his emphasis upon the developmental links between Aristotle, Rome, Machiavelli and indeed the American Revolution. The substance of this link or tradition consists in the idealization of the citizen as an active agent who forms himself by virtue of civic engagement, thereby keeping despotism and corruption at bay. If Pocock, like Skinner, prefers contexts to texts, he also prefers great, vertical shafts of time to Skinner's local, horizontal clearings of understanding.

If we take Quentin Skinner's most extended work, *The Foundations of Modern Political Thought* we find he avows that he has 'tried not to concentrate so exclusively on the leading theorists' and has 'focused instead on the more general social matrix out of which their works arose'. He discusses texts only in regard to the social and intellectual framework or social base out of which they emerge. This framework in which texts are set is itself devised from such evidence. Skinner's intellectual context', accordingly, is secondary, supplementary, background noises.

Skinner seems concerned to close the door, which Pocock leaves open. He seems to take the view that it is not tenable to suppose that the logic of any text can supply its own context. Skinner's reason is not that one can infer the context from the text but that the context imposes a lid, an ultimate framework on the range of conventional meanings that it was possible for an author to have entertained and articulated.

Skinner's Method

Skinner is a leading light among the Cambridge 'new historians' who, since the 1960s, have advanced a distinctive programme of historians' research and textual interpretation. Its origins may be traced in part to R.G. Collingswood's approach to the history of philosophy. That history, he said was not about an eternal but finite set of questions to which different philosophers have proposed different answers. It was rather about historically variable problems to which particular philosophers proposed particular answers. In his *Autobiography*, Collingswood wrote:

> If there were a permanent problem P, we could ask what did Kant, or Leibniz, or Berkeley, think about P? But what is thought to be a permanent problem P is really a number of transitory problems p, p, p, whose individual peculiarities are blurred by the historical myopia of the person who lump them together under the one name P.

In contrast to those who claim that there are 'perennial' questions or problems in philosophy and political theory, Collingswood argued that the questions themselves change in subtle but significant ways. If we are to understand the meaning of something that a particular political theorist wrote, we must first understand the problem they were addressing and attempting to solve.

Something like this Collingswoodian approach informs Peter Laslett's lengthy and learned introduction to his edition of John Locke's *Two Treaties of Government* which restored Locke's political treatise to its political and historical context in the Exclusion Crisis of the early 1680s. Far from having his head in the clouds of philosophical abstraction, Locke was deeply involved in the radical parliamentary politics of the Shaftsbury circle. By means of some brilliant historical detective work, Laslett showed that Locke's *Two Treatises* had been written near a decade earlier than anyone has heretofore supposed and that from offering a post hoc justification of the Glorious Revolution, Locke was prescribing and legitimizing just that sort of revolutionary action, and well before the fact. Laslett's scholarly sleuthing paved the way for subsequent interpretations of Locke by John Dunn, James Tully and Richard Ashcraft in particular and of other works of political theory more generally.

If Laslett was circumspect about articulating and defending his method of historical investigation and textual interpretation, others were not. J. G. A. Pocock, John Dunn and most especially and extensively Quentin Skinner mounted deflationary critiques of traditional 'textbook' approaches to the interpretation of works of political theory. Despite minor disagreements, they agreed that most of what has heretofore passed as the history of political theory has been insufficiently historical-concerned with the context and situation in which Locke and others found themselves and the problems with which they dealt. Skinner and his fellow Cambridge historians view works of political theory as forms of political action, grasping the point or meaning of which requires that one recover the intentions of the actor/ author and the linguistic resources and conventions available to him or her.

One of Skinner's principal innovations has been to incorporate 'speech act' theory, as formulated by J. L. Austin and further developed by John Searle and others, into the interpretation of texts in political theory. According to this view, a work of political theory is itself a political act or intervention consisting of a series of interconnected actions with words-speech acts in Austin's sense-that are intended to produce certain effects in the reader: to warn, to persuade, to criticize, to frighten, to encourage, to console, etc. Political theorists have not, by and large, been armchair philosophers engaged in abstract thinking; they have been political actors engaged in high-level propaganda and persuasion on behalf of this or that political cause: the critique or defense of democracy; the critique or defense of royal absolutism; likewise for religious toleration, resistance and regicide, the French or other revolutions, capitalism, the emancipation of slaves and/or women, and so on, through a rather long list of political causes and campaigns. Textual interpretation is largely a matter of restoring a text to the historical context in which it was composed and the questions to which it was offered as an answer or the problems to which it was proposed as a solution.

Skinner argues that we modern interpreters ought not to impose our own concepts, categories and concerns upon texts written by authors long dead. Rather we should, in so far as possible, try to inhabit their world instead of making them inhabit ours and forcing them to address questions and concerns that they would have found alien if not incomprehensible. Skinner's conception of historical understanding bears more than a passing resemblance to the late Clifford Greetz's view of anthropological explanation in the latter's 'From the Natives' Point of View' and other seminal essays. To 'see things their way' is not somehow to read their minds or to walk in their shoes; it is, rather, to reconstruct the conceptual and imaginative framework through which they view the world and act in it through deeds and with words that are deeds. What concepts and categories are available to political thinkers and actors in a particular culture and age? How do they use particular words to perform this or that speech act? What for example is Hobbes doing when in Leviathan he defines liberty as 'the absence of external impediments' to motion. He was in fact repudiating and attempting to replace the old civic republican understanding of liberty as requiring self-rule. What at first sight looks like a descriptive scientific definition of a term actually has a political and polemical intention? How are we to understand puzzling silences or omissions -as when, for example, Machiavelli omits any mention of 'justice'? These are among the questions that are to be addressed and answered if we are to 'see things their way'.

A good many of Skinner's critics have not seen fit to see things his way. Margaret Leslie and Joseph Femia, among others, have taken Skinner to task for his critique of anachronistic readings of texts and have mounted their own defense of anachronism. Strained anlogies, and even anachronisms, as Femia and Leslie aver, may in the hands of an ingenious writer such as Antonio Gramsci, prove to be politically persuasive when addressed to a certain sort of audience. In redscribing the Communist party as the 'modern prince', Gramsci adapted and made creative use of what he took to be Machiavellian notion of a ruthless and all-powerful prince. On Gramsci's reading, the party, like Machiavellian prince, must be prepared to use guile, cunning, deceit and violence to achieve worthy ends. By substituting 'party ' for 'prince' Gramsci was able to adapt Machiavellian arguments to a more modern context.

Skinner's rejoinder, in effect, is that no such license is granted to historians of political thought. For if we are to understand the meaning that particular terms, utterances, claims and arguments had for certain authors and their audiences then surely we must, at a minimum, know something about the linguistic conventions of the day and the political concepts, languages of idioms available to them. Thus it would in this instance be important to note, for example, that the modern concept of the 'political party', as understood by Gramsci and his audience, was not available to Machiavelli and his contemporaries. One might also note that certain key concepts in Machiavellian vocabulary, such as fortune, have no place in, and are indeed at odds with, Gramsci's own rather more deterministic Marxian framework. To make these observations is of course to take nothing away from Gramsci who wrote not as a scholar or historian but as an engaged political actor and activist. An interpretation may be adjudged innovative, ingenious, path-breaking, and persuasive on political grounds even as it is adjudged deficient on scholarly grounds, and vice versa. In short, Skinner draws a fairly sharp distinction between historians of political thought like himself and "innovating ideologists' such as Machiavelli and Gramsci. An innovating ideologist attempts, via a variety of rhetorical stratagems and other ploys to legitimize some form of social behavior generally agreed to be questionable.

We must remember that political actors, past and present, are apt to fight dirty by, for example, misrepresenting views, constructing arguments and using almost any rhetorical weapon that comes to hand. And success in such endeavours depends, as often as not, upon one side's skill or sheer good luck in hitting upon an illuminating image or telling metaphor to make its case persuasive or at least palatable. But it is also important, as Skinner reminds us repeatedly, to note that such arguments and appeals must be tailored to the tastes, standards and outlook of the audience at which they are aimed. If one fails to take one's audience's attitudes, beliefs and standards into account, one runs the grave risk of having one's actions viewed as unintelligible and /or illegitimate.

Another criticism leveled repeatedly against Skinner is that the recovery of authorial intention, even if possible in principle, is unimportant or irrelevant in interpretive practice. For, these critics contend, even if we accept Skinner's claim that political writing is species of action, the fact remains that these sorts of actions like all human actions sometimes misfire and produce consequences unintended, unforeseen and perhaps even unforeseeable by the actor/author. Hence to recover an author's aims or intentions, even if possible, is beside the point. The history of political thought is, or at any rate should be, about the consequences of actions, i.e. the use to which an author's ideas were later put by actors whose interpretation of the meaning of a term (utterance, phrase, passage or entire text) may not and need not accord with the author's own intentions. Or, to put it another way, the historian's task is to trace the unintended consequences of purposive political action, in this instance the action of writing a political tract or treatise.

A further criticism commonly leveled against Skinner's method is that it produces purely 'antiquarian' accounts of political theories past that have no bearing on present-day political theorizing. Skinner resolutely rejects that charge, arguing that framework, concepts and categories change over time as authors and audiences attempt to come with changing circumstances and new problems of political and social life. Any attempt to devise a theory that purports to freeze historical time is a misguided and mistaken denial of the reality of 'conceptual change', the fact that concepts have historically mutable meanings. Skinner comes out openly against all those neo-Kantian projects of our time in which we encounter an aspiration to halt the flux of politics by trying definitively to fix the analysis of key moral terms [e.g. justice]. Skinner continues to harbor a special prejudice against those who, in adopting this approach, imagine an ideal speech situation in which everyone would make the same moral and cognitive judgments. There are no moral and cognitive judgments, which are not mediated by our concepts, and it seems to that even our most apparently abstract concepts are historical through and through.

Thus Skinner's method leads not only to a concern with understanding theories past, but with politics and political theorizing in the present and pungent proscriptions about how not to theories. But the merit of any method is to be found in what it does yield in actual historical and interpretive practice.

Contexts are as various and encompassing as are any other propositions, including texts. The need to recover the context is consistent with recruiting any thing at all that is additional to the text. Logically, the context could be the recent past or the distant past, the near future or the distant future. One may reflect upon a text in the context of its past or present or future. Nor is there anything at all problematic about reflecting on a text in the context of its future. Indeed, we who reflect upon any text always and necessarily do so subsequent to its appearance, are associated with its future, and thus create for it a future context. The context then is virtually all encompassing. It extends front and back, chronologically speaking of any designated text. There is no field whether science, architecture, social structure, economics, politics or philosophy which can be excluded from it in principle.

The contention that one can never take the meaning of a text as given, even where the text seems perfectly perspicuous. Of course, apparent clarity may mislead. The use of context seems most appropriate, in the sense of an emphasis upon contemporary background, not where the text appears perfectly clear and sensible, but precisely where it does not. First-year students reading Plato's *Republic* may find his text highly unpersuasive. It is in this circumstance that the instructor rightly resorts to contextual reconstructions, so to portray the text as more coherent than it can possibly appear to be in the light of present day understanding.

Historical contexualism, conceived as a methodological demand, seems hopelessly circular. The trouble is that it is logically and physically impossible for any observer endlessly to contexualize the context of the context....of the context. A 'context' is nothing more than a text which, by virtue of being last in place, has not yet been and cannot itself yet be contextualized. The construction of a context is never conclusive, nor logically sounder, by virtue of being a context.

The context is not magically self-revealing or methodologically privileged. It supplies no miracle cures or instant restoratives. It may mark a direction in which one might explore. It may advise where to look outside the text – but not how to render the text more or less valid. Contexts and texts are not distinguishable in terms of truth-claims. The preference for context over text is not the same as a preference for a valid over an invalid claim. The relational order of context to text does not correlate with any order of superior to inferior validity. It involves nothing more than a matter of logical sequence, where text is antecedent to context and may serve it accordingly as an object of attention.

We may encounter a difficulty in a text, then it may be wise to look elsewhere for solutions to it. But if one has not looked closely enough at a text to determine the problems, then to look at context is bound to be a bootless business. The context after all is as large as life itself, and as unrelenting. Nor is it just one: contexts are irresistibly plural. If one has no sense of what the text is about, if one does not first take from it some sense of what is to be pursued, then the context in turn, unbounded as it is, neither will nor can reveal anything of relevance. The preference for context over text only presumably makes sense on the misleading assumption that texts, as distinct from contexts, are necessarily unclear or incomplete, or on the assumption that more data always make for greater clarity.

The trouble is, that if all texts, are necessarily unclear or incomplete, then all contexts, we advance to explain or embellish text – are equally unclear and incomplete. If all texts are defective, then so are all contexts defective. But more detail does not necessarily get us closer to the truth. Most detail is irrelevant to what we can or seek or need to learn. A contextualizing procedure, which perhaps asks us to inspect the views of Hobbes's contemporaries, rather than the text of *Leviathan*, may well take us further from, not closer to, what we can or seek or need to grasp.

Ideas reflect historical stages in the growth of society. They arise because there is a tension, which has to be resolved. But they have an autonomy of their own. The history of ideas has its own momentum. Doubtless ideas are influenced by developments in society but they also influence society. It is true that while the Greeks of their time found Plato and Aristotle largely irrelevant, yet their ideas caught fire in thirteenth century Europe to shape a new civilization. But one can never be sure that the same ideas will influence all societies in the same way. For instance, Aristotle came to India during the same period through Islamic writings but the influence took an altogether different form. The contextual approach has recently found much support in historical conferences. The attempt here is to look at philosophers in the context of special situations and specific audiences to which these writes were addressing themselves. It is believed that great writings do not always have a universal message. They are not always a search for Platonic 'essence' or 'forms'. One must, argues Skinner, go beyond the text and context and recover the authors' intention; the historian must have insight into the language, ideas and symbols of the time because philosophy is expressed through words which are located in the language of a particular time. This philosophical position is right in so far as it insists on the importance of context, but it ignores the fact that the history of ideas in due course acquires its own autonomy and whatever the language or words or historical context, certain ideas or concepts are common to all humankind. They persist across time. Otherwise Plato's *Republic*, Kautilya's *Arthasastra* would be simply incommunicable to us. The dilemma which haunted Arjun on the battle-field still confronts us. We are able to appreciate and identitfy with it and it is this which explains the enduring influence of these classics and provides a legitimacy to all attempts to seek cosmos amidst chaos.

It is one thing to emphasize the importance of context and another to make the context absolute at the expense of the text. The context is important because it helps us in two ways. First, it throws a new light on some hidden meaning in the book, which would not otherwise be revealed. Secondly, it is important insofar as it emphasizes the totality of social process in which the world is integrally related to consciousness as a part of this process. Political thought cannot be divorced from political experience. Therefore, it is incumbent on us to understand the context of ideas and issues in their age if we wish to properly appreciate Kautilya, Rammohun Roy or Gandhi or Ambedkar. They were debating issues, which were important to their contemporaries. In that sense, they were addressing particular audiences of their time. To this extent, the totality of historical process provided the background to their political thought. It would, for example, make no sense to argue about imperial administration before Kautilya or about liberal democracy before the modern experience. The emphasis on the context of the historical process must make us very careful in our evaluation of historical actores. Righthy V.R. Mehta has argued that Rana Pratap and Shivaji might appear as reactionaries from the point of view of the present but in the context to which they were responding, their struggles had a definite revolutionary significance and meaning.

Context has two aspects. First comes objective and subjective apparatus and second, the intellectual history of the society. We must affirm that while the objective and subjective factors condition men, they do not condition all that they do. Though human condition may not provide much choice, man has a certain autonomy and responsibility for conscious action. Political thinkers like individuals are moral beings insofar as they make conscious decision and are responsible for these decisions. They cannot be condoned on the pretext that they thought in a particular way because of the logic of the situation in which they were located. Rules and institutions of society may be laid down but human beings are endowed with the capacity for making conscious choices, either of conforming to these rules or changing them. The historical process has its own flow out of which individuals have the capacity to give it new direction. The individual may not always succeed. There may be, as the ancients believed, an inexorable destiny or cunningness of circumstances.

Every writer or thinker struggles with this to find out where changes or jumps are possible. In that sense while every man is a creature of his age, he is also a creator. There are so many instances of people who were weak in their personal life yet became most powerful and positive leaders, heroes or philosophers. There is a need to explain for this incongruity in their lives. We have to pay more importance to the value of his personal or historical experience in terms of search for permanence. The greater his effort to transcend the immediate in order to change, revitalize or reshape it, the greater is his stature as a thinker. This is what is meant by great thinker or hero. Both often appear irrelevant to their contemporaries. A great thinker is indeed one who transcends the immediate constraints to create something, which connects him to the past, the present and the future. Of course even here there are limits beyond which thinker cannot go. But between these two points of immediate environment and historical sweep, there are many options and choices available to thinkers in terms of which they can communicate their message. The cherished ideals of truth, justice, freedom, equality may vary from society to society but there is hardly a society, which would deny the importance of these ideals. Certainly some ideas are more important in one tradition than in another and author must be related to this distinctness in their traditions but the greater the attempt one makes to transcend the boundaries of one's tradition and formulate a universal discourse, the greater is one's stature as a thinker. That is why, Plato or Kautilya or Gandhi still makes sense to us.

Moreover, a purely historical approach will make us archivists rather than political theorists. As political theorists, we are interested in that past as far as it illumines our own situation and predicament, gives us new insights into the human condition. After all, the vision of a right order or dharma or a good person such as Rama has provided meaning and substance to the development of our national ethos. These visions grew in a particular historical setting constituted by both the material situation and the intellectual history of society. But once they arose, they acquired autonomy of their own, transcended history to become part of the ever-growing corpus of ideas and became integral to the intellectual background of every subsequent generation. It is in this sense that the ideal of Ramarajya in the *Ramayana* or of Karmayog in the *Gita* make sense to us; the principles of dharma or justice in the middle ages provide a background against which we react. It would be impossible to understand the integralism of Aurobindo or the notion of Ramarajya of Gandhi without understanding their basis in the ancient thought. Every age has its epochal characteristic, some of these features are given up in the course of historical development. Others are retained because they are found to be either useful or conforming to deeper human experiences. A sense of history is important because it help us disentangle these features. In the subsequent ages, we shall not be asking questions of past thinkers about things, which did not directly concern them, nor shall we quote them out of context. A historical sense makes us humble and more sympathetic to their predicament. It also helps us to identify those features of human situations, and consequently demands a new answer. In this respect, a study of history of political thought does two things; it gives us knowledge of the past, its ideas and their relationship to concrete political activity in terms of tradition and innovation. Second, it helps us understand ourselves and our predicament better by sharpening similarities and differences between the past epoch and ours and providing a vision for the future. It embodies traditions of society, its past aspirations and achievements, present crisis and future promises and possibilities.

2

Socrates

> I am wiser than this man; it is likely that neither of us knows anything worthwhile, but he thinks he knows something when he does not, whereas I do not know, neither do I think I know what I do not know.

Philosophy, as it is studied in the West today, is an invention of the ancient Greeks. Modern philosophers, by contrast, continue to discuss problems which were first raised some two thousand five hundred years ago, and they often do so in terms which their Greek predecessors would have found fully intelligible. For that reason, the ancient philosophers are not just historical figures; they are part of the living community of philosophical debate; and they have to be studied by anyone with a serious interest in the subject.

Unfortunately, much Greek philosophical writing has been irretrievably lost. The authors whose works survive in greatest bulk are Plato and Aristotle, both of whom left extensive writings, which, between them, cover virtually the whole range of philosophical problems. Plato has a greater claim than anyone else to be regarded as the founder of philosophy as we known it. His dialogues remain the starting-point for the study of logic, metaphysics, morals, and politics. He believed it important to separate knowledge from mere opinion; and he held that true knowledge would enable people to live well, for morality could be objective. He also believed that the soul was distinct from the body, and that there was a world of ideas separate from things in this world. His thought is often poetic and imaginative, with a mystical dimension, yet it also relates to highly practical issues in education and politics which continue to perplex us even today.

Aristotle was both philosopher and scientist. He was a polymath who provided organizing categories for the whole of human knowledge. He founded biology, reshaped logic and metaphysics, and determined the subsequent character of thinking about ethics, politics, psychology, and literary criticism. By laying down the principles of valid interference and explanation, he erected the foundations of scientific knowledge. His mind was balanced, and stunningly capacious.

Socrates (470 BC-399BC) left no writings whatsoever. He was Plato's teacher and he is known to us primarily as the dominant character in Plato's dialogues, particularly the earlier ones. It is impossible to distinguish between what Socrates thought and what Plato thought, but the individuality of Socrates is nevertheless brilliantly realized. The modern world accepts him as the enduring model of the great teacher, the questioner and sceptic who leads his pupils towards a solution by forcing them to see the inconsistencies in their own unconsidered and unexamined beliefs, opinions and assumptions.

Since the fifth and fourth centuries BC. when these men taught and wrote, there has never been a time when their ideas have been wholly without influence. Plato's thought underlay the neo-platonic movement of late Antiquity, but then went into a period of relative neglect until it was revived during the Italian Renaissance. It had a deep influence upon the Cambridge Platonists of the seventeenth century and the poets and philosophers of the Romantic period, entering modern philosophical discourse. Aristotle came into his own in the twelfth and thirteenth centuries, when the scholastic synthesis of his thought with the doctrines of medieval Christianity became the accepted intellectual orthodoxy. The scientific revolution of the seventeenth century shattered this tradition and relegated Aristotle's scientific works to oblivion, but his *Ethics, Politics,* and *Poetics* remained deeply influential. *The Ethics,* in particular, is still the indispensable starting point for anyone wishing to reflect upon morality, human nature, and human fulfillment. As for Socrates, his heroic death became a moving exemplar of intellectual integrity and total commitment to the intellectual life as the supreme human value. His questioning posture shaped the way in which philosophy was subsequently thought and numerous successive schools of philosophical thought have attempted to appropriate him as their patron saint.

The Greeks were a group of nomadic Indo-Europeans who came down from the north and replaced a people already settled by the Aegean Sea. They were not great innovators at first, but as they traded around the Mediterranean, the Greeks borrowed freely from other cultures. From the Phoenicians they borrowed an alphabet, some technology, and new religious ideas. From Egypt, they borrowed the models that came to define Greek architecture, the basics of geometry, and some of the more exotic ideas of early Greek "mystery" religion. From, Babylon (now Iraq) they borrowed astronomy, mathematics, geometry, and still more, religious ideas. The Egyptian God Oriris became the Greek Dionysos, and in the sixth century, the powerful mystery cult of Dionysos spread across Greece teaching that human nature is part nature, part divine.

Greek philosophy emerged from this mixture of mythology, mystery, and mathematics. The first Greek philosophers found themselves in both enviable and extremely vulnerable circumstances. Their culture was rich and creative, but they were surrounded by jealous and competitive enemies. It was not at all unusual for great cultures to be suddenly invaded and virtually wiped off the map of the known world, and what was not destroyed by war would often by devastated by nature. Epidemics swept through cities like silent armies. Life was unpredictable, often tragic, and therefore both precious and lamentable.

In a world in which people had so little control, the concept of fate naturally played an important role. The Greeks since Homer's time attributed fate to the whimsical decisions of the gods and goddesses, but the philosophers of the sixth century looked for an underlying order to things, some stable and comprehensible foundation. In place of the whims and passions of the gods and the uncertainties of fate, there had to be logos, some reason or underlying logic. Religion had opened the way to the "beyond" for thousands of years, but it was philosophy that would demand order in the beyond.

By sixth century, the traditional mythology of Greece was already becoming a bit tired and increasingly problematic. The stories of the gods and goddesses and their various victims and escorts were no longer taken all that seriously, much less literally, by sophisticated Greeks. In the gap between the mundane and the fantastic, the idea of "the Truth" emerged. We do not know how are these doubts extended through Greek society, but it is very clear that they were in the air. Monotheism was certainly known through the Hebrews, for there was considerable contact between the Hebrews and the Greeks. Monotheism must have also appealed to the Greek sense of unity, despite the plurality of Greek gods and goddesses. It was from such radical ideas that philosophy (from the Greek philein, love, and Sophia, wisdom) was born in Greece.

The founder of ethical philosophy in Western civilization was a short, ugly, snub-nosed, poor and unemployed, modestly dressed and barefooted man named Socrates. He lived in ancient Greece as a citizen of the city-state of Athens during the fifth century BC. He was ironically executed by his fellow Athenians on grounds of immorality. Socrates was not the first Western thinker to engage in ethical reflection about morality, but his ideas have been responsible for some of the main directions of thought about right and wrong and good and evil throughout the subsequent 2,500 years of Western philosophy. Furthermore, Socrates stands even today as a revered example of a person who truly lived the moral life. Although sometimes criticized for not doing enough to fight the injustices perpetrated by others, he was committed to never engaging in an unjust act himself. He always listened to his conscience and did what he thought was right – even when doing so put him in grave danger and defame. In fact, his insistence on never committing an unjust act provoked his own execution at the hands of the Athenians. Astonishingly, Socrates acceded to his execution on moral grounds.

Socrates died in the year 399 BC after being tried by the citizens of Athens for corrupting the youth and not believing in the gods of the Athenian city-state. He was seventy years of age at the time of his execution. He had been born an Athenian citizen – the son of a stonemason – and he spent almost all of his life within the city of Athens, a city he loved and to which he was always loyal. Although he served honorably and courageously as a soldier on several occasions and, in rare instances, as an official in the governance of the city, he never held a regular job or regular political office. Most of his time was spent talking to the people of Athens, young and old, citizens and visitors, about the meaning and course of their lives – usually urging them to change their ways. His message to them was: the unexamined life is not worth living for a human being. His counsel: pay attention to the most important thing in life, your soul or character; seek goodness and justice, for these alone benefit the soul. And he offered his fellow citizens the following assurance: nothing can harm the good and just person, while the wrongdoer courts unhappiness and misery. "For I go around doing nothing but persuading both young and old among you not to care for your body or your wealth in preference to or as strongly as for the best possible state of your soul".

Such a message was not well-received by all Athenians, many of whom came to resent his criticisms and to feel that his self-described role as a "gadfly" was detrimental to the city. But a handful of Athenians came to believe, as the Oracle at Delphi had in fact asserted, that no one was wiser than Socrates. When he was accused of the charges of impiety and corruption of youth, his friends came to him first pointing out how he could win acquittal and subsequently arranging for his escape. In response, in a moving and morally elevating series of discourses that have inspired readers throughout the ages, Socrates argued that it would be contrary to justice to engage in normal "courtroom" tactics or to escape from a state and a set of laws which he loved, to which he owed much, and to which he had sworn allegiance. He demanded and drank the cup of poisonous hemlock. And so he died one of the wisest, one of the most just, and one of the happiest of men.

M.W. Rowe has asked whether it is a merely contingent fact that the most famous practitioner of philosophy, Socrates, was a homosexual. Men who sometimes fell in love with their male students and were sometimes loved in return? Socrates clearly thinks that homosexuality and philosophical dialectic are internally related. At the beginning of the *Charmides,* he returns to Athens and inquiries about the 'present state of philosophy, and about the youth.' When the attractive Charmides is introduced, Socrates requests that he strip and show his soul by responding to questions before he reveals his naked body. In later dialogues, philosophy and youths remain intimately conjoined. In the *Gorgias,* Socrates describes himself as 'in love with two beloveds...of Alcibiades the son of Cleinias, and of philosophy; in the *Phaedrus,* the ban on returning to heaven within ten thousand years is waived for the 'man who has lived the philosophical life without guile or who has united his love for a boy with philosophy.'

The only place where he seems to suggest a reason for this conjunction is where he has Diotima argue that: "Those who procreancy is of the body turn to women as the object of their love and raise a family. But those whose procreancy is of the spirit rather than of the flesh conceive and bear the things of the spirit.' The clear implication being, in the context of the dialogue, that the latter turn to boys.

It may be possible to find better reasons for thinking that erotic attraction arises naturally from philosophical dialectic. Unlike writing a treatise or delivering a lecture, Socratic questioning has to be directed to an identifiable individual or individuals. The conversation that develops takes place over a protracted period of time, and the pupils are a great deal more involved in their task than the conventional reader or lecture audience. The pupils are part of the inquiry, they are not simply hearing a report of an inquiry, and this leads them to identify with their teacher and fellow pupils. As personnel manager knows, any joint task encourages unity and team spirit amongst the group undertaking it. However, the relationship can become closer than mere identification and team spirit suggests. Socratic questioning gets inside the interlocutor by bringing his own mind into operation, and thus the normal separation between the teacher's thought and the pupil's thought begins to disappear. The pupil finds his ideas subtly adjusted by his teacher's voice; the very act of thinking becomes collaboration and thoughts begun in one mind are finished in the other.

The intensity of emotion generated by the Socratic method enhances these feelings of oneness. Initially the pupil's soul is cramped and dreads philosophical conversation. During the conversation, because it involves mental action rather than simple receptivity, he will experience frustration, boredom and bafflement, and then, with luck, growing satisfaction and delight. At the end, ideally he should feel staggered bewitched, turned upside down. On seeing this, the teacher, who has been so closely involved in his pupil's mind, feels moved, pleased and excited by the pupil's responsiveness and wonder. This intensity of shared and novel emotion can only give rise to feelings of identification and gratitude; and this is fertile ground for erotic attraction.

Socratic conversation also demands a certain sincerity of utterance. Socrates insists you cannot just entertain a proposition in philosophical discussion, you have genuinely to assert it. This, of course, requires courage on the part of the speaker, and sympathy and understanding on the part of his hearers. Under the right conditions, however, it leads to an unusual degree of openness and trust. It would be strange to deny that love can begin in intense, protracted, personal and sincere conversation about the other person's mind, and perhaps it should be foreseeable that love can begin in philosophical conversations of this type.

As the mind of every pupil differs, the teacher must know each of his pupils' personalities well. Only then will he be able identify his pupil's temptations and work out the best route around his resistances. This of course means that there must be a personal as well as professional bond between master and pupil. In such circumstances, it is not altogether surprising that friendship and respect should become criticized. After all, Freud—who was engaged in a similar enterprise—thought it utterly natural that the patient should, at a certain point in his treatment fall in love with the therapist.

None of the foregoing suggests that philosophy is necessarily homosexual, but it may suggest that it is best conducted between people who are mutually attracted. The homosexual inflection of Socratic philosophy in 4th century Athens, may be due to social circumstances. Women in ancient Athens, unless they were courtesans or priestesses, were largely confined to the house, as Greece was thoroughly male-dominated society. Presumably Socrates talked to were young because they were students or not yet involved with careers. And they were upper-class, because those from other classes needed to work or could not afford higher education. These restrictions may well explain why the most effective practitioners of the Socratic method were homosexuals.

Socrates wrote nothing; he only talked. Our knowledge of his actions and ideas based on primarily in the writings of Plato, who had been his student and who went on to become one of the greatest philosophers of all time. Plato wrote dialogues, in almost all of which Socrates is the main speaker. Determining which ideas in the dialogues came from the historical Socrates and which came from Plato himself is referred to as "the Socratic problem." It is not a problem that has been resolved even today to the satisfaction of all scholars. Experts and scholars are generally agreed, however, that in the early dialogues, such as *Euthyphro*, *Apology*, *Protagoras* and *Crito*, and perhaps in the transitional *Meno*, Plato lets the character "Socrates" speak for the historical Socrates, expressing and defending beliefs that Socrates actually held. The so-called "middle dialogues," including the *Phaedo*, *Symposium*, and *Republic*, present Plato's own ideas even though the character "Socrates" continues to be their spokesperson but these ideas are not always clearly demarcated from those of Socrates. However in Plato's masterpiece, the *Republic*, the ideas are clearly his own, at least after the first book of this lengthy work.

The dialogues are artistic masterpieces, highly dramatic, beautifully written, engaging and enduring. Plato was not only a great artist but one of the greatest Greek prose writers. While we can and should appreciate his artistry, it does cause us difficulties in establishing the connection between the philosophical content of the dialogues and Plato's and Socrates' own views. Difficulties of interpretation often arise in the case of works having the form of dialogues, more so than with treatises. These difficulties are especially evident with regard to the actual thought of Socrates, as can be seen from the fact that subsequent philosophical schools equally claiming to follow Socrates – such as the Cyrenaics and Stoics – developed philosophies quite antithetical to one another.

In his youth, Socrates was taught by the scientist Archelaus. The latter was a pupil of the cosmologist Anaxagoras, and succeeded him when the older philosopher was forced to flee from Athens. Socrates duly became fascinated by scientific matters, and he recalls his interest in a lengthy autobiographical episode of the *Phaedo*. When he was young, he had an extraordinary passion for natural science. He was constantly veering to and fro, puzzling primarily over this of sort question. Then again, he would study celestial and terrestrial phenomena. However, Socrates later rejected the study of science and transferred his attention to the study of ethics and human action. Historically, this new subject matter and its new manner of treatment represented a radical departure from the way philosophy had previously been practiced. Socrates brought philosophy down from the sky and establish her in the towns and introduce her into homes and force her to investigate life, ethics, good and evil.

In the early Socratic dialogues, we find Socrates and his interlocutors attempting to arrive at definitions of important ethical concepts: 'friendship', 'temperance', 'courage', 'piety' and so no. The interlocutors produce putative definitions of these terms, and fictional counter-examples are produced to test their adequacy. The method is important because discovering a true definition of, for example, 'courage' could equally well be described as discovering what courage is. And the method is informative because one can know how to use a word in everyday contexts correctly, without being able to say that it is used in such and such a manner.

As Socrates' interest in science declined, his attitude to religion appears to have become more sympathetic. At his trial, Meletus accuses him of atheism and believing that the sun is a rock and the moon a clod of earth. Socrates rejects the charge, saying that his atheism may not have been quite so stupid or groundless as Meletus implies. He had been taught by a pupil of Anaxagoras, and had once conducted similar inquiries. It does not therefore seem unreasonable to assume that he had, in his youth, held similar religious views. Indeed, in the Aristophanes' *The Clouds*, performed in 423BC, he is shown teaching that Zeus has been dethroned by 'Vortex –motion' and swearing by a set of new deities including Chaos, Respiration and Aether. However, by the time of his trial he affirms that his belief in the standard Greek deities is even firmer than that of the man on the jury. While in the *Phaedrus*, he says that he is prepared to accept myths as he finds them: applying scientific standards of evidence to myths, he continues, is a fashionable waste of time, and only distracts us from the more important task of seeking self-knowledge. The mature Socrates could not be described as unequivocally religious, but he in later life, accepted and respected the religious life.

Knowledge of humanity has traditionally been the province of the arts, and one reason why scientific investigation may have lost its appeal for Socrates was because he had a strong artistic streak in his personality. In the *Phaedo,* Cebes says that he has heard that Socrates has composed some lyric poems while in prison. Socrates says this is true, and that during the course of his life he had a dream, which exhorted him to practice and cultivate the arts. Hitherto, Socrates says, he had thought he was doing just this, because he always thought philosophy the greatest of the arts. Since his trial, however, he had come to feel that perhaps the dream was referring to the popular conception of art, and he had therefore decided to put this new interpretation into practice by writing some poetry. According to Socrates' own report in the Menexenus he also studied music: 'I had Connus, the son of Metrobius as a master and he was my master in music'.

In the early part, Socrates lived in Athens, which was the capital of peaceful, secure and powerful empire. The hubris of this empire then provoked extended periods of warfare: the Peloponnesian War between Athens and Sparta from 431-404 BC. During the early years of hostilities, Socrates fought as frontline troops in defense of his empire but witnessed its destructions and saw a vast reduction in power. A similar view is asserted in even more brutal terms in the dialogue with the Malians just before the Athenian attack on Syracuse. It thus seems wholly understandable why Socrates felt true ethical values stood in urgent need of investigation and defense.

Once the war began, the moral crisis depended further. Commenting on events in 427 BC, Thucydides deplores the 'general deterioration of character throughout the Greek world' that had become all too obvious since the beginning of the conflict. Rivalry between democrats and oligarchs, he says, became increasingly violent, while love of power and love of pleasure became the dominant motives in all affairs. This corruption in politics and morals led to a new corruption of moral language: 'To fit with the change of events words, too, had to change their usual meanings.' Thus, aggression became 'courage', while moderation became 'unmanliness;. plotting and treachery grew synonymous with intelligence, while attempting to understand came to mean being unfitted for action. Considerations of justice and principle disappeared, and more interest was shown in 'those who could produce attractive arguments to justify some disgraceful action'. If the corruption of Athenian morals was sufficient to turn Socrates into the first moral philosopher, then the corruption of argument and language Thucydides diagnosed during the war must have confirmed the importance of his methods. For the rest of his life, using valid argument to arrive at a correct understanding of words like 'courage' and 'piety' would be Socrates' vocation.

War made Socrates philosophically aware of the human world. It also had an introverting effect on his personality. The first is that Socrates became preoccupied with the ethical life, but decided to take no part in politics. The second effect on his personality was that he became increasingly ascetic in outlook. Asceticism is clearly an intensely ethical form of life, and it is also a form of 'withdrawal'. The ascetic renounces any normal human desires and ambitions; he ceases to take part in the administration of his society; he no longer cares for its material goods; he lives in a certain place but he can live anywhere. It is a natural response to a society whose values and priorities have grown strange and alien. Consequently, Socrates gives the impression of a man who is subtly detached from the society around him; he has questioned its traditions, assumptions and values, and politely abstained from its most ardently pursued goals.

We do not know a great deal about Socrates; like Jesus, he wrote down nothing of his philosophy. What we do know about him comes primarily from Plato, his greatest student just as we know about Jesus from his followers who wrote the New Testament. The new testament of Greek philosophy is the Platonic dialogue, a series of dramatic confrontations that locates Socrates against a variety of protagonists, the most important of were a group of teachers known as the Sophists.

The Sophists were roving teachers who began to appear around the early fifth century BC. They went from city to city offering their services for a fee, and some of them, such as Gorgias and Protagoras were famous and eminent men. The Sophists taught young men from wealthy families who wanted to learn how to get ahead in life, and particularly those who wanted to learn how to get ahead in politics. Thus, the Sophists were the first political educators in Greece, and their teachings represented the first attempt to "philosophize" about politics, although it is not until Plato that we can speak in any real sense of a political philosophy.

Despite the fact that Socrates opposed the Sophists, they did have one thing in common. Both believed that the sixth century-philosophers' investigation of nature was leading nowhere and, more importantly, was not dealing with the significant questions. Even if it could be shown that the universe is composed of water or of atoms, or other substance, what difference would that make to human beings, they asked. For both the Sophists and Socrates the significant questions were questions of ethics: How should we live? What is important in life? What is the good life?

Of course, Socrates and the Sophists were aware of the earlier debate between being and becoming. The Sophists almost surely were influenced by Heraclitus. The link between Socrates and the pre-Socratics is more tenuous, but his greatest student, Plato, drew upon the work of such philosophers of being as Parmenides and Pythagoras. The point however, is that it was the concern with physical questions as such that Socrates and the Sophists rejected. They wanted to raise the ethical question of how human beings ought to live their lives.

Here we must briefly discuss what we mean by ethics. Ethics has to do with values that is, with whether or not an action or, more broadly, a way of life is good or evil, right or wrong. As such, ethical statements are immediately recognizable because they are always ought or should statements. "We ought not to commit murder" or "we should love our fellow human beings", are examples of such statements. When we make such assertions, we implicitly claim to have knowledge of what is right and what is wrong, what we ought or ought not to do.

There is another kind of statement we can make about reality based upon empirical observation is knowledge where attained by the senses. Such statements are is or are statements: "The earth is round," The flower is red," or "The material world is composed of atoms", are all empirical statements because they all assert knowledge attained either directly or indirectly through the senses. Modern science is an empirical discipline because it claims to deal with the world as perceived by the senses alone, with objects of knowledge that can be directly or indirectly observed. It is concerned with what is, not with what ought to be.

These distinctions between is and ought, empirical knowledge and normative knowledge as it is sometimes termed, are more clearly drawn in our own day than they were in Socrates' time. Our knowledge of these matters has expanded considerably since then. But we must bear in mind and this will become clearer as our analysis of Socrates ' philosophy proceeds, that Socrates did much to lay the basic framework of thought that eventually allowed these distinctions to be made.

It is important at this juncture to emphasize again that Socrates and the Sophists were interested in ethical or normative questions, not with the empirical questions that concerned the pre-Socratic physicists. And they realized, although again not as surely and consciously as we do today, that answering such questions required a way of thinking different from that needed to answer empirical questions of this variety. For in the case of ethical matters, whether we ought or ought not to do something depends upon the ends we wish to achieve. And in order to say that an end is good, we must first posit some ethical standard that establishes the validity of our end, goal, or objective. It is for reason that ethical questions always deal with ends. Empirical questions do not do this since they are concerned only with what in fact exists. In the broadest terms, all ethical questions deal with we ought to live our lives. All the ancient Greek thinkers including Socrates and the Sophists agreed that the ultimate end of human action should be happiness. Their disagreement was over the larger question: What is the human standard of happiness?

Even then, there was a superficial agreement. Both Socrates and the Sophists maintained that virtue which they both claimed to teach, ought to be the standard of happiness. They even agreed on the meaning of virtue in a general sense because it was a commonly used term. Virtue meant arête or excellence. Arête is related to the word aristocracy, which originally meant rule by the excellent. The Greeks employed this idea of virtue very broadly and comprehensively to describe a variety of human activities. They would say, for example, that the virtue of a shoemaker is his ability to know and use his materials to produce a fine product; the virtue of an athlete is his ability to use his body to its fullest potential. Thus, virtue presupposed some end and a standard of excellence. In other words, virtue or arête was the measure of a person's ability to perform well a specific function in life. And of course, the Greeks believed the ultimate end of virtue to be happiness. A shoemaker who cannot make good shoes or an athlete who cannot perform well will not be fulfilled, they would argue, and therefore will not be happy.

While the Greek idea of virtue is a standard of excellence, it does not appear from these examples to be strictly an ethical standard. But virtue does become an ethical standard when it is used to judge how human beings should live, not simply in narrow occupational terms, but in terms of the goodness or evilness of their lives. This is why Socrates came to insist that there is such a thing as moral excellence that will produce not simply the limited happiness of performing well a simple task, but the complete happiness of living life well.

More than anyone else, Socrates transformed virtue from a morally neutral term to one with moral connotations, because he discovered that being a good craftsman and being a good human being hold something in common. Socrates maintained unfortunately people that fail to recognize this shared quality. Thus, while they can easily agree about what constitutes virtue or excellence when it comes to making good shoes they cannot agree at all when it comes to the much more important matter of living a good life. In the first case, failure to know what virtue is simply means sore feet. In the second, it means an unhappy and unfulfilled life. That people should know how to make shoes and not know how to make their lives fulfilled is absurd and tragic, Socrates argued.

How then does Socrates define virtue, and how does his definition differ from that of the Sophists? Both definitions are at first sight, quite simple and quite understandable. This simplicity is deceptive, however, because behind the differing conceptions of virtue lie two profoundly contrary visions of society, and of politics. And here we must add yet another dimension to our discussion of ethics: ethical and political questions are intimately connected. Before Robinson Crusoe met his man Friday, he had a number of problems, but not ethical or political ones. People do not live as individuals on deserted islands however; they live among other human beings in political communities in which political decisions must be made. And political decisions involve questions of the ought variety: Ought we to make laws against abortion? Or ought we go to war? are typical political questions that directly affect people for good or evil.

The Sophists argued that virtue in general is the ability to acquire those things that people agree give pleasure- wealth, honor, status, and so on and that political virtue in particular is the ability to acquire these things by the successful use of power. If this seems a shocking definition of virtue, remember that virtue originally meant nothing more than the ability to attain a given end. If the end of politics is the acquisition of power as the Sophists belived, then the virtue of a politician is simply his ability to master the techniques of attaining it. Interestingly, the Sophists were the first teachers of rhetoric that is of the art of speaking well. They saw it as a most important technique for gaining power because it gave the politician the means to sway public opinion to his side. For this reason, the political education of the young men who came to the Sophists included lessons in rhetoric, and rhetoric was considered a prime component of political virtue.

The Sophists' definition of virtue clearly implies a particular conception of society and politics and a corresponding view of human nature. The Sophist view holds that society and the state are conventional, that they are nothing more than artificial arrangements created to serve limited purposes such as providing security and maintaining order. There is nothing natural about society and polity, the Sophists argued because human beings are not innately social creatures. They are rather individual egotists who are more concerned about themselves than about some larger social good. Behind the Sophists' philosophy of society and politics lay an individualistic and egotistical psychology or theory of human nature.

The conventionalist view of society and the state explains why the Sophists defined virtue as they did. Hence, the Sophists taught their students to use the social order to their own benefit. People are constrained by laws that are ethically meaningless, argued the Sophists.

Knowledge is not merely instrumental knowledge of how to attain power but a larger ethical knowledge of how we ought to live our lives. Just as we recognize that knowledge is required to exercise a craft, says Socrates, so too must we recognize that knowledge is required to learn the art - the arête of living an ethical life. This is why we find Socrates constantly making analogies between the good craftsman and the good man in his dispute with the Sophists.

The Socrates' trial was in fact a political trial aimed at preventing Socrates from continuing to teach his philosophy. When in the name of a higher duty to follow his philosophic conscience, Socrates refused to abide by the court's demand that he cease his teaching he was condemned to death. That Socrates chose to die rather than cease his teaching illuminates the real political meaning of his philosophical system. For Socrates death was a political act aimed at demonstrating that philosophy is not simply a set of ideas, but a way of life superior to that of politics, at least politics as conceived by the Sophists. The story of Socrates incarceration and death and the events leading up to it are told in several dialogues. One of these, the *Crito* best illustrates Socrates' position.

In this dialogue, Socrates friend Crito comes to his jail cell with a plan for escape. Socrates refused to flee, however, even though he knew that his sentence was utterly unjust. He based his refusal on the argument that the state had raised him back upon it. He owed obedience to it but only to a point. The state demanded that he stop teaching and he could not do that without violating his conscience. He could, however, affirm the right of the state to make laws and impose penalties by suffering the consequences of following his conscience.

We would today classify Socrates' decision as an act of civil disobedience. Civil disobedience is a political act that attempts to affirm the individual's conscience as the highest law yet at the same time recognizes the social necessity of civil law and order. This is accomplished by violating the law where it contradicts the urgings of conscience yet affirming the necessity of law by suffering willingly the consequences of one's acts. This was precisely Socrates' intent. In disobedience, Socrates had discovered a way to carry his philosophy into real life. By refusing to stop teaching, he affirmed the superiority of conscience and the philosophical life upon which it is based. By refusing to escape, he affirmed that the state is a natural and a necessary good even though specific laws and institutions may be only conventional, unjust and arbitrary.

Moreover, in choosing to die as he did, Socrates demonstrated the appropriate relationship between philosophy and politics. His teaching had been that the political sphere the state should be founded upon philosophical truths but in his own case the relationship seemed to Socrates to be breaking down. The men of thought and the men of action seemed to be of different minds. What to do? Given his situation Socrates only solution was to die. To live would be to concede that the commands of the state are superior to philosophical truth

There will be those who take exception to Socrates' reasoning, of couse It might be argued, for example, that if Socrates is correct in what he teaches, he is not correct whether he lives or not, and that had he chosen to live he could have had a continuing influence upon people. Crito made precisely these kinds of arguments, and others like him asked-What about your family, Socrates? –Your friends? but to no avail. Socrates refused to do the prudent thing, because prudence is not philosophical. Prudence demands action upon one's political judgment of the relative merits of a course of action. Philosophy demands to act strictly on the basis of truth, regardless of the consequences. This, at least, is what Socrates meant by philosophy. The philosopher must behave strictly according to knowledge of what is right and what is wrong. According to Socrates, if one knows, what is ethically correct, one cannot help but act accordingly, for no one would knowingly do something that produces unhappiness.

An epistemology is a theory of knowledge; it is a theory about what and how we can know. Every political theory, as with every other kind of theory, is based upon some kind of epistemology, if only implicitly. For it is impossible to assert knowledge about anything without first demonstrating that we know our knowledge to be a valid source of truth. This certainly is the case with Socrates whose epistemology is explicit and absolutely crucial to his whole philosophy of life. This is why the real dispute between Socrates and the Sophists is not simply over the purpose of life, but over how we know that we know that purpose. And this is why fundamental question here is epistemological: How does Socrates know that he has knowledge with such certainty that he is willing to die for it?

Socrates' answer is given in a number of dialogues, but it is best to begin with the *Apology*, the dialogue that deals with his trial and conviction. In this work, Socrates explains by way of a story the basis of his claim to possess knowledge or wisdom. A friend, he says, was told by the Oracle of Delphi that he, Socrates, is the wisest man in Greece. Now, Socrates did not believe that this was so and determined that if he could find someone wiser than himself he could refute the Oracle. "Accordingly," says Socrates "I went to one who had the reputation of wisdom and observed him - his name I need not mention, he was a politician." And I found, continues Socrates, that I was wiser than the politician, because " he knows nothing, and thinks that he knows; I neither know nor think that I know. In this one little point, I seem to have the advantage of him. "This same procedure, says Socrates, he followed with others, and the results were always the same. He found that he was wiser than others were because he alone seemed to know that he was ignorant.

Socrates' assertion that he is wiser than others "in this one little point " is not to be taken to mean that he believes knowledge is unattainable. It is simply that one must first admit ignorance in order to acquire knowledge. The ignorant who think they are wise are unreachable; those who know they are ignorant are willing to learn and in this Socratic sense, are already" wise."

It is of more than passing interest that Socrates initiates his experiment in wisdom with a politician. The politicians, like the Sophists, were not only the most arrogant in their ignorance, but the most dangerous. They were the teachers and leaders of society. Their ignorance, therefore, was a public concern. From the beginning, Socrates' theory of knowledge was, employed by himself and by his students in critiques of existing political practices. In such critiques, the ignorance of the Sophists and the leading politicians in Athens was demonstrated.

Meno

In the dialogue, Meno engages Socrates in a discussion about whether or not virtue can be taught. Socrates' response is at first perplexing, for he argues that it can neither be taught nor in the usual sense of the term, learned. It can however be drawn out, for knowledge of such matters is already within us. We need simply learn to know what we already know, a paradox that Socrates explains by way of a demonstration. He borrows one of Meno's slaves, a young boy who has had no formal education, and by a process of questioning gets him to discover for himself the Pythagorean theorem that the square of the hypotenuse of a right triangle is equal to the sum of the squares of the other two sides. Now Socrates asks, how could the boy have discovered the theorem without in some sense already knowing it? He had no mathematical training; there was nothing in his experience that could explain his knowledge. How, then, did he come by it except that he already knew it? And Socrates continues, what is true of mathematical knowledge is true of other branches of knowledge, including ethics. Just as the slave boy discovered for himself a principle of mathematics, in the same way we can discover for ourselves the principles of leading a good life. We need only look within ourselves.

Concealed in this simple analogy between mathematics and ethics is an epistemological discovery of momentous import in the development of Western thought. Socrates had discovered the concept, which is a generalized, abstract idea by which we classify and organize particular ideas about the world around us. For example, the slave boy in the Meno is able to recognize all three -sided polygons as triangles when he sees them. Socrates would argue, because he already has within him the concept -the generalized idea or ideal of "triangleness." In the same way, according to Socrates, people recognize courage, or temperance, or justice, or any other virtue because they have prior conceptual knowledge of what constitutes virtue. Philosophers would call this a priori knowledge.

It is this conceptual knowledge, that is already within us and because this knowledge is general and "ideal" it must be universal and unchanging. That is it must always be true, and it must be the same truth for all. There is one Pythagorean theorem, and it will be as true an infinite of tomorrows from now as it is today. In the same way, Socrates asserts, since ethical knowledge is also conceptual, it must be universally true and unchanging. It cannot be merely conventional as the Sophists claim.

It is clear that conceptual knowledge must be arrived at in a particular way. Since this knowledge is within us, it needs to be drawn out, it cannot be imposed. It does no good, Socrates would argue, to lecture to students about virtue. People already know what virtue is but must be helped to know that they know. This requires a form of questioning what the Greeks called the dialectic. Through dialectic the student's initial definition about what constitutes virtue is countered on the part of the teacher by critical questioning that demands a more inclusive definition. Seeing the inadequacy of a first opinion, the student will attempt to modify it in light of the teacher's questioning. The process continues until a definition is reached that is complete, inclusive, and genuinely conceptual. But it is the student who ultimately recognizes the inadequacy of the initial opinion and who, by the very logical structure of the mind, is forced to learn the truth. Thus Socrates' dialectical method of questioning is designed to tap this logical structure, not to impose the truth upon it.

The dialectic then is a method that begins with opinion and ends with knowledge. And herein lies a crucial distinction in Socrates' debate with the Sophists. For Socrates, opinion is the precise opposite of knowledge because it is not conceptual. Everyone has opinions, but the philosopher alone has knowledge, that is a conceptual grasp of the underlying order of things. He alone has an understanding of the nature of being, as opposed to that of becoming, which is in the realm of opinion.

Now it is Socrates' claim that the Sophists teach opinion, not knowledge. This is so, he argues, because they do not understand that opinion is simply ignorance masquerading as knowledge. And the reason they do not understand, Socrates insists, is that they have no concept of the concept. Hence, they never teach more than commonsense opinion about virtue. Their theory that virtue is pleasure is in reality an idea that has been accepted by every philistine throughout the ages. And the Sophists never go beyond this general and mistaken theory of virtue.

It is now clear why the Sophists taught rhetoric instead of dialectic. Rhetoric has to do with swaying public opinion not with the acquisition of genuine conceptual knowledge. The Sophists taught their students how to change people's opinions; Socrates taught his students how to rise above opinion. Clearly, the Sophists had the easier job of it. They only had to tell people that which they wanted to hear. Socrates taught what they should but would rather not hear. People do not willingly give up their opinions, as Socrates discovered. The dialectic works only if the student first commits to the quest for truth. Then and only then, will the logical structure of the mind come into play and the conceptual knowledge within emerge into full consciousness.

It is easy to see why classical thought, which begins with Socrates, was so easily absorbed by medieval Christianity. Socrates' moral universe could be construed as the mind of God, and his idea of inner knowledge could be seen as the illumination of God's divinity within the soul. In fact, Socrates believed something very much like this. His epistemology indicated to him the existence of God, of a soul, and of life after death and his belief in the immortality of the soul was linked to a theory of reincarnation. It seemed to Socrates that since knowledge is within us, we must have learned it somewhere in another life. Hence, he came to view learning as a recollection of that which we have forgotten in the process of being reborn.

Is this not ultimately Socrates' criticism of the Sophists? They recognize no order or purpose to anything, whether it be the universe, the state, or the individual. Hence, their idea of virtue where no ethical purpose or order exists reduces itself to a struggle for power and nothing more. But the other side of this inability to see order and purpose, Socrates maintained, is the Sophists' inability to understand the nature of knowledge. They have no concept of the concept. As a result, they have no conception of an inner order that would clue them to the existence of an outer order. And their political theories simply reflect this inability to conceptualize order. This is why they justify a politics of chaos, anarchy and disorder.

Socrates' insight into the nature of knowledge transformed Western consciousness. The central role accorded to reason in Western philosophy, and the idea that human institutions ought to reflect a larger rational order have become almost the sine qua non of Western thought we owe to Socrates. And while he was, from all we can surmise, a ceaseless critic of Athenian democracy, he never created a toughgoing political philosophy as an alternative to existing political practices. Ploto did. He picked up where his teacher left off. He united Socrates insights with those of pre-Socratic thinkers of being such as Pythagoras, who claimed that beneath everything we see is a prefect and unchangeable order. The result was not only great political philosophy, but the beginning of a tradition of political thought that extends to the present day.

Socrates is sometimes thought of as a man of the people but there is good evidence for supposing that his background was moderately wealthy. His father was an important stonemason at a period of extensive public building, and his son probably followed his father's trade. It was widely believed in the ancient world that Socrates was married twice: first to Myrto, daughter or grand daughter of Aristides and secondly to Xanthippe. The 'ipp' is in the aristocratic style, and many other names in his family imply aristocratic origins. This suggests that Socrates, like his father, was a successful member of the bourgeoisie, and that his wealth was sufficient to attract the attention of aristocratic fathers who wished their daughters to marry well.

Socrates always had ascetic tendencies. He went barefoot and wore the same old cloak in summer and winter, and his physical hardihood was the cause of comment during the Potidaea and Delium campaigns. However, the very fact he served as an infantry soldier to supply his own armor and weapons suggests that Socrates had a regular income, and work as a stonemason seems its mostly likely source.

The philosopher who perfected his asceticism by relinquishing his trade, came to rely on either his savings or the financial support of his friends. This later Socrates abjured "making money, having a comfortable home, high military or civil rank, and all the other activities, political appointments, party organizations. Even though he lived in poverty he refused to accept payment from his pupils. He prided himself on the simplicity of his way of life and used to say that those who want fewest things are closest to the Gods. Socrates' asceticism was reflected in his intellectual tastes, especially the hatred he shared with Plato for rhetoric and rhetoricians. The war and politics had shown all too clearly the damage that inflammatory language could do. Probably the most thoroughgoing attack is in the *Gorgias.*

Plato's image of the philosopher as midwife is the best known of the medical analogies for philosophy that thread their way through his works, but they can also be discovered in the Socratic dialogues. The idea of Socrates as mind doctor is a classical commonplace. Plutach, for example, remarks: 'Socrates used his negative critique as a kind of purgative medicine. Socrates' medical skill was not applied to the body; it was an antiseptic for a diseased and festering soul'. The reason for Socrates' shared medical imagery is that he aims at a healthy, integrated psyche. It is also the psyche of a real person, not an ideal reasoned who lacks the normal human portion of pride, prejudice, blindness, and faulty memory. This is why his techniques bear such a close relationship to psychoanalysis. At the beginning of philosophical inquiry the interlocutor's mind is in a state of cognitive dissonance; he does not know what he thinks he knows; he cannot make his implicit knowledge explicit; he has false beliefs about his beliefs. In exactly the same way, the psychoanalytic patient suffers from disharmony between his conscious and unconscious beliefs and desires. It is for the philosopher or analyst to resolve these intellectual tensions.

Because their aims are the same, their methods are similar; a talking cure is required. The Sophists placed great emphasis on rote learning and listening to lectures. Socrates, on the other hand, placed his faith in questioning, and in the power of questions to stimulate thought in the listener. What is original in Socrates' form of argument is not that he drew consequences from an interlocutor's position which eventually made the interlocutor want to revise or renounce his position. Socrates' originality lies in expecting the interlocutor, with suitable prompting to realize the implications of his own starting point, and therefore, its untenability himself. As in psychoanalysis and literary criticism, the interlocutor has to recognize the truth; merely being told what is true, or even the reason why it is true, is not good enough. Socrates connsidered philosophy as designed to relieve a certain kind of cognitive dissonance, and as well as guiding us from falsity to truth, it should lead us from pain and oppression to pleasure and enlightenment. In the *Apology,* Socrates says he is like the stinging gadfly; in the *Meno,* the eponymous questioner likens him to the numbing stingray. In the *Laches,* Niceas says that to enter into conversation with Socrates is to became a 'sufferer'.

Just as perplexity and the process of cure are deeply unpleasant so enlightenment brings jouissance and delight. The repetitious, open-ended, interrogative method—prompting people to self-knowledge—can generate a peculiar kind of intellectual excitement. The whole soul of man seems to be brought into activity. We do not merely register an answer or acquiesce to a piece of information. We are puzzled, we seek, we are disappointed, upset, and we retrace our steps and try again.

Enlightenment, when it comes, feels like a gift or revelation, and we feel grateful to and frequently amazed by the person who prompted us.

People tend to think the method is irrational, magical, illegitimate, and that the philosopher who practices it is some kind of magus or seducer. The parallel imagery witnesses the Socratic effect as very telling. The intoxicated Alcibiades opines: 'aren't you a piper…? I should think you were—and a far more wonderful piper than the satyr Marsyes who only had to put his flute to his lips to bewitch mankind. You can get just the same effect without any instrument at all—with nothing but a few simple words—not even poetry.'

Socrates rejected the model of the paid instructor the Sophists had developed, and he felt no inclination—as both Plato and Aristotle later did—to set up a formal school of his own. For the Socratic teacher, a formal pedagogic role is cramping or limiting. The success of the Socratic method does not only depend on the conscientiousness and cleverness of the teacher, but also on how sensitive he is to his pupils' personalities, and how responsive they are to him. It depends on tact, charm, insight, mutual liking and trust: it is thus impossible to draw a distinction between him and his role; between the professional and the personal. It is often a sign of Socratic success that the normal rules of engagement between teacher and pupil break down: they start to socialize together, meet outside of their institution, or outside of normal institutional times. They become more considerate or more fierce with one another than decorum usually allows. Education is not just part of the working day; it becomes woven into a whole manner of living. Accordingly, being a philosopher was not something Socrates did some of the time; it was something he was all the time; he lived exemplary philosophical life.

The extremely personal relationship the Socratic method requires means that there are other reasons it does not institutionalize easily. This divides students and colleagues into insiders and outsiders, disciples and skeptics, and provokes emotions which chafe against institutional notions of propriety. Equally awkward is the way the Socratic method sets out to question the beliefs, rules and authority on which all academic structures rely, and, for obvious reasons, it does not lend itself to syllabuses, timetables, lectures, lecture-notes and the standard institutional requirements. It is interesting that socrates avoided lecture halls, classrooms and other designated teaching spaces. Socrates liked friends' rooms or public space where friends could meet; this, not simply a role or job, but a natural extension of his personality.

Socrates saw difficulties with turning his philosophy into writing, and solved them by not doing any. Plato himself, despite being a copious writer, also felt equivocal about the written word, and gave a number of objections to the idea of written philosophy. In the *Phaedrus,* he remarks that the living, breathing philosopher can choose whom he speaks to; whereas a book can be read by anyone:

> Once a thing is put in writing, the composition, whatever it may be, drifts all over the place, getting into the hands not only of those who understand it but equally of those who have no business with it; it doesn't know how to address the right people, and not address the wrong. [But the] dialectician selects a soul of the right type and in it he plants and sows his words founded on knowledge.

In the *Seventh Letter*, Plato reports having heard that his former pupil, the tyrant Dionysius, is writing a book about Plato's philosophy. He then objects to the very idea of such a book in the follow way:

> Acquaintance with my philosophy must come rather after a long period of attendance on instruction in the subject itself and of close companionship, when suddenly, like a blaze kindled by a leaping spark; it is generated in the soul and at once becomes self-sustaining.

Plato's solution to these problems was to write in dialogue. Compared with living interlocutors and living speech, any form of philosophical writing must be frozen, calcified and inadequate, but it is evident that the dialogue—as a literary form—is slightly less inadequate than most other kinds of writing. It is by its nature social, and it is the form of writing that comes closest to spoken word. A dialogue can show how different interlocutors are to be treated and responded to; the interlocutor can demonstrate what intellectual sympathy is, and anticipate what readers would like to see explained or defended. Dialogue does not state its method but shows it; and the reader can learn by example. Also it does not merely present its conclusions and then run through the justifications; it develops the reader's acuity by allowing him to witness a process of thought. It presents many poor arguments, wrong turnings, digressions, and the reader has to select amongst these what he will take away. Consequently, truth will be something arrived at by the reader rather than something of which he is informed.

Socrates figures in the dialogues, especially the earlier ones, not primarily as a dogmatic philosopher but as a critic, eliciting opinions from his interlocutors and subjecting them to critical scrutiny, usually resulting in a refutation by showing the doctrine in question to be inconsistent with other propositions agreed by both parties to be true. This method of 'elenchus' has obvious affinities with the argumentative strategies employed and taught by the Sophists, and Plato is concerned to stress that in Socrates' hands it was intended not to produce victory in a debating contest, but to lead to genuine understanding by purging the person subjected to it of false beliefs. Philosophical inquiry conducted by this method is supposed to be not a contest between opponents (eristic), but a co-operative search for truth and understanding (dialectic).

Under the tyrannical regime which briefly ousted the democracy at the end of the Peloponnesian War, Socrates refused an order to participate in the arrest and subsequent death of an innocent man. Nonetheless, his association with notorious anti-democrats, especially Alcibiades and Plato's relatives Critias and Charmides, led to his accusation after the restoration of the democracy on vague charges of impiety and corruption of the young, and to his condemnation to death. The events of his trial and its aftermath are immortalized in three of Plato's works, the *Apology,* an idealized version of his defense at his trial, *Crito,* which gives his reasons for refusing to take the opportunity of escape from prison and subsequent exile, and *Phaedo,* a moving re-creation of his final hours, containing first a Platonic treatise on the philosophy of life, death, and immortality and then a depiction of the ideal philosophic death.

The average Athenian craftsman or tradesman could still remember for himself, or had heard from his elders about a man named Socrates who had been parodied in Aristophanes' comedy twenty years earlier. This was a man who studied everything on the earth's surface and all that was beneath it. He was a humorous charlatan, but he was also a dangerous corrupter of the young, giving them instructions on ways to deceive their creditors in court. Moreover, the old Socrates believed in some unknown gods—clouds perhaps, or thunder and storms. And he himself admitted to harboring inside his body something he called daemon, whose voice he unswervingly obeyed. If all that were not enough, the older generation remembered that at one time Alcibiades, Critias and Charmides had followed Socrates, proudly proclaiming to be his disciples. And everyone remembered the great harm Alcibiades and Critias inflicted upon Athens and how many innocent upstanding citizens were killed during the rule of the Thirty Tyrants. In light of all this, the threat Socrates faced was serious indeed.

The trial proceedings began in one of the ten divisions of juries, which was comprised of five thousand citizens and one thousand reserve jurors. There were five hundred men in the division trying Socrates' case. An odd number was needed, so one more juror was added before votes were to be cast. Socrates was to appear in court and conduct his own defence. The famous court orator Lysias offered his assistance and even wrote a speech for Socrates. But the old philosopher did not use Lysias' speech, though it was an accepted Athenian practice to ask an orator to prepare such speeches of defence, or as they were known in Greece, apologies. Socrates, however, was accustomed to speaking before people of various age groups, social position, wealth and education, and decided to convince the court of his innocence himself. Any Athenian citizen twenty years of age or older could sit in the court. The jurors were potters, weapon-makers, tailors, cooks ship-builders, coppersmiths, physicians, carpenters, tanners, small-scale traders and merchants, teachers, musicians, scribes, and many other people in Athenian society with whom Socrates had often spoken in the city's squares and markets.

Socrates was given the opportunity to speak after his accusers. However, a strict time limit was set for his apology, and a water clock, was placed in open view. Plato later sadly observed that there was much Socrates needed to say to answer the twenty-year-old accusations of Aristophanes and those that were being made by his present accusers. None of the accusations had any basis. As Socrates said, he had to deal with shadows and innuendos. But he well understood that those who were slandering him were either men whose insignificance and ignorance had been habitually disclosing for years, or naïve simpletons who were being influenced by rumors. During his speech, Socrates questioned Meletos in his usual ironic fashion; Meletos answered irrelevantly or did not answer at all.

Socrates, who had always tried to persuade people to seek virtue rather than fortune, conducted himself with dignity and asked for no condescension. He did not hope to arouse the pity of the jury with his poverty, old age or three children. He was certain of his righteousness, and stated that he would continue to teach the citizens of Athens in the future. He acknowledged that an oracle had proclaimed him to be the wisest of men, and that he listened to an inner voice, which restrained him from doing anything dishonourable. He stated that he had courageously resisted the tyranny of the Thirty, and that he had never given private lessons to any one person or taken money from anyone. As witnesses he called his friends: the elderly Criton and his son Critobulos, Aeschines of Sphetta and his father, Antiphon, Nicostratus, Apollodoros and his brother and Ariston's sons Adeimantus and Plato. Socrates did not ask the court to circumvent the truth or violate any oath; he merely sought justice.

After deliberating the case, the jurors brought back a guilty verdict. Some were irritated by Socrates' pride, by the fact that he did not weep before them and beg; others were intimidated by a man allegedly proclaimed by Apollo to be the wisest of all and one who listened to some kind of demonic inner voice; still others did not like Socrates equanimity, his steadfastness and confidence in his own righteousness. According to Plato, 221 votes were cast for Socrates, and 280 against him. He needed to win only 30 more votes, since a minimum of 251 out of the 501 jurors was necessary for exoneration.

In his written accusation Meletos demanded the death penalty for Socrates. But Athenian law stated that the defendant could suggest his own punishment. In his typically ironic manner, Socrates proposed that for an old man who had done so much to educate Athenian citizens, nothing would be so suitable as that he should be boarded free in the town hall, which he deserved more than anyone who had gained the prize at Olympia. The jurors were not amused by Socrates' mockery and voiced their indignation, as they had done several times before during his speech. But Socrates continued. He said he was prepared to pay a fine of one mina, for his entire property was approximately 5 minae. Socrates' friends Criton, Critobulos, Apollodorus and Plato were able to convince him to name a fine of 30 minae in order to placate the jurors. These were trustworthy men of some wealth, and they would see to it that the money was paid.

The court was not satisfied with the fine. The jurors were offended by Socrates' mockery, and this time when the votes were counted, 80 more men voted to sentence Socrates to death. Apollodoros wept and said: "But, Socrates, what I find it hardest to bear is that I see you being put to death unjustly." To which Socrates replied: "My beloved Apollodorus, was it your preference to see me put to death justly?" Before the final verdict was reached Plato tried to address the jurors. He mounted the platform and began: "Though I am the youngest men of Athens, of all who ever rose to address you, whereupon the judges shouted out, "Get down, Get down!". The court had no inclination to listen to the son of Ariston, a close relative of those who just recently headed the oligarchy.

Socrates was calm; he observed that nature had doomed him like everyone else to death from the day he was born. Moreover, death was a blessing, for it would give him the opportunity either to become nothing and feel nothing, or, if one were to believe in the afterlife, to meet the glorious wise men and heroes of old. Most important, he was prepared to seek out, even in hell, those who were really wise and who only claimed to be. Socrates accepted the decision of the Athenians, and left to their care his three sons that they might be guided down the path of virtue, just as he himself had guided his fellow-citizens. Before leaving the court he said:

"And now it is time to go, I to die, and you to live, but which of us goes to a better thing is unknown to all but God." Socrates predicted that those who had sentenced him would themselves be sentenced, and the younger the man, the harsher the sentence. Also, the injustices exposed would exceed those which Socrates had exposed. Those who punished Socrates would have to answer for their violation of justice, and the punishment they received would be harsher than the death to which they sentenced Socrates. According to legend, Socrates' prediction came true for his accusers. It is said that once the Athenians reflected upon what had happened, they drove these men out of the city, depriving them of "fire and water". The only thing they could do was hang themselves. Later generations wanted the murderers of Socrates to receive their just due, and so the legend was formed that Anytos the chief instigator of the deed and persecutor of Socrates, died an agonizing death by stoning.

But, at the time of his trial, what did Socrates care about the future legends about him? By the court's decision he was put in jail. Plato describes what happened. The sentence could not be carried out until the sacred delegation returned from its annual voyage to the island of Delos, the birthplace of the god Apollo. It was forbidden to put anyone to death while the delegation was on the island to honor the Athenian hero Theseus. Thus Socrates lived in prison for approximately a month awaiting his inevitable death. During this time his friends visited him daily. Criton tried to persuade him to flee far from Athens, perhaps to Thessaly, where he would be welcomed. Simmias and Cebes, well-known Pythagorean philosophers, were willing to help their friend by bribery if need be. Apparently, the jail-keepers were upset by the injustice of the court and therefore were less than diligent in guarding their prisoner.

Each day Socrates was visited by his loyal disciples. They would gather at the court, and, as soon as the jail opened, went in to see Socrates, spending the entire day with their teacher. Soon it was rumored that the ship was returning from Delos the next day. Criton now urged Socrates to make his decision, for everything had been prepared for his escape. But Socrates did not wish to flee. How, he exclaimed, could he leave the city of his birth, the city where he had grown up and been educated? And what about the ancestral laws? Could there be any forgiveness for him if he agreed to this cowardly act? And what would the people whom he had taught and enlightened think of him? No, it was better to meet death with dignity and to accept the evil done to him by his native city. One should never break the laws and customs and do evil in return for evil. In his heart, Socrates seemed to know what was right, and though he pitied old Criton he thought it best to wait for the ship with its sacred delegation to return to Athens.

The next day, when the ship returned, Socrates' friends gathered earlier than usual, wanting to prolong their last meeting with the philosopher. Present were Phaedo and Apollodorus, Critobulos and, his father, Hermogenes and Aeschines, Antisthenes and Menexenus, Epigenes and Ctesippus. Clombrotus and Aristippus were on the island of Aegina, and Plato was ill, evidently due to the strain of the events. But Simmias and Cebes came from Thebes, and Euclides and Terpsion arrived from Megara and there was another Phaedo. The Eleven jail wardens ordered that the death sentence be carried out that very day. Socrates was released from his fetters, which he had worn all the while he was in jail, and, sitting on his bed, he was happily massaging his leg. His wife, Xantippe, holding their youngest son in her arms, began to weep, and Socrates asked Criton to take her home.

Socrates calmly conversed with his friends about the immortality of the soul, the afterlife, and about how beautiful the real earth and sky seemed to him. He was certain that after drinking the hemlock that would kill him, he would enter a world of bliss. After making his ablution in the next room, he bid his children and relatives farewell and instructed that they be taken home. It was almost dusk when the Eleven sent in a servant to indicate that it was time for Socrates to die. A slave entered the room together with a man carrying a chalice with the poison. He instructed that after drinking the poison Socrates was to walk around the room until his legs felt stiff; then he was to lie on the bed and wait for the poison to work its way up to his heart. Socrates took the chalice in his hands and drank its contents. His friends who were present sobbed, especially Apollodorus, who cried as it his heart would break. Yet Socrates put them all to shame with his composure, remarking that death should occur in decent silence.

At first he walked around the room, then he lay down on the bed, now not feeling the hand of the servant who cautiously touched his increasingly numb body. Suddenly, as the deathly cold crept closer to his heart, he uttered his last words: "Criton, we owe a cock to Asclepius, pay it without fail." "That indeed shall be done, said Criton. "Have you anything more to say?" But there was no answer. Socrates was still. Criton closed his eyes and mouth. Socrates believed that in dying he was renewed; his soul would return to eternity, freed of earthly pain and misery. This was why his last words concerned the sacrifice of a cock to Asclepius, the god of health.

The Craft of Living

In discussing knowledge and happiness, Socrates frequently appeals to what scholars call his "craft analogy." Individuals who have mastered a craft possess a knowledge both of the ends of their activity and the means to achieving them. A shoemaker knows what a good shoe is, and how to make one. A horse breeder knows what kind of equestrian offspring is desirable, and how to breed horses in order to obtain this result. The captain of a ship knows the ends and means of sailing, and so on. In the case of a craft, there is an end product that is determinate and clearly defined; and there are agreed-upon procedures for obtaining this end product. No one disputes what being a good shoemaker or horse breeder is. For Socrates, living well or successfully requires that we see the activity of living as a craft, the end product of which is happiness. The procedures for attaining it are what he calls virtues, these being the modes of excellence, or excellent functioning of the various states and activities that make up a human person, both in body and soul.

At this point, we should take note of one way in which Socrates' thought rejects the popular Greek morality of his time. Ordinary Greek citizens frequently talked of virtue and identified five basic virtues: temperance, piety, courage, justice, and wisdom. Socrates agreed that these are virtues; much of his philosophical activity was aimed at trying to understand exactly what they are. In our discussion of the Euthyphro, we found Socrates and his friend discussing the question "What is piety?" and other dialogues deal with the virtues of courage and temperance in the same fashion. Most of the early dialogues consist of attempts to arrive at a definition of the virtue under discussion, as an account or identification of what all instances of it have in common and hence what can serve as a criterion or standard for saying that something is, or that someone has, this virtue. In these dialogues, Socrates wants to show several things about the virtues, one of which is the most people do not have a clear grasp of their nature. That their failure is worrisome results from the fact that, as the person in the street also vaguely realizes, each of the virtues is no more than a form of excellence, something of which everyone approves. Courage, for instance, is an excellence of behavior with respect to feelings of fear; temperance an excellence of behavior with respect to our appetites. What Socrates' friends do not fully realize is that these virtues are required for the attainment of happiness, and hence that practicing them is part of the craft of living a successful life. Most people, on the contrary, have picked up only superficial conceptions of the virtues that make up the common-sense morality of the society. Socrates' task is, first, to show them that these conceptions are inadequate and, second, to convince them that the virtuous life is the life that is required for happiness. His task is to demonstrate that the virtues, properly understood, are the tools or procedures of the craftsman's trade when the craft itself is life.

The Gadfly's Ignorance

But to succeed at this task of educating his fellow citizens, Socrates must first disabuse them of their conviction that they already know all there is to know about these matters. It is in this context that we find him making his famous claim in the *Apology* that he himself is unaware of having any wisdom – great or small. At his trial, as reported in the *Apology*, he tells the story of how his friend Chaerephon visited the Oracle of Delphi and the Oracle answered affirmatively that Socrates was the wise man. Socrates was astonished at this announcement, and he claims to have searched far and wide to see if he could refute the oracle by finding a person wiser than himself. But his search, he tells the trial judges, was unsuccessful. After approaching one reputedly wise person after another, conversations with them proved that they were not really wise at all but only thought they knew much. "I am wiser than this man; it is likely that neither of us knows anything worthwhile, but he thinks he knows something when he does not, whereas when I do not know, neither do I think I know what I do not know". Thus, Socrates concludes that insofar as he is conscious of his own ignorance, while the "wise men" think wrongly that they know a great deal, perhaps, he is in fact the wisest of the lot. As he says regarding any knowledge of the afterlife, "It is perhaps on this point and in this respect, gentlemen, that I differ from the majority of men, and if I were to claim that I am wiser than anyone in anything, it would be in this, that, as I have no adequate knowledge of things in the underworld, so I do not think I have".

Socrates himself never claims to have mastered the craft of living. After reducing his interlocutors to inconsistency and a state of confusion about particular virtues, he stops short of demonstrating the nature of these virtues. His primary aim is to show, through the practice of the 'elenchus' (cross-examination, the art of refutation), that others, in spite of their pretensions, fail to understand this craft of living. Such a philosophical demonstration is the service he as "gadfly" provides his fellow Athenians; he shows them their ignorance and thereby sets them on the path to self-knowledge. But doing so he remains faithful to his own claim to ignorance – although, some commentators think, without perfect consistency.

Virtue as Knowledge

Although Socrates seldom provides a positive account of any of the virtues, he does affirm and argue for several general propositions about virtue and human nature. Included among these propositions are those commonly referred to as the "Socratic paradoxes." The paradoxes certainly challenge us to think more deeply about human nature and action, so that whatever the final judgment as to their truth or falsity, they perform the Socratic "gadfly" function of pulling us to short and forcing us to reexamine some of our common-sense beliefs about morality.

Knowledge then, is a necessary condition of any activity being beneficial, since without knowledge an activity may turn out to be harmful. Virtue, it is agreed, is good, and beneficial. Since knowledge alone is always beneficial, virtue is knowledge. In claiming that virtue is knowledge, Socrates appears to be saying not only that knowledge is a necessary condition of virtue, something one must have in order to be virtuous, but also that knowledge is the very essence of virtue, that is, a necessary and sufficient condition of it. If one has knowledge, one will be virtuous; knowledge is all that is required. Such a strong thesis appears very dubious. It seems to fly in the face of our common-sense conviction that many knowledgeable individuals are not virtuous at all but on the contrary are scoundrels and criminals. Socrates' claim that virtue is knowledge, when knowledge is understood as a necessary and sufficient condition of virtue, is therefore a paradox.

The Unity of the Virtues

The equation of virtue and knowledge suggests that there really is only one virtue, or that all of the virtues normally distinguished are in fact one, namely knowledge or wisdom. Thus, we are led to the second Socratic paradox, the thesis of the unity of the virtues.

How can all the virtues be one? Can they be identical – courage, for instance, being the same virtue as temperance? Socrates himself, in seeking definitions of the various virtues, certainly suggests that these definitions, and hence these virtues, are quite different; he would not, for example, accept a plausible definition of courage – "knowledge of the fearful and the hopeful in war and in every other situation" – as the definition of justice, or as the definition of any of the other traditional virtues. In what sense, then, are the virtues one? Many commentators have found Socrates' thesis of the unity of the virtues so bizarre that they have in fact dismissed it.

Once again, the key to understanding such a claim is the emphasis Socrates places on the virtue of wisdom. All of the virtues, he maintains, are parts of wisdom. We have seen how knowledge is a necessary condition of any particular virtue;

one cannot be temperate without being wise, i.e., without curbing one's desires by the use of reason; one cannot be courageous without being wise, since knowledge what to fear and what not is clearly a form of wisdom. It follows that a courageous person cannot be foolish, a just person cannot be foolish, and likewise for all of the virtues. As Socrates puts it, folly is the opposite of both courage and temperance He then argues that two different things cannot have the same opposite, and he concludes from this claim that all of the virtues (courage, temperance, piety, justice, and wisdom) are the same, having as they do the same opposite, folly. Socrates' logic may be a bit shaky in this argument, but his line of thought clearly shows that he wishes to place all virtuous persons in one class, the class of individuals who are not foolish (lacking in wisdom). Thus if an individual person does not fall into the class of foolish persons, he will therefore be in the class of individuals who are courageous, temperate, pious, just, and – of course – wise. Thus, having one of the virtues, he will have them all.

No Harm Comes to the Just Person

Finally, let us turn to the last of the Socratic paradoxes, the claim that no harm can come to a good and just person. Unfortunately, this too seems to fly in the face of experience. How many decent, in many cases, noble individuals have been brought down by the powers of corruption and conspiring. Take the case of Socrates himself; he was condemmed by the Athenians on charges that contained little truth, having initially been brought to trial as the likely result of the resentment, felt toward him by individuals who had been "shown up" by his elenctic investigations. Here is a man who is good, decent, and just, but one who is being harmed in the extreme by unjust fellow citizens. Doesn't the case of Socrates refute his own theory?

Socrates certainly didn't think so. He maintained to the end that he was not being harmed by his accusers or by the verdict of the jury. Not only was he already old and likely to die soon anyway, death would only provide him with an occasion to answer some question which, as a philosopher, it was his business to answer. Furthermore, death was either a transition to an eternal life with the gods, which couldn't be very unpleasant, or an eternal dreamless sleep, which, if his previous experience held up, was one of the most important, however, Socrates claims to be happy because, throughout his life and then at his trial, he has always done his best to be a good and just person. He has obeyed his divine "sign" when it told him not to do certain things. He has honored the gods and served his city. He has led a life of virtue and for this reason he is a happy man. Nothing is more important than this. The virtuous person is the happy person, simply because he is virtuous, and no enemy arrows or fateful catastrophes can destroy such happiness. No harm can come to the virtuous individual.

Socrates clearly implies that the reverse of this proposition is also true; no happiness can come to an unjust man, to one who is not virtuous. Those who pursue a life of injustice may pile up riches and honors and enjoy abundant pleasures, but these do not make a happy life. The Greeks believed that virtue and excellence were the same thing, and that to live an excellent life is therefore to live a virtuous one. The excellent life is the one best suited to the attainment of the end of life, and it is agreed by all that this end is happiness. Hence it follows that the virtuous and just man, but not the unjust, is happy; the temperate, but not the profligate; the wise, but not the foolish. All of these virtues are simply specific manifestations of the knowledge of what is good and what is bad. The virtuous person is the one who knows what is good, and, knowing this, pursues the good and avoids the bad. In doing so, the virtuous person attains the end of his craft, the life of happiness. The person lacking virtue, on the contrary, acts from ignorance of good and bad. Not knowing the good, mistaking something else for it, he fails to pursue the good. And this amounts to his failure to obtain happiness, since the good is nothing more than happiness. The wrongdoer is therefore the miserable person.

Seen in this fashion, Socrates' thought ought to be remarkably consistent. Once we understand the nature of human action, as reflected in the so-called paradoxes, we shall see that the moral life is rationally justified. Any rational person, therefore, will lad a life of virtue and avoid a life of vice – ad thereby achieve happiness.

Socrates' ethical thinking was a response in large measure to ideas about morality that were prevalent in fifth-century Greece. Among these ideas were, in the first place, the concepts informing the popular culture, most of which came from the still influential Homeric myths. These myths, derived from Homer's eighth-century poems *The Iliad* and *The Odyssey*, perpetuated the cult of the hero, for whom personal honor and self-aggrandizement were the highest values. Secondly, in fifth-century Athens, ideas about morality emerged from political developments in Greece, ideas particularly about the rule of law and justice. These political/moral notions became particularly influential with the development of an early form of democratic government in Athens. Indirectly such ideas had flourished in the work of the pre-Socratic philosophers of nature such as Anaximander and Empedocles. They rejected the idea that human destiny was controlled by the whimsical and capricious decisions of the Olympian gods. They interpreted events in terms of an all-encompassing rational and intelligible order of nature. This philosophical development led to the notion that there might be a rational order of values as well. Finally, fifth-century Athens had a group of thinkers called the Sophists. They forcefully challenged the traditional Greek morality, taught techniques for political success within the Greek city-states. Practicality, success, and adaptability were central values for most of the Sophists, although the clacm of some of them that virtue can be taught led to the idea that there can be rational ethical discussions. Other Sophists preached a more radical doctrine praising immorality and self-indulgence. They rejected conventional morality by arguing that it is no more than a false story designed, in the interest of those holding power, to mislead the masses about the facts of human nature and conduct. In Socrates' eyes, both the conservative emphasis on success and conformity and the radical sophistic call to individual willfulness were dangerous. They constituted alternatives to true morality and threatened to undermine it.

Socrates' thought must be grasped in relation to all three of the above developments. First, he set out to repudiate some of the essential ingredients of Homeric morality. Second, he sought to describe the nature of true morality as a rational enterprise. And third, he mounted a defense of morality – morality as it ought to be understood against the influence and arguments of the Sophists. These challenges will give us a glimpse of Socrates' style and his famous devotion to reason. The first concerns the relationship between the gods and morality; the second, the issue of vengeance.

In the early dialogue *Euthyphro,* Socrates is engaged in a discussion with Euthyphro, a religious seer, about the nature of piety or godliness. Euthyphro is in the process of prosecuting his father for murder – on the grounds that his father tied up a house slave and left him out in the cold, with the result that the man soon died. In prosecuting his father, Euthyphro considers himself to be doing what is pious, and Socrates wants to know why he thinks this – especially in light of the fact that the bond between father and son was particularly important in the morality of the time, so much so that Euthyphro's act would be seen as highly questionable by most people. What, in other words, are the characteristics found in all pious actions by virtue of which they are pious and as a result of which they differ from all things that are impious. This is an example of Socrates' famous " What is it?" question: a demand for a definition of the subject matter under discussion and a question he thinks we must be able to answer if we are to know what we are talking about.

One of Euthyphro's attempts to comply with Socrates' request is as follows : "Well, then", he replies, "what is dear to the gods is pious, and what is not is impious". Socrates immediately points out that the gods often differ and disagree with one another. Given this fact, it follows that what is dear to or pleases one god often displeases another. Thus Euthyphro's definition would lead to the absurd conclusion that some things are both pious and impious – pious by virtue of being dear to some of the gods, and impious by virtue of being displeasing to others. But it cannot be the case that one and the same thing is both pious and impious. Such a state of affairs would be self-contradictory and therefore irrational.

When Euthyphro corrects his definition of the pious and states that it is what all the gods love, Socrates pursues the discussion by raising another famous question: "Is the pious loved by the gods because it is pious, or is it pious because it is loved by the gods." In order to answer this question, he inquires whether something's "being loved by the gods" results from the fact that the gods love it, or whether, on the contrary, they love it because it is loved. The latter option is an odd. Therefore, Euthyphro and Socrates agree that the gods love certain actions because those actions are pious; they are not pious because the gods love them. Piety has an objective nature independent of how it may be perceived or experienced. The god's love of a pious act is simply their response to the fact that this act has the essential properties that make an act pious.

Socrates continues to press for a definition of piety, understood now as the essential characteristic of pious actions by virtue of which the gods love them. Unfortunately; Euthyphro is unable to provide such an definition, and the dialogue ends with the religious spokesman in a state of confusion. Socrates then draws the telling moral : if Euthyphro had no clear knolwedge of piety and impiety, you would never have ventured to prosecute your old father for murder on behalf of a servant". Faced with such a predicament, Euthyphro takes quick leave of Socrates, saying that he will inform him of the nature of piety on another occasion. At this point the dialogue ends.

Socrates has raised a question in the *Euthyphro* that many of us might profitably ask even today. Is an action right because God commands it, or does he command it because it is right? Many believers in the Christian, Jewish, and Muslim traditions think God is the source of right and wrong, and one way of expressing this view is to see it as a version of the position rejected by Socrates : an act becomes right as a result of God's commanding it. Such a "divine-command" theory of ethics entails that such a thing, an act is right simply because God commands it. Anything he commands thereby becomes right, even if it is murder, rape, or theft ! Such a notion of God and rightness gives us pause, and becomes a problematic.

Socrates' secular temperament suggest becomes that moral truths are independent of God, and that if an all-good God commands an act, it is because the act is itself right or obligatory. From which it would follow, that God commands an act because it is right; it is not right because God commands it. God should have a reason for what he commands, and the very best reason is that he knows that act he commands is, in accordance with morality, objectively right.

A person who raises questions like the above may easily by regarded with suspicion – and perhaps seen as undermining the belief in the gods or God. In fact, Socrates was a religious believer although not necessarily a believer in the traditional Greek gods; he was not the atheist he was accused of during his trial. He worshiped the gods and lived a life of piety. At the same time, he considered it his duty to provide the most rational interpretation possible of the gods. It is inconsistent, he maintained, to think of the gods as the most perfect being and also to view them– as most Greeks did – as acting capriciously or immorally.

Another disagreement Socrates had with the longstanding popular morality of the Greek people relates to the issue of vengeance. Most Greeks simply took it for granted that if a person harms you, you should harm that person in return. Indeed, a favorite conception of justice, one which Socrates wished to rebut, was that it consists in helping your friends and harming your enemies. Socrates disagreed vigorously and is the first major figure in Western philosophy to do so.

His argument against vengeance is found in the dialogue *Crito*. Early in this dialogue he obtains agreement from Crito that, just as some things harm the body and make it "corrupted," so injustice harms the "higher part of man" – the soul – while justice "improves" or benefits it.

Crito agrees that the "health" of the soul in which right and wrong operate is just as important as the health of the body. Socrates and Crito then agree that "the most important thing is not life, but the good life", and Socrates is also able to gain Crito's assent to the proposition that the good life is the same as the just life. It follows from these agreements that "wrongdoing is in every way harmful and shameful to the wrongdoer". Crito is led to accept Socrates' conclusion that one should never do wrong in return, nor injure any man, whatever injury one has suffered at his hands. Vengeance, in other words, is always wrong: the age-old doctrine of an eye for an eye must be rejected.

The repudiation of vengeance gives us a good example of Socrates' moral methodology. He starts from an assumption that many of his fellow Athenians would accept – the goodness of justice. He then interprets this goodness as a benefit to the soul, with the corollary that injustice is harmful to the soul. Insofar as an act of vengeance involves harming others, it is a case of wrongdoing. Such an act is harmful even to the soul of the perpetrator of vengeance. Thus, contrary to popular opinion, vengeance is wrong. Common morality is inconsistent in approving vengeance and at the same time applauding the goodness of justice. A more rational morality would repudiate vengeance.

"The unexamined life is not worth living for a human being." Nowhere else in Western literature has the call to ethical inquiry and philosophical reflection been expressed more forcefully. According to Socrates, not to reflect on the question of how to live one's life amounts to living a worthless life, and, as he also argues, an unhappy one. Unfortunately, most people spend little if any time examining their lives. All of us enter a world populated by other people and dominated by society. Our parents, our relatives and neighbors, and our fellow citizens constantly tell us what to do, what to seek, how to run our lives. And so, in spite of the usual teenage rebellion, we normally grow up accepting the ideas of the society we inherit. Almost without exception, we emerge from our early period of socialization unhesitatingly and unreflectively subscribing to these ideals. In short, most of us live our lives in conformity to our society and culture. This is the kind of unexamined life that Socrates deems unworthy of a human being. Why?

Because few of us in such a condition pay any attention to our character or our spiritual life – what Socrates calls our soul. For the most part, we seek pleasure, wealth, or fame, but we are seldom aware of precisely what motivates us and we seldom question the direction of our lives or make deeply informed choices about our goals. We are simply pushed and pulled by social pressures and by our own inchoate and impetuous desires. Although we may think otherwise, we are hardly in control of ourselves. Such an unexamined life, according to Socrates, is a sure recipe for disaster; it leads inevitably to unhappiness.

Although Socrates was a religious person, he did not accept the religious conception of an afterlife, but it is uncertain whether or not Socrates believed in immortality. Death, he claimed in the *Apology*; is one of two possibilities: (a) a transition to life in another world, or (b) eternal sleep – and he appears to accept the second option as being just as likely as the first. The soul for Socrates, and for most Greeks and Greek philosophers, is the animated "part" of a person that feels, desires, suffers, thinks, and acts. It is more than one's body, to be sure, but not something that is necessarily independent of one's body. Our soul is the locus of happiness or, unhappiness, and because our happiness is supremely valuable to us, we must tend to this soul. Tending to it requires knowing it. The motto inscribed over the entrance to the temple of Apollo admonished each of those who entered to "Know Thyself," The person who lives the examined life is the one who knows himself.

3

Plato

> I was forced in fact, to the belief that the only hope of finding justice for society or for the individual lay in true philosophy, and that mankind will have no respite from trouble until either real philosophers gain political power or politicians become by some miracle true philosophers.

Plato (427BC-347BC) was born in 427 BC in Athens which had already been engaged in the Peloponnesian War with Sparta for thirty years. Pericles, the great aristocratic leader of the Athenian democracy, had died the previous year. Plato therefore grew up in interesting times, and he came of age while the war was ending disastrously for Athens with the humiliation of a Spartan garrison on the Acropolis and some vicious political infighting between the oligarchic and democratic factions for control of the city's politics.

By family connections, Plato seemed destined for a political career. His father, Ariston claimed descent from Codrus, the legendary last king of Athens. The family of Perictione, his mother was connected with Solon, one of Athens greatest statesmen, and contained two of the Thirty Tyrants, Critias, her cousin, and Charimides, her brother. Both of them were killed in the fighting in 403 when the democracy regained power. But despite their bad end, Plato apparently took pride in Critias and Charmides.

As he stood on the sidelines, Plato's political interests found expression in his writings. Though politics and political theory are not the only concern of the dialogues, they are an important concern at all stages of his career, most clearly in such works as the *Gorgias, Republic, Statesman* and *Laws*. In addition, Plato made three voyages to Sicily, in the hope of converting the tyrants of Syracuse, Dionysius I, and later his son Dionysius II, to philosophy. These attempts failed, but Plato was closely associated with Dion, who in 357 successfully invaded and took control of Syracuse—for a time. Finally, Plato opened the Academy, which was intended as a training ground for future statesmen and advisers of rulers. Several of Plato's students did manage to achieve positions as advisers to rulers or teachers of future rulers, the most important of whom was Aristotle, who became tutor to the young Alexander of Macedon.

Plato had family connections with both the oligarchic and democratic parties, as a well-born youth with a connection in both camps, it was natural for him to consider a political career. The politics of a city at war was no doubt the staple of conversation in his youth. Contemporary witness suggests that the Athenian democracy changed its nature as the war went on. Pericles took Athens and her allies into the war because he thought Athens had no option, and his control of the popular assembly meant that he could confine Athenian strategy and expenditure within the bounds of the possible. After Pericles, the Athenian assembly began to listen to ill-bred demagogues who were willing to tell the assembly only what it wanted to hear. Athens became less cautious in its policy towards its own allies, whom it began to treat as part of an Athenian empire, and much less cautious in strategy, which eventually led to the debacle of the expedition to take Syracuse. The rich saw themselves as being bled while to pay for a badly conducted democratic war, while their democratic enemies began to suspect that the oligarchs might be moving towards defeatism because victory against aristocratic Sparta would be a victory for the Athenian demos, and its leaders.

The last years of the Peloponnesian War were years of bitter party strife in Athens, oligarchy alternating with democracy, but the problem was virtually impossible to solve while the Athenian army consisted of the better-off hoplites and the equally important navy relied on the poor for its manpower as rowers. Athens lost the war, and an oligarchic government of the Thirty came to power partly with the help of Spartan arms. The government of the Thirty was vicious to its democratic enemies but it did not last long, democracy being quickly restored. In 399 it executed Plato's mentor, Socrates, on a charge of impiety and corrupting the young, and this despite a famous pronouncement by the Delphic Oracle that Socrates was the wisest man in Greece.

The political experience of the Athens of his youth and early manhood appears to have sickened Plato. Plato is reported to save said spuriously in the autobiographical *Seventh Letter*, 'I was forced, in fact to the belief that the only hope of finding justice for society or for the individual lay in true philosophy, and that mankind will have no respite from trouble until either real philosophers gain political power or politicians become by some miracle true philosophers.' Plato traveled widely after the death of Socrates; made an unsuccessful attempt to convert a tyrant of Syracuse into a philosopher-ruler, and eventually founded the Academy in Athens in 386 where he taught for the rest of his life. He died in 347 BC.

According to legend, Plato died on the day of his birth, the day of the birth of Apollo. He left a very modest will, instructing that his nephew Speusippus and six other executors fulfill his last wishes. During the course of his long life Plato had acquired two estates. One he left to his kinsman Adeimantus and the other to his friends. As for valuables, he had only 3 minae in money, two silver goblets, a gold signet ring and a gold earring. He left four slaves and instructed that the female slave Artemis be freed. The words, "I owe no one anything," were also affixed to his will.

Plato was buried on the grounds of the Academy; no other place on earth was dearer to him. The philosopher was right in saying that the yearning for glory was the last vestment we cast off in dying. Mithradates, a Persian king, placed a statue of Plato in the Academy with the inscription: "Mithradates the Persian, the son of Ornobates, dedicated to Muses a likeness of Plato made by Silanion." The Athenians erected a statue to Plato not far from the Academy.

Besides the *Republic* Plato wrote two other books on politics, *The Statesman* and *The Laws* which are considered to be an account of Plato's second best state. His famous account of a drinking party, *The Symposium*, celebrates homosexual love in a way once thought to be mildly scandalous.

History and Social Structure

It was not until the fifth century BC. that anything like a historical record of events was written down by the Greeks. Herodotus, the first historian, born about in 490 BC, surveyed the history and ethnography of many parts of Asia, as well as Egypt, Libya, and southern Russia. In the first part of his history he traced the growth of the Persian Empire and the development of Greece from the middle of the sixth century BC.–although the latter was accomplished quite unsystematically. In the second part of his work, Herodotus provided an account of the Greco-Persian wars from the Ionian revolt of 499 BC. to the repulsion of Xerxes' invasion of Greece in 479BC.

The second pioneer Greek historian was Thucydides, an upper class Athenian intellectual born 460 BC. It is to him that we have our knowledge about the first twenty years of the Peloponnesian war between Sparta and Athens. As we read Thucydides, we sense throughout that he tries to be objective by carefully sifting reports from any sides. He is concerned with causes and consequences, and he effectively conveys the temper of the times by means of elaborately composed speeches delivered, presumably, by leading historical individuals. For the remaining years of the Peloponnesian War, we rely on a rather selective historical account by Xenlophone, another Athenian. These histories, together with the surviving comedies of the playwright, Aristophanes, various inscriptions which the Athenian state engraved on stone, and a sprinkling of inscriptions from other cities, enables us to be reasonably well informed about Greece during the fifth and fourth centuries BC.

By the end of the eighth century BC. the primitive Greek monarchy depicted in the Homeric epics was no more. Although there remained some hereditary kings who held office for life, they were actually little more than magistrates with limited authority. Most often kings reduced to magistrates no longer held their positions for life. The hereditary privilege was removed from the family in which it had originally resided, and magistracy became an annual office open to the families of the ruling nobility. At the same time the king's role was reduced and restricted to sacred functions. In Athens, for instance, the king was only one of nine archons (chief magistrate), and his sole responsibility was to oversee and administer the cultic ceremonies.

The weakening and gradual breakdown of the primitive monarchy turned to the advantage of the powerful noble chiefs who had been working toward that end for some time. It was they who now became the masters of the city-states (polis) and remained so for centuries. Tracing their origin to some deity and taking immense pride in their noble blood, these chiefs carefully preserved their genealogical tree and the traditional history of their house. They belonged to illustrious families and clans who controlled land and revenues from sizable domains and who enjoyed the riches won at the point of the sword over many generations.

In the seventh century BC however, the expansion of commerce, and with it mining, manufacturing, and ship-building, brought about significant social and political changes. Money increasingly replaced the old natural economy. The large, noble land-owners, who were used to taking the lion's share of the booty through raids on land and piracy at sea, were advantageously situated to gain from the new commercial developments. They owned and controlled fields, forests, vineyards, olive groves, mines, and quarries. They built ships, made forays into foreign lands, and, through trade or piracy, brought back wealth in many forms. In this way, the noble aristocracy changed its character. It was money and not only landed wealth that now gave the nobles their power.

They however, were not the only ones to benefit from the large volume of trade stretching from one end of the Mediterranean to the other. In most city-states the artisans and traders were able to take a portion of the profits and thus to form an intermediary class between the nobility and the hired laborers. Although the new commercial class owned neither land nor horses, they had sufficient wealth to arm themselves and thus to form a heavy infantry. In time they became sufficiently numerous and strong to threaten the position of the knights, and even to defeat them in battle.

In many city-states affected by such economic and social developments, power was always concentrated in the hands of a few, it was for this reason that the Greeks gave this form of government the name of oligarchy. The meaning of oligarchy for the Greeks was very different from that of aristocracy—a term that earlier had referred to the "best men," the ancient nobility, but which the future philosophers Plato and Aristotle would reserve for those who were morally and intellectually the best. Oligarchy meant the division of the populace into two classes, only one of which had the right to participate in government. Participation varied with the city, depending on the size of the upper class and thus extending either to a large minority or to a small and exclusive one. The major defect of the system was that it created more and more inequality, even among the privileged. The monopoly control of the magistracies gave to certain families and circles such power that the majority of the economically privileged, who were excluded from government, refused to submit to this state of affairs.

The Emergence of Democracy

While the great noble families of the eighth century BC. were monopolizing power in the polis, what was the condition of the people? The less-skilled artisans struggled to make a living, and the unskilled were even worse off. And judging from Hesiod's description of the lot of the peasants, their position was steadily worsening. Their small patches of land that barely sufficed for scratching out the necessities of life were increasingly swallowed up by the giant estates. On the other hand, the land of the nobles was expanding, protected as it was from permanent alienation by the kinsmen's right to buy back any portion of the original inheritance that might have been sold. On top of that the nobles had successfully encroached on the traditionally common pasture grounds Hesiod reflects the plight of the oppressed peasants of Greece. He does so, however, in a pessimistic philosophy of life, expressed in his myth of the five ages of the world, in which there has been a continuing moral deterioration of humanity. It has gone so far that Shame, Righteousness, and Justice have fled to Olympus, have found no abode on earth. Hesiod's pessimism results from the belief that humanity has degenerated from the Golden Age to the Iron Age and that he himself now lives in that era of rapacious landlords and their accomplices, the crooked judges.

When democracy was first organized as a political party, it therefore, sought to counteract the iniquity of the magistrates by demanding the publication of the laws. Virtually all of the opponents of oligarchy were united on this point. The people had enough of the crooked judicial sentences that the hereditary aristocrat handed down as the presumed expression of the divine will, but which were all too often a cynical exploitation of their power. Many generations had waited in vain for the judges, delivering sentences under solemn oath, to remember Orcas, the avenger of perjury. Patience had run out. Now the people demanded to know the laws and the have them written down.

Little wonder, then, that neither Solon nor any of the other legislators were able to do their work free from the raging passions of civil conflict. The mandate of the legislator was precisely to put an end to the bloodshed by bringing about reconciliation. It was his task to intervene and mediate between the warring factions by proposing a compromise. In any event, the legislator's mission was considered temporary, either for an indeterminate period until the task was accomplished, or for a fixed period of one, five, or even ten years. In all cases it placed supreme authority in the hands of a single man. Aristotle called it an "elective tyranny". Once the society had been saved by the elected tyrant, he returned to private life. Not surprisingly, the nobility and the other wealthy elements did not always submit to the legislator and accept compromise. In such cases, the people had recourse to an extreme expedient. They placed themselves in the hands of a tyrant, hoping thereby to gain some material improvement of their lot.

The term "tyrant" probably originated in the East and signified master or king. On account of its origin, however, and because of its association with the despots of the East, the term was applied by the adversaries of tyranny in a derogatory sense to those who had gained absolute power unlawfully, by insurrection. An aspiring tyrant typically began his career as a demagogue leading the discontented poor against the rich or the common people against the nobles. The multitude followed him blindly as long as he promoted its welfare. Tyranny did not establish itself throughout Greece, but only in those cities where commercial and manufacturing interests had created a markedly oppressive regime and where, therefore, a persuasive demagogue could mobilize the masses for an assault upon the privileged classes.

Tyrants who made themselves champions of the lower classes, were generally speaking, restless, ambitious, and discontented members of the privileged camp.

By virtue of the fact that they already held an office of state or a military command, aspiring tyrants, seizing an opportune moment, could mobilize armed partisans and succeed in ousting the reigning monarch. Once in power, a tyrant usually left the civil laws intact and remained content with adapting the existing governmental administration to his own interests. Tyrants frequently disdained public offices for themselves, preferring to turn them over to their sons, relatives, and friends. In this way, a tyranny that began with the usurpation of power soon tended to become a family affair, a dynastic regime. The general principle guiding tyrannical rule was to humble the nobility and appease the lower classes.

In addition to disposing in this manner of their actual and potential enemies, the tyrants constantly preoccupied themselves with the task or appeasing the masses by improving their material condition. The urgent agrarian problem of restoring land to the impoverished and indebted peasants may have been dealt with at lest partially by distributing the property of the banished nobles. Solon, rejected the peasants' demand for the redistribution of landed property; but we no longer hear such a demand after the rule of the tyrant Pisistratus.

Tyranny was a system directed against oligarchy; it persisted, therefore, as long as it had the support of the people, for whom it was a temporary expedient. The people used it as a weapon with which to demolish the strongholds of the oligarchs; and once this had been achieved they destroyed the weapon. The founding tyrant, placed on the pinnacle of power by the multitude, was almost always succeeded by a more harsh and less capable ruler. For as tyranny became less useful to the people, it also became more oppressive and thus doomed to death. And yet, it had fulfilled a historic role in activating the people and thereby contributing to the birth of democracy.

Athenian Democracy

By the close of the sixth century BC, then, the people had stirred in some city-states and moved into history-albelt under the leadership of tyrants. In other states, however, the large noble families succeeded once again in seizing power and restoring their hereditary prerogatives. The Greece from the fifth century on was shaped by a struggle between competing and even antagonistic socio-political systems. For although the wars between Persia and Greece, as related by Herodotus, were struggle for territory and spheres of influence, they also represented a struggle between "Oriental Despotism," and Athenian demo croc. Aristotle, recognizing that the Oriental monarchy was significantly different from that of the Greeks, remarked that because the Asiatics were more servile than the Europeans, "they endure despotic rule without any resentment". And Herodotus, in his discussions of Egypt, Babylon, and Persia, provides some insight into the political system that scholars, from the time of Montesquieu, have called "Oriental Despotism" –a highly centralized agrarian bureaucracy of which pharaonic Egypt was the prototype. Often but not always, the economic corollary of this political system was a vast and complex system of artificial irrigation. As the Persian-Greek wars represented a struggle between two opposing socio-political systems, so did the Peloponnesian

War, which was at one and the same time an ideological struggle between oligarchy and democracy. This is a fact that Thucydides repeatedly stresses.

Thucydides thus makes it clear that Athens everywhere encouraged democracies, and Sparta encouraged oligarchies; and though there were exceptions, the rule cannot be denied. The propertied classes, generally fearing and distrusting the people, regarded the imposition of democracy as an act of tyranny; but the lower classes looked forward to Athenian victory as offering at least some protection against their native oligarchs. Sparta, as the leader of the Peloponnesian League, commanded enormous forces—so enormous, in fact, that there was no question that she would lead the Greek army and navy in the conflict against the Medes and Persians. The Spartan warrior-aristocracy was, of course, an oligarchy, its economic and social system resting on the subjugation of a large population of peasant cultivators. The aim of the Spartan warriors' education was to train them to fulfill two functions, preparedness for war and internal security—keeping the peasant cultivators under control.

Athens, in contrast, prided herself from earliest times on having neither a dominant ethnic group nor a subjugated one in her midst. Nevertheless, a modicum of the ancient political equality had prevailed for a time both among the clans and within them. For beneath the nobles the common people—composed of freeholders, shepherds, artisans, fishermen, and sailors—had been accustomed to deliberating and having a say in matters of common interest. The ancient, communal traditions were undermined, however, as the nobility became more and more oppressive. The rural poor, in particular, were subjected to debt-bondage by the rich landlords. The poor were called dependents and "sixth-parters," because it was for a sixth of the yield that they worked the land of the rich. Much if not all of the best land was concentrated in the hands of a few powerful families; and if the poor failed to pay their rents, both they and their children were liable to seizure as debt-slaves. At this time, before the reforms of Solon, all loans were made on the security of the person. As one would expect, political power was likewise concentrated in the hands of the well-born and the very rich. They ruled through the nine archonships and the council of the Areopagus. The Athenian political structure had become an oligarchy; and strife between the nobles and the people had become the rule.

In these circumstances a mediator and lawgiver emerged. Deeply disturbed by the prevailing social conflict, and inspired by the ethical teachings of Delphi, Solon sought to apply the lessons of limit and moderation to social and political life, and thereby to restore social peace and unity. Solon reintroduced the ideal of social equality and made a real effort to prevent the rich from exerting their power without limit. At the same time he tried to soften the burden on the poor by canceling the debts accumulated on mortgages by the impoverished peasantry. He imposed a limit on the extent of landed properties, and he restricted, by means of sumptuary laws, the ability of the rich to flaunt their wealth. In addition, he attempted to reestablish the peasants as freeholders on their own farms. Equally important for the future of Athens, Solon provided legislation permitting foreign, skilled craftsmen to settle in Attica, thereby encouraging the rise of manufacturing. In the long run this proved to be a safety it for the poor, since it rescued them from the misery of exclusive dependence on a strictly agrarian source of livelihood. In his zeal to protect the weak and needy, Solon stipulated that any Athenian citizen might undertake, on another's behalf, to prosecute a criminal offender, thus enabling the common people to take a large stride forward in ensuring evenhanded justice. But Solon's work went even further. His aim was to institute a general rule of balanced equality in which no class could claim either social superiority or undue political privilege.

Since Solon was a great mediator, it turned out that the nobles were disappointed with him because of his cancellation of debts and that, indeed, both the rich and the poor came to regret his appointment because his reforms were contrary to their expectations. The common people had wanted him to carry out a complete redistribution of property, while the notables had assumed that he would make only small changes. But Solon was in principle opposed to the extremes of both parties; and though he was in a position to align himself with either one and become a tyrant, he followed his principles instead and incurred the hostility of both. In the face of such ingratitude and animosity, Solon left his homeland to trade and travel in Egypt, declaring that he would stay away for ten years. In his lifetime, then, Solon incurred hostility because he conceived of the neutral, mediator state as a means of moderating the strife raging between the nobles and the people. But by the end of the fifth century BC; some 200 years after his reforms, he was honored by both. On the one hand, the democratic party claimed him as the father of Periclean democracy; on the other hand, the oligarchical party that attempted a political revolution in the year 411 BC.—regarded Solon as the father of an "ancestral constitution" of a mixed type, neither democratic nor oligarchical, to which they urged, Athens ought to return. And Aristotle appears to have perceived both the aristocratic and democratic elements in Solon's constitution.

But Solon's reforms failed to achieve their aim, and it was not for long that Athens remained free of civil discord. Since none of the conflicting parties had achieved full satisfaction, they refused to lay down their arms. There were three factions in conflict, each representing a socio-economic class and a distinct areas of the land, and each having at its head a powerful family: the nobility of the plains the merchants and fishermen of the coast the small peasants of the mountains. Pisistratus won the day by seizing the tyranny, which the lower classes had offered to Solon in vain. Pisistratus introduced far-reaching agrarian reforms. He distributed the wasteland and the large estates confiscated from the nobles, and thus created again a vigorous class of small-holders who came to play a significant part in the affairs of Athens. He encouraged maritime commerce. At the same time he created to the rural and urban masses by means of festivals in honor of Dionysius, as well as theatrical productions and the construction of magnificent buildings. And since he allowed the Athenian constitution to remain in effect, he fostered among the people valuable political experience in the sessions of the Assembly and in the courts. On the whole, Pisistratus appears to have enjoyed the support of the masses. Consequently, he remained in power for a long time, and when he was expelled he easily recovered his position. He had many supporters both among the nobles and among the ordinary people: he won over the notables by his friendly dealings with them, and the people by his help for their private concerns, and he behaved honorably to both.

Philosophers, poets and politicians enormously admired the ancient Greeks. Their art, philosophy, religion and mode of life were, in a way unsurpassed and they occupied a large part of their attention and writings. The Greeks were the ethical people par excellence. In contrast to earlier societies, Greek society was a humanized society, in which natural forces were felt to have been tamed and subdued. Their gods were of a human form; their sculpture portrayed human and not animal figures. The world of the Greeks was familiar and friendly to its inhabitants. The chaos of nature was held at bay by social norms and institutions, which were recognizably the product of men and in which men felt at home. The Greeks had not yet come to regard their social norms and institutions as alien and oppressive. They acted out their appointed roles without question.

In this rather idealized picture of them, the Greeks simply read off their duties and their rights from their social institutions. In an ethical community, it is easy to say what man must do, what are the duties he has to fulfil in order to be virtuous : he has simply to follow the well-known and explicit rules of his own situation. The ethical Greek does not reflect upon his society and his activities to the point of asking why he should follow the laws and customs or accept the religion of his society. This naive, pre-reflective faith goes together with an undeveloped awareness of oneself as an individual. The Greek does not and cannot draw a sufficiently sharp distinction between himself and others to enable him to ask: 'Why should I do what they do or believe what they believe?' Such differences are explicable in terms of their socially assigned role and class, whether they are men or women, parents or children, warriors or craftsmen, not in terms of the deliberate adoption of a mode of behaviour or life. Men share the same norms, institutions, gods and cultic activities, and cannot raise the questions why they do so or whether they should do so.

The harmony of Greek life is, however marred by three features. Firstly, different aspects of ethical life are in potential conflict with one another. Antigone, for example, who wishes to bury her rebellious brother is acting in accordance with the norms of the family. King Creon, who opposes this, adheres to the norms of public, civil life. The parties do not question the laws and customs of their society as a whole, but each identifies himself with one aspect of them to the exclusion of the other. In any case, within drama, the conflicts are resolved, and the performance of dramas portraying them might assist their containment and resolution in real life. Secondly, some men, notably Socrates, began to look into themselves for the right way to behave and not to social norms and institutions. They distanced themselves from accepted values and insisted that any particular course of action should meet their own approval before they embarked on it. The tendency to question accepted values and to decide for oneself is accompanied by a heightened self-awareness. As Hegel notes, this is the beginning of a self-knowing and so of a genuine freedom. Finally, individual Greeks began in the late fifth and the fourth centuries BC. to serve their own interests, disregarding the larger interests of their society and the accepted values of their time.

These three types of case are distinct, but connected. Presumably, Greeks, like other men, had always pursued their own interests, but, Hegel might argue, they had done so within the accepted rules, and had appealed to generally accepted values in order to justify their demands. Again, although Socrates wants to work out for himself what he ought to do, this does not necessarily mean that he acts in a self-interested way. In Plato's dialogue, *Crito*, Socrates decides, on rational grounds, to obey the laws of Athens against his immediate interests. What is important about Socrates is that he reflects on the rules, asks why they should be as they are and why we should follow them. His particular answers to these questions are less significant than that he raised them at all.

Nevertheless, these three features as connected. Value-conflicts of the first type might eventually give rise to a questioning of the norms as a whole. Again, the view that one should 'know and determine from within oneself what is right and good' easily degenerates in less scrupulous men than Socrates into the view that one can do what one likes. What most men like is what serves their own ambitions and desires. The testing of external constraints by internal constraints leads to the dissolution of all constraints. Thus, the growth of purely self-interested conduct goes hand in hand with the emergence of reflective moral autonomy.

It is at this point that Plato, Socrates' pupil and the source of most of our knowledge of Socrates' doctrines, enters the scene. Hegel draws a sharp distinction between the ethical views of Socrates and Plato. Socrates was a self-conscious individualist, whose moral questioning introduced an alien and disruptive element into Greek life. Plato attempted to meet this challenge by proposing to extrude moral questioning, as well as self-interested conduct, from Greek society and restore the harmony of Greek society. Socrates constituted, as much as raised, the problem, which Plato was trying to solve, and the fate of Greek society depended on whether or not some solution could be produced.

Plato's *Republic* is overly concerned with the questions: 'what is it for a man to be just? And 'why should he be just?' To answer these questions we should first try to see what it is for a state to be just. For the justice of a state will be analogous to the justice of a man, and yet, since a state is larger than a man, it will be easier to see what its justice consists in. The just state is introduced only to enable us to see more clearly what a just man is like. Plato answers that an ideally just state is one which is ruled by a class of trained philosophers, assisted by a class of warriors, neither of these classes is to own property or engage in trade, manufacturing or agriculture. These tasks are assigned to a subordinate class of workers. None of these three classes is to encroach on the tasks of any other; each class is to do only its own job. The state is just if and only if it consists of three such classes, each of which does its job and keeps to its position in the hierarchy. Similarly a man's soul consists of three elements, a rational element, a spirited element and an appetitive element. these correspond respectively to the philosophers, the warriors and the workers. A man is just if and only if these three elements are ordered in the correct manner, that is, if the rational element, assisted by the spirited, is dominant over the appetitive element.

Plato takes the substantial, the universal social norms and institutions as basic. The individual has the universal as his aim, custom and spirit; he acts, wills for the state. The state is his second nature, his usage and custom. The members of his society are permeated by the social forms. Their desires and purposes are supplied by their society. They follow without question the norms and customs of their society. And they act for the state, they aim at the well-being of their society. Moreover, Plato regards his state as a sort of organism: The ethical substance constitutes the spirit, life and essence of individuality and is the foundation. It systematizes itself in a living organic whole; The activity of these members is the producing of the whole. The parts of this whole cannot be separated from one another and still remain what they were.

An important feature of Hegel's account of Plato is that he does not accept the orthodox view that Plato was proposing an unrealizable ideal. In Hegel's words: 'Plato's *Republic,* which passes proverbially as an empty ideal, is in essence nothing but an interpretation of the nature of Greek ethical life'. In his *Republic,* Plato displays the substance of ethical life in its ideal beauty and truth. This accords with Hegel's view of philosophy in general, particularly with the memorable pronouncements that what is rational is actual and what is actual is rational, and that 'when philosophy paints its grey in grey, then has a shape of life grown old'. But it is not easy to see what these doctrines mean or why Hegel accepted them. Hegel sometimes speaks as if Plato were merely giving a brief, generalized description of actual Greek society, analyzing, but not prescribing. 'Plato does not preach morals, he shows how the ethical moves vitally within itself, displays its functions, its viscera'.

Nevertheless, Hegel insists, 'the true ideal is not what ought to be actual; it is actual'. Plato's state is actual. What he seems to mean by this is that the fundamental structure of existing Greek society remained unchanged in Plato's ideal. Such alterations as are introduced are minor reforms of the surface features of Greek life, reforms which will eliminate destructive tensions and conflict. It would not be too great an over-simplification to suggest that in Hegel's eyes Plato's state is related to existing Greek states as a healthy fully-developed oak tree is related to an underdeveloped, stunted or deformed one. Plato himself thinks of his state as the paradigm of a state, as a proper, healthy state as opposed to diseased or deformed ones. Hegel felt not only that this was the nature of Plato's enterprise, but that this was the only philosophically respectable enterprise open to him, or, indeed, to any political philosopher. 'No one can overleap his time. Its spirit is also his spirit. The point is to know this spirit in its content'.

It does not follow, however, that a philosopher must simply describe, still less accept, these values and institutions as they stand. For the values and institutions of a society are unlikely to be wholly coherent and they are often seriously discordant with one another. This, according to Hegel, was true of Greek society in Plato's time. Plato's state is designed to suppress and exclude an element of Greek life, which was in conflict with Greek ethical life. This element was 'the subjective self-will of individuals, do not act out of respect, reverence for the state, the fatherland, but from their own conviction, according to a moral reflection they grasp a decision from themselves and determine themselves in accordance with it-the modern principle of subjective freedom'. Hegel tends to equate this with acting in one's own interests. Though it may lead to this, it should no more be identified with it. Nevertheless, this principle, on Hegel's view, led to the corruption of Greek state and life. The Greek constitution, law and customs were unable to accommodate it and eventually the customs had to succumb. Greek life in its purity lacked this principle, the emergence of the principle ended Greek life in its purity. Greek society was unable to withstand, that is either to accommodate or to suppress, this principle and the self-seeking and ambition to which it gave rise, it declined to the point where it could be dominated and supplanted by the Macedonian and Roman empires.

Plato proposes to maintain his state by education, by imbuing individuals with the appropriate norms so that they become customary, a sort of second nature. The rulers both undertake this education and have earlier undergone it. Hegel stresses here Plato's banning of poets, which was proposed in part because their ideas of god were unworthy. Since this measure is not presented by Hegel as primarily intended to suppress subjective freedom, it presents a problem for his view that Plato is not proposing an unrealized ideal. For poetry was an integral part of Greek life and was not excluded from Greek societies. Hegel wants to imply that whereas the poets were once appropriate to Greek ethical life, they no longer were by Plato's time. By then they were taken as an authoritative source of 'universal maxims', as the 'basis of the truth of the ethical'. Earlier they hand not been taken in this way and were therefore harmless, but the time had now come for them to be reduced to something 'past, merely historical'. Plato's exclusion of them is seen, then, simply as a logical next step in the development of Greek society. But some of Plato's arguments, for example those based on the degraded picture of the gods presented by the poets, would clearly warrant the banning of poetry at any earlier time and not simply in Plato's own time. Plato is not merely bringing Greek society up to date, but is proposing, in this respect, a radical reform of it.

Three measures in particular are, on Hegel's view, intended to suppress subjective freedom. The suppression of such freedom is what Hegel objects to in Plato's state, but it is not entirely clear what he means by it. Apart from the confusion between acting according to one's conscience and acting self-interestedly, it is uncertain whether he meant that Plato sought to render men psychologically incapable of making up their own minds or whether he meant that Plato would prevent men from doing what they would like to do.

The first measure, that men cannot choose the class to which they are to belong, but are assigned to the appropriate class by the rulers, is taken by Hegel as a straightforward infringement of liberty. It prevents men from doing what they want. Hegel believes on the contrary that a man should be allowed a free choice of occupation or at least, should be permitted to follow his inclinations. Hegel's account of the second, the banning of private property, is more complicated. He does not object to it on the ground that it prevents men from doing what they want to do, namely to acquire property. Plato, as he concedes, wanted to exclude property because it was a source of conflict, but more important for Hegel is that private property elevates the individual to independent status and therefore promotes Socratic individualism.

Finally, Plato abolishes marriage. It is perhaps odd that Hegel should interpret this as a measure devised to stabilized Greek chital life since elsewhere he regards the family as one of the pillars of ethical life. There are two distinct strands in Hegel's thought here. Firstly, the family is seen as a source of individualism in much the same way as property is. A man and his wife are related to each other solely in virtue of their past personal histories and personal affection and not because of any special features which they have. Similarly a person is attached to a particular family and is valued by its other members for himself, just as that individual and not as any particular sort of individual. Secondly, a family is an 'independent whole', an 'extended personality', which may come into conflict both with other families and with the state. This happens in the Antigone, where the ethical requirements of the family are at odds with those of the state. Such a situation does not necessarily give rise to individualism, but the conflicts which result from it may, in any case, be damaging, and Hegel does suggest that it is in part through such conflicts of values that men learn to question law and custom and to make conscious decisions whether or not to obey.

By these measures, then, Plato intended to eliminate subjective freedom from Greek life. On Hegel's view, it was neither possible nor desirable that he should succeed. One obstacle to clarity is perhaps Hegel's belief that Plato was not an impractical idealist. For any attempt to show that Plato's state would not work tends to undermine this belief. An example of unclarity is Hegel's attempt to distinguish between Plato's time and modern times. Plato's state, he stresses, is a purely Greek ideal, suitable only for the Greeks at that stage of their history. It is fruitless to ask whether such a state is desirable or possible today, because 'in modern states there is freedom of conscience; each individual can demand to follow his own interests'. But whether this means that we are now psychologically capable of making up our own minds or that modern states permit us to act on the conclusions we reach, the argument is uncoupling. Modern states are as capable as ancient ones of forbidding or preventing us from acting as we wish, and even of indoctrinating us so that we become incapable of thinking for ourselves.

The main reason for Hegel's failure to criticize Plato's state effectively was perhaps his reluctance to concede that Plato was an innovator, proposing an ideal which was not put into practice. Unable to resist the temptation to regard Plato as describing Greek society rather than recommending its reform, he does not clearly distinguish the question whether and why Greek society in fact broke down from the question whether and why Plato's state would have broken down, had it been implemented. Having said that the growth of subjective freedom was the downfall of Greece, he does not seriously confront the question whether the growth of subjective freedom could have been suppressed. In this way Hegel runs together his criticism of Plato with his post mortem on Greek society.

Justice

The Republic is written in the form of a long conversation between Socrates and his interlocutors. The tone becomes less conversational as the work goes on, and by the end it has virtually become a Socratic monologue. Some commentators have concluded that *the Republic* as we have it must be a composite of two works because the first at least of its ten Books is so unlike the rest; but no one denies that there is a single connecting argument which goes right through it. Perhaps the best way of looking at the relationship between the beginning of the *Republic* and the rest of it is to see the First and Second books as setting the scene for the arguments in a straightforwardly dramatic sense.

The theme of *The Republic* is the nature of justice. The Greek word is dikaiosune. In English versions of Plato the term is standardly translated as 'justice', but the Greek concept is somewhat wider than that. The English word 'justice' primarily refers to ethical principles regulating the distribution of social benefits and burdens. It suggests the idea of people receiving their fair share or their appropriate deserts, and is closely linked also with the idea of law. Dikaiosune sometimes carries similarly specific connotations, but is also used more widely so that it almost amounts to something like 'the disposition to act rightly' –to act richly, that is, in one's dealings with other people, for dikaiosune is the social virtue par excellence. Often we could translate it as 'morality' and not be far off the mark. As Plato says, typical manifestations of injustice would be committing sacrilege or theft, betraying one's friends or one's country, breaking promises, committing adultery, and neglecting one's duties to one's parents and to the gods.

The account of justice in *The Republic* is built upon a comparison between the just individual and the just society. The work therefore deals not only with ethics or moral philosophy in the strict sense, but also with social and political philosophy and indeed with metaphysics, the theory of knowledge, the theory of art—it is Plato's most comprehensive treatment of all his various philosophical interests. Much of the work is taken up with Plato's account of the organization of his ideal society, and with a discussion of how the existing societies of his day deviated from this ideal. How successfully Plato integrates his moral philosophy with his social philosophy is a matter for debate.

Traditional School

The Republic opens with Socrates walking back from the Piraeus to Athens after a religious festival when he is persuaded by Polemarchus, the son of Cephalus, to come home with him and meet a gathering of friends. Socrates is greeted by Cephalus, who seems to have aged since Socrates saw him last, and the talk quickly turns to the question of what it is like to be old. In the course of that discussion Plato allows us to find out a good deal about Cephalus and about the way he looks back on his own life. Cephalus has lived a good life according to his delights. He has told the truth, he paid his debts; unlike the other old men of his acquaintance, he does not regret the passing of youth and its pleasures, and he does not take a jaundiced view of the young. He has been a business person. He inherited a diminished family capital and increased it, which enabled him to look forward to leaving his sons more than his father left him, though less than his grandfather left his father. He has been able to make money without having to struggle; he has never been tempted to lie and cheat for it, and he has not become over-fond of money. He has heard tales about the punishments which might be visited upon the wicked after death, but when he looks back on his life he sees no cause for alarm. Socrates finds his serenity in the face of death admirable.

Cephalus' goodness lies in his consistency. His is a business person's ethic, giving every man what he is owed. He has done his duty to his fellow men and to his own sons. When Socrates meets him he has been sacrificing to the gods, for Cephalus will leave no debts unpaid. If he has a fault, it is that he is not very reflective about his own ethics, though Socrates does not chide him for that. Socrates does ask him what he thinks goodness is, and Cephalus answers that it is telling the truth, helping friends and paying debts. Cephalus has expressed the conventional understanding of the moral life; it is a matter of not doing such things as deceiving and defrauding others. Socrates wishes to look deeper.

He points out very gently that there may be cases where that definition might cause a problem as when a friend has lent you a knife and gone mad in the meantime. Would it be just to return the knife in these circumstances? Well, probably not, because that would hardly be helping your friend, though it would certainly be paying your debt. Cephalus can see no way out of the difficulties; Socrates does not press him, and anyway Cephalus has more important things to do because he hasn't finished his sacrificing yet. Obviously there is more to be said. He bequeaths the argument to the young men and quietly shuffles off the scene, never to be heard again. Socrates then asks Polemarchus, Cephalus's son, for a better definition of justice. In the discussion that follows, Polemarchus offers another traditional conception of justice – doing good to one's friends and evil to one's enemies. This is also to be rejected by Socrates. "Is it, then, the role of a just man to harm anyone?"

The scene is charming, but at the same time puzzling. One of the pleasures of old age that Cephalus mentions to Socrates is a delight in intelligent conversation, yet Plato does not keep Cephalus in the dialogue very long. Plato has even prepared us for his exit right at the beginning of the scene where Cephalus is found resting in a chair with a garland round his neck; plainly Cephalus has unfinished business on hand. Cephalus is dismissed because his is not an example to be followed. *The Republic* is a book about justice, and Plato could have said: Being just is being like Cephalus; his life is admirable, so imitate him. When Cephalus leaves the scene the moral authority of a lived life leaves too; justice is to be found elsewhere, in the present, not the past. Perhaps the dismissal of Cephalus is also meant to tell us that the gods can no longer be relied on to provide answers to questions about how we ought to organize our lives. Religion is no longer center stage; it has lost the moral authority it once had. What old men and the gods have to say is still worth listening to but what is said has to be examined on its merits. Nothing is to be taken at face value.

Radical School

Cephalus is replaced by the arrogant sophist Thrasymachus, and the scene has been carefully set for him too. The rejection of ancestral wisdom and the wisdom of the gods is meant to tell us that the world has lost its way. Moral authority is no longer adequate; everything is questionable and there are no obvious answers. The greatly danger in a world like that is the man who peddles easy answers to complex questions, and the greatest danger of all is the man who has only one answer to a host of different questions. Thrasymachus stands for both.

Perhaps the most famous sophistic theory of ethics is the one often attributed to Thrasymachus: "might makes right". Thrasymachus's actual statement, as reported in Plato's dialogue *Republic* is "I say that justice is nothing other than the advantage of the stronger". In this dialogue, moral skeptic Thrasymachus blasts Socrates for his pious messages, lambasts his character, and loudly affirms "the facts", viz., what rules the world is power; government is simply the control of the weak by the strong; rulers develop laws to further their own interests; and whatever the rulers demand is just and right. According to belligerent Thrasymachus, rulers govern, not in order to improve the condition of their people but to better their own lives. In fact, he argues, the greater the amount of control they exercise over people, the greater their own gain-hence tyranny, he thinks, is the best form of government. The tyrant, whose control over the people is absolute, is actually praised and applauded by the people far more than is the democratic ruler – out of fear.

Socrates has little difficulty identifying problems with the "might makes right" ethic. He asks Thrasymachus if the rulers can ever make mistakes about their advantage and their interests, and helpless Thrasymachus has no choice but to agree that they can. Rulers are, after all, human and fallible. Thrasymachus had already claimed that. But this claim, together with the admission that the rulers can make mistakes and formulate laws against their advantage or real interests, generates an inconsistency. What if the citizens determine that one of the laws of the state is, in fact, not to the advantage of the rulers? Should they obey it? If they do not do so, they violate the claim that obedience to the ruler is just; if they obey this law, then they do not act in the interest of the rulers, and hence they violate the claim that what is right is what is to the advantage of the stronger party. Insofar as the fundamental principle of Thrasymachus's theory generates this contradiction, the principle that might makes right must be rejected as false.

It is unclear whether or not Thrasymachus perceives the power of Socrates' argument, but for one reason or another he soon changes his tune. He begins to speak of the stronger party, not as the one who is just and right because of his power and might, but as the unjust person who happens to gain more out of life, precisely because of his injustices, than does the individual who always follows the precepts of justice. In the competition of life, he now claims, injustice pays better than justice. The unjust person will cheat on his taxes when he realizes there is little chance of being caught; the just person will never do this – consequently the unjust individual comes away from the tax season with more money in the bank. If elected to political office, the unjust person will have no scruples about taking bribes and will anger her constituents, who want a favor from him or a "piece of the action." Thrasymachus affirms that the greater the injustice, the greater the payoff : the more power, strength, and freedom it brings. But he is quick to say that even bag-snatching pays if you aren't caught at it.

Justice is the interest of the stronger and injustice pays; remember that and life becomes simple; you will get through and you will never have to think again. Thrasymachus gets a real drubbing from Socrates. What happens when the strong tell you to do something, which is obviously not in their interest? Is it then right to do what they tell you? Thrasymachus wriggles by saying that rulers as rulers never make mistakes. We do not call a mathematician a mathematician by virtue of his mistakes and the same is true of rulers: they are called rulers to the extent that they get things right. This is the moment when Socrates begins to duff Thrasymachus up. On Thrasymachus' own account of it, ruling is a skill like other skills. Socrates has no trouble in showing that skills like medicine are praised for the good of the patient, not for the good of the practitioner. The relationship between doctor and patient is one between superior and inferior but the doctor has the good of the patient's health at heart and not his own. It follows from that all skills are practiced for the good of the their object; ruling is a skill, therefore its purpose is the good of the ruled, not the ruler. Therefore justice is the interest of the weak, not the strong. Thrasymachus does not give up easily, although in the end he concedes defeat; but unlike Cephalus, he is not dismissed from the dialogue. He is tamed and allowed to remain, but to remain in silence. It might have made more sense to keep Cephalus and let Thrasymachus go. Thrasymachus is exactly the kind of false philosopher that Plato despises. After Socrates has finished with him, he really ought to go off in a huff. Cephalus ought to stay; Yet, Cephalus goes and Thrasymachus stays.

Why? The answer is probably age. The theory of justice which Socrates will eventually offer in the *Republic* is a theory of self-control. Cephalus is a man with all passion spent. One of the advantages of old age that Cephalus mentions to Socrates is the freedom from the tyranny of desire. That is what makes Cephalus unreachable; there is nothing left to be controlled. Thrasymachus is still vigorous. Thrasymachus cares about money and the others agree to pay for him. Thrasymachus is worthy of his hire. He has a reputation as someone worth listening to and we can assume that he has done well in this kind of art before. Thrasymachus is worldly. He makes a claim to an expertise which looks as if it is based on experience of the political world: no matter where you go you will find that all states are in fact divided into the powerful and the weak, no mater how that fact is disguised. Thrasymachus' claim to his expertise is never seriously disputed. Socrates' refutation of Thrasymachus is inferior to the knowledge possessed by true philosophers, but Thrasymachus' claim to knowledge is left substantially intact. Plato probably wants us to think that what Thrasymachus has to tell us about the world of politics is substantially correct, and Plato in fact returns to a power theory of politics in Book IX of *The Republic* where he discusses imperfect forms of rule. His objection to Thrasymachus is not just that he is dangerous because like all sophists he peddles false ideas about justice. Rather, it is the claim of Thrasymachus to have been beyond the appearances to the reality of politics. Thrasymachus says that justice is always the interest of the stronger, and that would be the case even where the interest of the stronger is publicly proclaimed as the interest of everybody. Thrasymachus claims a knowledge, which is worldly knowledge, but not everyday knowledge. In *The Republic* Socrates is also laying claim to knowledge beyond the appearances, and so it is important for Plato to distinguish between 'real' real knowledge beyond the appearances and bogus real knowledge beyond the appearances of the kind that Thrasymachus possesses. This makes for a certain complication, and it is well to understand clearly that knowledge for Plato is divided into three classes, not two: first, ordinary knowledge as it appears to men living ordinary lives in the world; second, knowledge of the Thrasymachus kind which avoids the deceptions practiced by the world on the perceptions of ordinary men; and third, a true knowledge which sees beyond what Thrasymachus has seen.

Perhaps inadvertently, brash Thrasymachus has put his finger on something, which always causes trouble in states. Things are not always, as they seem to be; the strong do not always proclaim openly that what they say justice is, is really only their own self-interest. Ways can always be found of softening the message. Ideological forms can easily conceal the reality of power, and power itself can always find proxies. It can be difficult in states to get to the bottom of the question: who rules? We sometimes forget that the oppressiveness of government is not the only thing about it which causes discontent. Often a sense of alienation arises from not knowing who it is who really does call the tune. If those who apparently rule are in fact the agents of others, then discontent can be compounded with frustration: Some one is being badly treated and he does not even know by whom. Political science since Thrasymachus, and especially modern political science, has importantly concerned itself with questions of this kind: Who really rules? The Ideal State of Plato's *Republic* is designed to bring the realities of power out into the open. Plato's Guardians rule and are seen to be doing so. There is no place in *The Republic* for informal oligarchs of wealth and influence. Guardians rule, and that's it. Plato knows that family, caste, and class based on wealth, are often the bases of disproportionate power in states, and the purpose of the political engineering in *The Republic* is to neutralize them. Rulers are denied wealth and family life so that they can control the deleterious effects of wealth and family loyalty in others on the state, and the military caste is kept in strict subordination. He is not trying to stop family life, or to prevent people from loving honour; rather he devises arrangements, which will make them a source of unity, not of division.

The final problem which Thrasymachus leaves unresolved, is the problem of divided states. The state as it exists in the world is not one state but two. All cities are divided. Plato could either try to construct a state in which the causes of those divisions were eradicated or try to construct a state in which the causes remain but the effects are not divisive. Plato takes the second course by making sure that the causes of division, where they operate at all, always have the effect of dividing the ruled and not the rulers. He has at least as sure a grasp as Aristotle of the principle that the cause of political instability and changes of regime is disunity in the ruling group, and he adds the twist that the ideal recipe for political stability is unity above and disunity below. If all the material wealth in a society is possessed by the ruled class, then they can quarrel about it to their hearts' content provided only that wealth is not concentrated in too few hands. The same is true of honour. Provided that competition for honour is confined to a military caste who are kept from the highest positions in the state, then the military are unlikely to compete with their rulers, who are above such things, and they are unlikely to be united as a group except on the battlefield. The problem then becomes one of finding a principle, which can keep the ruling group itself united, and this Plato thinks he has found in the principle of justice.

Almost all of Plato's philosophical writings take the form of dramatized discussions, and in most of them the main participant is Socrates. The life and thought of Socrates exercised an enormous influence on Plato. In the minds of many of his contemporaries Socrates was identified with the Sophists. He was not however, a professional teacher, indeed he claimed he had nothing to teach. He simply questioned people. He would engage in discussion with those of his fellow citizens who had a reputation for piety, courage, moderation, or some other virtue. Like the Sophists, Socrates thereby raises the basic questions of ethics. What is the good life, and how should we live it? But in contrast to the Sophists, Socrates' intent was much less negative and much more serious. He was not concerned to dismiss the possibility of ethical knowledge. On the contrary, he maintained that though he himself did not posses it, such knowledge was attainable, and was by far the most important thing to strive for. The form of Plato's dialogues presents us with a problem. In a work like *The Republic*, all the important philosophical ideas are put into the mouth of Socrates. Do these ides represent the philosophy of the historical Socrates, or the philosophy of Plato? The question is a disputed one. In some of his earlier and shorter dialogues Plato may give us a fairly accurate picture of the historical Socrates, in major works like *The Republic* the philosophy presented in Plato's own, using Socrates as his mouthpiece.

The *Republic* is in part an attack on the immoralism of Thrasymachus and his claims to be realistic about human nature and human behavior. Plato's masterpiece is a passionate attempt to show that justice really does pay that the life of the just person is better and happier than the life of the unjust person, and, indeed, that the life of the unjust person is in reality a miserable one.

Pragmatist School

The Republic is also an attack on conventionalism, the view that moral distinctions are created by human beings and do not reflect any real distinctions in nature. At most, obedience to conventional moral rules work to one's advantage by earning one protection and public admiration and acclaim. There is no deeper justification for these rules. In Book II of *the Republic,* Plato has two of the participants in the discussion, Glaucon and Adeimantus, state as forcefully as possible the pragmatist case against Socrates and the moral life. Glaucon and Adeimantus are in fact friends of Socrates and are inclined to think him correct about morality, but so far they have not been convinced by what he has to say. Hence they pose objections in order to prompt him to come up with more convincing counter-arguments. One of their arguments consists of a recounting of the famous story of Gyges' Ring. As narrated by Glaucon, Gyges is a simple, modest, law-abiding shepherd who tends to his flock, gets along reasonably well with his fellow shepherds, and generally stays out of trouble. One day, while looking for a stray sheep, he stumbles across a skeleton which has a ring placed on one of its fingers. Thinking no harm will be done, he takes the ring and places it on his own finger. Later, while in the midst of other shepherds, Gyges notices that when he turns the setting of the ring inside his hand, his companions pay no more attention to him and in fact appear to think he is no longer there. Subsequent experimentation proves that turning the ring in this fashion actually renders him invisible, and he quickly sees the advantages he can reap from the possession of this marvelous magic instrument. So, quickly he leaves the company and simple life of the shepherds and, with the help of his ring, goes to the royal court, slays the king, seduces the queen, takes over the throne, and lives ever after with great wealth, fame, and power.

And the moral of the story for us listeners and readers is—wouldn't we do the same things if we came to possess this ring, if we could get away with them as Gyges did? Would any person continue to obey the principles of morality if he could break them without being caught and punished? Would he not, on the contrary, follow in the path of Gyges? More importantly, would any person have any reason to behave morally if he could get away with behaving immorally? The cynical suggestion behind this story is that people are just only because they are afraid of being caught and punished if they disobey society's moral rules. The normative lesson of the story is that if behaving justly is only a means to staying out of trouble, has no intrinsic value, no value in itself—just behavior can reasonably be put aside if no longer needed. Justice, the suggestion goes, rather than being something desirable in itself – as Socrates had argued – is in fact something quite burdensome. We tolerate it only because it is the lesser of two evils – it frequently prevents others from harming us. Why should the just person continue to be just if he comes to have the powers signified by Gyges' ring? Why should he do so, when he would be able to enjoy with impunity all the powers and pleasures he could wish for?

The story of Gyges' ring is a dramatic presentation of the skeptical point of view regarding morality and shows that Plato fully understands the appeal of such skepticism and the philosophical positions that sustain it. Plato sets for himself the demanding task of demonstrating that, in spite of the attractions of moral cynicism, the truly moral life is better than the immoral life. He seeks to prove that the life of a just person – even if devoid of the rewards often attaching to just behavior – is a happier life than that of an unjust person. He also wants to show that the unjust life is an unhappy one – that Gyges would be miserable as he sits on his throne with all the world bowing before him. Plato attempts to justify the moral life by proving that it is superior to its alternatives, including both the calculating life of self-interest and the life of conformity to the social conventions of the day. Plato knows very well that to prove these things is a tall order, but Plato sets out to do so He admits the difficulty of his task, as is shown by the fact that Socrates constantly expresses uncertainty, gropes for answers, and offers the listener and reader, as the best he can come up with more images and analogies.

The pragmatist position subsequently put forward by Glaucon, and elaborated by his brother Adeimantus, can usefully be seen as a compromise between nature and convention, between traditional school and sophistic school. They present it not as their own view, but as one, which is very widely held. According to this common opinion, they say, the way of life advocated by Thrasymachus would be the best if one could get away with it. If one possessed the mythical ring of Gyges, which could render one invisible, this would be possible. But as things are, if you simply pursue your own interests and entirely disregard the interests of others, inflicting harm, and injury on them whenever it suits you, then others will act in the same way towards you, and you are likely to end up the loser. When people realize this, they come to an understanding with one another that each will as far as possible refrain from inflicting harm on others, provided everyone else likewise refrains. Justice, then, is indeed a convention, but it is the best available approximation to that self-interest which all naturally pursues as good. Adeimantus adds that conventional justice has the further advantage of securing the favour of the gods as well as that of our fellow humans.

These ethical positions, put forward by Thrasymachus and by Glaucon and Adeimantus, set the scene for the dialogue. Socrates will confront them and attempt to refute them. It cannot be emphasized too strongly that they are not merely 'straw men'. Commentators on *The Republic* are tempted to treat Thrasymachus, in particular, as someone who is quite obviously wrong. We should on the contrary, take very seriously the possibility that he may be right. Certainly the position presented by Glaucon as the popular view is as widely held in our own day as it was in his. The question, 'Why should I pursue my own interests?' seems redundant; such action has an obvious rationality. On the other hand the question , 'Why should I heed other people's interests?' does seem to require an answer. And in view of the obvious rationality of pursuing my own interests, the most plausible answer would seem to be that it is rational for me to heed other people's interests, just in so far as I need to do so for the sake of my own interests. This is the plausibility in Glaucon's view. And if there is that degree of truth in it, then there may be an equal degree of truth in Thrasymachus' view. For, though there are some cases where we cannot get away with injustice, there are surely other cases where we can, and is it not then rational to do so? We do not have to choose between total justice and total injustice. If the only test of rationality is self-interest, then one can save one's reputation—in a shady business deal, perhaps, or minor pilfering from one's place of work, or a host of other everyday situations where a little bit of injustice would come in handy.

Can Thrasymachus be answered? Plato, through Socrates, intends to do so. His response to Thrasymachus, and to the sophists generally, is threefold. He rejects the antithesis of nature and convention. He wishes to link the two more closely than Glaucon does. Conventional justice is not simply the best available approximation to the dictates of nature. It is itself grounded in nature, that is, in human nature. If we understand our own nature as human beings, we shall see that the life of conventional justice is thoroughly in accordance with that nature. He rejects the opposition between conventional justice and personal benefit. A life lived in accordance with conventional justice will itself be the happiest and most worthwhile kind of life. Again the link between justice and well-being is closer than that posited by Glaucon. For Glaucon the relation between justice and happiness is that of means and ends; justice is not desirable in itself, but it secures happiness as a consequence, because it ensures that other people will be just towards oneself. For Plato the life of justice is by its very nature the happiest life. He rejects Protragoras' view that there are no objective ethical truths or values. Since justice is grounded in human nature, we can establish an objective truth that there are good reasons for living the life of justice.

In Plato's attempted refutation of the Sophists, the crucial role is played by the definition of justice. Justice in society has been defined as a harmonious relation between the three main social classes: the guardians, the auxiliaries, and the economic class. When each class performs its proper function—when the guardians rule, the auxiliaries defend the society against its enemies, and the economic class engages in production and exchange—the society as a whole will be a harmonious unity and will be perfectly just. Socrates now suggests that to these social classes three correspond their parts of the soul, three aspects of the human personality. These are reason, spirit, and desire. Socrates proposes that, as justice in society is a harmonious relation between classes, so justice in the individual consists in a harmonious relation between the different aspects of the personality. Reason must rule, spirit must assist reason by providing the required emotional qualities of self-control and strength of will, and through their combined efforts desire must be inhibited so that it seeks no more than the satisfaction of essential physical needs.

Plato has to convince his audience that justice really is what he says it is and then he has to show that audience that we have good reasons for wanting justice. Justice is obviously a very odd virtue, different in kind from wisdom, courage and self-control, which, with justice, go up to make the catalogue of the virtues. The difference between justice and the other virtues is that the other virtues are worth practicing even though others do not practice them. It is to my advantage to be wise if others are foolish, brave if others are timid and temperate if others are profligates. At the very least, these virtues do not make vulnerable and they might enable to protect from others. These virtues are directly and positively related to the power relations between men, while justice can hardly be recommended as a course of life and as a prescription for happiness. In the *Republic* Plato argues the reverse. He argues that justice is a political virtue in a sense in which the others are not. The other virtues are certainly worth having, and Plato will end up by showing that the just man will in fact possess all the other virtues, but he wants us to believe that justice is the central political virtue; useful in politics in a way the others are not.

Justice is necessarily a political virtue because it has to be widely practiced for the just to survive. The just have an interest in the spread of justice, in making others in the image of themselves. Wise men may want others to be wise, but a selfish man who was also wise might well want to restrict wisdom to himself and a few friends for the advantages it brings. A just man in an unjust society would always be at risk unless he could persuade others to share his justice, but problems immediately begin to arise when one begins to ask whether or not all men are capable of being just. If the answer is that all men are capable of being just, then the additional question has to be asked: if that is so, why is it the case that so few are just in fact? If justice is so generally accessible, why is it so rare? Wisdom, courage and temperance, are spread fairly wide, so why is the same not true of justice? Partly, no doubt, the rarity of justice is to be explained by the fact that it is usually inexpedient to be just, but it might also be that being just is in itself harder than practicing any of the other virtues and it will be even harder after Plato has made justice include all the other virtues as well.

An inferior virtue like courage, while admirable in itself, fails to engage the whole personality. Plato divides the human psyche into three faculties reason, passion and appetite. And he thinks that there are virtues appropriate to each. Courage is a passionate virtue, and has as its object military honour and the passionate virtues in general are directed towards everything, which concerns a good reputation. The pursuit of a good reputation is admirable because it requires the sacrifice of inclination; honourable men do not break the line by running away from the battle, and they are prepared to forego self-indulgence to maintain the state of physical fitness required by the military life. Base appetite is therefore controlled for some higher good. Plato believes that courage is a limited virtue because the man of honour has a limited understanding of his own virtue. The courageous man is not always very clear about why he pursues honour, and the proof of this is that he is kept to the path of honour by the opinion of others with whom he competes for honor's prize. This leads to a certain moral emptiness, especially, when the courageous man is away from the censuring gaze of his peers. He is likely to be self-indulgent in secret, and to be jealous of others fame and so he hides this jealousy. He is also prone to admiration of the other things, which men do in fact admire, like wealth, but he also conceals this admiration because the soldierly character is supposed to care only for honour. The secret life of the man of honour means that he is never really at peace with himself. There is always something puzzling to him about his life, which he does not wish to examine too closely. This can make the man of honour appear to be unreflecting, and it explains the attractions of the battlefield; there the call of duty is pure and simple: at war with his enemies, he finds that he is at peace with himself.

There is also a subordinate virtue associated with the appetites. By appetites, Plato means desires directed towards things, which are neither true nor good in themselves. That definition is negative but it is not meant to be evasive. Plato deliberately refuses to give a list of the appetites beyond the most obvious –food, drink and sex – because he thinks that the desires multiply, and the more they multiply the more difficult they are to satisfy and the worse they become. A taste for this leads to a taste for that, until the man dominated by his appetites finds himself in a state of siege, surrounded by clamoring desires each yelling out to be satisfied. He cannot satisfy them all, and he might not even know which to satisfy first. The only way out of the dilemma is to become a tyrant. He would then have all the resources of his state to satisfy his desires. If a man can only live a life of appetite then the best thing he can do is to subordinate as many different appetites as possible to a single appetites – say the love of money. Miserliness is about the best that the appetites can offer. The miser denies himself other indulgences so he can indulge his love of money to the full. He does not care who knows that he is a miser; in fact, he might take a perverse pride in it; unlike the honourable man, he does not need the good opinion of others, and he could easily spend his life in lonely contemplation of his hoard. It never occurs to him to ask himself why he wants more money; he simply does, and finds it odd that not everybody else does too.

Reason in Plato's sense is not involved in the lesser virtues of courage and self-control. This is not to say that the lesser virtues can be practiced without some kind of knowledge. A courageous man has to be good at being a soldier, which involves training in a skill and in the kind of knowledge, which comes from knowing the dangles to be faced in war. Likewise, the moneymaker must know something, otherwise we could not distinguish between those who make money and those who try to but don't. In Plato's view reason is directed towards true knowledge. By reason, he sometimes means what we mean by reasoning, or judgment, or contemplation, but reason is to be thought of as unitary because it is directed towards a single object. Of course, not everything we call knowledge is true knowledge in Plato's special sense and not all knowing is done by those who possess true knowledge. There is a rough, everyday knowledge, which Plato does not always despise in the way he despises moneymaking – craftsman's knowledge for instance – but that is not the true knowledge which reason seeks. That everyday knowledge , while not despicable, can easily get in the way of the acquisition of true knowledge and can even be mistaken for it. Much more insidious are the bastard claims to true knowledge peddled by Sophists. The mind's search for true knowledge is made that much easier by emptying the mind of these other kinds of knowledge at the start. Part of this mistaken knowledge is about justice; at Sparta, courage was reckoned the supreme good, and at Carthage, wealth. Part of true knowledge is the recognition of the limitations of other views of justice. The practice of the virtues is supposed to bring happiness, but the happiness which' courage and self-control bring is always incomplete. The courageous man has his self-doubt and the miser always wants more. Only reason can complete the happiness of the other virtues, and reason does this partly through its relationship with the other faculties and partly through the pursuit of the true knowledge. Reason supplies a kind of control to the other faculties, which they cannot provide the themselves. The self-control exercised by the lower faculties, while useful, only tells a man how to control himself, and never why. Only reason can tell us why control of the other faculties is good. Reason's first job is therefore self-knowledge, an awareness of the right ordering of the soul.

Like the other faculties, reason is active. It works out what the soul's order should be and it is the guarantor of the order. Reason's knowledge is its title to rule the rest of the self, and that knowledge, together with the rule, which it justifies, makes up the kingly science. What is true for each man within himself is also true for the relations between men. The man who is himself properly self-controlled is fit to command other unlike himself. His relations with others like himself will be friendly and co-operative, but his relations with others unlike himself will be relations of rulership. Plato sees a very close connection between instability of character and political instability. An unstable character is one where are the naturally ruling part is not in control, and an unstable state is one where men who are not naturally in control of themselves control public affairs. In both cases, an inherent instability will cause unhappiness sooner or later; much better to get things properly organized at the outset. The *Republic* is largely an attempt to show how just men can be produced and how advantageous it would be if they were to rule a polis.

Justice as Mental Health

Anthony Kenny has pointed out interesting similarities between Plato's theory and Freudian psychology. Both of them offer an account of mental health in terms of a harmony between the three parts of the personality. Freud, in his later works, divided the psyche into the ego, the super-ego, and the id. The ego and the id correspond very closely to Plato's reason and desire. What Freud understands by 'the super-ego' is rather narrower than Plato's 'spirit'. The super-ego is a specifically moral phenomenon. It is, in effect, the conscience created by the internalization of parental and social authority. It is akin to Plato's 'spirit', however, in that its characteristic function is to assist the ego (reason), by providing the emotional force which will keep in check the id (desire).In a at this point the comparison between him and Plato is useful because it alerts us to the general significance of Plato's theory. The concept of mental health was Plato's invention', and in introducing it into ethical theory, Plato was the forerunner of those who in our own day have suggested that ethical questions can be illuminated by a psychology of mental health and illness. The comparison of Plato with Freud should remind us of Freud's insistence on the continuous spectrum that extends from psychic harmony to mental breakdown. The analogy with physical health should point us towards the same recognition. Most of us are neither sick nor perfectly healthy. We are healthy enough to function at a basic level, but not fully fit, and we can recognize the desirability of improving our health to the level of positive physical harmony and well-being. Similarly with psychic health, Plato's account attempts to establish, on the continuum between health and insanity, a close affinity between the thoroughly unjust person and the madman, and then to locate lesser degrees of injustice as intermediate points on the spectrum.

For Plato, then, the main similarity between injustice and insanity lies in the obsessive or compulsive nature of the desire, which dominates such a person. A particular desire has grown out of all proportion, and lost touch with reality. If Plato can indeed establish that this is the typical feature of injustice, the continuity with insanity will be clear, and especially with that form of mental illness known as obsessional neurosis, which consists precisely in a person's behaviour being dominated by a compulsive wish, fear, or belief whose expressions are widely irrational.

Plato's psychology, like his politics, has an authoritarian cast. He believes that, for the proper inner harmony to be achieved, reason, in alliance with spirit, must exercise a strict control over the desires, inhibiting some, and eliminating others. Just as we might question Plato's authoritarian politics from a democratic standard point, so also we might question Plato's authoritarian conception of psychic health, and attempt to make a case for what might be called a more 'democratic' character-structure. The reference to Freud could again help us here. Freud's account of mental health and illness exhibits a much greater ambivalence about the repression of desires. Like Plato, Freud sees such repression as inescapable, both the repression of society and within the individual if civilized human life is to be viable. However, Freud also recognizes that, beyond a certain point, excessive repression becomes harmful and self-defeating. Desires which are repressed do not simply disappear, they continue to exist, but remain unconscious, they become all the more difficult to control, and the ways in which they find expression, and resist the attempt to block them, may well give rise to mental illness. Thus the control of the desires which Plato equates with mental health can, on Freud's account, itself be a cause of mental illness, and conversely mental health may actually require the gratification of those instinctual desires which Plato wants to inhibit.

Justice and Happiness

We saw that Plato wishes to meet Thrasymachus' challenge by showing that the just life is the happiest and most fulfilling. Initially this is held to have been demonstrated as a direct consequence of a definition of justice as mental health. For men don't reckon that life is worth living when their physical health breaks down, even though they have all the food and drink and wealth and power in the world. So we can hardly reckon it worth living when the principle of life breaks down in confusion, and a man willfully avoids the one thing that will rid him of vice and crime, the acquisition of justice and virtue in the sense which we have shown them to bear.

The claim is further substantiated in Book IX, where three arguments are offered. The first is a further elaboration of the appeal to the idea of mental health. Plato has suggested that the tyrannical personality is one which is dominated by a single obsessive and compulsive desire. It follows, he claims, that though such a person may appear to be happy when that desire is gratified, he is in reality enslaved to the desire. The crucial point here is that satisfaction of the desire does not necessary mean satisfaction of the person, as a whole self. Plato is appealing to the idea of the self as a unity, not just a bundle of desires, and consequently whether a person is happy must be determined by considering not his or her superficial satisfactions, but the deeper harmony that underlies them.

The second argument appeals to the idea that each of the three parts of the personality has its own characteristic pleasures. There are the pleasures of reason, of spirit, and of desire. Persons in whom reason is the dominant faculty value most highly the pleasures of reason, and likewise those dominated by spirit or desire will value their own respective pleasure. The question, then, is to how to decide between these three estimates of the value of the different kinds of pleasure. Plato argues that the person dominated by reason possesses in the greatest measure the very qualities of knowledge and rationality, which are needed to make a correct estimate. Moreover, only such persons have fully experienced all three kinds of pleasure and are in a position to judge between them, whereas the person dominated by desire knows only his own kinds of pleasure, and cannot appreciate the value of higher kinds. Therefore, when the person dominated by reason asserts from his experience that his own kind of life, the life of justice, is the happiest, he must be right.

Plato's final argument is that our pleasures are unreal when we take pleasure in things which are themselves unreal. For Plato it follows that physical pleasures, the pleasures of food and drink and sex, are unreal, since the physical world is unreal. The only fully real world is the world of ideal forms known by the intellect, and therefore the only true pleasures are the pleasures of reason. Here we are entering Plato's metaphysics. Can I really be said to be happy, if my happiness depends on illusion? Plato's answer is unequivocal: if my happiness is based on a false belief, it is a false happiness, that is, it is not really happiness at all. Can we accept such a simple answer? There are problems in doing so, for against Plato one is inclined to say that if a person really does feel happy, then as a matter of plain psychological fact that person surely is happy, whether or not he or she ought to be. And yet one is also inclined to agree with Plato, at least to the extent that there is something defective or degenerate about a happiness based on illusions, however secure those illusions are form being shattered.

In general, Plato offers a subtle and complex conception of happiness, which is clearly distinguished from the mere satisfaction of immediate desires. We have seen that, according to Plato, whether one is truly and fully happy will depend not only on the degree of immediate satisfaction, but on the degree of unity and harmony in one's life, on the range of one's experience, and the extent to which one has acquaintance with different possibilities, and on the depth and veracity of one's knowledge of oneself and one's world. Plato, inserts the mindless pleasures of the media-drugged zombie are not true happiness. We shall appreciate more fully the richness of Plato's account of happiness when we come to compare it with other accounts, such as those of some Utilitarian philosophers, but in the meantime we can also see that it stands in marked contrast to the conceptions of happiness invoked by Threasymachus, by Glaucon and Adeimantus, and by many of the sophists.

Objective Values and the Theory of Forms

As the third of Plato's responses to the Sophists, we listed his assertion of the objectivity of ethical values. Implicitly this is embodied in Plato's account of justice as mental health. When articulated as an explicit theory, it becomes Plato's famous 'theory of forms' or 'theory of ideas' When does this theory assert? To begin with let us take it that among these 'forms' or 'ideas' Plato includes values such as goodness, justice, and beauty. Minimally, then, the theory is the assertion that there are such things as goodness, justice, and beauty. More substantially, what Plato maintains is that goodness itself is something distinct and separate from the many individual things which are good, that in addition to all the various just individuals and just acts and just societies, and in addition to all the various beautiful sights and sounds, there are also justice itself and beauty itself. It amounts to a separation between two distinct worlds, the everyday physical world and the world of the forms. The language of 'two worlds' is to be found especially in the analogy of the cave, where the interior of the cave represents the everyday physical world, and only the enlightened few can ascend to the world of true reality outside the cave, which is the world of the forms.

This talk of the separation of two worlds should not be understood too crudely. It is not a spatial separation between two different locations—the world of the forms is not literally 'up there' above the heavens. This would be too crude, because the forms, not being physical things, are not in space at all. This indeed is the real nature of the separation. The many good things exist in the physical world of space and time, whereas goodness itself is not a physical thing, and does not exist in space or time. It makes no sense to say of it that it exists 'here' or 'there', that it existed or will exist at this or that time.

In the first place, it indicates the contrast between the perfection of the forms and the imperfection of their exemplifications and manifestations. Justice itself cannot be equated with the sum of individual just persons and societies, because none of these are ever fully and perfectly just. Even the best of them fall short of the ideal in some respect. Plato regularly puts this in terms of a contrast between 'being' and 'becoming'. The world of forms is the world of being; the world of physical exemplifications is the world of becoming. In part, 'becoming' signifies literal change. Individual good things come into existence at a certain time and cease to exist at a later time, and their goodness is therefore transitory. But their instability is also a matter of changes of aspect. Any particular good thing wills also, at the same time, be bad in some respect that is to say it changes according to how you look at it. To say that it 'becomes' is therefore to say that it is never fully and completely good in all respects, and in that sense is variable. The 'being'/'becoming' contrast also serves to indicate that objectivity of the forms which was our starting-point. Any particular good thing is subject to becoming, not only in the sense that it is good in some respects and not others, but also in the sense that it will seem good to some people and not others. Goodness itself, however, cannot vary. It is what it is independent of the beliefs of individual human beings.

A further aspect of the separation of forms and their exemplifications is the contrast between the kinds of knowledge we have of each. Individual good things, since they exist in the physical world, must be known by the sense. However, since their goodness is necessarily an imperfect approximation to an ideal, we could not recognize them as good unless we already had a perhaps prior knowledge of the ideal itself. We could not derive our knowledge of goodness itself from our sensory experience of its instances, just because these are all imperfect. Sense-experience can awaken our knowledge of goodness, but that knowledge must be something, which we already possessed prior to all sense-experience. Strictly speaking, therefore, when we speak of 'coming to know' goodness, this 'coming to know' must really be a kind of 'recollection', a re-awakening of that innate knowledge of goodness which we already possessed at birth, before all our sensor experience, and which has lain dormant in us since then. This innate knowledge, since it is not sensory perceptual knowledge, must be what we know by pure reason, by thought, by the intellect alone. In modern philosophical terminology, it is *a priori* knowledge, as contrasted with the empirical knowledge acquired through sense-experience. The forms are therefore objects of pure thought, and in that respect the modern English word 'idea' is an appropriate one by which to refer to them. In calling goodness, justice, and the rest 'ideas', however, we should not give the impression that they exist only 'in the mind'. They are known by the mind, but can exist quite independently of any mind. Goodness would be what it is, even though no human minds had ever existed or had ever thought about it.

Communism

It is not by means of education alone that Plato hopes to ensure the devotion and dedication of the philosopher-Kings. They are denied the pleasure of charms of both family and private property and are enjoined to form among themselves an ascetic communistic regime. This material and economic provision, far from being the main focus, is an auxiliary to the spiritual changes—the basic changes in human character—which he sought to achieve. Plato was concerned with the question of how the rulers would transform themselves from benign "helpers" of society into savage masters of the State. For Plato, moral education is the chief safeguard against such an eventuality. But though material conditions are not the main thing, a thoughtful person would affirm that in addition to the right education, the houses and possessions of the rulers "ought to be such as not to interfere with the best performance of their own work as guardians and not to prompt them to wrong the other citizens". The idea of communal solidarity and basic economic equality was not entirely foreign to the Greek world. There is reason to believe that in very ancient times, before the Greeks turned to agriculture, land was held in common by the tribes and clans. Even in historical times, in a rather individualistic city like Athens, the State still exercised some control over private property and retained the institution of public or state-owned property in forests, quarries, and mines. And in Sparta, though the land of a Spartan citizen was tilled by helots, the produce went to supply the common tables at which the citizens had their meals. And even later, in Aristotle's time, there was a mixture of both common and private property. It was believed that virtue will result in making friends' good common goods. In Sparta people were using one another's slaves as virtually their own, as well as horses and hounds, and also used the produced in the fields throughout their country if they needed provisions on a journey. It is clear therefore that it is better for possessions to be privately owned, but to make them common property in use; and to train the citizens to this is the special task of the legislator. It can be safely associated that Spartan and other Doric institutions most probably inspired Plato's adoption of the idea.

In keeping with the central theme of the *Republic*, Plato's advocacy of communal property is directed against a conception according to which the self is an isolated atomistic unit, which is and should be primarily concerned with its own satisfaction. Plato's aim is to supersede that notion and to put in its place a conception of the individual as part of a system—an individual who derives his or her satisfaction from fulfilling a function in that system.

It thus followed for Plato that communism is a necessary condition of justice; for if the first two classes, the rulers and the warriors, are to do their work wisely and unselfishly, they must live under a communistic discipline. In the life of the society, these two classes represent the soul-elements of Reason and Spirit. In order to fulfill the special responsibility of these elements, they must forego the element of appetite, which has been relegated to the third class—all the participants in the economy whom Plato lumps together under the heading of producers. A life in which the economic motive plays no role is the only proper regime for the ruling classes representing the higher elements of the soul. Communism thus enables reason to govern the State untroubled by appetite, which, in the absence of communism, would distract reason and make it work for selfish ends. Reason, thus liberated from appetite, motivates the philosopher-ruler to work for the well-being of society as a whole.

There is, however, another important reason for Plato's advocacy of communism for the rulers. The experience of history had demonstrated beyond a shadow of doubt that the concentration of political and economic power in the same hands will surely lead to tyranny. It was time to learn this lesson: Economic power must be separated from political power, or corruption of social order is inevitable. Whenever the two forms of power are combined in rulers, they transform themselves form helpers of their fellow citizens into their enemies and masters; and so in hating and being hated, conspiring and being conspired against, they will spend their days fearing far more their own subjects than the enemies without, thus preparing the way for the destruction of both themselves and the ship of state.

No communism is advocated for the third class of citizens—the producers. They will retain private property but even for this class Plato proposes that precautions be taken to prevent extremes of wealth and poverty, since such extremes create social strife that necessarily destabilizes the entire social order. Hence, the philosopher-governors must regulate the economy. This is to be done not by means of legislation but solely by their wisdom. Plato fails to provide any specific suggestions as to how the rulers would accomplish this. For this reason and others, Plato's third class creates difficulties for his entire scheme. In the first place, Plato is so preoccupied with the rulers and guardians that he assigns no special virtues to the producers. The ruler's virtue is wisdom and the soldier's virtue is courage; but the producers, having no special virtue of their own, can only share "justice" with the first two classes—the meaning of justice being, of course, that the producers specialize in their respective arts and achieve competence or expertise in them. The minds of the producers, being dominated by the appetitive elements, are restricted to their economic functions and assigned no role whatsoever in the polity of the ideal State. Little wonder that they have been compared to serfs and helots despite the fact that the land and its products are in their hands. It is noteworthy that despite the precautions proposed in order to prevent extreme of wealth and poverty in the producing class, Plato does not rule out the possibility of rebellion on their part. He represents Socrates as advising that when the rulers choose the site for their encampment, it should be a position form which they could best put down rebellion against the laws from within and repel aggression from without.

The rulers, owning no property—neither land nor houses nor gold nor silver—live encamped in common barracks. They subsist on "wages" paid in kind by the producer class and consisting of food and other necessities of life that are consumed at common tables. All this again strikes a Spartan note. Plato himself raises the question of whether the philosopher-guardians can be happy under such circumstances. He argues that they can, but what he means is that they achieve happiness only through the happiness of the whole. Plato's aim in proposing the ideal state was not the happiness of any one class, but the greatest possible happiness of the society as a whole. The philosopher-rulers must therefore be persuaded and constrained to do what will make them the best craftsmen in their own work, even if they must forego those things which most human beings regarded as essential for happiness.

For all of his insistence throughout the *Republic* that the just individual is the happier, it needs to be said that Plato never quite proves this central thesis. Or, if the thesis is demonstrated, it is only by defining justice in the individual as a harmonious relation of the parts of the soul. But this doles not accord with the social quality inherent in the term of justice. Social justice, for Plato, is synonymous with specialization in a division of labor; but specialization in the three classes compels the members of each also to act with only one part of their souls and to renounced the use of the other parts. Given such renunciation, Plato has hardly demonstrated that justice in the city as a whole necessarily means that the just individual (the specialized individual) is the happier.

There are also other problems. As Aristotle observed, that there will inevitably be two states in one, and these antagonistic to one another. Socrates makes one set of individuals guardians, a sort of garrison, and another set farmers and artisans of other sorts. But quarrels and lawsuits and all the other evils, which according to Socrates exist in actual state, will all be found among his citizens too. Again, he makes the farmers the masters of the estates, for which they pay rent; but they are likely to be far more unmanageable and rebellious than the classes of helots, serfs, and slaves. Aristotle has not quite finished with his criticisms. He questions Plato's method of appointing the philosopher-guardians, suggesting that it is unsafe and unlikely to achieve his aim because Plato makes the same persons hold office always; but this occasions rebellion even among people of no special distinction, and all the more so among high-spirited and warlike men. Finally, Aristotle asks, what class will be happy in the Socratic-Platonic Ideal State? Although Plato deprives the Guardians of happiness, he says it is the duty of the philosopher-guardian to make the whole city happy. But it is not possible for the whole to be happy unless most or all of its parts possess happiness. For happiness is not a thing of the same sort as being an even number; that may belong to a whole but not to either of its parts, but happiness cannot belong to the whole and not to its parts.

So Plato has left unexplained how one can have a system of communism in one part of society joined in practice with a system of private property in the other part. Plato wants to get rid of the prevalent condition in which the typical State is actually "two states" antagonistic to each other. And yet his ideal State is surely vulnerable to such a division against itself. If, as Plato believed, gross inequalities in property and income tend to produce dissension and disunity, what is there to prevent such results among producer class? That such inequalities would breed strife and rebellion, as Aristotle observed, there can be no doubt. And if that is the case, another interesting question suggests itself: how would the philosopher-guardians, deprived of property and other economic means of exercising their authority, control both the internal strife and rebellious conduct of the third class? If we assumed that the rulers are a strictly spiritual elite, we would find it impossible to explain how they would control the third class. But we must remember that the rulers, far from being a mere spiritual elite, are also a military elite holding a monopoly over the most efficient instruments of violence and methods of warfare. It is a monopoly because there is no people's militia in Plato's scheme, which means that the producer class has been effectively separated—at least in theory – from control of the means of violence. In this light, we can see rather clearly, how Plato intends ultimately to control the third class—by force and the threat of force. In this fundamental respect, Plato's ideal State is no different from actual states, not of his time nor of our own.

Communism of Wives

Plato's proposal for the communism of wives is advocated for the same reason that he proposes for communal property. The rulers must not be distracted from their work by temptations of self-interest. Depriving them of property, Plato recognizes, would not accomplish the desired aim if the institution of the family were left intact. Private property and the family are interdependent institutions. Fathers and mothers, in their anxiety for the future of their children, may be easily tempted to become self-seeking. The prevalent form of the Greek family, with all the weaknesses of a male-dominated society, was nevertheless too strong and exclusive to fit into Plato's ideal State. The Greek family implied private household, secluded women, accumulated property, and, in general, too narrow a focus of life to be compatible with the unity of the ideal society Plato envisioned. He therefore rejects the existing situation in which men drag off to their own houses anything they are able to acquire, and have women and children apart, thus introducing to society private pleasures and pains. He wants to abolish the troubles the private property and family life entail, such as the conceit of the rich and the distress of the poor as they struggle to procure the necessities of life for their children and for themselves. This, of course, refers exclusively to the first and second classes of citizens, since the producing class retains home and family, just as it retains private property.

Plato's approach to the problem of the family begins with an argument for the emancipation of women. Employing the analogy of watchdogs again, Plato has Socrates ask Glaucon whether we expect the female to join the male in guarding and haunting and other tasks or whether we expect her to remain indoors, presumably incapacitated by the bearing and breeding of children. The answer being obvious, Socrates goes on to establish that it is impossible to employ any creature for the same task as another, if we do not assign it the same nurture and education. Then the question is raised whether female nature is capable of sharing with the male all tasks or none at all or some but not others. And it is clear that Socrates is heading in the direction of insisting that the women is in fact capable of sharing all tasks with the men.

Just as some men have the requisite qualities for guardianship and others do not, the same is true of women. It follows that the capacities of men and women are, on the average, equal, except for brute strength. With this exception, there is no duty we would demand from the philosopher-guardians which an equally gifted and equally trained woman could not fulfill as well as a man. Plato therefore proposes that such women be selected to mate with their male equals and to serve with them as guardians. To deny an equally gifted woman access to the philosopher-guardian class would be a violation of justice in Plato's sense, for she would then be denied the possibility of fulfilling the proper function for which she is qualified by nature.

Female guardians are to be the common wives of the male guardians, and the children shall also be common, but no parent shall know its offspring and no child its parent. Men and women will have barracks and meals in common, will participate together in sexual union. It is stressed that the innate necessity is that of erotic love and that promiscuity would not be tolerated. Nevertheless, intercourse must be regulated with the aim of yielding the greatest benefit to the State. Plato argues that as many cases as possible the best men must be coupled with the best women for the purpose of procreation, while the worst are coupled with the worst in as few instances as possible. And in order to prevent the conflict and dissension, which would otherwise arise from the pursuit of such a policy, the method by which it is implemented must be kept secret from everyone but the rulers. He further argues that the sound offspring of the best couples will be taken to the nurses' quarter in a separate areas of the city, but the offspring of the worst and any of the others born with defects will be disposed of in secret to ensure that what has been done with them will not become generally known.

There is, then, a strong eugenic element in Plato's program for the philosopher-guardians. He wants to regulate marriages so as to produce "good stock." He not only advocates the disposal of defective infants but also opposes the prolongation by medical means of the life of the chronically handicapped; and he allows for abortion when pregnancy has resulted from intercourse that has taken place outside the prescribed age limits: for men between the ages of twenty-five and fifty-five, and for women between the ages of twenty and forty. All of this Plato envisions as a means of ensuring the solidarity of the rulers of the State. And it is noteworthy that the principle of Plato's eugenics appears to be that there is no "right to life" in the individual as such; there is only such a right in the individual as a citizen able to serve the State.

Apart from the eugenic element, however, there are other serious problems with Plato's scheme of temporary and State-controlled liaisons. He tempers with certain fundamental human relationship, such as that of husband and wife and mother and child. In Plato's communistic scheme men and women come together for sexual intercourse, and then go their separate ways immediately afterwards. There is no provision in this scheme of things of conjugal affection, friendship, and love between parent and child, which Aristotle regarded as fundamental human needs. Aristotle has directed his guns against Plato by arguing that the friendship between husband and wife appears to be a natural instinct; since man is by nature a pairing creature even more than he is a political creature, inasmuch as the family is an earlier and more fundamental institution than the State, and the procreation of offspring a more general characteristic of the animal creation. So whereas with the other animals the association of the sexes aims only at continuing the species, human beings cohabit not only for the sake of begetting children but also to provide the needs of life; for with the human race division of labor begins at the outset, and man and woman have different functions; thus they supply each other's wants desires and seeds putting their special capacities into the common stock. Plato, in contrast, abstracts the sexual motive from the total relationship and turns the individual into a mere means to the State's ends. He thus denies to the whole personality the love and friendship and personal parental experience that are so essential to the happiness of a family.

More generally, one can question the underlying assumption of Plato's ascetic communism, namely that material conditions are the cause of political corruption and other evils. Plato subjects his rulers to extreme deprivation in the hope that this will produce a totally new human character. Thus, for all of his emphasis on spirit, Plato tends to belittle spirit. He does not fully trust education to change attitude of mind and character so that the very same material conditions that in others were connected with corruption would have an entirely opposite effect on the philosopher-rulers. Aristotle, on the other hand, seeing things quite differently, recognizes that although material conditions may often be associated with evil, they are not causes or active forces. He therefore justifies private property, in spite of its temptations, as a basis of personality and as an instrument of action.

Similarly, the family may have limitations, but it is an indispensable nursery in which the child develops his or her sense of self. In abolishing the family, then, Plato effectively destroys the context in which human beings first come to know themselves as distinct individuals, and in which they learn to think, act, and exercise their will. It is not only the family but also other small groups that Plato abolishes. There is no intermediate association, lower than the State, with which individuals can identify themselves. Plato is zealous in his commitment to the creation of a perfectly integrated organic unity. For him there is no greater evil for a state than its differentiation into a plurality of associations. For Plato the best society is that whose State is most like that of an individual human being. In the Greece of Plato's time there were, of course, families, clans, prairies, tribes and demes, religious associations, manufacturing and trading groups, and other organizations intermediate between the individual and the state. These are genuine historical institutions that find no place in Plato's scheme, although they do find recognition in the theory of Aristotle who regards households and villages as constituent elements of society and who speaks of tribesmen and demes men as forming associations which are essential parts of it. Plato so thoroughly identifies the guardian with the state that the result, as Aristotle remarks, is not one which Plato would wish for. The unity of the state which Socrates praises most highly, both appears to be the effect of friendship, just as we know that Aristophanes in the discourse on love describes how the lovers owing to their extreme affection desire to grow together and both become one instead of being two. In such a union both personalities, and at least one, would be bound to be obliterated. Social unity, for Plato, often appears to be an end in itself rather than a quality that society must possess in order to attain a worthwhile end. So the personalities of the guardians are severely diminished, if not obliterated, in their fusion with the state.

Education

However much importance Plato attached to communism as a means for removing obstacles from steep path of the philosopher-ruler, it was not upon communism but on education that he placed his confidence. So striking is the part played in Plato's ideal state by education that Rousseau considered the *Republic* as hardly a political work at all but was the greatest work on education ever written.

The first stage in the education of the youth, the stage through which the majority of the class of soldiers pass, is, of course, military training. Here, the aim is to produce a certain temper of "high-spiritedness" and not merely to teach fighting skills. The second stage, which comes in the matured years, is only for those who will be able to prove their fitness for membership in the class of "perfect guardians," the philosopher-rulers. The curriculum, accordingly, consists of science and philosophy. Plato's first stage is an adaptation of Athenian elementary school studies in which he emphasizes gymnastics and music. Gymnastics included dietary and medical studies as well as physical exercise and competitive athletic games. Music, similarly, was broader than the modern sense of the term, including as it did music per se and other media of expression such as the plastic arts and speech.

Gymnastics was more than a training of the body. It was intended to improve the mind and produce a certain strength of character; just as the athletic games had a moral value in enhancing social solidarity. Music, poetry, literature, and art are also to be taught more for their moral value than for their own sake. The Greek poets who were at the forefront of literary education were also the teachers of religion. Hence, moral education being Plato's primary aim, he proposes a re-editing of Homer and the Greek dramatists to expunge from their works representations of the gods that Plato finds offensive and that, he assumes, would undermine reverence for them. Plato's ideal State thus controls education and, through education, religion and literature as well, because certain forms of poetic expression might have an undesirable moral influence on the young. Plato assumes that the soul absorbs everything with which it comes in contact. Drams, therefore, is especially threatening to his ideal society. The essence of drama is that it is made up of different characters-some good and some bad. As the youth read and observe dramatic plays, they will identify with this one and that, play one character and then another. Clearly, this is quite antithetical to Plato's fundamental principle, that an individual should "play" the one part to which he or she is called and that part only. Plato perceives drama to be the literary form of democracy, where each individual plays several parts. Drama, therefore, has no place at all in the ideal State. The State, in a word is the critic and censor of all artistic expressions, including even music. Music, especially, its innovations in music run counter to the long established norms. New songs may be permitted, but not new ways of singing. For it is Plato's view that one can never disturb the established musical modes without undermining the most fundamental political and social institutions.

Plato's attitude toward music, literature, and the arts seems to be characterized by a severe asceticism in which art must always serve a higher purpose—moral and even political ones. Against this attitude it might be argued that the artistic impulse needs free play, and if it is restricted by the state it will lose its appeal to the emotions and even fail in its ethical function of orienting individuals toward the Good. Some scholars, however, have defended Plato, maintaining that for him art was no mere servant of the state. His theory of art, it is argued, is governed by his doctrine of the True and the Good. Art is or should be a representation of life, and as such must be faithful to the original. An artistic expression must capture the Good that pervades the world. If, therefore, the poets, for instance, portray the gods and humans in such a manner as to ignore the good in them, they have produced caricatures, not true representations. This defense tries sympathetically to understand Plato's theory as he had intended it to be understood; and to that extent it sheds some positive light on his view of the role of art in society. However, that this defense glosses over Plato's subjection of art to the state and his apparent lack of concern for freedom of expression.

In the light of Plato's very broad conception of education, we can better understand why a system of laws finds no place in his scheme. In modern theories such as those of Hobbes, Locke, and Rousseau, the state is formed in order to institute or improve a system of legal justice. Such a system is indispensable in mediating the claims of individuals and classes. But Plato will not provide for such institutions for the same reason that he will not provide for the institution of medicine. The presence of physicians, surgeons, and drugs is a sign of disease of the body; just as law courts are a sign of disease of the soul. Plato wants nothing to do with all those matters that ordinarily require legal regulation. For Plato, right education in the state will make laws superfluous, for the true "lawgiver" is not a legislator but a philosophic educator. Once the proper moral values are instilled in members of the ideal state, reasonable individuals will find themselves capable of solving all problems. Here as elsewhere, Plato pushes a truth to an extreme, which makes it untrue. As he himself later recognizes, the spiritual basis of laws—moral and ethical principles—can never suffice in and of itself and therefore require an external expression of that spirit in a code of laws.

Education of the Philosopher-Rulers

To understand Plato's program for the education of the philosopher-rulers, we need to return to his theory of the Forms. Plato was under Pythagorean influence, and it was the Pythagoreans more than any other Greek thinkers who placed the greatest emphasis on mathematical studies as the key for unlocking the secrets of reality. Like them, Plato firmly believed that mathematics was the proper preparation for philosophy, especially for comprehending the Socratic theory of the Forms. Truth, for Plato and his master, Socrates, resides not in sensible particulars—this chair, this table, that book, man, woman, or whatever. These are only images cast by the perfect universals of which they partake, and by their partaking of which, they possess such truth as is in them. Reality, as distinct from that which appears to be, cannot be seen heard, touched, smelled, or tasted; it has to be grasped by the mind. And mathematics, Plato recognized, is the preeminent discipline that directly concerns itself not at all with concrete particulars. Arithmetical numbers, for instance, are not apprehended by the sense; they are the products of reason. Hence, mathematics is an indispensable branch of study since it compels the mind to employ pure thought in order to attain truth and knowledge. The study of mathematics sharpens the intelligence for other studies as well.

The real object of mathematical studies is pure knowledge—knowledge, , moreover, of that which always exists and not of things that come into being and pass away. Mathematics is knowledge of the eternally existent. On the other hand, of course, mathematics has an obvious practical value, especially in military matters.

Precisely because it has this two fold character, capable of satisfying everyday needs as well as preparing the way for philosophy, mathematics must be studied by those who are going to be the rulers of the state. But the real value of mathematics in all its forms is that it facilitates the apprehension of the Form of the Good. Thus, Plato adds to the curriculum plane solid geometry, astronomy, and harmonics. Astronomy, however, must not be merely the observation of the heavenly bodies, nor harmonics an attempt to distinguish musical notes by ear.

Such studies, beginning at the age twenty, when the youth has completed his earlier studies and his two years of military training, would last until the age thirty. Only those who had shown the most promise at the earlier stage would be admitted to the higher stage. The education of the rest would be completed and they would remain in the ranks of the army. The chosen few who will be trained for the function of "Perfect Guardian" (philosopher-ruler) will no longer devote themselves to the pursuit of knowledge in separate subjects, for they will not concern themselves with bringing things together and seeing the relations between them. They will be trained, in a word, to become dialecticians.

They have been prepared for dialectics by the study of mathematics, the main goal of which is the discovery of the common principles of all the subjects previously studied. Dialectics stands above mathematics. The latter trains students to ascend from objects of sense to objects of thought. Dialectics, however, is the means by which we attain the knowledge of the objects of thought themselves—the absolute or pure Forms and, ultimately, the final object of thought, the Form of the Good. The dialectician is one "who is able to provide an account of the essence of each thing", and who is able to bring this account together with others to yield a comprehensive view of the nature of things. All this will take trainees to the age of thirty-five and if they have passed all the tests and trials, they will be admitted to the elite ranks of the philosopher-kings, the Perfect Guardians of the state. From the age of thirty-five to age fifty, they will devote themselves to the service of the state, holding the command posts in both the civilian government and the military. But even at this stage the rulers cannot rest on their laurels since they will continue to be tried and tested. All this applies equally to those women who possess the requisite qualities. When these men and women have reached the age of fifty and have demonstrated their superior statesmanship, they will not rest, but rather they will be required to turn their gaze upward in order to hold the Good itself and to use it as a pattern for the right ordering of the state, devoting most of their time to their continuing studies in philosophy but also toiling in the service of the State when their turn comes. And when they have successfully educated a new generation to take their place, they will depart to the 'Islands of the Blessed' where public memorials and sacrifices will be established in their honour.

Although some readers of *the Republic* have imputed to Plato a certain wavering between the ideal of contemplation and that of action, there can be little doubt that the two ideals were united in this work, though not in Plato's own life. His personal disillusionment with politics, which he conveys in his *Seventh Letter*, does not prevent him from proclaiming that philosophers can only do their greatest work in the service of society. For those who have proved themselves to be the wisest and have scaled the ascent which permitted them to attain the vision of the Good must go down again into the cave and share their wisdom and labors with others.

This brings us to Plato's conception of government in the ideal State. Plato's rulers, as we see, emerge out of his educational scheme. Government is a creation of the educational system because government must be guided by knowledge; and in-asmuch as true knowledge is gained only by rigorously trained lovers of wisdom, government must be guided by philosophers. Either philosopher must become kings, or kings must become lovers of wisdom and the other virtues. There must be a fusion of political power and philosophical understanding which will preclude the pursuit of either one apart from the other. Otherwise, there will be no end of troubles for states and for the entire human race. Only thus can an end be made to incompetence and self-seeking among politicians; only thus can states gain wise and unselfish rulers who regard political office not as a perquisite but as a duty to be fulfilled for the common good of all.

Now, because these philosopher-rulers have seen the Truth or the Good—words to which Plato characteristically never gives substantive content—the rulers constitute either a monarchy or an aristocracy, and eventually they are treated as one, "if we assume the identity of the aristocrat and the king". In any case, whether it is government by one or by several, it is absolute in the sense that the governing authority is totally unrestrained by any code of law. Plato thus departs from the traditional Greek conception of the State as an association of equals, in which the first among equals is simply the guardian and instrument of the law, which was the true sovereign. Among the Greeks the departure from this tradition was called tyranny, a form of government in which personal rule abolished the sovereignty of the law. In *the Republic* Plato, in effect, advocates tyranny, the most unpopular form of government in the Greek world. And though he is careful to dissociate his new form of rule from typical tyranny, which he regards as the last and most degraded form of government, he appears to recognize that he is proposing a dangerous doctrine.

Philosopher-King

The rule of the philosopher-king is arguably the most important and distinctive feature of Plato's political theory. When Plato addresses the question of the reliability of the ideal state, in The *Republic*, he says that it can be brought into existence only if political power and philosophical wisdom can somehow be united in the same hands. The ideal state requires the philosopher's unique wisdom as well as their special personalities. Throughout the *Republic,* Plato repeatedly notes the importance of having philosophers who know the Form of the Good. Because it is through their relationship to the Good that justice and everything else of value becomes useful and beneficial, Plato holds that knowledge of the Good is indispensable. By virtue of being ruled by philosophers who know the Good, that state as a whole is rendered wise.

We have already encountered Plato's simile of the philosopher-king and the artist. In the *Gorgias,* the true politician is compared to painters, builders, shipwrights and other craftsmen. Since the virtue of the soul, like that of anything else, "is a matter of regular and orderly arrangement", it is the job of a true ruler to impose this order upon the souls entrusted to him. The parallel between ruler and craftsman is extended in the *Republic.* Returning to Plato's account of the philosophers' knowledge we find that Plato does not explain exactly how this is beneficial to the state. This is not surprising in light of the remoteness of absolute goodness from the lives and concerns of ordinary human beings.

Though we are able to say little about the precise contents of the philosophers' knowledge or exactly how it is applicable to their concerns as rulers, we do know one crucial thing: it supplies the state with an active, probing, critical intelligence. This is an important theme in the political theory of the *Republic*. We will see some good reasons why the philosophers must have the most exalted knowledge possible—regardless of the precise contents of that knowledge—and so understand why Plato insists that they know the Good.

With the introduction of the philosophical system of the middle dialogues, Plato moves on to a very different conception of what it is to care for one's soul. Because an individual can achieve this condition only through intensive conditioning, the Socratic ideal of each individual caring for his own soul must be cast aside. The introduction of the theory of Forms also leads Plato to oppose Socrates' belief in the limited power of human knowledge. According to the epistemological views of the middle dialogues, the most exalted truths are accessible to man, but only to the highly privileged few. Since only the philosopher can reach such heights, the many must be enslaved to the few if they are to partake at all of divine intelligence. Accordingly Plato's epistemological views entail a renunciation of the Socratic faith in moral autonomy. Because the many can never know for themselves, they must live according to principles they are taught to believe. The state as a whole is wise only through the wisdom of its philosophers.

Because of these radically different psychological and epistemological views, Plato must depart from Socrates' commitment to critical rationalism. The philosophers know the truths of "all time and all existence". It is hard to conceive how they would be able to maintain a detached, critical attitude towards such knowledge. What is more, Plato clearly believes that the philosopher-kings will bring such knowledge to bear in ruling the state. Plato repeatedly depicts them as doing their job with an eye to the heavens, governing the state according to the dictates of their exalted knowledge.

Not surprisingly, many scholars have attacked Plato's this sort of depiction of the philosopher-king's activity. Popper, for instance, draws a sharp contrast between Socrates in the *Apology* and Plato in the *Republic*. Whereas he sees the former as a great figure in the history of rationalism and open philosophic inquiry, Popper grants Plato an equally prominent place in the history of irrationality and oppressive social thought. He says that the *Republic* reveals a "magical attitude" towards social laws and conventions, which must make them rigid and all but impossible to change. Popper is not alone in this conviction; scholars more kindly disposed towards Plato are willing to concede much of the same ground. For instance, R.S. Block, writing to defend Plato against some of Popper's more, outrageous allegations, describes the ideal state in the *Republic* as a theocracy. Block locates the central feature of a theocracy in the fact that "the ultimate author of all law, whether written or unwritten," must be divine. Thus, he believes that Plato wishes for the state to be founded on divine truths, in keeping with which the Guardians are to legislate. In Block's words: "the ideal state should acknowledge a divine force external to itself not only as the sanction of its laws, but also as the ever-present guide to interpretation of them, and its Guardians, having constant reference to it, should put these into effect.

Thus according to the view upheld by Popper and Block, the ideal state is founded upon some divinely sanctioned blueprint or plan of the state. Only the philosophers can have intellectual access to this plan, while clearly, according to this view, their role is to mold political reality according to its dictates. This would appear to be the basic meaning of the simile of the philosopher-king and the artist: the philosophers' main intellectual activity is seeing the Forms, according to the dictates of which they are to shape the state. Because this construal of the philosopher-kings' political activity rests heavily on divinely grounded truths, we can refer to it as the "mystical" conception of their activity.

Even though mystical interpretations of the *Republic* are widely held, Klosko believes that such views are actually misguided and should be qualified in important respects. Both Block and Popper overlook the extent to which Plato shapes the ideal state around the presence of an active, critical intelligence. In order to see this more clearly, and in order to see exactly how the mystical view neglects it, we must examine an important distinction Plato introduces in the *Statesman.* And so there is strong evidence that the philosophers are to play the role of an active, critical intelligence in governing the state. To employ the analogies of the *Statesman,* the philosophers have the knowledge of the doctor, who writes prescriptions, not merely of the pharmacist, who carries them out. They are not merely to shape their surroundings according to a blueprint that is given. They must take appropriate measures where the blueprint is found to be incomplete or faulty, and presumably when circumstances change as well.

There are, however, problems with this view. Probably the most serious is the fact that some element of the mystical interpretation of the philosophers' activity is undoubtedly true. The philosophers' attainment of supreme knowledge is generally described in terms of direct visual apprehension. This conception of knowledge as arising in a sudden burst of light has strong mystical or religious overtones and has commonly been interpreted along these lines. Similarly, the philosopher-rulers are repeatedly described in mystical terms, doing their work within an eye to the Forms, shaping the state according to the dictates of a divinely grounded pattern. It seems difficult to imagine how the philosopher could maintain an open, critical attitude toward knowledge that comes to them in a sudden burst of light. But to this troubling objection there is a reply.

It seems that Block is incorrect in his assertion that the ideal state is a theocracy in which divine forces are responsible for all laws. A more proper view is that the philosopher-king is given an end at which to aim, while his political task lies in devising proper means. Though the end perhaps is rooted in mystically apprehended truths, the question of devising means involves prototypically rational considerations. Insofar as the philosophers act in this capacity their role does not appear to be different kind from the Bentham's lawgiver, who must devise the optimal means to the greatest good for the greatest number.

Thus the central motif of the political theory of the *Republic* is putting philosophical intelligence in sewice of the state. Though Plato never explains exactly how the philosophers' supreme wisdom is beneficial to the state, his insistence that they possess this appears to express the ideal that the state be governed by the highest Truths. We have seen above that there is a tension in Socrates' thought between his desires (a) that individuals discover their own moral principles, (b) that the principles they discover be compatible with those he himself accepts as true. A similar tension is seen in the *Republic*. The philosophers possess the highest knowledge. They are able to glimpse the Forms and to see the necessity of shaping the state. Like Socrates, Plato makes the highly optimistic assumption that the truths the philosophers will discover are those he himself holds sacred.

It is with trepidation that Plato approaches the question of implementing the just state. But Plato is not interested in compromise; the ideal state can come into existence only through radical reform. Plato, however, realizes that the reformer of an actual state must settle for some approximation of the ideal. The problem, then, is to discover "how the administration of a city can come closest to our theories". This is answered by the paradox of the philosopher-king. There is one change, says Socrates, that is "certainly neither small nor easy, but it is possible."

> Cities will have no respite from evil nor will the human race I think, unless philosophers rule as kings in the cities, or those whom we now call kings and rulers genuinely and adequately study philosophy, until that is, political power and philosophy coalesce.

The paradox of the philosopher-king is familiar. It is restated a number of times in the central books of the *Republic,* and found in the *Seventh Epistle* as well. It contained Plato's prescription; philosophy and political power must coalesce. This can happen in either of two says: if kings become philosophers, or if philosophers become kings. Although once the ideal state has been established, it will not matter in which of the two ways it was founded, insofar as the actual realization of the state is concerned, it makes all the difference in the world. Two entirely different sets of political problems are involved. Transforming a king into a philosopher involves convincing one man, who is already in power, to follow the path of justice. Transforming a philosopher into a king involves the political problems: a specific individual or group of individuals must overcome in order to secure power. Although either way the problems are virtually insoluble, Plato realizes that these are political problems. They are not to be overcome in the world of rarified deductions, but in the world of facts.

In all probability, Plato arrived at the paradox of the philosopher-king as the result of a process of elimination: he had nowhere else to turn. The major trouble with the paradox is that it too is virtually impossible to achieve. But this is not to say that Plato was not interested in establishing the ideal state. Rather, it is only to realize that because of intractable political obstacles, its realization must wait upon the intervention of more than human forces. Thus the philosopher in politics is no better off than the philosopher outside politics. In the *Seventh Epistle,* we see that Plato arrived at his paradox of the philosopher-king when he realized that ordinary political solutions could not work.

In this *Epistles,* Plato explains how he came to be disillusioned with Athenian politics. He was bitterly disappointed in the reign of the Thirty and in the returning of democracy as well. The miraculous remedy in which Plato comes to lodge his hopes was the convergences of political power and philosophy, i.e., the philosopher-king. In this passage, Plato so much tells the reader that his reliance on the philosopher-king was forced upon him by the sorry state of ordinary political affairs.

The problem of how a philosopher attains political power is one that Plato does not consider in the *Republic*. Because he says nothing about the use of violent means to attain it—the means attempted in Syracuse by his friend and pupil, Dion—it seems probably that he would not approve of their use. But it is not possible to state Plato's position on this question with assurance. There is good evidence that Socrates was opposed to the use of violence to accomplish reform—especially violence directed at one's homeland. In a well-known passage in the Crito, Socrates says that, when someone disagrees with an ordinance of his city, he must either convince his city through persuasion that he is right, or if he is unable, he must submit. This position on the question of violence is in keeping with Socrates' attempt to reform his fellow citizens through the use of persuasive means alone. But it is more difficult to say whether this was the attitude of Plato as well.

From the evidence of the *Seventh Epistle,* it would seem that Plato remained faithful to the position of his teacher. In this *Epistle* he asserts that one should attempt to warn his city if he thinks it corrupt "and there is a prospect that his words will be listened to and not put him in danger of his life". But if persuasion will not work, "let him not use violence upon his fatherland to bring about a change of constitution. If what he thinks is best can only be accomplished by the exile and slaughter of men, let him keep his peace and pray for the welfare of himself and his city". It is worth noting that the last lines of this quotation almost echo the prescription Plato offers the true philosopher in the *Republic.* The problem, however, is that, in the *Statesman,* written some time during the period between the composition of the *Republic* and that of the *Seventh Epistle;* Plato is less squeamish about philosophic violence. The basic argument here is that in question of government, the betterment of the people is the only factor to be considered and so how this is to be achieved is open. Among the means Plato allows ideal rulers are putting citizens to death or banishing them. An indication that this was Plato's attitude when he wrote the *Republic* is the fact that, he is willing to resort to drastic measures against the population of the reformed state.

In the *Republic* Plato does not say anything about the philosopher using force to seize power. It is, however, interesting that Plato seems to shy away from this alternative. If the philosopher requires political power, why doesn't he attempt to take it? Had Plato followed the implications of this line of argument, he would have found himself on territory very lose to that of the more traditional political theorists of radical reform. But for whatever reasons, Plato rejects this alternative. Perhaps he does so for moral reasons, disapproving of "the exile and slaughter of men" on principle, or perhaps because in his youth he saw in the Thirty Tyrants, how political coups tend to end up—while the fate of Dion in Sicily would have more than confirmed his darkest fears, and perhaps explains his further retreat from violence in the *Law*. In any event, deprived of the resort to force, the philosopher is placed in an impossible position. He cannot undertake a Socratic-type mission of reform, nor can he hope to wield influence within the political system. If he cannot attempt a seizure of power, he must indeed, "keep quite and mind his own business"; all other options are closed to him.

There is, however, one remaining possibility, and this takes us to the other main alternative. Even if the philosopher cannot hope to rise to power, he can hope to influence those who are in power—even granted the severe difficulties he would encounter. It is apparently upon this alternative that Plato lodges his hopes for less dramatic political transformations in the founding of the "second-best city" in the *Laws* and in his dealings with Dionysus II, tyrant of Syracuse. But Plato does not pursue this line of approach in the *Republic*, probably because he does not think it can yield the thoroughly radical reform he has in mind.

Plato divides the population into three categories: lovers of wisdom, lovers of honor, and lovers of gain or those with gold, silver and bronze in their souls. Justice in the state requires that the principle of specialization be maintained, that each type of man be located in his proper class and perform his function. Plato puts considerable emphasis upon this, at one point calling it "the first and most important command of the god to the rulers". It should be pointed out that this principle pertains much more to classes than to individuals. Plato does not believe that each individual is able to perform only one task in the state, which only he can do. Indeed, he says that no great harm comes from a carpenter doing the work of a cobbler or a cobbler that of a carpenter. The danger is if individuals are not assigned to appropriate classes. But this real fear is seeing an inferior nature somehow rise to the ruling elite. Should this happen, Plato prophesies, it would spell the end of the state. Correspondingly, Plato depicts the decline of the ideal state as beginning when inferior natures comes to rule.

On the whole, Plato does not seem to value justice, the maintenance of the system of classes, greatly for its own sake. Rather, it is necessary if the other virtues are to flourish. Justice assures that the state will be wise through the wisdom of the philosophers, brave through the courage of the auxiliaries, and free from faction. The virtue of temperance will spread throughout the three classes, bringing with it general agreement as to who should rule.

In accordance with a proper distribution of civic functions, only true philosophers are to rule. He does not provide any institutional safeguards—checks and balances—to prevent the philosophers from abusing their power. He relies instead on their education. It is in reference to this problem that the question of educating the Guardians is first raised in *Republic*. Socrates notes that, in order to be a suitable fighting force, the Guardians must be brave and high-spirited, but they must not be savage or brutal in their dealings with each other or with the citizens they are to protect. Should the Guardians behave in this fashion, they would bring about the ruin of the city.

Plato realizes that he faces a universal political problem here. In the myth that closes the Gorgias he remarks that power corrupts; the Under-world is filled with the souls of earthly rulers who, having the ability to do wrong with impunity, could not restrain themselves. Plato notes that it is rare to find a good man among the powerful, and more than once in the *Republic* he displays a full awareness of the consequences of being ruled by lesser men. Accordingly, he argues that every precaution must be taken to insure that the Guardians behave properly towards the citizenry. The best means of accomplishing this is through education.

The testing of the future rulers does not stop with the virtues of right opinion. It continues as they embark upon their exclusive program of higher studies. As they were tested in regard to "toils, fears, and pleasures" during their early years, now they must be examined in regard to intellectual matters. Even when the future rulers have completed their course of abstract studies and are spending the requisite fifteen years doing administrative work in the city, they are subjected to additional tests. Only those who pass these as well will be led to look upon the Good. The intensive program of testing prescribed for the Guardians indicates Plato's desire to exploit the possibilities of an exceptional type of personality. Plato wants to make sure that his rulers have a divine nature that their souls are naturally akin to the Forms. Through the process of erotic sublimation that accompanies their rise to the world of the Forms, the philosophers gain more than knowledge.

Thus, we see the beauty of Plato's solution to the problem of insuring that rulers do not abuse their power. The key is to make sure that they are the kind of people who would gain nothing by doing so. Plato is aware that most rulers of actual states rule for the sake of gain. They are like shepherds who treat their subjects as sheep to be slaughtered and fleeced. The problem of getting better rulers can be solved only by finding men who view ruling as a burden and so do not wish to rule, and forcing them to do so, either through their fear of being ruled by lesser men, or because they know it is their duty to the city that has raised and educated them.

Plato presents an inverse proportion: a city in which the prospective rulers desire least to rule should be governed best and experience the least strife, while a city with the opposite kind of rulers should end up governed in the opposite way. The question why the philosophers are willing to rule has been much debated by recent scholars. Part of the problem is caused by Plato's saying that philosophers who have escaped from the cave and seen the light must be forced to descend once again to aid their fellows. It should be noted that this only pertains to philosophers who have not been formally educated by their societies. Those who have been so educated are obligated to govern out of gratitude. There are, however, at least three reasons why philosophers should be willing to rule.

First, as Plato says if they do not rule, other people will, in which case the philosophers pay the severe price of being ruled by lesser men. In other words, they are forced to rule as the lesser of two evils. Second, Plato puts great store in the tran formatives effects of philosophic wisdom. Even having ascended the ladder of love, the philosopher still craves immortality, which in his case assumes the form of a desire to inculcate virtue in other people. In order to satisfy this desire, he must rule. It is not entirely clear why Plato believes that the desire to propagate virtue is one effect of the highest wisdom.

Popper's Critique of Plato

Plato is often criticized for his radical approach to political reform. In his famous work, *The Open Society and Its Enemies*, Karl Popper especially questions Plato's support of radical measures, instead of what Popper calls "piecemeal social engineering." Piecemeal social engineering entails thoroughly rational approach to social problems. Rather than attempting to reconstruct society as a whole after the pattern of a fully worked out blueprint, piecemeal reform advocates attempting to relating specific social evils within the framework of existing society. Piecemeal reform would alleviate real suffering, while each attempted change would also be an experiment. By observing the effects of such actions, reformers would be able to learn about the working of society, thereby increasing their effectiveness in the future.

Popper defends the modesty of piecemeal reform as having several advantages. First, it is based on a body of information built up in the past by similar practices. Second, since such reforms are of modest scope, the damage caused by failed attempts and unforeseen consequences should also be minimally modest and therefore relatively easy to contain. Third, piecemeal reforms are directed against obvious, known evils, and so constituencies in their favor can be mustered within the open political process of a democratic society. Finally, since the consequences of any specific measure should be tolerable to society, the reformers need not shrink from public disclosure and discussion of their work, against making their policy suitable for democracies.

Popper rejects total reform irrational. He believes that there are no precedents for such actions, and so little practical knowledge to guide the former. Moreover, any attempt to change society as a whole goes far beyond the elimination of obvious evils. Popper questions the feasibility of the reformers' alternative blueprint. Since it does not arise from actual experience, it must have some other source. He believes that Plato's blueprint is unworldly, based on revelation, and so not easily adapted to inevitable changes in the political environment. Because access to the blueprint depends on privileged knowledge, Popper sees no way that disagreements and conflicts about the blueprint could be settled – or future rulers trained to perceive it. Furthermore if the blueprint is not available to large segments of the population, a constituency in favor of democratic deliberation and discussion. The reformers will require political power, absolute authority in order to achieve their ends.

Popper believes that the scale of such reform raises additional problems. Any attempt to reconstruct society as a whole will come into conflict with members of the existing order who do not wish to be uprooted. Such individuals are likely to resist and so the reformer's power must be sufficient to overcome them, while a high degree of conflict and strife seems inevitable. Mistakes made during wholesale reform will probably be far-reaching; unintended consequences will be similarly grave, while such problems will inevitably engender up further resistance. Thus, the reformers would be tempted to limit knowledge of their actions, and so would resist open disclosure and examination of their work.

Popper cites other difficulties: experience reveals clear dangers inherent in radical reform. The combination of difficulty in enlisting popular support, resistance by powerfully entrenched interests, and the need to limit disclosure of what is actually being done, will lead the reformers towards dictatorial methods. They will tighten their hold on political power and use it to crush dissent. The political history of the twentieth century—which is the source of Popper's fears—certainly bears out much of his concern.

This brief look at Popper's arguments should be sufficient to show the extent to which his basic assumptions about policies differ from Plato's. But because Plato's views are so different, he is able to respond. In fact, we will see that reasons similar to those Popper cites lead Plato to believe that the state is unlikely to be realized in practice. We will also see that the kind of blueprint upon which Plato bases his state is neither quite as rigid nor quite as irrational as Popper argues. One can offer Plato's replies to several of Popper's specific criticisms of radical reform.

First, Plato was in fact able to base his plans upon a substantial body of precedents, of the founding of new ones. In discussing Plato's political theory in the *Republic*, it must be borne in mind that the city he envisions is small; it is a polis, not a modern nation-state. The problems of reconstructing such a society are vastly more manageable then those confronted in the radical reform of modern countries like those faced by the leaders of the French and Russian Revolutions. There were also abundant precedents. Given the instability of much of Greek political life, cities were constantly beset by revolution and consequently by large scale political changes. More important, through mechanisms such as colonization, entire cities were founded from scratch. Thus, Plato's idea that the philosopher-rulers would be able to reconstruct their city from the ground up is not nearly as impossible or unprecedented as Popper makes it seem.

Secondly, Plato differs sharply with Popper concerning the nature of the existing political order. Popper finds much of value in existing society, and so is content to work on solving problems on a piecemeal basis. Plato, on the other hand, is thoroughly disenchanted with the existing order and wants it wiped away. Seeing the existing order so differently, Plato and Popper differ sharply in their accounts of the irrational and unpredictable elements encountered in political life. While Popper tends to emphasize the unforeseen consequences of actions not yet taken, Plato is confident of the ideal ruler's ability to manage in the future. Plato believes that existing societies are chaotic and irrational. They are the domains of appetitive men, built up in the pursuit of worthless aims. Thus, Plato believes it is a great boon to be able wipe away with a single stroke the residue of centuries of aimless activity. This also benefits the rulers, in that the leveling of existing society will eliminate all possibility of resistance by conservative elements.

Because he views society so differently from Popper, Plato castigates piecemeal reform. He believes that the ills that beset existing societies lie at their very heart and that these will thwart separate attempts to deal with them. Laws passed to correct specific ills will simply be corrupted and rendered ineffective. Plato compares such measures to cutting off a hydra's heads for every one removed, two more grow back in its place. The existing order will be defended by entrenched voted interests, not only in spite of its abuses but because of them. Those who profit from the way things are will resist meaningful reform. Plato is skeptical about the amount of real reform that could be accomplished with popular consent.

Thirdly, though the ideal state may have some features in common with the "totalitarian" societies that arose earlier this century, it is also different in crucial respects, especially its lack of a system of "terroristic police control" to keep its population in check. The security of the ideal state is to rest on voluntary harmony, not informers, systematic purges and concentration camps. Though the Guardians have the means to terrorize the population, the explicit purpose behind their education and renunciation of private property is to make sure that they will not do so. A comparison between inter-class relations in Plato's state and Sparta is instructive here. In Sparta, the helots were constantly in revolt or threatening revolt. Accordingly, the Spartans adopted severe tactics, going so far as annually declaring war on them in order to legitimize killing them. Spartan youths were commonly sent out to stalk and murder helots they encountered. On one occasion reported by Thucydides, when the Spartans were especially fearful of revolt during the Peloponnesian War, they rounded up some two thousand of the bravest helots, supposedly to free them. Instead the helots were massacred, under precise circumstances that have never come to light.

Needless to say, tactics of this sort are not what Plato has in mind. Though at one point he says that the lower kinds of men must be enslaved to the higher, this expresses a moral rather than political proposal. The philosophers are to govern—unwillingly—in the interests of their subjects, not in order to exploit them. Plato says that members of all classes should as far as possible be alike and philoi. Philos, the Greek word usually translated as "friend," connotes more than "friendship." It is also the emotional tie between close family members, in this sense covering emotional we would call "love." But at least insofar as Plato's intentions are concerned, there can be no doubt that in this crucial respect his ideal state is not totalitarian.

Fourth, the ideal state is not racist either. One of Popper's most inflammatory charges is that Plato advocates the subordination of the lowest class to the rulers because of their racial inferiority. But this allegation is groundless; class membership is based on merit not birth. One of the rulers' chief responsibilities is insuring that individuals born unsuited to their classes are moved accordingly. Though Plato does not provide the details concerning how that is to be accomplished, there can be no doubt that considerations of merit are intended to outweigh considerations of blood.

In regard to how the ideal state treats its individual members, the system must on balance be deemed fair. The guardians do not use their political power to monopolize life's goods. In fact, they make substantial sacrifices in order to be worthy of political trust. Though the lowest class is excluded from politics, it controls all the state's property. Because members of this class are appetitive oriented, they care more about economic goods than political goods and so would perhaps be unwilling to exchange places with their rulers.

Gregory Vlastos has rightly argued that the principle of distribution Plato follows in the *Republic* is granting goods solely with an eye to the welfare of the state. The principle of specialization, according to which each individual is to stick to the one task for which he is naturally suited, is obviously based on maximizing the well-being of the state. The consistent thread running through all the measures is distribution of various goods in accordance with the interest of the state, while all inhabitants are treated impartially according to this principle. Moreover, as Vlastos shows, it is not part of Plato's political theory that the state is something over the individuals who inhabit it, with rights that take precedence over theirs. Rather, the interest of the state is identical to the best interests of their individuals who inhabit it.

Fifth, Popper attacks Plato for his anti-humanist, anti-democratic political ideas on the ground that Plato's does not grant freedom. To a certain extent Plato's disregard for individual freedom can be explained by his historical background. It is to be argued that the time Plato wrote, "the individual" as he exists in modern Western society, and as he has existed from roughly the seventeenth century on, did not yet exist. Though the Greek cities of course recognized rights belonging to individuals, in general these did not belong to them by virtue of their humanity, considered apart from any social role. Individuals had rights in connection with their positions in society, e.g., their citizenship , but the notion of natural rights was largely absent from Greek political discourse. The view expressed in the USA Declaration of Independence, that all men are created equal and are endowed with inalienable rights to life, liberty and the pursuit of happiness," would have struck the Greeks as odd. The polis did not sharply differentiate between society and the state, or between the individual and the community.

The relationship between individual and society in Greece was complex. Certain cities, especially Athens, were known for granting individuals a large measure of freedom. Thus in his funeral speech, Pericles comment upon the openness of Athens: "We do not look down on our neighbor if he enjoys himself in his own way. We are free and tolerant in our private lives". Similarly, Nicias says of Athens that "all who lived there had liberty to live their own lives in their own way". Plato reports something similar in the *Republic*, where he critiques democracy for its extreme openness and permissiveness. Thus, it is clear that at least some Greek cities recognized the importance of allowing individuals to live as they please—to pursue their good own way, which Mill calls "the only freedom which deserves the name." We must ask, then, what reasons other than concern with the traditional polis led Plato not to follow this example. Plato's overall position on the freedom of the individual can be traced back to the two-world view underlying his philosophy as a whole. According to Plato's Orphic psychological views, the soul is in essence simple, uniform and pure, only temporarily imprisoned in the body. The entire subject matter of moral psychology—and the rationale for political theory as well—is occasioned by the soul's imprisonment. Though it is difficult to know how seriously to take this theme, at the very least it sets a tone of disdain for people's bodies and their desires that permeates Plato's moral and political philosophy. The image of the Cave is telling here. Since ordinary lives are devoted to the pursuit of illusory goals, Plato shows little hesitancy in wiping them away. The theory of Forms supports this orientation, by posing a counterpart of perfection to existing imperfection. The forms supply the only proper answers to all moral questions. People who hold values removed from the Forms are simply wrong. As Plato says, they unsuccessfully strive to hit the mark which they know is there but are unable to perceive.

The political implications of Plato's belief in objectively grounded moral truths are that man as he is corrupt, and so removed from the realm of absolute value and truth. Accordingly, the individual can have no moral claim to protest against them being educated by the state. Because the goal of the education process is objectively good, his reasons for resisting can only lie in his corrupting flesh—all the more reason to help him. Again, Plato does not believe that grown up adults can be reshaped, and so questions of moral reform do not arise in regard to them..

Plato's attitude toward individual liberty demands a closer scrutiny. The kind of liberty that concerns us here is so-called "negative freedom," the kind of freedom most closely associated with the liberal political tradition. This is basically freedom from coercive interference by other individuals. It entails some autonomous area in which an individual can be assured of being so free. Now, it is clear that the inhabitants of the ideal state are granted very little of this. Those liberties that liberals believe to constitute the autonomy of the individual—freedom of though, of speech, of worship, freedom to live as one pleases—are almost completely denied to the inhabitants of the ideal state.

This is seen perhaps most clearly in regard to what they believe. The cohesiveness and stability of the ideal state rest on its members agreeing as to rulers and ruled. Plato is more than willing to have this assent result from a ruthless process of indoctrination. In Book III he declares that falsehoods can often be useful, as a kind of medicine or drug, which the rulers can employ for the good of the state. In two contexts, he recommends that specific deceptions be employed. First is the rigged lottery used to deceive the inferior Guardians. They are to believe that their ability to reproduce is curtailed by chance rather than by the rulers. What is striking here is that such deception is advocated for Guardians, not for craftsmen.

Guardians are also to be deceived by the notorious "myth of the metals" encountered in Book III. The myth is intended to foster unity in the city. It is made up of two parts. First, all citizens—including the rulers and auxiliaries—should be made to believe though they are brothers; they fall naturally into three classes. Some were born with gold in their souls and should rule; others have silver and should be Auxiliaries, while the rest have bronze and should be farmers and craftsmen. He believes the natural differences between the three main kinds of men. But there is no doubt that even if the myth did not express basic truths, Plato would uphold its use anyway, if he believed it to be for the good of the state.

Much more important than Plato's willingness to play deception is his advocacy of intensive education. Such education should be regarded as interfering with the freedom of the state's inhabitants. But basically, though once the inhabitants' beliefs have been formed physically, force will not be needed to get them to behave in the prescribed fashion, the fact that the state has so tightly controlled what they have been made to think should be regarded as a deprivation of freedom. By educating them in this way, the state has sharply limited the range of their possible choices, just as surely as if it had blocked them off with armed guards.

Plato clearly sees little reason not to interfere with the liberty of the inhabitants. Unlike recent liberal political thinkers, he does not see such freedom as an essential component of human dignity. In his classic work, *Four Essays on Liberty,* Isaiah Berlin defends the opposite position: "to be free to choose, and not be chosen for, is an inalienable ingredient in what make human beings human." Plato does not see things in this light; he does not consider freedom as an end in itself. But even more, he does not believe it is an important instrument to the realization of other values. Plato believes that freedom to choose between different values or styles of life loses much of its importance if one set of ideas is believed to be correct or one mode of life demonstrably best. In these cases the freedom to think differently would boil down to the freedom to be incorrect, and freedom to live differently to freedom to follow an inferior course. Because Plato believes in objectively grounded moral truths and in the demonstrable superiority of a relatively set way of life based upon them, he sees little reason to grant individuals the ability to think or to live differently. Berlin spells out the connection between freedom and objective values—grounded in his conviction that there is no single set of all-encompassing, absolutely valid moral truths. Because Plato believes that there is a single solution to all human problems, that the universe as a whole is divinely directed towards a single goal, he does not see the need to provide individuals with the opportunity to think or to choose differently.

Interestingly enough, in a crucial passage in Book IX Plato explicitly declares that the citizens of his state will be set free. Plato states that individuals who reasoning faculties are not naturally strong enough to rule the beast within must be enslaved to and molded by the rulers of the state, so that all can be "alike and friendly and governed by the same principle". The implication of this passage is that, after undergoing some finite period of training under the Guardians, individuals will be removed from their control. Exactly what this means is not indicated. But surely Plato is presenting a contrast between the treatment of children and of adults. This sort of contrast is familiar. Since children, especially younger children, are neither fully rational nor in possession of the elementary knowledge needed to survive on their own, it is generally recognized that they must be placed under the supervision of adults until they reach the age of maturity. It is also widely recognized that once individuals achieve maturity, this period of subordination comes to an end, and individuals must begin to lead their own lives.

What distinguishes Plato's case is that, aside from the rulers, the citizens of the ideal state never seem to come of age. Certainly, they will never be free to choose from among a variety of kinds of art or from competing philosophical belief systems. The intellectual life of the state is rigidly controlled, with censorship applied to all artistic or other creations that deviate from the one true path. In these important respects, and no doubt in others also, the state never stops exercising parental control over its citizens. In a word, Plato has too little faith in the ability and character of human beings to allow them freely to lead their own lives. Plato sees the vast majority of people as somewhat less than human—as the philosopher-rulers are regarded as almost more than human. As one commentator says: "Plato's estimate of the human race is at once incredibly low and incredibly high. Between the wisdom of the few and the docility of the rest the human race has never been so exalted or so abased."

Karl Popper was revered by politicians on both the right and left for his passionate arguments against Marxism and all other 'totalitarian' doctrines. The central idea he defended against such doctrines was that of democratic governance. In his 'intellectual autobiography' entitled *Untended Quest.* Popper tells us that at 17 he regarded himself as a communist, but after three months he was 'disenchanted'. What upset him was that he had so far 'accepted a dangerous creed uncritically, dogmatically' – the creed that by knowledge of the laws of historical development one could create a better world. He soon realized ' the incredible arrogance' of Marxism, the arrogant to oneself' a kind of knowledge which made it a duty to risk the lives of other people... for a dream which might turn out not to be realizable.

His horror of such a creed resulted, 50 years ago, in *The Poverty of Historicism* and *the Open Society and Its Enemies.* The first volume of *The Open Society* was called 'The Spell of Plato'. Popper traced the Marxist creed 2,000 years back to Plato. Popper was not revolted by Plato's advocacy of a limited communism in the *Republic* – that the small class of the state's rulers should have all things in common, including women and children. That the children should be produced and reared entirely for the sake of the state. These measures do not apply to the rest of the citizens. What draws Popper's ire is Plato's wider political theory – his 'holism', his blueprint for an ideal state, his concept of governance and his dislike of democracy.

Plato, deeply concerned about the ills of his own society, held that an ideal state would be one where one or more persons of sterling intellectual and moral worth would be appointed rulers after being put through a rigorous training. These guardians would look after the welfare and stability of the state and defend it against any threats, external or internal. Once installed, they must be given absolute power to act without any interference or criticism from the citizens for, says Plato, 'no wrong can possibly be done' by such good, wise and well-trained rulers. They could do just anything for the good of the state, even to the extent of eliminating anyone likely to be a hindrance or unlikely to contribute to the welfare of the state.

Admitting Plato's brilliant analysis of the ills of society, Popper is still to a large extent justified in condemning many of Plato's remedies. To those brought up on democratic ideals, a first reading of the *Republic* is indeed disturbing. In Plato, Popper sees the genesis of modern totalitarianism. Plato and Marxism taught him lessons he has never forgotten. 'They made me the value of intellectual modesty and made me most conscious of the differences between dogmatic and critical thinking'. Suspicious of grand utopian planning, he strongly recommends piecemeal social engineering. It has been admitted even by Popper's admirers that 'the depth of passion which informs his defense of liberty' makes him less than fair to his adversaries. He quotes out of context and, though he learnt Greek to read Plato in the original, the accuracy of his translations and the correctness of his interpretations have been challenged. It must also be noted that even in the *Republic,* suspicious as he was of democracy as he knew it Plato, is dead against power-mad dictators, whom he refers to as the 'most miserable of men'. His philosopher-kings are quite different from the type of dictators the world has always known.

Plato's description of democratic society and the democratic individual is an indictment of the citizens and political life of Athens. It is an accurate picture, it is a portrait of Athens at the end of the fifth century, after her defeat at the hands of Sparta in the Peloponnesian War. It is emphatically not a recognizable account of Athenian life at the time of the Persian invasions or even at the beginning of the Peloponnesian War. Plato's picture is not a fair or objective account of democratic government as such and it was probably not intended to be. If all the citizens of a state manifested the virtues of the philosopher-king, Plato would not object to their use of democratic decision procedures. The real object of his scorn is the careless hedonism of his "democratic man."

Unlike the personal characteristic of the other forms of government, the "democratic man" is not depicted as a ruler in his society, but that is no surprise, for democracy as Plato describes it is a government in which no one rules, but each individual may "take to politics" on occasion and say "whatever comes into his head." This is not fair description of the democratic leadership of Pericles, but the Athenian assembly did allow all citizens to speak on topics of public policy. Of course, unbridled exercise of that right would lead to anarchy, but anarchy is not, in Plato's mind, very different from democracy.

How much of what he says applies to modern western democracy? That is a question for the reader to determine, but there are some disturbing parallels between his account and contemporary life. Today's democratic citizens often seem as unconcerned with the public good and as devoted to the pursuit of the latest trend in pleasure-seeking as Plato claims and, like his "democratic man," many find nothing in principle wrong with such self-absorbed hedonism. To the extent that Plato's character resembles the citizens of a modern democracy, his criticisms are not one we can simply dismiss as irrelevant to our current condition.

Plato thought that democracy degenerates into tyranny. As each successive government is ruled by progressively worse elements in the state, tyranny is the government of the worst cut-throats in the criminal class. Ironically, Plato thinks it is the extreme love of liberty among democrats that gives these "stinging drones" a chance to gain power. When they are in charge, they introduce a reign of terror, killing their enemies and confiscating the property of the rich. In order to remain in power, the tyrant must eliminate every person of virtue from the society, for such persons constitute a threat to his rule. The tyrant, Plato says, is the opposite of the good physician who administers a purge to his patient: "for doctors remove the worst element and leave the best, but he does the opposite".

As the tyrannical state is ruled by the worst elements in it, so the tyrannical individual is ruled by the worst elements in his soul. Like the oligarch and the democrat, the tyrant is devoted to pleasure, but unlike them, he knows no moderation or subordination in its pursuit. He pursues the most lawless and violent of the unnecessary pleasures

The waking life of the tyrant, however, resembles the worst nightmares of the philosopher. The tyrant is enslaved to some violent and lawless passion, which he will do anything to satisfy. Plato's tyrant, in other words, is an addict, though the object of his addiction may vary. The depiction of such a person is realistic enough, and contains some impressive anticipations of Freudian psychology, but it is not easy to see a person of this sort as the leader of a state, because the addiction would make normal political activity impossible for him. The tyrant would be unable to rule by virtue of mental illness. Nonetheless, it must be said that ancient tyrants were known to perform many of the violent and lawless acts Plato mentions, and at least Stalin and Hitler among modern tyrants seem to have been in the grip of some sort of psychopathology, if not quite that Plato describes.

Once the life of the tyrant has been described as a life of addictive pursuit of lawless pleasures, it is clear that every one would prefer to the life of the philosopher. The earlier attractiveness of such a life is now seen to be a sham, based on external appearances only. Plato, however, adds several arguments to show that the philosopher is happier than the tyrant. The first is based on the analogy between the city and individual. Tyranny is clearly the worst of states, so the tyrant should be unhappiest of people. As the populace of a tyranny is enslaved to the worst element in it so is the tyrant. As the tyrannical state is impoverished so is the life of the tyrant. Finally, as the citizens of a tyranny live in fear and anguish, so much the tyrant, who must live in constant fear of being overthrown. Once Plato's hostility and contempt for the tyrannical state is known, it will not be fair to attract Plato as the father of modern totalitarianism.

To some extent Plato's hostility to the democracy can be attributed to his economic and social background. The conservative land-holding classes from which he came saw the rise of the commercial economy as a threat to their economic position and political aspirations. Democratic government undermined their traditional claims to political domination while militant, expansionist imperial foreign policies also threatened their economic interest. Being the wealthier elements in society, they had the most to lose through war. War taxes fell upon them especially hard, and during the Peloponnesian War, when Athens retreated behind its walls; it was their land that was ravaged by the Spartans. Aristophanes describes what happens when a new military venture is proposed. Someone brings a proposal that the fleets be launched; the poor vote "Yes", and the rich determined farmers "No". Faced with the need to protect their class interests, conservative elements were delimited to subvert the democratic system. In the closing years of the Peloponnesian War two such attempts were made.

Throughout his writings Plato reveals many of his class's attitudes and biases. Many of his criticisms of the Athenian system and of democracy in general—were common to his class, and it should be realized that much of what he says along these lines is colored by an almost inbred hatred of these features of his state. Supporters and defenders of the Athenian system have long accused him of unfairness and have amassed considerable evidence to counter his depiction of the democratic regime.

Plato's criticism of the Athenian democracy is carried on in many of his works. The *Republic* and *Gorgias* contain direct political critiques, but in addition to what is said in these works is what is implied. The fact that Plato does not talk about alliances or other forms of cooperation between cities in his political works is significant, as is his low opinion of inter-city commerce. It is significant that the ideal states in the *Republic* and *Laws* are to be without commercial relations with other states. According to Plato, not only does foreign trade foster undesirable customs and beliefs, but it also upsets the economic balance of a city, enriching some and impoverishing others. In the *Laws*, Plato says that commerce makes a city unfriendly within itself and to other cities. In his political dialogues he turns his back on the world in which he lives in order to promote the merits of something closer to an ideal-type polis, rooted in political and economic authonomy. He retreats from the Greek world of his own time to an earlier, more ideal situation—perhaps one that never fully existed—in which the polis was able to do its job of forming and morally educating its inhabitants, free from outside interference.

In another respect as well, the political view expressed in the *Republic* and *Laws* represents a return to earlier times. As the separate Greek cities retreated from economic and political isolation, the ties binding the citizen to his community weakened. The communal spirit idealized by many Greek political philosophers took a reheat before ever-growing individualism. The religious underpinning of the state's laws was widely questioned, and individuals more frequently put their own welfare before the welfare of their cities. Such individualism is reflected in numerous changes in the political scene. One important development is the rise of mercenary soldiers. Whereas in former times, cities had been defended by armies of citizen soldiers, during the fourth century they increasingly turned to hired spleens. Other forms of public service were also on the wane. In Athens, citizens increasingly demanded payment for performing state functions, while the conduct of political affairs passed into the hands of a class of professional politicians. During the fifth century, pay was introduced for serving in the Assmbly and on jury duty. During subsequent decades the practice of state pay expanded, as citizens began to receive payment for attending state festivals. In the year 358 a special fund, the theoric fund, was set up to provide poor relief on a regular basis. Management of the theoric fund became a locus of power in Athenian politics, eventually coming to control state finances as a whole.

These changes are indicative of important changes in the nature of the polis itself. From a moral community, it was evolving in the direction of an association of individuals interested primarily in their own well-being. Thus in *Republic* Glaucon presents the view that justice was founded by individuals motivated by selfinterest, a view that approaches liberal, social contract theory. Along similar lines, the sophist Lycophron asserted that the polis exists merely to protect the rights of its citizens. The degree of self-interest in Athenes is attested to by the orator Aeschines. "You leave the Assembly," he said to his fellow citizens, "not after deliberating but after dividing up the surplus like shareholders". Here too Plato's political writings contain an implicit critique and a return to an earlier state of affairs. In the ideal cities described in the *Republic* and *Laws,* the polis reasserts its claims upon the individual. The primary task of the polis is to promote the virtue of its citizens, while the sharp divided between economic and politics in both works marks another return to an earlier, more ideal era.

> For with the human race division of labor begins at the outset, and man and woman have different functions; thus, they supply each other's wants, putting their special capacities into the common stock. Hence, the friendship of man and wife seems to be one of utility and pleasure combined. But it may be based on virtue, if the partners be of high moral character; for either sex has its special virtue, and this may be the ground of attraction. Children, too, seem to be a bond of union, and therefore childless marriages are more easily dissolved; for children are a good possessed by both parents in common, and common property holds people together.

Plato, in contrast, abstracts the sexual motive from the total relationship and turns the individual into a mere means to the State's ends. He thus denies to the whole personality the love and friendship and personal parental experience that are so essential to the happiness of a family.

More generally, one can question the underlying assumption of Plato's ascetic communism, namely that material conditions are the cause of political corruption and other evils. Plato subjects his rulers to extreme deprivation in the hope that this will produce a to tally new human character. Thus, for all of his emphasis on spirit, Plato tends to belittle spirit. He does not fully trust education to change attitude of mind and character so that the very same material conditions that in others were connected with corruption would have an entirely opposite effect on the philosopher-rulers.

Aristotle, on the other hand, seeing things quite differently, recognizes that although material conditions may often be associated with evil, they are not causes or active forces. He therefore justifies private property, in spite of its temptations, as a basis of personality and as an instrument of action.

Similarly, the family may have limitations, but it is an indispensable nursery in which the child develops his or her sense of self. In abolishing the family, then, Plato effectively destroys the context in which human beings first come to know themselves as distinct individuals, and in which they learn to think, act, and exercise their will.

It is not only the family but also other small groups that Plato abolishes. There is no intermediate association, lower than the State, with which individuals can identity themselves. Plato is zealous in his, commitment to the creation of a perfectly integrated organic unity. For him I there is no greater evil for a State than its differentiation into a plurality of associations. For Plato the best society is that, whose State is "most like that of an individual human being". In the Greece of Plato's time there were, of course, families, clans, phratries, tribes and demes, religious associations, manufacturing and trading groups, and other organizations intermediate between the individual and the State. These are genuine historical institutions that find no place in Plato's scheme, although they do find recognition in the theory of Aristotle who regards households and villages as constituent elements of society and who speaks of tribesmen and demesmen as forming associations which are essential parts of it. Plato so thoroughly identifies the guardian with the State that the result, as Aristotle remarks, is not one which Plato would wish for:

> The unity of the state which Socrates praises most highly, both appears to be and is said by him to be the effect of friendship, just as we know that Aristophanes [in Plato's *Symposium*] in the discourse on love describes how the lovers owing to their extreme affection desire to grow together and both become one instead of being two. In such a union both personalities, or at least one, would be bound to be obliterated....

Social unity, for Plato, often appears to be an end in itself rather than a quality that society must possess in order to attain a worthwhile end. So the personalities of the guardians are severely diminished, if not obliterated, in their fusion with the State; and the individual members of the third class of citizens are also reduced to just one part of their minds and personalities—the appetitive.

The Republic: Utopia or Reality

In the light of the criticisms, which from the time of Aristotle have been made of Plato's ideal state, it might well be asked whether he had intended this work to influence actual life. There are passages suggesting that although Plato recognized difficulties in implementing his program, he believed it was practicable. Greece of Plato's time was torn by factions that created enmity among the city-states. One major aim of the *Republic,* then, was to teach the Greeks how to found cities which would be fundamentally different, cities without internal strife and in which the citizens would be *philhellenes*, or lovers of Greeks, and who would therefore regard all of Greece as their homeland and revere the holy places common to all Greeks. Such cities would refuse to make war upon one another, and would settle all quarrels amicably, striving for reconciliation. This is Plato's pan-Hellenism, which never became a universal vision.

Plato acknowledges that the realization of his ideal state would be difficult, but he maintains that it is not impossible and that the social and political structure he has outlined would yield the best society and state known to humanity. In order to realize it, however, the Philosophical Muse would have to gain control of the state—the state would have to be mastered by real philosophers for whom justice is the chief and indispensable concern. Yet the difficulties of which Plato speaks are such that the project must begin with a social *tabula rasa.* This would mean that all the inhabitants over the age of ten would be sent out into the country where the guardians will take over the children, remove them from the old customs and habits of their parents, and bring them up in accordance with the guardians' teachings and rules.

There are, however, other passages which occur late in the *Republic,* in the Ninth Book, suggesting that the work was in fact intended as an ideal. In response to Socrates' detailed description of the new society and the role of the wise ruler in it, Glaucon says he understands that the city just described is one whose home is in the ideal, "for I think that it can be found nowhere on earth." And Socrates comments that perhaps it is only an extraterrestrial pattern existing for those who wish to contemplate it and strive to become its citizen. But whether it exists now or ever will is immaterial, since it is only that city's politics, which the lover of wisdom will call his own. So the *Republic* is an ideal construction, after all, and it will have accomplished its purpose, in Plato's view, if it exists as an influence on our thoughts and actions.

The *Republic* is an inquiry into the nature of justice, in Plato's peculiar meaning of the term. And once the nature of ideal justice is discovered, the point is not to attain it, which is impossible, but only to approximate it as nearly as possible. "Ideal Justice" is a "Pattern" or "Form" that Plato seeks, asking what would be the character of the perfectly just individual and, conversely, the character of the totally unjust individual.

> These are types or models, as it were, so that whatever is discerned in them as happiness or the opposite would necessarily apply to us as we fashioned our lives after one or the other. But our aim was not to demonstrate the possibility of the realization of these ideals.

Practice must fall short of theory in approximating the ideal; for it is in the nature of things "that action partakes of exact truth less than speech". Plato's method assumes that principles exist, but that limiting conditions prevent the principles from producing the desired results. A thought-experiment is therefore required in which one thinks away the limiting conditions and replaces them with favorable ones. Plato is right to say that the picture emerging with this method is no daydream. It is an abstraction that can be fruitful even if it cannot be realized, for it helps us to think through the fundamental question of whether certain institutions are necessary, or merely institutions that have been with us for a long time and to which we have grown accustomed.

His communism, is problematic throughout. His ideal state is a three-class system in which the members of each are permitted to use only one part of their minds. It subjects the first two classes to an unbearably ascetic regime in which they are deprived of family and property and turned into one large single "family" with wives and children in common. And the third class, although it retains family and property, is not permitted to participation in government. And although Plato urges his rulers to guard against the development of extremes of wealth and poverty in the third class, he fails to explain how they are to guard against it in the absence of laws by which to regulate the economy. One seeks in vain for answers to other important questions as well: What advantage will members of the third class gain by submitting to the rule of the philosopher-guardians? If they will gain no advantage, what will induce them to submit? What will prevent the development in the third class of substantial social inequalities and the corresponding social conflicts? In the absence of laws regulating the economic life of the society, what is there to prevent the dispersion of interests—the unrelenting pursuit of self-interest by each of the specialized occupations, resulting in a Hobbesian war? And to repeat questions if the third class sees no advantage in submitting passively to the rulers, will they not tend to rebel? And how would the rulers deal with rebellion? In the absence of a legal and judicial system, it would seem that force and the threat of force would loom large in Plato's scheme.

In the Eighth and Ninth Books of the *Republic,* Plato seeks to measure actual states by the extent to which they depart from his ideal. As he traces successive stages in the corruption of the ideal, Plato explicitly states that even his ideal state is subject to change and, indeed, to the laws of dissolution, since everything that has come into being must also pass away. Strictly speaking, however, Plato's conception of growth and change is cyclical and logical rather than historical. Neither he nor Aristotle had a genuinely historical approach to social change. As Plato studies the four successive corruptions of the ideal state—timocracy, oligarchy, democracy, and tyranny—he follows the same logical procedure in each case, describing the origin and attributes of the corrupt form and then portraying the type of individual character to which it corresponds and from which it emerges.

Mind or soul being the criterion, Plato begins with the ideal state in which the three elements of mind—reason, spirit, and appetite—are brought into a harmonious relationship through the hegemony of reason. Just beneath the ideal state is one in which reason has lost its dominant position to spirit, which has now gained control. The next three forms of the state—oligarchy, democracy, and tyranny—are all based on the supremacy of appetite and the resulting discord in the elements of the soul.

Plato next proceeds to distinguish types of appetite—the necessary, which is beneficial, and the unnecessary, which is not—linking both to the different types of states. This yields the notion that both oligarchy and democracy rest on appetites conducive to production, although democracy represents, in addition, appetites lacking in thrift. In the Ninth Book of the *Republic* Plato goes on to make the distinction between natural and legitimate appetites and desires, and unnatural and illegitimate ones, anticipating Freud almost verbatim.

> manifest themselves while we are asleep when the rational part of the soul slumbers but the beastly and savage part asserts itself, endeavoring to satisfy its own desires. In such cases there is no sense of guilt or shame, for it does not inhibit itself from trying in our dreams, to be with a mother or with anyone else—man, god or animal; nor does it shy away from bloodshed and other foul deeds.

And it is this lawless part of our nature that is embodied in tyranny.

The other factor Plato employs to explain the corruption of states is excess and engendering a reaction in the opposite division what might be called the principle of "contradiction," anticipating Hegel and Marx:

> When an oligarchy, for instance, concentrates property and other forms of wealth in the hands of the few while the great mass of the populace suffers chronic impoverishment, the poor begin to recognize, affirm, and demand their rights as human beings. Soon a kind of "class consciousness" emerges and with it class warfare and revolution, which is easily touched off by the slightest impulse. Thus oligarchy is transformed into democracy.

The democratic city is full of liberty and freedom of speech, and individuals have license to do as they choose, to lead their own lives the way they please. Plato likens democracy to a "multicolored garment embroidered with a variety of fibers so that this multifarious society with every type of character would appear to be the best and the most beautiful". But democracy has a basic defect in that it tramples under foot Plato's ideals and allows individuals from any walk of life to participate in politics and to hold office. Democracy, for Plato, merely appears to be a wonderful form of government and society; but actually it is unjust and anarchic, granting equality to equals and unequals alike say they love the people. Thus Plato gives us something like an economic interpretation of the structural changes which polities and societies undergo. Changes in the distribution of wealth tend to produce political changes. The state declines into inferior forms once the ideal communism of the ideal state is disturbed. The timocracy introduces private property as a prerequisite for political office; and the oligarchy makes the accumulation of private property and wealth its sole object, which gives rise to a struggle for the redistribution of wealth, to revolution, and to democracy.

Plato's first and least corrupt form of state is a timocracy, from the Greek word *time* meaning honor. In Greece it meant that power was given on the basis of a property qualification. Sparta appears to have been the model for Plato's conception of the timocratic State. It is a mixed structure of good and evil, but its most conspicuous feature is its "high-spiritedness," its contentiousness and covetousness of honor. The timocratic man is harsh to his slaves, gentle with fellow citizens, and submissive to officials. He loves political office and honor, basing his claim to them on his military prowess and exploits in war, and on his excellence in competitive athletics and hunting. The soldier, in a word, has dethroned the philosopher.

In oligarchy—the second logical stage in the decline from the ideal state—the military elite has been corrupted by the commercial motive. The appetite for wealth, which had already existed in the timocracy, becomes the dominant motive. Property and wealth are the sole qualifications for holding political office, so that the rich hold power and the poor are excluded and the rich put through laws claiming legitimacy for their power by force of arms and by the threat of force. Such a city is not one but two, "a city of the rich and a city of the poor, dwelling together, but always conspiring against one another". And worst of all, such cities produce impoverished, dependent proletarians, beggars, thieves, purse-snatchers, temple robbers, and other artists in crime.

The third stage of decline is democracy; and here we find that all of the features of democracy which Pericles lauded in his funeral oration that Plato views as evil. Plato and Socrates before him had somehow failed to see that it is precisely a democracy which can best combine individual initiative with a common social purpose; that differentiation and specialization of natural capacity, which Plato himself held to be a necessary condition of justice—nay, justice itself—can be most readily achieved in the state in which there exists the most freedom of opportunity to discover one's capacities and thus one's calling. What democracy meant in ancient Greece and still means today is government by the common mind and will of a free citizenry. For Plato, however, democracy is anarchism pure and simple. Liberty and equality, far from being goods, principles, or self-evident truths, were rather the negation of principles, since they ignored the proper hierarchical basis of social order. Worse, democracy is in its very essence the negation of "justice" in Plato's sense, for it rests on the absolute rejection of the principle of specific function, which is shown most clearly in its refusal to choose its leaders from among the philosophers.

In the history of ancient Greece tyranny arose as a reaction to oligarchy, a rigid and oppressive aristocratic regime. The people, weary of poverty and oppression, gave themselves over to a strongman who seized power by force and maintained the allegiance of the people, at least temporarily, by improving their lot at the expense of the wealthy. In Plato's view, in contrast, it is democracy, with its excess of liberty, or more precisely its excessive thirst for liberty, that produces tyranny. Plato arrives at this position by arguing that when the people of a democratic city athirst for liberty get bad leaders who disappoint them, they accuse them of being oligarchs. Plato thus represents Socrates as asserting that tyranny arose not in reaction to oligarchy or out of it, but out of democracy. In a democratic city, Plato sardonically comments, even the dogs, horses, and asses exude the spirit of liberty, jostling anyone who does not readily step aside.

It is quite likely that Plato's conception of tyranny—the lowest and most degraded form of the state—was derived from his reflections on the history of Syracuse and the regime of Dionysius I. At first the tyrant is like the young lion-cub in Aeschylus' *Agamemnon,* smiling on the people's hand that feeds him for need of its support. When he has entrenched himself in power, he embarks on a policy of war, which makes his leadership necessary and distracts the people's attention from their troubles. Then when his old associates who helped him seize power begin to criticize his rule, the tyrant ruthlessly removes them from his path. This proves inadequate as criticism mounts, so he hires mercenaries to protect him; to maintain his power he not only confiscates the estates of the wealthy but also intensifies his oppression of the people, the very power that created him.

Conclusion

Any final assessment of the *Republic* is very difficult. The older generations of commentators were perhaps too apt to idealize Plato; they partly ignored and partly excused anything with which they disagreed, and it is sometimes not easy to discover from them that Plato was not a good nineteenth-century liberal. Hardly a note of criticism will be found for example, in such an admirable standard commentary as A.E. Taylor's *Plato*. Commentators during the last fifty years have become more critical. Fite, in *The Platonic Legend,* deconstructs and deprecates earlier idealization, and finds Plato to be an aristocrat, something of a snob, and the advocate of a restrictively organized society. With the growth of totalitarian regimes, criticism became sharper but often, because of contemporary anxieties, less balanced. Crossman, trying in his *Plato Today* to assess how Plato would have looked at our contemporary world, sums him up as a reactionary who encouraged in practice the 'dictatorship of the virtuous Right" and who advocated the unscrupulous use of propaganda. Karl Popper's criticisms are even more formidable, both because of their weight of detail and their wide currency. Plato is a totalitarian opposed to all liberal or humanitarian ideas. He is a Utopian, in the sense that his method of approach to political problems is to prepare in advance a blueprint of the society at which we aim and then be ruthless in putting it into effect; he similarly supposes that politics can be reduced to an exact science, a view for which he is also criticized by Weldon and Fite who speak of his 'illusion of geometrical method and 'scientific prepossession' And Popper has further charges. Plato advocates the use by his rulers of the unscrupulous lie, is a 'historicist' and a 'racialist'.

These charges are, of course, not entirely groundless. But it is important to distinguish those which have some basis from those which are due to misunderstanding or which reflect contemporary modern anxieties rather than what Plato said or meant. Thus the charge of countenancing the unscrupulous use of propaganda rests partly on the mistranslation of the Greek *gennaion pseudos* as 'noble lie.' The Foundation Myth is clearly intended to express in fictional form essential truths about the new society, just as the myths on which we bring up children express—or should express—truths about God and human behaviour. It is not a piece of propaganda in any proper sense of the word. Plato is of course aware that in some circumstances it may not be desirable to tell the exact truth; there are 'medicinal lies', which rulers may on occasion use, as ordinary people use them. But the only use actually recommended in the *Republic* is to deceive those who are 'unlucky' in the eugenically rigged lots at the marriage festivals and here there is perhaps a certain irony. The charge of racism is even more questionable. Racism is an emotive issue today, and it is important first to state clearly what it entails. A racist must assume that birth into a particular racial group in itself confers superiority, he must despise other racial groups to a greater or lesser extent, and be ready to persecute them or ill-treat them. How far are these attitudes to be found among the Greeks generally and in Plato in particular? The Greeks were certainly conscious of their difference from other peoples, whom they called collectively 'barbarians.' But as a Greek scholar has pointed out, the term 'barbarian' was not one of loathing or contempt; it was simply a general term for those who did not speak Greek, but made odd 'bar-bar' noises. The Greeks knew very well that this included both comparatively primitive peoples, and peoples such as the Persians and Egyptians who had established civilizations which many of them admired. Not unnaturally they preferred their own way of life and culture, and after the Persian wars they were conscious of a certain enmity between themselves and the 'barbarian' world. But it is extremely doubtful whether the term 'racism can be used with any propriety of this general attitude. It is an attitude, which Plato seems largely to have shared. 'Barbarians' arc foreigners in a sense that fellow-Greeks are not, and if Greeks do fight each other, they should exercise greater restraint than they would in wars with foreigners.

Indeed, though Plato to a great extent shared the ordinary Greek attitude, he expresses admiration in the *Laws* for the Egyptians, he can express in the *Theaetetus* a contemptuous opinion of the advantages of birth, and allow the possibility of his ideal state being realized among 'barbarians'. And there is one point at which Popper's anxiety to press home the charge of racism leads him to positive misstatement. Having described the "foundation myth", in emotive and misleading terms, as the myth of Blood and Soil, he proceeds to treat the 'metals' as 'racial characteristics'. This is sheer nonsense. Plato's citizens are all Greeks—the section on warfare emphatically describes them as such and the qualities symbolized by the metals are therefore not racial at all. Plato was, as has so often been observed, temperamentally an aristocrat. And he believed that the qualities needed in his rulers were, in general, hereditary and that given knowledge and opportunity one could deliberately breed for them. But belief in a hereditary class of rulers, though it may be mistaken or even, wicked, is not a form of racism, any more than was the concern in the past of so many English parents that their children should marry into 'good families'. Plato is emphatic that exceptions occur and that promotion and demotion are a necessary part of his scheme. The charge of racism hardly sticks. Nor, if we consider the Greek background, does the charge of historicism, by which Popper means a belief in historical inevitability, the doctrine that there are predictable regularities in the course of human history which the historical and social sciences can discover. It is true that Plato in VII Book speaks as if there were an inevitable process of degeneration in human society; and that in the *Timaeus* and *Laws* he speaks of recurrent natural catastrophes after which the arts and sciences have painfully to be relearned. But a belief in decline from a golden age and belief in recurrent cycles were not uncommon in antiquity, and it is doubtful how far, even in Plato, they reached the level of serious philosophical doctrine. Most peoples have views about the past, expressed in stories; but these hardly rank with the theories of Hegel and Marx.

In other charges there is more substance. Plato had little sympathy with democracy as he had seen it in Athens nor would he have had much sympathy with any regime in which popular approval was an important factor in selecting those who are to direct the workings of society. If government is, as it must be, operated by a chosen minority, then the people's choice is liable to be a bad choice because the people are so easily deceived. This may show an aristocratic bias; but Plato's basic preference was not for an aristocracy in the common sense, but for trained expertise. It is true that he thinks this is likely to be provided by heredity guided by eugenics; but expertise and trained ability are the guiding criteria. Crossman thinks that the result would be a dictatorship of the virtuous Right. But Plato, as Popper rightly points out, is a Utopian and a planner; and that approach is more characteristic of the virtuous Left, as perhaps Bertrand Russell and Fite were suggesting when they pointed to Soviet Russia as the state most nearly run on Platonic principles. Was Plato then a totalitarian—Popper's main charge? If by a 'totalitarian' we mean one for whom the state is everything, the individual nothing, then, great as is his interest in people and personalities in much of what he wrote, when he turned explicitly to society and politics the individual seems to count for very little. There seem to be two approaches to the consideration of social and political issues. One, remembering the importance of order and coherence in society, stresses the need for planning and central authority. The other, remembering the diversity of human beings, stresses the need for a variety of institutions and a diversity of pattern. We may call them the centralist and the pluralist views. One will tend to overstress authority and order, the other to degenerate in practice into chaos. Plato was a centralist, partly because he was also a Utopian and thought, as his critics charge, that politics could be a much more exact study than it is. He wanted a plan, he wanted power to order society according to it, and he had, perhaps, a touch of the ruthlessness-which this kind of approach often engenders. You only have to be determined enough to realize heaven on earth to be sure of raising hell.

The *Republic,* in fact, is a long book, covering many topics, and the impression it makes on us depends to some extent on the eyes with which we look at it. Let us be critical; Plato would have wished it. But let us keep a sense of proportion and not ride our own political hobby-horses too hard. Let us remember that a great deal of the *Republic* is not about politics at all. A large part of it is about education, and has been a continued source of stimulus to educational thinking and pedagogic practice; there is a great deal about individual morality-the balance of impulses under the control of reason, the passionate desire for truth, the underlying religious seriousness. There is literary criticism, there is philosophy, there is a wealth of incidental comment on many things. When we do come to politics we find that Plato has little sympathy with the kind of outlook we should call democratic. He had seen democracy at work in Athens, and was too deeply critical of its faults to regard it as a desirable form of government. And if we disagree with him, we should start by trying to understand his criticisms and the problems he was trying to solve. The Philosopher Ruler is a mirage, a product of the kind of idealism which asks too much of human nature and is then disappointed by what it finds; but he does stand for a set of problems which are real, and to which every society must find its answer.

The *Republic* is traditionally divided into ten books. But this division, as has often been pointed out, was dictated rather by the technicalities of book-production in the ancient world, than by the sequence of the argument. It is in dialogue form and its style is conversational. The dialogue form was used by some of Plato's contemporaries, Xenophon, for example, as well as by Plato himself; and many have used it since his day. But in the hands of his successors and imitators it is often more formal than dramatic, more a device for much detail as possible from one language to another. The approach has its advantages because it is clearly desirable to lose as little as possible in the transfer. But there are many authors, Plato among them, who cannot properly be translated word for word. The result is too often 'tedious, or grotesque, or silly, or pompous and verbose'. The method adopted by Cornford has produced a version in natural and readable English, but to be fairly free in rendering the Greek, and to cut and compress if the original seems tedious. It is of course true that Plato, one of the most readable of authors, ought not to be represented in English by a version which has the defects which Cornford censures.

This is partly because of the particular conditions under which Plato wrote. The Athenians loved an argument; their political life was one of constant discussion in Assembly and law court, and they spent most of their spare time in the public places of Athens gossiping, debating, discussing, or listening to other. The activity of Socrates fitted naturally into this context, and though a discussion with him must surely have been, in reality as well as in Plato's representation, a rather one-sided affair, yet those who took part in it undoubtedly felt that they had taken part in a genuine argument. Socrates was a conversationalist, not a lecturer.

It is this conversational atmosphere that Plato reproduces in his dialogues. Their style, of course, varies with the turns of the argument; it can be light-hearted or serious, philosophical or descriptive or dramatic according to the context. And in a work of the length of the *Republic* the dramatic and conversational element can vary; in much of the argument there is very little of it. But nonetheless the general impression left is that of a conversation and the style at which the translator must aim is that of an intelligent discussion; he must use the kind of language that people really do use when they are talking about the sort of topics with which the *Republic* deals.

Plato wrote nothing about himself, and mentioned his name in his works only twice—in *Apology* and *Phaedo*. But when he was asked if there would be any memoirs of him, he replied: "A man must first make a name, and he will have no lack of memoirs." Plato's stature increased with passing generations. Brutus, who murdered Caesar because he deplored any form of tyranny, received a Platonic education. Plato was dead, but people still came to the Academy realizing that what was important was not the acquirement of knowledge but the eternal quest for it. Why has Plato exercised such a tremendous influence and why do the problems he considered continue to disturb us more than two thousand years later? Plato was the founder of what we now call objective idealism. This is why he continues to have such a great influence on the development of philosophy. Lenin wrote: "Could the struggle between materialism and idealism, the struggle between the tendencies or lines of Plato or Democritus in philosophy, the struggle between religion and science, the denial of objective truth and its assertion, the struggle between the adherents of supersensible knowledge and its adversaries, have become antiquated during the two thousand years of the development of philosophy?" But Plato's objective idealism as a world-view is the least of his contributions to the history of philosophy.

It should also be noted that readers of Plato invariably find in his works some form of support for their own philosophical strivings. We all find something of value, something that tell us we are not alone in our confusion, in our rambling and digression, that this was something familiar even to the "divine" Plato. And this means that this is permissible, even necessary, in order to understand the essential.

Almost all the better known modern philosophers present their philosophical theories in a complete and well thought out form. Usually it is impossible to ascertain how they arrived at their system and what doubts plagued them before this discovery. We are called upon to simply accept the system. This is not the case with Plato, who compels the reader to reflect upon his system as he himself has done. Plato does not conceal his doubts, uncertainty or weaknesses. This is democracy in thought, and as such it has proved attractive to numerous people in different eras and different parts of the world. Plato always keeps us in suspense, waiting for that decisive and final statement that he continues to postpone pronouncing. Then there are times when he disperses all our doubts and confusion with a single phrase. Plato's philosophical system is composed of separate and often contradictory judgements. Also, the terminology he uses generally has multiple meaning; even his famous "idea" can be construed in different ways. Plato can never be accused of being dogmatic. His philosophy is the path of sharp criticism and never-ending dialectics.

The truly great individual fears neither bitter denunciation nor effusive praise. Plato was a great man not just because he was the source of a phenomenal philosophical movement but because he was a complex and contradictory individual often at conflict with himself, his surroundings and even with his own epoch.

The European philosophical tradition indebted hugely to Plato. In the words of Whitehead:

> The safest general characterization of the European philosophical tradition is that it consists of a series of footnotes to Plato. I do not mean the systematic scheme of thought which scholars have doubtfully extracted from his writings allude to the wealth of general ideas scattered through them. His personal endowments, his wide opportunities for experience at a great period of civilization, his inheritance of an intellectual tradition not yet stiffened by excessive systematization, have made his writing an inexhaustible mine of suggestion.

The creation of philosophy was not simply a matter of giving name to a new method of inequiry and argumentation. Rather, philosophy had to make a case for itself as a discipline that offered a unique kind of wisdom, which rivaled the other brands on offer. This was by no means a simple enterprise, as Plato's frequent attempts to define and legitimize philosophy clearly attest. Plato defined philosophy at least in part by way of the rhetoric of invective and exclusion-rhetoric which had a specific valence in the context of the social and political structures of democratic Athens. But he did not rest content with explicit definitions and denunciations. For Plato also marked the boundaries of philosophy by scripting intertextual encounters with traditional genres of poetry and rhetoric. Although Plato is famous for his quarrels with "poetry" and "rhetoric" as super genres, his parodic attacks invariably focus on individual genres of literature. Why did Plato opt for the intertextual mode? And what is distinctive about Plato's use of intertextuality? First of all, Plato regularly chooses to interact with the texts of genres other than his own. His target, moreover, is never simply an individual author or text. For, when he incorporates a particular work of poetry or rhetoric into a dialogue, he invariably treats it as the representative of a genre. In fact, the incorporated texts are often composed by Plato himself: take, for example, the funeral oration in the *Menexenus,* or the encomiastic speeches in the *Symposium.* Since Plato is concerned not so much with a specific author or text as with the genre as a whole, it makes little difference whether the subtext is written by Plato or by someone else. It should be emphasized that Plato targets genres that have currency in classical Athens-genres which make some claim to wisdom or authority. Not surprisingly, then, when Plato engages with a given genre of discourse, his stance is usually adversarial. Plato uses intertextuality as a vehicle for criticizing traditional genres of discourse and, what is more important, for introducing and defining a radically different discursive practice, which he calls "philosophy". Plato incorporates other texts and genres into his dialogues in a number of different ways. He can, first of all, borrow or compose a complete text from a given genre and transplant it in his own composition: an example of this approach is the funeral oration in the *Menexenus,* which is a finished text that faithfully represents the genre of the *epitaphist.* Alternatively, a text can be incorporated by way of allusion: the numerous allusions to Euripides' *Antiope* in the *Gorgias,* for example, conjure up the themes and structure of that play together with the genre of tragedy as a whole. Finally, Plato can target a genre by incorporating the discourse, *topoi,* or themes that are peculiar to it and readily identified as such: when Callas' slave slams the door in Socrates' face at the opening of the *Protagoras,* for example, we are confronted with a *topos* from the genre of comedy.

When one genre enters into the text of another genre, it both acts and is acted upon. In this encounter, the targeted genre may be granted more or less authority. A useful discussion of this complex phenomenon is found in Bakhtin's analysis of intertextuality or "hybridization" in the genre of the novel. According to Bakhtin, the author of a "hybrid" text make use of someone else's discourse for his own purposes, by inserting a new semantic direction into a discourse which already has, and which retains, an intention of Its own. Such a discourse must be perceived as belonging to someone else. In one discourse, two semantic intentions appear, two voices, are heard.

In such cases, then, the audience or reader "is meant to hear both a version of the original utterance as the embodiment of its speaker's point of view and the second speaker's evaluation of that utterance from a different point of view. Given that Bakhtin considered the Socratic dialogue a "precursor" to the dialogic novel, it comes as no surprise that so many of Plato's texts meet Bakhtin's criteria for the "novelistic hybrid": "an artistically organized system for bringing different discourses in contact with one another, a system having as its goal the illumination of one discourse by means of anther. Plato was concerned with the discourse and the dissemination of the poetic and rhetorical genres he interrogated: these genres are criticized both as literary forms and as discursive practices, which played specific roles in the social and political life of Athens. It should come as no surprise, then that Plato introduces "philosophy" not just as an intellectual activity but as a new kind of social practice. For philosophy as Plato conceived it was not simply a distinctive mode of inquiry and argument, but rather a unique way of living based on specific ethical and political commitments.

It should go without saying that there are many aspect of Plato's effort to define philosophy, which are not addressed in this study. A more comprehensive examination would have to deal, first of all, with all of the dialogues, which define or investigate the nature of philosophy. In each dialogue, the interpreter would have to analyze both what Plato is saying about philosophy and the various methods of inquiry used by the individuals who are doing philosophy. In such a study, considerations of dating and of development would also have to be addressed. Finally, it would be necessary to examine Aristotle's conceptualization of philosophy (which differs from Plato's on a number of fundamental points), especially since it was Aristotle who composed the first and, indeed, the most influential account of the beginnings of philosophy in the West. It is precisely because Aristotle's definitions and classifications of "philosophical" thinking have come to seem so natural, in fact, that the construction of these categories requires examination.

The differentiation of literature and philosophy would indeed be absolute were it not for the fact that philosophy is itself unable to produce a coherent theory of the differences that separate it from literature. Plato's a various attempts to define philosophy examines the differentiation between literature and philosophy in the very period when the boundaries of these disciplines were first demarcated in an explicit and systematic way. As when Plato constructed the specialized discipline of philosophy, he defined it in opposition to other genres of discourse. But while Plato separated philosophy from its adversaries, he did not sequester it. Rather, he staged an ongoing dialogue between philosophy and its "other". To be sure, Plato's "conversations" with alien genres were not always friendly; parody, as we have seen, is the norm in the Platonic dialogues. But the parodies themselves, which offer painstaking and penetrating criticisms of the genres that they target, testify that Plato took "alien" genres very seriously indeed. The fact that Plato continued to compose "mixed" texts - texts in which poetic, rhetorical, and philosophical discourse are interwoven and or juxtaposed - may indicate that he considered his many attempts to offer a coherent theory of "differences" insufficient. Alternatively, he may have sensed that a complete divorce from poetry and rhetoric was unnecessary or, indeed, undesirable.

What is at stake when professional philosophers insist that certain thinkers are no philosophers? Many scholars in recent decades have suggested that philosophy is either dead or in desperate need of transformation. Not surprisingly, a number contemporary philosophers are turning to literature in their attempts to stake out new ground for philosophy (e.g. Rorty, Cavell, Williams, Nussbaum). After effacing the boundaries that have traditionally separated philosophy from other discursive practices, of course, scholars must confront a new set of problems. In particular, we need to ask whether the notion of argumentative reason can be loosened up enough to incorporate the rhetorical and figurative aspects of philosophy, discourse, while being kept tight enough to allow for its demarcation from, say, literature or non argumentative forms of persuasion.

Plato does not proceed by "loosening up" the notion of argumentative reason. But his approach to literary discourse is in many ways instructive. For, though he defines philosophy in opposition to poetry and rhetoric, Plato deliberately violates the borders, which he himself has drawn. The boundaries between philosophy and alien genres of discourse are created, deconstructed, disrupted, and created afresh. The ambivalence of this originary gesture is perhaps appropriate, since philosophy in the West has persisted by reinventing itself again and again. And this reinvention is surely necessary, since the discipline must respond to the socio-political practices as well as the intellectual developments of its respective culture. If one conceives philosophy as a discipline whose boundaries are flexible rather than fixed, its present "crisis" may be but one more round in the ongoing reconstruction of this protean discipline.

4

Aristotle

> It is evident that a city-state is among the things that exist by nature, that a human being is by nature a political animal, and that anyone who is without a city-state, not by luck but by nature, is either a god or beast.

Aristotle (384BC- 322 BC) was born at Stagira, a Macedonian city some two hundred miles to the north of Athens, in the year 384 B.C. His father was friend and physician to Amentias, King of Macedon and grandfather of Alexander. Aristotle himself seems to have become a member of the great medical fraternity of Asclepiads. He had every opportunity and encouragement to develop a scientific bent of mind: he was prepared from the beginning to become the founder of science.

We have number of stories for his youth. One narrative represents him as squandering his patrimony in riotous living, joining the army to avoid starvation, returning to Stagira to practice medicine, and going to Athens at the age of thirty to study philosophy under Plato. A more dignified story takes him to Athens at the age of eighteen, and puts him at once under the tutelage of the great master; but even in this fascinating account there is sufficient echo of a reckless and irregular youth, living rapidly.

Under Plato he studied twenty years; and indeed the pervasive Platonism of Aristotle's speculations—even of those most anti-Platonic—suggests the longer period. One would like to imagine these as very happy years; a brilliant pupil guided by an incomparable teacher, walking like Greek lovers in the gardens of philosophy. But they were both geniuses; and it is notorious that geniuses accord with one another as harmoniously as dynamite with fire. Almost half a century separated them; it was difficult for understanding to bridge the gap of years and cancel the incompatibility of souls. Plato recognized the greatness of this strange new pupil from the supposedly barbarian north. Aristotle had spent money lavishly in the collection of books. He was the first, after Euripides, to gather a library; and the foundation of the principles of library classification was among his many contributions to scholarship. A more authentic quarrel seems to have arisen towards the end of Plato's life. Our ambitious youth apparently developed an "Oedipus complex" against his spiritual father for the favors and affections of philosophy, and began to hint that wisdom would not die with Plato; while the old sage spoke of his pupil as a foal that kicks his a mother after draining her dry.

The other incidents of his Athenian period are still more problematical. Some biographers tell us that Aristotle founded a school of oratory to rival Isocratic; and that he had among his pupils in this school the wealthy Hernias, who was soon to become autocrat of the city-state. After reaching this elevation Hernias invited Aristotle to his court; and in the year 344B.C. he rewarded his teacher for past favors by bestowing upon him a sister in marriage. One might suspect this as a Greek gift; but the historians hasten to assure us that Aristotle, despite his genius, lived happily enough with his wife, and spoke of her most affectionately in his will. It was just a year later that Philip, king of Macedon, called Aristotle to the court to undertake the education of Alexander. It bespeaks the rising repute of our philosopher that the greatest monarch of the time, looking about for the greatest teacher, should single out Aristotle to be the tutor of the future master of the world.

Alexander, when Aristotle came, was a wild youth of thirteen; passionate, epileptic, almost alcoholic; it was his pastime to tame horses untamable by men. The efforts of the philosopher to cool the fires of this budding volcano were not of much avail. Alexander left philosophy after two years to mount the throne and ride the world. History leaves us free to believe that grandeur form his teacher, the most synthetic thinker in the history of thought; and that the conquest of order in the political realm by the pupil, and in the philosophic realm by the master, were but diverse sides of one noble and epic project—two magnificent Macedonians unifying two chaotic worlds.

Setting out to conquer Asia, Alexander left behind him, in the cities of Greece, governments favorable to him but populations resolutely hostile. The long tradition of a free and once imperial Athens made subjection—even to a brilliant world-conquering despot-intolerable; and the bitter eloquence of Remoistens kept the Assembly always on the edge of revolt against the "Macedonian party" that held the reins of city power. Now when Aristotle, after another period of travel, returned to Athens in the year 334 B.C., he very naturally associated with this Macedonian group, and took no pains to conceal his approval of Alexander's unifying rule.

Meanwhile life had become unmanageably complicated for Aritotle. He found himself on the one hand embroiled with Alexander for protesting against the execution of his nephew Calisthenics who had refused to worship Alexander as a god; and Alexander had answered the protest by hinting that it was quite within his omnipotence to put even philosophers to death. At the same time Aristotle was busy defending Alexander among the Athenians. He preferred Greek solidarity to city patriotism, and thought culture and science would flourish better when petty sovereignties and disputes were ended; and he saw in Alexander what Goethe was to see in Napoleon-the philosophic unity of a chaotic and intolerably manifold world. The Athenians, hungering for liberty, growled at Aristotle, and became bitter when Alexander had a statue of the philosopher put up in the heart of the hostile city. The angry crowds intrigued and clamored for his exile or his death.

And then, suddenly, Alexander died. Athens went wild with patriotic joy; the Macedonian party was overthrown, and Athenian independence was proclaimed. Antipatter, successor of Alexander and intimate friend of Aristotle, marched upon the rebellious city. Most of the Macedonian party fled. Eurymedon, a chief priest, brought in an indictment against Aristotle, charging him with having taught that prayer and sacrifice were of no avail. Aristotle saw himself fated to be tried by juries and crowd incomparably more hostile than those that had murdered Socrates. Very wisely, he left the city, saying that he would not give Athens a chance to sin a second time against philosophy. There was no cowardice in this; an accused person at Athens had always the option of preferring exile. Arrived at Chalices, Aristotle fell ill; it has been reported that the old philosopher, in utter disappointment with the turn of all things against him, committed suicide by drinking hemlock. However, induced, his illness proved fatal; and a few months after leaving Athens the lonely Aristotle died in 322BC.

Aristotle worked within the severest limitations. He was an astronomer without a telescope, a biologist without a laboratory, a physiologist and psychologist without apparatus. He was a natural historian who had to rely for his data partly on hearsay and tradition, partly on the miscellaneous specimens and prodigies that reached him from the itinerant agents of Alexander the Great. In an age when written records were few, he devoted himself to placing phenomena in historical and causal perspective. Aristotle was also among the first to study comparative government to analyze the life history of institutions. In his attempt to relate the individual to the state, and education to law, he became an ethical theorist of prime importance. He was a literary and dramatic critic of rare insight. And underlying all these achievements was this: he was a logician of subtlety and strength, and a searcher after the knowledge that transcends and exists independent of all other knowledge. He called this knowledge "first philosophy" or "wisdom," and it has since become known as metaphysics.

Many of the questions Aristotle asked—about the nature of man and society, science and knowledge and art—are very much alive today. But it cannot be denied that some of the answers he gave are no longer valid. His aristocratic bias and his relative insularity now seem to vitiate some of his conclusions about ethical, social, and political goals, while his particular scientific conclusions have since been denied by fact and experience. The keystone of Aristotle's logic, the syllogism now has little real function, even though for centuries it was regarded as one of the more potent instruments of human inquiry. Similarly, Aristotle's doctrine of causes, which he considered his chief and distinctive contribution to philosophy, has lost its usefulness, even though its schematic and semantic beauty is still appealing.

Aristotle's Criticism of Plato

In the first part of Book II of *Politics* Aristotle examines the best political proposals made by past thinkers but he is most concerned with Plato's proposals in the *Republic*. His criticism focuses on the institution of communism, which he believes illustrates the mistaken assumptions the *Republic* makes about politics.

The early books of the *Ethics* contain, alongside discussions on the proper method of ethical investigation. Aristotle divided the sciences into three kinds: theoretical sciences, such as mathematics, physics and metaphysics; practical sciences, which include ethics and politics; and productive sciences, such as carpentry or pottery. The theoretical sciences deal with matters that are eternal and, unchanging necessarily the way they are. This unchanging subject matter gives the theoretical sciences, in his view, a stability and precision not to be found in either the practical or productive sciences. The practical and productive sciences, on the other hand, deal with matters that can be changed by our own efforts. In the practical sciences actions are performed and the character of the agent is developed. Because the subject matter of the practical sciences is changeable, Aristotle thinks that these sciences themselves must be less precise than the theoretical sciences.

These remarks point out a major difference between Aristotle's concept of ethics and Plato's. Plato would have rejected the distinction Aristotle insists on between the theoretical and practical sciences, and the corresponding difference in precision between them. As the discussion between Socrates and Cephalus in the *Republic* shows, Plato would not have been satisfied with ethical principles that hold only as a general rule, rather, he sought as respectable as anything in mathematics. Ethics was for Plato the investigation of certain eternal, unchanging forms, an enterprise as "theoretical" as any of Aristotle's theoretical sciences. This difference in methodology leads to one of Aristotle's criticism of Plato. Aristotle discusses Plato's view of the good. The good of Platonic philosophy, he states, "evidently is something which cannot be realized in action or attained by man. But the good which we are now seeking must be attainable".

This difference in methodology has practical consequences. Plato, believing he had access to an independent standard by which human actions could be judged, was quite willing to reject ordinary views as misguided. Thus he was able to reach radical conclusions, for instance on the equality of women and the abolition of the family, which were often quite at variance with the beliefs of Greeks of his time. No such radical conclusions will be found in Aristotle, precisely because of his reliance on the views of ordinary Greeks.

Aristotle begins by observing that Plato's purpose in establishing communism is the unification of the city to the greatest extent possible. This excessive unity, Aristotle claims, is a mistaken goal, for it eliminates the distinctions among the particular beings that necessarily comprise any city. Contrary to Plato's, a city should not be homogeneous but is, of necessity, made up of diversity. To unify the city completely is to destroy it. Aristotle implies that when a ruler unifies the city, he imposes an artificial unity upon it, constraining the growth of its parts and forcing them toward sameness.

In Book I of the *Politics*, Aristotle finds the origin of the city in the association of human beings differing in kind: master and slave come together for the sake of security, man and woman come together for the sake of procreation. These relationships, as well as that between parents and children, comprise the household out of which the city develops. The city is based on the differences between men and women, who have characteristically different virtues.

Man's origins in the family, for example, should teach him that it is impossible for him to transcend altogether his particular, contingent existence. The natural diversity that Aristotle thinks politics should recognize and preserve, thus acts as a restraint on man's tendency toward the abstractions. The diversity upon which Aristotle's politics is based, however, does not merely act as a limit or restraint. A man's particular contingent existence is the condition for his growth. The differences among men, most obvious in their bodies, become manifest in their characters as they mature through their exercise of speech and reason, their choices, and their relationship with other. By denying natural diversity, the *Republic's* city not only removes men from nature's limits, but also forecloses to them nature's complex possibilities. For Aristotle, nature is both more closed and more open than the *Republic's* city admits.

Aristotle therefore criticizes Plato for imposing a particular role on men which stifles growth and prevents development in a variety of directions. As he points out, no man is a shoemaker by nature. Although men do better jobs when they have only one job to do, nature does not endow men with the capacity for only one particular job. Nor does she always divide men into rulers and ruled. Although it would be better for cities if they had permanent rulers, this is not possible in a city of free and equal men. For them it is just to rule and be ruled in turn. The distinctions that do exist in the city, the differences among artisans and the division into classes, are not the natural differences that Aristotle is seeking as a guide to political life. From Aristotle's point of view, these radical distinctions make political community impossible. While the *Republics'* communism assumes too great an identity among men, its artificial class structure assumes too great a disparity among them.

Aristotle calls the situation in which men rule and are ruled in turn—the situation he contrasts with the rule in the *Republic's* city—by the name of "political rule". It is the kind of authority which is most appropriate to political life and which characterizes political life at its best. Aristotle distinguishes political rule from the despotic rule of a master over his slaves and even from the rule of a father over his children. Political rule is rule among equals—men who, although they may not be absolutely equal, are never as unequal as masters and slaves or fathers and children. It is because political rule occurs among men who are more or less equal that it is just that ruler and ruled rule in turn. Thus, while he rules them, he is also ruled by them—his rule is only partial. He is limited by his subjects' desires and opinions, which he must take into account in his choices and actions. The ruled are independent of rulers in a way that a slave is not independent of his master or a child of his father. Just as the *Republic's* city does not recognize the independence of the city's parts, no political rule is to be found there.

Aristotle contends that it is mistaken not only in believing that the greatest possible unity should be the city's goal, but also in supposing that such unity is possible. Communism is not a good means to unity. "Men care most for their private things, and less for the common ones". Communism has deprived men of everything that is exclusively their own. Aristotle prefers the way "it is now in cities": the same person is called son by one man, nephew by another, and designated by different names according to a variety of relationships, whether of blood, of marriage, or of political fellowships. A man is known through the variety of particular relationships that he has some existing by kinship, others by choice.

Just as the city in the *Republic* ignores men's connections to their parents, the friendship it tries to produce through communism destroys men's separate identities. It resembles the friendship, Aristotle says, that Plato has Aristophanes describe in the *Symposium* in which lovers desire to become one: "in such a relation," according to Aristotle, "both or at least one must be destroyed," for by becoming one they cease to exist as two discrete individuals. Aristotle gives another model for friendship when he discusses communism of property. Instead of common possession of property, he recommends that the legislator encourage the common use of property by inclining citizens to friendship. Friends will choose to use their property in common while its ownership remains private. Possessing something of one's own makes an inexpressible difference in the pleasure one derives from it, Aristotle says. Moreover, to please and help friends, visitors, and comrades is very pleasant, but this can take place only when men have private property. Friends have something of their own which they are able to share with friends.

Private property makes possible not only friendship but the virtues of moderation and liberality. Moderation is the proper restraint toward what is not one's own, while liberality is the proper use of one's own in relation to others. The practice of these virtues therefore assumes a distinction between one's own and what belongs to others. With moderation, a man is free from the compulsion to take something from another in order to make it his own. With liberality, a man gives away something of his own; he does not have to keep everything in order to satisfy basic needs. Like friendship itself, a man's practice of these virtues manifests his freedom.

Aristotle next argues that, had communism been a good device, it would have been discovered in the past. He implies that the ideal city does not sufficiently take into account what has happened in the world. In prescribing its institutions, Plato does not build on what has occurred in the past; rather, he reasons about what is good in theory from what has come into being. He acts as if reason were free from experience. Aristotle's next point is that the worth of Plato's proposals would become evident if we could see his regime being formed from practice.

When one tries to see Plato's city in action, one sees the disruptive force of the city's parts, which, after all, it must contain. Plato in his drive toward unity, has paid little attention to them, but, according to Aristotle, they threaten to break the city apart. The military class, "spirited and war-like men," will not tolerate being ruled by others. And the members of the lowest class in the republic's city are likely to be more difficult and full of conceit than the helots and the serfs and the slaves in some cities. Plato has not said whether communism will apply to them. If it does, nothing will distinguish them from the upper classes. Why, then, should they submit to being ruled? If communism does not apply to them, the city will be two cities, antagonistic to each other because they have very little in common. The city does not satisfy men's pride or their desire to share in governing themselves. It seems to provide only the bare necessities. Plato has tried to form a whole, ignoring the tensions that make wholeness problematic.

There are therefore two sides to Aristotle's criticism of Plato's proposals in the *Republic*. First, Plato encounters no natural limits when he arranges the city: he ignores the family, the physical resemblances between parents and offspring, and the irreducible diversity out of which the city is composed. Similarly, there is no political rule in the city, for political rule encounters natural limits in the independence of the ruled. On the other hand, when Plato arranges the city, he imposes an artificial unity on human beings, constraining the development through which men attain freedom. He goes too far in unifying the city; he limits men to one art; he deprives them of the independence implied in self-government; in general, he takes from them their capacity to exercise in their relationships and through their activities the virtues that free them from the compulsions of their bodies.

Aristotle prefers the regime in the *Laws* to the one in the *Republic* because it attempts to bring various classes into the regime without assimilating them to one another and because it permits the existence of families and private property. Aristotle thus criticizes Plato for presenting a politics that insufficiently allows for the private dimensions of human life. According to Aristotle, Plato's political thought does not deal sufficiently with the problems that private life necessarily poses for politics nor does his thought incorporate into politics the benefits man's private life could provide. Like Adeimantus in the *Republic*, Aristotle claims that the communistic city does not make its guardians happy. He does not accept Plato's answer to Adeimantus—that the city is a whole that can be happy even though none of its parts are. The happiness of a city, Aristotle says, is not like a number, which could be even although all of its parts are odd. A city can be said to be happy only if all, or most, or at least some of its parts are happy. Although man is a political animal and therefore dependent on the city for his happiness, he should not be entirely assimilated into the city. Plato presents a politics that does not recognize the independence of the parts that compose the political community.

Aristotle's criticism of Plato does not mention the institution of philosopher-kings. His silence raises the question of whether he found nothing to criticize in this institution. Aristotle's objection to Plato for not allowing political rule, however, is an implicit objection to his philosopher-kings, who rule the members of the city as masters do slaves. Moreover, Aristotle's criticism of communism makes further criticism of its philosophy redundant. To criticize the republic's communism in the name of diversity is to criticizes its philosophy in the name of heterogeneity. Indeed, Aristotle did make this very criticism of Plato's philosophy in Book I of his *Nicomachean Ethics* in arguing against Plato's ideas of the good.

When Aristotle criticizes Plato's philosophy in his *Politics*, he is objecting to Plato's description of politics rather than to his philosophic activities. He tries to treat each man in accordance with his distinctive character, potentials, and desires. Plato does recognizes the differences among men when he composes dialogues between different human beings. However, Socrates and Plato saw too great a disproportion between politics and their own philosophic activities to suppose that cities could imitate philosophy in recognizing the independence of men and in allowing the diversity and change that their independence implies. Through politics, they thought men seek permanence, simplicity, and certainty. Aristotle claims, in contrast, that their independence implies, in contrast, that cities are composed of diversity.

Aristotle therefore is seeking addresses who recognize the impossibility of perfect political solutions. He is seeking such addresses, not because they are most likely to be turned away from political life to something higher, but because such men of mature character will make the best political leaders. Aristotle's politics urges statesmen to work with what is given, arranging the different parts of the community and improving the relations among them without destroying their differences. Aristotle teaches not only the numerous ways statesmen can do this but also the nobility of the task. His intention in the *Politics* is to correct what might to be effect of the *Republic* –discouraging men from participating in political life.

Aristotle makes political life attractive to men by explaining the way in which it fulfills man's nature. Because the city encompasses all other associations and their ends, its end, Aristotle says, is the supreme good. Cities come into existence for the sake of life; they continue to exist for the sake of the good life. Aristotle indicates the good life that the city makes possible when he explains that man is a political animal. He argues that man is political by nature because he alone of the animals possesses reason or speech. Speech indicates not merely pleasure and pain, which other animals indicate through mere voice, but the good and the bad, the just and the unjust. Since a city is a partnership in these things, man's speech or reason indicates that he is naturally suited to political life. At its best, politics involves communal action based on reasonable discussion of the alternatives possible at the time. They must rule and be ruled in turn, that is, they must contribute to political knowledge and action, just as their own knowledge and action must include the contributions of others. Political rule, which characterizes political life, is consequently an ongoing process.

Aristotle's view of the rationality of politics, however, does not imply that men are not motivated by passion and interest. Men must reason about what is beneficial to them and persuade others that what they want is just and good for the city. Men's selfishness leads them to considerations of justice, just as their attempt to preserve their lives by living in cities makes possible their attaining a good life. Political life is noble because of its ability to elevate men.

Plato's politics allows no room for the elevation of men through their discussion of the benefits and justice of what they desire. There we find no reasonable discussion of alternatives undertaken by a group of dissimilar individuals, each of whom makes distinctive contributions. Rather, in the city, philosopher-kings impose general conceptions upon the community, without taking individual opinions, desires, and choices into account. Indeed, rulers treat their subjects as slaves. There is no political rule in the *Republic's* city; rulers are not ruled "in turn" by those they rule.

Aristotle can teach that politics is noble in a way that Plato cannot, because he shows that politics can combine many of the goods Plato's presented as conflicting. The city, Aristotle says in objection to the excessive unity of the Plato's city, is a heterogeneous whole. Although it is definitely a community—its members to a greater or lesser degree share a view of justice and nobility, the city is made of a variety of human beings and groups who differ from one another. Unity or community, does not require uniformity. Nor does diversity give rise to degeneration and chaos.

Plato's Socrates also avoids the two extremes to which he thought man's politics was inclined. Aristotle thus shows how a political community can do what Socrates did in his own philosophic life. Indeed, one can understand Aristotle's city as its best aims at the supreme good for man, or the good life. That life, like the life of Aristotle's city at its best, consists of reasonable discussion among dissimilar human beings about what is beneficial and just for them. Like the men in the city as Aristotle sees them, the discussants in a Socratic conversation are motivated by passion and interest, but they are led to give reasons for the positions to which their passions and interests incline them. In the best case, they modify their positions as a result of other considerations that their discussion with one another brings to light. So also does Socrates listen to the opinions of others, and his arguments take their contributions into account. He modifies his argument in light of the particular individuals with whom he converses, treating each of them differently. Socrates' treatment of others therefore is reminiscent of Aristotle's concept of equality. Socrates modifies his arguments in light of the individuals with whom he speaks, and he tries to treat each as he deserves, just as the man who practices equity modifies his general rule in light of the individual cases to which he applies it.

Moreover, because his conversations involve others who have independent opinions and interests which they often try to promote, Socrates cannot entirely direct the outcome. His discussions might involve surprises. Like Aristotle's city, Socrates' way of life is open to change. His knowledge is partial, constantly modified by new considerations, even imagines that he might learn more about justice, for example, after death, if he has the opportunity to talk to the heroes of the past about their experiences. Like political rule, Socrates' philosophizing is an endless affair, modified continually by the particular individuals and circumstances he encounters.

Aristotle unites philosophy and politics in his political science so that each compensates for the defects of the other. He tries to curb the dangerous propensities of philosophy toward abstract thought—which Aristophanes emphasized and Aristotle acknowledges in his criticism of Socrates' understanding of politics—by binding thought to the necessities of action. Because action involves particulars, thought will not bypass or deny such things as a man's love of his own, family life or political tradition. Aristotle provides a more adequate defense of politics than Plato did. Aristotle's political community incorporates the diversity which Socrates' political philosophy recognizes but which Socrates did not make politically efficacious. It resembles less the communistic city of the *Republic* than the community formed by Socrates and his interlocutors, in which the independence of each is preserved as they pursue a common discourse or dialagne.

Aristotle's political science is based on the view that man is a political animal. Man develops his full potential only by participating in a community in which he pursues with others what is advantageous and just. He may initially participate in a community in order to foster his individual goals, but his interactions with others compel him to use his abilities as a rational beings. He consequently changes or grows through his relationship with others. Man is not a self-contained whole who is merely protected through his membership in civil society. He is an incomplete being who becomes more complete through political activity.

Because Aristotle views man as both a communal and a private being, his political science is a complex attempt to reconcile individuality and community. These two sides of Aristotle's political science can be seen, in his criticism of Plato for neglecting man's desire for honor and preeminence, on the one hand, and in his criticism of Hippocampus for trying to give that very desire too great a place in the city, on the other. Aristotle distinguishes himself from both these men by means of his political science: his political science allows change and individual achievement by encouraging statesmen to improve their regimes, at the same time that it respects the role of regimes in providing continuity for the lives of their members.

Aristotle's statement that man is a political animal thus does not deny that there is a private element to human life. In fact, it is only because a man has something of his own to contribute to politics that it is good for the community that he participates in its ongoing search for the advantageous and the just. For Aristotle, the political community is a heterogeneous whole. Because the political community is a heterogeneous whole, Aristotle can find a place within it for philosophy, not merely as one element along side the many others necessary for community, but also as the human capacity to see the possible relations between the diverse elements of the community and the different orders that might be formed out of them.

Even if Aristotle's political science constitutes a successful attempt to give importance to political life, it does not satisfy modern political thinkers. When they object to the political thought of antiquity, they make no exception for Aristotle. Machiavelli, for example, objects to the imaginary republics and principalities of the past that turn men's attention toward ideals that cannot be realized and away from men's actual behavior. The political thought of the past, from his point of view, ill equips men to live in this world. Hobbes, similarly, claims that the ancients aim too high in that they hold up to men an imaginary *Summum Bonum* and make them unfit to enjoy the low but solid pleasures available to them.

From Hobbes' point of view, the Socratic political philosophy presented by Plato is as ethereal as political communities aiming at justice and the good life. Socrates' exploration of tensions, such as that between the community and the individual, or the whole and the parts, does not permit him to establish a political science. His philosophizing is not sufficiently useful to men. Though Hobbes also resembles Aristotle in his concern that theory have a direct bearing on practice, rejects community in the Aristotelian sense as one of those imaginary goods, like the ideal principalities of the ancients or the *Summum Bonum*. By grounding his political science on man's desire for self-preservation and limiting the end of politics to the protection of life, Hobbes asserts that men are not parts of a whole. To the contrary he views men as self-contained wholes, which political life protects, rather than as beings completed by their political activities. Only when their pride is held in check by their fear of an absolute sovereign can, men escape the deadly conflict resulting from their selfish or apolitical natures. Only thus can men find the security necessary for life and comfortable living. In this conception of government, liberal regimes find their origin. Instead of promoting friendship or community as political ends, rulers, imitating Hobbes' political science, are supposed to administer to the personal or private needs of men. Even when living in political society, men are not to be citizens in the ancient sense. They remain fundamentally private individuals.

Later modern thinkers find Hobbes' rejection of community for the sake of peace inadequate. They nevertheless accept one fundamental premise of Hobbes—the apolitical character of man. While denying that men are naturally directed toward community, they propose that men might attain community through the will or history or some combination of the two. Rousseau teaches. that men might become citizens, as opposed to private individuals, by an act of the will. The man who wills the general will thus overcomes his particular interests and desires, or all the attributes that belong to him as a particular being, in order to act simply as citizen. As citizens, men are not distinct from one another, for their wills are identical.

Similarly, for Marx, man must evolve beyond the stage of "an isolated monad withdrawn into himself;" when man has "in his everyday life, his individual work, and his individual relationship, become a species-being, only then is human emancipation complete". We can see that early moderns try to secure individualism at the expense of community, later moderns try to secure community at the expense of individualism. And just as in early modernity, so also in later modernity, philosophy or theory becomes active in the achievement of this end. Kant's theories of history, for example, are intended to encourage men to work for historical progress, just as Marx's theories provide men with models of philosophic activity intended to change the world, rather than merely contemplate it.

Aristotle's political science is superior to the major modern alternatives precisely because it offers a perspective from which the partial truths embodied in modern thought can be understood and reconciled. Because early moderns emphasize individuality, and later moderns community, they stand in unrelieved opposition to each other. Each offers a vision of human life that fails to do justice to the complexity of human nature. Aristotle's political science suggests a basis for reconciling the poles of modern political thought.

Reason—Theoretical, Productive and Practical

By distinguishing between theory and practice, the school, family and the city, the intellectual and the moral virtues, Aristotle attempted to focus upon that which is distinctly political and to create, thereby, a distinctly appropriate science for the investigation of the political. Although in Aristotle's scheme philosophy is no longer an immediate requirement for the creation of political order, some form of knowledge is. And in his effort to demonstrate what is required, Aristotle introduced his distinction among the theoretical, instrumental and practical reason.

Theoretical Reason

It remains for us to examine the virtues of the other aspect of reason, the part is theoretical rather than practical: reason aimed at ascertaining the truth about the nature of things. In order to understand the virtues of theoretical reason, we must briefly describe the way in which Aristotle pictures the operation of this form of reason. Science, the knowledge of reality, he views as a deductive system of propositions similar in structure to the deductive system of geometry. In the case of geometry, we have a system of propositions- theorems; they are called-which follow logically or deductively from a set of propositions referred to as axioms.

In a deductive system, the truth of the axioms is transferred to the theorems that follow from them. What about the axioms themselves? These propositions are usually characterized as self-evident, so that their denial in necessarily false.

According to Aristotle, the science of nature has the same structure. It consists of a set of axiomatic laws about the very general nature of things, together with more specific laws that follow deductively from the axioms. Given this understanding of natural science, theoretical knowledge will be achieved through the exercise of two epistemic capacities. First there is the ability to think logically and derive theorems from axiom and then to derive still more specific theorems from the more general ones. Aristotle calls this "scientific knowledge." Additionally, there must be the capacity to see that the axioms are evidently true. This is done through a kind of intellectual intuition or mental perception. Aristotle refers to the exercise of this capacity as understanding. Theoretical knowledge, then, consists of understanding plus scientific knowledge. When reason in its theoretical capacity is functioning well, achieving both understanding and scientific knowledge, it is manifesting the virtue of wisdom *(Sophia).*

Aristotle makes it clear that Sophia is concerned only with knowing the nature of things, not with productive knowledge, technology or with action. It consists of knowledge of universals—propositions about general types of things holding true universally—rather than, as is the case with practical reason, particulars. Scientific, theoretical knowledge aims at truth, at demonstrating what the general nature of things is. Practical reason, concerned as it is with action, aims at the good, the object of intelligent desire and feeling.

In his *Metaphysics,* Aristotle attempts to explain those criteria by which it is possible to distinguish among the three forms of rational inquiry. Each form or type can be characterized both by the nature of the object it investigates and by the investigator's concern or intention while undertaking the inquiry. For example, the theoretical sciences study unchanging principles. As such, the realities structured by these principles exist independently of humanity and are thus beyond any control.

Aristotle lists mathematics, physics, and metaphysics as examples of theoretical science. In each case, the investigators are concerned with understanding principles over which they have no influence. According to Aristotle, for example, both physical nature and being as such are the kinds of substance which have the principle of their movement and their rest present within themselves. Inasmuch as human being cannot hope to alter the fundamental structure of nature or of being, their motive for engaging in purely theoretical inquiry is essentially that of intellectual interest. The theoretical sciences seek knowledge for its own sake. They arise out of a sense of wonder and culminate in a moment of understanding. Although the theoretical sciences do not present us with "results" in a pragmatic sense, they do allow humanity to share in an activity which is ultimately divine in nature. As such, theoretical inquiry represents the highest and most noble form of human endeavor.

Instrumental Reason

The productive sciences are quite different. They are, in effect, all those skills, crafts, and arts which people employ in the self-conscious making of things. Thus their character is primarily technological and instrumental. Unlike the theoretical sciences, the productive sciences deal with those objects over which humans do exercise some control. Generally this control is guided by the artisan's concern for utility. For example, carpenters work with wood in order to make it usable as a desk, a boat, or a house. In each case, they are taking the material at hand and forming it in such a way as to meet their own purposes. It is as if they are imposing a form upon the material, and, in so doing, are using the object for a purpose which they bring to it. This is so inasmuch as it is a carpenter who ultimately decides if a particular piece of wood will become a desk, a chair, or a house. Whereas the theoretical sciences emerge from a sense of wonder, the productive sciences are born out of need. And, when theoretical sciences seek wisdom, the productive sciences are concerned with efficiency. In short, they are the arts which guide one in the human action of making.

Practical Reason

Aristotle divides the soul into irrational and rational parts. So far, we have considered the virtues of the irrational soul or at least that segment of it capable of listening to and following reason. Now we need to consider the rational soul itself and to identify its virtues, its ways of performing excellently so as to fulfill its function. These virtues are wisdom, intelligence, understanding and comprehension.

In general, the function of the rational soul is the intellectual one of reasoning. But reasoning, according to Aristotle, comes in two forms. First, there is pure theoretical reasoning whose aim is to ascertain the essential, unchanging laws of the universe. This is the activity of the "scientific part" of reason. Its task is to grasp truths about eternal things that could not be otherwise. Second, there is what Aristotle calls the "rationally calculating part," the part often referred to today as practical reason. Its job is to assist the soul in attaining *eudaimonia*. Practical reason investigates what is "up to us," what is temporal and variable, namely the actions we may or may not perform and it advises us of the rational course of action. The virtues of reason in general will be those modes of thought which permit it to perform its scientific and practical tasks in the most excellent fashion. Theoretical reasoning will achieve virtue when it grasps the truth about the way things in the world are and cannot fail to be. It will then manifest *Sophia,* theoretical wisdom. The goal of practical reason being to assist the individual in attaining eudaimonia, it will manifest its virtues when it assists the character of a person in making correct decisions and engaging in correct actions. In doing so, it will reveal practical wisdom or *phronesis.*

There are two ways in which practical reason operates in the pursuit of *eudaimonia.* Practical reason manifests itself in deliberation, and it functions well when its activity expresses the virtue of intelligence. "It seems proper to an intelligent person to be able to deliberate finely about what is good and beneficial for himself, not [merely] about some restricted area—e.g., about what promotes health or strength but about what promotes living well in general". Thus the intelligent person does not have a narrow focus but rather is able to take whole life into consideration. The end is the attainment of happiness. Unlike craft-knowledge, which aims at producing some object, intelligence aims only at producing the correct action. Actions are those things that are up to us and may or may not occur. Intelligence, then, is neither science nor craft-knowledge. Deliberation yields decision and this decision is the origin of action. Aristotle defines decision as "a deliberative desire" since action, he maintains, is always motivated by desire, never by thought or belief alone—"Thought by itself moves nothing". As Aristotle claims at the very beginning of the book, we always act to attain an end, and desire or wish is "for the end" or as he tells us later, "desire is for the goal". But thought or reason must enter the picture as we deliberate over what to desire.

The first job of practical reason is to give guidance to the appetites, feelings, and emotions of the irrational soul, to direct this soul to those feelings and actions that constitute the mean in particular situations. There is, Aristotle believes, a sort of natural virtue in us that inclines us toward virtuous actions, but natural virtue is not virtue in the fullest and most precise sense. To attain the latter, deliberation is required. Deliberation involves an interplay of reason and desire. For one thing, reason can prioritize ends and thereby realign desires. Deliberation thus leads to desire molded or directed by reason, and when a decision is reached, the resultant deliberative desire is what moves one to act. When the decision is excellent "the reason must be true and the desire correct, so the what reason asserts is what desire pursues".

When well done, deliberation will include the virtues of comprehension and understanding. One role of deliberation is to determine the mean with regard to feelings or actions in specific contexts. To do this, it must be able to grasp or take into account all relevant aspects of the situation the agent finds himself in, thereby ascertaining the nature of the circumstances which bear upon proper or virtuous action. Doing this well amounts to comprehension, putting together the components of a complex situation in their proper relationships. Comprehension provides us with correct judgments about the nature and context of actions and feelings. Once a situation is comprehended in this fashion, the agent must be able to see what the moral demands of the situation are, i.e., what the proportionate action or feeling would be. Here, Aristotle thinks, we manifest intelligence if we come up with the correct decision or, as he sometimes expresses it, the correct prescription to action. General rules or principles of action may be appealed to in arriving at this decision, but since practical reason is concerned with particulars-particular situations and particular acts- we cannot simply rely on general rules to tell us what to do. There are three reasons for this. First, rules, being general, do not by themselves identify what specific action we are to take. Second, no rules can encompass all the specific and changing detail of the circumstances of action. Third, rules must be applied to particular situations, and because of the first two factors, their application is never "mechanical" but demands an "eye" for what is required in the particular situation, i.e., for seeing this situation "aright." In order to arrive at a correct decision we must rely on a form of direct insight which, in light of the picture of the complex particulars already achieved through comprehension, yields an indication of what act or feeling would be the mean. We see, that is to say, what the overall situation demands of us with respect to the mean. Aristotle refers to this direct insight as a form of perception. He also suggests that it is the manifestation of the virtue of understanding in the practical sphere. So, comprehension and understanding cooperate to determine the virtuous act. Together they constitute *phronesis.*

Aristotle is notorious for his claim that deliberation is always focused on means, never on ends: "We deliberate not about ends, but about what promotes ends" His thinking here is not easy to understand, but it does suggest that in all deliberation there is some end that is presupposed and not itself debated. In our discussion above regarding deliberations aimed at identifying the mean feeling and action, the end presupposed is that of happiness, since pursuing the mean is the way to promote happiness. Happiness itself is not in dispute: we do not deliberate over whether to be happy; we don't decide to be happy.

It may appear to us today that the employment of reason in its practical and productive modes is at least as important, if not more so, than the operation of theoretical reason. Just the opposite was the case for Aristotle. He suggests that the life devoted to scientific knowledge, is the highest form of life, and, when it achieves the virtue of wisdom, the highest form of happiness. Indeed, in Book X of the *Ethics* he implies that the perfect life would be one devoted to study alone, with only minimal attention given to the nutritive and appetitive dimensions of the soul — just enough to allow a person to concentrate on the important matter of study. Clearly he himself, being the great philosopher he was, preferred the life of study, the life of philosophizing and the pursuit of theoretical knowledge. He also notes that theoretical reason is godlike in nature, and hence it is what places us closest to the gods. He concludes in Book X of the *Ethics* that the excellence of contemplation is the best of the various excellences and thus should be the dominant end we seek. But in other passages he explicitly recognizes that happiness pertains to the human being as a whole. From this perspective, while theoretical wisdom may still be thought of as the highest virtue, it is not the equivalent of happiness since it is not self-sufficient. We are agents as well as thinkers, and from the perspective of the whole person, the virtues of character and the intellectual virtues constituting *phronesis* are as essential as the virtue of theoretical wisdom.

The practical is reason in some respects similar to the productive sciences. Aristotle emphasizes this similarity by treating them both as forms of calculation, which is knowledge guided by a concern for action. That is like the productive sciences, the practical sciences deal with realities over which humans exercise some control. Yet, unlike the productive sciences, the practical sciences are not concerned with the activity of making; rather they seek to inform human doing. They reflect, therefore, the differences between making and doing.

Perhaps this distinction can best be illustrated by examining Aristotle's two major examples of practical reason-ethics and politics. For purposes of illustration, ethics can be understood as that practical reason concerned with the direction of one's personal life. As such it deals with a realty over which people have some control; for each person determines to an extent who he or she will become. Ethical knowledge, accordingly, is concerned with the problems of living. It is, in effect, an applied science. Yet even though it is an applied science, it is different from the productive science. This difference is rooted in the fact that, unlike the productive sciences, the reality governed by ethics already carries with it its own purposes. Thus, rather than attempting to impose a purpose on human life, ethics is concerned with nurturing and developing that purpose which is already given in the structure of human nature itself. For Aristotle people are not free to make of themselves anything they wish. Rather they are to do those things appropriate to their human nature. Unlike the artisans who bend their material to fit their own design, ethical actors seek to fulfill the potential of their humanity by conforming to those principles inherent within human nature as such. Consequently, the science of ethics is concerned with happiness how to act in light of a sufficient understanding of such principles. Its goal is happiness, not efficiency.

Politics is another example of practical reason. As such, it is concerned with guiding society in such a way as to allow it to fulfill the natural purposes of political existence. Aristotle believes that there is a proper purpose implied by the very structure of a political association itself. Accordingly, regimes are not free to use society for any purpose whatsoever. Rather societies which are true to their nature must seek the common good. Political science, in turn, is that practical science concerned precisely with such matter. Like ethics, it seeks happiness, and inasmuch as Aristotle associates happiness with action, it goes beyond a concern for knowledge simply for its own sake.

Aristotle's distinction among the theoretical, productive and practical sciences should not be interpreted simply as an attempt to achieve an academic division of labor. Rather these distinctions, made at the level of rational inquiry, reflect, in turn, deeper distinctions within Aristotle's understanding of the human soul. The various types of science actually represent various forms of excellence within the human psyche. They are not dry epistemological categories but rather the means by which various elements of the soul articulate their proper and peculiar function. For example, a life concerned with theoretical science achieves the fundamental excellence of humanity's godlike nature. Similarly, the doing of practical science attests to the psyche excellence of the person of moral virtue Thus our discussion of Aristotle's understanding of science will not be complete until it incorporates his analysis of the human soul and its particular needs. Such an analysis is a central concern of both his *Ethics* and *Politics.*

State

The agenda that Aristotle lays down for politics is thus much broader than in Plato's *Republic*. Where Plato believed that this is a world of appearance and thus unworthy of serious study, Aristotle believes this is the world in which nature realizes its purposes and therefore deserves close attention; it is a testing ground for any theorizing about politics.

Not only is Aristotle a great intellect; he also respects common sense. Practical wisdom is as important as theoretical speculation. Thus his attitude to Plato is one which reflects his rejection of a revolutionary departure in favors of reform consistent with Greek reality. He constantly insists that practice must be used to test theory; experience limits our possibilities. His polis he believes is closer to the real world of individuals and families and their property and affections, than is Plato's which negates rather than includes the individual, which denies the plurality of the polis in its search for perfection. The point for Aristotle is to improve the present not to destroy it; the future is immanent in the present. Plato's clean canvas on which the philosopher-artist paints gives way to Aristotle's world of experience in which the statesmen must practice. The real world is no longer the ideal world as it was with Plato, though the ideal does illuminate features of the real world and their potential for improvement.

In the real world the most important unit is made up of smaller parts – the household and groups of households (villages), all natural and aiming at providing existence, a subordinate role to that of the polis which aims at some version of the good life. The household, in addition to its head, has three subordinates parts – children, women and slaves – all under he authority of the head as the natural superior. The household as an economic and family unit is inferior to the polis which is morally superior in terms of its superior goal of human fulfillment; the citizen who participates freely and equally in the polis is nevertheless the undisputed master of his own household. In Aristotle's ideal polis only those shall be citizens who pursue the good life – that is true distributive justice. Equality is not sameness; it leads to differences. Thus the democrats and oligarchs have only partial and inadequate conceptions of justice. Justice is about equality but only for equals; it is about inequality but only for unequals. Who counts as equal or unequal can only be decided in the light of a standard of judge, and that true standard is virtue, not freedom or wealth.

The claim that we need to focus on is that politics is natural to man and that man's happiness is dependent upon being a citizen of a polis or city-state. It is for this argument, above all else, that Aristotle is famous. The argument here is opposed to the claim that politics is an artificial construct designed to curb the worst excesses of human nature. In Aristotle's time, this position was held by some of the Sophists who were also protagonists in the Platonic dialogues. But this debate is not merely some ancient Greek curiosity. In the modern period, it formed the core of the arguments between Hobbes, Locke and Rousseau: even today, this debate is still vital. It is certainly the case that this discussion is culturally informed and therefore differently nuance in each incarnation. But the question of whether we have politics to constrain the actions of human beings or to enable human beings to flourish must still inform our view of what the best sort of political arrangement is. Understanding the arguments that provide the foundation for this claim will require that we explore questions concerning human nature, human happiness, the nature of ethics, the constitutional possibilities of politics and the idea of justice.

The *Ethics*, then, treats of real people and their actual behavior, but within the context of Aristotle's metaphysical system. The employment of this system requires

Aristotle to begin with basic theoretical questions. First, he asks, what is the Good? It is, he says, "that at which all things aim." What do people aim at above all else? Happiness, says Aristotle. The end or telos of humans as ethical beings is happiness, and here of course, he is in perfect agreement with Socrates and Plato, But what makes for happiness in human terms? It must be something that is unique to humans. This something, Aristotle argues, is people's capacity to reason and to carry what they reason into practice. This being the case, happiness must be related to people's capacity to act appropriately upon a rational basis, and to shape their behavior according to the dictates of reason. Happiness, in a word, is virtue, which means, the ability to perform a specific function well. And for people to perform well, their actions must have a rational basis.

The Ethics is a treatise on the whole variety of virtues (liberality, courage, temperance, justice, and so on) that people praise as good and necessary for a genuinely human and happy life. But Aristotle's method of analyzing these virtues, owing to his modified theory of form, is radically different from Plato's. Aristotle develops his catalogue of virtues from what people actually say about courage, or temperance, and so on. Unlike Plato, he does not reject as mere opinion, commonsense beliefs about these matters. People practice virtue because they recognize that it contributes to happiness they recognize that a courageous person is happy; a coward, miserable and they philosophize about virtue because they understand the enormous importance of it to their development as adult human beings. In other words, virtue is not something that exists in the sky attainable only by the few. For Aristotle, virtue is precisely the proper end of the human being, and it exists as an integral part of the development of each of us. How we actually behave and what we say about that behavior are part of our end or telos and, therefore, virtue must be understood as part of this human context.

Moreover, Aristotle cannot accept Plato's assertion that moral virtue is strictly identical to knowledge. Again, if we look at real people and how they actually develop to their end as ethical beings, says Aristotle, that habit and training play a profoundly important role. By and large, we learn to be virtuous by practicing virtue. Aristotle argues this point with an analogy that should be familiar by now:

> The moral virtues we do acquire by first exercising them. The same is true of the arts and crafts in general. The craftsman has to learn how to make things, but he learns in the process of making them. So men become builders by building, harp players by playing their harp. By similar process, we become just by performing temperate actions, brave by performing brave actions.

This emphasis on practice as opposed to pure reason in the development of a virtuous life is uniquely Aristotelian. Human happiness for Aristotle is the result of reason plus action, not reason alone. People act to shape their lives and institutions to a given end; it is through action that they actualize the form of virtue. Moreover, Aristotle's conclusion about virtue in general is also uniquely his own, and quite different from that of Plato. Virtue, says Aristotle, is a mean. Again, if one looks at the real human meaning of any given virtue, we find that it is equidistant between extremes. For example, courage is a mean between cowardice on the one hand and foolhardiness on the other. Courage involves knowing what is and is not to be feared and acting upon that knowledge. Cowards fear everything because they do not know what is not to be feared; the foolhardy fears nothing for the opposite reason, and therefore neither develops in their behavior the proper habit of courage. We may surmise that Aristotle thought he struck the mean when he fled Athens.

When Aristotle's theory of ethics is taken as a whole, we note the profound influence of his notion of immanent form. His idea that practice and habit are essential in the development of virtue is in accord with the idea that the form of virtue is immanent within people's lives and can be actualized only through real, concrete action. It is for this reason that Aristotle believes that the function of social and political philosophy is to modify and perfect commonsense notions of what constitutes a virtuous life, not automatically to reject people's opinions.

These ideas lead directly to Aristotle's theory of politics because politics is a collective form of reasoned action. Like Plato, Aristotle believes the primary function of the state to be the inculcation of virtue in its citizenry in order to achieve human happiness and fulfillment. But given Aristotle's philosophy of form, we find that his theory of the state differs from Plato's in a number of important respects. His starting point in the opening pages of *Politics*, nevertheless, is perfectly compatible with Plato's views:

> Every state is a community of some kind, and every community is established with a view to some good; for humankind always acts in order to obtain that which they think good. But, if all communities aim at some good, the state or political community, which is the highest of all, and which embraces all the rest, aims at a good in a greater degree than any other, and at the highest good.

Note Aristotle's claim that the state, like every other human community, aims at some good. This logically follows from his premise in *Ethics* that all things aim at the good. The good at which the state aims is the virtue and happiness of the whole community. But why is the state's end the hightest good? Partly, of course, because it is concerned with the whole community, which is more important than the individual. But the reasons go deeper than this, for the state, Aristotle insists, allows people to acquire virtue to a higher degree than in any subordinate community.

We can understand Aristotle's argument if we put it in the context of his larger theory of community. According to Aristotle, the human community is complex interrelationship of three different kinds of communities, the simplest of them evolving teleologically into the more complex. The primary social unit is the household or family. Over time, various families unite to form the village that, in turn, unites with other villages to form the state or polis. In historical terms, of course, the household and village are prior to the state. In teleological terms the opposite is the case. Teleologically, the state is the end toward which people's social life ultimately aims. Since the state is our final end, or telos, other kinds of communities are subordinate to it and are simply stages leading to this most complete form of community. This is why, despite the historical reality, Aristotle insists that the state is prior to the household and village.

It is apparent from this analysis that Aristotle considers the state as well as the subordinate communities to be natural. Like Socrates and Plato, Aristotle rejects the Sophist argument that people are naturally self-interested individuals, and that the state is a mere convention designed to frustrate the desires of the "superior man." Human beings are above all social animals for Aristotle; they are naturally political animals as well. Politics is simply the highest expression of humanity's sociability. Because politics is the highest expression of human sociability the polis or city-state is able to inculcate virtue in its citizenry to a greater degree than the household or village. This is so because it allows for the expression of reasoned action to a greater degree. This is why Aristotle argues that slaves and animals cannot form a state. They lack free choice and, therefore, cannot engage in reasoned action. As a consequence, they cannot attain virtue. And since a virtuous life is the basis for a happy life, slaves or animals can have no share in genuine human happiness. Aristotle says:

> A state exists for the sake of a good life, and not for the sake of life only: if life only were the object, slaves and brute animals might form a state, but they can not, for they have no share in happiness or in a life of free choice.

But why does Aristotle assume that reasoned action can occur only within the state? Why not within the household or village? The reason is that in subordinate communities, particularly the household, free choice is severely limited. The function of the household is to maintain biological existence and there are no "free biological choices." Survival dictates that people eat, sleep, and procreate, and it dictates the means by which to do these things as well. To live, people must make a living somehow; they must labor, acquire property, and manage the household. All these activities are economic and all are rooted in biological necessity. And these activities, Aristotle argues, require strict hierarchical relationships. The husband must rule like a monarch and the children must obey their parents.

The state, however, is above mere biology, argues Aristotle. Unlike the private domain of the household, the state is a public arena in which people come together to make decisions affecting the whole community for good or evil. This requires debate, hence free speech. This is why speech is the preeminent political virtue for Aristotle. Politics could not exist without it, although a primitive form of social organization could. Aristotle distinguishes between animals and human beings precisely on this crucial point. Bees, he notes, have an elaborate social organization, but no politics. Their sociability is purely instinctual; they have no free choice about how they shall live because they have no capacity to speak to the issue. This is why animals cannot attain virtue. Virtue comes from reasoned action, and speech is simply reason made active.

The necessity of free speech, further, means that the state must be organized differently from the household. The public sphere can function only where there is equality, says Aristotle. The words of one person must count as much as those of another, otherwise there would be no equality of speech and no genuine debate. Thus Aristotle insists that rulership of the state is distinctly different from management of the household. The state must be ruled constitutionally, which means that the whole citizenry must in some way participate in an equality of ruler ship, whereas the inequality of the household demands the rule of one person. This is why Aristotle believes that only in the state, only in the public arena of political action, can people acquire virtue and thereby attain genuine human happiness and fulfillment. And this is why he believes that, among all the kinds of communities, the state alone aims at the highest good.

Aristotle's analysis, once again, is thoroughly teleological. The historical development of household, village, and state is teleologically conceived, a movement from necessity to freedom being the distinguishing telos of human beings because it is the condition necessary for their happiness. Grasping the teleological nature of this development, people should understand, says Aristotle, that their true home lays in the public arena. Unless people devote themselves to political activity, they will not be genuinely free. They will be incapable, therefore, of the highest form of human happiness. In fact, they will be no better than slaves, because slaves are distinguished precisely by their inability to enter the political arena, the only arena in which they can be treated as equal and free members of the community. The slave is tied to the household, like women and children, and subject to the rule of the household activity to provide the necessities so that people will have leisure for political activity. Those who spend their lives acquiring wealth and property as an end in itself, therefore, are really no different from slaves. Their idea of freedom, Aristotle argues, is not genuine human freedom at all.

Unfortunately, Aristotle believed that slavery and male supremacy are natural. This is why he justified the exclusion of slaves and women from the political arena. And since this arena alone allowed for reasoned action, it was a logical step to conclude that slaves and women, like children, are not fully rational. The legacy of this kind of reasoning is still with us. But it is legacy that has no necessary connection to Aristotle's political theory. We now know that slavery and male supremacy are purely conventional, and we can eliminate Aristotle's defense of them without rejecting the whole of his political thought. Indeed, to the extent that Aristotle's theory is valid, to that same extent, we should encourage women and others traditionally excluded from the public arena to engage in politics. In this way alone, if Aristotle is correct, will their full humanity be recognized.

Having established the importance of political life, Aristotle turns to classifying and then analyzing forms of the state. His classification is premised upon his theory of form. The structure of the state is determined by its constitution, and the constitution of a state, says Aristotle, is nothing other than its form. We can best explain Aristotle's reasoning by way of an analogy. Recall that the form of anything for Aristotle is its final end, its actualization, which occurs after a period of development. Thus, species refers to the form immanent within a given biological category. A constitution is a kind of "political species," and it emerges or becomes actualized only at the end of a period of social development that begins in the household and culminates in the state.

We must be very careful with this analogy, however, because there is a fundamental difference between a biological species and a political constitution. Biologically there is no choice. A dog, for example, cannot choose to be other than a dog. But human beings are not merely biological creatures. They live among other human beings in elaborate social arrangements and, ideally, they choose freely the kinds of social and political organizations they wish to have. Here we come full circle back to Aristotle's starting point: Humans are ultimately ethical beings who may choose or choose not to become virtuous through reasoned action. It is people to make moral choices, and the choice of a constitution is the most important choice they make because a constitution determines to what extent they can collectively attain a life of virtue and happiness.

But what, precisely, is a constitution? According to Aristotle, it is an arrangement of political offices that effectively determines who shall be allowed to participate in ruling the state. Obviously, as we expand or circumscribe the number of those engaged in rulership we alter the character of the state. But Aristotle's classification of states, or constitutions, involves more than mere numbers. We may have two different states, each ruled by one person, but the quality of rule in one state may be quite different from that in the other. One person may rule to his own advantage, the other to the public's advantage. Thus, Aristotle argues that the simplest and most basic classification of states must involve two considerations-the number of rulers and the quality of rulership.

Given these considerations, Aristotle proposes a six-fold classification of states three good and three bad. The three good states are monarchy (rule by one), aristocracy (rule by the few), and polity (rule by the many). The corresponding types of perverted states are tyranny, oligarchy, and democracy. In this scheme, the absolute best kind of consituation is monarchy, the absolute worst is tyranny. Here, Aristotle agrees almost exactly with Plato's classification of constitutions developed in the *Republic*. Note that his six basic constitutional types closely rescmble to those discussed by Plato in his theory of the decline of the ideal state.

But in the *Politics* Aristotle focuses on the best possible constitution under the variety of circumstances that confront people most of the time. Thus, when Aristotle agrees with Plato that monarchy is the ideal constitution, he does not thereby dismiss all other constitutions as inferior or relegate them to the shadow world of the cave. Justice is the key to Aristotle's classification of constitutions, and constitutions are more or less good to the extent that they embody the ideal of justice. The tendency of Plato to see an irreconcilable gap between the ideal and the real is thereby overcome by Aristotle. This is why the theory of immanent form is so much more practically useful in political science than the theory of transcendent form. If justice is immanent within people's political arrangements, then they always have the possibility of further actualizing justice in their political communities. Life is movement, not stasis, Aristotle insists. We must look at the variety of constitutions on a continuum of worst to best, therefore, not simply at the ideal or final point. This is why Aristotle's initial classification soon gives way to a much more complex system. In reality, there are various types of monarchies, democracies, oligarchies, tyrannies, and so on. Moreover, it follows that if justice is a continuum, then some oligarchies or tyrannies are better then others. Even the perverted states can be made better or more just according to Aristotle, and it is the task of political leaders, no matter what kind of state they live in, to move toward the ideal within the limits of possibility.

For Aristotle, then, rule by a philosopher-king is a purely theoretical possibility that is, for all practical purposes, impossible to realize. But other types of states face real practical limitations as well. Aristocracy is close to the ideal, but it is not always possible to attain. In ordering the constitutional structure of the state, the limitations that leaders face is, in fact, many: the size of the population, the temperament of the people, their geographical location, and so on. But above all else, Aristotle focuses on social class as the most important factor in determining what is constitutionally possible.

Aristotle was exceedingly sensitive to the economic basis of politics, so much so that some have seen in him the anticipation of Karl Marx. This goes a bit too far, but it emphasizes the enormous importance Aristotle attached to the economic class system in his analysis of various states. He argues that the fundamental conflict in all societies is the conflict between rich and poor. It is thus the distribution of wealth and property that really determines the character of perverted constitutions. Oligarchy really means rule by the few rich in their own class interest; democracy means the equivalent rule by the many poor; and tyranny means the self-interested rule by one who comes to power when either the poor or the rich cannot maintain control. Aristotle's economic analysis constitutes a clear admission that people will tend to seek their own class advantage at the expense of the public good. How, then, can he speaks of any form of just constitution as a real possibility? It was precisely this pessimistic assessment that drove Plato to his extreme political solution: institute a philosophical ruling class that is propertyless and that will have, therefore, neither the desire nor the opportunity to rule unjustly in its own class interest.

Aristotle's solution is radically different from Plato's. He regards property as natural and as a means to people's ethical betterment if used appropriately. Plato's communist ideal is not, therefore, acceptable to Aristotle. At the same time, he takes it as given that people tend to seek their own economic advantage and that, therefore, class conflict undergirds any political system. But there is no contradiction here. We find in human institutions both the bad and the good, argues Aristotle. Property is both an ethical good and a potential evil. The function of leadership is to draw out the good and to direct people's institutions toward the just and the virtuous.

Thus, Aristotle advocates not the elimination of economic classes but rather a balancing of one against the other. This idea is particularly applicable to polity, the lowest form of just state. Polity is Aristotle's best average constitution under most circumstances. It is a form of democracy in which the many participate in ruling but, unlike pure democracy, under the constraints of the public good. Polity is created by combining the principles of democracy and oligarchy -that is, by constitutionally balancing the rich and the poor such that neither group is able to grasp control of the state to further its own ends at the expense of the other.

How, then, do we know who has the greatest political virtue? Quite simply by observing how people speak and act in their public lives. Politics for Aristotle is not only a means to solve pressing social problems, it is a testing ground -a process in which we select as rulers those who demonstrate the greatest political abilities. And, Aristotle argues, this principle of proportional equality is intimately connected to the rule of law. A state in which equals rule and are ruled in turn is by definition a state organized around the principle of rule of law. Law regulates who will rule and in what manner they will rule. In this way, those such as Thrasymachus who want power for its own sake, will be kept in check. The principle of proportional equality, regulated by the rule of law, will ensure that public spirited people attain the important offices of state. Unless they demonstrate public spiritedness and political virtue, they will not be chosen to rule. And once chosen, the rule of law will constrain the rulers to rule legally and rightfully, if not philosophically.

Aristotle's emphasis upon rule of law and the corresponding ideal of a proportional equality of political participation points to an interesting conclusion about his political ideal. Clearly, these ideas fit precisely his notion that the necessary condition for a virtuous life is reasoned action within a public arena. Yet in his classification of constitutions Aristotle put monarchy forward as theoretically best. Here there is an apparent contradiction because rule by monarch excludes others from political activity. We must keep in mind, however, that for Aristotle monarchy, although ideal, is not a practical possibility in most circumstances; and he therefore feels free to advocate aristocracy and polity, which do allow for wider political participation. And it is apparent from a close reading of the *Politics* that Aristotle in fact prefers aristocracy rather than an ideal monarchy because it does provide people with a genuine life of political action; and he considers that polity best that comes closest to aristocracy. Conversely, since polity gives the greatest scope to political action, Aristotle prefers those aristocratic constitutions that embody some of the democratic principle of polity.

Such then is the basic outline of Aristotle's political philosophy, a philosophy that has become an enduring part of the Western tradition of political thought. The ideals of political participation, rule of law, the mixed constitution, and so on have become such an unconsciously accepted part of Western tradition of political discourse that we sometimes forget their initial originality.

Teleology sounds like an intimidating concept but it is not. The word comes from the Greek 'telos', meaning 'end' or 'goal'. For Aristotle the final goal or endpoint of a thing is also its formal cause, through which we can understand its purpose. Focusing on the goal of a thing offers us a way to understand its nature. For example, the purpose of an acorn is to become an oak tree. We know that not all acorns become oak tree but nevertheless we could not understand what an acorn is if we did not have a grasp of its telos. An acorn that falls on barren ground or that ends up as squirrel food is not uncommon but in one fundamental sense, it is a failed acorn. In thinking about acorns this way, we have a grasp of what an acorn should be and what conditions contribute to the realization of its potential. This teleological way of thinking about things is characteristic of Aristotle's political theory. The only real difference is that human beings are more complicated than acorn. But the *Politics* and the *Ethics* are teleological in that Aristotle argues that questions concerning the best life for man can be understood by looking at his nature-endpoint. At its simplest Aristotle's question is 'what conditions allow man to reach his full potential? The answer is equally-simple 'being a citizen of a just polis'.

We can understand human potential by looking at what makes people happy. The main reason for this is that eudemonia is a more sophisticated notion than basic happiness. Sometimes this notion is described as activity of the soul in accordance with virtue. The essence of the notion is that true happiness stems from being the best human being we can be, making the most of all our capacities. Politics is the key to man's happiness. Politics is natural. These are massive claims and, if proven, will confirm politics as the master science. Aristotle's fundamental claim, the foundation for all of his political thought, is laid out clearly in what must be one of the most famous quotations of all time: "It is evident that a city -state is among the things that exist by nature, that a human being is by nature political animal, and that anyone who is without a city-state, not by luck but by nature, is either a beast or a god".

We already have the intellectual tools to understand this as the foundation of Aristotle's politics. The first idea, 'that a city-state exists by nature, that a human being is by nature a political animal', is an expression of man's telos. The second idea, as Aristotle puts it another way: 'anyone who cannot form a community with others, or who does not need it because he is self-sufficient is no part of a city-state-he is either a beast or a god.

Beasts do not have the capacity to live politically even if they do live socially. They lack the power of speech and reason that enable human to live this way. Gods, we can assume or believe, do not need the benefits of political society as they are self-sufficient. We can all think of examples of humans who are bestial and human who shun the benefits of society. Humans who are incapable of living in decent society, perhaps because they follow their base desires in an unconstrained way, we do think of as somehow not being fully human. Sometimes we lock them up as criminals or treat them as sociopath. At other times, we censure them as 'vulgar ' or 'immoral'. At the other end of the scale, we can imagine hermits, examples of the ascetic saints who engage in a life of spiritual contemplation in the deserts of Rajasthan or in the caves of the Himalayas. Be they saintly or otherwise, it does not take a comic genius to draw out the absurdity in this way of life. Similarly, the idea that philosophy is the perfect way of life for man does not seem to capture the full human experience. Pure reason is too high a life for man. We are capable of philosophical reasoning. It is an important part of what and who we are. But if a life of contemplation is perfection how do we ensure we have enough to eat or propagate the species? Human virtue lies in finding the mean, a balance between the animal part and the rational part of our nature.

Returning now to the first idea that 'man is political animal', we begin to get an idea of how we find this balance between our animal and rational sides. Aristotle's claim is that the balance is struck in becoming a citizen of the polis. The idea of citizenship is vital here. It is not enough for man to simply live in a polis. He must be a citizen. This is not true of all men or any women. Happiness depends upon citizenship or full membership of political society. Our nature dictates that we are type of animal that is suited by nature for life in a polis.

It is here that the acorn / oak tree-human/polis analogy begins to break down. Acorns never existed without oak trees; the whole (the tree) is necessarily prior to the part (the acorn). It fact, Aristotle's claim is even stronger then this His claim is not that citizenship is the key to happiness but that citizenship in the polis is the key to happiness. Life before the ancient Greek city-state, or outside it in confederations or nations, or beyond it in the modern nation-state, is not conducive to happiness.

What evidence does Aristotle use to fill in his claims about man's telos? He begins by arguing that there is a series of natural relationships between a man and a woman and a man and his slave. There is, Aristotle generously admits a difference between a woman and a slave but they are similar in that a man needs them for survival. Women are needed for the sake of procreation and slaves are needed for manual work. Man, the natural ruler, can organize these resources in a way that is beneficial to all this is not the sort of beginning likely to endear Aristotle to the modern reader. In our view, most of this comes under the 'cultural baggage' category. The important claim is that the family or the household is a basic natural unit among humans. The fact that the ancient Greek household included slaves and assumed that women should be subservient to men is as culturally relative as the nuclear family of modern western societies. Nevertheless, Aristotle expends considerable energy showing that neither woman nor slaves can run their own lives and so they fit in his scheme of things in a manner that supports the eudemonia of the full citizen.

It is also clear why a human being is more of a political animal than a bee or other gregarious animal. Nature makes nothing pointlessly, as we say, and no animal has speech except a human being. A voice is a signifier of what is pleasant or painful. But speech is for making clear what is beneficial or harmful, and hence also what is just and unjust, and the rest. And it is community in these that makes a household and a city-state. Aristotle's initial definition of a citizen seems clearly empirical-anyone who is eligible to participate in deliberative and judicial office. This is a definition that gives us a small insight into life in the polis of ancient Greece. Aristotle valued communal participation in society. This meant participation in military, judicial and political decision-making and action. Such a huge personal investment in one's society was fostered by the limited size of the polis; It is for this reason that Aristotle favored a small political unit limited by 'self-sufficiency'.

Aristotle encourages a citizen to participate fully in his own community and notes that how one achieves this depends on the sort of constitution that governs the polis. A good citizen respects the norms and customs of his community and takes his turn at ruling and being ruled. The key to grasping this part of Aristotle's theory is to notice that good citizenship is relative to the constitution the citizen lives under. Here, in his practical advice citizenship does not necessarily entail participation in ruling. Rather it is reduced to sharing in the benefits of membership of a state. To elaborate freely on Aristotle's theme: there are several types of states and many cultures in the world. Different religious backgrounds, different ethno-cultural heritages, different socio-economic conditions, different human resources and different geographical situations: all place their own demands on a community and have to be managed in different ways. Politics is a practical thing and we have developed a number of different ways of managing our lives. We have to acknowledge the validity of these different structures for their own citizens. Being a good citizen means being a good citizen within these constraints.

Nevertheless, reflection on the basic elements of Aristotle's work offers a series of important insights into politics. We could develop this basic argument in any number of ways, drawing on Aristotle's theory in some parts and challenging him in others. Political theory does not really offer us complete set answers. Instead, it offers an entry into some of the most complex and pressing problems we face. Aristotle's longevity stems from the way he helps us think about what he termed the master science. It is clear that his legacy is wealth of conceptual tools that offer us an introduction to ourselves.

One of the first key insights that Aristotle gives us concerns the nature of political theory itself. The claim that politics is the master science may be little arrogant but politics is about living well or managing our lives to get the best out of them. Everything else is geared to this end. The big claim is that we are political animals. Aristotle's reflection on this leads him to suggest that citizenship is the key mode of human life and that the state is the key context in which we can achieve our potential. Thinking about how a state should be organized and how we are to live as citizens is thus hugely important. Without the state, without community in citizenship, we are nothing. Politics is a practical science and there are many ways to pursue happiness but the basic context is membership of a just state.

Ideal State

The constitution which is best for most cities and most men is the polity. It is inferior to the ideal constitutions of true kingship and aristocracy though still superior to the three perverted forms of constitution—oligarchy, democracy, and tyranny. Initially, polity is the good form of democracy but it later becomes a mixture of, or compromise between, oligarchy and democracy and it is its intermediate or moderate status which provides the reasons for its relative value. In the world of ordinary politics, the choice is between moderate or mixed constitutions, which are preferable, and pure, unadulterated constitutions, which are all inferior. The polity is not the only type of mixed constitution mentioned by Aristotle. There is also so-called aristocracy which differs from the polity by giving weight to the principle of merit or virtue as well as the principles of wealth and freedom. This difference, together with Aristotle's statement in criticism of Plato that the more constitutions are included as ingredients the better the mixture might lead us to expect that pride of place would be given to so-called aristocracy in Aristotle's account of the relatively best constitution. However, though so called aristocracy might have a claim to be superior to the polity, Aristotle does not accept it as a candidate for the best constitution for most cities and men. It either lies beyond the reach of most states or else is very close in nature to the polity and need not be discussed separately from the polity. Another reason for ignoring so called aristocracy, which Aristotle does not mention explicitly, is that it upsets the theoretical symmetry and elegance of his account. Given that oligarchy and democracy are the commonest forms of constitution, an assumption which runs through the central books of the *Politics*, it is logically simpler and more satisfying to concentrate on the constitution which is a mixture of these two forms alone.

Aristotle has several reasons for believing in the relative value of the mixed or moderate constitution. His discussion of equality and distributive justice in Book Three provides a justification for such a constitution. Both the oligarch and the democrat are criticized for ignoring all claims except those of wealth and freedom respectively. By referring to the purpose of the state, Aristotle argues that honour and power should be distributed in accordance with both wealth and freedom as well as virtue. In a non-ideal state, where these qualities are possessed not by one group, but by different, though overlapping, groups, distributive justice will demand that all groups have a share in the constitution. Aristotle also examines two arguments for democracy which seem to contain some difficulty and perhaps some truth. In his opinion they justify not the complete sovereignty of the many, but rather the right of the many to a share in the constitution and they therefore support a mixed constitution which contains some democratic elements but is not completely democratic. These arguments are of particular interest for democratic theory. The first may be called the argument of collective wisdom. A large body of men who are inferior as separate individuals may collectively be superior because each individual contributes his own share of virtue and practical wisdom to the group. When these contributions are added up the group will be found to possess a greater sum of virtue and wisdom than a smaller number of individually wiser and more virtuous individuals. As with Aristotle's other 'mathematical' doctrines in ethics and politics, for example his theory of distributive justice in terms of proportion, we should not press the quantitative implications too far. He recognizes that ethics and politics are not capable of the same degree of precision as mathematics and is unlikely to have considered that the merits of individuals or groups can be mathematically calculated and compared. The addition is a metaphorical, not a literal, sum, a way of illustrating the belief that 'two heads are better than one.' Aristotle's belief in collective wisdom fits with his general respect for public opinion. But he does not claim that the many are invariably superior, only that they may be sometimes superior. Moreover, the collective superiority of the many, when it exists, will not give them a right to monopolize the functions of government. Magistracies, for example, must be held by a small number of individuals and here the many cannot exercise their superiority. The argument justifies the limited participation of the many in functions such as deliberation and adjudication and therefore provides support for the mixed constitution, which Aristotle, on this occasion, particularly associates with the Athenian lawgiver, Solon.

> It was to avoid this that Solon and some of the other lawgivers gave to the people power to elect officers of government and to demand an account from them at the end of their tenure, but no right individually to hold such offices. This was in accord with our principle that the whole body of citizens acting together have the necessary understanding, even though each is individually not qualified to decide. By thus cooperating with the better sort of citizen the people can render some good service in their cities, in something like the same way that a combination of coarse foods with refined renders the whole diet more nutritious as well as more bulky.

Aristotle justifies the collective wisdom of the many by the analogy of the feast to which many contribute. This will be a better feast than one provided by a single individual, even if the many are individually poorer and their contributions inferior to that of a single individual. The quality of the feast is assumed to consist of a certain quantity of consumable objects such as food and drink and we can readily see how this can be made up of a large number of small ii dividable contributions. This analogy may illustrate but it does not prove the collective superiority of the many, because there does not seem to be any similarly simple way of aggregating the individual contributions of virtue and wisdom. Aristotle also uses the analogy of aesthetic judgement.

> The general public is a better judge of works of music and poetry, some judge some parts, some others, but their joint pronouncement is a verdict upon the whole.

Aristotle adds another argument which is more convincing. According to Socrates and Plato, ruling was a skill like medicine or navigation, which implied that government, like these other skills was a matter for properly trained and educated experts. Furthermore, just as the work of a doctor can only be properly assessed by other doctors, so in politics only the expert in the statesman's art can properly appoint or judge statesmen. Aristotle mentions this argument as a possible objection to the previous argument that the collective wisdom of the many may entitle them to a share in the deliberative or judicial functions and, in particular, to elect magistrates and call them to account. He meets the objection by saying that in some arts and skills the expert is not necessarily the best judge.

> There are tasks of which the actual doer is not either the best or the only judge, cases in which even those who do not possess the operative skill pronounce an opinion on the finished product. An obvious example is house-building; the builder certainly can judge a house, but the user, owner or tenant, will be a better judge. So too the user of a rudder, the helmsman, is a better judge of it than the carpenter who made it and it is the diner not the cook that pronounces upon the merits of the dinner.

This argument concedes that the expert has specialized knowledge and skills, but refuses him the right to be above criticism or control. In the political sphere it means that those who are actually making decisions and carrying out the business of government should have specialized capacities and training but are not therefore exempt from public control. Though they alone may have the ability to devise and administer policy, they are not the ultimate judges of whether these policies are the right ones. It is the individual citizen who feels the effect of government action who can provide the final judgement on its merits. Like the argument of collective wisdom, this argument justifies a mixture of democracy and some more restrictive and elitist type of government. It is, however, a much better argument. The collective wisdom argument assumes that political decisions are like assessments of works of art, which Aristotle saw as empirical judgements about independent matters of fact. On this view, it is difficult to argue that the population as a whole are likely to have opinions superior to those of the expert few. On the other hand, if political decisions are seen as decisions which affect the population and if the individual is assumed to be he best judge of how he ought to be effected, then the case for democratic rather than expert government is much stinger. Aristotle seems to hesitate about accepting this argument, perhaps because in the ideal state it is the rulers not the subjects who know best. But even if his support is partial and hesitant, he has at least recognized and understood an argument which can be used to rebut the more authoritarian implications of the view that politics is a skill.

Aristotle offers the argument which favours both democratic and oligarchic and combines both democratic and oligarchic institutions. In Book Four, however, the arguments depend more on the social composition of the polity and from this point of view the polity is more a moderate than a mixed constitution. In institutional structure it may by a mixture of oligarchic and democratic principles and institutions but socially it is not a mixture or balance between rich pour but a constitution in which the middle class dominate. In Book Four, therefore, Aristotle argues for the relative superiority of the polity in tens of the superiority of the middle class over the rich and the poor and not in terms of the superiorly of a mixture of democracy and oligarch over either of these constitutions in an unmixed form. Aristotle's middle class is defined with reference to the amount of their property. When talking of the middle class', we should remember that Aristotle's term is 'those in the middle' and we must not import any modem, Marxist connotations of the bourgeoisie or of a specific relation to the means of production. 'Those in the middle' are simply those of moderate or medium wealth. They are the men who could afford the armour of the hoplite or heavy-armed infantryman and thus formed the core of the city's military power on land.

Aristotle gives a number of arguments, of varying cogency, in favour of the superiority of the middle class. First, he draws an analogy with the doctrine of the mean from the *Ethics.*

> If we were right when in our Ethics we stated that virtue is a mean and that the happy life is life "free and unhindered and according to virtue, then the best life must be the middle way, consisting in a mean between two extremes which it is possible for each individual to attain. And the same principle must be applicable to the goodness or badness of states and constitutions.

This illustrates Aristotle's general preference for moderation and the middle way in ethics and politics but it does not prove that the rule of the middle class is best. The doctrine of the mean in the *Ethics* is concerned with the individual's disposition to act. The character of the ethically virtuous man is such that he has his emotions in balance and does not act or even wish to act with extremes of pity, fear, amusement, and so on. For example, the courageous man avoids the twin extremes of rashness and cowardice. But even if we accept this doctrine as an analysis of ethical action, Aristotle's use of it to prove the superiority of the middle class is invalid. It should not for example, be too adventurous or too cautious in its policies. But this does not prove that the constitution should be in the hands of the middle class.

Secondly, Aristotle claims that those who have a moderate amount of gifts of fortune, including wealth, are more likely to follow reason. The wealthy are inclined to arrogance and great crimes and the poor to roguery and petty crimes. As insolence and roguery are the two sources of crime, the middle class are most likely to be law-abiding and therefore reasonable. It might be objected that, if the rich tend to commit great crimes and the poor petty crimes, then the middle class will commit middling crimes which would not make them especially reasonable and law-abiding. But Aristotle may intend this argument not as a proof but as a statement of sociological fact; extremes of wealth or poverty are likely to prevent the development of virtue. Admittedly, he does not believe that moderate wealth is a sufficient condition or guarantee of virtue. As he said in criticism of Phaleas, it is not enough to ensure a moderate amount of property for the citizens; one must educate them to obey the laws. But he certainly believes that poverty is a bar to virtue and reasonableness and that great wealth is unnecessary and unnatural. In their level of material prosperity, if not in their moral development, the middle class match the citizens of the ideal state.

The other arguments in favour of the middle class point to their more specifically political qualities. A city in which the middle class dominate is more likely to have free government and is also most likely to incorporate friendship and equality:

> Those who have a super-abundance of all that makes for success, strength, riches, friends, and so forth, neither wish to be ruled nor understand how to be; and this is ingrained in them from childhood on; even at school they are so full of their superiority that they have never learned to do what they are told. Those on the other hand who are greatly deficient in these qualities are too subservient. So they cannot command and can only obey in a servile regime, while the others cannot obey in any regime and can command only in a master-slave relationship. The results is a state not of free men but of salves and masters, the one full of envy, the other of contempt. Nothing could be farther removed from friendship or from the whole idea of a shared partnership in a state. Sharing is a token of friendship; one does not share even a journey with people one does not like. The state aims to consist as far as possible of those who are like and equal, a condition found chiefly among the middle section. And so the best government is certain to be found in this kind of city, whose composition is, we maintain, a natural one.

The argument of this section is important and requires careful analysis. It may be summarized as follows: the rich are unaccustomed to being ruled but accustomed to ruling despotically; the poor are unaccustomed to ruling but accustomed to being ruled despotically; the rich and the poor will therefore together form a city of masters and slaves not of free men; a city should have friendship and equality which come most from the middle class; therefore the rule of the middle class is best. We may perhaps agree that the rich are unlikely to accept the rule of another less wealthy group and that their rule will tend to be selfish and therefore despotic. But the second point is more dubious. Is Aristotle right in thinking that the poor are unable to exercise rule and are fit only for being ruled as slaves? Elsewhere in the *Politics* he does not see the poor in such a docile and servile light; as a group, they tend to aim for power and domination in a way similar to, rather than opposite from, the rich. In this passage he has assumed a false opposition between rich and poor in order to argue that the middle class occupy a middle and mean position: they neither rule despotically nor obey slavishly but alternate between ruling and being ruled in a free and undisputed manner. He thus attempts to establish an intrinsic political superiority for the members of the middle class.

What is more likely to make the rule of the middle class less despotic and more equal is the fact that, given a division of society into rich, poor, and middle class, there is no class as opposed to the middle class as the rich and the poor are to one another. The middle class can be expected to treat the poor more leniently than the rich do and the rich more leniently than the poor do. But in this case, the superiority of the middle class, if it exists, is a product not of their intrinsic qualities but of their relative position in the social structure.

There will be no equality and friendship between rich and poor. It does not follow that there will be no equality and friendship between members of the same class, between rich men or between poor men. Yet this is what Aristotle implies. He says that friendship and equality exist especially among members of the middle class whereas he is entitled to say only that there will be more friendship and equality in a state where there is a large dominant middle class.

Aristotle also argues that a state dominated by the middle class is more likely to achieve stability, a political goal which he values very highly, especially for ordinary, non-ideal states. The middle class is the most secure and stable group in the community in that its members do not have enough wealth to be the object of envy or attack while they are sufficiently well off not to wish to attack the rich. The observation that the middle class is least likely to be a cause of economic grievance and conflict seems a reasonable one. It stems from the fact that the middle class in general is not opposed to either the rich or the poor to the same extent that the rich and the poor are opposed to one another. The existence of a strong middle class can therefore prevent the antagonism of the rich and the poor from causing strife and revolution. The middle class thus acts as a buffer between the rich and the poor. It also provides the only hope of a government consented to by all the citizens. The rich and the poor will not consent to be ruled by one another but they are both likely to consent to be ruled by the middle class who play the role of arbiter or mediator. But on all occasions the mediator is well trusted and the one in the middle is mediator.

These arguments, which depend on the central, balancing role of the middle class, are theoretically plausible and appear to be confirmed by experience. Communities which are polarized into two groups of rich and poor do appear to be less stable politically than those in which there is a substantial middle class. Though a balance between opposing political principles may produce stability, as in the mixed constitution of Sparta, famous for its resistance to change, a balance between opposing classes without any middle class, will lead to instability. Aristotle rightly recognizes the importance of economic divisions in political conflict and the need to reduce and blur these divisions in order to achieve political harmony and stability. Though he sometimes overstates the virtues of the middle class, he is right to recognize its stabilizing influence in the community.

With his awareness of the intimate connection between political institutions and the underlying social structure, he recognizes that it is useless to impose a constitution on a society, which cannot support it or make it work. Given the socio-economic structure of most Greek states, either democracy or oligarchy is likely to be the most appropriate form of constitution. But the legislator should make every attempt to temper the constitution by involving the middle class in it. As far as their social composition will allow, all states should aim to possess at least some of the characteristics of the polity.

Aristotle's theory of the polity is different in several respects from later theories of the mixed constitution. Aristotle does not like Polybius and Cicero, support a mixture of the three main types, rule of the one, of the few, and of the many, but of only two. Nor, like Montesquieu and the founders of the American constitution, does he argue for a balance between the different powers or functions of government that is the legislature, the executive, and the judiciary. Institutionally the polity is a mixture of, or compromise between the procedures and principles of different types of constitution. Again, Aristotle's theory is concerned not just with institutions but also with the social structure which supports them and which they serve. On this level it is less a theory of mixture than of moderation. The polity does not rest on a balance between rich and poor but on the dominance of the middle class. Nonetheless, though the account of the polity is unique in many of its details, it is similar to subsequent theories of the mixed constitution in its assumption of the value of moderation and of the need to avoid political extremes. In general inspiration, then, it may be said to belong to the tradition of the mixed constitution.

Though Aristotle's account of the polity is open to certain objections, they should not be allowed to obscure the real and lasting value of this part of his political theory. Its importance has to some extent been masked by a shift in our political terminology. What many people today describe and defend as 'democracy' has more in common with Aristotle's polity than with his democracy. For instance, those who hold that there should be regular elections every few years but would not approve of annual elections or of submitting all major decisions to referenda are really subscribing to Aristotle's view that the best constitution in the non-ideal world is one which combines oligarchic and democratic procedures. Furthermore, research by political sociologists has tended to confirm Aristotle's observation that stability is unlikely to be achieved in states where there is a sharp division into rich and poor. There is a much greater chance of avoiding dissidence and revolution when the government is in the hands of, or at least has the support of, a large middle class. More generally, Aristotle is to be commended for making a clear distinction between the ideal constitution and the constitution which may serve as a standard and model for ordinary constitutions. Great harm can and has been done by using utopian standards to judge ordinary situations and by trying to impose political institutions which may be suitable for an ideal situation, in which men have achieved their full moral and intellectual potential, on people and societies whose characters and needs are far from ideal. Aristotle takes great care to avoid this mistake. He distinguishes the ideally best from the practicable best and also points out that the practicable best, the polity, is not suited to all situations; there will be cases where it would be wrong to impose a polity rather than an oligarchy or a democracy.

Slavery

Of the two lesser communities, the household and the village, which are parts of the poils and precede it in time, the household is much more important in Aristotle's ethical and political theory. Though the village provides a necessary link between the household and the polis in the chain of historical development, Aristotle ignores it as an integral part of the fully developed polis. The household, on the other hand, continues to have important functions. Its origins lie in the instincts of reproduction and self-preservation and in the need to provide the basic necessities of life and it remains, as it was in Greek society of Aristotle's time, the institution which provides for the procreation and rearing of children and which produces much of the economic wealth of the polis. Once it has become part of the *polis,* the household is also closely involved in the aims of the larger community, It is very important as an educational institution, introducing children into the morality of the community. It is, moreover, the centre of life for over half the population of the city, that is for women, children, and slaves. Plato, realising moral influence of the household and fearing that it would conflict with, and undermine the public-spiritedness of the rulers, had advocated in the *Republic* the abolition of the household for the ruling class. Wives were to be held in common and there was to be no private property. He hoped to remove the conflict between public and private interest by the highly radical device of removing private interest altogether. Aristotle disagrees with these proposals very strongly and his criticism of the *Republic* in Book Two is largely taken up with objections to the community of wives and property. Many of his arguments are now part of the stock-in-trade of conservative opposition to communism. For example, disputes about property are due not to the existence of private property but to human wickedness. Indeed, sharing property may oven lead to an increase in disputes. More generally, Aristotle considers that people will not extend to the wives, children, and property held in common the same feelings of possession and affection that they have held for their personal family and property: Communism, in short, is contrary to human nature. Aristotle says:

> Moreover there is an immense amount of pleasure to be derived from the sense of ownership; every man bears love towards himself and 1 am sure that nature meant this to be so.

Communism of families and property also destroys the possibility of exercising certain ethical virtues, for example temperance towards other men's wives and personal generosity and liberality. Similarly, abolition of the family will cause problems in relation to such immoral acts as incest and parricide.

Though Aristotle rejects Plato's communism, he does not dismiss the problem which Plato was trying to solve. He recognizes that the private interests of the household and its members may clash with the interests of the *polis* as a whole. Hence the importance which he attaches to the household as an institution of moral education and his belief that the organization of *the* household is a matter of vital public concern and therefore a proper part of the subject matter of political science.

> Every household is part of a polis; and the virtue of the part ought to be examined in relation to the virtue of the whole. This means that children, and women too, must be educated with an eye to the whole constitution of the polis-at least if it is true to say that it makes a difference to the goodness of a state that its children should be good and its

women good. And it must make a difference; for women make up half the adult free population and from children come those who will participate in the constitution.

The pivotal figure is the head of the household who acts as a link-between the political community and the smaller community of the household. He will typically be a citizen and therefore a full member of the polis and will also be in charge of the other members of his household as well as of the family property. Control of the other members of the household will be exercised through the three household relationships of husband and wife, father and children, master and slave. Each of these relationships includes the head of the household as ruler but each involves a different type of rule.

Fundamental to everything that Aristotle thinks about politics is the idea that some ways of ordering human life are natural and others not. Aristotle's teleological biology informs his view that only some kinds of human relationship are as nature intended them to be and his treatment of rulership is largely concerned with untangling the natural forms of the ruler-ruled relationship from the unnatural. In the *Politics* Aristotle establishes the criteria for naturalness in the context of his treatment of slavery in Book 1. Aristotle begins the discussion by identifying what he calls 'natural pairs', one half of which rules the other. Rulership, he thinks, exists in any relationship between superior and inferior. Rulership includes commanding, but it also included directing, guiding and educating. Aristotle thinks that masters and slaves, husbands and wives, fathers and children, and rulers and ruled, are all natural pair for the straightforward reason that each needs the other to be what it is. This is more than a matter of definition; of course, fathers cannot be fathers without children and children cannot be children without fathers, but Aristotle also means that neither can begin to be self-sufficient without the other, and neither can perform its function without the other. The ruling of one of a natural pair by the other must be in the interest of both. The rule of men over animals qualifies as natural. Men are naturally at war with wild animals, as they are with wild men, so it is highly advantageous for animals to become domesticated. They are then fed and watered, are protected by their owners, and, most importantly, are protected from other men, so it is highly advantageous for animals to become domesticated. Domestic animals have the stamp of ownership on them, so that men who are not their owners have no reason to fear them because the animals, being at home somewhere, can be assumed to be tame.

Rulership is exercised in different ways. Aristotle gives two illuminating examples: mind over body and intelligence over the desires. The rule of mind over body is absolute or despotic in the interests of both, while the rule of intelligence over the desires is constitutional and royal. By this Aristotle means that the mind does not negotiate with the body. The desires arise naturally, and some, like the desires for food, drink and rest, have to be satisfied sometimes or the body would die and the desires would die with it. The desires are best thought of as subjects petitioning a king. They ask to be satisfied, but the king decides if and when. Constitutional monarchy for Aristotle is kingship exercised through laws, and a wise king would outlaw some desires as being too unruly, and would establish some kind of orderly programmer for the satisfaction of the reasonable desires, say three meals a day, none in excess, and regular hours of sleep. The desires would then know where they stand like the subjects of a king ruling through law. Like Plato, Aristotle does not think that the desires are fixed either in number or in intensity. New desires arise, or old desires assert themselves with a new intensity; a wise mind considers the first kind on their merits and puts down the rebellion of the second. Endless self-indulgence kills desire, dulls the intelligence and threatens the body.

All forms of rulership are limited by the end for which rulership is exercised. Rule is not domination for its own sake; abuse of power for Aristotle means something very close to what we mean by 'drug abuse', the use of something which has no end and which can only lead on to disaster because it has no end. Husbands must remember that sexuality is for procreation and not for mere enjoyment, father must remember that children will one day be like themselves, and masters of slaves must remember that slaves are for use and not for exploitation or profit. Slaves exist to free masters from the menial occupations. Free men need the leisure for virtue and so have not got the time to get their own living. Aristotle is careful to say that slaves are a part of wealth and not a means towards the increase of wealth, by which he means that it is no part of a master's business to squeeze the last ounce of labour out of his slaves. Some commentators think that in making this distinction Aristotle was already being a little old-fashioned in his treatment of slavery, defending a traditional form of household slavery in the face of a new kind of slavery which saw slaves as an investment on which their masters demanded the highest possible return. Aristotle says that a slave is like a bed, not a shuttle. In principle, there is no limit to the use of a shuttle, which could be used to weave day and night; beds are for sleeping in, not for sleeping in all day, and the bed does not produce anything else. Likewise the slave. He is not for increasing his master's wealth; he must, of course, reproduce his own kind, but slave-breeding for profit would be ruled out.

The ends of human relationships put their places in a hierarchy of ends. Nature's pattern is a pattern of subordination, otherwise no form of rule would itself be natural and men would not even rule over animals by nature, and this hierarchical pattern extends to the ends for which forms of rule exist. The relationship between husband and wife makes the continuation of the species possible; the rule of the head of a household over wife, children and slaves has as its end the social unit which, together with others like itself, goes to make up economically self-sufficient village communities, and it is a group of these self-sufficient communities which makes up the supreme community, the polis, which has as its end not just self-sufficient life but the good life. The end of the family and the village lead naturally to the supreme end which is life in a properly constituted polis.

No doctrine, so the argument goes, which justifies slavery can be taken seriously. Nonetheless, Aristotle himself plainly takes his argument for slavery seriously, though some commentators have argued that he is especially worried by slavery to take the matter too far. A rational account of slavery is necessary, just as a rational account is necessary of any other kind of relationship between rulers and ruled; Aristotle is worried about slavery only in the sense that he is worried about all possible abuses of power there is no special worry about slavery, though there is a special technical difficulty. Nature has made the difference between men and animals, male and female, children and adults, very clear, and it is this clarity which enables Aristotle to speak of nature's intentions. Nature does nothing without a purpose, and there must, therefore, be a purpose in these distinctions.

In the case of the distinction between free men by nature and slaves by nature a clear-cut distinction is not so easily made. The problem is compounded by the obvious fact that in the world of the Greek cities some obviously superior men ended up by being slaves and some obviously inferior men ended up as the masters of slaves, and the cleaver slave who outwitted and manipulated his dull master was to become one of the stock figures of ancient comedy. Who then, is fit to be a master and who a slave? Aristotle says that those who are fit to direct themselves are fit to direct those who are incapable of self-direction. The ability to rule a household is part of intelligence; being good at running a household is part of goodness, so the claims of masters to rule slaves are partly managerial and partly moral. Ideally, the master's intelligence should take the place of the absent intelligence of the slave, but unfortunately slaves, even slaves by nature, are not always entirely stupid. There is something in the slave which corresponds to intelligence in the master, and the fact of the matter is that slaves are treated differently from tools or from beasts of burden. Masters talk to slaves and give them orders, and slaves are capable of being trained to do fairly sophisticated jobs.

So what is the proper relationship between the slave's intelligence and the master's intelligence? The master is fit to rule the slave because he is himself self-directed. This would be true of the master even if he had no slaves. He is capable of a rational course of life; he is a man who knows what his life should be and is capable of sticking to what he knows it should be like. Not so the slave. Left to his own devices he would probably descend to a level of swinish idleness; much better for him to be part of a well-run operation under a master's direction. These generalities are not really very helpful in deciding who should be a slave, and Aristotle provides a sliding scale of suitability from nobly born Greeks, who are the least suitable, to base-born barbarians, who are the most suitable. Base-born Greek and nobly born barbarians come somewhere in between, and Olympic victors should probably not be made slaves. Barbarians make the best slaves because they have never known the rational liberty which only a polis can provide. The classification is meant to show that it does a master no favors to have as his slave someone who is unsuitable, and a master who has a better man than him for his slave would look ridiculous. Aristotle knows that slaves are frequently slaves by accident, and he has heard the Sophist argument that all power relations are the result of more or less arbitrary convention. What bothers Aristotle about the Sophist position is that if every ruler-ruled relationship is conventional only, then nobody would ever have cause for complaint. Nothing would ever be unnatural. If there are no slaves by nature, then there are no free men by nature and the world become meaningless, fit only for those capable of a stoical indifference.

Four consecutive chapters of Book-1of the *Politics* are devoted to a thematic discussion of despotic rule. The first of these, Chapter 4 raises the subject in the context of the household manager's need for property and tools. Both property and tools are understood in the broad sense as including animate as well as inanimate members. The slave is a living tool for the use of his master, the household manager. While it is possible to see here an argument for the necessity of slavery, Aristotle's primary concern is to disclose the nature and capacity of the slave.

Resisting the temptation to say that slavery is necessary or just before saying what a slave is, Aristotle includes these points in his discussion of the slave: the slave is a kind of property and a kind of tool he is, in particular, a human tool and one which is oriented towards life and action. He is thus similar to the assistants of the various artisans, for all these are also human tools but he is unlike them in that they are tools for production whereas he is a tool for action.

Aristotle's definition of the slave is not understood by its author as setting the question of the existence of the slave as defined. Rather, the definition of the slave establishes the various criteria. A slave by nature, a human being who belongs not to himself but to another human being. This is taken to require that he be a part of another human being, perhaps this is what it would mean to say that one by nature belongs to another. As the property of his master the slave must also be separable from him and be useful as a tool for action.

Aristotle's examples of actual slaves show them to be employed as tools for production. There is thus a gulf between the nature of the slave as defined by Aristotle and the use to which actual slaves are often put. Immediately following Aristotle's confident assertion that the nature of the slave is clear, we come upon the following lines, which introduce Chapter 5:

> One must consider that this whether or not there is any such slave by nature, and whether or not it is better and just for anyone to serve as a slave, but every servitude is against nature.

Aristotle may have seemed to have been assimilating natural and actual slavery, but the above passage suggests that he is proceeding with considerable caution. Not only does he not assume that actual slaves are natural slaves, he does not even assume that natural slaves exist. The precise wording of the question is also worth nothing. Aristotle distinguishes the question of the existence of the natural slave from the question of whether it is "better and just for anyone to serve as a slave." Perhaps Aristotle is ready to suggest that if there were no natural slave, it may still be wondered whether it is better and just for someone to serve in this capacity of its utility. More simply, one should notice that the question implies that the real problem is whether all slavery is unjust, not whether any is unjust. This is not the question of a dogmatic defender of slavery.

The allegedly easy question of whether there exists a natural slave appears to be answered by an easy "yes." This shows Aristotle's aristocratic pride and prejudice. He is least bothered about humanist and egalitarian values. Ruling and being ruled are announced as being not only necessary but also advantageous. Moreover, in one of those famous passages that proclaim nature's harmony and design, Aristotle says that some things, even from the moment of their origin, are designated for ruling, while others are marked out for being ruled. The reader will note, however that Aristotle has evaded an important part of the question: we are seeking to learn not whether ruling and being ruled are necessary, advantageous, but whether servitude, a distinct kind of being ruled, is ever good, just and natural among men. Aristotle eventually addresses this objection, however, and affirms that despotic rule does indeed exist and, moreover, is advantageous not only for the ruler but also for the ruled. True, he does not say that this instance of despotic rule is just, but perhaps the problem of justice disappears with the assertion that this despotism is advantageous for both parties and that its dissolution would be attended by harm for all.

Aristotle is very bold and arrogant in making this explicit and unambiguous statement that rule and even despotic rule are sometimes natural and advantageous for all. But we are forced to wonder whether Aristotle is not teasing us a bit, for his illustration of natural rule is drawn not from Spartan rule over Helots, or Greek rule over barbarians, or even from some legendary regime of distant past. Rather, after putting aside the example of the natural rule present in a musical harmony on the grounds that this may not be adequate defense to the present inquiry, Aristotle chooses another strategy. He mobilizes all his resources to convince his readers. He settles on the rule of soul over body as the example of a natural despotism and on the rule of reason over passion as the example of political and kingly rule. Thus the view implicit from the beginning of Aristotle's discussion of slavery is now explicit: despotic rule is indeed natural and beneficial.

Once having established the rule of soul over body as the paradigm of natural despotic rule, one would expect Aristotle to examine directly the bearing of this paradigm on actual slavery. This examination is deferred and complicated by the introduction of a new paradigm, that of man's rule over animals. Although man's rule over the animals is not immediately identified as despotic, it is termed with that of soul and body to illustrate the difference that must exist between natural masters and slaves. But if natural despotic rule is exemplified well by the rule of soul over body, why has Aristotle introduced a second metaphor.

The analogy of man's rule over animals seeks to effect a transition from the paradigmatic rule of soul over body to the rule of human masters over slaves. It suggests that the paradigm can be applied to cases between unlike beings as well as within a given being. It leads one to consider whether the relationship that exists between soul and body might not be approached by that between man and the animals, and this in turn prepares us to wonder whether certain man might not be separated as far from each other as is man from beast. Indeed, after moving from the case of soul/body to that of man/beast, Aristotle moves briefly to that of male/female. The evident progression here is from the problem of rule between parts of the same being, to the problem of rule between different species, to the problem of rule between different members of the same species. This progression illustrates two different aspects of the general problem of rule. It compels us to ask whether there in truly a common good as Aristotle is at pains to assert in the case of man/beast. Is there truly a natural superiority of rule over ruled as Aristotle is at pains to assert in the case of male/female? Both of these problems become more acute and complicated as we approach the case of despotic rule as actually practiced among men.

Aristotle is not offering dogmatic defense of actual slavery, his conclusion is entirely circumspect. It merely reiterates the criteria for natural despotic rule and leaves it to the reader to apply these criteria. If the reader believes the actual slaves are mere beasts or body, he will doubtless see here a defense of actual slavery on the grounds that it is natural' but Aristotle himself refrains from offering such a defense. He changes his paradigms of natural rule so that they seem to reach down toward the case of actual slavery, but whether they ever reach far enough is a matter of doubt. He reinforces these doubts by dropping the paradigm for natural rule within a species, the rule of male over female from his conclusion. This encourages us to doubt that the human species is so divided that it is, in effect, two species, of which one deserves to rule the other despotically.

In the light of the problem that natural masters and slaves must in effect be members of a different species, it makes sense to ask how it is that they are not so readily distinguishable from each other as are beasts from men or even males from females. The consequence of this failure is not simply that certain slaves and free men have bodies ill-designed for their work; but because men make their judgments about who does and who does not deserve to be a slave in large part on the basis of bodily appearance, the confusion among bodies would lead to a departure of the actual from the natural order even men with the best of intentions. A similar result might be encouraged by the distribution of warlike bodies of slaves and of unwarlike bodies to free men. It seems, then, that even if nature is to be credited with making clear distinctions between the mastering and the servile in bodies, souls, and even in this inanimate, Aristotle shows that the actual household must often fail to observe these distinctions.

Aristotle has consistently argued about slavery as though it exists by nature, and he has advanced no open attack on actual slavery. He twice indicated that the naturalness of slavery was indeed an issue, but only in the case of the corrupt rule of body over soul did he ever use the phrase "against nature". It is thus not surprising that his defense of natural slavery, combined with his restraint in openly attacking actual slavery, should be taken as a sign of support for the institution as it then existed. He explains this paradox by noting that "enslaving" and "slave" are equivocal terms in this way: for there is also a slave according to law and a being enslaved according to law. Only now is Aristotle directly introducing actual or conventional slavery into his discussion, and the manner of its introduction emphasizes how different it is from natural slavery.

After introducing the new theme of the slave according to law, Aristotle offers this explanation of what law is as it pertains to slavery: "The law is a certain agreement in which men say that what is conquered through war belongs to the conquerors". Further it generality reminds us that the investigation of lawful slavery is also, in part, an investigation of law.

After defending only the servitude of natural slave to natural master, Aristotle's now mentions two other arguments that attempt more generous defenses of conventional slavery. The first of these argues that because force is not without virtue, then enforced servitude is justified by the virtue of the enforcer. The second argues that because the law is just, then the lawful enslaving of captives is also just. Aristotle has doubts about both of these defenses of conventional slavery. The ambivalence or complexity of his position is thus not visible.

Aristotle's dissatisfaction with the first defense of conventional slavery is not made explicit. In the first place, this defense of slavery looks at the qualities of the conqueror only in relation to those of the conquered. It says nothing about the general requirements of ruling or the particular requirements of ruling despotically. Even if it could be established that the conqueror is always superior to the conquered in all virtues, it would not follow that the conqueror was so far superior as to deserve to rule despotically. In other words, Aristotle's own paradigms for the relationship between master and slave were soul to body and man to beast. The defenders of conventional slavery who search for some standard behind the law look to virtue and vice. They do not deny that slaves are human or have reason, whereas Aristotle's account of the natural slave demanded that he be as beast as to man. Indeed, this defense of conventional slavery might well justify the barbarian practice of treating women as slaves.

In the second place, when Aristotle explains why this view has arisen, he notes that "in a certain way, when it obtains equipment, virtue is especially capable even of using force". Aristotle is thus careful not to grant that virtue is the primary or exclusive component of force; virtue needs equipment, and its link to force is qualified by "in a certain way." Aristotle leaves it quite open that virtue can be unarmed and that unarmed virtue can be vanquished.

Aristotle's irritation and uneasiness with the second defense of conventional slavery is explicit. Its defenders maintain that the man captured in war is justly a slave because the law says he is a slave and the law is just. Aristotle attacks this attempt to justify slavery on two grounds. In the first place, the origin of the war might not be just. Conceivably, this objection would indeed prove problematic even for the strict defender of the law, for wars can be begun or prolonged in contravention of the law. Thus the position that the just is the legal must face the problem that the legal may be ambiguous or self-contradictory in some cases.

Aristotle's skeptical look at attempts to justify conventional slavery gives rise to a skeptical glance at the claims of the well-born. He shows his skepticism in part by not taking seriously the well born Greek claim to have had gods for parents. Beasts are born from beasts, human beings from human beings. The claim of the well-born should not be that they are of divine birth but that they are superior in virtue. Unfortunately, however, one's superiority in virtue is not well demonstrated by appealing to the virtue of one's birth.

We have seen that Aristotle's discussion suggests that there are such things as the natural master and the natural slave, but we have also seen they only establish a standard by which actual slavery must be judged. Natural slavery is evident in the rule of the soul over the body, but this sort of rule appears to be unlike that of captors over their captives, and it is especially this latter sort of slavery that we find in cities. Lawful slavery might be found to be just if it could be established either that it were just for the stronger to rule the weaker or that laws sanctioning slavery were just simply in virtue of their being laws, but Aristotle raises series of doubts about both of these positions.

When Aristotle discusses questions regarding the actual institution of slavery, in both actual and proposed regimes, his main point concern the usefulness of slaves in providing leisure and the problems and tensions arising out of keeping slaves in disciplinary control. He does not give practical advice on the detection or recruitment of natural slaves or masters. Even in the case of his own best regime, Aristotle does not mention that natural slaves should be sought. He mentions instead that the slaves ought to be useful as regards their works and safe in the sense of not being prone to revolution. Aristotle advices against spirited slaves, because they are prone to innovation, but he does not advice against intelligent slaves. His advice is thus quite open to the outcome that those who are not natural slaves would be enslaved in his own best regime, while those who come close to being natural slaves would be passed over as troublesome and useless. Indeed, in offering to slaves the promise of liberation, Aristotle tacitly admits that they are not natural slaves. It seems puzzling that Aristotle advancing a teaching on the natural slave, does not allow this teaching to guide his remarks on slavery as a practical problem. The tension between Aristotle's practical remarks and his theory of natural slavery looks ominous as well as puzzling. If natural slavery remains the standard for just slavery, must we not conclude that Aristotle's practical remarks about slavery show a marked disregard for social justice?

For properly understood, Aristotle's view of slaves and women is neither the sophistry of a prejudiced Greek male enjoying a privileged position nor simply the product of a misguided biologist who assumes uncritically that nature's way is identical with the status quo. Rather it is also and even primarily a political application of what was unquestionably an important advance in philosophical psychology. Aristotle was able to accept the demand of Plato that a difference in role or pursuit be tied to a relevant difference in nature and at the same time to reassert the claim of Gorgias that the virtues of slaves and women are different from those of free men because their activities or roles are different.

Aristotle's remarks on slavery are admittedly difficult and controversial. He seems not only to be on the wrong side of a convention versus nature controversy but also to express himself in a way that threatens the very humanity of slaves. He emphasizes their capacity for bodily labour comparing their utility to that of tame animals and says that slaves differ from masters to the same extent that bodies differ from souls and beasts from men. Such remarks closely relate slaves to animals, so that it is at least understandable why difficulties have been felt as to whether Aristotle classes them as human. But Aristotle is quite explicit in classifying slaves as men and if we understand that Aristotle's idea of the natural slave is based upon his newly developed political and ethical psychology, we can see quite easily how slaves qualify as human beings. Aristotle denies slaves the capacity to deliberate but he never denies them the capacity of emotional response. In more technical language, Aristotle denies them the logical or reasoning half of the bipartite soul but not the alogical or emotional half. This means that slaves can make the judgments involved in emotional responses and therefore have at least a minimum share in the cognitive capacity peculiar to men in relation to other animals.

In denying slaves the capacity to deliberate Aristotle is not robbing them of their humanity. Rather he is meeting Plato's demand for relevant differences and so explaining and justifying a peculiarly servile activity and virtue. Slaves lack the ability to deliberate, that is to say the ability to act with forethought. When this deficiency is combined with bodily strength suitable for necessary tasks then a role of obedient services seems proper. Natural slaves must have a measure of temperance and courage and in general be properly disposed toward their masters. But they are not expected to have practical wisdom or in general the virtue demanded of a master.

Aristotle's view of slavery is neither psychologically foolish nor morally repulsive. Of course, there are not natural slaves in the world, so that the view remains theoretical. But as theory it has the merit of running a middle course between the opposing views recognized by Plato in the *Laws*. It neither allows the possibility of slaves excelling in regard to all virtue nor despises them as if they were animals. Instead it seems to take a hint from Homer to the effect that slaves lack half their wits. They lack the capacity to deliberate but are in other respects cognitive creature. Such a view may not be altogether novel at least in the *Laws*.

Women and Children

The head of the household also rules his wife and children. Whereas the rule over slaves is despotic or in the master's own interests, rule over both wives and children is free and is exercised in their interests not those of the head of the household. Women and children are not however treated in precisely the same way. Rule of the father over his children is similar to kingly rule because the father, though ruling in his children's interests, is naturally superior to them. Children have the deliberative faculty in their soul which makes them, unlike slaves, fully human and entitled to respect as people of independent value. But this faculty is undeveloped or incomplete and so children are still dependent on their parents. Aristotle thus adopts the familiar and relatively uncontentious position that the immaturity of children requires them to be disciplined for their own good.

His attitude towards the role and status of women reflects the attitudes prevalent in his own society. The proper area of women's activity is the and biases house. Greek women had no political and few legal rights and even within the house were under the general supervision of their husbands. Hence, male courage is shown in commanding female courage in obeying. Aristotle's one criticism of current attitudes to women is that the need to educate women in the values of the community has been neglected. Women constitute, after all, one-half of the free population. The Spartans, who are commended for the public concern they show for education, are said to have suffered defeat partly because of their failure to educate their women. The education of women, however, is not intended to take them out of their traditionally domestic and subservient role; it is to ensure that they perform this role effectively and in harmony with the general aims of the polis.

Aristotle's attempts to justify such a role for women are brief and unsatisfactory. Though he usually parades his differences with Plato, he gives very little attention to Plato's radical suggestion that women should be politically and socially equal except in so far as their physical difference from men is strictly relevant. Plato's justification of the equality of women is closely connected with, indeed is only made possible by his abolition of the household. Aristotle, by supporting the retention of the household on the grounds of the value of personal family relationships and private property, is thereby committed to opposing the equality of women. He admits this openly:

> To argue from an analogy with beasts and say that male and female ought to engage in the same occupations is futile: beasts do not have household.

If the household is natural, so too must be the inferior status of women. As in the case of slaves and children, we would expect Aristotle to support such a belief by identifying the particular natural difference, which makes women inferior to men. This he does only once and inadequately; whereas the slave has no deliberative faculty and the child has a deliberative faculty which is undeveloped, woman has a deliberative faculty which lacks authority. Aristotle gives us no reason why women's deliberative faculty should be without authority and completely ignores Plato's arguments about the intellectual equality of men and women. To the critical reader it seems that Aristotle is simply arguing from the fact of subjection to the existence of a natural inferiority which justifies subjection, an inference of right from might which he usually deplores.

The same difficulty occurs with Aristotle's description of the rule of husband over wife as 'political' in contrast to the 'kingly' rule of father over children. Political rule involves a relationship of equality between ruler and ruled and therefore implies an alternation of ruling and being ruled. But in the case of husband and wife there is no such alternation; the husband always rules. Aristotle tries to reconcile this permanent inequality with the equality implied by political rule by pointing out that whenever there is a relationship of ruler and ruled, even among equals, the ruler will always, by the very fact of his ruling, be distinct from and superior to the ruled. This distinction is usually accentuated by a difference of 'outward dignity, style of address and honour paid', and it is this difference which is said to exist between males and females. It is true that all forms of control by definition involve inequality, that when a leader is selected from a group of equals the previous equality has necessarily been destroyed and that the difference is commonly reinforced and increased by the symbols and trappings of authority. But if the inequality between husband and wife is due solely to the fact that one always rules while the other is always ruled, what prior justification is there for this permanent subjection of the one to the other? If there is no prior inequality, why should there not be, as in other types of political rule, an alternation of ruling and being ruled? Aristotle avoids this particular problem in the *Ethics* by comparing the role of husband over wife with aristocratic rather than political rule; aristocracy clearly implies superior virtue on the part of the ruler, though Aristotle admits that the husband will hand over to his wife responsibility for matters for which women are suited.

In some respects, Aristotle's treatment of the position of women is more culpable than his more commonly castigated justification of slavery. There, at least, the counter arguments are admitted and argued against, however unsuccessfully; here he is content with dogmatic assertion. In both cases we see how unshakeable is his belief in the value of the household and the family. Initially he derives the naturalness of the household from the supposed fact that the rule of husband over wife and of master over slave accord with innate characteristics in human beings. We can now see that he offers no convincing empirical evidence for the existence of these innate characteristics. Instead his belief in them seems to depend on the assumption that the household itself must be natural. Because the household meets what to Aristotle are essential human needs, its relationships must be founded on natural differences, even if these are not readily discoverable by empirical observation.

In discussing women Aristotle leaves no doubt about their subordinate and domestic role. He states clearly that men are better fitted to command than women and that the role of women is not the bodily service characteristic of slaves but rather the preservation of goods procured by men. Moreover, since Aristotle relates virtue to function he demands of women a virtue which reflects their domestic role. They will need, Aristotle tells us, less courage than men and not the courage of command but rather the courage of subordination.

So far Aristotle's account of women is based upon his conception of their role within the household. But his account goes deeper than this. It also relates women to the distinction between logical and alogical halves of the soul and contrasts the psychic capacities of women with those of both slaves and children. Salves are said not to possess the deliberative faculty at all; women are said to possess it, but without authority; and children are said to possess it imperfectly. The alogical or emotional half of the soul is prior in generation to the logical or reasoning half. Children will develop the capacity to deliberate, but during their immaturity they live emotionally and without reflection. However, the case of women is more obscure. At first glance it may appear that Aristotle is simply referring to the subordinate position of women. He may seem to be saying that while women possess reason, it does not prevail in the society of men. Women lacked authority both in actual Greek city states and in the society recommended by Aristotle.

It is important to emphasise that in calling the deliberative capacity of a women as without authority, Aristotle is not impugning the cleverness of women. He recognizes that women can think through and even give reasoned advice. He would see not absurdity, for example, in Ajax praising the forethought of Tecemssa or Crone fearing the cleverness of Medea. His point is not that women deliberate only in some vague and illogical way, but that their deliberative reflections are likely not to control their emotions. This view is, of course, not an original Aristotelian creation. It is common view of women and one that is illustrated often in Greek literature. Medea is a celebrated case. Deserted by Jason for another women, she is angered and plans to take revenge by killing the children born to her and Jason. Reflection tells Medea that such an act of revenge is excessive and against her own interests. She hesitates but ultimately her anger is stronger than her deliberations. In Aristotelian terminology her deliberative capacity is without authority. Her deliberative faculty cannot control her anger so that she acts emotionally and unreasonably, but not without considerable cleverness. Women are most clever contrivers of every evil. In the service of emotion their deliberative faculties lack authority. Medea understands that she is about to do something terrible, but she is not deterred by this understanding.

Aristotle's view of women may be false. Certainly the exceptional behavior of a tragic heroine cannot decide what is in the end an empirical issue. But it would be mistake to think that Aristotle's view is simply the creation of a prejudiced male or, more charitably, the product of an overly keen biologist. On the contrary, it is a thoughtful view that well illustrates how investigations within one sphere of philosophical enquiry can determine developments within another. Aristotle investigated emotional response and drew a fundamental distinction between reason and emotion. He then applied this distinction to the field of political theory, formulated a bipartite psychology and used this psychology to explain the role of women within society. He credited women with reason and therefore distinguished them from natural slaves who lack reason altogether and from children who have not yet acquired reason. Aristotle recognized that women merit a role that is neither "servile nor puerile," but he was prepared to assign them a subordinate role on the grounds that their reason or logical side is without in relation to their emotional or irrational side.

In the work of many philosophers, conceptions of what is a good life for human beings are anchored in conceptions of what it is to be 'fully human'. Sometimes this humanness has been characterised by trying to identify what are seen to be the distinguishing marks of human beings - those things which differentiate human beings from other species. Aristotle is a case in point. Much of his philosophy is based on the assumption that everything which exists can be seen as existing for a reason or an end. To understand this end, we have to identify *the function* of a thing, and its function resides in its nature, in that which distinguishes it from other things and makes it the sort of thing that it is. Aristotle assumes that, just as the individual parts of the human body have a function, or just as the harp player has a function -namely, to play the harp as well as possible - so human beings have a function, which is to develop their special talent or excellence. We will find what this function is when we find what it is that distinguishes human beings from other species.

There were however, according to Aristotle, certain classes of human beings who were excluded from the full exercise of human reason; namely, slaves and women. Slaves he regarded basically as a form of property: 'Any piece of property can be regarded as a tool enabling a man to live, and his property is an assemblage of such tools; a slave is a sort of living piece of property, and like any other servant is a tool in charge of other tools'. The life of a slave is simply a means to an end, that of enabling the master to pursue a life of freedom and virtue among the other male citizens of the city state or polis. The life of a woman was similarly functional; the wife of a male citizen was needed to produce heirs and, like slaves, to play a part in providing the necessities of life. Aristotle also expressed this by saying that the family or household, existed 'for the sake of the *polis*. It was an inferior though necessary form of association, whose rationale lay in its providing the means for free males to live a life devoted to intellectual and political pursuits. Aristotle, however, recognised a difficulty with his exclusion of women and slaves from the life of reason, and the way in which he tried to cope with it is revealing of the assumptions from which he starts.

The problem is this. Women and slaves are, after all, human beings. They do not lack speech, and the adequate performance of their functions will surely require capacities for reason, and perhaps certain virtues. Here Aristotle faces problem. Aristotle's solution to this problem is to argue that the type of knowledge possessed by slaves and women was a special type. The fully rational part of the soul, the 'deliberative faculty' was not present at all in slaves and was ineffective in females. The knowledge and virtue of slaves and women consisted in knowing how to be ruled and how to perform their allotted tasks, and this did not qualify as fully rational.

Now this view of women and slaves, combined with Aristotle's belief that it is 'natural' for the rational part of the soul to rule the irrational, generates an anomaly in Aristotle's philosophy and points to some assumptions that underly it. Aristotle compared the rule of the mind over the body to the rule of a master or free man over a slave. He believed that there was a class of 'natural rulers; that is to say, those whom nature had intended to rule. But he did not believe that everyone who was born into this natural ruling class necessarily possessed the qualities of mind and character to fit them for this task. There were free males in whom the rational part of the soul did not rule. In the case of such people, Aristotle would argue that the rational part of the soul should rule the irrational, that it was natural and fitting that this should be so. He could not, however, argue this in the case of women or slaves, since this would be undermining the sharp distinction between the rulers and those who should be ruled. This is tantamount, to saying that women are by nature unnatural. What Aristotle does is to offer a general theory of human nature and about the proper relationship between body and soul, and then simply excludes certain classes of human beings from this 'human nature' in ways which cannot be explained at all within the theory, and which generate the sort of anomaly.

The whole of Aristotle's political philosophy is based on the assumption that one class of human beings — namely free males — should lead a life that he sees as self-justifying or as lived for its own sake, and that others should lead a life that is merely a means to this. And he consistently regards women as defective, inferior beings, almost as a degenerate form of human life. This comes out very clearly in his biology. Aristotle believed that the female supplied the 'matter' in conception, and he thought this to consist of the menstrual fluid. The male, on the other hand, supplied the 'form'[1] or 'soul', via the emission of semen. He believed the male to be superior in possessing more 'vital heat' than the female; semen, he thought, was a 'concoction' of the blood which was superior in all respects to the menstrual fluid.

Females were inferior because of their inability to 'concoct' semen. Female embryos were inferior to male ones; if a girl child was born, it was an indication of the inferiority of the state of the uterus. Aristotle regarded the female state as being a sort of deformity, although one which occurred in the ordinary course of nature. Aristotle, of course, did not possess modern biological knowledge about conception. But the assumption of the inferiority of the female in no way follows from his purely biological assumptions; these would have been quite compatible with the assumption of an equally important part played by both males and females in conception.

Aristotle therefore sees women as inferior and deficient. But there is sometimes a tension between this and the fact that he also wants to see women as fitted or suited for the roles that they play. This tension is very common in the history of philosophy. On the one hand, women arc seen as inferior, as lacking whatever capacities it is supposed exemplify some ideal of excellence. On the other hand, women are seen as possessing their own virtues, or their own special forms of skill or excellence. These special female virtues or skills are seen as necessary for the female role. They may also be seen as charming or delightful or valuable, they may even sometimes be praised to the skies, and not .apparently or officially regarded as inferior at all. If one reads such views of women, however, in the context of more general assumptions about human nature or morality or social life, it is usually the case that women's virtues are seen as lesser, and that the fullest or truest forms of excellence are reserved for men. Conversely, if one reads some philosophical accounts of these in the light of a philosopher's views about women, it can be argued that they are 'gendered.'

Property and Wealth

Apart from the personal relationships of husband and wife, father and children, and master and slave, the other essential element of the household is the possession and acquisition of wealth. Though property is to be left in private hands, it is still the concern of political science and the statesman. Like the moral behaviour of the members of the household, the economic activity of the household may affect the values and behaviour of the polis as a whole. Because the political community, in the sense of the institutions of government, has a responsibility for the over-all good of the polis it must ensure that the methods of using and acquiring wealth do not conflict with the public good. Private ownership of property does not entail complete economic freedom or *laissez faire.*

The principles which should govern the production of wealth are discussed in Book One in terms of the relation of the art of acquisition to household management. The question appears to be rather abstract, dealing with the relation of two branches of knowledge or skill, but it also has a more concrete application; it is another way of asking to what extent the head of the household should engage in acquiring material wealth. Aristotle considers three possibilities. First, the art of acquisition may be identical with household management; secondly, the art of acquisition may be part of household management; thirdly, the art of acquisition may be subordinate to household management. Of these possibilities, Aristotle immediately rejects the first and supports the second though he later seems to move towards the third. The head of the household will be concerned with acquiring wealth for his household but it will not be one of his major interests. He will be concerned more with the use of wealth than with its actual acquisition. He will oversee his own property but will leave most of the actual work to others in the same way as he will be generally concerned for the health of his family but will employ a doctor to minister to them. This is the conclusion we should expect from Aristotle's conception of the good life which places no value on work in the sense of economic activity but does require, as a necessary condition, a certain level of material prosperity.

During his discussion of the art of acquisition, Aristotle distinguishes between acquisition, which is justified and should properly be a concern of the head of the household and acquisition, which should be avoided. This distinction is elaborated at some length and is the most important part of his theory of property. It depends, like so many of the arguments of Book One, on his view of nature. The natural world and all the natural species which it contains are organized according to a rational plan or order; 'nature does nothing without purpose. All living things are provided by nature with the means of their own sustenance. Thus plants exist, at least in part, for the purpose of feeding animals and animals exist, at least in part, for the purpose of feeding and clothing human beings." 'Natural' wealth is property which is naturally provided in this way for men and is confined to the products of land and sea, such as farm animals and their by products, crops, fruits, and fish; it exists 'naturally' while unnatural wealth is 'gained by experience and skill. 'Unnatural' wealth is derived from exchange, from buying and selling and other commercial activities such as usury. In Aristotle's sketch of its development, exchange began as a method of acquiring necessary and natural goods, for example exchanging wine for corn. This type of barter is justifiable because it is aimed at satisfying men's natural wants. But the expansion of trade led to the development of money which greatly facilitated the exchange of products; with the invention of money came the illegitimate and unnatural use of exchange which is aimed not at meeting essential needs but at acquiring the maximum financial profit.

Aristotle's disapproval of this type of commercial exchange seems to rest partly on the objection that money is itself not intrinsically or naturally valuable but derives its value from mere convention; he quotes the story of Midas, who turned everything to gold, as an example of the folly of thinking that money is true wealth. It is on these grounds that he singles out the usurer for special condemnation. Usury, the lending of money for interest, is the making of money from money itself. It is therefore even more unnatural than other forms of trade because it is a step further removed from nature. Retailers are at least using money to buy and sell objects of natural wealth but the usurer has lost even this contact with natural wealth. But Aristotle's major objection is that commercial exchange is aimed at unlimited wealth. He assumes that there is a limit to the amount of agricultural wealth which can be stored. Once money becomes the measure of wealth, this constraint is removed because there is no limit to the amount of money that can be accumulated. Traders are therefore induced to pursue unlimited wealth. Aristotle's objection to the unlimited pursuit of wealth is essentially moral. Though material prosperity is a necessary condition of the good life, a limited amount of wealth is quite sufficient. Any attempt to seek more than is necessary or to elevate the acquisition of wealth into an end in itself will confuse the necessities of life with the real purpose of life. In terms of Aristotle's familiar distinction it is to concentrate on 'life but not the good life.' Aristotle also connects the pursuit of money with the pursuit of physical pleasure; excessive wealth is chiefly sought and used for gratifying bodily pleasure. The pursuit of money may corrupt the whole ethical character of men who pervert all virtues and skills by turning them into means of gaining wealth. He is especially critical of small businessmen of shopkeepers rather than merchants, of petty usurers rather than bankers, and seems to consider that they are the people most corrupted by the desire for financial gain. These arguments are of interest as an expression of the aristocratic attitude towards wealth, with its preference for landed property and its prejudice against trade and commerce; they have also been influential in the history of economic and social thought. But we need to ask whether they do more than express an attitude and bias and whether they have any validity as arguments. The claim that agriculture is closer than commerce to nature carries conviction if we mean that it is concerned more directly with products and processes of natural growth which do not depend on human technology. Aristotle, it is true, underestimates the extent to which, even in his day, farming made use of technology. The grinding of corn, the making of wine, and the catching of fish all require some tools and techniques.

Aristotle often assumes that what is natural is best but it does not follow, even from his own theory of nature, that what is natural in the sense of primitive or unaffected by human technology is therefore best for man. When arguing that the polis or the relationships of the household are natural, he tries to show that they are in accordance with certain innate needs and capacities but he does not deny a role to human contrivance. He approves of civilization as the Greeks understood it and does not advocate any turn to nature in the sense of a rejection of civilized life. Yet the logical implication of the argument about natural property would be a complete rejection of civilization and a return to the primitive. We must assume that the desire to prove that agricultural wealth is morally superior has led him to adopt a view of nature, which he would normally disown. The other main argument is that agricultural wealth is limited whereas the profits of commerce are unlimited. Though we may grant that it is much easier to go on accumulating wealth in money than in produce, it is quite possible to continue increasing holdings of land and it is not impossible to hoard unlimited amounts of some types of agricultural produce, such as corn. Aristotle is also wrong in equating the products of farming with basic human necessities as if farmers were never concerned with the production of luxuries. If he believes on ethical grounds that it is wrong to pursue more than a certain level of material prosperity, then he would have done better to argue for a limit to the general acquisition of wealth instead of trying to maintain that one type of acquisition is intrinsically limited. Similarly, if money is not the only type of wealth which may be accumulated in greater quantity than is necessary or proper, there is no justification for singling out the trader as the man who pursues unlimited profit. Indeed, even if this were the only pursuit in which unlimited profit were possible, this would not prove that he actually does aim at unlimited wealth. Thus, Aristotle's attempt to prove that traders are more concerned with profit and material gain than farmers is unsuccessful. This does not mean, however, that his conclusion is false. The view that farming, especially when relatively primitive in technology, is less oriented than retailing and commerce, towards profit is one that has been widely held in different historical periods, not just by aristocrats but, more recently, by radical critics of modern capitalism. But though it may contain an element of truth, it needs to be tested by sociological investigation not proved by *a priori* argument.

Aristotle's arguments against retailing and commerce seem to imply that such activities are to be completely banished from the polis. Yet the level of civilization necessary for the good life could hardly be provided without some reliance on traders. Indeed, in Book Seven, when describing the ideal polis, Aristotle admits that there will be trading, both internally within the city and externally with other states. He does not try to exclude traders altogether but confines himself to limiting their influence within the state. In Book One, however, he is not asking whether trading is necessary for the polis as a whole but whether the head of the household will engage in trade. He is concerned with the personal conduct of the head of the household who, ideally, will be someone who has achieved human happiness and is living the good life. The conclusion that such people should possess agricultural wealth and not engage in trade does not necessarily imply that no trading should be conducted at all. In the ideal state there are many functions which are necessary but which, because they are in some way not worthy of the character and abilities of the good man, should be performed by people who are not full members of the state and do not share fully in the purposes for which the city exists. It is therefore beside the point to criticize Aristotle for ignoring or misinterpreting the social function of trade in Book One. He is not concerned with the social usefulness of trade, which he elsewhere acknowledges, but with its effect on the individual, which he deplores. This focus on ethical effect rather than social function explains why Aristotle is particularly contemptuous of the small-scale businessman in modern terms the petit bourgeois. Such a person though engaged in the same economic activity as the wealthy businessman has to spend more of his time directly involved with his business and his character is therefore likely to be more infected by business values.

It is significant that the longest section in the *Politics* which Aristotle devotes to what we would call 'economies' is primarily ethical in approach. He seems to be very aware of the influence of economic factors on human behaviour, both on the personal and on the political level; he considers that the major political conflict in the states of his time is between the rich and the poor and that the regulation of production and wealth is one of the major functions of the statesman. But though he is aware of economic factors, he does not see them as such. He does not think, of the economy' as something separate and independent which may affect or be affected by politics. Indeed, he does not have the concept of an economy of a pattern or structure of behaviour concerned solely with production and wealth and operating, least in the abstract, according to its own independent rules. This is a modern concept, which was unknown to the Greeks and to Aristotle. For Aristotle, 'economies' *(oikonomike)* still carries its original meaning of household management and is not exclusively concerned with economic questions. Wealth and production are aspects of the general life of the polis like education, warfare, or drama and so are equally subject to ethical evaluation and political control. The question of 'economies' in Aristotle illustrates a more general difficulty which we face when we try to understand Greek political thought. We tend to divide our thoughts and activities into different, autonomous categories such as the economic, the religious, the moral, the legal, the political, and the educational. For the Greeks some of these distinctions did not exist and those that did were much more blurred than they are for us. Greek society was more integrated less differentiated than our own. Aristotle's approach to politics reminds us that the spheres of economics, law, morality, and education are not isolated but closely interdependent.

According to the teaching of Aristotle's *Politics*, the polis "comes into being for the sake of life but is for the sake of living well". The role of property in Aristotelian political science may be explained in relation to the two parts of this utterance. The pursuit of self-sufficiency through household and village which obtains its end in the polis is a satisfaction of daily and more than daily needs by acquisition; those goods acquired in this way so as to satisfy the needs of life with others are natural objects of the polis, the most important good obtained through the polis is a share in living well or nobly. As the polis is the most comprehensive of human associations, the good towards which it is directed must be a more comprehensive or final good than those sought by lesser or more partial associations; that greatest or most final good which is also the object of political science is happiness - the activity of the soul in accordance with its own greatest excellence or virtue. Property is connected to this most important good for the sake of which the political community exists, but the complex relation between the ends of life and living well render the role of property especially problematic.

Happiness as full activity of the soul in accordance with its greatest virtues surely requires equipment and this includes external goods and hence property, but the pursuit of property is itself no part of virtuous activity. Although a certain material prosperity may be a necessary condition for the activity of the moral virtues generally and, indeed, it entailed in the very exercise of certain virtues, these virtues are manifested in the use of, not the acquisition of property. These virtues, on Aristotle's account, may even be said to consist in a kind of indifference to property. The greater vice associated with liberality is not prodigality but parsimony.

Though property may be a necessary condition of virtuous activity, it seems that the virtuous or serious man is as such not very serious about the acquisition of property. Even those who aim at living well often see this as a life of bodily enjoyments and, as this seems to consist in acquiring and possessing, devote all their efforts to acquiring money. Property is then a necessary condition of virtuous activity but its pursuit is not itself a virtuous activity nor perhaps even consistent with virtuous activity.

For an understanding of Aristotle's teaching on property, we must consider two distinct discussions that occur in the text of the *Politics*. Property and its acquisition, various modes of obtaining money or those needful and useful things "whose worth is measured by money", and economic activity in general are examined in the First Book of the *Politics* in relation to the household and its management, while Aristotle's consideration of whether property and possessions are best owned and used separately or in common is set out in the Second Book. Aristotle's case for a modified form of private ownership is chiefly developed through his critical examination of the communism of Plato's *Republic.*

Property and acquiring are discussed most generally in relation to household management. The household and the relations that belong to it, as also the question of whether and how the acquiring of property or wealth is related to household management, are considered within a part of Aristotle's political teaching apparently intended to show that the polis exists by nature and that political rule must be distinguished from kingly rule, the rule of the head of a household, and the rule of a master of slaves. Economic activity is examined as part of a discussion intended to manifest the distinctness and accordance with nature of the political. Further, as Aristotle initially seeks to show that the city is by nature, so the entire discussion of Book One is guided by the standard of nature; the discussion proceeds from the demonstration that the city is by nature through the question of whether the master-slave relation may be by nature, to the effort to distinguish between forms of acquisition and exchange as these accord with, or are contrary to nature.

In order to understand that part of Aristotle's account of property which belongs to this most general treatment of economic activity, we must examine the relation between household and polis as this is set out in the First Book of the *Politics*. This relation is important to our understanding of the Aristotelian account of property because the concept of "economics" have developed out of some specific modifications of the Greek and Aristotelian term for the art of household management. Aristotle's account of property, wealth, acquisition and exchange is primarily developed in relation to household management.

The *Politics* begins with the argument that the political community as the most comprehensive of human associations must aim at the most authoritative of human goods. This statement is presented as a refutation of the claim that statesman, king, head of the household, and master of slaves are the same. Household and polis are distinguished, in the first place, by the fact that the former seeks a partial, the latter the most authoritative human good. If the greatest good sought by the polis is living well, or happiness, or the complete exercise of what is specifically human in man, what is the partial good sought by the household ? In the passage that follows, as we watch the polis "growing from its beginnings," we learn that the household is the community that is formed according to nature for the satisfaction of daily needs; the village is on the other hand made up of several households for the satisfaction of "more than daily needs," while the polis obtains complete self-sufficiency. Yet we cannot suppose that the household continues to be for the satisfaction of the daily necessities for which it comes into being any more than we may suppose that the city continues to be defined by that same kind of self-sufficiency for which it comes into being.

As Aristotle's refutation of the conventionalist thesis affirms the natural character of the city both as the result of a natural growth from sexual union and master-slave relation to household, village, and polis, and as the community within which man's capacity for reasoned speech and even for distinguishing the just and unjust finds expression, so the household may be understood in two ways: either as a community for the satisfaction of daily needs and the joint result of the union of male and female for procreation and natural ruler and naturally ruled for security, or as a constituent of the polis. The household may be understood as a natural unit as it is the product of two natural relations. On this understanding, the polis is natural unit. Yet the household so understood is not the perfected household of the perfected polis; the household in the latter sense is a natural unit only because it is a necessary constituent of the city which is itself by nature, not because it arises out of the natural association of natural units but because it is the necessary condition or sphere of a fully human life.

Following the demonstration that the city is by nature as natural growth and/or as condition of the fully human, Aristotle says we have first to discuss household management since "every polis is comprised of households;" it therefore becomes necessary to examine the relation of master and slave, husband and wife, and father and children. The art of obtaining wealth, or those things the value of which is expressed by money, must also belong to this discussion because some consider this art as identical with household management, others as the greatest part of it. The household and the relations that belong to it as well as the acquiring of wealth must be examined "before going on to speak of the polis."

Why the household, the relations that belong to it, and the acquiring of property should be discussed before turning to the regimes is not immediately clear. It is, of course, true that John Locke examines the question of property, as also that of the family, before turning to the forms of the commonwealth; but this does not explain the perplexing character of Aristotle's procedure, for Locke, unlike Aristotle, seeks to indicate the priority of property to government i.e., to show that the latter is instituted for the sake of the former. Aristotelian political science, on the contrary, seems to argue the primacy of the political or the regime.

Having introduced the money-making art which some identify with household management Aristotle turns to the question of master and slave, what the slave by nature is and whether such exists. It has been suggested that Aristotle examines this question before money-making, or property in general, both because it is his initial aim to show that the master of slaves and statesman are different and because the slave is a part of property and "the part should be studied before the whole." It is true that Aristotle speaks of property in general in the context of the discussion of slavery, but his procedure suggests that the slave constitutes an especially important kind of property. Aristotle steers a course between those who see the rule of a master of slaves as based upon the same science of ruling exercised by household head, statesman, and king and those who suppose one man can be master of another only by convention.

Property is, according to Aristotle, "a part of the household and the art of acquiring property is therefore a part of household management, for without the necessary things living and living well are impossible". Like the practitioners of the arts with specific ends, the head of the household must have the use of appropriate tools in order to accomplish his specific work. An article of property, including the slave as one such article, is to be understood as a tool - a slave is a live article of property. Property is not, however, any multitude of tools or instruments; it does not consist of instruments of production but of instruments for living, or action. From tools or instruments of production we get products as a consequence of their use, while property as a number of tools for living or activity furnishes nothing beyond the actual use of these - we simply wear a garment and sleep in a bed. An article of property is, according to Aristotle's conclusion, "a separable instrument for action".

As a definition of property this Aristotelian account has seemed particularly narrow to many because it considers property only as a part of the household. As an examination of slavery the discussion similarly confines the sphere of the slave to that of domestic service by ruling out the use of slaves in production. The present account thus precludes the use of slaves in farming, though the primary union of slave and master for security described earlier suggested the employment of slaves in farming. These two restrictions seem to be related. As property is exclusively a part of the household, the employment of slaves as property must belong to the sphere of the household and so to activity rather than to production. As Barker notes, property is not seen as "capital for the production of commodities" but as a source of services consumed by its owner in the sustenance of life.

Aristotle discusses the relation between an art of acquisition that is in accordance with nature and another sort of acquisition "especially and justly called money-making". The difference between the two might be understood in relation to the primacy of oikonomike; the notion of wealth as an object of unlimited pursuit belongs to the acquisitive art that is contrary to nature, and we might reasonably suppose that it is precisely this which makes that art contrary to nature. This is not, however, the only sense in which Aristotle distinguishes natural and non-natural acquisition. The account of acquisition begins with an enumeration of modes of obtaining food or nurture and corresponding ways of life which are natural since in such settings food is not obtained from others by retail trade; these ways of life "whose work or operation arises naturally by itself" are those of nomadic herdsmen, farmers, robbers or pirates, fishermen and hunters.

These natural or independent ways of life are explicitly compared with the variety of modes of nurture among animals, implying that the lives of men differ in accordance with the food they seek just as the solitary or herd-living propensities of various animal species differ in accordance with the source of nurture set out for each by nature. Those engaged in these ways of life seek and obtain self-sufficiency without entering into retail exchange; if necessary such men combine these pursuits.

One kind of property and form of acquisition may be understood on the basis of this account of natural modes of nurture and further consideration of the generous sustenance afforded men by nature. Such property as is obtained through each of these modes "seems to be rendered to all by nature itself". Aristotle further leads us to reflect that nature furnishes sustenance for many species from birth until the offspring of those species are able to provide for themselves while others that are viviparous have milk for their young. on the basis of such reflections Aristotle says "one ought to suppose" that nature provides generally for men through the plants and other animals. Acquisition in accordance with this understanding of the natural provision for man's welfare is that form of acquisition which belongs to the household; to the extent that sufficient is not at hand, the household should provide a supply of such goods as are "necessary for life, capable of being stored, and useful for the community of the household and city". True wealth consists in this sufficient supply afforded by nature with the help of household.

In addition to this natural form of acquisition which is subordinate to the household and polis and entails a limited notion of wealth, there is a kind of acquisition which "men justly call money making par excellence." The opinion that wealth and property have no limit results from the existence of this wealth making as also from the fact that the two forms of acquisition are sufficiently similar as to be often confused. This second kind of acquisition is not in accordance with nature because it has come into being through some sort of experience and art. To understand the origin and non-natural character of this art, recall that every item of property has two modes. A shoe may be worn or exchanged. In both cases, according to Aristotle, the shoe is used as a shoe; but where the shoe is exchanged it is used in a way other than that for which it was made - it is not used according to its proper use. The possibility of exchange, and through exchange of an art and activity directed to the pursuit of wealth without limit, is grounded in the fact that every item of property may be used for exchange; but how or why is this possibility realized?

Although money-making is contrary to nature, the exchange out of which it emerges is not itself contrary to nature. Rather, we learn now that nature's providence was less adequate than we had previously been required to suppose; it is also by nature that men have "more than enough of some things and less than enough of others". Barter, the first and most natural mode of exchange, emerged out of this imperfection of nature's provision only when the association of several households had come into being; there is not need for exchange within a single household where all things are shared. In any case, barter as such remains natural because items of property are still traded for other items of property strictly with a view to use. Such barter remains common among many barbarian races. From this form of barter to replenish natural self-sufficiency which is "according to reason", the art of money-making par excellence arose through the invention of currency.

According to Aristotle the use of money resulted from the practice of trade with more foreign ports; money was devised because not every thing that is a necessity by nature is portable. At first a metal employed as something useful, money finally acquired a conventional value. With this development the obtaining of wealth through exchange became possible- "through experience money-making became more artful, discovering whence and how to make to greatest profit by exchange". Thus, out of barter which is itself natural and reasonable and through the more or less necessary invention of currency arose that form of money-making properly called such, which is itself contrary to nature and gives rise to the notion that property and wealth are unlimited.

Against the view that wealth is a multitude of tools for living and living well or a multitude of those things necessary for life and useful for household and polis, money-making regards wealth as a quantity of money. The acquiring of wealth so understood becomes an activity without limit. Some apparently question this notion of wealth precisely because of the conventional character of currency and its inability to satisfy the needs connected with life directly. These critics of money-making point out that one could, like Midas, starve while possessing great sums of gold and that those who have established the value of a currency may alter it. The latter objection suggests the dependence of economics upon politics but, as generally in this part of the discussion, Aristotle emphasizes the natural account of wealth acquiring and the subordination of these to the management of the household.

As a consequence of the invention of currency and subsequent discovery through experience of how one's wealth might be augmented most by exchange, an art of money-making has come into existence. Like medicine, or any other art, the new art of money-making is "concerned with its end without limit". Such an art becomes possible once wealth is defined no longer as a multitude of tools for living but as a quantity of money. Money-making is unlike the other arts and uniquely problematic, however, both because there's a powerful propensity to the unlimited pursuit of this art's end in human nature and because of the comprehensive sphere within which it may be exercised. Money-making is an art whose end is likely to be pursued without limit because of its similarity to that natural and necessary art of acquiring to complete nature's provision that belongs to and serves household management. Proceeding from a proper concern to supply the things necessary for life, men are likely to regard it as the work of household management "to preserve or augment without limit the substance of the household". They devote themselves to the unlimited pursuit of wealth because they associate living well with an excess of bodily enjoyments.

We have seen that in the First Book of the *Politics* Aristotle develops a notion of property and acquiring as natural in opposition to that non-natural and unlimited mode of acquiring that emerges after the development of currency. In large part Aristotle develops this standard, in the light of which unlimited wealth-seeking is seen as deplorable, through an appeal to the providence and generosity of the natural order. He barely alludes to the questionable aspects of this standard by identifying piracy as the central natural mode of acquiring and nothing that it is among the barbarians that the natural form of exchange is still practiced. He also remarks on the failure of nature to accomplish its intention with respect to natural slavery and acknowledges the basis in nature and reason of that very art of money-making he deplores as against nature. The difficulty to which Aristotle's insistence upon a large and somewhat unwarranted supposition as to nature's providence responds is perhaps that acquisitiveness and a serious concern for mere life obstruct and distort concern for living well and yet contribute to that situation within which a life of noble activity becomes possible.

Turning to the question of property as such, Aristotle argues that the common ownership of possessions proposed by Socrates would be inferior to the existing system of private ownership, especially since the existing system might be modified by "good habituation and the regulation of correct laws" so as to promote the common use of such possessions. Thus modified, the present system would avoid the problems generated where use and ownership are common, benefit from the fact that men generally display greater care for what is their own, and still obtain the advantages of common use. The thought that something is one's own also contributes greatly to the pleasure that something can yield and is based upon a love of self that is natural. Further, the exercise of temperance and liberality as well as the legitimate pleasure derived from benefiting others, whether friends, strangers, or fellow citizens require the separateness of households and possessions. Finally, such a system is consistent with the way in which the polis is one and many. The city, according to Aristotle's account, should remain "a many" while being "made common and one" in and through education, "habits, philosophy, and laws".

The polis is "many" and must remain so if it is to continue to exist as a city and if virtuous activity is to remain possible for its members. Separateness of households and property must continue as the foundation of this "manyness." On the other hand, the polis can and should become "one" in a certain sense through habits, philosophy, and laws; the fostering of this "sharing in use" is, indeed, "the distinctive work of the legislator". "The "oneness" of the polis is consistent with its "manyness" insofar as that "oneness" is constituted by the virtuous activity of the members of the polis and insofar as a necessary condition of that virtuous activity is the continued separateness of property and households.

We have dealt exclusively with Aristotle's treatment of property and acquisition in the First Book of the *Politics* and his argument for the separateness of property and households in the Second. Though these together constitute the chief Aristotelian account of property and provide a proper starting point for any analysis of this subject, they do not yield a complete account of the role of property in Aristotle's political science. This is so because the two discussions occur somewhat in abstraction from the regime, which is the central concern of Aristotelian political science. Precisely in light of this fact, we may conclude this discussion by reflecting briefly upon the relation between property and acquisition and Aristotle's chief political question of regimes.

In the first place, government for Aristotle does not exist to secure property, much less to secure men's unequal abilities to acquire it. The proper aim of lawmaker and government is rather the promotion of happiness through the possession and exercise of the moral virtues. Though some measure of wealth may be necessary equipment for virtuous activity so understood, Aristotle barely acknowledges any responsibility of the statesman to furnish such wealth. On the other hand, it is for Aristotle an indictment of a certain case for the rule of the many that it could authorize an expropriation of the possessions of the wealthy. Aristotle's account of distributive justice does not authorize a redistribution of existing wealth. The separate and probably unequal ownership of property is for Aristotle a necessary condition of virtuous activity; in any case, he does not regard an equalization of possessions as a proposal that would eliminate the major causes of injustice.

In the second place, though the Aristotelian political science of regimes acknowledges and even stresses the importance of that difference between rich and poor generated by the existence of property and men's varying success in acquiring it, that political science continues to assert the primacy of the political. The complex relation between the property question and the question of regimes as well as the final primacy of the political is suggested both by Aristotle's treatment of wealth, freedom and virtues as claims to rule and by his attempt to promote the cause of polity. Thus the claim of virtue permits an otherwise unobtainable reconciliation of the claims of wealth and poverty and erects a standard in terms of which the partisans of both must begin to act. So too, polity must satisfy rich and poor with their share in the regime but in doing so may also create an opportunity for virtuous activity.

Revolution

In Books Five and Six Aristotle deals with the protection of particular constitutions against constitutional change and disorder. These books have often been neglected because of a tendency to concentrate on Aristotle's political ideals and on the contrast between these ideals and those of Plato's *Republic,* Yet they contain much that is of more than historical interest not just in matters of substance but also in general method and approach. In several respects they come closest to Aristotle's view of political science as an intellectual discipline. In the first place, the method of exposition is more straightforward, especially in Book Five, than in most of the other books. There is less dialectical discussion of problems or of his predecessor's views. Instead, the evidence and conclusions are set out in a logical order, and criticism of Plato, for example, is postponed to what amounts to an appendix. These books, however, are by no means completely finished. Both end abruptly as if they were meant to be continued.

Secondly, these books make most use of the research into the history and workings of individual constitutions which was carried out by Aristotle and his pupils. Political science, if it is a science, must deal with the general rather than the particular case but its generalizations must be based on empirical evidence; hence the need to organize research into individual constitutions. The empirical research was thus inspired by the demands of theory and both the questions asked and the answers discovered would have been influenced by theoretical preoccupations. Aristotle was not interested in facts for their own sake. At the same time his preoccupations were themselves based on a deep acquaintance with Greek political life and we cannot say that theory is completely prior to fact.

The final respect in which these books illustrate Aristotle's view of political science is that the empirical discussion of political behaviour is clearly related to a practical purpose, the securing of political stability. The phenomena of political disorder and constitutional change are investigated not simply as objects of scientific interest but in order that the statesman may learn how to avoid and prevent them. The analysis of causes leads directly to the giving of advice to the statesman, just as the explanation of disease helps the doctor to administer the cure. Political science is thus clearly seen to be a practical science. This does not mean that Aristotle's causal analysis is necessarily value-laden or distorted by the practical aim. He recognizes that the two aspects of analysis and advice are conceptually distinct. Though his analysis may sometimes have been influenced by his political preferences, this is not an inevitable consequence of his use of his results for a practical purpose. Similar distortion may be found in the work of political scientists whose aims are purely academic. What the practical purpose determines is not the analysis of the phenomena but rather the choice of what phenomena to analyse. Political instability is chosen as a subject of study because it is bad and ought to be avoided. Thus, though Books Five and Six are rightly called the most scientific or empirical books of the *Politics*, we must not forget that their ultimate purpose is moral and practical.

Constitutional Change and Political Disorder

Aristotle announces his subject at the beginning of Book Five as the investigation of constitutional change. We have still to discuss what are the causes of change in constitutions, their nature and number, what are the destructive agencies that affect each constitution, and from what kinds into what kinds they generally change. We must likewise consider what factors make for the preservation of constitutions, both in general and of each kind separately, also by .what means each of the types of constitution could best be preserved.

Almost immediately, however, the area of inquiry is broadened to include the causes not only of constitutional change but also of 'stasis.' Stasis is a term which cannot be satisfactorily translated into English. It is used by Aristotle to refer to a certain type of political conflict within a state. Not all internal conflict, however, counts as stasis. It is distinguished from the milder 'rivalry' or competition for office between individuals and groups and also from outright warfare. A common synonym for stasis is 'disorder' or 'confusion and, in its political connotation, close to the Irish troubles. Roughly speaking, the essence of stasis is that it involves the attempt to seize power by those who are prepared to use violence or other illegal means.

Though stasis and constitutional change usually go together, each can occur without the other. First, stasis need not involve constitutional change. It may be aimed simply at the gaining of power within the existing constitutional framework or at a minor modification rather than a full scale change in the constitution. Secondly, constitutional change may occur without stasis. The change may be brought about peacefully by a deliberate decision on the part of the governing body to alter the rules determining their own composition and so alter the constitution itself. Alternatively, the constitution may change accidentally when no one has deliberately intended a change. For example, if there is a change in the general level of economic wealth in a community, a property qualification, though itself unaltered, may produce a change in the relative size of the governing body. Because Aristotle includes this unintentional type of constitutional change, it is misleading to use the word revolution as an equivalent for 'constitutional change.

'Revolution' usually implies the use of violence or at least a conscious intent to change the constitution.

Thus the subject matter of Books Five and Six includes two separate phenomena, stasis and constitutional change. Because each can occur without the other, neither can be classed as a species or type of the other. Yet it was natural for Aristotle to treat them together. Both are types of what we may call general political 'instability' or 'disorder' which threaten the pursuit of Aristotle's good life and which he considers most rulers are anxious to avoid. Moreover, in most cases they do accompany one another; stasis usually leads to a constitutional change and constitutional change is usually brought about by stasis. These central cases which include both phenomena may properly be called 'revolutionary'. The fact that Aristotle does not restrict himself to this central core but also includes non-revolutionary constitutional change and non-revolutionary stasis might be thought to blur the focus of his investigation. Yet the modern study of revolution shows that great problems are caused by attempts to define the phenomenon too closely. This appears to be a case where Aristotle's lack of precision pays dividends. By not defining his terms too precisely, he is not forced arbitrarily to exclude evidence which is relevant to his central theme.

The General Causes of Disorder

In describing the causes of constitutional change and political disorder Aristotle begins with those which apply generally to all constitutions before describing causes which are peculiar to individual types. This method fits with his view of the proper logical order for scientific knowledge.

Political disorder is analysed in three such stages. Aristotle begins with what applies to all constitutions, though he does not include all six types of constitution under this heading but makes a broad distinction between 'constitutions', covering oligarchy, democracy, polity, and aristocracy, and 'monarchies', that is kingship and tyranny. The next stage involves causes in the four main types of constitution, and later, in the two types of monarchy. This is as far as Aristotle goes in Book five. In Book Six, however, a third stage of particularity is introduced in the discussion of separate sub-types, though the discussion is confined to the sub-types of democracy and oligarchy and is directed less to the reasons for instability than to the methods of preventing it. Of causes applying generally to all constitutions the most important is differing conceptions of justice and equality. At the beginning of Book Five he repeats his distinction between arithmetic and geometric equality, that is between absolute and proportionate equality. Though all men agree in the abstract that justice is proportionate, that goods and political power should be distributed equally according to merit and desert, they disagree about the nature of such merit and desert. In particular, some people (democrats) consider that as they are equal in one respect (free birth) they should be equal in all, while others (oligarchs) think that as they are unequal in one respect (wealth) they should be unequal in all. Aristotle considers the conflict between the oligarchic and democratic principles of justice to be the most widespread and most important. Democracy and oligarchy were the two commonest forms of constitution in Greece and the opposition between them, is one of the underlying themes of the central books of the *Politics*. Differing conceptions of justice, which lead to differing criteria for the distribution of office and political power and hence to different constitutions, are the basic cause of political disorder and constitutional change. When men are excluded from power and wish to seize it for themselves, they do so in the belief that the existing distribution of power is unjust.

But if this were a necessary condition political disorder and change, there could be no instability where power was justly distributed. This would be a somewhat naive position which Aristotle does not adopt. He later makes it clear that a subjective feeling of injustice is sufficient as a cause of dissidence though we may assume that such a feeling of injustice is more likely to be produced where actual injustice exists.

By making this cause the first and most fundamental Aristotle again moves from the more general to the more particular in the way that is proper for scientific knowledge. Distributive justice is part of the essential core not only of all constitutions but also of all social groups. He also wishes to make an important, substantial point about dissident and revolutionary movements. Such individuals or groups usually act in pursuit of a general principle. Admittedly, they are seldom purely idealistic in the sense of having no thought for their own personal and material interests; as Aristotle constantly emphasizes, there is a close connection between a man's social and economic status within the community and his political principles, especially his conception of political justice. On the other hand, successful movements are rarely based on purely selfish motives without any concern for moral principles. Aristotle would disagree with those political analysts who argue that the appeal to moral principle is merely hypocrisy, a mark to gain support. By making the sense of injustice the fundamental cause he implies that the revolutionary is motivated by genuine feelings of injustice.

He adds two further causes which apply in all cases. One is the end or goal of the dissidents. Aristotle considers the object aimed at, or the final cause, to be an important part of the explanation of any movement, whether human, animal, or even inanimate. Though we may agree with philosophers of science who criticize him for including goals and purposes in his scientific explanations of physical phenomena, we may be more prepared to accept them in explanations of deliberate human action. The dissident's object is profit and honour or their opposities; men revolt either to acquire profit and honour, which includes political power, or to avoid being deprived of them. Profit and honour embrace two aspects of social life, the economic and the political. Modern political scientists sometimes argue about which of these two aims is to be given priority. Do men seek wealth in order to gain political power or political power in order to gain wealth? For Aristotle, both are desired for their own sake.

The third general cause is really a number of more specific causes. While the sense of injustice and the desire for profit and honour are common to all, there are other causes which may affect any type of constitution, yet are not found in all or even in most instances. As causes in the third group they are properties belonging to those in power who provoke rebellion by the fact that they possess honour and wealth and by the way they use them. The difference is a real one: men's desire for profit and honour may be intensified and activated by seeing their rulers possessing them. The next cause is '*hybris*' (3) usually translated as 'insolence' or 'hubris' but in Greek a wider and stronger term, covering not only arrogance towards subordinates but also acts of violence and sexual violation and having strong overtones of contempt for religion. The fourth cause is pre-eminence, not simply the pre-eminence that any rulers must have but the excessive superiority when one or more individuals exercise power out of all proportion to the state or to the power of the citizen body. This sort of excess of power may lead to a monarchy or family oligarchy and justifies the institution of ostracism by which such people are banished. The next two causes are fear (5) and contempt (6), fear operates, for example, when men expect to be punished for some crime and aim to seize power in order to avoid punishment; or when they expect injury from those in power and seek to prevent it. Contempt refers not to the attitude of rulers to ruled which is covered by '*hybrds*,' but that of ruled to rulers when subjects despise those in power and therefore reject their claim to rule. The seventh cause is disproportionate increase (7), which Aristotle describes by means of a biological analogy. If a part of the body increases in size relatively to the other parts, the form and nature of the animal will change. Similarly, if one social class grows in relation to the other classes, the constitution will no longer fit the social composition of the state. The relative increase may be caused either by the actual growth or by the actual decrease of one class or section of the community. When it occurs the newly predominate class will agitate for change. This cause of stasis and constitutional change is similar to the fourth cause, pre-eminence. The difference between them is partly one of degree. Whereas pre-eminence refers to the relative superiority of an individual or small group of people, disproportionate increase refers .to whole classes, especially the rich and the poor. Moreover, pre-eminence appears to be restricted to those already in power, whereas disproportionate increase is typically a growth in a class excluded from power.

Aristotle adds four more to the above seven causes. Three are causes which produce constitutional change without political disorder: election contests (8), carelessness (9), when, for example, someone who is disloyal to the constitution is inadvertently appointed to a position of power in the normal way; and neglect of small matters (10), such as gradual decrease in a property qualification leading eventually to a qualitative change in the constitution. The last is dissimilarity of elements (11). This is a broad category including a number of different dissimilarities, which can produce friction and disorder within a community. The main one is difference in tribe or stock. The existence of groups of dissimilar origins within a community provides a focus for political strife. Aristotle is not thinking here of racial differences, such as the difference between Greeks and barbarians, though such divisions would certainly cause difficulties within a community, but is referring to the differences that can exist between Greeks of different cities, with different tribal origins and communal traditions. When colonies or new cities are formed with citizens from more than one city, this difference in background may be perpetuated in political factions and may prevent the citizens from uniting into a harmonious civic body. Another difference which may cause dissension is that of geographical terrain. In the stale of Athens, for example, there is tension because the inhabitants of the port, Piraeus, are more democratic in outlook than the inhabitants of the city itself.

It may be more useful to classify the different causes into the following three groups: first, those causes which depend on the particular behaviour of the rulers and on the emotional response of their subjects; for example, '*hybris*', contempt, or fear; secondly, what may be called social causes, where dissidence is caused by some factor in the basic social structure of the community, for example a citizen body drawn from members of incompatible populations or the relative increase of one class from economic or other reasons; thirdly those causes which operate almost unnoticed because of the negligence of the rulers or the gradualness of the change. Again, the classification is not clear cut and we must remember that it is not made by Aristotle himself. But it does at least indicate the great variety of the causes he lists. One of the main purposes of his account of political disorder and change is to point out the variety of their origins. That his list of causesdefies clear and systematic classification either by himself or by his commentators may perhaps be seen as a measure of his success in demonstrating the complexity of the subject.

Aristotle's analysis of the general causes of political disorder and constitutional change does not as we might expect end at this point. He adds a further chapter which includes a number of supplementary observations in a somewhat random order. For example, he cites more examples of how relative growth of one part of the community may lead to a change in the constitution and emphasizes the ways in which members of groups who have achieved positions of power may provoke opposition and rebellions. But new material is also introduced. A new and important distinction is made between the origins or occasions of political disorder and the issues at stake. The former may be small but the latter are always great and Aristotle gives some interesting examples of revolutions which have begun from trivial incidents such as marriages or lovers' tiffs. These incidents are both more immediate and at the same time less obviously causes of stasis than any of the earlier eleven causes. The distinction between occasions and issues is still a useful one when accounting for some major political upheaval, we shall often want to distinguish the major, underlying causes from the more immediate occasions or trigger-factors. Aristotle also distinguishes between the different means by which changes may be effected or power seized. The main means are force and fraud, each of which is then further subdivided. Force may be used either from the beginning or later; fraud may be used initially and then the people held down by force or persuasion may be sufficient both for the seizure and for the subsequent maintenance of power.

The next stage is to list causes for individual types of constitution. Democracy and oligarchy, as the two commonest forms of constitution, are treated first and at greatest length. Aristocracy and polity are then taken together. By aristocracy Aristotle means not the ideal rule of the virtuous but so-called aristocracy, the mixture of birth, wealth, and poverty. He can thus include aristocracy with polity because both are species of mixed constitution and are closely related. Thus, in the chapter on democracy, we hear much of the activity of the demagogue, the popular leader particularly associated with democracy, though Aristotle later broadens the concept of demagogy to include similar behaviour within a more restricted group than the people as a whole. In the case of oligarchy, he emphasizes dissension within the ruling class, a fault to which he thinks oligarchies are especially prone. In the case of aristocracies and polities, the mixed constitutions, he concentrates on factors, which may change the constitution by altering the balance of the mixture, for example, grasping behaviour of the nobles. Some factors are mentioned which might have qualified as general causes. In particular, he refers for the first time to external factors, the influence of foreign states:

> Constitutions may be changed from the outside as well as from within; for example, if a neighboring constitution is of the opposite kind and is not far away, or, if far a way, especially powerful. Both the Athenians and the Spartans illustrate this in their history; the Athenians everywhere brought low the oligarchies, the Spartans the popular governments.

The bulk of his analysis is taken up with historical examples which demonstrate Aristotle's wide knowledge of Greek politics and his ability to marshall this knowledge to illustrate general points. In general, the same causes which affect the other constitutions also affect kingship and tyranny for example, '*hybris*,' fear and contempt. Individual ambition is also a cause, especially the ambition to win glory by the assassination of a tyrant. Tyranny is particularly susceptible to external attack from hostile neighbours. Those tyrants who have not won their position for themselves but have inherited it from someone else are likely to be overthrown because they have been brought up in softness and curry. Because tyranny combines the evils of both extreme democracy and extreme oligarchy it is liable to be overthrown by the same causes as each of these types, presumably by the oppression of the rich or of the poor, the respective vices of extreme democracy and extreme oligarchy. In kingship, which is less open to external attack, there are two main causes of change: conflict within the royal family and illegal action by the king himself. Again, as with the other constitutions, the major interest lies in the wealth of examples Aristotle has amassed even of forms of government which he admits are relatively rare in his own time.

During the discussion of causes in particular types of constitution, Aristotle also refers to possible patterns or cycles of change. Plato, in the *Republic*, had described a pattern of change from timocracy on the Spartan model through oligarchy and democracy to tyranny and the question of what constitutions tend to change into what other constitutions is one of the general topics announced at the beginning of Book Five. Aristotle has already given two generalized accounts, broadly similar, of Greek constitutional development from kingship to democracy. But they are historical in purpose and are not meant to leave theoretical or predictive value. He is aware of the great variety of actual and possible changes and is skeptical of simple schemes like Plato's. His general principle is that the commonest type of constitutional change is change into the opposite form, though it is not always clear precisely what this means. 'Opposite' is sometimes to be understood in terms of the distinction between normal or perverted constitutions; a constitution's opposite form is a constitution with a ruling group of the same size (one, few or many) but normal instead of perverted or *vice versa*. This type of change into opposites appears in the *Ethics* where Aristotle describes how kingship passes into tyranny, aristocracy into oligarchy, and polity into democracy. Change of this type is easy because it requires little if any structural change in the legal or constitutional machinery of government but is simply a result of a change in the moral character of the rulers. He does not mention the possibility of a reverse change, from the perverted to the normal, which would be just as easy constitutionally. In general, he tends to share Plato's pessimism about people in power and believes that change is usually for the worse. In the *Politics* 'opposite' sometimes refers to the division between rich and poor; change to an opposite constitution is thus change from aristocracy and oligarchy to democracy or from polity and democracy to oligarchy.

When he is explicitly arguing against Plato he is particularly hostile towards the notion of universal patterns of change. Democracy may change into oligarchy instead of into tyranny; oligarchy may change into tyranny rather than to democracy; history shows that tyranny may change into another tyranny or into oligarchy or into democracy or into aristocracy. We are left with the impression that any simple cycle or scheme, even the one he himself describes in the *Ethics*, will be so riddled with qualifications and exceptions as to be virtually worthless.

Methods of Prevention

The main purpose of analysing the causes of constitutional change and political disorder is to teach the statesman how to preserve the stability of his constitution. The discussion of causes is followed immediately by discussion of methods of prevention and almost all the advice that Aristotle gives can be traced directly back to statements in the analysis of causes. Indeed, there are occasions during the causal analysis itself when the practical consequences are referred to immediately. Like the causes, the preventive measures come in differing degrees of generality. Aristotle begins with general principles affecting all constitutions and then refers to the major types of constitution, especially oligarchy and democracy. Next, after discussing the causes of change and disorder in monarchies, he gives advice about how to preserve the types of monarchy, kingship and. tyranny. Finally, in Book Six, he recommends measures for preserving the different species of democracy and oligarchy.

That he recommends methods of preserving all types of constitution, even those which he considers most pernicious, may seem surprising and requires some explanation. He certainly adopts an attitude of strict ethical neutrality and seems to have relished the intellectual challenge of entering into the spirit of different types of constitution. On the surface, then, he appears to be the complete 'machiavel' and to have altogether suppressed his own moral convictions. But this picture is not completely accurate. Political disorder threatens the life and property of individuals and therefore prevents them from living the good life, as Aristotle conceives it. Political stability is therefore closely linked to his own values. But this general preference for stability may not be sufficient to justify the preservation of all regimes regardless of their merit. There will surely be some political situations where the security of individual citizens will be better protected, at least in the long run, by an improvement and therefore a change in the type of government. The worst forms of constitution, such as tyranny or extreme oligarchy or extreme democracy, are essentially hostile to the life and property of their subjects; we would therefore expect Aristotle to be in favour of the destruction not the preservation of such regimes. He himself provides two indirect answers to this objection. First, outright rebellion and seizure of power by the men of virtue, though justifiable, is not a practical possibility. He argues that those members who are of outstanding merit would have by far the greatest justification for rebelling, but they least often do so.

Thus the prevention of all revolution will not prevent revolution by the virtuous because such men will not rebel anyway. Secondly, much of the advice he gives, especially to the worst forms of government, requires the use of measures which will in fact make the regimes better by his own standards. Though he argues that the reason for adopting such measures is that they preserve the particular constitutions and are therefore in the ruler's own interests, the fact that they are also measures which improve the constitution lessens the apparent inconsistency between his own values and those of the rulers he advises. The inconsistency is not removed completely but it is not as glaring as it at first sight appears.

The main principle to be followed in preserving constitutions is to ensure that the loyal citizens should be stronger than the disloyal. This is closely connected with the principle of moderation, because many of the methods recommended for gaining loyalty and consent amount to the pursuit of moderation and the avoidance of extremes. The surest way for rulers to make their subjects loyal is to treat them well. For example, in oligarchies the rich should not maltreat the poor and should be particularly careful not to enrich themselves by virtue of their position of power. Oligarchies should also be prepared to admit deserving individuals to their ranks. Conversely, democracies should treat the rich well. The rich will be content if their property is not divided among the poor and if they are not heavily taxed or made to undertake expensive public services. Similar advice is given in Book Six in the discussion of how to preserve the different species of democracy and oligarchy. Democracies should avoid confiscating the property of the rich or victimizing them in public trials. Oligarchs should willingly accept onerous public services and should placate the people with generous public expenditure on such things as festivals and public buildings.

The general effect of these measures, which are aimed at gaining the support of those excluded from power, will be to temper the constitution by moderating the divisions and conflicts between the opposing groups of rich and poor. This illustrates an important distinction: the principles which support and preserve a constitution are not necessarily the same as those on which the constitution is itself based and which determine the distribution of power and the values of the ruling class. Indeed the dominant principles of the constitution may work against its continued existence.

> Many steps, apparently democratic, may be taken that lead to the fall of a democracy and the same may happen in oligarchies. Therefore both the lawgivers and the practicing politician must learn to distinguish between those democratic measures which preserve and those which undermine democracy and oligarchic measures in the same way.

To make their subjects contented and loyal democrats must in certain respects become less democratic and oligarchs less oligarchic.

Aristotle is opposed to any dishonest engineering of the subjects' consent and refers to his earlier criticism of the clever devices or 'sophistries' by which oligarchs deceive the poor and democrats the rich. For example, oligarchs may make the assembly or the courts open to all but at the same time may impose a fine on those wealthy men who do not attend, thus ensuring a proportionately higher attendance from the rich than from the poor. Conversely, democracies, by offering payment for attendance but not fining the rich for non-attendance, ensure an assembly dominated by the poor though they claim it is open to all. Aristotle claims that such deceit, which gives the appearance, but not the reality, of power, will be useless presumably because people will see through it. But he does not give any supporting evidence and we may wonder whether the claim is justified. The example he gives of a democratic device, payment for attendance without a corresponding fine for the rich, was the normal practice in democratic Athens which was a relatively stable constitution by Greek standards. Aristotle's objections may be moral rather than empirical. Because he disapproves of such measures he may be too ready to believe that they are in fact useless as means of ensuring consent and stability. Some of the measures that he himself later recommends come very close to being deceptive. For example,

> Constitutions last longer not only when any possible destroyers are at a distance, but sometimes just because they are close by; for through fear of them men keep a firm hold on their own constitution. So it becomes the duty of those who have the interests of the constitution at heart to create fear on its behalf, so that all may be on the lookout and not allow their watch on the constitution to disperse like sentries at night; the distant fear must be brought home.

This device of exaggerating the threat from outside in order to increase internal unity is surely deceitful. In his advice to the tyrant Aristotle is also forced to rely to a considerable extent on measures involving deception. On the whole however he keeps to the principle that a government, to be secure, should not just appear to treat its subjects well but should actually do so.

As well as protecting the material condition of their subjects, the rulers should also pay attention to their values and attitudes. Ideas or behaviour which may lead to disrespect for the constitution and its laws are to be avoided. The system of education, which most states ignore, must be made to support and not undermine the constitution. Education is a vital factor not only in the ideal state but in any state which wishes to preserve its constitution.

> It is useless to have the most beneficial rules of society fully agreed upon by all members of the constitution, if individuals are not going to be trained and have their habits formed for that constitution, that is to live democratically if the laws of society are democratic, oligarchically if they are oligarchic.

Though education should be relative to the constitution concerned, this does not mean that it should concentrate solely on inculcating the values of the ruling class. Again the rulers must distinguish between those of their principles which preserve, and those which destroy, their constitution. Aristotle does not give any details of what should be included in the proper education for each constitution but he does mention certain ideas and values which are to be avoided. Oligarchs, for example, should be wary of educating their own sons to a life of luxury. Such a life may accord with the oligarchic emphasis on the value of wealth but it will make the ruling class soft and liable to be overthrown, especially if the poor are at the same time being toughened by hard work and exercise. It is in this context that he makes his well-known criticism of the democratic conception of freedom. The democratic notion that freedom is doing what one likes may work against democracy and lead to the destruction of the constitution, by encouraging anarchy and disrespect for the law.

> It ought not to be regarded as slavery to have to live according to the constitution but rather as self-preservation.

Thus Aristotle's advice to oligarchs and democrats of the more extreme type is that they should become more moderate. Such advice fits with his general conviction that, ideal situations excepted, political extremism is inherently more unstable than government based on a mixture of principles. This conviction, which provides one of the main reasons for the relative superiority of the polity in comparison with the unmixed forms of oligarchy and democracy, may have some empirical, justification and Aristotle's advice may be politically sound.

Change or perish may be the right political advice for such regimes but can a constitution be said to be preserved by being changed? The problem does not arise sharply so long as Aristotle confines his remarks to the general categories of oligarchy and democracy. At this level of generality, a moderate oligarchy is still an oligarchy and a moderate democracy still a democracy and Aristotle sometimes does not consider the change from one another to be a genuine instance of constitutional change.

The same problem arises, with the other type of extreme and perverted rule, tyranny. Aristotle describes two contrasting methods of preserving tyranny, of which the first is derived from the practice of the tyrants of early Greek history and of the Persian kings. It involves such expedients as the assassination of rivals, depriving the citizens of their wealth and keeping them hard at work without leisure or education, encouraging flatterers, and despising people of noble character. It can be summed up in three precepts: humiliate one's subjects, make them distrust one another and make them incapable of action. The second, opposite, method follows from Aristotle's own inquiry into the causes of political disorder and constitutional change in monarchies. Just as a kingship is destroyed by tending towards tyranny, so a tyranny will be preserved by tending towards kingship. The tyrant must behave like a king, provided that he keeps sufficient power to dominate his subjects whether they like him or not; if he abandons this power, he will no longer be a tyrant. He should therefore avoid acts of *hubris* and sexual violation of his subjects and should maintain the appearance of personal virtue and respect for public funds. He should honour the virtuous among his subjects and should administer justice through the courts. Of these two opposing methods, the first is described, somewhat dismissively, as the traditional method and Aristotle does not himself vouch for its efficacy. It is the second method, derived from his own causal analysis, which he supports. Not only will it make tyrannies more lasting; it will also make them better. The tyrant's rule will therefore be better and more enviable; it will not be hated and feared and it will be exercised over better men, not men reduced to impotent submission.

Thus, as in the cases of extreme oligarchy and democracy, the regime is to be maintained by being made more moderate. The difference is that Aristotle is aware of an alternative method which would tend to make the tyrant's regime not less but more extreme. Perhaps he is too ready to dismiss this method as ineffective. Like many who oppose police states on moral grounds, he is eager to believe that such regimes are unlikely to last and that it is in the rulers' own interests to treat their subjects more liberally and justly. Even if we accept that moderation is more effective than ruthless extremism for preserving the tyrant, the problem of identity and change remains: is the moderate tyrant still a tyrant? Aristotle himself seems to recognize the difficulty and is careful to insist that the moderate tyrant must retain some tyrannical characteristics. He must keep enough power to control his subjects should they not consent to his rule. Also, the virtue and generosity of the moderate tyrant is to be apparent and not genuine. He must give the appearance of being concerned for the public funds, a brave soldier, self-controlled and respectful of religion. But even if he retains power and lacks genuine virtue, the character of his rule will still have been substantially altered. His behaviour, if not his motives, will be kingly rather than tyrannical. Above all, his subjects will consent to his rule and the difference between rule with and without consent is the main criterion for distinguishing kingship from tyranny, The task that Aristotle has set himself is in fact impossible. Believing that extreme constitutions are inherently unstable, he is unwilling to support means of making them stable which do not also involve making them less extreme and so altering their character. One wishes that he had recognized this inconsistency and had consciously abandoned the attempt to preserve every type of constitution whatsoever. By so doing, he would not have been abandoning his aim of showing that political science has advice to give the statesman in every type of political situation. He certainly has advice to give extreme oligarchs, democrats, and tyrants but he should have admitted more openly that he considers their position untenable and that they must change the nature of their rule or be overthrown. The same variety and attention to detail which mark the causal analysis are evident in the methods of preservation. Two points may be briefly mentioned to illustrate the close correspondence between the causes and the recommendations and also the difficulty of preventing all constitutional change.

First, as change often starts from small beginnings, the rulers must be on their watch for apparently innocuous incidents. This requires exceptional skill and vigilance because only a real statesman can discern in its early stages harm that is being done.

Secondly, the ruler's must also guard against changes which occur, often gradually, in the general economic and social structure of the community. Where there are property qualifications for office, the level of the qualifications should be frequently reviewed in order to prevent any change in the composition of the ruling class caused by alteration in the general economic wealth of the community. Relative changes in the prosperity of individuals or classes must be watched. In the case of individuals who become excessively prosperous, Aristotle recommends banishment as a last resort and again shows his willingness to sacrifice the individual for the general good of the community. Where a considerable section of the community becomes relatively more wealthy the drastic measure of banishment is not possible. Instead, he suggests a number of general measures, all of which have the effect of making the constitution a mixed one:

> The danger can be met by not entrusting assignments and responsibilities to one section alone but to different and opposing sections. (I am opposing the educated class to the generality and the wealthy to the more indigent.) An endeavor should be made either to merge the poorer with the richer or to augment the number of those of medium wealth.

By recommending a mixture of elements in the constitution, Aristotle implies that the way to deal with the relative growth of one section of the community will be to give this section a greater share in the constitution. In effect, if the community is to remain politically stable, the constitution will have to be changed. This fits with his belief that political stability is possible only if the distribution of power is in harmony with the genera! social and economic structure of the community. But, though his advice may make good political sense, he is again implicitly recognized that not all constitutions are salvageable. Because the statesman cannot exercise complete control over the relative distribution of wealth, he is not always free to preserve the relative distribution of power.

Aristotle's recommendations about the preservation of constitutions accord both with his analysis of the causes of political disorder and constitutional change and with his convictions about the conditions necessary for political stability. Though he deals with the politics of the Greek city-states much of his advice may be readily transferred to other political contexts which indicates both the continuity of political experience and Aristotle's success in generalizing from his evidence. Two major objections have emerged. First, he is perhaps too sanguine about the inability of political regimes to perpetuate their rule by immoderate and unjust means. But this question is at least open to debate and his liberal conviction that terror and oppression are not in the ultimate interests of those who use them may have empirical as well as moral justification.

The second objection is more serious because it involves an internal inconsistency in his theory. If he believes that certain constitutions are unavoidably unstable and can only be preserved by being changed, he should have been prepared to qualify his aim of preserving any constitution whatsoever. The qualification required would be only slight; the number of irretrievable situations is comparatively small and even there the rulers are shown how they may still retain some, if not all, of their power.

This interest in everyday politics is one of Aristotle's most important innovations in political science and forms the basis for the realistic books of the *Politics*: books Four to Six. In them, he considers three main topics or groups of questions. The first concerns the number of different types of constitution; the second concerns the relative merits of non-ideal constitutions; the third, about the causes and prevention of political instability.

All living substances change. In Aristotle's view of the nature of things, they either grow or decay. Things grow when they are realizing their natural potential and begin to decay when they cease to do so. This is as true of human beings as oak trees, and it is also true of political communities. The "efficient" causes of political change are too varied to consider here, but the "material" and "formal" causes are everywhere the same. The former are simply the stakes of public affairs, which can always be reduced to either honor, in the case of real political communities, or profit, in the case of perverted ones. The formal cause is invariably a sense of justice or injustice, which controls the extent to which the allocation of honor or profit is considered acceptable.

Conclusion

Among students of political theory, Aristotle is probably best known and most appreciated for his insistence upon the naturalness of human political association. "Man is by nature an animal intended to live in the polis," he declares at the beginning of his lectures on politics. Aristotle's political theory will be subjected to critical scrutiny primarily through analysis of his account of the origins and nature of the polis and the oikos in Book I of the *Politics.* The questions around which this analysis revolves are three: What are the features of man and of the polis that so perfectly suit each other and only each other? Why must men be members of a political community to be complete as men and what is it about others in the population that does not require this membership? What is the character of the politicalness Aristotle takes to be man's natural inclisation?

An appropriate place to begin an interpretation of Aristotle's *Politics* is with that which most bothered Hannah Aendt about his account of the polis: "he tentatively assumed that at least the historical origins of the polis must be concerned with the necessities of life. For Aristotle indeed attempts to derive the polis from the "pre-political" associations of household and village, even as he seeks to establish the polis as a transcendent and self-sufficient association. The polis emerges out of household and village but comes into existence to serve entirely different ends.

There is a foreshadowing in this passage of what is to come in Aristotle's discourse on oikos life—that it is the very capacity to work that renders one vulnerable to being enslaved. Just one chapter later, Aristotle declares; "a man is thus by nature a slave if he is capable of becoming the property of another." The mere capacity for work contains the potential for "becoming the property of another," for becoming an "instrument" of someone else's needs. Since Aristotle's epistemology and ontology involve imbuing "what is" with rationality, he does not leave this matter at the level of potential. Indeed, the "naturalness" and hence justification of the unfree realm of the oikos depends upon turning the potential for alienation inherent in labor into a metaphysical necessity and good. The lack of freedom associated with work issues less from the fact that it is bound up with nature or necessity than from the institutionalization of workers as the property of from Aristotle's discussion of slaves and women, we may deduce that the superiority of tame animals ties in their obedience, a quality that depends upon the rule of their minds over their appetites and bodies. Aristotle approves tame animals because they, like men of virtuous nature, have mostly quelled their instincts. Of course, the tame were not born that way but were coerced, bribed, and punished into their tame state by man. The taming of an animal depends upon making it fear for its own preservation and teaching it through any number of clever, coercive, or barbarous means that filtered reservation in the master's hands. The tame are thus in a condition of forced dependence, a condition that, filtered through Aristotle's theory of nature and observational method of inquiry, is then rendered as their essential nature. In this way, the "second nature"—the learned dependence and subservience—of a tame animal, male slave, or woman is presented as its "first nature," its true being and function.

In this process of double alienation, i.e., of surrendering self-directed minds as well as bodily instincts and needs to a master, a new creature may indeed emerge—a tame or crippled one. As long as these creatures are deprived of the means of their own self-sufficiency and hence, of their own survival, it may appear "natural" that free men should rule them, extract benefit from them, and protect them. And here, in microcosm, is the essence of Aristotle's formulation of the "natural" relationship between master and slave, husband and family, man and animal, the realm of politics and the realm of necessity. The politics of domination and exploitation are converted ideologically as well as institutionally into what is given and natural.

One reason, then, for Aristotle's concern that men of the polis avoid direct involvement with the realm of necessity pertains to the potential in work for alienation leading to domination, that is, the potential for labor to be appropriated and for laborers to be enslaved. Through the practice of slavery and the subjugation of women in ancient Greece, this potential was actualized in Aristotle's milieu and he treated its actualized state as natural and necessary. The second reason for Aristotle's concern to establish distance between polis and oikos pertains to the elements of violence and domination in the oikos. The significance of this will become clear through an integration of the foregoing discussion of Aristotle's account of man's command over slaves, women, and tame animals with his general philosophy of rule.

Not only, then, are those bound to nature and necessity unfit for higher things, the higher thing itself is threatened by proximity to or involvement with lower things. The fear, noted in Arendt's thought, of letting the most valued things and activities touch anything else now appears in Aristotle. For him the public realm must be literally separated and insulated from the realm of necessity. What this implies is the irony that the best of men and highest of activities—manhood and politics—are actually extremely fragile, easily threatened or contaminated by the inferior elements supporting them and giving them life. These men who are so superior to all others and who inhabit the most superior association, who determine all matters of right order and justice, must be physically and sprritually sequestered from the contaminating effects of those who receive the benefit of their rule.

Aristotle refus to grant political standing to a realm that provides for the polis and is organized politically, that is, through systematic and institutional relations of power. Yet Aristotle does not successfully establish that politics begins only where the force and violence of the pre-political ends. His discussion of the oikos is replete with analogies between husband and statesman slave master and monarch; he introduces his discussion of slavery with considerations of justice—a supremely political referent; and he devotes the first section of Politics to the nature and structure of the household. Aristotle recognizes that those elements and activities that are mere "conditions" of the polis have a political character and must be dealt with by the political theorist; indeed this is precisely what was insisted upon by Plato, his teacher and predecessor. But Aristotle's strategy in dealing with these elements and activities is to depoliticize them, both ideologically and practically. He asserts the politicalness of these relations and then proclaims them natural. He reminds their threat to polis life and demands their exclussion from the realm called politics.

In his discussion of political ideals, Aristotle explicitly poses the question, "what is political association for" and links the problem of discerning the telos of politics to questions about the telos of man. In this regard, Aristotle returns to Plato's indentification of the nature of the polis with the nature of the soul yet as he does so, he creates difficulties for himself insofar as he seeks to avoid the profoundly critical conclusions Plato drew about extant political life. In asserting that the "true end for any state of society is the enjoyment of partnership in a good life and the felicity thereby attainable," Aristotle must confront the fact that much of the activity of the Greek polis revolves around war and defense and that these things are not directly constitutive of partnership in a good life and felicity. Moreover, in establishing *eudaimonia* as the telos of man and the polis, Aristotle raises the problem of whether political life itself fulfills this end or whether it is only a means to the higher good of contemplative life. He introduces the problem this way.

Here Aristotle appears to be trying to compel an answer to the action-contemplation problem through recalling that goodness—with which both rightly practiced action and contemplation are infused-must be active. Goodness by itself is not enough: there must also be capacity for being active in doing good. Thus, felicity should be held to consist in 'well-doing' and it follows that the life of action is best, alike for-every state as a whole and for each individual in his own conduct. Yet precisely at the moment Aristotle seems to have resolved the dilemma between action and contemplation in favor of action, he snatches away the solution. Contemplation rightly pursued, it turns out, is also a kind of action. In fact, it is the highest sort of action, for it is the most rational and the most god-like.

Aristotle's originality lay in his recognition that the complexity of life required plurality in politics, and that plurality is not something that contradicts the theory of form. Thus, in uniting matter and form, being and becoming, Aristotle was able to bring together the reality of politics with a genuine ethical standard. This is something Plato could never quite do. Even in his later works, such as the *Statesman* and the *Laws,* where he more directly confronts the complexities of the human condition than he does in the *Republic,* the spell of the ideal of justice still holds sway over the real world of politics. Yet, it must not be thought that Aristotle's realism is irreconcilable with Plato's idealism. His originality lay in uniting Plato's, ideal with an appreciation for the real. Without Plato, Aristotle's work would not have been possible. Aristotle made his teacher's philosophy of form and his theory of justice more compatible with the everyday worlds. He did not reject Plato's philosophy so much as modify it.

Does this modification make Aristotle's theory superior to Plato's? Here we enter the realm of judgment. Whether or not one finds one thinker preferable to another is really a matter of intellectual temperament. Those with a pragmatic bent will likely appreciate Aristotle's grasp of the complexity and plurality of politics. Those who are inveterate rationalists, who love the abstractions of pure theory, will probably prefer Plato. In political philosophy, these two tendencies are usually described generically as conservatism and radicalism. Seen in this light, the real political difference between Plato and Aristotle becomes apparent. Almost invariably, rationalists are radicals. Like Plato, they want politics to correspond to an ideal, and they are impatient with anything less than the ideal. For this reason, radicals of all stripes, whether of the right or of the left, typically dislike real politics because it seldom, if ever, corresponds to the ideal.

Pragmatists are conservative. They have their ideals, of course, but they have perhaps a greater appreciation of the limits of the ideal, and they tend to be more comfortable with and have a greater appreciation for the imperfect world around them. Moreover, conservatives are even a little distrustful of the ideal. This is why Aristotle, the conservative, argues in what has become the rallying cry of conservatives throughout the centuries, "that we should not disregard the experience of the ages."

Clearly then, whether or not Plato is superior to Aristotle depends upon one's most fundamental intellectual and political convictions. But from a theoretical point of view the question of which thinker is superior does not really apply. The most basic level Plato and Aristotle work from the same assumptions. Both are convinced that ethics and politics are one, and that politics is a human affair that ought to contribute to a human good. The difference between them is a difference of emphasis only, and the serious thinker ought to read, appreciate, and criticize both rather than reject one for the other.

In the case of Aristotle, our criticism of his political philosophy is connected precisely to his conservative point view. We know from our analysis of Plato that one of the dangers of radicalism is that in striving for the ideal the radical thinker may fail to take into account the realities of the human condition and, therefore, propose reforms that may be destructive of important human values. But conservatism has the opposite fault. In accepting the concrete and the real, the conservative thinker frequently accepts without questioning things that perhaps ought to be changed. The ideal may not always be right or proper for human beings, but the same can be said about the real. Sometimes the ideal would be better and more workable than the real.

This criticism of conservatism applies directly to Aristotle because in accepting the good around him, he also accepted the bad. Recall that, unlike Plato, he defended male supremacy and slavery as natural, and he did so precisely because he did accept "the experienceof the ages." He fell into the conservative fallacy of assuming that because a particular social practice or institution has existed over time, it therefore ought to exist. Radicals escape this fallacy because the logic of the rational ideal is, in their mind, superior to the irrationalities of the real.

The lesson we learn from reading Plato and Aristotle, then, is that both have their virtues and their defects, and that therefore to temper our own political attitudes with a healthy dose of the point of view opposite to our own. Radicals ought to listen carefully to the conservatives who warn us of the dangers of the ideal. And conservative are to take seriously the opposite advice from the radicals. Throughout the history of political thought, we will come across many extremely persuasive stories and narratives about politics and ethics and it is easy to get carried away with the basic intuitive sense in each one. But it is important to remember that each story is the product of an argument that we are being asked to judge. Every story retold here has been persuasive enough to convince history to remember it. Our task is to learn how to discriminate between convincing stories and the best way to begin to do that is to learn how to uncover what supports each of the most important steps in the story.

5

St. Augustine

> The earthly city, which does not live by faith, seeks an earthly peace, and the end it proposes in the well-ordered concord of civic obedience and rule, is the combination of men's wills to attain the things which are helpful to this life. The heavenly city, or rather that part of it which sojourns on earth and lives by faith, makes use of this peace only because it must, until this mortal condition which necessitates it shall pass away. So long as it lives like a captive and a stranger in the earthly city, though it has already received the promise of redemption, and the gift of the Spirit as the earnest of it, it makes no scruple to obey the laws of the earthly city, whereby the things necessary for the maintenance of this mortal life are administered; and thus, as this life is common to both cities, so there is a harmony between them in regard to what belongs to it.

St. Augustine (354-430) was born in 354 in the North African town of Thagaste what is now in Algeria. His mother Monica was a Christian but his father Patricius remained a pagan. Given the forceful personality of Monica, Augustine and his brother and sister became believers early on, but Augustine, as he vividly describes in his masterful *Confessions,* soon strayed from the fold. First at the neighboring University of Madaura and then at the University at Carthage, he succumbed to the pleasures of the flesh, living to the hilt the bawdy and sensual life of a student. Later he began to cohabit with a concubine and fathered a son by her. But there was more to the young Augustine than the pleasure-seeker and libertine. Attracted to the intellectual life by the work of Cicero, he soon fell under the influence of a heretical Christian sect called the Manichaeans. The Manichaeans preached a dualistic doctrine in which the forces of good (God) are pitted against the forces of evil (the Devil). It seemed to the young Augustine that this doctrine provided the best explanation available for the existence of evil in the world, including his own ever apparent sin. How could a good God be responsible for so much evil? Is it not more reasonable to think that an independent force of evil exists in the world and competes with God?

After his student days, Augustine became a teacher of rhetoric at Carthage and then moved to Rome to continue his academic career. Never far away lurked the indomitable Monica, worked there hoping and attempting to dissuade him from his sinful and heretical life. It was in Rome that Augustine was introduced to the work of the Neoplatonists, the result being that he began to question and then to abandon the Manichaean and Ciceronian views he had previously held. More positively, under the influence of the Neoplatonists he began to appreciate the reality of the immaterial dimension of life and world. The writings of the Neoplatonists directed his attention inward, to his soul, to his innermost, intangible being, and to the reality of the spiritual realm. Augustine was particularly attracted to Plotinus for resolution of the problem of evil, the problem of reconciling the existence of evil in the world with the reality of a good and omnipotent deity. Plotinus's theory of evil as privation claims that evil is not something that exists as a positive factor in the world but signifies only a lack of being resulting from the inferior status of the created world. By denying that evil is some entity for whose existence God must be held responsible and blamed, Plotinus demonstrates that God is wholly good.

Later, when Augustine took a professorship at Milan, he was introduced to the great Christian bishop Ambrose, with whom he was greatly impressed both intellectually and spiritually. It was in this context that he underwent his famous conversion to Christianity. The conversion occurred in a garden, where he overheard a child say, "pick it up and read it, pick it up and read it". He took this to mean the Bible, and on opening it to one of St Paul's epistles, he read: "No reveling or drunkenness, no debauchery or vice, no quarrels or jealousies. Let Christ Jesus himself be the armour that you wear; give no more thought to satisfying the bodily appetites". He immediately came to see that no effort of will or intellect could save him from sin, and the realization dawned that his only hope lay through the power of God's grace. He came to understand that by God's grace he could turn his attention wholly to God and away from worldly desires and ambitions. He soon returned to North Africa in 388 where before long he was installed as the Christian Bishop of the town of Hippo. He remained in this post until his death many years later 430, serving both as a beloved pastor and as a highly esteemed Christian intellectual who was in the vanguard of many efforts to stem the tide of heretical doctrine. He was a prodigious and prolific writer, and he left us with an enormous body of books and pamphlets which have become seminal works of early Christian literature. In addition to his *Confessions,* his *The City of God* still ranks as one of the classics of Western civilization.

The attempt by Christian thinkers in the West to provide an account of the nature of political society draws upon a number of different sources. Christianity was born into a world dominated by Roman institutions, including Roman law, and by Greek philosophical concepts. Roman ideas on the nature of the civitas defined political society as a community under 'the rule of law'. Plato and Aristotle, on the other hand, saw the polis as an agency of moral education and formation since for them it was impossible to live a fully human life outside society. Only beasts and gods, Aristotle said, live outside the polis: beasts because they are sub-human and gods because they are superhuman. For the Greeks the civil law must always be in accordance with the moral law, otherwise tyranny ensues. Tyranny is that form of government where the naked will and power of the ruler prevails – in other words, where might is right.

The Christians of the first three centuries took an ambivalent attitude to the Roman State. Some were convinced that the end of the world and the advent of the kingdom of God were ineritable so that for them it was not a pressing concern to elaborate a Christian theory of the State. Others identified the State with the anti-

Christian and pagan Roman State and rejected it completely. For them the Church, the community of believers, was the only true society. Just as the Christian philosophers had no need of pagan wisdom since the Scriptures were sufficient for them, so also Christians had no need of Greek and Roman political concepts and institutions. The 'City of God', the Church, was sufficient for them. Theocracy and fideism tend to go hand in hand. Other Christians recognized the role of the State and groped tentatively towards some kind of theory about the relationship that ought to obtain between the Church and the State – the supernatural society and the natural society – just as in the sphere of knowledge certain Christian thinkers attempted to define the relationship between what is known by 'faith' through revelation and what is known by 'natural reason' alone.

With the advent of the medieval period, we enter the world of Christianity. The West did not however, entirely abandon the modes of thought developed and perfected in ancient Greece. The two greatest Christian thinkers of all times, St. Augustine in the fourth and fifth centuries and St. Thomas Aquinas in the thirteenth, developed theologies and philosophies that attempted syntheses of the Christian message with Greek philosophy. Augustine was heavily influenced by Plato and the Platonist thinkers who followed him, especially the great Neoplatonist philosopher Plotinus. And Aquinas resurrected Aristotle and incorporated his thought into an explicit amalgam of Aristotelian and Christian beliefs. In one way or another, all of the medieval philosophers were concerned with issues whose origins were Greek. But, of course, the main and driving element in the philosophies of Augustine and Aquinas as well as of the other thinkers of this period is the Christian message itself, the doctrine of the one eternal God who is creator of the world and of humanity, the loving God who sent his son Jesus Christ to save human beings from sin, and the judgmental God who assigns his human creatures to heaven or hell as a result of the kinds of lives they live during their earthly sojourns. The Platonic and Aristotelian concepts are used to articulate and interpret this message. They also provide it with universal scope or application. Augustine, Aquinas, and the other medieval thinkers see their philosophies as offering truths about humankind in general.

The Genesis of Being

The things we project into the porous text of Eden tell as much about our hopes, fears, anxieties, and animosities as they do about necessities installed in the story. But the vantage point from which the projections of another are assessed is similarly informative. Where is the transcendental place from which these projections and counter-projections might be assessed? What if there is no such place? These questions may be borne in mind as we consider Augustine's brief on Eden.

Augustine must not allow a limited or blundering or amoral god to enter Eden. He recognies an allegorical dimension in the myth, but he also insists that these events actually occurred in history. "There is no prohibition against such allegorical exegesis, provided we also believe in the truth of the story as a faithful record of historical fact." He must be alert to control the interpretation of key metaphors in this creation story so that no trace of the limitation in them sticks to the creator.

Thus, though man is fashioned out of the "dust of the earth," this does not mean that the god worked as an artist works, with limited materials at his disposal. He worked as an omnipotent god works, achieving visible results by invisible means.

In Augustine's Eden, the god created Adam with free will. Adam acted through free will to disobey the single command issued by this god. And the god then delivered a punishment proportionate to the crime. The will of Adam is thus the window through which evil enters the world. This act makes Adam responsible for evil and deserving of punishment. The original sin of Adam created the divided will that humans experience thereafter through inheritance of the first sin. This inheritance makes the grace of the god indispensable to a healing of the will and the possibility of salvation. The woman named Eve is a subordinate figure in Augustine's presentation, more like a transmission belt than an active agent.

If we read Augustine as a sovereign politician of Scripture who constructs a sovereign, beneficent, salvational god out of scriptural materials, it is not too difficult to ascertain the imperatives governing his construction. Ho must drive a firm wedge between the god and the introduction of evil to preserve omnipotence and innocence together in the same divinity. Indeed, he must drive two wedges, one separating the will of Adam from god's responsibility, the other separating the will of the snake from god's responsibility. The gap between the god and evil is produced by the free will he attributes to the first two actors. The human will is invented to protect a willful god above all, but it is presented as an intrinsic property of human being that lifts it to the highest position among god's creatures because its composition reflects the image of the god's will. The attribution of evil to these first acts flows from the way they deviate from the intrinsic moral order Augustine identifies in Eden. Let's examine these strategic moments.

Our first parents, says Augustine, disobeyed the god's commandments and for the first time felt a novel disturbance in their disobedient flesh, as a punishment which answered to their own disobedience. The disobcdience of the god's command is an act of will attributed solely to them. The soul, in fact, rejoiced in its own freedom to act perversely and disdained to be God's servant; and so it was deprived of obedient service which its body had first rendered. At its own pleasure the soul deserted its superior and master; and so it no longer retained its inferior and servant obedient to its will. It did not keep its own flesh subject to it in all respects, as it could have kept it forever if it had itself continued in subjection to God.

Augustine needs and asserts the absolute freedom of Adam. For if God "created man aright," as Augustine insists, the rift in being for which humans are "justly and rightly condemned" must come from "defects" for which Adam is responsible. Adam "could have kept" this state of bliss forever, but acted freely not to. And inheritance of this "first sin" by all succeeding humans, who "were that one man who fell into sin through the woman who was made from him before the first sin," enables Augustine to explain the human experience of a divided will thereafter. The first, pristine act of will separates the god from evil by devolving evil on man; the resultant punishment of death, labor, and a divided will explains the common condition of humanity afterward.

The inheritance of original sin can be seen to be essential to Augustine's doctrine of Eden, once one begins to appreciate the profundity in his understanding of the role obdurate habit plays in shaping human conduct after the fall. Original sin is a softening agent in the Augustinian narrative. It offers a weak excuse for the repetition of sin through recourse to the inheritance of a divided will; and it provides a miserable explanation for the human experience of dissonance within life that this god must not be held responsible for. But a poor excuse and a miserable explanation may be better than none, when the stakes are infinitely high. The inheritance of original sin is functionally indispensable to the protection of Augustine's conception of divinity; and it also provides humans living under the gaze of this omnipotent being with the hope that the baleful effects of obdurate and sinful habits might be redeemed by its abundant grace. Omnipotence, original sin, divided will, obduracy of habit, and grace go together in this system. Within this complex, the inheritance of obdurate tendencies to sinfulness suggests the need for grace; grace is the hope of hopes for those who blame themselves for the rift, fear eternal damnation, and hold salvation to be beyond the capacity of their own wills alone. It would h psychologically intolerable to retain the other elements of the doctrine while dropping original sin and grace, for the experience of habit, sin, and divided will would then defeat every hope for salvation. The doctrine of original sin is often presented as the one element in Augustinianism most in need of revision because of the sense of injustice that attaches to it. But again within the hard compound into which it is mixed, it is a softening agent. But, granting that these elements (a pristine act of pure will, human guilt for the rift in being, the inheritance of original sin, the pure separation of good from evil, the desert of divine punishment, the role of grace) are functionally indispensable to Augustine's concept of omnipotent divinity, how could the very first human act have been an act of will? For something can be functionally indispensable to a faith or practice and nonetheless highly problematic in its credibility.

Augustine insists not only that Adam's act is the only pure act before the introduction of the divided will, but that the punishment meted out by the god for this pure act of disobedience is proportionate to the crime. The crime is willful rebellion, willful disobedience to the will of the god. The penalties are severe: a slimy life for the snake, labor in childbirth for women, toilsome work for men, a divided will for humans in general, a first death for the twosome followed by a second death that takes the form of damnation. The punishment may seem a little excessive to some. But Augustine finds it appropriate because the pristine act of will generates such a fundamental rift in being and because the rift would have been so easy to avoid.

The injunction was so easy to observe, so brief to remember; above all, it was given at a time when desire was not yet in opposition to the will. Therefore the unrighteousness of violating the prohibition was so much the greater, in proportion to the ease with which it could have been observed and fulfilled.

An omnipotent, benevolent, salvational god; an unnecessary rift in being created through the pristine will of the first human; an original fall into sinfulness inherited by every human to follow; severe and deserved punishment for the act; obedience to the god as the sign of a healed will; the grace of the god as crucial to healing of the divided will; salvation as the hope attached to grace. This is the logic governing the Augustinian reading of Eden. Suffering is explained by making human beings primordially responsible for it. Human responsibility is explained through the doctrine of pristine will. The god is protected from responsibility for evil through the introduction of human will into the order of being. All these effects ensue, that is as long as this slender will can bear the load Augustine imposes on it.

What role does the snake play here? Do its actions not recoil back on the divinity that created it? Augustine's reading of the snake provides the second wedge between his god and responsibility for evil. The snake is a mask worn by Lucifer. Lucifer, an angel who fell from this god through a previous, proud act of willful disobedience, enters Eden in a fallen state. The snake form is particularly appropriate to Lucifer because of its "slippery body, moving along in tortuous twists and turns.' Lucifer, crawling along in Eden, envies the unfilled state of the first two humans. It knows it cannot fool Adam directly—the superior human in this twosome of Adam and Eve because his will is given the purest form—so it practices its powers of seduction on the woman, the subordinate, seducible creature. This snake is very sly, supposing that man would not be trapped by a false move on his own part, but only if he yielded to another's mistake. Eve is successfully deceived. Adam, in his turn, yields to her suggestion, not because he too is deceived, but because he does not want to forfeit the pleasure promised. It is clear why this highest human in the intrinsic order of things Adam must not be deceived by the snake, for otherwise he would not be blameworthy enough and the god would not be pushed far enough away from implication in responsibility for evil.

But it is still not clear why Eve, the one being in this foursome (the god, the snake. Adam, Eve) not said by Augustine to act with full and deliberate will, deserves the harsh punishment visited upon her—unless her subordination in the intrinsic order of things makes the sins of males automatically recoil on the females dependent on them.

Now the structure of the story is set. The god is protected by two pristine acts of will creating a gap between it and the inception of evil, suffering, divided will, labor in childbirth, and imposition of a double death. Humanity is guilty. Its future salvation is preserved as a possibility. Good is separated cleanly from evil in the intrinsic order of things. Augustine knows how to construct a reading producing the effect he demands. This creative theologization of Eden, prepared to some degree by Paul's writings before Augustine, delivers rich dividends for the faith that energizes it.

Two sores, however, begin to fester within the bowels of this story. First if an omnipotent god created these beings and an omniscient, moral god possesses foreknowledge of these events, how can it avoid moral implication in the acts for which it holds them responsible? Second, how can the first acts of evil by Lucifer and Adam, respectively, be attributed to their wills without any responsibility flowing back to the god who created these willful beings? These questions do not stare out as directly as others would have had Augustine confessed his god without intervening in the story of Eden. They displace a blunt question: How could or would an omnipotent, omniscient, moral god ever allow suffering and punishment to enter the world? The more subtle questions generated by Augustine's rewriting of Eden are posed above all by those who wish to remain within the folds of this faith but find themselves troubled by nagging doubts as they study its details. The faithful can be counseled to renew their faith as they ponder these puzzles, and to treat insistent reiteration of them as possible signs of a lack of piety that impedes the very understanding sought. These displaced questions are thus politically less disruptive. The Augustinian theologization of Eden depoliticizes difficulties that might otherwise destabilize its faith; but this strategy of deferral and displacement is susceptible to destabilization in its turn. That's politics.

Augustine's god must have foreknowledge of everything that will occur, or else it would not be omniscient. But foreknowledge of these fateful events in Eden so close to the creative moment seems to implicate it in them, and his combination of benevolence and omnipotence would seem to require that he act to circumvent these effects if their implications were clear to him in advance. "God was well aware that man would sin," and he was equally aware of the effects of this sin. But he also knew that through them a process would be set in motion in which the good would eventually "enter into fellowship with the holy angels in eternal peace, when the 'last enemy,' death, had been destroyed. Here Augustine invokes a Hegelian conception before Hegel of historical progress through the providential effects of suffering. But Augustine also evinces awareness that the treatment of evil as a vehicle of future perfection cannot be satisfying to those who take god's omnipotence seriously. They will ask: "Why could your perfect god not come up with a better way that did not involve so much suffering and punishment?" So this theme of the providential effects of evil, often introduced as a palliative, is superseded by a more fundamental assertion. The god foresees and foreknows everything in all time without being responsible for the evil events foreknown.

How? The question forms part of a more general issue as to how the god could know the future if the future does not take the form of a return of the past. The cyclical theory of return had been introduced by Stoics to answer the question skeptics posed to them: What was god doing before it invented the world? This question is an embarrassment to both Augustine and the Stoics. Its embarrassment to Augustine resides, first, in the suggestion that there was a time before his god invented time and, second, in the judgment that his god created this world because of some deficit in itself before the creation. Perhaps it was bored or lazy or needy or incomplete before it created the world, and the creation was designed to fill one or more of those lacks. The Stoic answer to such charges: There was no time before the world because the world is governed by long cycles that eternally recur. The god knows each cycle because it has lived through the preceding ones. But this resolves the problem of the god/time relation by introducing a world in which the god is now limited by the eternal return of the same cycle of events. The notion of eternal return, Augustine insists, is thus "blasphemous." Augustine rejects the Stoic solution while retaining god's omnipotence, timelessness, benevolence, and foreknowledge of all events. He says,

> Who are we mere men to presume to set limits to his knowledge, by saying that if temporal things, and events are not repeated in periodic cycles, God cannot foreknow all things which he makes. In fact his wisdom is multiple in its simplicity, and multiform in uniformity. It comprehends all incomprehensible things with such incomprehensible comprehension that if he wished always to create new things of every possible kind, each of them unlike its predecessor, none of them could be for him undersigned and unforeseen. God's wisdom would contain each and all of them in his eternal prescience.

It is reasonable enough to point to the incomprehensible comprehension of an incomprehensible god—that is, to mystery—in presenting a god who is by definition mysterious to finite humanity. But Augustine reverts to mystery only after evincing authoritative certainty about so many things: the omnipotence, omniscience, and benevolence of a salvational god, an intrinsic moral order against which sin is defined, a free will that makes humans responsible for the fault in the intrinsic order, the snake as Lucifer, the justice of the god's penalties, and so on, and so on. A series of absolute injunctions followed by the strategic deployment of mystery to protect them. Why not invoke the incomprehensibility of this god earlier, with respect to some of the above formulations? Why first insist so fervently on these basic elements of faith and then invoke mystery authoritatively wherever it is required to save them?

Augustine's vaunted celebrations of mystery are deployed to depoliticize theological issues; The selective presentations of authoritative faith at some junctions, mystery at others, and heresy at still others, function to conceal, control, and occlude the corrosive effects of mystery on the certainty and authoritativeness of the primary doctrine. The strategic introduction of blasphemy in his critique of the Stoic conception of eternal return parallels strategic invocations of heresy in other delicate places. "If men can say this, it only remains for them to plunge into the depths of blasphemy by daring to allege that God does not know all the numbers." Is Augustine's deployment of mystery as a political resource of theology driven by an urge to universalize a moral, salvational god who rewards and punishes after life as well as during it? Are the putative risks of questioning presumption of an omnipotent, salvational god too severe to encourage appreciation of agonistic diversity on these matters? Are these stakes and responses echoed in contemporary doctrines that insist on the certainty and universality of those claims to self-identity they cherish the most? Would only a snake pose such questions?

The point here is not a rationalist one in which Augustine is to be criticized for invoking mystery because everything important must be assumed to fall within the scope of possible knowledge. Augustine has excellent replies to the sufficiency of this sort of rationalism. The point, rather, is that he deploys mystery as a dogmatic instrument of power, refusing to qualify denunciations of alternative doctrines through reference to deep mysteries in his own. His method for reading Scripture, presents such a demand as a criterion of good exegesis.

Augustine contributes significantly to future reflection through his confessions of the persistence of mystery. The persistence of mystery may show faith to be an incorrigible precondition of human action. This is a fundamental and durable insight. But an affirmative appreciation of the incorrigibility of mystery might also spawn a more generous appreciation of the virtue of regular contestation over fundamental questions. The very first question posed at the inception of human life may indicate that there are numerous mysteries, including a persistent mystery over a fundamental rift in being. Augustine's selective invocations of mystery arc balanced by a refusal to celebrate the creativity of this very first question about the mystery of being. Today, though, it may be timely to take the monopoly of mystery away from monotonists and monotheists.

Augustine insists that Adam "fell" from unity and bliss through a pure act of "will" and that this willful fall makes us responsible for evil. Through Adam we are all guilty, and through Lucifer's prior fall from grace we learn something about the character of Adam's will. How could Adam and Lucifer perform acts of will separating them from the will of the creator if they themselves are at different "times," pristine products of its creation?

Augustine avoids detailed discussion of this issue in the case of Adam, who appears, more as a child in Eden than a mature adult in the world. This avoidance is tactical. It shifts the issue to a setting before Eden in which Lucifer falls from grace as an angel and to a chapter in *The City of God* before the crucial chapter on Eden. It shifts it to a place where its potential volatility is more manageable. The will of Lucifer is already formed when it makes its contribution to the drama of Eden through the mask of a snake. If human will is crucial to Augustine's conception of human agency, responsibility, and guilt, then certain features of Lucifer's will serve as a model for the will of Adam.

The question pressing against the Augustinian doctrine is this. How can that act by which a created being first falls away from god be an act of will for which it is responsible? If it possessed sufficient density of character before the act to act willfully (such as language, intelligence, experience, maturity of judgment, knowledge of good and bad, the capacity to coordinate its intentions with its actions, etc.), the elements installed in its character during creation would recoil back on the god who created it. But if it lacked such a density of character, it would seem that its action could not be an act of will, but either an arbitrary deed or a determined event: If arbitrary, only the omnipotent god could be responsible for it; if determined, only the omnipotent god could be responsible for it. With respect to either alternative, then—density or its absence prior to the act—the assertion of willful responsibility becomes highly problematic. But Augustine needs the wedge of pure will to drive the crucial gap between this god and responsibility for evil. He takes up the issue by considering the fall of the bad angels from the grace of his god. The angels are not responsible for the bliss they receive. That is the gift of a god who is responsible for everything good. Angels and humans can only act independently of the god to produce evil, to turn away from its grace; everything good they do is a result of the grace of a god who is responsible for all good. Okay. But what makes this fall away from the god an evil act of will?

> If you try to find the efficient cause of this evil choice, there is none to be found. For nothing causes an evil will, since it is the evil will itself which causes the evil act if any thing exists, it either has, or has not, a will. If it has, that will is either good or bad; and if it is good, will anyone be fool enough to say that a good will causes an evil will?

This rules out the god as an efficient cause of the evil choice, and it rules out any cause exterior to the will itself. Still, the key question remains, What makes this fateful fall an act of pure will and not something else? Here Augustine turns to an argument by elimination, an argument that supports the desired answer, not by showing affirmatively how the will works in its pure state, but by eliminating all other alternatives as incredible. Although the case before us is now Lucifer—the paradigm case of a fallen angel—Augustine clarifies this case through a hypothetical example of two men who are exactly alike in their physical and mental makeup. They are both tempted by an attractive woman. One of them follows by acting on an unlawful desire, while the other remains steadfast in his chastity. What is the source of difference between them? It could not be the flesh of the first, for they have the same physical composition; it could not be the mind of the first, for they are alike in mind. And a temptation presented to one by a malignant spirit is not enough either, for that would imply that his deed was determined by an external influence.

Now if both experienced the same temptation, and one succumbed and consented to it, while the other remained unmoved, the only way to solve the difficulty is evidently to say that one refused and the other agreed to lose his chastity. What other reason could there be than this personal decision, given that their dispositions were precisely the same, in body and mind?

The very first act of perversity is not clarified here; it is named an act of consent or will and presented as a necessary assumption. Augustine concedes that he cannot resolve the mystery residing within the Augustinian Imperative of a pure will by the argument through which he asserts its necessity. The doctrine of will is necessary to save this god's omnipotence and innocence. So, in conceding the will to be filled with mystery while asserting its necessity through an argument by elimination, Augustine implicitly builds upon an edifice of authority already established by political means. For this conclusion through elimination gains its necessity only because a series of other possible answers have been ruled out by prior acts of authority.

There would be numerous other possibilities to consider at this point. Manicheans could introduce a war of two cosmic forces; tragedians might speak metaphorically of demons in the self that move it mysteriously and variably at passionate moments; those who revere a limited god might speak of rifts in the initial design of the world to which the passions respond in unpredictable ways; those who express godless wonder for the wonder of being might construe the moment to be an index of mystery in the problematical constitution of agency; those who discern tragedy in the very inception of being might compare the social indispensability of responsibility to the problematical desert of those to whom it is applied; those who appreciate the beauty of sensuality in a world without an intrinsic moral order might celebrate the act while confessing wonder at the forces drawing the parties together; those impressed by the volatile energy of sexuality but worried about a potential for violence residing in it might look for ways to manage its dangers without destroying its beauty; and so on. Augustine's argument by elimination does its work only because he has already set up the situation to be one in which the rift in being must be a fault in the agents who have fallen from an omnipotent, innocent god. Take that imperative away and a lot of other mysterious alternatives appear. "What else could it be?" Many things, all of them containing their portions of mystery too.

Augustine's reading of Eden postulates two originary acts of pure will as mysterious in operation as they are indispensable to the reading. The fact that the act of Adam had only to occur once, and that it is followed thereafter by a more familiar, cloudy mode of willfulness, helps to divert attention from its profoundly problematical character. As in the case of his god's necessary foreknowledge of suffering, Augustine defines the place of mystery through authoritative stratagems that subdue its disruptive effects on core dimensions of his faith.

A question posed by a snake to the first woman, a feeling of shame by two humans who view their nudity for the first time, a whirlwind from which a divine voice speaks, a cultural slash in the gender of a young teenager, the experience of a divided will—all of these seem to register a gap or rift or fault or rent in being that must somehow be engaged. Readings of the myth of Eden most typically present this gap as a "fault." as Augustine does. The idea of a fault is suggestive because it contains several dimensions contending with and against one another. It can be located on a moral register, an existential register, a theological register, a geological register, or several of them together. A fault might exist in the will of human being or in the order in which it is set; it might invoke a failing that warrants punishment or an incompleteness that engenders effects; it might indicate a break that injures life or an opening that releases possibilities.

Paul Ricoeur, a Christian philosopher appalled by the Augustinian reading of Eden, introduces a couple of possibilities here. In the *Symbolism of Evil,* his opposition to Augustine revolves around the doctrine of original sin. "The harm that has been done to souls, during the centuries of Christianity, first by the literal interpretation of the story of Adam, and then by the confusion of this myth, treated as history, with later speculations, principally Augustinian about original sin, will never be adequately told." Ricoeur suggests that human consciousness of responsibility for a "fault" in being precedes historical consolidation of the theme of human will. Such a primordial sense of mysterious responsibility seems to circulate in Genesis. It sets the stage upon which Augustine constructs his plot of original sin and finds people ready enough to believe it.

The Problem of Evil

The problem of evil has remained as one of the dominant and perplexing themes in the West. This problem has arisen because of the felt inexplicability of evil. Through his agony and suffering, reflective man has from time to time raised his head to ask "why?" and it is during these reflective moments that this problem has evolved around suffering animals and angels. It is sufficient now to say merely that in the history of man on the planet there is abundant historical evidence that he has reflected on the apparent inexplicability of evil on the felt suffering and pain.

The most frequent, and probably the most poignant form it has taken is the theological one, arising when in the course of reflecting on human suffering, violence and death, it is recalled that there is, together with this evil, a deity or deities with powers to prevent that evil. Thus it becomes a theological problem, when deity, with certain properties, omniscience, and benevolence, perhaps, exists, and simultaneously with human evil. For those who believe that there is such a God, and that there is evil which that deity could overcome if He wanted to, for such persons this problem becomes especially distressing. Indeed the disappointment that such a deity does not act is reflected in the oldest expression of the theological problem that has come down to us, the dilemma probably first formulated by Epicurus (341-270 BC).

God either wishes to take away evils and is unable; or "He is able, and is unwilling; or He is neither willing nor able, or He is both willing and able. If he is willing, and is unable, He is feeble, which is not in accordance with the character of God; if he is able and unwilling, He is envious, which is equally at variance with God; if he is neither willing nor able, He is both envious and feeble, and therefore not God; if he is both willing and able, which alone is suitable to God, from what source then are evils? Or why does He not remove them"?

The point to be made about the dilemma is that while the entire argument appears to be valid, one can still say that it may not be a sound argument for the premises may not all be true. More on this to follow. Before Epicurus, Plato had taken up the problem which is the first distinct statement in Greek literature of the problem of evil. Socrates is speaking, and absolving Zeus from all wrong doing in the ills that befall man:

> Neither, then, could God, said I, since he is good, be, as the multitude say, the cause of all things, but for making he is the cause of few things, but of many things not the cause. For good things are far fewer with us than evil, and for the good we must assume no other cause than God, but the cause of evil we must look for in other things and not in God.

The history of the problem from this point on becomes a history of solutions. Indeed, we can deduce from Plato's perfunctory jab at the puzzle that the Greek knows a good God could not cause evil. But then the puzzle looms all that larger. For if God, who is good, didn't produce the evil and if God, who could presumably stop the evil, doesn't, we have two questions to ask, and each is tied to the other to haunt the theist who puzzles about human suffering: First, where did evil come from? and second, why doesn't God stop it, lessen it, or makes us able to bear it? Thus we are back again to the dilemma raised by Epicurus: and there the matter seems to have lain in the sense that no serious work was done on the problem until it was taken up with a vengeance by Augustine. The totality for problem and its solution really commence with Augustine, and we will begin our historical investigations with him. Whatever else may have driven Augustine in his theologically voluminous life, the problem of evil must rank first. Unlike Leibniz who surely saw evil as an interesting philosophical puzzle to be handled with logic and a cool brain, Augustine saw it as one of the major challenges to his and apparently to all Christians' belief in God. Consequently, he deliberately eschews the niceties of systematic argument, and as often as not, writes and argues with hot passion and a frenzy that leads this reader to the conclusion that solving the problem of evil was the most significant theological event in the good saint's entire life.

The principal source for our discussion of Augustine's understanding of and attempted solutions to the problem: *Divine Providence and the Problem of Evil, The Free Choice of the Will, Confessions, The City of God* and finally *Faith, Hope, and Charity.*

Augustine gives us, in these works, what seems to be a nearly complete list of all future possible solutions to the problem, some of which he rejects, such as the Manichean doctrine of two opposed powers, one malevolent, the other benovolent fighting for control of man and the world. Thus, it is fair to say that Augustine's treatment of the problem becomes the paradigm for all-future philosophical handling of the problem, because all the major figures who took the issue to their mind relied on Augustine for advice and solace, as well as in theory, for nearly all future solutions.

In Book One of *Divine Providence,* Augustine sets forth the problem of evil as a dilemma, reminiscent of the dilemma proposed previously by Epicurus:

> Wherefore, those who ponder these matters are seemingly forced to believe either that Divine Providence does not reach to these outer limits of things (where evil is) or that surely all evils are committed by the will of God. Both horns of this dilemma are impious, but particularly the latter (for) the imputing of negligence is indeed much more pardonable than the charge of ill will or cruelty.

We can identify the first horn of this dilemma 'the negligence horn' and the second 'the cruelty horn'. If evil is generated by assuming that God is all-powerful, 'the omnipotence thesis', and that God is all good, what will be called 'the ethical thesis', and by assuming and then denying one or the other of these, then it is plain that Augustine's formulation of the dilemma attempts precisely that, viz., the negligence horn attacks the omnipotence thesis and the cruelty horn the ethical thesis. Either way we produce evil. The solution proposed to explain the presence of evil under the very nose of an all powerful, all good deity is the start of Augustine's theodicy; it comes essentially to saying, both here in *Divine Providence* as well as throughout the other writings, that the evil we see is seen narrowly and myopically. We need but apprehend the whole creation to realize three things: first, that while the separate parts of the creation may here and there be apparently evil, the whole is nonetheless good; second, that tremendous good comes out of evil; and third, this evil is necessary to the full harmony and goodness of the whole. Thus in Book Two of *Divine Providence,* these three solutions are proposed, and are worth quoting both for the historical interest they afford. Augustine begins with 'the-whole-is-good solution', or 'the aesthetic solution':

> Thus it happens that whoever narrow-mindedly considers this life by itself alone is repelled by its enormous foulness, and turns away in sheer disgust. But, if he raises the eyes of the mind and broadens his field of vision and surveys all things as a whole, then he will find nothing unarranged, unclasped or unassigned to its own place.

Augustine follows this by showing that good arises within the whole and for the whole by the presence of these separate evils; and we might call this 'the good-comes-from-evil solution' or 'the theological solution'. He gives a very suggestive and philosophical example:

> What more hideous than a hangman? What more cruel and ferocious than his character? Yet he holds a necessary post in the very midst of laws, and he is incorporated into the order of a well-regulated state.

Finally, Augustine seems to argue that the evils present in the society, the particular whole that he chooses in analogy with the universe, are necessary in order to prevent greater evils that could come about without them. Augustine's delightful example follows:

> What can be mentioned more sordid, more bereft of decency, or more full of turpitude than prostitutes, procurers, and the other pests of that sort? Remove prostitutes from human affairs, and you will unsettle everything because of lusts.

Finally, in *Divine Providence*, there is one other solution proposed, which will have important defenders. Augustine speaks of a barnyard cock fight in which one of the combatants emerges battered, torn and bloody. While this might fall under the category of animal evil, it is plainly meant to apply, again by analogy, to the struggle for good going on within, and finally emerging from the whole. The production of good wouldn't be good unless there were evil. The dialetical struggle establishes the goodness of the good. Thus, beauty exists by contrast with the ugly.

In this rather hasty review of *Divine Providence*, then, at least four solutions to the problem emerge the aesthetic solution, the theological solution, the prevention solution, and the contrast solution.

In *Free Choice,* the problem receives its shortest formulation. The dialogue between Augustine and one Evodius opens with the latter asking: Tell me, please, whether God is not the cause of evil? But it is not until Book Three, some 100 pages later on, that the question is answered. In Book One, however, Augustine distinguishes two kinds of evil, which will have important applications in the later literature. We usually speak of evil in two ways: first, when we say that someone has done evil; second, when someone has suffered something evil: Now, the evil that man does is, for Augustine, sin and the evil that man suffers is punishment. But we have at this stage a distinction later to be called "moral evil" as opposed to "physical evil", respectively.

In Book Three, a number of new solutions and themes predominate along with ones already introduced. Evil is complicated, first of all by the introduction of a new premise, the omniscience of God. Following the distinction between sin and punishment as two meanings of evil, we can introduce two causes of evil, one of which might even be taken for a solution to the problem. Thus if sin is the evil that man does, then surely man is the cause of evil, i.e., if man is free to do the evil that he does, then man is the cause of evil and not God. So the man's-free will is the cause of evil. But the solution runs into trouble if God is all knowing. The trouble develops if the omniscience assumption is added to the omnipotence thesis. Augustine argues that God is all knowing in the sense that He knows events that have happened, that are happening, and that will happen; call this in turn 'the omniscience thesis'. But Augustine is at pains to point out that there is a seeming contradiction between the man is free solution and the omniscience thesis. A second cause of evil, evil as punishment, would seem to directly implicate God in the production of evil; so whether we understand evil as sin which man does, and involve God indirectly as the knower of what sins one would do, or understand evil as God's punishment for sin, and involve God directly, in either case God emerges as a causer, *at two removes or at one remove,* of evil.

In *The Confessions*, the problem of is peremptorily treated but one theme that will subsequently predominate Western theodicies is mentioned. God is all good and superior to his creation. God's omniscience is not mentioned, but perhaps assumed. Augustine states the problem as follows:

"Here is God and here is what God has created. God is good...and by far superior to these things. Yet, as a good Being he created them good. Whence then, is evil"?

Earlier he had responded to the problem in the *Confessions* by resorting to the now familiar aesthetic solution, e.g.,

"While the higher things are better than the lower still I decided by a sounder judgment that all things together are better than the higher things alone".

That is to say, evil and the good are better together than the good would be alone: That whole is better than either of its parts then.

In the gigantic The *City of God,* written between 413 and 426, Augustine reiterates themes previously developed, the theme that good comes out of evil, and that the whole is better with its evil parts than without:

> God would never have created a single angel not even a single man whose future wickedness He foresaw, unless, at the same time, He knew of the good which could come of this evil. It was as though He meant the harmony of history, like the beauty of a poem to be enriched by antithetical elements.
>
> And not even the sinfulness of a will refusing to preserve the order of its nature can lessen the beauty of God's total order. For as the beauty of a picture is not dimmed by the dark colors, in their proper place, so the beauty of the universe of creatures, if one has insight to discern it, is not marred by sins even though sin itself is an ugly blotch.

But the question remains, why did God create human ugly blotches. In other words, why did not God create man free of sin and suffering? One answer appears through the aesthetic solution and the teleological solution, i.e., that thing, the whole in the long run, just look better that way. Another is that man himself causes some evil, sin, and others are sent to him by God as punishment.

This justice solution appears to take two forms in rationalizing evil. Thus on the one hand the suffering we get is deserved, because God is an avenger and on the other, the suffering we get could be worse but isn't because God is just. In Augustine's opinion, condone the suffering that befalls man: This is precisely what the justice solution comes to.

In the fifth and final work, the written about 421, there are the usual references to the teleological solutions. *Faith, Hope and Charity* the theme is generally that even out of evil He can do good:

> Nor would He who is good permit evil to be done unless in His omnipotence He could turn evil to good

But amid this is the theme, again, that evil is necessary to contrast with good, in which it seems plain that the contrast solution is implied by the aesthetic solution since there could be no aesthetically beautiful whole in Augustine's sense, unless the parts, good and evil, beauty and blotches, harmony and antithetical elements, somehow contrasted with each other. And this in turn implies the teleological solution. They are all bound together here:

> In this whole even that which is called evil, well regulated and confined to its own place, serves to give higher commendation to the good, making it, in comparison with the evil, more pleasing and worthy of praise.

But now another notion emerges. That not only are these contraries dependent on each other but further that evil, would not exist without good, while, oddly, good can exist without evil:

> Yet, although there is no doubt that good and evil are contraries not only can they exist together, but evil without good and in anything that is not good cannot exist at all; good, however, can exist without evil.

This leads us around again to the privation solution, and dangerously close to the theory that evil is an illusion.

That Augustine realizes that he is close to the brink of heterodoxy results in his immediately quoting Isaiah just in case anyone should accuse him of confounding good and evil.

"Woe unto them that call evil good and good evil: that put darkness for light, and light for darkness" and he repeatedly enunciates his belief in the reality of evil, but not its ontological equality with nor superiority over the good. He argues that God judged it better to bring good out of evil than not to permit evil to exist at all'.

However, Augustine has a problem with evil. For on the one hand he wants to admit that evil is real, and on the other, it is a privation of good. How can these be reconciled? He wants to say that man's nature is not neutral, but basically good, and that he chooses freely to sin or not to sin.

Placing responsibility for evil on the shoulders of human beings solves for Augustine a problem that had haunted him from the beginning of his intellectual carrier, indeed long before the time he was converted to Christianity. The basic puzzle for him is how there can be evil in a world created by God. The Christian God is supposed to create all things out of nothing, from which it seems to follow that this God is responsible for everything that exists in the world, including evil. But God is also supposed to be supremely good, supremely powerful, and supremely wise. Thus, he would know how to create a world without evil; he would be able to do so; and given his goodness or beneficence, he would will to do so. How, then, can there be evil in the world?

The Manicheans whose doctrines Augustine embraced as a young man had an answer to this puzzle. God is not responsible for evil. God for them is not the only principle of creation. There is also the Devil, the principle of darkness and evil, who operates in influencing the affairs of the world. It is this negative source, therefore, which is responsible for evil. Such a theory, while highly plausible to some minds, including that of the young Augustine, achieves the goal of explaining evil only by limiting God. God is no longer thought of as infinite but rather as only one of two creative sources, which produce and control the inhabitants and events in the material world. Thus, God cannot be seen as the totally powerful being in whom orthodox Christians believe. Manichaeanism was therefore branded a heresy, and after his conversion, Augustine was a leader in the fight against this heresy.

There is one thing that Augustine professes to know with certainty: 'this I do know, that the nature of God can never be defective'. God cannot be responsible for evil, but created things as defective that Augustine finally comes to perceive the answer to the puzzle of evil. If there were some positive aspect of human nature that led individuals to act in ways that bring evil into the world, then we could ask why God created human beings with this characteristic. If say, human nature is essentially aggressive, why does God create essentially aggressive human beings? God does create us, and he deliberately creates us with all the positive characteristics we have. Thus if evil is the product of one of these characteristics, the fault really lies with God. He should not have created us with this characteristic. But evil results not from positive feature but from a lack. The human sinner is a creature, not the creator. God is perfect being, human beings, being created out of nothing, will be less than perfect being. They will lack perfect being. Their sin can then be understood to be the result of creaturehood; of the distance creatures are in their very being from the perfect reality of God. We cannot blame God for creating human beings with this lack, for they would not be creatures if they did not have this defect. Creatures could not have been created otherwise thus we cannot consider God's creation of them, with all their defects, to have been the product of any lack of knowledge, power, or goodness on his part. Here we find Plotinus evil as privation argument and Plato's doctrine of degrees of reality expressed in Christian terms.

Augustine's solution to the problem of evil, then, is his negative theory of sin and evil. Evil is not a positive reality, for which causal blame can be attributed to whomever or whatever brings it into existence. It is simply the lack of fully positive reality, the distance from God. Augustine frequently uses metaphors of light and darkness, and of sound and silence, to illustrate his theory. God is light, but creatures, being at such a far remove from God, are darkness. This darkness, however, is merely the absence of light. Likewise, silence is not a form of sound, a positive aural reality, but the lack of sound, it is not something we actually hear but rather the lack of hearing.

But, Augustine seems to have solved the problem of evil and his answer is that human beings are given the power of choice by God. Because they are defective, they can choose evil, but they also have the ability to perceive the moral law and act on it. They have the ability to love inferior things and in doing so create evil, but they also have the ability to direct their love toward God and thus pursue the good. By virtue of the freedom of their wills, their ability to choose either man or God, good or evil, human beings themselves are responsible for the existence of evil. They are created because God wants to have the opportunity to love him, and receive his grace and in granting them free will, he gives them his opportunity. But if they do not avail themselves of it voluntarily, as a result of their own choices, then, being creatures, they will not rise above their defective nature, and sin and evil will be the result.

Free Will

Few today find the negative theory of evil convincing, but there are those who appeal to human freedom in attempting to show how the fact of evil can be reconciled with the notion of an all-good creator. In fact, the free-will defense, attributing evil to the free acts of human agents, is part of a very common theodicy found in recent philosophy of religion. For one thing, much of the evil in the world does not appear to be the result of human agency at all. Consider all the evil resulting from hurricanes, tidal waves, volcanic eruptions, sumani plague and dreadful dilease Aids and the like. Surely these events are not the result of the perverted human will. Can't God prevent these natural disasters from happening? If so, why doesn't he do so? If he cannot prevent them, doesn't this show him to be limited in ability or knowledge and hence imperfect? With respect to the negative theory of evil, we might agree that natural disasters are the inevitable aspect of a created world, but we might still ask whether a created world, a created physical environment, must have all or so many of these dangers just because it is created? Unless we share Augustine's extreme Platonism, with its doctrine of levels of reality, an affirmative answer sounds very weak.

Augustine also struggles with the problem of how human beings can be thought to have free will if they are created by God and if God knows for all eternity what they will do. If God knows that a person will sin at a certain time, this person has no choice, no options he must sin at that time, in which case it is difficult to see how such a choice is free. Augustine answers these skeptical objections in ways that have become part of standard Christian apologetics. With regard to the claim that God's creation of human beings undermines their free will, he responds by saying that indeed God creates human beings, but he creates them with freedom of the will. It is this free will, not God, that leads to sin. With regard to the objection that God's omniscience is incompatible with human freedom, Augustine counters that one of the things God knows, in knowing everything, is that human beings will to sin and that they do so freely. Insofar as God knows this, it must be so and thus it follows that it is true that human beings freely will either to engage in sin or to be virtuous. Again, these solutions of Augustine's to the problems of divine omnipotence and omniscience are quite controversial.

Weak or strong, Augustine's answers to the problems inherent in the theistic world-view he adopts stand as major efforts of a Christian thinker to deal with these ethical and metaphysical questions. And his ethical theory as a whole, with its focus on love, stands as one of the major Christian attempts to answer Socrates' question about how we are to live our lives. Augustine shows how theists can be philosophical ethicists.

Chief Good

We have to see what does Augustine have to tell us about how we ought to live our lives. His ethics begins with a clearly recognizable Greek doctrine: we all certainly desire to live happily; and there is no human being but assents to this statement almost before it is made. Happiness is the aim of life for all human beings, the goal toward which, as human beings, they naturally strive. But Augustine immediately asks, just as had Aristotle, what this happiness consists in. It is important to note the terms used by Augustine in describing the possibilities of achieving happiness. The central term is love, a term he employs very generally to include all forms of desire and striving what we love is what we want and what we try to obtain through our actions. Consequently we are not happy if we do not obtain what we love; we are not happy if what we love turns out to be hurtful either because it harms us or fails to satisfy us; and we are not happy if, while possessing what is good in perfection, we fail to love it. What is good in perfection is designated by Augustine as a human being's chief good, and thus happiness exists when that which is man's chief good is both loved and possessed.

Augustine invokes the picture of the world embodied in the basic Christian conception of reality. This picture is a hierarchical one, incorporating, in Platonic fashion, the notion of levels of reality and perfection. All things have a place, a rank and species, assigned to them by the order of their nature. God is the being having perfect reality; the material world, being at distance from God, has least reality and is accordingly much inferior to God in its being. In between these two extremes, we find human beings. Made up of body and soul, they share the materiality of the physical world but also the spirituality of the higher domain. As a material being, the human person has a large number of physical wants and desires, the objects of which are themselves material. Clearly, these objects of love are inferior to the spiritual things that are closer in reality to God. But as soul, the human person has the ability to love these higher things, and indeed to love God, the perfect being.

The Order of Love

The levels of reality are distinguished by Augustine, again in good Platonic fashion, in terms of their susceptibility to change. All things in the created world of space and time are in constant change, and all of them come to exist and subsequently perish. God, on the other hand, is immutable, unchanging and eternally existing. Change and perishing are signs of inferiority, while immutability is the mark of perfect being. God is perfect being, and the material world imperfect being. Human beings have a perishable body but an immortal soul; thus they are intermediate on the scale of being. This metaphysical conception gives substance to Augustine's distinction between kinds of love. To love that which is eternal is to love that which will always be present and will always satisfy one's desires, whereas to love that which is mutable and perishable will disappoint as a result of change, or cause grief as a result of perishing. Thus it is only rational to love the souls of other human beings. It is certainly more rational to love God than to love perishing material objects and the perishing body.

The hierarchical structure of reality, together with the conception of the human being as possessing different degrees of reality within himself sets the stage for defining man's chief good. The notion that a thing's chief good is something superior to it, leads Augustine to claim that the chief good of the body is not the bodily states of pleasure, but rather the higher reality, the soul. By this he means that the best condition of the body is to be ruled over by the soul. Hence the more virtuous the soul, the better off the body. When we love God, we love that which is superior to us. God already dwells within us, but we may not in fact love this perfect good. If we turn our love away from inferior, material objects and redirect it toward this perfect being, we shall embrace the perfection of all good things. God, then, is our greatest good, and we attain it, and consequently happiness, by loving him.

Augustine frequently expresses this doctrine in terms of the Biblical notion of beatitude: the striving after God is, therefore, the desire of beatitude; the attainment of God is beatitude itself. Beatitude is a state of happiness, more specifically the happiness of the virtuous person. Such happiness is not an Aristotelian theoretical contemplation rather it is a loving union with God, a fulfilment of one's entire intellectual and emotional needs and desires. This must be kept in mind, since Augustine the philosopher often uses intellectual terms in describing beatitude: The happy life consists in rejoicing in the truth. Beatitude is the love of this absolute truth with all one's heart.

Peace

A central concept used by Augustine in describing the happiness of human beings is that of peace. Peace, he maintains, is desired by everyone. Whoever gives even moderate attention to human affairs and to our common nature, will recognize that there is no man who does not wish to be joyful, neither is there any one who does not wish to have peace. For even they who make war desire nothing but victory, desire, that is to say, to attain to peace with glory. For even they who intentionally interrupt the peace in which they are living have no hatred of peace, but wish it changed into a peace that suits them better. Thus, the universal desire for happiness is revealed as a universal desire of peace. And peace is achieved through establishing order, an arrangement of human beings with harmony among them. The peace of all things is the tranquillity of order. And order, Augustine tells us, is the distribution, which allots things equal and unequal, each to its own place.

Through war and aggression, wicked human beings may create a form of peace among themselves, but this peace is an unjust peace. The order achieved and enforced in this fashion is a perversion of the natural order of the universe. Human beings, in their pride, their self-centeredness, are paining God. Abhorring equality with other human beings under God, evil individuals impose a rule of their own over their equals-they reject the just peace of God and love their own unjust peace. Clearly, then, to achieve the just peace, human beings must order themselves individually and collectively so as to achieve the natural order of things.

The peace, then, that truly satisfies, that brings true happiness, is the peace which prevails when God's created order is preserved. It is a peace, which exists when our loves are ordered according to the place, the equality and inequality, of the objects of those loves. We must love God more than our fellow human beings; we must love all human beings equally creatures of God; we must love material objects in the order and degree dictated by the rational soul, and we must love them less than we love the spiritual life of the soul and our fellow human beings. By ordering our loves in this fashion, we attain harmony within the individual soul, within the community of human beings, and within our relationship to God. Such harmony is perfect repose, such repose is perfect and just peace, such peace is true happiness.

The Two Cities

The failure of the will to acknowledge and honour the natural order of the objects of love is widespread, so much so as to generate a community of people whose loves are disarranged in the same manner. All of them can be said to love themselves more than they love God. This commonality crosses all ethnic and national boundaries and generates a city not in a civic, political sense but in a psychological or moral/religious one. The common object of love of all sinners is themselves and their material reality. In this way, sinners distinguish themselves from all those human beings who love God more than themselves. These latter individuals also, given their common object of love, create a city. And so we find the basis for Augustine's celebrated distinction between the earthly city and the heavenly city, the 'City of Man' and the 'City of God:' Accordingly, two cities have been formed by two loves: the earthly by the love of self, even to the contempt of God; the heavenly by the love of God, even to the contempt of self. The former, in a word, glories in itself, the latter in the lord. While the 'City of God' has existed throughout all eternity, the 'City of Man' came into existence with the 'fall' of human beings through Adam's disgrace and sin. Throughout human history the two cities have been intertwined, some members of every nation being citizens of the one and others members of the other. Augustine also suggests that in this life we all at best possess dual citizenship. As fallen creatures, we are spiritual beings in conflict with our bodily vessels. We are all sinners, and as such none of us in this life can ever be fully and exclusively members of the 'City of God'. As history unfolds, each city tries to vanquish the other and recruit its citizens. But the division will continue until Judgment Day, when God will separate the cities and send their respective citizens either to heaven or hell, in accordance with their final choice of membership in the 'City of Man' or the 'City of God'.

Moral Law

All human beings are capable of being citizens of the 'City of God', since all human beings, possessed of a rational soul, can know the laws of God and hence can love and rejoice in the Truth. These laws, which make up the Eternal Law in distinction from the laws human beings created for the purpose of bringing order among themselves on earth' are known by human beings as the moral law. Recognition of the moral law by means of the rational soul is recognition of it through conscience. The moral law is simply an expression of the nature of God. It is God's sovereign reason. Hence, far from being arbitrary, it is totally objective and universal. It contains, among other injunctions, the laws of justice designed to order the relationships among human beings.

Through conscience, we can know the moral law, but we cannot know it through our own efforts alone. It is only God's grace that permits finite mortals to comprehend the infinite truth. The law was therefore given that grace might be sought; grace was given that the law might be fulfilled. This grace is manifested through the divine illumination of our minds. It is God who illumines our minds and impresses upon conscience the contents of the moral law. Augustine uses such phrases as the law being transcribed on to the human mind and its notion being impressed on us, to describe this mysterious manner in which God as light allows our conscience, our reason, to be illumined and to grasp the truth. The mind informs itself by the divine light through reason. What the moral law prescribes first and foremost is the love of God. The virtuous person is the wise individual who knows the moral law and follows it in his actions. And, as Socrates, Plato, and Aristotle had stressed, virtue leads to happiness:

Women and Sexuality

Feminists have attacked Augustine for his views of women and sexuality. In Greek religion and philosophy, woman represented the pollution associated with the body and sexuality because of their role in giving birth to life, which brings with it the threat of death. Both Plato and Aristolte denigrate women as the embodiment of the dangers posed to reason by sexuality. Since women are considered to be ruled primarily by passions, they are deemed unsuited for rational pursuits. A similar alignment appears in Christian views about women and sexuality, stemming from both Greek and Hebrew religions.

Augustine was one of the most influential figures of the early Church. His views about sexuality, lust, women, and embodiment constituted an important dimension of Christian teachings. Not only did he figure prominently among his contemporaries, but his stature and influence increased through the Middle Ages. In the fifteenth century, he was described by the Bishop of Florence as a luminary in Church history: What the sun is to the sky, St. Augustine is to the doctors and fathers of the Church.

Augustine's treatment of sexuality is intimately linked to his understanding of man's fall from grace. Sexual desire is one form of the more general state of desiring that Augustine calls concupiscence, or lust. In *The City of God*, Augustine comments that concupiscence is the generic word for all desires. The pleasures of all the senses-taste, hearing, smell, touch and sight-readily pose the dangers of temptation and desire to the soul. The general state of desire whether it is lust for sensual gratification, for money, or for power is itself the punishment man bears for his disobedience to God. In *The City of God,* Augustine notes that man's failure in paradise to abstain from one kind of food is all the greater since he was not yet compelled by lust to violate this command. He writes that man found no resistance to its observance in lust, which only afterwards sprung up as the penal consequence of sin. Consequently, all forms of lust are viewed as the punishment for the evil will, which initiated the human fall from grace. With the onset of desire, the senses pose the constant temptation of pleasure. Although hunger is no sin when we need to satisfy our appetite for our health, generally we are tempted to eat, not just to preserve health, but for the sake of pleasure itself. Thus, in the process of satisfying our needs we are caught in the snare of concupiscence in which we experience the ominous enjoyment of gratifying our greed.

Although concupiscence is a general term referring to all desires, sexual desire remains the preeminent form of lust. In *The City of God* Augustine comments that lust may have many objects, yet when no object is specified, the word lust usually suggests to the mind the lustful excitement of the organs of generation. The bodily movements that signify sexual desire were the first consequences of human's loss of grace. Not only is sexual desire the most immediate sign of corruption, but it also incarnates, as no other desire does, the act of disobedience for which mankind is punished. Because of man's disobedience to God, he now suffers disobedience within himself, for neither his mind nor his flesh obey his will. In sexual desire, the soul can neither master itself, so as to eliminate the temptation, nor master the body, so as to keep the members under the control of the will. Whereas in other forms of desire, resistance occurs within the soul, in sexual desire the body itself resists the mastery of the soul. Sexual lust is most shameful because the soul's will and order are resisted by the body, which is distinct from and inferior to it, and dependent on it for life. Thus, sexual desire embodies the disobedience that precipitated and forever marks man's fall from grace.

Thus, Augustine speaks as a man, addressing other men, regarding the need to eliminate sexual desire. Women appear primarily as the objects that incite men's desire. For example, Augustine's discussion of resurrection contrasts the natural female body, which will not excite lust but instead will call forth praise, with the body that occurs in our unrestricted state. Augustine argues against the view that women would be resurrected as men. This latter view implies that women's body is intrinsically a corruption that would be eradicated in the state of blessedness. Instead, Augustine argues that the vice in women's bodies lies in carnal intercourse and childbearing. Thus, Augustine condemns women's provocative and procreative body because it is a source of transgression for man. Since women arouse desire in men, their earthly bodies are deemed unnatural.

Augustine's treatment of sexuality in the states of blessedness, corruption, and resurrection indicates that ideal human relations are devoid of desire. Moreover, it implies that sexuality cannot be a vehicle for human love but serves only as an interference with it. Consequently, Augustine maintains a place for sexuality in human life only as a narrow and corrupted form of human expression. Augustine's conception that sexuality should be only a vehicle for procreation is part of his more general desensualization of the body. The ideal body, as Augustine's condemnation of concupiscence makes clear, is devoid of desire for sensual pleasures.

However, Augustine's appreciation is for the ideal body that is purified of all desire, and in every respect subject to the spirit. The mortal body that human beings have in this worldly existence is condemned in Augustine's philosophy. Only when we transcend our present mortal existence well our flesh be transformed to a wholly spiritual being. Thus, the body is valued insofar as it serves as an instrument of the soul, and it can be infused throughout with a spiritual nature. The body does not contain its good in itself, but the soul is the good of the body.

Although Augustine suggests that the body in general must be subject to the rule of the soul, he also implies that women are less suited to fulfilling this task than men. In a manner reminiscent of early scapegoat rituals, Augustine resolves his own ambivalence about sexual desire by banishing women from his presence. As in Greek religion and philosophy, by heaping the pollution of sexuality onto woman as the source of temptation, man thereby purifies himself of this contamination. Consequently, Augustine's interpretation of female sexuality as a danger signifies above all a conflict about male sexuality. Augustine's view that women are more closely linked to the corrupt body than men makes their subordination to men both natural and commendable. In his eulogy of the present order Augustine treats woman as existing exclusively for man. He describes man as made in the image and likeness of God because he has the power of reason and understanding.

Since Augustine views the physical world as a representation of God's spirit, the proper ordering of this realm must conform to the divinely ordained rule of reason over natural impulses. The subjugation of woman to man incarnates, in Augustine's view, the spiritual hierarchy that man must strive to achieve within his own soul. Since women's physical existence is designed for men, this external embodiment of the rule of the higher over the lower elements of the soul must enhance men's ability to achieve rational self-control. By means of their domination over women, men can learn to achieve that domination of reason within their own soul required for spiritual purity. However, Augustine does not identify women exclusively with the body, as does Orphic thought. He notes that in her mind and her rational intelligence, woman has a nature equal to man's. Despite this admission of women's rationality, women became, in Augustine's view, symbolically identified with the lower, instrumental uses of reason. Thus, women remain associated with those functions of the soul that signify the dimension of human existence that is not made in God's image. Ultimately, although Augustine acknowledges women's rational intelligence, the domination of male over female remains a natural dimension of human existence, which is overcome only with resurrection.

Thus, as Simone de Beuvoir has argued, woman is represented as other in the Christian tradition. She is created for man, and she embodies the aspects of human nature more closely identified with the sensibility of the body. Augustine's dual conception of women's spiritual and physical being leads him attribute conflicting qualities to women's nature. He writes that a good Christian is found in one and the same woman to love the creature of God whom he desires to be transformed and renewed, but to hate in her the corruptible and moral conjugal connection, sexual intercourse and all that pertains to her as wife. A Christian man must love woman, the creature of God who must be transformed, but he must hate her wifely, sexual nature. Augustine also compares the relation of husband to wife to the mandate to love one's enemies. Augustine's identification of women's function with procreation, which inevitably is imbued with sin, reveals an androcentric bias in his analysis. Since woman symbolizes the element of existence that precipitates us into lust, man can identify himself with the superior aspect of rationality. Augustine's ascription of different natures to male and female provides a theoretical rationale for men's dominance over women. Although woman also is rational, women's body appears as the symbolic representation of irrationality, whereas man's body appears as the symbol of rationality. Thus, the rational control that ascetic thinkers have sought as a religious and philosophical goal becomes incarnate in a physical existence that demands the social exercise of power. Augustine prefigures the identification of reason with mastery that became pronounced in the modern philosophical tradition since Bacon and Descartes. As in Augustine's writing, reason in modern philosophy is linked not only rational control within the soul, but also with men's control over women in the social world.

Some authors have suggested that the extremely personal origin of Augustine's theory of sexuality discounts it as representative of Christian attitudes. Although Augustine's views on sexuality reflect his own struggle to control sin, redemption, and the relations between men and women, which remained highly influential until the twelfth century. Moreover, Augustine's own conflict between the desire for sexual love and the legitimacy promised by the marriage union was not idiosyncratic. In an age in which it was common for men of thirty, forty, or even sixty to marry girls of fifteen. Augustine's view of marriage as primarily a union for the procreation of children would accord with contemporary practices. The enormous historical impact of Augustine's thoughts on sexuality indicates that his personal experience found resonance in the culture that embraced his ideas. As Lucien Goldman suggests in *The Hidden God*, the very prominence of certain thinkers indicates that their ideas originate in a common social experience. Goldman writes that the men who express the vision of their social class on an imaginative or conceptual plane are writers and philosophers, and their work expresses this vision in its complete and integral form. Viewed in this light, the preeminence of Augustine's thought about sexuality and women indicates how profoundly he articulates commonly held beliefs and practices. Thus, Augustine construes the sexual identity of men in the form of domination and the identity of women in the form of submission. Although for Augustine both men and women possess rational souls, the social relationships between the sexes are determined not by rational equality but by sexual inequality. Augustine's drive to conquer sexuality motivates him to institutionalize a sexual hierarchy as determinative of human relations.

Augustine's commitment to the natural hierarchy between the sexes, which is only overcome with resurrection, derives from his view of sexual desire as a disease, his identification of women with both physical and spiritual sources of temptation, and his imperative to establish a chaste and pure heart. Men's willful control of their bodily passions is necessary for spiritual purity, and the exercise of their authority over women is requisite for such self-control. This commitment to the values of purity and control ultimately becomes transferred in the modern period from the religious to the philosophical domain. The opposition between purity and sensual desire expressed by Augustine is reiterated in prevailing philosophical conceptions of rationality, which have devalued the role of feeling and desire. This detachment from the body is historically grounded, as Augustine demonstrates, in a distinctly andocentric perspective. From this standpoint, men provide the standard of purity against which women are constantly found lacking. Women face the impossible task of becoming pure in the midst of their intrinsically defiling nature. Although this association of embodiment, pollution, and women reflects a distinctly male perspective, it has been presented in both religious and philosophical traditions as an unbiased, all-encompassing truth. Consequently, the origin of this ascetic commitment to purity in a particularly male-centered world has been lost from view.

Conclusion

The troubled centuries that followed the establishment of imperial monarchy at Rome found the tradition of Western political thought at its most impoverished state. There had been failure all along the line-failure to face the implications of concentrated power, failure to indicate ways and means for recapturing a sense of participating membership, and failure to preserve the distinctive integrity of political knowledge. Hellenistic and Roman thinkers had struggled to account for the new magnitudes of politics, the extension of space, the centralization of power, and the unprecedented enlargement of the constituency, but in the end they had confessed to being unable to supply new theoretical constructs that were both political and intelligible. The attempted ordering of political phenomena through cosmological categories suggests that the newly enlarged magnitudes of politics had so far outdistanced the political understanding that only cosmic concepts appeared pertinent.

The reconstruction of political thought proved to be a long and arduous process extending over several centuries and manifesting odd twists and turns. It was a "process that began in paradox and ended in irony." With the default of philosophy, it fell to Christianity to revivify political thought. This may seem paradoxical in the light of the common belief that in its early phase Christianity professed a resolute indifference to political and social affairs and its followers appeared absorbed in "otherworldly" concerns. Admittedly, there is no difficulty in mustering evidence to show that in the first two centuries the Christians believed political affairs highly irrelevant to the fundamental problem of human existence. Their hopes were high that the "last days" were imminent, hence what need was there for Christians to turn to politics when the political order was part of a scheme destined to disappear in the Apocalypse.

Given these strongly apolitical tendencies, the thesis that the new religion contributed substantially to the revitalization of political theory can be sustained only by adopting a somewhat unorthodox approach. The significance of Christian thought for the Western political tradition lies not so much in what it had to say about the political order, but primarily in what it had to say about the religious order. The attempt of Christians to understand their own group life provided a new source of ideas for Western political thought. Christianity succeeded where the Hellenistic and late classical philosophies had failed, because it put forward a new and powerful ideal of community, which recalled men to a life of meaningful participation.

There was irony too in these developments. The remarkable spread of Christianity and the evolution of its complex institutional life were accompanied by a politicization of the Church, both in behavior and in language, which had the unintended effect of continuing the political education of the West. In pursuing religious ends, the leadership of the Church was compelled to adopt political ways of behavior and political modes of thought. The long tradition of civility which was built up "inside" the Church, and which became all the more important as the Church acted as residuary legatee of the Roman Empire, put the West eternally in debt; for the experience meant nothing less than that political ways of thought and action were preserved. The irony, however, lies in the fact that the Church paid a price, one that was strictly exacted at the Reformation, of a loss in religious vitality. The weakening of the Church not only allowed temporal rulers to establish their freedom of action and to prove how well they had learned their political lessons, but the politicization of religious thought, which had all along accompanied the merging of the purely religious identity of the Church into a politico-religious compound, opened the way for the development of an autonomous body of political theory which a compromised theology could not contain.

These developments had their beginnings in an event that is often overlooked in political theory but was crucial from the viewpoint of the early Christians. The drama of the Crucifixion had been enacted against a political backdrop; the Lord of the Christians had been put to death at the command of a political regime. This act made it impossible for Christians to take a strictly neutral attitude towards the political order. In addition, the complicated view that the Christian took of his own condition compelled him to confront the political order. Although he expressed contempt for the "world" and his conviction of its impermanency was strengthened by periods of Roman persecution.

The most comprehensive attempt at dealing with these problems is to be found in the writings of St. Augustine the first and perhaps the greatest of Christian synthesizers. The significance of his work was not that it solved any of the political ambiguities in Christianity but rather that it supplied a depth and sharpness, which rooted them more firmly into the western tradition. He made the supreme efiort to construct in the sharpest possible relief the religious identity of Christianity, its way of life and mission, its complex nature as an existential society as well as an intimation of a celestial society, its involvement in history and its ultimate triumph over time. Yet the ambiguities persisted; he recognized that at the existential level the Christian was politically implicated and crucially dependent on political society, so much so that the Augustine who could write of the notion of love with an unmatched passion and profundity was also the theorist of power, supplying the most persuasive case for coercing men's minds. These were ambiguities deeply rooted in Augustine's own life and personality; almost everything that he wrote carries the tensions of a passionate mind longing to rise above finite existence, and by the continued soaring of the mind, to attain to the unchangeable substance of God. The culmination of this system, woven of the most exquisite contraries found expression in the vivid symbolism of the two cities, of "the holy society" sustained by Christian virtues and the "earthly society" rent by human nature.

It is important not to be misled by the powerful antithesis of the two cities into concluding that Augustine was interested in manipulating the political order only as a convenient foil for the superiorities of the Church and the glories of the celestial city. Augustine could dwell on the bitter quarrels racked the earthly city and could speak of a deep enmity between the two e cities, but he was also prepared to allow that society was natural to man, than far from being an unmitigated evil, it was "better than all other human good," and that even a society "alienated from the true God" possessed degree of value.

Once the complexity of Augustine's ideas is recognized that the promise of a heavenly city was not taken by him to mean the political order had shrunk to insignificance, then we can better appreciate that the dualism of the two societies functioned to establish the identity: the political as well as the religious order. The intricate pattern of religion and politics, intersecting but not absorbing, was fashioned to teach that political and the spiritual were distinctive, however complementary might be at certain points; that while each ought to benefit the other, could achieve the other's salvation; and since it followed that the one not to be judged totally by the mission of the other, each had to be understood to an important degree in its own terms.

This problem assumed central importance in Augustine's famous discussion of whether the Roman state could be considered a true commonwealth. It provided a classic example of how the Christian adopted the older political concepts only to transform them. Augustine took Cicero's definition of a commonwealth—an association based on a common agreement concerning 'right and on a community of interests—and then raised the question of when conditions a commonwealth must satisfy before it could be considered just. Now the classical political writers, such as Plato and Aristotle, did not deny the existence of an absolute justice, but they did assume that an inquiry into the relationship between the "political" and the just ought to be directed at the kind of justice that was relevant to the peculiar nature of the political community. Augustine, however, followed a quite different method. Instead of seeking to discover what kind of justice a political order was capable he argued that Rome could never qualify under the Ciceronian definition because true justice had never been recognized. "Justice which is true justice resides only in that commonwealth whose founder and governor is Christ." But this conclusion obviously turned on a different definition of justice and a different conception of commonwealth than that of classical political theory, a definition of Christian righteousness founded on the love of God, and conception of a commonwealth transcending any human city.

It is a mark of Augustine's greatness that he was sensitive to the limitations inherent in this procedure. Augustine provided a detinition of commonwealth remarkable for its naturalism: "A people is a gathering of a multitude of rational beings united in fellowship by sharing a common love of the same things. This presented a striking contrast to the moral rigidity of the first definition where "true" justice had been restricted to the City of God and where every political society, past, present, or future, could be found deficient. This did not mean that the first definition was abandoned; it served instead as an absolute standard of justice. On the other hand, the naturalistic definition pointed to the possibility of establishing a gradation of commonwealth.

This can be stated differently by saying that Augustine's political theory contained a strong dialectical element in which the polarities of good and evil, flesh and spirit, Church and political society were lodged within a comprehensive and powerfully structured order which contained and directed these dynamics their predestined end.

6

Thomas Aquinas

> The government of any city-state or kingdom is best ordered when somebody appointed by virtue of personal excellence presides over everyone, with subordinates similarly governing by virtue of and in accordance with their true merits, and yet rulership belongs to everyone because anyone is eligible to be elected and each ruler is elected by everyone.

Thomas Aquinas (1225-1274) was born in Roccasecca, Italy near Naples. The son of a count and a member of a long-established feudal family, he outraged his family members when he entered the Dominican Order. At one point they went so far as to kidnap him and hold him prisoner in order to prevent his ordination. He studied and then taught theology in Paris, and his later career as a theologian included stays in Italy and then Paris again. Some of his writings were condemned by the Church soon after his death in 1274, but shortly thereafter, given the shifting winds of religious politics, he was canonized. He is reputed to have been the first person raised to sainthood by virtue of his teachings and his thought rather than by virtue of the performance of miracles. His philosophy is considered to be one of the glories of the high Middle Ages, and he ranks even today as one of the most important philosophers in the history of Western civilization.

It is obvious in reading Aquinas that he was considerably under the influence of Aristotle. His admiration for Aristotle was so great that he referred to this Greek thinker simply as 'The Philosopher'. Aquinas's own philosophy is a synthesis of Christian doctrine and Aristotelian thought. It has been claimed by some that his philosophy is merely eclectic and hence unoriginal, but this judgment ignores the genius involved in elaborating a systematic theory in which Aristotelian naturalism sits comfortably with the otherworldly attitudes of Christianity. As Aquinas saw it, Aristotle's work gives us deep insight into the secular dimension of human nature and the natural world. This secular view is not so much false as limited. Aristotle had no conception of the personal, providential God of Christianity, his deity being an entity who engages eternally in pure thought and pure thought alone. To attain an understanding of the Christian God, revelation is also required and hence pure or natural philosophy is not enough. Since, the natural power of understanding is not sufficient to see the essence of God, this power of understanding must come to it by divine grace. But admitting this does not diminish the importance of Aristotle's thought in understanding the natural order.

An Aristotelian Approach to Ethics

Aquinas's debt to Aristotle is perhaps even more apparent in his ethics than in other parts of his philosophy. As one commentator has put it, the theological ethics of Aristotle was, in general, sound, and that the Greek philosopher's way of thinking provided a philosophical backbone for a Christian ethics. Aquinas, like Aristotle, begins ethical inquiry with the question what is the good for human beings. Thus the notion of goodness is central to his ethics, as is the conviction that action is always aimed at an end or good, and ultimately aimed at the greatest, highest, most final good. But Aquinas's answer to the question of the good for human beings, while still very much Aristotelian in nature, has an obvious religious connotation, for the final good for a person turns out to be his perfection. Human perfection is what human fulfillment becomes when it is viewed as attaining a higher level of existence that puts human beings in touch with God and brings to completion God's plan for them. Life is seen by both Aristotle and Aquinas as a striving after the good, an attempt to achieve one's final end which alone brings fulfillment, the realization of one's potentialities, and happiness. But whereas for Aristotle one attains this end and lives the happy life in the natural world, among one's fellow citizens, for Aquinas the earthly life is but a preliminary step on the way to true happiness, achieved in the next life through union with God.

In his reading of human life and human nature, Aquinas reveals his religious perspective most clearly when he argues that nothing in the natural world totally satisfies our desires. A life of worldly goods, even a life of worldly virtue, leaves one dissatisfied and incomplete, with a sense that one has not made the most of one's life and not truly fulfilled one's inner nature and true purpose in life. Our desires remain unsatisfied by all temporal goods and accomplishments, and hence these desires reach beyond the temporal domain. Human beings are most strongly drawn to what fulfills and perfects them. As Aquinas puts it: Because in all things whatsoever there is an appetite for completion, the final end to which each moves marks its own perfect and fulfilling good. It turns out that this final end for human beings is God himself. Our ultimate end is uncreated good, namely God, who alone can fill our will to the brim because of his infinite goodness. We desire, most ultimately, to be united with God, to become one with him, to find our own joy and completion in him. Thus, complete and self- sufficient happiness is possible for us only in the next life when, through the grace of God, we are united with him, behold him, and enjoy his infinite goodness. God alone, the infinite good, will quiet the human heart.

But in this life, as we live in preparation for the next, it is human reason, which provides the tutelage and guidance required to attain earthly happiness. Although reason cannot grasp man's supernatural end or define the life by which it is to be attained, it can enable a human being to live the type of natural life ordained for him by God. And the picture Aquinas gives us of his life is essentially Aristotelian in nature. Human beings have a property or characteristic which sets them apart from all other things in the created universe: they are rational. The proper life for them to lead, then, is the life of reason. Reason is able to discern the ethical principles by means of which God intends us to live our lives. Furthermore, in living the life of reason, we are enabled to fulfill our potentialities, to actualize the modes of existence, which moves us closer to our final end, God. Reason permits us to grasp human nature and to live a life that accords with it.

In doing so, reason puts us in touch with natural law, the law that reflects in human nature the eternal law of God.

Natural Law and Human Behavior

Aquinas asserts that human beings are purposive beings: they act in order to attain goals; their desires move them toward ends that will satisfy these desires. According to Aquinas, there are three kinds of desires, which he also refers to as appetites or inclinations. First, there are natural inclinations shared with all other creatures. Second, there are sense appetites, among which are both concupiscible appetites for love and desire for pleasure and irascible appetites for fear and the desire to shun the harmful. These are shared with animals. Then, third, there are rational appetites whose object is the good as apprehended by reason. The latter appetites are conscious tendencies and ones over which we exercise control. In fact, in pursuing the objects of rational appetite, we manifest voluntary behavior or freedom of will, which sets us apart form the rest of nature. Free action is of the essence of human nature. We express this nature when our sense appetites are molded and guided by reason.

Aquinas raises the fundamental questions as to how does reason or will direct our activities. He wants to know the source of guidance concerning what things we ought to desire and pursue. These questions take us to the heart of the doctrine of natural law, a doctrine which, although it did not originate with Aquinas, is closely connected throughout subsequent history with his name and philosophy. The concept of natural law needs to be understood in terms of Aquinas's general definition of law and in relation to the concepts of eternal law and civil law. Law Aquinas defines as an ordinance of reason for the common good, promulgated by him who has the care of the community. This definition is most easily applied to the case of civil law, what Aquinas calls human law or positive law. A legislature is charged with the care of the community of citizens under its jurisdiction, and the legislators attempt, using their reason, to create laws that protect the public and provide it with the essentials of life. Such a law is backed up by sanctions, incentives to obey it most fundamentally the punishments that attach to any infringements of it. The existence of civil law is a fact of life in any form of organized social existence, but it is not, according to Christian believers, the only law. There is also the law of God, the rules expressing the divine reason which manifest themselves in the divine providence ruling the world. Aquinas expresses this notion of a higher law in the following passage:

> Granted that the world is ruled by divine Providence, it is evident that the whole community of the universe is governed by God's mind. Since God's mind does not conceive in time, but has an eternal concept, it follows that this law should be called eternal. Through his wisdom God is the founder of the universe of things and in relation to them he is like an artist with regard to the things he makes. Also he is the governor of all acts and notions to be found in each and every creature.

Aquinas and other orthodox Christians deny that the corporeal human being, whose soul in this life is housed within the material body, can directly understand the mind of God. Fortunately, however, God's laws have been incorporated into human nature, which therefore reflects them. The goals that God would have us seek, the forms of behavior he would have us follow-all these are built into the behavior that is natural for us. Thus, the percepts of eternal law correspond to the basic tendencies and inclinations of human beings. Natural inclinations direct us to goods, to those ends that God ordains as goods for human beings, as ways of perfecting human nature. By reflecting on these natural inclinations we become aware of what God has intended for us; we become aware of the human essence or ideal in accord with which God made us. And to this extent we come to appreciate God's Eternal Law. Now this sharing in the Eternal Law by intelligent creatures is what we call 'natural law'. Natural law is a dictate of reason, emanating from God's mind, reflected in natural inclinations, and apprehensible by human reason. Not all of God's laws, however, are reflected in human nature; those having to do with the religious obligations especially imposed on Christians are revealed by revelation. This subset of God's laws is referred to by Aquinas as Divine Law. But human nature embodies the laws that govern the activities of all human being qua natural creatures. Thus, it embodies the laws that can be directly grasped by reason without the aid of revelation laws dictating how all natural creatures should behave.

Natural Inclinations

What are these natural inclinations that reflect God's eternal laws? Given Aquinas's teleological conception of human nature, it follows that a basic inclination of all human beings is to seek the good together with an equally basic inclination to avoid what is not good, i.e., what is evil. Thus the first, most general principle of natural law is desire the good and shun evil. This principle has an ontological foundation in the nature of human beings, revealing as it does their most basic natural inclinations. Just as, Aquinas thinks, from the fundamental concept of being in the speculative or theoretical sphere we can derive the principle of non-contradiction, so from the fundamental practical concept of good we can derive the principle commanding us to seek the good and avoid evil. All other practical principles must be consistent with the basis demand that we seek good and avoid will, just as all theoretical principles must be consistent with the principle of non-contradiction.

Other general natural inclinations or tendencies can be noted reflecting the fact that human beings are simultaneously parts of physical nature, parts of the animal kingdom, and rational creatures. These inclinations yield additional general principles of natural law. First, all human beings attempt to sustain their existence, from which natural fact we can derive the law Conserve life and protect health. Some commentators have thought that the universal inclination to continue on existence yields the law that all life is to be respected and preserved. Second, being animals, humans naturally seek to propagate, from which inclination Aquinas derives the law commanding one to marry and multiply, or, more abstract put, bring order into one's sexual activities and relations. Third, as rational creatures, human beings are subject to still other precepts: There is in people an appetite for the good of their nature as rational, and thus it is proper to them, for instance, that they should know truths about God and about living in society. Correspondingly whatever this involves is a matter of natural law, for instance that people should shun ignorance, not offending others with whom they ought to live in civility, and other such related requirements. As rational creatures, we desire to know, and this inclination leads us to attempt to know the world and God. Moreover, human beings are social creatures who band together and live life as members of a group hence the command of natural law to live peacefully in a civic community, as well as the commands not to injure others and not to higher or obstruct their lawful activities. In general, natural law commands extend to all doing or avoiding of things recognized by the practical reason itself as being human goods.

Primary and Secondary Precepts

In both his early writing on natural law in the *Commentary of the Sentences* and in his late, mature writing on the subject in the *Summa Theologize* Aquinas makes a distinction between primary and secondary percepts of natural law. The basis for distinction changes to some extent from the early statement to the later one. In the *Commentary on the Sentences*, Aquinas relates the distinction between primary and secondary precepts to another distinction between primary and secondary ends of human action. Any action that circumvents one of the primary ends of action will violate a primary precept of natural law, whereas any action preventing the realization of a secondary end, but not circumventing the primary end, will violate a secondary percept. For instance, the primary end of the matrimonial state is the propagation of the species, while the secondary end is domestic harmony or tranquility. Monogamy serves both the primary and secondary ends. But, according to Aquinas, there may be circumstances in which polygamy is the best arrangement for ensuring the propagation of the species. In such cases, polygamy, even though it may violate the secondary end of matrimony, may still be approved as in accord with a primary precept of natural law. Accordingly, the moral demand for monogamous marriages is only a secondary percept. It appears that Aquinas made the distinction between primary and secondary ends of action in order to justify the fact that in the *Old Testament* the patriarchs are allowed to have more than one wife.

The natural distinction between primary and secondary precepts of moral law, although already present to some degree in the earlier commentary, as fully developed in the *Summa Theologize*. Here we are told that secondary precepts are those that are derived from primary precepts, either by a process of reasoning or a process of specification by which the general primary percepts are made concrete and determinate. Moreover, primary precepts are always true they hold universally, which is to say, without exception, e.g., it is always wrong not to place some restrictions on one's sexual relations. Secondary precepts may not hold in some circumstances, so they are not strictly the universal demand for monogamy is, therefore, a secondary, not a primary precept. Moreover, the primary precepts are self-evident. Any mind that understands the terms in which the primary precepts are expressed will grasp immediately that they are, and must be, true. Thus it is self-evident that human beings must live in society, and that they cannot do this if they harm one another and obstruct one another's lawful activities. Secondary precepts, on the contrary, are known in a manner subject to error. One may make a mistake in reasoning; for instance, one may make a mistake in deriving the secondary from the primary precepts. Although some experience of the world is necessary in order to understand any of the natural law precepts, none of them, therefore, is innate rendering the vague primary principles specific and determinate requires considerable experience with human life and the world. It follows that the secondary precepts do not possess the self-evidence of the primary ones.

In making the distinction between primary and secondary precepts, Aquinas shows that he is sensitive to the complexity of moral decision-making and understands the difficulty of arriving at moral judgments in the actual course of human life. While we do have the primary precepts as certain foundries and invariant guides, they do not address the detail of much actual moral experience. In concrete situations reason is to be our guide, but self-evidence is unavailable and error always possible. Rational reflection on our actual experience is essential for determining what we ought to do in these concrete situations. Different situations may require different solutions, and we must always be on the lookout for mistakes, blindness, and bias in our experience and the judgments based on it. Furthermore, when one turns from the derivation of secondary precepts of natural law to the application of one of these precepts to a particular case, Aquinas follows Aristotle closely in emphasizing the need for what Aristotle called 'perception'. It is the individual person who must judge whether or not the precept applies. Thus natural law doctrine, as taught by Aquinas, is not as rigid and formalistic as it is sometimes made out to be.

Reason, Human Goods, and the Will

It must be stressed that for Aquinas natural law is a dictate of reason, not a physical law. For one thing, we are accustomed to think of physical laws as making it impossible for material things to act inconsistently with them. Stones and human bodies have no choice but to obey the physical laws of gravity. A dictate of reason, however, can be disobeyed. Hence, in saying that humankind is governed by natural law, Aquinas is not claiming that we always in point of fact act in accordance with this law. Often, being the sinners we are, we fail to do so. Our failure is one of not living up to the dictates of reason as these dictates are embodied in what it is natural for us to desire and do.

Natural law prescribes the proper goods for human beings, the proper objects of desire, striving, and action. These goods include some that we share with animals, e.g., propagation. Animals, however, act in this fashion without choice, which is to say, without reason. Rational human beings, on the contrary, are under an obligation to follow reason, their characteristic feature. Hence, they should maintain themselves in existence and engage in sexual activities because natural law demands it. Physical goods thus become part of human good by virtue of being required by reason, by natural law. Thus, as one Theistic philosopher has expressed it, Sex is a human good, not just as such but insofar as it is engaged in consciously, purposively, and responsibly.

Natural law is the set of propensities built into our nature which followed, will lead to the perfection of our being. Hence, in seeking to fulfill or perfect ourselves, we must follow his law. The cardinal virtues, including temperance, courage, and justice, are in effect ways of following natural law and thus ways of perfecting our nature as with Aristotle, they promote what we all seek: happiness. Aquinas follows Aristotle in thinking of a virtue as a habit or disposition, not in the sense of an unreflective, unreasoning pattern of behavior but rather as an active tendency reflecting rational deliberation. Aquinas also follows Aristotle in believing that thought alone is not enough to produce actions and, ipso facto, good actions. The appetites or desires must be trained so as to follow reason and seek the good. The virtues include these trained, reflective desires, namely the concupiscible and irascible sense appetites transformed by the influence of reason into rational appetites or will. Once we have attained the virtues, they direct us in accordance with the precepts of natural law. Thus, the guides to a proper, fulfilling and perceptive human life are the law without and the virtues within.

The notion of the will plays an important role in Aquinas's thought. Will is that faculty in us which tends toward or desires God, being, our best good, our ultimate, self-sufficient, and complete good. Will is an intellectual power that directs one to one's end. The use of reason in the determination of means to one's end is a matter of choice. In manifesting rational appetite, will expresses itself as love of the good, and hence love of God. Although in this life, we cannot have complete or adequate knowledge of God, in knowing what we do about him through the use of reason we can grasp him as our greatest good, and hence we can love him. It is in loving him that we come closest to him in this life, reaching out to him with our will in an effort to imitate him and ultimately to be united with him.

One of the essential aspects of the human will is that it is free. It has the capacity to seek and love God, but it also has the capacity to turn away from him and love the things of this world more than his, pleasure, say, or power. It has the capacity to follow virtue, but also the capacity to sin. It can follow natural law, or repudiate it. One exercises free will when one's actions proceed from the will in pursuit of ends apprehended by reason. Thus, one's actions are voluntary when one knows what one is doing and when one desires the objects or ends of one's actions in light of one's knowledge of them. Again, the influence of Aristotle is apparent. It is also noteworthy that Aquinas's concept of free will is not that of some interior and mysterious action of mind. It is, on the contrary, more like informed desire issuing in overt behavior.

Moral Knowledge

Central to Aquinas's vision of human nature is his belief that human reason is capable of apprehending basic ethical principles and articulating an ethical system based on rational reflection. Reason accomplishes this task by considering the nature of man in society and understanding the natural inclinations built into this nature by God. Part of the task involves grasping the first principles of natural law; another part consists in the deduction of more specific precepts from the first principles. According to Aquinas, rational human beings have the ability to recognize immediately that certain moral principles are true this, for instance, is the case with the most general principle of natural law, Seek good and avoid evil. This immediate grasp of truth is referred to by Aquinas as synergetic. It is the result of a natural disposition or tendency built into human nature, and it is the practical equivalent of the disposition to grasp in an immediate and infallible manner the basic truths of logic and the first principles of theoretical reason. Sundress is infallible; it provides a certain, indubitable insight into truth and therefore cannot be in error or lead us astray. It is the foundation of all moral knowledge, for if we could not apprehend with certainty morality's fundamental principles, there would be no moral knowledge at all.

Interestingly, Aquinas describes the deduction of specific moral precepts from the first principles as an exercise of conscience. Today most people think of conscience as a sort of immediate vision of what is right or wrong, and they might be tempted to equate conscience with Aquinas's sundress. But for Aquinas conscience is a matter of reasoning: the application of general principles to concrete situations. Conscience, for instance, will tell us how to conduct our sexual lives in the particular circumstances in which we find ourselves. The operation of conscience requires that we put together general principles and statements of fact that describe particular circumstances; with the principles and statements of fact as premises, we exercise conscience in deriving the conclusions that deductively follow from these premises. Mistakes are possible in such a process mistakes not only about the matters of fact but about the logical relations between premises and conclusion. Conscience, then, is not infallible, but, according to Aquinas, it should nevertheless be our guide. It would be wrong for us not to follow it, even if it turns out to be in error.

A person who has perfected the power of practical reasoning has thereby developed a virtue, a habit. This virtue is an intellectual one, designated by Aquinas as prudence. Prudence amounts to right reason about action, the tendency to think correctly about what ought to be done. But prudence is not simply an intellectual virtue; it is also a moral one. This reflects Aquinas's view that for people to act well, it is requisite that not only their reason be well disposed through a habits of intellectual virtue, but also that there appetite be well disposed through habit of moral virtue. The prudent person is more, then, one who possesses practical knowledge. Appetite, the will, must be shaped or molded by moral virtue, so that practical knowledge is put to use in action. Thus, the prudent person is one who chooses well in accordance with practical reason.

Aquinas's system of philosophy permits the expansion of the above accounts of virtue and goodness in many directions and in great detail. Enough has been said, however, to give one a sense of how, borrowing from Aristotle, he developed a highly sophisticated Christian moral philosophy. Because of its elaborate and detailed metaphysical and epistemological dimensions, it appeals greatly to Christians who would not sacrifice reason as they pursue their faith and act as natural creatures in a providential world. Theistic ethics in large part remains with us today in the form of the ethics of Roman Catholicism. And its doctrine of natural law has been of immense significance in Western culture since the time of Aquinas. Given this significance, it is appropriate that we conclude with a brief critical discussion of the notion of natural law.

Criticisms of Natural Law Theory

Many philosophers believe that the concept of natural law illegitimately combines a normative and a descriptive account of human behavior. Natural law is supposed to reflect our natural inclinations, the ways in which we tend to behave. In this sense, statements of natural law are descriptive accounts, and they are true to the extent that they describe our natural inclinations correctly. In doing so they give us an account of our essential human nature. But these natural inclinations also amount to ways in which we ought to behave if we are to behave as God commands or as divine reason demands. Hence, to postulate natural inclinations is to put forward norms for behaviour. These norms may or may not be met by actual behavior, insofar as, being creatures of free will, we may choose not to follow God's commands and thus may behave in ways inconsistent with natural law. Thus, statements of natural law are normative, telling us how we ought to behave. In this way, the theory of natural law combines both descriptive and normative accounts of human behavior. The question is whether this combination of factual and evaluative statements is a coherent one.

The concept of natural law offers the promise of providing a factual, objective basis for moral precepts. The argument of natural law theory goes like this: human nature being of a certain kind, it follows that deviations from the natural course of behavior and perverse and hence evil. As one commentator has put it the idea here is that human beings are fulfilled or made happy in ways which can be seen by noting what they are But if human beings often do not act as natural law prescribes, then actual human nature is not reflected in natural law. Understood descriptively, statements of natural law are often false. In that case, natural law theory does not succeed in grounding moral precepts in human nature. Natural law theory may give us a normative set of moral principles, but it does not show how these principles are justified in light of human nature for the good reason that natural law does not tell us the way human nature always in fact is. Thus the attempt of natural law theory to depict natural law as both normative and descriptive to provide moral norms and their grounding in human nature is perceived by many ethical thinkers to be incoherent and hence to fail.

A proponent of natural law theory might response by claiming that the above argument fails to acknowledge the place of reason in natural law theory. Human beings are rational animals, which does not mean that they always follow reason but that they have a capacity, and, indeed, a natural inclination to do so. When human beings act in ways inconsistent with natural law, they are acting contrary to their rational inclinations. We all have a natural inclination to band together into social groups, but we do not always act in ways consistent with the rational insight that being social animals requires that we not harm others or infringe their lawful rights. We all have a natural sexual drive, but we do not always act in ways consistent with the rational insight that the good aimed at by the sexual drive are not best achieved by a life of sexual promiscuity. Thus our rational inclinations, which are part of our nature as rational beings, can and do ground the normative imperatives of natural law.

But who, the critic might respond, is to say what ends and goods of human life are rational and thereby natural? How does reason determine, for instance, that the propagation of the species is the end of sexual activity, or of marriage? In calling such an end rational, isn't the natural law theorist simply assuming his own value judgments? Implicit, undefended value judgments may slip in at other junctures as well. It has been argued, for instance, that one cannot simply derive by reason the secondary precept one must not kill from the primary precept one must not harm another person. The inference from the one precept to the other requires the additional value judgment that killing a person is harming her. While many people may accept this judgment, many would not do so in an unqualified manner. What about euthanasia, for instance? This is an instance of killing a person, but is it also an instance of harming a person? Defenders of euthanasia would say no. Hence, one might agree that one ought not harm an individual without agreeing that one ought not to kill that individual. Which is to say that not everyone agrees with the implicit judgment that killing a person is a matter of harming him. Reason and nature do not speak with an unequivocal voice with respect to the moral relation between harming and killing.

While such an argument is a strong one against a rigid doctrine of natural law, we have seen that Aquinas admits considerable flexibility into his account of natural law, specifically where it comes to the derivation of secondary natural law precepts and the application of these precepts to individual cases.

But Aquinas is a good essentialist. He follows Plato and Aristotle in believing that human beings have an essence. Hence, the ends at which human natural inclinations aim are essential ends, those that comprise the human essence. Reason is a faculty that allows us to comprehend essences, including our own, and hence to see that some ends are fulfilling of the human essence and for this reason are perfecting ends. If one rejects essentialism, as many philosophers today do so, especially those who subscribe to the later philosophy of Wittgenstein, then the notion that some ends are natural and essential will be uninviting. A critic of essentialism would maintain that human nature does not have neatly identifiable boundaries there is no set of necessary and sufficient conditions for someone being a human being, or for some activity being distinctively human. Human beings and their activities come in a variety of shapes and forms, and it is we, not human nature itself, who decide what is and what is not human or natural. And different people may decide differently, so that there is no objective answer to the question of what a human being essentially is. But essentialism is by no means philosophically moribund, which means that natural law theory will still be with us for a while.

The big question, which Aquinas leaves unresolved, is who is to interpret the moral law and judge when there is a conflict between it and the civil law. In the middle Ages from time to time the Church tended to claim to be the interpreter of the moral law and the judge of any conflicts between it and the law of the State. But there is nothing in Aquinas' theory, which gives the Church this, right. The interpretation of the moral law is the business of 'natural reason' and the Church authorities have to use the ordinary processes of reason just like the rest of us.

Later Catholic thinkers distinguish between the 'direct power' of the Church over the political order, and what they call the 'indirect power' of the Church vis-à-vis the State. They reject the first, but they argue that in pursuit of its proper spiritual and religious purposes the Church may sometimes run up against the certain law of the State. Thus for example the Church might, in pursuit of its religious mission, set up its own educational system; but then it might come into conflict with a law of the State decreeing that only a State-controlled education system will be tolerated. In this case the Church may, in defence of its own proper religious interests, legitimately protest against the policy of the State. Clearly the theory of the 'indirect power' of the Church can be interpreted in a very permissive way so that the Church is allowed a good deal of interference in politics. But, by and large Catholic thinkers, including the nineteenth and twentieth century Popes in their statements on social question have resisted this temptation and kept fairly closely to the position established by Aquinas.

Aquinas' ideas have also been developed by certain twentieth century Catholic thinkers with reference to liberal democratic 'pluralist' societies where the State largely opts out of the realm of private morality and restricts itself to providing a framework of peace and order within which people can, as Mill puts it, follow out their own 'experiments in living'. Catholic political philosophers such as John Courtney Murray welcome the advent of the liberal democratic state in that it has no religious or anti-religious commitment. The Church, like any other group, is free to live within such a society and to fulfill its specific religious task without being tempted to play politics. In the older 'confessional' societies in which the Church had a privileged place, the Church's religious mission was often compromised by its political commitments. In modern liberal democratic societies, the Church cannot demand any special or favoured place: it must take its chance in promulgating its views with other groups. But because of this the Church's essential spiritual mission is more clearly manifested.

What point do the ideas of Augustine and Aquinas have for contemporary political theory? No doubt, the medieval debates over the relations between Church and State do not now have much application in modern liberal democratic societies where the Christian churches have for the most part lost their special and favoured position and churchmen no longer wish to 'play politics'. There are, still some like the 'Moral Majority' in the United States who argue that the State should actively espouse specific religious views, and in Islamic societies such as Iran there is a strong tendency towards theocracy with the religious authorities assuming political power and using the law to enforce Islamic beliefs and precepts. The theory for the two societies elaborated by Augustine and Aquinas obviously has something to say with regard to these theocratic tendencies.

In more general terms, Augustine's political 'realism' has continuing relevance in that it reminds us that in practice in the political order self-interest remain a pervasive factor, and in that it warns us not to expect too much from politics. Augustine lentando that the two major defects of fallen man, perversity of will and ignorance infect every action that the State takes through its all too human agents. Since all those who bear political power- rulers, officials, judges, policemen, soldiers – are only men, their judgment is fallible, their information is inevitably inadequate and often incorrect, and their decisions are frequently biased by passion and self-interest. their actions, even when they are successful never dispose of the problems that they face, whether these be domestic issues or foreign relations.

Aquinas' relevance lies in a different direction. As we have seen, Aquinas insists that the main instrument of the State, law, necessarily has a moral basis. Any positivistic theory of law, which defines it merely in terms of the will of the 'sovereign' – whatever the state decrees through its duly appointed legislative and judicial bodies – is defective for Aquinas and his followers. Thus, it has been argued that it is only on a natural law basis that a justification can be provided for human rights claims by the individual against the decrees of the State and for international law a legal system which transcends particular State systems. The contemporary rejuvenation of Aquinas' natural law theory by Finnish and others shows how much point and meaning it still has even for those who do not subscribe to Aquinas' Christian world-view.

State and Church

Aquinas argued that our conceptual reach exceeds our practical grasp, and this enabled him to go on to speak of the complementarily of the philosophical and theological ends of man. Hence, as a Christian theologian, Aquinas finds a place for the role of the church as well as the 'state' and he adds: 'But God promised us complete happiness when we shall be like the angels in heaven'. Without God's promise, Aquinas seems to suggest that humans will never be completely at peace because their minds will always be thinking and their wills desiring infinitely. Under such conditions, and with intellectual effort, imperfect social and political happiness is man's lot. Aquinas claims that the activities of thinking a mind's natural object is the universal and unqualified good. Conceptualizing and willing are not engaged in a void and men can only be moral deliberators and agents within moral communities. The promise of the extrinsic good comes through the teachings of the church. In this way, the natural and supernatural ends of man are harmonized.

For Aquinas, men are so constituted as to be capable, through deliberative choice, to follow through their reasoning by means of intentional acts. And human acts are judged by their ends. Aquinas concludes that killing a man can be ordered to diverse ends, for instance, upholding justice or satisfying anger. In the first way, it will be an act of virtue, in the second, of vice. Human acts, which are deliberately willed, by definition, have as their natural ends the unqualified, universal good. If someone acts for an end that is not the good, he acts against his nature and is to be held morally responsible for so doing.

In the language of the two-sword theory, the ideal state's rational laws punish the vicious and irrational by coercive or rehabilitating means. But behind the function of the 'state' as directing and co-ordinating the common good, the church guards the vision of men acting to secure the unqualified, universal good and the natural order of reason. Positive civil law is trumped by natural law. Since through virtuous living man is further ordained to a higher end which consists in the enjoyment of God, then temporal government is subject in spiritual things to priests, most importantly to the successor of St. Peter, the vicar of Christ, the pope, as to

Christ. It pertains to the office of public authority and therefore political rule, to promote the good life of the multitude in such a way as to make it suitable for the attainment of salvation. Since what pertains to beatitude is learned from God's law, scripture, the church is universal educator, and the state is charged with finding the means to secure the end taught. Aquinas does not, thereafter, indicate that should a state not function in way that suit its role of directing men to their ultimate goal, the institutional church has coercive ways and means of responding. Nor does he think a ruler can impose on individual subjects or citizens a legal duty to pursue their ultimate ends. But he does imply that a multitude that is church-educated and state–governed will itself be capable of judging that its ends are not being adequately pursued, and it will devise the way and means of removing public officials who do not serve the common good in its ultimate, Selvific sense.

The nature of man realizes itself through action. No creature can attain its natural end without some activity natural to its by which it tends towards its ends. Deeds on the part of man are therefore required for happiness, says Aquinas, not because of any inadequacy of the divine power that bestows happiness, but for preserving the order of things, that is, for maintaining reality. And there is a crucial role for a 'state' that is devoted to the common good to play in enabling them to conform to their natures and act according to reason.

Free Will and Responsibility

When Aquinas insisted that whatever we choose, we as humans are the initiating and controlling principles of our individual and collective futures, precisely because we deliberate and act in whatever ways we do. As far as human affairs are concerned, Aquinas following Aristotle human beings are the originating principle of those things in the future they do as the controllers of their own acts, and that they have in their powers to do or not to do. They do not only act by natural instinct but by deliberating and judging what is to be done. People who do what they do not want to do', he says, 'may not have freedom of action but they do have freedom of choice.' And Aquinas makes it clear that 'if lives in a society whose customs and traditions are not in accord with what a reasonable nature would consider appropriate, then by deliberating, a person who is accustomed to do something can, indeed should, act against custom and tradition'. Humans are not obliged to obey irrational laws, which, he argues, are not even worthy of being called 'laws'. In this life, humans are obliged by reason. We shall see how far he takes this theory of resistance to irrationality.

In his treatise on the laws, Aquinas discussed the four laws that govern an individual's ethical behaviour and the community's political practices. Instead of socializing public power, as had some contemporary theologians who followed an Augustinian tendency, Aquinas emphasized the autonomy of the natural order in a universe of secondary causes that leads, ultimately, to the primary cause, God. Hence, he showed no interest in empires as products of force and conquest, nor was he concerned with a notion of government as the product of human artifice. Government is natural. Philosophically, he showed very little interest in historical kingdoms or republics, although he provides examples of current practices or he cites Roman history, to illustrate his philosophical arguments. He is directly interested in the common good and the mean to its realization by a multitude of men who, as free subjects, find themselves together with common interests which require direction.

Thirteenth-century theological works also began to include a distinct section on the laws. When Aquinas included his own 'treatise on the laws' in his *Summa Theologize* he drew on the canon and Roman law tradition in a selective way. Aquinas preferred the understanding of Ulpian, for whom three laws could be distinguished: a natural law, separate from the law of nations, which could be described as that which nature teaches all animals, and it therefore applied to man's as well as animals' instincts. Aquinas adapts Stoic principles, Aristotle's teleology, and a neo-patronized Christian metaphysics of participation. In an age when the rational aspect of the natural law had become dominant, commentators have observed the distinctiveness of Aquinas's positing in his wishing to accommodate irrational instinctive aspects of natural behaviour in his understanding of the natural law. He would emphasize an intrinsic natural instinct or principle in men, which consists in the dictates of natural reason in matters common to man and animals. This enables irrational animals as well as humans to participate in their respective ways in the eternal law or reason, an extrinsic principle with a divine purpose. Rational creatures participate in a distinctive way – intellectually and rationally – in the divine purposes, but they also participate by natural instincts in that purpose, just as irrational creatures participate in the divine purpose by natural instinct.

Natural Human Community

As a Christian Aristotelian, Aquinas was interested in community (civitas) as a system of relations between individual men and groups thereof. The relationship is based on the naturalness of linguistic communication. He underlined the communicative dimension of political groupings, especially when he commented on Aristotle's discussion of language. In his unfinished Commentary on Aristotle's *Politics,* he absorbed word communication, communities, communion political and its synonym civitas to correspond to Aristotle's polis. He says that language has been given to men by nature, which does nothing in vain, and it is designed for what men communicate between one another regarding the useful and not useful, the just and the unjust. It therefore follows that since communication on these points constitutes the domain of the city, man is an animal, naturally domestic and political, and this demonstrates the natural character of 'the political communication' or the political community, this resting on the natural character of linguistic communication. Indeed, unlike Augustine's view of the extraordinary lack of success in linguistic communication, for both Aristotle and Aquinas communication presupposes stable, shared assumptions about the way things are and the kinds of agents we are.

In his *Summa Theologian's* treatise on the laws, Aquinas calls natural laws those stable, underlying principles of moral practices that always lie beneath the more plural variations that emerge in cultural living. Behind the customs and civil laws that are particular to historical communities, lays a moral perception that to engage in certain behaviour as right or wrong, whatever the independent sanction in the civil or customary law. These primary practical principles are arrived at by induction and are naturally known ends prior to the development of any virtue as means to them. Human moral discourse, then, is constructed on a set of foundational principles, which may be encapsulated as: 'the good is to be pursued and done and the evil avoided'. Thereafter, whatever thing prudence, or practical reason, naturally grasps to be particular human goods as means to the human end, fall under the already known precept of the natural law as to what is to be done or avoided. As with Aristotle, humans do not know which inclinations are natural prior to an understanding of what the human good is. Like animals, humans have sexual inclinations, and inclination to care for their young. But to humans alone belong the further inclinations to know, converse and to live in society together.

None of these inclinations is a matter of choice. They are the natural law, and the human species has its own mode of participation in the divine ordering of things, the eternal law. The whole community of the universe is governed by divine reason, which Aquinas calls the eternal law, and the rational guidance of created things on the part of god has the quality of law. All created things, and not simply humans, participate to some degree in this eternal law.

In sum, all laws, divine, natural and civil are interlinked. Every species has its own nature or end, and man achieves his specific end, his characteristic virtue or excellence, by acting according to reason. Through a rational consideration of his natural instincts, man comes to learn the general principles of the law of nature, and hence this knowledge is not the consequence of Christian revelation: natural reason is a sufficient guide. But the law of nature is also to be found in divine law, scripture, and, for Aquinas, there is no contradiction between the positive law contained in scripture and the law of nature as it applies to man. The foundation of human morality is the natural law, and in grace not abolishing but perfecting nature, revelation is joined to nature. But it is the natural law, and hence natural reason, that is the standard by which all civil, positive laws of any state may be judged. In the particular circumstances of a historical community, human lawmakers are allowed certain latitude to establish in detail, and according to changing circumstances, what is ordained by the natural law.

Aquinas says that a king who is concerned for his own well-being and not for the common good is a tyrant, by definition. And he says that a scheme should be carefully worked out which would prevent the multitude ruled by a king from falling into the hands of a tyrant. In particular, once the king is established, the government of the kingdom must be so arranged that opportunity to tyrannize is removed. Furthermore, his power is to be tempered. The details are not elaborated in these fragments. Should the king stray into tyranny, but if not to excess, then he is to be tolerated; but if to excess, then the multitude maintains the right to depose him, for he has not kept the covenant with his subject and did not act faithfully as the office of a king demands. Public office is a fiduciary power, and its incumbent is open to removal if the common good is not pursued.

Aquinas is theorizing in the midst of a society with a multitude of consensual practices. Hence, he says that to order affairs to the common good, by law, is the task either of the whole community or of some one person who represents it. And the promulgation of the law is the business either of the whole community or of that public person whose duty is the care of the common good. Not only should all have some share in sovereignty in order to maintain peace and stability, but all should have some share in sovereignty because of the principle that every man, in so far as he is rational, participates somehow in government according to the judgment of his reason. Human laws are never infallible since they are not the conclusions of demonstrative science, but rather, deal with contingent thing that are possible. Hence, human laws are continuously open to rational scrutiny and change. The validity of the civil law depends on its being just, that is, reasonable. And an irrational law is not obliging on the individual. However, the consequences, for the individual who judges that promulgated law is not rational and therefore not binding, are not always clear.

In his early *Commentary* Aquinas argued that irrational laws established by self-seeking tyrants rather than by community-minded sovereigns are not obliging and that the overthrow of such government is praiseworthy and not to be considered seditious. But he added in the later *Summa* that unjust positive laws do not oblige in the forum of reasonable conscience, unless, perhaps, to avoid scandal or riot; on this account a man may be called to yield his rights. And if the disorder and scandal that weal result from the toppling of a tyrant by the community were likely to lead to even greater harm and disturbance than already existed, then overthrowing the government is not advisable. There is never, for Aquinas, a private right to depose or kill tyrants. There is, however, a public right to perform such action, a deed that may only be carried out by public authority. This is an idea with an important future in Western political theory.

Aquinas is clear, however, that should one be commanded by public authority to commit sin, one is obliged not to obey the command, and he cites the Acts of the Apostles: 'we must obey God rather than man'. The kinds of unjust laws he has in mind here are laws of tyrants, which promote idolatry or something else against divine law. Such laws exceed the power of public authority and are to be resisted.

The Mixed Constitution

It seems that Aquinas modified his idea of public duty with the notion of utility, but a doctrine of subjective, individual rights exercisable in the public sphere is not elaborated. Yet, he insisted that all human law must be directed to the common welfare of the city or state. Human law is promulgated by the ruler of t he community according to the particular regime that has been established. He is most in favour of monarchy, but one which has the characteristics of a mixed government that is constituted by and takes advice from the feudal nobility and reflects the opinions of the wise, and wealthy, and the entire people. Aquinas therefore revises the contemporary neo-Platonist support for 'feudal, absolute' monarchy. He looks to a state's unification in a sovereign who directs the common good as a public official with law-making powers. These powers are derived from the represented will of member's mixed constitution. The mixed constitution is Aquinas's interpretation of Aristotle's polity, but its characteristics conform more to the operations of medieval communities, legally redefined in Roman law terms.

According to the standard view, by nature all things are common, but Aquinas asks whether natural law can be changed. He argued that many things over and above natural law have been added, by divine law and by human laws, which are useful to social life. Common possession and universal liberty are said to be of natural law put private possession and slavery exist, not by natural law but by rational human contrivance for the utility of human life. Private property according to civil law is therefore permissible and is a conclusion of natural law. The division of the community into spheres of private is, no more than a utilitarian conclusion of reason in the circumstances to further peace and commerce. It results from human agreement, which, thereafter, is enshrined in positive law. but beyond the satisfaction of limited human needs and modest profit, the superabundance possessed by any individual is owed to the poor by natural right and it is to be used for the common welfare. It is left to individuals to make provision for the poor from their own wealth, except in cases of urgent necessity when a starving person may take what legally belongs to another and not be considered to have obtained such through robbery. For what is taken by God's command, God being the owner of the universe, cannot be against the owner's will, and hence cannot be considered theft. Private property is therefore circumscribed by a prior natural necessity and morality.

Conclusion

Is Aquinas's political theory new? And it is penetrated by Aristotelian insights, which were not, yet, taken up by all theorists, so that Aquinas would, for some time to come, be of immense influence largely within his own order alone. While there also is a Ciceronian legacy that has been absorbed into Aquinas's perspective, it is not as pure or pervasive as is Aristotle's overall influence. Cicero and other Roman moralists are, in Aquinas's writings, always filtered through canonist and civilian discourse, where they are given either a Christian or an Aristotelian 'spin'.

Cicero's condemnation of a state that redistributed property was rejected not only by radical fringe groups in medieval society. Aquinas in particular understood there to be a natural claim on anyone's superfluity of property, not least, the claim of a poor man who ought not to be considered to have stolen from a legitimate owner what he needs to keep himself alive. For Aquinas, this indicated that the particular conclusions of primary moral law were to be taught both by church and state' and were meant to be a part of the moralizing perspective of state. Although, like Aristotle, he did not think the 'state' has moral responsibilities in actively creating an ambience where men do choose to share their possessions with others.

The newness in Aquinas's approach to ethics and politics, then, is the newness of the twelfth-and thirteenth-century naturalism. It is the newness of the scholastics' recognition of the comprehensive perspective of Aristotle, brought into a systematic whole for Christians by Aquinas's efforts. But it goes beyond contemporary naturalism by reinstating rational man in the order of nature and thereby finding a place for man both as body and mind, as a creature of natural instinct and rational deliberation. Consequently, it affirms that man, as that kind of being, is to be actively involved in shaping and sustaining the polity as a means to his final end.

7

Niccolo Machiavelli

> I am well aware that many have held and still hold the opinion, that the affairs of this world are so controlled by fortune and by the divine power that human wisdom and foresight cannot modify them; that, in fact, there is no remedy against the decrees of fate, and that therefore it is not worthwhile to make any effort, but to yield unconditionally to the power of fortune. This opinion has been generally accepted in our times because of the great changes that have taken place, are still being witnessed every day, and are beyond all human conjecture. In reflecting upon this at times, I am myself in some measure inclined to that belief; nevertheless, as our free will is not entirely destroyed, I judge that it may be assumed as true that fortune to the extent of one half is the arbiter of our actions, but that she permits us to direct the other half, or perhaps a little less, ourselves.

Machiavelli (1469-1527) descended from a Florentine family, which had risen to major public office during the fourteenth century, but he was not a member of the Great Council or could hope to be elected to the civic magistracies. Machiavelli was concerned intimately and passionately with the political life of his time. His father was a Florentine lawyer of ancient family and moderate means and he grew up during the golden age of Florentine culture under Lorenzo Medici. When the French rode into the city unopposed Machiavelli was still an unknown young man yet unnoticed by his literary contemporaries and apparently with no writing of his own to show. The events of the last years of the fifteenth century made a deep and lasting impression on him. He saw the collapse of the Medici and was impressed by the instability of a government not based on the good will of the people. He witnessed the strife of the Florentine factions during the stormy period of Savonarola's domination and realized the need for powerful government based on internal unity. Very soon, he was to wrestle political problems at close hand.

The Florentines followed the sensible practice of giving state employment to men of letters. In 1498 when he was about thirty he was appointed secretary and second chancellor becoming in effect a fairly senior civil servant whose duty it was to serve the executive committees of the government; his work brought him mainly diplomatic responsibilities although he was also employed on administrative and military errands. Machiavelli held office fourteen years until the downfall of the republic in 1512.

Machiavelli was not an outstandingly successful diplomat. In any case, despite the importance of those to whom he was sent he was never in a position to negotiate with decisive authority. But he traveled widely and kept his eyes open and in his letters, dispatches and commentaries of this period can be found the ideas based on shrewd observation which he later developed in his major works. In particular, he showed his genius for grasping the fundamental political condition of the states he visited basing characteristic generalizations on a multitude of carefully observed details. It was during this period too that he becomes increasingly obsessed by the need for Florence to control a strong militia of her own instead of relying on mercenary troops or the fluctuating help of allies.

In November 1512 after he had already hopefully written letters of advice on government to the Medici his movements were restricted. A few months later suspected of being involved in a conspiracy against the new rulers he was imprisoned and tortured but subsequently exonerated and released. He retired to his small family property at San Casino he could just see the buildings of Florence from there and wonder what was going on and an intense period of literary activity began.

He was also introduced to the Medici household and his hopes of office revived. After carrying out a few commercial commissions of little importance, he at last enjoyed a brief return to public life. He visited Rome where he received a subsidy from Pope Clement for writing the history of Florence. He failed to persuade the Pope to do anything practical about his plan for establishing a militia but was then give responsibility for a scheme to fortify the walls of Florence. Ironically his craving for official employment meant that when the republic was restored Machiavelli was to some extent identified with the Medici and was therefore suspected and ignored. Soon after he fell ill with violent stomach trouble and he died in June 1527. According to his son, he left his family in considerderable poverty.

We know comparatively little about Machiavelli's family life. About 1502 he married a Marietta Cosine by whom he had six children. She seems to have been devoted to him ands probably to have been sadly neglected by a husband whose heart was in political affairs. It is doubtful if he was as loose -living as he has been supposed. One notorious letter which he wrote to his friend Francesco Vector describing an encounter with a hideous prostitute was perhaps more a literary adventure than anything else.

He was certainly a man of strong emotions far removed from the cold calculating deceiver of the legend. But if he could be passionate when aroused, the general impression left by his life and work is of a man withdrawn from the crowd standing aside with a slight contemptuous smile on his face. It is surely possible to reconcile an intellectual aloofness and arrogance with a restless urge for active participation in political life.

We have a picture of young Machiavelli as a man of middle height, slender figure, sparkling eyes, dark hair rather a small head, a slightly aquiline nose, a tightly closed mouth. All about him bore the impress of a very acute observer and thinker but not that of one ankle to wield much influence over other. He could not cagily rid himself of the sarcastic expression continually playing round his mouth and flashing from his eyes which gave him the air of a cold and impassible calculator while nevertheless he was frequently ruled by his powerful imagination some time led away by it to an extent befitting the most fantastic of visionaries.

He was a man too capable of great exertions. Because of its shrewd psychological insight, its prophetic quality and its hard vehement prose *The Prince* has never lost the power to shock. The artist in Machiavelli as much as the analyst is often responsible for the shocks. He loved antithesis and generalization; he was intuitive rather than logical. He constantly dramatized his remarks and exaggerated his conclusions for the sake of impact. His delight in bold sweeping statements, his admiration of efficiency at all costs and his admonitions to the Italian princes to respond to foreign ruthlessness with equal toughness almost account for the indignation which the book has aroused throghout the centurics.

The language of *The Prince* is not as modern as many of its sentiments. Some words and phrases are repeated frequently in all Machiavelli's writings: words like Onore, Gloria, Fortuna, Necessity and Virtue. These are key words both for Machiavelli and for other Renaissance writers. They are often too employed very judiciously as for example in chapter VIII of *The Prince* where Machiavelli uses the word *onore* again and again with mounting irony to describe how Oliver Otto tricked his uncle. A great deal has been written about the Renaissance concept of Virtue, But Machiavelli like his contemporaries seems to have used it freely and loosely nearly always in antithesis to Fortuna sometime with the sense of will power, sometimes efficiency, sometimes even with the sense of virtue.

Decade was swept away. During the years of enforced political idleness he produced a series of works which place him securely among the masters of Italian prose. His versatility and erudition were considerable and it is now commonplace to say that *The Prince* alone unjustly carries the burden of representing his genius. But it is not so unfair that he should be judged by *The Prince* which after all is his supreme masterpiece and which contains the essence of his political thought. It is also a book, which still arouses men's passions and around which controversy still rages. Its meaning, its purpose, even the date of its composition and whether it was first composed without its traditional dedication and last chapter are still matters on which no final unchallenged judgment has been given.

Machiavelli would spend years in enforced retirement reflecting on precisely the issue of statecraft for he had come to know the Florentines, their characters and their ambitions exceedingly well. He had also read enough ancient Roman history to insist that it should be used, indeed its successes imitated, rather than simply admired. To organize a republic or rule a kingdom requires knowledge of the character of the people to be ruled and sufficient knowledge of history so that its lessons might be applied to contemporary problems concerning the governance of men and the maintenance of states, be they princedoms or republics. In his dedicatory preface to *the Prince* he says that his dearest possession is his knowledge of the action of great men, which he has acquired in two ways: through long experience of contemporary events learnt at the cost of personal privation and danger, and through a constant reading of antiquity. Just as those who draw maps, station themselves on the plains to consider the mountains, and then take up a position on high ground in order to get a good view of the plains below, so it is necessary for a prince to know the nature of the people and to be of the people to know the nature of princes. The traditions, circumstances and character of the people would determine the nature of that state.

By the end of his career, he would have a wealth of experiences. Like other civil servants, he undertook missions as a negotiator and diplomat, within Florentine territories, elsewhere in Italy, to the papal court in Rome under Pope Alexander VI and Pope Julius II, and to the former's ambitious son Cesare Borgia, abroad to the king of France and to the Holy Roman Emperor. He proved himself to be by far the most active among the chancery officials who wanted to keep his jobs despite changes in regimes, he has been described as a political fence sitter. He also made enemies because he allowed himself to be seen as too independent and arrogant. When in 1512, Spanish troops attacked Florentine territory, the republican regime dissolved and the Medici returned to power, Machiavelli would be dismissed from office. In 1513, he was accused of a role in an anti-Medici conspiracy. He was tried, tortured and imprisoned, and upon his release he retired to his farm seven miles outside of Florence and composed a draft of the text we call *The Prince.*

Machiavelli's experience of the Florentine republic in its various reformulations had begun during the 1480s at the time when Lorenzo Medici was in position, and ended with the return in 1512 of another Medici, Galliano, who was in turn replaced by his nephew, the younger Lorenzo in 1515. *The Prince* was originally dedicated to Galliano and re-dedicated to junior Lorenzo in 1515. It was aimed at a Medici with princely ambitions. By this time, Italy had been subjected to a succession of foreign invasions and Machiavelli would include as his final chapter of *The Prince* an exhortation that such a man free Italy from the stench of foreign domination. Machiavelli would still be alive in 1527 when Rome was sacked by the forces of Charles V, King of Spain and Holy Roman Emperor and Florence revolted against the Medici, establishing a new republic. But by then he was viewed as a Medici collaborator, and he died shortly thereafter, in poverty.

Bitter factionalism within the ruling elite ensued from 1494-98, during which Florence saw the guiding influence on politics of the Medici replaced by Savonarola. It is too infrequently mentioned in general histories of the Renaissance that religion and rhetoric interacted in preaching; indeed, that religious preaching remained the universal form of contemporary oratory and was often influenced by humanist theory and practice. As a friar who not only lacked political rights as a foreigner but whose religious status prevented him from direct participation in government, Savonarola was a powerful preacher who condemned the Medici as tyrants dominating a free republic. He came to play an exceptional role in Florentine republican politics when the government invited him to advise the citizens on constitutional reform. Instead, he argued in true Dominican fashion that since neither God nor Christ were heads of state, then it must be 'the people' who were lord of Florence: 'government is in the hands of the people which is the true and legitimate Lord of our city', not the Signori but the Great Council as sovereign legislator. The Great Council, comprising some three and a half thousand citizens who themselves, their parents or grandparents, had held one of the three major offices of state, were to be advised by Savonarola. He spoke of himself as a new

Moses, a prophet, legislator and disciplinary leader of his people. This was Savonarola's popular republicanism, preaching popular participation in discussion and voting to Florentines in the great Council.

Savonarola did hold skeptical view of the people's right reason. Hence, he modifies the vision of the natural rationality of the 'human legislator' in the Great Council. His language was penetrated by a prophetic quasi-royal imperative that can also be found in contemporary discourse on mixed constitutions, not least based on the Venetian model of an aristocratic republic. Savonarola first favored the Venetian model but then changed to popular government. He thought the character of the Florentine people did not suit them for monarchy, although his early preaching indicates that princely government, superficially along the lines presented by Thomas Aquinas, was his ideal. And so, like the Medici before him, who used the language of the Platonic philosopher-king to justify their arbitrary power, Savonarola appropriated for himself the regal role in the mixed government. It was through him as judge and prophet, as their Moses, that Florentines in their Great Council were, in effect, counseled by God. Like Moses, Savonarola was believed to talk with God. Led by its prophet-king, Savonarola saw this as a true republican regime.

Machiavelli had heard Savonarola's sermons and summarized the sermons for the Florentine ambassador in Rome, saying that Savonarola kept digressing and changing with the times, telling the people lies to suit them. In 1498, Savonarola's regime ended and Savonarola was tried and executed, having been excommunicated by church authorities for his criticism of Catholic corruption. During the next fourteen years, Machiavelli worked for the Republic. In 1502, the republican constitution was again modified. Soderine was elected to this position, but he refused to accept the addition of a Senate of aristocrats curtailing his position. It was Soderine regime that collapsed largely through aristocratic hostility in 1512. Machiavelli served him well and reached a position of diplomatic importance that was unusual for his social rank. While there is no evidence that Machiavelli played any role as Soderine's political agent, and there is evidence that he manicured among the various political factions, it is known that he expressed intense hatred for the aristocrats who destroyed Soderine's government.

Just before he entered the Florentine chancery, Machiavelli had heard Savonarola preach, like Moses, of the importance of arms for success, but he was aware that unlike Moses, Savonarola was an unarmed preacher who lost control of his followers after they ceased to believe him. He observed that Moses got his laws adopted by murdering men opposed to him, and Savonarola said it was necessary to murder the sons of Brutus – but he never did it. Machiavelli came to the view that oratory was necessary but not sufficient either to motivate men to action or to maintain them in that motivation. Machiavelli was on his way to formulating his theory of political success based, in part, on the lesson of violence and the need for arms. Skinner has observed that Machiavelli challenged his own humanist heritage in denouncing the humanists' failure to emphasize the significance of sheer power in political life. They misunderstood the scope of necessity. Not only is it not enough to devote oneself either to ancient or Christian virtue. The maintenance of successful government also depends on an unflinching willingness to supplement the arts of persuasion with the employment of effective military force.

Machiavelli's political theory would eventually surface in his *Prince* and *Discourses.* These two works in particular provide two perspectives on government, princely and republican. Most analysts have observed that there are fundamental differences between these two works, Skinner arguing in particular that *The Prince* is organized around the basic value of security, and the *Discourses* around the value of liberty. Like other humanists, Machiavelli wrote a tract in the tradition of the mirrors for princes, and one on republics, both works taking up the agendas revealed in contemporary writing on monarchies and republics by civic humanists. But in shifting humanist priorities, both works display a belief that history, one's own, can teach us, if we read it correctly, that success comes not through persuasion or even good laws, in the first instance, but rather comes through the prudential deployment of force responding to necessity.

Machiavelli and the Renaissance

Machiavelli is a child of the Renaissance. Against scholars who argue that the Renaissance never happened, or that the tern is too vague to denote any historical reality, or that it is an academic myth created by historical fancy, Skinner says that 'there is no escaping the fact that there was something that was undoubtedly reborn and restored'. He hastens to add that we of course cannot point to a determinate moment at which the dark ages ended and a new light began to dawn. While there was no sudden and decisive break between the Middle Ages and the Renaissance, there was arguably a gradual rebirth of classical learning. If there was a rebirth, it was protracted and difficult one. It began in the twelfth century when the Italian universities emerged as centers for the teaching of Roman law and the humanites, which included rhetoric, history and moral philosophy. Unlike the schoolmen of the Middle Ages, whose teaching relied on reason and demonstrative proofs, Renaissance humanists emphasized the rhetoric and the indispensability of eloquence and persuasion. They also espoused a Ciceronian-humanist view of history, viz. that one studies the past in order to learn lessons concerning the conduct of political life in the present. Sallust, Livy and other Roman historians were read as teacher's of prudence and the other political virtue. And, not least, Renaissance humanists turned to classical moral theory for advice and guidance.

This was also the period in which 'republican values' were being 'rediscovered' in Italy and 'the state' was beginning to acquire its modern meaning. In the eleventh century the city-states of Italy began to develop a recognizably 'republican' form of government that required legitimating, in as much as church orthodoxy ordained that monarchy was the best regime and that 'all governments are imposed by God's ordnance as a remedy for human sinfulness'. Aristotle gave a new confidence as well as a new armory of concepts with which they challenged church orthodoxy and created or rather recreated republican political discourse. Republican political practice proved a bit more problematic, however, because at the end of the thirteenth century it appeared to many commentators that self-government had simply proved a recipe for endless civil strife and that it will always be safer to entrust our community to the strong government of a hereditary prince. In this atmosphere, the ancient philosopher-hero was not Aristotle but his teacher Plato and his Italian political progeny who mounted a 'defense of the despotism of the wise'. It was this mantle that the Medici, among others, assumed. Machiavelli stands astride the divide between monarchists and republicans, having written advice books for both.

Our modern concept of 'the state' is so common and so pervasive that we are apt to overlook the fact that it once represented a rather startling innovation in political theory and practice. Before the advent of 'the state', the sovereignty of the ruler resided in his person and the loyalty of subjects was owed not to an abstract institution but to the person of the ruler. When Machiavelli advised a prince to maintain the state, he did not mean to 'maintain the state' but rather to maintain or uphold the status or standing of the ruler. In the century following Thomas Hobbes was among the first to speak of 'the state' as an agency distinct from the 'natural person' of the ruler, and, indeed, as an ' artificial person' in its own right.

Before we compare and contrast *The Prince* with views expressed in his *Discourses*, we must observe that in neither of these tracts is there counsel to call what is evil, good, or the vicious, virtuous. Neither tract is skeptical of the moral domain. In neither tract is there a redescription of injustice as justice. The underlying political morality of both works is the same. Machiavelli, when speaking of Agathocles who rose from a lowly position as the son of a potter to become king, tells how he called the people and Senate together and killed the senators and the rich. Machiavelli observes that it cannot be called virtue to kill one's fellow citizens, betray one's friends, be without faith, without pity and without religion; by these methods one may indeed gain power but not glory. The barbarous cruelty of Agathocles does not permit him being named among the most famous men and we cannot attribute to fortune or virtue that which he achieved without either. True princely virtue will have to include capacities other than the unrestrained and continuous use of force. Machiavelli advocates 'an economy of violence'. Therefore, Skinner is correct in arguing that 'the difference between Machiavelli and his contemporaries cannot adequately be characterized as a difference between a moral view of politics and a view of politics as divorced from morality. The essential contrast is rather between two different moralities, 'two rival and incompatible accounts of what ought ultimately to be done'.

What Machiavelli teaches is an understanding that 'evil', 'good', 'vicious', 'virtuous', 'justice' and 'injustice' are always determined by circumstances. Skinner has an interesting discussion on rhetorical redescription, and he analyses Machiavelli as a master of redescription. Machiavelli is making the Aristotelian rhetorical point that virtue and vices exist but what they mean to any agent depends on the circumstances in which acts are performed and characters are then subsequently judged. Virtues are not judged as such by theoretical reason but rather by practical reason, prudence. Prudence deals with the unintended consequences of necessity, opportunistically. In both works there is a sustained observation that past successful leaders and peoples could never have been successful in maintaining appearances had virtue and vice not been understood by all men as determined by circumstances. Modes of behavior are always to be determined and displayed by the quality of the times. Machiavelli is not preaching about moral relativism; rather, it is the classical, rhetorical understanding of prudent choice, in particular and contingent circumstances, that a prudent man, or people, determine what is the right thing to do, at the right time. In the *Discourses*, Machiavelli advises a republic:

> When the safety of one's country wholly depends on the decision to be taken, no attention would be paid either to justice or to injustice, to kindness or cruelty, or to its being praiseworthy or ignominious. On the contrary, every other consideration being set aside, that alternative should be wholeheartedly adopted which will save the life and preserve the freedom of one's country.

This recalls Cicero's appeal to an argument which we have come to call raison detat, reason of state. From antiquity one learns that to preserve Rome's newly recovered liberty, the sons of Brutus had to be killed; in contemporary times, Machiavelli thought Soderine should have taken extra-legal action to secure his hold on power and crush Medici supporters.

Statecraft

The new prince's statecraft is expounded in Chapter XII-XXIII. Exposition has led us, via the *Discourses* and *The Prince,* to recognize the theoretical problem on which Machiavelli's whole reflection is focused: namely, the beginnings of a state that endures the conditions for the foundation and duration of this state – a problem that takes the political form of the new prince. In this analysis, Machiavelli puts aside the problem of the original founding moment for practical purposes. He assumes that things have already begun, and that the conjoint process of becoming the prince and becoming the state is under way. The issue he poses and treats is the political practice that the prince must employ to see this process through to a successful conclusion in the first instance.

Machiavelli begins in chapter 1of *The Prince* by asserting that all states and dominions, which hold or have held sway over mankind, are either republics or monarchies. He distinguishes between monarchies as (a) hereditary or (b) of recent foundation. Monarchies of recent or new foundation rule over a people who either (1) have been previously accustomed to the rule of another prince, and hence, having no tradition of self-rule, the new prince simply grafts them on to his own possessions, or (2) have themselves constituted free states, that have been accustomed to self-rule. In this case, free states, that is those with a tradition of self-rule and a tradition of their own liberties, must be conquered by force, fortune or a prince's special ability. It is the latter, the prince's special ability, which Machiavelli will call princely virtue. Just as Aristotle had drawn the distinction between making and doing and the different but related skills required for each, so Machiavelli says that there is a difference between establishing a princedom by force, fortune or virtu, and governing or maintaining it. If the main foundations of every state are good laws and good arms, then, according to Machiavelli, where there are good arms, good laws inevitably follow. And the good arms must be one's own army and never hired mercenaries.

The Fixity of Human Nature

We are being forewarned by Machiavelli that an individual's and a people's character is open to manipulation, while man's nature is fixed. We must remain alive to the distinction between character formation and man's nature. Man's nature is fixed for the species and is universally shared. Man's characters however, the consequence of habits built up by experience. For Machiavelli and all ancient, medieval and Renaissance thinkers, man's nature does not change over time: hence, ancient, medieval and Renaissance men share the same natures. In all societies throughout history, men can be observed to have demonstrated through their actions the same kind of nature, a nature that is specific to humans.

It is to this fixed model of human nature that modern political scientists find themselves attracted, thinking it to be evidence of Machiavelli's 'modern' approach to man from which he and they can induce the universal 'law of politics'. But this is not a modern position. Some of the universally shared characteristics which Machiavelli attributes to human nature as such may be listed as follows: men change their masters voluntarily, believing they can better themselves; men walk almost always in paths trodden by others, proceeding in their actions by imitation, men are incredulous, not truly believing in anything new until they have had an actual experience of it; men commit injuries either through fear or through hate; it is the nature of men to be as much bound by the benefits that they confer as by those they receive; for it may be said of men in general that they are ungrateful, voluble dissemblers, anxious to avoid danger and covetous of gain; love is held by a chain of obligations which, men being selfish, is broken whenever it serves their purposes; fear is maintained by a dread of punishment which never fail; men forget more easily the death of their father than the loss of their patrimony; men love at their own free will but fear at the will of the prince, men are bad and would not observe their faith with you; men are so simple and so ready to obey necessities that one who deceives will always find those who allow themselves to be deceived; men in general judge more by the eyes than by the hands, that is, men see appearances but do not feel what things are; the common people are always taken by appearances and the occurrence of events, and the world consists only of the common people; there are three 'breeds' of human brains: one which understands things by itself, another which learns what others understand, and a third which understands neither by itself nor by other: the first is excellent, the second also excellent but the third is useless; men are much more taken by present than by past things and when they find themselves well off in the present they enjoy it and seek nothing more: a common fault of men is not to reckon on storms in fair weather; all men aim at glory and wealth but proceed in different ways to achieve their aims.

In short, men are by nature primarily self-interested and what they take to be their interest is material wealth and glory. The desire to acquire possessions is a very natural and ordinary thing. All their actions are aimed at self-betterment, as they perceive it. This is an Aristotelian observation as Aristotle explained it not only in his *Rhetoric* but also when he spoke about less than ideal constitutions, democracies and oligarchies, in *Politics* IV. Like Aristotle, Machiavelli does not picture man's self-interest as characteristic of an atomistic isolate, calculating utility maximization prior to his social embeddedness. Rather, he describes humans as inclined by their nature to live in societies. Machiavelli has learned this not only from the ancients but from his own experiences in Florence. His picture of society is conflictual along the lines of Aristotle who had emphasized the prime division of the state into the poor and the rich so that in such cases there seem to be two constitutions, 'democracy' and 'oligarchy', where the interests of the poor are 'freedom' and those of the rich are 'wealth'.

Indeed, Machiavelli acknowledged, as did Savonarola, the notion that Florentine politics was and always had been a contest for the power between the people and nobles. Society is natural and it consists of natural enmities between the people and nobles, caused by the desire of the later to command and the former not to obey. These natural enmities continue to exist in civil principalities and in civil republics. In both, there is more danger from the noble than from the people. The naturalness of societies with its natural enmities remained in all his writings an organizing principle for the interpretation of politics in city states: the enmities are the cause of all the ills, but he would read Roman history to show that in ancient Rome the contest had beneficial results, whereas in Florence the struggle between noble and people had perhaps less happy consequences. Given the natural enmities in society, 'all the qualities that are reputed good cannot all be possessed or observed, human conditions not permitting it'. As a consequence, men are not grateful or faithful to others unless necessity forces them to be.

Character Formation

The stability of human nature, however, is distinguished from character. Individually and collectively as culture, men develop their universally shared human natures so that they come to have the discrete characters they have, such characters being the consequence of their individual and collective experiences. These experiences are not random and unconscious events, which happen to men. It is true that men cannot control contingencies, that is, the times and circumstances they are born in, no matter how prudent they may be. Machiavelli says that 'time brings with it all things and may produce indifferently either good or evil'. But experiences are the psyche's responses to the world of times and circumstances, and experiences have effects on men's characters. Men are agents and their experiences are their willed responses to contingent events, so that from these willed responses characteristic habits of behavior become fixed. Hence, he notes that the character of different peoples varies.

A new prince who confronts a free people is obliged for his own security to take some drastic steps to reformulate their character, turning them initially into passive subjects rather than active citizens and thereafter allowing them to develop different characters by habituating them through good laws to proceed cautiously towards their perceived self-interest.

Fortune is a Woman

The more traditional 'mirrors for princes' spoke of the forces that opposed the heroic prince despite his plans, notably the capricious force of fortune which can do irreparably harm even to the most prudent man. But fortune can also permit a man to achieve great things. Machiavelli speaks of his hero Cesare Borgia, who acquired his state through good fortune but even he could not rely on fortune's support to maintain it. Machiavelli tells us that Cesare found the opportunity to appoint Ramiro, who exercised the necessary hatred and harsh authority in his lands, but Cesare wished to show the people that Ramiro's cruelty was not his own. He had him cut in half and placed in the public square this, for Machiavelli, being a lesson in how to exploit cruelties well. A successful prince must therefore be sufficiently experienced so that he is prepared to seize opportunities that require that he does what is necessary before adverse times come upon him. Machiavelli makes it clear, however, that experience is a necessary but insufficient ingredient of success. To recognize what is necessary before adverse times come is a characteristic of prudence, a practical reasoning based on experience of men and things, which enables him to recognize troubles in his state as, or before they arise.

Machiavelli is aware that many believe that fortune and God rule worldly events to such an extent that a man's own prudence cannot change things. They are resigned to the view that things are ruled by chance. But Machiavelli seeks to show how human free will may not altogether be extinguished and proposes as plausible the view that the goddess fortune is the arbiter of half the things we do, but the other half is within our own control. Perhaps the most important distinction a prince must be able to make is between what is necessary and what are the opportunities that flow from it as unintended consequences. It is possible to understand Machiavelli's argument as the standard one that necessity is outside of anyone's deliberation, but that his innovation is in proposing that one overcomes necessity not by fighting it, but by imitating it, creating artificial or political necessities. But no man is ever found so prudent as to be able to adapt himself to all times and all circumstances. Hence, the fortunes of states follow the qualities of their times. Of course, it is advantageous to 'tame' fortune and make her serve you, but Machiavelli believes that those who have less fortune have maintained themselves best, and have come to power through their own merits, like Moses, Cyrus and Romulus.

Machiavelli's Fortuna is equated to the sum of forces lying beyond one's abilities, a prince's virtue. Good luck cannot be guaranteed and both bad luck and the changes in fortune from good to bad cannot be overcome by remaining steadfast in adverse circumstances. Machiavelli rejects Cicero's injunction that one consistently pursue what is honorable. For Machiavelli it is dangerous to remain steadfast, a paragon of Christian or classical virtue. Continuing the metaphor of the goddess Fortuna as a women, Machiavelli advises that it is better to be impetuous than cautious, for fortune, as a woman, lets herself be overcome by youthful force and boldness. Machiavelli advises that if a ruler wishes to maintain his state and achieve the goals of honor, glory and fame, he must be prepared to go beyond the traditional range of Christian and moral virtues; indeed, he must forgo ethical and political habituation and, in his own case alone, actively prevent the acquisition of settled dispositions. He should not maintain steadfastness but rather a prudential restlessness and impetuosity.

Learn to Imitate Foxes and Lions

Machiavelli famously proposes that a prince must learn how to imitate both the lion and the fox, learning how to recognize traps, as does the fox and to frighten away wolves, as does the lion. A prince must learn the skills of both beasts as well as employing the human means of regulating the environment by law. Using laws is appropriate for men, and using force is appropriate to animals. Laws, however, are often ineffective and one needs to have recourse to force and animal cunning as well. Ancient writers speak of how rulers, like Achilles, were entrusted to Chiron the centaur, to be raised by him, Chiron being half-man and half-beast. A ruler needs to learn how to use both natures, and that one without the other is ineffective.

It is not accident, says Machiavelli, that the ancients made the Centaur the political teacher of their great men, suggesting that rulers should become like this strange being: half-man, half-beast. In fact, the prince must have a dual nature. Why? Because there are two ways of contending: one by using laws, the other, force. The first is appropriate for men, the second for animals; but because the former is often ineffective, one must have recourse to the latter. Therefore, a ruler must know well how to imitate beasts as well as employing properly human means. We are on familiar territory: the state's political practice must combine force (animal) and consent (human). But let us examine this more closely.

What does it mean to employ human means? It means to govern by laws in respecting the moral laws of kindness, fidelity, generosity, keeping one's word, and so on. It is thereby specified that in order to obtain the people's consent, it is indispensable to practice the moral virtue, which act on attitudes by their prestige and their recognition, without any violence. But when the laws are impotent one must also be able to resort to force, employ animal means. This is the other aspect of the statecraft. Here it is no longer a matter of moral virtue, but of violence, whose result alone counts, 'because one should reproach a man who is violent in order to ruin things, not one who is so in order to set them aright'. Employment of force is forging to morality: it is the converse of the use of legal means. There are two types of practice, and they are conjointly necessary: a ruler needs to use both natures and one without the other is not effective.

However, there is a considerable surprise in store for us. For the animal that is intended to represent force, just as man was intended to represent laws, is divided in two. The prince who is to imitate beasts must take two animals, not one, as models – the lion and the fox: 'one needs to be a fox to recognize traps, and a lion to frighten away wolves. "The lion is 'very fierce', while the fox is 'very cunning'. The context leaves no room for doubt: to be a fox is to be the master of fraud- both the fraud played on you, so that you can recognize its traps, and the fraud you must be able to perform, so as to entrap others. It is to be the master of guile and deception – not only in acts of war, traps, feigns, and so on, but in the government of men generally. Now what is astonishing in this division, this dual personality, of the beast is precisely that the beast, which is force, is divided into force (the lion) and fraud (the fox); whereas fraud – the art of deception – apparently has nothing to do with force, is not a division of force, but something quite different.

First, of all, we can say this: there are not two ways of governing men – by laws and by force – but three – by laws, force and fraud. But as soon as this statement has been made, we realize that fraud is not a mode of government like the others; it is not on the same level. Laws exist – let us say as human institutions, recognized rules, and opinions; force exists – let us say as the army. In contrast, however, fraud possesses no objective existence: it does not exist. If fraud is a way of governing, given that it has no existence, it can be employed only when it is based on laws or force. Fraud, then, is not a third form of government; it is government to the second degree, a manner of governing the other two forms of government: force and laws. When it utilizes the army, fraud is stratagem; when it utilizes laws, it is political guile. Fraud thus opens up a space, beyond force and laws, for diverting their existence – a space, in which force and law are substituted for, feigned, deformed, and circumvented. Mastery of fraud in the prince is the distance that allows him to play at will on the existence of force and laws, to exploit and, in the strongest sense of the word, feign them.

The chapter where Machiavelli discusses the Centaur, the prince who is both man and beast, opens with these words: 'Everyone knows how praiseworthy it is for a ruler to keep his promises, and live uprightly and not by trickery.' The opposition between laws (morals) /deception is blatant here. Machiavelli adds: 'Nevertheless, experience shows that in our times the rulers who have done great things are those who have set little store by keeping their word, being skilful rather in cunningly deceiving men.' The opposition laws/deception thus discloses two limit-cases: that of the prince who governs exclusively by laws and that of the prince who governs by deception, tricking men's minds. The first is laudable. What of the second?

The opposition laws/deception contains precisely the answer to this question. Deception is counterposed to laws as immorality to morality. To engage in trickery with the law is, in effect, to get around people; it is to load the dice by lies and deception. We now understand why Machiavelli assigns fraud to the category of the animal, rather than the human. To employ human means is to exercise the moral virtue; to play the fox is to exercise the vice of all vices: untrustworthiness, deceit. And we then grasp why fraud, an animal faculty aligned with force on account of its immorality, is paired with laws as their opposite, and is a form of government to the second degree: in effect, it is the capacity to govern by laws immorally; it is the art of affecting to abide by laws while violating or circumventing them.

A prudent ruler then, ought not to keep faith when by so doing it would be against his interest and when the reasons which made him bind himself no longer exist. Here one should imitate the fox's cunning but conceal it, men being so dominated by immediate necessities that a skilful deceiver always finds people who will allow themselves to be deceived. Plausible reasons can always be found as to why a prince failed to keep his promises. He must have a mind disposed to adapt himself according to the wind and as the variations of fortune dictate, not deviating from what is good if possible, but being able to do evil if necessary. A prince should therefore seem to be merciful, trustworthy, full of integrity, humane and religiously devout; he must especially appear to be pious, for men judge more by the eyes than by the hands, all see what a prince appears to be, few feel what he is, and those few will not dare oppose themselves to the many when the opinion of the majority of the common people is sustained by the majesty of the political community and regime.

It is here that we have wrongly become accustomed to the translation that 'the end justifies the means'. Rather, Machiavelli says that in all human action and especially actions of princes, where there is no appeal to higher judgment, one looks to the result. Humans, in always judging particular actions in the circumstances and men's characters by appearances, have no access to an agent's intentions or higher reasons: they show themselves to the consequentiality. The end does not justify the means; they have no access to the means, which may have been many and various, and only see the end, judging it against what appears to be their self-interest.

Better to be feared than hated

A prince should avoid being hated by the people, but if he cannot be both loved and feared, it is safer to be feared if one must make the choice. Nonetheless, Machiavelli stresses that the best fortress is to be found in the love of the people, for fortresses will not save you if you are hated by them. Avoid being hated and despised, largely by not attacking the property and honor of the people, for the generality of men will then live contented. Well-ordered regimes and wise princes have always studied diligently not to drive the nobles to desperation and to satisfy the people and keep them contented. Hence, the skills needed to cultivate appearances, a reputation for being great and excellent, are the skills that will encourage a people's love. Machiavelli insists that no one ever judges anyone's intentions or intrinsic qualities, but rather, judgment is always to appearances. And this advice, to develop the art of dissimulation and concealment, is not a simple message but rather to external performances in the circumstances. These are not illusions but they are appearances.

Theory of State

Machiavelli's theory of state merits our attention on three points. First, the state is led by a prince, but the prince's practice is unintelligible if it is not appreciated that this state is a state rooted in the people, a popular state. The popular character of the state determines the prince's political practice. Second, what is involved in the prince's political practice is not the state in the broad sense – namely, the social organization of a people in all its manifestations: economic, political and so on. It is the state in the narrow, political sense as a form of state power, as state power held by an individual and exercised by what the marxist tradition has called the state apparatus. For Machiavelli, the prince's political practice, is the practice of the holder of state power, and therefore, Machiavelli analyses the means that the prince fashions or employs, constitutes and implements, in order to exercise state power – in other words, what we can call the state apparatus. Third, at one extreme, the apparatus of force, represented by the army; at the other, the apparatus of consent, represented by religion and the entire system of ideas and, between the two, the politico-juridical apparatus represented by the 'system of laws', the provisional outcome and institutional framework of the struggle between social classes. In Machiavelli the instruments of force, the army, the instruments of consent, religion and the prince's reputation, and the instruments for the channeling of conflicting interests laws, are component parts of the state; they constitute its means, substance and mechanism. It is because these three instruments feature in the state, and in particular because force does not figure there alone but combines with laws and popular consent, that the state is the converse of a tyranny, and hence can be popular. This was clearly appreciated by Gramsci, who discovered in the combination of force and consent notions that referred him back to the marxist definition of the state: 'hegemony [consent] protected by the armour of coercion [force]'.

Machiavelli's theses on the army are impressive – not only in their consistency, but above all for their incisiveness and political acuteness. They anticipate not only the Jacobin positions of the French Revolution, but also the well-known theses of Clausewitz, Engels and Mao on armies and war. Obviously, Machiavelli speaks a language whose terminology is not identical to that of the Jacobins or the marxists. But his principal theses are incisive, and of an astonishing political and theoretical penetration. Machiavelli's understanding of the state can be explained by the following four theses.

First, the army is the number one quintessential state apparatus, constituting the state as force, endowing it with a real historical and political existence. A prince without an army is merely an unarmed prophet, like Savanorola. However much he resorted to ideology, he lacked the absolute precondition, the state apparatus of armed force. Consequently, all armed prophets succeed whereas unarmed ones fail. This brings out the double function of the state – of force and ideological consent – but under the primacy of force: hence the primacy of the army as state apparatus over ideology and laws.

Second, the army, its constitution, formation and utilization, must be considered predominantly from the viewpoint of politics. It is necessary to regard war as the continuation of politics by other means; and to put politics in command in military matters. Machiavelli is the first conscious, explicit and consistent theorist of the primacy of the political over the military in military matters themselves; of the primacy of politics over military technique. He is the first theorist consciously and systematically to subordinate technical questions regarding armies and war to the primacy of politics. He is equally well known for having subjected the use of castles and fortresses to a radical critique: they are not solutions because they are political mistakes. Fortresses are monuments not to architecture, but to political error. Castles of brick and iron are dangerous expedients: a ruler's real citadels are his people, his soldiers, his people in arms. Machiavellis is known for having denounced the ideology of contemporary military experts, who believed that the ultimate weapon of artillery was going to overturn all the rules of war. Against them Machiavelli maintained that virtue– political and military velour – would always have the last word on the battlefield, even if the intervention of artillery had the effect of compelling soldiers to engage in close combat.

Third, we have seen that Machiavelli first asserted the primacy of force over consent, the primacy of the army over ideology, in the state. Now, we have just seen that in respect of this same army, the second thesis asserted the primacy of politics. The first thesis is thus subordinate to the second. The primary of the first thesis would, in effect, have reduced state power to the exercise of naked force, to the technical employment of the army, combined with the subsidiary effects of consent. The second thesis rectifies this potential error, since it defines force, the army, as subordinate to politics. The upshot is that armed force is simply the realization of politics in the region of the state that employs violence. Now, the same politics is realized in laws and ideology. The force/consent, army/ideology, duality is thus not an antagonistic one: it is not a case of violence on the one hand, persuasion on the other. This duality realizes two necessary forms of state power under a single rule: that of the prince's popular and national politics.

Fourth, the system thus specified – the unity of armed force, laws and forms of popular consent, hence the system of military and ideology politics in the popular state – can be characterized by a slogan that commands everything: the prince must rely on his own forces. His forces mean in the narrow sense – his army – and his forces in the broad sense popular support. They are one and the same: the prince's forces are those of his people. The prince must fashion forces that are strictly his own; he must rely on his own forces, count on his own forces, be 'the complete master of his own forces'.

Once these indicators have been offered, Machiavelli's theory of the new prince can be understood without difficulty. But it contains some surprises. Here are the essential moments. Machiavelli begins by rejecting three types of troops or army that share a single and unique feature: namely that in three cases the prince cannot count on as his own forces, his own troops. These three types of army are mercenaries, auxiliaries, and mixed troops. Mercenaries are 'useless' and 'dangerous'. Why? Because they are retained solely by money. Machiavelli satirically comments that they have no affection for you any other reason to induce them to fight for you, except a trifling wage, which is not sufficient to make them want to risk their lives for you. They are very glad to be in your service as long as you do not wage war, but in time of war they either flee or desert. Accordingly, they are useless. But they are also dangerous. For if they chance to have a good mercenary leader, he can turn them against the prince. And if they do not turn against the prince, they form bands that proceed to pillage the country.

Auxiliary troops are 'much more dangerous than mercenaries', since they are not even dependent upon the prince for their wage. They are dispatched by a foreign ruler; they have another master, triggering another sequence of events. In themselves, these auxiliaries can be capable and effective but they are almost always harmful to those who use them; for if they lose you will be ruined, and if you win, you will be at their mercy. So true is this that is preferable 'to lose using your own troops than to conquer through using foreign troops', for 'weapons and armour belonging to others fall off you or weigh you drown or constrict your movements."

In the case of mercenaries, they have no master at all; they are not of the people, but are retained solely by money, which only encourages them to pillage and cannot bind them either to their employear to his country. In the case of auxiliaries, they have a master and a country, but it is not the prince: it is someone else. They are bound to their external master, and he who resorts to them is caught in another's trap: if he relies on someone else's troops, he is liable to be delivered over his political designs. This is why auxiliaries are even more dangerous than mercenaries.

Mixed armies comprise native and mercenary troops. An example is France. Charles VII was able to liberate France from the English because he recognized the need for France to be defended by national troops, and formed an army composed of cavalry and infantry. But his son Louis XI abolished the infantry and hired Swiss as infantry men. This was a serious blunder, for in disbanding the infantry he made his own cavalry dependent on foreign soldiers. In decreasing order of disadvantage, then, there are four types of army: auxiliaries and mercenaries – both definitively condemned, this condemnation being accompanied by numerous examples from the history of Italy, whose rulers committed the unpardonable blunder of trusting in them; then the intermediate form of mixed armies, which are part native, part mercenary; and finally, purely national armies – the only good ones.

What is an army of one's own? One's own forces are those composed of subject or citizens or of one's dependents all the others are either mercenaries or auxiliaries. The new army will therefore be a popular army. This involves not merely a generic denomination, but a political determination. Machiavelli's notion consists not simply in rejecting mercenaries or someone else's weapons, but in a new political conception of the army's recruitment and organization. To constitute a popular army is to arm a section of the population that had not hitherto possessed weapons. Furthermore, it is to have the people in arms play a new role in the army's organization and operation. This objective is attained by two measures. Recruitment of the army from the popular strata of town and country, in the form of standing popular militias. Machiavelli's essential innovation in this respect is massively to extend recruitment to the peasantry, and to have them enroll in the standing militias. This constitutes the blending of towns and country. A reorganization of the army that ensures a preponderance of infantry over cavalry. This represents the primacy of infantry.

On these two counts, Machiavelli overturns prevailing opinion, and introduces revolutionary innovations whose political import is obvious. It involves imparting a popular content to the army and, at the same time, making it the school and crucible of popular unity, by reversing the political balance of forces within it. To have peasants enroll in the army en masse undermines the power of the feudal lords. To unite the popular strata of town and country in the infantry, and prioritize it over cavalry, initiates a process of social and political amalgamation that simultaneously challenges the hierarchies sanctioned by the feudal order and its military organization. Not only does the lofty reign of the cavalryman come to an end, but a new form of popular unity, hitherto nonexistent, takes shape: in the army common to them, the men of the towns and countryside begin to become – learn to become – one and the same people. Gramsci was especially sensitive to this political objective of Machiavelli. Gramsci argues that any formation of national-popular collective will is impossible, unless the great mass of peasant farmers bursts simultaneously into political life. That was Machiavelli's intention through the reform of the militia, and it was achieved by the Jacobins in the French Revolution. That Machiavelli understood it reveals a precocious Jacobinism that is the fertile germ of his conception of national revolution. The conception of the army in Machiavelli then appears in all its clarity and truly revolutionary audacity.

In a first moment, we learnt and appreciated that the army was to serve to build the new state – that is to say, serve as a means to national and popular ends. But it was open to us to think that the relation of means to ends was one of exteriority, the army being a neutral technical instrument, a force organized according to the rules of existing military technique and serving authority purely as a means to attainment of its ends. Machiavelli plunges us into a quite different universe. The existing army, the forms of its employment, recruitment and organization, all existing military techniques – these he condemns and repudiates as politically incompatible with attainment of his political objective. To this new end, a new army is required, one that is politically compatible with that new goal and, like it, popular and national. This is the second moment, when Machiavelli declares that the prince equips himself with forces that are his own and, to fashion them, arm his own subjects. On this condition, the means – the army – will no longer be external to the end – the nation – since the army will be national.

But here is the third moment, when we discover that the forms of army recruitment and organization have the effect of making the end internal to the army itself; and that creation of the army is already in itself accomplishment of the goal. Not only are the means not external to the end, but the end is internal to the means. For Machiavelli's army – with its popular recruitment, amalgamation of town and country, and supremacy of infantry over cavalry unites the people whom the state is assigned the goal of uniting and expanding, simply by virtue of being constituted. The military apparatus simultaneously exercises an ideological function. Ideology thus figures in the army itself, as the prince's other means of power.

Machiavelli's conviction is that there is no escaping the reign of men's opinion, beliefs and judgments. Political relations have two aspects: on one side is force, on the other, opinion. In Machiavelli, it is not a matter of such and such an individual's opinion. His purpose is not to elaborate an anthropology or psychology of individual passions and opinions. His target is the mass. He states it categorically: 'the common people are the vast majority'. The only object that could be of concern to be prince's political practice is the opinion of the people in its mass: for the common people are impressed by appearances and results. Everywhere the common people are the vast majority, and the few are isolated when the majority and the government are at one.

Machiavelli insists that while founding the new principality the new prince had to ignore every actually existing political form. For wherever he establishes himself, the new prince will encounter men who possess their own customs and obey religious and moral laws: in short, men subject to ideologies. It is not a matter of such and such an individual's opinion, but of the opinion of the mass. Such is the reality that dominates everything in this domain: the existence of a mass religious and moral ideology. The implication is obvious: to achieve his national and popular goals, the Prince must start out by respecting the people's ideology, even if he wants to transform it. He must take care that every political act, each form of political practice, intervenes and resonates as a matter of fact in the element of this ideology. He must therefore, take charge of it, accept responsibility for the ideological effects of his own political practice, anticipate them, and inscribe them in it. And since the prince is literally the public face of the state, he must take care that the people's representation of his figure is inscribed in popular ideology, so as to produce effects beneficial to his politics. For this representation plays a key role in the state's constitution, in the association of subjects and their education. Now, it is here that fraud comes in, and in the first instance, it can intervene because the people are so disposed that they trust appearances more than reality:

> Most men judge more by their eyes than by their hands. For everyone is capable of seeing you, but few can touch you. Everyone can see what you appear to be, whereas few have experience of what you really are; and those few will not dare to challenge the popular view.

That men believe in appearances was already inherent in their attachment to the obvious facts of religion, rites of worship, true or false miracles, as to the self-evidence of customs and morality. It follows that nothing is easier than deceiving them: 'men are so naïve, and so much dominated by immediate needs, that a skilful deceiver always finds plenty of people who will let themselves be deceived."

We thus return to the relation between deception and laws, and, before that, to the relation between moral virtue and political virtue. Machiavelli's precept that fraud 'should be well concealed: one must be a great feigner and dissembler'. The prince must know how not to be good. To appreciate the necessity of fraud, we must revert to the prince's historical task, the exceptional situation imposed on him, the means he is compelled to employ, and his virtue. If we might consider the two extremes of his practice, we find, on the one hand, that he must be good and virtuous so far is feasible; and on the other, that he must learn not to be good, and thus to do evil. But even when he is reduced to this extremity, the prince must, if he can, 'disguise' his immoral conduct as moral conduct, feigning virtue:

> A ruler need not actually possess all the above-named qualities, but he must certainly seem to. Indeed, I shall be bold as to say that having and always cultivating them is harmful, whereas seeming to have them is useful; for instance, to seem merciful, trustworthy, humane, upright and devout, and also to be so. But if it becomes necessary to refrain, you must be prepared to act in the opposite way, and be capable of doing it.

It may be characterized by saying that this ideological policy must be subject to the primacy of politics tout court. The prince must take the reality of popular ideology into account, and inscribe therein his own representation, which is the public face of the state. But his ideological policy must be a politics, not an ideological demagogy. There is no question of the prince conforming to the spontaneous ideology of the people in every detail of his conduct and practice. He must compose, and politically control his conduct and its representation. At one extreme, he must know that there are 'vices that enable him to rule', such as being cruel and harsh at the state's inception. At the other extreme, he must be apprised that there are virtue's that enable him to rule: mercy, trustworthiness, humanity, uprightness, piety. These must be either possessed or affected, because their reputation is politically operative.

But he must not ensure himself in them, or be bound to them, because necessity might demand their renunciation. Politics is in command in everything; as a function of its goal, it dictates the selection of political vices and virtue alike, and their affection when required.

The objective is to establish a correct ideological relation between prince and people. As always, Machiavelli proceeds by examining extremes: on one side, hatred and contempt; on the other, love. He completely rules out the first extreme: the prince must at all costs avoid being hated and scorned. If he were hated, he would be in the condition of a tyrant, at the mercy of popular rebellion; if he were scorned, he would not be a ruler, but at the mercy of the nobility's insurrection. Let us translate: the prince must not at any price find himself in the position of having the people against him. But what of love? Is it not the fondest wish of a popular ruler? Machiavelli rejects love as incapable of guaranteeing stable relations between prince and people on its own. For love is inconstant: 'whether men bear affection depends on themselves'. 'While you benefit them,' Machiavelli writes, 'they are all devoted to you: they would shed their blood for you; they offer you their possessions, their lives, and their sons when the need to do so is far off. But when you are hard pressed, they turn away.' A more reliable bond must be found: fear. In Chapter XVII of *The Prince*, Machiavelli writes:

> A controversy has arisen about this: whether it is better to be loved than feared or vice versa. My view is that it is desirable to be both loved and feared; but it is difficult to achieve both and, if one of them has to be lacking, it is much safer to be feared than loved.

The advantage of fear is that it persists. But it persists because it is the creation of the prince, who controls its cause – something that is not the cause with love: 'whether men bear affection depends on themselves, but whether they are afraid will depend on what the ruler does." A wise ruler should rely on what is under his control, not on what is under the control of others. The formula – fear without hatred – might seem harsh for the people of a popular prince. But to give it its precise meaning, it must be developed. That the prince must at all costs avoid being hated by his people obviously signifies that he must be-ware of alienating the people at the greatest peril. But there is more: hatred in Machiavelli has a precise connotation. Above all, it is the people's hatred of the nobles. In connection with the kingdom of France, for instance, we are told that Louis IX 'was well aware of the ambition and arrogance of the nobles; on the other hand, he knew that the people hated the nobles.' The founder of the kingdom therefore established the parliament 'to restrain the nobles and favor the people'. Hatred thus possesses a class signification. In the formula 'fear without hatred', the phrase 'without hatred' signifies that the prince demarcates himself from the nobles and sides with the people against them.

But there is still more: fear without hatred closes down one space and opens up another, specific space: the minimal political base from which the people's friendship – an expression Machiavelli prefers to the people's love – becomes the decisive political objective. In effect, what is ruled out is the people's undiluted love, without coercion, since it is precarious and capricious. What is aimed at instead is the people's friendship, 'popular goodwill' on the basis of state coercion. Machiavelli constantly return to this theme, which gives explicit expression to his own position. A further twenty examples could be cited that leave no room for doubt. The theory of fear without hatred is the theory of the political precondition for 'popular good will' towards the prince. It is also factually an acknowledgement of the popular state's doublet function: the unity of coercion and popular consent that so struck Gramsci in Machiavelli.

Finally, to appreciate this policy of 'fear without hatred' properly, it must be called by its name: it is an ideological politics, politics in ideology. It must also be remembered that this representation of the prince's figure in the people, on the basis of religion, accounts for only one component of the means of the state power, the other component comprising the army. It must be remembered that of the two the dominant means is the army, whose role in the unification, formation and constitution of the people as a people we have observed. Finally, it must be recalled that state ideology and force alike are subordinate as means to one and the same end: the constitution of a new, popular state that must face up to its historical task: unifying Italy.

Let us go back a little further. The Italian situation was of extreme misery and depletion. Italy is a 'matter' awaiting only a suitable form to unify it; but on the other hand, nothing is to be expected of the political forms it is decked out in and cursed with, because they are all old, feudal forms. That is why the prince must be completely new, and begin to execute his historical task starting out from a completely new principality. This involves creating a political base. While it must be completely new, and sweep away the old political forms, this political base is not going to be constituted in a vacuum. The prince will have to 'mould' existing men, who bear the scars of feudal forms of political domination, in their customs, and their religious and moral laws. Once again, Machiavelli's political objective is not to reform the constitution of a state, or even to take power in the formal framework of an existing state, but to constitute a radically new political base. This base must be imposed and be expanded by force to be capable of enduring; it must fell all the wretched Italian states one after the other, and be defended by force against foreign states.

We then appreciate the political nature of that strange relation of people to prince: fear without hatred. It is indispensable to the constitution of the new principality, which has to be popular if it is to resist assaults from without and wrest the means of building the national state from the old states; it is indispensable to the education of the populations of conquered principalities and republics. If the prince knows how to inspire fear without hatred in his subjects, he guarantees himself the time required for his grand design, and will be able to win over populations acquired by war or guile. But there again, this is only a beginning. For fear without hatred is simply the means to an end that surpasses it: the ideological base from which 'popular goodwill' will little by little, be won.

The guiding thread of Machiavelli's thought is to be found in the concept of political virtue, which is synonymous neither with moral virtue nor with its negation. It sometimes seems that there were several sixteenth-century Florentine writers, all named Machiavelli but sharing little else in common. The most famous, or notorious, is the 'murderous Machiavelli' mentioned by Shakespeare and, as 'Old Nick', decried as the devil himself. An apostle of violence and advocate of murder in the name of political expediency, Machiavelli has been vilified and roundly condemned by critics from Frederick the Great until the present. He has been called everything from a proto-Nazi and a 'teacher of evil' to a misogynist. But there are also other, ostensibly more benign Machiavellis: the first 'scientific' political analyst to focus on 'facts' while forgoing 'values', the resuscitator of republican political ideals, a skilful satirist of political folly, a proto-liberal, who was perhaps the first to recognize the irreducible plurality of values, a cunning deceiver and trapper of Princes, and many others besides. These interpretations and assessments are remarkable not only for their variety but for their ingenuity.

Of course it used to be fashionable to say that Machiavelli was immoral, or at any rate amoral; but now it is more fashionable—and arguably more accurate—to suggest that he did in fact subscribe to a system of morality, even if there is as yet no consensus about what this code consists of. Our aim here is to attempt to deconstruct this code, or at lest one part of it. In making, this attempt we hope to shed some light on Machiavelli's morals and along the way to say something about the mutability of our own moral concepts and convictions.

The moral codes and concepts of different nations and cultures are radically different. And yet we consider them to be moral codes because they are all concerned, in their very different way, with shaping and directing the course of human conduct. Moral codes set standards by reference to which conduct can be praised or blamed, criticized and condemned, judged and justified. And it is for this reason that Machiavelli can be considered a moralist. For he, too, stipulates standards and criteria of virtuous conduct, not for human beings generally but at least for princes in particular. There are, in Machiavelli's view at least two different varieties of virtue—one for private persons, another for princes. Machiavelli's conception of princely virtue is entirely consistent with the brutal precepts and practices prescribed in *The Prince*, and for which his own and succeeding generations have roundly condemned him.

Machiavelli's model prince, like Don Quixote, attempts, not to create a new conception of morality but, in effect, to resurrect and revive an archaic one. Machiavelli's manifest intention in writing *The Prince* was not set out to compose a comedy or a satire either. On the contrary, he seriously meant to add his own unorthodox contribution to and perhaps the subversion or the deconstruction of the already well-established mirror-of-princes genre. Like other writers in this genre, Machiavelli offered guidance and advice to princes, particularly to new ones who are most obviously in need of it. Machiavelli's advice to aspiring princes has a decidedly quixotic character and tenor. To the new prince Machiavelli says, in effect: if you wish to acquire and hold political power you must not think and act within the moral framework of our own age, but in that of another, earlier time. The dominant moral framework of our corrupt and effeminate age, he continues, is Christian, and its listing and ordering of the virtue is a veritable recipe for the prince's political suicide. And since no one should, morally speaking, be required to commit suicide, there is good reason to believe that the princely virtue are not identical with the virtue by the Church. A good prince, he insists, must 'learn to be not good'. By this Machiavelli does not mean that the prince must learn to be evil, but that he must, in his role as prince, unlearn the Christian virtues, substituting in their place virtue of another variety entirely. These distinctly political or princely virtues, Machiavelli designates by the single word, *virtu*.

The word virtu recurs in Machiavelli's political writings. Indeed, one might even read his three best-known works—*The Prince, The Discourses,* and *The Art of War*—as explications of three varieties of virtue. *The Prince* explicates and illustrates the concept of princely virtue; *The Discourses* that of civic virtue; and *The Art of War* that of military virtue.

Virtu is among the most contested and controversial concept in Machiavelli's moral lexicon. *Virtu*, as Maschiavelli uses the term, has no exact English equivalent. Nor, for that matter, is it exactly equivalent to the Latin virtue from which it ostensibly derives. Virtu is, however, clearly connected to its Latin antecedent in at least one respect. *Virtu* derives from vir, or 'man'. *Virtu* refer to the qualities and character traits to be found in the vir, the free male citizen. It is indeed the possession of particular *virtu*—courage, temperance, prudence, and justice—which distinguish the true, vie from slaves or ordinary laborers or even, from women. The etymological point here is that Machiavelli's concept of *virtu*, like its Latin antecedent, refers not to qualities or characteristics of human beings as such but to those qualities displayed by virile in their respective roles. *Virtu*, like virtues, is a role-related concept; in this, the two differ radically from the Christian virtue, which all human beings, regardless of role or rank, are at least potentially capable of exhibiting, especially in interpersonal or intimate interactions. The Christian virtues—humility, charity, meekness, piety, and the rest—can as well be characteristic of the attitudes and actions of women and slaves. Nietzsche severally characterized Christianity as a 'slave morality'. The Christian concept of virtue, in other words, has no necessary connection with public or political life. Political power and position are not goods to be actively sought after by the virtuous Christian but are, rather, evils inflicted upon and endured patiently by passive subjects.

That Machiavelli's *virtu* bears scant resemblance to the Christian conception of virtue should now be clear. There are the pronounced and profound differences between the Ciceronian-humanist concept of virtue and the Machiavellian concept of *virtu*. The qualities ascribed by Cicero to the virtuous stateman are not those ascribed by Machiavelli to the prince. Machiavelli's prince is at least prepared to act in ways that Cicero and his humanist successors would have thought disgusting and distasteful. Cicero requires that one might on occasion achieve one's ends more efficiently by resorting to force or fraud. It might even appear to be rational to resort to such means. But the appearance, says Cicero, is misleading. He forcefully insists that to be fully rational is to be most fully human and therefore not at all 'bestial'. Force and fraud are ruled out as being 'unworthy of man' inasmuch as they are characteristic of the behaviors of beasts—force being characteristic of the lion and fraud of the fox.

Machiavelli explicitly rejects the Ciceronian view that the best and most rational human action differs categorically from the behaviors of the beasts. Tweaking the Roman nose of the humanists, he says that the prince must learn to imitate both beasts by combining the cunning of the fox with the forceful courage of the lion. We may conjecture is that Machiavelli's conception of princely *virtu*—which encompasses lying, deceit, treachery, cunning and so on – has obvious but unnoticed affinities with a much older conception of *'virtue'*. Machiavelli's *Virtue,* shares certain crucial conceptual affinities with the Homeric conception of *Virtue* found in the *Iliad* and the *Odyssey.*

Arête is that quality or set of qualities, which enables one to play a particular role and to discharge its duties. From this follows: arête does not and cannot refer to the excellence of man qua man but of man qua role-bearer in relation to other role-bearers. However, *arête* need not denote specifically human qualities at all. The *arête* of a sword, for example, is its sharpness, the *arête* of a racehorse, its speed; the arête of a guard-dog, its ferocity and loyalty to its master. Thus Odysseus's faithful dog Argos exhibits canine arête by remaining fiercely loyal, by recognizing his returning master, despite his disguise, and by staying alive long enough to welcome him home before dying, his duty done, from a combination of delight, relief, and old age.

Homeric virtue requires on occasion that one act in ways that are by our normal standards, immoral and vicious. Thus, Penelope's role permits, or perhaps even requires, her to deceive the suitors. Similarly, Odysseus's role requires that he do everything and anything within his power to protect his men and return them safely to Ithaca. There is nothing of the Golden Rule, the Kantian categorical imperative, in Homeric ethics. Odysseus has no scruples about ordering his men to plug their ears and lash him to the mast so that he can listen to and be tempted by the Sirens' song. Nor does he entertain any doubts about the appropriateness of deceiving the drunken Cyclops Polyphemus, and blinding him into the bargain. Arête is the ability to discharge one's role-related functions in a particularly ingenious or cunning way to enhance one's glory or fame.

It is Machiarvilli's strange assertion that to seize the day, to act boldly and even ruthlessly, is the only way in which fickle fortune (Fortuna) can be tamed and genuine glory (Gloria) and lasting fame (Fam) secured. Machiavelli's metaphor is instructive. 'Fortune', he says in a now-notorious misogynist tone 'is a woman, and it is necessary, if you wish to master her, to conquer her by force; she lets herself to be overcome by the bold rather than by those who proceed coldly'. Virtue is to politics what virility is to sex: it is the congeries of qualities that bring success in the activities in which the manly man, the virile vir — and the virtuoso prince— are respectively engaged. Princely virtue is, in effect, Machiavelli's modernized and politicized rendering of the archaic arête.

Some objections have been raised against Homeric reading of Machiavelli's concept of virtue because Machiavelli's models, personas, examples, and illustrations are almost invariably drawn, not from Homeric Greece but from Rome; Machiavelli's stock of examples and illustrations comes from Roman history, it does not follow that his categorical framework—his most basic concepts, categories, and criteria-is itself Roman. Clearly the virtue praised by Cicero and other humanist writers—are in Machiavelli's views, vices leading to political ruin and suicide. The copious use of Roman examples of political success and failure by an ardent Italian patriot and proto-nationalist is scarcely surprising: not only were such examples likely to be more familiar to his reader; they might also serve to remind them that Italy had once been the unified center of the civilized world. For Machiavelli, who confesses that 'I love my native city more than my own soul', this is not a neutral historical fact but a pertinent political reminder. Not for nothing does *The Prince* conclude with a call to arms and an exhortation to drive the barbarians out of Italy. The instrument of this exorcism is to be the man of heroic action and imaginative vision. That man is, of course, the prince. And because unarmed princes do not succeed in this world, the prince must resort to armed force to gain his ends and thereby exhibit his virtue for all to see. It is surely significant that Machiavelli singles out for special mention one of the heroes of the *Iliad*. Achilles was imitated by Caesar. Thus, the arête of this Homeric hero had once served—and might again serve—as a model and inspiration for an Italian warrior-prince. Machiavelli's moral code is, in a word, heroic; it rests upon an archaic ethic of emulation, not upon reasoned reflection on the right, the just, and the goods.

The second objection one might raise against Homeric reading of Machiavelli is that his prince, unlike Homer's heroes—Achilles or Odysseus—is entirely self-serving. His prince seeks, not the good of others, but his own fame and glory. Thus, Machiavelli appeals solely to the vanity of the upstart and usurper. Homer's heroes, it will be recalled, won honors, fame, and glory by excelling in their respective roles. The majesty of their deeds is attested to by the fact that they are remembered; their stories are celebrated in song and verse, told and retold; they are held up as models worthy of imitation; and in this way they live on long after their deaths, thereby enjoying the only measure of immorality of which human beings in this world are capable.

It is just this sort of fame to which Machiavelli's model prince aspires. Pure self-aggrandizement, unconnected to the founding of cities, princedoms, and republics, is mere notoriety; it is not genuine glory or true fame. As an example of the former, Machiavelli cites the case of Agathocles, the tyrant of Syracuse. At first sight Agathocles looks like Machiavelli's model prince. Through trickery and treachery of the basest sort he defeated his enemies, betrayed his friends, and concentrated all power in his own hands. And yet Machiavelli denies that Agathocles exhibited princely virtue. Why? Because, he tells us, Agathocles is remembered not with the awe and affection accorded to founders but with the disgust and loathing reserved for wanton destroyers and tyrants. It cannot be called virtue to kill one's fellow citizens, betray one's friends, be without faith, without pity, and without religion; by these methods one may indeed gain power but not glory. Despite his military virtue, the fact remains that, as a prince, Agathocles's 'barbarous cruelty and inhumanity, together with his countless atrocities, do not permit him being named among the most famous men'.

Not that Machiavelli has anything against atrocities or acts of princely cruelty; but such deeds are for him morally and politically permissible only when they are dictated by necessity, the crime directed against vicissitudes of Fortuna. This body political is, as the Greeks would have said, a civil cosmos created out of a corrupt, pre-political chaos by a solitary law-givers, a Solon, a Lycurgus, or a Draco. The draconian measures to which the prince has recourse are not freely chosen but are, on the contrary, dictated by necessity and are required for anyone who chooses to play that particular role. And that peculiarly ruthless role is in turn called into being by time and circumstance. The prince makes his appearance in a society so thoroughly corrupt that its inhabitants long ago ceased to be citizens. A people possessing and exhibiting civic virtu would hardly have need of such a prince. But a people conquered and despoiled, sunk in dissension, depravity, and corruption, stand in dire need of his harsh but transforming praxis. A lasting legal and political order can be created only by a singular man of princely virtue and vision. Nothing does so much honors to a newly risen man, Machiavelli writes, than the new laws and measures which he introduces. These measures when they are well based and have greatness in them render him revered and admired.

Although Agathocles was not such a man, Romulus was. Agathocles had no objective other than keeping himself in power; all his dastardly deeds were directed to this end. Romulus, though he murdered Remus and acquiesced in the death of Titus should not be censured or criticized as Agathocles deservedly is. For we must, as Machiavelli says in *The Discourses*, 'take into consideration the object which Romulus had in view in committing that homicide'. Romulus, unlike Agathocles, acted not out of a selfish regard for his own good but from a solicitous regard for the public good. A wise mind, he continues, will never censure anyone for having employed any extraordinary means for the purpose of establishing a kingdom or constituting a republic. It is well that, when the act accuses him, the result should excuse him; when the result is good, as in the case of Romulus, it will always absolve him from blame. For he is to be r reprehended who commits violence for the purpose of destroying, and not he who employs it for creative and generalive purposes.

This is to miss Machiavelli's point, which is that, the citizen's shared remembrance of their polity's founding is a central component of civic virtue. Civic virtue is that collection of qualities required for the role of the free citizen of a republic. Here it is enough to suggest that one of the components of civic virtue is civic memory—that is, the stock of common memories which bind citizens together, giving them a common sense of who they are, where they have come from, and what they are collectively capable of achieving. For the Romans, this came in large part from Virgil, who told the story of Rome's founding; its heroes are Aeneas, Romulus, and Numa. For the Greeks, this common sense and shared sensibility stemmed from Homeric tales and traditions; its heroes are Achilles, Odysseus, and other exemplary figures. What we now lack, Machiavelli says in effect, is a shared civic memory; because it—and the civic virtue of which it is a part—does not now exist, it must be created ex nihilo; creation requires a creator, and to create something from nothing is bound to be a violent process.

Machiavelli's prince is a comic character on a quixotic quest for two reasons. The first is that his prince would have to think and act within the confines of a framework that is utterly foreign, not to say unintelligible, to his subjects; little wonder that their relations should be so strained and violent. Little wonder, too, that he thinks it better for a Prince to be feared than loved. Secondly, he is, in effect, trying to turn back the clock, to resurrect an archaic and long-lost moral framework. Despite his copious use of historical examples, Machiavelli is not a historically minded thinker. He sees the world as having its cycles, its ups and downs, its fallings possibilities and returns; but because human nature remains essentially unchanged, the maxims applicable in one age are applicable in another.

Machiavelli's archaic ethic of emulation is, in the end, profoundly ahistorical. For it fails to recognize that the concepts constitutive of our moral codes and practices have historically mutable meanings. The mutability of moral codes and concepts is a pervasive theme in much of modern literature, if not in moral philosophy. It might, therefore, be instructive to conclude by contrasting Machiavelli's ahistorical ethics of emulation with the more modern view that there is nothing deader than the ethics of a bygone era, and nothing deadlier, more dangerous—or more futile— than the hope of reviving the dead and reliving the past. They had lived so long ago, their time was so unlike the present, their hopes and motives were so widely removed from ours, that between them and the living there seemed to stretch a gulf too wide for even a spirit to pass.

Machiavelli denies this. The gulf between past and present is not, in his view, impassable. The spirit can pass if the flesh is willing; past practices can be revived and exemplary actions emulated. The agent of this revival is to be the virtuous prince. But Machiavelli's prince aspires to the doubly difficult, if not indeed impossible feat of resurrecting the dead and turning the vinegar of violence into the wine of civic harmony. Machiavelli alone is not in believing that such political alchemy is indeed possible. Robespierre attempted to revive the patriotic and patriarchal moral values –all shared something with Machiavelli's quixotic hope of reviving the past and resurrecting the dead. All are alike in their failure to understand Marx's admonition that if indeed history repeats itself, it does so the first time as tragedy and the second time as farce.

Machiavelli's Republicanism

Machiavelli has been given due honour for his republicanism and nationalism. There was nothing in Machiavelli's account of the absolute monarchy corresponding to his obviously sincere enthusiasm for the liberty and self-government of the Roman Republic. The preservation of the state, as distinct from its founding, depends upon excellence of its law, for this is the source of all the civic virtues of its citizens. Even in a monarchy the prime condition of stable government is that it should be regulated by law. Thus Machiavelli insisted upon the need for legal remedies against official abuses in order to prevent illegal violence and pointed out the political dangers of lawlessness in rulers and the folly of vexatious and harassing policies. In particular, the prudent ruler will abstain from the property and the women of his subjects, since these are the matters on which men are most easily stirred to resistance. He favored a gentle rule wherever possible and the use of severity only in moderation. He said explicitly that government is more stable where it is shared by .the many and he preferred election to heredity as a mode of choosing rulers. He spoke for a general freedom to propose measures for the public good and for liberty of discussion, in order that both sides of every question may be heard before a decision is reached. He believed that the people must be independent and strong, because there is no way to make them warlike without giving them the means of rebellion. Finally, he had a high opinion both of the virtue and the judgment of an uncorrupted people as compared with those of the prince.

In both *The Prince* and the *Discourses,* he praises popular judgment, but his confidence is always in those who can manipulate that judgment for the good of the state. A multitude without a head is useless. He notes that those who have been present at any deliberative assemblies of men will have observed how erroneous their opinions often are; and in fact, unless they are directed by superior men, they are apt to be contrary to all reason. The strength of the people comes from their being led and thereby united, and states, by they monarchies or republics, need skilled rhetoricians who can persuade men into seeing what is right in the circumstances. To elevate popular judgment is to elevate the skill of the leaders in manipulating that judgment. We shall see that the people's skill is limited to maintaining the state, not founding it, and to judging good proposals, not inventing them. The people's skill is the skill of a good audience judging.

Machiavelli means by liberty independence from external, barbaric, foreign aggression and tyranny. He also means the habitual capacities that accrue to a people having been accustomed to self-government. Using Roman examples, he says that ancient history shows how difficult it is for a people that has been accustomed to live under the government of a prince to preserve its liberty, if by some accident it has recovered it. He makes it clear that such a prince is a tyrant and not a constitutional monarch. Liberty is a condition that is contrasted with corruption. When liberty is preserved, he says the good prevails over the bad. A state is defined as having a free government when it bestows honors and rewards according to certain honest and fixed rules, so that those who obtain such honors and rewards do not consider themselves under obligations to anyone, believing that they were entitled to them by their merits. Free government then, is government under law, with constitutional provisions and institutional arrangements that ensure stability. Free government benefits the mass of people, enabling them to enjoy their own property without any apprehensions; neither have they anything to fear for the honor of their wives, daughters or themselves. It is clear that Machiavelli's prince was advised to provide precisely this: free government under a monarchy.

In *Discourses* I, chapter 16 Machiavelli speaks of a prince who wishes the good will of an initially hostile people. He advises that such a prince—tyrant should discover what people really desire and it is two things: to revenge themselves on those who have enslaved them, and to recover their liberty. The prince can satisfy the first desire because, as Machiavelli makes clear, those who enslaved the people were the noble and rich, and a prince can follow the example of the tyrant Clichés and massacre the nobility to the great satisfaction of the people who desired revenge. But about the other popular desire, the recovery of their liberty, he will discover two things. He will find that a small part of the people wish to be free for the purpose of commanding, while all the others – who constitute an immense majority - desire liberty so as to be able to live in greater security. In all states, however organized, there are never more than forty or fifty citizens who attain a position that entitles them to command. A prince can either put them out of the way or give them a share in public honors and offices, according to their social status. This will content them. The rest, who only care to live in security, are easily satisfied by institutions and laws that confirm at the same time the general security of the people and the power of the prince.

Machiavelli has accepted the Ciceronian belief that the vast majority of the people want their liberty, meaning nothing more than security against the oppression of the wealthy and more powerful. What sustains liberty is rule by law and institutions. Corruption is the lack of both and where this is the case, there is no constitution at all, only despotic pride vanity and whim. For Machiavelli it is clear that despotic whim can be expressed by a tyrant or by a people. He thinks Rome under Caesar had a people that was thoroughly corrupt, a faction, and hence, tyrannical. In the case of ancient Rome, Machiavelli thinks that kings had to be extinguished because they had become corrupt, while the people remained to some degree honest, their customs and institutions remaining alive. But a corrupt people living under the rule of a prince can never become free even should the prince be removed. A corrupt people is one without regulated customs and traditions. A corrupt people can only become settled if a new prince is created, whose own qualities and virtues can maintain their liberty.

Where there is corruption there is an incapacity to maintain free institutions, and such corruption results from there being a great inequality in a state. To reduce inhabitants to equality requires the application of extraordinary measures which few know how or are willing to employ. It would require the complete destruction of gentlemen or nobility. It is beyond doubt that Machiavelli is no proto-democrat; he is speaking of creating equality before the law and not of reduction of all citizens to the same social equality. His interest is in equality before the law while sustaining differentials in public honors and status. Indeed, he argues that free cities need to be rich in the sense that profits, say from military campaigns, are left to the public treasury, but their individual inhabitants ought to be kept poor. Machiavelli's attitude to the populace is that they require relatively little to keep them content and that if properly guided, that is, controlled by laws, they are neither servile nor do they command with insolence.

Machiavelli is not giving the people an opportunity to be involved in shaping legislation but rather in consenting to laws proposed by experts. Hence, he says that princes show themselves superior in making laws and in forming civil institutions and new statutes and ordinances, while the people are superior in maintaining those institutions, laws and ordinances. What does it mean for Machiavelli to say that since every republic is composed of nobles and people, the protection of liberty is best confided to those who have least desire in violating it? Remember that republic is the well-established humanist Latin word for any good constitution. Included in Machiavelli's examples of republics are Sparta, Venice and Rome – all ' mixed regimes' – and both Sparta and Venice lasted longer than Rome. All states, whatever their constitutional forms, are comprised of the rich and poor, the nobles and the people. Now the nobles have always had a desire to dominate, while the people only have the wish not to be dominated. Hence, it is the people who have the greater desire to live in the enjoyment of liberty. Machiavelli trusts the people because their only desire is to preserve that which they already possess. Machiavelli insists that the people as a whole are better guardians of liberty. The nobles must have their aggression turned to conquering neighbous. Given that states naturally rise or decline and can never remain stable, Machiavelli takes ancient Rome's constitution as a model of success and despite all the difficulties, he is prepared to tolerate the unavoidable conflicts between the nobles in the Senate and the people. This is because the natural enmities between rich and poor can never be eliminated. Instead of trying to eliminate them, they can be made to creatively serve the public good. Hence, Rome's historical genius consisted in recognizing that the divided power of a mixed regime is naturally more effective than the concentrated power of a simple regime.

Machiavelli believed that anyone who would foresee what has to be, should reflect on what has been for everything that happens in the world has a genuine resemblance to what happened in ancient times. This is because agents who bring such things about are men, and he insisted that men have and always have had the same passions. Machiavelli, in looking old liberties, was not nostalgically escaping to the past but attempting to establish continuities in the present with that past. He was certainly not looking forward to what would become a new, arbitrary and conventionally established autonomy of subjects, a new individual liberty that would come into existence. Machiavelli's liberty was not Hobbes's liberty. Machiavelli's was perhaps one of the last great statements about the liberty that medieval theorists and practitioners, in successful monarchies and city-state republics, believed was natural to men and which the state, monarchy or republic was meant to acknowledge and secure.

Religion and Politics

The eclipse in the West of the ideal of the active citizen, is hard to explain fully. But it is clear enough that the antithesis of homo politicus is the homo credenza of the Christian faith; the citizen whose active judgment is essential is displaced by the true believer. While it would be quite misleading to suggest that the rise of Christianity effectively banished secular considerations from the life of rulers and ruled, it unquestionably shifted the source of authority and wisdom from the citizen to otherworldly representatives. The Christian worldview transformed the rationale of political action from that of the polis to a theological framework. The Hellenic view of man as formed to live in a city was replaced by a preoccupation with how humans could live in communion with God. In sharp contrast to the Greek view that the polis was the embodiment of political good, the Christian worldview insisted that the good lay in submission to God's will. How the will of God was to be interpreted, and articulated with systems of secular power, preoccupied Christian Europe for centuries, until the very notion of a single religious truth was shattered by the Reformation.

Christianity certainly did not ignore questions about the rules and goals that humans ought to accept in order to live a productive life. Although Christianity was imposed on many communities, it could scarcely have become a world religion unless it bore values and aspirations, which commended themselves to some extent by virtue of their role in human affairs. Moreover, it would be wrong to regard Christianity as a complete retreat from ideals, which had been so central to parts of the ancient world. The ideal of equality, for example, was to a degree preserved in Christianity, despite being embedded in a wholly different context. It has been suggested that the Christian affirmation of the equality of men before God, with its gesture to the possibility of a community in which nobody has superior moral or political rights, was the only basis on which values of equality could be preserved for society where the mass of people lived at near or below subsistence level. Under such conditions, the religious vision of equality was, at least a way of maintaining the vision. Clearly, Christianity was used to justify a diverse array of institutions, including slavery and serfdom. But it contained contradictory elements, some of which were later to become seeds of its own supercession.

St. Augustine's *The City of God,* written between 410 and 423 AD, has frequently been regarded as the most authoritative statement of the superiority of ecclesiastical power over the secular. Augustine's insistence that the history of the Church was the march of God in the world and that the true Christian ought not to focus on the problems of this temporal life was immensely influential in medieval Europe. Written during the early stages of the fall of the Roman Empire, *The City of God* recommended firmly the harnessing of 'the desire for earthly things to the desire for the heavenly city. The illumination offered by God could guide the true believer to the everlasting blessings that are promised for the future.

The Middle Ages did not give rise to extensive reflection on the nature of political community that could become central to political philosophy. While there were some important political innovations in Europe, these did not crystallize into a major new form of democratic system. Undoubtedly, the Eurocentric nature of much contemporary political theory has prevented an adequate grasp of important developments outside Europe during medieval times; and no doubt a great deal has been lost to the historical record. But until the work of Thomas Aquinas in the thirteenth century, the influence of the Church Fathers, and of Augustine in particular, on political thought was profound, and an important factor in explaining its relative stagnation.

The distinction between the spheres of secular and spiritual jurisdiction was re-examined by Aquinas, who attempted to integrate the rediscovered work of Aristotle with the central teachings of Christianity. Among the many unsettling aspects of his writings was the best form of government it ought not to be ascribed unlimited authority. In his view, a monarch's rule was legitimate only to the extent that it upheld natural law – that part of the 'eternal law' disclosed to human reason. Since the state had no authority in the interpretation of religious doctrine, the Church could 'stand in judgment' over rulers. Moreover, rebellion against a ruler was justified if natural law was repeatedly violated. Thus, the idea of limited, constitutional government central to the development of the liberal democratic tradition – was anticipated by Aquinas, despite his ultimate overriding concern for the development of the Christian community.

So much was the medieval view of society conceived as a whole-a divinely ordained hierarchy of rank and order in the 'Great Chain of Being'–that the idea of the state, in anything like its modern form, could not be found. In modern Western political thought, the idea of the state is often linked to the notion of an impersonal and privileged legal or constitutional order with the capability of administering and controlling a given territory. While this notion found its earliest expression in the ancient world especially in Rome, it did not become a major object of concern until the late sixteenth century. It was not an element of medieval political thinking. The idea of an impersonal and sovereign political order could not predominate while political rights, obligations and duties were closely tied to religious tradition and the feudal system of property rights. Similarly, the idea that human beings were individuals or a people, with a right to be citizens of their state, could not develop under the constraining influences of the closed circle of medieval intellectual life.

The historical changes that contributed to the transformation of medieval notions of politics were immensely complicated. Struggles between monarchs and barons over the domain of rightful authority; peasant rebellions against the weight of excess taxation and social obligation, the spread of trade, commerce and market relations; the flourishing of Renaissance culture with its renewed interest in classical political ideas including Athenian democracy and Roman law; the consolidation of national monarchies and the absolutist state system in Europe notably in England, France and Spain; religious strife and the challenge to the universal claims of Catholicism; the struggle between church and state–all played a part. As the grip of feudal traditions and customs was loosened, the nature and limits of political authority, law, rights and obedience emerged as a preoccupation of European political thought. Not until the end of the sixteenth century did the concept of the state, became a central object of political analysis.

Of all the developments that helped trigger new ways of thinking about the proper form of the state, it was perhaps the Protestant Reformation that was the most significant. The Reformation did more than just challenge papal jurisdiction and authority across Europe; it raised questions about political obligation and obedience in a most stark manner. To whom allegiance was owed – the Catholic Church, a Protestan ruler, particular religious sects – was an issue that did not easily resolve itself. The bitter struggle between religious factions, which spread across Europe during the last half of the sixteenth century, and reached their most intensive expression during the Thirty Years War in Germany, made it clear that religion was becoming a highly divisive force. Very gradually, it became apparent that the powers of the state would have to be separated from the duty of rulers to uphold any particular faith. This conclusion alone offered a way forward through the dilemmas of rule created by competing religions, all seeking to secure for themselves the kind of privileges claimed by the medieval Church.

But it was not just the strife created by the Reformation movements that had a lasting impact on political thought. For the teachings of Luther and Calvin contained at their very heart a new conception of the person as 'an individual'. In the new doctrines, the individual was conceived as alone before God, the sovereign judge of all conduct and directly responsible for the interpretation and enactment of God's will. This was a notion with profound and dynamic consequences. In the first instance, it loosened the individual from the direct institutional support of the Church and, in so doing, helped stimulate the notion of the individual agent as master of its destiny, the centerpiece of much later political reflection. It directly sanctioned, in addition, the autonomy of secular activity in all domains, which did not directly conflict with moral and religious practice. The development, when joined with the momentum for political change initiated by the struggle among religions, and between religious and secular powers, constituted a major new impetus to re-examine the nature of society and state.

This is Machiavelli's way of getting the contemporary church, with its theological intrusion into men's inner intentions and its presumed monopoly of the moral domain, out of politics. He thought that what the contemporary Church taught had actually deprived Italy of religion. Had the Christian religion from the beginning been maintained according to the principles of its founder, then Christian states and republics would have been much more united and happy than they are. To Machiavelli, the Christian religion is now corrupt, and the court of the Church of Rome has destroyed all piety and religion in Italy. Not only had the current church presided over the replacement of ancient religious customs with a humility that prevented Italians from securing their civic well-being. The church as a temporal power, in not having been powerful enough to master all Italy, nor having permitted any other power to do so, has been the cause of Italy not having been united under one head, thereby becoming prey to powerful barbarians.

Like most Italians of his day, Machiavelli held the church to be peculiarly responsible for this state of affairs. Too weak to unite Italy himself, the pope was still strong enough to prevent any other ruler from doing so, while his international relationships made him a leader in the vicious policy of inviting foreign intervention. This is the reason for the bitter irony with which Machiavelli so frequently assails the church:

> We Italians then owe to the Church of Rome and to her priests our having become irreligious and bad; but we owe her a still greater debt, and one that will be the cause of our ruin namely, that the Church has kept and still keeps our country divided became a prey not only to the powerful barbarians, but of whoever chose to assail her.

Apart from a common hatred of the papacy as the cause of Italian disunion, which Machiavelli shared with Marsilio, the two men had substantially similar idea about the political utility which religion ought to have as its secular consequence. Machiavelli's secularism, however, goes much beyond Marsilio's and is free from all the sophistications imposed by the twofold truth. Marsilio defended the autonomy of reason by making Christian morals otherworldly; Machiavelli condemns them because they are otherworldly. The Christian virtues he believed to be servile in their effects on character and be contrasted Christianity unfavorably in this respect with the more virile pagan religions of antiquity:

> Our religion places the supreme happiness in humility, lowliness, and a contempt for wordly object, whilst the other, on the contrary, places the supreme good in grandeur of soul, strength of body, and all such other qualities as render men formidable. These

> principles seem to me to have made men feeble, and caused them to become an easy prey to evil-minded men, who can control them more securely, seeing that the great body of men, for the sake of gaining paradise, are more disposed to endure injuries than to avenge them.

As this passage suggests, Machiavelli was not indifferent to the effects which morals and religion, in the masses of mankind, have upon social and political life. He sanctioned the use of immoral means by rulers to gain an end, but he never doubted that moral corruption in a people makes good government impossible. He had nothing but admiration for the civic virtues of the ancient Romans and of the Swiss in his own day, and he believed that these grew out of purity in the family, independence and sturdiness in private life, simplicity and frugality of manners, and loyalty and trustworthiness in performing public duties. But this does not mean that the ruler must believe in the religion of his subjects or practice their virtues. Machiavelli was by no means blind to imponderable forces in politics, but the imponderables were still for him merely forces. An army fights with morale as truly as with guns, and the wise ruler sees that both are of the best quality. Machiavelli offers an extreme example of a double standard of morals, one for the ruler and another for the private citizen. The first is judged by success in keeping and increasing his power; the second, by the strength which his conduct imparts to the social group. Since the ruler is outside the group, or at least in a very special relation to it, he is above the morality to be enforced within the group. His two books were written within ten years of the day on which Martin Luther nailed his theses to the door of the church in Wittenberg, and it was the effect of the Protestant Reformation to involve politics and political thought more closely with religion and with differences of religious faith than had been the case during most of the Middle Ages. Machiavelli's indifference to the truth of religion became in the end a common characteristic of modern thought, but it was emphatically not true of the two centuries after he wrote. In this sense his philosophy as Sabine has commentated was both 'narrowly local and narrowly dated'. Had he written in any country except Italy or had he written in Italy after the beginning of the Reformation, and still more after the beginning of the Counter Reformation in the Roman church, it is impossible to suppose that he would have treated religion as he did.

Machiavelli undoubtedly believed that where religion exists appeal by rulers to divine authority gives rise to good laws, and good laws bring good fortune and from good fortune results happy success in all enterprises. But where men do not fear God, a country will come to ruin unless it be sustained by the fear of the Prince, which may temporarily supply the want of religion. Savonarola had been successful in persuading his subjects that he conversed with God. Machiavelli thinks Savonarola's success was the consequence of how he appeared to Florentines: living a pure life, and choosing with skill the subjects of his discourses. But when appearances and persuasion fail to maintain men in their faith then recourse must be had to force in order to maintain them in that faith. States that cannot rely on their unity being maintained by ancient religious customs and the fear of God had better discover ways and means of establishing political customs which will similarly providing security and contentment.

Machivalli followed an established tradition of discourse on the autonomy of the political. Although it has often been observed that Machiavelli returns to a pagan morality of the ancients, his is a new version of that morality adapting selected old virtue to new times. John of Paris, Marsilio of Padua and William of Ockham each in their own way contributed their different views on this. Like Marsilio, Machiavelli puts forth the view that it may not in the circumstances be prudent for a prince to be a Christian, it is prudent in the circumstances to persuade others that he is. Each of these medieval theorists agreed that men structure and orders their collective wellbeing, de facto by otherwise unauthorized practices, then by custom and laws. So did Machiavelli.

Machiavelli says that everyone, presumably including himself, will admit that it would be highly praiseworthy in a prince actually to possess all the qualities that are reputed to be good, but as they cannot be possessed or observed, human conditions not permitting it, it is necessary that he should be prudent enough to avoid the scandal of those vices without which it would be difficult to save the state. The real skill is in judging which apparent vices and virtues really are vices and virtues in the circumstances.

We have seen that many civic humanists believed that the mass of men were irrational and evil, but the nobility pressed rare attributes of rationality and conventional virtue; Machiavelli, however, express no illusions about a rational and virtuous nobility. The heavens are not open to human scrutiny and the world of action is not open to knowledge of intentions or higher truths. Some see this as a kind of atheism. But a reading of the vast literature on the relation of Fortuna, divine providence, the scope of human free will and divine foreknowledge, written during the fourteenth and fifteenth centuries, would demonstrate the extraordinary extent to which these subjects were on the Christian agenda, dealt with by scholastics and humanists alike. Others argued that philosophy and theology could not be reconciled and the religion did not need the protection of philosophy. Here, in an undoubtedly religious society, was the range of debates on necessity and fortune, knowledge of future contingents and the possibility, or otherwise, of man's penetration of providence and the divine will. Any student who wishes to read one particularly original example of this genre can turn to Lorenzo Villa's *Dialogue on Free Will*. Villa wrote in his concluding exhortation that 'we stand by faith and not by the probability of reason'. In matters of civil science, Machiavelli argued that the probability of reason was sufficient.

The end of the fifteenth century in Europe saw the beginnings of the military revolution and the emergence of the modern state, two developments which set off long crisis in European society, government and political thought. At a geopolitical level, the Ottoman Turks had finally recovered from the long succession crisis following the death of Mohamed II in 1481 and were renewing their assault on eastern Europe and the Mediterranean; many western commentators, observing the political divisions and the lack of credible religious leadership in the West, believed that the final extinction of Christendom had now become a real possibility. The European crisis was particularly acute in northern and central Italy, an area which lost its dominant position in the European economy soon after 1500 and for the first time since the mid thirteenth century came under the control of non-Italian powers. The disastrous decades around 1500 shattered the cultural self confidence of some Italians, particularly in Florence, and led to some serious questioning of their cultural traditions. The naïve claim of the humanists that political reform could be effected through moral uplift among the political classes came to be regarded with skepticism.

That Machiavelli was himself a humanist, in the most concrete professional sense, can no longer be denied. His relation to the previous tradition of humanist thought, however, is more complex. Certainly, he inherited that flexibility of political loyalties characteristics of humanists in general; what he wanted was power, and he did not much care whether he enjoyed it under a princely or a republican regime. Like the humanists, he believed that encouraging virtue among the ruling classes was the most effective means of reform. He was interested more in changing political culture than political institutions. He believed that the study of classical antiquity held lessons for the modern world and that the Roman Empire had a special exemplary status as the most successful polity in world history. He was certainly realistic in his political analysis; he eschewed teleology in historical explanation; and he was a frank critic of contemporary Christianity.

Machiavelli wrote treatises to curry favors both with the Medici and with their republican opponents, but when writing as a republican, he was far more populist in his outlook than his humanist predecessors. This was because the regime he served before 1512 and the regime he aspired to serve in the later 1520s both aimed at wide participation; the regime that ruled Florence between 1494 and 1512, indeed, enjoyed the widest extent of popular participation of any government in Florentine history. Whatever might be said about his own commitment to republicanism, Machiavelli was the first Renaissance humanist to defend popular government in his published writings.

Secondly, Machiavelli's critique of Christianity is far more radical than anything in the humanist traditions. Previous humanists, aware of the conflict between pagan and Christian values, try either like Valla to recast current Christianity in light of pagan values; or like Ficino to minimize the differences between high pagan and Christian theology; or like Bruni to make a sharp distinction between political and religious values, assigning to each its proper sphere. Machiavelli makes no attempt to hide the fact that Christian morality is inconsistent with the morality needed to create a successful polity along the lines of the Roman republic. He boldly subordinates religion to the interests of civil society. His instrumental and functionalist view of religion, surely incompatible with religious belief, has no parallel in earlier western political thought.

Machiavelli also breaks with humanist tradition in the way he uses classical authorities. Earlier humanists had advocated external imitation of the ancient: the reproduction of speech, actions, artifacts and virtue. Machiavelli rejects this kind of imitation altogether as superficial. What he wants to know from the past, and especially from the Roman past, are the secrets of power, glory and success. To do this he needs to get beyond the pieties of ancient and modern moralists. One had to study the actions of the ancients as well as the moderns to discover, not their moral beliefs, but how they had actually behaved, and why this behavior had failed or proved successful. One could then derive certain rules of conduct, which would limit the role of fortune and increase the chances of success. By following these rules one would acquire, not the four cardinal virtue of traditional morality, but Virtue in Machiavelli's special sense of the word: strength, prowess, ability, power.

In *The Prince* especially, but also in the *Discourses,* Machiavelli stresses the rules of behavior inculcated by traditional morality. It is here that Machiavelli challenges a set of assumptions fundamental to western political thought and unquestioned by any earlier humanists. From the time of Plato, philosophers had agreed that there was an unbreakable connection between nature, happiness and virtue. Nature, it was held, wanted human beings to be happy; she was designed in such a way as to produce happiness for those who followed the rules of correct behavior. The rules of correct behavior, the laws of nature for mankind, were the virtue and were discoverable by reason. The exercise of the virtue led to happiness. An analogous system governed political life. States were natural institutions. The whole art of politics consisted in producing and conserving virtue in those who ruled the polity. Even Augustine, though he transposed the rewards of virtue of the next life, did not deny the ultimate connection between creation, goodness and happiness. The part of nature we experience in this life, subject to time and change, might be defective in the sense of not rewarding virtue with happiness. but virtue aided by grace would ultimately enjoy beatitude when the soul escaped from temporal to eternal creation. It is precisely this connection between nature, happiness and traditional virtue that Machiavelli denies. His reason for doing so is stated bluntly in the famous fifteenth chapter of *The Prince:*

> Because there is so much difference between how men live and how they ought to live, the ruler who forsakes what is usually done for what ought to be done invite ruin, not self-preservation. For a man who wants to take a vow of goodness in all things, must come to ruin among so many who are not good. Therefore, a prince who wishes to remain in power must necessarily acquire the ability to do evil, using it or not using it as necessity requires.

It has been argued by Isaiah Berlin that what Machiavelli is actually doing is reviving a pagan morality to oppose to the Christian morality of his time and that his originality consists in his recognizing the incommensurability of these two moral systems. But this cannot be the case. There are no ancient moralists – with the exception, perhaps, of Gorgias and Thrasymachus – who would condone the kind of behaviors Machiavelli calls for in his two famous political treatises. The wicked no doubt prospered in the ancient as in the modern world, but there was no pagan code of morality that sanctioned vice in the interests of political power. Equally mistaken is the contention of Benedetto Croce and his many followers that Machiavelli divorced politics from morality. What Machiavelli has in fact done, in effect, is to recognize the moral heteronomy of ends and means: that not all good ends can be secured by good means, that not all good means issue in good ends. In so doing he has left behind the unified eudemonistic and teleological ethics of older western thought and has embraced the dilemmas of modern ethics, where being good and doing good are often seen to be in conflict. On the one hand, a 'consequentiality' ethics where the goodness of ends must be allowed to trump the goodness of means; on the other, a Kantian 'deontological' ethics where the goodness of an act is dependent on its being free from the interests of the actor: this is the new ethical world that Machiavelli began to explore in the second decade of the sixteenth century.

Machiavelli is sometimes called the father of political science, and it can now be seen why this is so. He argues that political life is subject to a different kind of moral calculus, one in which an actor must be held responsible for the result even of good acts. The prince who allows disorders to arise because he shrinks from cruelty is responsible for the evils resulting from his goodness. What this consequentiality ethics presupposes, however, is that we can predict accurately the full results of our actions in any given set of circumstances. Without a reasonable certainty about the consequences of our acts, no moral principle can be derived; unless we know cruelty will suppress disorders, there can be no possible justification for it. The claim, then, that a consequentiality ethics can be valid is tantamount to a claim that we have a scientific knowledge of human behaviors, taking scientific in the sense of being able to predict behaviors according to known laws of human nature. This kind of knowledge-claim is one that Machiavelli makes over and over again in *The Prince* and *The Discourse*. Again and again he says that if rulers act in a given way, certain results must necessarily follow. He assumes (1) that human nature is uniform in time and space, (2) that human beings act nearly always from selfish motives and (3) that they act rationally. Applying these principles to particular circumstances, rigorously ignoring issues of right and wrong, will enable the experienced observer to predict the behaviors of political actors and hence to make the correct decisions and moves so as to avoid undesirable outcome. The structure of consequentiality ethics and Machiavelli's political science thus require the observer to make a rigid distinction between the descriptive and the normative. This distinction, too, is one of the characteristic marks of modern moral and scientific reasoning, distinguishing it from the teleological reasoning of the pre-modern West, in which value may be derived from fact and fact from value.

In Machiavelli the problem of political ideology and the political practice of ideology is centered on two themes, one of which – religion – is relatively straightforward, whereas the other – the representation of the prince's person in popular opinion – is highly complex. Machiavelli starts out from religion as a given which is absolutely impossible to ignore, since it is the existing dominant mass ideology. But he does not accept it at face value. He categorically does not confront religion with the question of its origin and religious credentials. He considers it from an exclusively political, factual point of view, as an instrument, alongside the army, for the foundation, constitution and duration of the state. He treats it as an existing reality defined by its political function. Machiavelli discusses religion in Book I of the *Discourses,* immediately after elaborating his theory of the foundation of a new state by a single individual, and devotes several chapters to the Romans' religion. His basic theme is as follows: Romulus had only laid the initial foundations of Rome and designed its laws; having found a very fierce people and wishing to bring them to civil obedience with the arts and peace, Numa Pompilius turned to religion as an absolutely necessary support for maintaining a civilized society. The text goes on to show the function of religion: it is the precondition for military and legal obedience and, through recourse to God's authority, induces the people to accept the introduction of new institutions, as well as the crucial decisions required at critical moments. Thus, it is because they knew how to make themselves masters of the art of manipulating oracles – and, on the eve of battles, interpreting the behavior of sacred fowl not always desirous of pecking! – that Roman kings, consuls and commanders could secure the support of the people or soldiers.

Machiavelli fell that religion is an absolutely necessary support for maintaining a civilized society. Religion plays an ideological function. Religion rallies the people to existing institutions; it secures their obedience and submission to military and legal regulations. This adhesion, this popular consent, is indispensable to the functioning of the army and laws. Without religion, no army or law signifies: without the support of ideology, no popular consent to the state. It is indeed a question of ideology, since religion elicits such popular consent without violence, in and through the simple idea and fear of the gods:

> Just as the observance of divine worship is the cause of the greatness of republics, so the disregard of divine worship is the cause of their ruin, because where fear of God is lacking, that kingdom must either come to ruin or be sustained through fear of a Prince who makes up for the shortcomings in its religion.

So the essence of religion is fear, which is the most economical and reliable form of ideology. But at the same time religion is the most necessary support because, when it comes to fear, fear of the gods has the immense advantage over fear of the prince that it is constant, not exposed to the vicissitudes of the political existence of an individual who might not only die, but also commit blunders. Hence the fundamental political rule:

> The rulers of a republic or a kingdom must uphold the foundations of the religion they profess; and having done this, they will find it an easy matter for them to maintain a devout republic and, consequently, one that is good and united. They must also encourage and support all those things that arise in favor of this religion, even those they judge to be false.

Considering the volley of blows Machivelli delivered to the Papal states, and what he regarded as the papacy's political treason, it will be appreciated that these lines on religion are truly those of a great politician. From them a certain conception of religion emerges, as two dimensional, mass political and moral ideology: on the one hand, fear, keeping subjects obedient; on the other, virtue, inspiring them to conduct and action worthy of the state. The prince is not some ordinary, private individual. We recall Machiavelli's little phrase on the 'adventure' involved in making the transition from private individual to prince. This process of becoming-a prince demands prolonged practice. But in his essence, even as a novice, the prince is no longer a private individual: he is a political individual, wholly defined by his political function, by the necessary existence of the state in the guise of an individual.

The private individual seeks satisfaction of his needs or passions; he is subject to the categories of religion and morality. He is judged according to the terms of the moral alternative: vices and virtue. His perfection is defined by moral virtue. For his part, the prince belongs to a different realm of existence. It is not satisfaction of his needs that motivates him, or assuagement of his passions that should guide him. He is beyond the moral categories of vice and virtue beyond good and evil. For he pursues a completely distinct goal: a historical goal – founding, consolidating and expanding a state that endures. His perfection resides not in moral virtue, but in political virtue–that is to say, in the excellence of all the political virtue–of character, intelligence, etc.–appropriate to accomplishment of his historic task.

At this level of existence, the prince can be judged by only one criterion: success. The adage 'the result alone counts' can be literally applied to him in all its rigour. This is so, however, on condition that it is understood that the result is itself defined by the prince's historical task–that it is only this result that counts; all the rest are condemned. We are at the antipodes of any vulgar pragmatism. The result alone counts: but the goal is the sole arbiter of the result that counts.

It is form this perspective that the relation between political virtue and moral virtue and vice can be considered. Political virtue is not the opposite of moral virtue: it is of a different order. It does not exclude moral virtue; Political virtue is so positioned vis-à-vis moral virtue that it can include it, yet simultaneously exceed it. Thus, political virtue can take the form of moral virtue. But it must then be said that the prince is morally virtuous through political virtue, and Machiavelli would like him to be so as often as possible.

But political virtue is so positioned relative to virtue that it makes the prince 'prepared to act immorally', as Machiavelli puts it – even capable of committing a crime, a parricide (Romulus), an assassination, a breach of trust (Borgia), and so-on. Once again, it is the result alone that counts – that is to say the historical task with which we are acquainted. Thus, it cannot be called virtue to kill one's fellow-citizens, to betray one's friends, to be treacherous, merciless and irreligious', writes Machiavelli of Agathocles' appallingly cruel and inhumane conduct, and countless wicked deeds'. Machiavelli returns to this theme in connection with cruelty. When it is employed continuously, it goes on increasing, in a spiral of violence, and is bad. By contrast, when, at the state's inception, it is imperative to strike a blow, cruelty may be necessary and good.

Founding the state, seeking and achieving the well-being of one's subjects: this is the result that counts and judges virtue, as it judges the moral virtue and vices the prince has assumed and practiced the virtue. Moral as often as possible, immoral when the political result dictates it. This is why the virtue of the prince-individual has nothing to do with some individualism of moral conscience. While it is the attribute of an individual, virtue is not the intrinsic essence of individuality; it is merely the reflection, as conscious and responsible as possible of the objective conditions for accomplishment of the historical task of the hour in a prince-individual.

Machiavelli's readers often take at face value his claim that Christianity has weakened Italy's civic spirit and martial valor, leaving it open to priestcraft and foreign invasion. Some scholars see this critique of Christianity as an expression of the irreligious, immoral, non-pagan, or scientific Machiavelli, making it the chief index of his modernity. One subset within this group treats Machiavelli's anthropology as a secularized version of Augustine on original sin, an Eden behind it and redemption before it. Another view of Machiavelli on religion sees him as treating religion, whatever its teachings, functionally, as an instrument promoting desirable political behavior. This is why they regard Machiavelli as original and modern; although some argue rightly that Machiavelli is here simply imitating the ancient Roman historians, who all treat religion in just this way. For some proponents of the functionalist interpretation, it does not preclude Christian belief on Machiavelli's part. For them his brief is not against Christianity itself but against clericalism, the papacy, and Christianity as it is currently interpreted and practiced. Still others recognize Machiavelli's acceptance of signs and portents, saintly behavior and miracles, and other indices of God's existence and action in human history. They also note Machiavelli's praise of biblical leaders seen as divinely inspired and his inclusion of them among the founders of religions and states who head his list of heroes. Going farther, some scholars argue that Machiavelli was a conventional, if not an ardent or impeccable Christian, who joined a religious confraternity before which he preached his Exhortation of Penitence, and the apparent recipient of the last rites of his church after a deathbed confession.

Can these conflicting assessments of Machiavelli on religion be integrated? To some extent, yes. Machiavelli recognizes that the foreigners who have overrun Italy are as Christian as the Italians. At home and abroad, their Christianity has not undermined their military strength or the civic virtue Machiavelli associates with republics, seemed to have preempted Machiavelli's own anti-clerical, anti-papal, anti oligarchic, and anti-Medician positions. If we foreground Machiavelli's desire to defend his own version of republicanism by undermining the Savonarolan alternative and if we recall that he treats Christianity positively in other contexts, it becomes possible to read those passages where he criticizes Christianity as practiced in Italy as texts with an anti-Savonarolan subtext. Read this way, they are not incompatible with his acceptance of Christianity as true or as politically constructive elsewhere. In approaching this topic, we should also remember the longstanding associations that bound Christianity to politics and warfare.

Addressing this last point first, the claim that Christianity induces pacifism would have raised eyebrows in Machiavelli's day. For throughout the Middle Ages religious wars had been fought on the authority of Christian leaders. 'Just War' theories had proliferated and were expressed in liturgy, theology, popular preaching, vernacular literature, and visual art. In the Middle Ages, church leaders had abandoned the effort to mitigate warfare through the Peace of God and Truce of God. Now, they baptized the sword, canonized military saints, founded military religious orders, used them to fight the Reconquest and the Crusades, labeled any war against enemies of the faith, and even enemies of the papacy, a Crusade, and elaborated indulgence theory to promote participation in and support of such wars. St Francis and St. Dominic may have interacted peaceably with heretics or non-Christians; but by the later thirteenth century mendicants joined other religious orders in preaching the Crusades and in helping participants financed their campaigns. This mandate returned with new urgency in the early sixteenth century, with conquistadors recycling Crusade rhetoric and Pope Leo X calling for a Crusade against the Turks in Eastern Europe.

Machiavelli's charge that Christianity had unmanned them and his laying the blame on the friars must have sounded bizarre. Yet, he makes this claim. While he states that Christianity "shows us the truth and is the true way," he ads that it "makes us esteem less the honor of the world," causing Christians to shun resolute action and avenging wrongs in favor of a passivity, sloth, humility, abjectness, and contempt for human things that makes them prey to military defeats and the dominion of the wicked. All this, he argues, is a misreading of Christianity. But it leads Christians to disdain the lessons of antiquity and it impairs their efficacy in both offensive and defensive war. And who is responsible? Machiavelli says that Francis and Dominic brought the church back to first principles; without them, Christianity "would have disappeared." But the result of this mendicant salvage operation was to make the laity supine and uncritical of nefarious prelates. While for numerous reason Popes rank high on Machiavelli's list of corrupts churchmen, his insistence on the critical role of the friars as agents of demoralization strongly suggests that these texts bear a coded meaning.

Catholics before, during, and after Machiavelli's time have been able to mix anti-clericalism of the Popes with sincere religious belief, and there is good evidence to suggest that Machiavelli is one of them. He makes straightforward references to Christian beliefs as normal and expresses Christian sentiments himself. He recognizes that Christianity can have positive as well as negative effects on politics. Machiavelli recognizes the liberty of the church as a legal reality, For better or worse, ecclesiastical principalities are a fact of life and they are instituted by higher power. For Machiavelli, God acts in history and his intervention and providence are forces to be reckoned with fortune and necessity. This principle applies to the gentiles as well as to Jews and Christians. God sent great leaders, like Numa and Scorpio Africans, to the Romans; most recently, the hand of God is visible in the Turkish victory at Mochas. The political interaction between God and man is a two-way street. In serving their communities' common good, Machiavelli states, leaders also serve God; politics offers the greatest opportunity to do so. In addition to intervening directly, God manifests His will through sign and portents; according to Machiavelli, nothing important happens without them. These phenomena not only presage coming events but also motivate people, as did the miracles that persuaded imperial Rome and her Germanic invaders to accept Christianity. God also manifests His power in His saints through their holy lives. Machiavelli's calendar of saints includes Augustine, Boethius, Benedict of Nurse, early Popes before they started encroaching on secular affairs, benefactors of the church like the Holy Roman Emperor Henry I and his consort. Crusade preachers like Peter the Hermit, the martyred Thomas Becket, Copestone V, whose holiness can be seen in his rejection of papal honors.

Machiavelli expresses conventional Christian ideas in a number of his minor works; he refers to God's creation of the universe and mankind, original sin and the banishment of the primal parents from Eden, and the Cain and Abel story.

Machiavelli's state papers and letters also make conventional reference to Christianity. Some are doubtless formulaic, as with his expressed hope, in his report on Cesare Borgia's movements in 1503, Machiavelli's main point is that Christians should do more than lament their sins. The introspection enabling them to recognize their faults should lead to action. Penitents should change their outlook and accept self-discipline.

Machiavelli makes this point repeatedly by comparing Hannibal and Scorpio the former acting with harshness and cruelty and the later acting with compassion, chastity, humanity, and religion. Both were successful. On balance, Machiavelli thinks that the ancients used religion well, recognizing its utility in promoting support for the leader's program. But it is not necessary to return to paganism in order to apply this lesson of antiquity, for Jewish and Christian leaders also teach what to follow and what to avoid in the political use of religion.

Machiavelli's most sweeping praise of religion is in the *Discourses*: "Among all famous men those are most famous who have been heads and organizers of religions," and the most "infamous and detestable are those who have been destroyers of religions." His roster of great men starts with Moses. Machiavelli presents Moses as an arch-hero not only because he enforced the law harshly when necessary and because he had the executive ability to lead the unruly Israelites through the desert but also because he was divinely commissioned. Machiavelli likewise praises his successor, Joshua, a general notorious for his take-no-prisoners policy in the battles through which Israel won the Promised Land. Another Old Testament exemplar is David. In *The Prince* Machiavelli describes not the repentant adulterer but the king who defeated his neighbors using his own troops, sometimes, forcibly shifting entire conquered populations, while on the domestic front he defeated expectations, making the fortunes of his people depend on his own and ruling with learning and judgment.

Among Christians, too, religion can promote good arms. Machiavelli states that the Greeks were defeated by the Turks because the Greeks lacked, among other things, religion. On the other hand, the Christian defenders of Rhodes forced the Turks to abandon their siege. Throughout the Florentine histories, Machiavelli presents crusading and the Christian bellicosity it involves as normal and laudable. Fibrosis Colonna, his spokesperson in *The Art of War*, amplifies the point. Commenting on the staffing of citizen militias, he proposes the exclusion of irreligious men; they will make bad soldiers. Religion, he adds, supplies an important sanction to the oaths men swear when they join the army and its ceremonies promote military discipline. When challenged for failing to create the citizen militia he advocates, Colonna gives as a major reason the blasphemous, licentious, and irreligious nature of the manpower at his disposal: "By what God or by what saint can I have them take the oath?" he asks; "how can those who feel contempt for God respect men?"

Good laws no less than good arms depend on religion. Machiavelli states this general rule in considering the institutions of the Roman Numa. But he also applies it to Christian politicians. Fear of the Lord is not only the beginning of wisdom; it also promotes respect for the rule of law. Religion helps undercut Machiavelli's bets noire, factionalism. He cites a speaker addressing the Florentine Signori in 1372, who observes that the city does not live free but is divided into factions. In part, the speaker attributes this problem to the fact that "religion and the fear of God have been extinguished in all men"; hence, oaths have no force and pledges are broken, civic virtue is abandoned, and corruption so acute sets in that good laws cannot correct it. Most heinous to the speaker are people who mask their partisan ambitions in pious words while actually seeking their own and not the common good. A particularly noxious example in Florentine history is the Duke of Athens, who, intending to make himself prince of Florence, concealed his true motives by faking an appearance of piety and kindness.

Machiavelli and the Idea of the Political

The independent life of European cities was weakened markedly with the fall of the Roman Empire. But it was not undermined entirely, especially in Italy. It is perhaps not surprising, then, to find, with the renewed development of city life during the Renaissance, a revival of interest in the republican thought of ancient Greece and Rome. The ideal of active citizenship in a republic became an abiding concern in the new climate of the independent city-states. Although the thinkers of this period by no means simply endorsed the Athenian conception of democracy, the classical concept of the polis became central to the political theory of Italian cities, preeminently in Florence. The particular problem that had to be faced, however, was how the ideas of the polis could be realized in the particular circumstances of Italy, circumstances that were highly unstable. Since the ancient civilizations had suffered decline and defeat, the question was how could certain of their values be upheld in radically changed historical circumstances. There could be no simple adoption of past models of government. Few understood this better than Machiavelli.

Machiavelli, often regarded as the first theorist of the modern state, sought to explore how a proper balance might be found between the powers of the state and the powers of the citizen in two key texts, *The Prince* and *The Discourses.* For too long *The Prince* has been taken as Machiavelli's major contribution, and this has led to a quite distorted reading of his work. If one places greater stress on *The Discourses*, as contemporary scholars argue, then a distinctive and, in some respects, compelling position emerges. The study of classical history reveals, Machiavelli argued, that the three major constitutional forms of government – monarchy, aristocracy and democracy – are inherently unstable and tend to create a cycle of degeneration and corruption. In passages which parallel elements of Plato and Aristotle, Machiavelli held that after an initial period of positive development monarchy tends to decay into tyranny, aristocracy into oligarchy and democracy into anarchy, which then tends to be overturned in favor of monarchy again.

Machiavelli points directly to Athens as an example of a democracy, which degenerated because of its inability to protect itself from 'the arrogance of the upper class' and 'the licentiousness of the public'. The political world, he contended, was always one of flux and potential chaos. Unlike Plato and Aristotle before him, and Hobbes and Locke after him, Machiavelli did not believe that there was a given or fixed principle of organization which it was the task of government to articulate and sustain. There was no natural or God-given framework to order political life. Rather, it was the task of politics to create order in the world. Machiavelli conceived politics as the struggle to win, utilize and contain power. Politics is thus ascribed a pre-eminent position in life as the chief constitutive element of society. Like so many political thinkers from Plato onwards, Machiavelli conceived of 'the generality of men as self-seeking, lazy, suspicious and incapable of doing anything good unless constrained by necessity. The question was: under what circumstances might people support political order and commit themselves to the state? Or, to put the question in more Machiavellian terms, how might virtue, 'a willingness to do whatever may be necessary for the pursuit of civic glory', be instilled in people?

Machiavelli stressed two key institutional devices as critical to the inculcation of virtue: upholding religious worship and the enforcement of law. The latter, in particular, provides the basis to compel people to place the interests of the community above their own interests: the law can 'make citizens good'. But how can good and bad laws be distinguished? The answer is disclosed by historical investigation into the ways the law has been used to foster civic culture and greatness. The instability of all singular constitutional forms suggests that only governmental system-combining elements of monarchy, aristocracy and democracy can promote the kind of culture on which virtue depends. The best example of such a government was, in Machiavelli's opinion, Rome. Rome's creation of a 'mixed government' was directly linked to its sustained achievement of glory.

It is not only the historical route to this conclusion that is important; Machiavelli's reasoning is theoretical innovation as well. A 'mixed government', structured to compensate for the defects of individual constitutional forms, is most likely to be able to balance the interests of rival social groupings, particularly those of the rich and the poor. Machiavelli's argument should not be confused with later arguments for the state and for representative government based on party competition. Nonetheless, his argument is a precursor of them, anticipating important aspects of their rationale. If the rich and the poor can be drawn into the process of government, and their interests found a legitimate avenue of expression through a division of offices between them, then they will be forced into some form of mutual accommodation. Even watchful of their own positions, they will expand great efforts to ensure that no laws are passed that are detrimental to their interests. The outcome of such efforts is likely to be a body of law that all parties can agree on in the end. Against the dominant traditions of his time, Machiavelli contended that the existence of factions and dissension, far from eroding all possibility of good and effective laws, might be the condition of them. A quite unconventional conclusion was reached: the basis of liberty may be conflict and disagreement.

Writing against the background of competition and war between sixteenth-century Italian city-states, Machiavelli's views were of particular significance; for his argument was that communities have never increased in 'dominion or wealth' except when they have been able to enjoy liberty. Under tyranny, whether imposed by an external power or by a local tyrant, cities or states degenerate in the long run. This means that to say of a city or state that it possesses its liberty is equivalent to saying that it holds itself independent of any authority save that of the community itself. Liberty thus comes to be equated with self-government. If a community can enjoy liberty, as Machiavelli hoped a united Italy would do in the future, it is likely that it will flourish. Machiavelli sought to reinforce this point by referring to classical Athens with its factional disputes and Rome with its conflicts between Senate and Commons as examples of cities, which enjoyed liberty and grew enormously in relatively short periods of time.

The preservation of liberty, however, depended on something more than just a mixed constitution: 'eternal vigilance'. There are always threats to liberty posed by, on the one hand, the particular interests of factions and, on the other hand, competing states. While a mixed constitution is essential to containing the former, the best way of meeting the challenge of competing states is to contain them before one is contained. A policy of expansion is therefore a necessary prerequisite to the preservation of a collectivity's liberty: the application of force is integral to the maintenance of freedom. In so arguing, Machiavelli was firmly placing the ends of the state or community above those of the individual, both at home and abroad; 'reasons of state' held priority over the rights of individuals. A person's duties were first and foremost those required by citizenship. However, Machiavelli linked this classical emphasis on the primacy of civic life directly to the requirements of power politics. Accordingly, 'Machiavellianism' in its more popular contemporary sense emerged: the politics of statecraft and the relentless pursuit of power had priority over individual interests and private morality. Machiavelli thus anticipated certain of the dilemmas of liberalism, but resolved them ultimately in a profoundly anti-liberal way, by granting priority to the preservation of society by whatever means necessary.

Political life is ambiguous. In order to create liberty and political stability, it may not always be possible to resort to law and the minimum use of force. Machiavelli unquestionably preferred liberty to tyranny, but he thought the latter might often be necessary to sustain the former. His judgment hovered uneasily between admiration of a free, self-governing people and of a powerful leader able to create and defend the law. He tentatively sought to reconcile these preferences by distinguishing between, on the one hand, the kind of politics necessary for the inauguration of a state or for the liberation of a state from corruption and, on the other hand, the kind of politics necessary for the maintenance of a state once it had been properly established. An element of democracy was essential to the latter, but quite inappropriate to the former.

In general, however, Machiavelli believed that free government was difficult if not impossible to sustain in the actual political circumstances of Europe. Thus, there was a clear necessity for the resourceful despot to impose his vision of state and society and to create the possibility of order and harmony. The free state would depend on the strong expansionary state to secure the conditions of its existence. The good state was first and foremost the secure and stable state. Therefore, while we find in Machiavelli the germs of a theory of democracy – elements of democracy are necessary to protect the governed from the governors and to protect the governed from each other they have a very precarious existence in the context of other aspects of his thought. What emerges most strongly in his writings is the necessity of an organized political force, supreme in its own territory and actively pursuing a policy of aggrandizement. These ideas were decisive to the development of the notion of the modern state, but there will be a considerable distance from a fully coherent conception of democracy.

Finally, when Machiavelli is said to defend elements of democratic government, it is very important to be clear what is meant. By the standards of his day, he was, it should be stressed, a democrat; that is, he conceived of political participation in broader terms than simply the involvement of the wealthy and/or noble in public affairs. Along with the ancient Greek democrats, he wanted the process of government to include artisans and small traders. The people or citizenry were to be those with independent means who might be expected to have substantial interests in public affairs. Foreigners, laborers, servants and dependents were not, however, regarded as having such an interest. Citizens were men with a stake in the country of unambiguously local descent. Public affairs were their affairs. Freedom, as he understood it, did not entail rights of free speech, expression, belief and association; that is, in his hands it did not yet embrace many of the elements that became central to modern liberalism.

Among the traditions of political thought that emerged during these times two were to become central: the 'civic humanist' or 'classical republican' tradition represented here, above all, by the thought of Machiavelli which maintained a firm foot both in the political theory of the ancient world and in that of the new emerging European order; and the liberal tradition of which Thomas Hobbes and, above all John Locke were among the first exponents. Hobbes marks an interesting point of transition between a commitment to the absolutist state and the struggle of liberalism against tyranny. Locke, by contrast, signals the clear beginnings of the liberal constitutionalist tradition.

However, it is not possible to ignore the 'Machiavellian moment' in these developments and hence it is first necessary to address Machiavelli's thought. Machiavelli provides a context that helps us grasp many later developments. These developments themselves culminated in a new model of democracy – referred to here as 'protective democracy ' – which received its fullest exposition in the work of Jeremy Bentham and James Mill. Protective democracy emphasized the centrality of democratic institutions to safeguard the governed from tyranny of all kinds and form oppression by the state in particular.

Machiavelli And The Modern Prince

Gramsci's Italian background leads him to draw on the ideas of Niccolo Machiavelli in order to develop a practical and action-based approach to polities and history. His approach is one of 'immediate political action' and Gramsci claims that Machiavelli's conception of the world is based on a philosophy of praxis which emphasizes the role of purposeful action. This might be contrasted with the mechanical, deterministic marxism that Gramsci was criticizing. While these views left little scope for human action or creativity, Machiavelli's approach is described as a 'neo-humanism' which 'bases itself entirely on the concrete action of man, who, impelled by historical necessity, works and transforms reality'. This helps enforce Gramsci's belief in human will as Machiavelli is not merely a scientist; he is a partisan, a man of powerful passions, an active politician, who wishes to create a new balance of forces and therefore cannot help concerning himself with what "ought to be".

The Florentine diplomat was concerned with the instability of the Italian city-states and wished to see Italy restored to its former greatness. This requires the rulers to adopt a clear strategy that can create civil unity and order. To do so, the ruler may draw upon different tactics, employing both force and consent in order to maintain power and influence. It appears that Machiavelli favours force when he writes that 'it is desirable to be both loved and feared; but it is difficult to achieve both and, if one of them has to be lacking, it is much safer to be feared than loved'. However, his examples of force are almost exclusively derived from ancient society whereas his discussion of his own society draws much more on the idea of consent or 'civil principality'. Despite his best-known work being called *The Prince*, Machiavelli's writings, in particular *The Discourses*, reveal him to be a modern republican who is interested in less direct forms of rulership and is concerned about popular governance. A broader consent can be developed on the basis of custom and tradition, laws and justice, the dominance of the towns and the middle classes and, above all, through civic virtue and the institutionalization of popular power. Power should operate though various social institutions and through civil society. In this way, states can develop their roots, trunks and branches, and will not be destroyed by the first chill winds of adversity. Here we find a clear precursor to Gramsci's concept of hegemony.

Machiavelli inspires the practical aspect of Gramsci's marxism, but this has its limitations. Just as Marx found inspiration from Hegel, so Gramsci is influenced by the Italian Hegelian philosopher Benedetto Croce. Through Croce Gramsci is able to situate practical activity within a wider context; history is the dialectic between the practical and the ideal, it is unified by spirit and represented by the progress of liberty. Gramsci also draws on the one notable Italian marxist of this time, Antonio Labriola, who introduces the term 'philosophy of praxis' to describe marxism. Gramsci later uses this term in his *Prison Notebooks* in order to evade the prison censors; however, it also captures the spirit of Gramsci's approach, which is to reject the mechanical or scientific aspect of marxism in favour of an emphasis on historical actions and human will. This emphasis is also derived from Georges Sorel, whose conception of revolutionary activity is based the spontaneity of the masses. His notion of myth describes the ideal that inspires the masses to overcome society. Gramsci believed that Sorel's notion of myth could be combined with Machiavelli politics. He angued that Machiavelli's *Prince* could be studied as an historical exemplification of the Sorelian myth – i.e., of a political ideology expressed neither in the form of a cold utopia nor as learned theorizing but rather by the creation of a concrete fantasy which acts on a dispersed and shattered people to arouse and organize its collective will.

The prince in Machiavelli's work is not a real prince but a theoretical abstraction or ideal type. His intention is to form a collective will out of the mass of the people but under the clear direction of a leadership and programme. Gramsci believed that this factor was missing from Italian history and that the prince's task to unify society was still to be achieved. In this sense the role of Machiavelli's prince must now pass on the communist party or 'modern Prince', which must attempt to awaken and develop a national-popular collective will based on its political and ethical leadership.

We can see, therefore, how Gramsci shifts emphasis away from mechanistic marxism towards an active and dynamic politics. Machiavelli is not a cold-blooded political scientist but an advocate of moral and political action. Politics, for Machiavelli, is the art of the possible. What Machiavelli brings to marxism is a politics of statecraft, of tactics and strategy. Power will not fall into the hands of the communist party as a result of objective economic developments, but may be won through conflict and consent. The communist party must turn itself into an intellectual force capable of forging a new political will that is universal and total. It must first bind together an alliance of different groups and interests and offer a leadership which will lay the basis for a new state power. The modern prince must be the proclaimer and organizer of an intellectual and moral reform, which also means creating the terrain for a subsequent development of the national popular collective will towards the realization of a superior, form of modern civilization.

The clear difference between the two philosophers is that Machiavelli's prince is already in power whereas Gramsci's 'modern prince' must struggle to gain that position. Machiavelli advocates a strategy for the ruling class in order to modernize Italy, while Gramsci's modern prince is initially only an aspiring ruler although it must also learn how to maintain power once it is won. Philosophies, Gramsci believes, reflect the class standpoint of the bearer, and in this sense there is a radical distinction between the philosophies of the two thinkers. The philosophy of the modern prince is marxism. However, marxism must win support from the masses. In creating a counter-hegemonic force, the communist party transform existing consciousness and gain an acceptance of the communist worldview. This corresponds to Machiavelli's emphasis on the need to develop a popular will. But it must be combined with the more calculating aspects of Machiavelli's advice so that the 'modern prince' can assess the possibilities inherent in a given situation and decide how best to act. The prince gives way to the party, but the party must learn how to replace the state.

In the history of Western political thought, 'Machiavellianism' has come to signify the principle of realpolitik, that expediency is always preferable to morality in statecraft. As Machiavelli exhorted his prince in the treatise of the same name, a leader should not deviate from what is good if possible, but he should know how to do evil if that is necessary. Irrespective of whether or not Machiavelli deserves his reputation as a teacher of evil, his thought does rest on a profoundly anti-Christian understanding of social life, which had a powerful influence on Nietzsche's philosophy of 'beyond good and evil'. Nietzsche derives to important conceptions from Machiavelli. Firstly, he accepts what he calls 'the Machiavelliism of power that is, the view that morality can always be seen to have been built on 'immoral' foundations; in other words Nietzsche is tremendously influenced by Machiavelli's notion of virtue, a notion which he constantly counterposes to the Christian understanding of virtuous action.

Sheldon Wolin points out that the modernity of Machiavelli consists in his rejection of natural law as a moral standard for judging political life, and in the construction of a pragmatic method in focusing on questions of power. Machiavelli's notion of politics is predominantly an aesthetic one in which the prince experiences the aesthetic exhilaration of stamping reality with his own personality. Machiavelli promulgates a new kind of political knowledge in that he recognizes that evil is implicated in the possibilities for creative political action. Contrary to Plato's positing of a world of forms, Machiavelli grasps that reality is movement. Because humanity finds it difficult to live in a world of becoming, it creates an illusory transcendental world, treating it as a real basis for action. In Machiavelli the emphasis is not so much on the moral basis of political legitimacy, as on achieving political stability and order through a proper understanding of the mechanics of power, 'the ability to exert mastery by controlling an unstable complex of moving forces'. That the application of violence is regarded as abnormal represents, Wolin argues, a significant achievement of the Western political tradition. He argues that Machiavelli's economy of violence aims at the 'pure' use of power undefiled by pride, ambition, or motives of petty revenge. In his writings we do not find any child-like delight in the contemplation of the barbarous and savagely destructive potentialities of power. Concerning Machiavelli's reputation as an immoralist, Wolin's perception that his conception of politics amounts to the view that politics is not to be conducted without ethical criteria, but that the criteria are not to be imported from outside. Machiavelli rejects the idea of any literal translation of ethical acts into political situations, and replaces it with a notion of political irony by introducing an appreciation of the alchemy of the political in which good is transmuted into evil, and evil into good.

Nietzsche was in fact a great admirer of Machiavelli's *The Prince*. On a number of occasions he refers to 'the grand politics of virtue' in terms highly reminiscent of Machiavelli's fundamental insight that legitimacy has its roots in illegitimacy, that civil society has its roots not in justice but in injustice, and that all social orders have been established with the aid of morally questionable means. Nietzsche writes, for example: 'By which means does a virtue come to power? By exactly the same means as a political party: the slandering, inculpation, undermining of virtue that oppose it and are already in power, by robotizing them, by systematic persecution and mockery. Therefore, through sheer "immorality"'. The victory of a moral ideal is achieved by the same 'immoral' means victory, namely, force, lies slander, injustice.

There are a number of similarities between Machiavelli's notion of 'virtue' and Nietzsche's notion of 'will to power'. Both notions refer to creative public action that is beyond the opposition of 'good' and 'evil'. There is no satisfactory equivalent in English of 'virtue' as the word 'virtue' has been translated in a variety of ways as prowess, ability, strength of character, and talent. The word comes from the Roman *vir* (man) and *virtue* (what is proper to man). As one commentator has noted the word has nothing to do with Christian notions of virtue and virtuousness; rather, courage, fortitude, audacity, skill and civil spirit – a whole classical and Renaissance theory of man and culture underlies the world. Whatever translation is used, one must appreciate the creativity the notion attributes to human action. It is this aspect of the notion which so appealed to Nietzsche, for creative and courageous action implies that a person may find it necessary to defy established convention of good and evil. Thus, Nietzsche's use of the notion removes it from its overtly political context and provides it with an aesthetic meaning denoting any kind of action, which is based on the creative entwinement of good and evil. Thus, for example, Nietzsche argues that for every strong and natural species of man, love and hate, gratitude and revenge, good nature and anger, affirmative acts and negative acts, belong together. One is good on condition one also knows how to be evil; one is evil because otherwise one would not understand how to be good. Nietzsche interprets the nineteenth-century picture of man as a triumph over the sentimental portrait of man in the eighteenth century which he finds in Rousseau. What Nietzsche seeks to undermine is the notion that the ideal man is always the one who is 'good':

Rousseau was also a great admirer of Machiavelli, and regarded his masterpiece *The Prince* as a satirical work in which Machiavelli, for certain practical reasons concealed his real political morality, which for Rousseau was one of patriotism and republicanism. There is no doubt that Machiavelli's realism served to temper the idealism of Rousseau's political philosophy. In the first chapter of Book Three of *The Social Contract*, for example, Rousseau acknowledges that there is no single unique and absolute form of government that can be regarded as valid for all communities at all times. Rousseau agrees with Machiavelli that Christianity has done great damage to political life. His statement that 'true Christians are made to be slaves' echoes Machiavelli's claim that whereas paganism praised greatness of soul – magnanimity, physical vigour, and everything that serves to make individuals bold and courageous – Christianity preaches humility, abjection, contempt for human things, and glorifies humble and contemplative human beings, not human beings of action and great deeds.

But how genuine is Rousseau's appreciation of Machiavelli? One commentator has argued that Rousseau's approval of Machiavelli in the *Social Contract*, serves to conceal his divergence from a Machiavelli inspired politics of virtue. In Rousseau, for example, the lawgiver is to respond to public opinion, not establish it. Perhaps the major source of their disagreement from which the rest spring, is Machiavelli's view that whoever founds a State and gives a people laws must assume that human nature is intrinsically weak and wicked, a view which clearly clashes with Rousseau's belief in humanity's natural goodness. Thus, the main difference between Rousseau and Nietzsche in their appropriation of Machievelli is that that whereas Nietzsche is prepared to accept Machiavelli's radical concessions to immorality in the reform of political life, Rousseau is not. One commentator has recently argued that Rousseau never seriously confronts the tragic dimension of politics, which is so central to Machiavelli's concerns. Informing such a tragic conception of politics is the view shared by Nietzsche–that power can never ultimately be justified but only creatively used and abused. In an early, unpublished essay on the Greek State, for example, Nietzsche puts forward the view that 'power gives the first law and there is no law which is not in its fundamental presumption a usurpation of this act of power.'

Nietzsche's critique of modernity is informed by an appreciation of the Renaissance. If ages are to be assessed according to their positive forces, then, Nietzsche says, the age of the Renaissance appears as the last great age. 'We moderns', he writes, 'with our anxious care for ourselves and love of our neighbor, with our virtue of works, of unpretentiousness, of fair play, of scientifically – acquisitive, economic, machine-minded – appear as a weak age'. The modern age is lacking in 'stern and frightful customs'. The cult of equality and demand for equal rights is a sign of decline and exhaustion, for 'the chasm between man and man, class and class, the multiplicity of types, the will to be oneself, to stand out – that which I call the pathos of distance – characterizes every strong age'. For Nietzsche, the Renaissance represented the revaluation of Christian values in order to bring about the triumph of the opposing values, 'noble values': 'I behold a spectacle at once so meaningful and so strangely paradoxical', Nietzsche tells us, that 'it would have given all the gods of Olympus an opportunity for an immortal roar of laughter – Cesare Borgia as Pope and decadence.

Pitkin's assessment that Machiavelli presents a political universe that is neither a fixed, sacred order nor a meaningless accident seems plausible. We face neither eternally valid abstract standards of right that it is our duty to try to approximate, nor inevitable forces moving to predestined goals, nor yet a randomness that defies understanding and effort. It is like dealing with a person, to be sure, and one large and more powerful than ourselves, but nevertheless a being with personality like ours, intention like ours, moods and foibles like ours, open to influence to some extent and in some ways, just as we are, yet never wholly within our control.

Doubts expressed by Hannah Arendt regarding Machiavelli's modernity appear to be persuasive: "In my opinion the scientific character of Machiavelli's theories is often greatly exaggerated." Indeed, one is led to the conclusion that the true prince does not have rational knowledge at all but has, rather and at best, some kind of inexplicable gift or knack, a peculiar genius that defies analysis, an awareness that resists discourse. In a standard formulation, a person has knowledge if the following three conditions obtain: (1) there is a fact about the world; (2) the person believes that, (3) the person is justified in having that belief. In Machiavelli's account of virtue, conditions 1 and 2 might hold, but condition 3 does not, since princely knowledge seems to defy anything that would qualify as justification.

The result is a kind of mysticism. The image is of a world filled with "occult signs and mysterious portents, decipherable by auguries, and haunted by unpredictable Fortuna, a political universe inhabited at its very center by magic. No mere philosopher, no rational human, could operate successfully in this kind of world. Politics is an "art", and the actor who would decide wisely must have the inexplicable, miraculous gifts of a great artist. According to Pocock, this is clearly true of the prophet and the legislator, each of whom is attempting "a task beyond normal human powers."

One plausible line of thought argues that Machiavelli in effect has no philosophical or discursive pretensions, properly understood, and that his method of presentation—his method of thought—is primarily imaginative, figurative, and literary. If politics is an art, then the political thinker must be an aesthete. Thus, we are told that "Machiavelli is an artist as much as he is an historian." His writing is steeped in metaphor, in allusion, and in irony. His methods are fundamentally literary, and his precise intentions are often "obscured by his love of paradox." Indeed, "he was less concerned with the explanation of facts than with making an impressive argument." According to Federico Chabod, Machiavelli relied on "the sudden flash of intuition, identical with that of the great poet, who in any single event detects that ever-recurring workings of a universal process that is part and parcel of the human story." He is not, then, primarily a logician, working from principles from which, by a continuous process of reasoning, rigorous and slavish, he deduces a complete "system." He is first and foremost a man of imagination, who sees his truth in a flash, with blinding clarity. Machiavelli, in common with the greatest politicians—who, like him, so resemble the artist in that their logic and their dogma are completely subordinte to their intuition—has what may literally be termed initial inner illuminations, immediate, intuitive visions of events and their significance. Such, then, is the genius of Machiavelli—a potent genius, peerless in the realm of political thought, consisting entirely of sudden, immediate flashes of insight, coupled with an almost miraculous natural dynamism and the manner and imagery of a great poet. When confronted with a world bereft of natural law, steeped in particularity, and ruled by capricious fortune, the political thinker/ political actor seeks glory in miracles—in explicable flashes of insight and sudden illuminations that far transcend the "slavishness" of logic. Presumably, such illuminations constitute a special kind of wisdom or knowledge. It is a knowledge that emerges out of the exceptional ambition for glory that is a mark of virtue.

Conclusion

In the porch of the 16th century, enigmatic Machiavelli stands as a rock of sinister abuse and offence. We doubt whether any name in literary history to be so generally odious as that of Machiavelli. The sheer volume of Machiavelli commentary testifies to the continuous importance of what he wrote about politics. There has always been something about Machiavelli's political writings, which his readers have found attractive or repulsive, but it is far from easy to pin down exactly what it is. There seem to be, broadly speaking, five distinct possibilities for explaining the perennial interest in Machiavelli's political thought, though to say that there are five is, in a sense, simply to restate that there is a Machiavelli problem.

The first possibility is that what Machiavelli wrote about politics is profoundly shocking. This is the stock Machiavelli of the Elizabethan dramatists, the Machiavelli of 'Machiavelliism'. In this view, Machiavelli is the teacher of lago in *Othello* or Edmund in *King Lear*, the advocate of utterly ruthless and devious methods for the acquisition of power or the doing down of one's enemies. This can even be made into a game played for its own sake, the game of power politics and intrigue played for enjoyment like game of chess, with no other object than to keep playing the great game. The Machiavelli of Machiavellianism certainly exists. His hands are not bloodless. *The Prince* is full of hard and calculated advice about how a new prince should act to establish himself in a recently conquered princedom, and a good deal of the advice is about the use of violence and deceit. So much is clear, but what is not so clear is why the advice should be considered to be especially shocking.

Machiavelli is always careful to cite modern and ancient precedents for what he advises, not to excuse what he has to say but to convince us that his advice would work. His advice to new princes is an extrapolation from the actions of already successful princes, so it is hard to see what was so 'shocking' at least in the sense of being 'shock news'. Machiavelli seems to be saying to princes: 'do what others have already done', only choose your precedents carefully to make sure that you imitate the right Prince in the right circumstances. And the notion that princes might have to do some pretty nasty things now and again to save their states had been a commonplace since ancient times. The ancient Romans, so much admired by the Renaissance humanists, had thought nothing of massacring whole peoples, would put their own surrendered armies to the sword to encourage the others, and would decimate a legion before breakfast. Aristotle himself had said that it was a part of political science to advise a tyrant how to survive, and Aristotle's own advice is straightforwardly Machiavellian: he tells the tyrant to 'act like a king' –that is, to deceive.

From this unlikely but always possible eventuality comes another of Machiavelli's political axioms for a prudent prince: treat everybody as a potential assassin. It can't matter to the prince that he has to operate on the basis of an assumption about human beings which is not true. Machiavelli is perfectly aware of the fact that assassins prepared to risk horrible deaths to kill princes are very rare. The point is rather that the only safe assumption a prince can make is that he is surrounded by assassins. From this follows a third Machiavelli axiom: dissemble affability. Princes are expected to be friendly to their subjects and all princes have to live in courts among friends, family and advisers. The prince must wear the mask while unmasking others, concealing his inner malevolence while seeing through his familiars to the inner malevolence if he is going to survive. Part of Machiavelli's message is that those who wish above all things for a quiet life have no business going into the prince business in the first place.

What does matter a great deal is the way the prince has to think, or the way an adviser to princes has to think on the prince's behalf. If there is a general message in *The Prince*, it is that the prudent prince will always think the worst of those by whom he is surrounded. It follows from this that thinking about politics and thinking about ethics involve profoundly different ways of looking at the world. Thinking about ethics at all requires that we think of our fellow men as neither very good nor very wicked. If men were very good by nature, then thinking about ethics would be superfluous because men could always be relied upon to act well. If men were very bad, then thinking about ethics would be redundant because men could always be relied upon to act badly. Thinking about ethics is thinking about the 'in between' the very good and very bad, on the assumption that saintliness and devilishness are both very rare. Machiavelli seems to be saying that useful thinking about politics can only proceed on the basis on the assumption that men are always very bad. If the prince acts on the assumption of the universality of human wickedness, it is a case of heads he wins and tails he doesn't lose. It must be stressed that this is a special kind of thinking, which applies to politics only. Ordinary family life, or ordinary human life in general, would become impossibly miserable and diminished if it were to be conducted on the basis of the political axioms of Machiavelli. People living their ordinary lives have a choice about what assumptions to act upon as the occasion demands. Sometimes they will assume the best, sometimes the worst, and mostly they will make assumptions which fall somewhere in between.

One of the annoying things about Machiavelli is that he refuses to argue that Christian ethics as conventionally conceived are not ethics at all. We would not have the problems we do have with reading Machiavelli if he would just say with an insider's wink that we all really know that the Christian virtue of the Sermon on the Mount aren't really virtue at all, or that they are pseudo-virtue for popular consumption, useful for keeping the plebs in their place but of no use at all to thinking men. But Machiavelli refuses to be Gibbon or Voltaire. The Christian virtues are virtues, and we are to take seriously Machiavelli's famous assertion that he was quite looking forward to going to hell because there he could enjoy for eternity the conversation of the ancient sages. Behind the moral bravado lies a real belief in hell's existence and a real sense of his own sin.

Machiavelli is probably a Christian about everything important except politics. Commentators have not always emphasized enough just how political Machiavelli's political thought actually is. Thinking about politics is different from thinking abut anything else. When we say that Machiavelli separates thinking about politics from thinking about ethics, we should add that thinking about politics is different from thinking about lots of other things as well as thinking about ethics. There may be a Machiavelli 'worldview' because nothing is easier to attribute to a great thinker than a view of everything. But what should not be assumed is that whatever Machiavelli thinks about things in general is necessarily 'Machiavelli'. His view of politics is, but it simply does not follow that his view of everything is 'Machiavelli'. Commentators on Machiavelli have always been impressed by his intellectual range. Machiavelli might be Renaissance man writ very large indeed, but that does not mean that he has to be Machiavelli over the whole range; nor does it even mean that his thoughts about everything have to be particularly original. It may even be that Machiavelli is a rather conventional kind of Renaissance humanist in everything except politics.

The successful new prince is a man who is consistently lucky. Machiavelli invokes the ancient Roman goddess of luck, *Fortuna,* as the successful prince's guiding spirit. Fortuna is a woman, so she likes her votaries to be young, handsome and masterly, combining the warlike quality of Achilles with the cunning persistence of Odysseus. Fortuna is a bit of a bitch, flighty and treacherous; she needs constant wooing, and sometimes she needs to be roughed up, but keep her sweet and there is nothing she won't do for you. Fortune becomes the ideal mate for a prince on the make in the rough business of state making. Fortuna can take the chance element out of luck, at least for a time – and perhaps for a long time as she did with her ancient Roman favorites. Some princes are so consistently lucky that their luck begins to appear to be uncanny. Observers begin to think that there is something not quite human, or at least quite out of the ordinary, about the prince whose luck holds through all the vicissitudes of high politics. It also does the prince no harm to spread the word that more than human agency is at work in his career. By degrees, Fortuna begins to show that her favorites are men apart. They become like the ancient heroes in whose fate the gods took an immediate and constant interest. Indeed, that is what made them heroes and created the distance between them and ordinary men. Who accepts another hero would dare to tangle with Hector? Only a fool would stand up to Achilles without some kind of divine protection. Successful princes are a bit like that taking them on is to take more on then a mere human being, and you would yourself have to be very sure of your own exceptional abilities before you even tried.

The word 'citizens' is used deliberately here as a substitute for 'subjects' because it is a feature of good princely rule that there should be a transition from the one to the other. Subjects in original subjection are supposed to feel the prince's yoke less and less, until they begin to feel like citizens of a state, which is truly theirs. This is, of course, highly advantageous to the prince. He gets soldiers free who feel that their country is worth fighting for. The Prince begins to thank God he took Machiavelli's advice and did not enslave his people.

A citizen army returning victorious from its country's wars will not put up with being bossed about at home. Tyranny of a petty-minded and rapacious kind would be the least appropriate form of government for men conscious of their own strength and who had arms in their hands. The fact that a prince can trust his people enough to arm them shows they have become partners. Partners regulate their relations with each other on the basis of consent. Machiavelli knows his ancient authors well enough to know that government by consent means government by law in the interests of all, and not government by force in the interest of the tyrant only. Good arms and good laws entail and imply each other, and a wise prince would be well pleased when his people began to think of the laws as their laws. That is one of the why Machiavelli thinks a prudent new Prince should alter the existing laws as little as possible. There is nothing people find more irksome than having laws imposed on them by foreigners. A prince should add to existing law whenever possible, and should be glad to acquiesce in the continuance of those local customs which over time have acquired the force of law.

Properly considered, princely government consists of the union of the interests of Prince and people. Machiavelli anticipates Hobbes in believing that the glory of a prince can consist of nothing but the prosperity and contentment of his people. Simple common sense might dictate that it is men with nothing to lose who will cheerfully put their lives at risk on the battlefield, but this is just another case where Machiavelli thinks that common sense is wrong. It is citizens with a good deal to lose that you can lead to war with confidence, and even losing cannot alter the fact that a citizen army still has a good deal left which is worth defending. Citizen armies cannot simply melt away after a defeat. Quite the reverse. They reform with renewed determination to defend what is theirs, and the chances are that, if their Prince has not been cowardly or incompetent, the citizen army will reform around him.

Machiavelli thinks that there is no reason in principle why a prince well-versed in statecraft and with luck on his side should not be able to unite the warring principalities of Italy. The kings of the French have managed to unite the various French provinces into a single kingdom, so why not Italy? The short answer is, of course, the papacy, which Machiavelli regards as the real Italian problem. The papacy enjoys a prestige so enormous that even Borgia Popes have failed to destroy it. On the other hand, the papacy has no real forces of its own. Even Cesare Borgia ultimately failed to produce a militia out of the peasantry of the Papal States. Popes, as secular princes, have their wars to fight. The only way they can do this is to invite allies to invade Italy, and the papal allies are no less dangerous than the allies of other princes. The French, the Spanish, the Swiss and the Germans do nothing but follow Machiavelli's own advice to princes when they descend upon Italy: they come by plausible invitation and they fight on another's land. In Machiavelli's own terms the foreigners would be fools not to come. What Italy needs is a prince who can knock some sense into Italy as a whole, perhaps forming an alliance strong enough to expel all the barbarians. No wonder that Machiavelli was to be a hero of Italian national unification in the nineteenth century. The history of the eventual unification of Italy could be written on the Machiavelli theme: When will the prince come and who will it be? Garibaldi? Cavor? Even Mussolini claiming to complete the Risorgimento?

It has been commented *The Prince* is a book inspired by the Devil. The legend of Machiavelli's depravity was already established by the time the first English translation appeared in 1640 .The Elizabethan dramatists found suitably exotic setting for their tragedies in Renaissance Italy and Machiavelli supplied them with a useful cliché to describe enormities they would have depicted without his help. Old Nick was identified with Niccolo Machiavelli though that name for Satan existed before Machiavelli's evil reputation reached and it became as acceptable to call the devil Machiavelli, as it was to call Machiavelli diabolical.

The English man Cardinal Pope was one of Machiavelli's earliest and sternest critics probably the first to bring the devil into it but the legend of Machiavelli's reputation as an evil counselor of princes came here from France where it was fostered by hostility to the rule of Catherine de Medici. From the very start Machiavelli was a scapegoat for religious controversies. He had never attacked the dogmas of the Catholic Church but he was a bitter anti-clerical and his scathing attacks on the papacy were naturally intolerable to Catholics of the Counter-Reformation. For Protestants he was the tutor of the Catholic kings whose teaching was for example responsible for the massacre of sanity Bartholomew day. With passions so aroused, it is little wonder that the legend soon obscured the man and his work. Parts of *The Prince* quoted out of context convincingly demonstrated the author's wicked condemnation of the prince led to glib distortion of the facts of his life.

The Prince was received at first almost with indifference: its immediate reception can hardly called favorable. It made its way slowly until it was printed. Then religion raised its voice, efforts were made to defend the book on the hypothesis of a secret meaning, then criticism looked back to the author and drew a fancy picture of a cynic and a rogue. *The Prince* still has a bad reputation partly because of tradition partly because it is more often cited than read and partly because it is frequently approached as an impassioned tract for the time. Of course, it is more than journalism but like journalism, it cannot be understood without reference to the circumstances in which it was written. It is necessary to go back beyond the legend to the condition of Italy in Machiavelli's time and to the mood in which it was hurriedly canonized. The book was a product of personal and national tragedy created however in a spirit of hope. During Machiavelli's lifetime, Italy suffered from incessant and often brutal warfare. The Italian states were crushed between the rival ambitions of foreign powers.

It is still widely accepted that Machiavelli's little work on principalities *The Prince* was started after he had written part of his discourses on Livy that he started writing it in july1513 and finished it early in 1514. Almost all the observations and maxims in *The Prince* are to be found elaborated in the discourses but there is a marvelous difference of perspective between the two books. The discourses were written with no less vehemence but are more discursive and crucially constitute a commentary on all forms of government from the viewpoint of an ardent republican. From the pages of the *Prince* emerges the figure of the autocrat-the new man, ruthless, efficient and defiant-the literary forerunner of the new monarchs of the sixteenth century. Why should Machiavelli have moved from the *Discourses* to create this apparent monster?

Machiavelli was fundamentally interested in the state rather than in the form of its government and in the state as a self-sufficient entity in continual conflict with other states and therefore in need of power. The new prince he created personified the state and enabled Machiavelli to try to please the Medici while dramatizing his views on the supreme political challenge of an effective foreign policy. What Machiavelli has to say concerning foreign policy could be applied by a republic every bit as much as by an autocracy. And Machiavelli's autocrat must not be thought of as an irresponsible tyrant. He continually stresses that the prince must build his state on the good will of the people. He must respect his subjects susceptibilities being ready for cruelty only because in the long run it is often wiser to be cruel than weak.

Machiavelli wanted a strong state capable of imposing its authority on a hopelessly divided Italy. The condition of Italy in his time demanded ruthlessness on the part of any Italian state seeking to resist foreign domination. At the same time he had a philosophy by no means an original one which saw the history of a nation in terms of an inevitable cyclical progression, a descent from prosperity to adversity, a rise again from adversity to prosperity. Nations inevitably become corrupted but when this happened the greatness of the states could still be restared by a man comparable in stature to the states original founder.

For the type of man needed, Machiavelli looked first to the Romans. Here he was perhaps most typical of his time assuming that human nature remained constant and that the ancients had attained a political and artistic grandeur never since equaled. From the ancient world was derived the idea of the legislator, the founder of the state and of the reformer of the state, the dictator not in his modern guise but as a political genius who takes power in an emergency sometimes with the assent of his fellow-citizens in order to restore order and renew the nation's strength.

Machiavelli looked back to the past for inspiration but his method of arriving at what he thought were universally valid generalizations governing political behavior entailed a comparison of the past with the present. And the typical modem rulers in Machiavelli's Italy were usurpers who had climbed to power when the cities grew corrupt and feeble during the century before the French invasions. In his sketch of Cesare Borgia Machiavelli's idea of the reformer of the state and his vision of the possibilities open to an efficient Italian usurper were fused. He well remembered how Cesare had with the backing of his father Pope Alexander and with ruthless will power carved out a state for himself in the center of Italy. When years before he had been sent to Cesare by the republican government of Florence he had viewed him as a dangerous potential enemy. But in *The Prince* he uses him as a flesh and blood example of what an Italian ruler starting almost from scratch can achieve if he repudiates half-measures and he is untroubled by the contrast between the historical Cesare and the Cesare he sets before the Medici as an ideal.

Machiavelli claimed that he was writing on politics in a new fashion. He would base his conclusions about the way princes should govern not on abstract considerations but on analysis of historical facts. Here *The Prince* becomes more than a tract for the times and takes its place as an important treatise on the art of government. Whether or not his method was as revolutionary or as scientific as he thought is undoubtedly the Prince marks an important stage in the development of political science. Most of the excitement and repulsion, which the prince has generated, comes from its frank acknowledgement that in practice successful governments are always ready to act ruthlessly to attain their ends. We are nowadays probably less inclined to quarrel with Machiavelli's low opinion of humankind than our ancestors were. Where he is being descriptive, he raises no question of principle. But the *Prince* is something more than a commentary on how rulers in fact behave. Machiavelli was not a dispassionate observer: he wanted to be taken as guide and he was offering advice. Although he sometimes tried to dodge the issue he could plead necessity for the stern measures in the final resort. He taught that in politics whether an action is evil or not can only be decided in the light of what it is meant to achieve and whether it successfully achieves it. Here Machiavellism is as potent and controversial today as it ever was.

In Machiavelli's most famous political work *The Prince* the following passage ends irrevocably the classical and medieval traditions of political discourse and ushered in the age of modern political thought:

> My intention being to write something of use to those who understand it appears to me more proper to go to the real truth of the matter than to its imagination and many have imagined republics and principalities which have never been seen or known to exist in reality; for how we live is so far removed from how we ought to live that he who abandons what is done for what ought to be done will rather learn to bring about his own ruin than his preservation.

There are a number of things about this statement that mark it as modern. In the most general sense, we note a new spirit of realism and empiricism. Machiavelli is telling his readers that the appropriate way to understand politics is to eschew ideals and to look directly at the empirical reality of human behavior. For this reason

Machiavelli is considered one of the great theorists of real politics so much so that his name has become almost synonymous with the term.

Machiavelli's new spirit of political inquiry was but one reflection of even deeper intellectual changes associated with the Renaissance-a period that lasted from roughly the late fourteenth into the seventeenth century. The Renaissance which marks the end of the medieval period and the beginning of the modern involved major transformation in the way people thought of themselves and of the world around them. In fact, the Renaissance produced an entirely new intellectual class: the humanists. Humanists were scholars and men of letters who attempted to revive the ideals of classical antiquity by reemphasizing the great literature of the past. These ideals were essentially secular; they glorified man and his works rather than God. Humanist ideals thus embodied that same spirit of empiricism and realism that Machiavelli brought to his political theory. Indeed, Machiavelli himself returned to the classical past particularly to those political ideals of ancient Rome that emphasized the importance of the state and the practical political skills required to maintain it. However, at a deeper metaphysical and epistemological level he rejected the completely classical heritage and in the process laid the foundation of modern political thought.

But there is much more to the Renaissance than a new intellectual vision. All social relationships underwent major transformations as the medieval order crumbled. In place of the old static and hierarchical society of the medieval world, there emerged a new and dynamic social order. The beginning of modern capitalism can be traced back to the Renaissance when a new moneyed economy emerged in connection with the discovery of new markets. Along with economic change came a new sort of man-the entrepreneur-the self-made man who made his fortune through his own skill, and effort. In fact, all spheres of society began to open up to those who in the medieval world would' have been consigned by birth to a particular role or status. Corresponding to the new economic man of the Renaissance we find for the first time the political entrepreneur the self-made political who by dint of his skill enterprise and daring could wrest a state for him self. At least this was possible in Machiavelli's Italy, which was divided into a series of small states, or principalities that frequently changed hands.

We have already seen how this opening up of the medieval social order had begun in embryo form even in Thomas Acquinas's time. This process involved the checking of the power of the Church by other emerging political units. By Maachiavelli's time the process which culminated in the Reformation and the defeat of feudalism a system of political organization that dominated Europe from about the ninth century up to the Renaissance. The feudal system was characterized, by the existence of a host of different political communities, towns, principalities, baronies and other small feudatory states each claiming the right to rule its subjects. Exactly which community had ultimate authority and exactly where the territory of one community ended and the other began was no easy matter to determine. This is what made the Church so politically crucial prior to the Renaissance. It was one organization capable of giving somekind of coherence to an otherwise fragmented social order.

Eventually a new type of polity-the nation state emerged from the wreckage of feudalism. We may define nation-states a form of polity in which people live within a legally defined territory and give their allegiance to one centralized government that has the power to enforce laws. The United States fits this definition as does France, Great Britain, Sweden and so no. Historically these political entities are quite modern. Indeed some countries such as Germany and Italy were not fully consolidated into nation-states until the late nineteenth century and many countries in the third world are still very much in the process of becoming nation-states.

It Western Europe the issue was resolved more or less by the end of the sixteenth century when the nation-state had emerged in clear form. This occurred under the leadership of absolute monarchs who by appealing to new nationalist ideals consolidated and centralized power at the expense of the Church and other institutions of feudal society. It is for this reason that the initial stages of the formation of the nation-state system have been called the age of absolute monarchy and age that was bloody and violent in the extreme.

Machiavelli had some idea albeit a very, imperfect one of this new emerging political order. In this sense, Machiavelli's genius was the opposite of Aristotle's. Aristotle summed up the political experience of the polis a form of political organization that was waning in his own day. Machiavelli on the other hand grasped the new forms of political action that would be required to found the modern state. Before Machiavelli no thinker was able to take this step out of the feudal framework although another Italian of the fourteenth century Marcillus of Padua came very close to doing so.

It is difficult to put Machiavelli's thought in historical perspective. He is a transitional figure standing midway between the medieval and modern eras. He speaks of the state in an almost modern way, yet possesses little idea of how it will be organized. He recognizes that absolute monarchy will be required to unify the state into a coherent national entity but he has little appreciation for the other factors that will be necessary for unification. And while he had a vision of the unification of Italy he was not yet fully a modern nationalist although he has traditionally been considered the first thinker to give expression to what we would now recognize as nationalistic ideals. Despite these qualifications, we must nevertheless emphasize Machiavelli's essential originality. He went further in this regard than any of his contemporaries. And he most certainly grasped that the old order was crumbling and that new modes of political thought and action would be required to transform the chaotic corrupt and increasingly violent political order of Renaissance Italy in to a stable and unified polity.

It is important to keep in mind this less attractive side of the Renaissance for it is this side that interested Machiavelli as a political thinker. The social and political chaos of the times compelled him to approach his study of politics with a new spirit of empiricism and realism. Machiavelli's claim that how we live is far removed from how we ought to live was never more true than during the Renaissance. So he was forced to look at politics without illusions and without the moribund ideals of the medieval world. This lack of illusion was especially strong in Machiavelli because he was personally caught up in the conflicts and passions of the times. Almost all of his writings his literary works included have a political tone to them for Machiavelli saw all human relationships as pervaded by politics. He was the most political of men in the most political of times and had he had the choice he would have preferred being in politics to philosophizing about it. But fate or fortune as Machiavelli called it, determined that he would make his name as a political theorist rather than as a politician.

Machiavelli reverses the whole Platonic order of things. In this sense, the *Prince* is the reverse image of the *Republic.* It was quite clear to the disputants in Plato's *Republic* that if justice has no ultimate reality, if it is simply a word that the politician invokes for the sake of appearance, then indeed might makes right is the essence of political ethics. In reducing politics to appearances, Machiavelli clearly returns to sophistic political principles. Not only does he emphasize the struggle for power but also he describes that activity in much the same way, as did the Sophists of Plato's day. For the ability to successfully acquire and maintain power an ability that requires appearing just while behaving unjustly Machiavelli like the early Sophists.

Who is correct-Plato or Machiavelli? Once again, we note the intimate connection between epistemology and political theory. If like Plato one accepts the existence of an objective moral order that people can know and incorporate into their lives, then clearly Machiavelli's prince is evil. But if like Machiavelli one does not accept the notion of such an order, there is nothing to know in the Platonic sense. What is knowable is nothing more than what we would now call the real empirical world what Plato had described as the cave-world of appearances. In Platonic terms we could say that Machiavelli's virtuous prince is one who grasps that he is in the cave that there is no leaving it and that knowledge must be confined merely to using and manipulating those shadows and illusions that bind human beings and their societies together.

It follows that Machiavelli's rejection of the Platonic theory of knowledge applies equally to Aristotle and Cicero; while their political theories are secular and empirical they presume a connection between the real world and larger ethical purpose. Aristotle's empiricism for example is embedded in a teleological system. Machiavelli is anti-teleological; he admits no larger purpose to human events than that which is observable. Indeed in Machiavelli's political universe there is no form, no natural law, no teleology operating in the affairs of human beings. There is nothing but the empirical reality of politics as given to the observation.

This is the real import of Machiavelli's claim that it is useless to study "republics and principalities which have never been seen or known to exist in reality ". His claim is a clear rejection of Plato and of that whole genre of classical and medieval political thought that was premised upon an ethical or utopian standard. It is not simply the *Prince's* emphasis upon real politics then that makes Machiavelli a revolutionary thinker for there is in this nothing new. St Augustine had long before developed a theory of political realism. Rather it is Machiavelli's insistence upon studying politics without any ethical standard at all that makes him the first genuinely modern political thinker.

It is part of Machiavelli's political genius to have recognized that the medieval world could not be put back together again nor could the political ideals upon which it was based. He understood that the political reality of the modern world would require a new science of politics that would no longer conceive of politics from the perspective of ethical ideals. The triumph of a purely secular state would inevitably generate purely secular theories of politics that would go well beyond a mere separation of sacred and secular. The sacred itself would become secularized; it would become merely another illusion to be manipulated by those who understand. Herein lies the genuinely revolutionary character of Machiavelli's political thought. In conceiving of ethical ideals as mere illusions, he breaks asunder the classical unity of ethics and politics. In contemporary terms, we would say that Machiavelli attempts to study the empirical facts of politics in isolation from any consideration of ethical values. His empiricism and naturalism for example are the consequence of his interest in studying real politics firsthand not of any philosophical principle. Whereas a Plato or an Aristotle began with metaphysical and epistemological concepts from which they derived their philosophies of politics, Machiavelli begins with politics and end there, leaving his assumptions about the nature of reality and the basis of knowledge implicit in his political analysis.

Machiavelli grasped that a republican Italy required in the first instance a united Italy that could withstand the outrages of foreign invasion. But he further grasped that Italian unification would require the leadership of one strong man who possessed a new political vision and who had the political skills requisite to implement it. Thus, *The Prince* opens with a dedication to the Medici ruler of Florence who would be required to unite Italy. And what Machiavelli proposes in the dedication is to teach Lorenzo Medici those political skills necessary to found a united Italy. He proposes in short to teach Lorenzo the rules of power politics.

It is this focus on power that in large part marks Machiavelli as the first genuinely modern thinker and it is a focus intimately connected to the rise of the modern secular nation-state. Following Machiavelli power becomes a key variable of political analysis. This is not to suggest that medieval or classical thinkers were iqnorant of it. But they did not, with some rare exceptions such as St. Augustine, believe power to be the defining characteristic of political activity. Aristotle for example viewed politics as a key source of friendship and as an arena in which moral excellence could be acquired and displayed. He recognized the reality of power to be sure but he did not take it to be the defining reality of political life.

Machiavelli and so many political thinkers following him view power as the essence of politics. Power may be defined as the ability to control others by compelling their obedience. The key word here is to make people obey whether they want or not. Clearly, violence is a form of power, indeed the most extreme form for it is the extreme kind of compulsion. But power can be manifested in much more subtle forms as well. A threat of violence may be just as effective as its actual exercise. And even apparent acts of friendship such as the granting of gifts and favors may actually be a manifestation of power. Those who become dependent upon receiving favors from the political leader for example must constantly face the possibility that they will suffer the loss of their favored status if they cease to obey. This is why it is apparent that at bottom power no matter how subtly applied is a form of coercion. And this is why the essence of power if it is not always violence in the strictest sense is something very close to it.

It is clear that Machiavelli's emphasis no power implies a particular and essentially modern view of human nature. That view is that human beings are essentially self-interested and self-regarding. Clearly, power would not be an effective influence unless self-interest was the defining characteristic of the human personality. Violence would not be capable of compelling obedience if it did not appeal to the individual's fear of death or bodily harm.

Of course, not all relationships based upon self -interest are power relationship but power is always based upon self-interest. But for human being could transcend self-interest for some higher purpose, power relationships would not exist because neither the threat of death nor the granting of favors could compel obedience. Politics as we know it would disappear and Plato's *Republic* or something like it would become a real possibility. Machiavelli is convinced that no such possibility exists because his analysis of human behavior convinces him that self-interest is the essence of human nature. What makes Machiavelli's views genuinely modern however is the attitude he adopts toward these "facts" of human nature and the corresponding reality of power politics. For unlike St. Augustine who also focused self-interest, self-regarding behavior to be sinful Machiavelli is an empiricist. His psychology is derived from observation of how people actually behave. He means to make no moral or religious judgment. Being bad for Machiavelli does not mean being sinful; it simply means what humans naturally are. There is no more sin involved in humans acting self- interestedly for Machiavelli than there is in the earth revolving around the sun. Both are simply following their "nature."

Given Machiavelli's view of human nature, his emphases on power as the key variable in political behavior makes eminent sense. The political analysis that he employs to comprehend that behavior makes equally good sense. Machiavelli proposes to describe the logic of power for he views power as something uniquely amenable to logical analysis. Power has to do with the manipulation of people's self-interest. Later thinkers who followed Machiavelli's pioneering efforts in this regard most notably Thomas Hobbes in the seventeenth century attempted to transform the logic of power into a comprehensive science of power. We need only recognize that *The Prince* is a technical manual on the logic of acquiring and maintaining political power. We should add that it was written essentially for a new type of ruler rather than for the hereditary leader, who were becoming increasingly common in Renaissance Italy, who lacked the support of tradition and was required therefore to rely upon the effective use of power in gaining and maintaining his political position.

In *The Prince*, Machiavelli advocates two intimately related rules of power politics that are clearly the most important of all because they are the basis for learning and applying all the other rules necessary to gain and maintain a principality. First, Machiavelli says the prince must learn to think about politics in a new way. He must be strictly empirical in his political analysis. This requires that he eschews all ethical ideals for it is precisely such ideals that blind the political leader to the reality of politics. And second the prince must act as logically as he thinks even if this means violating generally held moral values. For recalling that how we live is so far removed from how we ought to live that he who abandons what is done for what ought to be done will wishe to make a profession of goodness in everything must necessarily come to grief among so many who are not good. In short if the prince expects to maintain his power he cannot himself always behave "ideally"; he cannot approach his task as if he were conducting a Sunday school. The dictates of power require cold-blooded logic in action no less than in theory.

The subsequent rules of power politics follow logically from these first two. Most important, says Machiavelli, the wise prince must keep power in his own hands and he must never be the cause of another becoming more powerful than himself. Given the inherent workings of human nature, power that is shared or given to another will likely be turned against the prince. It is therefore logically imperative that insofar as possible power not be shared.

The problem, of course is that it is impossible for the prince to keep power totally within his own grasp since he must rely upon others both in its creation and in its implementation. He must rely upon the police, the military, the population at large, his own advisors and perhaps foreign allies if he is to be effective. Consequently, the prince must find mechanisms for maximizing his control over these various forces for they are as much a potential threat to his power as they are the source of it. He must therefore keep others dependent upon him and not the other way around. He must be willing in short to employ power whether in its extreme or subtle forms. In its most extreme form the prince may be called to kill his opposition in which case he need no longer fear them at all or he may manipulate them with favors and thereby make them dependent and subject to his control.

We need go further than this to see why Machiavelli has the bad reputation. It is not surprising that the Catholic Church put Machiavelli's writing on the index of forbidden books or that generations of scholars, political leaders and assorted thinkers have raised their voices against the "frightful Machiavelli." No charge has seemed to extreme. Frederick the Great of Prussia, for example, wrote a famous attack on *the Prince* in 1739 in which he called Machiavelli a criminal, a monster and an enemy of humanity. So intense has the opposition to Machiavelli been that the word Machiavellism has become a general term for the evils of power politics. Frederick's attack upon the prince is typical of much anti-Machiavelli liter afure Actually Machivelli in that work for nowhere does praise the exercise of power for its own sake nor does he advocate its unlimited use. Quite the contrary. In fact, Machiavelli considers such behavior to be self-defeating. Nevertheless, a serious study of this strain of literature merits a sevious explanation.

Given the condition of the times the idea that people must be caressed or annihilated is logically at least indisputable. If people will not obey willingly then they must be forced or manipulated to obeying. This is a strictly empirical and logical conclusion. Machiavelli's justification of violence is not an end in itself. The prince must exercise power in order to maintain his position and violence is one of the tools for exercising power. As such it must be employed when needed. The only real question for Machiavelli then is—How can violence be used most effectively? Not is it ethical to employ it? Indeed the wise prince must not even ask such a question for to the extent that he concerns himself with ethical issues he will fail to use violence appropriately if at all when needed. Ethical concerns induce moral squeamishness, a condition not conducive to the effective use of violence.

How then is the prince to employ violence for maximum effectiveness? Once again, we may note some general rules. In the first place, it ought not to be used at all, unless absolutely necessary because it tends to engender resistance and thereby pose a threat to the prince's security. In the second place if violence must be employed it must be used quickly and mercilessly. The injury we do to man must be such that we need not fear his vengeance, says Machiavelli. Machiavelli offers the inexorable logic–if violence engenders resistance then clearly it should be avoided if at all possible. And if it must be employed then logically it should be done in such a way that it minimizes resistance. Clearly killing one's enemy is in order since a dead man is by definition incapable of resistance. Machiavelli's analysis is based upon a crucially important insight into human nature when people are subjected to violence short of being destroyed they will seek revenge. This is because violence has the unfortunate quality of engendering hatred. Hatred transports people outside of themselves and causes them not to calculate their self- interest. Thus, the prince who has caused himself to be hated is in the unfortunate position of having to deal with people he can no longer control.

This analysis of violence points out something about the nonviolent form of power classified as manipulation. And indoctrination-the rules of manipulation, Machiavelli argue's are exactly the opposite of the rules of violence although the underlying principle is the same. That principle to reiterate is that the prince must appeal to the self-interest of others such that they remain dependent upon him and not the other way around. This means that violence must be used quickly and mercilessly. Nonviolent forms of power on the other hand such as giving gifts or granting favors should be applied over a long period of time so as to maintain dependency upon the prince. Thus Machiavelli concludes "injuries should be done altogether so that being less tasted they will give less offense. Benefits should be granted little by little so that they may be better enjoyed".

This brings us to the third rule of violence, which logically follows from the second rule that "injuries should be done altogether." Insofar as possible, says Machiavelli, the prince should get someone else to do the injuries for him. Any hatred that might arise will then be directed at the perpetrator of the violence not at the prince. Moreover, once the violence has been committed the prince may reap a further advantage by employing a particularly devious tactic that Machiavelli describes by way of an example drawn from the life of Cesare Borgia his contemporary and his ideal of the wise prince. In the following example Borgia had recently gained control of a small principality that had been poorly governed. Consequently, he judged it necessity to give them a good government in order to make them peaceful and obedient to his rule. For this purpose, he appointed Ramiro a cruel and able man to whom he gave the fullest authority. This man in a short time was highly successful in rendering the country orderly and united whereupon the duke not deeming such excessive authority expedient lest it should become hateful appointed a civil court of justice in the center of the province under an excellent president to which each city appointed its own advocate. And as he knew that the harshness of the past had engendered some amount of hatred in order to purge the minds of the people and to win them over completely he resolved to show that if any cruelty had taken place it was not by his orders but through the harsh disposition of his minister. And having found the opportunity he had him cut in half and placed one morning in the public square with a piece of wood and bloodstained knife by his side. The ferocity of this spectacle caused the people both satisfaction and amazement.

Even violence that generates hatred then may under certain circumstances work to the advantage of the prince if he uses it wisely. But as the example clearly shows the prince can use violence wisely only if he is utterly cold-blooded and unscrupulous that is only if he employs violence logically to attain his desired end without letting moral scruples cloud his judgment. This is quite different from using violence for its own sake. Cesare Borgia is not praised by Machiavelli because he was violent but because he used violence coolly and logically to attain his objective. Once again, Machiavelli does not advocate the unlimited use violence but it's very opposite.

Machiavelli's emphasis upon religion as a necessary condition for a stable democratic system brings to mind Aristotle's discussion of polity as does his recognition that a stable and lawful republican regime requires a whole complex of viable social institutions to undergird the state and its laws: like the classical thinkers Machiavelli understand that a mere legal structure is not sufficient. A workable legal constitution requires a corresponding social constitution that is a network of social institutions, says Machiavelli, none is more important than that of religion.

Such a view seems at first surprising given Machiavelli's secularism and the fact that he was personally irreligious. But his interest in religion is political not theological and as a political realist Machiavelli is the first to recognize the political importance of religion. Religion, he says, gives a divine sanction to the laws without which the people would have no reason to obey. This is why he argues that the observance of divine institutions is the cause of the greatness of republics, the disregard of them produces their ruin; unless it be sustained by the fear of the Prince which may temporarily supply the want of religion. But as the lives of Princes are short the kingdom will of necessity perish as the prince fails in virtue. From political point of view, Machiavelli would wholeheartedly agree with Voltaire's statement that if God did not exist it would be necessary to invent him. Since the people lack sophistication, they require a supernatural agency to stands behind the laws and indeed behind all of their social institutions. But question of precisely what form God takes or how religious institutions are structured are of concern to Machiavelli only in terms of the impact for good or evil upon the political sphere. It is for this political reason that Machiavelli insists that the state must control the Church and its teachings.

Machiavelli criticized the Church of his day precisely for political and not religious reasons. He recognized that the existence of the papal state and its ceaseless struggle to dominate political affairs was a primary cause of Italy's inability to unite into one political unit. But Machiavelli's political critique of the Church went beyond a condemnation of its involvement in secular affairs. He was critical of its teachings again not for religious but for political reasons. And politically Machiavelli was at best ambivalent about Christianity for it taught the otherworldly virtue of meekness and humility rather than the political virtue of strength and courage, virtue that he insists are required to maintain the state be it a principality or a republic. Christian principles, he argues, have made men feeble and caused them to become an easy prey to evil-minded men who can control them more securely seeing that the great body of men for the sake of gaining paradise are more disposed to endure injuries than to avenge them.

Machiavelli's religious preference for the pagan religion of antiquity which he says;" deified only men who had achieved great glory such as commanders of armies and chiefs of republics whilst ours glorifies more the humble and contemplative men than the men of action". A religion of man, a theology of action in short a political religion, this was Machiavelli's ideal–an ideal that had not existed since the days of classical antiquity. In making the sacred superior to the secular Christianity had subordinated the state to the church it. In returning to the classical ideal Machiavelli rectified if only theoretically the modern divorce between religious ands political ideals.

Such then is Machiavelli's republican ideal: a liberal and democratic government constrained by the rule of law and undergirded by deeply held social and religious values that encourage civic virtue and love of country. His ideal clearly is drawn from the Roman Republic to which he refers again and again in the *Discourses* just as other Renaissance thinkers drew their ideals from classical antiquity. And while Machiavelli understood that his " Roman ideal" in no way corresponded to the actual conditions of Renaissance Italy it was his hope that the great political leader might create the conditions for it.

Machiavelli clearly believes that in a well–founded republic obedience to the laws need not be coerced but should result almost naturally from the people's belief in their social order and those cultural traditions upon which it is based. Leader of a republic need not be ceaselessly coercing or manipulating. In short, the whole basis of obedience to law is more secure in a republic than in a principality. In a republic it is not primarily power that creates obedience but authority. Authority like power does how and why people obey their laws and support their political institutions. Unlike power however authority exists where people obey because they believe obedience to be morally appropriate not because it is simply in their self -interest to obey. Unquestionably most long lived political systems are based upon authority In those that are not the leadership is driven to apply the rules of power politics that Machiavelli recommends in *The Prince* for where internal moral controls are lacking the law can be enforced only by force.

Machiavelli clearly prefers authority to power and for a very pragmatic reason: power particularly explicit coercive power is a terribly inefficient method by which to compel obedience. It requires enormous resources to hold a gun against the heads of an entire population military-personnel, police, domestic spies and so on. Even then, raw power is frequently ineffective because it is simply impossible in most cases to hold a whole population in line by the use of force. Moreover, Machiavelli emphasizes again and again that the excessive use of force is self-defeating .He shows that the more it is used the more resistance it engenders. There is one other great disadvantage of power to which Machiavelli draws our attention. It lasts only so long as the prince survives or is able to maintain his position. But authority transcends the life or effectiveness of the prince because it is a moral position on the part of the people to obey the law regardless of who is ruling or how effectively the prince enforces the law through threats of punishment.

More dramatically Machiavlli presents the importance of religious institutions. Recall his statement that while the feat of a prince may temporally supply the wand of religion the kingdom will of necessity perish as the prince fails in virtue. Fear is effective only so long as the prince is effective but religion fosters moral predisposition to obey the law and to support the social order that transcends the life or effectiveness of the Prince. Religion in other words is the primary basis of authority for Machiavelli .It is for this reason that he accords an even higher status to founders of religions than to founders of states.

Thus, we conclude that an analysis of the *Discourses* and its republican ideal with a picture of Machiavelli that utterly contradicts the popular image shaped by centuries of anti-Machiavellianism. It is perfectly accurate to say that Machiavelli was a democrat and a libertarian who believed the state should be bound by authority based upon rule of law fostered by religious institutions supported by an equality of citizenship and ruled by those with a conception of the public good. Much anti–Machiavellianism has been based oven an intuitive sense of this more radical aspect of Machiavelli's theory of politics but it has failed to direct its criticism at this the real issue. It has criticized his modernity indirectly by way of a superficial and quite mistaken analysis of what he says about power and violence and the relationship of means to political ends.

The modern state came out of the feudal order. Of course it is a long story, but we can trace its progress from about 1500 to about1800 in the works of Machiavelli, Bodin, Hobbes and Adam Smith. In Machiavelli there is no trace of the idea that the political order is part of the God-given order of things. Machiavelli thinks that a state is a radically created order, not a differentiated social whole entrusted to and presided over by a king. The Machiavellian prince is a creator, an artist who designs and builds the state which he is to govern, and the artistic gift is not given to all men. A king of ordinary abilities who is not too lazy to deal with problems as they arise and who has no spectacular vices might do very well in keeping up his state in a hereditary realm whose subjects have become accustomed to being ruled by their princely family, but the creation of new kingdoms is the task of the specially gifted. There is nothing feudal about Machiavelli's account of the princely state, no mediating institutions between prince and people. Rivals in the feudal sense are killed off, for there must be no notable figures around which resistance to a new prince might consolidate itself. The prince gathers up all the reins of power into his own hands, and Machiavelli has lots of advice for princes who want to keep power out of the hands, of others. Authority in Machiavelli's scheme of things must have a spatial as well as a personal center. Princely government represents the victory of the city over the countryside. A prudent prince would do well to build solid walls a round his capital, and to build a solid citadel for himself within the walls. There is to be none of the local self-government which is a characteristic of feudal societies. All decisions are to be the prince's decisions, and they have to be the right decisions, otherwise the prince might lose his state, because what can be won can always be lost again. What this means in the modern idiom is that policy has to be right, and that includes foreign policy. War is the trade of princes with armies of their own making, not the affair of a knightly class. Mercenaries are one possibility, but a prince who knows his business would do well to imitate the ancient Romans and go to war with his own citizen militia who feel that the prince is their prince and the state their state.

For all the rigour of Machiavelli's advice to princes, there is still something ad hoc about his political theory, which is really a tissue of expedients for princes to use in emergencies. Princely life for Machiavelli is a series of such emergencies. The last thing a prince should do is to dream of retiring to a little kingdom by the sea. Machiavelli does in fact admire the great law-givers as well as the great improvisers, but he talks of the great law-givers as if they were the successful devisers of expedients which lasted. The rules of necessity do not operate at those stages of history in which there is such great need for law-givers. Law-givers, like Moses are the founders of peoples which survive for centuries as viable political units, but Machiavelli can give no coherent set of reasons why such law-givers should appear, beyond saying that in the case of Moses we can see the have of God. Law for Machiavelli is only one of the ways, though the best way, that a people should be made to feel that it is being ruled, but, the reiteration of ancient pieties apart, it is obvious that for Machiavelli law is only one arm in the armories of princes, and it is certainly not the means by which a prince in a newly acquired state should begin to make his new people feel the force of his rule. When Machiavelli speaks of law-giving, what he really means is not legislation where legislation means generally accepted laws according to some generally recognized standard, but the whipping –in of a lawless people, as with the Roman people under Romulus and Numa Pumpilius.

Yet what makes Machiavelli modern, or what makes Machiavelli's political thought speak to a world which is no longer medieval, is his recognition that a particular kind of people, living at a particular time and subject to particular circumstances, needs a particular from of rule. Machiavelli's political thought is cast in generalizations about the universal character of human nature, but it does not take much of an effort of hindsight to see that princely government is being offered as the proper form of government for Renaissance men who are particularly hard to rule. The men that Machiavelli's prince has to confront are self-assertive, egotistical and opportunist, but they also have the obverse qualities of diffidence, gullibility and indolence. Such men may have a natural longing for democratic, that is republican, government; they are naturally citizens rather than subjects, but when men like these get themselves into a political mess, then princely government is the only answer. Despite his admiration for the ancient law-givers, Machiavelli in fact thinks that law and princely force are alternatives in the world in which he thinks he is living.

In Italy the forces of a new commercial and industrial system had been especially destructive of older institutions, but for reasons implicit in the political situation, the constructive forces were peculiarly feeble neutralized and retarded. The free cities of northern Italy had become political and economic anachronisms, unable to cope with a situation which required concentrated power, a citizen-soldiery, and a larger and more vigorous foreign policy. When Machiavelli wrote Italy was divided among five larger states: the kingdom of Naples in the south, the duchy of Milan in the northwest, the aristocratic republic of Venice in the northeast, and the republic of Florence and the Papal State in the center of Rome. The downfall of the Florentine republic in 1512—which produced in Machiavelli's life the enforced period of idleness responsible for his political writing—illustrated the fate awaiting a form of government which was incapable of coping with the political forces of its day. The popes of Machiavelli's time, "scoundrels and profligates" though they often were, succeeded in making their state the best consolidated and the most permanent in Italy. Nothing perhaps is more significant of the change in European politics than this, which transformed the pope into one Italian ruler among others. The old ambition to stand as arbiter of all the quarrels of Christendom had dwindled to the more practicable, but more worldly ambition to retain the sovereignty of central Italy.

But though consolidation had begun, it could not be completed, an this left Italy, as Machiavelli saw it, in a state of arrested political development. In Italy no power appeared great enough to unite the whole peninsula. Italians suffered all the degradation and oppression of tyranny with few of its compensations, and divisions among the tyrants left the land a prey to the French, the Spanish, and the Germans. In the chessboard of Eurepean politics Italy simply has become a pawn.

The closest analogue to Machiavelli's separation of political expedience from morality is probably to be found in some parts of Aristotle's *Politics*, where Aristotle considers the preservation of states without reference to their goodness or badness. It is not at all certain, however, that Machiavelli took these passages as his model. It is not likely that he was conscious of following anyone, though there may possibly have been a connection between his secularism and the naturalization Aristotelianism.

The character of Machiavelli and the true meaning of his philosophy have been one of the enigmas of modern history. In the words of Sabine he has been represented as an utter cynic, an impassioned patriot, an ardent nationalist, a republican, a convinced democrat, and an unscrupulous seeker after the favor of despots. In each of these views, incompatible as they are, there is probably an element of truth. What is emphatically true is that none of them gives a complete picture of either Machiavelli or his thought. His thought was truly empiric, the result of a wide range of political observation and a still wider range of reading in political history; it has in it no general system to which he tried to relate all his observations. In the same way his character, have been most complex. Sabine has rightly observed that "Machiavelli writes about nothing and thinks about nothing except politics, statecraft, and the art of war. For deeper-lying social questions, economic or religious, he had no interest except as they bore upon politics. He was perhaps too practical to be philosophically profound, but in politics pure and simple he had of all his contemporaries the greatest breadth of view and the clearest insight into the general tendency of European evolution".

Machiavelli more than any other political thinker created the meaning that has been attached to the state in modern political usage. Even the word itself, as the name of a sovereign political body, appears to have been made current in the modern languages largely by his writings. The state as an organized force, supreme in its own territory and pursuing a conscious policy of aggrandizement in its relations with other states, became not only the typical modern political institution but increasingly the most powerful institution in modern society. It acquired more and none power to regulate and control all the other institutions of society, and to direct them on lines overtly set by the interests of the state itself. The part that the state has played in modern politics is an index of the clearness with which Machiavelli grasped the drift of political evolution.

Yet it would be hard to say whether the intense brilliance that Machiavelli's genius cast on the statecraft of the despots and of the national states which followed them did not hide at much as it revealed. A philosophy which attributes the successes and failures of politics chiefly to the astuteness or the ineptitude of statesman is bound to be superficial. Machiavelli thought of moral, religious, and economic factors in society as forces which a clever politician can turn to the advantage of the state, or which he can even produce for the sake of the state. At all events it is certain that Machiavelli misrepresented completely the state of European thought at the beginning of the sixteenth century. Machiavelli was not detached; he was merely interested in a single end, political power, and indifferent to all others. He never hesitated to express sweeping judgments of rulers who allowed their states to grow weak. Moreover, he was in no definite sense scientific, though his judgment was formed empirically by the observation of rulers that he had himself known or by studying historical examples. But his empiricism was that of common sense or of shrewd practical foresight rather than an inductive empiricism controlled by the wish to test theories or general principles. Sabine contends that it is misleading to argue that Machiavelli followed an "historical" method, just because his examples were often drawn from the past. He used history exactly as he used his own observation to illustrate or support a conclusion that he had already reached quite without reference to history. He asserted explicitly that human nature is always and everywhere the same, and for this reason he took examples where he found them. His method, as far as he had one, was observation guided by shrewdness and common sense. The most telling description of his accomplishment is that given by Janet, that he translated politics into the vernacular. Machiavelli's political theories were not developed in a systematic manner, but in the form of remarks upon particular situations behind them, or implicit in them, however, there often was a consistent point of view, which might be developed into a political theory and in fact was so developed after his time. Machiavelli was not much interested in philosophy and not much inclined to generalize beyond maxims useful to a statesman. He sometimes merely stated his principles, often merely took them for granted; practically never did he try to give any proof of them.

Behind nearly everything that Machiavelli said about the political was the assumption that human nature is essentially selfish, and that the effective motives on which a statesman masterly are egoistic, such as the desire for security in the masses and the desire for power in rulers. Government is really founded upon the weakness and insufficiency of the individual, who is unable to protect himself against aggression of other individuals unless supported by the power of the state. Human nature, moreover, is profoundly aggressive and acquisitive; men aim to keep what they have and to acquire more. Neither in power nor in possessions is there any normal limit to human desires, while both power and possessions are always in fact limited by natural scarcity. Accordingly, men are always in a condition of strife and competition which threatens open anarchy unless restrained by the force behind the law, while the power of the ruler is built upon the very imminence of anarchy and the fact that security is possible only when government is strong. He frequently remarks, however, that men are in general bad and that the wise ruler will construct his policies on this stark assumption. In particular, he insists that successful government must aim at security of property and of life before everything else, since these are the most universal desires in human nature. Hence his cynical remark that a man more readily forgets and forgives the patricede than the confiscation of his patrimony. The prudent ruler may kill but he will not plunder. When completed by a systematic psychology to explain and justify it, this phase of Machiavelli became the political philosophy of Hobbes. Machiavelli, however, is not so much concerned with badness or egoism as a general human motive as with its prevalence in Italy as a symptom of social decadence. Italy stands to him as the example of a corrupt society, with no such partial mitigation as the monarchy brings in France and Spain.

The problem in Italy, then, is to found a state in a corrupt society and Machiavelli was convinced that, in such circumstances, no effective government was possible except absolute monarchy. This explains why he was a once an enthusiastic admirer of the Roman Republic and an advocate of despotism. By corruption Machiavelli means in general that decay of private virtue and civic probity and devotion that renders popular government impossible. It includes all sorts of license and violence, great inequalities of wealth and power, the destruction of peace and justice, the growth of disorderly ambition, disunion, lawlessness, dishonesty, and contempt for religion. A republican form of government, he believed, still to be possible in Switzerland and some parts of Germany, where a vigorous civic life had been preserved, but not in Italy. When the necessary virtues have decayed, there is no possibility either of restoring them or of carrying on orderly government without them, except by despotic power.

Apart from moral corruption, however, the natural aggressiveness of human nature makes struggle and competition a normal feature of every society. This explains, on the one hand, the defeat that dogs the steps of every government: not knowing when to limit their hopes. But on the other hand, it explains also the stability of a healthy society in which opposing interests are held in equilibrium. The rivalry of patricians and plebians in Rome Machiavelli regarded as the secret of Roman strength. From it was born the independence and sturdiness of character that supported the greatness of Rome. When directed by wise rulers, having great but lawful authority, the virility that made turbulence possible became a chief reason why the Romans were a war-like, conquering people. For this reason Machiavelli faroured the ancient theory of the mixed or balanced constitution. The balance which he had in mind, however, was not political but social or economic—an equilibrium of competing interests held in check by a powerful sovereign.

Another general principle that is continually assumed by Machiavelli is the supreme importance in society of the lawgiver. A successful state must be founded by a single man, and the laws and government which he creates determine the national character of his people. Moral and civic virtues grow out of law, and when a society has become corrupt, it can never reform itself but must be taken in hand by one lawgiver, who can restore it to the healthy principles set up by its founder. Machiavelli was not thinking of political organization, but of the whole moral and social constitution of a people, which he conceived to grow out of the law and from the wisdom and foresight of the lawgiver. There is practically no limit to what a statesman can do, provided he understands the rules of his art. He can tear down old states and build newones, change forms of government, transplant populations, and build new virtues into the characters of his subjects. The lawgiver is the architect not only of the state but of society as well, with all its moral, religious, and economic institutions.

This exaggerated notion of what a ruler and a state can do had several causes. In part it merely reproduced the ancient myth of the lawgiver which Machiavelli found in writers like Cicero and Polybius. In part it reflected his understanding of the problem that confronted a ruler amid the corruption of sixteenth-century Italy. By sheer political genius a successful ruler had to create a military power strong enough to overcome the disorderly little cities and principalities and in the end to evolve a new public spirit and civic loyalty. All the circumstances of his time conspired to make him see in an absolute ruler the arbiter of a nation's fate. But beside these historical circumstances, the logic of his own political philosophy weighed heavily in the same direction. In this respect also it was Hobbes who gave a systematic statement of what Machiavelli suggested.

From this point of view it is easier to understand the double standard of conduct for the statesman and the private citizen which forms the main connotation of what is called "Machiavellianism." The ruler, as the creator of the state, is not only outside the law, but if law enacts morals, he is outside morality as well. There is no standard to judge his acts except the success of his political expedients for enlarging and perpetuating the power of his state. The frankness with which Machiavelli accepted this conclusion and included it in his advice to rulers is the chief reason for the evil reputation, though the *Discourses* were really no better. He openly sanctioned the use of cruelty, perfidy, murder, or any other means, provided only they are used with sufficient intelligence and secrecy to achieve their ends.

Machiavelli's prince, the perfect embodiment of shrewdness and self-control, who makes political capital alike of his virtues and his vices, was little more than an idealized picture of the Italian tyrant of the sixteenth century. He is a true, if exaggerated, picture of the kind of man that the age of the despots threw into the forefront of political life. Though .the most extreme examples occurred in Italy, Ferdinand of Spain, Louis XI of France, and Henry VIII of England were of the same type. There is no doubt that Machiavelli had a temperamental admiration for the resourceful, if unscrupulous type of ruler and a deep distrust of half-way measures in politics, which he rightly believed to be due to weakness more often than to moral scruple.

Machiavelli never based his belief in the omnipotent lawgiver into a general theory of political absolutism, as Hobbes did later. His judgment produced two positions—for the resourceful despot and for the free, self-governing people—which were not consistent. He patched the two together, rather precariously, as the theories respectively of founding a state and of preserving it after it is founded. In more modern terms it might be said that he had one theory for revolutions and another for government. Hence he recommended despotism only in two somewhat special cases, the making of a state and the reforming of a corrupt state. Once founded, a state can be made permanent only if the people are admitted to some share in the government and if the prince conducts the ordinary business of the state in accordance with law and with a due regard for the property and rights of his subjects. Despotic violence is a powerful political medicine needed in corrupt states and for special contingencies in all states but still a poison which must be adminisbred with the greatest caution.

Catastrophic changes occurring in society throughout Europe produced as a matter of course an equal change in political theory. And in the opening years of the sixteenth century this change found its brilliant expression in the difficult—almost the contradictory figure of Machiavelli. Sabine's this lyrical passage captures brilliantly that genius of Machiavelli:

> No man of his age saw so clearly the direction that political evolution was taking throughout Europe. No man knew better than he the archaism of the institutions that were being displaced or accepted more readily the part that naked force was playing in the process. Yet no one in that age appreciated more highly the inchoate sense of national unity on which this force was obscurely based. No one was more clearly aware of the moral and political corruption that went with the decay of long-accustomed loyalties and pieties, yet no one, perhaps, felt a keener nostalgia for a healthier social life, such as was typified in his mind by ancient Rome. Certainly no one knew Italy as Machiavelli did.

And yet, writing on the even of protestant Reformation, he was almost blind to the part that religion was to play in the politics of the next two centuries. Indoctrinated as he was in the pagan revival in Italy, he was unable both by training and temperament to grasp the constitutional and the moral ideals that European politics would carry over from the Middle Ages. Clear and broad as his vision of politics was, Machiavelli was still in a peculiar sense an Italian of the first quarter of the sixteenth century. Had he written in any other time and place, his conception of politics must have been significantly different.

Italian society and politics, as Machiavelli conceived them and as historians have for the most part agreed to picture them, were peculiarly illustrative of a state of institutional decay. It was a society intellectually brilliant and artistically creative, more emancipated than any in Europe from the trammels of authority, and prepared to face the world in a coolly rational and empirical spirit, yet it was a prey to the worst political corruption and moral degradation. The older civic institutions were dead; medieval ideas like the church and the empire were no longer even memories. Cruelty and murder had become normal; agencies of government, good faith and truthfulness had become childish scruples to which an enlightened man would hardly give lip-service; force and craft had become the keys to success; profligacy and debauchery had become too frequent to need comment and selfishness, naked and unadorned, to supply its own justification. It was a period truly called the age of "bastards and adventurers," a society created as if to illustrate Aristotle's saying that "man, when separated from law and justice, is the worst of all animals." Machiavelli is, therefore, in a peculiar sense, the political theorist of the "masterless man," of society in which the individual stands alone, with no motives and no interests except those supplied by his own egoism. Sabine has aptly observed that in this Machiavelli represents a phase of all modern society, but he represents it in the exaggerated form appropriate to Italy in the sixteenth century.

The political theorists before Machiavelli would have contested the elementary that "security for man is impossible unless it be conjoined with power the dominant mark of the state. Indeed, it has been and remains one of the abiding concern of the Western political theorist to weave ingenious veils of euphemism to conceal the ugly fact of violence. At times he has talked too sonorously "authority," "justice," and "law," as though these honorific expression alone could transform coercion into simple restraint. That the application of violence is regarded as abnormal represents a significant achievement of the Western political tradition, yet if it is accepted too casually it may lead to neglect of the primordial fact that the hard core of power is violence and to exercise power is often to bring violence to bear on someone else's or possessions. Writers before Machiavelli cannot be accused of having ignored power. The classical and medieval theorists had spoken long and eloquently of its brutalizing and corrupting effects on those who were called to exercise it. They rarely faced up, however, to the problem of the cumulative effect on society of the consistent application of coercion and the not infrequent use of violence. This evasion had come about largely because attentive to power had arisen primarily in connection with the establishment or reform of a political system. It had been assumed that once affairs were set in along the prescribed paths, once proper education, the spread of knowledge or of faith, the improvement of social morality, and all of the other pressure flowing from a rightly ordered environment had begun to operate, then would be progressively less need for the systematic application of force.

With Machiavelli the euphemisms were cast aside and the state was directly confronted as an aggregate of power. Its profile was that of violence. Machiavelli believed that the vitalities of politics could not be controlled and directed without application of force and the threat at least of violence. The new prince above all other princes, cannot possibly avoid the name of cruel. Even when the political actor was not faced with the task of creating a tabul rasa, he could not avoid inflicting injuries on some one. His hands are brend to be bloody and dirliy. He must act while hemmed in by vested interests and expectations, privileges and rights, ambitions and hopes, all demanding preferential access to a limited number of goods.

But Machiavelli tried to create an 'economy of violence', a science of the controlled application of force. The task of such a science would be to preserve the distinguishing line between political creativity and destruction. "For it is the man who uses violence to spoil things, not the man who uses it to mend them, that is blameworthy". The control of violence was dependent upon the new science's being able to administer the precise dosage appropriate to specific situations. In corrupt societies, for example, violence represented the only means of arresting decadence, a brief but severe shock treatment to restore the civic consciousness of the citizenry. In other situations there might well be a diminishing need for cruel actions; men could be managed by playing on their fears, by using the threat rather than the actuality of coercion. But every application had to be considered judiciously, because the indiscriminate exercise of force and the constant revival of fear could provoke the greatest of all dangers for any.

This preoccupation with economy of violence was manifest also in Machiavelli's discussion of the external forms of violence—war, imperialism, and colonialism. One of the basic aims of the *Art of War* was to demonstrate that, while military action remained an unavoidable fact of the political condition, its costliness could be reduced by proper attention to strategy, discipline, and organization. *The Prince* and *The Discourses* followed the same theme of economy with counsels like these: a prince ought carefully to consider his resources, because, while a war may be started out of whim, it could not be as easily stopped; an unreliable army was an inefficient instrument of violence because it multiplied devastation without any of the compensations of victory; to avoid a necessary war was costly, but to prolong it was equally prodigal; a prince who found his position weakened by a victory had over–estimated his power resources.

In the matter of imperialism Machiavelli adverted to the example of Rome for the significant reason that Roman imperial policy had sought to preserve the wealth of the subject populations and their native institutions, thereby limiting the cost in devastations for both conqueror and conquered. If imperialism were handled efficiently the destructive consequences could be minimized, and the whole transaction reduced to a mere change in power. In contrast to Rome's controlled use of violence were those destructive wars which had been compelled by necessities, such as hunger, plague, or overpopulation.

While Machiavelli's economy of violence subsumed both domestic and external actions, it never seriously entertained the proposition that the incidence of force could be appreciably lessened in international politics. The effects of violence might be controlled, but the resort to it would not diminish. He saw quite clearly that the absence of arbitrating arrangements, such as law and institutional procedure, left the international field more exposed than the domestic to conflicts of interest and the drives of ambition. On the other hand, he believed that the internal politics of society could be structured by a variety of methods aimed at minimizing the need for extreme acts of repression. The importance of law, political institutions, and habits of civility was that in regularizing human behavior they helped to reduce the number of instances in which force and fear had to be applied.

Machiavelli's most important insight into the problem of internal power politics came when he began to explore the implications of a political system based on the active support of its members. He grasped the fact that popular consent represented a form of social power which, if properly exploited, reduced the amount of violence directed at society as a whole. One reason for the superiority of the republican system consisted in its being maintained by the force of the populace, rather than by force over the populace. The economy of violence which resulted from the people's feeling a sense of common involvement with the political order made it in the interests of the prince to cultivate and garner their support. Lacking this, he would have to draw on his fund of violence and the eventual result would be abnormal measures of repression. The greater his cruelty, the weaker does his regime become. Far from limiting his initiative, popular approval could be utilized to depreciate the great cost in violence of radical reforms. In a revolution by consent only the few had to be harmed.

In evaluating Machiavelli's economy of violence it is easy to criticize it as being the product of a technician's admiration for efficient means. A century like ours, which has witnessed the unparalleled efficiency displayed by totalitarian regimes in the use of terror and coercion, experiences difficulty in being tolerant on the subject. Machiavelli regarded the science of violence as the means for reducing the amount of suffering in the political condition, but that he was clearly aware of the dangers of entrusting its use to the morally obtuse. What he hoped to further by his economy of violence was the pure use of power, undefiled by pride, ambition, or motives of petty revenge. In contrast, there was no hint of child-like delight when Machiavelli contemplated the barbarous and savage destructiveness of the new prince, sweeping away the settled arrangements of society and leaving nothing intact. There was, however, the laconic remark that it was better to be a private citizen than to embark on a career which involved the ruin of men. Sheldon Wolin has rightty observed that the theorist like Machiavelli, who was aware of the limited efficacy of force and who devoted himself to showing how its technique could be used more efficiently, was far more sensitive to the moral dilemmas of politics and far more committed to the preservation of man than those theorists who, obssessed with moral indignation eager for heroic regeneration, preach purification by the holy flame of violence.

Of course, if one reads his *Prince*, knowing nothing about the late fifteenth and early sixteenth-century Florentine milieu in which it emerged and for which it was meant to provide solutions, knowing nothing about the traditions of humanist discourses and the patrons who were meant to receive their tracts, knowing nothing about the various medieval and early Renaissance discourses concerning motivation to civic action, he may be shocked by Machiavelli's pessimism or realism about human greed, self-interest and the apparent human inability to sustain moral obligations when confronted by foreign invasions, one constitutional reform after another, and a factionalism especially among a rapacious ruling elite. But no political theorist especially from the Middle Ages, would have said anything different about corrupt societies where the common good is daily seen to be destroyed. *The Prince* was written for a dysfunctional society and suggested ways in which a people could be brought back to health that is, to acting for the common good. In this, it was innovatory as political theory because every other theorist whom we have discussed wrote about collective, consensual customs and laws, which worked.

We live today in the shadow of Machiavelli the man who above all others taught the world to think in terms of cold political power. He was one of those rare intellectuals who wrote about politics because they have had a hand in politics and learned what it is about. His portraits show a thin-faced, pale little man, with a sharp nose, sunken cheeks, subtle lips, a discreet and enigmatic smile, and piercing black eyes that look as if they knew much more than they were willing to tell.

What gives *The Prince* its greatness? It is not a great formal treatise on politics. It is bare of any genuine insights into social organization as the basis of politics. It has very little passion in it—so little that, because the final chapter crackles and glows with Machiavelli's fervor for the unification of Italy, some commentators have suggested that it is not an organic part of the book but was added as an afterthought. It has been pretty well proved, moreover, by recent scholarship that Machiavelli's little pamphlet on princes is not even original in form. It is part of a whole traditional literature on princes that stretches back to the Middle Ages. The structure of the book, its division into chapters and even some of the chapter headings follow the conventional form of what has been called the 'mirror-of-princes' literature; the discussion of how to rule conquered territory, what advisers a prince should rely on, how he should conduct himself among the intrigues of diplomacy, whether he should depend mainly on fortified castles or entrenched camps in warfare.

But the intellectual spirit that pervades the book is quite another matter. Here we are in the presence of something little short of a revolution in political thinking. The humanists who had written books about princes had written in the idealistic and scholastic medieval tradition; they were ridden by theology and metaphysics. Machiavelli rejected metaphysics, theology, idealism. The whole drift of his work is toward a political realism, unknown to the formal writing of his time. When Machiavelli wrote thus he was not creating a new ethos, whatever we may think of it; he was expressing the ethos of the late *quattrocento* and the early *cinquecento* not only in Florence but in the whole of Italy. Machiavelli was, in short, the child of his time—neither better nor worse than the other intellectuals, politicians, diplomats and civil servants of his time.

He was able, using the traditional humanist literary forms, to pour into them a realistic political spirit which his age was acting on but which had never before been so well expressed in political thought. He had the daring to turn against the whole idealistic preoccupation of the humanists. He had the clear-eyed capacity to distinguish between man as he ought to be and man as he actually is—between the ideal form of institutions and the pragmatic conditions under which they operate.

But if we have come close to his greatness here, we have not wholly succeeded in ensnaring it. There have been other men who have expressed the consciousness of their period. They have in very few instances achieved the highest rank in the history of ideas. And while those who content themselves with seeing Machiavelli thus in the context of his time, may succeed thereby in countering the charges made against him of being a sort of anti-Christ who had created a new immorality, they do not thereby get at the roots of his greatness.

To take a further step in our analysis, we must see that Machiavelli, while he expressed the ethical consciousness of his time, was also a good deal ahead of his time in other respects. He lived in a period when economic growth had gone so far as to burst the bounds of existing political forms. What gave the city-states of Italy their Renaissance grandeur was not some mysterious flowering of the humanist spirit at the time. It was the fact that with the opening of the East by the crusades, the breakup of the manorial economy and the growth of trade and handicraft manufacture, the cities of Italy found themselves strategically placed with respect to the world trade routes. There followed what amounted to a communal retribution in Italy and a reorganization of the government of the Italian city-states under democratic and guild forms. The expansion of the economic power of these cities went on apace into the end of the fifteenth century by the time Machiavelli came to the maturity of his powers. The expansion had gone as far as the political limits of the communal organization allowed.

If the Italian city-states had been able to adjust themselves to the needs of an expanding economy by resolving their rivalries and joining in a united political structure, Italy might have been spared the two and a half centuries of political humiliation, economic backwardness and cultural aridness which followed the fall of the communes. Elsewhere however, in France, in England, in Spain, the expansion of political forms kept pace with the economic expansion. Machiavelli lived in what, with our historical perspective, we now say to have been the beginnings of the Western nation-state system. He was himself only dimly aware of it. He was in no sense an articulate nationalist, and the fervor of his national feeling has probably been overestimated by commentators. But two elements were historically to enter into the composition of the Western nation–state. One was national unity and the idea of a common tongue, common culture and common economic limits. The second was a realistic concentration of power at the center in order to break down divisive barriers. Machiavelli only dimly foresaw nationalism, but he very clearly expressed the second element—the realistic use of power from the center, the methods by which unity could be achieved.

Therein lies the importance of *The Prince* in the subsequent history of the Western world. Machiavelli wrote a grammar of power, not only for the sixteenth century, but for the ages that have followed. Read *The Prince* today and we will be struck by the detonations which its sentences set off in the corridors of our experiences with present-day rulers. Machiavelli seen only in his historical context does become intelligible; but his greatness does not emerge until we see that when he wrote his grammar of power he came close to setting down the imperatives by which men govern, and are governed in political communities, whatever the epoch and whatever the governmental structure.

The Prince has become, for better or worse, a symbol of a whole body of literature and a whole approach to politics. Just as in literature and art we mast always face, under whatever names, the polar conflict of classic and romantic, so in the history of political thinking we have always to face the polar conflict between the ethical and the ruthlessly realistic. *The Prince* is part of the world's polemical literature because it places itself squarely in the ranks of realism. It brushes aside, with an impatience in which Machiavelli scarcely cares to conceal his disdain, the tender-mindedness of reformers and idealists.

There is in all of us, along with the ethical and normative strain, a strain of hard-headedness and of the acceptance of the framework of human passions and social reality within which we have to work. One can trace it back to Aristophanes and the way in which he always deflated contemporary dreams and illusions by getting back to the essential limits of the human reason. In every generation since him the young men have been divided between the pursuit of some passionate ideal and the hard-bitten inquiry into how things actually get accomplished in a real political world. It is to that pole of our political thinking that *The Prince* gravitates. As long as this strain will remain in- political thinking, so long will *The Prince* be found to have expressed in undying prose its intensity and its temper.

Very few who talk of *The Prince* have ever read more than a few sentences in it. But fewer still have read the saner, the more rounded the more comprehensive work *The Discourses* of Machiavelli.

It was the longer work on which Machiavelli was engaged when, because of political opportunism, he made a sudden sortie to finish *The Prince.* He came back to it later. He seems to have worked on it intermittently for the better part of a decade. It bears to *The Prince* much the same relation that Marx's *Capital* bears to the *Communist Manifesto*. It is the considered, comprehensive treatise. Outwardly an unfinished commentary on the first ten books of Livy's *History of Rome*–reflections on politics which use Roman history as a point of departure. It is clearly not a book which ever had a chance for real fame. The very people who have written most about *The Prince* seem to have neglected *The Discourses,* and very few seem to have read it. When we talk of Machiavellianism, it is *The Prince* we have in mind. And that is perhaps as it should be. But when we talk of Machiavelli, we must have *The Discourses* in mind as well. For if we are to judge a man it is fairer to judge him by the book into which he sought to put his whole system of politics rather than by the pamphlet which he dashed off to win a friend and influence a personage.

Scholarship has not done well by *The Discourses.* The scholars pay lip service to it as the larger frame of reference within which *The Prince* can be understood. What was the intellectual tradition that lay back of *The Discourses*? In the case of *The Prince,* it was the mirror of prince's medieval and humanist literature. Felix Gilbert has suggested that research into the literature of "the good state," both in Italian and in European thought, might yield exciting results for an understanding of *The Discourses.*

However that may be, what are the basic ideas of *The Discourses*? We should say the following: first, the-superiority of the democratic republic to every other political form; second, the ultimate reliance even of despotic and authoritanan regimes on mass consent; third, the primary political imperative of cohesiveness, organic unity in a state, stability and survival; fourth, the great role of leadership in achieving this cohesiveness and survival; fifth, the imperative of military power in insuring survival and the need for putting it on a mass base; sixth, the use of a national religion for state purposes, and the choice of one not for its supernatural validity, but for its power as a myth in unifying the masses and cementing their morale; seventh, the need in the conduct even of a democratic state for the will to survive, and therefore for ruthless instead of half-hearted measures when ruthless measures were necessary; eighth, the idea—later to be found in Vico and in our day in Spengler—of the cyclical rise and fall of civilizations due to the decadence and corruption of the old and the reinvigoration of the new.

The Prince is great because of its intensity, *The Discourses* are great because of their variety; if *The Prince* is great because it is polemical, *The Discourses* are great because they have balance; and if *The Prince* is great because it gives us the grammar of power for a government, *The Discourses* are great because they give us the philosophy of organic unity not in a government but It in a state, and the condones under which it alone can survive.

"The authentic interpreter of Machiavelli", Lord Acton in his erudite preface to Burd's *The Prince* is the whole of later history. Acton strings out a remarkable series of quotations from the great writers and statesmen of the last three or four centuries which show the impact that Machiavelli had on the European mind. The history of that impact may be called the history of Machiavellianism.

It is clear that one element in the denunciation of Machiavellianism was the use of that symbol as a weapon of the Counter-Reformation. Machiavelli was utterly secular in his thinking. And when the Church in assuming the aggressive against the religious reformers, sought something that could be set up as a secular devil-symbol in contrast to the ethical teachings of religion, it easily found what it sought in Machiavelli's writings. At the same time also the same symbol could serve to brand with infamy the methods that were being used to set up and consolidate the new nation-states of Europe, the power of whose sovereigns was one of the great threats to Church power. And so the Church statesmen who had at first accepted *The Prince,* then ignored it, finally decided to attack it. Under Leo, Clement, Paul III, it was tolerated. But under Paul IV, in 1557, a generation after the Florentine's death, Machiavelli was put on the Index. What is somewhat ironic about this is that the Church princes, like the secular princes, were among the principal followers of Machiavelli's precepts. As Lord Acton points out, the arguments used to excuse the massacres of the religious wars were drawn from Machiavelli.

There is another important element in the history of Machiavellianism—so far, at least, as the English-speaking secular world is concerned. Machiavelli entered our consciousliess large]y through the Elizabethan drama. Wyndham Lewis has written a provocative, although erratic, book with the title The *Lion and the Fox*. It takes its point of departure, from a fact spelled out by scholars like Edward Meyer and Mario Praz—that the figure of Machiavelli dominated the imagination of the Tudor dramatists. The meeting between Italian Renaissance culture and the Tudor mind contained an element of shock arising from novelty. The English were, as is true of all cultural borrowers, at once attracted and repelled by Italians. More over, Tudor drama was enormously sensitive to world currents. The result was that not only were there, as Meyer has pointed out, some 400 direct references to Machiavelli in the Elizabethan literature; but the Machiavelli figure, whether directly or indirectly, dominates it as does no other. Iago was drawn from Machiavelli, as was Barabas. Webster, Massinger, Ford, Marston, Ben Jonson, Shakespeare—they were all fascinated by the image they constructed of subtle cunning, of treachery, of the gap between outward seeming and inward being, all of which they thought of as Machiavellianism. To the Tudor imagination, which has in turn so influenced our own, Machiavelli was the symbol that stood for the decadence, the corruption, the unfathomable depths of Renaissance Italy. It was probably due to the fusion of the influence of Church and stage that Machiavelli became associated in the popular mind with the Devil himself. "Old Nick" became an epithet equally applicable to both.

It may therefore seem surprising that Tudor England had scarcely read Machiavelli at all. *The Discourses* were not translated into English until 1636, *The Prince* until 1640. The Elizabethans got their knowledge of Machiavelli from a French book attacking him, Gentillet's *Anti-Machiavel.* And Gentillet gave just enough of Machiavelli to distort him, and not enough to make him either comprehensible or human. This should not surprise us. It is the essence of a symbol that its outlines should be shadowy. What has first been sifted through the intellect is unlikely to ensnare the imagination. Had the Elizabethans really read *The Discourses* and *The Prince,* they would no doubt have been more just to the author, but their drama would have suffered and one of its type figures would have had to be scrapped. By the time the translations were made it was unfortunately too late to affect either their intelligence or their art. The symbol had become fixed and frozen.

But Machiavelli became the subject of attack from still another source—the seventeenth and eighteenth-century absolute monarchy. We have a long roster of despots—benevolent and otherwise— who are reputed to have drunk in Machiavelli with their mother's milk and were know as "Machiavellistae." But we must remember, so black had Machiavelli's reputation become, that if you wanted to hit at a monarch, you had only to start a whispering campaign to the effect that he ruled according to Machiavelli's grammar. The supreme irony was that Frederick the Great of Prussia, while still a young man, wrote a refutation of Machiavelli. As Frederick's later career showed, Machiavelli had adumbrated the methods of the benevolent despots only too well. His offense had been only to unmask them, to lay bare to the world the mechanisms of power which were behind the authority of the ruler.

But if Machiavelli was a butt and a tool in the Age of Reason, he came into his own in the nineteenth century in the age of new nationalism. Men rediscovered Machiavelli the liberal, Machiavelli the democrat, Machiavelli the nationalist patriot. In Germany, during and after the Napoleonic wars, the intellectuals rediscovered Machiavelli, and turned their fine gifts of scholarship toward him, with the characteristic result of a spate of Machiavelli studies. The leader was Fichte, who made an analysis of Machiavelli part of his famous Address to the German Nation; and Hegel, who following Machiavelli made a cult of the state, taught that the course of world history stands outside of virtue, blame and justice. And in Italy Cavour and the leaders of the Risorgimento found in Machiavelli their ideal symbol. What both the Italians and the Germans sought in him was what they needed for their movements of national liberation: the stress on cohesiveness, the pursuit of the main chance, the prime virtue of political survival. The Germans took from him the concept of *Statrason*—opportunism justified by reasons of state policy; and in the field of foreign affairs, *Realpolitik*.

In country after country the rediscovery of Machiavelli seems to have had an almost magical efficacy in stirring latent national and even reformist energies. To complete the history of Machiavellianism, need only point out that for the recent collectivist movements as well he became an evocative figure. H. G. Wells, in what is one of his really first-rate political novels, *The New Machiavelli*, dreamed of a strengthened and perfected state that blends Machiavelli with English Fabian humanitarianism. Both Lenin and Musolini did their work in the shadow of the Florentine. The old Bolshevik Kamenev published a volume of Machiavelli selections with a sympathetic Introduction under the Soviet regime. Some years later, when he was tried and conevicted in the purge trials, the public prosecutor used his Machiavelli editing job against him. Mussolini also wrote an introductory essay to an edition of The *Prince*. Rauschning in his *Voice of Destruction*, which recounts his conversations with Hitler, asserts that Hitler ranked Machiavelli with Wagner as among the influences shaping his thought; and that he used to keep a copy of the prince by his bedside.

It has become a truism to point out that Machiavelli is the father of power politics. Whether a truism or not, it is still true. Machiavelli as ambassador and administrator could not afford to do any wishful thinking. But to say that he was the father of power politics may have curiously erroneous implications—as if we were to say that Harvey was the father of the circulation of the blood. Power politics existed before Machiavelli was ever heard of; it will exist long after his name is only a faint memory. What he did, like Harvey, was to recognize its existence and subject it to scientific study. And so his name has come to be associated with it. To be sure, Machiavelli's role is not wholly innocent. His grammar of power brought a whole new world to consciousness. Frederick, Richelieu, Napoleon, Bismarck, Clemenceau, Lenin, Mussolini, Hitler, Stalin, and others have gone to school to Machiavelli, But, by bringing the world to this awareness Machiavelli did what every creative figure does. We might as well blame Shakespeare because, by creating Hamlet, he has intensified the agony of the indecisive and divided liberal.

Machiavelli has also been accused and it is true, of being the father of the martial spirit, of propaganda techniques and of the totalitarian spirit. But here again he anticipated things latent in the very texture of society and the state. A reading of *The Discourses* should show that his thinking fathered many movements, democratic as well as dictatorial. The common meaning he has for democrats and dictators, alike is that, whatever your ends, you must be clear-eyed and unsentimental in pursuit of them and you must rest your power ultimately on a cohesive principle.

May we venture a guess as to the reason why we still shudder slightly at Machiavelli's name? It is our recognition that the realities he described are realities; that men, whether in politics, in business or in private life, do not act according to their professions of virtue; that leaders in every field seek ruthlessly and hold on to it tenaciously; that the masses who are coerced in a dictatorship have to be wooed and duped in a democracy; that deceit and ruthlessness invariably crop up in every state; and that while the art of being ruled has always been a relatively easy one, the art of ruling ourselves is monstrously difficult. Machiavelli today confronts us with the major dilemma of how to adapt our democratic techniques and concepts to the demands of a world in which as never before naked power politics dominates the foreign field and determined oligarchies struggle for power internally. It is not an easy dilemma to resolve. And in a sense, just as the seventeenth and eighteenth-century monarchs hated and feared Machiavelli because he had exposed their authority to the world, so today we hate and fear him because he has exposed our dilemma and made it visible to ourselves and the world.

Let us be clear about one thing: ideals and ethics are important in politics as norms but they are scarcely effective as techniques. The successful statesman is an artist, concerned with nuances of public mood, approximations of operative motives, guesswork as to the tactics of his opponents, back breaking work in unifying his own side by compromise and concession. Religious reformers have often succeeded in bringing public morale closer to some ethical norm; they have never succeeded as statesmen. Even in the theocracies of Savonarola in Florence, Cromwell and the Puritans in England, men in New England colonies, the men of God, when they came to power, learned to play the game of power. The only difference between them and others is that, since they had a certitude of having a pipeline to God, they did not have to reckon at all with the uneasy factor of their conscience. The most destructive imperialisms of the world have been those of men who have elevated their preferences to the pinnacle of moral imperatives and who have then confidently proceeded to impose those imperatives on others.

Today, as in Machiavelli day, our world has become a collection of principalities struggling for survival, maneuvering for position, fighting over spoils. The scale is bigger but the proportions are the same. The strong men have come forward in every state, using the rhetoric of mass interest and national glory to extend their power and entrench their class. The first law of internal policy is to hold on to power, it external policy it is to extend your imperialism. Like Machiavelli, we live in a time of the breaking of nations.

Let it be said that Machiavelli in his day blundered as we are doing in ours. He could not make up his mind whether what he wanted was a democratic Florence of a unified Italy. We think he must have felt, when he wrote *The Prince,* that democracy would somehow follow if unity was achieved. There are others who feel that no integration is worth the candle if democratic rights and human decencies are scrapped in the process. In Machiavelli's writing you will find both attitudes, but more often the first.

This raises sharply, of course, the interminable question of ends and means. Machiavelli would shrug his shoulders at the whole problem. He himself, he would say, was an observer of politics. And as such he would find it irrelevant to impose his own ethical patterns on the torrential flow of world history. It is for that very reason that Machiavellianism, after everything has been said about it, fails to be an adequate philosophy for a way of life. Men are not only observers, not only participants; they are also valuing individuals. Without judgments, life loses its hierarchial quality of being a choice between preferences. And losing that, it loses its savor.

Machiavelli sought to distinguish the realm, of what ought to be and the realm of what is. He rejected the first for the second. But there is a third realm; the realm of what can be. It is in that realm that what one might call a humanist realism can lie. The measure of man is his ability to extend this sphere of the socially possible. We can start with our democratic values, and we can start with Machiavelli's realism about tough-minded methods. To be realistic about methods in the politics of a democracy at home does not mean that you throw away all scruples, accept the superior force of "reason of state", or embrace the police state crushing of constitutional liberties. To be realistic about the massing of power abroad in the economic and ideological struggle for the support of men and women throughout the world does not mean that you abandon the struggle for peace and for a constitutional emporium that can grow into a world republic. We may yet find that an effective pursuit of democratic values is possible, within the scope of a strong social democratic state and an unsentimental realism about human motives.

Machiavelli's understanding of politics stands in sharp contrast to that of Aristotle. Machiavelli makes no grand claims for the exalted nature of man, he does not cast political life as the whole of life, he is infamous for having divorced politics from ethics and for distinguishing the virtues of the political man from virtue itself. In the tradition of political theory, Machiavelli is unique by dint of his passionate devotion to political action. He loved the subject matter of political theory—politics itself—to a degree unparalleled by any other. theorist of equal repute. Ironically, the consequence is that through five hundred years of interpretation, Machiavelli has probably been more maligned and disparaged than any of his fellows in the tradition of political theory. In fierce and uncompromising fashion, Machiavelli pierced to the quick of Western politics and the men who comprise it; weaker hearts have rebelled.

Above all, Machiavelli reincorporated into political thought that which we watched the Greeks try to eliminate—the body. For Machiavelli, politics is a visceral, earthly, flesh and blood affair. His is a politics seething with irrepressible drives and urges a politics that transpires on earth and through the body. There are no unchanging forms or spiritual ideals in Machiavelli's political world, no ultimate telos that man fulfills, no gods to whom he pays homage with his political activity. Politics is not an aesthetic ideal, but life itself. However, the particular constructions of body, desire, and need in Machiavelli's politics are profoundly gendered. The life in which this politics is situated is the life of men bent upon control and domination, the life of communities ruled by those who care for ruling and the expansion of their power above all else. Similarly, while "necessity" figures largely in Machiavelli's musings on politics, this necessity too is narrow and one-sided, signifying for Machiavelli the limitations and dangers to one's quest for power and, conversely, the spur to glony—it has little to do with daily, concrete human needs.

Machiavelli's sharply gendered view of human beings and politics led him to subvert some of his own understandings about the political world. Despite his attunement to the intricacy and complexity of political life, he often urges the political actor to use the bluntest of instruments and force in this realm, advice that secures fleeting victories at best and more often increases the actor's vulnerability to threatening and incomprehensible forces *(fortuna).* Similarly, Machiavelli's commitment to demystifying the political would is thwarted by his own reification of power's consequences in the character of fortuna.

For Machiavelli, politics emerges from what he takes to be the nature of man and, develops men into creatures of true manliness. In contrast to the Greeks, this development docs not involve bringing man's nature to "perfection" through political life, but transforming, overcoming, or harnessing to specifically political purposes a number of the unwieldy qualities he perceives as indigenous to man. For Machiavelli, men are the raw material of politics and require a form superior to that which naturally inheres in them if political life is to nourish and if they are to achieve individual and collective glory. This superior form embodies the Machiavellian ideal of manhood that, in urn, provides the shape of Machiavellian politics. Moreover, for Machiavelli, politics always bears the limitations of the tranformative possibilities for man's nature. Machiavelli harbors no illusions about the usefulness of a political theory based upon men as they ought be rather than men as they are or can be.

It will be that a evident close inspection of the nature of "unmodified" Machiavellian man suggests that while Machiavelli has much to say about human nature and identifies human beings as creatures of the natural world, his exploration of human nature is based upon a very particular kind of man. From the beginning, Machiavelli assumes men to be alienated from themselves and their surroundings, driven by a kind of random desire for power and conquest, inherently short-sighted and frustrated in their aims and ambitions.

Machiavelli's writings are replete with remarks about man's nature. Most of his political advice begins from or culminates in statements about one or more immutable characteristics of man. Thus, for example, when discussing Scipio's failure to quell rebellion in his troops, Machiavelli concludes, "this came from nothing else than not fearing him, because men are so restless that if the slightest door is opened to their ambition, they at once forget all love for a prince. Enumerating the difficulties of political innovation, Machiavelli cautions, "men don't really believe in anything new until they have had solid experience of it." His teachings to the would-be leader of an insurrection are capsulated in the doctrine, "men are driven by two things: love and fear." Nowhere, however, does Machiavelli offer a comprehensive portrait of man's nature. Rather, his ruminations on this subject are scattered throughout his writings and are synopsized only in the repeated declaration, "the nature of man is everywhere and always the same. Thus, we must elicit a composite drawing of Machiavellian man from the diverse and partial testimony Machiavelli offers throughout his literary and political works.

We begin with Machiavelli's appreciation of man's animality. In contrast with the many political theorists who arrive at a definition of man by distinguishing him from other animals, Machiavelli suggests a very close and by no means unfortunate kinship between man and beast. Most familiar in this regard is chapter eighteen of *The Prince* in which he praises ancient allegory for its frequent depiction of the apprenticeship of would-be princes to Chiron, the centaur. The mythical creature who is half-man, half-beast, is the symbolic figure of perfection in *The Prince*, a book of teachings and models for political success. On a first reading, it would seem that the most effective political actor is he who draws closest to his animal nature. On the other hand, the discussion of Chiron and the "lion and fox" allegory that follows might be read as an attempt to distinguish the nature of animals from the nature of man. Identifying man as a "creature of law" in this discussion, Machiavelli appears to make this distinction explicitly. We need to know that there are two ways of fighting: one according to the laws, the other with force. The first is suited to man, the second to animals; but because the first is often not sufficient, a prince must resort to the second. Therefore, he needs to know well how to use the traits of animal and man.

By Machiavelli's time, these ideas and practices have been largely cut loose from their formally ethical foundations and gave rise to a world in which power is quite starkly pursued for its own sake. Political rationality has grown more forthrightly instrumental, and the ends of politics pertain to a relatively narrow conception of political glory by comparison with the rich conception of the "good life" cherished by the ancient Greeks. For Machiavelli, woman, nature, and the uncontrollable are bound together in the guise of *fortuna* and are cast as the explicit antagonist of political men in search of political glory, freedom, and power.

If Machiavelli were pressed to capture in a word that feature of man least shared by other animals and most salient as a political quality, inarguably the word would be "ambition." "What province or what city escapes it? What village, what hovel? Everywhere ambition and avarice penetrate." These two furies sent to dwell on earth are the source of nearly all that man does or creates, especially that which is destructive or self-destructive. If they had no existence, happy enough would be our condition but they deprive us of peace set us at war and take away from us all quiet and all good. Ambition and avarice never arrive anywhere alone but bring their necessary companions, Envy, both, and Hatred, who in turn are always accompanied by cruelty, ride, and Jesuit. Machiavelli considers ambition an utterly ineradicable feature of individuals and of the human condition as a whole: when man was born into the world, ambition was born too. And in the *Discourses* he says, "whenever men cease fighting through necessity, they go to fighting through ambition, which is so powerful in human breasts that what ever high rank men climb to, never does ambition abandon them. Machiavelli does not have moral objections to the drive he has labelled ambition; indeed, he considers it the spark and fire of political life. But he does identify a number of problems created by is the development of a particular kind of man first uncovered in ancient Greek political life. The Greek alienate his head from his body, once he conceives of the body as something to be mastered, once he institutionalizes that conception in the organization of social life, he is set upon a course in which he strives to conquer, master, dominate, or control all that threatens his precarious freedom from the body. The head that is separate from the body and subjugates the body is threatened and spooked by what it has suppressed, and it must be eternally vigilant in sustaining its achievement. The mastery is never complete, never final, and the amorphous drive for power at the center of Machiavelli's conception of man is at least in part a consequence of this dynamic.

One of the most striking features of the distorting effect ambition has upon perception and judgement is formulated by Machiavelli as a tendency to reify gaps or failures in one's 0wn understanding of the world. An excessive emphasis upon appearance—a confusion of appearances with reality—is one manifestation of this reification. A man blinded by ambition is too caught up his own desires to perceive what lies underneath superficial appearances. But by far the most extreme expression of this reification is that which Machiavelli joins with his predecessors in denoting *as fortuna.*

While Machiavelli often portrays *fortuna* as a goddess with mind, will, and intentions of her own, he also declares that *fortuna* is nothing other than man's inadequate grasp of his circumstances. The former is how Machiavelli knows most men regard *fortuna* while the latter is his own view of her existence.

Necessity's nurturance of virtue is a central concern for Machiavelli because of its role in the development or political *strength* and *power.* This is most apparent in his praise of the "tumults of Rome" chronicled by Livy, In the chapter title of this discussion, Machiavelli declares that "the discord between the people and the Roman Senate made that republic free and powerful"—free because the people had to exercise their freedom in order to maintain it and powerful because the ceaseless discords and quests for power within the city made the people into citizen-warriors of the strongest sort imaginable. Forced daily to fight for their civic status in order to maintain or enhance it, plebeians and patricians alike contributed to the enormous strength and vitality of the Roman state. Necessity unities and focuses ambition and it cultivates vigor where its opposite threatens. "That kingdom which is pushed on to action by energy or necessity will always go upward."

Ambition generates striving, striving breeds competition, competition nourishes *virtu,* the existence of *virtu* intensifies man's experience of scarcity, narrowed options or necessity. Myths, deceptions and fabrications become a second-order environment for political action and further complicate the actor's struggle with knowing where he is, what time it is, and where he stands in relation to enemies, allies and objectives. Hence, political life is not only several paces removed from human or social "needs" but also from any autonomous political "reality." In Machiavelli's account, politics transpires in the frenzied realm of appearances—a realm in which the political actor is half-blinded by his own ambitions but is also threatened by camouflaged mine fields and false images of insurmountable passes constructed by his adversaries.

One modern interpretation of Machiavelli stands out amidst the massive literature on his thought. This is a reading that casts him neither as political scientist nor philosopher, but as political playwright. According to Norman Jacobson,

> Someone once inquired of Demosthenes, "What is the chief part of an orator?" "Acting," replied Demosthenes. "What next?" "Acting." "What next again?" "Acting!" . . . Were we to inquire of Machiavelli the chief part of his *Prince,* we would undoubtedly receive the identical reply: acting.

For Machiavelli, so this interpretation goes, the political realm is a stage, there is no essential reality more important than appearance, there is real political power in symbolic action and events, in myth, faith, exuberance, good scenes or bad. Moreover, there is no authentic man but only the masks that he wears—predictable and transparent if he is a poor actor-politician and many, varied, and fluid if he is a clever and successful one.

Machiavelli's new political art is utterly devoid of content, its teaching precisely the opposite of "Be yourself." Its precept is instead "Be your roles." The object is to create a man of a thousand faces, a master performer who eventually does become his roles.

"After all, says Merleau-Ponty in his kindred reading of Machiavelli, "a face is only shadows, lights and colors." And Jacobson corroborates, "in *The Prince*, political art is the capacity of the unique man to transmute words and events into appearance. From Machiavelli's oft-quoted precept, "in general men judge more with their eyes than with their hands, everyone sees what you appear to be, few perceive what you are." K. R. Minogue surmises "politics is then, in a deep sense, an exercise in theatricality." Hannah Arendt develops the theatrical aspect of politics discerned by Machiavelli into a metaphysical principle. Genuine politics, she argues, can only occur in a bounded pubic realm where "appearance— something that is being seen and heard by others as well as ourselves—constitutes reality.

The characterization of the theatrical dimension of politics is not quite true to Machiavelli whose political world includes, but is not wholly constituted by the realm of appearances. Machiavelli does not give us inauthentic man, pure role-player, and from him reach inauthentic politics, a politics of nothing but roles and seeming. To the contrary, Machiavelli begins with men who distinctly crave power but must re-order reality, dissimulate, and fabricate appearances to reach their desires. Machiavellian man is a creature of intense subjectivity and identity — he does not blend easily into the roles and forces that political success demands. He climbs into the realm of appearances for purposes instrumental to his real ends or is caught up in the order of appearances because he does not know better. But he cannot possibly hope to succeed in his endeavors if he takes events, conditions, or individuals at face value. Political man must constantly strive to pierce the appearances thrown up by others while creating appearances useful to his own ends. Thus, while Machiavellian politics has a theatrical element, it contains elements the theater does not–unmasking the rest of the world while masking one's own character and plans.

Machiavellian politics is never quite real, it is never quite about real things. The spur of politics—ambition or the amorphous quest for power—is itself of an ultimately intangible quality and spins a world of unreality. In the Western tradition of "masculine" politics, political life is always at some level a game played by juvenile delinquents, and this is precisely what Machiavelli confesses as he portrays politics in dramaturgical terms. Still, Machiavelli's concern with the problem of appearances in politics is also about that most concrete of political goods—the construction and wielding of political power. That something so ephemeral as contrived appearances could be partly constitutive of something so tangible and determinate as power is not only an intriguing enigma but one that opens up clever prince arranges and rearranges appearances—his own and that of his surroundings or adversaries—for the purpose of securing or mobilizing power. Religious rituals as well as purely secular proclamations are useful to this end, and Machiavelli bears no scruples about mixing one with the other.

A prince also builds power within his state through careful attention to his reputation. Not what he is but what he seems to be determines the extent to which he is in control of his dominion, and in turn, the extent to which his state is a powerful one.

What makes the prince contemptible is being considered changeable, trifling, effeminate, cowardly, or indecisive; he should avoid this as a pilot does a reef and make sure that his actions bespeak greatness, courage, seriousness of purpose and strength Any prince who gives such an impression is bound to be highly esteemed, and a man with such a reputation is hard to conspire against, hard to assail, as long as everyone knows he is a man of character and respected by his own people.

What is eclipsed by these interpretations is Machiavelli's repeated insistence that the successful politician must be able to distinguish what seems to be the case from what is in fact the situation; he must be able to pierce the order of appearances if he is to work that realm in his own advantage. No one is more ill-fated than a prince who responds to the reputation rather than to the concrete power of another prince, or who makes the error of trying to be what he must appear to be. Whether external conditions or his own image are at issue, a prince who is duped by either is bound to fail, Machiavelli advises the political actor to play the game of appearances from outside of its clutches for political phenomena have an underlying reality even if few can grasp it and even though false appearances can transmute into power.

The Machiavellian political actor cannot pierce appearances to grasp what lies beneath them because he is not capable of such judgement, because the underlying reality of men questing voraciously and blindly after power is what has given rise to the game that is politics, if the political world is full of illusions, political man is also a creature of delusions. Important as it is for him to see through the fabrications thrown up by others, his judgement is cloaked by its own particular burden, its inseparability from the distorting effects of the intentions and passions that focus it. Add to this the tremendous pace of political events making thoughtful inspection of motives, actions and circumstances so difficult, and we have a picture of Machiavelli's political men incapable of the necessary, doomed by the impossible.

Ruled by time and conditions distorted and manipulated by all, politics is a race through a riot by half-blind men who must plow through this chaos in order to face and create still more chaos at the next turn.

Neal Wood has suggested that "Machiavelli's politics is cast in the mould of the warrior" and that war is the paradigmatic scenario for expression of *virtu*. Wood's insight is accurate enough, but he fails to stretch its implications toward an even more fundamental feature of Machiavellian politics: politics is utterly dependent upon the presence of an enemy, it is at all times a fight, and dissolves when opposition is not present or is too weak to inspire consolidated struggle. This is why Machiavelli insists that peace always give rise to laziness, decadence, or a state of effeminacy. Politics manifests itself only when necessity is present and politics is experienced only as against something or someone. Thus, the frequent observation that Machiavellian political thought is relevant only to kill-or-be-killed circumstances is actually the wrong way of putting the matter. For Machiavelli, the apparent or actual existence of a kill-or-be-killed environment is the precondition for politics as well as the *raison detre* of politics. This is not merely to say that "politics is struggle" for, in Machiavelli's account, struggle without an end is as corrupting of *virtu* and political life as is idleness or passivity. "The vigor that in other countries is usually destroyed by long peace was in Italy was destroyed by the cowardice of those ceaseless wars from 1434 to 1494." Rather, it is to say that politics only appears when there is something to conquer, overcome, ambush or resist. Wars, Machiavelli writes in the *History of Florence*, are not for purposes of peace but for the enlargement of power and thus necessarily entail resolution through total conquest rather than truces or compromises. Peace, besides being an intangible good, is the death of politics. War, by contrast, presents what Wood calls "the archetypal battle between virtu and fortuna," a battle, of course, which is itself the archetype of Machiavellian politics and political action. War is the contest between all that is manly, and all that is changeable, unpredictable, and capricious, a struggle between masculine rational control and feminine irrationality.

The power of mental and physical force are man's greatest weapons in this kind of politics. The shortage of these powers, by comparison with other animals, was precisely what weakened and disadvantaged Machiavellian man in the wilderness. But in politics, his vulnerability is turned to aggression, his blindness is compensated by brutality, his precarious bearing in the world is cloaked by his *virtu*. Unfit to live in the jungle of the natural world, Machiavellian man creates a jungle of his own in civilization: Machiavellian politics.

Perhaps this explains the priority he gave to what today may seem a peripheral issue: it provided an opportunity for theoretical advances, which was unavailable in overtly political discourse. By thus attempting to reform long-established, customary behavior while lacking a theoretical justification for political innovation, Savonarola soon made himself unpopular, and he was overthrown and executed in 1498. A younger Florentine, Niccolo Machiavelli, drew from this the conclusion that an innovative ruler must disseminate a systematic illusion among his subjects if he is to retain power. Savonarola, declares Machiavelli in *The Prince*, was an– 'unarmed prophet' 'who was ruined in his new orders when the multitude began not to believe in him, and he had not the means of keeping firm those who had believed, or to make unbelievers believe'.

The Prince considers the question of how a reforming ruler can legitimate his reign. Machiavelli claims that the issue does not arise in the case of hereditary princes, or with regard to a ruler who does not seek to introduce social or cultural change. In such circumstances, an appeal to custom is sufficient to forestall rebellion. Machiavelli rightly has observed that it is enough, not to transgress the arrangements of their ancestors; it is reasonable that the prince will be well liked by his subjects, and the memories and causes of innovations are lost in the ancientness of the continuation of his dominion in maintaining their old condition, and there not being differences in customs, men will live quietly.

The question raised by the recent history of Florence, however, was how a government which desires to abolish old customs and introduce new ones might justify itself in the eyes of its subjects. Obviously, such a government cannot honestly invoke established custom. And yet Machiavelli did not have access to any other vocabulary in which power could be legitimated. The only possible solution for an innovative government, he concludes, is to deceive the people. As he puts it in *The Discourse*.

> He who desires or wants to reform the State of a City, and wishes that it may be accepted and capable of maintaining itself to everyone's satisfaction, it is necessary for him at least to retain the shadow of the ancient forms, so that it does not appear to the people that the institutions have been changed, even though in fact the new institutions should be entirely different from the past ones, for the general mass of men are satisfied with appearances, as if it exists and many times are moved by the things which appear to be rather than by the things that are.

When skilfully deployed, it seems, mere representations can pass themselves off as reality. Machiavelli has thus described two distinct forms of false consciousness. There is, first of all, the tendency of the people to make a fetish out of their past modes of behaviour, or custom. Machiavelli perceives a natural human urge to continue doing things as they have, apparently, always been done. This essentially involves mistaking the second nature for the first nature. It is as if the actions people have performed in the past acquire an animate power in the present and work to frustrate progress and disguise society's real interests, so that, as Machiavelli puts it later, 'the people desire their own ruin'. But this self-deception on the part of the people necessitates a second deception which is deliberately instigated by their ruler, who must falsely represent any innovations as if they were continuations of established practice. It thus appears that ideology can arise spontaneously out of quotidian social life, and that it can also be inculcated through a conscious manipulation of 'appearances' by the rulers. This attribution of a deceptive element to the civil power was so shocking to Renaissance sensibilities that Machiavelli's name soon became a byword for cunning, deception and intrigue in general. Thus, in Marlowe's *The Jew of Malta* [1590], the prologue uses the Florentine's name as a noun, which tells the audience all they need to know about the villainous protagonist, Barabas: 'you shall find him still in all his projects a sound Machiavelli. And that's his character.

Despite his unsavory reputation over the century following his death, Machiavelli's work both described and facilitated a radical change in political thought. The ideas that the people's attachment to custom can constitute brake on good government, and that it can be desirable for the government to deceive the people, amounted to a transformation in the conventional conception of civil power. One good reason for locating the decisive historical break between the 'medieval' and the 'modern' worlds in the early sixteenth century is the fact that an analogous development in religious thought took place simultaneously with Machiavelli's breakthrough in the secular realm. *The Prince* was written in 1512, and in 1517 Martin Luther nailed his ninety–five theses to the church door at Wittenberg.

Niccolo Machiavelli may well be the most political of all the great political theorists; and, like politics itself, Machiavelli horrifies and repels us, yet also attracts and fascinates. We do not know what to make of him, or how to think rightly about political life. We know that politics matters profoundly, perhaps more in our time than even before; we suspect that somehow we have gotten it terribly wrong; but we feel powerless to change, or even fully to understand our situation. It in true thinking about politics and thinking about Machiavelli have become in terconnected enterprises, each illuminating and obscuring the other.

Machiavelli's thought is as problematic as politics itself, presenting a different face to each observer. Thus, he is also one of the most misunderstood of political theorists, or at any rate the most subject to conflicting interpretations. Some see him as a tough-minded advocate of *raison detat*, others as a romantic who idealized ancient Rome; some see him as a passionate patriot, others as a cynic; some as a detached, objective observer, others as a teacher of evil; some as republican, others as worshiping strong leaders and military might. Each reading claims foundation in the texts, yet none has ever succeeded in displacing the others.

Often the problem of interpreting Machiavelli is formulated in terms of a conflict between his two best-known works, *The Prince* and *The Discourses*. The former is seen as favoring one-man rule, the latter a republic; the former is seen as cynical, the latter idealistic. But although there are important differences between these two works, the fundamental tensions in Machiavelli's thought lie not between these works but within each of them, and indeed within all his writings. *The Discourses,* too, are studded with cynical advice to princes and disparaging remarks about human nature; *The Prince,* too, gives indications of a devoted, patriotic concern for republican virture.

In our understanding, Machiavelli was committed, lifelong republican and Florentine patriot. He served the republic loyally in office, mourned its fall, and meditated on ways to restore it or to create a more viable version of it for the whole of Italy. Unemployed, he also tried to get a job with those who had over thrown the republic; that may or may not be considered cynical or evil. But Machiavelli also despised utopian idealism, and relished the tough, reeking realities of political power. He admired success, skill, strength, power; he revered the ruthless, heroic leader, the effective military force, the conquering empire of ancient Rome. He was then, both a republican and something like a protofascist.

With respect to Machiavelli himself, some have suggested that the tensions and ambiguities in his thought simply indicate the carelessness of a second-rate mind. Others regard them as evidence of duplicity, of an effort to convey simultaneously an esoteric and exoteric message. The initial suggestion of this book will be that the apparent contradictions in Machiavelli's thought arise neither from ineptitude nor from manipulative cleverness, but from ambivalence–intense but incompatible feelings that can be neither given up nor reconciled.

Machiavelli's fame as a republican theorist came relatively late. His contemporary fellow-Florentinces did not trust his republican faith, and when a republican government was restored in 1527, they did not return him to the post of Secretary that he had lost in 1512. What damaged him was not so much the fact that he had served the Medici in few humble affairs and had written the Florentine Histories for Medici, but the authorship of *The Prince:* Everyone hated him because of the *Prince*. The rich thought that his *Prince* was document written to teach the Duke how to take away all their property. Church regarded him as a heretic, the good thought him sinful, the wicked thought him more wicked; so all hated him. Giovanbattista Busini, the author of this well-known judgement was notoriously malicious and hostile to Machiavelli but his words render well the mood of the Florentines, including Florentine republicans.

The restoration of Machiavelli's reputation as a tepublican thinker began with Oxford professor Alberico Gentili. In 1585, he wrote an eloquent eulogy of Machiavelli, whom he praises as the author of the golden observations on Livy and as a man of unique prudence and learning. Those who have written against him, Gentili claims, have not understood Machiavelli's ideas at all, and have indeed slandered him. The truth is that Machiavelli was a strong supporter and enthusiast for democracy. He was born, educated and received public honours in a Republic. He was extremely hostile to tyranny. Therefore he did not help the tyrant; his intention was not to instruct the tyrant, but by making all his secrets clear and openly displaying the degree of wretchedness to the people. He excelled all other men in wisdom and while appearing to instruct the prince he was actually educating the people.

Almost a century later, the interpretation of Machiavelli as a champion of liberty was resumed by Spinoza. The opinions of that 'wise man' wrote Spinoza, seem to me particularly attractive in view of the well-known fact that he was an advocate of freedom and also 'gave some very sound advice for preserving it. After Spinoza, the idea of Machiavelli as a misunderstood republican was authoritatively endorsed by Pierre Bayle and by Diderot and it received its final sanction in the well-known lines of Rousseau's Social Contract. While appearing to instruct kings he has done much to educate the people. Machiavelli's *Prince* is the book of Republicans.

For us, though we may not believe that *The Prince* is the book of republicans, Machiavelli's reputation as a republican theorist is a solid acquisition. We still debate how the same person could have been a republican citizen and the author of *The Prince* but contemporary scholars all agree that Machiavelli was an advocate of republican constitution. A number of scholars seem to agree, however that Machiavelli's republicanism was of a rather special sort because it contained a strain of monarchism, in so far as he believed that even republics could not come into existence without the help of great individual personalities, as Friedrich Meinecke put it, or because it is in truth a 'mixture of republicanism and tyranny', as Harvey Mansfield and Nathan Tarcov have recently written. Others have remarked that the distinctive aspect of Machiavelli's republicanism was his commitment to civic and military virtue, even to its most unpleasant manifestations—war and conquest.

8

Thomas Hobbes

> The passions that incline men to peace, are fear of death; desire of such things as are necessary to commodious living; and a hope by their industry to obtain them. And reason suggested convenient articles of peace, upon which men may be drawn to agreement. These articles are they which otherwise are called the Laws of Nature.

Thomas Hobbes (1588-1679) was beyond doubt the first great English philosopher. He is arguably the greatest of all that followed. He stands out as a titan for at least four reasons: first, the sweep and coherence of his analysis; second, the energy and vividness with which he expressed his views; third, the detailed and inventive development of argument, without reverting to rhetoric and fourth, simple, pellucid conclusions, thoroughly unsettling to both contemporaries and successors, and so virtually impossible to ignore. What cannot be denied is that Hobbes's work has been paid more sustained critical attention in the twentieth than in any preceding century, with the possible exception of his own. It can scarcely be doubted, given the attention Hobbes commands, that he speaks to us, and proves, in various ways, significant and relevant to our concerns.

Hobbes was born prematurely in 1588, his mother's labour, it is said, being brought on by news of the Armada ('Hobbes and Fear were born twins') but he survived all the vicissitudes of seventeenth-century English politics to die in his bed at the age of ninety-one in 1679. Hobbes was an Oxford man who found the prevailing Aristotelian scholastic philosophy little to his taste. He was recommended as tutor to the Cavendish who became the second Duke of Devonshire. He spent most of his life in the houses of noblemen. He discovered the new science on the Grand tour in 1610, and in the early 1620s he became the friend and amanuensis of Francis Bacon. Hobbes was a staunch Royalist. By 1641, when he fled to France to escape the coming Civil War, he had met Galileo and many of the most noted scientists and men of letters of his day.

Hobbes spent some of his time in exile in France (1641-51) as mathematics tutor to the future Charles II. He also worked on *Leviathan*, which was published in London on Hobbes's return to England to make his peace with the Commonwealth. There is some mystery about why he actually came back when he did, though the probability is a combination of homesickness and his growing reputation in émigré circles for religious unorthodoxy, if not downright atheism. Charles II, in his good-natured way, always retained a soft spot for Hobbes. He was invited back to Court after the Restoration and given a royal pension of £100 a year.

Hobbes had no direct family, no wife, no progeny. Nor had his parents any standing in a country, in an era immensely conscious of class, or status. He was bright boy whose work was furthered by powerful protectors, who made good use of him. He was a man in service to the Cavendishs. He was a tutor to their young children. He was a dependent, with an intellect dazzlingly, but never proudly independent. Hobbes was, in short, a loyal retainer. He theorized both equality and subjection, but was more familiar with the second than the first. His theory could be said to reflect his condition: he knew his worth, but he also knew his place. In this, we are to distinguish between social inequality and intellectual superiority. It was Hobbes's intellect and that only which made him sovereign.

We have not enough knowledge of Hobbes's personality. But we do know that he was orderly, efficient, quick, productive, restrained and curious, with an immense interest in science. Science is an established means of escaping class hierarchies. Hobbes's most important, if not his only experience of class equality was among savants, where it was more the argument than the person that mattered. Hobbes's arguments were convenient to the powerful, even while removing from these some of their luster. On Hobbes's account, even if he was a servant and he were – then so were those who were less than sovereign. Not only did Hobbes's intellect make him equal to his betters, but he employed his intelligence to illuminate the principle of equal subjection by all strata to Leviathan. The sovereign, following Hobbes, was not sovereign due to any special virtue attaching to him or her or a few to wear the crown. No divinity doth hedge Hobbes's king, only a prudent and mutual need for common authority. Were Hobbes's tastes and sympathies more bourgeois, or more aristocratic? Among those prepared to supply an answer we may identify Macpherson and Wood.

In England, Hobbes functioned as the dependent of a noble family. He voted with them, as required. He served them, as they saw fit. Hobbes's later irascibility may well have kept him out of the Royal Society. Hobbes's exclusion on class grounds is all the more plausible, if we take the Royal Society as a microcosmic representation of society as a whole.

He was more analytical than Machiavelli, more concise that Bodin, more historical than Descartes, more insightful than Spinoza, more coherent than Locke, and perhaps more 'modern' than any of them. He was able to argue powerfully on virtually any plane, scriptural, logical or historical. If Hobbes's greatness is now universally agreed, the reasons informing the conclusion vary from critic to critic to entice the next. For C.B. Macpherson, Hobbes reflected a new bourgeois market mentality. Leo Strauss, more broadly, saw Hobbes as a 'modern'. Lubienski took Hobbes to supply 'the first great effort' to turn ethics and politics into a science without the help of reason. It is in a way unfortunate for the history of political thought that the first masterpiece of social contract theory, Thomas Hobbes's *Leviathan*, should be so untypical of social contract theorising. Social contract was invented to support the case for disobedience to authority. In *Leviathan* Hobbes makes out a social contract case for the absolute government which social contract had been invented to undermine. Hobbes is a masterly political arguer because he meets and beats his opponents on their own ground. He uses social contract's own language to drive a coach through all the libertarian conclusions which previous social contract thinkers had come to. Hobbes is also subtle. He wrote at the time of the English Civil War (*Leviathan* was published in 1651), and his more acute readers soon realized that his arguments are double-edged. What would have been an argument for Cromwell's power in 1651, and again for Charles II in 1660. Hobbes pleased neither the Royalists nor the Parliamentarians, though Cromwell left him alone, and Charles II received him at court.

Hobbes's universe, human and natural, is subject to uniform explanation. No item requiring explanation can receive this without being resolved into its component parts. The ultimate components of human society, for Hobbes, are individuals. The ultimate components of the universe are atoms. And what governs these is motion. The individual moves and is moved, in the manner of one atom striking another. But the individual is moved not just physically, it is also moved psychologically perplexed by desires passions and drives. Indeed, physical determination is largely a function of psychological direction. The chief motive which determines human action, is that of self-preservation. Whether this is to be read as a mere factual datum, or as a moral principle, is subject to dispute. But self-preservation, for Hobbes, is the underlying desideratum.

Although human individuals, for Hobbes, may be solipsistic, or self-contained, they are not self-sufficient. Indeed, one of the major difficulties for Hobbes is to determine how solipsistic parasitic individuals overcome their neurosis sufficiently to be able to establish orderly social relations. Hobbes's view of self-preservation is far more complex than at first appears. He is more likely to mean, not that the individual's first and only concern is and ought to be to preserve the self, but that the individual is, as a matter of fact, governed by an underlying fear of premature death and that this fact is not to be regarded as inconsistent with a proper morality. Indeed, Hobbes hoped to show how self-preservation was consistent with a morally grounded submission to the state, or how fear of authority was consistent with a morally grounded obedience to it.

Hobbes insists that both regulated and intuited trains of thought were caused, were determinate. But in some cases, the cause laid within, in other cases outside, the agent affected. Regulated thought was that which obtained when the process was regulated by some desire, some design. Humans, for Hobbes, enjoyed an enormous capacity for internalizing causes, which is to say for thinking in a highly regulated or rational way. The first problem was not to establish human causal control over nature but to set up regulated or rational communication among men. This, for Hobbes, was the job of language.

Language was not a by-producet but a precondition of human organization. For Hobbes, humans relate to one another, not so much by empathy, as Rousseau would later maintain, but by speech. It is by language, as Hobbes sees it, that we 'make known to others our wills and purposes'. Here, too, in discussing the reach of regulated thought, there is room for debate. Either Hobbes showed that (1) all dispute can be resolved rationally, or that (2) public authority has to be blindly obeyed since there can be no such authority if every subject keeps his own counsel. The difficulty is that (2) sounds like a paradoxical variant of (1), which Hobbes was determined to refute.

Reason is a form of regulated thought available to humans. Reason is a form of language, and is not altogether independent of it. It is the instrument by which humans understand, and thus combine one with another. Language has no preordained meaning or purpose but that which individuals individually give it. Hence the importance of human nature, of human will and of social contract. A society for Hobbes is a form of verbal order. It expresses a convergence of wills. Individuals are not just social creatures, but self-interested solipsists, who enter into society as part of an express or tacit desire for personal good and gain. They accordingly do not exist for society, but society for individuals. For Hobbes, however, the ultimate achievement of human rationality is a firm recognition of the limits of rationality, and consequently of the need for authority. Rationality, for Hobbes, leads to the conclusion that order, which he assumes all humans to desire, can only be purchased at the cost of submission to some external authority. Here again there is much room for dispute as to how consistently authoritarian Hobbes's conclusion actually proves.

Hobbes's overall philosophy provides both an explanation and a justification for the emergence of the state, and for the consolidation and concentration of state power. It is in part because he does this so powerfully and coherently, and in the apparently neutral, scientific language of modernity, that Hobbes is rightly taken to be so great a figure. He establishes from the outset continuity between natural and social science. He insists upon individual difference, in the form of divergent perceptions and interests, even while insisting upon equality of human condition. It is indeed this very equality, which for Hobbes supplies the ground for a legitimate mutual fear. For Hobbes, it is this fear, which contradicts prospects of social peace and simultaneously foreshadows the logic of its accomplishment.

Since there is no natural accord, and everyone cannot be sovereign, the security to which reason and speech point is submission to some individual or group among them. Thus does Hobbes take up from Bodin the logic of the idea of sovereignty – the logic of establishing an ultimate and all-powerful arbiter. But again there are interpretive difficulties: what are the limits that Hobbes may or may not have intended to apply to sovereign authority? If the individual's own interest – self-preservation – is paramount, then how can this interest be meaningfully protected without legal constraints of any kind upon the sovereign? There is the inevitable problem about empowering a Leviathan to protect interests, which he, at the same time, cannot be legally bound to respect. There is the puzzle as to how a sovereign with no legal obligation to subjects may be consistently viewed as the equal defender of the natural rights of each and every one of them.

During the past decades the literature devoted to Hobbes has expanded rapidly both in volume and in breadth of focus, covering the most diverse topics of his natural and civil philosophy. The reasons for this preoccupation are complex and elusive. To some extent the pre-occupation may stem from the fact that Hobbes stood at the beginning of various intellectual and social trends that have culminated or have been eclipsed in our own time. According to C.B. Macpherson, Hobbes was one of the first advocates of "possessive individualism," an anthropological doctrine that concentrated on the accumulation and protection of property as man's primary motives and became a cornerstone of the market economy and modern industrial society. Taking a broader view, Jurgen Habermas identified Hobbes as one of the ancestors of technological rationalism, a rationalism that in its combination of rigorous analysis and technical invention continues to animate the "scientific revolution" of our age. These and similar interpretations undoubtedly possess great plausibility and persuasiveness, but they hardly tell the whole story. Neither Hobbes's vocabulary nor our own seems restricted to this range of discourse. While attractive to the scientific mentality of a technological era, Hobbes's voice also reaches us on a different level of frequency—the level of basic human experience. From this vantage point, one may legitimately query whether and to what extent Hobbes's idiom bears resemblance to that of contemporary existentialist literature.

After having delineated principles of analysis and the basic properties of inanimate and animate bodies, Hobbes embarks on an examination of human attitudes and dispositions in their natural state or in the absence of a civil community. Some of the propositions advanced at this point have received wide currency as distinctive trademarks of his thought, but their basis is less frequently explored. The thesis of man's "perpetual and restless desire of power after power, that ceases only in death" and the portrayal of natural human life as "solitary, poor, nasty, brutish, and short" are sometimes ascribed to the pessimism, if not the base disposition of the philosopher. His anthropology is thus reduced to a personal idiosyncrasy. To be sure, the context in which these propositions are advanced does not always enhance their persuasiveness.

In the first sketch of his philosophical position, the thesis of the dependence of human motivation and of animal motion in general on external impacts was joined almost abruptly with the conception of a restless competition and discord; the nexus remained largely implicit. Yet, the treatment of human sensation in terms of quasi-mechanical motion seemed to preclude at least the metaphysical notion of a human essence, of a preordained teleology gently directing man's path with the promise of fulfillment. Some implications of man's predicament were developed in *De Cive.* Arguing against Aristotle's view of man as a "political animal," Hobbes in the opening chapter maintained that nature had not provided man so conveniently with a goal. He insisted that man's inclinations and desires, even when ultimately directed at social commerce, did not by themselves procure peace. Civil society was, in short, the result less of natural inclination than of design and planning. The nexus between natural inclinations and human discord was explored more fully in the *Leviathan*. Thus while signals of command were found to be intelligible to most animate creatures, man was assigned the special capacity of "understanding not only his will, but his conceptions and thoughts, by the sequel and contexture of the names of things into affirmations, negations and other forms of speech." Moreover, man could go beyond the immediate confines of perception by trying to determine the likely consequences and possible uses of an object—a faculty, Hobbes writes, "of which I have not at any time seen any sign but in many only; for this is a curiosity hardly incident to the nature of any living creature that has no other passion but sensual." Coupled with this inventiveness was man's rational potential, his ability developed through training to "reduce the consequences he finds to general rules," to "reason or reckon, not only in number, but in all other things."

Largely on the basis of these arguments Hobbes then advanced his general thesis of the deficiency and restlessness of human life. The absence of a preordained essence and the incongruity between man's imagination and the world supported the conclusion that man on earth could not find ultimate fulfillment that the "felicity of this life" resided not "in the repose of a mind satisfied" nor in the attainment of an object, but rather in the "continual progress of the desire from one object to another, the attaining of the former being still but the way to the latter." The further proposition of human conflict and discord could be attached to this thesis without great difficulty, for in the pursuit of his goals man cannot avoid encountering others engaged in a similar endeavor. This general search or race, however, is dominated not only by scarcity of desired goods, but above all a scarcity of positions in front or on top, and from this scarcity derives the danger of hostility and even physical destruction. Moreover, man in the pursuit of his ends has to assure himself constantly of the necessary means, and, due to their diverse abilities, other human beings are liable to be employed as such objects or instruments or to be subdued or destroyed in case of resistance. As Hobbes suggests, there are three principal sources of human conflict—competition, diffidence, and resentment: competition to use and subdue others as objects, diffidence of being used or subdued as such, and resentment for being valued more as an object than as a person.

Bacon embodies empiricism, and subscribes to ontological individualism. But for a really thorough and systematic exposition of both we must turn to a far more formidable thinker, Thomas Hobbes. The one thing which everyone knows about Hobbes is the conclusion to his argument in *Leviathan*: that to establish human society on a basis of lasting security, it is necessary to place 'an absolute and arbitrary legislative power' in the hands of a single sovereign. Divided authority, or divided sovereignty is a recipe for insecurity and conflict. It is this conclusion which has led to Hobbes being associated with theorists of absolutism like Bodin, and to his being charged, rather vaguely, with authoritarianism.

Human Nature

But what is chiefly interesting and significant about *Leviathan* is not so much the conclusions, as the process and arguments through which they are reached. And these are so radical, so untraditional, that it is not surprising that despite his apparently reassuring conclusions, Hobbes was mistrusted and condemned by contemporary monarchists. Robert Filmier, who attacked him from that angle, commented 'It may seem strange that I should praise his building but dislike his foundations – but so it is '. It was not strange at all. Hobbes's arguments have nothing in common with those of the divine right theorists. The structure of his case does not rely upon the quotation of authorities or the citing of precedents. His method is to start from what he takes to be empirical premises – factual truths about human nature – and arrive at his conclusions by deductive arguments based upon these premises: 'For I ground the Civil Right of Sovereigns, and both the Duty and Liberty of Subjects, upon the known natural Inclinations of Mankind, and upon the Articles of the Law of Nature'. He wished to construct a science of politics, or a civil philosophy, analogous to what was currently being achieved in natural science.

To realize this scientific ambition, it was necessary to see human beings themselves as parts of nature, subject to the same fundamental laws as all other natural beings. Hobbes does this by applying to human motivation and action Galileo's law of inertia – proposition that 'When a Body is once in motion, it moved (unless something else hinder it) eternally'. The types of motion which animate human behavior displays 'to have no Desire, is to be Dead' – Hobbes repeatedly makes this point. There is no point of rest on this side of the grave: 'For there is no such thing as perpetual Tranquility of mind, while we live here; because Life it self is but Motion, and can never be without Desire, nor without fear, no more than without Fear no more than without Sense'. As soon as one desire, or appetite, is gratified, we move on in search of a further satisfaction: 'So that in the first place, I put for a general inclination of all mankind, a perpetual and restless desire of power after power, the ceased only in Death.'

With the possible exception of Bentham, no writer brings out more clearly than Hobbes the central role played by desires in the liberal theory of human nature. It is these which animate and dominate our actions. In relation to them reason and thought are purely instrumental: 'the Thoughts, are to the Desires, so Scouts, and Spies, to range abroad, and find the way to the things desired'. Hobbes whose capacity for clear and logical thought most of us can only envy, yet believed that reason was the 'slave of the passions', and that reason meant little more than 'reckoning', a fundamentally calculating ability of the mind. And not only reason, but also ethics, are subordinated to the desires. For it is Hobbes's view that 'good' and 'evil' are simply the names we give to the objects of our particular individual appetites and aversions. There cannot be 'any common Rule of Good and Evil, to be taken from the nature of the objects themselves; but from the Person of the man' who uses the terms.

Hobbes's ethical reductivism derives in part from his nominalism. For him, words are names, and the naming quality of language is linked in turn to his ontological individualim. Common or general names, as opposed to proper names, do not refer to single objects, despite their singular form, but to many individual objects grouped under a single heading or name. These 'universals' have, therefore, no real existence – 'there being nothing in the world universal but names; for the things named, are every one of them individual and singular'.

This ontological individualism, which Hobbes shares with Bacon, Locke and the other liberal empiricists, provides the general philosophical foundation for his individualistic conception of human beings. For the natural world is composed of unique and discrete individual bodies, and human beings conform to this principle. Each of them is a self-contained, self-moving and totally self-orientated being. There is nothing naturally social about Hobbesian man: 'We do not by nature seek society for its own sake, but that we may receive some honour or profit from it; those we desire primarily, that secondarily.' Hobbes explicitly distinguishes human being from such naturally social creatures as bees and ants, and further denies that there is in human affairs the same coincidence of the common good with private interests as there is in the worlds of these insects. 'every man is presumed to do all things in order to his own benefit', and this egoism leads directly to competition, rivalry, perpetual insecurity and, at worst, to unrestrained physical conflict. This is one of those several points at which Hobbes is in conflict with later and more optimistic versions of liberal theory. Hobbes, like Sade, does not make the bland assumption that all humankind's desires are directed towards ends, which are in themselves rational, civilized and moderate. Nor does he postulate a hidden hand, which ensures that individuals pursuing their own interests automatically furthers the general good at the same time.

But what is the basis of Hobbes's presumption of universal self-interest? Here Hobbes follows the method adopted by Montaigne and Descartes: 'know thyself', or 'Read thyself. It is possible to generalize from observation of oneself and others, because people are much the same, despite the varieties of time and place. Hobbes gives to this 'sameness' a democratic or egalitarian dimension by claiming that taking one thing with another, men are about equal in their natural endowments: 'nature hath made men so equal, in the faculties of body, and mind; as that when all is reckoned together, the difference between man, and man, is not so considerable, as that one man can thereupon claim to himself any benefit, to which another may not pretend, as well as he'. Indeed, Hobbes like Descartes suggests that just because 'the common-peoples minds' are not 'scribbled over with the opinions of their Doctors (meaning the traditionalist university teachers) they may be more receptive to new ideas. But just at this point Hobbes once again undercuts later liberal optimism which interpreted the 'blank sheet' or tabula rasa theory of the mind as the basis for the transforming potential of education, by pointing out that those whose minds are like 'clean paper', are also 'fit to receive whatsoever by Publicque Authority shall be imprinted in them'. It is an opportunity for manipulation and indoctrination as much as for education.

Hobbes's conception of human nature illustrates the change in the concept of nature itself which took place in this period. From being a moral category, which signified the divinely appointed ends or purposes which each natural being was supposed to fulfil it has been changed into the concept of an irreducible, amoral and even anti-social bedrock of urges and passions which any realistic social and political theory and prescriptions must, however, regretfully, take account of. It followed from this conception of human nature that the supposed 'state of nature' is simply a condition of unrestrained competition, of what Hobbes call 'war of every man against every man' though he is careful to point out that by this he means not necessarily open conflict, but that condition of insecurity which is always apt to break out in war.

There are, however, some distinctive aspects of Hobbes's version of this myth which expose some of the most problematic assumptions of liberal theory. Hobbes adopts the view which the authorial protagonist in Buchanan's dialogue many critics have rejected that the creation of society and government is inspired purely by considerations of self-centered utility. Their argument is that such a motive tends to dissolve rather than unite society, and it tells powerfully against Hobbes, as it does against Bentham. But there is a sense in which Hobbes, like Bentham, sidesteps this criticism by postulating a society which remains little more than a collection of self-seeking atoms, and therefore never achieves the coherence which more traditional theorists saw as essential to the very concept of society.

Alasdair MacIntyre is therefore wrong to suggest that it is 'confusion' on Hobbes's part 'to make political authority constitutive of social life'. This, on the contrary, is the logical consequence of his throughgoing individualism. Only an all-powerful sovereign can prevent these jostling atoms from destroying each other. Hence, Hobbes's absolutism is the necessary response to his individualism, and reflects a tendency within liberal thought to negate itself by pushing individualism to the point where authoritarianism seems to be the only possible political answer. But Hobbes is consistent in both his absolutism and his individualism. On the one hand he denies to the individual the right to follow his conscience, since this might then imply a right of resistance or opposition to the sovereign. Similarly there can be no question of the sovereign being limited by a pre-existing constitution or set of laws, since this makes the constitution or the laws the actual sovereign. For Hobbes, law is what the sovereign decrees, and justice is synonymous with law. All this is decidedly anti-liberal.

On the other hand, since the purpose of each individual in joining the compact to establish the sovereign is to further his own self-preservation, it follows that the individual does retain the right to defend his own life. Hobbes therefore allows the right of resistance to 'private and particular men', the very thing that earlier and more traditional theorists ruled out. In this, he exemplifies a more modern and individualistic kind of political thought – although the individual right he allows would, of course, be of little practical use against the might of Leviathan. Hobbes is equally consistent in allowing that it is no crime for a starving person to steal food, 'because no law can oblige a man to abandon his own preservation'. Hobbes, unlike Locke, was not so attached to the institution of property as to allow its protection to distort his central argument.

Against Hobbes's radical and drastic individualism, several recent writers have been concerned to emphasize the more traditional elements in Hobbes thought. It is not at all surprising that his thinking incorporated 'feudal' as well as 'bourgeois' elements, and Keith Thomas, perhaps following Leo Strauss, was right to point to Hobbes's stress on honor and glory than a bourgeois scale of values. It is notable, too, that Hobbes does not altogether adopt the harsh attitude towards the unemployed which was to become the orthodoxy among liberal thinkers. Those who, by no fault of their own, 'by accident inevitable' find themselves 'unable to maintain themselves by their labor', ought not to be left to the uncertain fortunes of 'the Charity of private persons', but should be 'provided for (as farforth as the necessities of Nature require) by the Laws of the Commonwealth'.

There are, however, two further elements in Hobbes's contribution to developing liberal thought which must be mentioned. The first is his philosophical empiricism: that is, the stress on sense-experience as the source of knowledge: 'for there is no conception in a man's mind, which hath not at first, totally, or by parts, been begotten upon the organs of Sense'. Hobbes extends this analysis of mental activity to cover imagination, which he describes as 'nothing but decaying sense', the fading image of what has already been experienced. 'imagination and memory are but one thing' for Hobbes.

Secondly, Hobbes offers what is to become a classic statement of the liberal conception of liberty, or freedom, to be quoted with approval by leading liberals even in our own time. Hobbes's first definition is 'the absence of external impediments', and he returns to the subject to elaborate on this. An internal impediment, that is to say something that is 'in the constitution of the thing itself' does not imply a want of liberty, but of power. It is quite consistent with this definition that Hobbes should assert that 'Fear and liberty are consistent', because a person who throws his goods overboard to prevent the ship he is on from sinking, or pays a debt in order to avoid going to prison, can act otherwise. His action is therefore that 'of a man at liberty'.

That Hobbes should provide such examples, which expose the narrowness and strictness of his notion of freedom, is typical of his honesty and precision as a thinker. Hobbes's thoroughness makes him an especially revealing, and so especially valuable writer for the student of political ideas.

Equality and Security

Hobbes has offered a radical view on human equality. He observes:

> The question who is the better man, has no place in the condition of mere Nature; where. all men are equal. The inequality that now has been introduced by the Laws civil. I know that Aristotle in the first books of his Politics, for a foundation of his doctrine, maketh men by Nature, some more worthy to command, meaning the wiser sort (such as he thought himself to be for his Philosophy;) others to serve, (meaning those that had strong bodies, but were not philosophers as he;) as if Master and Servant were not introduced by consent of men, but by difference of Wit: which is not only against reason; but also against experience. For there are very few so foolish, that had not rather governed themselves, than be governed by others: Nor when the wise in their own conceit, contend by force, with them who distrust their owned, do they always, or often or almost at any time get the victory. If Nature therefore have made men equal, that equalities is to be acknowledged: or if Nature have made men unequal; yet because men that think themselves equal, will not enter into conditions of peace, but upon equal terms, such equalities must be admitted. Therefore, for the ninth law of Nature, I put this, that every man acknowledges other for his equal by Nature The breach of this precept is pride.

The Levellers extended Lutheran egalitarianism into politics, and it remained for Hobbes to expound a political version of Calvin's conception. He did so, however, in the process of a restatement of political philosophy intended to supplant religion and theology. This restatement consisted of an attempt to formulate a science of politics using the "clear and exact method" of geometric logic and a philosophic justification of authority and obedience founded on purely secularist, natural set of values. As Raymond Polin has suggested, Hobbes "seems to be one of the first philosophers, like Machiavelli to conceive a politics with the clear intention of excluding the divine from its principles, and the influence of religions and churches from its practice". Indeed, perhaps the most profound motive of Hobbes's work is the desire to sever political philosophy and political science from theology and the church and to anchor them instead in the methods of seventeenth century natural science and the institutions of civil society.

In view of this underlying motivation, it is interesting that Hobbes should have retained at least the rhetoric of theology, even while he was introducing into political philosophy the mechanistic imagery of the science of his day. The Leviathan is described both as an "Artificial Man" and as a "Mortal God": and the sovereign is designated, in a metaphor compounded of both styles of thought, as the "Artificial Soul" of the commonwealth. It is easy to imagine why Hobbes did not discard the rhetoric of theology along with the theological mode of analysis and the conception of society as an expression of a divinely ordered universe. Hobbes felt that the message of his philosophy could be broached in more familiar terms. As a clever polemicist, Hobbes also must have recognized that the surest way to cut the ground out from under his theological opponents was to turn their own sources against them, even if this tactic required tortuous exegesis, to say the least.

Like Hobbes, Machiavelli faced a similar problem in his effort to replace Christian values by an ethics of secular survival and fulfillment. It is therefore instructive for the understanding of Hobbes's use of theological rhetoric to note that Machiavelli employed classical props such as the glory of the Roman past and the Roman conception of virtue as a substitute for the emotional symbols of religion. For Hobbes theological rhetoric serves a similar purpose. By retaining the rhetoric but infusing it with an entirely different set of values, Hobbes could hope to transfer to his secularist philosophy the sense of importance and the will and dedication, which were ordinarily invested in religion. Hobbes deliberately drew his description of government from the *Book of Job*, described the sovereign as the "Mortal God," and sought in numerous other ways to hang the trappings of religion on his political philosophy.

The really striking feature of Hobbesian thought in this connection is its similarity both to Calvin's anthropology and to his understanding of authority and obedience. It would be patently erroneous to hold Calvin responsible for Hobboism or to identify Calvin with the motives and values of Hobbes. Two theorists could scarcely be father apart in their conceptions of the purpose of human life. There is certainly more than a superficial resemblance between Calvin's understanding of human nature and the portrait Hobbes paints of man as a creature trapped in a jungle of passions. Calvin had argued that, because of human depravity, life on earth was bound to be afflicted with anxiety and insecurity so long as man attempted to live by his own resources. Since he could no longer hope to merit salvation, all that man could realistically strive to achieve by his own efforts was an inner tranquility in the face of the torments of the world. To secure tranquility it was necessary to surrender all pride, to forego all claims of self-sufficiency, and to become the obedient servant of an omnipotent divine authority the justice of whose ways man could not understand.

Upon all these points, Hobbes recapitulates the arguments of Calvin in political terms, except that he makes several substitutions. For inner tranquility, he substitutes physical and psychological security. For the omnipotent authority of the creator God, he substitutes the power of an earthly protector. For Christian eschatology, he substitutes an equation of earthly security with salvation and of civil order with the kingdom of God. Thus secularized, the conceptions of human nature, which had served Calvin in the effort to exalt God and remind man of his humble station become for Hobbes the basis of a civil authoritarianism. For Hobbes, however, obedience is no mere surrender. The recognition of depravity is now designed to lead to a kind of redemption by man of himself. The creation of order by humankind, through a universal submission to the "King of the Proud," who is "made so as not to be afraid," is the symbol and manifest of this self-redemption.

Hobbes set forth his dialectic of depravity and redemption both in philosophical form and in his analysis of Scripture. The appearance of human depravity is confirmed both in the Scriptural account of the fall from grace and in the fall from innocence described in pagan mythology. In the *De Cive,* he alludes to an age of innocence when "it was peace and a golden age". In this golden age, men were not equal in authority: some held power and others obeyed. There was no disorder because the right of the rulers to command went unchallenged. In this presumably idyllic state "princes kept their empires entire, not by arguments, but by punishing the wicked and protecting the good." Men were kept in peace "not by disputations, but by power and authority", and the "science of justice" was "wrapped up in fables" rather than "openly exposed to disputation". It was inevitable, however, that this dubious bliss should end, because men is the only one of the creatures endowed with the faculty of speech. He would begin by assigning names to things and would advance from this simple but momentous step to the very heights of philosophy; from reason, according to Hobbes, is precisely the establishment of logical relationships among named objects. Out of this development of reason as an instrument of desire must have arisen that dramatic and revolutionary phenomenon, the private judgment of good and evil.

The theological parallel is here obvious and intended. God gave Adam the power to name all the things of the earth. Adam was bound to use this power, once he had learned to employ reasoning, to question the myths, which governed Paradise. In raising his questions, he committed an act of disobedience, expressing a will to raise himself to the level of God. In eating the fruit of the forbidden tree, Adam asserted the right of each man to make his own private judgment of good and evil, thus denying God's sovereignty in favor of the equal sovereignty of men. The immortality lost upon the fall is reinstated along with the permanent restoration of civil society; but this immortality is now not granted to men as individuals but to society as a whole through the succession of its rulers, which Hobbes designates an "Artificial Eternity."

Hobbes redefines traditional Christian eschatology to make the advent of Christ a final restoration of primitive innocence and immorality on earth. By redeeming the sins of man, Christ gained a "victory over death" and established the "Kingdom of God on Earth." This kingdom is the civil commonwealth in which God "reigned by his Vicar, or Lieutenant," the civil sovereign. As the commonwealth is the kingdom of God, salvation is the participation in this commonwealth. Salvation is achieved not in an afterlife but on earth whenever there is order and security. "To be saved is to be secured, either respectively, against special Evils, or absolutely, against all Evil, comprehending want, sicknesses, and death itself." Hobbes admits the difficulty in establishing from Scripture the place in which salvation is to be located, but it seems to him that because the kingdom of God is "an estate ordained by men for their perpetual security against enemies and want, this salvation should be on Earth."

In expounding his mechanistic theory of political psychology, Hobbes presents essentially the same case in other terms. Through the use of the resolutive-compositive method he dissolves the relations of civil society into the elements of human nature, and constructs civil society out of these elements as he observes them. Formally, this provides two intellectual models—the state of nature and the state of civil society. All actual historical social relations fit into either one or the other category. In nature, as distinguished from civil society, men follow not only their own private judgment but also their own immediate self-interest. In this respect, they are alike: each strives as best he is able to maximize his satisfactions. Moreover, they are all endowed by nature with roughly the same advantages. "Nature," Hobbes writes,

> Hath made men so equal, in the faculties of the body, and mind that the difference between man and man is not so considerable, as that any one man can thereupon claim to himself any benefit, to which another may not pretend, as well as he.

Strength of body in some is balanced by the "secret machination" or confederacy of others physically weaker. Men are equal not only in their ability to work their will, but also in being driven by the same passion of power. All of their actions can be accounted for as expressions of the motions of desire and aversion. For Hobbes the role of the passions is so important that he associates desire with life itself: "for as to have no desire, is to be dead." Reason has no role but that of an instrument of the passions; unlike the theological right reason, which Hobbes rejects as entirely subjective, it does not contribute to the creation of value, but only to the fulfillment of desire. Human values are determined by the passions: that for which we have a desire is esteemed good; that toward which we feel aversion is evil. The function of reason is to indicate a way of fulfillment to the passions, or to check the expression of a less intense passion for the sake of a more intense passion whenever there is conflict. This kind of reason, which is the reason that is operative in society, is common to all men:

> Prudence is but Experience; which equal time, equally bestows on all men, in those things they equally apply themselves unto. That which may perhaps make such equality incredible, is but a vain concept of ones own wisdom.

Men do not admit their natural equality precisely because they are all given up to self-love. All the pleasures sought by natural man express his supreme evaluation of the exercise of power over others. Beauty and "general reputation amongst those of the other sex" are considered honorable because they are sings of "power generative." Physical strength is honorable as a sign of "power motive", the ability to persuade is honorable because persuasion is accomplished by "a certain violence of the mind"; riches are a sign of "the power that acquired them"; nobility shows "signs of power in the ancestors." Humility is the fear of power, laughter the result of a sudden recognition of our own pre-eminence, as weeping is the result of a "sudden conception of defect." Lust is not only an appetite for sexual pleasure, but a desire to be recognized as the possessor of a power "so much to please." Charity is the greatest of virtues because it is the greatest "argument to a man of his own power" to find himself "able, not only to accomplish his own desires, but also to assist other men in theirs."

Thus, men are naturally equal in two respects. They are all driven by the same passion for self-glorification, and in the pursuit of this goal, they are all equipped with roughly the same abilities to attain it. The life of man can be compared to a race, which "we must suppose to have no other garland, but being foremost; and in it. Continually to out-go the next before is felicity. And to forsake the course, is to die." From the equality of desire and ability their arises a competition among men, which threatens the overthrow of equality and the ultimate destruction of the competitors. "There is no way for any man to secure himself" so that he may pursue his desires in peace except "to master the persons of all men he can, so long till he sees no other power great enough to endanger him." Indeed some men set out to dominate others without the ulterior motive of security simply because they take pleasure in contemplating their own power. Success in such a competition is out of the question, because no man can tolerate sign, that another undervalues him, and because wherever any particular good is in scarce supply, contention and strife are bound to arise. As results, the life of man in the state of nature is bound to be a life of perpetual fear and insecurity.

In the state of civil society, a new artificial equality replaces the equality of nature. In nature, men are equal in their common addiction to the pursuit of power and in their possession of an identical ability to achieve power. In society they are equal because there are all equally powerless and because they have recognized this new equality in making the covenant Given Hobbes's description of human nature it is remarkable that he should consider it possible for humankind to achieve a renunciation of the quest for personal power. Indeed, Hobbes does not expect that this renunciation will be maintained by the force of promises alone. There are, in human nature, "two imaginable helps to strength" the keeping of covenants:

> Either a fear of the consequences of breaking their word; or a glory, or pride in appearing not to need to break it. This later is a necessity too rarely found to presumed on, especially in the pursuers of wealth, command, or sensual pleasure; which are the greatest part of mankind.

To the covenant, therefore, must be added the power of the sword. But there is a sense in which Hobbes attempts to compensate subjects for their renunciation of personal power. Hobbes's theory of representation permits the citizen to ignore his actual inferiority to the sovereign in favor of a psychological identification with him. As the universal persona, the sovereign is the projection of every member of society. Whereas in the state of nature each individual had seen himself as the only sovereign, in civil society he would be able to bask in the reflected glory of an omnipotent ruler, participating, like all the other citizens, in the power and freedom from restraint enjoyed by the sovereign. Through this identification with the sovereign, the citizen would consider himself the source of command and the recipient of obedience. Representation provides a benign psychological satisfaction of the desire for power in lieu of the destructive outlets available in the state of nature. The original frontispiece of the Leviathan captures the peculiar character of Hobbesian political representation in portraying the sovereign as a giant man holding in either hand a sword and a scepter; inscribed in his body, like so many homunculi, are the smaller figures of the citizens.

On the one hand, then, Hobbes wished to come to terms with the passions by providing them with a limited but secure opportunity for gratification. On the other hand, as his theory of representation indicates, he was also anxious to forge an identification of the citizen with his society beyond self-interest. Surely, it is not simply an inability to follow his own logic, which leads Hobbes to conclude that a soldier may not refuse to go to war on behalf of his sovereign, even though no man can be compelled to forfeit his life. For Hobbes as for Machiavelli, the establishment and preservation of a stable and strong society is an achievement of the highest order and not merely a utilitarian alternative to the anarchy of complete individual autonomy. Stability in civil society represents the ability of an admittedly depraved species to overcome its own inherent weaknesses sufficiently to exercise a continuous control over itself. Hobbes was quite conscious of this motive in undertaking to develop a civil science. To understand the cause of social antagonism, he declared, it was not necessary to seek the help of transcendental knowledge. "Because we make the commonwealth ourselves." If it were be made to last and to act with vigor, the raw material of human nature expressed in the will to power would somehow have to be transformed into an instrument of peace. The Hobbesian sovereign, recognized and obeyed, is the depravity of man made legitimate and constructive.

The equality of the Hobbesian civil society is in this sense an equality of domination, which is sustained, at least in part, by an identification of those dominated with the holder of authority. It is this psychological relation, which is the major expression of social equality. With Hobbes the conservative theory for equality, which in its classical formulation had associated equality with tyranny, is made into an advocacy of psychological equality as the counterpart of actual domination. It is a matter of indifference, from the point of view of this conservative egalitarianism, in what proportions property is distributed. The sovereign is to decide the division of meum and teum in whatever way he believes best suited to the preservation of society. Because the sovereign is the personification of the citizens, they all are considered to be equally the authors of any such distinction.

Measured by liberal or socialist standards, such a conception of equality is neither valid nor truly egalitarian. Given the assumptions of Hobbes concerning human nature, however, equality can take only two forms: either an equality of depravity, which produces insecurity, or a psychological equality made effective by actual domination, which provides security.

Hobbes's New Science of Politics

Among Thomas Hobbes's many boasts, none was prouder than his claim to be the first scientific thinker for providing a new science of politics. Placing himself in some very impressive company, he compared his achievement with those of Galileo and Harvey. Physical science or 'natural philosophy', he continues, 'is therefore but young; but civil philosophy is yet much younger, as being no older than my own book *De Cive*'. Hobbes's own assessment of his achievement has been widely accepted at face value. J. S. Mill's remark that Hobbes was the first to view 'the methods of physical science as the proper models for the political science" anticipates the claims of later commentators. According to this view, Hobbes attempted to apply the methodological canons and criteria of the natural sciences to the study of social and political phenomena. And being both a materialist and a determinist, Hobbes conceived human actions to be ultimately describable as physical matter in motion, and explainable via general laws governing the motion of all matter. He compares his science to Galileo's; but he avers that it is the use and abuse of speech that characterizes the sentient subject matter of civil philosophy, and this makes his science quite unlike that of Galileo or Harvey. Yet, this tension goes almost wholly unrecognized and unprepared because of our penchant for ransacking the past in search of like-minded predecessors and precursors. This results in textbook history of the simplest sort. The history of political science is supposedly the story of the forward march of science, as it progressively discards the excess baggage of philosophy and assumes a surer scientific aspect. Thus, for example, Plato's 'preference for imaginative and somewhat rigid theoretical notions drawn from brilliant fancy rather than hard fact' gives way to the 'solid good sense' of Aristotle, 'the first great behavioral scientist'.

In Hobbes's case this progressive move is effected by dividing his life and work into two stages. The divide is marked by Hobbes's discovery of geometry. After discovering Euclid, Hobbes discarded Thucydides; he ceased being the historically minded humanist who translated Thucydides and became the mathematically minded social scientist who wrote the *Leviathan*. Hobbes's translation of *Thucydides' History* in 1629 contains an illuminating preface in which he calls special attention to the constitutive role of speech in political affairs. It is through the medium of language that societies exist and through their speech that men reason, rule, lay, command, calculate, dissimulate, deceive, justify, persuade and dissuade, accuse and excuse, commend and condemn. It is, therefore, no accident that a series of speeches should occupy pride of place in *Thucydides' History*. These speeches were not verbatim reports but were instead imaginative reconstructions in which he makes the speakers say what was in demanded of them by the various occasions.

Thucydides' account of the revolution at Corcoran, in which the conceptual and communicative basis of political order is most fully and dramatically exemplified. When words lose their meaning, communication—and therefore community—is impossible. Conceptual confusion and political chaos are the same. Ambiguity and anarchy go to gether . Point for point, feature for feature, Hobbes's state of nature parallels Thucydides' description of the Coreyraian revolution. More striking still, Hobbes follows Thucydides' account of the essentially conceptual character of political conflict.

Both Hobbes and Thucydides are in effect agreed that politics are the collective communicative creation of their members. The role of Thucydides' theory is to expose, criticize, and attempt to remove the sources of blocked or systematically distorted communication. Political theory therefore answers to a 'practical' interest in human understanding rather than to a 'technical' interest in control. This is, of course, to speak in the idiom of Habermas and not of Thucydides and Hobbes, who say nothing at all about distorted communication, technical and practical knowledge constitutive of interests, and the like.

Man in the state of nature is scarcely more than a body bent upon preserving itself from annihilation; the instinct for self-preservation is natural, and shared with all other animals. 'Every man', says Hobbes, 'is desirous of what is good for him and shuns what is evil, but chiefly the chiefs of natural evils, which is death; and this he doth by a certain impulsion of nature no less than that whereby a stone moves downward. Although their fear of violent death 'inclines men to Peace', they repeatedly risk death for the sake of 'honor' and other 'trifles'. Thus the natural instinct of self-preservation is occasionally overridden by vain and prideful men. At the very least, it would seem that this general law would have to be restricted to the explanation of rational behavior.

The difficulty with this move is, however, immediately apparent. For to be rational, Hobbes avers, is to have the use of speech: 'in reasoning, a man must take heed of words. Since without language there is no reason, only humans can be said to be fully rational. But ironically it is language—the medium of reason itself which feeds vanity and inflames the passions. To reason with loose and imprecisely defined concepts just is to act in inflammatory, irrational, and self-destructive ways. That we are language using and abusing creatures makes us, unlike stones, ill-suited to be subjects of a natural science. And this difference in subject matter dictates a difference in method.

The 'most notable and profitable invention of all other', Hobbes says, 'was that of speech without which, there had been amongst men, neither commonwealth, nor society, nor contract, nor peace, no more than amongst lions, Bears, and Wolves'. Language is a blessing, in that it is the medium that makes reason and science possible; but also a bane, because of our penchant for using words loosely and according to our own momentary appetites and inclinations. For every good use of language there is a corresponding abuse; and it is our penchant for abusing language—for making false statements, lying, making insincere promises, speaking metaphorically, boasting, insulting our fellows, and the like—that makes us wary and distrustful and that puts us, in short, in that 'state of war' that is the state of nature.

State of Nature

The state of nature is for Hobbes both a description of dire political possibility and an ingenious methodological device according to which 'we feign the world to be annihilated'. The wolrd thus methodologically dissolved is the common world of mutual meanings and shared significations. The state of nature is a condition of complete communicative breakdown, a veritable Babel of mutually incomprehensible voices and tongues. The tragedy of the state of nature is that, although its inhabitants are linguistically competent (in Chomsky's sense), they are not yet communicatively competent (in Habermas's sense). They have the capacity to speak, to construct and utter well-formed sentences, but still are apt to speak insincerely, self-interestedly, untruthfully, and the like. Each attempts the impossible feat of speaking a private language; each tries, in Humpty-Dumpty fashion, to make words mean whatever he wishes them to mean. The upshot is that the concepts constitutive of civil order—'right' and 'justice', for example—are meaningless sounds, signifying nothing. 'to this war of every man against every man, this also is consequent; that nothing can be unjust. The notions of right and wrong, justice and injustice have there no place.' In this natural state there is 'no propriety, no dominion, no mine and thine distinct; but only that to be every mans that he can get; and for so long, as he can keep it'.

A civil war was in the nature of a "break" in social existence, a suspended moment which threatened to initiate a reversal of time. The links between past, present, and future had been snapped, and men were left alone in an awful stillness.

> In such condition, there is no place for industry; because the fruit thereof is uncertain; and consequently no culture of the earth; no navigation; nor use of the commodities that may be imported by sea; no commodious building; no instruments of moving, and removing; no knowledge of the face of the earth; no account of time; no arts; no letters; no society.

When contrasted with this condition, political society symbolized humanity triumph over nature, and, since nature had no history in the human society also marked man's creation of history, or more precisely, his very of it. The re-establishment of order changed man's relationship to time. The human animal alone was conscious of living amidst a succession if fleeting moments, and because of the fears and anxieties aroused by life in the state of nature he became a time-haunted creature—viewing the time with "a perpetual solicitude of the time to come." Conversely, the carting of the political order, which made possible a "commodious" life and all of the arts of civilization, meant that man could face the future without perpetual solicitude." For Hobbes, as for Marx later on, the "future" become meaningful by means of an act essentially political in nature.

The natural state of humankind is, however, quite unlike the natural condition in which the other animals find themselves. And this difference is again due to our being language using creatures. Hobbes has several answers. For one, the concepts of honor, dignity, and envy are not available to ants and bees; for another, 'they want that art of words, by which some men can represent to others, that which is Good, in the likeness of Evil; and Evil, in the likenesses of Good'. Because we can speak, we can communicate our false beliefs, thereby deceiving others and, no less often, ourselves: 'man, alone among the animals can devise errors and pass them on for the use of others. Therefore, man errs more widely and dangerously than can other animals.' Moreover, 'because of the ease of speech, the man who truly doth not think, speaks; and since what he says, he believes to be true, he, unlike a beast, can deceive himself. Therefore by speech man is not made better but merely given greater possibilities.' Thus, the task of the zoologist, and indeed the natural philosopher generally is easier and more straightforward than that of the civil philosopher or political scientist. The former need not concern himself with the linguistic and conceptual reconstitution of his science's object-domain; his subjects cannot lie, dissimulate, and mislead, for they lack the use of language altogether. The civil philosopher, by contrast, deals with a wily subject made the more canny by his capacity to acquire, to use—and above all to abuse—language. Thus, civil philosophy necessarily takes a sharp turn—a linguistic turn—away from natural philosophy.

Hobbes's civil philosophy differs from natural philosophy in several significant respects. Natural philosophy deals in probabilities, civil philosophy in certainties; natural philosophy studies nature—the art of God—while civil philosophy studies the art of man. Since the causes of natural things are not in our power, but in God's, we cannot deduce their qualities from their causes.' We can only 'demonstrate that such and such could have been their causes. This kind of demonstration is called a posteriori, and its science physics.' By contrast, 'politics and ethics can be demonstrated a priori; because we ourselves make the principles—that is, the cause of 'justice—whereby it is known what justice and equity and their opposites injustice and inequity, are'. Civil philosophy, in other words, deals with the commonwealth, that most human of creations. Our knowledge of matters political is more certain than our knowledge of natural phenomena, for we have made the former but not the latter. The creator's knowledge of his own creation is unique and privileged. And just as God has perfect knowledge of his own creation, so may man have perfect knowledge of his own creation.

The language devised by Adam was lost after Babel and must now be created anew. Words and concepts are our inventions and have only such meaning as we give to them. Because the world of mutual meanings and shared significations—our world—is our own creation, we can know it in a way that we can never know the world of nature. Hobbes's new science of politics takes geometry as its model. The civil philosopher's knowledge of matters political is every bit as certain as the geometer's, and for precisely the same reason: geometry is, in Hobbes's view, the product—indeed, the very paradigm of human art and artifice. 'Geometry, therefore is demonstrable, for the lines and figures from which we reason, are drawn and described by ourselves; and civil philosophy is demonstrable because we make the commonwealth ourselves.' Because the commonwealth is created by its members, they alone can have perfect knowledge of its structure and operation.

Any science worthy of the name, Hobbes suggests, must yield perfect, and not merely provisional or contingent knowledge. Until civil philosophy was bestowed upon mankind by Hobbes, geometry was 'the only science that it hath pleased God hitherto to bestow on mankind.' The striking oddity of this claim is lessened somewhat by attending to Hobbes's distinction between two kinds of knowledge—roughly, that which we acquire through observation of fact and that which we gain through deduction.

Thus, natural philosophy and civil philosophy are both scientific, but in different senses. For civil philosophy can follow, as physics cannot, the lead of the geometer. True philosophy consists of reasoning, which Hobbes contrasts with empirical observation. What has heretofore passed for moral or civil philosophy has not, however, been genuinely scientific. 'What hath hitherto been written by moral philosophers, hath not made any progress in the knowledge of the truth,' says Hobbes, because they have not defined their terms precisely and deduced their conclusions accordingl

But the pretence for civil war stems less from the crude views of the vulgar than from the pretentious and ostensibly earned opinions of the philosophers. And it is their failure to be 'scientific' that is, in Hobbes's view, the root of almost all political evils. Loose concepts, imprecisely defined terms, metaphors, tropes, and figurative speech of all sorts are the sources of sedition. And these are all the more pernicious because they purportedly derive their authority from philosophy itself.

Hobbes's complaint is not merely a methodological but a political one. The concepts spun by earlier philosophers—'law', 'justice', 'right'—pose a political danger of the first magnitude. In the conceptual confusions, contentions, and disagreements of the philosophers we find the first stirrings of sedition and discord. Philosophers have heretofore lived in world of words whose meanings they refuse to define; 'and as men abound in copiousness of language, so they become more wise, or more mad than ordinary'. Such learned madness must sooner or later affect the multitude of the vulgar who further fuel and legitimize their private appetites by appealing to ill-defined notions of justice and right. Abandon Aristotle, and Cicero, and all previous philosophers so-called, counsels Hobbes, and take the rigorous road of science. From conceptual confusion comes political chaos.

The England of Hobbes's day, like his hypothetical state of nature, was populated by madmen, each hearing his own particular voice distilled from one or another academic scribbler. The only cure for conceptual-cum-political chaos was to be found, Hobbes thought, in civil philosophy of a more surely scientific stripe. A veritable conceptual purge, amounting to nothing less than the complete schematization of the political vocabulary, seemed the only solution. Just as geometers could not calculate without first agreeing on definitions, so citizens cannot live together without sharing a common vocabulary of concepts whose meanings are fixed in advance. To the civil philosopher, and to the sovereign who follows his lead, falls the task of purging the political and moral vocabulary of the citizenry. By fixing once and for all the meanings of the concepts constitutive of the commonwealth itself, he dampens political conflict. By linguistic art and artifice is created the great Leviathan.

The first step to be taken by Hobbes's 'mortal God' is to undo the damage done at Babel, when the immortal God decreed that 'every man be stricken for his rebellion, with an oblivion of his former language'. The damage is to be undone by creating a new language, its concepts strictly and scientifically defined. Thus the sovereign must purge the philosophically tainted vocabulary of his subjects: the conceptual contests fomented by all previous philosophers must be terminated by sovereign fiat, and true philosophy or 'civil science' sent to rule Leviathan-like over the children of pride. But this conceptual-cum-political purge does not end here. Besides ridding our vocabulary of the last vestiges of philosophy, Hobbes would purge it of poetry and literature as well. Hobbes, no mean poet himself vents his wrath upon metaphor and other 'abuse of speech'. Into the fire go 'obscure, confused, and ambiguous expressions, also all metaphorical speeches, tending to the stirring up of passion.' Political science or civil philosophy offers nothing less than a political purgative.

This purge cannot be politically neutral, for science itself has an intrinsic interest in social stability and political pacification. There is indeed a symbiotic relationship between Hobbes's science of politics and the pacific polity envisioned in the Leviathan. There can be no science, Hobbes avers, where there is no safety, and conversely no lasting security, without the aid of science, rightly understood and applied. Science promotes, and is itself part of 'commodious living'. Without a thorough cleansing of the stables of philosophy, men cannot live commodiously.

Hobbes's defense of linguistic austerity must be viewed against the background of an older rhetorical tradition in which the aim of political speech is to kindle the passions and direct the interests of the audience. Hobbes is as critical as Plato of appeals to the passions and mere 'opinions' of the masses. But of course Hobbes's approach and his appeals are no less 'rhetorical'. He relies upon-indeed he virtually invents—a new rhetorical form. Hobbes appeals not to the panoply of the passions but to our fear of death and our corresponding interest in physical safety and self-preservation. This rhetoric of sobriety is not so much a result of Hobbes's civil philosophy as it is a requirement for it. For it is only by assuming certain sorts of interests to be 'natural' that his science acquires its intelligibility. It is by first assuming and then appealing to these natural interests that Hobbes is able to cast his arguments in ostensibly scientific form. But Hobbes's explicit epistemological and methodological presuppositions matter less than his own covertly rhetorical strategy. The persuasiveness of Hobbes's science relies a good deal less upon his definitions and deductions than upon his metaphors. What, after all, is his state of nature if not an extended metaphor in which men are beasts, life is war, war is hell, and so on? And who is the sovereign if not a secular savior, a 'mortal god' sent not from heaven but sprung, Athena-like, from the head of the civil philosopher himself? Hobbes was always more adapt at detecting the mote of metaphor in another's eye than the beam in his own.

Leaving aside Hobbes's reliance upon metaphor, analogy, allegory, and other rhetorical stratagems, there are still other reasons for viewing his science with a skeptical eye. Consider, for example, his definitions of 'law' and allied concepts like 'justice'. 'Law in general', Hobbes says, 'is not counsel, but command; nor a command of any man to any man; but only of him whose command is addressed to one formerly obliged to obey him.' Thus no law, provided that it has been duly promulgated and pronounced by the sovereign, can ever be unjust. To speak of an 'unjust law' would be to contradict oneself. For sovereigns, says Hobbes, 'make the things they command just, by commanding them, and those which they forbid, unjust, by forbidding them'. From this it follows that the only operation or test by which we can determine whether a particular command is indeed a law, and therefore just, is to see whether it in fact issues from the sovereign. His science is not a neutral broom for sweeping semantic rubbish into the dustbin, but is, on the contrary, clearly prescriptive, and pregnant with a peculiar vision of the good society.

But civil peace comes at a price. There can in Hobbes's commonwealth be no fundamental dissent. There can be no criticism to the effect that, for example, the sovereign is acting illegally or that the laws he has enacted are unjust, because there is no vocabulary in which dissent is intelligible and criticism communicable. Hobbes's model commonwealth is a conceptually closed society. Reason having been defined in terms of discourse duly schematized, political dissent is perforce indicative of irrationality of insanity. His is a vision not of an imaginary nightmare world but of a technocratic dream capable of coming all too true in our own time. The precursor of a conceptually sanitized and schematized society largely immune from internal criticism and deaf to dissent, Hobbes has proved to be a prescient prophet. The scientist appropriation of the linguistic turn was, for Hobbes, an act of hope. For us it stands as a warning.

The realization of this contradiction—indifferent to nature—becomes a sting to man's awareness and the first signal of rebellion: the signal for an attempt to overcome nature's haphazard condition through creative design, through the establishment of a peaceful and civilized life.

Hobbes's Argument

From ancient times it has been observed that human beings are social creatures: we are not hermits; we naturally live together in groups, wanting and needing the company of others of our own kind. Some philosophers have thought that this fact is the key to understanding morality. Morality, they say, arises when people are brought to accept the rules that are necessary for social living.

The line of reasoning that leads to this conclusion begins by asking what it would be like if there were no social rules and no commonly accepted mechanism for enforcing them. Imagine, if you will, that there were no such thing as government —no laws, no police, and no courts. In this situation, each of us would be free to do as we pleased; there would be no one to tell us we couldn't do this or that. We might call this the state of nature. What would it be like?

Thomas Hobbes, the foremost British philosopher of the seventeenth century, thought it would be dreadful. In the *Leviathan* he wrote that there would be

> No place for industry, because the fruit there of is uncertain: and consequently no culture of the earth; no navigation, not or use of the commodities that may be imprted by sea; no commodious building; no instruments of moving, and removing, such things as require much force; no knowledge of the face of the earth; no account of time, no arts, no letters, no society and which is worst of all, continual fear, and danger of violent death; and the life of man solitary, poor, nasty brutish, and short.

Why would things be so bad? It is not because people are bad. Rather, it is because of certain basic facts about the conditions of human life. Hobbes appeals to four such facts in arguing that the state of nature would be intolerable.

1. First, there is the fact of equality of need. Each of us needs the same basic things in order to survive—food, clothing, shelter. Although we may differ in some of our needs, we are all essentially very much alike.

2. Second, there is the fact of scarcity. We do not live in the Garden of Eden, where milk flows in streams and every tree hangs heavy with fruit. The world is a hard, inhospitable place, where the things we need to survive do not exist in plentiful supply. We have to work hard to produce them, and even then, there often is not enough to go around.

3. Since there are not enough essential goods to go around, and each of us wants to live, and to live as well as possible, each of us will want as much as we can get. But will we be able to prevail over the others, who also want the scarce goods? Hobbes thinks not, because of the third fact about our condition, the fact of the essential equality of human power. No one is so superior to everyone else, in strength and cunning, that he or she can prevail over them indefinitely. Of course, some people are smarter and stronger than others; but even the strongest can be brought down by several others acting in concert.

4. If we cannot prevail by our own strength, what hope do we have? Can we, for example, rely on the charity or good will of other people to help us? We cannot. The fourth and final fact is the fact of limited altruism. Even if people are nor wholly selfish, they nevertheless care very much about themselves; and you cannot simply assume that whenever your vital interests conflict with their vital interests, they will step aside.

When we put these four facts together, a grim picture emerges. We all need the same basic things, and there aren't enough of them to go around. Therefore, we will be in a kind of competition, and no one—or almost no one—will be willing to forgo the satisfaction of his needs in favor of others. The result, as Hobbes puts it, is a "constant state of war, of one with all." And it is a war no one can hope to win. The reasonable person who wants to survive will try to seize what he needs and prepare to defend it from attack. But others will be doing the same thing. This is why life in the state of nature would be insurable.

Hobbes did not think this a mere speculation. He pointed out that this is what actually happens when governments collapse, as during a civil insurrection. People begin desperately to hoard food, arm themselves, and lock out their neighbors. Moreover, the nations of the world, without any meaningful international law, exist in relation to one another very much like individuals in the "state of nature", and they are constantly at one another's throats, armed and distrustful.

Clearly, what is needed to escape the state of nature is some way for people to cooperate with one anther. By cooperating, and dividing the labor,, the amount of essential goods could be increased and distributed to all who need them. But two things are required for this to happen. First, there must be guarantees that people will not harm one another —people must be able to work together without fear of attack, theft, or treachery. And second, people must be able to rely on one another builds houses—with each expecting to share in the benefits created by the others —each person in the chain must be able to count on the others to perform as expected.

Once these assurances are in place, a society can develop in which everyone is better off than they were in the state of nature. There can then be "commodities imported by the sea, commodious building, arts, letters," and the like. But—and this is one of Hobbes's main points—in order for this to happen, government must be established; for it is government, with its system of laws, police, and courts, that ensures that people can live with a minimum fear of attack and that people will have to keep their bargains with one another. Government is an indispensable part of the scheme.

To escape the state of nature, then, people must agree to the establishment of rules to govern their relations with one another, and they must agree to the establishment of an agency—the state—with the power necessary to enforce those rules. According to Hobbes, such an agreement actually exists, and that is what makes social living possible. This agreement, to which every citizen is a party, is called the social contract.

In addition to explaining the purpose of the state, the social contract theory also explains the nature of morality. The two are closely linked: the state exists to enforce the most important rules necessary for social living, while morality can sists in the whole set of rule that enhance social living.

Moreover, it is only within the context of the social contract that we can become moral agents, because the contract creates the conditions under which we can afford to care about others. In the state of nature, it is every man for himself; it would be foolish for anyone to adopt the policy of "looking out for others," because one could do so only at the cost of putting one's own interests in continual jeopardy. But in society, altruism becomes possible. By releasing us from "the continual fear of violent death," the social contract frees us to take heed of others.

Social Contract

In the area of ethics, Descartes had little to contribute, whereas Hobbes developed a theory that is still considered one of the live options among ethical theories today. He is the father of the form of ethical theory known as "contractarianism,' the view that our moral and political obligations arise out of a contract we human beings make with one another as a means of fostering our survival and achieving a contented life. Reason, according to Hobbes, counsels us to enter into a contract whereby we give up our unlimited liberties and place ourselves under the authority of a central power. Having made this contract, we subsequently find ourselves under an obligation to abide by it. Herein lies the origin of morality: obligation is a bond we create through voluntary contract.

For Hobbes, moral obligation and moral rules are necessary means for avoiding the horrifying consequences that would result from the absence of them. They are not desirable in and of themselves. "Obligation is thralldom," Hobbes tells us, and much of his moral philosophy consists in showing us why we should voluntarily accept such an undesirable thing as thralldom. His answer, in essence, is that the constraint of obligation is the lesser of two evils. The alternative, a life free from the bonds of contract and morality, turns out to be a life that is "solitary, poor, nasty, brutish, and short". The moral life, restrictive though it may be because of the obligations imposed on us, permits us not only to survive but also offers us our best chance for living a 'commodious life'. Morality is simply the better bargain.

Hobbes's conception of morality is clearly different from that of many of the thinkers we have considered hitherto. Plato and Aristotle, and many of their medieval followers, thought that the dictates of morality were intrinsic to human nature: to be fully human, or to achieve the human telos, requires that one follow the laws of morality. The moral life, in other words, is constitutive of human nature. Not so for Hobbes. Human nature can be understood without any appeal to morality. The problem, as Hobbes sees it, is that, given human nature, we won't survive and certainly won't prosper unless we enter into a contract and thereby bind ourselves to fulfill the obligations we ourselves create. Morality is a means to a highly desirable end: survival and contentment. If in some sense virtue is its own reward for Plato and Aristotle, it is decidedly not its own reward for Hobbes. It is simple the only way we can attain those other things we most fundamentally desire.

The Way Out: The Laws of Nature

Fortunately, even in the state of nature, we would retain our reason, and it is reason that would show us what to do in order to leave behind our desperate and pitiable condition. Reason, according to Hobbes, is able to grasp general precepts or rules that instruct a person in what must be done in order to preserve his life. Such rules he calls laws of nature: "A Law of Nature is a precept or general rule, found out by reason, by which a man is forbidden to do that which is destructive of his life or teeth away the means of preserving the same, and to omit that by which he thicket it may be best preserved". The law of nature is the laws of prudence. They indicate what actions must be taken to serve the individual's self-interest, the most important aspect of which is his very survival. These laws, being discovered by reason, are objective reflections of the causal relationship between certain classes of actions and individual survival and well-being. Reason shows us the way out of our predicament in the state of nature.

Hobbes introduces the notion of a law of nature by way of contrast with the notion of a right. A right, he tells us, "consists in liberty to do or to forbear", liberty in turn being "the absence of external impediments, which impediments may oft take away part of a man's power to do what he would". One has a right, in other words, if there are no external impediments to his doing what he wants to do. Hobbes clearly has in mind the kind of impediments found within society: laws, rules regulations, and the enforcement thereof. These normative requirements limit a person's power to do what he would want to do. In the state of nature, there are, by definition, no social constraints on action and the expression of power. Thus in the state of nature, a person has what Hobbes calls the "Right of Nature": "the liberty each man hath to use his own power, as he will himself, for the preservation of his own nature, that is to say, of his own life, and consequently of doing anything which, in his own judgment and reason, he shall conceive to be the aptest means thereunto". This Right of Nature, this liberty of every person, is unlimited in scope. In the state of nature, "every man has a right to everything, even to one another's body". There are no impediments – no civic rules and regulations – to one person taking the life of another or enslaving another. The Right of Nature gives each one of us unlimited liberty to do as we please, so long as we see our actions as being necessary to protect and enhance our lives. The problems of life in the state of nature can be traced to the fact in it each inhabitant possesses the Right of Nature.

This right, this unlimited liberty, disappears as soon as reason grasps and subscribes to the laws of nature, for laws, according to Hobbes, "determinith and bindeth". A law places one under an obligation, thereby imposing limits on one's liberty. A law of nature places one under an obligation to do certain things and not to do other things. Law involves the "thralldom".

The First Law: Seek Peace

It is by limiting our liberty through the acknowledgement of the laws of nature and by replacing our unlimited liberty with obedience to these laws that we raise ourselves out of the state of nature. Reason sees what must be done:

> And consequently it is a precept, or general rule of reason that every man ought to endeavor peace, as far as he has hope of attaining it, and when he cannot obtain it, that he may seek and use all helps and advantages of war. The first branch of which rule contained the first and fundamental law of nature, which is to seek peace, and follow it. The second, the sum of the right of nature, which is by all means we can, do defend ourselves.

We are instructed by reason to seek and to pursue peace to give up our warlike condition in the state of nature, but we are also advised that if we have no reason to think that peace is possible we should revert to the strategies of war. If peace is not possible, the Right of Nature once again takes priority, and we have the right to defend ourselves by any action whatsoever. The first law of nature – "Seek peace" - is our best hope for survival, but the ever-realistic Hobbes recognizes that such a strategy may not work.

The Second Law: Lay Down the Right of Nature

Hobbes immediately proceeds to describe the second law of nature, the second general rule laid down by reason for defending ourselves:

> From this fundamental law of nature, by which men are commanded to endeavor peace, is derived this second law: that a man be willing, when others are so too, as far-forth as for peace and defense of himself he shall think it necessary, to lay down this right to all things, and be contented with so much liberty against other men, as he would allow other men against himself.

In seeking peace, we are seeking to escape from the state of nature, "the condition of war of everyone against everyone". This war results from our unlimited liberty in the state of nature combined with our more or less equal power. Thus, the only way to escape the condition of war is to give up, to renounce our unlimited liberty, our right to all things. This is what the second law of nature commands of us. It does so, again, with certain conditions attached. We are to lay down our right to all things if others are willing to do so too. It would be foolish to do so unilaterally, for that would simply be to open ourselves to attack. Each of us is to renounce the Right of Nature if everyone else is willing to do so. Moreover, we are to renounce this right only to the extent necessary to attain peace and thereby protect ourselves. In ascertaining the amount of liberty we are to give up, Hobbes appeals to the law of the Gospel commonly known as the Golden Rule! Whatsoever you require that others should do you, that do you to them. In Hobbes's appropriation of this rule, it requires each of us to be satisfied with as much liberty toward other human beings as we are willing to allow them with respect to ourselves.

Hobbes finds the source of both obligation and justice in the laying down of the Right of Nature:

> And when a man hath in either manner abandoned or granted away his right, then is he said to be obliged or bound not to hinder those to whom such right is granted or abandoned from the benefit of it; and it is said that he ought, and it is his duty not to avoid that voluntary act of his own, and that such hindrance is injustice, and injury, as being without right the right being before renounced transferred.

There is no morality in the state of nature, since in that condition everyone has a right to everything whatsoever. As we have seen, having this right is a way of saying that there are no impediments, no restrictions, no laws, and no obligations standing in the way of a person appropriating and doing what he wants. But if I give up my right, I commit myself not to exercise it, and thus I am restricted in what I can do by the impediment I myself create, namely my promise not to exercise my right. Thus, my duties and obligations arise from my laying down of the Right of Nature.

Contracts and Covenants

The laws of nature recommend themselves to all rational human beings in the state of nature, and so all of them can be expected to lay down the unlimited rights they have in this state. Hence there will be mutual renunciation or transference of rights. This mutual interaction Hobbes calls a contract. When two or more individuals engage in a contract that commits them to future actions, they have formed a covenant, or a covenant of mutual trust. He notes that the contract or covenant need not be express, that is to say, it need not be explicitly conveyed and acknowledged by words. The sign or indication of a contract may be "by inference," and thus implicit or explicit Hobbes does not indicate exactly what such a covert contract might consist in, other than to say, "Generally a sign by inference of any contract is whatsoever sufficiently argues the will of the contractor". Thus we can assume that a contract has been entered into if we have reason to think that such is the will of the parties involved. Insofar as human beings in the state of nature are rational, we do in fact have reason to believe that they have contracted with one other in the way needed to emerge from this untenable situation. We have reason to believe that they have agreed, even if not explicitly, to live within the moral limits they themselves, if as rational agents, impose on themselves.

In engaging in a contract or covenant with one another, there are limits to the rights the parties can renounce or transfer, so that the contract itself is a limited one. A person cannot give up the right to resist any who 'assault him by fore, to take away his life." The very purpose of the contract is to protect one's life, hence giving up the right to defend this life would be inconsistent with the purpose of the mutual transference of right. Likewise, a person cannot give up the right to resist and avoid wounds, or to resist imprisonment. Hobbes emphasizes that "Whosoever a man transferred his right or renounced it, it is either in consideration of some right reciprocally transferred to himself or for some other good he hoped for thereby". A person enters into the social contract as a means of attaining "the security of a man's person, in his life and in the means of so preserving life as not to be weary of it". No person, therefore, can be expected to contract away his right to security of person or to the means needed to preserve life in a manner minimally acceptable to him. Even in the commonwealth created by the contract, a human being maintains the basic rights to these things.

The Third Law: Perform Covenants

Hobbes turns next to the third law of nature:

> From that law of nature by which we are obliged to transfer to another such rights as, being retained, hinder the peace of mankind, there followeth a third, which is this that men perform their covenants made, without which covenants are in vain, and but empty words, and the right of all men to all things remaining, we are still in the condition of war.

The second law of nature required us to make covenants, to agree to give up our unlimited liberty on the condition that other individuals would do so as well. And having made this covenant, each of us thereby incurs the obligation to do what we have contracted to do. But while reason may require us to enter into a contract, does it also require that we live up to this contract? In setting forth the third law of nature, Hobbes answers this question in the affirmative. Peace will not be attained and the war of all against all avoided unless people perform their obligations. Hobbes reminds that "the definition of justice is no other than the not performance of convent'. Thus, justice requires that we live up to our covenants.

Other Laws of Nature

Having articulated the first three laws of nature (to seek peace, to enter into a contract with others to give up the universal Right of Nature, and to keep one's covenants) Hobbes proceeds to identify and justify sixteen other such laws. In describing these various obligations and rights, Hobbes sees himself as engaged in moral philosophy. And the science of them [the laws of nature] is the true and only moral philosophy. Morality is conceived to be a science, is the set of human desires and aversions-what we want, covet and hate. We are led to engage in moral philosophy because of the simple and inescapable fact that this disagreement leads to conflict and, without much ado, the conditions of the state of nature. Hobbes's well-know expression of this conception of morality is as follows:

> Good and evil are names that signify our appetites and aversions, which in different tempers, customs, and doctrines of men are different and diverse men differ not only in their judgment on the senses of what is pleasant and unpleasant to the taste smell, hearing, touch, and sight...And therefore so long a man is in the condition of mere nature (which is a condition of war) as private appetite is the measure of good and evil; and consequently, all men agree on this, that peace is good; and therefore also the way or means of peace (which, as I have showed before) are justice, gratitude, modesty, equity, mercy, and the rest of the laws of nature are good (that is to say, moral virtues) and their contrary vices, evil.

The Sovereign

It is time now to turn our attention, to the idea of the commonwealth and to Hobbes's account of the creation, powers, and functions of the sovereign. We begin by recalling the situation that leads to the necessity for a commonwealth. It will not be enough, Hobbes claims, simply to join together with family and friends in a defensive association. Others might do the same and the war of all against all would continue – now with the various associations at odds with one another. Nor is it enough simply to band together as a great multitude, for the conflicting voices within the multitude would cause any such coalition to collapse and them embers to turn on one another. There is, Hobbes maintains, one option.

We agree among ourselves, that is to say, that we must give to one person (such as a king or a group of individuals (such as Parliament), the power to control our lives and enforce the conditions of peace. We contract with one another, each saying in effect to all the others.

> I authorize and give up my right to governing myself to this man, or to this assembly of men, or this condition, that thou give up thy right to him, and authorize all his actions in like manner". This done, we have created a commonwealth: "This is the generation of that great Leviathan, or rather (to speak more reverently) of that Mortal God to which we owe, under the Immortal God, our peace and defense.

The civil society we have created has the unity that we as separate individuals with conflicting goals do not possess in the state of nature. The unity resides in the singleness of power, whether that power be placed in the hands of one person or an assembly. We have created an artificial person as opposed to a natural one, and this artificial person is the sovereign. We have also bestowed authority on this person or the assembly. This authority is our own authority willingly transferred to the sovereign. The sovereign's actions henceforward are our actions; he is our agent who represents us. When the sovereign restrains us, it is in reality we who restrain ourselves. In obeying the sovereign we are simply following our own collective will. And it is by obedience to the sovereign that we are able to live in a condition of peace and prosperity.

Since society depends on mutual trust, the next step is evidently to explain how this is reasonably possible, and this brings Hobbes to his theory of sovereignty. Because of the unsocial inclination of men, Iris hopeless to expect them to agree spontaneously to respect each other's rights, and unless all do so, it is unreasonable for any to forego self-help. The performance of covenants may be reasonably expected only if there is an effective government which will punish non-performance.

> Covenants, without the sword, are but words, and of no strength to secure a man at all. The bonds of words are too weak to bridle men's ambition, avarice, anger, and other passions, without the fear of some coercive power

Security depends upon the existence of a government having the power to keep the peace and to apply the sanctions needed to curb man's Innately unsocial inclinations. The effective motive by which men are socialized is the fear of punishment, and the authority of law extends only so far as its enforcement is able to reach. Just how this motive Stands in relation to the reasonableness of performing covenants is not quite clear. Apparently Hobbes meant that reason provides a sufficient ground for mutual accord but is too weak to offset the avarice of men In the mass. In substance his theory amounted to identifying government with force; at least, the force must always be present in the background whether it has to be applied or not.

To justify force Hobbes retained the ancient device of a contract, though he carefully excluded the implication of a contract binding upon the ruler. He described it as a covenant between individuals by which all resign self-help and subject themselves to a sovereign. He stated it as follows:

> I authorize and give up my right of governing myself, to this man, or to this assembly of men, on this condition, that thou give up thy right to him, and authorize all his actions in tike manner. This is the generation of that great Leviathan rather (to speak more reverently) of that Mortal Cod, to we owe under the Immortal God, our peace and defence.

Since the right resigned is merely the use of natural strength and "covenants without the sword are but words," this is a contract only in a manner of speaking. Properly it is a logical fiction to offset the anti-social fiction of his psychology. Undoubtedly it helped him to import the notion of moral obligation into social relations, and this added a good deal of plausibility to his argument. Strictly speaking he is saying merely that in order to cooperate men must do what they dislike to do, on pain of consequences which they dislike still more. In no other sense is there logically any obligation whatever in Hobbes's system.

Hobbes's thought on this point can be stated, perhaps more accurately, by using the legal conception of a corporation instead of contract, as he did in *De Cive*. A mere multitude, he argues, cannot have rights and cannot act; only individual men can do this, a conclusion which follows from the proposition that any collective body is merely artificial. Consequently, to say that a body of men acts collectively really means that some individual acts in the name of the whole group as its accredited agent or representative. Unless there is such an agent the body has no collective existence whatever. Hence Hobbes argues with perfect logic, if his premises be admitted, that it is not consent but union which makes a corporation, and union means the submission of the wills of all to the will of one. A corporation is not really a collective body at all but one person, its head or director, whose will is to be received for the will of all its members. On this analogy it follows, of course, that society is a mere fiction. Tangibly it can mean only the sovereign, for unless there be a sovereign there is no society. This theory is applied consistently by Hobbes to all corporations. Any other theory, he holds, would make them "lesser commonwealths," "like worms in the entrails of a natural man." The state is unique only in having no superior, while other corporations exist by its permission.

From this view of the matter follow some of Hobbes's most characteristic conclusions. Any distinction between society and the state is a mere confusion, and the same is true of a distinction between the state and its government. Except there be a tangible government—individuals with the power to enforce their will—

there is neither state nor society but a literally headless multitude. Few writers have held this opinion as consistently as Hobbes. It follows also that any distinction between law and morals is a confusion. For society has only one voice with which it can speak and one will which it can enforce, that of the sovereign who makes it a society. Very properly Hobbes calls his sovereign a "mortal God" and unite in his hands both the sword and the crosier.

This theory of corporate bodies lies also at the root of Hobbes's absolutism. For him there is no choice except between absolute power and complete anarchy, between an omnipotent sovereign and no society whatever. For a social body has no existence except through its constituted authorities, and its members no rights except by delegation. All social authority must accordingly be concentrated in the sovereign. Law and morals are merely his will, and his authority is unlimited, or is limited only by his power for the good reason that there is no other authority except by his permission. Evidently, also, sovereignty is indivisible and inalienable, for either his authority is recognized and a state exists or it is not recognized and anarchy exists. All the necessary powers of government are inherent in the sovereign, such as legislation, the administration of justice, the exercise of force, and the organization of inferior magistracies. Hobbes relieved sovereignty completely from the disabilities which Bodin had inconsistently left standing. But his disjunctions have nothing to do with the nuances of actual political power. His theory was pure logical analysis.

There was another side to his theory of sovereign power which Hobbes emphasized less but to which he was by no means blind. For controversial purposes he stressed the fact that resistance to authority can never be justified, since justification would require the approval of authority itself. It followed equally, however, that resistance will in fact occur wherever government fails to produce that security which is the only reason for subjects' submission. The only argument for government is that it does in fact govern. Hence if resistance is successful and the sovereign loses his power, he ipso facto ceases to be sovereign and his subjects cease to be subjects. They are then thrown back upon their individual resources for self-protection and may rightly give their obedience to a new sovereign who can protect them. There was no room in Hobbes's theory for any claim of legitimacy without power, and it was this which gave offense to royalists. 'This consequence of his theory was most clearly stated in *Leviathan*-the only one of his books on politics written after the execution of Charles and when, as Clarendon says, Hobbes had "a mind to go home." But it was at all times a perfectly evident implication of his principles and he had referred to it in *De Cive*. On utilitarian grounds government—any government better than anarchy. Monarchical government he thought more to be effective than any other kind, but the theory is equally good for any government that can preserve peace and order. Later thinkers had no difficulty, therefore in adapting it to a republican or parliamentary form of government.

Since government consists essentially in the existence of sovereign power, it follows for Hobbes *as* for Bodin that the difference between forms of government lays solely in the location of sovereign. There are no perverted forms of government. People impute perversion, with such terms as tyranny or oligarchy, only because they dislike the exercise of a power, just as they use terms of approval, like monarchy or democracy, if they like it. There is certain to be sovereign power somewhere in every government and the only question is who has it. For the same reason there is no mixed government and no limited government, since the sovereign power is indivisible. Someone must have the last decision and whoever has it and can make it good has sovereign power. Probably there is nothing in political literature that more perfectly illustrates the inability of a congenital utilitarian enter into the spirit of a revolutionary age than these chapters in winch Hobbes argues that all governments which keep order come to the same thing in the end. The aspiration for more justice and right summed to him merely an intellectual confusion. Hatred of tyranny seemed mere dislike of a particular exercise of power, and enthusiasm for liberty seemed either sentimental vaporing or outright hypocrisy. Hobbes's account of the civil wars in his *Behemoth* makes them a strange mixture of villainy and wrong-headedness. The clarity of his political system had nothing to do with understanding human nature in politics.

From the theory of sovereignty, it is only a step to that of the civil law. In the proper sense of the word, law is the command of that person whose precept contains in it the reason of obedience. It is to every subject, those rules, which the commonwealth has commanded him, by word, writing, or offers sufficient sign of the will, to make use of, for the distinction of right, and wrong. He was careful to point out that this definition sharply distinguishes civil from natural law, for the former is a command sanctioned by enforcement while the latter is a dictate of reason. The law of nature is law only in a figurative sense, for the imperative or coercive aspect of civil law is the essence of it. This, Hobbes explains, is the confusion in the position both of parliamentarians and of common lawyers like Coke. The former imagines that there is some virtue in the consent of a representave body and the latter that there is some validity in custom. In fact it is the enforcing power that makes the precept binding and the law is his who has the power. He may allow custom to persist, but it is his tacit consent which gives it the force of law. Doubly absurd is Coke's superstitution that the common law has a reason of its own. Similarly, the sovereign may consult parliament or permit it to frame statutes, but the enforcement is what makes them law. Hobbes assumes that enforcement takes place in the king's name, but there is nothing in his theory contrary to the sovereignty of parliament, provided that body can both make the law and control its administration and execution. Hobbes was wrong in thinking that he could bolster up absolute monarchy but he was not mistaken in believing that centralized authority in some form was to be a chief mark of modern states.

Since the laws of nature merely state the rational principles upon which a state can be constructed, they are not limitations on the authority of the sovereign. Hobbes's argument sounds like a quibble but there was reason behind it. No civil law, he says, ever can be contrary to the law of nature; property may be a natural right but the civil law defines property, and if a particular right is extinguished, it simply ceases to be property and so is no longer included under the law of nature. What limits the sovereign is not the law of nature but the pepper of his subjects. Hobbes's sovereign is faced by a condition and not a theory, but there can be no limitation of the civil law in its own field. Bodin's conception of a constitutional law limiting the competence of the sovereign has disappeared entirely.

The State and the Church

Hobbes's theory of sovereignty brings to completion of subordinating the church to the civil power which was begun when Marsilio of Padua carried through to its logical conclusion the separation of the spiritual and temporal authorities. For a materialist like Hobbes the spiritual becomes a mere ghost, a figment of the imagination. He does not deny that there is such a thing as revelation or as spiritual truths but he is clear that there is nothing to say about them. Hobbes remarks:

> For it is with the mysteries of our religion, as with wholesome pills for the sick, which swallowed whole have the virtue to cure; but chewed are for the most part cast up again without effect.

The very belief in non-material substances he regarded as a cardinal error derived from Aristotle and propagated by the clergy for their own advantage; it is the metaphysical side of that other cardinal error the belief that the church is the kingdom of God and so endowed with an authority other than that of the state. Hobbes still affects to think that belief cannot be forced, but the profession of belief is an overt act and therefore falls within the province of law. Freedom of belief is completely inoperative so far as external consequences are concerned All observance and profession, the canon of religious books, the creed, and the government of the church, if they have any authority are authorized by the sovereign. Since there is no objective standard of religious truth, the establishment of any belief or form of worship must be an act of sovereign will.

A church therefore is for Hobbes merely a corporation. Like any corporation, it must have a head and the head is the sovereign. It is a company of men united in the person of one sovereign and therefore indistinguishable from the commonwealth itself. Temporal and spiritual government are identical. Hobbes still holds, like Marsilio, that it is the duty of the church to teach, but he adds that no teaching is lawful unless the sovereign authorizes it. Excommunication or any other ecclesiastical penalty is inflicted by the authority of the sovereign. Obviously enough, then, as Hobbes concludes, there cannot be any conflict between divine and human law. In every sense that counts, religion is completely under the sway of law and government. One easily conjectures that religion was not a matter of vital moment in Hobbes's experience. He attributed less moral weight to it than Machiavelli. The desire for freedom of conscience, like the desire for political freedom, seems to have figured in his mind merely as an evidence of intellectual confusion, and the force of a genuine religious conviction must have been quite unknown to him. At the same time ecclesiastical questions still bulked very large in his political outlook. Nearly half of *Leviathan* is devoted to them. In this respect English thought must have moved rapidly between 1650 and the end of the century. When Locke wrote forty years later he could assume far more actual separation of political and religious questions than Hobbes ever imagined.

Powers of the Sovereign

When Hobbes delineates the rights and powers of the sovereign, it is important to remember that he views the sovereign as an artificial person who is the representative of the people, who by contracting among themselves, create the commonwealth. Otherwise, one has the impression that Hobbes is recommending a highly repressive form of dictatorship or tyranny. Moreover, Hobbes's arguments for specific rights and powers often depend upon his conception of the sovereign as artificial person.

Once constituted, Hobbes tells us, a sovereign cannot be deposed, for the following reason: "And they have also every man given the sovereignty to him that beareth their person; and therefore if they depose him, they take from him that which is his own and so it is injustice". In deposing the sovereign the members of the commonwealth would be taking from the sovereign what they themselves have given – the sovereign's authority – and Hobbes sees this as the kind of inconsistency he has labeled injustice. Moreover, the citizens, having instituted one form of government – a democracy or aristocracy, say – cannot then force the sovereign to change this form to some other.

Second, the sovereign himself, or the sovereign assembly, cannot be in breach of the contract that created sovereignty, this for the reason that the sovereign was not party to the contract. The people contracted among themselves to lay down their universal right to all things and to institute a sovereign in order to ensure that their covenants are kept. The sovereign did not exist until called into being by the contract and hence could not have been party to the contract. Therefore the sovereign has not made a promise to the people or a covenant with them; there is no commitment on his part, then, that he might break.

Hobbes argues that a person, having agreed voluntarily to contract with others in giving up the Right of Nature, in seeking peace, and in agreeing to generate a sovereign, may not then reject the sovereign selected by the majority, even if this person had supported someone else to be sovereign or had advocated a different form of sovereignty: "For if he voluntarily entered into the congregation of them were assembled, he sufficiently declared thereby his will (and therefore tacitly covenanted) to stand to what the major part should ordain". Here one of the basic principles of majoritarian democracy seems to find expression. One cannot willfully do injury to oneself, because, according to Hobbes, one always wills one's own good. And just as the sovereign cannot harm his citizens, the citizens cannot harm him. They cannot punish him and they cannot put him to death.

Duties of the Sovereign

The sovereign's duties are derived from his function, which is to further peace, survival, and commodious living. Thus, he is the person who judges what must be done in order to attain peace and avoid war. Moreover, given the great importance of public opinion concerning matters of war and peace – given the fact that these opinions can incite the populace to unreasonable stances, both warlike and peaceful –the sovereign is the judge of what opinions the populace shall have concerning these matters. The sovereign establishes a censor who 'shall examine the doctrines of all books before they be published". Hobbes seems aware of the dangers of such censorship, and he engages in some sophistical reasoning in order to blunt the impact of his doctrine: "And though in matter of doctrine nothing ought to be regarded but the truth, yet this is not repugnant to regulating of the same by peace.

For doctrine repugnant to peace can no more be true than peace and concord can be against the law of nature". Moreover, if people are willing to take up arms to ensure the acceptance of an unorthodox opinion, this only shows that they are not members of the commonwealth in the first place, and therefore are not governed by a legitimate sovereign who can establish orthodoxy for them. In reality they are still in the state of nature and war.

It is important to note that the sovereign establishes the rules of what Hobbes calls propriety, what we might think of as private property and the realm of privacy. These rules dictate "what goods a person may enjoy, and what actions he may do, without being molested by any of his fellow subjects". That which is mine and that which is yours, that which is good and that which is evil – these are all established by the laws set forth by the sovereign. Moreover, the sovereign exercises judicial power, applying the laws he has created and deciding controversies in light of them. And the sovereign can both reward the law keepers and punish the lawbreakers.

In an executive capacity, the sovereign has the right to declare and conduct war, to call up a military for this purpose, and levy taxes on the people in order to pay for the effort. In times of peace as well as war, he appoints all "counselors, ministers, and officers", and he establishes the 'titles of honor" that are awarded to those who deserve well of the commonwealth.

According to Hobbes, the rights of the sovereign are "incommunicable and inseparable": they cannot be given away by the sovereign to someone else and they cannot be divided up. The sovereign cannot, for instance, retain his judicial powers and give up his control over the military, for without the military he could not ensure that the laws would be executed. His undivided power is close to absolute. He cannot do anything that infringes on the rights citizens – the right to defend themselves, – but these are but meager limits considering what the sovereign can and must do in order to achieve the very goal for which he was established: "But a man may here object that the condition of subjects is very miserable, as being obnoxious to the lusts and other irregular passions of him or them that have so unlimited a power in their hands". But such complaints have no merit – those who complain exaggerate their small payments by the magnifying glasses of self-love and passion. They lack the telescope of moral and civil science that would allow them to see what miseries would hang over their heads if they did not to make these small payments. Enlightened self-interest can look beyond the inconveniences of the moment and acknowledge that life in the commonwealth, even with its rules, laws, and limits, is the very best bargain a person can strike.

It is worth briefly reviewing here Hobbes's impact on contemporary political thought. This will not only help us to appreciate the depth of his influence, but also bring to life what is often seen as a highly abstract and remote political philosophy. And the influence of Hobbes's thought has been perhaps more on the realist school of thought, for its basic vision of international politics is essentially Hobbesian. The realists, for example, maintain that the international arena perfectly corresponds to Hobbes's description of the state of nature. There exists no sovereign authority, hence no overarching system of law. As a consequence, there is no way to constrain individual nation-states that are concerned only with their own national interest just as Hobbes's "natural man" is concerned only with his own self-interest. Each state thus finds itself in a perpetual struggle of "power after power," with the result that each finds itself in a chronic condition of war. The realists follow Hobbes as well in insisting that the international state of war could be eliminated only by nation-states mutually laying down all rights and powers and turning them over to a common power that can unite their wills "unto one will." In Hobbes's terms, they agree that each nation-state would have to contract out of the state of nature and create a world sovereign power if lasting peace were to be attained.

Furthermore, the facts of international life bear out Hobbes's thesis that the ultimate power of any world government cannot be limited. In Hobbes's terms, they agree that the contract cannot be a reciprocal agreement between the world sovereign and the subject states. The United Nations has largely failed as a peace keeping institution, they argue, precisely because each nation retains its powers or rights. Hence, the United Nations does not possess sovereignty and, consequently, cannot translate its laws into commands. And until some world sovereign power is created, say the realists, we will continue to be in an international state of war, just as Hobbes's political theory would predict.

But there are an increasing number of thinkers, the "neo-Hobbesians," who now argue that Hobbes's political theory is also born out by the reality of domestic politics. While the brute facts of political power may not be as easily perceived domestically because the state of nature has been abolished, they are still very real according to the neo-Hobbesians. For while our civilized order often hides these facts from us, that order can exist only so long as the state remains sovereign and the laws have the power to command.

Moreover, from a Hobbesian perspective, it is mere pretense to believe that constitutional rights really limit the power of government. These rights and liberties are granted by government and can be taken away whenever government sees fit, although our constitutional mythology supposes otherwise. In the meantime, the contemporary Hobbesian will argue that the existence of extensive rights and liberties is simply a reflection of the fact that the power of the state is sufficiently secure that freedom of expression poses no threat to the effective functioning of government. Once these conditions cease, as they often do during times of crisis, the real power of government become manifest. Yet, here we must conclude our discussion of Hobbes with what seems to be a contradiction. Hobbes himself did not advocate the extensive exercise of power over the individual that some now say is necessary. Quite the contrary, Hobbes argued that the sovereign power need not interfere in most spheres of life, and that in most circumstances people should have the liberty to buy and sell and otherwise contract with one another; to choose their own abode, their own diet, their own trade of life, and institute their children as they themselves think fit; and the like.

Clearly Hobbes is in no sense the father of modern totalitarianism as he is sometimes quite mistakenly said to be. Ironically, the great proponent of absolute sovereignty laid the foundations for the liberal theory of the negative state. For now, it is sufficient to note that the theory claims that the state's functions ought to be confined to maintaining law and order, and that the other spheres of life ought to be left free from political constraint. For Hobbes those other areas comprise for the most part the economic aspects of human activity, what Aristotle referred to as the household or private domain. And it was part of Hobbes's political insight to recognize not only that the state need not interfere in people's private lives in order to maintain control, but that people would be less likely to meddle in affairs of state if they were left free to pursuer their economic interests.

Herein lies a paradox of the first order. Hobbes at one and the same time advocates a sovereign state with negative functions—that is, a state possessing ultimate power yet limiting the exercise of that power over the individual. But he was perhaps the first to have understood that the enormous centralization and consolidation of political power that is the essence of the modern nation-state is actually conducive to the liberation of the individual from social and political constraints. For to consolidate power into one unit is to take it from others and thus leave the individual free from the control of subordinate powers. Historically, the formation of the centralized nation-state involved just this, for it not only destroyed the church as a political power, but the whole range of feudal entities that had far constrained the individual. Thus, just as Hobbes's concept of sovereignty is the theoretical reflection of the new nation-state, so too is his idea, paradoxical though it may seem at first, granted a large measure of social and economic liberty.

Viewed from this perspective, we can now see that while power is the basis of Hobbes's nation-state, it is not power in the narrow sense of force or violence. Hobbes expects very little actual force to be used by the sovereign power, except against the criminal class that exists in every society. Rather, the Hobbesian system is to be held together by the mutual self-interest each individual has in maintaining that system. Each will have an interest in obeying the law, since disobedience will result in some form of punishment. But even more important, each individual will have a personal stake in maintaining a system of governance that grants extensive liberty to pursue private social and economic interests. The negative state, in other words, allows individuals to pursue their self-interest in a way that would have been impossible in the feudal system, yet it ensures that political control will be maintained.

In the same way, it is in the self-interest of the sovereign body to limit the scope of its power in order to maintain the continued support of the subjects. If government were to abuse its powers by violating people's lives and liberties, the whole purpose of the contract would be vitiated. Carried to its logical extreme, the abuse of power might lead people to revolt in the false belief that a condition of war could be no worse than their present condition. Thus, in limiting the exercise of power particularly in the economic domain, the sovereign authority actually ensures its continued existence.

Hobbes's Individualism

Hobbes's political philosophy is beyond all comparison the most imposing structure that the period of the English civil wars produced. It is notable chiefly for the logical clarity of the argument and the consistency with which it carried through the presumptions from which it started. It was in no sense a product of realistic political observation.

The actual motives which sway men in civil life were largely opaque to Hobbes, and his interpretation of the characters of his contemporaries was often grotesque. His psychology was not conceived by him to be the product of observation. It was not so much a description of men as they are as a demonstration of what they must be in the light of general principles. This was what science meant to Hobbes—a rational construction of the complex by means of the simple, as exemplified by geometry. The resulting estimate of government was wholly secular and quite coolly utilitarian. Its value consists solely in what it does, but since the alternative is anarchy, there can be no doubt, which a utilitarian will choose. The choice has little sentiment behind it. The advantages of government are tangible and they must accrue quite tangibly to individuals, in the form of peace and comfort and security of person and property. This is the only ground upon which government can be justified or even exist. A general or public good, like a public will, is a figment of the imagination; there are merely individuals who desire to live and to enjoy protection for the means of life.

This individualism is the thoroughly modern element in Hobbes and the respect in which he caught most clearly the note of the coming age. For two centuries after him self-interest seemed to most thinkers a more obvious motive than disinterestedness, and enlightened self-interest a more applicable remedy for social ills than any form of collective action. The absolute power of the sovereign a theory with which Hobbes's name is more generally associated—was really the necessary complement of his individualism. Except as there is a tangible superior to whom men render obedience and who can, if necessary enforce obedience, there are only individual human beings, each actuated by his private interests. There is no middle ground between humanity as a sand-heap of separate organisms and the state as an outside power holding them precariously together by the sanctions with which it supplements individual motives. All the rich variety of associations disappears, or is admitted suspiciously and grudgingly as carrying a threat to the power of the state. It is a theory natural to an age which saw the wreck of so many of the traditional associations and institutions of economical and religious life and which saw above all the emergence of powerful state in which the making of law became the typical activity. These tendencies—the increase of legal power and the recognition of self-interest as the dominant motive in life—have been among the most pervasive in modern times. That Hobbes made them the premises of his system and followed them through with relentless logic is the true measure of his philosophical insight and of his greatness as a political thinker.

It is this clear-cut individualism which makes Hobbes's philosophy the most revolutionary theory of the age. Beside this his defense of monarchy was superficial. Well might Clarendon wish that Hobbes had never been born to defend his royal pupil with this sort of argument. For it is a perfect solvent of all the loyalty and reverance and sentiment upon which the monarchy had rested. With Hobbes the power of tradition is for the first time fully broken by a clear-headed and cold-hearted rationalism. The state is a Leviathan, but no man loves or reveres a

Leviathan. It is reduced to a utility, good for what it woes, but merely the servant of private security. In this argument Hobbes summed up a view of human nature which resulted from two centuries of decadence in customary economic and social institutions. Moreover, he caught the spirit which was to animate social thinking for at least two centuries more, the spirit of laissez faire.

Here we may begin our critical analysis of Hobbes's political theory. The problem is that Hobbes is such a complex and provocative thinker that there is hardly an aspect of his thought that does not invite a challenge. Down to our own day, political theorists have attempted to refute him on almost every point. We cannot, however, look at what is potentially the most devastating criticism that has been made of his political theory: that he renders his mighty sovereign weak and ineffective by divesting it of any real authority.

Both power and authority are terms we use to describe forms of political obedience. Power in the narrow sense is that which compels obedience by the use of force or by the threat of its use. In the broadest sense, however, power is based upon an appeal to self-interest. Thus, "caressing" people is no less a form of power than "annihilating" them. And while it is clear from our analysis that Hobbes's sovereign is much more a caresser than an annihilator, his caress is still very much an expression of power.

Authority, on the other hand, is that form of obedience that is inwardly willed because the citizen feels he or she ought to obey the law. It is not self-interest, but a moral predisposition to obey. And, Hobbes's critics argue, it is precisely the lack of this form of obedience that renders his sovereign ultimately weak, because mere power and self-interest are incapable of holding together any polity.

Hobbes, of course, is in perfect agreement with Machiavelli that ethical values, in the sense most people think of such values, are illusions. If justice is but a word, and natural law merely another term for self-interest, we are no longer speaking of ethics as an objective reality. But Hobbes goes one step further than Machiavelli; he strips not only the political leader of ethical illusions, something that Machiavelli considers essential, but the people themselves. For to organize the polity strictly upon the basis of self-interest is to train the citizens to view their relationship to the state in these same terms. Thus, in Hobbes's state, the subject obeys largely because of the felicity that can be attained by being left free to pursue pleasure in the social and economic domains. Obedience does not derive from any deeply felt moral purpose.

Herein lies the problem, say Hobbes's critics. His sovereign retains the ability to command only so long as it can continuously create the conditions for felicity. Should these conditions cease, as in times of extreme ad protracted economic hardship, for example, resistance to the sovereign is inevitable because people will have no stake in the system or each other beyond their own individual self-interest. And the sovereign will be incapable of calling the people to a higher public purpose because the sovereign power itself is not based upon a higher purpose and is incapable of even creating the illusion of one.

This criticism is not merely academic. Quite the contrary; it goes to the very heart of our modern politics. It touches one of the deepest problems inherent in the

Western industrialized nation-states. For to an amazing degree we have come to accept the basic political assumptions that lie behind Hobbes's theory of sovereignty, even though we do not accept his monarchical conclusions. Thus, if Hobbes's critics are correct, our modern democratic state, despite its outward appearance of awesome power, is in reality internally weak because it cannot create real authority.

Applied to modern nation-states the argument is that we have gone a long way toward replacing a public spirited community with a collection of self-interested individuals held together only by contractual ties and legal constrains. Thus, what binds our country together is merely the self-interest each has in supporting a political order that allows for an extensive degree of economic gratification. So long as we are able as a nation to continue expanding the gross national product, thus perpetuating the satisfaction of "desire upon desire" for material things, we support the political order. But if the condition of affluence should end, it is argued, support will be withdrawn and the country may well break into that "war of everyone against everyone" that Hobbes so feared. It is precisely this possibility that lies behind the neo-Hobbesian argument that the implementation of state power, that is, power in the narrow sense of force or violence, will be increasingly necessary as affluence declines.

The road leading from conflict to peace, however, is slow and arduous. In Hobbes's argument, reason never rises far above nature's contradiction; rational awareness remained linked to the contingency of existence and human passion. Even when designing a civil remedy, man does not simply abandon his natural inclinations; rather, compelled to seek his own preservation by an apparently careless nature, he can be reconciled with himself and his awareness only in a condition in which nature's aim is more stably secured against avoidable dangers. Moreover, the realization of nature's contradiction is not an inspiration with the power of sudden transformation. Although implanted in man by nature, reason in Hobbes's view is a tender faculty requiring cultivation and industry. Especially in the state of nature where passions abound, rational awareness is liable to be a fragile gift. If reason requires cultivation, the pursuit of its precept demands diligence and foresight, for reason cannot effect the immediate removal of nature's dilemma. It is only with a view toward the future or in the context of time that this dilemma can be remedied, because only in this context is man able to subordinate his short-range good to the long-range good of a more secure life. Finally, in Hobbes's argument, the task of building a civil life is not assigned to reason alone but is shared by various natural inclinations, which can be enlisted in support of the enterprise. Despite its fragile condition, rational awareness nevertheless imposes on man the burden of responsibility. Once this voice of consciousness is perceived, man can no longer in good faith pretend his utter helplessness at the hand of nature, he can no longer blame his acts entirely on nature without offending his consciousness or conscience. To be sure, in the absence of further safeguards, man's outward conduct cannot entirely follow the precepts of peace without endangering his life and thereby continuing the contradiction; however, good faith requires man even under these circumstances to abstain from senseless violence and to direct his endeavors—and his actions to the extent that safety permits—toward the emancipation from nature's dilemma.

Hobbes's theory of sovereignty and the commonwealth, can only be sketched at this point. In the absence of further safeguards, moral rules are in Hobbes's view unable to extricate man from nature's dilemma, from the conflict of preservation and destruction. To remedy this conflict, a further step is required—the establishment of a civil society and a common government. Except in case of immediate danger or overwhelming force, this undertaking is the work of foresight and design. Properly speaking, civil authority is always the result of conscious assent and recognition, regardless of whether assent precedes the exercise of power (government "by institution") or follows after the fact (government "by acquisition"). It should be noted, however, that in Hobbes's theory mutual recognition or understanding does not simply emanate from a transcendent source, nor is it by itself a secure basis of civil life. Agreement is commonly accompanied or encouraged by natural inclination, especially by fear of harm. In this respect, the main types of government differ only in the source of danger and in the origin and immediacy of possible violence. Yet apprehension, while active as midwife, is not properly the parent of the civil bond. All social or civil obligation involves an act of consciousness and mutual consent, which requires at least some degree of trust, but neither trust nor consent are unmotivated. In addition, mutual agreement alone does not sufficiently guarantee the observation of its terms. In Hobbes's poignant phrase, "covenants without the sword are but words, and of no strength to secure a man at all". Thus, having prodded the growth of social concord, natural inclination—especially fear of sanctions and retaliation—becomes also its jealous protector and guardian. In times of excitement, it is true, a multitude may gather and, without established authority, jointly perform actions that seem to proceed from a common will; this union, however, is the result of quick disintegration. To overcome this hazard a more durable type of commitment is required, a commitment that combines the expression of mutual consent with the simultaneous appointment or acceptance of a common power of whose actions every partner considers himself the joint author. This commitment, writes Hobbes, is "the generation of that great Leviathan, or rather (to speak more reverently) of that mortal god," the civil community or commonwealth.

In Hobbes's presentation, the establishment of a common power seems to inaugurate a reign of relative tranquility and rationality, a reign whose continued maintenance depends chiefly on the skill and circumspection of the sovereign. It is true that he rejects the possibility of complete security and describes the commonwealth as a "moral god"; but the sources of this mortality or vulnerability remain largely obscure. Despite the restraining impact of the common power, the exercise of this power obviously requires at least the tacit consensus or acquiescence of the majority of the population. Yet, while Hobbes notes the ineradicable flux of passions and sentiments, he simply appeals to the ready intelligibility of the advantage of public order without specifying how abstract understanding and acceptance are translated into practical loyalty in concrete situations. Moreover, acceptance and consensus are conditioned by governmental performance. Again, Hobbes acknowledges that governments and representative bodies are by no means "free from human passions and infirmities"; but in discussing the "internal causes tending to the dissolution of any government," he concentrates almost entirely on seditious opinions and erratic emotions of the people. It is at this point that Hobbes seems to have left or abandoned his argument without pursuing its further implications. The stipulation of a common power whose decisions ultimately derive from human will clearly introduces an element of contingency into the operation of the commonwealth. Far from embodying a transcendent or perennial rationality, governments inevitably pursue particular human designs and programs; likewise, popular loyalty and obedience are due not to authority in general but to actual rulers with concrete policies. Thus, rather than reflecting solely the immaturity and flightiness of the people, a measure of discord and change seems to be endemic to political communities.

The ambiguity and effervescence of political life, only implicit in Hobbes's argument, have been eloquently stressed by existentialist writers. In Sartre's argument, political communities are engaged in a constant search for synthesis and unity, without being able to accomplish this goal on a permanent basis. The process of organization and institutionalization injects into group relations an element of rigidity and confinement. While acting as supreme regulator, the sovereign remains a human individual with special goals and ambitions; governmental decisions are thus necessarily limited both in objective and appeal. To an even greater degree, Merleau-Ponty has been sensitive to the elusive character of political efforts. "Our times," he observes at one point, "have experienced and are experiencing, more perhaps than any other contingency." There is no assurance of the success of the human adventure, of the quest for a properly human society; one cannot even "exclude in principle the possibility that humanity, like a sentence which does not succeed in drawing to a close, will suffer shipwreck on its way." But though unaided by a preordained destiny and plagued with constant reversals, men can remain guardians of their future "provided they will measure the dangers and the task." Viewed in this subdued light, Hobbes's writings may still speak to us with the voice of a contemporary. From the distant shores of Stuart England Thomas Hobbes still speak to us in a strangely familiar and captivating idiom. Having traversed the rugged expanse of three centuries, some of his words are obviously muffled and obscure, but whatever the obstacles, our generation seems willing to strain in order to perceive more clearly the subtle inflections of this voice. Our generation, like his, has been nearly overwhelmed by violence. How can we fail to appreciate his serenity and quiet perseverance in an age in which the potential of destruction has reached global proportions and in which civil life reveals more than ever its extreme fragility?

Political obligation

No part of Hobbes's writing is more intensely controversial than his theory of political obligation. Lodged at the juncture between the "state of nature" and the commonwealth, his moral philosophy clearly occupies a crucial place in his entire argument. Broadly speaking, two main alternative interpretations have emerged in this area—interpretations that, though conceived as radical opposites, are perhaps not entirely incompatible. According to the first and more traditional view, Hobbes's moral theory coincides with his psychology of natural dispositions and constitutes in essence a doctrine of self-interest adorned with prudential admonitions. The second view originating in the "Taylor thesis" last warregards Hobbes's moral tenets as entirely divorced from his psychology or anthropology, as a true deontology based on no empirical, transcendent values.

The first wedge was driven between Hobbes's philosophic materialism and his political theory. Some of the best-known students of Hobbes have taken the view that his political theory was not derived form his materialism or decisively affected by his concept of science. This view reached its culmination in the influential study published by Leo Strauss in 1936. This line of interpretation, however, did not require any extensive revision of Hobbes's political theory. For while Hobbes had spoken of the possibility of deducing his psychological principles and hence his political theory from the geometrical and physical first principles of matter and motion, he did not in fact try to make any such deduction. He pointed out that the psychological principles from which a political science could be deduced need not themselves be deduced from the laws of motion of material but could be reached directly by self-observation, and this was the method he used. Hence, to set aside Hobbes's materialism is not necessarily to undermine his political theory, although argued that the political theory requires the materialism for another reason.

More recently, a new wedge has been driven this time between Hobbes's psychological principles and his political theory, and this has had the more far-reaching consequence of requiring a virtual reconstruction of his political theory. The new view was put forward by A.E. Taylor in 1938. Hobbes's theory of political obligation, it was argued, had no logically necessary connection with his propositions about the psychological nature of man. This view has been widely accepted. Since its publication, outstanding students of Hobbes have tried to construct out of Hobbes's writings a theory they could regard as logically coherent and as being what Hobbes really meant. In doing so they have had put aside Hobbes's own statement that he was deducing his political theory from his premises about human nature, and to find some other basis in Hobbes for the theory of political obligation.

Thus Oakeshott, after disarmingly remarking that we should not expect a coherence in Hobbes's moral thinking which is foreign to the idea of any seventeenth-century writer, and that we should not attempt to create such a coherence by extracting some consistent doctrine from his writings, rejects the theory of political obligation in terms of self-interest, and goes on to offer an interpretation which will give 'as coherent a view as is consistent with all of what Hobbes actually wrote'. This view is that Hobbes's political obligation a mixture of physical obligation (submission to the superior force of the sovereign), rational obligation, which prevents a man from willing an action the probable consequences of which he rationally perceives to be likely to be harmful to himself (which is based on self-interest), and moral obligation, which is created by the voluntary act of authorizing the sovereign, and consists of obedience to the commands of the authorized sovereign (which is not based on self interest).

This degree of coherence has not satisfied other scholars. Warrender, sharing the view that Hobbes's theory of political obligation is not sufficiently based on self-interest, rejects Oakeshott's cautionary admonitions and constructs from Hobbes a highly coherent theory of obligation, in which political obligation is moral obligation and is deduced not form the postulates about man's nature but from the will or command of God, or from a body of natural law which bears its own authority. This construction has in turn been found unsatisfactory by other critics; its very excellence and thoroughness in developing the implications of the Taylor thesis has led to the whole thesis being called into question.

But if we reject the Taylor thesis and return to the traditional view that Hobbes was deducing his theory of political obligation from postulates about human nature which he held to be self-evident to any thoughtful observer, we are faced again with the old difficulties which the Taylor thesis had the merit of avoiding or resolving. Two difficulties particularly may be noticed.

First, Hobbes's theory of human nature has seemed so unacceptable, at least as the universal theory Hobbes claimed it to be, that unless the political theory could be logically detached from it, the political theory did not seem to be worth serious consideration; yet the political theory continues to haunt Hobbes's critics as worth serious consideration. Hobbes's theory of human nature is indeed difficult to accept entirely. Apart from the fact that it is apt to arouse strong emotional resentment, and so to be rejected out of hand, it may be rejected on various reasoned grounds. Its mechanical materialism may be held to be untenable. Or it may be rejected empirically: if the theory of human nature were valid, then the political conclusions he drew should have been acceptable to the men for and about whom he was writing, whereas in fact they have never been accepted. It is probably because Hobbes's theory of human nature is considered to be untenable while yet his prowess as a thinker is admired and his conclusions are uneasily felt to have considerable force, that searches are made for some other basis for his conclusions about political obligation. But admiration for Hobbes as a thinker need not drive us to such lengths.

This difficulty can be disposed of without going to the extreme of jettisoning Hobbes's theory of human nature or denying its essential place in his deductive system. When we see his theory of human nature as a reflection of his insight into the behavior of men towards each other in a specific kind of society, we can see why Hobbes thought his propositions about human nature would be self-evident to all honest contemporary observers once he had set them out 'orderly and perspicuously'. We can see also that, while his propositions are not universally valid, they are more nearly valid for his and our time. Nor is there any difficulty in showing why his propositions, in spite of their high degree of accuracy and adequacy, were not acceptable to his contemporaries. In short, when Hobbes's universal claims are reduced to an historical measure, there is no need to divorce his theory of human nature from his political theory in order to rescue the latter; both theories are seen to have a specific historical validity, and to be consistent with each other.

A second difficulty with the traditional view is that it presents Hobbes as having committed what is now said to be a grave logical error, namely, as having tried to deduce moral obligation from empirical postulates of fact. The core of his theory of human nature is undoubtedly a series of postulates of supposed fact. And the political theory is certainly presented in terms of moral obligation. If the political theory was intended to be a strict deduction from the theory of human nature, Hobbes is convicted of having deduced what ought to be form what is; convicted, because it is now held that it is logically improper to deduce 'ought' from 'is'. To rescue Hobbes from this position it has seemed necessary to detach his theory of obligation from his theory of human nature and to find some other basis for the former, or else to deny that his theory of obligation is a moral rather than merely a prudential theory of obligation.

But here, as with the first difficulty, an historical view of Hobbes's thought may show us that it is not necessary to go to such extremes. Why should we impose on Hobbes logical canons, which are post-Hobbesian? It may be said that we must still do so if we are to satisfy ourselves to what extent his political theory is logically sound and can properly be built upon today. But the rule that obligation cannot be deduced from fact is itself historically questionable. We shall suggest that when Hobbes's historically conditioned assumptions are given adequate recognition there is some reason to think that Hobbes had struck through several layers of philosophical confusion and hit on a relation between fact and obligation which has or better a logical standing than the modern rule. we shall argue that his penetrating vision into his own society enabled him to make a philosophic leap which, because of the demands society then made on political philosophy, was not taken up, and was soon lost sight of. Here, without anticipating the argument, it need only be said that in view of the difficulties we have seen to be involved in imposing post-Hobbesian logical requirements on Hobbes, there is a prima facie case for turning to social and historical considerations when we confront problems of Hobbes's logical consistency or adequacy.

We shall perhaps be told that logical and historical enquiries are each autonomous and that no historical interpretation, however acceptable, can affect the question of a theory's consistency and logical adequacy. It is true enough that no amount of historical evidence or conjecture about an author's motives or idiosyncrasies can be expected to contribute to a judgment of the logical adequacy of his system; though even that sort of historical inquiry, by drawing attention to the purpose for which and the audience to which he was writing, may save us from attributing to him philosophical questions he was not asking, and from searching his work for answers he was not seeking. The sort of historical interpretation, however, is not concerned with motives. It considers historically the probable content of unstated or unclear assumptions that are contained or necessarily implied in the theory itself. We see no reason to fence this off from philosophical inquiry. There has indeed been an increasingly sharp division of labor between philosophers and political theorists in recent years, especially since philosophers have turned to linguistic analysis. This has reached the point where it can seriously be proposed by the most able recent philosophic writer about Hobbes, that historical consideration are irrelevant to the establishment of Hobbes's meaning: 'the problem of how Hobbes's theory originated or how it is to be explained' is put in a separate compartment. It may equally well be that one cannot establish what the theory is without making historical as well as logical conjectures about Hobbes's unclear or unstated assumptions. In any case, it seems worth trying whether an inquiry at once logical and historical can throw a different light on Hobbes's theory, and can bring out essentials of it that have been left in the shadows by the prevailing sorts of logical analysis.

In the inquiry it may be assumed that Hobbes was trying to do what he said he was doing, i.e., deducing political obligation from the supposed or observed facts of man's nature. Instead of putting his theory immediately to post-Hobbesian tests of logical consistency in the matter of ought and is, and then trying to construct from his writings a theory which will pass the tests, or excusing him on the ground that no seventeenth-century thinker should be put to such tests, and then making out the best case one can for him as a thinker handicapped by the philosophical shortcomings of his time, we set aside temporarily the question of these tests and move directly to the social content of some of his assumptions.

We have seen so far how Hobbes's recognition of the essential attributes of market society led him to believe that the facts about society contained all that was needed for the deduction of a political obligation that would be morally binding on rational men.

Hobbes market assumptions provided two separate reasons for his thinking that he could deduce moral obligation and right from the facts. First, the facts of man's condition in society, as he analyzed them, included an equal need for continued motion, a universal opposition of motions, and hence an equal insecurity. The equality of need and of insecurity, being on his analysis more fundamental than any inequalities, enabled him to assume equal moral rights, and hence the possibility of moral obligation, without postulating any purpose or will outside of the individuals themselves. Secondly, the facts as he analyzed them included an objective but not supernatural standard of right.

The idea that obligation cannot deduced from fact is a comparatively recent innovation. It is commonly attributed to Hume, although it is doubtful if it goes back that far. Earlier political philosophers, including those before Hobbes and some after him, had genially derived moral and political obligation and rights from the observed and capacities of men. But they had done so only with the aid of some postulate as to the purpose or will of Nature or God. With such a postulate they could proceed to argue from men's capacities and needs to a system of obligations and rights. The argument appeared to be a deduction of right from fact, though it was not, and it was generally accepted in principle that obligation and right could be deduced from fact.

Since Hume, critics have seen that the earlier philosophers were not doing what they had thought they were not doing what they had thought they were doing, or what they had been thought to be doing it was seen that they had not been logically deducing obligation from fact, but had been bringing in an extraneous postulate. This point has been seized by modern critics, most emphatically by the linguistic analysts.

Now a system of obligation that is, or can become morally binding on all individuals in a society, must be one which all of them are capable of accepting as binding. One of the facts that must be present before such obligation can be deduced from the facts, is that individuals are capable of a acknowledging such obligation. This condition can be met if the society is one in which individuation can be met if the society is one in which individuals are capable of seeing themselves as equal in some reportant than all the respects in which they are unequal. Only in such a society can it be said, and accepted, that there is no reason why any man should claim superior rights. For if men do not acknowledge such equality they can claim unlimited superiority claiming this, they cannot be morally bound by any non-supernatural system of obligation. A factual equality, which men can see as overriding all their factual inequalities, is thus a prerequisite of deducing, from the facts alone, morally binding obligation.

Hobbes grasped this. It was, from his postulate of equality that he argued that there was no reason why anyone should have more rights than others, and from this to the possibility and necessity of obligation. The supposed factual equality from which he argued directly to the necessity of political obligation was the equal ability of men to kill each other, which in the hypothetical state of nature entailed an equal insecurity of life and possessions. This supposed equality is not, however, a sufficient basis for political obligation of men in society.

In Hobbes's model of society, as it can be collected from his analyses of power, honour, value, and justice, there may be said to be two kinds of equality: equal insecurity and equal subordination to the market. Everyone is necessarily pulled into the competition for power over others. Everyone seeks to acquire more power than he naturally has, and can do so only by converting to his own use some of the power of others. Hence everyone is liable to incessant invasion of his powers by others. Hobbes treated this as an equality of insecurity. He saw this equality of insecurity as so close to the surface of men's lives that any rational man could see it and acknowledge its necessary consequences as soon as it was pointed out. But the only society in which there can be this incessant invasion of every man's power by others is the possessive market society. We have therefore to ask whether the insecurity of every man in possessive market society can accurately be treated as equal insecurity.

It is immediately apparent that while every individual in that society is insecure they are far from equal in insecurity. For the possessive market, society requires a substantial inequality of command over resources. There must be a class of men with sufficient resources to employ the labour of others, and a class of men with so little resources as to offer themselves for employment. While the members of each class are insecure, i.e. open to invasion of their powers through the market, the insecurity of the two classes is quite unequal. They cannot therefore be expected to perceive themselves so equal in insecurity as to acknowledge, on that ground alone, a binding obligation to a common authority. Thus Hobbes failed to allow in his model for the inequality of insecurity which the other attributes of his model necessarily imply.

However, there is in his model of society another feature which may, be considered a kind of equality: the equal sub-ordination of every individual to the to the laws of the market. In Hobbes's model, in which in this respect coincides with the model of possessive market society everyone is subject to the determination of the competitive market for powers. Hobbes saw, accurately, that in a possessive market society all values and entitlements are in fact established by the operation of the market, and all morality tends to be the morality of the market. The possessive market society does establish rights by facts; every man's entitlements are determined by the actual competitive relationship between the powers of individuals.

Yet it must be allowed that in assuming the inevitable dominance of possessive market values Hobbes had the facts on facts on his side. He was perhaps a little ahead of his time, for there were still substantial numbers in English society who rejected. The Civil War, on Hobbes's own interpretation of it, was a contest between those who supported traditional values and those who aligned themselves with the morality of the market.

Locke tried to combine traditional and market morality; so did Burke, in a more fundamental and more desperate way, a century later. But by that time the morality of the market had come to prevail, it was not seriously challenged again until well on in the nineteenth century, Hobbes, then, was substantially right after all, at least for as far ahead as he could see, which turned out to be about two centuries, m assuming that the market system once established was so powerful that no individual in it could escape from it, and hence that all rational men in it had to accept the market concept of justice as the only possible one.

So Hobbes appears to have found a basis for a rational obligation for all members of a possessive market society. In other words, every individual in it can and must in his own interest acknowledge obligation to a political authority with enough power to enforce the rules of a competitive society. And this obligation may as well be called moral as prudential; it is the highest morality of which market men are capable.

Macpherson has argued that the difference between moral and prudential obligation becomes insignificant as soon as reliance on some transcendental will or purpose is rejected; that when it is rejected the significant question is whether any obligation that can be expected to be binding on rational individuals is possible; that such obligation is possible if men see themselves, or can be expected to come to see themselves, as equal in some respect more vital than all their inequalities; that Hobbes grasped this; and that the equal subservience of all men to the determination of the market which he put in his model of society, and which is an attribute of possessive market societies, is a sufficient basis for the deduction of obligation binding on all rational men in that society, so long as possessive market relations prevail and are thought inevitable.

This is a greater measure of validity than is usually allowed Hobbes's system, though it would not have satisfied. The fact that English society soon came to be adequately governed by a sovereign body without self-perpetuating power shows that Hobbes's full prescription was not necessary for the maintenance of a stable society. It shows also that, in the measure that English society was then a possessive market society, Hobbes's prescription was not necessary for possessive market society.

The source of the error was in the one significant shortcoming of Hobbes's model. His model failed to correspond to the possessive market model in that he did not allow for the existence of politically significant unequal classes. He saw society as so necessarily fragmented by the struggle of each for power of each for power over others that all were equal in insecurity. He failed to see that the very same characteristic of a society, which makes it an incessant competition of each for power over others, makes it also an unequal class-divided society. It was Hobbes's failure to see this that led him to see society as so completely fragmented. And it was from his view of society as so completely fragmented that he deduced the need for a self- perpetuating sovereign person or body.

What Hobbes missed, then, was the possibility of class cohesion offsetting the fragmenting forces in market society. Hobbes was not so blind as to have missed the fact that there was a class division in England, as is evident from his remarks in *Behemoth.* He saw, too, that the growth of the market relation had undermined the old values, and that the new men of mercantile wealth had enough cohesion to foment a civil war. But he was apparently more impressed with the divisive effects of the loss of old values, and with the contests for power between different groups on the parliamentary side which broke out as soon as the monarchy had been thrown over, than by the cohesion that had enabled the opponents of the old structure to overthrow it. Hobbes's model failed to correspond, in this one essential, to the model of possessive market society as well as to the actual English society.

This shortcoming in Hobbes's model of society was what misled him to conclude that a self-perpetuating sovereign body was necessary. It made his conclusions inapplicable to the possessive market society, and unacceptable to the proponents of market society in seventeenth-century England. Since he left class division and class cohesion out of his model, there was no place in his conclusions for a sovereign body tied to one class. Those who possess substantial property need a sovereign state to sanction the right of possession. They must therefore authorize a sovereign body to do whatever is necessary to maintain the right of possession, and the sovereign body must have the right to decide what is necessary. But the men of property need not give up their right or power to choose the persons who shall from time to time be the members of the sovereign body.

The argument on which Hobbes rested the necessity of a self-perpetuating sovereign body is thus without basis in a class-divided society with a cohesive possessing class; and the very fact that a society is so divided tends to give a sufficient degree of cohesion to the possessing.

Macpherson has righthy commented that Hobbes, in building on the compulsions and morality of the market, penetrated to the heart of the problem of obligation in modern possessive societies. The paradox of Hobbes's individualism, which starts with equal rational individuals and demonstrates that they must submit themselves wholly to a power outside themselves, is a paradox not of his construction but of the market society. The market makes men free; it requires for its effective operation that all men be free and rational; yet, the independent rational decisions of each man produce at every moment a configuration of forces, which confronts each man compulsively. All men's choices determine, and each man's choice is determined by the market. Hobbes caught both the freedom and the compulsion of possessive market society.

The English possessing class, however, did not need Hobbes's full prescription. And they had some reason to be displeased with his portrait of themselves: no reader, except the fashionably flippant, could relish such an exposure of himself and his fellows, especially when it was presented as science. Before the end of the century, the men of property lad come to terms with the more ambiguous, and more agreeable, doctrine of Locke.

It is one of the oddities of Western political thought that the critics' image of the Hobbesian theory of sovereignty should have been anticipated in the famous frontispiece adorning the 1651 edition of the *Leviathan*. The drawing shows the sovereign as a huge figure towering above his surroundings like some regal Gulliver, brandishing in one hand the military sword, in the other the sceptre of justice. Nestled in the valley below lies a tiny, thriving city, its geometrical tidiness clearly symbolizing the peace and order made possible by the giant looming in the background. Thus the picture seems perfect summary of Hobbes's thought: the blessings of peace are assured only when society is in total subjection to an absolute authority. This impression of the awesome power of the sovereign seems further confirmed by the vivid language with which Hobbes described his Leviathan: moral god, "the greatest of human powers," the greatest dominion that can be granted limited only by the strength and forces of the city itself, and by nothing else in the world.

Yet there is another feature of the frontispiece worth noting. The sovereign's powerful body is, so to speak, not his own; its outline is completely filled in by the miniature figures of his subjects. He exists, in other words, only through them. Equally important, each subject is clearly discernible in the body of the sovereign. The citizens are not swallowed up in an anonymous mass, nor sacramentally merged into a mystical body. Each remain a discrete individual and each retains his identity in an absolute way. What is suggested here is that the substance of power assigned the sovereign less impressive than the rhetoric surrounding it. This is not to say that Hobbes sought consciously to mislead his audience, for in a very special sense his awesome language was quite justified. Within the confines of the Hobbesian view that political philosophy dealt with the construction of non-empirical, logically consistent system of propositions, the Hobbesian sovereign occupied a truly awesome position. He was the unchallengeable master of the system of rules or stipulative definitions fundamental to political peace.

The argument from the physiological nature of man to men's necessary behavior towards each other, from which behavior the need for a sovereign follows, is not the simple deduction from physiological postulates. Hobbes's argument from the physiological to the social motion of man is often seen less clearly than it might be because it is usually taken as culminating in the hypothetical state of nature, which itself is often not clearly understood. We therefore proceed by trying to put the state of nature in focus, first by showing that it is about social, not natural men and then by showing that it is in any case not the culminating point of the argument from physiology to the behaviour of men towards each other, but that before Hobbes uses the state of nature hypothesis at all he has developed a theory of the necessary relations of men in society. This is later reproduced with variations in the state of nature hypothesis. This is what Macpherson has done. He has argued that phobia theory of the necessary relations of men in society requires the assumption of a certain kind of society. The question, how far back in his argument from the physiological to the social motion of man he put the necessary social assumptions, is less important than the other question, with what kind of society is the social motion at which he arrives consistently? Both questions, however, are worth consideration. The first admits of more than one answer, depending on one's reading of some possibly inconsistent statement by Hobbes about what is innate and what is acquired in man's nature. This difficulty is noticed, and the reasons for preferring one reading are given. The second question is then shown to admit of only one answer on either reading of the passages relevant to the first question.

Having thus shown that Hobbes's theory of the social motion of man requires the assumption of a certain kind of society, Macpherson examines some models of society, in order to demonstrate more precisely, what kind of society is required? Macpherson argues that Hobbes did more or less consciously construct such a model, and that the model did correspond in large measure to seventeenth-century English market society. The recognition of Hobbes's social assumptions, and of the consequent completeness of his deduction of men's need for a sovereign, does not in itself dispose of the philosophic question whether the political obligation whose necessity Hobbes has thus demonstrated is properly moral obligation or merely expedient and prudential obligation, but it does put that question in a different perspective.

In the light of Hobbes's assumptions, his deduction of obligation from fact must be allowed a logical validity as well as a striking novelty. It is argued that because of the assumption he made about the nature of society, which he saw as a series of competitive relations between naturally dissociated and independently self-moving individuals, with no natural order of subordination, he was able to deduce a moral obligation from the supposed facts, without importing hierarchical moral values or teleological principles; that his materialism was an integral part of that deduction; and that the deduction of obligation directly from the supposed facts about the nature of man and the necessary relations between man is not illogical in principle but requires conditions which were not clearly satisfied before Hobbes's time. We conclude, from a reconsideration of Hobbes's originality, and of the reasons for his doctrine being so generally unacceptable, that he was much less in error, and that his theory has a much greater relevance to modern society than is usually allowed.

In turning to the moral philosophy of Thomas Hobbes, we enter for the first time into the period of modern philosophy. Hobbes, an Englishman, and his French contemporary Rene Descartes are the founders of modern philosophical thought. Their differences, however, are more noticeable than their similarities. Both stress the ability of unfettered reason – unaided by faith – to ascertain the nature of reality, but the pictures of reality they draw are dramatically different. Descartes is immortalized in the annals of thought for his mind/body dualism, according to which there are two fundamentally distinct kinds of things in reality, bodily or physical substances, on the one hand and mental entities – minds or souls – on the other. in a living human being, these two metaphysically distinct things are joined together and even interact with one another. Death, however, involves the separation of a person's soul from his body. While it inhabits and interacts with the body, the Cartesian mind engages in acts of thinking, feeling, and willing; it is, in short, a thinking thing, without which the body is incapable of cognitive, affective, or voluntary activities. But for Hobbes, all reality inducing the consign mind is physical. The activities of thinking, feeling, and willing are no more than motions of the physical body, movements that occur as a result of the body's interaction with objects in the surrounding physical world. Hobbes's materialism – or more developed, sophisticated forms of it – is highly popular today, although Descartes' dualism had more impact on the thought of the seventeenth and eighteenth centuries.

Still, the empirical approach to rights has its origins in the work of Thomas Hobbes, whom Hegel regarded as the "revolutionary" founder of the completely modern tradition. The novel and shocking character of Hobbes's insights consisted in the fact that he was the first to derive a teaching about political obligation from a doctrine of the will alone. The state for Hobbes is no longer conceived as it was by Plato and Aristotle, as a duplication of principles already "out there" in nature that can be discovered by dint of human reason. rather, for Hobbes, the state is the result of an active choice by which we impose our wills upon nature. This emphasis on the active role of choice or will is what distinguishes ancient from modern conceptions of right. Indeed, nature is on longer able to provide a ground for political obligation precisely because the idea of nature has undergone a radical change. Nature is no longer regarded as beneficently organized for human ends and purposes. Rather, it is seen as something indifferent or even hostile to human life, devoid of what Nietzsche would call "metaphysical comfort," and therefore something to be "conquered." It is necessary, then, to "construct" social reality out of the raw materials provided by nature, "to the end of securing as far as matter, and human force permit, such ends as human life requiretch".

The Prisoner's Dilemma

Hobbes's argument is one way of arriving at The Social Contract Theory. There is another line of thought, however, that has also impressed many philosophers in recent years. This line of thought is connected with a problem in decision theory known as The Prisoner's Dilemma. The prisoner's dilemma may be stated first in the form of a puzzle; you may want to see if you can solve it before looking at the answer.

Suppose you live in a totalitarian society, and one day, to your astonishment, you are arrested and charged with treason. The police say that you have been plotting against the government with a man named Smith, who has also been arrested and is being held in separate cell. The interrogator demands that you confess. You protest your innocence; you say that you don't even know Smith. But this does no good. It soon becomes clear your captors are not interested in the truth—you are going to be sent to prison no matter what you say but the length of your sentence will depend on whether you can fess. You are given the following information:

* If you confess and Smith does not, you will get one year in prison and Smith will get ten. (You get one year—this is the you can hope for.)
* If neither of you confesses, you will each be sentenced to two years in prison. (You get two years—this is second best.)
* If you both confess, you will each be sentenced to five years in prison. (You get five years—this is third best.)
* If Samarith confesses and you do not, you will get the ten years and he will get only one. (You get ten years—this is the worst thing that could happen to you.)

Finally, you are told that Smith is being offered the same deal; but you cannot communicate with him and you have no way of knowing what he will do.

The problem is this: assuming that your only goal is to protect your own interests, what should you do? Confess, or not confess? For the purposes of this problem, you should forget about maintaining your dignity, up for your right, and other such notions. That is not what this problem is about. You should also forget about trying to help Smith. This problem is strictly about calculating what is in your own interests. The question is: what will get you the shortest sentence? Confessing or not confessing?

And now the answer: At first glance it may seem that the question cannot be answered unless you know what Smith will do. But that is an illusion. Actually, the problem has a perfectly clear solution: no matter what Smith does, you should confess. This can be shown by the following reasoning.

Remember that Smith is being offered the same deal. Assuming that he is not stupid, he will also conclude from the very same reasoning that he should confess. Thus the outcome will be that you will both confess, and this means that you will both be given five-year sentences. But if you had both done the opposite, each of you would have gotten only two years. That's the catch. By rationally pursuing your own interests, you both end up worse off than if you had acted differently. That is what makes the Prisoner's Dilemma a dilemma. It is paradoxical situation: you will both be better off if you simultaneously do what is not in your own individual self-interests.

By cooperating you would both be better off than if you acted independently. Cooperating will not get either of you the optimum result—the one-year sentence—but it will get both of you a better result than either of you could obtain if you did not cooperate. Such a bargain, you would have to be assured that he will have to keep his part. Only an enforceable agreement could provide a way out of the dilemma, for either of you.

In living together with other people, you could adopt either of two strategies. First, you could pursue your own self-interests exclusively—in every situation, you could do whatever will benefit yourself, taking no notice of how others might be affected. Let us call this "acting egoistically." Alternatively, you could be concerned with other people's welfare as well as your own, balancing the two against one another, and sometimes forgoing your own interests one another, and sometimes forgoing your own interests in order to benefit them. Let us call this strategy "acting benevolently."

But it is not only you who has to make this decision. Other people will also have to decide which policy to adopt. There are four possibilities: first, you could be an egoist while other people are benevolent; second, others could be egoistic while you are benevolent; third, everyone could be egoistic; and fourth, everyone could be benevolent. You must consider how you would fare in each of these situations. Purely from the point of view of advancing your own welfare, you might assess the possibilities like this:

* You would be best off in a situation in which you were an egoist while other people were benevolent. Other people would faithfully respect your interests, but you would be free to ignore theirs whenever it was to your advantage to do so. (In this situation you would be, in the terminology of decision theory, a "free rider".)
* The next best situation for you would be one in which everyone was benevolent. You would no longer have the advantage of being able to ignore other people's interests, but at least you would have the advantages that go with considerate treatment by others. (This is the situation of "ordinary morality.")
* A bad situation, but not the worst, would be one in which everyone was egoistic. You would try to protect your own interests, although you would get little help from anyone else. (This is Hobbes's "state of nature.")
* And finally, you would be worst off in a situation in which you are benevolent and other people are egoistic. You respect other people's interests but they ignore yours. Other people could knife you in the back when it was to their advantage, but you would not like to do the same to them. You would come out on the short end every time. (Making up our own terminology, we might say that in this situation you are easily tricked. You are a "sucker.")

We end up back in Hobbes's state of nature, with everyone willing to knife everyone else whenever they see some advantage in it for themselves. And in this situation each of us is obviously worse off than we would be if we cooperated. To escape the dilemma, we need another enforceable agreement, this time an agreement to obey the rules of mutually respectful social living. Cooperation would not yield the optimum outcome but it would lead to a better result than could be obtained by each of us independently pursuing our own interests. We need, in David Gauthier's words, to "bargain our way into morality." We can do that if we can establish sufficient sanctions to ensure that, if we respect other people's interests, they must respect ours as well.

Conclusion

Thomas Hobbes is the most systematic seventeenth-century critic of civic humanism and Renaissance republican political thought. Skinner is particularly concerned to trace the twists and turns in Hobbes's thought. Very roughly and crudely, Skinner discerns three fairly distinct periods in Hobbes' life. Hobbes began as a humanistic scholer as exemplified by his translation of and introduction to *Thucydides' History* in 1629. Hobbes' introduction is the very model of a humanist text, employing all the conventions and practices of the rhetoric to make an eloquent and persuasive case that the study of history provides the surest guide to the present and future. In the second phase of his life Hobbes repudiated the classical Ciceronian conception of *sciatica civilize* which combined reason with rhetoric in favor of a more truly 'scientific' approach involving deductive reasoning from first premises, and primly eschewing 'eloquence' and the tricks of the rhetorician's trade, the practice of arguing both sides of any question with equal persuasive force. Demonstrative reasoning would henceforth replace rhetoric. This middle period saw the publication of *The Elements of Law* in 1640 ad more especially *De Cive* in 1642, both of which are spare and shorn of rhetorical color and flourish. In Hobbes' third period he came to recognize that 'science is small power' in comparison with rhetoric or eloquence, and averred that the latter must henceforth serve the former. Eloquence in the service of science produced Hobbes's greatest and most memorable work, *Leviathan*, which Skinner reckons was written in a mere eighteen months.

In 'Hobbes and the Purely Artificial Person of the State' Skinner further develops his interpretation of a major conceptual innovation–'the state'–which has loomed large in the discourse of modern politics and political theory. In the emergence of 'the state' Hobbes, though hardly alone, was innovator-in-chief. Before the invention of 'the state', the sovereignty of the ruler resided in his person and his subjects owed allegiance not to the abstract institution of the state but to the person of the ruler.

Hobbes' conception of the state relies in large part upon the distinction he draws between 'natural' and 'artificial' persons in chapter 16 of *Leviathan:*

> A person, is he whose words or actions are considered, either as his own, or as representing the words or actions of another man, or of any other thing, to whom they are attributed, whether truly or by fiction. When they considered as his own, then he is called a natural person: and when they are considered as representing the words and actions of another, then is he a feigned or artificial person.

After quoting this passage Skinner writes:

> Since the distinction between natural and artificial persons turns out to be fundamental to Hobbes' theory of the state, it is unfortunate that he introduces it in such an ambiguous way. In the second paragraph, strict grammar requires that the referent of the final 'he' should be 'another'.

And yet, Skinner continues, the sentence as written 'suggests that the referent of "he" must be the natural person mentioned at the start of the first paragraph in which case the artificial person must be the representative'. He goes on to say that, 'Hobbes initially resolved the ambiguity by endorsing the latter alternative'. However, in the Latin *Leviathan*, written shortly after the restoration, Hobbes deletes 'the passage from chapter 16 in which Hobbes lays it down that representatives are artificial person.

Some sixteen years after its publication, and seven years after the restoration, *Leviathan* was still sufficiently controversial to be banned and burned publicly by parliamentary order. Not content with that mild measure, some clerical critics, as John Aubrey 'made a motion to have the good old Gentleman burnt for a Heretique'.

This and other attacks might help explain why in the Latin Leviathan Hobbes' strictures regarding religion were toned down or eliminated entirely. It might also shed some light on the intentionally ambiguous wording used by Hobbes in drawing the distinction between 'natural' and 'artificial' persons at the beginning of chapter 16 of Leviathan, and its subsequent deletion from the Latin version. Ambiguity is without doubt a logical vice, but it may prove to be a personal and political virtue; and silence is positively golden. Perhaps Hobbes was hedging his bets, at least so far as his personal safety was concerned. Skinner cautions that we should not make too much of Hobbes' fear for his personal safety. But Skinner sometimes makes too little of the fear felt by a man who was by his own admission the most fearful of men.

Hobbes' conception of the state as an 'artificial person' offered an answer to a question posed forcefully during the *Interregnum,* and most especially during the Oath of Engagement controversy – viz. to whom is allegiance owed of to the 'natural person' of the king, the loyal royalist is in a quandary, since one king is dead and the other had fled, replaced by a regicide regime. If to the natural person of Cromwell and the Protectorate he heads, then allegiance is owned to a regicide and usurper – and that is both immoral and absurd. Hobbes' answer is: allegiance is owned to neither natural person but to the artificial person of the state, whose head can be either a hereditary monarch or a Lord Protector. This supplies a neat and even elegant solution for people with 'tender consciences' and royalist sympathies who resided in Cromwell's commonwealth and who, on the one hand, did not wish to endanger their liberty or their property by defying the edict to swear allegiance to the new republic but, on the other, did not wish to lend legitimacy to the new regime. Under Hobbes' new and ingenious theory of political obligation they could in good conscience swear the oath, since allegiance was owed to no natural person but to the purely artificial person of the state. Hobbes civil science is concerned mainly his conception of liberty and his theory of political obligation. It concludes, however, on a less lofty and more personal plane with accounts of Hobbes' disciples in France and England and of the reasons for his having failed to become a member of the Royal Society.

Lamprecht contends that Hobbes's bad press was, in effect, latent in the position which Hobbes himself had detailed a position which attacked every major Reformation interest, including the Papacy, Presbyterians, the clergy in general, religion as such, the gentry, the royalists and the universities. Lamprecht implies that had Hobbes been less well known for the more polemical Leviathan, and better known for the more moderate *De Cive*, the distorted perception of his purpose, as passed down to later generations, would not have been so marked. Perhaps Lamprecht himself began to overdraw the case. His reconstruction of Hobbes, in any event, hints more fully at the latter as a precursor of a proto-liberal position. Through Lamprecht's eyes, though Hobbes's absolutism remains, it takes on a much less threatening aspect than hitherto.

Curtis draws us back to Hobbes's attacks upon Oxford and Cambridge, institutions disseminating Greek and Roman philosophy, extolling the ancients, supposedly inculcating the promotion of 'popular government "by the glorious name of liberty'". The Presbyterian ministers trained by these institutions, following Hobbes, encouraged a view of themselves as ambassadors of God. They attacked the monarchy as tyrannous and in this bread sedition. Curtis suggests that 'one would have to be as authoritarian as Hobbes himself' to adopt so unbalanced a perspective. For Curtis, the universities were not 'the core of rebellion'. Puritanism, moreover, 'led few if any men before 1646 to adopt republican views'. The explanation, argues Curtis, lay elsewhere – in the fact, simply that the universities 'prepared too many men for too few places'. They gave young men a sense of destiny, of 'high calling' in the service of the monarch, hopes dashed in a real world of limited openings. The universities, in short, by overproducing, 'precipitated an insoluble group of alienated intellectuals who individually and collectively became troublemakers'.

Where Hobbes explains rebellion in terms of a free market in ideas, or simply by reference to the course of study on offer at Oxford and Cambridge, Curtis counterpoises more material considerations, earlier hit upon by Tocqueville, and subsequently referred to as 'revolutions of rising expectations'. It will be obvious that Curtis's purpose is not so much to explain Hobbes as to correct him.

Macpherson was not concerned with whether Hobbes was more of an absolutist or liberal. He scrambled these concerns. He interpreted Hobbes as a child of his time, one reflecting powerful contemporary social forces. Macpherson read Hobbes's position, not as an abstractly logical claim about the theoretical relations between humans and society, but as a reflection of Hobbes's concrete commitment to or awareness of a newly emerging competitive capitalist order in which an earlier medieval corporatism had dissolved. Macpherson portrayed Hobbes's state of nature, not as a system of universally autonomous individuals, but as a new set of social relations instituted in seventeenth-century England. In this setting, following Macpherson, individuals were cut adrift from one another; each man had his price; each played an animate calculus of self-interest; labour and skill had become commodities; and out-and-out competition required the vigorous imposition of state authority.

For Macpherson, the chief oversight of Hobbes lay in supposing that it would be more a powerful individual than a propertied class that would play the role of sovereign. In all this, Macpherson moved a confusingly great way from assessing Hobbes's position in straight-forwardly logical terms. He generated considerable heat from the attempt to make sense of a set of universal claims by reducing them to the contours of a specific historical context. Macpherson's approach was 'confusing' in the sense that he was a man of the left who none the less avoided a conventionally liberal attack upon Hobbes; confusing too in that, while his politics were idealistic, his methodology was plainly materialist, even determinist.

There were many objections to Macpherson's claims. The lines of attack were basically two. First, there was the concern that the views Macpherson attributed to Hobbes were not in fact grounded in what Hobbes himself said. Second, there was the concern that the historical perception which Macpherson entertained of Hobbes's time was unrealiable or illusory. Isaiah Berlin was one of the first to rehearse one or both of these claims.

The first complaint that Berlin lodges is precisely the claim that Macpherson paid insufficient attention to Hobbes's text, to what Hobbes himself wrote. Berlin insists against Macpherson, that 'a political theory stands or falls by what it says and omits to say'. It does not depend on the manner in which we may suppose a context to condition or occasion an authors errors or obscurities. For Berlin, those writers whom we consider great, and whom we research most voluminously, are the exceptional thinkers least engaged in merely mirroring their own conditions or crises. The idea then is that one cannot really come to grips with Hobbes merely by study of his background. More broadly, the 'vitlity of the classics springs from some quality that transcends their times'. Berlin thus detects in Macpherson an historicist tendency, and objects to the idea that the logical coherence of an author should be made to turn round the supposed match between his or her views and the material conditions of the time. The claim by Skinner that the logical meaning of a text cannot be divorced from the historical context in which it is lodged directly counters the independence of the text, as advanced by Berlin. Skinner has attracted considerable attention and respect in virtue of his sustained effort to press this case. Hobbes's philosophy was long regarded as sufficiently comprehensive and coherent to warrant primary regard for what he himself wrote his texts. Many important studies of Hobbes by Taylor, Warrender, Strauss and Goldsmith inter alia proceeded in this way. They projected it as their problem to establish the most credible reading of Hobbes, less by reconstructing his background than by concentrating on his books. Such formulated an approach was by Berlin. When Skinner turned to Macpherson, the burden of the position seemed to be not so much that Macpherson read the texts in some given way, but that he placed too great emphasis by reading texts as such.

Hood proposed, by means of a close examination of the relevant texts to show that Hobbes was not a proponent of a utilitarian calculus, but rather of an abstract and universal duty, contained in natural law, as dictated by God and reason. Hood's proposal would represent the significant rejection of an anti-traditional view, first broached by A.E. Taylor, on the thrust of Hobbes's ethical and political doctrine.

Skinner, in contending Hood, argues that the latter's position does not logically derive from Hobbes's text, but from, a sequence of textual misunderstandings and even from a failure to recognize the logical structure of Hobbes's work. What is of interest in Skinner's 1964 review of Hood is that there is nothing new to be remarked in the critical method resorted to, adhering as it does to a traditional, which is to say a mostly textual approach. Nor does skinner's substantive judgment jumps the queer, representing a position behind which most scholars at the time would have lined up. What is distinctive is Skinner's intimation – and it is here little more than that of an inclination to declare against textual analysis as such.

Hood's analysis of *Leviathan* falters basically on textual, not on contextual grounds. Skinner, however, attributes the difficulty not merely to faulty interpretation, but also and possibly more importantly, to faulty method. He taxes Hood, in short, with the adoption of an insufficiently historical or contextual approach. Skinner does not fully argue the case, but he does broaden it. In accusing Hood of a necessarily faulty textualism, Skinner extends his attack to Macpherson, although Macpherson, like Skinner, is himself in essentials a historicist or materialist or contextualist. It follows that those whom Skinner accuses of adopting a textual approach are not necessarily distinguished by this strategy. It is only safe to say they are marked off by their embrace of conclusions with which Skinner has found it difficult to concur.

In his more straightforward historical essays, Skinner reveals, far more symphathetically than elsewhere, something of the concrete nature of his concern. The problem that he specifically locates is that of political ideologists concocting and espousing a particular theory about history which is entirely devoid of any historical foundation. Skinner's attention is caught by the 'Whig view' of history. It was a view universally accepted by parliamentarians and monarchists, because it suited the different purposes of both. Seventeenth-century parliamentarians could not acknowledge William's 1066 conquest of England as conquest, since this would imply for them that parliamentary 'sovereignty' was derived from the pleasure, and prior title of the monarch. Nor could monarchists acknowledge 1066 as an act of conquest, since this would imply for them that the title of the monarch was grounded in usurpation as by Cromwell.

E.G. Jacoby displays a great degree of understandable impatience with the inclination to interpret Hobbes from an exclusively political perspective. The inclination is generated in part, but only in part, by the contemporary emphasis upon contextual approaches. The preferred outcome of such an emphasis is the disposition to apprehend the writer more as a political agent than as a philosophical thinker. Conceptualism stresses the point of an act, as opposed to the logic of an idea. In these circumstances, virtually anything that the writer qua agent thinker must be brought back to the political color of his purpose. Jacoby is, then, moved by a concern to remind us that *De Cive* presented itself as the third part of a system, in which natural philosophy was central. He notes and favours recent discoveries by 'French and Italian scholars whose work was less focused on the isolated political science context.

Gavre's approach reduces to a distinct type of conceptualism. Yet, it is markedly more ecumenical than many. For it insists, not just upon knowledge of contemporary understanding which a writer like Hobbes would have been countering or confirming, but equally upon sensitivity to multiple audiences, or multiple arguments, to very different layers and styles of debate, thus serving to highlight rather than to obscure the singularity and enduring value of a given writer's contribution. Any approach which simply reduces an author to his background, as Berlin thinks Macpherson tends to do, or which merely insists upon those gross similarities which a figure shares with his contemporaries, which Wiener takes to be Skinner's inclination, must ride roughshod over these subtle but all important nuances constitutive of philosophical genius. Although Gavre's broader, historical approach is satisfying for its breadth and suppleness, it is still not demonstrated that the supply of greater historical detail in this way directly or logically assists in testing any one of the possibly several Hobbesian 'justifications for political authoritarianism.

Warrender's approach to Hobbes was philosophical, analytical and textual. His book on Hobbes's political philosophy was the most important and tightly reasoned study of its subject in the three decades following World War II, attracted counter-argument from a variety of observers, among them Thomas Nagel, D.D. Raphael and Brian Barry. Following the surge of conceptualism and the declining favor of philosophy in Britain, Warrender's work has been increasingly neglected.

Richard Ashcraft in contrast to Jacoby, insists that 'Hobbes was, in the first instance, a political theorist'. Whether Hobbes was or was not primarily a political theorist may not be crucially relevant, if the question is really whether Hobbes's political conclusions derive from his metaphysics, or, by contrast, rest upon an independent experiential ground. Ashcraft, like Skinner, Wiener and Gave, is concerned generally with Hobbes's historical context, but more specifically with 'the political importance of Hobbes's thought to his contemporaries'. Ashcraft wishes to go beyond opaque claims to the effect that Hobbes's political thought was a 'product of civil war and strife', in order to link context to text, 'the historical genesis of a theory and its substantive content'. The link for Ashcraft is not between the geometry, on the one hand, and an emergent Leviathan on the other. It is Hobbes's metaphysics and his politics. It is between England's history of civil strife and Hobbes's resultant absolutism.

Neal Wood contends that Macpherson's portrayal of Hobbes as a theorist of bourgeois society and market morality is not covincing. Wood does not disavow Macpherson's method; rather he dispels its results. For Wood, as for Macpherson, Hobbes is allowed to be little more than a child of his times. The Hobbesian absolutist state, far from constituting 'a complex machine to prevent the self-destruction of bourgeois man', as in Macpherson's account, becomes rather 'a masterful project', as Wood would have it, to salvage the aristocracy. Leviathan was devised as a means of curbing, not the 'money-makers and merchant', but 'the English landed gentlemen in their frenetic pursuit of honours'. Wood's intriguing historical case then is that Hobbes 'generalized the outlook and conduct of that specific class into the bellum osmium contra omens... he transmuted the crisis of the aristocracy into the universal condition of humanity'. The approach, the method, is exactly parallel to Macpherson's and is significant precisely because of the divergent conclusion which Wood is able to extract from it.

J.C. Carmichael argues that Macpherson's account of Hobbes as a possessive individualist is brilliant, original, lucid and meticulous, but nothing to do with Hobbes. Carmichael's complaint, like Berlin's, is that Macpherson's contextual assumptions simply do not fit well with what Hobbes says. One unenunciated implication underlying this is that the deciphering of a context can prove every bit as thorny as the decoding of a text. Where the text is difficult, the context may prove equally or more so. It may indeed be that the context is nothing more than another sort of text, such that neither of these can be viewed as representing a 'final solution' to the other, with each in various ways replicating the problems of the other.

Where Skinner complained that Macpherson paid insufficient attention to Hobbes's context, Carmichael protests that Macpherson's difficulty derives from insufficient attention to the texts. Hence Carmichael's axiom: 'Hobbes's text is the basis on which Macpherson's interpretation must eventually be judged'. C.B.Macpherson in turn counters Carmichael textually, adjudges his claims to be hasty and ill-founded, and concedes not the slightest bit of ground to his adversary. Carmichael's reply briefly replays the dominant themes of the original argument to the effect that Machpherson's interpretation depends essentially upon reading into Leviathan's postulates which it does not state explicitly'. Carmichael renews his plea that 'the text should be read more exactly, with greater respect for its precision'.

Just as Macpherson proposed to decipher Hobbes with reference to his context, so did Skinner. But the context which absorbed the one differed radically from that which attracted the other. Where Wood attacked Macpherson more for his result than for his method. Skinner attacked him more for his supposedly textual method than for his (possessive-individualist) result. It is not that Skinner agreed with this result.

Skinner understands Hobbes as a 'rationalist-utilitarian' whose talk of a 'natural law duty to God' is mere 'window-dressing'. Skinner is made to endorse Hobbes as a 'utilitarian' in order to dismiss claims for him as a 'deontologist'. The chosen approach is not new, however, from the vantage point of Hobbes's texts, but from that of his context, engaging specially the views entertained of Hobbes by his contemporaries, including, on Skinner's account, a host of 'disciples'. Tuck records it as 'an extraordinary fact that there has been hitherto no proper modern edition of the works of Thomas Hobbes', with 'many letters to him and even some written by him' still unpublished. Tuck views this as 'testimony to the unhistorical character of so much philosophical writing in England'.

Tuck's brief discussion is revealing. He argues that a contextual reconstruction can apparently aid in deciphering the meaning of a text. Two texts by the same author appear more or less simultaneously in 1651 one being the new *Leviathan*, the other a new version of *De Cive*. These texts make different and opposing claims about the role of the Church. One gives the sovereign greater power over it; the other accords the sovereign less. The question arises, Was the author confused? Or can one of these texts be conceded precedence over the other? The substantive difficulty centers on the degree of absoluteness concretely accorded by Hobbes to the sovereign. Tuck prepares an excellent case, on the basis of external evidence, for granting precedence to Leviathan.

Brain Trainer performs a service in bringing together the two apparently inconsistent perspectives on Hobbes, textual and contextual, by Warrender and Skinner, respectively. As suggested earlier, Warrender's textual concern fixes upon the logical coherence of Hobbes's position, and argues for Hobbesian political obligation being grounded ultimately in natural law. Skinner's problem has been to offer contextual evidence to demonstrate that Hobbesian duty is derived from a prudential calculation of self-interest. Trainer seeks to show that the mostly contextual criticism of the textual analysis is largely 'wide of the mark'. His attack on Skinner is similar to that of Carmichael on Macpherson; the charge in each case is that insufficient attention is paid to Hobbes's text.

Trainer contends that Skinner's characterization of Hobbes, as a non-natural-law thinker is untenable. Trainer concludes that 'if we wish to discover the intellectual and ethical foundations of the Hobbesian doctrine... then with Warrender, we will seek full supporting arguments in Hobbes's published text's, for which Hobbes was 'fully responsible', rather than in 'the real historical world', implicitly immersed in ambiguity, confusion and incomprehension, and which lay 'beyond Hobbes's control'. Quentin Skinner in a brief reply, acknowledges it to be Warender's view that the laws of nature derive their obligatory force as 'the command of God'. But against this view he contends that 'Hobbes never advances this argument at any point in any of his political works'.

Mark Whitaker is dissatisfied both with Macpherson's 'ahistorical model of seventeenth-century English society' and with Skinner's propensity to connect 'a great text of political philosophy to "real politics" only through the writings of its imitators and borrowers'. Whitaker takes it that, before 1649. Hobbes was concerned to explain civil war in general, but that the task of *Leviathan* in 1651 was to 'respond to the specific character of the English conflict'. Whitaker, in short, is less concerned with the logical complexity of Hobbes's argument than with the rhetorical and political purpose which inspired Hobbes to advance the argument as and when he did. Whitaker thus sees Leviathan 'not as an act of philosophical reflection on England's chaos, but as an intervention into English revolutionary politics'.

If indeed, *Leviathan* is a revolutionary act or engagement of some kind, it directly forms a part of the context, so that the distinction between text and context now necessarily becomes blurred. And if the text is the context, there can be no complaint about studying it on its own, since 'it can never be said to be 'on its own': to study a text is always simultaneously to study that by which it is occasioned and that to which it adverts. He embodied these references and connections must obviously within the text itself and therefore, the text happens to be the more elaborate, sophisticated, self-conscious and coherent. Indeed, in this sense, a text may be understood to supply its own context, such that the latter cannot be regarded as some species of inert externality.

What is remarkable about Hobbes's account of the state in *Leviathan* is that the political order is natural only in a very extended sense because on Hobbes's account of the matter men would be very reluctant to give another power over themselves. The state is an artificial creation which is not derivable from human nature but which is made necessary by human nature. The political order is a radically created order, and Hobbes thinks that even if we could go back to the beginning, rational men would create absolute sovereignty because their own self-knowledge would prompt them to it. There is something miraculous about the existence of the Hobbesian state, but it is not miraculous in the sense of supernatural. There is nothing mysterious about Hobbes's political theory at all.

It is sometimes said that Hobbes's sociology and his political theory do not go well together because competitive, striving men intent on increasing their market value would be unlikely to put up with the absolute state which Hobbes constructs for them. Hobbes seems to be inviting men to enrich themselves but not to expect a share of the human when we remember how innately aggressive Hobbes thinks men are. In the State of Nature, that imagined state of men without government, diffident men realise that their only hope of safety would lie in their being able to dominate all other men. Of course, they cannot do that in the State of Nature, because men are roughly equal, and it is this perception which Hobbes thinks would induce rational men to give to one man, the Sovereign, that power over others which all men would have, but recognise that only one man can have. Hobbesian men do not change their nature when they come into civil society, and so it is reasonable to assume that they will be jealous of their Sovereign because he is the one man who got what all the others would have had if they could. A rising bourgeoisie, it is said, would want that share of the sovereignty which they would feel their wealth would entitle them to. However, this is to misunderstand the full force of the Hobbesian theory of sovereignty. The sovereign does not necessarily have to be one man. It could be a body of men, an aristocracy or even a democracy. What is startling about the Hobbesian theory of sovereignty is that its nature as sovereignty does not alter with the manner of its exercise. A state could be the purest democracy but its sovereignty would still be absolute sovereignty.

The anti-feudal thrust of Hobbes's argument is unmistakable. Sovereignty, being indivisible, does not have to be shared with hereditary estates or parliaments. We sometimes forget just how much feudal societies were riddled with ideas and practices of representation, and how much modern theories and practices of representation derive from them. From the Hobbesian point of view, political representation as a form of power-sharing could easily seem to be some kind of feudal remnant getting in the way of the exercise of pure sovereignty. When feudal ideas of representation were converted in the modern world into ideas of democratic representation, the political legitimacy they produced in its turn produced an idea of sovereignty which nobody could challenge because each has a part, however remote, in that sovereignty's exercise. Hobbes and Rousseau may be worlds apart about everything else, but they are in close agreement about what sovereignty means. The main difference between Hobbes and Rousseau as theorists of the state becoming modern is that Rousseau's version of the state requires it to be the vehicle of a collective moral enterprise. Hobbes sees the state as the expression of civil, not social, association.

It is easy to see how difficult it would be for Hobbesian men to come together for any common social purpose if they cannot even be induced to obey the law except by fear of punishment. Social peace is no doubt a 'good' end, but our natures are so constituted that only the absolute Sovereign can guarantee it and them only if he is efficient. The social peace is fragile because we are like we are, and it is really a miracle of human contrivance that there is any social peace at all. We notes above that a change takes pave in social theory after Hobbes as men become less chary about human sociability, and Hobbes's obsession about the constant possibility of a return to a State of Nature very quickly begins to look dated. None the less, he goes a considerable way beyond Bodin towards modernity by firmly rooting his theory of the state in coherent view of human nature as expresses itself in social life. Hobbes has a firm theoretical grasp of the problem which all modern political thinkers have to face, which is that only particular form of the political order will suit a particular form of social order. In effect, Hobbes separates the two long before the world had heard of liberalism, the rests on the fundamental distinction between state and society.

Hobbes puts his finger inadvertently on the problems which are going to concern political thinkers in the future when the theory of the natural sociability of essentially egotistical men was to become the commonplace it was already in Rousseau's day. What Hobbes does not spell out is what the mechanisms of modern government are going to have to be like. It is enough for him simply to say that the Sovereign's writ runs unimpeded throughout the realm. Hobbes seems to assume that the Sovereign's unimpeded writ and efficient government are the same thing. By the end of the eighteenth century, much more self-consciously sociological theories of modern society had appeared, so that the problem of defining what kind of state suited what kind of society at what stage of that society's development became much more explicit. By the time Adam Smith came to write his Wealth of Nations a particular view of the state is tied to a specific economic and social analysis of 'commercial' and 'opulent', that is to say capitalist, society.

The old Augustinian view that human nature was fundamentally anti-social because of original sin had received a notable boost in the seventeenth century from the political theory of Hobbes. Hobbesianism was the old Augustinian theory dressed up in the very latest concepts of seventeenth-century rationalism. God did not get a look-in with Hobbes except as an afterthought; his was Augustinianism expressed in the clear language of reason, the language of Enlightenment itself. Eighteenth-century enlightened thinkers had to dig very deep into the Augustinian and Hobbesian view of the human condition to come up with an answer to the assertion of the natural unsociability of man. Why is it, enlightened thinkers began to ask, that human beings have this tendency to prey on one another which makes social and political repression so apparently necessary? They found the answer in economics. Original sinfulness was really a theological gloss on a scarcity economy. The first thing God did after the Fall was to proclaim the brute fact that man was always going to find it hard to get his sustenance out of a barely yielding nature. Work was a curse laid on mankind. Bread was going to be earned in the sweat of men's faces. There was always going to be barely enough to go round, and human covetousness was going to extend beyond neighbours' wives to neighbours' goods. Therefore, a repressive social order was required to make men labour, and a repressive state order was required to batten down the effects of human envy.

The antidote to this appeared to be straightforward. Technology, the application of reason as science to nature, could show that scarcity was not a brute fact at all but the product of particular human circumstances. Economic change lay at the bottom of political change. The merest glance at Diderot's Encyclopedia, the great intellectual compendium of the age, shows how much Enlightenment wanted to spread the latest technical accomplishments in agriculture and industry. The thrust was profoundly political. Control of industry and trade by the state, and of agriculture by the servants of the aristocracy, was a bar to those improvements without which the creation of vastly increased national wealth was made immeasurably more difficult. Britain took the lead largely by ignoring in practice the superstructure of laws which was meant to regulate economic life, though it was the attempt to put them rigorously into practice again which was to cause the trouble with her American colonies. There seemed to be growing consensus among advanced thinkers that the way to wealth lay with the freeing of trade and the gradual emancipation of economic life from state encumbrances, so that when Adam Smith published the first volume *The Wealth of Nation* in 1776 he was speaking with something like the voice of the whole Enlightenment.

Michael Ryan has offered a deconstructive reading of Hobbess's theory of sovereignty. He argues that Hobbes's *Leviathan,* it is possible to see the sort of metaphysical operations which deconstruction attacks at work as political ideology. He suggests that deconstructive analysis can be used to reveal the metaphysical underpinnings of the political theory of conservative liberalism, that amalgam of possessive individualism, philosophic and scientific rationalism, authoritarian statism, and natural law market economics which has served so well as the philosophy of the capitalist class, as well as to reveal the ideological nature of intellectual enterprises that give themselves out to be rational, scientific, axiomatic, and self-evident. Deconstruction teaches one to attend to gestures of exclusion. What is the operation of exclusion in a philosophy that permits one group, or value, or idea to be kept out so that another can be safeguarded internally and turned into a norm? How is that norm impossible without an excluded other that is inferior, derivative, and secondary in relation to the primary value?

Hobbes not only cloaks and masks class interests in the assumptions of universal reason and natural law; he goes one step further: he lays claim to absolute knowledge, and he identifies the deductive reasoning procedure with the presumption of axiomatic authority in the absolutist state. This is fertile ground indeed for articulating a critique of philosophical procedures with a critique of political institutions. For Hobbes demonstrates the relationship between the metaphysical concept of the logos as a point of absolute cognitive authority, from which laws issue in an unequivocal language that excludes all possibility of ambiguity of intention or interpretation, and the absolutist political concept of a sovereign who represents the whole state and who is the unique source of laws whose authority is incontestable. In Hobbes, metaphysical rationalism and political absolutism are mutually supporting, and this is made clear in the way an absolutist theory of meaning in language hinges with an authoritarian theory of law. The authority of the sovereign's law depends on the establishing of unambiguous proper meanings for words. Perhaps this why Hobbes associates ambiguity, equivocation, and improper metaphor with sedition. Such absolute meaning requires the possibility of absolute knowledge of a logos in which meaning and word coalesce as law. The absolute political state is necessarily logocentric because it depends on law, which in turn depends on the univocal meaning of words, which can be guaranteed only by the metaphysical concept of the logos, a point at which knowledge and language attain an identity that can serve as an absolute source of authority. This is why Hobbes began by defining terms, the first of which is the mind when, he wrote the *Leviathan.*

Philosophical deconstruction usually focuses on assumptions which privilege the absoluteness of proper meaning and of the knowledge proper meanings afford metaphysical philosophy. In this case, it would ask what is excluded by this norm, and the answer would be metaphor, the "illegitimate" and unsanctioned transfer of meaning, improper analogy. A metaphor says one thing is something quite different; it implies the possibility of transformation and change, a questioning of the absoluteness of proper meaning and, consequently, of law. Metaphors lead astray; in metaphor, a thing becomes other than itself. The law of identity, which is the law of all sovereignty, be it of meaning or of the state, is broken. Such transformations of supposedly self-identical things into different things are irrational; hence, they trouble the rationalism of fixed, legitimate, proper meaning. And, according to Hobbes, metaphors arouse passion by inciting feelings that may not be compatible with a political institution whose laws require a rational acceptance of unequivocal definitions of words.

Derrida would argue that metaphor might in fact name an actual state of things, characterized by transformation, alteration, relationality, displacement, substitution, errancy, equivocation, plurality, impropriety, or nonownership, against which Hobbes's doctrine of proper meaning and his institution of propriety or ownership, to which meaning is linked, as antidotes. Might it not be that impropriety is fundamental, that metaphor founds language instead of being a derivative accident in relation to an absolutely univocal language? Given the dependence of Hobbes's political theory on the doctrine of absolute meaning, the consequences of such a conclusion would indeed be grave. If metaphor and sedition are interrelated, then sedition and civil disobedience rather than absolute sovereignty would be the foundation upon which political theory should be built. In other words, we would be on our way toward a theory of popular sovereignty and a functional theory of the state—not a goal Hobbes would cherish. And yet the deconstructive argument would establish that Hobbes's own text permits such a conclusion. For what is the "Leviathan," the analogy between the state and a natural being, but a metaphor? "For by art is created that great Leviathan called a Commonwealth, or State, in Latin *Civitas*, which is but an artificial man." Hobbes's entire theory, then, rests on a linguistic form—metaphorical displacement, transposition, and analogy—that he will later exclude and banish as seditious. Does this seemingly unavoidable metaphoricity indicate a necessity that has implications for the political theory itself? Is the unavoidability of metaphor also the unavoidability of sedition? And is the naturalness of absolute meaning thus transformed into the mere forceful repression of a force and a necessity that works against the absoluteness of meaning, conceived as absolute propriety purged of all metaphorical displacement? Does this suggest that natural sovereignty is also the forced repression of sedition? And if the possibility of sedition indicates the permanently open possibility of an alternate form of popular sovereignty, does this imply that Hobbes's sovereign is himself seditious of that popular sovereignty? Metaphor against metaphor, force against force, sedition against sedition—these differences do indeed trouble the supposedly seamless universality which absolutism, in language and in the state, assumes. If Hobbes's incapacity to avoid what he condemns indicates the work of a norm of metaphoricity and, by Hobbes's own logic, of sedition and civil disobedience, then

Hobbes's theory consists not of an absolute truth shining through exact, proper names which preexists the workings of metaphor, but instead of concepts produced by the impropriety of metaphoric displacement; not of a doctrine of universal sovereigmy supported by "scientific" and "rational" principles, but of a particularistic class interest that seditiously displaces all other possible types of sovereignty by placing itself at the center; not of a norm, but of a deviation from a norm of displacement, of permanent revolution.

Derrida says that such displacernent, which is a force of difference that resists the desire in metaphysical thinking for identity is usually excluded by metaphysics in the name of some norm or value such as, in Hobbes's case, proper meaning or absolute sovereignty. The open possibility of displacement which metaphor represents makes the absolute propriety of meaning and of sovereignty impossible. This is why it must be banished. Like sedition, it indicates a fissure in the supposed plenitude and universality sovereign meaning. Where the possibility of sedition manifests itself, there sovereignty is shown its limit. Where metaphoric displacement begins, there also the power o£ sovereign law as the absolutely proper name of a universal meaning is shown its limit. Both of these limits are necessarily internal; their very possibility retroactively conditions what they limit. There is no sovereign meaning outside of the possibility of displacement, which is therefore a condition of possibility of sovereign meaning. And there is no political sovereignty outside of the possibility of sedition. Without sedition, there would be no necessity for sovereignty. The name for that state and sovereignty would be revolutionary democracy, purely participatory self-government, without delegational representational mediation.

Both absolute meaning and absolute sovereignty thus lose their generality and their power. Hobbes's absolute sovereignty itself is simply displacement among others in a potentially infinite series. This is what he fears, and this is why Derrida speaks of the deconstructive affirmation of the ever-open possibility of displacement as hope or trust. The assertion of absolute sovereignty in meaning in the state is always an economy of distrust, desire, and fear. Like the presence of white blood cells, it is the best indicator of disease, in this case a force of displacement that undermines sovereignty and makes antidotes necessary. Hobbes's own theory is a negative affirmation of the open possibility of displacement, both in meaning and in politics, a possibility of irreducible, repetitive difference.

Standard philosophic deconstruction consists of showing how what a norm of sovereignty or identity excludes is in fact an internal necessity for that norm. Usually, what is excluded is some sort of crisis that could befall the norm. Metaphysical thought would say that this eventuality is absolutely external to the norm; the deconstructive argument consists of saying that if it could happen (sedition or metaphor, say), then it must necessarily be part of the internal structure of the norm it eventually disrupts, as a latent possibility. Furthermore, the crisis is usually something that would make the norm impossible. The displacement of metaphor and the impropriety of sedition make absolute meaning and absolute sovereignty impossible; their very existence indicates non-absoluteness; hence, Hobbes rightly declares, they must be banished. The final point of a deconstructive analysis would be to say that sovereignty is itself merely a form of displacement, that it can not define itself other than as the displacement of the ever open possibility of displacement. Absolute meaning is the displacement of metaphor, is in other words, the metaphor of metaphor. As the displacement of displacement, absolutely proper meaning becomes a name for metaphor. The part turns out to exceed the whole, and the whole becomes a point in a seriality it was supposed to transcend. Absolute political sovereignty, in turn, is the displacement of sedition, is in other words, the sedition of sedition. What Hobbes's political sovereignty excludes is civil war; the sovereign demands obedience in return for security against the civil war in nature of all against all others. The deconstructive argument asserts that rather than be the purgation of civil war, absolute sovereignty is itself a form of civil war in that it must be defined as the suppression of sedition. The exclusion of civil war must take the from of a civil war; against civil war; the attempt to exclude division absolutely is the absolute internalization of division. Intended to transcend difference, sovereignty instead is situated within difference, as a form of difference. The limit to its absoluteness is internal. Absolute transcendence, in meaning or in \the state, is impossible as what it claims to be; universal transcendence is itself merely a situated point in the seriality it is supposed to encompass. What Hobbes excludes as that which makes sovereignty impossible is in fact the condition of possibility of sovereignty.

Derrida's work focuses in part on the side of this argument that shows the way supposedly sovereign or proper meaning is situated within an open seriality of metaphoric displacement. The norm is displacement; hence, all attempts to establish a normative identity of meaning which transcends and regulates that seriality as a sort of all encompassing paradigm that excludes further metaphoric displacement can be shown to be a construct, a fiction. This is the meaning of the word deconstruction to show the fictive nature of such constructs. Derrida occasionally suggests that this argument has implications for political, sexual, and economic institutions, and Hobbes certainly allows one to see how this might very well be the case. Rather than to anarchism as some might contend, this critique leads to a radical socialism that is more akin to the participatory and egalitarian models of self-government and self-management proposed by democratic socialists, feminists, and autonomists than to the hierarchical and party-elitist, central state, Leninist variety that exists in the East. Concretely, the critique of political sovereignty implies that all representational government that necessarily must present itself as the whole state is a fictive construct. The people who rule are merely people with common particularistic interests that attain uncommon propriety and universality only as a socially sanctioned fiction. They are inscribed in a cultural and historical seriality that prevents them from attaining the transcendence that is the claim of sovereignty. This critique points toward a necessary displacement of all such fictions toward a political institutional form that would be predicated upon the ever-open possibility of a displacement along a serial chain that could not be transcended by any kind of sovereignty that is not itself inscribed in the chain, that, in other words, is not sovereign: permanent revolution, continuous discontinuity, radical difference, but also, more concretely, a governmental form that does not pretend to be sovereign, perhaps something like the sort of alternating representation, subject to immediate recall, in which the represented and the represented are interchangeable because equal, which Marx describes in the Paris Commune.

Hobbes, then permits us to see how language and politics, metaphor and sedition, an absolutist theory of meaning and an authoritarian theory of the state, a deconstructive critique of meaning and a political critique of absolute sovereignty, might be articulated. In such a slightly more liberal thinker as John Locke one encounters a sense of the antiabsolutist historicity and contextuality of meaning and of words. To pursue the equation, one could say that Derrida's sense of the open dissemination of meaning and the infinite extendability of reference, which is resistant to the sublative paternalism of politically conservative, idealist theories of meaning, is the philosophical accompaniment of a radically democratic and egalitarian socialism, in the same way that Hobbes's nominal absolutism balances his theory of absolute political sovereignty.

Deconstruction designates a state of things in materiality which resists the desire for conscious categorical mastery of the sort at work in Hobbes. There is no such thing as an absolutely proper meaning word, which is not made possible by the very impropriety of metrical displacement it seeks to exclude. That impropriety of displace ability of meaning and of the infinite openness of syntactic reference beyond that circumscribed by proper meaning is a material force. The imposition of a conclusive, self-identical meaning that transcends the seriality of displacement is therefore metaphysical or idealist. Its political equivalent is the absolute state (be it dictatorial or liberal) that imposes order on the displaceability of power through sedition. The political equivalent of displacement—that force deconstruction foregrounds against absolutist philosophies of identity—is continuous and plural revolutions, the openness of material forces which exceeds the imposition of power.

The domain of philosophy articulates with the various ways power is exercised; concepts are also forces. But equally, the deconstructive critique of absolutist concepts in the theory of meaning can be said to have a political-institutional corollary, 'which is the continuous revolutionary displacement of power toward radical egalitarianism and the plural defusion of all forms of macro and micro-domination. In many ways deconstruction is the development in philosophy which most closely parallels such events in recent critical Marxism as solidarity, autonomy, and socialist feminism. It marks a critical opening, a reexamination of the conceptual infrastructure which informs institutions and practices, a reexamination which is necessary if the other openings are to be given a theoretical basis and a justification against the mobilization of reactive, hierarchal-absolutist concepts of socialism against them. Deconstruction both opens the possibility of an infinite analytical regress in the determination of final, absolute truths and implicitly promotes an infinite progress in socially reconstructive action. It opens the possibility of further special, political-economic, sexual-political, and cultural revolutions, as opposed to closing them off in the aprioristic monumentality of a formal scheme, or in the generality of a universally inclusive institution, or through the coercive power of a norm of transcendental science conceived as absolute knowledge.

Hobbes occupies a huge space in political science like Adam Smith in economics. The judgment on Hobbes have varied from time to time. While his materialist utilitarianism has been a strong current since he propounded it, Hobbes's modern reputation dates from the re-emphasis on sovereignty and utilitarian morals by the Benthamists. The reaction against Benthamism led to strong criticism of Hobbes by English idealists such as T. H. Green. Their criticism of his materialist metaphysics and of his behaviorist ethics set the tone of the standard treatment of Hobbes, and seemed to have rendered his political views harmless. As long as Hobbes was regarded as primarily materialist arid his political doctrines were seen as consistent deductions from his materialist position, it was relatively easy to dispose of his unpleasant theory of the state, for materialism has had little standing in English political thinking since the eighteenth century when the historical materialism of Millar, Ferguson, and Robertson enjoyed some prestige.

Hobbes's stature, however, was too great for his political ideas to be tidied away in this fashion. Later generations of scholars set out to detach Hobbes's political theory from his materialism. Robertson in 1886, John Laird in 1934, and Leo Strauss in 1936 have taken the position that Hobbes's political philosophy was not derived from his materialism or decisively influenced by his concept of science. While it is possible to show that Hobbes might have reached his political conclusions from certain moral attitudes and preconceptions unrelated to materialism or science, this position raises other difficulties. In view of the emphasis which Hobbes placed on his materialism and in view of his insistence on the scientific nature of his method, it seems unsatisfactory to dismiss these attributes of his thought as merely his share in the current intellectual fashion, especially when the result is to say, as does John Laird that his thought is medieval, or, as with some urgent text-book writers, to leave his theory rootless and unexplained except as the reaction of a timid man to the disturbed political conditions of his time.

A clue to a different understanding of these matters is to be found in all three of Hobbes's constructions of his political philosophy. It is the fact remarked by Macpherson and Leo Strauss that Hobbes's morality is essentially a bourgeois morality. When this is followed back it can be seen that Hobbes's analysis of human nature, from which his whole political theory is derived, is really an analysis of bourgeois man; that the assumptions, explicit and implicit, upon which his psychological conclusions depend are assumptions peculiarly valid for bourgeois society. Considered from this point of view, his materialism falls into place understandably. It is not necessary either to minimize its place in his thought or to make it the whole explanation. And this approach may afford a new view of the strength and weakness of his political thinking and of its relevance today.

Even those who disagree fundamentally with Hobbes's analysis show a remarkable respect for it. We do well to be afraid of Hobbes; he knows too much about us. What more accurate and more displeasing picture of ourselves could we have than that which Hobbes says,

> How, by what advice, men do meet, will be best known by observing those things which they do when they are met. For if they meet for traffic, it is plain every man regards not his fellow, but his business; if to discharge some office, a certain market-friendship is begotten, which hath more of jealousy in that it than true love, and whence factions sometimes may arise, but good will never; if for pleasure and recreation of

> mind, every man is wont to please himself most with those things which stir up laughter, whence he may, according to the nature of that which is ridiculous, by comparison of another man's defects and infirmities, pass the more current in his own opinion. And although this be sometimes innocent and without offence, yet it is manifest they are not so much delighted with the society, as their own vain glory.

This passage shows to indicate the emphasis which Hobbes puts on pride, or vainglory, as a basic drive of the individual. For Hobbes is here not merely describing the character of men as he found them in contemporary society; he is attributing these characteristics to man's eternal nature. The point he is making is that man is not by nature a social animal. "We do not by nature seek society for its own sake, but that we may receive some honour or profit from it; those we desire primarily, that secondarily. Again, 'all free congress ariseth either from mutual poverty, or from vain glory."

All society therefore is either for gain or for glory. But no society can be great or lasting which begins from vain glory. Because that glory is like honour; if all men have it no man has it, for they consist in comparison and precellence. Though the benefits of this life may be much furthered by mutual help. Yet those may be better attained to by dominion than by the society of others.

Dominion therefore, not society, is natural; without fear there could be no society but only the struggle of each for power over others. "We must therefore resolve, that the original of all great and lasting societies consisted not in the mutual good will men had towards each other, but in the mutual fear they had of each other".

In all his treatments of motivation, Hobbes gives roughly equal prominence to gain and glory, concupiscence and vanity. These he postulates as the basic drives which lie behind that search for power and its obverse, the fear of others from which Hobbes's political theory directly flows. Vanity or vainglory is no doubt an old trait, yet it is difficult to read Hobbes's various treatments of the theme without seeing in them a generalization of the specifically modern form: the incessant desire for recognition as an individual superior to others. Not only does glory consist in 'comparison and precellence', but the individual search for glory knows no bounds. Hobbes is attributing to human nature in the abstract a quality which is largely a product of the social relations set up among members of the upper classes by the Renaissance encroachments of capitalism on the older society. With the development of capitalist relations, with the freeing of more classes of men from the old social bonds, this ambition or striving for vainglory has become a widespread characteristic. So, Hobbes's picture may be called an unpleasantly accurate analysis not of man as such, but of man since the rise of bourgeois society.

It is, not merely that men *seek* material gain, but that the competitive search for gain is a constant drive dominating the whole character of the individual. The most frequent reason why men desire to hurt each other, arises hence, that many men at the same time have an appetite to the same thing which yet very often they can neither enjoy in common, nor yet divide it; whence it follows that the strongest must have it, and who is strongest is decided by the sword. Hence again the fear each has of the other where there is no power able to overawe them all, and hence each man's need to be a member of a society which will have that power. The postulate of the dominance of competitive material appetites is crucial to Hobbes's theory of the state. And it is clearly derived from the behaviour of man in bourgeois society. The argument is that men are fundamentally hostile to each other because they have appetites for things which they cannot enjoy m common, and of which there is such scarcity that all who want them cannot have them. It may be said that this scarcity has always existed, but Hobbes's assumption is that men are so conscious of it, and are so determined to avoid it for their part their actions are dominated by this consciousness. This is the mark of bourgeois society, in contrast to pre-capitalist societies.

We need not be surprised, that to Hobbes, all the relations between men tend to be the relations of the market. 'The value, or worth of a man, is as of all other things, his price that is to say, so much as would be given for the use of his power: and therefore is not absolute; but a thing dependant on the need and judgement of another. And as in other things, so in men, not the seller, but the buyer determines the price, And again: The manifestation of the value we set on one another is that which is commonly called honoring, and dishonoring. To value a man at a high rate, is to honour him. Nor does it alter the case of honour, whether an action be just or unjust for honor consist only in the opinion of power." Thus the relations of power between men are seen in terms of the market.

Hobbes remarks that virtues are internal standards, self-imposed in the quest for goodness or the good life and absolute, values, in contrast, are externally determined or imposed and relative. What makes an object or quality valuable (instead of virtuous) is the demand for it, how much people are willing to pay for it, relative to other objects or qualities. Thus, the transition from the terminology of virtues to that of values entailed the loss of the concept of intrinsic worth. Virtues is a transcendent standard; value arises from the marketplace.

The much deplored devaluation of all things, that is, the loss of all intrinsic worth, begins with their transformation into values or commodities, for from this moment on they exist only in relation to some other thing which can be acquired in their stead.

One of the earliest philosophers to use this terminology of market and values when speaking of what were formerly known as virtues was Thomas Hobbes. He defines virtues, referring to intellectual virtue, as "somewhat that is valued for eminence; and consisteth in comparison." In saying that "consisteth in comparison," Hobbes is stating that virtue is relative to some thing else. It chapter 10 of *Leviathan* Hobbes enumerates list of powers that enable a person to obtain some future good for himself. Among these power are items that might have been included in some form in Aristotle's list of virtues from the *Nicomachean Ethics*. These include "riches joined with liberality," "reputation of love of a man's country," and "what quality soever maketh a man beloved, of feared by many." By subordinating the worth of these qualities to their ability to obtain power or some other good for the possessor, Hobbes effectively denies that anything could have absolute value or worth. Instead of advocating patriotism as a attribute worthy for its own sake, Hobbes recommends the reputation of patriotism in order to gain more power. And the kind of power

Hobbes is referring to is not so much 'political power' as 'purchasing power.' In other words, these qualities are desirable only insofar as they enable one to purchase the support of other people.

The most ominous consequence of this switch from virtues to values was Hobbes's challenge to the very notion of the absolute worth and dignity of a human being, when he declared that "the value or worth of a man, is as of all other things, his prince; that is to say, so much as would be given for the use of his power: and therefore is not absolute; but a thing dependent on the need and judgement of another." Hobbes's philosophy sets market value, the prince someone would be willing to pay according to supply and demand, as the moral standard for both human beings and their actions. As Arendt remarked ironically, "There is hardly a single bourgeois moral standard which has not been anticipated by the unequaled magnificence of Hobbes' logic."

There is much other evidence that Hobbes's morality is the morality of the bourgeois world and that his state is the bourgeois state. There is his attitude towards the poor, his view of thrift and extravagance, his insistence that the state should institute private property and provide freedom for individual enrichment, his expectation that the sovereign will provide for equality before the law. And while he was critical of the concentration of wealth by monopolies and of the great number of corporations, he took it for granted that the sovereign state would permit individuals such bourgeois freedoms as 'the liberty to buy, and sell, and otherwise contract with one another; to choose their own aboad, their own diet, their own trade of life, and institute their children as they themselves think fit; and the like.

The fact that Hobbes's thought does not reflect the self-regulating market economy must not be allowed to obscure the fact that it does reflect the capitalist market economy. He sees men as freed from those relations of status and reciprocal aid which had given each of them a relatively secure and understandable place in the world before the rise of capitalism. He sees them instead, engaged in a naked individual struggle for place and power and a foothold on security. What he did not see as social force, and what bourgeois thought for the next two centuries generally overlooked, was that the individual in capitalist society is brought under new relations of superiority and subservience, apart from the state, in the measure that the old relations are dissolved. The new relations are largely interned by the individual's relation to capital. Those who control capital have power over those who do not; the latter can only use their labour as a commodity, offering it on the market to those who have capital. This is a relation of social dependence of some individuals on others as real, if not as cohesive, as the feudal relations. But it is not so obvious. The relation between persons in capitalist society, as Marx emphasized in his concept of 'commodity fetishism' is disguised as a relation between commodities. Production is carried by individuals or groups for exchange, the producers significant dealings with each other are through the market; in the market the individuals are related only as commodity owners, whether the commodity is labour-power, capital, land, or a product. As commodity-owners they are free and equal; each sells his commodity for its value, and the he turn gets is determined by the apparently impersonal return relations of the market. Thus in a developed capitalist economy the relations of dependence between persons have the appearance of impersonal relations between things, The acceptance of this appearance as the reality is one aspect of what Marx called commodity fetishism.

So a coercive state built from a multitude of isolated wills is necessary. Fear of death and desire for more commodious living drive the individuals to it; their ability to calculate the consequences of continuous atomic competition makes them capable of it; but only a coercive state can prevent them backsliding from it.

The illusion that individuals are naturally free of all social ties and are constituted primarily for struggle is the illusion created by developed form of commodity fetishism. The difficulties and contradictions in Hobbes's theory of political obligation which have been pointed out by idealist philosophers might all be traced back to it. In Hobbes the illusion is so closely related to mechanical materialism that it seems to be the result of it, but both are the result of his appreciation of only one aspect of capitalist social relations. The faults in his political theory which appear to be the result of his rigid mechanical materialism and his one-sided notion of scientific method may better be explained as the result of his imperfect appreciation of the social relations of bourgeois society. The explanations are not inconsistent. For the extent to which his materialism was rigid and mechanical corresponds to the extent of his failure to see society as more than an artificial construction of isolated wills. In his natural as in his social philosophy, his failure was to see only an agglomeration of equal discrete units as the basis of relations.

C.B. Macphersam has rightly argued that in spite of this failure, Hobbes understood the essential nature bourgeois of society more thoroughly than most of his contemporaries and many of his successors. The continuing strength and the present pertinence of his political theory are due to this. For it is not entirely an illusion that in a capitalist society men are free from normal social ties except those imposed by the state. There is an obvious sense in which the individual in capitalist society is freer from social ties than the individual in any society based on status. The greater insecurity of men is a measure of their greater freedom. The social ties in capitalist society are real, being largely determined by the individual's relation to capital, but are not as cohesive as the social ties of other societies. The result is that on the whole a stronger state is necessary to maintain a capitalist society than is needed to maintain a society in which the social relations are more obviously personal, or more obviously purposeful,' and so more easily understandable. The latter society can be kept going by customary moral codes the strength of which is automatically renewed because the relations are visible and their value is readily perceptible. A capitalist society needs stronger political sanctions. It was Hobbes's supreme merit to see this and to urge it relentlessly.

If it is the acuteness of Hobbes's analysis of bourgeois man which made him the profoundest political thinker of the seventeenth century, it was the same acuteness that led his political theory to be forgotten in favour of Locke's from the Whig Revolution through the eighteenth century, and that led to the revival of his concept of sovereignty by the Benthamists. The Whig Revolution had secured the political power of the eighteenth-century bourgeoisie and there was no need or desire to raise the fundamental questions of political authority as long as that state was satisfactory. But when the Industrial Revolution brought a new section of industrial capital to the fore and revealed the Whig state to be inadequate to the market relations which the new capitalism required, fundamental questions had again to be raised. They were raised by insisting again on the atomic competitive individual as the basic unit of society. The confusion in the Benthamist theory of society, between the assumption of a natural harmony and the need for the state to create an artificial harmony between conflicting self-interests, comes from the Benthamist failure to resolve into a consistent theory the two views of society, one inherited from Hobbes, the other from the eighteenth-century optimists. The failure is understandable, reflecting a contradiction in the society they were analysing. The idealists reaction against the crudities of nineteenth-century industrial society and of Benthamist theory drove them to a refutation of Hobbes which neglected the profundity of his analysis of bourgeois society. Hobbes's insight is more relevant in the twentieth century than at any time since he produced *Leviathan.* Modern attempts to go beyond Hobbes in the study of political obligation must still reckon with the basis of his argument.

Breaking away from traditional hierarchical natural law and reciprocal natural rights, Hobbes put every man on his own in a market society, and provided a sovereign state strong enough to keep them all in order. In doing this, Hobbes was refleeting the new seventeenth-century demands for bourgeois equality. He does not rest his case on a simple assertion that men are equal, in the sense of being equally in mechanical need of continuous motion and equally liable to destruction, but on the observation that, whether or not men are naturally equal, they think themselves equal. 'If nature therefore have made men unequal; yet because men that think themselves equal, will not enter into conditions of peace, but upon equal terms, such equality must be admitted.

For Hobbes, moral and political philosophy were not merely academic exercises; he believed that they could be of tremendous practical importance. He held that 'questions concerning the rights of dominion, and the obedience due from subjects were the true forerunners of an approaching war.' And he explains his writing of *De Cive* prior to the works that should have preceded it as an attempt to forestall that war. Hobbes's moral and political philosophy is informed by a purpose: the attainment of peace and the avoidance of war, especially civil war. When he errs, it is generally is his attempt to state the cause of peace in the strongest possible form. In this day of nuclear weapons, when whole nations can be destroyed almost easily as a single person in Hobbes's day, we would do well to pay increased attention to the one philosopher for whom the attainment of peace was the primary goal of moral and political philosophy.

9

John Locke

> The great and chief end therefore, of mens uniting into commonwealths and putting themselves under Government, is the preservation of their property.

John Locke (1632-1704) was born in 1632 and grew up with the seventeenth-century scientific revolution. He the foremost English philosopher of the early period of modern post-Cartesian philosophy was educated at Westminster School and Christ Church, Oxford. Besides studying and then teaching subjects such as logic, moral philosophy, rhetoric, and Greek, he had a deep and abiding interest in medicine, which brought him into the service of the Earl of Shaftesbury. As secretary to Shaftesbury he became involved in Protestant politics. This involvement resulted in an exile in Holland from 1683 to 1689, when, shortly after William of Orange took the thorne, he returned to England and led a life of private study and public service. He wrote widely—not only on various branches of philosophy, but also on education, economics, theology, and medicine. He is best known for his anonymously published Two *Treatises of Government* (1690) and his *Essay Concerning Human Understanding* (1690). He came from an upwardly mobile Somersetshire family who made it into the gentry class. Though not particularly forward at his books, Locke decided early on an academic career. He became a don at Christ Church College, Oxford, until he was illegally rejected for his allegedly subversive opinions in 1684. He was outwardly not much concerned with philosophy and political theory during his Oxford years, teaching some law and a lot of medicine. The young Locke even seems to have been a bit of a Tory, believing that non-resistance to established authority was the just price of political and social stability.

Locke's friendship with the first Earl of Shaftesbury, whose life he saved with a miraculous operation on the liver, changed him from a mildly subversive Oxford don into a meddler in high politics as adviser and confidant to highly placed plotters against the Divine Right monarchy of the Stuarts. He no doubt provided Shaftesbury with arguments to use in the everyday political battle of the Exclusionist Whigs who wished to exclude James II when he was still only the Duke of York from the succession to the throne on the grounds that he was a Roman Catholic against their Tory opponents in the last years of the reign of Charles II. It was probably inevitable either that Shaftesbury would eventually ask Locke's opinions on the most important political question of all, the question of the grounds for legitimate resistance to government, or that Locke's own position in Shaftesbury's circle would eventually lead him without prodding to consider that question. It was in these circumstances that Locke wrote his famous *Two Treatises of Government* (the exact date of the works is still not certain, but a good guess would be 1679-80). It was while enjoying the patronage of Shaftesbury that Locke worked on the ideas which would see the light of day as *An Essay Concerning Human Understanding*. It was also about this time that Locke turned his attention to economics, education and questions of colonial government.

Locke's *Two Treatises* were published to justify the Glorious Revolution of 1688, in which Locke was involved as the friend and adviser to a leading Whig, Lord Somers. Locke's own attitude to his famous political treatises appears to have been decidedly odd, not to say shifty. He never acknowledged his authorship of the treatises, but was very keen that they should be available in a true text. Editions were mangled by printers, and it may also be that Locke was worried that opinions more radical than his own would be attributed to him. On the other hand, it may simply be that there was an impenetrably secretive side to Locke's character which will always hide his true teasons for publicly denying his authorship of such famous books.

The Treatises, which contain Locke's political philosophy, were composed in the years of the Exclusion Crisis, during which Locke's patron, Shaftesbury, and others, sought to exclude James, then Duke of York, from the succession to the throne, and argued for government by consent and for the right to religious dissent. *The First Treatise* less studied now than the *Second*, consists mainly of criticism of Robert Filmer's *Patriarcha* (1680) of absolute monarchy and the divine right of kings. Locke found this account of political authority, according to which God granted Adam absolute and total political authority, unworkable. It could not be used to justify any actual political authority, since it is impossible to show of any particular ruler that he is one of Adam's heirs. In an alternative account *The Second Treatise* argues that though subjects do have a duty to God to obey their ruler, their ruler's power is not God-given or absolute, and it goes along with duties to his subjects. If a ruler's commands do not deserve obedience, resistance to them might be justified.

State of Nature

Locke develops his account from the idea of people living in a state of nature free from external authority, in families and loose groups. In this state, each person has a duty to God not to 'harm another in his life, liberty or goods' and so has a parallel right to defend against such attack. But it does not follow that these rights and duties are actually respected and obeyed. Someone may lack the power to defend his rights, or he may go too far in his own defense. For such reason people agree to unite, and to 'enter into society to make one people, one body politic, under one supreme government'. Leaving the state of nature, they set up a judge with authority to determine all the controversies and redress the injuries that may happen to any member of the commonwealth. But this authority is not absolute in his dealings and decisions; he is answerable to the will and determination of the majority. The views and wishes of the people form a possible court of appeal against the ruler. Popular consent not only creates, but also produces the continued existence of a Lockean political society.

A distinction between tacit and explicit consent provides Locke's answer to the objections that there is no historical evidence for his account for the creation of political authority, and that people are simply born into civil societies and come under their law and authority without choice. By remaining in society, one gives one's tacit consent to it. Locke's suggestion that one is always at liberty to incorporate himself into any other community, or to begin a new one is even less plausible now than then. But his whole account can be seen as a picturesque way of analyzing the structure of legitimate political authority, and of revealing it to be essentially based on the consent of the governed. The notion of tacit consent is given further substance by Locke's allowing the possibility of legitimate resistance or revolution. The community perpetually retains a supreme power of saving themselves from their legislators, whenever they shall be so foolish or so wicked, as to lay and carry on designs against their liberties and properties.

Hobbes, seeing the danger in the distinction between justice and law, proposes an absolute sovereign created by contract as a solution. This not only gives preference to consent; it also makes it the sole condition of law, because the sovereign is a vessel into which almost all natural rights are poured. Since the sovereign who has a monopoly of rights, is the full vessel, and his will is law. Hobbes thus impales himself on the consent horn of the dilemma, but in so doing, he apparently solves the problem by making law and justice identical. Justice is keeping one's contracts. John Locke does not accept Hobbes's solution to the problem. He rejects the absolute sovereign, the rule of men, and he proposes instead the rule of law, but a rule of law in which consent is the sole condition of legimate government and disagree with Hobbes regarding absolute government.

An answer to these questions is not easily found, for one of the obvious and frequently noted problems in Locke's *Second Treatise of Government* is that Locke's argument does not move with mathematical precision. In a word, he is not consistent. He does not, as does Hobbes, begin with first principles, and then carefully deduce from those first premises. Rather, he often employees the technique of gradually retracted assertion. The most obvious cause is his initial assertion that the state of nature is a 'state of plenty' and his retraction through the chapter on property to the point where he contradicts his original premise and asserts that the state of nature is a 'state of penury'. In analyzing Locke it is important, therefore, to find a base position from which he never retracts. There is general agreement that Locke never retracts from his assertion that absolute government is worse than the state of nature. This is the most obvious point of his disagreement with Hobbes. Further, Hobbes, following Machiavellian advice that we learn most from the worst case, the state of nature.

In the beginning of his chapter on the state of nature, Locke asserts that there is a natural law and, on the implicit principle that every real law must be enforced, that there is an executive power in the state of nature. This is followed by a fairly extensive argument that the executive power is universal, "put into every man's hand." After describing and defining the executive power of nature, Locke calls it a "strange doctrine," one that is not only foreign, belonging to a different place, but also one that excites astonishment and objection because of its apparent unreasonableness, because it makes men judges in their own cases.

Locke's response is that absolute monarchy is more unreasonable. This response is not a rebuttal; it is a retort. Talk about the pot calling the kettle black! However, to say that B is more unreasonable than A does not make A reasonable. Locke, of course, knows this, and, therefore, he silently concedes that the objection to the universality of the executive power is correct. But is absolute government actually more unreasonable? Are many bad judges better than one? Are a thousand tyrants better than one? We can almost hear Hobbes's voice leading the objections. If there is only one bad judge, there is only one source of danger. A man has only one flank to protect. He does not have to worry about a multiform war. If there are many bad judges, a man has an unlimited problem of defense; he has to watch all corners.

In the both his chapters on slavery and on the despotic power, Locke finds the source of the despotic power to be forfeiture, to be a penalty for offense. In the chapter on slavery, Locke declares flatly that absolute government is not based on consent, "for a man not having the power of his own life cannot by compact or his own consent enslave himself to any one, nor put himself under the absolute arbitrary power of another to take away his life when he pleases." He repeats the point later in his chapter on the despotic power:

> For man, not having such an arbitrary power over his own life, gives another man such power over it; but it is the effect only of forfeiture which the aggressor make of his own life when he puts himself into the state of war with another.

An aggressor, one who makes war on another, literally gives up his own property rights. To put it in Locke's more legalistic language, the executive power of nature, belonging to all land including the right of reparation, permits "the injured person and the rest of mankind that will joint with him in the execution of justice," to destroy the aggressor. As an example he cites "captives takesn in a just and lawful war" and concludes, therefore, that the despotic power does not arise from compact. This argument, which is fairly convincing regarding compact, tends to undermine the assertion that nature gives no right of despotic power since it is based on the natural right of reparation and the executive power of nature. Rather than be captious, we can solve this problem by qualifying the assertion: Nature gives no despotic power over the innocent. In fact, this is Locke's point, and he is quite insistent that the rights of nature are the rights of the innocent. Nature, he says, prefers the innocent. After asserting that the executive power is universal, he states that this is to "preserve the innocent and restrain offenders." In his chapter on the state of war, he mentions the innocent four times. In the first case he declares their value: "By the fundamental law of nature, man being to be preserved as much as possible when all cannot be preserved, the safety of the innocent is to be preferred." Later in the chapter he speaks of the "right to the innocent party to destroy the other whenever he can, until the aggressor offers peace and desires reconciliation on such terms as may repair any wrongs he has already done and secure the innocent for the future." Finally, he directly connects the civil law with the innocent, "For wherever violence is used and injury done, though by hands appointed to administer justice, it is still violence and injury, however colored with the name, pretenses, or forms of law, the end where of being to protect and redress the innocent."

Initially one is rather troubled by Locke's claim that nature places a higher value on the innocent, because it seems to patently contradict his basic premise of natural equality. How can there be a natural equality and a natural priority at the same time? Inconsistent or not, the assertion is appealing because it appears to introduce a qualitative element. It appears that nature prefers a certain quality of life over mere life.

Who are the innocent? And why is it that the innocent are to be preferred: why not the good or the just? The innocent are the law-abiding, those who abide by the law of nature. Locke's use of the word innocent here is precise and fully in keeping with his definition of the law of nature: "The state of nature has a law of nature to govern it, which obliges everyone; and reason which is that law, teaches all mankind who will but consult it, that being all equal and independent, no one ought to harm another in his life, health, liberty, or possessions." The innocent are those who do no harm, who are not disposed to do harm, and thus who are free from guilt and not deserving of suffering. Under this first definition, the law does not prescribe positive action; it does not require that one assert one's self or perform any deeds of beneficence. It merely proscribes actions that harm others. It requires that one forbear and abstain. The term innocent is much more appropriate to describe those who have priority of nature than either the good or the just, terms that suggest excellence or virtue in a positive-action rather than a negative-passive sense. At the end of this section, Locke restates the law of nature, this time giving it a slightly more active, less passive prescription.

> Everyone, as he is bound to preserve himself and not to quite his station willfully, so by the like reason, when his own preservation comes not in competition, ought he, as much as he can, to preserve the rest of mankind, and may not, unless it be to do justice to an offender, take away or impair the life, or what tends to the preservation of the life, the liberty, health, limb, or goods of another.

Whereas the initial passive prescription (harm no one, thou salt not be an aggressor) is unconditional, the second and more active prescription (help others, punish aggressors) is conditional upon one's own safety. Since the acts of punishing aggressors must usually if not always, involve risk to one's safety, the obligation to actively, as opposed to passively, preserve others is insubstantial. The innocent are not the peacemakers; they are the peaceful. The innocent are preferred not because nature esteems the actively worthy or noble, a qualitative form of life, but rather because nature will preservation, mere life, and peace as the condition of preservation. Nature prefers the peaceful to the peacebreakers because of the equality of the natural right to life.

Even if we accept nature's preference for the innocent and agree that the despotic power arises by the forfeiture of the aggressors, it still does not solve the problem of how an absolute ruler comes to be. The tempting solution is that it is some kind of compact, but not a political compact, Locke, indeed, argues that "it is not every compact that puts an end to the state of nature between men, but only this one of agreeing together mutually to enter into one community and make one body politic; other promises and compacts men may make one with another and yet still be in the state of nature." Since Locke's clearly stated purpose in the *Second Treatise* is to define political power and to distinguish it from all other kinds of power, it might follow that an absolute sovereign is created by compact, but this compact is not a political compact.

A political compact properly so called has common good as its end, not the private good of the ruler. It is tempting to conclude that an absolute monarch is created by those "other promises and compacts men may make with one another." This, however, is a dead end. Such a contract, according to Locke, cannot be made. It is irrational to worsen one's condition. The creation of an absolute sovereign does worsen one's condition. Such a contract is not a real contract; that is, it is not obligatory. By such a contract the innocent enslave themselves; they subject themselves to the despotic power. Nature permits that only the guilty be subject to the despotic power. The innocent cannot and do not forfeit their rights.

An absolute government over the innocent does not exist by any right of nature, certainly does not exist by political compact properly defined, and cannot exist by any kind of compact. Locke's argument seems to have led to the absurd conclusion that absolute government over the innocent does not exist. The simple solution is that the innocent may be under absolute government by natural power as distinguished from natural right, that is, by just conquest. However, the conqueror having no right or title, the innocent are not bound to obedience. The practical problem is that the innocent often believe themselves bound. The innocent often give either direct or tacit consent to an absolute ruler. Locke's statements that they cannot do so seem to be contrary to fact. They do so. It is unreasonable to consent to absolute government, but that doesn't make it impossible. Locke, of course, knows that they do and sees that as the essential problem.

In his extended analysis of absolute government in the chapter on political society, Locke suggests that absolute government may have begun when chief rule without caution devolved out of the deference given to and the faith in "some good and excellent man." This lack of "caution," he ascribes to "the negligent and unforeseeing innocence of the first ages." The innocent are not merely the harmless, the nonaggressors; they are also those lacking in worldly knowledge and common sense. In a word, they are the ignorant. The law of nature forbids consent to absolute government, but men are "ignorant for want of studying it." This answers the question of how absolute monarchs come to be. They come to be on the basis of unsuspecting innocence; absolute monarchs command multitudes of ignorant; nay foolish men.

> As if when men, quitting the state of nature, entered into society, they agreed that all of them but one should be under the restraint of laws, but that he should still retain all the liberty of the state of nature, increased with power and made licentious by impunity. This is to think that men are so foolish that they take care to avoid what mischiefs may be done them by polecats or foxes, but are content nay, think it safe, to be devoured by lions.

At this point one is inclined to wonder if absolute government is the penalty for ignorance. Criminals incur the penalty of subjection to the despotic power because of their aggression. The ignorant incur the penalty of subjection to absolute government because of their ignorance. Still it does seem rather harsh! Absolute government being worse than the state of nature, the penalty for ignorance would be more severe than the penalty for willful violation of the law of nature. Nature's preference for the innocent does not seem to have given them any real advantage. It is on a par with God's gift of the earth to all mankind—worthless. Even if the innocent can be said to break the law of nature by consenting to absolute government, they do this out of ignorance. Isn't ignorance an excuse? Ignorance is an excuse if the law of nature is not promulgated, available to everyone. No man can be expected to obey a law he cannot know. Locke begins by asserting that the law is available to everyone and, then characteristically, gradually retracts the assertion. In his chapter on the state of nature, he says, "It is certain there is such a law, and that, too, as intelligible and plain to a rational creature.

This assertion is immediately followed by his critique of Hobbes's proposal for absolute government. Hobbes was surely a close student of the law of nature and just as surely was an intelligent and logical man. If the law of nature is so "intelligible and plain" and so easily understood by a close student, why does Hobbes make such a grievous error in interpreting it? Few men have studied it as diligently as he. If he could misinterpret it, what hope is there for the rest of us? The law of nature is a defective law; it is not fully known to all, and it is not fully known even to all scholars. Locke eventually concedes that the law is not fully promulgated. When he lists the things wanting in the state of nature, he lists first the lack of "an established, settled, known law." Ignorance of the law of nature is indeed an excuse.

In the chapter on the paternal power, Locke says that children, because they are born "ignorant and without the use of reason, they were not presently under the law, for nobody can be under a law which is not promulgated to him." But how is the law promulgated? Locke answers that "it is made known by reason only." Those who are without reason are not under the law." He that is not come to the use of his reason cannot be said to be under this law. The law of nature is reason, and it is promulgated by reason. Reason is only known to those who have it. Only those who have reason are rational it would seem that Locke is begging the question with a vengeance. Why does he beg the question? What is the point of this circular argument? What do we learn from it? We learn that the law of nature is not only defective; it is also not a real law; that is, it is not prescriptive, but rather descriptive. Rational man act rationally. We learn that nature's greatest preference is not for the innocent, who have been transformed before our eyes into the ignorant, rather nature prefers the rational. The rational are the free. Or freedom is a product of rationally. "We are born free as we are born rational, not that we have actually the exercise of either; age that brings one brings with it the other too." The will is bound; rationality is a condition of freedom. "The freedom then of man, and liberty of acting according to his own will, is grounded on his having reason."

The innocent are the "law-abiding," but the law they keep is a defective law. Innocence is not enough; like the law of nature itself, innocence is defective. It is negative-passive, and because it is, it cannot fulfill the will of nature—"the peace and preservation of all mankind." Only the rational can actualize, or actualize as much as possible, nature's will. The law of nature is inherent in the rational. Rationality is positive-active; it directly affirms nature's will. The argument is indeed circular, but there is method in its superficial madness. Nature will the preservation of all men, but if all men cannot be preserved, then the preservation of the innocent has priority. However, the innocent cannot preserve themselves because they are largely ignorant. They are unlikely "to be free from restraint and violence," from the "arbitrary will of another." The real issue is not who is to be preserved, but how are men to be preserved. The innocent may be the "law-abiding," but the rational are the true lawmakers. The rational are preferred because they create the rule of law that fulfills the will of nature.

Nature's preference for the rational is not a contradiction of natural equality, not does it indicate a greater esteem for a certain quality of life. Nature's preference for the rational is merely the means or method by which nature "enforces" its law, by which nature allows for the observance and actualization of its law. Just as the possibility of human labor converts a worthless gift, the earth, into a plenty, so the possibility of human rationality converts a worthless freedom into an actual freedom. Consent to absolute government is the heart of the problem for Locke. If all legitimate government rests on consent and if, further, the historical fact is that men have consented to absolute government, then it would follow that consent is not a sufficient basis for government Locke's answer is to collapse the distinction between rationality and consent. He merges and fuses reason into consent. Men have the liberty to consent only to what is rational. Consent is not simply a procedure; it has a substance. It is not just form, a manner of acting, of decision making. It also has matter; it includes the content of the decisions to be made. Its matter, or substance, is natural right. Consent is more than agreement; it is more than an act of will. It is an act of determinate will, an agreement to a specific thing: the protection of natural rights. Consent is, therefore, both the necessary and sufficient condition of legitimate government.

The ancients faced with the conflict of wisdom and consent tried to bring off a compromise in which the status of law is consent, and the quality of law is its relative degree of wisdom. Thus, the ancients drew a distinction between good law and bad law. Consent, for the ancients, is the power of the many provided to wisdom. Locke, faced with a conflict of reason and consent, tried to fuse the status and quality by making reason a prerequisite, an antecedent of the will. He injects reason into consent, thereby making a distinction between law and no law. All true law, law properly so called, is good law. "for law in its true notion is not so much the limitation as the direction of a free and intelligent agent to his proper interest, and prescribes no further than is for the general good of those under that law." This welding of reason and consent that gave consent, a content was very functional for Locke's purpose of justifying a revolution and identifying the limits of government.

When Locke, in his attack upon Hobbes, raises the rhetorical question, "I desire to know what kind of government that is, and how much better it is than the state of nature, where one man commanding a multitude, has liberty to be the judge in his own case, and may do to all his subjects whatever he pleases." He does not imply, as some have suggested, that the answer is that this is bad government. Locke's answer is that this is not government at all. In his chapter on political society, Locke states, "Absolute monarchy, which by some men is counted the only government in the world, is indeed inconsistent with civil society, and so can be no form of civil government at all." Government, Locke clearly believes, is the appointed remedy for the "inconveniences" of the state of nature.

Since absolute government is not government at all, it is clear that men are not bound to obey it. Men are bound only when they have consented. They cannot consent to absolute government; thus, they did not do so. "Revolution," resistance to a "government" that does not protect natural rights, does not have to be justified because it is not revolution. There is no government overthrown because there was no true government in the first place. There is no duty to obey; men have not reneged or rebelled because true consent could not have been given. In preaching resistance to kings, Milton at one point argued that revolution may be much the lesser of two evils. To counter the suggestion that the people's consent to and election of a king is a sign of divine will and therefore that revolution is a sin, Milton said, "If it needs must be a sin in them to depose, it may as likely be a sin to have elected." Under this justification, revolution may be a form of penance for a prior Vice. But Locke absolves the people completely. Ignorance of the law of nature is not simply an excuse; it is an exculpation. The people cannot sin in this way.

The collapse of the distinction between reason and consent was functional for Locke's purposes and remains functional as long as men recognize Locke' point that consent has a content, and that mere procedural agreement and the preservation of natural rights are both conditions of legitimate government. Our Founders knew it and did not forget it. They knew that to be rightful, and consent of the people must be reasonable. They knew that the proposition can not be converted; they knew that what the people agree to is not necessarily reasonable. The problem inherent in Locke's collapse of the distinction between reason and consent is that men may forget that consent has a content, that they may come to believe that democratic majoritarianism or popular sovereignty is the sole condition of legitimacies.

The clearest illustration of the fact that men do forget that consent has a content is Stephen Douglas's position on popular sovereignty. His proposal that the inhabitants of a territory should decide the slavery question for the themselves is an endorsement of the Hobbesian principle that there are no inherent limits on consent, that consent is an act of sheer will. Fortunately for us all, Abraham Lincoln was alive, and he understood the natural rights content of consent. It was Lincoln who agreed with Locke that it is *sales popular supreme lax*, not *vex popular supreme lax*. And so it was he, above all men of his time, who fought against the debasement of the concept of consent, who argued that no man had the right to agree to slavery for himself or others. It was Lincoln who recognized the difference between choosing and choosing well.

Locke presented at the opening of the *Treatise* is that men are naturally able to govern themselves by the law of nature, or reason. The state of nature, we are told, has a law of nature to govern it, which is reason. The state of nature, is flatly contrasted to the state of war: the two are 'as far distant, as a State of Peace, Good will, mutual assistance, and preservation, and a state of emnity, malice, violence, and mutual destruction are one from another. Men living together according to reason, without a common superior on earth, with authority to judge between them, is properly the state of nature.

It is no derogation from this view of the state of nature to allow, as Locke does, that there are in it some men who will not follow the law of nature. The law of nature teaches only those 'who will but consult it'; some men transgress it and, by doing so, declare themselves 'to live by another Role, than that of reason and common equity' and so become 'dangerous to "mankind; a man who violates the law of nature becomes degenerate, and declares himself to quit the principles of human nature, and to be a noxious creature'. There are, then, some natural criminals amongst the natural law-abiding people of the state of nature. But Locke's description of these men as 'noxious', 'degenerate', and having 'quit the principles of human nature' makes it apparent that he wants his readers to regard them as an exceptional few. The extravagance of his language might even be taken to suggest that Locke was anxious to convince himself of the prevailing decency of the state of nature.

But this is only one of two opposite pictures Locke has of the state of nature. As early as chapter 3 of the *Treatise,* only a page after the distinction between the state of nature and the state of war, we read that where there is no authority to decide between contenders 'every the least difference is apt to end' in the 'state of war', and that 'one great reason of men putting themselves into society and quitting the state of nature is 'to avoid this state of war. The difference between the state of nature and the Hobbesian state of war has virtually disappeared. We read further, some chapters later, that the state of nature is 'very unsafe, very unsecured' that in it the enjoyment of individual rights is 'very uncertain, and constantly exposed to the Invasion of others', and that it is 'full of fears and continual dangers' and all this because 'the greater part are no strict observers of equity and justice'. What makes the state of nature unliveable, according to this account, is not the viciousness of the few but the disposition of 'the greater part' to depart from the law of reason. The state of nature is now for deferent from the state of war.

The contradiction between Locke's two sets of statements about natural man is fundamental. The state of nature is sometimes the opposite of the state of war, sometimes identical with it. This is the central contradiction in the explicit postulates on which Locke's political theory is built. It will not do to say that it is simply an echo of the traditional Christian conception of man as a contradictory mixture of appetite and reason. One might of course say that he had to take both in order to make his case as against Hobbes that he had to make men so rational as not to require a Hobbesian sovereign, yet had to make them contentious enough to require heir handing over their natural rights and powers to a civil society. But to say this would be to accuse Locke, quite unjustly and unnecessarily, either of intellectual dishonesty or of extraordinary superficiality; and would, besides, imply an lender estimate of the extent to which Locke did subordinate the individual to the state.

We have seen how Locke, by carrying into the postulates of the *Second Treatise* the implicit assumptions of class differential rationality and rights reached an ambiguous theory of differential membership in civil society, a theory which justified a class state from postulates of equal individual natural rights. The ambiguity about membership concealed the contradiction in his individualism, in which full individuality for some was produced by consuming the individuality of others. Locke could not have been conscious that the individuality he championed was at the same time a denial of individuality. Such consciousness was not to be found in men who were just beginning to grasp the great possibilities of individual freedom that lay in the advancement of capitalist society. The contradiction was there, but it was impossible for them to recognize it, let alone to resolve it. Locke was indeed at the fountainhead of English liberalism. The greatness of seventeenth-century liberalism was its assertion of the free rational individual as the criterion of the good society; its tragedy was that this very assertion was necessarily a denial of individualism to half the nation.

The social and political norms embodied in this ideal state of nature were given a sharper outline through contrast with another model condition, the state of war. The identifying marks here were a "declared design of force" aimed at reducing someone to the "absolute" power of another, and the absence of a "common superior on earth to appeal to for relief." While the state of nature was confined to a purely pre-civil stage, the state of war represented an aberration potentially present in both the ideal state of nature and civil society, an aberration in the sense that it destroyed the distinctive element of community common to both: the agreement to live by a common law, the law of nature in the one case, the positive law of the state in the other.

The next step in Locke's argument has always presented puzzling problems in interpretation. Did Locke conceive of political society as originating in the state nature or in the state of war? If the first explanation is adopted the individual's decision to enter political society appears either inexplicable or superfluous. For if political society is an improvement over nature what are we to make of Locke's description of the state of nature as idyllic? If the natural condition were generally harmonious, peaceful, and rational, why leave it? If it is marred only by "inconveniences," is this sufficient cause for choosing another mode of life? On the other hand, if political society is to be deduced from the state of war, how is it possible to resist the logic of Hobbes and its conclusion that political society necessarily involves a structure of power and authority sufficient to overcome anarchy and its recurrent possibility? Since most interpretations have assumed that Locke derived political society from one or the other of these conditions, they have concluded that his political state was achieve despite the careless reasoning of its author—which to rank Locke as a philosopher less by grace than for his good works More it has been fashionable to argue, especially among those who find Lockian political society originating in the state of war that Locke is really Hobbes in liberal clothing—which is sort of political version of the Baconfinkedspear controversy.

These interpretations appear to be faulty because they fail to pay sufficiently close attention to Locke's language. What Locke did was to interject in third condition, one distinct from what he called the "perfect state of nature" and the state of war. For purposes of clarity we shall designate it be 'fallen state of nature' because it has certain suggestive similarities to Foreltsch's distinction between the Christian conception of the natural law haeavailing before the fall from grace and the "fallen" natural law regnant war the sinful state which followed. Were it not for the corruption and viciousness of degenerate men, there would be no need of any other [society] no necessity that men should separate from this great and natural community and by positive agreements combine into smaller and divided associations.

That Locke meant to convey the impression of a different situation from that in the ideal state of nature, and yet one not to be confounded with the that in the ideal state of war, is indicated by the ominous language which he employed in repeating a plausible context for the contract. The natural condition, he tells us, is "full of fears and continual dangers," and "the greater part' of its inhabitants, far from being rational interpreters of the law of nature, as we had been led to suppose, are described as "no strict observers of equity and success. Men are impelled towards civil society because they are anxiety-trodden, "uncertain" about their rights, "full of fears." But since they are having the fallen state of nature—for the ideal state by definition has no inconveniences"—their search for a better arrangement will of necessity be guided by knowledge of the ideal condition; that is, by the norms which allow them to recognize the "deficiencies" of the fallen state. In short, the 'defects' that rendered the fallen state intolerable were cognizable only in the "remedies" for the fallen condition. These are: a common law, a method for impartial judgment, and an enforcing power: and all three hark back to arrangements which had been in force in the ideal state.

Citizenship and the Constitutional State

Locke's famous objection to the Hobbesian argument that individuals could only find a 'peaceful and commodious' life with one another if they were governed by the dictates of an indivisible sovereign, anticipated the whole tradition of protective democracy. He said of this type of argument: 'This is to think that men are so foolish that they take care to avoid what mischief's may be done them by polecats, or foxes, but are content, nay think it safety, to be devoured by lions". In other words, it is hardly credible that people who do not fully trust each other would place their trust in an all-powerful ruler to look after their interests. Locke approved of the revolution and settlement of 1688 in England, which imposed certain constitutional limits on the authority of the Crown. He rejected the notion of a great state pre-eminent in all spheres. For him, the institution of government can and should be conceived as an 'instrument' for the defense of the 'life, liberty and estate' of its citizens; that is, government's raison detat is the protection of individuals' rights as laid down by God's will and as enshrined in law.

Locke thought, as Hobbes had done, that the establishment of the political world followed from the prior existence of individuals endowed with natural rights. Like Hobbes, he was concerned about what form legitimate government should take and about the conditions for security, peace and freedom. But the way he conceived of these things was considerably different. In the important second of the *Two Treatises of Government* Locke starts with the proposition that individuals are originally in a state of nature, a 'State of perfect Freedom to order their Actions, and dispose of their Possessions and Persons as they think fit, within the bounds of the Law of Nature, without asking leave, or depending upon the will of any other Man'. This state of nature – the basic form of human association ' is a state of liberty' but not 'a state of license'. Individuals are bound by duty to God and governed only by the law of nature. The law of nature specifies basic principles of morality: individuals should not take their own lives; they should try to preserve each other and should not infringe upon one another's liberty. The law can be grasped by human reason but it is the creation of God, the 'infinitely wise Maker'.

Within the state of nature, men are free and equal because reason makes them capable of rationality, of following the law of nature. They enjoy natural rights. The right of governing one's affairs and enforcing the law of nature against transgressors is presupposed, as is the obligation to respect the rights of others. Individuals have the right to dispose of their own labor and to possess property. The right to property is a right to 'life, liberty and estate', though Locke also uses 'property' in the narrower sense to mean the exclusive use of objects.

Locke argues that adherence to the law of nature ensures that the state of nature is not a state of war. However, the natural rights of individuals are not always safeguarded in the state of nature because of existence and occurrence of certain 'inconveniences' exist: not all individuals fully respect the rights of others; when it is left to each individual to enforce the law of nature there are too many judges and hence conflicts of interpretation about the meaning of the law; and when people are loosely organized they are vulnerable to aggression from abroad. The central 'inconvenience' suffered can be summarized as the inadequate regulation of property in its broad sense: the right to' life, liberty and estate'. Property is prior to both society and the state; and the difficulty of its regulation is the critical reason which compels 'equally free men' to the establishment of both. Thus, the remedy for the inconveniences of the state of nature is an agreement or contract to create, first, an independent society and, secondly, a political society or government. The distinction between these two agreement is important, for it makes clear that authority is bestowed by individuals in society on government for the purpose of pursuing the ends of the governed; and should these ends fail to be represented adequately, the final judges are the people – the citizens of the state – who can dispense both with their deputies and, if need be, with the existing form of government itself.

In Locke's opinion, it should be stressed, the formation of the state does not signal the transfer of the subjects' rights to the state. The rights of law-making and low enforcement (legislative and executive rights) are transferred, but the whole process is conditional upon the state adhering to its essential purpose: the preservation of 'life, liberty and estate'. Sovereign power remains ultimately with the people. The legislative body enacts rules as the people's agent in accordance with the law of nature, and the executive power (to which Locke also tied the judiciary) enforces the legal system. This separation of powers was important because: it may be too great a temptation to humane frailty apt to grasp at Power, for the same Persons who have the power of making laws, to have also in their hands the power to execute them, whereby they may exempt themselves from obedience to the laws they make, and suit the law, both in its making and execution, to their own private advantage, and thereby come to have a distinct interest from the rest of the community, contrary to the end of society and government.

Thus, the integrity and ultimate ends of society require a constitutional state in which public power is legally circumscribed and divided. Locke believed in the desirability of a constitutional monarchy holding executive power and a parliamentary assembly holding the rights of legislation, although he did not think this was the only form of government and his views are compatible with a variety of other conceptions of political institutions.

The government rules and its legitimacy is sustained by the consent of individuals. Consent is a crucial and difficult notion in Locke's writings. It could be interpreted to suggest that only the continually active personal agreement of individuals would be sufficient to ensure a government's authority and legitimacy. However, Locke seems to have thought of the active consent of individuals as being crucial only to the initial inauguration of a legitimate state. Thereafter, consent ought to follow from majority decisions of 'the people's representatives, so long as they, the trustees of the governed, maintain the original contract and its covenants to guarantee 'life, liberty and estate'. If they honour the contract there is a duty on the part of the people to obey the law. It the government flout the terms of the contract with a series of tyrannical political acts, rebellion to form a new government, Locke contended, might not only be unavoidable but justified.

Political activity for Locke is instrumental; it secures the framework or conditions for freedom so that the private ends of individuals might be met in civil society. The creation of a political community or government is the burden individuals have to bear to secure their ends. Thus, membership of a political community, i.e., citizenship bestows upon the individual both responsibilities and rights, duties and powers, constraints and liberties. In relation to Hobbes's ideas, this was a most significant and radical view. For it helped inaugurate one of the most central tenets of modern European liberalism; that is, that the state exists to safeguard the rights and liberties of citizens who are ultimately the best judges of their own interests; and that accordingly the state must be restricted in scope and constrained in practice in order to ensure the maximum possible freedom of every citizen. In most respects it was Locke's rather than Hobbes's they that helped lay the foundation for the development of liberalism and prepared the way for the tradition of popular representative government. Compared to Hobbes, Locke's influence on the world of practical politics has been considerable.

Locke's writings seem to point in a number of directions at once. They suggest the importance of securing the rights of individuals, popular sovereignty, majority rule, a division of powers within the state, constitutional monarchy and a representative system of parliamentary government: a direct anticipation of key aspects of British government as it developed in the nineteenth and early twentieth centuries, and of the central tenets of the modern representative state. But, at best, most of these ideas are only in rudimentary form, and it is certain that Locke did not foresee many of the vital components of democratic representative government, for instance, competitive parties, party rule and the maintenance of political liberties irrespective of class, sex, colour and creed. It is not a condition of legitimate government or government by consent, in Locke's account, that there be regular periodic elections of a legislative assembly, let alone universal suffrage. Locke would almost certainly not have dissented from a franchise based strictly on the property holdings of male adults. Moreover, he did not develop a detailed account of what the limits might be to state interference in people's lives and under what conditions civil disobedience is justified. He thought that political power was held 'on trust' by and for the people, but failed to specify adequately who were to count as 'the people' and under what conditions 'trust' should be bestowed. He certainly did not think that such power might be exercised directly by the citizens themselves, i.e., in some form of direct or self-government. While Locke was unquestionably one of the first great champions of liberalism – and although his works clearly stimulated the development of both liberal and democratic government, what we may call liberal democracy, especially its 'protective' variant – he cannot, in the end, be considered a democrat without careful qualification.

Natural Rights in Locke

Locke's claim as a natural rights theorist is generally thought to be much clearer than Hobbes's. Locke's claim is, in important ways, less clear than Hobbes's; particularly, in that Locke, after, beginning with a beautiful set of natural rights, which are said to be effectively sanctioned as well as limited by natural law, then goes on to override one of the most important limits (the limit on infinite appropriation), thus removing the equality of natural rights, and ends by admitting that natural law is a wholly ineffective guarantor of natural rights, which therefore lose the original character he had given them.

The grounds for claiming Locke as a genuine natural rights philosopher are apparently clear: (i) His natural rights are presented as effective rights; rights which others have a natural obligation to respect (ii) His natural rights, being less wholesale than Hobbes's, are more meaningful and more specific (e.g. the right of private appropriation and the right of inheritance). (iii) Locke uses natural rights to establish a case for limited government, and to set up a right to revolution. In these respects, Locke's natural rights are different from, even opposite to, Hobbes's natural right. All these differences may be said to be based on the logically prior difference that Locke derives his natural rights from natural law: it is 'Reason, which is that Law', that establishes the rights and the corresponding obligations: whereas for Hobbes the rights are logically prior, and the natural law is derived from them. Yet when

Locke's natural rights are examined more closely, they have more in common with Hobbes's than is generally allowed.

(i) The Right to Life

The first natural right we hear of is the right 'to make use of those things, that were necessary or useful to his being or serviceable for his subsistence and means of his preservation'. This right is later called the right a man has to subsist and enjoy the conveniences of life. Here, as in the *Second Treatise,* Locke asserts a natural right to preservation of one's life, and hence to the means of subsistence and even 'conveniences' And this right to life and the means of life is deduced from the need or 'strong desire' every man has 'of reserving his life and being'. The first and strongest desire being that of self-preservation, that is the foundation of a right to the inferior creatures, for the particular support and use of each individual person himself.

Is this deduction of right from the strong desire of self-preservation at all different from Hobbes's deduction? There is a difference, and it is characteristic of Locke: he deduces the right not directly from the fact of desire but from the intention of the Creator, which intention is deduced from the fact of desire.

A second right is deduced in the same indirect way from observed desire. The natural right of children to inherit the possessions of their parents is deduced from the strong desire men have of propagating their kind, and continuing themselves in their posterity. If this desire is to be fulfilled, children must be allowed to have a right to a share of their parents' property. It is the strong desire that gives the right, but apparently only because God planted the desire in men.

(ii) The Right to Freedom

The *Second Treatise* opens with an assertion of a natural right to freedom from the arbitary wills of others. It is a right not to be interfered with, except when one has transgressed natural law: a right of freedom to order their actions, and dispose of their possessions and persons as they think fit, within the bounds of the law of nature, without asking leave, or depending upon the will of any other man. This is first introduced simply as a freedom, but is later referred to as a right. From this right follows the right to execute the Law of Nature, which includes two distinct Rights the one of punishing the crime for restraint, the other of taking reparation. There also follows the right to destroy an aggressor who would take away my liberty.

The basic right to freedom is deduced (a) negatively from the intentions of the Creator and (b) positively from the need for self-preservation. Thus (a), since men are fundamentally members of the same species, and since there is no evidence that some of the species were intended to be subordinate to others, they must be assumed to be equal in jurisdiction, equally free from the will of others. And (b), 'This freedom from absolute, arbitrary power is so necessary to, and closely joined with a man's preservation, that he cannot part with it, but by what forfeits his preservation and life together.

We may now ask how different is Locke's natural right to freedom from Hobbes's natural right? Both are deduced from the need for self-preservation. And the equality of natural right is in both cases deduced from the species-similarity, i.e. the organic or mechanical sameness of the beings; both writers start from the assumption that men are equal in need and capacity, and deduce natural equal right from that equality.

The great difference, of course, is that whereas Hobbes finds a natural right of every man to every thing, Locke's natural right to freedom is limited by the law of nature, which teaches that 'no one ought to harm another in his life, health, liberty, or possessions.' It is because 'the state of nature has a law of nature to govern it, which obliges every one that men do not need, and cannot be allowed, the right to every thing.

A further difference, less often noticed, is that Locke's natural right to defend oneself, although based like Hobbes's on the need for self-preservation, is not entirely inalienable as Hobbes's is the freedom from absolute, arbitrary power, which Locke finds is so necessary to a man's preservation, can be forfeited, as can the right to life itself, by the commission of some act that deserves death. From this it appears that the source of Locke's natural right is not the need for self-preservation but is the moral law of nature which is superior to the right to life.

(iii) The Right to Property

Let us look finally at Locke's natural right to individual appropriation of the fruits of the earth and the earth itself. For Locke, a property in a thing is a right to exclude others from it, to use, enjoy, consume, or exchange it. The purpose of the chapter on property of the *Second Treatise* is to show that individuals have a natural right to property, a right prior to civil society and government, and not dependent on the consent of others to it. The right to property is deduced from (a) the right of self-preservation, and (b) the property in, or right, to, one's own person—'the labour of his body, and the work his hands, we may say, are properly his. The right to property is limited, by this derivation, to as much as leaves enough for others, since all have an equal right to subsistence.

Locke turned this limited natural right into an unlimited natural right, and justified the appropriation of all the land by some men, in amounts exceeding the requirements of their comfortable subsistence, leaving others with no land on which to labour for themselves. This extended right is said to be established without express compact. But it does require one kind of consent, i.e. tacit consent to the use of money, which consent Locke assumes men are naturally capable of giving. The extended property right is not, as pure a natural right as the others, for the others do not require any consent. And it is less pure in another respect: it is established by means of utilitarian argument to productivity. It is the greater productivity of labour on appropriated land that justifies its appropriation beyond the amount which would leave as much and as good for others. Because of the greater productivity, those who are left without any land can get a better subsistence than they would have had if no land were appropriated.

But if the extended property right is less pure than the other rights, because it requires consent, it is none the less natural. It follows from the nature of man, because Locke puts into the nature of man the capacity of making agreements and the desire of having more than he needs. The latter desire, Locke admits, is not present in the most primitive stage of human life: there was a time, in the beginning, when this desire was absent. But the desire did arise and flourish in the state of nature: it came with the use of money, which inaugurated the second stage of the state of nature.

It has often been pointed out that Locke's state of nature is a social state, that his natural man is social man. What is more to the point is that his natural man is a man with a socially acquired desire for more wealth than he can use, 'more land than he himself can use the product of, to draw money to him by the sale of the product. Locke's natural man is bourgeois man: his rational man is man with a propensity to capital accumulation. He is even an infinite appropriator.

Because Locke's natural men are capable of understanding the law of nature, and because they desire not only to preserve their lives, and not only to maintain their comfortable living, but also to accumulate property beyond the amount required for such living, their natural rights are both less and more than the natural rights of Hobbes's men. Less, in that Locke's men are forbidden by the law of nature to invade the lives, liberties, and properties of other men; more, in that they have a natural right, which others must respect, to unlimited accumulation of wealth.

Locke, then, seems to have reverted to a more traditional notion of natural right, in postulating the social nature of man and hence the existence of a law of nature. It is the law of nature that both limits men's natural rights and, by imposing obligation on the others to respect rights, makes the rights more effective than Hobbes's rights. But Locke has not returned to the traditional natural law: he has put into it quite a new content, the right to unlimited accumulation.

And because he has done so, he is forced to admit that men are not naturally as social as he first said they were. He is forced to admit that men are naturally so contentious and invasive that they do not follow the law of nature. If the logical consequences of this admission are allowed, all the effective differences between Locke's natural rights and Hobbes's disappear, for the differences all depended on Locke's assertion that natural law limits do confine men's natural rights and do render them naturally effective. It is perhaps not too much to say that, as soon as Locke had shown how the original natural law limits on private appropriation were made ineffective by men's consent within the state of nature to the use of money, he logically destroyed his natural law system. It might be better to say that in thus subordinating natural Jaw to natural consent, he revealed that the natural propensity to unlimited accumulation was inconsistent with his natural law. In spite of this, Locke maintained the reality of his natural law. He had to do so, because it was only from the natural law which gave every man the right not to be harmed by others, that he deduced the limited powers of governments and the right of revolution against arbitrary government. Only if men's rightful natural powers are limited, as Locke limits them by natural law, can it be argued, as Locke argues, that the government's power is limited.

Property

Central to the political thought of Locke, is the concept of property, which immodestly said, 'I have nowhere found more clearly explained, than in a book entitled, Two *Treatises of Government.*' In the *Second Treatise* Locke argues that the reason that men set up government, and therefore, the purpose for which government exist, is 'the Preservation of their Property'. Exactly what Locke means by property is a complex matter. In so far as he means land and goods, he devoted an important chapter to discussing what gives an individual the right to claim sole ownership of a piece of land. This is a problem, for Locke begins by accepting the traditional biblical view that God gave the world 'to mankind in common.' He then argues that the right to self-preservation, and the implied need to consume or use the fruits of the earth, lead inevitably to individual ownership. He even argues that cultivation and use necessarily depend upon individual possession, as if common ownership was synonymous with neglect – a view taken, not surprisingly, by many advocates of enclosure:

> God gave the world to men in common; but it cannot be supposed he meant it should always remain common and uncultivated. He gave it to the use of the industrious and rational. Self–preservation, the need to consume, and finally labour, are what create the right to property. A man who works his patch of earth is thereby entitled to its product. A man owns his labour, because 'every man has a property in his own person', and so 'the labour of his body, and the work of his hands, we may say, are properly his.

The right to property derived from labour implies, however, a corresponding limitation: a man may not own more than he can cultivate through his own labour. This limitation is reinforced by a second and similar one: we may not own anything that we let go to waste, for 'Nothing was made by God for man to spoil or destroy'. Finally, the equal right of all to self-preservation implies; that there must be 'enough, and as good left in common for others'. Such a justificatory theory of ownership is strongly egalitarian in principle, and the assertion that labors in itself confers a right to ownership is particularly radical in its implications.

But Locke immediately retreats from these radical implications of what he has written. The limitations on property ownership which he has set out, he then negates, principally by the device of money: the invention of money introduced by consent. For money enables an owner to sell off such products, as he cannot himself consume; in this way he evades the limitations imposed by the criteria of use and non-spoilage. Money does not spoil, and is always useful. As for the labour limitation, it vanishes almost as soon as it is introduced. In the second of the paragraphs in which Locke discusses the rights conferred by labour, he makes it embarrassingly clear that he does not really mean what he says: 'Thus the grass my horse has bit; the turfs my servant has cut; and the ore I have digg'd in any place where I have a right to them in common with others, become my property, without the assignation or consent of any body'. Apart from the oddity of assuming the existence of servants in which is supposed to be the 'state of nature', Locke assumes, naturally and without feeling any need to argue the point, that a servant does not own the fruits of his/her labour: either employer does. Just because I 'own' my labour, I can sell it, and its product to another. The 'right' goes with the property (labour), not with the person who labours.

The third requirement, that there should be 'enough, and as good' left for others, imposes no restraint on accumulation, since the increased productivity of privately-owned or 'enclosed' land is of greater benefit to mankind than if it were left 'lyeing waste in common'. God created men and gave them the world in common. By this, Locke meant not positive but negative communism, that is, the world was not a collective human property to be used for collective well-being, but rather it belonged to no one and was available to all for their individual use. God's gift entailed both rights and duties. Every man had a right to mix his labour with nature, and to use its fruits to satisfy his needs consistently with a due regard for others. Since God wanted man 'to be fruitful and multiply', every man also had a duty to develop the earthly resources to the full and maximize the conveniences of life. As Locke put it, 'God gave the world to man in common, but it cannot be supposed he meant it should always remain common and uncultivated. He gave it to the use of the industrious and rational'. Locke's juxtaposition of 'Industrious and 'Rational' is striking.

A truly rational society established the institution of private property and provided incentives for industry and the accumulation of wealth, without both of which men could not discharge their duty to develop the earth's resources and create a prosperous society. Locke was deeply haunted by the idea of waste and wanted all the material potentialities of the earth to be fully realized. The duty to be fruitful and multiply 'contains in it the improvement too of arts and sciences', and hence a truly rational society encouraged these as well.

Locke analyzed English colonialism in America in terms of his theory of man and society. He argued that since the American Indians roamed freely over the land and did not enclose it, it was not 'their land'; they used it as one would use a common land, but they had no property in it. The land was therefore free, empty, vacant, wild and could be taken over without their consent. This was odd for, although the Indians did not build fences or barriers to demarcate their land, they knew what land was their and what belonged to their neighbors, and had thus enclosed it in a manner intelligible to them. That was not acceptable to Locke, who only recognized the European sense of enclosure. Even then, Locke faced a difficulty. Whilst some Indians did not enclose their land in Locke's sense, the coastal Indians who lived in villages and engaged in no sedentary agriculture did enclose. English settlers were covetous of these lands and sought to take them over to avoid the hard labour of clearing land themselves. They had argued that although the Indians enclosed and owned the land, their practice of letting it rot and compost every three years for soil enrichment demonstrated that they did not make rational use of it. Locke agreed that enclosure was not enough. He observed:

> ...if either the grass or his inclosure rotted on the ground, or the fruit of his planting perished without gathering, and laying up, this part of Earth, notwithstanding his Enclosure, was still to be looked on as waste, and might be the possession of any other.

Even when Indians enclosed and cultivated land, they were not industrious and advanced enough to make the best possible use of it and produce as much as the English could. Indeed, since they produced not even one hundredth of what the latter could, they were for all practical purposes guilty of wasting the land. In Locke's view, the trouble with the Indians was that they had very few desires and were easily contented. Since they lacked the desire to accumulate wealth, engaged in commerce, produce for an international market, and so on, they had no interest in exploiting the earth's potential to the fullest. In this regard the English settlers were vastly superior and had a much better claim to the land. After all, since God Himself had imposed on man the duty to maximize the conveniences of life, the English had both a right and a duty to replace the Indians.

But even this was not the end of the problem. Locke had hitherto discussed America as if it were no more than a mass of land, and the Indian tribes as if they were no more than a collection of individuals, vacant lands in Locke's sense existed in several parts of Europe as well, but he would not allow their colonization because they fell within the boundaries of specific political societies, whose independence and territorial integrity had to be respected under international law. The vacant lands in a political society were under the jurisdiction of the law of the land and not available to all mankind but contended that this could not be true of the Indians. Their vacant lands could not be seen as part of their territory, and hence available for colonization. He acknowledged that the Indians called themselves nations and were ruled by elected kings, but argued that it was a misleading way of describing their society, which was not really a political society at all.

For Locke, Indians were 'wild' like savages, and devoid of the capacity to raise themselves unaided to the level of the 'civilized part of mankind'. Since they lacked the basic drive to accumulate wealth and engage in international commerce, without which property, the arts and sciences and political society were impossible, they would if left to themselves, forever remain in the state of nature. The English guardianship was indispensable for their historical transition to civility and civilization.

Locke distinguished two modes of colonization, one based on 'conquest by sword' and represented by the Spanish, the other based on 'commerce' and represented by the English. He unreservedly condemned the former and welcomed the latter. Spanish colonialism violated the natural rights of the natives, and additionally failed to establish a civilized way of life in the colonies. In Locke's view it was also self-contradictory, for the colonial expansion was motivated by a desire for economic gain, whereas the right of conquest on which it rested 'extends only to the lives of the conquered' and did not give the conqueror a right over the latter's property. English colonialism was not open to these objections. It respected the natural equality of Indians, it was relatively peaceful, it used force only when they did not voluntarily part with their vacant and wasted lands, it civilized or morally uplifted them and drew them into an economically interdependent world, and it furthered the interests of mankind. Locke had not doubt at all that in colonizing America, the English performed the remarkable moral miracle of serving God, mankind, Indians and themselves.

Locke assumed a natural identity between individual profit and the general welfare. It turns out, too, that unequal property ownership, like government itself, developed by consent. For since money only has value by consent, 'it is plain, that Men have agreed to disproportionate and unequal Possession of the Earth'. In this way, in the course of a few paragraphs, Locke moves from egalitarian premises to anti-egalitarian conclusions. Later on, he took a further step away from his original individualistic analysis by adding a further right that 'every man is born with 'a right, before any other Man, to inherit, with his brethren, his father's goods'.

Clearly, if Locke was to produce a defense of existing property and property rights, his conclusions were necessary. But why then does he choose such an obviously contradictory starting point, and proceed by such unconvincing routes? Here, we find the conflict between Locke the theorist, anxious to explore fundamentals, and Locke the ideologist. But it is also a conflict between his concern with universal, individual rights, which is an inheritance from the time of the Levelers, and his need to endorse Whig orthodoxy, which defended property regardless of the gross inequality of its distribution.

Locke's treatment of the notion of 'consent' is very similar. Consciously or not, he follows Hobbes in arguing that the legitimacy of government derives from the fact that it is set up by agreement among persons who voluntarily divest themselves of their natural liberty. But Locke undermines the principle of individual consent by suggesting that government can be set up by the consent of a majority. Further dilutions follow. In response to the criticism that few societies are actually created in this manner and that men are in fact 'born under Government', Locke replies that 'the consent of free-men' is given by each individually as he comes of age, which is why it goes unnoticed. A child, he is bound logically to admit, 'is born a subject of no country or Government'.

But Locke knows very well that few societies require a formal or explicit declaration of consent or allegiance: he therefore introduces the notion of tacit consent, which is judged to be given by a person's mere presence in a particular state: 'in effect, it reaches as far as the very being of any one within the territories of that government'. Thus, the fundamental requirement of individual consent turns out to mean very little in practice. Even by 'traveling freely on the Highway,' a man 'doth thereby given his tacit consent'. It is disturbing to find a key democratic idea like consent so diluted and distorted so early in the evolution of liberal thought.

Returning now, to Locke's use of the term property', we find that it is given two meanings, one broad and one narrow. But at other points in the Second Treatise Locke suggests that by property he means 'Lives, Liberties and Estates'. However, it is by no means as certain, as Laslett suggests, that the term is usually to be read in this latter sense. Section 138 is one of the clearest examples of the term being used ambiguously. In it, Locke repeats his view that 'the preservation of property' is the end of government, and that for which men enter into society', but this time without specifying the wider meaning. He then goes on to speak of property synonymously with estates'. In this section he also makes the point that if men enter into society to preserve their property, this implies that they have some property to preserve.

Now if Locke here is speaking of estates alone, rather than life and liberty as well, then the inference is that the state exists for property-owners rather than for all. Locke's meaning is unclear, and it is therefore, quite fair for Macpherson to argue that 'men without estate or goods, that is, without property in the ordinary sense, are rightfully both in and not in civil society', since the ambiguity is there in Locke himself. It is any case indicative of his thoroughly bourgeois frame of mind that he should think of life, liberty and labour as essentially possessions, and subsume them under the single heading of 'property'. It says much about liberalism that the philosopher who is often said to be its 'founder' or 'father' should have placed property, even as a metaphor, at the heart of his philosophy of government and human rights.

The relation between freedom and laws is another major issue on which Locke again tries to have it both ways. On this issue Hobbes is absolutely clear: freedom consists in the absence of external restraints or impediments, in 'the silence of the law'. Locke's account, by comparison, is totally confused. On the one hand he values the Hobbesian type of liberty: 'A liberty to follow my own will in all things, where the rule prescribes not.' Yet in the same sentence he suggests that the rule of law is itself a form of freedom: 'freedom of men under government, is to have a standing rule to live by, common to every one of that society and made by the legislative power erected in it'. Later he extends this line of argument by suggesting that law itself is not really a restriction: 'that ill deserves the name of confinement which hedges us in only from bogs and precipices. There is a good case to be made for saying that law and liberty are not inherently in conflict, but it is not made by Locke, since he wishes also to argue that a concern for liberty requires that laws should be kept to a minimum.

The confusions and ambiguities in the *Second Treatise* over property, labour rights, consent and freedom, are confusions and ambiguities at the heart of liberalism. For they reveal simultaneously both the democratic, egalitarian and even anarchist potentialities in the liberal idea of individual rights, together with the bourgeois liberal's anxious recoil from those alarming tendencies. In the 1660s, when his political views were more authoritarian, Locke had written of the maxim vex popular, vex die, 'Surely we have been taught by a most unhappy lesson how doubtful, how fallacious is this maxim.' By 1680 the threat of 'popular tyrannies' had long receded, and it was hardly necessary to say that by 'the people' was meant only the political nation of already enfranchised property owners. In case it was Locke's friend James Tyrell spelt it out: 'when I make use of the word people, I do not mean the vulgar or mixed multitude, but in the state of nature the whole body of free-men and women, especially, the fathers and masters of families; and in the civil state all degrees of men, as well the nobility and clergy as the common people'.

Cranston has referred to Locke's 'revolutionary liberalism', but this is only appropriate if taken as a reference to Locke's identification with the events of 1688-89. most of Locke's opinions were not notably radical by the standards of his time. *His Letter on Toleration* is conventional and restricted in its recommendations. Locke rules out toleration for Catholics on the ground that they owe their allegiance to 'another prince' and for atheists since 'promises, covenants, and oaths, which are the bonds of human society' supposedly have no hold on them. Nor should anyone be allowed to preach with impunity 'things which manifestly undermine the foundations of society'. What such doctrines might be, Locke does not say, but such a limitation could be interpreted in a very restrictive manner. Locke's *Letter*, wrote a recent historian of toleration, was 'neither as original nor liberal as several earlier defenses.

Even the momentous events of 1688-89, Locke is concerned to stress, were not so much a revolution as the preservation of the 'Just and Natural Rights' of 'the People of England', which saved the nation when it was on the very brink of slavery and ruin'. It was James II who had threatened innovation, while the Whigs had successfully defended the traditional rights of the people. But this had involved resistance, and Locke in common with all the Whigs was torn between the need to offer a theory of legitimate resistance to 'tyranny', while ensuring that such a theory gave no encouragement to any further popular uprisings, like those of the 1640s, and that of Monmouth in 1685. caution and compromise were the keynotes of Lockean liberalism. Even Lord Acton, who worked in the grand tradition of Whig history, and who regarded 'the Revolution of 1688, as 'the greatest thing done by the English nation', could not muster much enthusiasm for Locke and his party: 'The very essence of the new Party was compromise, they were a little disappointing, a little too fond of the halt-way house. Their philosophy, or rather their philosopher, John Locke, is always reasonable and sensible, but diluted and pedestrian and poor.'

The 'Glorious Revolution' of 1688 came to be seen as the central and greatest achievement of the Whigs. The protracted political conflicts of the century had finally been resolved in a gratifyingly moderate manner: the tendency towards absolutism and Catholicism had been decisively checked, while the equally frightening prospect of popular republicanism had also been averted, once Monmouth's rising with its alarming echoes of the Levellers, had been defeated and savagely punished. The way was clear for a century of more or less undisputed dominance by the landed aristocracy and gentry.

The process by which this occurred was not particularly glorious, nor did it amount to a revolution. It was more likely a nearly bloodless coup detat engineered by a united ruling class, against the final Stuart bid for absolutism. But by calling this coup a revolution, the prestige of radicalism was appropriated for an essentially conservative achievement, and radicalism itself was partially disarmed. Nor did the Whigs wish to set any kind of precedent. As Bruce rightly said, a century later, 'the great men who influenced the conduct of affairs at that great event, were anxious 'to make the Revolution a parent of settlement, and not a nursery of future revolutions.' The majority of the Whigs were from the beginning determined to minimize the radical implications of what they had done. They shrank from any outright assertion of popular or even parliamentary sovereignty. Therefore the fiction was maintained that James II had not been deposed, but had abdicated, leaving the throne vacant and needing to be filled. It was only the radicals, who in this case included Locke, who wished to define the displacement of James on such general grounds as the ultimate sovereignty of the people, or the right of resistance of tyranny. And not even they wished to revive Milton's argument that the people had the right to change their government or form of government whenever they chose. So for nearly a quarter of a century after 1688 the 'Glorious Revolution' was as much a source of weakness as of strength of the Whigs. They had constantly to rebuff Tory accusations that what they had done, or claimed to have done, provided not just the political nation but also the 'lower orders' with a license for disaffection and rebellion. So even Locke's limited and qualified arguments were too radical for the ascendant Whig oligarchy. From the very moment of their triumph in 1689 there began a withdrawal from the principles commonly associated with the term 'Whig', until with Walpole's ascendancy in the 1720s and 1730s, nothing remained but an appetite for power, office and their many advantages.

The Whig triumph in 1689 nor the establishment of their ascendancy after 1715, led to any further political progress. In fact their success resulted in political reaction. For example, the tendency in the first half of the seventeenth century to resolve electoral disputes in favors of a wider rather than a narrower franchise was not sustained after the Restoration, and was, decisively reversed after 1688. At the same time a considerable number of borough with tiny franchises were created. Attempts were made in 1696 and 1729 to freeze electorates; but the most blatant Whig attack on the still very limited right to vote was the City Elections Act of 1725, whereby at a stroke 3,000 freemen of the City of London were deprived of their voting rights, thus greatly enhancing the power of the rich City aldermen.

Meanwhile, the Septennial Act of 1716 had extended the length of each parliament, including the one that passed the Act, from three to seven years; and in 1721 Walpole favored a Bill to reintroduce parliaments with no limit on their duration, although Lord Molesworth, an 'old' Whig had pronounced 'frequent parliaments' to be an absolutely 'fundamental part of the constitution'. The logic of these tendencies, together with the government's extensive methods for the control and management of parliament and elections, was that an increasing number of parliamentary seats went uncontested, particularly the country seats. It was Walpole's achievement to turn the country into what was effectively a one-party state, in which the opposition could not hope to match the government's vast powers of manipulation and patronage.

Meanwhile admiring foreigners and self-congratulatory natives praised the extent of British freedom and toleration. But both these had their limits, which the Whigs did nothing to extend. The Whigs were supposed to be committed to the principle of toleration for dissenters. Yet Walpole evaded every pressure from dissenters to remove some of the civic disabilities from which they continued to suffer. And it was Walpole who, to prevent satirical attacks upon himself, introduced in 1737 the system of censorship over the theatre which was then not finally abolished until 230 years later.

It may perhaps be asked what this dismal record of political stagnation has to do with the principles of liberalism. Surely, it might be said, what is illustrated here is the abandonment of Whig principles by those who called themselves Whigs – a phenomenon with many political parallels, and no more to be laid at the door of liberalism than, say, the crimes of Stalin are to be imputed to socialism or Marxism, per se. Two considerations weigh against this argument. The first is that in exploring and evaluating an ideology, we have always to consider not only its professed values and principles, but also those which it adherents exemplify in their lives and actions. The second is that practice affects principles, particularly in the case of a movement of ideas with a long history and a complex evolution.

Above all, there is continuity in relation to the issue of property. And where property is concerned, Whig practice is an important, and revealing as Whig theory. Not that there was a great disjunction between them. For while the Whigs might seem to have abandoned the old principle that those who own land should govern, they did not neglect to extend the rights of landowners. Their alliance with the moneyed men simply reflected their recognition that the forms of property and wealth were changing, and that land was no longer the only form of property of source of wealth and power. As Marx observed: 'the new landed aristocracy was the natural ally of the new bankocracy of newly-hatched high finance, and of the large manufactures, at that time dependent on protective duties. It was the Tories who identified themselves with landed property, while the more flexible Whigs emerged as the defenders of property in all its forms, commercial and financial as well landed.

The Whig hegemony inaugurates a golden age of property rights. Back in the days of the Commonwealth, 'elective parliaments' became the bulwark of property'. That is what they became after the Restoration. A great battery of new laws were passed which extended the rights of the propertied at the expense, directly or indirectly, of the traditional rights and customs of the poor majority of the people. The most striking demonstration of this was the great increase in the number of offences for which the prescribed penalty was death. These are estimated to have increased from about 50 in 1688, to over 200 by 1820 and almost all of them were offenses against property: 'A man was hanged for stealing one shilling, a boy of sixteen for stealing 3s.6d. And a penknife, a girl for a handkerchief. A boy of eleven was hanged for setting his master's house on fire. Many more were sentenced to transportation.' The ferocity of the British laws became a by-word, and Kenyon describes capital punishment in eighteenth-century England as 'not so much a way of government as a way of life, enforcing by fear an increasingly stratified class system.'

Just as significant was the extension of the rights of property-owners into areas where such exclusiveness was a novelty. The Game Laws of 1670 made it an offence for all except the very rich to kill birds and animals even on their own land, the basic qualification being an income of 100 a year from freehold property, fifty times greater than the property qualification needed to vote in a country election. The same set of laws gave to gamekeepers the right to search people's houses and confiscate weapons. Wild birds and animals, which had not been thought to 'belong' to anyone, and which had provided meat for the rural poor, were now declared to be the property of the large landowners. In this way some of the traditional rights of the poor were 'simply redefined as crimes: poaching, wood-theft, trespass'.

Even many aspects of what 'rational' economists and economic historians have always interpreted as 'improvement', such as the large-scale reclamation of the fens, were no gain to the poor and landless, who lost food resources as a result.

And this was generally true of enclosure. Daniel Defoe and William Petty, were among those who urged that the whole process should be speeded up by the passing of general acts for enclosure. This was not to happen until 1801, but Parliament was never reluctant to pass legislation for specific enclosures: 2,000 such acts were passed between 1750 and 1800, and another 900 in the following decade. Under these acts between six and seven million acres were enclosed, about a fifty of the whole land, and a quarter of all cultivated land. Two-thirds of that total was not waste, as writers like Locke implied, but land which was already cultivated and used under the old open field system. Legislation was needed for enclosure because landowners were usually unable to get villagers to agree voluntarily to the loss of their traditional common lands. It was little more than legalized robbery. The advance made by the eighteenth century shows itself in this, that the law itself now becomes the instrument by which the people's land is stolen. The Parliamentary robbery is that of 'Bills for Enclosure of Commons', in other words decrees by which the landowners grant themselves the people's land as private property, decrees of expropriation of the people. Enclosure was not a new phenomenon, of course. It had provoked much protest in the sixteenth and early seventeenth centuries. But the last parliamentary bid to restrain the process was made unsuccessfully in 1656. After that, Parliament reflected only the interests and ideology of the substantial property-owners.

The speed with which the process of enclosure went ahead after about 1760 reflects not only the power of property, but also the growing ascendancy of a new kind of economic rationality. It was economic in a very pure sense, in that it was only economic gains and losses which were taken into account: social gains and losses, being less measurable, were left out of the account. Modern economic historians, imbued with the same kind of rationality, have endorsed the view that enclosure was beneficial. The usual argument has then that enclosure, and hence the landlord, stand acquitted of most of the charges brought against them because enclosure greatly helped in the increase of output, so necessary in the age of growing population, and the expansion of cultivation and wider use of improved techniques helped to absorbed the rising labour force.

The Highland clearances of the late eighteenth and nineteenth centuries, and the consequent enforced emigration of thousands of the Highlanders to Canada and elsewhere, was no doubt a special case of enclosure. From the generally accepted axiom that those who had property should govern, it was not a long step to arguing that the function of government was the protection of property. Defoe argued this way in 1706:

> Here all the governments in the world began: the right of possession always had the right of government, which is the band and guard of that possession. Reason, thus finding itself possessed of property, dictated government for its regulation and security, and this is a right whose divinity cannot be disputed.

The theoretical justification for this was that the property alone gave a man the material basis of independence necessary if he was to act as a free person. Those without property were necessarily dependent, and could not therefore be relied on to vote freely. They were easily bribed with promises of money, food, or employment by unscrupulous political adventures or radical agitators. Hence, the poor constituted a threat to freedom as well as to property. An abiding fear and mistrust of the poor was the corollary of the dominant commitment of property.

Critics of English colonization have attacked Locke for his views private property. They argue that it violated the rights of the American Indians to their property and territorial integrity. The Indians had cultivated and lived on their land for centuries and it was their rightful inheritance. They had also established stable societies which, like their counterparts elsewhere, were entitled to non-interference by outsiders. England had no 'right or warrant' to enter into, let alone 'go and live in the heathen's country', and was acting in an immoral and un-Christian manner.

Locke, who had both a philosophical and a financial interest in the Americans, was greatly interested in the controversy. He asked the English settlers for information about the American Indian way of life, and built up an impressive collection of books dealing with the European exploration of the Americans. His philosophical interest sprang from the fact that unlike Hobbes's largely imaginary state of nature, the Indian way of life offered a realistic contrast to, and provided most valuable insights into the nature and structure of political society. Locke's interest was not entirely intellectual. His patron the Earl of Shafesbury had strong financial interests in the New World. Locke played an important part in formulating colonial policies. He was in no doubt that English colonization of North America was fully justified, and provided its most articulate and influential philosophical defense.

Locke stressed human equality yet justified the English subjugation of Indians, including annexation of their land. How could an egalitarian premises yield such patently inegalitarian conclusions? Only two explanations are possible. First, Locke's thought rested on a narrow view of human nature. For him, man was essentially rational; reason had a natural and uniform structure and mode of operation; reason was detachable from, and functioned best when insulated from feelings and passions; man had a natural desire to accumulate wealth and enjoy a life of plentiful material comforts; and so on. Judged by such a view of man, Indians appeared defective and not fully human. Locke was not wrong to assume that human beings shared several basic capacities, needs and desires in common. His mistake was twofold. First, his list of universal human capacities and desires was narrow, and uncritically universalized those characteristic of the Englishmen of his time. The desires to accumulate wealth, enjoy maximum comforts and master nature are historically contingent, and there is no obvious reason why all human beings should develop them or why these desires should be given the importance that Locke gave them. Again, Locke was right to stress human rationality, but wrong to think that reason is inherently calculating, utilitarian, result-oriented or concerned to obtain the maximum possible advantages from a given unit of human effort. Second, Locke did not appreciate that even the universally shared human capacities and desires are shaped, structured, related and valued differently in different societies. All men reason, but they do not do so in an identical manner, nor do they all dissociate reason from feelings and sentiments, nor do they all give reason the same importance.

Given these and related assumptions, it is easy to see how Locke deduced his defense of English colonialism from an egalitarian premises. Indians were human beings, and like the rest, entitled to protection of their basic rights and interests. This is why Locke condemned in the strongest possible terms the outrageous Spanish treatment of the Indians, and took great pains to show that English colonization was in their ultimate interest. Precisely because Indians were human beings, they were expected to live up to the rational and moral imperatives of their human status. Since they had not fully yet developed their rational capacity and lacked an adequate understanding of what it was to be human, they were not equipped to define their interest themselves and could not be allowed to lead their self-chosen way of life. Locke's principle of equality accepted them and other 'savage' people as equal objects of concern, but not as self-defining subjects entitled to full and equal determination. The manner in which Locke defined and defended equality thus had both egalitarian and inegalitarian implications, and both justified colonialism and regulated its excesses. It had an egalitarian form but its inegalitarian assumptions gave it an inegalitarian content, and it legitimized violence against the poor at home and the savages abroad provided, of course, that the violence did not exceed certain limits and served their long-term interests as defined by their masters.

Liberalism is full of strange paradoxes and reveals living contradictions. It offers one of the most inspiring statements of human equality, yet some of the greatest liberal philosophers justified colonialism with a clear conscience. Liberals condemned racist prejudices and misuse of political power in the colonies, but endorsed both the economic exploitation of the colonies and arrogant assertions of cultural superiority. The contradiction is not just between liberal thought and liberal practice, but within liberal thought itself. Liberalism is both egalitarian and inegalitarian, it stresses both the unity of mankind and the hierarchy of cultures, it is both tolerant and intolerant, peaceful and violent, pragmatic and dogmatic, skeptical and self-righteous. The origins of its contradictory impulses, the way it accommodates and reconciles them in different contexts, the tensions they create in liberal thought and practice, and so on, raise fascinating questions.

In normal cases, a contract may involve a surrender not merely of freedoms, but of rights – in exchange for rights of another kind. It is therefore open to someone to argue that the citizens of Locke's community have bargained away many of their rights in exchange for civil protection – perhaps even the rights to life, limb and property. Locke wished to avoid such a result – for he believed that natural rights set limits to government, thereby giving grounds for rebellion should they be violated. He argued, therefore, on grounds that are none too clear, that natural rights are inalienable: even if one seeks to bargain them away, one cannot succeed, since they are not the kind of thing that can be bargained.

There is another difficulty for social contract theories of Locke's variety. On what grounds do we infer the existence of a social contract in any given society? Certainly there is seldom, if ever, an explicit contract; and how can we infer an implicit contract in so complex a case? Locke's answer is that a civil society, when legitimate, is made so by the 'tacit consent' of its citizens, a consent which could be represented, for clarity's sake, in the form of an explicit compact defining the rights and duties of the parties in the manner of a contract at law. Unfortunately, as Hume pointed out in an essay on the 'Original Contract', the metaphor begins to look precarious. For what is the criterion through a country tacitly consents to the civil order there prevailing – otherwise how could he be bound by its laws? This seems counter intuitive. Even more counter-intuitive, Hume argued, is the suggestion that ordinary people, born into a situation from which they lack the means to escape, have tacitly consented to all the burdens which they inherit.

Locke introduced into political thought another highly influential conception, that of the separation of powers. Hobbes's sovereign is the single autonomous fount from which all the actions for the commonwealth take their origin. His powers are legislative, military and domestic at once. Locke argued that, even if such powers are in practice, exercised together or by a single authority, they are separable in theory, and can be both exercised and justified independently. He went further, arguing that these powers were in fact already separated – at least to some extent – in the constitution of England, and that they ought to be separated if that constitution were to command the consent of its subjects. He proposed that the powers which sometimes are, and always ought to be, so separated are the following: the legislative, the executive and the federative involving the making of treaties and the waging of war.

The theory of the separation of powers is familiar from the American constitution, which explicitly acknowledges it as one of its foundations. It was adopted and refined by the eighteenth-century political theorist Montesquieu (1689-1755), in his *Spirit of Laws* (1748), a vivid celebration of principles which he thought to be enacted in the English constitution and which he recommended as the only certain salvation for a society adapted to the complex pursuits of contemporary man. Such a society must combine the strongest possible safeguards of liberty with the greatest internal cohesion, and it was through the separation of powers, Montesquieu argued, that this could be achieved. Such a separation in Montesquieu's theory, between the executive, the legislative, and the judiciary guarantees the individual liberty, by ensuring that each power can be curtailed by the others. It also ensures cohesion, through the internal relations between the powers, which make it impossible that any of them should be exercised without the elaborate co-operation of the other two. Discussion of this intriguing conception has continued unabated to the present day, so much so that it is now very difficult to separate the basic philosophical ideas from the manifold prejudices, which have woven themselves into them. Nevertheless, it is another of the achievements of Locke's varied genius that he should have discovered the way in which to decompose, the Hobbes Ian conception of sovereignty, and to give to it at least the semblance of a reasoned basis.

Locke and the Foundations of Liberalism

Liberals have always shown a certain fondness for Locke, and it is easy to see why. Certain assumptions which Locke makes, certain attitudes which he held, and certain arguments which he uses, fit in well with the doctrine which at the beginning of the nineteenth century came to be called liberalism. Some commentators go further, and say that Locke invented liberalism practically single-handedly, but that is to exaggerate. Too much of at least English liberalism came out of utilitarianism, a doctrine antithetical to Natural Rights, for this claim on Locke's behalf to be sustained.

The first liberal-looking assertion in Locke is the naturalness of property and the inviolability of property right except by free and voluntary consent: what we have come to call consent to taxation. Nine points of positive law will be about who rightfully owns what. What makes something mine is either that I have inherited it or, better still, that I have worked for it. Mixing one's labour with something is that surest title to possession of all. Locke is certainly not hostile to aristocracy, and he looks with favour on self-made men, the traditional alliance between Whig aristocracy and industrial wealth which was to form the basis of the English Liberal Party after 1859.

Locke wrote famous *Letter Concerning Toleration* which still strikes a liberal chord. Locke's plea for toleration is an appeal for the privacy of the individual's own mind. The law should never be used to proceed against a man for what he thinks, but only for what he does or might be about to do. The exceptions are Catholics, a potential fifth column in the service of the nation's Catholic enemies, and atheists because, have no fear of hell-fire, they cannot be expected to tell the truth on oath in courts of law, Locke's appeal for toleration is, then, a plea for toleration of every kind of Protestant and dissenting sect, a view of toleration which seems unduly restricted in the light of the classic liberal statement on toleration, J.S. Mill's essay *On Liberty* (1859). but on the way there. What the state must never do is try to change men's opinions on the rack. The man may be coerced, but not the conscience, which is by its nature free, a doctrine surprisingly reminiscent of Hobbes's dictum that the will cannot be coerced.

Liberals like to think of themselves as putting a high value on human rationality, and this is an attitude they share with Locke. In the *Second Treatise* Locke is careful to argue against the naturalness of patriarchy in Filmer. Children only owe a duty of obedience to natural fathers who keep their children's Natural Rights in trust for them until they reach the age of consent. As soon as children know what they are doing, they become adults as fully endowed with Natural Rights as anybody else. Locke is very sensible here. The existence of a moral sense, which plainly exists even in very small children, is not enough to put a child in full possession of his Natural Rights. Rationality is still crucial; children have got to be able to understand that rights imply duties, especially the duty to recognize the same rights in others. Living with others means accepting mutual obligations, and failure to recognize this is a failure of understanding, either through incapacity or willful obtuseness. Some such plea underlies the Lockean theory of punishment: a thief who denies the Natural Rights of others has failed to act a as rational man, and so must be corrected. A useful analogy would be with membership of a club. We would say that a member of a club who said that its rules did not apply to them would simply be failing to understanding what being a member of a club entails. Rationality also extends to the public reasonableness of positive laws: everything is to be out in the open. Marxist commentators on social contract theory have always detected a bourgeois flavour in the liberal conception of law as being fixed, knowable and known, because these are exactly the conditions in which commercial judgements about the future can be made. If law is vague, or can change arbitrarily and quickly say changes of the place where customs duties are to be collected, or constant variations in the rate of taxation, then the conditions for commerce worsen.

The Lockean model of society is a competitive, capitalist model. Men are free to acquire, and are encouraged by God to do so. There will be winners and losers, rich and poor. Strange, therefore, that Locke fails to mention class, which on Locke's own account, would exist even in the state of nature where there is buying and selling. What all individualistic theorists of society tend to forget is that there may be an important difference between acquisition and the defence of what has been acquired. Men may acquire as individuals, either through luck, effort or inheritance, but they tend to defend what they have as a group, which is class by any other name. Is Locke's state a class state in the way that his society is a class society? Locke never tells us in the *Second Treatise*, but there are broad hints elsewhere in his works, especially in his draft *Constitution for the Carolinas*, where he refers to his American polity as 'a democracy of God's proprietors'.

The idea of government as a trust which can be betrayed speaks of the liberal distrust of political power a century and a half before Lord acton: 'All power corrupts, and absolute power corrupts absolutely.' Plato apart, political theorists before Locke, are notoriously reluctant to tackle the question of why it is that men want power. Most would agree with Machiavelli that power aggrandizement is a fact of human nature as it applies to princes, or with Hobbes when he intimates that any man would agree to be sovereign if the change came his way. Locke at least has some feeling for what love of power can do to a man, hence his constitutionalism, and hence his emphasis on government as a trust. Perhaps Locke wishes us to think that, like the best trustees, the best governors would be those who get very little out of governing beyond the satisfaction of doing it well. The characteristic trait of men acting politically is not the desire for dominion over others but protection from them, and that obviously includes government. The worst rulers would be the grabbers for power, a view Locke does share with Plato.

Locke plainly thinks that there is a tendency, if it is no more, to harmony in human social life. This harmony is not perfect, otherwise political society would not be necessary. The state is therefore, society's regulating mechanism, essentially extra-society, not its vital spring. Free activity will be the norm, coercion the exception in the cases of thieves and vagabonds. As a Christian, Locke believes that God's intentions for his Creation are benevolent: he did not put men in the world so that they would continually be at one another's throats. Government is 'outside' society in the same way as the governor of an engine is not part of the engine, but extraneous to it. The governor of an engine is there to stop the engine overheating, and only starts working when there is a danger of that. Government regulates but does not initiate. The perfect image of Lockean sovereignty would be the stamping of a Sovereign's head on a pre-existing gold coinage, thus creating sovereigns.

Locke's famous *Essay Concerning Human Understanding* shows him to be cautious, and to a degree skeptical as an epistemologist. Locke believes that the only form of knowledge we can properly trust is the knowledge gained through the perception of the senses. This denial of the trusts of metaphysics (but not of religion because Locke believed in 'natural religion', the belief that the reasonableness of Christianity could be demonstrated) passes over into Locke's political theory in the form of a reluctance on Locke's part to attribute to the state any high, transcendent purpose beyond the peace and security of its citizens. Locke is no Rousseau, let alone Hegel. A certain becoming modesty informs Locke's view of politics. We must not expect too much of it: restricted political means for restricted social ends has a classically liberal ring to it. The only place in which Locke even approaches a higher raison d'etat is in his discussion of the residual power which inheres in all government, but his treatment of its is characteristically low-key. Everyone could agree that government has to act swiftly in emergencies from time to time, and everyone could agree to that, provided only that 'national security' is not invoked too often or on trivial occasions. Otherwise people will begin to smell a rat. Besides, good government would always be prepared to justify its emergency actions ex post facto.

Allied to the skeptical epistemology, and in part deriving from it, is a certain reasonableness about Locke's political theory. There is no urgency about it, nothing raucous or shrill. Locke does not ask us to believe anything which a reasonable Protestant English man might not already be prepared to think. Locke is writing for an audience in a society which is fast becoming commercial, and which is already involved in colonization in America. Even Locke's legalistic tone would have helped, because ownership in the seventeenth century, especially ownership of land, often brought litigation with it, and the fact that making money is second nature to busy men in commercial society needs no emphasis.

What really dates Locke is his account of the social contract itself, which liberalism later sloughed off in favour of the natural sociability of man and therefore his natural tendency to construct political communities. Under the influence of the thinkers of the Scottish Enlightenment, and especially of Adam Smith, liberalism found that it did not need a theory of origins at all. The justification for social and political arrangements shifted from Natural Rights to the principle of utility, which cut across a notion of rights at many crucial points. Locke's plea that free men should keep their government under constant scrutiny, to make sure that it does not overstep the mark finds its echo in the utilitarian idea that a government is more or less legitimate, depending on whether it increases or decreases the greatest happiness of the greatest number. Checking up on this should be almost a daily task for free men, but what utilitarian like Bentham lack in the suspicion of power itself, as distinct from a concern that power should be used for socially useful ends.

The other thing which dates Locke, though it doesn't disqualify him from being one of the main inspirers of liberalism, is the idea that we really could disobey the state by refusing to be bond by its laws. Perhaps in Locke's day it was possible to disobey the state without social chaos, because state did not in fact ask much of most of their citizens most of the time. Occasional service on a jury, occasional taxation, the old turning out to parade in the militia was all the government demanded of those who were not its servants. By comparison, modern states are miracles of complication, because many of them provide a myriad of services of which seventeenth-century defenders of wide scope for government never dreamt. Perhaps in the modern state disobedience is impossible in a much more technical sense. Disobedience to laws at least implies some kind of rough knowledge of what those laws are. The modern world is an age of intense legal specialization among lawyers, and it is technically impossible to disobey the laws because it is perfectly possible that one might think he was disobeying the laws while he was in fact continuing to obey some laws whose existence he did not even suspect. States in Locke's day didn't mange economics and they did not even know the names, or even the number, their own citizens. In circumstances like these, disobedience would not mean so much in social terms, and certainly no social chaos. This is part of what Locke means when he says that the state of nature is a state of liberty, not licence. Rebellion and revolutuion are very different things, and the day was far distant when men would make a rebellion to remodel society, though there had been hints of that during the Interregnum. This is not to say that Locke on disobedience is completely irrelevant to the modern world. Civil disobedience, to make government take notice, is at least in the sprit of Locke. Civil disobedience relies for its moral force on being the very opposite of a return to any kind of state of nature. It relies on very law-abiding people disobeying that law on that occasion. Locke might have liked that.

Through Hooker Locke political thought, back to St. Thomas, in which the reality of moral restraints on power, the responsibility of rulers to the communities which they ruled, and the subordination of government to law were axiomatic. It was not that Locke was in any sense an antiquarian. The chief mark of his genius, as Sabine has argued, "was neither learning nor logic but an incomparable common sense by which he gathered together the chief convictions in philosophy, politics, morals, and education that the experience of the past had generated in the more enlightened minds of his generation. By giving to these a simple and sober yet persuasive statement, he passed them on to the eighteenth century, where they became the matrix from which grew the later political philosophy both of England and the Continent".

Of all the figures in this intervening century, incomparably the most important for the development of a consistent political theory had been Thomas Hobbes. Hobbes, with his clear-cut proof that political absolutism can be deduced from rigidly individualist principles, was the opponent whom Locke should have undertaken to refute if he were to give an equally penetrating defense of constitutional government. Unfortunately he did not assume this obligation in his second treatise but continued his refutation of Filmer. In view of Locke's controversial purpose this is understandable, for his royalist opponents were far from identifying themselves with Hobbes, who was unpopular with both sides. Moreover, they had revived Filmer and had thus made him an obvious target. Filmer had the merit, also, for controversial purpose.

The medieval tradition that reached Locke through Hooker, and the constitutional ideals followed in the settlement of 1688, held that government—the king specifically but not less parliament itself and every political agency—is responsible to the people or the community which it governs; its power is limited both by moral law and by the constitutional traditions and conventions inherent in the history of the realm. Government is indispensable and its right is therefore in a sense indefeasible, but it is also derivative in the sense that it exists for the well-being of the nation. The main result of Hobbes's analysis, however, had been to show that a community as such is a pure fiction, that it has no existence except in the cooperation of its members, that this cooperation is always due to advantages enjoyed by its members individually, and that it becomes a community only because some individual is able to exercise sovereign power. Upon this analysis, Hobbes had based his conclusion that subjection is unavoidable in any form of government, and that ideas such as contract, representation and responsibility are meaningless unless backed by a sovereign's power. Hence they are valid within the state but not for the state.

The logical opposition between these two points of view is extreme. The first is stated in terms of functions. It conceives both individuals and institutions as doing a socially valuable work, regulated by government for the good of all, and within the framework of the Jaw which makes the group a community. The second is stated in terms of individual self-satisfaction. It conceives society as composed of persons, actuated by selfish motives, looking to law and government for security against their equally selfish fellows, and seeking the largest amount of private good consistent with keeping the peace. If Locke could have' adopted either point of view and rejected the other, he would have been more consistent than he was. The circumstances under which he required him to adopt both, and this ought to have entailed an examination of principles and a synthesis of the highest order. It was in fact a task that exceeded Locke's powers. His defense of the Revolution was practically upon the lines marked out by Hooker and already adopted in substance by Halifax. On the other hand, there were urgent reasons why Locke had to adopt into his social philosophy a large part of Hobbes's premises. With or without Hobbes's systematically egoistic psychology a theory of society in terms of individual interests was in Locke's day a foregone assumption. The whole drift of the theory of natural law was in this direction and to this tendency Locke made no small contribution. For he interpreted natural law as a claim to innate, indefeasible rights inherent in each individual. Of such rights that of private property is the typical case. Consequently his theory was by implication as the typical of Hobbes. Both government and society exist to preserve the individual's rights, and the indefeasibility of such rights is a limitation on the authority of both. In one part of Locke's theory, therefore, the individual and his rights figure as ultimate principles; in another society itself plays this part. There is nothing which adequately explains how both can be absolute.

Though Locke was not directly criticizing Hobbes, he attacked some ideas more typical of him than of Filmer, notably the theory that the state of nature is a war of all against all. Locke held that the state of nature is one of "peace, good will, mutual assistance and preservation." This is defended on the ground that the law of nature provides a complete equipment of human rights and duties. The defect of the state of nature lies merely in the fact that it has no organization, such as magistrates, written law, and fixed penalties, to give effect to the rules of right. Everything that is ever right or wrong is so eternally; positive law adds nothing to the ethical quality of different kinds of conduct but merely provides an apparatus for effective enforcement. In the state of nature every man must protect his own as best he can, but his right to his own and his duty to respect what is another's are as complete as ever they can become under government.

On the whole Locke regarded the setting up of a government as a much less important event than the original compact that makes a civil society. Once a majority has agreed to form a government, the whole power of the community is naturally in them. The form of the government depends upon what disposition the majority, or other wise the community, makes of its power. It may be retained or it may be delegated to a legislative body of one form or another. Following the. experience of the English Revolution, Locke assumed that the legislative power is supreme in government, though he admitted the possibility that the executive may share in lawmaking. Both powers, however, are limited. Legislative power can never be arbitrary, for even the people who set it up had no such power; it cannot rule by extemporary decrees, since men unite to have known law and judges; it cannot take property without consent, which Locke interprets to mean by majority-vote; and it cannot delegate its legislative power, since this is unalterably in the hands where the community has placed it. In general, its power is fiduciary, since the people have supreme power to alter the legislature when it acts contrary to the trust reposed in it. The executive is further limited by a general dependence on the legislature and also because the prerogative is limited by law. For the sake of freedom it is important that legislative and executive power should not be in the same hands. Every detail of Locke's account of the relation between legislatures and executives reflects some phase of the controversy between the king and the parliament.

At whatever date his treatises were written, Locke's purpose was to defend the moral right of revolution; hence at the end of his *Second Treatise* he discussed the right to resist tyranny. His most effective arguments depended on principles taken from Hooker. In substance it amounts to this: English society and English government are two different things. The second exists for the well-being of the first, and a government which seriously jeopardizes social interests is rightly changed. This argument is supported by a rather lengthy examination of the right which can be gained by conquest. Locke here distinguished between just and unjust warfare. A mere aggressor gains no right, and even a conqueror in a just war can never establish a right which contravenes the right of the conquered to their liberty and property. The argument is directed against any theory that a government can derive a just power merely from conquest or from success in the use of force. The principle of Locke's argument is essentially the same as that later developed by Rousseau, that moral validity and force are two distinct things, the latter being incapable of giving rise to the former. Consequently a government which begins in force can be justified, as all governments are justified, only by its recognition and support of the moral rights inherent in persons and communities. In other words, the moral order is permanent and self-perpetuating, and governments are only factors in the moral order. In this sense natural law meant for Locke substantially what it had meant for Cicero and Seneca and the whole of the Middle Ages.

A government, as distinct from a society, is dissolved either by a change in the location of legislative power or by a violation of the trust which the people have reposed in it. Locke contemplated two cases, both drawn from English experience in the preceding fifty years. He wished to show that the king had been the real author of the Revolution by attempting to stretch the prerogative and to rule without parliament; this was a dislocation of the supreme legislative power vested by the people in their representatives. He had also a retentive memory for the misbehavior of the Long Parliament and accordingly he had no thought of leaving the legislature unfettered. Any invasion of the life, liberty, or property of subjects is *ipso facto* void, and a legislature which attempts these wrongs forfeits its power. In this case power reverts to the people, who must provide by a new act of constitutional legislation for a new legislature. As in all such arguments, Locke created a considerable, and perhaps needless confusion by his use of the word "lawful." He continually speaks of unlawful acts of the executive or legislature when he well knows that there is no legal remedy, and of lawful resistance to tyranny when he means resort to an extra-legal but morally defensible remedy. Broadly speaking he used lawful as synonymous with just or right and made no distinction between what is morally just and what is legally permissible. This usage grew from and perpetuated the traditional belief that law—natural, positive, and moral—is all of a piece, and that there are therefore "fundamental" laws not made even by the supreme legislature.

Conclusion

In one sense, a critical appreciation of the *Two Treatises of Government* developed within a very short time following its publication, and Lockean political ideas form one of the undercurrents of political discussion in the early eighteenth century in the writings of individuals as diverse as Addison, Defoe, Bolingbroke or Mandeville. But while it is true to say that interpretations of Locke's political thought can be found in the works of eighteenth-century thinkers such as Rousseau, Burke and Hume, it seems preferable to view Locke's ideas as an integral element of liberalism. The foundations of modern Lockean scholarship were laid in Victorian England; that is, in the view that developed as to what kind of person Locke was and how his ideas might be related to this conception of Locke the individual. Locke was presented as the philosopher who provided the general principles for Whig political theory and the *Two Treatises* – but especially the *Second Treatise* – ought therefore to be read as a compendium of those commonsensical beliefs which comprise the political doctrine of liberalism.

Of course, on some level, this is still the dominant interpretative framework with respect to any discussion of Locke's political ideas. Yet the particular emphasis accorded to the philosophical dimensions of Locke's political thought and to the *Two Treatises* as a source of Whig orthodoxy by Fox Bourne, Macaulay and Lassies Stephen has in recent years lost its appeal. This decline is largely due to the same factors that supplied the basis for the Victorian view of Locke, namely, the appearance of previously unknown manuscripts by Locke, along with new biographical information concerning his activities and a general reassessment of the historical period in which Locke lived. Thus, certain religious and political beliefs have displaced philosophical concept as the interpretative prism through which the arguments of the *Two Treatises* are seen to be significant.

Sterling Lamprecht presented Locke as a resolute defender of rationalism. Locke's 'supreme trust in reason', Lamprecht maintained, was nowhere better displayed than in the *Two Treatises*. Lamprecht recognized Locke's failure to develop 'a purely rationalistic ethics' and he conceded that Locke's treatment of natural law displayed an unresolved tension between a rationalistic and a hedonistic ethics, but in the end Lamprecht situated Locke squarely within the rationalist camp. This interpretative battle, however, was fought over the status of Locke's moral philosophy, for Lamprecht showed no interest in challenging Stephen's identification of Locke with Whig political orthodoxies or the interests of the aristocratic landed class in seventeenth-century England.

Like Lamprecht, Harold Laski portrayed Locke as an exponent of a 'thoroughgoing rationalism'. Locke's political argument, Laski asserted, was structured around a secular view of life, a mechanistic conception of the state and an economic philosophy of 'narrow individualism'. Laski identified Locke as 'the theorist' of the Glorious Revolution and the Whig party.

George Sabine has been much less sympathetic towards Locke's efforts to formulate a consistent political philosophy than they had been. He sharpened the philosophical conflict and contradiction in Locke's thought between rationalism and empiricism, contending that it was virtually impossible to reconcile Locke's political theory with his general philosophical position. At its core, therefore, Locke's political thought, as expressed in the *Two Treatises*, was vitiated by logical difficulties. Not surprisingly, Sabine adopted a critical attitude towards the abstractions which he believed were prevalent in Locke's political thought. Thus, Locke's endorsement of the fiction of a social contract, his atomistic portrayal of the state of nature, and, in general, his ahistorical and asocial approach to politics, his defense of egoistic individualism and the economic interest of the ruling class were ultimately traceable to his philosophical confusion, which left Locke's political theory without any 'logical structure'. Of course, Locke's political ideas were immensely influential – in part, precisely because of their commonsensical appeal and absence of analytical rigour– but there had never been any serious doubt, Sabine insists, that if Locke was 'the ideal spokesman of a middle-class revolution' that he 'was the most conservative of revolutionists'.

The standard view of Locke prior to the 1950s – was that of a confused philosopher with confidence in rationalism, and a selfish pursuit of material interests. While this perspective had much to recommend it, practically speaking, to the Whig party politicians and the landed property-holders whose political revolution the *Two Tratise* dutifully defended, the philosophical approach to Locke certainly did not present him as being a profound or compellingly attractive thinker.

The most interesting, and almost the only departure from this interpretative orthodoxy, was Wilmoore Kendall. According to Kendall, Locke was really democrat, advocating manhood suffrage and popular sovereignty. Hence the collective consent of the community is not only paramount with respect to any determination of property right; but Kendall went so far as to identify the Law of Nature with majority consent. For Kendall, Locke appeared to be more like Rousseau and much less like Hooker or Hobbes than previous Locke scholars had supposed. Certainly this made Locke a more interesting intellectual and political figure. Purely from the standpoint of diversity of views, the 1950s were clearly a high-water mark of Lockean scholarship. Leo Strauss revived an earlier theme in the secondary literature associating Locke with Hobbes, but Strauss pressed the issue beyond mere association; for him, Locke's teachings were those of Hobbes, though disguised in order to appear more palatable to a seventeenth-century audience.

Macpherson presented Locke as the more or less conscious defender of exploitative capitalist relations. This, too, was an old theme in the secondary literature, but Macpherson – as Strauss had done with Locke's intellectual association with Hobbes – transformed a passing allusion into a major interpretative axis, according to which Locke's thought could be entirely revaluated. In other word, it was not only that the appearance in print of the *Two Treatises* was a convenient circumstance so far as the Whig property-holders of the Glorious Revolution were concerned, but, Macpherson argued, Locke consciously structured the arguments in the work in such a manner that any recovery of their meaning required a reading of the *Two Treatises* in which this imputed intention is given a central place of importance. Macpherson identified Locke as an exponent of the unlimited appropriation of property and of the view that members of the labouring class were sub-rational individuals. Locke's rationalism is thus employed in defence of the political and economic relations of capitalist society, while his writings on religion serve ideologically to secure the complaint obedience of non-rational individuals to a system that exploits their labour. The ownership and rights of property, taken in its narrowest sense, are what Locke's political theory –and the *Two Treatises* – is all about. Many critics of Macpherson has charged him for his failure to provide the historical and sociological evidence necessary to establish his claims regarding the existence of the market society in seventeenth-century England since the more inappropriate 'model' of society formulated by Macpherson is as a descriptive characterization of Locke's environment, the more difficult it becomes to associate that model with Locke's intentional purposes in writing the *Two Treatises.*

Since the older approaches to Locke had concentrated upon ascertaining the correctness of his philosophical position, based upon some reordering of concepts drawn from his writings, neither Locke's intentions nor the social context within which he wrote had counted for much in these interpretations. The shift in perspective demanded a type of evidence that could not simply be extracted from the *Two Treatises* itself. Thus, the interpretations of Strauss and Macpherson shared a common problem in that they were both dependent upon certain assumptions about the nature of seventeenth-century England and a set of intentions imputed to Locke that assumed significance in relation to that social context, but neither the nature of the context nor Locke's intentions were established by the evidence presented in their books.

Sheldon Wolin offered arguments to situate Locke's thought in its proper historical context than it was to present a sketch of the social psychology of liberalism. Locke's thought formed an essential element in the reconstruction of a social consciousness compatible with a liberal bourgeois society. Plamenatz's treatment of Locke represented a continuation of the philosophical approach, now accompanied by a polemical defence justifying the exclusion of historical evidence. All that was required of an interpreter, Plamenatz argued, was that he/she read the text over and over again until the meaning of the author became transparently clear in the interpreter's mind. Unfortunately, the *Two Treatises* proved a rather recalcitrant example for this approach since, as Plamenatz's predecessors had noted, it was not a profound, consistent or carefully constructed work of philosophy. Riddled as it was with ambiguities and contradictions, Locke's work might never yield a plain meaning. Notwithstanding his methodological pronouncements Plamenatz's interpretation of Locke is filled with assumptions about Locke's intentions, the expectations and beliefs held by his readers, the nature of English society in the seventeenth century, and so on, which are employed to elucidate the meaning of the text. Yet no references are supplied by Plamenatz's to indicate from where he derived these assumptions, no evidence is offered to support them.

Maurice Cranston's biography, the first in nearly a century, was notable for its failure to shed any light upon the intellectual dimensions of Locke's thought. The predominant conclusion one derived from a reading of Cranston's Locke is that he was an exceedingly secretive person. However, drawing upon the recently discovered Locke's manuscripts and Peter Laslett's argument concerning the composition of the *Two Treatises*, Cranston's work did extend our knowledge of Locke's activities, especially during the period of his association with the first Earl of Shafesbury. In an early (1956) article, but much more fully in his introduction to the critical edition of the *Two Treatises*, Laslett saw the association of Locke and Shafesbury as a fact of central importance to the writing of the *Two Treatises of Government*. Locke wrote that work, Laslett argued, 'for Shafesbury's purposes'. The general proposition that the *Two Treatises* should be read primarily as a political and not as a philosophical work was clear enough, but precisely how this affected one's view of the specific arguments advanced by Locke was less easy to discern. Laslett's dating of the *Two Treatises* as an Exclusion tract appeared to dislodge the long-standing orthodoxy that Locke wrote the work as a defense of the 1689 Revolution. Laslett maintained that Locke was not writing as a philosopher applying to politics his view of reality as a whole. Von Lynden's interpretation revived an earlier emphasis upon Locke's hedonistic ethics and the conflict between rationalism and empiricism in his treatment of natural law. Martin Seliger offered a reading of the *Two Treatises* that made Locke an authoritarian liberal, a champion of executive power and prerogative, and a reluctant revolutionary.

With John Dunn's interpretation, Lockean scholarship reached a significant turning-point in its evolution. This was due not so much to Dunn's resolution of old interpretative problem as it was to his methodological insistence upon paying attention to Locke's own meaning' in the *Two Treatises* rather than imposing twentieth-century meaning (for example, Strauss, Macpherson) upon that work. What Dunn sought to achieve was a more coherent and historically accurate account of what Locke was maintaining in the *Two Treatises* than has yet been given. The most important conclusion to emerge from Dunn's study as he himself noted, was 'the theoretical centrality of Locke's religious preoccupations' to any understanding of his political thought.

Notwithstanding the correctness of Dunn's reconstruction of the theoretical hierarchy of Locke's thought, its operative function in political thought as a guide to the *Two Treatises* seemed more adapted to evaluating alternative readings of that work than to clarify Locke's own intellectual or political objectives. For Dunn, the state of nature is purely an ahistorical construct, the nature of legitimate political society is merely a formal exercise in reasoning sanctioning an almost infinite variety of forms of government, Locke's treatment of consent is a case of muddled reasoning, and his discussion of revolution is actually a reassuring endorsement of the legitimacy of the English polity in the 1680s. to say that it is difficult to extract a clear or concise picture of Locke's political theory from Dunn's book is to understate the problem. Moreover, if the *Two Treatises* was written as an Exclusion tract (pace Laslett), Dunn observes, it was certainly an ineffective or poorly organized political tract.

The Locke industry shows little sign of succumbing to intellectual bankruptcy, thought it is difficult to forecast the direction of its future development. There now appears to be a secure and historically grounded niche for the message of political radicalism of the *Two Treatises*, located in various ways by Franklin, Tully, Kenyon, Goldie and in Richard Ashcraft. This extension of the political dimensions of the structure of Locke's thought is refreshingly fascinating. In both respects, therefore, the 'historical' Locke–Locke the seventeenth-century political and religious dissident – has finally achieved a place of prominence within the framework of Lockean scholarship. Today John Locke, or perhaps rather his reputation as a major philosopher, presents a puzzle. His influence in the eighteenth century is well-attested. He enjoyed extraordinary prestige as one of the liberators of the human mind, and one of those who, in Hume's words, 'began to put the science of man on a new footing'. What is more, modern commentators seem agreed on his centrality to the liberal tradition. Bertrand Russell described him as 'the founder of empiricism', and Trevor-Roper has called him 'the greatest of liberal philosophers'. Yet in what, precisely, does this greatness consist?

Many modern critics have pointed out that he is confused and inconsistent, and that he often fails to pursue his line of thought back to first principles. At one crux of his argument about the reliability of the senses as sources of knowledge, he falls back on bluff common-sense assertions in the manner of Dr. Johnson. It may well be, as Isaiah Berlin has suggested, that 'Locke may almost be said to have invented the notion of common sense', but one function of philosophy is to penetrate into and behind common sense, and this Locke often damagingly fails to do. Locke lacks the rigour and probing thoroughness of the very greatest philosophers. And his political philosophy lacks the systematic constructiveness of Hobbes, or Bentham. Locke is, as Macpherson aptly put it, 'the confused man's Hobbes'.

Confusion and inconsistency, so far from being obstacles to influence and popularity, may be aids to them, especially if they reflect the interests and prejudices of the dominant class. On the whole that class in eighteenth-century Western Europe found Locke very much to their taste, while the remorselessly logical reasoning of Hobbes made them distinctly uncomfortable – if they ever encountered them. But it is not only Locke in his role as the ideologist of the Whig settlement of 1688-89 who is important to liberalism. It is also by virtue of his empiricist philosophy of knowledge that he takes his place among the principal philosophers of liberalism.

Locke was the first to work out a whole theory of knowledge based on the empiricist principle – the contention that such knowledge as we have or can have, of the external world, can only come from sense-experience. The theory against which he argued was that there were certain ideas innate or inherent in the mind, 'which the soul receives in its very first Being, and brings into the world with it.' Locke thought that this was a quite unnecessary hypothesis: 'Men, barely by the use of their natural faculties, may attain to all the knowledge they have, without the help of any innate impressions'. Instead, Locke proposed a picture of the mind as an empty room, *tabul rasa* or a blank sheet or 'white paper void of all characters, without any Ideas'.

Noam Chomsky's view that certain common features of human language indicate something akin to innate ideas in human mind or thought processes, and the vehement reactions to that view, suggest that this philosophical issue is by no means settled. But whatever opinions may be held on the subject today, Locke's attack on innate ideas was a liberating step at that moment in history. It cut away the ground from those who claimed that certain traditional ideas, beliefs and dogmas were beyond test or question because they were part of the permanent furniture of the mind placed there by God. The dangers of Locke's theory were very quickly spotted by his religious contemporaries, one of whom, William Sherlock, wrote: 'if all the knowledge we have of God, and of good and evil, be made by ourselves, atheists will easily conclude that it is only the effect of education and superstitious fears.' At the same time the notion of the mind as a blank sheet or empty room became the ground for a optimism about the potentialities of education. Yet it was a further consequence of this blank sheet theory that the idea of the personality as a stable center of the individual tends to dissolve, and is eventually replaced by Hume's disturbing picture of the human being as nothing more than a 'bundle of sensations'. At this point liberal atomism succeeds in dissolving the very notion of personality.

Locke believes that each of us can be quite certain of the validity of our own experience. Other people's reports may be fabrication, but our sense cannot, in the last analysis, seriously mislead us. Trust your own experience above all, rather than any kind of report, authority, tradition or established belief. Many people had already begun to do this in matters of religion. Locke provided a ground for doing so in every aspect of life.

The world of which our senses provide us with knowledge is individualistic, too. Just as sensations, or sense-experiences, are particular and unique, so the world itself is made up of things which are also separate, individual and unique – 'All Things, that exist, being Particulars'. It is true that language is not made up of the names of particular things and beings, but of general names. But it is a mistake to confuse the pattern of language with that of reality. For although 'words are general', 'universality belongs not to things themselves, which are all of them particular in their existence'. The implication is that the world is a chaos of individual entities, while the order implied in the general names and categories which human beings use is something 'in the mind', invented and imposed on the world from outside. This atomizing approach was to be extended by David Hume. We perceive only conjunctions of events or things, and from regular conjunctions, we infer a chain of causes and effects: 'all our distinct perceptions are distinct existences, and the mind never perceives any real connexion among distinct existences'. Thus, 'all events seem entirely loose and separate'. There is a gap between the order upon which the mind insists, and the disorder of reality itself.

Locke was interpreted by the eighteenth century as providing a foundation for a general optimism about the potentialities of both science and education. Retrospectively, this looks like a misinterpretation, because Locke himself did not see the area or potential human knowledge as all that wide. He claims that reason must evaluate the claims of faith and revelation, and that nothing in faith should be contrary to reason. this is the predictable encroachment on the domain of faith which was, sooner or later, bound to follow from the Baconian separation of the two territories. But he is anything but dogmatic about matters of religious belief, and strongly aware of the vast areas in which opinion rather than knowledge must prevail. His arguments for toleration are classically liberal, in so far as they are based at the most fundamental level upon skepticism about the possibility of resolving disputes over religious beliefs. Locke's name is so closely associated with the intellectual history of the eighteenth century, and with the political settlement of 1688 and after, that it can be something of a shock to realize that he was involved in politics for more than 20 years before William III was brought to the English throne, principally as a member of the household of, the first Earl of Shafesbury, and effective leader of the Whig aristocratic opposition to Charles II.

It now seems clear that Locke's *Two Treatises of Government* were first drafted during the Exclusion crisis, even though they were not published until 1690, with a preface in which the anonymous author offered them specifically as a justification of the 'Revolution' of 1688-89. Thus Locke was closer to being a professional political propagandist, like Milton, than a scholarly recluse like Hobbes or Spinoza. His biographer, Maurice Cranston, has even asserted that the whole of Locke's political philosophy was called into being by the exigencies of the time he lived through and the circumstances of his being in the household of the opposition leader. Locke deploys general arguments, not for academic purposes, but to provide a theoretical basis for specific political ideology. It is these practical pressures which provide one clue to his notorious confusions and inconsistencies.

Locke's political philosophy can hardly be represented in a simple and straightforward exposition because of the logical difficulties which it reveals when it is subjected to analysis. This was due to the fact that Locke saw with great clarity a multitude of issues involved in the politics of the seventeenth century and tried conscientiously to combine them all. But his theory had no logical structure elaborate enough to contain so complicated a subject-matter. Though circumstances made him the defender of a revolution, he was by no means a radical, and in intellectual temperament he was the least doctrinaire of philosophers. His principles he mainly inherited and he never examined them very thoroughly. But he was extraordinarily sensitive to realities and absolutely candid in trying to face them. The mid-period of the seventeenth century had changed enormously both English politics and English thought, and yet it had not broken continuity with the days before the civil wars. Locke's political philosophy was an effort to combine past and present and also to find a nucleus of agreement for reasonable men of all parties, but he did not synthetize all that he combined.

Sabine reasons that the defects of logical structure in Locke's political theory arose from the fact that he never made up his mind what exactly was fundamental and what was derivative. There are in fact no less than four levels in his account of civil society, and the last three are represented as successfully derivative from the first. Yet Locke never hesitated, if it was convenient, to impute a kind of absoluteness to each of the four. The foundation of the whole system was represented as being the individual and his rights, especially that of property. On the whole this must be regarded as the most significant phase of his political theory, which made it primarily a defense of individual liberty against political oppression. Second, men are also members of a community, and though Locke described society as depending on tacit consent and as meaning effectively a majority, he constantly spoke of the community as a definite unit and the trustee of the individual's rights. Third, beyond society there is government, which is trustee for the community, somewhat as the latter is for the individual. Finally, within government the executive is less important and less authoritative than the legislature. Yet Locke certainly did not regard the king and his ministers as merely a committee of parliament. In the defense of liberty and property the legislature controls the executive, and the community controls government. Only in the remote event that society itself is dissolved, a contingency which Locke never seriously contemplated, does the defense of liberty revert to self-help. Society, the legislature, and even the king were all treated as having a kind of vested right, or permanent authority, only to be forfeited for cause, though the individual rights of property and liberty were the only rights which Locke declared to be absolutely indefeasible.

The greatest importance of Locke's philosophy, therefore, lay beyond the contemporary English settlement in the political thought of America and France which culminated in the great revolutions at the end of the eighteenth century. Here Locke's defense of resistance in the name of inalienable rights of personal liberty, consent, and freedom to acquire and enjoy property had their full effect. Because all these conceptions were in germ much older than Locke and had been the birthright of all European peoples since the sixteenth century, it is impossible to attribute their existence in America and in France to him alone, but he was known to everyone who gave any attention to political philosophy. In Sabine's words,

"Locke's sincerity, his profound moral conviction, his genuine belief in liberty, in human rights, and in the dignity of human nature, united with his moderation and good sense, made him the ideal spokesman of a middle-class revolution". Even his more doubtful ideas, such as the separation of powers and the inevitable wisdom of majority-decisions, remained a part of the democratic creed.

About the middle of the century Hume showed that this development, if logically carried through, made it possible to dispense with the theory of natural law altogether. The internal structure of Locke's political philosophy was thus completely destroyed. Yet most of its practical purposes and much of its inward spirit passed over to utilitarianism. Though less explicitly a defense of revolution, it continued Locke's spirit of cautious but radical reform. Its program continued the same gloritication of individual rights, the same optimism in liberalism as a panacea for political ills, the same commitment for the rights of property, and the same logic that public interests must be conceived in terms of private well-being.

Foundations of
Western Political Thought

Books by B.N. Ray

Tradition and Innovation in Indian Political Thought
Political Theory : Interrogations and Interventions
Critical Theory : The Marx-Marcuse Encounter
Liberalism and the Communitarian Challenge
John Rawls and the Agenda of Social Justice
C.B. Macpherson and Liberalism
Contemporary Political Thinking
Nietzsche After Hundred Years
Citizenship in a Globalising World
Gandhigiri
Reading Gandhi

Foundations of

Western Political Thought

Volume 2

B.N. Ray

Kaveri Books

New Delhi - 110 002

First Published in 2009
Second Impression 2023

ISBN: 978-81-7479-097-2 (Set)
ISBN: 978-81-7479-098-9 (Vol. 1)
ISBN: 978-81-7479-099-6 (Vol. 2)

Published by
Kaveri Books
4832/24, Ansari Road
New Delhi - 110 002 (India)
Ph.: 011-2328 8140, 4707 2321
E-mail: kaveribooks@gmail.com
info@kaveribooks.com
www.kaveribooks.com

Laser Typesetting by
Aarati Computers, Delhi - 110 009

PRINTED IN INDIA

In memory

of my

mother Kshetramani Ray

and

father Binod Bihari Ray

Preface

There are many books on Western Political Thought. All have something in common, yet all are different in important respects. If all political theories and ideologies had a single uncontroversial character there would be far fewer books and much less for political theorists to do. Fortunately, political theories do not have such a stable character. There is always room for contestation revisionism deconstruction and redescription and this suggests that there is indeed scope for yet another book.

For a number of years, my own students at Delhi University have sought such a text, book-length account of Western political thought. This book has emerged out of lectures and seminars given at the Delhi University and universities in Pondicherry Rajasthan, Udaipur, Baroda, Mizoram, Berhampur, Sambalpur, Utkal, Symbiosis, NEHU, BHU, and many colleges of Orissa. I have been privileged to test my arguments on a number of equally helpful audiences outside my own university. The experience in all these venues encouraged me to think that the ideas that are at the heart of Western political thought are not solely the fantasies of privileged ivory-tower academics. I am grateful to my hosts on these occasions. I am particularly grateful for their generosity-something increasingly difficult to reciprocate. Though the book is by no means a publication of lectures I have greatly profited from the stimulating and insightful contribution of my political science students in a course on Western political thought. I have tried to respont their anxities, even if on some issues I have remained obstinate.

Political thought extends over a vast domain and no anthology, however generously conceived, could present more than a very small fraction of it. For this then I make no apology, but the reader is entitled to be given some sense of the principles on which my inevitably ruthless selection was made. I own up to three biases, which, I recognize, not everyone will share.

The first is towards continuity. I have presented a diversity of thinkers as addressing, over the centuries, a range of broadly characterized, but recognizably continuous, issues. This is not to pretend, of course, that the positions taken towards those issues have themselves been stable—on the contrary I hope that the anthology will illustrate how radically attitudes to many fundamental political questions have changed—or that the thinkers of the past did not also concern themselves with issues and problems that now seem very urgent to us. Even so, to treat texts in this way is to cut oneself off from those layers of significance that can only be revealed by a proper appreciation of their historical context. An anthology with a different purpose might have presented the same authors very differently.

My second bias is towards argument. I have selected not only striking and significant positions taken in relation to political issues but looked for arguments to support them. To do so is to suppose that political discourse involves more than stirring rhetoric or appeals to self-interest. That the latter play a great role it would, of course, be foolish to deny, but argument too, if less spectacularly, plays its part, I believe, and I have allowed my selections to favour those who back up their views with evidence and reasoning.

Finally, I must confess to a certain bias towards issues of contemporary relevance. So, for instance, we have looked at what ancient authors had to say about the proper place of women in society rather than the justification of slavery, not because the authors themselves would have regarded the former question as any more interesting or important than the latter but quite simply, because it is contentious for us in a way that the question of slavery is not. Of course, issues come and go in surprising ways and so I have tried to be inclusive rather than narrow in my selection. Nevertheless, although many of the authors represented here are of timeless value, this is an anthology that does, to some extent, reflect the preoccupations of its own time. I hope that, in consequence, readers will find that the questions it addresses are ones whose importance they can easily recognize and that the arguments contained in it will help them to broaden and sharpen their own views on the subject.

Western political thought, from its inception to the present time, constitutes the subject matter of this book. Not all of the political thinkers who have contributed to the historical evolution of that tradition are included in this text but many of the most important are. Those who are discussed have been chosen for two reasons. First, they raise the perennial issues of politics and as such are most useful to the student who is just beginning to study political theory seriously. Second, they seem to best embody the changing relationship of ethics and politics in Western political thought. The book will argue that all political theories establish explicitly or implicitly some thesis about the relationship of ethics and politics. At a deeper level it will be argued that the relationship of ethics and political is a theme that defines key historical junctures in Western political thought and more importantly that explains certain crucial dilemmas within that tradition of discourse.

This book has been organized around a theme to adopt a particular perspective, a certain "point of view" that will differ from the perspective of others within the field of political thought. This is inevitable for there simply is no scholarly agreement that any perspective best characterizes the western tradition of political discourse. Indeed there is not even universal agreement that there is a tradition of discourse from which themes and perspectives can be derived. The issue is resolved in recognizing that it is precisely in contestation not consensus that our understanding of political matters has evolved. What ultimately is significant is not whether or not a perspective is valid in some absolute sense but whether or not that perspective enlarges our understanding and expands our horizon. Political theorists are important not because what they say is necessarily "True " with a capital "T" but because what they say enlarges our understanding of politics.

The following chapters, it is hoped, will offer numerous examples of thinkers with whom students will disagree but from whom they will also find new insights despite indeed often because of that disagreement. In the same way it is hoped that the student's understanding of political theory will be enlarged and deepened whether there is agreement with the premises of this work or not. Certainly, the theme of this book and the interpretations and arguments that follow are presented in this spirit.

I do not pretend originality for everything argued here. Various intellectual influences on my argument will be apparent, of which some deserve particular acknowledgement. I would single out for special mention the works of Amartya Sen Randhir Singh, O.P. Bakshi, Jurgen Habermas Bhikhu Parekh, V.R. Mehta, Pratap Bhanu Mehta, Quentin Skinner, Neal Wood, James Tully, Ruth Grant, Hanna Pitkin, Herbert Marcuse, C.B. Macpherson, George Sabine, Sheldon Wolin, Karl Popper, and Hannah Arendt.

I count myself very fortunate in the academic institution with which I am associated for four decades. I am deeply indebted to my friend Rajendra Prasad, the principal of Ramjas College, for providing me with generous academic and institutional support.

I will fail in my duty if I do not thank my host Mr. Ashok Gupta in whose home I have been living as a guest, not as a tenant. He has been my friend, philosopher and guide who has provided me with constant inspiration and encouragement to pursue my philosophical interests without fear or favour.

Finally, and perhaps curiously for a book on political thought family played an important part in this endeavour. Over many years now, I have been engaged in a continuing argument with them often about issues addressed in this book. They were my first teachers in moral and political thinking and I continue to learn from them. They instilled a passionate interest in what turned out to be political theory and they have remained interested in, if not always convinced by, what I have learnt along the way. This book is for them. I have also learnt from my own children, Lipika and Ayush as they become adults. They have discussed and argued over many of the issues in this book. Although they may not be able to see where I have tried to answer their questions, yet I have endeavoured to address their anxieties. My family continues to be the mainstay and support of all that I do. This is perhaps a pretty poor return for good humour, support and patience. Yet family is not everything; in writing this book I enjoyed the companionship of friends and students. They contributed immensely to this book in ways that only companions can.

For any errors that remain I am alone responsible. Much of the book was written during a period of 'involuntary leisure' from Ramjas College, it would have taken a lot longer time otherwise. To all, my thanks.

BN Ray
Ramjas College
University of Delhi

Contents

Volume - 2

10

Rousseau

> The body politic, taken individually, may be considered as an organized living body, resembling that of man. It is also a moral being possessed of a will, and this General Will, which tends always to the preservation and welfare of the whole and of every part, is the source of the laws..,... supreme direction of the general will, and, in our corporate capacity, we receive each member as an indivisible part of the whole.

Jean-Jacques Rousseau (1712-1778) supposed that he was a very remarkable man and he has right. We can gain something of an insight into his character, as he wanted us to, by reading his autobiography *The Confessions,* which he wrote between 1765and1770 and which was published four years after his death on 2 July 1778.

> I know my own heart and understand my fellow man. But I am unlike any one I have ever met: I will even venture to say that I am like no one in the whole world. I may be no better, but at least I am different. Whether nature did well or ill in breaking the mould in which she formed me, is a question which can only be resolved after the reading of my book.

Rousseau's mother died a few days after his birth in Geneva in 1712, and because of it, 'so my birth was the first of my misfortunes'. A sister of his father Isaac, an indulgent, erratic and irascible man, assisted in his early upbringing, his parents having left him only one endowment-a sensitive heart. 'It had been the making of their happiness, but for me it has been the cause of all the misfortunes in my life'.

On the same page of his autobiography, he tells us that his suffering, like most of his experiences, was unique: 'I suffered before I began to think: which is the common fate of man, though crueler in my case than in another's.' Why this should be so he does not tell us. He does however tell us about many of his other characteristics:

> My warm-heartedness, my acute sensibility, the ease with which I formed friendships, the hold they experienced over me, and the cruel wrench when they had to be broken; my innate goodwill towards my fellow men; my burning desire for the great, the true, the beautiful, and the just, my horror of evil in every form. I have told the truth. If anyone knows anything contrary to what I have here recorded, though he proves it a thousand times, his knowledge is a lie and an imposture; and if he refuses to investigate and inquire into it during my lifetime, he is no lover of justice or truth. For my part, I publicly and fearlessly declare that anyone, even if he has not read my writings, who will examine my nature, my character, my morals, my likings, my pleasures, and my habits with his own eyes and can still believe me a dishonorable man, is a man who deserves to be stifled.

While one may not agree with Rousseau that he was 'like no one else in the whole world', one can see even from these declarations that he was probably exceptional as a man-introspective, egocentric, passionate, uncomfortable and prickly and that he was certainly exciting as an essayist, sensitive, extravagant, elegant, energetic and pugnacious. All of this makes it easier to be excited than to be rationally persuaded by him. A prolific litterateur, Rousseau also wrote musical opera, one of which was performed in 1752 at court before Louis XV, his Queen, and family. His knowledge of musical composition and theory may have assisted the production of his political theory. Rousseau was a Swiss, born in Geneva in 1712 and brought up a Calvinist. His father Isaac was a watchmaker but did not flourish in his trade, being a troublemaker, often involved in violence and riots. His mother, Suzanne Bernard, came from a wealthy family, but died of puerperal fever shortly after Rousseau's birth. Neither parent came from the tight circle of families which formed the ruling oligarchy of Geneva. But they had full voting and legal privileges and Rousseau was always very conscious of his superior status. It made him a natural conservative by interest and gave him a lifelong contempt for the voteless mob. There was also a substantial amount of money in the family.

Rousseau had no sisters but a brother, seven years his senior. He himself strongly resembled his mother, and thus became the favorite of his widowed father. Isaac's treatment of him oscillated between lachrymose affection and frightening violence and even the favoured Jean-Jacques deplored the way his father brought him up, later complaining in Emile: The ambition, greed, tyranny and misguided foresight of fathers, their negligence and brutal in sensitivity, are a hundred times more harmful to children than the unthinking tenderness of mothers. However, it was the elder brother who became the chief victim of the father's savagery. In 1718 he was sent to a reformatory, at the father's request, on the grounds that he was incorrigibly wicked; in 1723 he ran away and was never seen again. Rousseau was thus, in effect, an only child, a situation he shared with many other modern intellectual leaders. But, though indulged in some ways, he emerged from childhood with a strong sense of deprivation and - perhaps his most marked personal characteristic- self-pity.

Death deprived him quickly of both his father and his foster-mother. He disliked the trade of engraving to which he was apprenticed. So in 1728, aged fifteen, he ran away and became a convert to Catholicism, in order to obtain the protection of Madame Warens, who lived in Annecy. The details of Rousseau's early career, as recorded in his Confessions, cannot be trusted. But his own letters, and the vast resources of the immense Rousseau industry, have been used to establish the salient facts. Madame Warens lived on a French royal pension and seems to have been an agent both of the French government and of the Roman Catholic Church. Rousseau lived with her, at her expense, for the best part of fourteen years, 1728-42. For some of this time he was her lover; there were also periods when he wandered off in his own. Until he was well into his thirties, Rousseau led a life of failure and of dependence, especially on women. He tried at least thirteen jobs, as an engraver, lackey, seminary student, musician, civil servant, farmer, tutor, cashier, music-copier, writer and private secretary. In 1743 he was given what seemed the plum post of secretary to the French Ambassador in Venice, Montaigu. This lasted eleven months and ended in his dismissal and flight to avoid arrest by the Venetian authorities.

The Social Contract

The Social Contract, Rousseau's great masterpiece of political theory, was first published in 1762. By then, the "Citizen of Geneva" had become one of the most celebrated authors of his day. If his *First Discourse* had created a scandal, the *Second Discourse* had confirmed his notoriety. Both had won him the respect of his peers and the interest of a wider audience. The publication of the *Letter to d'Alembert* had sparked gossip about life among the savants of Paris. Above all, though, it was *La Nouvelle Heloise*, his epistolary romance of love and death in Switzerland, that transformed Rousseau into a figure to passionate importance to a broad mass of readers, as their sobbing, ecstatic letters to him reveal. Published in 1761, his novel became one of the best-selling books of the eighteenth century.

Rousseau, though, was not yet satisfied. Much of his time he devoted to finishing *Emile*, his vision of a perfect pedagogy. And in the *Confessions*, he recalled that of "the diverse works that I had in hand, the one which I had meditated on for the longest time, the one which I had devoted myself to with the greatest relish, the one on which I wanted to work ail my life, and the one which, in my opinion, ought to put the seal on my reputation was my Political Institutions—the work that became *The Social Contract*."

The initial impetus for this work had come in 1743 and 1744, during a visit to Venice, where he was a diplomatic secretary in the employ of the French ambassador. Venice had long occupied a place of pride within the republican tradition of political theory. In his *Discourses on Livy*, Machiavelli had cited it alongside Sparta as an archetype of republicanism in a small city-state. Rousseau himself mentions reading a history of Venice as a youth. By the middle of the eighteenth century, though, the city had fallen into a period of decline, and its government had become a narrow oligarchy. What Rousseau found in his daily chore of writing dispatches on affairs in the city was not the Venice eulogized in the history he had read in his youth or in the great republican treatises, but rather a "dissolute state" as warm with seedy courtiers seeking favors from a "hereditary aristocracy."

Disillusioned and cast out of Venice after a spat with the ambassador, Rousseau at first decided, almost instinctively, to repair to Geneva, apparently hoping to revive his spirits there. But he never forgot the disappointing institutions he had seen from the inside in Venice. "By observing the defects in that Government so vaunted," and by noting the discrepancies between the republican ideal he still felt drawn toward and a real political world that repelled him, Rousseau developed a sustaining interest in political institutions and their role in shaping men.

Over the next fifteen years, Rousseau periodically turned back to the difficult questions first raised by his experience in Venice: "What is the nature of Government proper to form a People who are the most virtuous, the most thoughtful, .the most wise, finally the best, taking this work in its most lofty sense.... What is the Government which by its nature always holds itself closest to the law? Moreover, what is the law?" In the meantime, his revelation on the road to Vincennes and his subsequent discourses on the sciences and on inequality had convinced him that the root of the ills he observed lay not in human nature, but rather in the institutions of modern society. "I had seen that all depended radically on politics, and that, in whatever way one set about it, no people would be anything but what the nature of its Government made it to be."

His trip to Geneva in 1754 had renewed his interest in these matters—especially since "the notions of law and freedom" prevalent there had seemed to him "neither just enough nor clear enough for my liking." Sensing that he had something to say about the principles at stake in Geneva's ongoing political debates, friends there pressed him to address these issues directly. By 1761, Rousseau was ready. Once again, a discrepancy between his imagined ideal and a contradictory reality motivated him to formulate "some great truths useful for the happiness of humankind, but above all for those in my homeland."

He had been working on his "Political Institutions" for some time. It had occupied his attention in Geneva in 1754, and he had also devoted thought to the project while living near Montmorency. Although several early fragments of this work survive, Rousseau himself reports that he destroyed most of the materials when he decided that the scope to his original plan was beyond his powers. Some idea of this scope may be gleaned not only from the image of Alpine democracy we have examined, but also from his subsequent political essays on Corsica and Poland. He came to realise that the whole of human existence was rooted in politics, and it should be the task of good political institutions not merely to secure the property and protect the person of each inhabitant, but also to cultivate the capacities and develop the good sense of each citizen. To these ends, the art of politics needed to consider the economy and constitution of the household, the beliefs of the civil religion, even the structure of public play. In a note among the surviving fragments, Rousseau lists some of the things that interested him: "the greatness of nations; government; of laws; of religion; of honor; of finance; of commerce; of travel; of sustenance; abuse of society; culture of sciences; examination of Plato's Republic."

What eventually appeared in 1762 as the *Social Contract* thus represents but fraction of a much larger work. It scarcely conveys the range of Rousseau' interests, the full depth of his thinking about politics. Yet in it, Rousseau display: and defends his original principles and labors to distil into ideas the essence of his thought.

The Principles of Political Right

The argument of the *Social Contract* may be briefly outlined. Since debate still surrounds its central categories, we must pay special attention to making plain the sense here given to his contested concepts—particularly his ideas about the contract, the general will, sovereignty, and government.

Rousseau assumes that all human beings are by nature free: "Man is born free," even if everywhere he appears in chains. By birth a "master of himself," no individual, "under any pretext whatever," can be legitimately subjected to another "without his consent." This natural law of freedom is insufficient, however, to found any "natural right." For a "right"—a binding entitlement—to obtain among men and to have any force, a shared moral sense and some ability to reason with ideas are required; in his undeveloped natural state, man lacks both. Man's natural freedom, coupled with his lack of natural rights, poses the problem the *Social Contract* sets out to solve. In order to establish right, man needs to observe conventions that can develop his morality and reason without stifling his free will. The "fundamental problem," then, is this: "'Find a form of association that defends and protects the person and goods of each associate with all the common force, and by means of which each one, uniting with all, nevertheless obeys only himself and remains as free as before."

His book takes its title from his solution. In his usage, the social contract is that act by which a people becomes a people, an act in which all unanimously agree to live together as a community. Through this act of mural consent, the possibility of cooperation and collective agency first arises. But why should an individual willingly set limits on his natural freedom and immerse himself in a community? Part of the answer is that only in cooperation with his fellows can the individual develop his powers and secure from others recognition for the goods in life he feels entitled to. Another part of the answer is that a genuine community, because it is based on "the most voluntary act in the world," because it i rooted in a unanimous consent that expresses a real common interest, because it "obligates or favors all citizens equally," and because the association has "no other object than the general goods can never appear to the associated individuals as an obstacle to their own free will. "As long as subjects are subordinated only to such conventions, they do not obey any one but solely their own will.

Human Nature and Civil Sociaty

In order to remedy the ills of society as it is, Rousseau looks to the "hypothetical: a conception of what man might have been prior to the social process makes possible a better understanding of what he ought to be. From the logical point of view, this is quite sound, since the social contract constitutes a synthesis of the hypothetical and the real. The ought comes after the recognition of a total incompatibility between the hypothetical and the real. Man cannot be what he is and cannot return to what he might have been; he therefore ought to be what he is on the basis of what he might have been. This, of course, points to a basic contradiction in Rousseau's social theory. It will be shown, there is an insurmountable opposition between the state of nature and the state of culture, how can Rousseau hope to synthesize the two? If one says culture, one cannot say nature, and vice versa. But one can refound culture on nature, as Rousseau believes he does in the *Social Contract*, if one reduces one member of the binary combination culture/nature to the other. If nature becomes culture or culture becomes nature, the contradiction is eliminated. Rousseau was totally unaware of the necessary reductiveness inherent's in his system.

Rousseau's disruption of this hypothetical state of nature looks like a historical phase since it itself undergoes an evolutionary process: while emphasising the non-possibility of the state of nature, Rousseau describes it in very vivid and realistic terms as though it happens. Rousseau himself is unclear about the ontological status of the state of nature, which is so crucial to his system. If vestiges of this state lave remained within modern man through some process of archetypal transfer, then the state must actually have existed in the distant past; and if it is not a historical phase, then how can one claim that man still retains some of its original characteristics?

Rousseau had doubts as to the hypothetical aspect of the state of nature. Critics have tended to support Rousseau's claim that the state of nature is merely a concept, a comparative tool, a model. Gouhier hesitates to accept the historicity of the state of nature. Ernst Cassier carries it a step further and brings into focus the impact Rousseau has had on recent anthropological and social theories. He claims that in order to distinguish the 'homme natural' from the 'homme artificec, we need neither to go back to epochs of the distant and dead past nor take a trip around the world. Every one carries a true archetype within himself; still, hardly anyone has been fortunate enough to discover it and to strip it of its artificial wrappings, its arbitrary and conventional trimmings. As opposed to Gouhier, Cassirer conceives of the state of nature as a possible historical phase, for the distant and dead past is within the historical process. This archetypal approach indicates what impact Rousseau has had on modern anthropological theories. And were we to find that archetype, which is hidden and hard to reach, we would be in a position to abstract the whole historical process since, in essence, no movement has taken place within man. There is therefore a relationship between the concept of 'archetype' and pure absence, to which Rousseau aspires. Levi-Strauss's 'universal unconscious' bears a strong resemblance to this archetype; hence he sees in Rousseau his mentor.

The fact remains, however, that Rousseau believes modern man to incorporate some of the traits of natural man; his educational theory as a whole is based on his conception of the state of nature and geared to the social praxis of his times. There were attempts to raise children a la *Emile*. Critics prefer to side with Rousseau on this issue, though it was not settled in his own mind, mainly because otherwise they would have to accept Voltaire's criticism that he felt like going on all fours after he read the *Discourse*, which would not sit very well with the writer of the *Social Contract*. The conception of the state of nature is itself ideologically motivated—that in effect, after an adequate analysis, it reflects the social structures prevalent in the enlightened ideology of the eighteenth century. Natural man is an interesting copy of social man but of course, with some differences: otherwise the concept would lose its mythical appeal.

According to Rousseau, before the process of socialization, man goes through two stages in the state of nature: first, the stage of each man under his tree, and secondly, the stage of small groups uniting for common interests. The first man interacted with his immediate environment; he was robust, surmounting harsh climates and danger from other animals. Being totally separated from other humans who might harm him, his only enemies were natural: childhood and helplessness, disease and old age. His mental activities were geared to his immediate well-being, his only preoccupations being the hunt and physical survival. Lacking a conception of time, he did not think ahead. Natural man spoke no language except a cry; he lacked reason, and was amoral because morality comes with standards of justice that society instils. Rousseau summarises the state of nature thus:

Thus natural man was, in a way, sui generis. That is, he was his own definition. But this definition of self is not mediated by reason. Not only was there no gap between natural men, but also no gap existed in their own being since they perceived themselves in the immediate Rousseau never thought of natural man in the plural. Natural man lived on the level of the senses and felt no division into matter and mind: he was an absolute whole—not a composite of various elements. Like the infant, natural man's universe took the dimensions of his own body: the world and self coincide. And this body-mind unit does not even need a language to assert itself; in its irreducible sensual being, it is its own definition.

Most crucial to this state of being is the compatibility between natural man and his environment which rules out any possibility of deprivation. The perfect equilibrium between desire and its compensation, needs and their satisfaction, makes for the absence of lack in the state of nature: everything is full, without gaps, everything continuous without change. Consciousness, Rousseau believes, can arise only at the point where a gap occurs between desire and its satisfaction, which is not the case of natural man. Though he is devoid of consciousness, natural man differs from the other beasts surrounding him: he is not a simple physical automaton Unlike the other animals, he is free; but he shares with them both an instinct for self-preservation and a feeling of pity for the suffering. And most important, natural man possesses a potential for change, which Rousseau terms 'perfectibility'. Here we see the contradiction inherent in Rousseau's system between a theory of evolution and a notion of prehistory.

However, how can one have a feeling of pity when one is totally separated from fellow humans? Rousseau posits the feeling of pity as active and not virtual in natural man. But if natural man is alone under his tree, he cannot have a feeling of pity for the Other: the Other is simply not there. And if natural man has a feeling of pity, perhaps he is not so natural. Here lies Rousseau's main difficulty: he introduces social elements in the natural order and natural elements in the social process, thus collapsing the distinction between the two. This points to the ideological presupposition which Rousseau shares with the social theorists of his time. The postulation of the order of nature imparts upon a historically contingent ideology the qualities of absoluteness and eternity. Natural man is eighteenth-century man disguised: they both partake in perfectibility and rationality. In effect, then, natural man is nonexistent; he is eighteenth-century man cloaked in the coat of nature to provide him with defence mechanisms against change.

The question is what brought about changes in this blessed non-historical state of being? Could it not have gone on for ever due to inertia? Man himself had no reason to alter this paradisiacal life, and the shift from this stage to the next remains problematic. First, the primary stage involves some kind of external time in which people evolve, grow old and die. The introduction of decay to the system is nothing new. One might claim, though, that despite this external time, natural man lives internally in eternity. Secondly, what motivated people to come and stay together if they had no reason to do so? The fortuitous relationships could go on forever, with each man under his tree. The answer lies in the concept of perfectibility. Man's potential for change is dormant in the natural state, but external circumstances cause it to awaken.

These small groups are family cells at first; due to climatic and natural disasters they swell to bigger groups that constitute, in Rousseau's scheme, the idea! society. But this society of the golden age contains the seeds of an irreversible process of degeneration: agriculture and metallurgy are the sources of all social malaise. The making of tools and the beginnings of agriculture meant that man had lost that primordial equilibrium between his needs and their fulfillment. The cultivation of pieces of land required the acquisition of property which was unnecessary to natural man since food was abundant. The establishment of property, in turn, necessitated some rules of equity for the fighting over land had to be stopped and justice instituted.

Rousseau shares Descartes's ideological predilection for individual achievement over group effort. In the last chapter we pointed to Descartes's preference for the exclusion of the Other, who constitutes a hindrance in any professional task. Rousseau takes this position a step further: perdition is the outcome of collaboration; the minute the Other was needed to compensate for individual weakness, inequality set in.

As this passage indicates, the need for the help of the Other is followed by the need for one to have provisions for two. The second need – to hoard a double quantity and deprive the Other – does not follow logically from the first need – to make use of the Other's help, yet Rousseau cannot conceive of a group effort for the common good; he seems to think that the need for the Other's help means an infringement on one's territory and consequently a master-slave relationship. In Rousseau's system, the alternative to self-sufficiency is inequality. The social contract is conceived in terms of this same ideological presupposition: men associate in order for each individual to preserve his own territory.

At take here is the concept of selfhood as denoted by these confessions and the autobiographical tradition as a whole. The *Social Contract* bears a direct relationship to the *Confessions*; in effect, the social contract as a discursive production of the eighteenth century is the signified of the *Confessions*. Autobiography as a form is the signifier of the social text which is filtered through Rousseau's mythical beginnings and his conception of the construal relationship between humans. In short, the reason why he conceives of himself as a unique individual is found in his social theory which proves to be consistent with his concept of selfhood.

With the gradual development of the second stage of the state of nature, man slowly becomes aware of his own consciousness and of the Other, not as a mere animal among others, but as a being endowed with a similar consciousness. The concepts of relationship and comparison are now established and with them the origins of inequality. Here Rousseau introduces the idea of competition, that is, artificial criteria are now instituted in order to differentiate between men. Natural equality could exist only in a world without comparison; with the introduction into the social body of principles of difference, civil inequality sets in—an inequality based on 'looks'.

Rousseau, then, presupposes that man 'is' something but due to social circumstances he 'appears to be' something else. And since society encourages appearances in its promotion of competitiveness, men started coveting appearances and left their true selves hidden behind masks. Again, Rousseau cannot conceive of a social situation without competition; the minute the Other appears he brings with him the destruction of my self because I must alter my behaviour in order to be-for-him. If I am-for-the-Other, I cannot be-for-myself. Freedom in the state of nature means therefore the total possession of self by self; I cannot belong totally to myself, my ego cannot be my own centre, when the Other's look is out there.

This point is crucial to the understanding of the social contract as a discursive elaboration of the eighteenth century: the source of inequality does not reside mainly in the material and quantitative differences between you and me. Although the size of property and material possessions constitute expressions of social inequality, its main motivation is the simple existence of the Other out there threatening my autonomy over myself; the road from myself to myself has to pass by the Other, who brings with him all social evils since reason itself develops together with comparativeness, with the kind of relationship one can entertain with the Other.

The State of Culture

Society has come and created civil man; it caused two major gaps in the being of man. First, the gap within himself: since he has perfected his reason, civil man must take a distance from himself, must divide himself in order to perceive his self, not as an absolute but as a cell in a social whole. So the creation of perspective through reason has generated a split in the basically spatial self of natural man. And secondly, there is now a gap between man and man, with the necessity of appearances and masks in social life.

Thus the psychological and the economic go together in Rousseau; the alienation one experiences in society has to do with material deprivation. The inequality in objects translates into a gap between minds; the physical barrier is also a psychological one. Objects constitute a division between consciousnesses, as though they blur the transparency of self to the Other. Rousseau, however, does not follow this point through to its logical conclusion, which is that communication comes at the expense of property, that collective ownership would be necessary to redress the economic disparities.

It is clear that beyond the detailed criticism of the societies of his time Rousseau is attempting a more basic criticism. To him, the social is corrupt by definition. The very existence of the social, and not merely the existence of a specific society, is here put into question. The comparison is between the absolute man of nature and the relative man of culture. Man, then, has lost both unity and innocence. And Rousseau's purpose in *Confession* is to remedy these two lacks within being, to recapture his lost innocence and unity. But though he can return to Bossey, to an individual paradisiacal state, the return of man to earlier times cannot be achieved in time. If there were such beginnings they would have to be extra-temporal, an immutable stage that calls for no changes and in such a case the return would be impossible. There is no reason why natural man changed and fell to become social man; there can be no return because man cannot do away with the historical steps he has already taken.

So where do we get at least an approximation of these hypothetical beginnings? If natural man never existed, we would have to create him, or rather Rousseau must create him through fiction. And if fiction and myth are resorted to, then natural man is given to interpretation. But that fictional man of nature bears a dialectical relationship to historical man. So, at least, Rousseau believes and exemplifies in his story. The problem that arises, however, is whether this process of fictionalization, this creation of a particular myth, can precede history. For this would amount to the claim that essence precedes existence. The very division of history into two periods, one of which is hypothetical, points to the necessary failure of Rousseau's venture. No doubt the ideological climate of his times prevented Rousseau from perceiving that any definition of man is an ongoing historical process and that myth itself is historically conditioned; in short, that the virtual is secondary and not primary.

To Rousseau, the formation of civil society rests on two acts of aggression and violence that combine into one: the enclosure of a piece of land and the declaration of ownership over it. Property, at least in the discourse, is the source of all evil because it takes violence to assert one's autonomy over a piece of land which one wrests from one's fellow men in the state of nature, where everything is at the disposal of everyone. From this first 'declaration' on, the hoarding of property continues unabated and a total war ensues which has to be stopped by a social agreement for the preservation of the species. However, the first society that followed this state of war was inequitable since it was formed on the request of those who hoarded a lot of property to the detriment of their fellow men; the rich manipulate the masses to agree to their demands. Rousseau illustrates this manipulation through a monologue spoken by a rich man who lures his fellows with impressive language:

But the pact that followed this agreement was one of submission, not association; natural equality disappeared to make room for civil inequality and the subjugation of the weak by the strong. This, then, is the evolution of civil society down to modern times; despotism is the latest manifestation of this civil tradition, according to Rousseau. And the only way to redress the wrong is through the replacement—at least in theoretical conception, for Rousseau was aware of the gap between theory and practice—of the contract of submission by a contract of association.

Rousseau's view on property, as set forth in the discourse not his final word on the matter; in his other writings, he seems to have adopted the exact reversal of this position, in line with the general approach to property in eighteenth-century France. We recall that Emile's first lesson out in the world, after he has gained some awareness of external phenomena, is a lesson in property rights. In Emile Book 11, the key scene is a conversation which takes place among Rousseau, Emile and Robert, the owner of a plot; Emile cultivates the plot to his own taste before inquiring about ownership. Ernile subsequently learns that ownership comes with labour, with the cultivation of the land which the stranger should not trespass once ownership has been thus claimed.

This is Rousseau's final position and it is consistent with the crucial role property plays in the social contract. We believe that the whole meaning of the social contract revolves around the concepts of property and ownership— both productions of the neo-classical discursive space. Freedom and equality —the other basic ingredients in Rousseau's social pact—are functional to ownership over land and over one's self. The social pact itself, the agreement by which a group of people comes together, has no meaning in a context where everyone comes into the group with no property at all or with equal amounts of property. And the most important point of the contract is the preservation of all the goods each member owns before he enters into the social order and his exercise of liberty over them. The need for an association is itself motivated by the need to keep to one's grounds; we would coin it 'the spreading of selfhood over property'. To have any meaning, the pact must sustain and reinforce all the fences that surround all properties for otherwise there would be no need for a pact since everyone would be entitled to roam freely without threatening the Other. The key word is 'trespassing', or infringing on what we term 'privacy'.

Who is to decide how much disparity it takes for slavery to come about? Is it a quantitative measurement? It is certain that the act of association preserves the status quo of the individual participant; the pact is one act by which I give everything I own to the state and at the same time recuperate immediately everything I give. The alienation and recuperation of my goods constitute unsigned act. In other words, I do not first alienate myself and my possessions to the state and then receive from the state an equitable share of all the accumulated common good. Rousseau repeatedly stresses the fact that the individual, in the end, obeys no one but himself. The individual never disappears behind the General Will; rather, it is the General will which manifests itself in the individual will. Ideology enters the picture at this point for the alienation of all individual goods to the social body should entail a collective ownership of all goods. Logic necessitates that if I give up something, I cannot claim to own it, or somebody else owns it, and in our case it should be the social body. Rousseau clearly does not follow this logic through.

Considering the formal side of the concept of equality, we end up with the exact reversal, and formal equality means inequality. For in saying that the same principle applies under the law to all citizens alike, one abstracts the basic differences among them and, in effect, reinforces the natural inequalities. If the purpose of society is to supplement natural inequalities which cannot be avoided, then it should rather consider the concept of inequality. By applying different standards to different men, society could compensate for the natural inequalities. Furthermore, Rousseau's concept of equality, as a discursive phenomenon in eighteenth-century political discourse, takes hold only within the existing class structure that is in a situation where the gap between the classes must be minimized. It is not a concept which attempts a radical transformation of the class structure itself; it merely attempts to modify the status quo. The transformation of the social structure was not the problem but, rather, how to raise the living standards of over 80 per cent of the population to a more humanly acceptable level.

This is in line with the passage relating to material equality quoted above. Rousseau was not indifferent to the masses; on the contrary, he was probably the only one among the philosophers of the Enlightenment who identified openly with the poor. We have already mentioned his dislike for high society and its manners. But regarding possible solutions to the social problem he remains captive to the hegemonic mode within which he produced. Rousseau, indeed, typifies the struggle between a subject's search for meaning and the mental structures of the period. In the end hegemony overcomes his lonely voice to the point where the only remaining solution was an individual one— madness — which he adopted with a vengeance.

Equality, then, means the value everyself attains in its exercise of autonomy over property and not the well-being of the individual in his contribution to the welfare of the social body as a whole. Rousseau's dream must therefore be the exercise by every individual of sovereignty over his own piece of land, the only guarantee that the individual will not become enslaved by the rich. But equality can reside only within a social body. If we look closely at his social theory we see that he does not depart from the view of the Other that he espoused in his autobiography. Here we see the interface between autobiography and social theory for the conception of subjectivity is germane to the conception of a social structure in any given discursive matrix. And Rousseau is but one voice, albeit a lucid one, within the Enlightened discursive matrix. If Rousseau rejects the Other, no room is left for the social body and the pact of association is nothing but an artificial construct.

Natural man exists for himself in a radically different way from the way in which others exist for him, for he possesses an identity for himself and yet does not recognize other men as similarly endowed with self-consciousness. Natural man in not being aware of others as centers of consciousness in the world cannot be aware of having an existence in their consciousness, of being somebody for them. Man's consciousness does not merely happen contingently to be non-social, while it could be social, but is necessarily non-social, for it is defined in such a way as to be incompatible with a social consciousness.

This is true of man both before and after he participates in the social contract; we recall that the fall of man, in Rousseau's vision, is due to his being perceived by the Other, to his being attributed certain characteristics from the outside: that is, to his dependence upon the opinions and judgements of the others. Therefore, in wanting to refound society on nature, Rousseau does not synthesise between the natural and the social but, rather, introduces his conception of natural man—as totally independent and self-sufficient—into the social, and this is a contradiction in terms. If in the social order there are not enough trees to accommodate everyone, a feeling of independence must be fostered in every consciousness and this can be done through a proper approach to education.

This is mile before he falls into the social Order. Rousseau differentiates between the education of man and the education of civil man in correspondence with the two inderfities of man. *Emile* is mostly a treatise on education of the firsts identity; towards the end of the book, when Emile is twenty-two and ripe for full social relations, he is given a talk on civil education and the laws of government. Rousseau's assumption is that contact with the corrupting effects of the social order must be delayed until the child has built up his natural defences. Until that point the child or adolescent is sheltered from the judgements and opinions of others in order not to hinder the development of his own natural view of himself. Rousseau's fundamental credo with regard to the education of man is liberty; however, liberty is not total since the child is dependent upon his mentor until he reaches the ripe age of twenty-four when he is ready for a wife. But even the educator does not interfere with the work of nature; authority is never exercised directly on the child through threats or punishment. The teacher never comes to a confrontation with Emile; he controls him negatively, by creating a climate in which Emile comes to the right conclusions. This negative approach, to Rousseau, will enable Emile to develop, first, a feeling of material independence and, second, a definition of self that does not lie outside himself. This type of education is in line with the instinct of natural man for self-preservation, that is, *amour de soi* as opposed to *amour proper* which one acquires with the social mask. But what about the second natural tendency in man, to abhor suffering in others? Is not pity a form of intercourse with the Other? If so, then perhaps Rousseau does posit the necessity of an external consciousness for self-definition.

Thus, in his process of socialisation man has denied nature; Rousseau's task is to negate what man has negated—a double negation. In opposition to social man, the man of nature did not have to conform to appearances, nor to wear a mask, because his existence has not mediated by another consciousness. But the man of nature still lives within social man. At the level of the individual, we can see how these two periods, or two men, coexist in social man and what kind of relationship they have, at least in Rousseau's case, which is, as he claims in his opening statement to the *Confessions*. This is the point at which autobiography coincides with history in Rousseau's worldview. The delineation between the two men, between society and nature, can be achieved best in autobiography because it is the ideal case study. The total knowledge Rousseau has of his own self allows for the differentiation between the states and the rediscovery of that veiled innocence.

Critics have referred to a double movement in Rousseau. We find in Rousseau on the one hand, the desire to immerse himself in the thickness of the social texture—a tendency to expansion; and on the other hand, the tendency to run away from it all and face himself in solitude—a phenomenon of rarefaction. Rousseau, however, seems to jump repeatedly from shrinkage to expansion. He oscillates from one pole to the other like a pendulum. The one movement takes the form of presence, the other of absence. We also have mixed phenomena where Rousseau experiences presence in terms of absence and absence in terms of presence. In the end, though, the balance seems to tilt in favour of absence in Rousseau's world, for his madness is an extreme form of absence.

From early childhood Jean-Jacques develops the concept of the double; his first experience of the mask comes, not surprisingly, with his exposure to the world of fiction. His father initiates him to books as a child, and in his readings, his self undergoes a gradual change; he becomes someone else. Role-playing can sometimes become an obsession. When Rousseau decides to become a reader, he cannot stop reading; the activity occupies him to the exclusion of all other occupations. And so it is with chess playing. A momentary whim turns into a manic idée fixed. He cannot stop playing chess and the act overtakes all his faculties as long as it lasts. This means that Rousseau wants to extend the whim into a durable present, or a succession of presents that lose none of their intensity. The whim does not fade away; it goes as it comes, in a minute. It disappears in forgetfulness. While it lasts, then, the persona occupies him totally. This phenomenon reflects the lack of consistency in Rousseau's personality, a lack he confesses to and in fact welcomes. Role-playing calls upon the acting self, but all these actions are non-committing since they vanish in no time. Rousseau hears a continual 'bourdonnement', and internal noise that hardly leaves room for an external message. Interestingly enough, this internal noise forces him to stay up at night and write his books. The inner noise hampers any communicative dispatch that comes from the outside. The internal noise, as it were, conditions the external silence.

Now what are the actions Rousseau undertakes in the world? His worldly acts illustrate in many ways the problematic of mediation which, we believe, is central to

Rousseau. After the episode of the comb, Rousseau discovers theft and becomes a kleptomaniac. But he is never tempted by money, because money stands between the subject and the object. The mediating effect minimises the power of immediate possession that one can have in the theft of an object. However, indulging in theft entails punishment. Indeed the purpose of the theft is not the object only, but the punishment that follows as well, for crime and punishment go together. Rousseau enjoyed the beatings administered by Mille Lambencies at Bossey, and actually encouraged them because they satisfied some childish eroticism in him. This first encounter with the Other seems to be repeated throughout Rousseau's life. Mille Lambercier can be replaced by Rousseau critics and contemporaries, those who persecute him. The sado-masochistic form of the relationship is common to both experiences; in both cases, Rousseau asks for the punishment. The *Confessions* constitutes an apology; Rousseau is asking for forgiveness, if not from his contemporaries, at least from the future reader.

At the beginning of Book III of *Confession* Rousseau describes the agitation caused by sexual deprivation, but instead of finding an object to remedy the erotic lack, he resorts to exhibitionism. The exhibitionist exposes his nudity in dark alleys but close enough to be seen by the other sex. On the face of it, this seems to be a transitive act, since the exhibitionist challenges the look of the other. But, as Starobinski suggests that such an act stands for the expression of a minimal presence to the world; it remains intransitive because it does not reach out. Rousseau wants to be seen on his own terms, not on the terms of the other. Rousseau's love affairs are significant in respect to their mediating factor. We find that love, the epitome of communication, of reaching out, is intransitive in Rousseau's case. He never concludes his love, and rarely consummates it. He can take pages to describe a look or a kiss, and drive as much pleasure from them as anyone who takes them as starting points. Why? Possession means total presence to the other and this is in opposition to Rousseau's mode of loving: in order to love, Jean-Jacques must be absent.

In absence, Rousseau creates a love that meets his heart's desire without being challenged by the Other. Other instances of Rousseau's refusal of mediation are seen in his being an autodidact—negating the teacher; submitting his five or seven children to Les Enfants Trouves—refusing parenthood; and rejecting a pension offered by the king. Neither the teacher, his children, nor the king can define Rousseau.

Rousseau's story is marked by numerous trips. Travel is a major activity, not only towards the end of the *Confession* when Rousseau is apparently forced to run for his life, but right from the start when he leaves Geneva. The trips he enjoys most are the ones he takes on foot. In fact, an ambulatory mania seems to have a hold on most of his faculties: he cannot think without walking, and most daydreams come with wandering. Starobinski claims that Rousseau's walking involves a process of self-hypnosis. The main characteristic of such wandering is its aimlessness; one goes everywhere and in all directions. It is also an action that forgets time: one does not wander for an hour. Both daydreaming and wandering are occupations with no end, devoid of moorings in reality.

Rousseau, then, must be absent in order to be present. But the absence is not the distance the artist takes from his object to achieve perspective. The absence to the object is total; perspective entails a divided consciousness which would not benefit Rousseau's quest to possess the immediate through sense perception. So closeness to the object is attained by wiping it out and recreating it anew through the process of fiction. Fiction seems to be the only mediator between Rousseau and the world. This equation becomes alarming when we realise that, in Rousseau's case, the ontological gap between fiction and the world is trespassed to the point of madness. How does Rousseau live the greatest love of his life? Neither he nor Sophie are present in this relationship, because Rousseau defined her long before he met her.

First, there is an objectless desire; then he meets Sophie, but he meets her in terms of Julie, the heroine of his *La Nouvelle Heloise*—the fictional fulfillment of his real desire.

Rousseau tries to penetrate the world of books at a tender age, and identifies with his heroes. Over the years this identification becomes internal, through the creation of his own fictional universe. Towards the end he cannot cope at all with the Other who becomes a pure anonymity, an omnimous hand lurking in the shadows. The Other remains transfigured through the process of fiction. But sometimes, in moments of lucidity, Rousseau catches himself at his own game: He is sometimes aware of his exaggeration in the portrayal of the Other. Diderot, Grimm, Holbach seem to spread their wings not only over the people Rousseau comes in contact with, but over all the spaces he lives in. The old friends become despicable enemies: they lose their names and identities; hence the plot that is being woven quietly in the dark.

There has to be some tension between shrinkage and expansion, between self-possession and social relation, but the permanent self takes meaning within the social context, to the extent that the subject assimilates the other. Otherwise the Other loses existence and must be created ex nihilo as a composite entity—all the enemies group into the one, an entity which in Rousseau's case, threatens the very existence of the subject.

This alienation is generated by one major act, the only mediation for Rousseau, the act of fiction. Although Rousseau's literary career is relatively short, its preparation and aftermath seem to take the parameters of his life. Writing has a beginning in childhood, but it seems to have no end, since writing is not an activity Rousseau undertakes at the table facing a blank sheet; he writes 'in his brain.'

It is the act of fiction which gives rise to the insoluble paradox in Rousseau's life: the expression of negation through a positive act, saying 'no' to the world through the book which is pure affirmation, writing for public consumption while one craves absence, which in itself is a curse since assertion becomes functional to negation. Rousseau gives a tragic qualification to his vocation: he 'fell in to it' unawares.

To write and to hide: two acts that combine to make Rousseau what he is, the only acts that define him. One should say 'to-write-and-to-hide', for indeed these two verbs are not consecutive: they are simultaneous, constituting one integrated act. To be present involves not only a disadvantage but a disfigurement as well, a metamorphosis of one's features, a total alienation.

But the discourse itself is problematic, for Rousseau holds the conviction that the immediate is speechless. In the immediate, the sign does not stand for the object but rather, the sign is inscribed in the body of the object; sign and object are one. In the immediate one can never be out of place, look awkward, or be at a disadvantage. Speech is replaced by a non-verbal sign language. Rousseau would have liked to be mute, to point to things rather than speak them. Repeatedly he indicates the limits of language and its inability to express meaning. We know of Rousseau's aversion to social verbiage; 'babiller' is a damaging occupation. The body can express meaning: meaning is literally squeezed out of the body through its immediate presence. A magnetic force causes the attraction of subject to object and vice versa. This is the level at which the body becomes text—hence exhibitionism or writing. Exhibitionism and writing are identical: to-write-and-to-hide constitutes an act of exhibitionism that calls for silence. The parade of one's words coincides with the parade of one's body.

How can one communicate in a language that erects walls, a language of divisions? But perhaps one can avoid the alienating word—lay down the pen and resort to an immediate mode of communication. Maybe one can carry a message through the language of the body. It is not without reason that Jean-Jacques starts his reform with his outside appearance. In discarding his watch and sword he performs two magical acts: he negates time, because in the immediate time is of no consequence, and he rejects his social status. The Armenian robe completes the a, b, c of his body language. Rousseau declares over and over that he was persecuted less for his literary fame than for his personal reform. But he seems to ask for it. For the change of clothes, the negation of the external definition, the postulation of difference, is achieved with pomp. He wants to retire to the woods but he makes enough noise for everyone to notice it. He plays the game of hide and seek.

In consequence, Rousseau is a double loser. Not only is he unable to communicate through his body, through the virtues he seeks in the act of reform, but the choice to retire is taken away from him: retirement is forced on him through persecution. Wandering turns into running, to the point where Jean-Jacques asks for imprisonment. The attack on his world coincides with the physical attack on his body.

The persecution Rousseau asks for is, to Starobinski, the panacea for all his troubles. For being persecuted, disfigured, alienated in voice and body, encourages one to seek inaction. By altering his words and feelings, by making him other than he is, the persecutors force him to enter the immediate. But since no kind of regression is possible in history, and since Rousseau of necessity was anchored in reality, the immediate becomes the realm of impotence and masturbation. For the only thing Rousseau can do is look at himself.

The domain of action is restricted to fiction, not fiction as mediation of the real world, but fiction as an end in itself. Deliric verbiage replaces social small talk. Fiction assumes the role of the mediator. This is the only compromise Rousseau is able to afford, but at what price!

Rousseau came upon this question propounded by the Dijon Academy for the next year's prize: "Has the progress of the sciences and arts done more to corrupt morals or to improve them?" He submitted the essay for the competition. Rousseau's essay won the prize. Its theme was that, so far from ennobling man, the sciences and the arts have corrupted him by replacing the innocence, simplicity, self-reliance and honesty of the ancients with the artificial and mannered dissembling of modern times.

In our day, now that more subtle study and more refined taste have reduced the art of pleasing to a system, there prevails in modern manners a servile and deceptive conformity, sincere friendship, real esteem, and perfect confidence are banished from among men. Jealousy, suspicion, fears, coldness, reserve, hate and fraud lie constantly concealed under that uniform and deceitful veil of politeness. Human nature is not worse now than it used to be, but it has been diseased by false culture to such a degree that the people, as if addicted to their baubles, have become enslaved by them and have lost their sense of their own natural and authentic worth.

The accusation that modern society distorts what it does not suppress of the best part of man had been made many times before and has been made many times since Rousseau's *Discourse on the Arts and Sciences*. The charge, however, became a theme to which he returned in all his later political works: man has been forced by social institutions to become less virtuous than he had been and less virtuous than he can be. In most of his subsequent writings, Rousseau seeks to give the true account of man's virtue, how it was lost and how it can be regained.

Following Aristotle, Rousseau supposes that man's virtue will be found not by looking at distorted men but examining men who are rightly ordered according to nature. Again the Academy of Dijon provided the occasion for a thesis, its question being: 'What is the Origin of Inequality among Men, and is it authorized by Natural Law?' In reply, Rousseau, who this time did not win the prize, distinguishes between natural or physical differences and moral or political inequalities and proceeds to discuss how the second type of inequalities came about and what if anything could justify them. He begins the account by writing of man's evolution from savagery to society.

Like Descartes and Hobbes before him, Rousseau regards an animal as merely an ingenious machine 'to which nature hath given senses to wind itself up, and to guard itself against anything that might tend to disorder or destroy it'. Humans were always distinguishable by their capacity to make free choices. 'Nature lays her command on every animal, and the brute obeys her voice. Man receives the same impulsion ,but at the same time knows himself at liberty to acquiesce or resist: and it is particularly in his consciousness of this liberty that the spirituality of his soul is displayed'.

In this, then, that man's natural liberty consists, that he is neither a mere object in the hands of nature nor the subject of the will of any other person. In these respects, he is his own master. Nature who gives the savage his appetites secures his autonomy by providing him with the objects of their satisfaction. Since all men possess natural liberty equally and since nature herself takes care of all alike, the savage 'breathes only peace and liberty', respecting his own self and feeling at home in his world, innocent of pride and greed, having compassion for all. Rousseau argued that Hobbes was wrong in supposing that savage man was rapacious and cruel, at war with all his fellows: 'nothing is more gentle than man in his primitive state, as he is placed by nature at an equal distance from the stupidity of brutes, and the fatal ingenuity of civilized man.'

Rousseau introduces the notions of *amour de soi, amour propre,* and *pitie,* in the context of his discussion of the way in which various thinkers have arrived at a definition of natural law from an account of human nature. He argues that philosophers have made the mistake of inquiring into the rules necessary which men must agree on for their common interest, and have then proceeded to ascribe the name of natural law to these rules without any real knowledge of human nature. He argues that so long as we are ignorant of natural man it is in vain for us to attempt to determine either the law originally prescribed to him, or that which is best adapted to his constitution. All we can know with any certainty is that, we will perceive in human soul two principles prior to reason, one of them deeply interesting us in our own welfare and preservation, and the other exciting a natural repugnance at seeing any other sentient being, and particularly any of our own species, suffer pain or death.

Although Rousseau agrees with Hobbes that natural man possesses an innate desire for his own welfare and preservation, he disagrees fundamentally with the argument that natural man also has an innate desire for glory. For Rousseau the latter is only possible in an advanced social condition. The life of natural man being solitary and unsociable, has no place in it for such comparative passions. In an important footnote in the *Discourse on Inequality* Rousseau elaborate on this crucial point of difference between himself and philosophers who attribute a natural wickedness to man:

> *Amour propre* should not be confused with *Amour de soi* for they differ both in their nature and in their effects.

Amour de soi is a natural feeling which leads every animal to look to its own preservation, and which, guided in man by reason and modified by compassion *pitie*, creates humanity and virtue. *Amour propre* is a purely relative and factitious feeling, which arises in society, and leads each individual to make more of himself than any other, causes all the mutual damage men inflict on one another, and is the real source of the sense of honor. This being so, maintains Rousseau, that in our primitive condition, in the true state of nature *amour propre* did not exist.

Amour propre represents a desire for recognition and the need for self-esteem, which can only be found in the evaluation of oneself by others. It is necessary to make a distinction between vanity and pride, for in his work Rousseau does not simply adopt a critical tone towards *amour propre,* but towards its excessive or inflamed manifestations. Where pride involves seeking recognition in the possession of qualities of intrinsic worth, and is suitable to the creation of a community since these are qualities, which are recognized when they are placed in the service of others, vanity consists in the individual attaching itself to objects of no intrinsic value.

In the state of nature, each human being is the judge of their own actions because they are the only observer of them. In other words, each person is not dependent on any other for their self-estimation. In the state of nature, there are no comparative assessments of value between human beings. For this reason, Rousseau argues, that natural man knows neither hatred nor the desire for revenge, as these are passions, which depend on a sense of injury. Rousseau argues that as it is the intention to hurt, and not the harm done, which constitutes the injury, human beings who neither valued nor compared themselves could do one another much violence when it suited them without experiencing a sense of injury. 'In a word', says Rousseau 'each man, regarding his fellows almost as he regarded animals of different species, might seize the prey of a weaker or yield up his own to a stronger, and yet consider these acts of violence as mere natural occurrences, without the slightest emotion of insolence or despite, or any other feeling than the joy or grief of success or failure'. Thus, Rousseau argues that to attribute intentions of wickedness or wrongdoing to human action presupposes the development of a moral sense, a sense which, according to Rousseau can only be the result of a long process of social development.

In the *Discourse* Rousseau speaks of compassion as the pure emotion of nature that is prior to all reflection and from which follows all the latter virtues which make social relationships possible. He argues that 'compassion is a natural sentiment which, by moderating the activity of *amour de soi* in each individual, contributes to the preservation of the whole species'. It is compassion which in the state of nature takes the place of laws, morals, and virtue.

Rousseau posits compassion *pitie* in terms of a natural law of the heart, a 'law' which is present in man prior to his reason and his socialization. But is there not a contradiction in Rousseau's account? If man in a state of nature possesses a natural goodness which means he is neither virtuous nor vicious, how is it possible for him to have this natural sentiment of pity which teaches him to pursue his self-preservation in such a way that he will do as little evil to others as possible? How, in the state of nature, will natural man know what 'evil' is?

In order to resolve the contradiction in Rousseau's account it is necessary to recognize a distinction between natural pity and social pity. The crucial difference between the two can be seen in the context in which pity operates and is drawn into play. In a natural state, for example, an individual's sense of itself as a creature of compassion does not arise out of a comparison with others, but out of a spontaneous self-affirmation while in society the individual's disposition to experiencing pity at the sight of pain and suffering is susceptible to corruption at the hands of a perverted *amour propre*. Here its original goodness is lost, for it only affirms itself by negating the other Nietzsche's type of slave morality. The natural pity does not arise from a comparison with others, but is a purely physical sensation accompanied by a spontaneous feeling of compassion.

In this state, 'the happiest and most stable of epochs' man is moved by two innate and complementary springs of action, healthy self love-*amour de soi* which motivates every person to seek his own good, and compassion – *pitie* which produces generosity and friendship and the general sentiment which we call love of humanity and which was also called fraternity.

Rousseau is unclear, though very eloquent, about some aspects of the nature and the life of savage man, as he also is about the evolution from savagery to society. Three slightly different but quite compatible accounts are given of the emergence of society and oppression. The first account proposes that men compared their skills with the animals and with those of the other men and began feeling pride and began behaving proudly, desiring and striving for what they had previously not wanted, reputation and glory, as the basis of their own self-respect. This foundation for self-worth was utterly treacherous because it required that every man depended upon the assessment of others for their valuation of his own worth. Vanity, the desire to be admired, was paid for by dissemblance, by appearing to be what one is not, and thus lying and deceit were fostered and grew with contempt, conspiracy, and vengeance. This vanity, which Rousseau calls *amour proper*-improper self-love, and unnatural since it did not exist in the true and happy state of nature. It is the source of man's corruption. It is this vanity, which is the cause of the ridiculous sense of honor, that potent and corrosive destroyer of fraternity and equality in society.

A second account is of contented hunters living independent lives in rustic huts who, having been beguiled by the apparent benefits of metallurgy and agriculture and needing the assistance of other people in developing these arts, began to dominate and be dominated by their fellows. Where some gained by co-operative work, some lost and natural equality disappeared. The more aggressive men prospered, appropriating not only the fruits of the earth but the earth itself. The enriched grew richer and squeezed out their partners who became their impoverished servants and at length their slaves.

The third account is that the believed claim to the ownership of land was the cause of humankind's misery. The first man who, having enclosed a piece of ground, bethought himself of saying 'This is mine,' and found people simple enough to believe him, was the real founder of civil society. From how many crimes, wars, and murders, from how many horrors and misfortunes one might not have saved mankind, by pulling up the stakes, nor filling up the ditch, and crying to his fellows: 'Beware of listening to this impostor; you are undone if you once forget that the fruits of the earth belong to us all, and the earth itself to nobody'. The greed and the power of landowners increased, as did the misery of those who were dispossessed both of the land and its wealth. This, not the earlier state, was the violent epoch, which Hobbes had so vividly described, as the war of every man against every man. 'Usurpations by the rich, robbery by the poor, and the unbridled passions of both, suppressed the cries of natural compassion and the still feeble voice of justice, and filled men with avarice, ambition, and vice.' The chaos and the terror united with self-interest so that the rich and corrupt proposed what the poor and wretched accepted the establishment of political society. 'Instead of turning our forces against ourselves, let us collect them in a supreme power which may govern us by wise laws, protect and defend all the members of the association, repulse their common enemies, and maintain eternal harmony among us.' The trick worked. 'All ran headlong to their chain in hopes of securing their liberty'.

Rousseau does not mind whether the account he has given is true or not. What matters to him is that he has given a plausible explanation for the origin of political societies and that in showing that savage man contentedly rabbiting about in the bush possessed natural liberty and equality, he has also shown that this liberty has been stolen from him by greedy society which has been founded upon the vanity (*amour propre*) of the rich instead of the healthy compassion (*pitie*) and self-love (*amour de soi*) of everyone.

Rousseau's account of the natural goodness of man and of his almost accidental yet almost historically inevitable departure from original innocence is confirmed in many of his other writings and, in the manner of many rationalists of the time, it challenged the orthodox Christian account that man's fall from grace and expulsion from Eden was the consequence of God's anger at the sin of disobedience of man. It was not disobedience, rebellion and ungodliness which caused the misery of humankind, as the theologians proposed, but unnatural and vicious social arrangements which produced the inequality, the injustice, the loss of freedom and the consequent degradation of civilized humankind.

The New Helios (1761), a novel immensely influential in shaping and invigorating the romantic movement, restates the view that freedom is impossible if one is dependent upon other persons' wills when they are tainted with vanity, as does *Emile* (1762). Always a stylish opener, Rousseau begins *Emile* in characteristic declamatory fashion: 'God makes all things good; man meddles with them and they become evil'. Again, the theme is that society has perverted humanity. In *Emile* Rousseau brings the good news of redemption for the child who will be a man. Rousseau's good news is that we can become perfect and that this will happen and that it will only happen in society, when we have transformed the chains of the present corrupt and corrupting society making from them fraternal bonds of liberty. The volume, which bears the good news of the liberation of all, is *The Social Contract* (1762), and its vehicle is the majestic chariot the General Will.

Rousseau's political philosophy attempts a novel solution to the antinomies of modern political life-the oppositions of man and citizen, desire and reason, freedom and necessity, individuality and community- and was to have a tremendous impact on modern German thought, notably Kant, Hegel, Schiller, and Marx. Rousseau's political philosophy is frequently presented in terms of either a liberal, or a totalitarian, response to modern political life. He is seen on the one hand, to extol the primacy of individual liberty, while, on the other, to sacrifice the liberty of the individual to the authority of the State. Thus, several commentators have argued that there is a contradiction within Rousseau's thinking on the individual and society. It has been suggested for example, that whereas the *Discourse on the Origin of Inequality* (1755) offers an eloquent account of the rights of the individual, the *Social Contract* (1762) proposes the total subordination of those rights to the demands of the State.

However, this construal of Rousseau's political thought fails to recognize its unique nature, which lies in the fact that although it begins with the same individualistic premises as the liberal tradition of modern political thought (namely, Hobbes and Locke), it sees the goal of the *res publica*, or commonwealth, not merely in prudential terms but, rather, in moral ones. For Rousseau the social contract, by which the individual elects to join society and obey its rules through an act of free choice, is premised not merely on an exchange basis where the individual agrees to become a member of society and consents to obey its laws in return for peace and security; rather the social contract is the means whereby isolated individuals come together through a creative political act and transform themselves into moral beings by becoming self-legislating citizens. Thus, Rousseau argues that society exists not only to provide individuals with peace and happiness, though this is one of its aims, but also to educate them into moral beings. With Rousseau, politics has become education. In contrast to Hobbes and Locke, the transition from the pre-political state of nature to civil society is construed by Rousseau in terms of process by which human beings forsake their natural liberty in exchange for a higher moral or ethical liberty. In other words, Rousseau's argument is that we only become truly free and independent when we become moral beings united in society. This is a fundamentally different account of political obligation to the one we find in the early liberal tradition of political theory. Rousseau is closest to Hobbes in holding that human beings become moral through political education; but he departs from Hobbes in holding that sovereignty cannot' be alienated.

The State of Nature

In the preface to his prize-winning *First Discourse on the Arts and Sciences*, Rousseau says that the audience of any published work can be divided into two, the pubic and a few wise men. He speaks of the volatility of public opinion, of the fact that men are tied to the opinions and prejudices of their century. The free thinker, therefore, must necessarily address his writing to a future audience if he wants to live beyond his century: he is condemned to unseemliness. Although the *Second Discourse* was also occasioned by a competition set by the Academy of Dijon, Rousseau this time felt free to give full vent to his feelings and did not feel the need to flatter the prejudices of his contemporaries. It is a discourse not addressed to the 'academicians' but to the 'human race'. It is a work which explicitly rejects divine revelation as a source for the authority of truth. It is Rousseau's testimony whose truthfulness can only be judged by whether it speaks to the hearts of men, that is, to our 'true selves'. Again, Rousseau's thought faces a crucial paradox: if we have been corrupted' if we are decadents, then how is it possible for us to rediscover our real selves? Rousseau will address himself to both the common man and to the philosopher. He will relate the history of the human species, as it should be read, not in the books of one's fellowmen who are al liars, but in the 'book of nature' itself which, we are told, 'never lies'. Rousseau's intention is to replace the written thought of men with nature as the true standard of human existence, a move which is only possible because man's degeneration is not yet complete.

The *Discourse on the Origin and Foundation of the Inequality of Mankind*, a work which continues to haunt the Occidental imagination in the way in which it shows that the cultural achievements and wealth of civilization rest on barbarism, poverty, and injustice, was published in 1755 as a response to the question set by the Academy concerning the origin of inequality among men, and whether or not it is sanctioned by natural law. For Rousseau the problem of civilization reduces itself to the task of determining what is original and what is artificial in the nature of man. However, an investigation into this problem is compounded, Rousseau tells us, by the problem of reflecting on a state of nature 'which no longer exists, perhaps never did exist, and probably never will exist', but of which it is necessary to have an idea in order to form a judgments of our present state. In reflecting on this problem Rousseau makes the point that the more the human race advances the more difficult it becomes to know the 'true nature' of man, and thus we are faced with the paradox that, 'it is, in one sense, by our very study of man, that the knowledge of him is put beyond our grasp'.

In the first part of the *Discourse* he contends that there must be two kinds of inequality among men, one which is natural or physical, and hence beyond our choice, the other social or political, because it depends upon human choice. There is, Rousseau observes, no fundamental link between these two types of inequality, for the claims to dominance put forward by the few who govern the many can have no force unless they are acknowledged to be proper, and that acknowledgement was granted by individuals to other persons rather than bestowed as a gift from Nature. The social and political divisions which obtain throughout the world are thus never to be justified with reference to any of the physical traits which mark individuals apart. If the opposite were true, then the exercise of force might itself create an obligation to obey, and men would somehow command the respect of their neighbours for the same reason that they arouse their fears. In the *Social Contract* Rousseau was to explain at greater length that force is not the foundation of right, and this is his position in the *Discourse on Inequality* as well. Together with other social contract theorists, he believed that the rules which differentiate persons in society could only come to prevail through their consent, so that the inequalities produced by Nature must have been transformed into such inequalities as were enjoined by man.

Rousseau conceived the central theme of his *Second Discourse* as an account of how the human race might have undergone a transformation of this sort. Since in their natural state our ancestors would have had only casual and infrequent contact with each other, he claims that the earliest distinctions between individuals would have been of no consequence. The inequalities established by men themselves, however, formed the dominant features of each community. In their original condition, our forebears could have had no moral relations with or determinate obligations to one another and since natural man had neither any need for the company of other creatures like himself, nor any wish to hurt them, it was only with the birth of social institutions that his weakness became timidity or his strength a menace to his neighbours. The inequalities, which have arisen between persons in society, by contrast, where fixed and determinate relations do prevail, bind individuals together permanently through channels of subservience and command.

Because they had been entirely mistaken in their conceptions of the state of nature, Hobbes, Pufendorf, and Locke, by contrast, had wrongly supposed that all individuals must there be equal in their powers, and each of these thinkers had imagined that as a consequence of this equality every person would be apprehensive of his neighbours and unable to live in safety among them. Men of equal abilities, Hobbes had alleged, could pursue the same objectives only at their peril, for without a common power to keep them in awe, they would be in a state of war. In order to achieve peace, he had supposed that men must institute an artificial superior or 'mortal god' with absolute authority to protect each person from the next, so that the pernicious effects of equality might be overcome through the subjection of the whole multitude to the Leviathan. Thus while for Rousseau the inequalities of the natural state must have been entirely without significance for mankind, according to Hobbes the fact that there must be equality in a masterless world was of great importance and was one of the reasons which made the attainment of peace there naturally impossible.

Pufendorf similarly argued that men must have been precariously equal in their original condition. Agreeing with Hobbes that we were motivated by selfishness rather than any impulse of benevolence or fellowship, he nevertheless contended that in the state of nature we would have been at the mercy of the elements and of fierce animals, drawn together on account of our frailty and timidity, not positively but negatively, in order to survive. This was Pufendorf's doctrine of natural sociability a trait which, he claimed, would have led our ancestors to form communities of ever increasing complexity and sophistication, on account of the limitless capacities and insatiable desires unique to our species. The growth of a political commonwealth would accordingly have been more gradual than Hobbes had imagined, but for Pufendorf it was similarly designed to overcome the perilous instability of our natural condition of equality through our acceptance of the rule of an absolute sovereign. Civil society or civilization, thus conceived, provided a remedy for the barbarous misery of our savage state. Kant would later term such a theory of the genesis of society the doctrine of 'unsocial sociability'.

For Locke, too, it had been the fundamental equality of men in their original condition, 'wherein all power and jurisdiction is reciprocal' which must have made the tenure of property there uncertain and insecure. Only in civil society, he supposed, where it was constantly defended by a superior power entrusted with its care, could property be safeguarded and our natural right enforced. While Hobbes 's central focus had been the political dimension of peace, Pufendorf's the collective need for security and Locke's the civil protection of property, the three writers appeared to be in agreement that individuals were naturally unable to survive in the absence of government, and thus that an artificial power must always be established to reduce the dangers which accompany the unfettered equality of mankind.

Rousseau's account of inequality's origins in his *Second Discourse* was at least partly designed to contradict these claims. In his view, the superior authorities conceived by Hobbes, Pufendorf, and Locke must have reinforced the antagonisms which set persons apart from one another, and did not overcome such differences. He believed it was impossible to discover from the works of any of these or other political thinkers *why* men in the state of nature should seek protection from their neighbours, but he thought their ideas collectively did none the less explain how individuals might have established as legitimate just those determinate and fixed relations which form the distinctions between them in corrupt society. According to Rousseau, confronting Hobbes in particular, it was true that men must have developed all their social obligations so as to protect their lives and their possessions, but since they could not have been at war, nor owned any property, nor had any ambitions to dominate or any reason to fear one another, ii their natural state, it was inconceivable that they should origin ally have felt the need for such security. The state of nature could have contained no endogenous factors to drive its inhabitants out of it, and sentiments of envy or distrust, which made persons apprehensive for their safety or fearful of losing their possessions, were, in his view, simply not appropriate to men who lived contentedly alone.

In the *Discourse on Inequality* he acknowledges that the idea of private property must have constituted the most fundamental principle of obligation, although in so for as savages could not originally have formulated principles of any kind, he insists that such an idea must have arisen some time after they had begun to settle in communities. Pufendorf had mistaken to suppose that men's natural sociability must have impelled them to live together, since society itself is unnatural and depends upon an agreed vocabulary of signs, that is, a language, which makes the shared framework of intelligible discourse possible. But language, in turn, could not have arisen without a pre-existent society, which shaped it and gave a commonly accepted meaning to individual utterances.

In the absence of both society and language from our most savage state, the establishment of a right of property, such as Locke had described it would also have been impossible there. No claims of ownership could have been expressed or understood by men and women until the linguistic rules of social life had first been established, for without some form of language individuals could not have had a convention of what was specifically their own, nor could they have undertaken to respect anything that belonged to others. In fact, the institution of private property, Rousseau remarks, must, have depended upon a whole variety of conventions and practices which had evolved in the course of human history. It required not only language but also industry, enterprise, progress, and enlightenment, so that it actually formed what he terms the 'last point of the state of nature' and the first point in the emergence of civil society.

The first man who, having enclosed a piece of ground, thought up the statement this is mine and found people simple enough to believe him was the real founder of civil society', Rousseau observes. Such an impostor, a savage forebear of our species inspired by Locke's perniciously cunning eloquence, would have driven mankind into social subjection, concealing the fact, which Locke had himself recognized before embarking on his case for private ownership, that 'the fruits of the earth belong to us all, and the earth itself to nobody'. If civil society had been initially formed to justify men's property relations, it must have been just *these* relations, moreover, which had given rise to war. Land would have become scarce through individual appropriation and inheritance, while there must have been an increase in population, leading to usurpations by the rich robbery by the poor, and the unbridled passions of both. Just as Locke had been mistaken, therefore, to suppose that men could have established territorial rights of exclusive use and occupancy before they had created any other social institutions, so too Hobbes had failed to see that the property relations formed by men in their communities must be the principal cause of war, Rousseau contends. Since individuals could have come to harm one another only after and because they had established divisive property relations, in their original propertyless state they plainly would have had no occasion to inflict injury upon one another or to suffer it at each other's hands.

It was thus Rousseau's view that the social contract devised by men in order to make their property secure could not have been formed in the state of nature, but, on the contrary, must have been a hoax perpetrated in society by the rich upon the poor. Its terms might have seemed superficially plausible because they would have referred to the impartial rule of law and to the security of every man, but its real aim would have been to establish such order as was necessary to preserve the estates of some persons at the expense of others. By their own agreement, the poor would have been required to repudiate their right to share the wealth which men of property enjoyed, with the effect that in exchange for peace and protection of their lives, as Rousseau puts it, 'All ran headlong to their chains, believing they had secured their liberty. The notion that 'property is theft', advanced by Proudhon and other socialists in the nineteenth century, owes much to this argument.

Because of the simplistic manner in which philosophers have dealt with this issue, Rousseau argues that the term 'natural law' is mystifying. They have attempted to define natural law by considering what rules are expedient for human beings to agree on for their common interest. The attempt to inquire into the philosophical foundations of society rests on the idea of a state of nature, but as Rousseau points out, the fact that so many conflicting accounts have been given of this state, shows that there exists no universally agreed upon definition of natural law. He makes the crucial point that, in concaving of man in the state of nature, philosophers have attributed to natural man qualities, which could only have been acquired in a social state. The focus of Rousseau's critique is Hobbes's depiction of the state of nature in terms of a war of all against all. Rousseau concentrates a great deal of attention on Hobbes's argument because of his depiction of human behavior in the state of nature as one of natural wickedness. Such an account of man's natural condition clearly poses a major challenge to Rousseau's belief in man's natural goodness.

The idea of the state of nature plays a double role in Rousseau's political thought. On the one hand, it is conceived in philosophical terms as a legal fiction, best conceived as a Kantian regulative idea which tells us that we must think as if such a state existed in order to understand the nature of social man, and, on the other hand, it is understood to be an actual historical condition which preceded the emergence of political man. Thus, for example, Rousseau argues that in answering the question set by the Academy we must begin 'by laying all facts aside, as they do not affect the question'. Furthermore, 'the investigations we may enter into, in treating this subject, must not be considered as historical truths, but only as mere conditional and hypothetical reasonings, calculated to explain the nature of things, than to ascertain their real origin'.

Rousseau's major argument with his predecessors is that they attribute to human beings in a state of nature qualities, which could only be, acquired via a process of socialization. The idea of man's natural goodness is a rebuttal of Hobbes's argument that human beings are inherently aggressive and possess an innate desire for dominion over others. Instead, Rousseau aims to show that the desire for power over others is a result of a certain historical development in which the rise of inequalities in social and political power have given birth to certain qualities such as vanity and pride. This is why, for example, Rousseau tells us that the precise subject of his investigation into the origins of inequality is to mark 'the moment at which right took the place of violence and nature become subject to law, and to explain by what sequence of miracles the strong came to submit to serve the weak, and the people to purchase imaginary repose at the expense of real felicity. Here we encounter a major problem of Rousseau-interpretation the question whether Rousseau provides a materialist, or an idealist account of the transformation from innocent 'primitive' man to corrupt social man.

Although Rousseau actually begins from very similar premises to Hobbes-the belief, for example, that man is not naturally sociable, and that the major motive of human action is a desire for self-preservation-he draws from them radically different conclusions. While in Rousseau the precise historical status of the idea of the state of nature is ambiguous, there is no such ambiguity in Hobbes. Where in Rousseau the account of the state of nature is given a historical form and placed in the remote past, with the evolution of man as a social animal described in terms of evolutionary stages, in Hobbes the state of nature is not a condition which lies in the remote past, but is rather a condition we are constantly liable to fall into. On this account the state of nature provides us with a picture of what life would be like in the absence of political authority: "Hereby it is manifest, that during the time men live without a common power to keep them all in awe, they are in that condition which is called War and such a war as is of every man against every man. In such a state, there are no notions of right and wrong, of justice and injustice because there is no common power, and where there is no law, there can be no injustice. The only law of life under such conditions is that of self-preservation".

In Hobbes the origins of society and of political obligation are to be accounted for through the exercise of human rationality by which individuals learn to recognize that the pursuit of power in the state of nature is self-defeating, and that their desire for self-preservation and fundamental fear of death would be best served by them coming together and creating a sovereign power, a commonwealth, which would guarantee them peace and security -in fact an end to the grim and terrible war of all against all-in exchange for their near-unconditional obedience. Individuals can achieve this, Hobbes argues, through recognizing the 'laws of nature'. Although Hobbes is following traditional usage in calling these laws of nature 'laws', his use of the term is merely metaphorical; they are best understood as prudential maxims of what is conducive to self- preservation, what Hobbes calls 'dictates of right reason'. All the laws of nature and all political obligations derived from the individual's right to self-preservation. Thus, Hobbes distinguishes between 'the right of nature' and 'the law of nature'. The right of nature is, defined as the liberty each man has to use his own power as he himself wills for the preservation of his own nature. By contrast, a law of nature is defined as precept or a general rule, discovered by reason, which forbids a human being to do anything, which would be destructive of its existence. So long as human beings possess their natural right to everything, which is necessary for their self-preservation in a state of nature, the state of war will persist in determining their fate.

From this argument on the state of nature, Hobbes derives his first two fundamental laws of nature. The first one stipulates that where possible human beings should exercise their reason in order to seek peace and follow it when they find it; the second law of nature stipulates that each person ought to be willing to divest itself of its right to all things when others are also willing, and that it ought to be satisfied with just as much liberty against others as it allows others against itself. This mutual renunciation of natural rights is accomplished by the social contract wherein each one of a multitude of people oblige themselves, by contract with each of the rest, not to resist the commands of the human being or the body they have recognized as their sovereign, a sovereign that is granted absolute power.

It is clear that in Hobbes's account of the foundations of civil society self-interest constitutes the basis of morality. Perhaps the most notable feature of his account lies in his formulation of the laws of nature. It is evident from his deduction of these laws that, although posited as laws of 'nature', they are in fact laws of 'reason'. The laws of nature are the means by which human beings overcome their irrational pursuit of self-preservation in the warlike state of nature, and act in accordance with rational maxims of action. The laws of nature are a set of rules according to which any rational being would pursue its own advantage if he were perfectly conscious of the circumstances in which he was acting, and had overcome the irrationality of his impulses. Moreover, the laws of nature are the postulates according to which a rational construction of society is to take place. As one commentator has noted, the laws of nature 'are at once the principle of perfect prudence and of social morality, and therefore they make possible the step from the psychological motives of individual action to the precepts and values of civilized law and morality'. In construing rationality in such terms, Hobbes anticipates both Rousseau's notion of the general will and Kant's notion of the categorical imperative in that the idea of the universalities of reason constitutes the basis of his account of political obligation. Of course, Kant's understanding of morality differs fundamentally from Hobbes's in that it allows no room for self-interest. Indeed, the sole moral world worth of human action, according to Kant, lies in whether it has been performed out of the motive of duty and not out of any heteronomous maxims of self-interest. In this respect, Rousseau is closer to Hobbes, for his notion of the formation of the moral-collective body appeals directly to the self-interest of the individual. Indeed, the novelty of Rousseau's deduction of the social contract lies in the fact that it seeks to educate the isolated individual as to the real basis of its self-interest, that is, it is best served by acting in concert with others through the general will. Both Hobbes and Rousseau justify the social contract by arguing that if individuals are left to define good and evil, justice and injustice on their own as private individuals, then society becomes impossible. The difference between them lies in their account of sovereignty. For Hobbes, sovereignty must reside in an absolute power on account, of the untrustworthiness of human nature, but for Rousseau, sovereignty is inalienable and must reside with each individual considered as a participant in the general will, that is, as a citizen.

In Hobbes, the state of nature does not mark the literal origins of political society, but denotes a relapse, a reversal of time. It is a fall from civilized society without any sacral overtones and without sin. Its condition is ahistorical in the sense that it is a condition, which exists outside of history. Political society represents the triumph of man over nature. Since nature has no history the birth of society marks man's creation of history. The establishment of social order fundamentally changes man's experience of time, since it brings about an end to the fear and anxiety of a state of nature and the uncertainty over the future.

Rousseau's relationship to natural law is an ambiguous one, which has been the source of much disagreement amongst scholars of his work. The debate is between those commentators who believe that Rousseau fundamentally breaks with the concept of natural law, and those who argue that he reformulates it. Put simply, the question can be asked, can there be a 'law' prior to a reflective, moral state? If the natural law is merely metaphorical, how can it obligate us? Is the law of nature simply a synonym for a shared sense of what is just and unjust which develops over time, or is it something which exists prior to social development, but which is dependent on the cultivation of reason in order for its binding nature to be recognized?

In his work, Rousseau makes a distinction between a primitive natural law, which exists prior to reason, and a fully realized rational natural law which can only be cultivated in a civil state. Thus, in the transition from a state of nature to civil society, natural law undergoes a similar transformation to that undergone by humanity. It is clear that Rousseau believes in moral order based on innate principles and recognized by all human beings independent of human conventions and customs. Indeed, it is only on such a basis that he is able to launch such a powerful attack on modern civilization whose mores and morals are criticized for not being in accordance with our true nature of goodness.

The role the concept of natural law plays in Rousseau's thought is, however, paradoxical, for in the state of nature it is present, but not known, while in civil society it is understood, but corrupted. In the just polity, its function as a rule of conduct is replaced by the will of the legitimate sovereign and by civil law. Rousseau thus does not deny the validity of natural law, but only its effectiveness, in that he does not regard it as sufficient for the establishment of social order. However, it is important to recognize that if the function of natural law is replaced by political education in Rousseau's thought, then this education must not violate the voice of nature, but develop in accordance with it, in spite of its impotence to generate itself. Thus, for Rousseau our notions of property, of obligations and rights, of exploitation and domination only become meaningful in the context of a moral and social development of the human animal.

In contrast to Hobbes, Rousseau argues that in a state of nature man is characterized by a natural goodness. His argument is that the qualities of intentional action, which Hobbes attributed to humanity in the state of nature, are qualities, which are only acquired through extensive and fairly, sophisticated social relationships. Rousseau agrees with Hobbes that life in the state of nature would be solitary and non-social. However, in contrast to Hobbes, and because he has a fundamentally different understanding of human nature, Rousseau does not deduce from this insight the claim that human beings would seek out of necessity the acquisition of more and more power. According to Rousseau there are only two natural per-political sentiments: self-preservation what he calls *amour de soi* literally love of self and pitie (compassion). Rousseau argues that in the state of nature men will only injure each other if it is absolutely necessary to their self-preservation. They will not act to take delight or joy in hurting others or by seeking glory. Indeed, passions like vanity or pride are completely alien to man' in the state of nature according to Rousseau.

The First Discourse is only passingly and tepidly interested in the arts and sciences as such and their negative role in human happiness. It is most deeply and pervasively an attack upon the values, institutions, and intimate social relationships of the society

Rousseau had as a young man in France. In this *Discourse,* we are given a picture of French society—with full implications reaching all civilized society—that is skillfully argued with the full range of tones and accents reaching from egoistic corruption of inauthenticity. The society around him, Rousseau tells us, is raven with "jealousy, suspicion, fear, coldness, reserve, hate, and fraud." But surmounting even these is "hypocrisy". Now, what is the cause of this hypocritical or inauthentic society? In a word "inequality." It is in this *Discourse*—that the leitmotiv is introduced. Listen to Rousseau on the source of the corruption that for him spreads through all society.

Dangerous indeed, for whatever else the ancien regime was, it was hierarchical: in social structure, in religion, and also, in the intellectual-philosopher community, one that as Rousseau learned to his occasional humiliation tended to regard equality as a virtue only insofar as it did not affect their own status in the salons of Paris. Inequality, then, for Rousseau in 1750—as for Christopher Jencks or John Rawls in the America of two centuries later—is the cause of the conflict, hypocrisy, the corruption he had in his own personal life come to hate and to feel humiliated. In a word, it was an existence of inaunheticity.

It is not true that for Rousseau the primal state of nature was mankind's happiest state of existence—it was a later one, after language, morality, and the elemental arts had come into being, that Rousseau thought probably the happiest for man. But it is true that this primal state, as best it could be reconstructed through a speculative, rationalist psychology and ethnology, was the one which Rousseau used as his "laboratory" in which to examine the true nature of man. There are many things to be found in *Second Discourse,* including a distinct pre-Marxian recognition of the curse placed upon mankind by the rise of private property and condemnation of man thereby to an alienated existence. The speculations on the origin and development of language, of morality, the arts, and the earliest forms of social structure are, without exception, ingenious and reflect a degree of learning Rousseau is not always credited with. That is the rise of social inequality, yes, but also the immediately precipitating conditions of inequality. And these are what Rousseau called "combinations", that is, social interdependences which involved authority, hierarchy, and other elements of the social bond that for Rousseau were chains upon man's true nature.

> So long as men undertook only what a single person could accomplish, and confined themselves to such arts as did not require the joint labour of several hands, they lived free, healthy, honest, and happy lives. But from the moment one man began to stand in need of the help of another; from the moment it appeared advantageous to any one man to have enough provisions for two, equality disappeared, property was introduced, work became indispensable, and vast forests became smiling fields which man had to water with the sweat of his brow, and where slavery and misery were soon seen to germinate and grow up with the crops.

It is quite evident that in that passage the emphasis is not upon property or work as such, but upon social interdependences, upon aspects of the social bond rising from work or mutual need, which refers to "combinations fatal to innocence and happiness." True, by Rousseau's own declaration, it was the discovery of agriculture and the metallurgical arts, and with these the rise of private property, which provide necessary background. It became the interest of men to appear what they really were not. To be and to seem became two totally different things; and from this distinction sprang insolent pomp and cheating trickery, with all the numerous vices that go in their train.

In that statement, obviously we are brought back to the theme of the *First Discourse*, the point of departure of the *Second*. In the first we were told that the hypocrisy, uncertainty, and corruption of the social order around him sprang from inequality. In the *Second Discourse*, we have a superlative essay in anthropology and social psychology that seeks to demonstrate how deep the roots of inequality are in the human condition and, therefore, how radical must be the remedy. That remedy is provided us in the *Third Discourse*. There is, however, an anticipatory statement in the *Discourse on Inequality* in which, noting the defects of all early efforts at the reform of the political state which time and again had brought social inequality, strife, and conflict, he writes prophetically:

> It [the state] was continually being patched up, when the first task should have been to get the site cleared and all the old materials removed, as was done by Lycurgus at Sparta, if a stable and lasting edifice was to be erected.

It has been so often said of Rousseau that his desire was to return men to the state of nature. Never anywhere did Rousseau express such hint at any desirability of mankind's abandoning of civil society and, in effect, returning to forests and fields of the primordial condition. The "state of nature" for Rousseau was never anything more than a term for the primal condition that has never ceased to fascinate philosophers and social scientists: and a touchstone of moral excellence that could be applied to existing societies.

What Rousseau sought, with powerful effect, was no retreat from civilization but, rather a form of government that would, at one and the same time, liberate man from social inequalities and their tyrannies and important, establish a form of association from which all such inequalities and tyrannies would be forever banned. Rousseau turned to politics as the redemptive means. More accurately Rousseau availed himself of the theme of political redemption that had been in his mind from his youth. In the *Confessions* he tells us that in 1743, while an aide in the French embassy at Venice, well before he commenced any of his important social and political writings, the thought came to him one day.

> That everything was radically connected with politics, and that however, one proceeded, no people would be other than the nature of its government made it.

Rousseau never deviated from that conviction. In the *First Discourse* there is adulation expressed for ancient Sparta, its people freed of the corrupting influences of the kind of society and culture Athens knew, and in another connection unmistakable admiration for "military virtues." In the *Second Discourse*, having made argument which Marx and Engel's must surely have studied with care a century later, that the political state came into being as the means of seeking to contain, to moderate the conflicts in society generated by social inequality, Rousseau emphasizes the destructive effects of the political state upon men's liberty.

> All ran headlong to their chains, in hopes of securing their liberty; for they had just wit enough to perceive the advantages of political institutions, without experience enough to foresee the dangers.

It is, however, in the *Third Discourse*, "On Political Economy", published shortly afterwards, that the inspiration of *Confessions* becomes fully articulated.

For at least fifteen years from when, Rousseau was an aide in Venice that theme had been virtually inseparable from Rousseau's passion for equality and his hatred of all the inequalities which are the very stuff of civil society. Precisely as the religious fathers know how indispensable is God the absolute sovereign—omnipotent, omniscient, omnipresent—to the salvation of man, so does Rousseau knew how vital is the absolute sovereign in political terms. Without it, as he recognized almost mystically and eschatologically, all talk of justice, liberty, virtue, and equality is but idle rhetoric. Rousseau would regard most writings on equality as lacking in essential substance, as being emasculated by refusal to deal candidly with the problems of political power and of political psychology necessarily involved in any forthright proposal for building the social order on the rock of equality. Very well indeed did Rousseau know how deeply rooted in man's character is the impulse to inequality and how diversely manifest in the entire social fabric is this impulse. As only a supreme power can save man from original sin in the religious realm, only a political power can save man from society's inherent and pervasive inequality.

What is this power? The General Will, a power absolute, total, and penetrating for its declared roots in the people—that is, the people first purified, cleansed of the false wills and desires and attitudes which history has implanted in their minds and personalities, and, as it were, psychologically reconstituted. By definition the General Will, in contrast to the will of all, is the will that emerges when the members of the political community are able to give their allegiances and their thoughts completely to the community, when they have become liberated from the false consciousness that directs them to think and act as individuals or as representatives of partial interests in the social order. The General Will has nothing to do with a majority as such, least of all with the mere counting of votes. "The first and most important rule of legitimate government", Rousseau tells us in the *Third Discourse*.

> that is, government whose object is the good of the people , is to follow in everything the General Will. How is the General will to be ascertained? Must the whole nation be assembled? Certainly not. It ought the less to be assembled, because it is by no means certain that its decision would be the expression of the General Will; besides, the method would be impracticable in a great people, and is hardly ever necessary where the government is hardly ever necessary where the government is well-intentioned: for the rulers well know that the General Will is always on the side which is most favourable to the public interest, that is, most equitable, so that it is needful only to act justly, to be certain of following the General Will.

Rousseau would adapt that somewhat in later writings, including the *Social Contract*, seeking a means whereby voting might reveal the General Will, even suggesting that the majority must be followed. But from beginning to end in Rousseau there is the clear distinction between the General Will, alone sovereign, incorruptible, and the guardian of public interest, discernible by its common interest rather than by number of heads, and what is revealed by voting and by representation. For representation Rousseau had only contempt. Correctly, he saw representative institutions as the yield of that feudalism he and other philosophers hated in all respects. It is impossible to read Rousseau—and this holds in such works as *Emile* and *La nouvelle Heloise,* in his *Draft of Constitutions for Corsica* and for Poland, in the famous diatribe against D'Alembert, as well in the *Social Contract*—without becoming aware of his obsession with political power: whether it is Rousseau in his role of tutor to Emile or of Legislator in the chapter of that title in the *Social contract*, or any of the other roles he assumed from time to time, power—cast in therapeutic terms, power as redeemer, purifier, guardian as well as sovereign in the ordinary sense, power above all as the community in which reconstituted human beings would have equal rights—is the indispensable element of a social order. But what separates Rousseau's envisagement of political power from that of anyone else is the linking of power with morality, with liberty, and, of course, with equality.

How profoundly the uses of power fascinate Rousseau in his character of political psychologist can be seen in a passage of the *Third Discourse* where he treats of the relation of public power to the family. The context is the system of education, which for Rousseau is total, beginning in infancy, not terminating until death.

> The government, should not abandon to the intelligence and prejudices of fathers the education of their children, as that education is of still greater importance to the State than to the fathers. Family's dissolve, but the State remains.

It is important, to keep in mind that what actuates Rousseau is not power for its own sake, not power as sole possible refuge from a Hobbesian state of nature, but power as the necessary instrument by which to liberate men from inequality and its myriad corruptions and conflicts and also to create for man an equalitarian community. Above anyone else in the history of political thought Rousseau gave to the word citizen a majesty previously reserved for such words as Father, Priest, King, and Lord. And, for Rousseau, the central essence of citizenship is equal participation in power—the power that suffuses the community, reaching every corner and crevice. Necessarily, attention must be given to matters of property and possessions in the political community. This we find in the final section of the *Third Discourse.*

"It is not enough to have citizens and to protect them, it is also necessary to consider their subsistence."

Rousseau does not ban property from personal possession; at least not the residual property, the necessary possessions, all men must have in their individual names.

"It is certain that the right of property is the most sacred of all the rights of citizenship, and even more important in some respects than liberty itself."

There is every reason to believe that Rousseau was profound by sincere in that statement. But neither is there any reason to believe that by "private property" he had much else in mind than what he further on calls "the common necessaries of life." Socialism would be too strong a word for the kind of public weal Rousseau describes in this section of the *Third Discourse,* but by the time one has finished reading. Rousseau's artful prescriptions for taxation, based as they are on his hatred of all luxuries and his passionate exclamations on behalf of the common man, one is obliged to come up with a conception very nearer to socialism; one that is in almost equal measure puritan and communal.

Equalitarianism is the warp, of course, on which his proposed system of taxation is woven. First, those who "possess only the common necessaries of life should pay nothing at all." But taxation should be extended to everything, to all the "superfluities" an individual might have over and above the common necessaries. Those who object on the ground that rank and social statues is not thereby taken into account receive short shrift from Rousseau. The "grandee has two legs just like a cowherd and, like him again, but one belly."

It is easy enough to withhold sympathy, of course, for what Rousseau calls a "grandee." Our sympathy might be stretched, though, when a little later in the discussion we find Rousseau treating just as sternly "the useless professions." Here he makes plain that among these are artists, dancers, singers, players and other involved in any way in "public entertainments". Rousseau's hatred of the public arts was almost total, as his notable *Letter to D'Alembert* (1758) suggests in detail and as his recommendations to the citizens of Corsica suggest in even more austere fashion. And we cannot forget Rousseau's jibes and jeers at the scholars of his day, those whom he contemptuously refers to in the *First Discourse* as comprising "herds of textbook writers", "mountebanks exhibiting themselves in public", and mere hawkers of wares. There is reason to believe that Rousseau would regard the arts and sciences as baneful manifestations of social inequality.

There is an interesting and brief discussion toward the end of the *Third Discourse* of a form of taxation that might be thought of as Rousseau's "difference principle", though it has little resemblance to Rawls' principle. The imposition of an equitable tax, Rousseau suggests, "ought not to be in simple ratio to the property of the contributors, but in compound ratio to the difference of their conditions and the superfluity of their possessions".

At no point did Rousseau ever imagine that the good society can be had for the asking, had for simple legislation and appeal to popular reason. There is a passage in the *Social Contract* one in the chapter on The Legislator, that gives awful emphasis to what Rousseau knew to be required in the way of psychological surgery and transplant. Here it will suffice to cite a few more words on the subject to the General Will in the *Third Discourse*. To follow the General Will,

> it is necessary to know it, and above all to distinguish it from the particular will, beginning with one's self: this distinction is always difficult to make, and only the most sublime virtue can afford sufficient illumination for it.

Many today might wonder from how many ill-fated, even tragic and destructive political designs we might have saved during the past two centuries if their architects had but paused to look for even a part of the "sublime virtue" in human consciousness that Rousseau had wisely made a condition of the good society, and for the achievement of which he was willing to declare what was in effect permanent revolution.

The *Social Contract* was treated with a good deal of indifference by the reading public when it appeared in 1762. one can easily see why. Too many of its electric and quite essential passages are separated by meandering stream of exposition and often-pedantic digression. The reason lies, no doubt, in the fact that the book was a kind of compromise between Rousseau's desire to publish a truly systematic work on "political institutions" and his unconquerable passion to instruct the public. Despite its classic status, its demonstrable influence upon the political mind in not merely the West but quite literally the entire world, the book is unsatisfactory in many ways.

Nevertheless, the *Social Contract* achieved, after Rousseau's death, a unique popularity by virtue of the magnetic appeal it exerted upon minds like Robespierre and Saint-Just. Apparently it even had substantial following among the rank-and-file of the Revolution. A contemporary tells us that hardly a paragraph in the book failed to be quoted at one time or other in the newspapers, and that excited groups of citizens could be seen reading and discussing the book on the streets of Paris. No matter what one may think of the work taken as a whole or set against the grand project Rousseau had wished to complete, it has some of the most brilliant passages and torch-like phrases to be found anywhere in the history of thought.

As in his earlier writings, the two themes of liberty and equality are dominating. And also as in these earlier writings, the referent of each theme is the individual in his relation to traditional society and all its hierarchies and networks of authority. "Man is born free; and everywhere he is in chains." Those are the thrilling words with which the first chapter begins. The chains are, of course, the interdependences founded on kinship, class, religion, work, and composed of the tiny but puissant links of friendship, mutual aid, social exchange, conformity, and other aspects of the social bond which Rousseau had come to detest for their generation of inequality, corruption, and conflict and their debasement of the individual. The problem, we are told, is "to find a form of association which will defend and protect with the whole common force the person and goods of each associate, and in which each, while uniting himself with all, may still obey himself alone, and remain as free as before."

> the total alienation of each associate, together with all his rights, to the whole community; for, in the first place, as each gives himself, absolutely, the conditions are the same for all; and, this being so, no one has any interest in making them burdensome to others.

That is the social contract—conceived in and dedicated to the absolute equality that Rousseau cherished in the deepest parts of his mind, capable of being fulfilled, as Rousseau well knew, only through the instrument of a profounder, more penetrating, more absolute power than any ever before knew in human society but a power, by its very nature, that could liberate man completely form all the tyrannical inequalities which he regarded as inseparable from traditional society.

Then comes, in full effect and brilliant clarity, the passage that lets us know precisely what the costs of equality must be:

> In order then that the social compact may not be an empty formula, it tacitly includes the undertaking, which alone can give force to the rest, that whoever refuses to obey the General Will shall be compelled to do so by the whole body. This means nothing less than that he will be forced to be free; for this is the condition which, by giving each citizen to his country, secures him against all personal dependence. In this lies the key to the working of the political machine; this alone legitimizes civil undertakings, which without it would be absurd, tyrannical, and liable to the most frightful abuses.

Once the social compact, resting on the absolute General Will, is established, "each citizen would then be perfectly independent of all the rest, and at the same time very dependent on the state." Like the egalitarian philosophers writing today, Rousseau prizes an equality that will exist irrespective of unequal faculties, motivations, and aspirations in life, based very often on natural differences among individuals. The fundamental social compact does not, Rousseau writes, destroy natural inequality. It instead "substitutes, for such physical inequality as nature may have set up between men, and equality that is moral and legitimate, and that men, who may be unequal in strength or intelligence, become every one equal by convention and legal right."

At no point does Rousseau imply that the social contract can be effected through other than means of the most revolutionary character. Rousseau wans to achieve equality more delicately here by not only politicizing the question of income inequality but altering people's basic assumptions about the extent to which they are responsible for their neighbors and their neighbors for them. Well, Rousseau knew that at the very outset of his labours, and the whole revolutionary strategy of the General Will was designed precisely to "alter people's basic assumptions" in this respect.

We knew this intent to "alter" had immense long-run consequences—the total politicization of life through the General Will, the abolition of all forms of association, including religion, which might militate against the dogmas of the social compact, the exclusion of the arts and sciences above the most primitive level, the willingness of man to surrender himself and all his rights to the total community, finding liberty in equality of participation in the General Will, and, above all else, the continuing refashioning of man's mind and character. In the chapter on "The Legislator" –who is for the work of politics what the tutor is for the work of individual development in *Emile*, what the chilling figure of Wolmer is for the work of human relationships in *La Nouvelle Heloise*—we have Rousseau's superbly candid statement of what must be done.

> He who dares to undertake the making of a people's institutions ought to feel himself capable, so to speak, of changing human nature, of transforming each individual, who is by himself a complete and solitary whole, into part of a greater whole... of altering man's constitution for the purpose of strengthening it and of substituting a partial and moral existence for the physical and independent existence nature has conferred on us all. He must, in a word, take away from man his own resources and give him new ones alien to him.

Finally, it must be said for Rousseau that he knew full well the necessity of giving equality, and with it the General Will and all the laws flowing from this will, the ineradicable cast of the sacred. Hence the brilliant penultimate chapter on the civil religion. Men must have a religion, Rousseau there tells us, for otherwise the political tie will not remain firm and close. None of traditional religions will do, however, for their attention is always on the supernatural. Christianity is particularly objectionable, for it lacks the martial virtues which must always be resplendent in the good society. Imagine, Rousseau tells us, "your Christian republic face to face with Sparta or Rome: the pious Christians will be beaten, crushed, and destroyed, before they know where they are, or will owe their safety one to the contempt their enemy will conceive for them..." And Christianity has the fatal political ethic of desiring a large measure of autonomy from the state, a condition clearly intolerable under the General Will.

There must, therefore, be instituted a civil religion, "a purely civil profession of faith." In no way, Rousseau tells us that this civil religion interferes with men's freedom of conscience in reference to their religious beliefs, Christian or other, "for, as the Sovereign has no authority in the other world, whatever the lot of its subjects may be in the life to come, that is not its business, provided they are good citizens in this life." Subjects owe the Sovereign "an account of their opinions only to such an extent as they matter to the community." But, as Rousseau must surely have recognized, all struggles between the religious and the political in history have concerned precisely religious opinions as they matter to the community. Not the most despotic of Roman emperors cared a fig for Christian beliefs about the next world. It was this world that mattered, and it was this world that primitive Christianity could only too often seem to be revolutionizing.

There is therefore a purely civil profession of faith of which the Sovereign should fix the articles, not exactly as religious dogmas, but as social sentiments without which a man cannot be a good citizen or faithful subject. While it can compel no one to believe them, it can banish from the state whoever does not believe them—it can banish him, not for impiety, but as an anti-social being, incapable of truly loving the laws and justice, and of sacrificing, at need, his life to his duty. If anyone, after publicly recognizing these dogmas, behaves as if he does not believe them, let him be punished by death: he has committed the worst of all crimes, that of lying before the law.

It comes almost as a shock, after that passage and its clearly forestated premises of the Sovereign's responsibility for opinions as they matter to the community, and not to be forgotten, of the infallibility and incorruptibility of the General Will, to be told in the next paragraph that among the dogmas of the civil religion is one forbidding intolerance. But such excess of political zeal should not cause us to lose sight of the overall shrewdness and brilliance of Rousseau's chapter on religion. He understood, as few if any equality intoxicated philosophers of our day seem to understand, that if the dogmas of equality is to be instituted and made to survive it must be buttressed by a form of power that draws as much from religious as political substance.

Jean-Jacques Rousseau is not likely to be the first choice of anyone who canvasses the history of political thought in search of exemplars of republican liberalism. Rousseau's republican credentials are good enough, to be sure, as a number of recent studies attest. The problem is that they may be too good to allow much hope of finding a significant strain of liberalism in his thought. Certainly his willingness to invoke a legislator who "should feel that he is capable of changing human nature," his call for a civil religion that requires "a purely civil profession of faith, the articles of which are for the sovereign to establish, and his declaration that people may "be forced to be free" seem to put him outside the bounds of most definitions of liberalism.

In the end, one may decide that other important political philosophers—Montesquieu or Tocqueville, perhaps, or John Start Mill or T.H. Green –are better examples of republican liberalism than Rousseau. Yet, none of these thinkers combined a republican commitment to civic virtue with the analytical device of the social contract—a device usually associated with liberalism. But Rousseau did this, in a remarkable way.

Rousseau's peculiar contractarian republicanism is valuable, first, because it suggests that republican ideals and liberal devices are not strictly incompatible. Quentin Skinner may be correct when he remarks that "the ideals of classical republicanism had largely been swallowed up by the rising tide of contractarian political thought" by the time of Montesquieu, and of fine "the concept of individual rights attained that hegemony which it has never subsequently lost." For Rousseau, the rising tide of contractarian ideals did not engulf them. The idea of the social contract may have encouraged people to think of government as a guarantor of their individual rights and liberty, but Rousseau saw that the idea also offered a means of their understanding of their duties and common interests.

By using the contractarian device in this way, Rousseau pointed to the reciprocity that should obtain between the members of a body politic. This concern for reciprocity or fair play is the second respect in which his brand of republican liberalism is worth exploring here. Rousseau recognized the need to make people aware of their reciprocal rights and obligations and to help them see the connection between their individual interests and the common good. He hoped to accomplish these goals—and thus to promote citizenship—by appealing to the idea of the "general will." Whether he succeeded or failed, there is much to learn about the plausibility of republican liberalism from a study of his attempt.

In order to understand how Rousseau's political thought provides an example, of republican liberalism, we must therefore comprehend the general will. Rousseau's attempt to formulate the general will is an attempt to provide the foundation for a body politic as a cooperative venture in which all citizens are treated fairly. More than that, Rousseau's polity would secure a substantial measure of autonomy for citizens in the form of "moral liberty." Whether they will recognize this, and understand that their rights and obligations are reciprocal—that their liberty as citizens rests on their duties as subjects—is another matter. Whether they will act on that sense is yet another. As Rousseau remarks,

> When our interest is involved, our sentiments are soon corrupted. It is not a necessary effect of the constitution of things that the vicious man profits doubly, from his injustice and the probity of other? What more advantageous treaty could he conclude than one obliging the whole world, excepting himself, to be just, so that everyone will faithfully render him what is due him, while he renders to no one what he owes? He loves virtue, unquestionably; but he loves it in others because he hopes to profit from it.

Once he has formulated it, then, Rousseau's task is to find ways to secure the general will. One way, he argued, is to force people to be free. Another is to cultivate the desire to act in accordance with the general will.

The General Will and Moral Freedom

The notion of the General Will is without doubt the most complex and controversial aspect of Rousseau's moral and political thought. To a certain extent it is fair to say that the role the notion of the General Will plays in Rousseau's political philosophy is the same as that which the notion of natural law plays in the political thought of Hobbes and Locke. For Rousseau it is the source of law and of sovereignty; indeed, it is, on his account, the basis of political right. The most controversial aspect of the notion of general will stems from Rousseau's argument, in the First Book of the *Social Contract*, that whoever refuses to obey the general will shall be 'forced to be free'. For many such a statement proves that the doctrine of the general will is a tyrannical one which prefigures the totalitarian regimes of the modern age, including that of the French Revolution during the reign of Terror.

The General Will seeks to establish society on the basis of common interest. It is the common element in these different interests of particular wills which constitutes the social tie or bond, and without which society could not exist. It is this idea of a general will as the will of the common interest, which Rousseau develops into a theory of sovereignty. 'I hold then', he writes,

> That sovereignty, being nothing less than the exercise of the general will, can never be alienated, and that the sovereign, who is less than a collective being, cannot be represented except by himself: the power may be transmitted but not the will.

Society on Rousseau's account is the product of the free rational will. This implies that the origins and foundations of society lie in a convention; in other words, society is a human artifact. However, this argument was not original to Rousseau, but is equally present in the deduction of civil society found in Hobbes and Locke. The originality of Rousseau's political philosophy lies in his argument contra Hobbes and Locke, that sovereignty is inalienable.

Rousseau's theory of sovereignty shows the importance he places on the problem of power in political theory. The notion of sovereignty refers to the ultimate source of political authority and power; it is the supreme power. As soon as society comes into existence as a moral-collective body, the question of power assumes paramount importance. It is from the establishment of this common force that society derives its stability and strength. The nature and source of sovereignty are determined by the kind of association which is created at the moment of the social contract. The freedom of each individual can only be guaranteed by the power of whole community understood as a common force. Sovereignty is essentially the power to make law. As laws are the conditions of civil association, the people who are subject to them must at the same time be their author. Sovereignty must lie with the whole body of citizens, and its interest must lie with the whole body of citizens, and its interest must always be general. Were sovereignty to be either alienated or divided, the association or community which has been set up would, in effect, be dissolved and human beings would return to the state of nature. Rousseau's notion of the general will would seem to present us not with the stark choice between Hobbesian absolutism and anarchism, but between the absolute sovereign powers of the general will and the amoral state of nature. Does this not show that the general will is indeed absolutist?

The idea of the general will rests on a fundamental distinction between two aspects of a person. According to Rousseau's, theory every person may be thought of as a man—an actual, identifiable empirical person—and, at least potentially, as a citizen. Insofar as we are men, we are each unique; and each of us, has a particular identity and set of interests. Insofar as we are citizens, however, we are alike in that we are members of the public, and as members of the public we share a common interest in the welfare of the body politic. Everyone consequently has both a particular interest as a man and a general interest as a citizen.

From the distinction between man and citizen, Rousseau moves to a corresponding distinction between the particular or private will, on the one hand, and the general will, on the other. The private will aims at the fulfillment of the particular interest of a man, of an actual individual, while the general will seeks to further the interest of the citizen. Because the interests of all citizens are the same, the object of the general will is the common good or public interest—the interest all share as members of the public. Rousseau distinguishes the private from the general will in this manner: "The private will tends by its nature toward preferences, and the general will toward equality". As men with private wills, we naturally tend to grant priority to our own interests and desires. The private will is partial both because it is the will of an identifiable individual, one who is only part of the body politic, and because it places a higher value on one's personal interests than on the interests of others. The general will, in contrast, tends toward equality because it necessarily grants equal consideration to the interests of every member of the body politic. Because it focuses on the common interest we share as citizens, the General Will is impartial: it considers only the interests of the abstract person Rousseau calls the citizen. Because we are all the same qua citizen, the general will is devoted equally to all.

A man who has the ability to be an adept thief for example, may well find it in his interest, as a man, to put his burgling skills to use. His private will may then be to steal from others in order to satisfy his own desires. The general will, however, directs the potential thief to obey the law. As the example illustrates, the general will performs much the same function as John Rawls's "veil of ignorance," which deprives the parties to a hypothetical social contract of most information about their personal identities. Behind the veil, the parties do not know what their social or economic positions are, what abilities or disabilities they have, what religious or philosophical views they hold, or even what their ages or sexes are. The veil thus forces the parties to the contract to adopt a common, and presumably morally neutral viewpoint. In Rousseau's terms, it leads the parties to promote their common interest as citizens rather than their private interests as men.

There is also a moral dimension to the general will, just as there is to the veil of ignorance. Rousseau does not invoke the general will simply as a counterweight to selfish interests. This would be futile, for one's interest as a person may well outweigh one's interest as a citizen. An industrialist may find, for instance, that it is not in his or her interest to install pollution-inhibiting devices in the factory's smokestacks, all things considered, even though it is in his or her interest as a citizen to reduce air pollution. Rousseau's claim, however, is that in some cases we ought to consider only our interests as citizens. The purpose of the general will, then, is to provide a principle that will lead to just public policy. From the standpoint of citizens—as members of the public—we share the same interests. Considered abstractly as citizens, the burglar and his victim share a common interest in the enforcement of a law against burglary. What Rousseau suggests, in sum, is that only the general will of the citizen and not the private will of the man should determine public policy.

Understood in this way, the general will operate as a moral imperative or principle; its purpose is to guarantee that the claims of no particular individuals are given preference. Everyone receives equal consideration because public decisions take into account only the viewpoint of the citizen. Any other perspective is at best morally irrelevant. Here we see the emphasis on equality that is such a marked characteristic of Rousseau's political philosophy. The social compact, according to Rousseau,

> Established an equality between the citizens such that they all engage themselves under the same rights. Thus by the very nature of the compact, every act of sovereignty, which is to say every authentic act of the general will, obligates or favors all citizens equally, so that the sovereign knows only the nation as a body and makes no distinctions between any of those who compose it.

A further implication is that laws established in accordance with the general will do more than grant equal consideration to everyone: they truly are in everyone's interest, for a law sanctioned by the general will promotes everyone's interest qua citizens. Such a law may not be the first choice of many individuals, but it is acceptable to all because it makes some contribution to everyone's well-being. According to Rousseau, moreover, the general will applies only to laws, not to decrees. A law is a general policy, a rule that governs the conduct of every member of the body politic, while a decree is an act that refers to particular identifiable individuals.

Understanding the General Will as a principle meant to guide public decisions is also consistent with what Rousseau has to say about groups within the body politic. There is a sense in which each of these groups, or "partial associations," has its own general will, for the individuals who compose each groups share a common interest in their capacities as members of that association. These groups, in other words, may be considered publics. When we regard them from the perspective of the body politic, however, it is clear that the will of each association is a private will—one that may be antagonistic to the general will of the community as a whole. Rousseau consequently disapproves of these associations because he fears that they will divide and divert the loyalty of the people, who will be more likely to think of themselves as merchants or farmers, or Catholics or Protestants than as citizens. When this happens, Rousseau warns, the private wills of these groups will prevent the general will from prevailing when the people vote. "In order for the general will to be well expressed," he concludes, "it is therefore important that there be no partial society in the State, and that each citizen give only his own opinion."

There is also a close connection between the general will and Rousseau's conception of moral freedom. There must be, if the social contract is to solve the "fundamental problem" that Rousseau sets himself: "'Find a form of association that defends and protects the person and goods of each associate with all the common force, and by means of which each one, uniting with all, nevertheless obeys only himself and remains as free as before'".

How can a man who enters into a contract to place himself under law be as free as he was before the contract? Rousseau's answer relies on a distinction between three kinds of freedom: natural, civil, and moral. The man who enters into the social contract may surrender the natural freedom of the state of nature, but he gains civil freedom and the opportunity for moral freedom in its places. Civil freedom, which secures "the proprietorship of everything he possesses," is "limited by the general will"; moral freedom, which overcomes the "impulse of appetite" and requires "obedience to the law one has prescribed for oneself," is expressed through it. They will then be free when they obey, for them will be obeying laws that they have prescribed for themselves.

This solution to Rousseau's "fundamental problem" is not to free the citizen and remove the chains. Nevertheless, it is a remarkable attempt to square autonomy with authority. For Rousseau, as for Kant, there is a close connection between freedom and law. Moral freedom consists of self-legislation, of obeying laws that one gives to oneself. Natural freedom is freedom from restraint, but moral freedom requires self-restraint. In order to formulate the laws that are to govern one's conduct, one must reflect on one's appetites, needs, and circumstances. To follow "the impulse of appetite alone is slavery," but the moral freedom that comes with self-legislation "makes man truly the master of himself'. Moral freedom, then, is a form of self-government or self-mastery—of autonomy—that is available only to those who belong to a polity in which men act as citizens by following their general will. In the state of nature, man may be free in one sense, but he is subject to the impulses of his appetites and the elusion of others. In the just society the individual enjoys a different kind of freedom—the kind that allows him to obey only himself as a citizen while uniting with others in a cooperative, law-governed enterprise.

In this way the social contract and the general will, understood as a principle akin to Kant's categorical imperative, represent what may be called the liberal side of Rousseau's political authority by showing how to reconcile "what right permits with what interest prescribes, so that justice and utility are not at variance"; they also show how the individual who enters the contract "obeys only himself and remains as free as before". Yet political authority is justified, on the other hand, only when the general will is operative and citizens are obeying laws that they prescribe for themselves. Thus, Rousseau conjoins autonomy with authority, moral freedom with political obligation.

There are, however, well-known problems with Rousseau's contractual argument, especially where freedom and obligation are concerned, the first, the complaint that it is self-contradictory, and perhaps tilts toward totalitarianism, when he claims that someone may be "forced to be free". How can one be forced to be free when freedom is the very absence of coercion? The obvious answer is that Rousseau is talking about moral freedom here, and he merely means that one may be compelled to obey a law to which one has consented. But this explanation does not meet all objections, for why should one have to be forced to obey a law to which one has consented? Here the answer lies in Rousseau's distinction between private wills and the general will. The private will of the lawbreaker—of a man who cheats on his taxes, for example—is likely to be in conflict with his general will as a citizen. The cheater may "view what he owes the common cause as a free contribution, the loss of which will harm others less than its payment burdens him," and consequently "wish to enjoy the rights of the citizen without wanting to fulfill the duties of a subject". These two wills are in conflict because the cheater wants to enjoy the benefits of the social order—"the rights of the citizens" –without contributing his shares to the maintenance of that order—"the duties of a subject." If he follows his private will, he acts against "the general will he has as a citizen". The spread of this kind of injustice, Rousseau observes, would cause the ruin of the body politic. Therefore, in order for the social compact not to be an ineffectual formula, it tacitly includes the following engagement, which alone can give force to the others: that whoever refuses to obey the general will shall be constrained to do so by the entire body; which means only that he will be forced to be free. For this is the condition that, by giving each citizen to the homeland, guarantees him against all personal dependence and alone gives legitimacy to civil engagements which without it would be absurd, tyrannical, and subject to the most enormous abuses. The body politic, according to the view set out here, is supposed to be a cooperative enterprise, and the citizens are all pledged to share its burdens. Only those who try to evade this obligation—those who "wish to enjoy the rights of the citizens without wanting to fulfill the duties of a subject"—must be "forced to be free." These individuals are free riders. Like the tax cheater, they want to receive the benefits of social cooperation without contributing their fair share toward the provision of those benefits.

There is still a second problem confronting Rousseau's attempt to join right and interest, freedom and obligation. This problem arises out of Rousseau's endorsement of majority rule, which appears to lead him again into a contradiction: How can someone remain as free as before he entered into the social contract if he is not subject to the will of the majority? Rousseau is aware of this problem, as his brief discussion of majority rules makes clear. He begins by acknowledging that the social contract requires unanimous consent: "Since every man is born free and master of himself, no one can subject him without his consent". But he soon goes on to say that "except for this primitive contract, the vote of the majority always obligates all the others". The problem is obvious—"How can the opponents be free yet subject to laws to which they have not consented?"—And Rousseau quickly offers this resolution:

> When a law is proposed in the assembly of the people, what they are being asked is not precisely whether they approve or reject the proposal, but whether it does or does not conform to the general will that is theirs. Each one expresses his opinion on this by voting , and the declaration of the general will is drawn from the counting of the votes.

These two sentences provide a good example of an important distinction, almost unmarked in Rousseau's writings, between the general will and 'a' general will. The proposal is to be approved if it conforms to the general will, that is, the principle that everyone should act as a citizen, not as a man; but a general will, a specific policy that satisfies this principle, is discovered only by counting votes. Votes are irrelevant to the general will, for principles are not discovered by voting, but a general will often cannot be ascertained without them. Were it not for the difference between the general will qua principle and policies that conform to that principle, Rousseau would not even need to discuss voting. The point of immediate importance, however, is brought out in the reminder of the paragraph:

> Therefore when the opinion contrary to mine prevails, that proves nothing except that I was mistaken, and what I thought to be the general will was not. If my private will had prevailed, I would have done something other than what I wanted. It is then that I would not have been free.

This explanation is complicated and paradoxical, but it is not simply nonsense. Rousseau admits that even the people as a whole may fail to discern the policy that accords with the general will, so the question here is, Why is the majority opinion less likely to be mistaken than that of the minority or of a solitary individuals? It is certainly possible for one person to be right while everyone else is wrong. But if we make certain assumptions then the opinion of the majority is more likely to be correct than that of the minority. This occurs when we assume, as Rousseau seems to do, that (1) there is a uniquely right answer, a specific policy in conformity with the general will, to be found; (2) everyone has an equal, better-than-even chance of discerning the right answer; and (3) everyone wants the right answer to prevail. It may be difficult to accept all of these assumptions, but they do indicate how one might be glad as a citizen, that his or her own point of view was not victorious. Rousseau's point, then, is not that whatever the majority wants is the general will but that the majority is simply more likely than the minority to have discovered the policy that conforms to the general will.

Making Citizens of Men

Beginning with the liberal device of the social contract, Rousseau's argument leads to conclusions usually associated with republican theorists—and occasionally, some critic's claims, with totalitarians. His definition of citizens not as mere bearer of privileges and immunities but as "participants in the sovereign authority" already moves in the republican direction. So does his argument that people must sometimes "be forced to be free" in order to prevent them from disobeying laws they have prescribed, as citizens, for themselves. One might object that the man who resolves always to act as a man rather than a citizen is in fact obeying a law he has prescribed for himself and is therefore morally free in Rousseau's sense. But Rousseau's response is that no one can enter the social contract on these terms, for no policy could survive if it allowed its members to disobey the laws whenever it suited their personal interests to do so.

Rousseau's argument thus rests on his conception of the political order as a cooperative practice subject to the principle of fair play. He does not use these terms, to be sure, but the logic of his argument clearly points to this conception of the political order. One important aspect of this conception is his desire to promote the spirit of cooperation by encouraging people to think of themselves as subjects who have an obligation to obey the laws they make as citizens.

Rousseau's abiding concern for equality is evidence of this desire. The great possibility of a political society, according to Rousseau, is that it "substitutes a moral and legitimate equality for whatever physical inequality nature may have placed between men." In a footnote to this statement, he connects the distribution of wealth and property to this "moral and legitimate equality" by observing that "the social state is only advantageous to men insofar as they all have something and none of them has anything superfluous". Rousseau goes on to argument for equality because "freedom cannot last without it." It is necessary, therefore, that no citizen should be so opulent that he can buy another, and none so poor that he is constrained to sell himself."

Equality thus promotes freedom, largely by securing people from personal dependence. Throughout his writings, Rousseau makes plain his hatred for personal dependence, which in true republican spirit, he deems a form of slavery. As he declares in *Emile*, to return to a passage quoted in Chapter 1, "Dependence on men engenders all the vices, and by it, master and slave are mutually corrupted." But if "all have something and none of them has anything superfluous," then no one will be "constrained to sell himself." Only in this condition, when no one is rich enough or powerful enough to corrupt the ideal of equality under law, can people be autonomous, or morally free, for only then can they obey laws that they prescribe for themselves. And only then are they likely to see themselves as citizens, sharing a common will in a cooperation enterprise.

Rousseau's devotion to the small community and his hatred of big cities also play a part here. More than mere nostalgia for the Geneva of his youth or for the city-states of antiquity, this concern for equality reflects his underlying conception of the political order as a cooperative practice. As the size of a cooperative practice grows, each person's contribution seems less and less significant, just as "the share of each member of the State" in "the sovereign authority" decreases. It also becomes more likely, to return to the "forced-to-be-free" argument, that the members will consider "the moral person of the state as an imaginary being" and "wish to enjoy the rights of the citizen without wanting to fulfill the duties of a subject". To avoid this and other "abuses of large state", we must recognize that "it is always an evil to unite several towns in a single City". Indeed, "a town, like a nation, cannot legitimately be the subject of another, because the essence of the body politic lies in the harmony of obedience and freedom; If we want to promote citizenship, then, we must establish and preserve the conditions that lead to the harmony of obedience and freedom. We must keep the polity small enough, that is, for its people to be able to see how important their cooperation, in the form of obedience to the laws, is to maintaining the freedom the cooperative enterprise makes possible.

Rousseau's discussion of education in *Emile* and elsewhere also aims at cultivating the cooperative attitude of the citizen-subject, as to do his supposedly totalitarian remarks on "the legislator" and civil religion in the *Social Contract*. In pagan antiquity each state had its own deities, Rousseau remarks in book iv, chapter 8 of the *Social Contract,* the authority its gods encompassed by its political frontiers. First the Jews, however, and then the Christians paid homage to a god whose kingdom was not of this earth, and whose temporal ascendancy sometimes failed to match his spiritual predominance, thereby giving rise to disunion in separating the state's theology from its politics. Having spread their faith with their empire, the Romans doubted the indifference to politics professed by other-worldly Christians and, fearing their eventual rebellion, persecuted them. In due course, observes Rousseau, Christians did indeed forsake their humility, and laying claim to God's earthly domains they established the most violent despotism of the modern world. In this own day, political and theological identities had come to be disjointed everywhere, even among the Muslims, so that 'the spirit of Christianity has won completely'. Where clergymen wield corporate power, they seek mastery over princes by the regimen their holy orders demand and through their rights of excommunication, civil religion selves misters of the Church, at the risk of equally precarious schism between sacred and temporal pretensions to sovereignty. Alone among Christian authors, Hobbes had recognized such threats to civil peace and had rightly proposed that secular and religious power be placed in the same hands. But he had failed to take account of the perils to his system posed by Christianity, and of the fact that, wherever power is concentrated, the particular interest of a prince will always be upheld by his government more vigorously than the common interest of the state.

Following these reflections on Christianity's subversion of the sacred foundations of civil authority, Rousseau distinguishes three main types of religious belief in its social dimension: religion of the man, religion of the citizen, and religion of the priest. The first, the simple faith of the Gospels, dissolves all allegiance to the state; the second, in joining divine worship to love of the law, makes men credulous and intolerant; and the third, in placing ' persons under contradictory obligations to priestcraft and princely government, sets individuals at odds with themselves and their neighbours. Each of these cults is harmful to the body politic, concludes, none more so than the first, wrongly supposed by others to be the best imaginable, because of its shared beliefs and profound piety. In fact, a society of true Christians would be so spiritually perfect that its members would be completely unconcerned with worldly success or failure. Citizens would perform their duties out of obedience, determined only to ensure the salvation of their souls. How could a Christian republic ever confront the patriotic warriors of Sparta or Rome, 'devoured by an ardent love of glory and their country? Rousseau asks. How indeed could a genuine republic ever be Christian for 'true Christians are made to be slaves', their faith more amenable to tyranny than to the pursuit of the public good.

For the state to draw real strength from its members it must be nurtured by a religion which makes each citizen love his duty without intruding upon his beliefs through canons, sacraments, and dogmas. It must require of its subjects a purely civil profession of faith, prescribed by the sovereign merely to excite a public sentiment of sociability, and its tenets should embrace only the existence of an omnipotent, intelligent, and beneficent divinity, the sanctity of the social contract and the low, and the proscription of intolerance. Since belief is not itself subject to injunction, the sovereign can do no more than banish from its territory all persons whose intolerance of others would inevitably threaten the fabric of society, It may even authorize the capital punishment of individuals who betray their civil oath of allegiance—that is, who lie before the law, and thereby display their willingness to break it and thus to commit acts not of impiety but of sedition, as Rousseau stresses most particularly in his remarks on the same subject, anticipating that passage of the *Social Contract*, in his letter to Voltaire on Providence of 1756 (L 424). Theological intolerance is bound to have sinister political consequences, Rousseau argues, and in a note appended to this chapter, which perhaps out of unaccustomed prudence he tried to suppress, even as his work was being printed, he complains of the threat to the very foundation of the state, by way of its regulation of public offices and private inheritances, posed by clerical control over the civil con tract of marriage.

In stressing the inappropriateness of Roman Catholicism as a state religion, Rousseau's plea for tolerance in the *Social Contract* bears some resemblance to Locke's

Letter on Toleration of 1689, although his chapter's emphasis on the politically consolidating ties forged by the legislators of ancient republics owes rather more to Plato's *Laws* and, above all, the *Discourses* of Machiavelli, who had similarly found the civil religion of Rome immeasurably more attractive than Roman Christianity's cult of the City of God. No other modern thinker so impressed Rousseau as did Machiavelli, not only for his love of liberty but also for his incisive understanding of the place of religion in public affairs. Yet at least as striking as their similarity is the main difference between their philosophies of religion, for while Machiavelli approved of religious faith just in so far as it promoted the patriotism citizens, Rousseau was also passionately concerned with the nature of religious belief. Unlike Machiavelli, he was inspired by the life and example of Jesus, by the Gospels, and by the teachings of at least some of the Apostles. He had been moved by bewilderment and wonder at his place in God's universe, such as had troubled St Augustine, whose *Confessions* his own autobiography would echo in a fresh idiom. If in his grasp of the political effects of religion he was plainly under Machiavelli's influence in his religious convictions themselves, and in his perception of clerical orders and churches, he was equally a child of the Reformation.

However, unappealing it may seem, the civil religion is "a purely civil profession of faith, the articles of which are for the sovereign to establish, not exactly as religious dogmas, but the sentiments of sociability without which it is impossible to be a good citizen or a faithful subject". Indeed, the doctrine of the civil religion exemplifies Rousseau's attempt to combine the republican emphasis on civic devotion with a concern, subsequently associated with liberalism, for tolerance and freedom of thought:

> Now it matters greatly to the State that each citizen have a religion that causes him to love his duties; but the dogmas of that religion are of no interest either to the State or to its members; except insofar as these dogmas relate to morality, and to the duties that anyone who professes it is obliged to fulfill toward others. Everyone can have whatever opinions he pleases beyond that, without the sovereign having to know what they are. For since the sovereign has no competence in the other world, whatever the fate of subjects in the life hereafter, it is none of its business, as long as they are good citizens in this one.

The civil religion consists, accordingly, of several "positive" dogmas—"the existence of powerful, intelligent, beneficent, foresighted, and providential divinity; the afterlife; the happiness of the just; the punishment of the wicked; the sanctity of the social contract and the laws" –and one "negative" dogma, or proscription—"intolerance. It belongs with the cults we have excluded".

The state must tolerate everyone, in other words, except for two categories of people. The first comprises those who lack the belief in divine retribution that discourages people from harming or exploiting others whenever it is to their earthly advantage to do so; the second comprises those whose "theological intolerance" sets people against each other and stands in the way of civic virtue. Against this latter group, and with Roman Catholicism clearly in mind, Rousseau's civil religion would ensure "that there is no longer and can never be again an exclusive national religion".

In these respects, of course, Rousseau's position is quite similar to the one John Locke advocates in his *Letter Concerning Toleration.* Where he and Locke part company with subsequent liberals is in their conviction that it is necessary, for purely civil reasons, to require the profession of some kind of belief in a God who rewards and punishes in an afterlife. Rousseau adds fuel to Locke's moreover, by proposing rather stringent measures to secure the civil religion and, through it, "the sanctity of the social contract and the law":

> Without being able to obligate anyone to believe [these dogmas], the Sovereign can banish from the State anyone who does not believe them. If some one who has publicly acknowledged these same dogmas behaves as though he does not believe them, he should be punished with death.

Whether they betray his totalitarian instincts or his pessimism about the possibility of finding less draconian ways to induce men to act as citizens, the penalties Rousseau prescribes here certainly seem harsh for someone whose aim is to promote religious tolerance.

As for the legislator, this extraordinary person who drafts the fundamental laws and establishes the basic institutions should feel that he is capable of changing human nature, so to speak; of transforming each individual, who by himself is a perfect and solitary whole, into a part of a larger whole from which this individual receives, in a sense, his life and his being; of substituting a partial and moral existence for the physical and independent existence we have all received from nature. Although he cannot himself enact the legislation he recommends, the legislator should feel capable of transforming human nature because such a transformation is necessary to replace the natural life of men with the moral life of the citizen. The legislator's task, in a sense, is to complete the passage from the state of nature to the civil state that Rousseau describes in the first book of the *Social Contract*:

This passage from the state of nature to the civil state produces a remarkable change in man, by substituting justice for instinct in his behavior and giving his actions the morality they previously lacked. Only then, when the voice of duty replaces physical impulse and right replaces appetite, does man, who until that time only considered himself, find himself forced to act upon other principles and to consult his reason before heeding his inclinations. Although in this state he deprives himself of several advantages given by nature, he gains such great ones, his faculties are exercised and developed, his ideas broadened, his feelings ennobled, and his whole soul elevated to such a point that if the abuses of this new condition did not often degrade him beneath the condition he left, he ought ceaselessly to bless the happy moment that tore him away from it forever, and that changed him from a stupid, limited animal into an intelligent being and man. The legislator's task, then, is to provide the legal and institutional foundation that will prevent the abuses of the civil state that degrade people below their natural condition. By doing this—by directing people toward the general will the legislator will complete the transformation of human nature begun when people first left the state of nature.

Through these and other measures, Rousseau sought to encourage men to act as citizens—to seek and follow the general will. If some of the measures seem excessive, it is probably because Rousseau regarded the challenge—reconciling "what right permits with what interest prescribes, as extraordinarily difficult. Some of these measures may now seem out of place or anachronistic—the innovation of the legislator, for instance—and others, such as the call for a civil religion, may fit better with a strong form of classical republicanism than with republican liberalism. There are other problems with Rousseau's theory as well, notably his exclusion of women from the public realm. This exclusion is objectionable for not only what seems to be his condescending attitude but also for the way it condemns women to the personal dependence he so frequently abhors.

In addition, some problems associated with Rousseau's formulation of the general will persist even when we understand it as a principle that requires us to act as citizens rather than as men. First is the question of how the general will is to be applied. What does it mean to say that public policy must attend to the common interest of citizens and ignore the private interests of men? Is the viewpoint of the citizens always readily apparent? Consider the case of a city, akin to the one depicted in Henrik Ibsen's *An Enemy of the People*, that finds its fortunes tied to a single industry. Cities of this sort often find themselves on the horns of a dilemma. There may be reliable evidence that pollution from the industry is hazardous to the health of those in the community, but eliminating that hazard may involve the loss of the industry with all of the money and jobs it directly and indirectly provides. Everyone in the community will suffer if the hazard is not eliminated, yet it is also conceivable that everyone will suffer if the industry leaves. In this case, is there a single viewpoint that is distinctly the citizen's? What would the general will have those these predicaments do?

By altering the example slightly, we can produce yet another problem for Rousseau. Suppose that many people in this city will suffer severe economic hardship if the industry leaves and that a few, for one reason or another, will not suffer at all. In this case all of the members of the community share an interest in eliminating the hazard, but all do not share an interest in keeping the industry in town. The General Will, presumably, would require the elimination of the hazard because that would be in the interest of the citizens, even though it might spell disaster for most of the men in the city. Given possibilities of this kind, is it clear that we should always ignore the private interests of men when deciding matters of public policy.

If domination and servitude cannot form a just basis for society, what principles can be discovered which sustain political right or legitimate authority? The answer, as Rousseau has in all his works is in the notion of a covenant willed by all. Nothing in nature legitimizes the rule of one over another; therefore, agreement is the only moral source for such a relationship.

The social contract involves the alienation by each, of himself and all his rights, to the community, and this takes place in three stages: each gives himself up absolutely; all do this unconditionally; each recovers the equivalent of everything he loses. Put differently, all equally give themselves to the community and all in giving themselves to all give themselves to no one; it is a unity of equal and reciprocal dependence, and in the body politic so formed all are equal participants. In this way, natural freedom is given up in exchange for social freedom, where no one is dependent on another and each obeys himself. Individual wills are unified into a General Will in which all men participate. This new General Will is the will of the whole which has been created from the many particulars; it alone is sovereign, and the individual is both a sharer in sovereignty – a citizen – and bound by its laws – a subject. This General Will, this joint and equal power of decision making, is concerned with the common good not with particular or private interests, for its concern is with unity not division morality not self-interest.

The General Will is thus the force in society whereby man in giving up his natural independence gains not a vicious, unequal and servile dependence, but an equal share in his own rule, and personal independence. Rousseau calls both these states, the natural and the social, 'free', and he is led to this by the argument that as man gives up equally and regains equally it must be the same or something similar which is being given up and regained. What is given up is natural independence; what is gained is personal independence through a freedom which involves a right of participation and the duty of obedience. Social freedom is thus more than exchanging one kind of independence for another; it involves a change in man such that his concern is now not for himself but for the unity into which he has placed himself. Participating in the General Will transforms man from a creature of instinct, concerned quite properly with his own preservation, to a moral being concerned with what is just and with where his duty lies. Thus not only has man gained civil liberty in place of natural liberty, but he can now develop his moral freedom, which involves mastering himself and controlling his appetites.

Where the state of nature saw man as essentially innocent, political society opens up for the first time the possibility of moral man, man who puts the common good before his narrow pursuit of passion. Individual interest and the vices to which it gives rise will be subordinated to the common good as directed by the General Will, the authority which resides in the people. Only it can achieve harmony to replace the conflict of private interests, which made civil society necessary to begin with. This governing Will, this bond between all, is the sovereign collective being, whose authority can never be alienated from a free people because that is exactly what makes them free and what makes them a people. While their private wills, which incline them to partiality, will not always coincide with the General Will directed towards have a right to participate. Once the people alienate this right or have it taken from them, sovereignty ceases and the body politic as a legitimate unity is effectively dissolved.

As it is inalienable, so is the General Will indivisible; if it is truly General its declaration is law, but if it is partial or divided it lacks such authority. Neither can sovereignty be divided into legislature, executive and judiciary, for its concern is to make law as the voice of the people, not to apply it or interpret it, which are subordinate roles not the sovereign one. Furthermore, the General Will as the principle of unity amongst a people is always rightful and tending towards the general good. It is always the expression of such good, not the expression of self-interest by groups or individuals. It may not always be discerned, for men can will selfishly, but if it emanates from concern for the common good, it is always right. Thus it is not to be identified with the will of all, the sum with the state rather than as individuals or sectional groups promoting their won private interest. It is the result not of discussion but of purpose as well as in its nature, if it springs from all and applies to all, then it has absolute power over all the members of the community in all matters which concern the community, for the members in the original contract agreed to such absolute alienation of themselves in return for their part in formulating the General Will.

However, though the people acting together in a spirit of unity always desire and will the good, they do not always see it, and just as the General Will must guide individuals who fail to follow it, so is the General Will in need of guidance so that it will and its understanding are brought into harmony. At the beginning, moral concern needs to be complemented by an insight provided from outside the body politic, and this role is provided by a lawgiver, a figure of superior intelligence who understands the nature and passions of men but who is not limited by them and whose prime concern is man's happiness. Such a figure has no place within a system where t he people are sovereign: rather he creates the system which enables men to be transformed from natural to moral and communal beings. His task is to provide the framework within which the will to be good can arise and be realized; goodness is a matter of will but reason must provide the structure for such a process to be possible. The social spirit or General Will which emerges once the political society is established cannot itself establish that society. The lawgiver, using not argument or force but divine authority, must therefore shape those institutions which will thereafter shape the people, and he must do this in such a way as to adapt and relate to people. Such an enlightened and wise constitution-maker and creator of construction to guide him, and who has a plan to implement, but who must take note of local conditions and available material. Once such a project is successful, the lawgiver's role is ended, and the General Will can come into existence and flourish within the structure of law designed for it.

Having established the origins, purpose and principles of the state, Rousseau proceeds to discuss the role of government within this structure. The General Will is sovereign, and to the people belongs the legislative power, but the state also needs an executive power, to be exercised in particular acts and which represents the strength by which to carry out the designs of the will. Government is simply a commission from the sovereign body; it cannot itself legislate and its existence is entirely a grant from the people. It is not to be confused with sovereignty, for unlike the latter it is not the result of a contract but is merely a subordinate means by which the citizens as sovereign body communicate with the citizens as subjects. This executive power can be in the hands of all, few, or one; in all cases there is the danger to be guarded against that government will usurp its limited role and thus threaten the constitutional supremacy of the people. However, there are also other considerations is examining the merits of these three types of government. Democracy is not a serious candidate because it denies Rousseau's principle that the legislative and executive powers should be kept separate; the one deals with the general and the other with the particular, and democracy would threaten to blur this important distinction. Legislation is the result of men acting as citizens with a moral concern for all, and this must be kept apart from administration, where people would be tempted to act as subjects concerned with their own interests. For democracy to work, people would have to permanently elevate their altruistic concerns above their selfish concerns and such demands are impossible for mere humans to meet.

As a number of commentators have pointed out, the inequality Rousseau attacks, is the type founded on accident and caprice, not merit and virtue. As Judith Shklar has shown, the societies Rousseau most admired, such as Sparta and Rome, were aristocracies based on a clear distinction between rulers and ruled, in which the striving for distinction formed an integral part of the public-spirited nature of their polities. Thus, it is not distinctions, which Rousseau attacks as such, but those based solely on wealth. 'The Will against inequality', Shklar argues, 'is Will against wealth and privilege, not against political rulership'. A recent commentator argues that the equality which Rousseau thinks necessary to a just society is not arithmetical, ascribing the same to everyone, but proportional or geometric. Thus, for example, public honor and esteem should be commensurate with the degree of individual merit. A major problem, however, facing Rousseau's thought, is that of how to make equal degrees of liberty compatible with a principle of hierarchy in which different degrees of honor and worth are recognized.

Both Rousseau and Kant reveal their modernity in the attempt to arrive at a notion of community from a basis in the individual, an individual who is conceived as free and autonomous. Rousseau defines liberty in terms of the individual freely prescribing laws to itself. This liberty is defined as 'moral' because the laws which the individual prescribes must be universal and rational. The definition of self-mastery is of someone who can transcend obedience to 'the mere impulse of appetite', and act politically in terms of voluntary obedience to a collective rational autonomy.

There are, however, a number of important differences between Rousseau and Kant in their accounts of a moral autonomy. A key difference between them is that whereas Rousseau bases morality on heteronomy, that is, on appeal to enlightened self-interest is best served by acting in accordance with the General Will, Kant makes no appeal to heteronomy in his deduction of the autonomous nature of human action. On the contrary, Kant rules out self-interest as a basis for morality. A moral action can only be defined as one which is performed out of the motive of duty, where duty makes no appeal to any gains or ends one may hope to achieve by performing the action. Another important difference concerns the emphasis each place on the element of universalization in human action. Although morality is a matter of generalization for both Rousseau and Kant, in the former it is only the proposed course of action that is generalized, while in the latter it is a necessary characteristic of the moral quality of an action that the agent must generalize its own point of view. One commentator has expressed Kant's position well by suggesting that the rational human agent must consider his proposed course of action not from his own viewpoint, but from that of all rational being considered as equally rational. In Rousseau's account of the General Will, on the other hand, only that which is of common interest to all is to be willed on a universal basis. This is important for understanding just how novel Rousseau's account of a free, rational will is.

This will not simply free in an ethical sense, but also in a political one: moral liberty is a precondition of civil or political liberty. It must not be supposed that Rousseau envisages the formation of the General Will in terms of universalization of selfishness. Rather, through the social compact the individual is to become a citizen who is both an active member of the sovereign body, and a subject of its will who must obey its commands. The citizen is a political actor who performs in the public arena in order to promote the common good, not simply the good of its own particular will.

Rousseau: Totalitarian or Democrat ?

A good deal of controversy continues to surround the interpretation of Rousseau's political philosophy. Of all its many troubling features, however, surely none is more problematic than his scheme for a civil religion. That proposal has been controversial from the beginning. It earned for Rousseau the wrath of the authorities at Geneva, who condemned the *Social Contract* in 1762, and it has incurred its share of censure ever since. In Rousseau's own day, Calvinists and Catholics alike condemned it for its impiety, and atheists for its religiosity. Many modern critics claim to have exposed its 'totalitarian' implications. And so, not surprisingly, Rousseau's short chapter on civil religion has been something of a burden for his latter-day defenders and admirers, and a continuing source of scholarly controversy.

Rousseau's critics, particularly those who view him as a precursor of totalitarianism, have brought their bill of indictment by focusing upon four features to be found in the *Social Contract*. The first is the idea of General Will, which is 'always right' and 'cannot err'. The second is the frequency with which such sinister-sounding phrase as people being 'forced to be free' recur throughout the text. The third is the ominous figure of the omniscient god-like legislator. Finally, and most sinister of all, is Rousseau's civil religion with its dogmas, oaths, religious tests, and its provisions for punishing unbelievers. Taken together, these four features of Rousseau's political philosophy, these critics contend, amount to a convincing case for the prosecution.

Those who have defended Rousseau against the charge that he is a proto-totalitarian, however, had some success in showing that the General Will is not necessarily totalitarian in either its suppositions or its implications. Nor do such phrases as 'forced to be free' have, when considered in context, the ominous overtones detected by Rousseau's detractors and critics. But Rousseau's defenders have had much more difficulty in dealing with his account of the role of the legislator and the civil religion, and more particularly with the charge that the latter is, in the hands of the former, an instrument of political indoctrination and totalitarian rule. Critics are apt to see in Rousseau's arguments concerning the need for a civil religion a very clear display of the totalitarian elements in his thinking.

It is easy to see why. Rousseau's civil religion does appear to modern—or at any rate to liberal and secular eyes as an aberrant attempt to combine religion and politics, Church and State, in a kind of holy alliance that is almost always dangerous to individual liberties. To see just where this danger lies, let us look briefly at the arguments advanced by Rousseau in support of a civil religion. In making his case for a civil religion Rousseau proceeds by attacking two very different targets. Against Bayle, who had held that 'religion is of no use to a body politic', Rousseau rejoins that 'no state has ever been founded without religion as its basis'. And against Warburton's assertion that Christianity is the only firm foundation of any state, Rousseau replies that 'Christian law is at bottom more injurious than useful to the strong constitution of the state'.

Christianity comes in two variants, the first being institutional Roman Christianity, the second the pure or true Christianity of the Gospels. The first undermines civic virtue. Roman Christianity provides its adherents with 'two codes of law, two rulers, two fatherlands, places them under contradictory duties, and prevents their being both believers and citizens'. But 'from a political point of view', the 'holy, sublime, and true religion' of the Gospels is no less defective. It holds that all mankind are the children of the same God and envisions a universal brotherhood composed of men of all nations, past and present, living and dead. Thus, 'this religion, having no particular connection with the body politic', Rousseau complains, 'leaves the law with no other force than its own' and thereby deprives it of an additional spiritual dimension. Worse still, 'instead of attaching the hearts of the citizens to the state', this religion distracts them from all worldly concerns, including civic ones. 'Christianity is a religion that is entirely spiritual', Rousseau asserts, and 'the fatherland of the Christian is not of this world'. Worst of all, however, is that the terms 'republic' and 'Christianity' are incompatible; each term includes the other. Christianity preaches only servitude and dependence. Its spirit is too favorable to tyranny. True Christians are moulded to be slaves' – that is, passive subjects rather than robust and active citizens.

Rousseau then looks for a religion fit for republic and citizens, and finds it in civil religion whose articles are to be arranged by the sovereign 'not exactly as dogmas of religion, but as sentiments of sociability without which it is impossible to be a good citizen or a faithful subject'. The sovereign, he says, 'cannot compel men to believe' these sentiments, but 'it can banish from the state anyone who does not believe them'. The unbeliever is banished not so much for impiety as for unsociability, having shown himself incapable of sincerely loving the laws and justice, and if need be to sacrifice his life to his duty. But if anyone, after having publicly agreed to these dogmas, shall behave as if he did not believe them, he is to be punished by death, for he has committed the greatest of all crimes: he has lied in the face of the law.

Rousseau's critics have been quick to seize upon several apparently slippery statements. He says, for instance, that the 'sentiments of sociability' are not exactly 'dogmas'; but then he proceeds to call them dogmas. The dogmas of the civil religion ought to be simple, few in number, precisely fixed, and without explanation or comment. The existence of a powerful, wise, and benevolent Deity who foresees and provides; the life to come; the happiness of the just; the punishment of the wicked; the sanctity of the social contract and the laws—these are its positive dogmas.

Modern critics complains that the State has a right to conclude from a person's action—or, implicitly, from his non-action—what his real beliefs or opinions are, to accuse him of perjury, and to put him to death. What is this, if not the doctrine of arrest on suspicion of wrong thinking. We need take only one further step to punish people for lack of enthusiasm. The effect of such a state of affairs on people's conduct can easily be imagined from similar situations in later history. This reading of Rousseau suggests that the civil religion is an indispensable cog in the totalitarian machinery. Without it the juggernaut could not function for long, if at all.

Rousseau's modern critics have accordingly had little difficulty in arriving at answers to the three questions. To the first—what place does the plan for a civil religion occupy in Rousseau's political philosophy? —They answer that it necessarily occupies a central place. For some sort of civil religion, they argue, would be indispensable to the continued functioning and legitimating of the totalitarian society envisioned in the *Social Contract.* As to what Rousseau was doing, these critics answer that he was advocating a conformitarian theocracy in which all debate, dissent, and disagreement are prohibited, ostensibly on religious though really on political grounds. Rousseau's reason for placing the chapter on the civil religion at the end of the *Social Contract* is accordingly quite clear. His concept of the General Will, his remarks about forcing people to be free, and the rest, lead logically and inexorably to just that kind of conclusion and that kind of institution. Ernest Barker contends that it is significant that the Social contract ends with the suggestion of religious persecution. This is a clear proof that 'in effect, and in the last resort, Rousseau is a totalitarian.

There is plainly some kind of democratic thrust in Rousseau's political thought, though whether it is the thrust of totalitarian democracy that Talmon would have us believe is another question. What is democratic about Rousseau's *Social Contract* is that massive consent is required before a state can be made legitimate. But the legitimacy of a political order, and how that political order actually functions in its daily practice, are two very different kinds of concern. The modern democratic state partly legitimizes itself through periodic elections, which are the palest of all the pale reflections of Rousseau's General Will, but it also partly legitimizes itself by providing them equally with those services, which make the idea of citizenship worthwhile. The history of political thought can be seen as the history of different legitimizing arguments for the state, and it may be that the democratic argument for legitimacy is the most powerful of all. Who, it might be asked, has the right to oppose what all have agreed to? Of course, this argument only applies to the state in general, and it has very little to say about government and nothing at all to say about the day-do-day running of government. Early democratic theory in modern Europe hardly distinguished between democratic legitimacy to democratic government. However, Rousseau himself plainly regards representation as a sham. It can't really be me that my representative represents. At best, it can only be his idea of me that he represents, and, much more likely, his own interest will interpose itself between him and those whom he only appears to represent. Ancient democracies never had this problem because, being small, the sovereign people could represent itself. It is only in modern democracies that the form of government is an issue, and Rousseau leaves the question of what kind of government could be a delegation from the General Will dangerously vague. We do know that it may decide anything it likes about anything. In principle at least, nothing is outside the legitimate concern of the sovereign people as legislators. What Rousseau leaves out of the account is the possibility that the General Will could be manipulated by government. Rousseau tends to take a very passive view of government, assuming with the ancients that a government dependent on the General Will of its citizens will not be stupid enough to do anything detrimental to the interests of the whole because, the whole once assembled, government as a delegated power from the whole will cease to exist, and those who exercised executive authority on the people's behalf will return to the condition of private citizens.

But a government acting as a delegation from the General Will in a large democratic republic would be in a very different position. Granted that constitutional conventions cannot meet very often, and granted that there would have to be meetings of delegates, and granted Rousseau's reservations about delegates following an interest of their own, and granted Rousseau's suspicion that government can always corrupt delegates through patronage, then it is hard to see what Rousseau's scheme of things has to offer to modern states, and very easy to see how Rousseau's own political theory could be used by a ruthless governing cite to manipulate 'public opinion' to agree, or at least not to disagree, with anything. That is the sense in which Talmon regards Rousseau as a totalitarian democrat: a manipulated General Will could be used to justify anything. One can only repeat that such a manipulation of the idea of the General Will is about as far from the original spirit of Rousseau as it is possible to be. Of course, it is possible that Rousseau himself is the cause of the trouble. For all his insistence that the state of the social contract lies in the future, Rousseau is really extremely backward looking as a political thinker. Ancient Sparta haunts everything he has to say about politics, and it may be that, in raising hopes for the future of European states, he raises them only to be dashed. Rousseau may not be so much mistaken as dangerous.

What about the coercion of minorities? Rousseau does not say that going along with the majority is the price the minority has to pay for living in a new kind of society. On the contrary, the minority is forced to go along with the majority decision, and Rousseau says that forcing them to do so is forcing them to be free, the most famous of all his paradoxes. What can that possibly mean? On the face of it, Rousseau appears to be making a difficulty for himself by not simply saying that minorities are always coerced in political communities, and that that's just the way things are. On the contrary, Rousseau seems to be saying that the minority really wanted to be concerned all along. The minority apparently suffers the double indignity of being coerced, and of being told that they are being coerced in the name of their own real freedom. Rousseau certainly accepts that all states coerce in the sense that in political communities everybody is expected to pay more than lip service to the prevailing system of public values, but he thinks that coercion under the General Will is so different that it is a mistake to call it coercion of minorities an coercion is traditionally conceived.

The main question about the General Will which has still to be answered is: Where is its content to come from? Rousseau himself confuses the issue because he sometimes talks as if the General Will is something like what the utilitarian were later to mean by the general happiness, and it is easy to see why what the general happiness is could ascertained by counting heads. At other times, Rousseau speaks of the General Will is what a majority just happens to want, because one of the things a majority could just happen to want would be the permanent subjugation of a minority. The problem of the content of the General Will is that Rousseau will not allow any kind of pre-existing moral law to given the General Will something to go by. Rousseau in fact suppressed a chapter on Natural Law which he included in the first draft of *The*

Social Contract because he realized that the pre-existence of a transcendental moral law would limit the freedom of choice of the sovereign people when it made laws for itself. The only other possibility is that the content of the General Will would be supplied out of the what we have come to call a national culture. Here we may trace the influence of Montesquieu's *The Spirit of the Laws* on Rousseau, especially on the *Project for a Constitution for Corsica* and the *Considerations on the Government of Poland*. In these works Rousseau shows his nationalist side, playing the outside legislator who can see so far into a people's spirit that he can give them laws. Perhaps he thought that every particular people had its own particular spirit, and that spirit ought to be embodied in its laws, that is its constitution. It would follow from this that no two peoples should have the same set of laws, and that would explain the suppression of the Natural Law chapter in *The Social Contract*: nothing ought to inhibit a free people from choosing its own laws.

The idea that it is a particular national culture which furnishes the content of the General Will might explain the figure of the Legislator in *The Social Contract*. Rousseau says that ideally he should be a foreigner who has no personal or family or party interest in the constitution which he helps the sovereign people to form for themselves. Perhaps Rousseau thought that the ideal person to give a people laws would be the ideal outside observer who, because he is an outsider, can see the main lines of a nation's culture more clearly than those who are themselves steeped in that culture. This is the reason the way that the best books about particular countries are often written by foreigners who often notice significant things about a national culture which natives miss. Rousseau certainly admired the great, god-like law-givers like Lycurgus and Solon, and his admiration for Calvin, the founder of Rousseau's own native city's laws, is a much based on what the foreigner Calvin did for Geneva government as on what he did for its religion.

In *The Social Contract* Rousseau has remarkably little to say about government, as distinct from what he calls legislation, and it is important to understand the difference. Legislation is what the General Will enacts when the sovereign people meet. Meetings of the sovereign people are not a legislature in the ordinary sense of the term, because the sovereign people can only make decisions of a very general kind which affect everybody equally. A meeting of the sovereign people is much more like a constitutional convention than a parliament. Its laws are much more like constitutional principles than what we mean by 'the details of legislation'. Rousseau calls what we would call 'government,' a 'delegation' from the General Will, and he is careful to distinguish between acts of the General Will and what he calls 'acts of magistracy'. What magistracy – that is government – is to be like is largely an open question. A government of the gods would no doubt be a democracy, but the actual government of men is a different case. Perhaps the best form of government would be a virtuous aristocracy, as in the best period of the Roman republic, or even government by a single respected family. Whatever form government is to take, as acts of the sovereign people, and being a delegation from the General Will, government automatically ceases to exist when the sovereign people assembles in its own right. Rousseau's sovereign people, therefore, is best conceived as a constitutional convention with the permanent right of assembly. In a well-regulated state it is safe to assume that such meetings will be infrequent, but governors are supposed to have the possibility always in mind, and this in its turn is supposed to make governors moderate and reasonable in exercising the function of rule.

When all is said and done, however, Rousseau has the mark of a truly great political thinker. Our criticisms take us to the very heart of his political theory and raise the perennial political issues. It does not really matter whether or not we agree fully with Rousseau. What matters is that his political analysis raises all the important political issues and makes us think about them from fresh perspectives. Most important, Rousseau alerts us to the contradictions inherent in Western political thought, and that he alone had the insight to recognize the contradictions that were reflected in his own personality and the personalities of all European peoples. Ethics versus politics, sovereignty versus freedom, the individual versus the state, and classical ideals versus modern ideas, all are encompassed in Rousseau's political thought. And while we may or may not agree that he overcomes these contradictions, we cannot deny that in his attempt to do so Rousseau raises the key issues in the long tradition of Western political thought and makes us think about them anew.

The opening lines of the first chapter of Rousseau's *Social Contract* can fairly be described as the motto which has inspired most the modern revolutionary spirit. 'Man is born free', Rousseau writes, 'and everywhere he is in chains'. In this work, Rousseau is less concerned with the origins of man's social slavery, than with how the social bond can be made legitimate. The idea that the famous opening sentence of the first chapter of the book advocates a return to nature is part of Rousseauian mythology. In fact, it is Rousseau's aim to show in what way the social bond can lay claim to a legitimate hold on men's hearts. The work is an inquiry into the principles of political right. In other word, Rousseau's concern is not so much with studying existing governments and social practices, but more importantly with examining the foundations of legitimate government and showing the legitimate basis of political obligation. The work is premised, therefore, on Rousseau's belief in man's natural goodness; without this belief such an inquiry would be neither possible nor worthwhile.

It has to be appreciated, however, that Rousseau's inquiry into political right is also premised on the claim that the social order although a sacred right is a right, which does not come from nature and must, therefore, be founded on conventions. This explains why the work is presented in terms of an inquiry into the principles of 'political' right, and not into principles of 'natural' right. Thus, in the opening chapters of the work Rousseau dismisses the claim that legitimate authority – political right – can be founded on notions such as the right of the strongest and slavery: 'Since no man has a natural authority over his follows', Rousseau writes, 'and force creates no right, we must conclude that conventions form the basis of all legitimate authority among men'. Against Hobbes, however, he argues that the social contract cannot be based on a renunciation of man's liberty to the authority of the state. To renounce liberty in this way is to renounce one's status as a human being, since it is one's capacity for free agency which gives a person their humanity. Moreover, such an alienation of one's liberty involves removing all morality from man's actions. He thus rejects Hobbes's solution to the problem of sovereignty, which presents us with a stark choice between absolute authority on the one side and anarchy on the other. In a condition in which a natural right of conquest or slavery lies at the foundation of political authority, Rousseau says, one sees no more than a master-slave relationship, not a people and its ruler, but an aggregation instead of an association of human beings. From this argument Rousseau informs us that he will move on to examine that act by which a people becomes an association, for this is the only true foundation of society. In attempting to overcome Hobbes's stark choice between absolutism and anarchism with the notion of the conventional General Will, however, Rousseau constructs a model of legitimate political authority which reveals both absolutist and anarchist tendencies.

In introducing a notion of the social compact, Rousseau supposes that individuals have reached the point at which the obstacles in the way of their preservation in the state of nature show their power of resistance to be greater than the resources at the disposal of each individual for his maintenance in that state'. In other words, Rousseau premises his argument on the belief that the individual can no longer subsist on its own in the state of nature and must out of necessity join with others to form a community. However, having made this point, Rousseau is immediately faced with a huge difficulty. If such a compact is to be formed, how can it be created in such a way that the individual finds in it not the sacrifice of its natural liberty, but its fulfillment? In other words, what moral reason can be given to the pre-political individual for leaving the state of nature and joining a society in which he will be brought into relationship resting on interdependence with others? This is the fundamental problem of which the social contract provides the solution.

Rousseau is attempting nothing less the resolution of the fundamental antinomies of modern political thought: liberty and authority, the individual and society man and citizen freedom and necessity, desire and reason. Through the social contract, man is to elevate himself into a moral being. Rousseau's argument presupposes that through this creative act of political formation there will no longer be any split between the interests of the individual and those of the community, but that they will now be identical. On account of this it is stated that, in constituting such a political form, the social contract should demand the, 'total alienation of each associate, together with all his rights, to the whole community; for in the first place, as each gives himself absolutely, the conditions are the same for all; and, this being the case, no one has any interest in making them burdensome to others'. In other words, the individual of the state of nature will not simply lose the independence he enjoyed in this state, but will gain another form of independence, the independence that is gained through dependence, through being a member of a moral community based on free and equal social relationship. With this account of the social contract Rousseau's inversion of Hobbes is complete.

Rousseau accomplishes this inversion of Hobbes by attributing to the 'moral-collective body', that has been set up through the act of association, the status of a sovereign power. He employs the term 'General Will' to describe this form of sovereignty in which there exists a complete identity between the individual and the moral collective body. Instead of the individual will being renounced as in Hobbes's account of sovereignty, it is claimed to be realized in Rousseau's account. In Hobbes, the problem of the existence of a plurality of wills is resolved by the creation of one particular will, which is vested with absolute power. By contrast, Rousseau seeks a solution in which the plurality of particular wills create a community in which there exists an identity between the individual and the universal in a General Will. In fact, as a number of commentators have noted, Rousseau's employment of the term 'social contract' is misleading in this respect, since the association that is to be created through it does not depend for its existence, on a contractual relationship between 'rulers' on the one hand and 'ruled' on the other. On Rousseau's social contract, there is no such distinction. In obeying the general, will, for example, the individuals of Rousseau's social contract are merely obeying themselves; in other words, they are not obeying at all but commanding, they are not enchained but free. The community that is created through the act of association is not itself party to the contract, as there is no exchange of power in this act of sovereignty between community and individuals.

Rousseau requires the notion of a social contract in order to account for the formation of the General Will in the first place. The most striking aspect of Rousseau's formulation of the problem of the social contract, however, is not that it advocates the subjugation of the particular will by the General Will, or that it rests on an abstract and purely formal unification of particular wills – but rather that it appeals directly to the isolated, autonomous self of civil society depicted by Hobbes and Locke as a way of constituting a new ethico-political community in which the particular and the universal are united in a common identity.

The transition from the state of nature to a civil state emancipates the individual from the tyranny of his desires and gives him the freedom of reason: 'Instead of a stupid and unimaginative animal', Rousseau informs us, society now provides us with 'an intelligent being and a man'. Rousseau explains the terms of the social contract by saying that while individuals lose through it their natural liberty and unlimited right to things, they gain by it civil liberty and the ownership of all they possess. In other words, it is only by participating in the making of a social contract based on the principles of liberty and equality that human beings can gain all the advantages which a thinker like Locke construes as already in existence in the state of nature. For Rousseau a human being's entrance into the social state entails a profound transformation in their nature. The most important thing he gains by undergoing this transformation, according to Rousseau, is the acquisition of moral liberty, which alone makes a person master of him – or herself. It is at this point in his argument that Rousseau offers his definition of moral liberty in terms of self-mastery: 'the mere impulse of our appetites is slavery, while obedience to a law we have prescribed to ourselves is liberty.

The opening sentence of Rousseau's inquiry into the principles of political right shows that his prime concern is with justice. Rousseau's intention is to inquire whether if 'in the civil order, there can be any sure and legitimate rule of administration, men being taken as they are and laws as they might be'. The aim is to unite 'right' and 'interest' so that justice and utility coincide, so that what the individual wills and achieves by self-mastery is both just and useful to its self-interest. The tension in Rousseau's model of the just polity stems from individualists premises, for it is a society in which the pursuit of virtue in public or civic affairs is not only recognized to be the highest good, but which requires the individual to constantly sacrifice their self-interest. It is thus the task of an education in citizenship and in civic virtues to persuade the strong, independent human being who believes he can attain freedom in his lofty isolation, that true liberty is attained when one becomes a moral agent, a citizen acting in society in accordance with the reign of virtue. Rousseau in fact is faced with the same problem which faces Socrates in the Republic, that of convincing the individual of the nobleness and rightness of the moral way of life. Natural law is completely ineffective simply because human beings do not naturally follow the precepts of justice, since they find it more profitable to do wrong than to lead a moral life.

Viroli wishes to defend Rousseau against Hegel's critique that he has failed to resolve the antinomies of modern political life. Hegel's argument contra Rousseau is that the notion of the General Will, in which the opposition between the particular and the universal has supposedly been overcome, is not a rational universal will, but little more than the sum of individual wills. Clearly, this is a distortion of Rousseau's position, which separates the idea of the 'will of all' from that of the 'General Will' properly understood. Viroli argues that Rousseau's politics are based on the principle of the sovereignty of law, and hence of the rational will, and not as Hegel supposes merely of the individual will.

The precise meaning and significance of Rousseau's notion of the General Will has been interpreted in different ways by different commentators. It would be foolish to arrive either at a complete acceptance of Rousseau's doctrine, or a complete and outright rejection. Instead, it is necessary to appreciate both its promise, and its danger, by recognizing that the General Will represents Rousseau's novel attempt to overcome the antinomies of modern political thought which insists on portraying the relationship between the individual and society in oppositional terms. Thus, what is taken to be fatal weakness in Rousseau's account could turn out to be the source of its strength. It must not be forgotten that Rousseau's political thought is directed towards finding a satisfactory solution to the peculiarly modern problem of political legitimacy. Rousseau's concern with the question of legitimacy is founded on his insight into the recession of the regulative role of custom in modern political life, and its replacement by the supremacy of law. Thus, instead of interpreting the General Will simply in terms of a mere regulatory, authoritarian power, it is possible to read the notion as denoting an active, dynamic political will. In order to do the notion 'justice', therefore, it would be necessary to make a distinction between a static conception and a dynamic one. A static General Will would be one in which the rules and conventions animating public life become rigidified and ossified, but cannot be challenged without either the will dissolving itself into anarchy, or without the will assuming a tyrannical, despotic form. A dynamic will, on the other hand, would be one in which political rule provides the space for, and encourages its members to, freely challenge social rules and norms. Thus one commentator, for example, has argued that the notion of a General Will must incorporate political discussion and debate within its definition. He thus reads Rousseau's notion of the General Will as one which envisages political life in terms of an 'agony' operating within an 'agora'.

Of course the great danger of the notion of the General Will is that instead of producing genuine independence by fostering identity in difference, it produces tyrannical uniformity by obliterating difference altogether. Thus, the main difficulty which faces Rousseau concerns how the General Will is actually formed. Many read Rousseau political thought as pointing in the direction of a simple tyranny of the majority. The General Will thus leads to the rule of the herd. Once formed the General Will is discovered in a decision of the majority. In the fourth book of the *Social Contract* Rousseau says that the individual who stands alone and apart from the voice of the majority is simply in error, and what he thought was the General Will has proved not to be. But, in sacrificing the General Will to a majoritarian principle, Rousseau destroys the agonal basis of social life by failing to recognize the tragic nature of politics, that is, that political life is conflictual. Any harmony must be fought for to be genuine, and consensus must be reached through struggle and combat, not simply artificially created by being imposed from outside.

The great strength of Rousseau's notion of the General Will is that it shows that an adequate response to the modern problem of legitimacy must lie in a theory of democratic participation. Its great weakness, however, especially when seen in the wider context of Rousseau's argument in the *Social Contract,* is that it is a notion which is forced to rely on conformity and uniformity, forced to obliterate conflict and dissent, in order to retain its purity. It is not difficult to sympathize with a recent commentator's judgment that the way in which a politics based on a notion of the General Will protects its purity is by presiding over a society in which it is seldom needed to call this will into play. It is one of the great paradoxes of Rousseau's political thought that, although it sets out to establish politics on the ethical principle of the free autonomous will, it is forced to fall back on notions of coercion and constraint in order to save its argument on the moral transfiguration of humanity from total collapse.

Indeed, it is with Hobbes in mind that Rousseau developed his theory of General Will. It is in essence a moral concept that illuminates what he believes to be the fundamental flaw in all modern states organized on Hobbesian or Lockean premises. They lack any genuine ethical basis and, as such, the citizens have no inner reason or self-imposed duty to obey the law. Law then becomes in Hobbes's words 'command," that is, a civilized canon of force or coercion. Thus, obedience to law ceases to be an act of freedom and genuine liberty is destroyed. The concept of the General Will indicates that it is the liberal state which is based upon force and coercion, not Rousseau's ideal polity where if force is employed it actually enhances freedom.

The first of these is the censorship, an institution, says Rousseau, established "to preserve morality by preventing the opinions of men from being corrupted." For Rousseau, opinion is really the most fundamental law of the state. It is the law "written" within the human heart without which civil laws can have no meaning. As such, morality is subverted and the state ceases to express the General Will if opinion is allowed to become corrupted, if, for example, people come to believe their individual interest is superior to the collective interest. The censorship is thus crucial to the maintenance of the public good. We, of course, are rather shocked by the notion of censorship since freedom of opinion is one of our most cherished values. But it bears repeating that Rousseau holds a positive view of liberty and a positive theory of the state. To his mind, it is precisely the object of the state to engage in moral education so that the liberty of the subject will conform to the General Will. Absolute freedom of opinion can no more exist in his ideal state than can an absolute right to the unlimited accumulation of property.

This same logic lies behind Rousseau's argument for the institution of civil religion. Clearly, religious opinions, as with any opinions that have social or political import, must be fixed in Rousseau's ideal state. Hence, he argues, there must be a purely civil profession of faith on the part of the citizens, the articles of which are to be determined by the sovereign. And while he is willing to tolerate other religions so long as they do not contradict the tenets of the civil faith it is clear that Rousseau prefers the civil religion to others. Rousseau's preference is again reminiscent of Machiavelli. Like Machiavelli, he criticizes Christianity and other such universalistic religions, what he calls the "religion of man," because their otherworldly orientation directs people's attention away from the political community and makes them concerned only with "the purely internal cult of the supreme God." Civil religion, or the "religion of the citizen," on the other hand, is an intimate part of the state and thus makes religious and political values compatible. Where Christianity teaches otherwordliness and humility, civil religion glorifies the state and teaches those political virtues that contribute to its survival.

All these various institutions as a whole suggest that the whole social infrastructure of his ideal polity is such as to direct the citizen's attention almost totally toward the state. Love of country is the inevitable result, and this is precisely what Rousseau intended, for political virtue, is patriotism. Because patriotism, says Rousseau, combines "the force of egoism with all the beauty of virtue!"

How, then, is the sovereign assembly to actually make laws that express the General Will? Quite simply, says Rousseau, by voting until a simple majority is reached. Like Locke, Rousseau insists that only the social contract that creates political society need be decided by unanimous consent; all subsequent decisions require only a majority. The objection will almost surely be raised here that a majority is not the whole community. Yet, there is no inconsistency in Rousseau's argument. To begin with, Rousseau roots his majority in the whole community rather than in a minority of legislators, as does Locke. Hence, Rousseau's majority is much more likely to reflect the real interests of the community. But, more important, Rousseau nowhere suggests that the majority is identical to the General Will. It is perfectly possible, that the majority will merely reflect the self-interest or individual wills of the larger number of citizens. Yet this is equally true of the "will of all," says Rousseau. An unanimous decision may reflect nothing more than the self-interest or private will of each voting citizen. For this reason, he argues, there is often a great difference between the will of all and the General Will: "The latter regards only the common interest; the former regards private interest, and is indeed but a sum of private wills: But remove from these same wills the pluses and minuses that cancel each other, and then the General Will remains the sum of the differences."

In other words, the General Will cannot be determined simply by counting votes. Even if the votes are unanimous, this does not in and of itself guarantee a moral decision. The decision in the public interest as opposed to one reflecting a collection of individual self-interest. The entire assembly, for example, may refuse to increase taxes it knows to be in the public interest simply because each member's selfish interest in paying lower taxes predominates. Thus, the General Will is expressed only when the voters, whatever their number, reflect the general or public interest of the whole community, a condition that Rousseau describes rather mechanically when he speaks of subtracting from each other the pluses and minuses of self-interest.

All that can be said about the number of votes, and this is all Rousseau does say, is that the larger the majority the greater the probability that it is an expression of the General Will. And the only general rule of number that Rousseau provides is that the more important the issue at stake the larger the majority should be, and the more immediately serious the issue—a crisis situation for example—the smaller it need be.

Such, then, are the basic organization principles of Rousseau's sovereign assembly. But the issue of government still remains: what is the appropriate relationship of the government to the sovereign, and what is the best form of government in maintaining this relationship? Put simply, what form of government is most compatible with the maintenance of the General Will? There are two points that must be made before we get to these specific issues.

First, Rousseau makes a great point of distinguishing government and sovereignty, a distinction that he believes some thinkers like Hobbes have confounded. For Rousseau, government refers to the executive power in the state, not the legislative or law-making power that belongs to the sovereign assembly alone. And, technically speaking, government does in fact refer to the executive. Three is a tendency in England to subsume under government the executive, legislative, and judicial functions. But in European parliamentary systems the term government is reserved for the executive power.

Second, Rousseau insists that the existence of government in no way violates the basic principle of sovereignty that the General Will is inalienable because, as he argues, "the power may well be transmitted but not the will." In other words, the essence of the General Will is precisely its will or moral capacity. This it cannot alienate without ceasing to be a General Will. In political terms, the legislative function of the whole community cannot be transmitted to any other body such as Locke's assembly of representatives. But power or the ability to enforce the laws can and must be transmitted, says Rousseau, since it would be undesirable, not to mention impossible in most cases, for the people as a whole to enforce the laws. The exercise of power, in other words, properly belongs to government.

This is not to suggest that government does not pose a potential threat to the sovereignty of the General Will. Quite the contrary—this is precisely the danger according to Rousseau: "Just as the private will continually act against the General Will, so the government makes an unremitted effort against the Sovereign" until the social contract is broken. And he continues, "this innate and inevitable vice tends, from the birth of the body politic, to destroy it, as old age and death do in the human frame." In other words, while government is necessary, it inevitably subverts the General Will. This is so because the government is itself a particular will, what Rousseau calls a group will, that stands as a constant threat to the General Will. But unlike the private will of the individual, or the corporate will of an interest group, the group will of government has real power behind it. Hence, of all the particular wills in the community, government is the most dangerous because it is most capable of asserting its prerogatives against the public interest.

One of the most profound thinkers of modern history, Jean-Jacques Rousseau was a central figure of the European Enlightenment. He was also its most formidable critic, condemning the political, economic, theological, and sexual trappings of civilization along lines that would excite the enthusiasm of individualists and radical revolutionaries alike. In his attempt reconcile the antagonism within man between the natural and the civil Rousseau proposes a re-evaluation of the social whole and the refounding of society upon the tenets of nature. The practicality of such a venture is hopelessly limited for no society would agree to change its status for an unfamiliar structure. But despite the theoretical nature of his contract, Rousseau had in mind the possibility of such a realisation; otherwise he would not have attempted to draw up constitutions for Poland and Corsica. Even if one doubts the possible application of his social theory, one must consider his statements at face value and look for the coherence of the system as well as the ideology which generates it.

In the *Social Contract* Rousseau departs from the view of the social that he advanced in his *Discours;* he believes that one can find a form of association in which the fusion of natural freedom and civil obedience is non-contradictory. Indeed he attacks Hobbes so forcefully in the *Contract* because Hobbes put the emphasis on the natural state of warfare to which the pact must put an end; in submitting themselves to a powerful authority by the contract of submission, men safeguard their lives and property. Hobbes's absolute monarch constitutes a kind of referee with an iron fist. Rousseau, on the other hand, denies the natural corruption of man as well as the natural state of war. 'The war of all against all' makes no sense to Rousseau, since in the state of nature man is free; he has no inclination to compete given that in his dispersion and isolation he has no contact with the Other.

The idea of struggle in Hobbes is fruitful but not in its ethico-metaphysical context; Hobbes seems to think that there is an innate evil in man, for the war of all against all connotes the existence of a predetermined moral essence in man before he appears on the social scene. In any case Hobbes is more of a realist than Rousseau and a correct reader of social phenomena. Struggle as a positive concept is inherent in the social object; in order for the body politic to achieve its ongoing realisation it must do it within tfie context of a moving contradiction. Contradiction is inherent to the structure of the social body itself; the movement in the dialectic from one stage to the next hypostatises this conception of the social dynamics.

If Rousseau negates Hobbes's postulate of natural war, he must find a reason for the social pact. The social pact is conceived to counteract civil inequality and to devise a means to recover man's lost natural freedom. This formula rests on a cold calculation; in giving oneself and one's property to the social whole, (me in effect loses nothing because one gains on the Other the rights he loses through the act of association. Rousseau assumes that his basic act itself is indicative of man's maturity, his willingness to do away with natural rights and to opt for an artificial order based on the tenets of reason. With evolution man has developed to the stage where he can encounter and accept the Other of his own free will and be accepted in return. And in creating an order of exchange with his fellow men, civil man in no way subjects himself to them, for that primordial act of association is voluntary and intentional. The total dependence of man on the state guarantees his independence from his fellow man. Rousseau's notion of freedom in submission is that, in partaking in the body politic, man adopts a new identity which asserts his initial act of participation and an ongoing free renewal of that primary act as long as the social body exists. The body politic is sovereign, one and indivisible, and expresses itself through the General Will. Rousseau differentiates clearly between the General Will and the will of all, that is, the sum total of all wills within the body politic. The General Will deals with the shared common interests of the whole whereas the will of all deals with the sum total of private interests.

The second part of this statement emphasises the qualitative difference of this contract from any other contract between two individuals. The social contract is not between every individual and every other individual—that would be merely a series of contracts without a binding element connecting all the contracting parties; the contract is between every member and the totality of the group. The body politic as a whole is taken as a party to the contract as if it were one person. This points to Rousseau's assumption that all civil identities cohere into one entity.

This illustrates what Rousseau claims to be the collective nature of the social body, so that the General Will is or is not it is inalienable; it cannot be divided for then we would fall back on a pact of submission and not one of association: certain elements of the body would be subjected to others because private interests never coincide. Rousseau insists everyone wants what everyone else wants; a moral imperative drives the collective body to seek its own welfare.

However, sometimes the general welfare is not fully understood by the collective body and the latter, according to Rousseau, might need some assistance in meeting its moral imperative. And when the social body is not fully aware of its intended goals due to collective ignorance or failure, it must appoint a Legislator, an enlightened man with the qualifications of a god because, although his will is private, in its perfect knowledge of the ethical directives of the body politic it coincides with the General Will. Rousseau will be criticised for this notion of the Legislator which clearly opens the door to totalitarianism.

Sovereignty is inalienable by definition, for when it disappears, the body politic as a whole disappears as well: if a people gives up its political authority it ceases to be a people. It is clear that there is nothing quantitative in the notion of sovereignty, nor is the General Will some kind of synthesis of the sum total of particular wills. The General Will coincides with earn particular's membership in the social body. We have here a double identity: first, every man is seen as an individual subject arid this identity is quantitative; second, we have the will of every citizen as member of the sovereign, that is, as embodying the General Will. Every one in his membership in the collectivity coincides with the sovereign. Although sovereignty is indivisible in principle, it is divisible as to its objects. Here Rousseau separates the executive from the legislative: no one can legislate but the body politic as a whole. Rousseau advocated direct participation over representation because the law is the purest expression of the General Will; hence his predilection for small states where direct participation can be realised. But the sovereign can appoint an executive body which will constitute a mere intermediary between individuals and itself, that is, between the subjects as private men and the subjects as the collective members of the sovereign. In short, the institution of government is not a contract — there is only one contract, that of association — but a law of the social body.

Despite the theoretical and absolute nature of the *Social Contract*, Rousseau believes that three kinds of political system are viable: democracy, aristocracy and monarchy. And these forms of government depend, among other things, upon natural causes and climate. Forms of government are therefore relative and the same one does not suit all peoples. One cannot doubt Rousseau's bias for democracy; he cannot be accused of supporting an absolute monarchy.

Rousseau's social theory constitutes a big step forward over any theory of submission. His grouping of political authority in the people themselves and his conception of equality among them deal a blow to the theory of authority by divine right which prevailed within the medieval discursive space. The *Social Contract* can provide a stepping-stone to an ideal and equitable society; indeed the bulk of the critical material on Rousseau sees him as the father of the modern democratic state, the reformer of society, the man of reason and order, and sometimes, even, the instigator of the French Revolution. This dominant trend in the critical tradition counteracts another trend which finds in Rousseau's notion of the General Will and his concept of the Legislator, as maker of constitutions, the basic ingredients for the totalitarian state. John W. Chapman analyses both sides of the coin and sees the possibility of a dual interpretation: 'Emphasis on his concern for, moral creativity makes Rousseau a liberal. If his willingness to impose order and value on human life is brought to the fore, he becomes a totalitarian. Rousseau's own famous phrase forced to be free accentuates the totalitarian aspects of his theory; freedom, he claims, can be forced upon any private will which is not in harmony with the General Will. The dominant rationalist-liberal critical tradition — which is at the centre of the discourse of modernism together with the production of self-hood — is best exemplified by the works of Cassirer and Derathé on Rousseau. According to Cassirer, the *Social Contract* proposes the absolute unity of the social body: in alienating their individual wills to the absolute power of the General Will, men join in a collective endeavor based on their autonomy and ethical reasoning. The state comprehends all its members and merges them into an indissoluble unity. Rousseau insists that freedom did not mean arbitrariness but the overcoming and elimination of all arbitrariness, the submission to a strict and inviolable law which the individual erects over himself. The state claims the individual completely and without reservations. However, in doing so, it does not act as a coercive institution but only puts the individual under an obligation which he himself recognizes as valid and necessary, and to which he therefore assents for its sake as well as for his own. It is not a question of emancipating and liberating the individual in the sense of releasing him from the form and order of the community; it rather, a question of finding the kind of community that will protect every individual with the whole concerted power of the political organization, so that the individual in uniting himself with all others nevertheless obeys only himself in this act of union.

Cassirer argues that Rousseau postulates integration in nullifying the contradiction between law and freedom; far from cancelling one another, in effect, law guarantees freedom, for without law' freedom would disappear and chaos would prevail. Rousseau's under sandpit low in its pure and strict sense is not a mere external bond that holds in individual wills and prevents their scattering; rather, it is the constituent principle of these wills, the element that confirms them spiritually. It wishes to rule subjects only inasmuch as, in its every act, it also makes and educates them into citizens.

Law, then, is part of the constitutive structure of the individual and therefore cannot be opposed to will; a harmony prevails between man's spiritual demands for order and his aspiration to freedom. It is clear that Cassirer is talking about law in the absolute and not about law as historical contingency. He also presupposes that what he terms freedom and order are in man before the is social; civil society, as it were, synthesises these two existing tendencies in man. This indicates Cassirer's bias and his own contribution to the tradition of the Enlightenment.

Derathé follows a similar line of argument: both reason and sociability are potential drives in man that develop with the termination of he natural state of isolation. Derathé gives an overview of the polemic surrounding Rousseau's rationality or lack thereof which constitutes a preparation for his approach to Rousseau's political theory. It seems to us that the argument over Rousseau's rationality or irrationality is of little importance given that Rousseau himself was never consistent: he tilted back and forth from feeling to reason and vice versa. Certainly, the first Discours is a strong condemnation of reason. Nevertheless, Derathé's analysis is interesting in that H lays out Rousseau's division of the age of reason into three phases: (a) the prerational which is limited to the passive recording of scattered sensations without connecting between them; (b) sensitive reason, which means the conception of simple ideas which compare between sensations; and (c) intellectual reason, or the generation of complex ideas on the basis of simple ones. Emile's education exemplifies movement from one stage to the next. This, then, places Rousseau in the Empiricist tradition: he conceives of reason in sensual terms, since even the final stage of intellectual reason is based on the previous stay which is sensitive reason.

Cassirer rejects the irrationalist thesis altogether: 'this supposed irrationalist ended up with the most belief in reason. For Rousseau, the belief in the victory of reason coincided with his belief in the victory of the genuine cosmopolitan constitution.

In order to achieve a proper perspective on his political philosophy, the mystification surrounding Rousseau and his social theories must be overcome. The question is not whether Rousseau is totalitarian or liberal but whether he believes altogether in the possibility of the social object; for Rousseau to posit a social being, he must first" accept the existence of the Other as external consciousness with whom he must interact. And as we have indicated, he negates mediation in his autobiographical venture: the Other is there to rob him of his identity. It remains to be seen whether this holds true in his social theory whether Rousseau is consistent throughout his writings.

The *Social Contract* is based on a logical circularity; we have said that an act of magic separates the pre-contract from the post contract phases, but Rousseau posits in the pre-contract phase elements of the post-contract one. The reason for coming together is a social one actively and not potentially, which means that there is a social contract before the social contract. This logic would carry us backwards in infinite regression.

Conclusion

The study of Rousseau's life and works shows how his philosophy of history, his theories of music and politics, his fiction, educational and religious writings, and even his botany, were all inspired by visionary ideals of mankind's self-realization in a condition of unfettered freedom. He explains how, in regressing to classical republicanism, ancient mythology, direct communion with God, and solitude, Rousseau anticipated some postmodernist rejections of the Enlightenment as well. Together with Montesquieu, Hume, Smith, and Kant among his contemporaries, Rousseau has exerted the most profound influence on modern European intellectual history, perhaps even surpassing anyone else of his day. No other eighteenth-century thinker contributed more major writings in so wide arrange of subjects and forms, nor wrote with such sustained passion and eloquence. No one else managed through both his works and his life to excite or disturb public imagination so deeply. Almost alone among the seminal figures of the Enlightenment, he subjected the main currents of the world he inhabited to the most inspired censure even while channeling their direction, and when French revolutionary leaders later seized their opportunity to ignite the unity of political practice and theory, it was to his doctrines above all that the professed their allegiance.

In his major writings, and the various disciplines they address, Rousseau sought to give substance to such ideals by expunging all the institutions which obstructed their fulfillment, so that through a process of sublime negativity he could illuminate realms of unprosaic speech and unembellished music, of human nature without society, an education without teachers, a city without theatres, a state without rulers, a divine presence without a church. By way of such regressions, Rousseau not only posited diverse visions of men's self-realization in a condition of unfettered freedom. He also disengaged himself more dramatically from his own age of Enlightenment, appearing less circumscribed by the presuppositions and conventions of its discourses than any other major thinker of his day. In some of its registers, his intransigently critical voice still speaks with undiminished vigour more than two hundred years after his death. Modern and postmodern philosophers and writers alike often owe a considerable debt to his works, which they are sometimes loath to acknowledge, and more often still, they espouse views to which, in earlier formulations, he had already objected himself. In Rousseau's pursuit of a language of pure sincerity, in his ideal of truly communicative agents, engaged by their speech acts, taking full part in the articulation of public choice, can be found anticipations of the political philosophy of Jurgen Habermas, for instance. In his perception of the suffocating, mutilating, and dehumanizing tyrannies of modem commercial society, portrayed as if it were the panopticon of a Procrustean rather than Promethean monster. Yet, as distinct from most postmodernist thinkers and their critics alike, Rousseau was to find refuge and achieve tranquillity, even while buffeted in a personal and political world of continual turbulence. From both introspection and good grace, the most formidable eighteenth-century critic of the trappings of civilization, and the most vivid illustrator of the textures of its despair and discontent, believed all his life, no less than did Anne Frank at the darkest moment of modem history, that human nature was still fundamentally good at heart.

Between the writers most characteristic of the French Enlightenment Jean Jacques Rousseau is fixed a great gulf. Its existence was patent to everyone concerned. Diderot describing it as "the vast chasm between heaven and land said that the very idea of Rousseau disturbed his work "as if I had a damned soul at my side.' His character, his outlook on life, his scale of values, his instinctive reactions, all differed essentially from that of the Enlightenment. The twelve years from 1744 to 1756 that he spent in Paris brought him into close association with the circle that wrote the Encyclopaedia but they only produced on both sides the conviction that Rousseau did not belong there.

This opposition, and indeed all that Rousseau wrote on philosophy and politics, grew in some devious way from his complex and unhappy personality. His *Confessions* gives a clear picture of a deeply divided personality, in which morbidities both of sex and religion played a large part. "My tastes and thoughts," he says, "always seemed to fluctuate between the noble and the base." His relations with women, both real and imaginary, display a violent sensuality failing alike of animal satisfaction or effective sublimation, but issuing in a riot of sentimental fancy and introspective mood which he once said was the fundamental principle of his ethical wrings, was less an intellectual conviction than a reversal of his fear that he was bad. By throwing the fault on society he was able once to satisfy his need for condemnation and to shelter himself in a comfortable myth.

This conflict in Rousseau's personality between the noble and base, the ideal and the real, robbed him of all satisfaction in his work or confidence in its value. The inception of an idea was like a light from heaven, resolving "all the contradictions of our social system." The expression conveyed not one-quarter of the vague but glitter vision. In social relations he labored under a painful sense of made quacy, stupidity, and self-distrust. He seems never to have been comfortable except with women and in relationships practically deviod of intellectual content. By inclination he was parasitic and during considerable periods he lived in a state of semi-dependence, but he could never accept dependence gracefully. Instead, he built around himself a myth of pseudo-stoicism and fictitious self-sufficiency, which expressed itself most definitely in suspicion of those who tried to friend him and in the discovery of elaborate plots, probably imagine to ruin and betray him. Before the end of his life these suspicions came well-defined delusions of persecution. Despite his years of uncongenial vagabondage, "he represented in taste and morals sentimentality of the lower middle class." Essentially, he was interested in homely things, was terrified of science and art, distrusted polished manners, sentimentalized commonplace virtues, and enthroned sense above intelligence.

More than most men Rousseau projected the contradictions to malajustments of his own nature upon the society about him and sought an anodyne for his own painful sensitivity. For this purpose he adopted the familiar contrast between the natural and the actual current in all the appeals to reason. But Rousseau did not appeal reason. On the contrary he turned the contrast into an attack up on reason. Against intelligence, the growth of knowledge, and the progress of science, which the Enlightenment believed to be the hope of civilization, he set amiable and benevolent sentiments good will, and reverence.

The hero of Rousseau's primitivism, as Sabine declares, was not the noble savage; it was 'irritated and bewildered bourgeois', at odds with a society that despised and looked down on him, conscious of his own purity of heart and the greatness of his own deserts, and profoundly shocked at the badness of the philosophers to whom nothing was sacred, Rousseau laments:

> These vain and futile declaimers [the philosophers] go forth on all sides, armed with their fatal paradoxes, to sap the foundations of our faith, and nullify virtue. They smile contemptuously at such old names as patriotism and religion, and consecrate their talents and philosophy to the destruction and defamation of all that men hold sacred.

Inshort, intelligence is dangerous because it undermines reverence, science is destructive because it takes away faith; reason is bad because it sets prudence against moral intuition. Without reverence, faith, and moral intuition there is neither character nor society. This was a note which the Enlightenment could not easily understand. The enormous importance of Rousseau lies in the fact that, broadly speaking, he carried philosophy with him against its own tradition. Kant acknowledged that Rousseau revealed to him the surpassing value of the moral will as compared with scientific inquiry, and Kant's philosophy, if not the beginning of a new age of faith, at least began a new division between science on the one site and religion and morals on the other. The social philosophy from which Rousseau had to disentangle himself was the systematic individualism which by the time he wrote was attributed to Locke. It held that the value of any social group consists in the happiness or self-satisfaction which it produces for it members, and especially in the protection of their inherent right to own and enjoy property.

The writer who did most to release Rousseau from this agoistic individualism was Plato. With Rousseau there begins, in fact, a new era of classical influence in political philosophy, which was extended through. Hegelianism and which was more genuinely Greek than the pseudo-classicism of the eighteenth century. What Rousseau got from Plato was a general outlook. It included, first, the conviction that political subjection is essentially ethical and only secondarily a matter of law and power. Second and more important, he took from Plato the presumption, implicit in all the philosophy of the city-state, that the community is itself the chief moralizing agency and therefore represents the highest moral values.

Rousseau discovered a new inner self of considerable moral substance. Descartes, of course, had put enormous emphasis on the substantial, subjective self—the self as a thinking thing—but his was a concept that satisfied an appeal to logic, not to empathy and human fellowship. Strolling in solitude through the lush forests of St

Germain during the early adolescence of the modern age, Jean-Jacques Rousseau made a miraculous discovery. It was his self. This self was not, as his more scholastic predecessor Descartes had thought, that thing merely logical self, a pure formality that presented itself indubitably whenever he reflected: 'I think, therefore I am." Nor was the frustrated, sceptical search that led his friend Hume to declare, paradoxically, that 'whenever I look inside myself, there is no self to be found'. What Rousseau discovered in the woods of France was a self so rich and substantial, so filled with good feelings and half-articulated good thoughts, so expansive, natural, and at peace with the universe, that he recognized it immediately as something much more than his singular self. It was rather the self as such, the soul of humanity. Looking deeply into himself Rousseau discovered the self that he shared with all men and women the world over, and declared that it was good—intrinsically good, despite all of the artifices and superficialities of the social whirl. In nearby Paris it might be difficult see past the corruption and vain conventionality of modern society, but out there, free, alone, and at peace with one's nature, it was rather our innocence that was so apparent, a natural goodness that survived the sins and humiliations of social life, a true and absolute self that was not each person's alone, but which was shared with all humanity.

What Rousseau discovered—or at any rate raised to the level of first-rate philosophy—was the transcendental pretence. It appeared as innocence and common sense, but it embodied a profound arrogance that promoted self-righteousness, prohibited mutual understanding, and belied human diversity. Fully developed, the transcendental pretence has two central components: first, the remarkable inner richness and expanse of the self, ultimately encompassing every consequent right to project from the subjective structures of one's own mind, and ascertain the nature of humanity as such. It is suggestive that the transcendental pretence was discovered by a sociopath, free and alone with his self-aggrandizement, but one who inspired some of the most spectacular and successful philosophy that the world has ever known.

Rousseau emphasized feeling rather than thought as the key to the self, and the private sense of goodness rather than the logic of self-reference was its justification. Locke too had developed an empirical concept of self as introspectible between individualism and communitarianism—the self as atomic and personal versus the self as irreducibly social. Rousseau emerges as the champion of free and natural living, and as one of the creators of the modern state based on popular representation rather than force or 'divine right' but no less powerful for that. The results of this conflict are sometimes shocking, as in Rousseau's infamous insistence that a citizen who refuses to co-operate with the General Will should be 'forced to be free.' But it is this same sense of the General Will and the ideal of a society of non-combative individuals that gives rise to Rousseau's distrust of private property, a view that would be an important influence on the French socialists, and especially on the young Karl Marx. In England and America the demand for freedom emerged in the concept of the individual, working, acquisitive self, but in Europe the concept of self that emerged in the name of freedom was a supra-human, non-individual self, like Rousseau's General Will.

Some years later, in book 3 of *Emile,* Rousseau declares that 'We are approaching a state of crisis and the age of revolutions'. 'I hold it to be impossible if that the great monarchies of Europe still have long to survive'. No political exhortation was intended in this claim, which was to be expressed with similar vigour by other figures of his day, who hoped that the civilized world might still avert upheaval. But if Rousseau himself both longed, and at the same time held scant hope for a wholly changed political future of mankind, the principles of his *Social Contract* would in the course of the French Revolution came to be esteemed as if they formed the Ten Commandments of the new Republic of France. This was recognized by Louis Sebastian Mernier, who considered Rousseau as one of the first authors of the Revolution as well as by Burke, who in his *Letter to a Member of the National Assembly* of the same year condemned the 'insane Socrates' who had inspired a wholly destructive regeneration men's moral constitution and in whose memory the foundries of Paris were then casting their statues with the kettles of their poor and the bells of their churches'. No other political thinker, ancient or modern, was to excite greater enthusiasm among revolutionaries of that period than Rousseau, and in 1794 his remains were to be disinterred from their grave on the Isle of Poplars at Ermenonville and brought to the Paris Pantheon where, with great celebration, he was acclaimed a hero of the nation whose politics, culture, and religion he had loathed above all others—to his eternal torment, furthermore, reburied opposite Voltaire.

In 1762, Rousseau had scant reason to anticipate such canonization. On its appearance his *Social Contract* caused an immediate scandal, its distribution in France was prohibited, and he was obliged to flee the country to escape imprisonment, only to find his way to Geneva barred because of equal public outrage there. Yet it was not his ideas on liberty or sovereignty which then occasioned real disquiet. He was judged a threat to civil order principally because the penultimate chapter of the *Social Contract* on the civil religion, together with similar ideas in his *Emile,* published at almost exactly the same time, were held to be blasphemous with his political system thereby deemed criminal and seditious only in consequence of its affront to Christianity.

Introspective, antisocial, and almost paranoid, Rousseau alone among the great philosophers of France made an enormous impact not only on the thinking of revolutionary France, but on the history of ideas. We still admire the wit and irony of Voltaire but he is rarely read for his ideas. The brilliance of Diderot is still insufficiently appreciated, and even Hume, often said to be the greatest philosopher of modern times, plays a role in philosophy that is more provocative than inspirational. Curiously, though the great impact of Rousseau in philosophy was not felt and expressed in France but rather in neighboring Germany. Indeed, it is almost as if French philosophy went into eclipse after the Enlightenment. Rousseau's inspirational discovery first came to fruition in the academic cloisters of provincial Prussia in the work of Kant, then through Schiller, Goethe, Hegel, and Marx it came to influence half of the civilized world.

Rousseau is a political chameleon. His political philosophy was so vague that it can hardly be said to point in any specific direction. Though he believed that free citizenship was impossible in any form of larger state, it was inevitable under the circumstances that the sentiment which he aroused should result mainly in idealizing national patriotism. Thus in his essay on Poland he might advise a policy of decentralization, but the only effect of the work must lie in its appeal to Polish nationalism. On the other hand, he persistently labelled the humanitarian and cosmopolitan ideals of the Enlightenment as a mere lack of moral principle:

> Today there are no longer Frenchmen, Germans, Spaniards, or even Englishmen there are only Europeans. They are at home wherever there is money to steal or women to seduce.

The net effect was a very uncritical adaptation of the ideal of citizenship as it had been in a city-state to the modern national state. Thus the state was idealized as including all the values of national civilization, much as the Greek city had overlapped nearly all phases of Greek sort. Thus without being himself a nationalist, Rousseau helped to recast the ancient ideal of citizenship in a form such that national sentiment could appropriate it. A society must have common possessions, such a common language and a common interest and well-being, which not a sum of private goods but the source of them. The human race as a whole has nothing of this sort in common. In the second place, absolutely false that reason by itself would ever bring men together, they were concerned only with their individual happiness. The whole argument is fictitious because all our ideas, even of self-interest, are drawn from the communities in which we live. Self-interest is not more natural or more than the social needs that draw men together in communities. Finally if there is any idea of a general human family, it arises from little communities in which men live instinctively; an international is the end and not the beginning.

Nationalism, however was not a simple force acting in a single direction or with a single motive. It might mean democracy and the rights of man, as in general it did in the age of the Revolution, but it might mean also an alliance between the landowning gentry and the new middle-class aristocracy of wealth. It might sweep away the remnants of feudal institutions only to build in their place new institutions.

> We conceive a general society according to our particular societies: the establishment of little states makes us think of large ones; and we begin properly to become men only after we have become citizens. This shows what we should think of those pretended cosmopolitans who, in justifying their love for their country by their love for the human race, make a boast of loving all the world in order to enjoy the privilege of loving no one.

Rousseau's idealizing of the moral feelings of the plain man found an immediate echo in the ethics of Kant. Its full significance, especially his idealizing of the collective will and of participation in the common life, appeared in German philosophy with the idealism of Hegel. Rousseau's collectivism, however, required drastic revaluation of custom, tradition, and the accumulating heritage of the national culture, without which the General Will, was nothing but an empty formula. This sentimentalism of Rousseau tacitly set aside. The idealism of Hegel tried to weave reason and tradition into a single unit—the expanding culture of a national spirit or consciousness. In effect reason was to be bent to the service of custom, tradition, and authority, with a corresponding emphasis on the values of stability, national unity, and continuity of development.

Hegel's philosophy conceived the General Will as the spirit of the nation, expanding and embodying itself in a national culture and creating its organs in an historical constitution. Apart from the incoherence of Rousseau's presentation of it, the obvious defect of the General Will as he left it was the extreme abstractness of the conception. It was the mere idea or form of a community, as Kant's categorical imperative was the mere form of a moral will. Rousseau's position as an alien in French national life, his moral incapacity to ally himself with any social cause, and the state of French politics when he wrote, all conspired to prevent him from giving to the General Will any concrete content and embodiment. This want however was at once supplied by Edmund Burke. For Burke the conventions of the constitution, the traditional rights and duties of Englishmen, the living presence of a rich national culture growing from generation to generation were not abstractions but real existences, suffused with the warmth of ardent patriotism and the glow of moral sentiment. In the later years of his life the shock and horror of the French Revolution forced him to break the habit of a lifetime and to state in general terms the philosophy upon which he had always acted. The result was at once a contrast and a supplement to Rousseau. In Burke, the corporate life of England became a conscious reality. The General Will was released from temporary bondage to Jacobinism and made a factor in conservative nationalism.

The development of the theory of the General Will was involved in paradoxes, partly because of the cloudiness of Rousseau's ideas but partly, it seems, because he had a rhetorician's liking for paradox. Manifestly, in view of his criticism of the natural man, he ought to have avoided the notion of contract altogether as both meaningless and misleading. Seemingly, he retained the phrase because he liked its popular appeal, and in order not to make the inconsistency too glaring, he deleted the criticism of the state of nature, which he had written against Diderot. Not content with this complication, after introducing the contract he explained it away, so far as any definite contractual meaning was concerned. In the first place, his contract has nothing to do with the rights and powers of government since the latter is merely the people's agent and is so devoid of independent power that it cannot be the subject of a contract. In the second place, the imaginary act by which a society is produced is not even remotely like a contract, because the rights and liberties of individuals have no existence at all except, as they are already members of the group. Rousseau's whole argument depended upon the fact that a community of citizens is unique and coeval with its member they neither make it nor have rights against it.

In fact, Rousseau moved back and forth at will between his own theory of the General Will and the indefeasible individual right which ostensibly he had abandoned.

> But the sovereign, for its part, cannot impose upon its subjects any fetters that are useless to the community.

We can see from this that the sovereign power absolute, sacred, and inviolable as it is, does not and cannot exceed the limits of general conventions, and that every man may dispose at will of such goods and liberty as these conventions leave him.

In itself the mere fact that rights of any sort require social recognition and can be defended only in terms of a common good signifies nothing about what individual rights a well-regulated community will give to its members. Since Rousseau believed as a matter of course that social well-being itself dictates some liberty of individual choice and action, wherever he meets this sort of case he sets it down as a limitation upon the General Will. On the other hand, Rousseau was quite capable of arguing that because there are no indefeasible right in defiance of the general good, there are no individual rights at all. This again was a logical confusion, unless one argues, as Rousseau certainly did not mean to do that all liberty is contrary to the social good. The truth is that the General Will is so abstract—asserting merely that rights are social—that it justified no inference at all about the extent to which individuals might wisely be left to their own devices within society.

This confusion in Rousseau's argument gave rise to another paradox which is especially important and especially irritating, the paradox of freedom. He began by assuming a burden that was incumbent on egoistic theories but not upon him, provided he meant really to reject egoism, namely, to prove that in society a man "may still obey himself alone". Consequently he undertook nothing less than to show that real coercion never occurs in society and that what is taken to be coercion is only apparently so, a paradox of the worst sort. Even a criminal wills his own punishment. Rousseau says:

> In order than that the social compact may not be an empty formula, it tacitly includes the undertaking that whoever refuses to obey the General Will shall be compelled to do so by the whole body This means nothing less than that he will be forced to be free. This alone legitimizes civil undertakings, which, without it, would be absurd, tyrannical and liable to the most frightful abuses.

In other words, coercion is not really coercion because when a man individually wants something different from what the social order gives him, he is merely capricious and does not rightly know his own good or his own desires. This kind of argument, in Rousseau and after him in Hegel was a dangerous experiment in juggling with ambiguities. Liberty had become an honorific word the name for a sentiment. It was perfectly legitimate to point out that some liberties are not good, that liberty in one direction may entail loss of liberty in another, or that there are other political values, which in some circumstances are more highly esteeming than liberty. Straining language to show that restricting liberty is really increasing it and that coercion is not really coercion merely made the vague language of politics still vaguer. But this was not the worst of it. What was almost inevitably implied was that a man whose moral convictions are against those commonly held in his community is merely capricious and ought to be suppressed. Forcing a man to be free is a euphemism for making him blindly obedient to the mass or the strongest party. Robespierre made the inevitable application when he said of the Jacobins, "our will is the General Will".

It is convenient to distinguish between two periods of Roussea's political writings, a formative period dated about 1754-55, in which he shaped his own ideas in opposition to Diderot, and the period in which the final version of the *Social Contract* was prepared for publication in 1762. Many critics have felt a fundamental logical discrepancy between the works of these two periods, described by Vaughan as "the defiant individualism of *Discourse on Ineguality* and the equally defiant collectivism of the *Social Contract*. It is certain that Rousseau himself felt no such opposition; in the *Confessions* he says that "every strong idea in the *Social Contract* had been before published in the *Discourse on Inequality.*" In general Rousseau's opinion was correct, though it is also true that incompatible ideas abound throughout his writings. Much that seems like "defiant individualism" persisted in the *Social Contract*, and none of his works can be reduced to a consistent system. The difference between the earlier works and the latter work is merely that in the former he was writing himself free from an uncongenial social philosophy and in the latter he was expressing, as clearly as he could, a counter-philosophy of his own.

Confusion has always surrounded Rousseau's political ideas because was in many respects an inconsistent and contradictory writer. One reason why the Rousseau industry has grown so gigantic is that academics thrive on resolving 'problems'. In some passages of his works he appears a conservative, strongly opposed to revolution: 'Think of the dangers of setting the masses in motion' 'People who make revolutions nearly always end by handing themselves over to tempters who make their chains heavier than before; "I would not have anything to do with revolutionary plots which always lead to disorder, violence and bloodshed." The liberty of the entire human race is not worth the life of a sin human being But his writings also abound with radical proclamations: "I hate the great, I hate their rank, their harshness, their prejudices, their pettiness all their vice." He wrote to one grand lady: 'It is the wealthy class, your class, that steals from mine the bread of my children and he admitted to 'a certain resentment against the rich and successful, as if their wealth and happiness had been gained at my expense'. "The rich were hungry wolves who, once having tasted human flesh, refuse any other nourishment'. His many powerful aphorisms, which make his books so sharply attractive especially to the young, are radical in tone. "The fruits of the earth belong to us all, the earth itself to none.' 'Man is born free and is everywhere in chains.' His entry in the Encyclopedia on 'Political Economy' sums up the attitude of the ruling class: 'You need me for I am rich and you are poor. Let us make an agreement: I will allow you to have the honour of serving me, provided you give me whatever you have left for the trouble I shall take to command you.'

However, once we understand the nature of the state Rousseau wished to create, his views begin to cohere. It was necessary to replace the existing society by something totally different and essentially egalitarian; but, this done, revolutionary disorder could not be permitted. The rich and the privileged, as the ordering force, would be replaced by the state, embodying the General Will, which all contracted to obey. Such obedience would become instinctive and voluntary since the state, by a systematic process of cultural engineering, would inculcate virtue in all. The state was the father, the patria, and all its citizens were the children of the paternal orphanage. It is true that the citizen-children, unlike Rousseau's own babies, originally agree to submit to the state orphanage by freely contracting into it. They thus constitute, through their collective will, its legitimacy, and thereafter they have no right to feel constrained, since, having wanted the laws, they must love the obligations they impose.

Though Rousseau writes about the General Will in terms of liberty, it is essentially an authoritarian instrument, an early adumbration of Lenin's 'democratic centralism'.

Laws made under the General Will must by definition, have moral authority. The people making laws for itself cannot be unjust. 'The General Will is always righteous.' Moreover, provided the state is 'well-intentioned', interpretation of the General Will can safely be left to the leaders since 'they know well that the General Will always favours the decision most conducive to the public interest.' Hence any individual who finds himself in opposition to the General Will is in error: 'When the opinion that is contrary to my own prevails, this simply proves that I was mistaken and that what I thought to be the General Will, was not so.' Indeed, 'if my particular opinion had carried the day I should have achieved the opposite of what was my will and I should not therefore have been free.' We are here almost in the chilly region of Arthur Koestrel's *Darkness at Noon* or George Orwell's 'Newspeak'.

Rousseau's state is not merely authoritarian: it is also totalitarian, since it orders every aspect of human activity, thought included. Under the social contract, the individual was obliged to 'alienate himself, with all his rights, to the whole of the community'—the state. Rousseau held that there was an ineradicable conflict between man's natural selfishness and his social duties, between the man and the citizen. And that made him miserable. The function of the social contract, and the state it brought into being, was to make man whole again: 'Make man one, and you will make him as happy as he can be. Give him all to the state, or leave him all to himself. But if you divide his heart, you tear him in two.' You must, therefore, treat citizens as children and control their upbringing and thoughts, planting 'the social law in the bottom of their hearts'. They then become 'social men by their natures and citizens by their inclinations; they will be one, they will be good, they will be happy, and their happiness will be that of the Republic'.

This procedure demanded total submission. The original social contract oath for his projected constitution for Corsica reads: 'I join myself, body, goods, will and all my powers, to the Corsican nation, granting her ownership of me, of myself and all who depend on me. The state would thus 'possess men and all their powers', and control every aspect of their economic and social life, which would be Spartan, anti-luxurious and anti-urban, the people being prevented from entering the towns except by special permission. In a number of ways the state Rousseau planned for Corsica anticipated the one Pol Pot regime actually tried to create in Cambodia, and this is not entirely surprising since the Paris-educated leaders of the regime had all absorbed Rousseau's ideas. Of course, Rousseau sincerely believed that such a State would be contented since the people would have been trained to like it. He did not use the word brainwash, but he wrote: 'Those who control a people's opinions control its actions.' Such control is established by treating citizens, from infancy, as children of the state, trained to 'consider themselves only in their relationship to the body of the state'. 'For being nothing except by it, they will be nothing except for it. It will have all they have and will be all they are.' Again, this anticipates Mussolini's central fascist doctrine: 'Everything within the state, nothing outside the state, nothing against the state.' The educational process was thus the key to the success of the cultural engineering needed to make the state acceptable and successful; the axis of Rousseau's ideas was the citizen as child and the state as parent, and he insisted the government should have complete charge of the upbringing of all children. Hence – and this is the true revolution

Rousseau's ideas brought about– he moved the political process to the very centre of human existence by making the legislator, who is also a pedagogue, into the new Messiah, capable of solving all human problems by creating new men. 'Everything,' he wrote, 'is at root dependent on politics.' Virtue is the product of good government, "Vices belong less to man, than to man badly governed.' The political process, and the new kind of state it brings into being, are the universal remedies for the ills of mankind. Politics will do all. Rousseau thus prepared the blueprint for the principal delusions and follies of the twentieth century.

Rousseau's reputation during his lifetime, and his influence after his death, raise disturbing questions about human gullibility, and indeed about the human propensity to reject evidence it does not wish to admit. The acceptability of what Rousseau wrote depended in great part on his strident claim to be not merely virtuous but the most virtuous man of his time. Why did not this claim collapse in ridicule and ignominy when his weaknesses and vices became not merely public knowledge but the subject of international debate? After all the people who assailed him were not strangers or political opponents but former friends and associates who had gone out of their way to assist him. Their charges were serious and the collective indictment devastating. Hume, who had once thought him 'gentle, modest, affectionate, disinterested and exquisitely sensitive', decided, from more extensive experience, that he was 'a monster who saw himself as the only important being in the universe'. Diderot, after long acquaintance, summed him up as 'deceitful, vain as Satan, ungrateful, cruel, hypocritical and full of malice'.

Grimm accused he was 'odious, monstrous'. Voltaire shouted that Rousseau a 'monster of vanity and vileness'. Saddest of all are the judgments passed on him by kind hearted women who helped him, like Madame Epinay, and her harmless husband, whose last words to Rousseau were 'I have nothing left for you but pity.' These judgments were based not on the man's words but on his deeds, and since that time, over two hundred years, the mass of material unearthed by scholars has tended relentlessly to substantiate them. One modern academic lists Rousseau's shortcomings as follows: he was a 'masochist, exhibitionist, neurasthenic, hypochondriac, onanist, latent homosexual afflicted by the typical urge for repeated displacements, incapable of normal or parental affection, incipient paranoiac, narcissistic introvert rendered unsocial by his illness, filled with guilt feelings, pathologically timid, a kleptomaniac, infantile, irritable and miserly'.

Such accusations, and extensive display of the evidence on which they are based, made very little difference to the regard in which Rousseau and his works were, and are, held by those for whom he has an intellectual and emotional attraction and fascination. During his life, no matter how many friendships he destroyed, he never found any difficulty in forming new ones and recruiting fresh admirers, disciples and grandees to provide him with houses, dinners and the incense he craved. When he died he was buried on the lake at Ermononville and this rapidly became a place of secular pilgrimage for men and women from all over Europe, like the shrine of a saint in the Middle Ages. Descriptions of the antics of these devotes make hilarious reading: "I dropped to my knees pressed my lips to the cold stone of the monument and kissed it repeatedly. Relics, such as his tobacco pouch and jar, were carefully preserved at 'the Sanctuary', as it was known. The plaudits continued long after the ashes were transferred to the Pantheon. To Kant he had 'a sensibility of soul of unequalled perfection'. To Shelley he was 'a sublime genius'. For Schiller "he was a Christ–like soul for whom only Heaven's angels are fit company." John Stuart Mill and George Eliot, Hugo and Lambert, paid deep homage. Tolstoy said that "Rousseau and the Gospel had been 'the two great and healthy influences of my life'. One of the most influential intellectuals of our own times, Claude Levi-Strauss hails him as 'our master and our brother . . . every page of this book could have been dedicated to him, had it not been unworthy of his great memory'.

It is all very baffling and suggests that intellectuals are as unreasonable, illogical and superstitious as anyone else. The truth seems to be that Rousseau was a writer of genius but fatally unbalanced both in his life and in his views. He is best summed up by the woman who, he said, was his only love, Sophie. She lived on until 1813 and, in extreme old age, delivered this verdict: 'He was ugly enough to frighten me and love did not make him more attractive. But he was a pathetic figure and I treated him with gentleness and kindness. He was an interesting madman."

In both the long and the short term his influence was enormous. He was the first of the modern intellectuals, their archetype and in many ways the most influential of them all. Older men like Voltaire had started the work of demolishing the altars and enthroning reason. But Rousseau was the first to combine all the salient characteristics of the modern Promethean: the assertion of his right to reject the existing order in its entirety; confidence in his capacity to refashion it from the bottom in accordance with principles of his own devising; belief that this could be achieved by the political process; and, not least, recognition of the huge part instinct, intuition and impulse play in human conduct. He believed he had a unique love for humanity and had been endowed with unprecedented gifts and insights to increase its felicity. An astonishing number of people, in his own day and since, have taken him at his own valuation.

In the generation after his death, he attained the status of a myth. He died a decade before the French Revolution of 1789 but many contemporaries held him responsible for it, and so for the demolition of the ancient regime in Europe. This view was shared by both Louis xvi and Napoleon. Edmund Burke said of the revolutionary elites: "There is a great dispute among their leaders which of them is the best resemblance of Rousseau. He is their standard figure of perfection. As the French revolutionary leader Robespierre himself put it: 'Rousseau is the one man who, through the loftiness of his soul and the grandeur of his character, showed himself worthy of the role of teacher of mankind." During the Revolution the National Convention voted to have his ashes transferred to the Pantheon. At the ceremony, its president declared: "It is to Rousseau that is due to the health-giving improvement that has transformed our morals, customs, laws, feelings and habits."

At a much deeper level, however, and over a far longer span of time, Rousseau altered some of the basic assumptions of civilized man and shifted around the furniture of the human mind. The span of his influence is dramatically wide but it can be grouped under five main headings. First, all our modern ideas of education are affected to some degree by Rousseau's doctrine, especially by his treatise *Emile* (1762). He popularized and to some extent invented the cult of nature, the taste for the open air, the quest for freshness, spontaneity, the invigorating and the natural. He introduced the critique of urban sophistication. He identified and branded the artificialities of civilization. He is the father of the cold bath, systematic exercise, sport as character-forming, the weekend cottage.

Second, and linked to his revaluation of nature, Rousseau taught distrust of the progressive, gradual improvements brought about by the slow march of materialist culture; in this sense he rejected the Enlightenment, of which he was part, and looked for a far more radical solution. He insisted that reason itself had severe limitations as the means to cure society. That did not mean, however, that the human mind was inadequate to bring about the necessary changes, because it has hidden, untapped resources of poetic insight and intuition which must be used to overrule the sterilizing dictates of reason. In pursuit of this line of thought, Rousseau wrote his Confessions, finished in 1770, though not published until after his death.

Third, Rousseau initiated the process was the beginning both of the Romantic movement and of modern introspective literature, for in it he took the discovery of the individual, the prime achievement of the Renaissance, a giant stage further, delving into the inner self and producing it for public inspection. For the first time readers were shown the inside of a heart, though and this too was to be a characteristic of modern literature the vision was deceptive, the heart thus exhibited misleading, outwardly frank, inwardly full of guile.

The fourth concept Rousseau popularized was in some ways the most pervasive of all. When society evolves from its primitive state of nature to urban sophistication, he argued, man is corrupted: his natural selfishness, which he *calls amour de soi*, is transformed into a far more pernicious instinct, *amour-propre*, which combines vanity and self-esteem, each man rating himself by what others think of him and thus seeking to impress them by his money, strength, brains and moral superiority. His natural selfishness becomes competitive and acquisitive, and so he becomes alienated not only from other men, whom he sees as competitors and not brothers, but from himself. Alienation induces a psychological sickness in man, characterized by a tragic divergence between appearance and reality. The evil of competition, as he saw it, which destroys man's inborn communal sense and encourages all his most evil traits, including his desire to exploit others, led Rousseau to distrust private property, as the source of social crime.

His fifth innovation, then, on the very eve of the Industrial Revolution, was to develop the elements of a critique of capitalism, both in the preface to his play *Narcisse* and in his *Discourse on Inequality*, by identifying property and the competition to acquire it as the primary cause of alienation. This was a thought-deposit Marx and others were to mine ruthlessly, together with Rousseau's related idea of cultural evolution. To him, 'natural' meant 'original' or pre-cultural. All culture brings problems since it is man's association with others which brings out his evil propensities: as he puts it in *Emile*, 'Man's breath is fatal to his fellow men.' Thus the culture in which man lived, itself an evolving, artificial construct, dictated man's behaviour, and we could improve, indeed totally transform, his behaviour by changing the culture and the competitive forces which produced it that is, by social engineering.

These ideas are so wide-ranging as to constitute, almost by themselves, an encyclopaedia of modern thought. It is true that not all of them were original to him.

His reading was wide: Descartes, Rabelais, Pascal, Leibnitz, Bayle, Fontenelle, Corneille, Petrarch, Tasso, and in particular he drew on Locke and Montaigne. Germaine de Stael, who believed he possessed 'the most sublime faculties ever bestowed on a man' declared: "He has invented nothing.' But, she added, 'he has infused all with fire.' It was the simple, direct, powerful, indeed passionate, manner in which Rousseau wrote which made his notions seem so vivid and fresh, so that they came to men and women with the shock of a revelation.

For almost two centuries the philosophy of Rousseau has perplexed its interpreters. Among the many critics who have tried to deal with it, one of the greatest—but for a long time one of the most neglected—was Jean-Jacques Rousseau himself. In his *Confessions* he emphasized that his writings, taken as a whole, revealed a consistent and coherent philosophy: "All that is daring in the *Social Contract* had previously appeared in the *Discourse on Inequality* all that is daring in *Emile* had previously appeared in *Julie*." The discrepancies that the reader might find in them were, he said, purely superficial. He reiterated this conviction, which must have been of great importance to him, as he came to reflect on his work once more near the end of his life: "One great principle," he maintained, was evident in all his books.

Only a handful of Rousseau's interpreters were to take this self-estimate seriously. Instead, the majority of his critics searched for, and pretended to find, the "essence of Rousseau" in one or the other of his major works or in some of his scintillating epigrams. Worse, a number of Rousseau scholars inferred the supposed confusion or self-contradictory character of his work from the undeniable fact that his writings served as the inspiration for widely divergent movements, overlooking the notorious tendency of disciples to distort the philosophy of their master by selecting only what they need. Many thinkers have suffered at the hands of commentators, but few have had to endure as much as Rousseau. Conflicting claims, pronounced with equal certitude, have obscured that integrity of his thought on which he had insisted so often.

The influence of Rousseau's doctrines has been immense— they left their mark on the most diverse spirits and movements. Burke execrated Rousseau as the very embodiment of the Age of Reason. De Maistre and Bonald condemned him as the advocate of an irresponsible individualism and as the philosopher of ruinous disorder. Later critics, such as Henry Maine, attacked him for establishing a "collective despot" and for reintroducing, in the *Social Contract* "the old divine right of kings in a new dress."

Rousseau's disciples contradicted each other as vigorously as his opponents did. The Jacobins established the Reign of Terror in his name; the German romantics hailed him as a liberator; Schiller pictured him as a martyr to wisdom. Edmund Burke, Rousseau's most formidable antagonist in the eighteenth century, was surely right when he said, "I believe, that, were Rousseau alive, and in one of his lucid intervals, he would be shocked at the practical frenzy of his scholars."

The conflict of interpretations by no means diminished after Rousseau had ceased to be a symbol in the political struggle. Long after the smoke of revolution and reaction had cleared away, Rousseau was still praised or condemned for the widest variety of reasons. Rousseau was called rationalist and irrationalist by turns; his economics was described as socialist or as founded on the sanctity of private property; his religion was seen as Deist, Catholic, or Protestant; his moral teachings were alternately held to be Puritanical or too emotional and relaxed. However, since most of his commentators have treated Rousseau as a political theorist, or have judged his thought in the light of his political philosophy, political categories will prove most useful in an analysis of the literature. Rousseau, it has been said, is an individualist—a collectivist—a writer whose doctrines are deeply self-contradictory—a man who shifted in mid-career from individualism to collectivism. In the first decades after Rousseau's death, both the counter–revolutionaries, and the radicals, considered Rousseau the exemplar of individualism. Holderlin, who called him a demigod, translated Rousseau's purported defiance of the chains of law into extravagant verse.

This conception of Rousseau as an individualist arose before the opposite point of view became popular and it has never gone wholly out of fashion. Several notable French commentators defended it skillfully. Thus Emile Fuguet argued that "all of Rousseau can be found in the *Discourse on Inequality*. That is a commonplace but I believe it to be true." And this "novel of humanity," as Faguet calls it, has one central theme: man is good and becomes evil by embracing society. Faguet felt constrained to admit that the *Social Contract* is "antiliberal" and that Rousseau's political thought contain "not an atom of liberty or security." But he explains this difficulty away: the *Social Contract* "seems an isolated part of Rousseau's work" and "contradicts his general ideas." Rousseau's political theory is but an aberration. On the other hand, the individualist conception of the *Second Discourse* "the antisocial idea", is fundamental—it runs through nearly all his writings and appears with particular impressiveness in *Emile*.

A quarter of a century later, Henri Sée arrived at a similar conclusion by a different logical path. "*The Discourse on Inequality*" he wrote in full agreement with Faguet, "is inspired by an individualist, indeed almost anarchist conception." But at this point he departs from Faguet, "in the *Social Contract* Rousseau remains an individualist, despite appearances to the contrary." Rousseau's political theory revolves around the attempt to "assure the individual the full development of his liberty," and, Sée concludes, "Rousseau appears to us as an individualist and a liberal. It is not true that he wants to give the state an absolute and aggressive authority."

Probably the most significant source for the opposite contention, that Rousseau is a collectivist, has come from Taine's. It was Taine's belief that the French Revolution—in which "brutal force placed itself at the disposal of radical dogma, and radical dogma placed itself at the disposal of brutal force,"— had largely been the work of intellectuals whose knowledge of the world of men was slight. Consequently, these intellectuals had indulged without restraint in abstract theorizing which eventually infected the French mind with the success of revolutionary ideas. Viewing Rousseau as the prototype of these pernicious philosophers, Taine gave a new twist to Rousseau criticism. Rousseau's political theory, he argued, had been designed as the supreme assault on law and the state and had resulted, paradoxically but inevitably, in tyranny: "The doctrine of popular sovereignty, interpreted by the masses, will produce perfect anarchy until the moment when, interpreted by the rulers, it will produce perfect despotism." Rousseau's state, as he put it, is a "layman's monastery," and in this democratic monastery which Rousseau establishes on the model of Sparta and Rome, the individual is nothing and the state everything."

This and similar views have now become predominant in the literature. We can hear echoes of it in Karl Popper's description of Rousseau's thought as "romantic collectivism" and in Ernest Barker's, "In effect, and in the last resort, Rousseau is a totalitarian. Imagine Rousseau a perfect democrat: his perfect democracy is still a multiple autocracy." Many, although certainly not all present-day readers of Rousseau, remembering the supremacy of the General Will, the forcing men .to be free, the civil religion, and forgetting the rest of his writings, will agree with Taine and Barker. The fashion in fact is to consider Rousseau a totalitarian—a "democratic totalitarian" perhaps, but a totalitarian nevertheless.

These two irreconcilable interpretations of Rousseau's thought have been supplemented by two other views: it has been argued that his doctrines are confused and rent by internal contradictions, or that they shifted from one extreme to the other as they were developed and elaborated. Faguet saves his interpretation of Rousseau as an individualist by writing off what he assumed to be the collectivist implications of the *Social Contract*. Barker, who after some hesitation ranks Rousseau among the collectivists, professes to be unable to find a real core in his thought: "You can find your own dogmas in Rousseau, whether you belong to the Left or whether you belong to the Right."

Much earlier, John Morley had made this point even more emphatically. He accused Rousseau of neglecting the only sources of evidence—history and experience—on which a sound social theory could be based. He derided Rousseau's "narrow, symmetrical, impatient humor" and the "desperate absurdity of the assumptions of the *Social Contract*.

This conception of the "confused" Rousseau has also gained wide currency, although the critics who espouse it have been unable to make up their minds whether Rousseau's doctrine is worthless because of the deductive and abstract logic from which it springs or whether, as Irving Babbitt was to argue, Rousseau was betrayed by lack of method and by romantic emotionalism.

This attitude toward Rousseau's thought is partly redeemed by C.E. Vaughn. Vaughn sees Rousseau's thought as a problem demanding solution rather than a dogma requiring exposition: "Strike out the *Discourse on Inequality* with the first few pages of the *Social Contract* and the 'individualism' of Rousseau will "be seen to be nothing better than a myth." While the *Discours on Inequality* "suggested if it did not explicitly proclaim, a more extreme form of individualism than any previous writer had ventured to set forth," the compact with which the *Social Contract* begins "forms the porch to a collectivism as absolute as the mind of man has ever conceived." Nor will it be easy to reconcile these two strands that lie side by side in Rousseau's political thought: "When all is said, the two rival elements, the individual and the community, are left not so much reconciled, as in ill-veiled hostility, to each other."

Vaughan believes that the chief task of Rousseau interpretation is to account for or to solve this conflict, for which he himself offers three separate explanations. First, he argues that the early *Discourses* were primarily moral in character, pointing to existing vices by means of extreme statement. This is a prescient hint to overcome the supposed contradictions in Rousseau's thought by viewing Rousseau as fundamentally a moralist. Secondly, Vaughan draws attention to the conflict between abstract and concrete thought in Rousseau. The former, derived largely from Plato, pushes him into extreme and unqualified statements; the latter, inherited from Montesquieu, leads him to the conviction that life is never clear-cut and that principles are modified by circumstances. Vaughan finds a growing concern with concreteness in Rousseau's work, a concern that gains the upper hand in the later chapters of the *Social Contract* and becomes fully dominant in his last political writings. Vaughan's third explanation, however, is far more important: Rousseau's intellectual labors must be understood as a journey of growth from individualism to collectivism.

The political work of Rousseau, when taken as a whole, presents an unbroken movement from one position almost to its opposite. He starts as the prophet of freedom, in the most abstract sense conceivable. His ideal, in the *Second Discourse*, is a state of things in which each individual is absolutely independent of the rest. Save for those opening sentences, the *Social Contract* represents a very different—and assuredly a less abstract, as well as a less individualist—idea. Here freedom is no longer conceived as the independence of the individual. It is rather to be sought in his total surrender to the service of the State.

Silent though it is, the change of tone and temper is complete. The abstract individualism of the *Second Discourse*, the abstract collectivism of the *Social Contract*, are alike forgotten in the last political writings. The long journey is at last ended. And Rousseau now stands at the opposite point of the compass from that at which he started.

The blame for the multiplicity of opinions in the Rousseau literature cannot be placed solely on his interpreters. Rousseau was, in fact, neither confused nor inconsistent; we may conclude that Rousseau, like Nietzsche after him, invited misunderstanding.

David Hume wrote about Rousseau in 1766: "Really his writings are so full of extravagance, that I cannot believe their eloquence alone will be able to support them." But it was Rousseau's eloquence rather than his extravagance that created difficulties for the commentators. Rousseau was, unhappily, the coiner of happy phrases. Read in context, they were usually elucidated by the argument in which they were embedded. Taken out of context, their rhetorical power obscured the fact that they were only elliptical pronouncements. Used as slogans, they twisted or destroyed his meaning.

A careful and sympathetic reading of his full work would remove the obstacles which such sentences introduce, but Rousseau rarely found such readers. Rousseau himself realized that his intensely personal style might offer difficulties to his readers, and what he wrote to Madame d'Epinay about his use of language in correspondence may be applied with equal force to the writings he intended for publication: "Learn my vocabulary better, my good friend, if you would, have us understand each other. Believe me, my terms rarely have the common meaning; it is always my heart that converses with you, and perhaps you will learn some day that it speaks not as others do."

It is true that the genetic explanation, the biographic approach, will give insight into the motives of a writer and aid inquiry into the personal or social origin of his doctrines. It will help to explain why an author writes a certain book, and why he holds certain beliefs—but the objective validity of his doctrines is unaffected by the personal history of their creator. The fact that Rousseau confesses to abandoning his five natural children at a foundling home does not affect the merits of the educational plan in Emile. His paranoid quarrels with the Encyclopedists may illuminate his motives for publishing the *Social Contract* but they do not invalidate or improve the logic of his political theory. These canons of interpretation have been disregarded by many of Rousseau's critics. Hearnshaw writes, for example "So intimately were Rousseau's writings associated with his life that it is impossible to comprehend them without a detailed knowledge of his curious and remarkable career." Fortified by this statement, he divides Rousseau's life into five periods: the undisciplined boy, the supertramp, the would-be man of the world, the inspired maniac, the hunted fugitive. Hearnshaw thus spared the necessity of seriously grappling with Rousseau's meaning, can sum up one of the greatest of all political theorists with these words: "He was an unsystematic thinker, untrained in formal logic. He was an omnivorous reader with undeveloped power of assimilation. He was an emotional enthusiast who spoke without due reflection. He was an irresponsible writer with a fatal gift for epigram."

Around the turn of this century a small band of scholars began to go back to Rousseau's work in its entirety and to extract from it the basic unity of his thought. These critics had not lost interest in the question of Rousseau's individualism or collectivism, but such political categories no longer held a central place in their attention. Instead, they sought to widen the horizon of interpretation. They did not deny the paradoxical character of many of Rousseau's pronouncements, but they agreed with Rousseau that these paradoxes do not impair his fundamental consistency. The most notable contributions to this search for Rousseau's "one great principle" were made by Lanson, Wright, and Ernst Cassirer.

Lanson, author of a celebrated history of French literature, describes Rousseau as an individualist. But, in full agreement with Wright, he does not regard this as the key to the unity of Rousseau's thought. Wright's penetrating comment on the *Social Contract*, that "the book is meant for neither individualist nor absolutist," could serve as the motto for both Wright's and Lanson's estimates of Rousseau's entire work. What is central to Lanson's view is Rousseau's own statement of his "great principle," enunciated in the first sentence of *Emile*, implied through all his works. This principle, Lanson holds, is the key to Rousseau's philosophy: the essential vice of society, the *Discours on Inequality* tells us, is an inequality that is not ordained by nature—the inequality created by wealth and poverty. The *Social Contract* exemplifies this principle in conjunction with another on which Rousseau always insisted: The natural man cannot escape society but must recreate it to recreate himself. The educational program of *Emile* follows logically it outlines the growth of the "natural man with all the advantages and without any of the vices of the civilized man." *The Nouvelle Heloise* furnishes further details on the same theme: it establishes the moral values of personal relations without which neither the individual nor society can become truly good. Finally, Rousseau's system includes God in its scheme: the Deity has made man good and has implanted in him the moral energy to overcome the evils of a society that has not been built on natural principles. In this manner, Lanson argues, all parts of Rousseau's philosophy hold together, supplement each other, and express the central doctrine from which issues all the power of Rousseau's vision—the belief that man, by nature good, can transform himself into the good citizen in the good society.

Rousseau's problem, in the light of which all his writings can be grasped, is stated thus: "How can civilized man recover the benefits of the natural man, so innocent and happy, without returning to the state of nature, without renouncing the advantages of the social state?" The early *Discourses*, then, are protests against all hitherto existing societies, whose evils they expose; *Emile* and the *Nouvelle Heloise* point the way to the reform of the individual in the spheres of personal morality, family relations, and education; the later political writings outline the kind of society in which the good man can properly live.

Cassirer's eminence as historian of ideas philosopher combined with his neo-Kantianism, has made him an ideal interpreter of Rousseau's work. Kant, as Cassirer was fond of pointing out, had been almost the only eighteenth-century reader of Rousseau to prize him for his real rather than his alleged virtues. Kant's ethical speculations had been profoundly enriched by Rousseau's philosophy, and Cassirer developed Kant's suggestive clue that the key to Rousseau lay in his rationalist conception of freedom.

Derathe considerably expands a number of points which Cassirer analyzed only briefly and he illuminates Rousseau's treatment of the relation of conscience to reason and the development of reason in man. His conclusion is: "Rousseau never believed that one should fail to employ one's reason. Quite to the contrary, he wanted to teach us how to use it well. Rousseau is a rationalist aware of the limits of reason."

We would suggest, then, that we draw a distinction between Rousseau's political theory as a critical instrument and as a constructive device. Used as a critical yard-stick, Rousseau's political thought has been invaluable to democratic movements; used as a political blueprint, it has had a pernicious effect on libertarian ideas and institutions.

Rousseau's "one great principle"—that man is good, that society makes him bad, but that only society, the agent of perdition, can be the agent of salvation—is a critical tool. It affirms not only that reform is desirable but more important, that it is possible, and it suggests that a society which creates only knaves and fools has forfeited its right to existence. But Rousseau is the philosopher of the democratic movement in an even more direct manner: throughout his writings he enumerates those features which make contemporary society evil and those features by which we may recognize the opposite, the good society, in which the General Will is supreme. The greatest social evil is inequality, the greatest social good is freedom. Rousseau makes these points—two powerful weapons in the democratic armory—again and in all his works. His most significant statements in social theory are critical devices. We need to recall only his demand that the General Will must be absolutely general ("All votes must be counted; any formal exclusion is a breach of generality") his criticism of representative government in which the sovereign people surrender what they ought to retain for themselves ("The moment a people gives itself representatives it is no longer free; it no longer exists") and his charge against French intellectual culture and the manners of his day—that they detract from, rather than enlarge, life.

For a party out of power or a philosopher in opposition, no theory could be more useful or consistent than Rousseau's. Once it is embodied in institutions, however, once the democratic party has gained power, the absolutist implications of his philosophy emerge. Rousseau attacks voluntary associations, deprecates dissent, imposes censorship, wishes to impose a civil religion which can be disobeyed only on pain of exile or death. This is consistent with the rest of his thought: the kind of citizen he wants to create—the new man of *Emile* who must be so carefully shielded from the society of his own day lest he be corrupted by it—would not desire to belong to any special interest group; he would have no inclination to disagree with the decisions of the General Will. Indeed, he would recognize the civil religion as a necessary cement and either believe in it or profess it without scruple.

It is this normative conception, this utopian tendency to reason from the perfectibility of man to the perfect state in which only the perfect man can live, that makes Rousseau's thought so great as criticism and so dangerous when taken as a guide for constitution making. Rousseau's critical principles turn into fetters once the rebel is transformed into the sovereign.

11

Edmund Burke

> Society is indeed a contract. Subordinate contracts for objects of mere occasional interest may be dissolved at pleasure—but the state ought not to be considered as nothing better than a partnership agreement in a trade of pepper and coffee, calico or tobacco, or some other such low concern, to be taken up for a little temporary interest, and to be dissolved by the fancy of the parties. It is to be looked on with other reverence; because it is not a partnership in things subservient only to the gross animal existence of a temporary and perishable nature. It is a partnership in all science; a partnership in every virtue and all perfection. As the ends of such a partnership can not be obtained in many generations, it becomes a partnership not only between those who are living, but between those who are living, those who are dead, and those who are to be born.

Edmund Burke (1729-1797) was born in Dublin, Ireland in 1729 to a Roman Catholic mother and a Protestant father. By all accounts, the family was not wealthy but was comfortable enough to allow Burke to attend Trinity College, Dublin where he took a first class honours degree in classics. He then displayed an inclination to follow his father's profession and commenced legal studies in London in 1750. These studies, however, were never completed and by the middle of the 1750s, Burke had seemingly settled upon a literary career. In 1757, he manifested the religious tolerance of his upbringing and married the daughter of an Irish, Roman Catholic physician. Burke's literary endeavours were soon coupled with an increasing interest and involvement in political affairs, which were to persist until his death in 1797. His formal political career commenced in 1765 when he was appointed secretary to the Marques of Rockingham. Britain in the eighteenth century possessed only an embryonic political party system. Lords and Commons were divided into Whigs and Tories. Party lines were never clearly drawn but the prominent, contentious issue was the relationship between king and parliament. Here the Whigs were the radicals wishing to curb the prerogative powers of the monarch and establish the constitutional dominance of parliament. Factions within the two 'parties' were usually centred around a prominent member of a traditional noble family. Lord Rockingham headed a liberal group within the Whigs to which Burke attached himself.

In 1774, at the age of forty-five, Burke entered the House of Commons as the member for Bristol, but he forfeited the seat at the elections of 1780. Through the grace and favour of Rockingham, he was then shifted to the constituency of Melton, which, unlike Bristol, was a 'rotten' or 'pocket' borough, requiring little but noble patronage to win and retain. He sat for Melton continuously until his retirement in 1794. Burke's twenty years of parliamentary experience placed him amongst that very small group of political thinkers who were also practising politicians. While he held governmental office for only two brief periods, Burke was an active and influential parliamentarian who was to be found at the centre of all the major political controversies of the later eighteenth century. Surprising as it may appear at first, Burke's political ideas and activities marked him as a progressive and, to some, even a radical.

Space does not permit a full account of Burke's political activities, but a brief summary of some of them is necessary better to understand his political beliefs. Burke was an admirer of the so-called Glorious Revolution of 1688–89 and sought regularly to defend and advance its achievements. These he believed involved the establishment in England of a balanced constitutional monarchy and the defeat of the tyrannical pretensions of despots such as James II. Burke has rightly been criticized for an excessive servility, and even sycophancy towards those he perceived as his superiors; yet, at the same time, he could be courageous in his championship of unpopular and even dangerous causes. He never forsook his heritage and was a regular critic of British policy in Ireland; even to the extent of questioning the wisdom of establishing the English church there. Another of his famous parliamentary crusades concerned the impeachment moves against Warren Hastings, who had been Governor General of Bengal (1772–1785), on the grounds that his application of British colonial policy usurped the traditional rights of the Indian inhabitants. His pursuit of Hastings, who was acquitted on all charges, was not totally altruistic since personal animosity and the desire to assist the dubious financial schemes of two relatives seem also to have been motivating factors.

Burke's opposition to the slave trade was, however, genuine and probably contributed to his electoral defeat in the slave port of Bristol in 1780. Similarly, he was a consistent and articulate advocate for the North American colonists in their disputes with the administration of George III. Burke believed them to be suffering genuine and serious grievances at the hands of an autocracy, which was contemptuous of their rights. His preferred solution was to extend to the colonists the privileges and responsibilities of the British constitution. When the government displayed little inclination to do so, Burke supported the revolution of 1776.

Critique of French Revolution

Burke's political career until the year 1790 well justifies his own remark that "almost the whole of my public exertion has been a struggle for the liberty of others"- an opinion that would have been shared by most of his political colleagues. Imagine then, their surprise when in November 1790 he published his major political work *Reflections on the Revolution in France,* which contained a thoroughgoing repudiation and condemnation of the revolution, which had broken out in the previous year. Enlightened opinion in Britain was generally approving of the revolution, seeing it as liberating France from the stifling political environment of the ancient regime. Most expected Burke to be of similar opinion, especially given his views on the earlier revolutions in England and America. The fact that he took the diametrically opposite position inevitably gave rise to accusations of inconsistency, which have persisted to the present. Burke anticipated such charges and sought to refute them in the *Reflections.* He distinguished the two earlier revolutions from that in progress in France by arguing that the former were embarked upon in order to protect 'ancient indisputable laws and liberties' against usurpatious tyrants whereas the latter was a 'revolution in sentiments, manners and moral opinions' certain to destroy all that was good in the old order.

Edmund Burke constructed a classic conservative critique of political radicalism. The chief immediate object of his attack was the radicalism of late eighteenth–century France and England. But he appealed to general principles, which though expressed in the language and with the concepts of his own time, are sufficiently similar to widely held conservative ideas of today. Burke's radicals were never the real radicals of his own time. Nowhere in his works can we find a scrupulous account of the ideas or actions of any particular radical thinker or politician. Burke attacked certain abstract radical ideas by means of certain abstract conservative arguments. These abstract ideas may be held by radicals in different times and places, facing different concrete problems.

Burke not only at times expressed a preference for intuition over reason but also advocated pragmatism against theory. Theory, he said, was speculative, not real. Theory was too broad and too deep. The real problems of society were particular and their remedies must therefore be particular. A theoretical approach to social problems led to the characteristic defects and dangers of radicalism: solutions too remote from reality and too big for the problems. But, although he did not present his ideas systematically and was far from consistent, he did have a theory of politics and of political radicalism. This political theory was based upon the metaphysical doctrine that nature was order. This doctrine had two meanings. Nature ordained stability: good order is the foundation of all good things. Nature is also regular. Thus politics is governed by discoverable laws. Because stability is natural, revolution is against nature. But, though revolution is unnatural, it is still governed by nature's laws. These dictate that revolution leads to anarchy, which in turn must lead to tyranny. Thus, for all his pragmatism, Burke proposed a law of revolution for us to assess, a law both general and normative, a law derived from a highly articulated political theory.

The project of revolution, he argues, presupposes a degree of reliable social knowledge which no individual or faction can reasonably claim. The radical is in his essence intellectually arrogant. As a theorist, he thinks big. As a radical, he applies his big theories without adequate knowledge of the probable consequences of his actions and with little understanding of the inadequacy of his knowledge. The identification of practical grievances or real abuses in government is easy. The cure of grievances and the correction of abuses is often possible and always desirable when possible. But the radical who attempts the reconstruction of society cannot achieve his goal. Where abuses are clear and great, and grievances strongly felt, destruction of old institutions may not be difficult. But building new order out of the chaos of destruction is a formidable task. Tyranny is the short cut.

But the radical does not always confront a stable society with an accidental blemish. He faces a society already in disorder, a society whose rulers cannot solve the problems before them. Burke did not believe that revolutions were caused by conspiracies of radical intellectuals. Rather, they were caused by the mistakes, stupidity, arrogance and oppression of rulers, and by the strains produced by social and economic development. In such a situation, radicals might make bad worse. But societies may disintegrate from their internal contradictions. Particular radical solutions may be ill-conceived and lead to new oppression. But in some circumstances no moderate solution may work. Caution may become a speculative ideal, not a practical method.

Because Burke held this view of the causes of revolution, he acknowledged that revolution might be justified by necessity. Whether any particular revolution is justified by necessity can only be answered by analysis of the particular circumstances. In the case of the French Revolution, he maintained that the revolutionaries proclaimed and then trampled on the rights of man. They promised freedom and happiness but delivered tyranny and terror. This was not due to bad luck nor merely to bad judgement. It was in the nature of things. The promise of radical emancipation from evil is an illusion which, if acted on, necessarily leads to radical evil.

Radical ideals, Burke freely acknowledges, are, in the abstract, extremely appealing. But abstract ideals are not only an inadequate substitute for practical remedies, they often mask vicious intent. Those who seek the support of others to further their own ambitions will state their aims in terms of the interests of those others, not of themselves. Thus, their ideals will appear altruistic and noble. The results may not match the stated aims because the stated aims were never the real aims. The radicals will manipulate popular-democratic symbols to secure popular support for their ambitions. Impatience imbued with a sense of justice becomes fanaticism. And fanaticism is a tyrant. Burke was the first conservative thinker who has seen political radicalism as a sort of fanatical secular religion. One of the stigmata of fanaticism is Manicheans: dividing the world into the just and the unjust, the saved and the damned. This Manicheans seem reasonable when the just are 'the people', the overwhelming majority, and the unjust their oppressors. But the radical is not humble before the popular will. He has a theory of the popular interest. He has a mission to bring the people happiness. Revolutions achieve the opposite of what they intend because what they intend – radical freedom, equality, democracy and perfect justice – cannot be achieved. Consequently, radicals must force through the impossible and the unpopular. The result can only be the negation of the freedom, equality, democracy and justice that they promised.

Burke opposed despotism but saw justifiable political change as the specific remedy of particular grievances and abuses. 'I would not exclude alteration neither; but even when I changed, it should be to preserve. Safe politics is slow, cautious and dull. This is not an easy course. The virtue of moderation requires a deep courage to be temperate when the multitude impatiently condemns you". Radicalism is more exciting. Self-restraint is necessary to resist the temptation of political radicalism. Time and again, he exposed the British Government as despotic, at home and abroad, but he continued to advocate a piecemeal, increamental patient reform which was hardly adequate to the objectives he set out. Burke's gradualist approach to slavery entailed complicity with despotism. So did his toleration of a society in which the wealthy fed their dogs and horses with the food which should have nourished the children of the poor. Burke acknowledged this difficulty for gradualism.

Burke still deserves our attention, therefore, because his arguments can be generalized. Burke was a much better sociologist of revolution than is usually recognized. He had an implicit general theory of revolution, which is superior to many recent theories of revolution in two important respects. Firstly, he had an integrated theory of the causes, processes and consequences of revolution while most modern theory is confined mainly to the causes and has little to say about the consequences. Secondly, he integrated empirical and normative theory while modern theorists tend to separate the two and largely ignore the latter.

Burke teaches that the business of political radicals-the uprooting of established political and social institutions - may lead to quite unexpected and undesired consequences, involving great human suffering. He rebuked radicals for dogmatism and frivolous adventurism. He called for realism, pragmatism and respect for persons.

> I must see with my own eyes, I must, in a manner, touch with my own hands, not only the fixed, but the momentary circumstances, before I could venture to suggest any political project whatsoever. I must see all the aids, and all the obstacles. I must see the means of correcting the plan, where correctives would be wanted. I must see the things; I must see the men. I never will act the tyrant for their amusement. If they will mix malice in their sports, I shall never consent to throw them any living, sentient creature whatsoever, not so much as a kittling to torment.

Thus, the debate between conservatives and radicals remains inconclusive. Burke is still worth our attention because his is a classic statement of conservatism. It has the classic strengths and weaknesses of that position. He offered eighteenth-century solutions to eighteenth-century problems. But those problems belong to a family whose descendants live still among us. We still do not have very good solutions. We must therefore come to grips with Burke.

In the 1770s Burke was much agitated with British policy on America, attacking the arguments of government spokesmen and urging a more conciliatory policy. His speeches and writings on this are notable for their appeal to experience, more than to principle. He opened his *Speech on American Taxation* in the House of Commons in April 1774 with a demonstration from recent experience, that the repeal of the Stamp Act by the Rockingham ministry in 1766 had not led the colonists to demand repeal of any other taxes: hence the repeal of the tax on tea, *a* motion which Burke was supporting and the ministry was opposing, could not be opposed on that ground. The rest of the long speech is on the same ground of experience: it is a detailed analysis of the shifts in British policy since the fall of the Rockingham administration eight years before, and of the uniformly unfortunate consequences of those shifts.

Burke closed with an appeal to the House not to stand on its sovereign right to tax the colonies never but to consider the consequences of exercising that right in the way they had recently done:

> I am not here going into the distinctions of rights, nor attempting to mark their boundaries. I do not enter into these metaphysical distractions; I hate the very sound of them. But if, intemperately, unwisely, fatally, you sophisticate and poison the very source of government, by urging subtle deductions, and consequences odious to those you govern, from the unlimited land illimitable nature of supreme sovereignty, you will teach them by these means to call that sovereignty itself in question. When you drive him hard, the boar will surely turn upon the hunters.

A year later, in the *Speech on Moving his Resolutions 'for Conciliation with the Colonies* (March 1775), he proceeds on the same grounds. He presents an array of facts about the American colonies, including the fact that the colonists were mainly Englishmen, devoted ever since the seventeenth-century emigration to the principle that in all monarchies the people must in effect themselves, immediately or immediately, possess the power of granting their own money, or no shadow of liberty could subsist. That principle Burke fully endorses, but he does not urge it as a morally desirable principle: he simply cites the colonists' attachment to it as an experiential fact. And he insists that utility, in the broadest sense, should take precedence over legal right:

> The question with me is, not whether you have a right to render your people miserable; but whether it is not your interest to make them happy. It is not, what a lawyer tells we, I may do; but what humanity, reason, and justice, tell me, I ought to do.

He closes with a last appeal against driving principles to their logical conclusion:

> All government, indeed every human benefit and enjoyment, every virtue, and every prudent act is founded on compromise and barter. We balance in conveniences; we give and take; we remit some rights that we may enjoy others; and, we choose rather to be happy citizens, than subtle disputants.

In all of this, the appeal is not to principle but to tire empirical fact of colonists' attachment to a principle rooted in British history since at least the seventeenth century. There is no appeal to Natural Law or to any universal principle other than utility in the broadest sense. The happiness of the people is the only criterion of policy, and how that is to be achieved can only be decided by painstaking attention to experience, to the fortunate and unfortunate consequences of various past governmental policies.

State

Burke's conception of state is probably the most puzzling feature of his political theory. Sometimes his state appears to be a superhuman authority to which man owes an involuntary obedience. At other times, it is a human institution that man has made and chosen to obey. If this is an inconsistency in his theory, it is not one that can be explained on the assumption that he thought different things at different times. For the contradiction can appear within the context of a single work. At one point in the *Reflections,* he wrote of God as the "institutor and author and protector of civil society". At another point, he described government as "a contrivance of human wisdom to provide for human wants." In *The Present Discontents* the contradiction was stated within the compass of a single sentence: "...government certainly is an institution of divine authority, yet its forms, and the persons who administer it, all originate from the people." It is possible, however, to study Burke's state without first determining its pedigree. Whether the state was made by God or by man, Burke thought of it as a legal institution. Sometimes he conceived of it as an agency, very often as a trust, and sometimes as a corporation or body politic. The first question we must ask ourselves in reading Burke is not who authorized his state but what its legal capacity was.

Of the three identities that Burke gave to the state that of agency was the least explicit and least fully developed. The evidence for its adoption is mainly confined to the Popery Laws. Here government tended to figure as an attorney. He described the King as the "national procurator." The authority of the people approximated the authority of a principal. Government had the power to legislate positive law; but the people had merely given up their judgement and not their right. "In all forms of government," Burke contended, "the people is the true legislator." Government was only "the immediate and instrumental cause of the law", the "remote and efficient cause" was the consent of the people. This consent might be either actual or implied; but it was "absolutely essential" to the validity of a law. Whenever a law benefited the people, their ratifying consent could be presumed. No consent could be presumed when a law injured them: .... "such a constitution cannot in propriety be a law at all." The notion that the validity of a law supposed the consent of the people in any form is not characteristic of Burke's later thought. Holding to this conception of the state, Burke would have found it very difficult either to justify the Declaratory Act or to attack the Jacobins.

In another sense, however, the conception of the state as agent was to prove more durable. He assumed that the state might commit the people to binding contracts. The contract which he defended in the Popery Laws was the Treaty of Limerick of 1691. In this treaty William III had guaranteed to the Irish Jacobites that Catholic rights would be respected. In making this guarantee, Burke argued, William represented "the whole contracting capacity of the nation." There was in the state no "dormant" or "irresistible" power that could absolve the people from the obligation that William had assumed on their behalf. The compact of the king acting constitutionally was the compact of the nation. On the assumption that the Treaty of Limerick was binding upon the nation, Burke could dispute the validity of the penal laws that Parliament had subsequently legislated.

The idea that the state could negotiate binding contracts never entirely vanished from Burke's theory. He acknowledges this capacity in the debate over Fox's India Bill. Although none too explicitly, it was assumed in his efforts to obtain a treaty for the American rebels. Yet, on these occasions Burke did not assert the authority of public contract with the same absoluteness that he exhibited in his defence of the Treaty of Limerick. The state in Burke's later conception, possessed rights and duties that it could not alienate by contract. The evidence for this shift in Burke's theory of civil society can be seen as early as 1772 in his interpretation of the Act of Union. If any public measure might be represented as a contractual bargain, the act, which united England and Scotland, certainly qualifies. Yet Burke refused to admit that the terms of union were either "eternally binding" or "absolutely irreversible" in any point. He acknowledged that the act was a solemn and important measure. It was not to be changed without weighty reasons. But he denied that it restricted Parliament's authority in any particular way. "The power of rectifying the most sacred laws must, by the every nature of things, be vested in the legislature; because every legislature must be supreme and omnipotent with respect to the law, which is its own creature." The only check that Burke acknowledged on the authority of Parliament arose from considerations of prudence. Clearly the state which Burke assumed here was not the same institution that he had assumed in the Popery Laws. In the Popery Laws, the state lacked dormant and irresistible powers; here it possessed them; in the Popery Laws, the state could limit its authority by its engagements; here it could not.

The new conception of the state that Burke had adopted was the conception of trust. In *The Present Discontents,* he wrote of King, Lords, and Commons as "trustees for the people." "No power," he added, "is given for the sole sake of the holder." In his speech on the surrender of St. Estates, he argued that "in all government there is a trust reposed. Shaw me a government and I will show a trust'". The trust figured in his speech on economic reform. Burke argued that the King's property was held in trust for the people. "The king was only a trustee for the public. Property and subjects existed before kings were elected, and endowed with a portion of the former for the protection of the latter." The trust appears in his Indian speeches. In the debate on Fox's East India Bill, Burke argued that no government possessed "original, self-derived rights." The rights and powers of government were all "in the strictest sense a trust. The trust was assumed in his earliest attacks on the French Revolution. He wrote in the *Reflections,* "All persons possessing any portion of power ought to be strongly and awfully impressed with an idea that they act in trust, and that they are to account for their conduct in that trust to the one great Master, Author, and Founder of society." In the later anti-Jacobin works the trust yielded to the corporation. But for all practical purposes the trust supplied Burke with his normal working-conception of what the state was.

Whether this trust is a temporal or a heavenly institution makes little difference for our understanding of its significance. It was not in any strict sense a democratic conception of the state. Even if we suppose that its origins were entirely temporal, Burke's trust does not become a democratic institution. It implies no right on the part of the people to govern, even if it was the people who had settled authority in trust to be administered for their own benefit. For the legal ownership of a trust, property belongs not to the settler, nor to the beneficiary, but to the trustee. Burke either's subject as settler or as beneficiary could not claim a right to administer the trust at will. Short of extraordinary occasions when the trust was betrayed and rebellion justified, Burke's trustee was not answerable to anyone's discretion for his management. Burke's governors had ceased to be procurators and agents acting on behalf of their subjects as principals. This is clear from the *Reflections* where we find Burke writing:

> What was true of the King was also true of the Lords and Commons. Moreover, what was true of government under the British constitution was true of all governments under any constitution. As long as the state survived, the supreme power was not answerable for its conduct in office.

This assumption of independence was crucial to Burke's theory of parliamentary representation. The member of Parliament was raised to a trust by his constituents. Yet, within the limits of his trust, Burke's member was not commanded by the wishes of his constituents. He could not in conscience be bound by their mandates or instructions. He was not to act as their agent, their ambassador, or their advocate. His duty extended to the welfare of the entire nation. He was a "trustee for the whole, and not for the parts." In the last resort the member could not sacrifice his judgment nor his responsibility to the will of the people. "We are not to go to school to them," Burke told the Commons, "to learn the principles of law and government. In doing so, we should not dutifully serve, but we should basely and scandalously betray the people, who are not capable of this service by nature, nor in any instance called to it by the Constitution."

"All political power which is set over men ought to be exercised ultimately for their benefit." On the assumption that government was a trust, Burke could argue that it was the exclusive right of the trustee to decide what was of advantage or benefit to the subject. But on the same assumption Burke could also argue that the subject had a right to whatever measures might be thought beneficial or advantageous. The subject possessed no legal right to prescribe policies to the sovereign; he had nevertheless an equitable right to those policies, which the sovereign had an obligation to adopt. By the assertion of this equitable right Burke's trust could supply arguments that appeared almost Jacobin in character. "The object of the state is the happiness of the whole and the happiness or misery of mankind, estimated by their feelings and sentiments, and not by any theories of their rights, is, and ought to be, the standard for the conduct of legislators towards the people." But this statement does not deprive the legislators of their formal authority; nor does it represent them as the agents of the people. Whatever equitable rights the people enjoyed under the trust, they did not possess the right to govern themselves.

To fulfill the purpose of this trust, Burke's sovereign commanded an almost unlimited discretion. At times, it was both his right and his duty to disregard the restrictions of positive law. On Burke's account, the public welfare was the cause and reason of all law. This discretionary jurisdiction extended even to the forms and the laws of the constitution itself. The constitution was not something that was specified in the terms of the sovereign might alter and perhaps was obliged to alter as circumstances dictated. In the American controversy, Burke argued that the constitution had undergone changes in the past. "This Constitution has admitted innumerable improvements, either for the correction of the original scheme or for bringing its principles better to suit those changes which have successively happened in the circumstances of the nation or in the manners of the people." The American crisis required Parliament to consider further changes in the form of the constitution. "Public troubles have often called upon this country to look into its Constitution. It has ever been bettered by such a revision." The trustee's discretion over the forms of the constitution even allowed him to make a valid delegation of his trust. In 1755, Burke urged Parliament to transfer its taxing powers to the colonial assemblies. "If parliament be the sovereign power of America," he argued, "parliament may, by its own act, for wise purposes, put the local power of the purse into other hands than its own, without disclaiming its just prerogative in other particulars." This argument clearly violated the legal maxim that a trustee could not delegate an authority that he possessed in trust. Burke was familiar with the maxim and on occasions appealed to it in argument. The American controversy, however, left Burke with little choice. Before 1775, Burke had insisted that the Parliament possessed the constitutional right to tax the colonies; after 1775, he attempted to persuade the Parliament to surrender this right on prudential ground. For the sake of consistency, he was forced to suppose that the Parliament possessed the authority to delegate its trust.

In the extent of his jurisdiction, Burke's sovereign resembled Hobbes's Leviathan. But here the resemblance ends. For Burke's sovereign unlike Hobbes's, possessed his authority in trust. He was under an obligation to use whatever rights he possessed on behalf of someone else. Even if Burke's sovereign did not exceed the limits of his jurisdiction, it was still possible to charge him with tyranny or breach of trust. The discretion that Burke allowed to the sovereign did not license him to commit arbitrary and lawless acts. For it was in the end a "moral," "virtuous," and "equitable" discretion. At the very least Burke's sovereign had to use his powers of discretion in the interest of his subjects; this obligation alone rendered him liable to judgment in equity. "All discretion must be referred to the conservation and benefit of those over whom power is exercised, and therefore must be guided by rules of sound political morality."

Like the trustee in English law, Burke's sovereign was required to show prudence in the administration of his office. The policy that served the advantage of the citizen could not be discovered without a prudential regard for all the circumstances. For this reason, Burke could require the sovereign to make utilitarian calculations in the administration of his authority. Men had a right to the advantages that government could confer. These advantages were often compromises sometimes between good and evil, and sometimes between evil and evil. What prudent policy required could not be abstractly stated nor prescribed before the event. It depended upon the circumstances of the moment; and as these circumstances changed, the dictates of prudence changed as well. Yet in all circumstances the obedience of the sovereign to the dictates of prudence was an obligation of his trust. "A statesman, never losing sight of principles, is to be guided by circumstances; and judging contrary to the exigencies of the moment, he may ruin his country forever." Under this obligation, the governor had a duty to behave in different ways at different times.

Burke tended to write like a utilitarian when he stressed the prudential duties of the state. The trust was not an idea that Burke had adopted before he entered politics. There is no evidence in his writings that explains how he discovered and why he continued to use it for most of his active political life. He challenged the right of the King to manage his own revenue, to choose his own servants, and to dissolve Parliament at will. Burke could hardly deny that these rights existed; nor could he deny the title of the authorities who exercised them. In some cases, the ownership of the right was manifestly provided for by the British constitution as he and his contemporaries understood it. That the King might appoint ministers or dissolve Parliament was not something that the eighteenth century was prepared to debate.

Burke could hardly reverse himself and argue that rights, which he had once defended, did not in fact exist. But he could argue, and argue without inconsistency, that these rights were held in trust. On each occasion, Burke could recognize the right and acknowledge its legal ownership, and then proceed to defeat the exercise of that right by asserting the equitable interest of the beneficiary.

Burke's reasons for adopting the conception of the corporation or body politic are more difficult to fathom. Doubtless, the change had something to do with the French Revolution. The use of the corporation was confined almost entirely to his anti-Jacobin works. Before the Revolution Burke had often used the trust on the popular side of public controversies. But it is unlikely that he discarded the trust because it committed him to democratic arguments. Clearly, the trust was a conception that could be worked on either side of a conflict between the government and the people. When he chose to dispute the sovereign's authority, he could plead the beneficiary's interest; and he could plead the trustee's legal right when it suited him to dispute the pretensions of the people.

To understand the limitations of the trust we must remember that Burke had two points to make about the French Revolution. The first was that man in civil society could not choose his governors by virtue of his natural rights. For this purpose, the assumption of the trust was presumably adequate. The second point was that the National Assembly had gained power by usurpation and that the legal government of France remained with the authorities in the old regime. Here it is possible that the trust proved to be an embarrassment. The two points, after all, were not identical. Without supposing that any democratic right resided in the people of France, it could have been argued that the National Assembly possessed a perfectly legitimate authority. The establishment of the Assembly had been consented to by the King and each of the three Estates. At the King's request, the nobility, the clergy, and the commoners had merged themselves into a single legislature. He needed a conception that would allow him to assert the authority of an ancient constitution, to assert it even against the discretion of the formal government. The trust that Burke had assumed in the American crisis, could not serve this purpose. On the assumption that the state was a trust, Burke had allowed the government to alter its constitution and to delegate its authority. Whatever the merits of this speculation may be, Burke first introduced his new definition of the state into the *Reflections* at a point where he argued that King, Lords, and Commons could not dissolve themselves nor abdicate their respective duties in the government of the realm. The argument was stated with explicit reference to what might happen in England; we may assume that it had some reference to what had actually happened in France.

In common law a corporation derives its being from the act of the sovereign. For obvious reasons, Burke's state as a corporation could not be explained as an institution, which had created itself. It arose from the act of the original corporations. Whatever part God played in its creation, man was at least its "proximate and efficient cause." In this sense, Burke could argue in the *Reflections,* "society is, indeed, a contract." He could go on to call society a partnership. But the institution he actually described in this famous passage was not a partnership nor in any strict sense a contractual association. But it was a corporation. Like a common-law corporation, Burke's state was subordinated to the ends and purposes of its institution.

Burke never wanted to accept the interference of abstract modes of thought into politics. We all know that he condemned in particular the idea that the duties of individuals can be exclusively or even mainly based on their will or consent. 'Duties are not voluntary', he wrote an *An Appeal from the New to the Old Whigs.* 'Duty and will', he added, 'are even contradictory terms. We have obligations to humankind at large, which are not in consequence of any special voluntary part. On the contrary, the force of all the pacts which we enter into with any particular person or number of persons amongst mankind depends upon those prior obligations'.

This view which could hardly be described as Lockean—does not seem to be distinctive of Burke. This view may be found, at first sight, in several, probably all, counter-revolutionary authors in continental Europe. But what is distinctive of Burke is that he—unlike continental counter-revolutionaries—does not proceed to define the source of duty in Government, or even in an alliance of Church and State, or, in short, in any strictly defined political realm. Burke saw the emergence of duty from a very special sort of contract which we could perhaps describe as tacit in any civil, order, in the spontaneous dealings between individuals—always rooted in their own ways of life—and between generations.

It is certainly true that Burke saw the state as playing a crucial role in this compact, but it is a 'great continental mistake', to infer from this that Burke's view of political arrangements is in any way similar to the views of continental counter-revolutionaries or even conservatives. Let us recall that famous passage from the *Reflections on the Revolution in France*:

> Society is indeed a contract. Subordinate contracts for objects of mere occasional interest may be dissolved at pleasure; but the state ought not to be considered as nothing better than a partnership agreement in a trade of pepper and coffee, calico or tobacco, or some other such low concern, to be taken up for a little temporary interest, and to be dissolved by the fancy of the parties. It is to be looked on with other reverence; because it is not a partnership in things subservient only to the gross animal existence of a temporary and perishable nature. It is a partnership in all science, a partnership in all art, a partnership in every virtue and in all perfection. As the end of such a partnership cannot be obtained in many generations, it becomes a partnership not only between those who are living, but between those who are living, those who are dead, and those who are to be born.

Burke argues that this contract is not made by political design and that government itself, or politics, are bound and limited by this very primeval contract and this limited government is a friend of the free market. By third step will consist of recalling that Burke insists that limited government is best limited when it is accountable to its subjects—and, in this sense, Burke can be seen as a democrat of sorts. Burke saw every attempt of government, or every political attempt to redesign spontaneous arrangements in order to make them conform to an abstract vision always is an abuse of power. In the letter to the sheriffs of Bristol, he wrote:

> I was persuaded that government was a practical thing made for the happiness of mankind and not to furnish out a spectacle of uniformity to gratify the schemes of visionary politicians. Our business was to rule, not to wrangle.

And he added in the same letter:

> As the Sabbath (though of divine institution) was made for man and not man for the Sabbath, government, in its exercise and at least, ought to conform to the exigencies of the time, and the temper and the character of the people with whom it is concerned, and not always to attempt to bend the people to their theories of subjection.

During the 1780s most of Burke's energy was devoted to his crusade against the East India Company. England's Indian empire was indeed, in Burke's view, a proper white man's burden, but he took strong exception to the way Parliament had allowed that burden to be exercised, with inadequate oversight or control, by the chartered East India Company. He compiled such a mass of evidence of the Company's dishonourable vicious, corrupt and genocidal behaviour, that he was able almost single-handedly, to persuade the House of Commons to impeach the chief architect and defender of the Company's policies, Warren Hastings, and thereby to bring those policies into a glare of publicity unprecedented in British parliamentary history. His speeches and reports on India take up seven volumes of his sixteen-volume collected works, and he said, towards the end of his life that he would rather be remembered for his efforts in defence of the Indian people than for anything else he had done.

What concerns us here is the extent to which Burke built his case against the Company, and for the impeachment of Hastings, on general principles of right. What we find is that he frequently invoked such general principles, but never defined them at all closely. He needed to invoke them, he knew he could not show that the Company's actions had been illegal, so his only recourse was to show that they offended against some more fundamental law. This law he sometimes described as divine, sometimes as natural, sometimes as moral. But he did not need to specify its content, for the activities of the Company and its servants, which Burke had put on record in enormous detail, were strikingly in defiance of the simplest principles of fairness and honesty.

In his *Speech on Fox's East India Bill,* (I December 1783), he undertook to demonstrate three propositions about those activities and their results:

> First, that there is not a single prince, state, or potentate, great or small, in India, with whom they have come into contact, whom they have not sold. I say sold though sometimes they have not been able to deliver according to their bargain. Secondly, I say, that there is not a single treaty they have ever made, which they have not broken. Thirdly, I say, that there is not a single prince or state, who ever put any trust in the company, who is not utterly ruined; and that none are in any degree secure or flourishing, but in the exact proportion to their settled distrust and irreconcilable enmity to this nation.

Moreover, in the whole internal administration the rule of law had been replaced by arbitrary rule:

> In effect, Sir, every legal regular authority in matters of revenue, of political administration, of criminal law, of civil law, in many of the most essential parts of military discipline, is laid level with the ground; and an oppressive, irregular, capricious, unsteady, rapacious, and peculating despotism, with a direct disavowal of obedience to any authority at home, and without any fixed maxim, principle, or rule of proceeding, to guide them in India, is at present the state of your charter-government over great kingdoms.

When Burke denounced the behaviour of the East India Company and of Warren Hastings he often paid tribute to India's old civilization:

> India is inhabited by a people for ages civilized and cultivated, cultivated by all the arts of polished life, whilst we were yet in the woods. It has its own princes, an ancient and venerable priesthood, the depository of their laws, learning and history, the guides of the people whilst living, and their consolation in death, as well as a nobility of great antiquity and renown. This civilization is being devastated by British.

Keeping the power of politics and government in due limits was always a first concern of Burke's and these limits were always in his view, related to a certain respect for the spontaneous arrangements of particular traditions. In a curious letter to Sir Hercules Languished, Burke explained that there a difference between absolute slavery and a degraded state of citizenship, where an hereditary nobility possess the exclusive rule. The latter, he explained, 'may be no bad mode of government (for those countries not blessed by British mixed government)—provided that the personal authority of individual nobles be kept in due bounds and that the people are subjected to but light impositions, and are otherwise treated with attention, and with indigenous to their humors and prejudices'.

It was of course the indignation against unlimited political power that led Burke to attack the French Revolution. He cannot admire the change of one piece of barbarism for another, and a worse. He cannot rejoice at the destruction of a monarchy, mitigated by manners, respectful of laws and usages, and attentive, perhaps but too attentive, to public opinion, in favour of the tyranny of a licentious, ferocious, and savage multitude without laws, manners or morals, and which, so far from respecting the general sense of mankind, insolently endeavors to alter all the principles and opinions which lave hitherto guided and contained the world, and to force them into a conformity to their views and actions.

This may suffice to recall that Burke has endorsed a certain type of limited government—without deducing it from Lockean first principles:

> That the state ought to confine itself to what regards the state or the creatures of the state: namely, the exterior establishment of its religion; its magistracy; its revenue; its military force by sea and land; the corporations that owe their existence to its fiat, in a word to everything that is truly and properly public, to the public peace, to the public safety, to the public order, to the public prosperity. My opinion is against an overdoing of any sort of administration, and more especially against this most momentous of all meddling on the part of authority, the meddling with the subsistence of the people.

Burke was a friend of representative government and, in this political sense, of government by consent. He certainly was against the so-called sovereignty of the people, because he perceived it as a threat to limited government. Burke avers the most secure form of limited government was government accountable to the people. Nowhere is this more clear than in his critique of royal favoritism which he brilliantly developed in his *Thoughts on the Cause of the Present Discontents*, published in 1770. This is considered to be Burke's first great political pamphlet and also the first systematic defence of what would become modern parliamentary political parties.

Finally, states like common law corporations could not dissolve themselves at pleasure. They are not "morally at liberty, at their pleasure, and on their speculations of a contingent improvement, wholly to separate and tear asunder the bands of their subordinate community, and to dissolve it into an unsocial, uncivil, unconnected chaos of elementary principles." In civil society the making and unmaking of corporations was regulated by rules of positive law. Similarly, higher justice regulated the state corporation. "Each contract of each particular state is but a clause in the great primeval contract of eternal society." Here, Burke supposed that the authority of natural law controlled the formation and dissolution of states. "This law is not subject to the will of those who, by an obligation above them, and infinitely superior, are bound to submit their will to that law." The only excuse which might justify the dissolution of the state was the necessity of the act. "It is the first and supreme necessity only, a necessity that is not chosen, but chooses, a necessity paramount to deliberation, that admits no discussion and demands no evidence, which alone can justify a resort to anarchy." But the right to dissolve the corporation under the license of necessity did not mean that its members possessed the right to dissolve it at their discretion. "...If that which is only submission to necessity should be made the object of choice, the law is broken, Nature is disobeyed, and the rebellious are outlawed, cast forth, and exiled, from this world of reason, and order."

Starting from the premise that the state was a corporation, Burke developed a powerful argument against the legitimacy of the National Assembly. The Assembly could claim no authority under the constitution of the old body politic. It was nothing more than "a voluntary association" of men who had usurped an unlawful power. "They have not the sanction and authority of the character under which they first met. They have assumed another of a very different nature, and have completely altered and inverted all the relations in which they originally stood. They do not hold the authority they exercise under any constitutional law of the state." In the *Appeal* Burke entertained the supposition that the old body politic had been validly dissolved and that the Assembly claimed legitimacy under the authority of a new incorporation. But even on this argument, it was still possible for Burke to charge the Assembly with usurpation. "When men break up the original compact or agreement which gives its corporate form and capacity to a state, they are no longer a people, — they have no longer a corporate existence, — they have no longer a legal coactive force to bind within, nor a claim to be recognized abroad. They are a number of vague, loose individuals, and nothing more."

Until his death, this argument dominated Burke's case against the French Revolution. Reduced to its simplest terms, it meant that constitutional authority resided with the brothers of Louis XVI and not with the de facto powers in Paris. The former were the legal representative of the French corporation; the latter were nothing more than usurpers. In a sense, Burke's argument against the revolutionaries never entirely depended upon their abuse of power. Their cruelties and follies may have in Burke's mind aggravated their original offence. But there remained, nevertheless, the original crime of having seized an authority to which they did not possess a valid title. Burke's case against the new regime in France, like Paine's case against the old regime in England, was essentially legitimist. Like Paine, and perhaps like everybody else in the eighteenth century, Burke cared too much about the merits of its policy.

Whatever part God played in the formation of Burke's state, it is clear that divine participation did not rule out the need for human volition and consent. Burke regarded states as artificial combinations; "in their proximate efficient cause," he spoke of them as "the arbitrary productions of the human mind. His state like Filmer's could figure as a supernatural authority, but the similarity between their conceptions is superficial. Filmer's state derived its authority as a direct and special delegation from God. Burke's state was a secular institution to the extent that it was made in history through the voluntary act of its founders. Burke called this voluntary act sometimes a contract, sometimes an agreement, sometimes a compact, and sometimes a trust. Although Burke might write of God as the author and founder of civil society, God was not in any mysterious sense a party to its institution. In the main, God assumes no more important a part in the formation of Burke's state than he does in Locke's.

Burke's supposition of human consent worked only for the first formation of the state. When he tried to account for the obligations of those citizens who were neither founding fathers nor express contractors, then the coherence of his explanation collapsed. In *The Conduct of the Minority*, it was argued that people submitted to old governments "not because they have chosen them, but because, they are born to them". The same argument was stated at greater length in the *Appeal.*

Here, Burke made an effort to keep up the authority of the original contract: the original covenant was said to endure and to attach to subsequent members of the state. The rights and duties of the son were presumably the same as the rights and duties of the father. The father's attachment to the covenant was voluntary; the son's was not. The son acquired the benefits and duties of civil society without choice; for him the authority of the original contract commenced at birth. In short, the first generation of Burke's citizens entered into civil society by virtue of their free consent; the second generation was conscripted into membership by the forces of nature and the will of God.

Whatever it may have been in its origins, Burke's state at this point ceases to be credible as the institution of human contract and consent. The inconsistency, however, cannot be read to prove that Burke rejected Locke or the characteristic assumptions of contract theory. For the inconsistency was not peculiar to Burke. It is evident in other contract theories; and is perhaps something that no contract theory can really avoid.

He had been born an Irish man and became an English man by choice. Throughout his life, he acknowledged that he owed duties to both England and Ireland. But the artificial and chosen duty to England took priority over his natural duty to Ireland. In 1780 he told his Bristol constituents, "I certainly have very warm good wishes for the place of my birth. But the sphere of my duties is my true country." Five years later, he made the same point in the Commons. It was true he was an Irishman; and he conceived much was due by everyman to the place of his nativity, but that this duty ought not to absorb every other. When another country was generous enough to receive a man into her bosom, and raise him from nothing to stations of honour and trust such a country had given him birth. In 1792, he again admitted the double obligation. But if the two countries should ever come into conflict, it was with England, "which was the country of his adoption, that he would take part. In Burke's own case the allegiance of choice finally superseded the allegiance of birth and inheritance.

If we consider Burke's theory of the state in its entirety, its basic incoherence cannot be denied. It is impossible to conceive of the citizen as being the principal of an agent, the beneficiary of a trust, and a corporate of a body politic. The legal relationships, which these figures imply, are radically different. The citizen cannot be all three things at once with respect to the same civil relationships. In a sense, Burke did not develop a consistent theory of the state, but adopted a succession of legal identities, which he introduced as logic of debate required. But if we admit this, we should also recognize that there were limits to Burke's powers of invention. However much he shifted and changed in his definition of the state, he never went beyond the truisms of eighteenth-century political speculation. Whether Burke's state stands as agent, trust, or corporation, it is an institution that man has made under the authority of higher justice. Doubtless the supposition of an agency, a trust, or a corporation is more elaborate than the supposition of a simple contract. Far from rejecting the distinctive principles of eighteenth-century political theory, Burke had retained them and used them to serve his polemical purposes.

At first glance, the distinction may appear thinly drawn but for Burke it was crucial. He opposed the French Revolution because he believed that it was caused principally by the teachings of abstract metaphysicians such as Rousseau who lacked empirical experience of political reality and who held false and dangerous ideas about rights, the state and democratic government. On a more parochial level, he feared that the French revolutionary idea, if it were not refuted, might spread like a contagion to England and destroy his much-cherished British constitution. In fact, the *Reflections* is as much a celebration and commendation of the British constitution as it is an attack on the French revolutionaries. He dismissed French attempts to 'make' a constitution since he believed such a task to be impossible; constitutions require time to evolve and grow, they cannot be cobbled together overnight. The concepts of state and constitution are central to Burke's political thinking. He favoured a strong centralized government and castigated the proposed federalist administrative arrangements of the French National Assembly because they would dismember the nation and render it impossible to govern 'as one body'. The organic analogy employed by Burke to refer to the state has remained popular with conservative writers to assert that 'the State is not a machine, but an organism – more, a person'.

Burke was grudgingly prepared to concede that the revolutionaries might succeed in crating a government and even that they must grant some degree of freedom to the people, but he insisted that their methods rendered them incapable of securing the elusive necessity of a civil society – a free government.

On the general issue of rights Burke appears most vulnerable to the charge of inconsistency; how could the defender of the rights of the Irish, Indians and Americans deny them to the French ? Because, for Burke, the French revolutionary theory of abstract rights was a chimera and quite foreign to those traditional liberties of which he prided himself as an advocate. Burke argued that while rights are 'indefinable, they are discernible' and he insisted that he loved 'a manly, moral, regulated liberty' as much as any supporter of the French revolution. Where he parted company with the revolutionaries was with his rejection of their theory that rights can and should be derived from metaphysical abstraction. He was thus at odds with the Enlightenment dictum that man can be liberated by reason alone. Rather, Burke on rights was a circumstantialist in that he held that enduring rights can emerge only within the protective environment of a well-ordered civil society. Government is as important as liberty for without stable government there can be no true liberty:

> I should therefore suspend my congratulations on the new liberty of France, until I was informed how it had been combined with government; with public force; with the discipline and obedience of armies; with the collection of an effective and well-distributed revenue; with morality and religion; with the solidity of property; with peace and order: with civil and social manners. All these (in their way) are good things too; and, without them, liberty is not a benefit whilst it lasts, and is not likely to continue long.

Because the concept of government was so important for Burke, he was naturally concerned with discovering which was the best form of government. Again, he was deeply suspicious of the French experiment. At the time the *Reflections* was being written the revolutionaries were in the process of dismantling the absolutist monarchy of the ancient regime and instituting a system of government, which they supposed democratic. While Burke was highly critical of this process, his position regarding the ideal form of government was more complex and sophisticated than might be imagined. In short, he preferred a constitutional monarchy of the British type in which sovereign, lords, church and commons occupied defined and balancing places under the law. While he was certainly capable of cloying sycophancy towards monarchs and held as subversive the view that all power should proceed from the people, he rejected the theories of those 'old fanatics of single arbitrary power' who insisted that a divinely-ordained, absolutist monarchy was the only legitimate form of authority. Again Burke was a circumstantialist constitutional monarchy is the desired form of government, but it is possible for monarchs to usurp the constitution and if they attempt to do so it is both necessary and desirable to replace them – as the English revolutionaries did in 1688.

The French revolutionaries of 1789 were not, however, similarly justified in rebelling against such a 'mild and lawful' monarch as Louis XVI. Burke was adamant that Louis and his queen, Marie Antoinette, were not 'inexorable and cruel tyrants'; had they been he would have agreed with their punishment for 'the punishment of real tyrants is a noble and awful act of justice'. Burke conceded that the French monarchy was not without fault but he denied that it was so corrupt as to justify its destruction – it could and should have been reformed. He accused the revolutionaries of maliciously exaggerating the failings of the monarchy as a contrivance to justify a revolution that was based on nothing more than the speculative theories of evil-intentioned metaphysicians.

Burke was equally trenchant in his criticisms of the French revolutionaries' advocacy of what he regarded as an extreme form of democracy. While perhaps not fully agreeing with his contemporary John Wesley's opinion that 'the greater the share the people have in government, the less liberty, civil or religious, does a nation enjoy', Burke warned against allowing 'the humbler part of the community' becoming the 'depositaries of all power' and he was a life-long opponent of attempts to extend the right to vote to the lower classes. Instead, he preferred a moderate democracy, in which the power of the 'people' was tempered by other constitutionally entrenched institutions of monarch, lords and church. For Burke the French revolutionaries embraced false panaceas such as extreme democracy because they were incapable of discerning the true nature and sources of tyranny: 'Pure' democracy, in Burke's view, meant unfettered democracy and was 'the most shameless thing in the world.' His case against democracy of this type was essentially a case against majoritarianism or tyranny by the majority.

Given these strongly held beliefs it is perhaps surprising to learn that Burke was nevertheless prepared to concede that occasions could arise when a purely democratic form of government may be both necessary and desirable. He explained this apparent contradiction by asserting that 'I reprobate no form of government merely upon abstract principles'. Pure democracy is clearly inferior to a mixed and balanced system of government, but what was required above all else was a legitimate government capable of creating and maintaining civil order; if in certain circumstances democracy was the only system capable of so doing then Burke was prepared to support it.

Legitimacy of government was a central concern of Burke's and he castigated the French revolutionaries for their foolish actions in 'having industriously destroyed all the opinions and prejudices which support government'. He proceeded to the prophetic observation that, in destroying the sources of governmental authority, the new rulers of France would soon be required to resort regularly to naked violence to enforce their decisions on the people. This, Burke predicted, would result in the army becoming a deliberative institution, thus promoting the degeneration of the state into the worst form of tyranny imaginable – a military democracy.

Edmund Burke has been described by Ian Gilmore as 'the most intensely religious of all British political writers'. This is not to imply that Burke derived his political principles solely and always from theological precepts. He did believe in the concept of original sin and thus held that the Enlightenment notion of man's perfectibility on earth was dangerous cant. Burke was, however, no bigot he practiced religious toleration in an age when to do so was unpopular in many quarters. His was a rational faith and he was coldly dismissive of superstition as 'the religion of feeble minds'. He held that man was a 'religious animal' and that 'religion is the basis of civil society'. Not surprisingly, Burke was highly critical of the French National Assembly's treatment of the Catholic clergy, in particular of its confiscation of church property. He was convinced that the revolutionaries, motivated by a naive faith in Reason alone, were planning the eradication of the Christian religion. The folly of such a course of action lay in the failure of the revolutionaries to comprehend that organized religion was an all-important force, which sustained the civil order by conferring legitimacy upon government. Burke leaves the reader in no doubt that he commends the English system of church establishment because.

It can be agued that Burke's political thinking was more subtle and complex than has often been imagined. Popular misconception of Burke's beliefs is nowhere more apparent than in regard to his theory of political change. Burke was an implacable opponent of the French Revolution of 1789, but he was not an opponent of all revolutions and he most certainly did not deprecate necessary processes of political transformation. This much is clear from his statement that 'a state without the means of some change is without the means of its conservation'. Burke's first priority was the preservation of the state and he opposed the French revolution because it was on a path, which would lead to the destruction of the civil order. Out of such chaos would emerge despotism immeasurably more terrible than that of the ancient regime. He chided the revolutionaries for witching to destroy the old order simply because it was old. On the contrary, Burke contended that the age of an institution constituted a prima facie case for its retention, since by its persistence it had demonstrated its utility. He cites as an example the English ecclesiastical forms and institutions, which, he proudly proclaims, have not, altered greatly since the fourteenth or fifteenth centuries. This reluctance to embrace every current and passing political fashion

Burke saw as the essential strength of Britain's constitution. He praised 'our old settled maxim, never entirely nor at once to depart from antiquity'.

Nonetheless, Burke was not so naive as to be ignorant of abuses and injustices within the civil order. But again the French revolutionaries were deserving of censure because they wrongly believed they could root out evil by destroying its ephemeral manifestations:

> You would not cure the evil by resolving, that there should be no more monarchs, nor ministers of state, nor of the gospel; no interpreters of law; no general officers; no public councils. You might change the names. The things in some shape must remain. A certain quantum of power must always exit in the community, in some hands, and under some appellation. Wise men will apply their remedies to vices, not to names; to the causes of evil, which are permanent, not to the occasional organs by which they act, and the transitory modes in which they appear.

Granted that political remedies are sometimes required, how, in Burke's opinion, should they properly be applied? Slowly and deliberately, because to act in haste will surely fail to achieve that 'union of minds which alone can produce all the good we aim at'. Since man is by nature imperfect so are his social and political organizations. The faults of the established political institutions are obvious and the irresponsible criticisms of speculative metaphysicians will easily destabilize them to the ultimate disadvantage of all:

> That he should never dream of beginning its reformation by its subversion; that he should approach to the faults of the state as to the wounds of a father, with pious awe and trembling solicitude. By this wise prejudice we are taught to look with horror on those children of their country who are prompt rashly to hack that aged parent in pieces, and put him into the kettle of magicians, in hopes that by their poisonous weeds, and wild incantations they may regenerate the paternal constitution, and renovate their father's life.

Because rage, and possion, fury will pull down more in half an hour, than prudence, deliberation and foresight can build up in a hundred years, the more difficult but essential task is 'at once to preserve and reform'. Change should occur when and because circumstances require, not in response to the speculations of political 'magicians' untutored in the practice of politics.

Given what has been revealed of Burke's political ideas is it profitable to label him a 'conservative'? In a literal sense, it is yes because he was forever at pains to defend what was valuable against those who, in their eagerness to reform the imperfect, were happy to destroy equally the good with the bad. In a contextual sense, it is no becouse the description fails to do him justice. During the nineteenth and twentieth centuries the term 'conservative' became debased and distorted by the actions and writings of a diverse assortment of absolute monarchists, reactionaries and racial supremacists many of whom were pleased to invoke Burke's name but whose ideas and methods would have appalled him. Burke has suffered by being associated with these later ideologues and it is for this reason that Charles Parking has argued that it would be preferable if we 'could break the association of his name with the conservative tradition' so that we can assess him free from the distorting preconceptions engendered by his later so-called disciples.

Nevertheless the central difficulty for Burke and Burkeans alike remains the question of political change. Burke's position of supporting change when and to the extent dictated by circumstance begs the question, how can we discern which circumstances require how much, if any, change? Burke is unhelpful here because he made no attempt to provide a set of criteria which might give guidance to the conservative reformer. Of course, it was completely in keeping with Burke's practical approach to politics that he would not regard it necessary to lay down such a scheme. His concern in the *Reflections* was to oppose the French revolutionary idea, not to develop an abstract theory of revolutions or political change.

Theory of Representation

Burke's theory of representation as is seen a special instance of a general theory of trusteeship. To say that government is a trust is to say that it must be conducted in the interest of the governed. This is not, however, to say that the government is to be popularly controlled. Burke does not, in Pitkin's view, believe that the trustees (representatives) are controlled by the people or accountable to them. The trustee is to use his own judgment to decide what is in the interest of his constituents, and he is then to enact it regardless of their opinions, for their opinions are quite likely to be wrong.

The key to Pitkin's interpretation of Burke's theory of representation is the concept of objective interest. She claims that, "for Burke, political representation is the representation of interest, and interest has an objective, impersonal, unattached reality." According to Pitkin, this is true not only on the national level but also on the district level. That is, the representative is chosen not for people but for interests. Thus, "Burke conceives of broad, relatively fixed interests, few in number and clearly defined, of which any group or locality has just one." Since it is interests which are represented and not people, it is not necessary that each district or group of people choose a member of Parliament; it is sufficient that their interest be represented, even if it is done by a representative chosen from some other geographical location. This, then, is the theory of virtual representation. A district is represented as long as its interest are protected by some member of Parliament. If this is so, what is the significance of election? Why must any of the member of Parliament be elected? Pitkin offers several reason. On the one hand, "elections are merely a means of finding the members of a natural aristocracy." Further, even virtual representation must have some basis in the actual. An interest must have somebody to protect it. It is not essential that every area which share the interest be represented, by some must or the interest's grievances will not be aired. Finally, there must be some bond of sympathy between the people and their rulers; this bond can only be maintained if at lest some of the rulers are directly elected. Yet, even in these cases of actual representation, the voters are not to seek to control the representatives through instructions, and they should be removed only for corruption or lack of ability.

Still, Pitkin's theory of representation has the considerable merit of being systematic and of recognizing the complexity of Burkes theory. Other more traditional approaches to Burke's thought fail to produce a coherent account of his theory of representation and are therefore inferior to Pitkin's discussion. Such commentators as O'Gorman,

Macon, and Chapman realize that Burke believes in conflict resolution through compromise and rejects the idea of a general good. On the other hand, their treatment of the issue of accountability—that is, of the relationship between the representative and his district—is totally inadequate, for they deny that Burke held the representative accountable at all. Burke believed that government should exist for the good of the people but not that it should be controlled by the people.

Why are the major accounts of Burke's position on representation so unsatisfactory? It seems that the causes are two: a general lack of familiarity with the political situation at Bristol at the time of Burke's speeches there, and a failure to place Burke's arguments on representation within the context of his theory of the state. Let us now begin to remedy these faults by taking a closer look at the Bristol speeches. Burke served as one of the two representatives in Parliament from Bristol from 1774 to 1780. He came to Bristol because he had lost the patronage of Lord Verne and with it his previous seat. Bristol was prepared to accept him, even though Burke was a Whig and the city usually voted Tory, out of a sense of rebellion against the government's American policy. Bristol, at the time the second largest city of the kingdom, had its wealth tied to the colonial trade. As one of the leading opponents of the administration's policy of repressing American trade, Burke seemed the perfect spokesman for Bristol's interests. Unfortunately, "the election of 1774 was like a sudden love-match, based on an ardent but ignorant affection, and divergences of views and of temper began to appear as soon as the marriage was celebrated." While the city had opposed the government's policy in America, once the war started, the city rallied to the Crown. Burke, however, continued to oppose the policy. At the same time, his stand on other issues created considerable opposition in Bristol. By 1780, Burke's chances for reelection were slight.

Of the four speeches Burke made at Bristol, the first, upon arrival in 1774, need not concern us here; the fourth admits the impossibility of winning the poll in 1780, and is except for one point, also of little importance. The second speech was delivered after the election 1774. In it Burke offers his most theoretical statement of the relationship between voters and their representatives. The issue which concerns Burke is that of instructions. The other successful candidate had endorsed the right of the constituents to instruct representatives how to vote in Parliament. Burke disagrees. He admits that a representative ought to be close to his constituents their wishes ought to have great weight with him and he should give comparative attention to their interests. Yet, what means is that the Government is not a question simply of will or inclination; it invoices judgment. It is not a mater of what people want, but of what is best to be done. It is quite possible, then, that judgments may be in error. Further, it is likely that the judgments most prone to error are those, which are most remote. The representative is the man on the scene; he is the political expert. Therefore, "your representative owes you, not his industry only, but his judgment; and he betrays, instead of serving you, if he sacrifices it to your opinion." Burke goes on to argue that a member of Parliament must participate in debate and discussion, study issues carefully, and consider the interests of the entire country before making up his mind how to vote. The will of his own district is only one of the factors he must keep in mind as he decides.

The second Bristol speech seems to support the view that Burke holds that representatives are not accountable to their districts. However, Burke goes on in the third speech to considerably modify that impression. The third speech opened Burke's campaign for reelection in 1780, and is, therefore, a detailed defense of his conduct in office. Indeed, while there is some discussion of the theory of representation, the vast bulk of the speech is a reply to four specific charges. The first of these is that Burke has neglected the affairs of the city. Burke agrees that he has spent little time in Bristol—he does not live there and has visited only twice in the last six years—but he denies that he has not served the city well. Indeed, he suggested, "I could hardly serve you as I have done, and court you too." Burke also quickly passes over the charge that his stand in favor of the reform of the laws requiring imprisonment for debt conflicts with Bristol's interest. He points out that an imprisoned person cannot repay the debt and suggests that debtors should be allowed their freedom so they can work to repay their obligations. To a third charge—that he has supported Irish trade—Burke pleads guilty. However, he maintains that his support of the Irish trade will benefit Bristol in the long run by preserving the Empire. This choice is, he claims, between liberalization and war. Look at America; there all concessions were refused. And the result was that "from war and blood we went to submission, and from submission plunged back again to war and blood, to desolate and be desolated, without measure, hope, or end." Surely, England can learn from experience to avoid such consequences. By far the largest section of the speech is taken up with the final issue: the question of Catholic emancipation. Bristol was a zealously Protestant city, but Burke had voted to repeal a series of anti-Catholic acts. His defense is simply that his action was correct. Considerations of religious toleration and practical political prudence combine, in his view, to legitimate his stand.

Careful consideration of the Bristol speeches thus produces the beginnings of a coherent theory of representation, but we are still in danger of misunderstanding that theory unless we also understand Burke's theory of the constitution and the place of Parliament in that theory. Burke's theory of the constitution is largely a defense of the settlement of 1688-90. The value of the constitution established then is, according to Burke that it created a government balanced between royal, aristocratic, and democratic elements, with the weight slightly in favor of monarchy. England is thus best described as a limited monarchy. The possession of such a system is quite fortunate, for "a monarchy is a thing perfectly susceptible to reform, perfectly susceptible of a balance of power, and that, when reformed and balanced, for a great country it is the best of all governments"

Burke believes that the success of Parliament in resisting the Crown is directly people and their representatives, the better able those representatives will be to stand against the persuasions of the ministers and the greater the opportunity of the constituents to notice any lapse in the zeal of their members. This is not, however, to argue that the people every wish is to be done. In Burke's view, "the people are the natural control on authority; but to exercise and to control together is people are to express their grievances and the representatives are to seek the actual remedies. Burk writes;

> The people are the masters. They have only to express their arts at large and in gross. We are the expert artists, we are the to shape their desires into perfect form, and to fit the utensils to their use. They are the sufferers, they tell the symptoms of the complaint; but we know the exact seat of the disease, and how to apply the remedy according to the rules of art.

Government, as Burke often notes, is a trusteeship. This means that the members of Parliament are to act in what they believe to be the best interests of the people, and, generally, the people are best served by leaving them broad leeway. Yet, at times of crisis, the people are well advised to be more careful. If there seems to be a threat to their liberty, "the people ought to be excited to a more strict and detailed attention to the conduct of their representatives." Even in the most peaceful of circumstances, the people have the right to remove representatives for whatever reason they choose. Burke never contests the right; at most, he questions the wisdom of exercising it for insufficient cause.

One of Burke's most often quoted principles comes from this same period, namely, his insistence, in his speech to the electors Bristol, that a Member of Parliament is not an instructed, delegate but a representative empowered to exercise his independent judgement:

> Your representative owes you, not his industry only, but his judgment and he betrays, instead of serving you if he sacrifices it to your opinion.

He further said:

> Parliament is not a congress of ambassadors from different and hostile interests; which interests each must maintain, as an agent and advocate, against other agents and advocates; but parliament is a deliberative assembly of one nation, with one interest, that of the whole; where, not local purposes, not local prejudices ought to guide, but the general good, resulting from the general reason of the whole. You chose a member indeed; but when you have chosen him is not a member of Bristol, but he is a member of parliament.

This commonsense principle, beloved of M.P.s ever since, was perfectly sensible at the time when M.P.s were not elected on clear party platforms. We cannot blame for the use which has sometimes been made of that principle in later times, to excuse members elected on a specific party platform from living up to their commitments.

This brings us to two constitutional issues concerning representation which require further discussion if Burke's theory is to be fully understood. The first is the question of majority rule. According to Burke, popular control of government is essential. In a speech on economical reforms, he argues in favor of a reform bill because "...it is necessary from the demands of the people, whose desires, when they do not militate with the stable and eternal rules of justice and reason ought to be as a law to a House of Commons." Again, in the *Thoughts on the Cause of the Present Discontents*, Burke can be found urging the strictest public scrutiny of the conduct of members of Parliament. Yet, it is equally clear that Burke does not extend his concept of popular control to include majority rule. In the "Appeal from the new to the Old Whigs," he writes, "the number engaged in crimes, instead of turning them into laudable acts, only augments the quantity and intensity of the guilt." In fact, a sizable section of the "Appeal" consists of a detailed, and theoretically impressive critique of majority rule. Burke develops his case through an analogy to the government of a corporation. He argues that if government is truly based on contract, there can be majority rule only if all the parties to the contract agree, but, given the general incapacity of the masses, they would be foolish to create a majoritarian government. If the original contract did not call for majority rule, it can be added only by unanimous agreement. Applying this abstract argument to England, Burke denies that the country was originally ruled by the majority or that the Revolution of 1688 added it to the political system.

What finally are we to make to Burke on representation? Given the context we have discussed, what emerges, as his view of the relationship between a representative and his constituents is indeed a kind of trusteeship. What this means is, first, like the trustee of a corporation, the representative must serve the interests of the constituents. He is to act in what he believes to be the best interest of his client. The representative ought to consult with his constituents, listen to their complaints, and be mindful of their needs. Of the constituents, Burke says, 'their wishes ought to have great weight with him; their opinions high respect; their business unmerited attention...." But, in the end, while the voter is fully capable of feeling a need for action, he is not competent to decide what that action should be. It is the duty of the representative to shape the vague feelings of a district into government policy. Generally speaking, then, it is up to the representative to decide what the interests of his constituents require. Further, when the representative acts in Parliament, he is to act for the good of the entire nation; where the interests of his district conflict with those of the notion, it is the latter which are to prevail. As Burke puts it, "if the local constituent should have an interest or should form a hasty opinion evidently opposed to the real good of the rest of the community, the member for that place ought to be as far as any other form any endeavor to give it effect." This is so, not as Pitkin would have it, because there is a clash of abstract objective interests or between particular and general wills, but simply because what benefits the country at large is preferable to what benefits a single district. Burke thinks in terms of groups with interests, material and otherwise, not in terms of objective goods. In his view, politics is based on compromise and bargaining rather than the search for some abstract right, and parliament is an arena for debate, and conciliation not a Platonic Academy.

However, discourse, discussion given that the representative ought to be allowed great freedom, given that he ought to be judged liberally, and given that he ought not to be removed for simple disagreement, he may yet be removed. At Bristol, Burke claims to take pride in being attacked, for "the charges against me, are all of one kind, that I have pushed the principles of general justice and benevolence too far." What is more, he promises that, if reelected, he will continue in the same way:

> It is certainly not pleasing to be put out of the public service. But I wish to be a Member of Parliament, to have my share of doing well and resisting evil. It would therefore be absurd to renounce my objects, in order to obtain my seat.

Viewed against the background of the politics of the late eighteenth century, the interpretation of Burke's view of representation as trusteeship must be qualified. It must be recognized that Burke does not think that the representative's role is exclusively or even principally legislative in nature. In his time, the role of Parliament as a legislature was just becoming more important than its role as an overseer of the ministries. These, in turn, were responsible to the King, not to Parliament. Thus, Burke believes that one of the most important ways in which Parliament serves the people's interest is through checking the authority of the crown by blocking improper actions of the administration. Indeed, it would be step toward tyranny for Parliament to become an active positive force in government. Among the complaints leveled against the court cabal in the *Thoughts on the Cause of the Present Discontents* is that "...the control of Parliament upon the executive power is lost; because Parliament is made to partake in every considerable act of government." The truly vital function of the representative is not to enact the will of his constituents; it is rather to protect their interests. And an important reason why it is unnecessary for voters to have the authority to instruct representatives is that the representatives, once in Parliament, are not really expected to initiate programs but to respond to actions taken by the administration. In short, the members of Parliament don't rule; they defend the people against royal misrule. If we are to describe Burke's position on representation as a form of trusteeship, we ought also to understand that it is a defensive trusteeship.

Burke's assertion that there has been a ruling class in England with claims to continuity need cause no surprises. What might cause a surprise is that Burke thinks that this ruling class has always had a care for the constitution. Surely, one might say, ruling classes since the world began have been keen to break out of the constitutional constraints on their own self-aggrandising behaviour. That has been a commonplace view of ruling classes since Plato's *Republic*. Burke thinks that the case of England is different. England has been fortunate in having a ruling class which has been divided in its political attitudes. For extremely complicated political reasons, part of the English ruling class always sees its own future advantage in supporting the royal prerogative, while the other part of the ruling class has always seen its own future advantage in supporting Parliament. This split got out of hand in the seventeenth century and in part caused the Civil War, but in general it has been healthy for the English constitution. The dialectical clash between king and Parliament, executive and legislature, has provided the continuous dynamic of English constitutional politics, and such a dynamic cannot fade away while there exist in England devoted defenders of the king's power and robust defenders of the rights of Parliament. Burke by no means thinks that the events of the Revolution of 1688 have settled the question of relationship between king and Parliament for ever.

This camouflaged internecine quarrel can only be productive of good. In ordinary times it preserves a balance between the authority of government and the liberties of the subject, and in times of crisis the ruling class has to make a decision about where the balance ought to be struck. The motive for the striking of those balances is always obvious. In England, the survival of the constitution, and with it the survival of the ruling class, depends on the ruling class, or a section of it, getting the balance right.

Burke's constitutionalism comes out of what is really a rather grand view of the continuity of English politics. The Whig view of the continuity of English politics was far from parochial. It holds that, since the Norman Conquest, English history has been one continuous constitutional history lesson taught by freedom-loving Englishmen to their foreign kings who have typically had too elevated an idea of the royal power. In England, the king is expected to share power with the other estates of the realm, nobility and commons, and the king is also expected to acknowledge that there is an English way of doing things which he may not alter at will. The royal prerogative, the power which the king has simply because he is king, is supposed to be extensive but at the same time limited by the powers and privileges of the other orders. In the ordinary course of government the various powers are supposed to act in partnership. Occasionally they come to be seen as rivals, and that is an indicator that things have begun to go wrong, a signal that one of those cases has arisen in which adjustments have to be made so that each of the powers can be returned to run in its proper track. A wise ruling class is the vehicle by which those skills are transmitted from one generation to the next. There is nothing mysterious about this, no aristocratic cult of noble blood. Aristocracy, according to Burke, is, in the modern idiom, a socializing agency, teaching the manners, morals, santiments and skills to each new generation of its members which will enable constitutional politics of the English kind to work. Such an aristocracy must never become a caste. It must keep at least a half-open door to outside talent and to new wealth. It would be both wasteful and dangerous if the spirit of caste were to exclude all the outsiders with a claim to joining the ruling class, and Burke knows perfectly well, though he doesn't mention it, that the history of aristocracy in England is not all that smooth, and that new ennoblement over the centuries has become a commonplace.

Inheritance is the key to Burke's politics. Everyone in England, from the king downwards, has something valuable to hand on to his children. The king inherits his crown, the nobility its privileges, and the common people their rights and liberties. Each of these three instances of inheritance is consistent with, and indeed bolsters up, the other. Every estate of the realm claims what is valuable to it by the same title, and so no estate can have a good reason for quarrelling with another. Each part of the realm is supposed to realise that, in denying its privileges to any other order, it begins to undermine its title to its own privileges.

Burke stresses the rights and liberties of all Englishmen as an antidote to the new-fangled doctrine of the rights of man which threatens to cause so much trouble in the world. Burke boxes very cleverly with the whole idea of rights. He recognises that the two questions which have to be answered above all others about rights are: What are they and Where do they come from? Natural rights are vulnerable to those questions. One of the real problems of natural rights theory is always knowing where to draw the line. Most lists of natural rights would include the rights to life, liberty and property, but why stop there? Why not natural rights to a whole host of other things, until the list gets very long? A list of natural rights which included everything that anybody had ever thought of as a natural right would be very long indeed. The problem would then be to decide which was natural right and which was not. This problem simply will not go away whenever natural rights are under discussion, and it is the problem which enables thinkers like Burke to regard natural rights as a rather airy-fairy concept, meaningless when it is not actually dangerous. The motive for making a list of natural rights is nearly always to contrast the rights which men have in principle with the rights which they are being denied in practice, a contrast in which the existing political order always comes out very badly. What Burke cannot stomach is the idea that an existing and successful political and social order should be threatened by belief in a concept of natural rights which is not itself solidly based.

The problem of what natural rights are pales when compared to the problem of where natural rights come from. The usual answer is: from God; but this does not really help much, because it is not clear on what occasion God actually made the gift. Holy Writ no more helps the believer in natural right than it helps the believer in the divine right of kinds. As far as one can tell, God gave neither the right to rule forever nor natural rights to Adam and his posterity.

Rights, for Burke, are rooted firmly in the processes of a society at a particular moment of that society's development. It is only by looking at rights in that way, that Burke thinks a reasonable answer to the two vital questions about rights can be answered : What are they and where do they come from? Established practice tells us what our rights are and we know where they come from because we have received them as an inheritance from our ancestors.

Burke's Conservatism

The basis of Burke's defence of aristocracy is a belief in the complication of the social and political order. Burke's knows perfectly well that the argument against aristocracy is that it is both expensive and useless. That argument was already commonplace in revolutionary France, and it was to be restated in Tom Paine's celebrated reply to Burke, *the Rights of Man*. The French Revolution is accounted as a bourgeois revolution because it attacked aristocracy as an unproductive estate foreign to the body politic. Aristocracy was a consumer, not a producer, the best the could be said for it was that it was decorative. Aristocracy, then, needlessly complicates the social order, and part of the purpose of revolution was to create a social order which would consist of the productive classes only. All early nineteenth-century radicalism was to take up the same cry. The societies of the future were to be simplified societies of the producers only. Societies of the producers, which mean societies of the buyers and sellers of labour were going to be naturally harmonious societies because everybody was going to work for their living.

Burke is notoriously hard to categorise politically because he began his political life as a Whig and continued to regard himself as a Whig to the end of his life. Whiggism was what we would call 'on the left', however vaguely, in the eighteenth century, yet Burke has been identified with conservatism ever since and we are used to thinking that conservatism is 'on the right'. The difficulty partly arises from Burke's use of arguments from history to bolster up his own political positions. We have become accustomed to thinking that political positions which look to history for their legitimations must somehow always be right-wing positions, but that was not necessarily the case in late eighteenth-century England. It needs to be emphasized that, in eighteenth –century England, it was the liberty-loving Whigs who typically used arguments from history. It was the Whigs who 'invented' the idea of the ancient English constitution which the king could not alter at will. Toryism was connected with the idea of the divine right of kings and therefore with Jacobitism. That meant an obsession with who was really king at the moment, and that in its turn meant he whose father had been king before him. We have become so used to the kind of

Burkean argument for monarchy, which emphasises the long possession of the Crown in a particular family as the legitimizing factor in monarchy that we have tended to forget the stress put on the presentness of kingship by eighteenth-century Jacobites. What Burke did was to provide Whig arguments for Tory things. Of course, the Tories had always defended the ancient institutions of Church and King, and of course one of the reasons for loving Church and king was that they were ancient, But Tory arguments had always rested on present legitimacy. Burke's arguments were instantly available to defend historically the established institutions of England, and that is in fact how Burke's arguments were used by those calling themselves Tory in the nineteenth century.

In his own day, Burke the Whig was often accused of inconsistency. Burke led the Whig charge against the policies of George III's government which eventually alienated the American colonists into their Declaration of Independence. As an MP for Bristol, whose commercial prosperity depended on its trade with America, Burke could hardly avoid some involvement in American affairs, but that does not explain the completeness of his commitment to the Americans' cause. How, then, could such a consistent defender of American liberties turn almost overnight into the scourge of the liberties of the French? Was not French Revolution a continuation of that revolution which had already taken place in America? Some of Burke's friends on the Whig side insisted that Burke had turned his coat.

Burke always said that the language of abstract right applied without a care for the circumstances in which that language is used is bound to lead to fatal consequences. The statesman looks to what is reasonable in the circumstances and leaves the dispute about the exact boundaries of rights to the schools, for there only may they be debated with safety.

There is an exact parallel between Burke's view of the rights question in the American and French cases. In both, it was the assertion of abstract right which caused the trouble. In the case of America, it was the assertion of the essentially abstract right of the British government to tax America by the principle of parliamentary sovereignty, which led the Americans into their assertion of the equally abstract right of no taxation without representation. The forms which these two opposed assertions of right took were abstract in the sense that they were new, thought out in the protagonists' heads in defiance of established practice. Each, in its way, was an assertion of right which would upset the present state of things. And so no to the French Revolution, where the whole of the existing social and political fabric of old Europe was threatened by the assertion of rights of so abstract a kind that a whole new set of social and political institutions would have to be created in which these new-fangled rights could be embodied.

Burke's claim to consistency over America and France is therefore a good claim. The cases of the American and French Revolutions both showed what could happen if political problems were not to be resolved within the existing framework of government. Both, in Burke's eyes, represented failures to exercise adequate political skills. Again, Burke cannot lay much emphasis on the French nobility's failure to make its constitution work by reforming it, because he realizes that old Europe is going to need all the allies it can get to combat the French Revolution, the French aristocracy included. Therefore he cannot say too openly that the French aristocracy has failed its own constitution, and therefore its own nation. Any example of ruling class failure is damaging to Burke's own case for government.

The intensity of the Indian teased may well be attributed to his reverence for traditional establishments. Much of his case against the East India Company was that it had deliberately set out to destroy the ancient constitutions, laws and customs of all the proud kingdoms of the Indian sub-continent. He argued also that the Company's rule in India was already endangering the authority of the established propertied classes at home, by creating a despicable new breed of nouveaux riches who were bringing home untold plunder from their service in India.

It is clear enough that Burke did not see the Revolution as a transfer of power to a substantial bourgeoisie, nor as removing feudal obstacles to a respectable bourgeois order that was waiting, to emerge. Indeed he argued that, on the contrary, Revolution might well be as damaging to commerce and industry as he expected it would be to the civilised arts and learning, since they had all grown to their present strength under the protection of the old regime:

> commerce, and trade, and manufacture, the gods of our oeconomical politicians certainly grew under the same shade in which learning flourished. They too may decay with their natural protecting principles. With you, for the present at least, they all threaten to disappear together.

The transfer of power to the pettyfogging National Assembly he saw as a threat to, not an instrument of, capitalist advance ill France. Besides, for all his historic bent, Burke believed at firmly as his very unhistorically minded contemporary, Bentham, that an attack on *any* established system of property was threat to *every* kind of property. The innate rapacity of those with small or no property must run wild when any established system was breached. The present breach must be as devastating to emergent capitalism in France as it would be to established capitalism in England if the revolution were copied there. This was no mere abstract speculation, nor was it based only on history: it was already happening in France where the revolutionary government, moving on from their confiscation of the church lands:

> have at length ventured completely to subvert all property of all descriptions throughout the extent of a great kingdom. They have compelled all men, in all transactions of commerce, in the disposal of lands, in civil dealing, and through the whole communion of life, to accept as perfect payment and good and lawful tender, the symbols speculations on a projected sale of their plunder.

Moreover, only on the assumption that Burke had some notion, however unclear, that there was in France a substantial bourgeois interest, is there any sense in his belief that the revolution in France could have been a mild Whig revolution. Yet that was his belief. The old French constitution, with its checks on royal power, could have been restored, as the English one had been in 1689.

> Had you made it to be understood that you were resolved to resume your ancient privileges, whilst you preserved the spirit of your ancient and your recent loyalty and honour; or, if diffident of yourselves, and not clearly discerning the almost obliterated

> constitution of your ancestors, you had looked to your neighbors in this land, who had kept alive the ancient principles and models of the old common law of Europe meliorated and adapted to its present state by following wise examples you would have given new examples of wisdom to the world.

The French monarchy was not incapable of reform. The wealth and the population of the country had been steadily increasing, evidence enough that its government was not

> So oppressive, or so corrupt, or so negligent, as to be utterly unfit for all reformation, I must think such a government well deserved to have its excellencies heightened; its faults corrected; and its capacities improved into a British constitution.

Burke's alarm about the French Revolution went deeper. He saw that the principles on which it was based would, if they were successfully exported, totally undermine the established order in England and the rest of Euroge. They must therefore be countered by principles more substantive than those he had so far deployed. The English ruling class had until now treated Burke's principles as a paper tiger. Now he had to persuade them that the threat was real, and that it was an immediate threat to their whole way of life, that is, to their property. To do this he had to invest his divine and natural law with some property substance. He did not abandon his rhetoric-it even reached new height but now he backed it with some down-to-earth economic principles.

Conclusion

Burke prided himself on being a hard-working practical politician, on exposing whatever abuses he found in the British system of government, and pressing for moderate reforms which would prevent future abuses whether at home or in the handling of the colonial empire in Ireland, America and India. His record of activity in this role is indeed impressive. But had he been no more than such an active politician his work would not now be of interest to any except eighteenth century historians. What more was there? Why should his speeches and writings, most of which were partisan pleadings on some issue of the day, still command attention?

There is no dispute about the wide variations in the way he has been seen and the grounds on which his writings have been celebrated. Through most of his active life his work had been valued by moderate reforming Whigs as a reasoned support of their position, as in his exposure of the inroads he saw being made on the independence of Parliament by the Court, his case against the government's policy on the American colonies, and his sustained attack on the arbitrary rule of the chartered East India Company. Then quite suddenly, in the last decade of his life he appeared in a new character, as the scourge of the liberal egalitarian ideas unleashed by the French Revolution, the great defender of traditional hierarchical society against die menacing theory and practice of that revolution. This brought him a much wider acclaim than any he had previously enjoyed, and from a different quarter. George III, of whose policies bad been a very vocal critic, went so far as to say, after publication of Burke's *Reflections on the Revolution in Franc* (1790), 'You have been of use to us all... I know that there *i* no Man who calls himself a Gentleman who must not think himself obliged to you, for you have supported the cause of the Gentlemen. Other crowned heads in Europe equally impressed. Even the rationalist Edward Gibbon, who could not have relished Burke's insistence that the Christ religion was the indispensable basis of political stability, congratulated Burke on his *Reflections* as 'a most admirable medicine against the French disease'. The impression of Burke as the arch-conservative seemed indelibly fixed: his crusade against the French Revolution had eclipsed all his other works.

But in the nineteenth century Burke was made over into a utilitarian liberal. His French crusade was set aside as something of an aberration. Attention was focused instead on his earlier writings and speeches. The record there was very different: vigorous foe of the Court party, of autocratic government, of the kinds of British imperialism then prevailing in America, Ireland and India; friend of the commercial interest, informed critic of economic policies, and advocate of a self-regulating market economy, friend of religious toleration; and of course defender of the Whig Revolution. Here then was a worthy successor to John Locke, the founding father of the Whig theory, whose work was now a century out of date. In that character he was held in contempt by Marx, who called him 'the celebrated sophist and sycophant' and 'an out and out vulgar bourgeois'; but the nineteenth-century liberals honoured him for that position.

But while Burke was merciless at that idle rich he was by on means a leveler. As Kramnick has pointed out, Burke's position then was substantially a bourgeois one: property should be secure, but the duty of proprietors was to improve their properties so as to increase the wealth of the nation to the benefit of all classes. It would not be too much to see in this undergraduate performance the manifesto of a thrusting young man who was aware that he had unusual talent but realised that his future could only be that of a self-made man. This would require coming to terms with the establishment and moving within it. But that prospect was not too daunting, since he already subscribed to its cardinal value, the sanctity of property. His task would be to persuade his betters that they would be still better if they would anchor their property in something other than absentee landlordism. Had he confined his efforts to Ireland this would have been difficult. But in England, where many of the great aristocratic landowners were already operating on improving commercial principles, this was not such a problem. This would give Burke the opening he needed, and not long afterwards he was able to tab advantage of it.

The liberal view in the nineteenth and twentieth centuries has been that his ideas rightly command our attention because Burke infused every particular issue with general principles. He is credited with raising politics far above the mean and unprincipled skirmishing for office and spoils which it had become in the mid-eighteenth century with the disappearance of the old difference of principle between Whigs and Tories. He insisted that every issue should be debated in terms of some standard of justice or right or long-run human benefit, rather than of mere legal rights or short-run expediency; and this insistence, in the House of Commons and in pamphlets and books and speeches outside the House, compelled his opponents to move to that higher ground. Nineteenth and twentieth century liberals, who were apt to think that the liberalism of their own time needed the same sort of moral injection, could not but regard this as a significant achievement. Thus John Morley in 1867 said: "Burke brought the dead Whig principles up from out of the grave, and kindled a life in them, which has only just flickered out forever in our own days'. And again:

> No one that ever lived used the general ideas of the thinker more successfully to judge the particular problems of the statesman. No one has ever come so close to the details of practical politics, and at the same time remembered that these can only be understood and only dealt with by the aid of the broad conceptions of political philosophy.

Similarly Harold Laski wrote:

> No English statesman has ever more firmly moved amid a mass of details to the principle they involve. He had an unerring eye for the eternal principles of politics. He knew that ideals must be harnessed to an Act of Parliament if they are not to cease their influence. Admitting while he did that politics must rest upon expediency, he never failed to find good reason why expediency should be identified with what he saw as right.

This liberal view of Burke, though couched in such extravagant terms, does not claim him as a great theorist or political philosopher: the only claim is that he revivified political practice bringing it back to some moral principles. The liberals did not inquire how thorough or consistent those principles were. They could not have claimed Burke as a theorist, for very good reason. During the whole period in which Burke could be claimed as a liberal, that is down to 1790, Burke neither was nor wished to be a political theorist, and even after 1790 it was only against his will that he was forced into theorising. Scorn for abstract theory was a constant refrain of his output as a reforming politician. Again and again he argued that it was unrealistic, even disastrous, to try to deduce practical policy from abstract principles. He wrote:

> It is melancholy as well as ridiculous, to observe the kind of reasoning with which the public has been amused, in order to divert our minds from the common sense of our American policy. There are people who have split and anatomised the doctrine of free government as if it were an abstract question concerning metaphysical liberty and necessity; and not a matter of moral prudence and natural feeling. They have disputed, whether liberty be a positive or a negative idea; whether it does not consist in being governed by laws; without considering what are the laws, or who are the makers; whether man has any rights by nature; and whether all the property he enjoys, be not the alms of his government, and his life itself their favour and indulgence of another kind, speculations are let loose as destructive to all authority, as the former are to all freedom; and every government is called tyranny and usurpation which is not formed on their fancies.

> Civil freedom, gentlemen, is not, as many have endeavoured to persuade you, a thing that lies hid in the depth of abstruse science. It a blessing and a benefit, not an abstract speculation; and all the just reasoning that can be upon it, is of so coarse a texture, as perfectly to suit the ordinary capacities of those who are to enjoy, and of those who are to defend it. Far from any resemblance to those propositions in geometry and metaphysics, which admit no medium, but must be true or false in all their latitude; social and civil freedom, all the other things in common life, are variously mixed and modified, enjoyed in very different degrees, and shaped into an infinite diversity of forms, according to the temper and circumstances of every community.

This particular rejection of abstract theory may well be ascribed to Burke's perception that its use by both sides in the war of American Independence had contributed to their intransigence and was impeding a rational peace:

> ... whether liberty be advantageous or not, (for I know it is a fashion to decry the very principle) none will dispute that peace is a blessing; and peace must in the course of human affairs be frequently bought by some indulgence and toleration at least to liberty.

Burke's appeal to the leaders of public opinion on both sides to abandon their stand on theory was the only way he could see to break out of the political impasse. Had he been a theorist, his appropriate response would have been to expose the fallacies of one or both of the two theoretical cases by a more adequate theoretical analysis; but that was not his way. Similarly, in his efforts to restore the 'true' principles of the Whig settlement of 1689, he was practitioner, not theorist. A theorist would have seen a need to reconstruct Locke's theoretical justification of the principles of 1689, to rework it so as to meet the damaging criticisms implicit in the work of Hume but again that was not Burke's way. The liberal view of Burke as a non-theorist seems amply vindicated. The twentieth-century neo-conservative readings of Burke, on the contrary, rank him as a masterly political philosopher. Thus Parkin says:

> ... while Burke's thought is by design a response to immediate contingencies, it is in no sense an uncontrolled or arbitrary response, but always, in his own eyes, under the guidance of moral principles, which represent themselves unchanging truths of human life and community. Burke's political thought always leans toward a still centre of the most general and absolute belief. His ideas carry all the marks and associations of their origin, but they converge on core of moral certainty freed finally from the relative and the contingent.

Similarly Stanlis, arguing that Burke's great achievement was to restore the classical and scholastic Natural Law to its rightful place as the fundamental moral principle of politics, holds that the true nature of Burke's cardinal political principles can not be understood apart from its connection with the Natural Law, and that his political philosophy supplies a superb solution to the persistent confusions and doubts of those who still rely on the utilitarian or positivist or materialist traditions. Stanlis goes on to assert:

> In every important political problem he ever faced, in Irish, American, constitutional, economic, Indian, and French affairs, Burke' always appealed to the Natural Law. What is more, by Natural Law Burke always meant essentially the same thing, and he applied it as ultimate test of justice and liberty in all human affairs.

But it is clear that for the neo-conservatives Burke was essentially a political philosopher. In view of this disparity between the liberal and conservative of Burke's stature as a thinker it seems worthwhile to examine with more care than has been usual, just how much appeal to principle there is in his work.

It is common ground among all students of Burke's work that such appeal to principle as he did make was, throughout his political career, only what he thought would be efficacious making his case on some current issue: British government policy in Ireland, America, India; the supposed assault of the Crown on British liberties; and finally, the menace of French Revolution principles, especially of their insidious influence in England, as in the propaganda of Priestley, Price, Paine, and their adherents.

Burke's denunciation of the French Revolution is thus not only consistent with, but logically follows from his praise of the Whig Revolution. And since he linked the Whig Revolution with the 'improved domestic prosperity that had then commenced in England, and condemned the French Revolution as having 'laid the axe to foe root of all property, and consequently of all national prosperity', it is perhaps not too much to see a bourgeois consistency in his treatment of the two revolutions.

However, to return to Burke's overriding concern with the situation in England, he was not entirely wrong in treating the capitalist society there as traditional society. It is true that the market was not yet absolutely triumphant in England. Humanitarian voices from within the establishment were still sometimes raised against it. This made it all the more important for Burke to try to prevent such voices being pressed into common cause with the much more dangerous new French ideology.

His genius was in seeing that the capitalist society of the late eighteenth century was still heavily dependent on the acceptance of status. Contract had not replaced status: it was dependent on status. Burke's historical view was, for his time at least, more valid than the view of nineteenth-century analysts such as Sir Henry Maine. Burke saw that, down to his own time, such movement as there had been was not from status to contract but from status to status, that is, from a feudal status differentiation, which rested on military capacity, to an internalized status differentiation, which rested on nothing more than habit and tradition, that is, on the subordinate class continuing to accept its traditional station in life. With no more solid basis than that, it could easily be undermined. Burke, recognizing that fragility, had no recourse except to enlist Christian Natural Law in its aid. And this did no violence to the Christian Natural Law. It had always upheld a traditional social order against any threats. Now the content of the social order had changed, and in England it had changed long enough ago that the new content had already become traditional. So the Natural Law could now appropriately be used to defend the new-traditional social order against new threats the more so since the new content utilised the old form seeing that he had put a new bourgeois content into Natural Law. That misses Burke's real insight. And it begs the question of how useful a return to Burke would be in the late twentieth century.

Burke's insistence on the rule of law, on constitutional versus arbitrary government, and on the respect due to property, is agreeable to both conservatives and liberals. And his case for letting a natural aristocracy interpret and implement the real will of the people would be welcome enough to both; though they might not be willing to avow it, it is not too far from the idea of meritocracy to which they both subscribe in some measure. The real difficulty seems to lie in Burke's idea of distributive justice: the just distribution of the national product is that which the free market allots to those who enter the market from positions of class domination and subordination. That concept of justice cannot now be accepted or avowed by either conservatives or liberals; and it seems to be especially obnoxious to welfare-state liberals, since they start from the postulate of equal natural rights.

Nevertheless, the most renowned current liberal theory of distributive justice, namely John Rawls's *A Theory of Justice* is not fundamentally different from Burke's. Rawls accepts the welfare-state distribution up to a certain limit, but the limit is set on precisely the same principle as Burke's zero limit, Rawls holds that state interference with the market, intended to be in the interests of the poor, must stop short of the point at which it would make everybody, including the poor, worse off; and that that point is reached when the degree of Interference would discourage enterprisers from continuing their work of maximising efficient production. This was also Burke's position. The only difference is that Burke argued that any interference would have this effect, whereas the twentieth century liberals have learned from experience that capitalist enterprise is still very active when it has to contend with the present quite substantial amount of interference. The difference is not one of principle but of empirical judgement. It appears, then that if current liberals were to point this out they might well enlist Burke, the more readily in view of Burke's lifelong insistence that circumstances alter cases and that statesmen and projectors should always devise their policies in the light of changing circumstances.

But the risks of enlisting Burke in this way would be considerable, for the change in circumstances between his time and ours is greater. The liberal task now is different from Burke's task. His was to persuade the English ruling class to resist any ideas which would weaken the still prevailing working-class acceptance of the established hierarchical order. He did not have to speak to the working class, nor did he do so. Now, however, the main liberal task is to legitimate the presently established modified capitalist order, or some variant of it, in the eyes of a somewhat politically conscious and quite strongly organised Western working class. And this has to be done in quite changed international circumstances.

No one was more aware than Burke that national policies needed to be framed in the light of the international situation. But when Burke died in 1797, the egalitarianism of the French revolutionary theory and practice, while it was indeed a menace to the established English and European order, was still just a menace. Its outcome was still uncertain. It is so no longer. Now, the egalitarian principle is the official ideology of the communist world and the Third World, and their acceptance of it lies uneasily on the conscience of liberals in the Western world, who are not at all sure that the Western devotion to the egalitarian principle is more than skin-deep.

The twentieth-century liberals' problem is compounded in so far as they recognise that the utilitarian case for capitalism is no longer morally adequate. Moral theorists and political economists in the eighteenth century and well into the nineteenth could make a reasonable case for capitalism on the ground that a system of competitive enterprise moved by capital's search for profit would maximize production and hence promote maximum general benefit. But as capitalism has moved away from pure competition to oligopoly and monopoly it has become evident that capital's devotion to profit no longer necessarily maximises production or general benefit: in the circumstances maximum profit is not tied to maximum productivity. To the extent that this is recognised, the potential usefulness of Burke's principles is further diminished. Not must a case be made to a different national and international audience, it must be made without one of the main moral props of the old case.

The twentieth-century democrats, both liberal and conservative, share with Burke, the non-democrat, the caption that what is at stake is the legitimating of a social and that this is ultimately a question of moral values share, also, some of Burke's most general moral values. Macpherson gives a caution that they heed Burke's warning about the vital necessity of adjusting principles to concrete circumstances and they must think twice about recruiting him. By his insistence on the importance of circumstances Burke ruled himself out of court for the late twentieth century.

12

Jeremy Bentham

> Indeed, pain and pleasure are the two 'sovereign masters' that govern us in all we do, in all we say, in all we think and it is for them alone to point out what we ought to do.

Jeremy Bentham (1748-1832) was born in 1748 into a Tory family at a time when Tories and Jacobites were indistinguishable in the eyes of their Whig opponents. These were not auspicious circumstances for the infant prodigy who was to become one of the great radical thinkers of the late eighteenth and early nineteenth centuries. Bentham went through the ordinary course of education of the comfortable bourgeoisie, first at home, then at Westminster School, and then at Queen's College, Oxford, which he left at the age of fifteen.

Like other fathers, Jeremiah Bentham wanted his son bred up in his own profession of the law, and so young Jeremy entered into Lincoln's Inn in 1763, but as things turned out, Bentham was less interested in laws than in legal science. Very early on Bentham conceived a plan of legal science on a vast scale, to which he devoted the whole of the rest of his long life.

Bentham was radical in the literal sense of going to the root. He thought that all law which had not been thought out from coherent first principle was in fact likely to be founded on nothing. Most law was therefore fraudulent. Law, to adapt an anachronism, was all superstructure with no basis. This was especially true of English law. English law was a lawyers' racket which needed root and branch reform. Law science was to be understood in the widest sense to include criminology and penology. This last was to connect Bentham's name for ever to the Panopticon, the famous design for a prison in which a single sharp-eyed gaoler could, as the spider at the center of the web, keep all the prisoners under constant supervision. Parliament shillied and shallied over the Panopticon, eventually buying Bentham off with the considerable sum for those days of £ 23,000, and the only Panopticon ever built was at Joliet for the use of the citizens of the progressive state of Illinois.

Bentham became convinced that a new science of law was impossible to construct using language inherited from unregenerated legal systems. His later writings are therefore much concerned with the invention of a new legal babble whose superiority to the old is by no means obvious. This did not affect his worldwide reputation as a legal reformer, and when Bentham died in 1832 he was one of the most famous Englishmen of his age.

Mad genius Bentham was working from six in the morning until ten at night with time out only to jog around his garden, writing 15 folio pages every day, yet virtually incapable of finishing anything; keeping a keyboard instrument in every room of his house; arranging that after his death his body should be preserved as an "auto-icon" to inspire his followers. Brilliantly inventive, he envisioned not only the notorious "panopticon" model prison, school, poor house, or whatever built like a spider-web with the "keeper" at its center – but also such devices as a primitive telephone, a system for multiple music printing, reforms for the London police, a central heating system, a law school run from his home; schemes for reducing the national debt, detecting forged bank notes, and securing low-interest loans for the poor; a national system of public education, a national health service, a national census; a "frigidarium" for storing food at low temperatures, and a canal to be dug through Central America to connect the Atlantic and Pacific Oceans. In love with words, Bentham bequeathed us an astonishing array of neologisms, including "maximize" and "minimize," "codify," "international", "rationale," "eulogistic," "demoralize," "deontology," and "false consciousness."

The early English liberal program sought to develop a political environment, which would stimulate and sustain the growth of individuality. Based upon a tradition of natural-rights speculation, early liberalism attempted to protect individuals by creating for them a private space within the public realm. The individual's right to property, the freedom of religious belief, and a citizen's right to resist governmental oppression functioned in such a way as to create for people a private sphere within which they could partially determine their own destiny while being shielded from social control. As England moved into the nineteenth century, however, certain changes occurred which disrupted the original equilibrium of the former age. One was at the theoretical level, where the natural-rights tradition, which had originally supplied the ethical basis for political liberalism, came under increasing strain and criticism. Inasmuch as natural-rights theory presupposed that human beings could know their original rights, it was based upon the rationalistic assumption that humans were capable of discovering specific universal principles, which existed independently of particular historical and social conditions.

The thinking of David Hume (1711-1776) was typical of this development. Hume radicalized the teachings of English empiricism by pushing them to their logical limits until he arrived at a thoroughgoing skepticism. According to Hume, the human mind can know neither cause nor effect, and without this knowledge it can never achieve an understanding of the nature of reality itself. While Hume's skepticism obviously challenged the rationalistic assumptions of modern science, it also served to undermine the very foundations of natural-rights philosophy. Hume argued that as the mind cannot know nature, it is at the same time incapable of knowing what is naturally right or what is naturally just. Thus, those moral doctrines which claimed a knowledge of the natural law were in fact mere fictions. Indeed, according to Hume, reason is incapable of judging the truth or falsity of any moral proposition. Reason cannot teach humanity how to act because it cannot know which desires are naturally good and which are by their nature evil. Thus rather than guiding the passions, reason is ultimately their slave.

Hume's analysis led to the obvious conclusion that natural rights do not exist. From his perspective, all morality was simply a matter of convention, and convention, in turn, was simply a matter of convenience. With this criticism, then, political liberalism faced a fundamental crisis. As the natural-rights tradition became increasingly questionable, liberalism was threatened with the eventual loss of its own ethical foundation. Thus if liberalism were to remain an ethically defensible political doctrine, it would have to develop a moral theory which could confront the challenge of a radically skeptical empiricism.

The second challenge to early liberalism come from changes in the English economic and social order. By the nineteenth century England was beginning to experience the first effects of the industrial revolution. The large scale introduction of machinery in the production process had a number of important, if unintended consequences. For example, mechanized technology increased the division of labor and, thereby, reutilized the tasks of production. The increased division of labor, however, required more planning and consequently encouraged the centralization of administrative authority. Similarly the use of coal power markedly increased the economy's productive capacities. This, in turn, created the need for more workers and eventually led to the rapid expansion of the urban areas. Rapidly growing cities, however, demanded new techniques of the municipal governance and soon challenged the adequacy of the traditional English system of political representation. Most importantly, however, the sudden development of industrial wealth led to the emergence of new classes whose appearance constituted a challenge to the older social order. The bourgeoisie not only threatened the prerogatives of the landed aristocracy, but at the same time it was separated from the working classes because of a growing disparity in wealth and social power. As this disparity increased, class antagonism intensified.

Each of these developments eventually created its own specific for the liberalism associated with such natural-rights theorists as John Locke. For Locke and others, government was to act both as an impartial judge and as a protector of individual rights. Therefore, it was to refrain as much as possible from intervening in the economic and social processes of its day. As the social and economic environment changed in response to industrialization, however, liberalism's formal commitment to the safeguarding of rights had the substantive effect of protecting and preserving distinct social and economic privileges. As a consequence, its theoretical impartiality actually appeared to favor the partisan interests of the commercial classes. As the demands upon government increased, it became more and more apparent that liberalism would have to assume an activist attitude towards social issues. Whereas the extremely individualistic perspective of the natural-rights tradition had only allowed for a minimal level of governmental involvement in economic affairs, the political realities of the day seemed to dictate a more positive proactive approach.

Given this situation, then utilitarianism may be understood as liberalism's response to the intellectual and social crises which were characteristic of nineteenth-century English society. Among the utilitarian reformers, were Jeremy Bentham, James Mill and his son John Stuart Mill. Utilitarianism is not, strictly speaking, a problem of philosophy, but it is a problematic approach to moral philosophy which has always attracted both ardent defenders and ardent opponents. Seen by its enthusiasts as a down-to earth and liberating theory which enjoins an empirical attitude to practical decision-making and refuses to accept the tyranny of questionable moral conventions, utilitarianism has been condemned by the more severe of its critics as a pernicious doctrine which treats our most precious values with scorn and prescribes the universal sacrifice to principle of expediency. Between the extremes, of course, there are more muted shades of opinion. Many philosophers have granted the intuitive appeal to core utilitarian idea while remaining dubious about the theory's ultimate adequacy. Perhaps the best that can currently be said about utilitarianism is that it is a very bad form of moral philosophy, but that all the others are so much worse. Some philosophers professed that the days of utilitarianism are numbered. Some wrote premature obituaries. Reports of the death, or imminent demise of utilitarianism have been greatly exaggerated. Utilitarianism is destroyed,' claimed John Plamenatz in 1949, and no part of it left standing. Yet there was still enough life left in the corpse a quarter of a century later. It is premature on part of Bernard Williams to hope that 'The day cannot be too far off in which we hear no more of it'. Twenty years further on we hear as much about utilitarianism as we ever did, and the flow of new writings on the subject is unceasing. For a viewpoint often accused of simple-mindedness, utilitarianism has demonstrated a striking ability and tenacity to go on stimulating forceful and subtle argument on both sides of the case. John Stuart Mill believed that the appeal of utilitarianism was perennial. In every age of philosophy, he thought, one of its schools had been utilitarian. But in every era too, the doctrine had provoked virulent opposition: from a very early period, the theory of utility had by some been designated as 'utterly mean and groveling and worthy only of swine'.

Utilitarianism during the Christian Middle Ages was not a philosophy; but it was occasionally a style of argument. St. Thomas Aquinas held that a state might legitimately permit prostitution to avert greater sin. Although it might sometimes be futile to the confessing person to reveal a sin disclosed under the seal of secrecy, it is more conducive to public good to maintain the absolute confidentiality of the sacrament. Such examples of utilitarian logic are fairly common, but they do not amount to an outlook on life. Whatever Christ himself may have thought, the medieval Church saw the present life as pre-eminently a period of probation determining man's destination for eternity. Happiness in the next world, not this, was what counted; and man's business on earth was to earn that happiness by scrupulous adherence to God's law. Saints took rejection of worldly happiness further still: they endeavored to earn extra merit by eschewing all earthly comforts and deliberately cultivating ascetism. Generally speaking, the Middle Ages was not a period of optimism about human possibilities; the perceived distance between divine perfection and human imperfection was simple too great.

The Renaissance initiated the long process of transition from a God-centred to a man-centred universe. Neoplatonist philosophers reacted against medieval notions of human worthlessness, and reasserted ancient ideas of the dignity of man, the uniquely rational animal. The seventeenth century also witnessed a revival of interest in the thought of Epicurus, culminating in France. Meanwhile in England Thomas Hobbes's *Leviathan* gave serious weight to the fact that people have an interest in being happy in the present life, and proposed political strategies for dealing with the conflicts of interests that inevitably arise from human insecurity, vanity and greed.

The eighteenth century was the green youth of utilitarianism, as the nineteenth was its prime. Almost of all the characteristic theses of utilitarianism had made their appearance by 1800, many of them before the advent of the term utilitarian. Utilitarianism has been justly called the dominant philosophy of the mature Enlightenment. It could also be seen a socially progressive philosophy, for many existing political, social, economic, legal and religious institutions loved by conservatives appeared plainly defective by the test of public happiness. Utilitarianism embodied, too, rationalism that seemed admirably fitted to sweep away moribund ideas and the profitless practices they sustained. It gave hope to men like Condercet who believed passionately in the perfectibility of man and the possibility of true human happiness on earth. Writing in the shadow of the guillotine, Condercet looked forward to a future epoch of the world in which no one would go hungry, when all illness could be cured and life expectancy increased without limit, slaves would be free and women gain equality with man, war would be abolished and the arts and education flourish.

Utilitarian ideas appealed also for their secular, this-worldly character, their unindebtedness to Jerusalem, Rome or Geneva. They answered to the philosophers' demand for a non-religious, rational morality, which would treat human being as ends in themselves in their lives as valuable irrespective of their place in a divine plan. Moreover, utilitarianism ascribed to all human beings an equal moral status, regardless of race, sex, age or class. Kant defined 'Enlightenment' as the 'exit by man from his own self-imposed minority', when he begins to rely on his own understanding and rejects the guidance of others. Utilitarian moral thought was enlightened in this Kantian sense: utilitarian refused to be guided by authority, and insisted on working out their own positions from first principles.

Chastellux and Helvetius exemplify perhaps better than any other writers the specific flavor of utilitarianism in pre-revolutionary France. Both were deeply committed to the improvement of the condition of the poor and believed that governments had a duty to foster the general good; both thought that as Helvetius put it, 'wise laws would be able without doubt to bring about the miracle of a universal happiness.' For these writers, as for others of their compatriots, utilitarianism was primarily a political philosophy and less a theory of personal morality. Further, it was a philosophy which offered what seemed to them a clear-cut and highly practical recipe for political action: government should first of all find out what makes people happy, then devise appropriate social strategies to bring about that happiness.

A more powerful thinker than Chastellux, Helvetius is the most important, and the most forthright of the Gallic utilitarians. Although some of his early readers objected to the relentlessly egoistic picture of human beings he painted, Helvetius believed that through carefully managed education individuals could be moulded into cooperative citizens of communities enjoying a high level of general happiness. Helvetius's intended target was not individuality, but the gross social disparities of rich and poor in eighteenth-century Europe. French utilitarianism was not so much careless of the individual, as careful of the mass of people whose interests were invariably subordinated to those of rich and powerful minorities. The clarion call of public happiness in a pre-democratic age evoked different emotions, and raised different conceptual issues. Our present worries about the interests of individuals and minorities are premised on the political power of the majority in modern western states. What rightly mattered more to an eighteenth-century utilitarian was the domination of the many by the few. All men, Helvetius believed, had a right to an 'equal felicity' and philosophers should help to ensure that they obtained it.

The Scottish philosopher Francis Hutcheson was the first to speak of the greatest happiness of the greatest number; more importantly, he bears the distinction of being their earliest writer to enunciate a philosophy that can without qualification be termed 'utilitarian'. Hutcheson wanted to accord a considerable role to consequentiality reasoning in the evaluation of actions. When we judge and compare actions, we need to weigh up rationally a number of factors: the amount of happiness or misery they will generate, the number of people potentially affected, and the dignity or moral importance of the persons, concerned.

Hutcheson believes that we are naturally inclined to want, and to work for our own happiness and that of other people. As for what happiness is, it consists for any being, 'in the full enjoyment of all the gratifications its desires and is capable of obtaining them.' But he immediately explains that pleasures can be divided into higher and lower categories, and that greater happiness ensures from pursuing the former than the latter. Higher pleasures tend to be more durable and more dignified than lower pleasures, though not always intense. Such passages look backward to Epicurus, as well as forward to J.S.Mill. But Hutcheson is at his most strikingly similar to J.S. Mill when he attempts to locate a criterion by which higher pleasures may be distinguished from lower ones. Like J.S.Mill, Hutcheson believes that people do not necessarily possess equal happiness when each can gratify all the desires and senses he has.

Pleasures can be meaningfully distinguished as higher and lower only by a criterion which makes reference to values other than pleasure alone. Hutcheson's socially elitist form of the criterion is no more satisfactory. Most eighteenth-century's 'superior people' preferred the delights of the hunting field or the ballroom to the pleasures of poetry and art. Hutcheson sometimes appears to abandon his social conception of superior beings, and consider them instead as the people who possess divine faculties and fuller knowledge. Hutcheson's moral philosophy is not always perfectly clear, consistent or cogent, but it is an intriguing and suggestive system which deserves closer attention than it usually receives. More than any other writer, Hutcheson deserves the title of father of British utilitarianism. His work contains, if sometimes in rudimentary form, most of the ideas which were characteristic of utilitarianism in its early period. All the leitmotifs of utilitarianism can be found in his books. Hutcheson was a consequentialist who believed that happiness was the proper target of human action. He never questioned both happiness and misery were aggregative commodities. And he held that we should always endeavor to maximize the happiness and minimize the misery of the largest number of people whom we are able to affect. Hutcheson did not grasp all the possibilities of utilitarianism, or foresee all of its problems. But his very considerable achievement was to lay the solid foundations on which others would build.

David Hume combined, in a highly original way, a theory of moral sense with a rejection of moral realism. By this Hume did not mean that things are determined as good or bad simply according to whether they give us pleasure or its opposite; rather, moral feeling are feelings of a special kind which we entertain about certain characters, actions and states of affairs. Moral judgments express these feelings of approbation and disapprobation; they do not ascribe objective moral qualities to things. Hume's theory of moral judgment has been very reasonably regarded as foreshadowing twentieth-century non-congnitivist theories of ethics. We are all, he thought, naturally capable of caring about the welfare of others, even if our benevolent and sympathetic sentiments are often overborne by our egoism. There is no such passion, he suggested, as the love of mankind, yet if we are not capable of loving humanity in the abstract, we are able to feel an altruistic concern even about total strangers once we are brought into contact with them: this ability to feel for the happiness and suffering of others, Hume believed, to be the psychological basis of our moral sentiments: 'we approve of voluntary actions which increase people's happiness; we disapprove of those which increase their misery'. Such 'principles of humanity' have a considerable influence on our actions. They likewise 'have some authority over our sentiments, and give us a general approbation of what is useful to society, and blame of what is dangerous or pernicious'. This notion of utility underpins our concepts of virtue and vice: 'we pronounce any quality of the mind virtuous, which causes love or pride; and any one vicious, which causes hatred or humility'.

Hume, unusually among the early utilitarians, was a conservative in politics, a Tory who disbelieved that the cause of public happiness required any substantial changes to the social status quo. But Hume contributed much more to the development of the theory. He demonstrated more forcefully than his predecessors had done how well utilitarian principles fitted into a demystified, naturalized conception of the moral life. His vigorous attack on moral realism and his subtle analysis of the psychology and phenomenology of moral experience indeed seemed to leave moral philosophy with nowhere else to go. Hume thought it a simple 'matter of fact that sentiments of humanity and sympathy lead human beings to approve or disapprove of actions, virtues and practices on the basis of their utility. Hence utility is the foundation of morals, which has a reference to mankind and our fellow creatures. Hume may have been no radical in politics, but he was uncompromising in his support for the central tenet of utilitarianism.

Bentham was the son and grandson of lawyers working in the City of London and was intended by his father to follow and surpass them as a practicing lawyer. However, while following his legal studies, Bentham became disgusted with the current state of English law and so, rather than making money by the practice of the law as it is, he turned instead to a study of what the law might be. This study formed the center of his long life, during which he wrote an enormous amount of manuscript material on law, economics, politics, and philosophy which naturally arises from these subjects.

His first important writing, the *Fragment on Government of* 1776, was an attack on William Blackstone's *Commentaries on the Laws of England* (1765-9), a work whose complacent satisfaction in the English statute book and legal system seemed to Bentham intolerable. Bentham's treatise, the opening salvo in his life-long campaign against the irrationalities of the law and the obscurantism and self-seeking of its practitioners, proclaimed on its very first page that: 'It is the greatest happiness of the greatest number that is the measure of right and wrong.' The prime task ahead, was to carry out a careful and methodical investigation of this 'fundamental axiom'. All his subsequent writings were contributions to this central project. With enormous singlemindedness and boundless energy, Bentham devoted the whole of his long career to spelling out the practical implications of the basic principles he had accepted in his youth. Before any proposals could be drawn upon for the reform of social institutions, he commenced his theorizing with an account of the nature of man. Works like *An Introduction to the Principles of Morals and Legislation (1780)* and *A Table of the Springs of Action (1815)* accordingly discuss the variety of human motivations, and attempt to demonstrate their reducibility to the promptings of the 'two sovereign masters', pleasure and pain. Bentham also interested himself in specific projects for criminological and penological reform, which the most notable was the scheme for a 'panopticon' model reformatory in which the inmates could be overseen and controlled by their jailers throughout all hours of the day and night. The essence of Bentham's view of right and wrong, from which he never deviated, was set out in a few brisk sentences of the *Fragment on Government*.

The Hedonic Calculus

Bentham thought that utility is something that is measurable, quantitative, scientific, and objective. Here we have the fundamentals of Bentham's quantitative hedonism. The aspect of pleasure primarily of concern to him is the amount of it, since quantity is something measurable. In examining the consequences of our possible action, we can determine the quantity of pain and pleasure produced by them and thereby determine which of the options open to us would bring about the greatest balance of pleasure over pain, or the smallest possible amount of pain. It is in Chapter 5 that Bentham develops what has come to be called the 'hedonic calculus'. This calculus is a quasi-mathematical system for measuring the amount of pleasure and pain brought about by an action, and thus is a system for determining the utilities that should guide our decisions to do one thing rather than another.

The key to the hedonic calculus is the recognition that pleasure and pain have different dimensions each of which is measurable. They may vary from one another in their duration: one of them may simply last longer than this, some pains dull or low level, others excruciating. Less obviously, pleasures and pains can be considered under the aspect of their certainty or uncertainty. Some actions will lead to pain with absolute certainty other actions are more problematic in this regard. Similarly, some actions will undoubtedly lead to pleasure while others may or may not do so. Furthermore, there is the fact that pleasures and pains may vary with regard to the time when they can be expected to occur: some actions lead to immediate pleasures, others to long-delayed ones. Pain follows immediately upon some actions; in other case it take a while before the pain occurs. Bentham refers to this aspect of pleasure and pain as their propinquity or remoteness. Thus the first four dimensions of pleasure/pain to be measured by the hedonic calculus are: intensity, duration, certainty, propinquity.

In applying the calculus, we are to measure each of the pleasures and pains consequent upon each of the several actions upon us. We do this by assigning a number registering the intensity, a number representing the duration, and number expressing the certainty / uncertainty and the propinquity / remoteness of each pleasure and pain. Positive numbers signify the amount of pleasure, negative numbers the amount of pain. The number representing the intensity and duration of a particular pleasure, insofar as the value of a pleasure is decreased by its uncertainty and remoteness and increased by its certainty and nearness, we can use fractions representing the degree of uncertainty and the distance to reduce the magnitude accordingly. Calculations of this sort will yield a value for each pleasure, and, mutatis mutandis, for each pain.

There are still other dimensions of pleasure/pain. Some pleasures have the tendency to produce in their turn, or to be, followed by, yet other pleasures, and some pains have the tendency to generate still other pains. The mild pleasures involved in studying or doing homework are likely to be followed by other pleasures that result from getting a good grade in class. The pain of a hangover is likely to lead to other pains – as when one takes an exam infirm with the hangover and gets a bad grade as a result. Thus a pleasure or pain has what Bentham calls its fecundity – "the chance it has of being followed by sensations of the same kind". Presumably, we can measure this "chance" and assign a number to it. Likewise, we can look at a pleasure or pain and determine the likelihood of its not being, followed by the opposite sensation. There is a great likelihood that some pleasures will not lead to subsequent pains, while other pleasures are highly likely to lead to pains Hence we must determine the purity of each pleasure and each pain consequent upon an action. It is clear that we should assign a high value to pleasures that are pure, but a low value to pains that are pure; and similarly, a low mark to pleasures that are impure, and a high mark to pains that are impure. Thus, in addition to measuring the pleasures and pains consequent upon an action ford dismissing we must also add two additional dimensions fecundity, and purity.

The resultant numbers assigned to each of the pleasures produced by an action can be added together to give one a sum representing the total amount of pleasure produced by this action. A similar number representing the total amount of pain this action produces can then be subtracted from the pleasure number, and the result will represent the overall balance of pleasure or pain produced by this action.

Greatest Happiness of the Greatest Number

According to Bentham, the above calculations should first be performed by a person with regard to the pleasures or pains that can be expected for himself. To put it in Bentham's own words: "Sum up all the values of all the pleasures on the one side, and those of the pains on the other. The balance, if it be on the side of pleasure, will give the good tendency of the act upon the whole, with respect to the interest of that individual person; if on the side of pain, the bad tendency of it upon the whole". But the calculation should also be undertaken with respect to the pleasure and pain that other people will experience because of each possible act. Thus, Bentham tells us, we must add a seventh dimension of extent of pleasure and pain to our considerations. The overall balance of pleasure or pain for each act will be a function of the amount of pleasure and pain experienced by everyone because of the act. When all these calculations are concluded, when we can ascertain which of the actions open to us will be right action, the one that ought to be performed: it will be the action measured as having the highest overall balance of pleasure over pain, or the least amount of pain, involved in its consequences – for all persons affected. The final calculation will demonstrate the impact of the right action on the general happiness.

Bentham recognizes that the decision procedure he has suggested is a very complex one, which would take a considerable amount of time and involve consideration of numerous consequences. And he admits that because of this complexity it is not to be expected that the process will occur prior to every moral judgment or legislative decision procedure to which one should appeal when necessary. The hedonic calculus is the ideal of reason. In other words, we already use the principle of utility and the hedonic calculus when we are rational about pursuing our own good or the good of the community. In his day and ever since, Bentham's proposals have served as a rallying cry for social reformers and philosophers who see the rational life. However impractical and difficult it may be, the use of the hedonic calculus represents for these individuals the ideal of rationality. There are, however, a number of problems with Bentham's proposals that must be overcome before one can have much confidence in his decision procedure.

The Principle of Asceticism

Philosophical defenders of the principle of asceticism according to Bentham, are motivated by hope, that by avoiding the pleasures of life they will attain "honors and reputation at the hand of man". Religious defenders are motivated more by fear, "the fear of future punishment at the hands of a splenetic and revengeful Deity". Men and women of education, Bentham avers, are usually those who subscribe philosophically to the principle primarily as the philosophical defenders of asceticism.

First, Bentham notes, they usually go no further than saying that pain is a matter of indifference; they do not actually say that it is good. Moreover, they seem to reject only some forms of pleasure, the gross "organically" kind, and even accept the more "refined" pleasures, which, of course, they call by another name: "the honorable, the glorious, the reputable, the becoming." In making the best point, Bentham is arguing that the philosophical advocates of asceticism in fact operate with something like the principle of utility, albeit under another name. His next criticism aims at an alleged inconsistency in their outlook. If pleasure is so abominable why restrict oneself, as the advocates of asceticism do, to avoiding it oneself? Why not do all one can to make other people as miserable as possible? It should seem, that if a certain quantity of misery were a thing so desirable, it would not matter much whether it were brought by each man upon himself, or by one man upon another." The religionists, he remarks, are more consistent in this regard. They are perfectly willing to make other people miserable, although they too offer the just punishments of heretics and infidels and are unwilling to endorse in general a policy of causing misery to other human beings. But why should an advocate of asceticism not pass laws to ensure the misery of all citizens, say by "stocking the body politic with the breed of highwaymen, housebreakers, or incendiaries"? Such action would be entirely consistent with their principle of asceticism, if they really believed in it. But of course they don't really believe in it, and the principle of asceticism cannot be consistently applied: "Let but one tenth part of the inhabitants of this earth pursue it consistently, and in a day's time they will have turned it into a hell". In fact, Bentham suggests, the original advocates of asceticism seem to have adopted the principle because they correctly say that some pleasures can lead to greater pains. They should have seen that this fact – and it certainly is a fact – proves not that pleasure is bad and pain good, but that one must look to the overall consequences of an act in order to judge it. That some pleasures lead to pains, in other words, is entirely consistent with the principle of utility, and only to a confused mind suggests the alterative principle of asceticism.

The Principle of Sympathy and Antipathy

Next there is the principle of sympathy and antipathy, which Bentham calls as a strange "principle," and he acknowledges that it is really the denial of all principles. According to it, right and wrong are not determined by external considerations that might warrant the internal sentiments; right and wrong are determined, rather, merely by the sentiments – "whatever you find in yourself a propensity to condemn, is wrong for that very reason". Advocating the principle of sympathy and antipathy, then, is really advocating extreme subjectivism, the view that feeling something right or wrong makes it so. Bentham characterizes such a subjectivism by pushing it to extreme lengths: "if you hate much, punish much: if you hate little, punish little: punish as you hate". In other words, degrees of right and wrong are reduced to degrees of feeling.

According to Bentham, many thinkers including many British moral philosophers such as, Lord Shaftesbury, Hutcheson, Hume, Beattie, Richard Price, and Samuel Clark and Butler belong to this category. But in Bentham's view such theories are a façade, a cover-up for a reliance on one's own sentiments as a guide to right and wrong. In other words, the high-blown rhetoric merely disguises an unabashed appeal to what the thinker himself likes or dislikes, approves or disapproves of, has sympathy with or antipathy for. The chief mischief of all these moral theories, Bentham remarks, is "their serving as a cloak, and pretence, and aliment to despotism". They simply disguise the acts of the despot who would impose his own feelings on other people.

Bentham singles out for special attention the strategy of those who appeal to the will of God as the basis of moral judgment. This appeal, he thinks, is just another instance of the principle of sympathy and antipathy, or the principle of asceticism at work. He notes that before the revealed will of God can be applied to practical matters and matters of private conduct, it must be interpreted. Taking the precepts of revelation literally, he argues, would be disastrous: "taken in a literal sense, they would overturn the world, annihilate self-defence, industry, commerce, reciprocal attachments". But if we do not interpret the will of God, such interpretations require some other standards or principles of right and wrong in order to be applied.

Utility and Motives

In concluding his discussion of the principle of sympathy and antipathy, Bentham warns us against confusing a motive of action with its ground or a reason for its being the right one to perform. A motive is what moves us to act; the ground of rightness is what justifies the action. Admittedly, when we act on certain motives we often do things that have desirable consequences and this frequently leads us to commend the motive itself. But a motive that sometimes yields good consequences may at other times yield undesirable ones, and so the motive itself is insufficient to justify any action.

> The only right ground of action that can possibly subsist, is after all the consideration of utility. Other principles in abundance, that is, other motives may be the reasons why such and such an act has been done: that is, the reasons or causes of its being done: but it is this alone that can be the reason why it might or ought to have been done.

The notion of a reason, Bentham is saying in effect, is ambiguous. The reason for an action may be the cause of it, its motive, or it may be the objective consideration that justifies it. In his view, we need always to look for objective considerations. And to his mind, the possession of utility is the only objective reason that renders an action justified. Utility was a principle, thought Bentham, which all men could readily see to be true. Moreover: 'The consequences, of any law, or of any act which is made the object of a law – the only consequences that men are at all interested in – what are they but pain and pleasure?'.

Bentham presented minute and painstaking application of the principle of utility to almost every aspect of the legal and political structures of his time. In J.S. Mill's opinion, Bentham's greatest service was to have 'deduced a set of subordinate generalities from utility alone, and by these consistently tested all particular questions. In other words, Mill thought Bentham important less for his account of the mainsprings of action than for his practical and commonsensical treatment of specific issues of public interest. His philosophy was best fitted to 'teach the means of organizing and regulating the merely business part of the social arrangements'. Stephen described Bentham as a "codifying animal". But we shall concentrate on three theoretical themes in Bentham's philosophy, which underpin everything he had to say about practice. These are: (a) his theory of pleasure and pain; (b) the explanation of the possibility of altruistic behavior; and (c) the rejection of all non-utilitarian standards of moral evaluation.

(a) Bentham's elaborate classification of the 'springs of action' and of the various categories and dimensions of pleasure and pain is wholly typical of him. He was a man who believed that analysis consisted in the making of lists. This passion for classifying things is often tedious and occasionally comic; but Bentham believed, with some justice, that a careful account of the species of pleasure and pain was a necessary preliminary to the construction of detailed rules of utility. The basic presupposition of the utility principle, he explained, is that every person is subject to the empire of pleasure and pain, the only determinants of human behaviour; the utilitarian objective must therefore be to 'rear the fabric of felicity by the hands of reason and law'. All actions should be approved or disapproved solely according to their tendency to promote or to oppose the utility (otherwise, the 'benefit', 'advantage', 'pleasure', 'good' or 'happiness') of the persons they affect.

Pleasure and pain are the instruments, which legislators have to work with; therefore it is crucial that they should understand how to measure their value.

Bentham considered that there were seven 'circumstances' which determined the value of a pleasure or a pain: its intensity; its duration; its certainty or uncertainty; its propinquity or remoteness; its fecundity, its purity and its extent. Bentham thought that numerical values could in principle be attached to these 'circumstances' and an arithmetical operation performed to determine the relative merits of different courses of action. The strategy is to sum up the numbers expressive of the degrees of good tendency which an act has with respect to each individual concerned, do the same with regard to its bad tendency, then calculate the balance with respect to the total number of community of individuals concerned. Bentham himself scarcely apprehended the severity of the technical problems involved in plotting the values of pleasures and pains on a numerical scale particularly when so many 'circumstances' contribute to determining that value and he underestimated the difficulty of interpersonal comparisons. Yet he did concede, with more realism that it is not to be expected, that this process should, however, always be kept in view as an ideal model of rational deliberation, to which actual deliberations should conform as closely as possible.

Ironically, Bentham himself unwittingly supplied a further ground for thinking that a felicific calculus would be at best extremely hard to operate. The more varieties of pleasant and painful activities there are, the more complex the task of measuring and comparing their quotients of pleasure and pain. But Bentham thought that the number of species of pleasure and pain was very large indeed, and in his inimitable style set out to list them. In the Principles we learn that there are fourteen kinds of simple pleasures and eleven of simple pains, all of which are carefully enumerated and discussed. Thus, the simple pleasures are said to be those of sense, of wealth, of skill, of amity, of a good name, of power, of piety, of benevolence, of malevolence, of memory, of imagination of expectation, of relief, and those dependent on the association of ideas. The first category of sensory pleasures is further distinguished into pleasures of the taste of intoxication, of smell, of touch, of hearing, of sight, of sex, of health and of novelty; and other categories of pleasures and pains are subdivided in a similar manner. Even this exhaustive natural history of human motives was not Bentham's last word on the subject. *A Table of the Springs of Action* contains a still more elaborate taxonomy of motives, supplying among other things fifty-four synonyms of the word pleasure' and sixty-seven of pain.

Despite the extraordinary labour, which Bentham spent on displaying the variety of pleasures and pains, he did not attempt to rank them, as some earlier utilitarian had done and many following J.S. Mill's lead, did later, according to a qualititative measure of value. He did not deny that some kinds of pleasant activity were usually more worth pursuing than others: benevolent deeds, for instance, tended to bring a person a greater and more pure satisfaction than malevolent ones, and were therefore preferable in point of pleasantness. The famous remark that pushpin is as good as poetry if it gives as much pleasure does not entail that pushpin is as pleasant as poetry though Bentham in a rare resemblance to Plato, suggested that poetry unlike pushpin, could disturb the soul in a way which was rather painful than otherwise. But he never supposed that some activities were necessarily more satisfying than others were because the pleasure they offered was of an intrinsically higher grade.

Bentham refused to 'cook' his theory of value to ensure that intellectual activities like reading philosophy would emerge superior activities to non-intellectual ones like sex or football.

(b) However, Bentham's view that pleasure and pain are the 'sovereign masters' of every human being leads to an awkward problem for his account of moral motivation. The very first paragraph of the Principles shows his commitment to a thoroughly deterministic picture of human nature. Pleasure and pain govern us in all we do, in all we say, in all we think: every effort we can make to throw off our subjection, will serve but to demonstrate and confirm it. In other words, a man may pretend to abjure their empire: but in reality he will remain subject to it all the while.

If the hold of pleasure and pain over us is really as absolute as this, the scope for genuinely moral action would seem to be nil. In everything we do we are simply seeking our own pleasure or avoiding our own pain, and any attempt to break away from these constraining forces and seek another's good instead of our own is futile. Bentham also claims that pleasure and pain 'point out what we ought to do, as well as determine what shall do'.

Bentham offered a somewhat complex response to this problem. Three separate lines of thought can be distinguished. Sometimes he seems inclined to moderate the egoism of his psychological theory and admit, alongside self-interested motives, altruistic ones as well. In the late work *Deontology* (1834) he conceded the existence of a human disposition to philanthropy and self-sacrifice. Even rulers sometimes acted in a benevolent manner, in the interests of their subjects. In addition, Bentham accepted the presence of what Bhikhu Parekh has termed 'semi-social' motives for promoting the public good though admittedly these appeal to selfish interests rather than to benevolence. A rational person realizes that it is in his own interests to act well towards others, who will act well towards him in return. Men who live in society need the assistance of others to fulfill their needs, and enlightened self-interest dictates that they display a cooperative spirit in order to secure this. Finally, Bentham claimed that benevolent actions can reward the actor with pleasure of an unusually intense kind.

It is sometimes objected that Bentham is too sanguine if he supposes that self-interest and utility will always coincide: no matter how great the pleasure of benevolence. A more serious point is that the coincidence of public and private utility provides no real evidence that people are not always narrowly self-interested; even doing good to others because of the pleasure it gives one seems to be a species of action from selfish motives. The situation would be saved if Bentham's recognition of a spirit of philanthropy in human beings were capable of filling the psychological gap. But while Bentham certainly believed that human beings are capable of forming a disposition to act for the good of others, the true selflessness of that disposition as he conceived it is open to question. Bentham never referred to any benevolent or self-sacrificing spirit without simultaneously emphasizing the pleasure to be derived from cultivating it. There were kings, he allowed, who did their utmost to promote their subjects' welfare – but they reaped great enjoyment from doing their duty. Philanthropy, for Bentham, was a real mental disposition, and not particularly rare;

but he seems to have seen its essential motivation as the satisfaction it engenders in the philanthropist.

(c) Bentham shrewdly rested the case for the utilitarian principle in part on the poverty of alternative moral theories. Most of these, he claimed, rely not on evidence but solely on their authors' prejudices. The moral-sense tradition in ethics he dismissed as a rhetorical exercise in which fine-sounding and empty phrases supplied the place of arguments. Other philosophers used different language to make the same claim: one referred to his common sense to show his moral truth; another to his understanding or to natural law or to the fitness of things'. Bentham thought that all these variant theories were caught on the horns of the same dilemma: either they represented nothing more substantial or they involved a tacit appeal to utility, which should have been made explicit. Bentham likewise criticized the language of rights popular with apologists for the American and French revolutions. This is condemned roundly as 'rhetorical nonsense – nonsense upon stilts'. Only by substituting the idea of utility for the high-sounding but meaningless notion of natural rights would one have a reasonable principle, which could be supported by experience.

Bentham's acute and often witty attack on rival theories was singled out for praise by J.S. Mill. Bentham, Mill said, always 'required something more than opinion as a reason for opinion'. Yet one might fairly ask whether the principle of utility is itself grounded on anything more solid than the opinion of utilitarian. Bentham believed that its superiority stemmed from its basis in a sound psychological theory of human motivation; but this is persuasive only if we grant the very dubious proposition that normative judgment can be derived from descriptive ones – that, in other words, an 'ought' can be deduced from an 'is'. That human beings naturally desires happiness does not entail that they ought to promote that happiness. A man may tell us, said Bentham,

> That there are certain practices conformable, and others repugnant, to the fitness of things; and then he tells you, at his leisure, what practices are conformable, and what repugnant: just as he happens to like a practice or dislike it.

The question we need to ask is: what prevents our substituting the word 'utility' for the phrase 'the fitness of things'? This is a question, which Bentham, unlike Mill, never faced squarely.

In his earlier years Bentham turned some of this manuscript into books, such as his *Fragment on Government* of 1776, or his *Introduction to the Principles of Morals and Legislation* of 1789. Later on, even the *Fragments* tended not to be published by him and were left for others to edit. In this manner, the first work which made his name was produced in French and published in Paris by his disciple, Etienne Dumont of Geneva. Dumont subsequently edited other works; these were translated into English by disciples, who also edited others directly. Therefore, much of the published text of Bentham has passed through the hands of others, and also sometimes been translated or retranslated prior to its publication. In fact, Bentham's greatest work on the philosophy of law was not published until the present century in its latest version, edited by H.L.A. Hart, under the title *On Law in General.*

Bentham's grand project was for legislation: the exploration and theoretical foundations of a perfect system of law and government. For this he needed a measure of perfection, and this for Bentham was the principle of utility, otherwise known as the greatest happiness principle. In his already mentioned *Introduction* to the subject, Bentham starts chapter with the rousing declaration that 'Nature has placed mankind under the governance of two sovereign masters, pain and pleasure.' This first paragraph ends with the statement that 'the principle of utility recognizes this subjection, and assumes it for the foundation of that system, the object of which is to rear the fabric of felicity by the hands of reason and of law'. Bentham's aim is to produce felicity, happiness. The means to be employed are 'reason and law': the right law will produce happiness, and the right law is one in accordance with reason. In Bentham's draft codes of law, each particular law was attached to a 'commentary of reasons on this law'. The commentary demonstrated its value and also, Bentham hoped, improved its effect.He says elsewhere, 'power gives reason to law for the moment, but it is upon reason that it must depend for its stability'.

Bentham explicitly states that by 'utility' he means that property in any object, whereby it tends to produce benefit, advantage, pleasure, good, or happiness or to prevent the happening of mischief, pain, evil, or unhappiness'. The rightness of actions depends on their utility; and the utility is measured by the consequences, which the actions tend to produce. Of all these varying terms describing the consequences, the most important for Bentham are pleasure and pain. For Bentham thinks that these are clear, easily understandable terms, which are therefore be used to give precise sense to the others. So the good, for Bentham, is the maximization of pleasure and the minimization of pain. Otherwise, as he puts it we would be dealing 'in sounds instead of sense, in caprice instead of reason, in darkness instead of light'. For Bentham the principle of utility, interpreted in terms of pleasure and pain, is the only appropriate measure of value because it is the only comprehensible one.

Bentham's aim of increasing happiness is a practical one; and he had many purely practical proposals. But the most famous and important of these particular practical proposals was for a prison, which he called the 'panopticon'. It was to be circular so that the warders could sit in the center and observe all the prisoners. It was also going to be privately run, by contract management with Bentham as its manager. Bentham therefore not only intended to produce what he called a mill for 'grinding rogues honest' but also to make money in the process. In fact, blocked by the interests of the landowners whose property fell under the site of the proposed prison he lost both money and time until, after twenty years' struggle, he was compensated by Parliament.

In his more general theory of government, just as in his more particular prison proposals, Bentham needed to rely on a psychology. This is that people tend to act in their own interests, where these are again understood in terms of pleasure and pain. People are understood to be seekers after pleasure and avoiders of pain. Given this knowledge of people's psychology, the benign legislator can so arrange his system of law that people seeking only their own interests, will in fact be led into doing what they are meant to do, which is to promote the general interest.

From this follows the Benthamite theory of punishment. It is a deterrent account. The proper aim of punishment, as of anything else, is to produce pleasure and prevent pain. Now all punishment is in itself a pain. So for Bentham, all punishment is in itself harm. Therefore, it can only be justified if this particular pain is outbalanced by the reduction in pain or increase of pleasure it causes. If people are deterred by punishment from doing things which would produce more pain for example, as rape, theft, or murder, then the punishment will be justified. If not, there is no point in punishment or retribution for its own sake. This defense of punishment not only justifies punishment but also enables in principle the precise calculation of how much punishment is appropriate.

Bentham's general account of law and punishment and his use of the principle of utility as a means of providing reasons for his particular codes of law is constant through out his life. However, his idea about the particular political system which should be the source of this law developed. At the start, he thought that he only needed to appeal to enlightened governments for such obviously beneficial arrangements to be put into effect. When he found that this did not happen he became a supporter of democracy. Not just the law had to be changed but also the system of government. He was accordingly active in the movement for the extension of the parliamentary franchise, which finally came into effect in the year he died. But Bentham wanted something considerably more radical than the extension, which actually happened: he wanted one man, one vote; and a secret ballot.

Such democratic proposals were in any case much more in accord with his general theories. If, according to the psychological theory, everyone acts in their own interests, so also do governments or governors. The classic eighteenth-century figure of the benevolent, semi-divine legislator has to be dispensed with. Dictators, kings, oligarchies cannot be trusted. The appropriate end of government, popularly sloganized by Bentham as 'the greatest happiness of the greatest number', is only safe in the hands of the greatest number of themselves. If the people as a whole are granted political power, they will merely by following their own interests, promote what is also the appropriate end. Just as in the right system of law, so in the right system of government, actual and appropriate action will coincide.

It can be seen that Bentham's project was centrally a project of clarification. He wanted to clarify values, to show at what we ought to aim. He wanted to devise the appropriate system of government, law, or punishment so that these two things could be placed in step. However, his interest in clarification went further. He also wanted to clarify the very idea of law; both as a whole and also in its central terms. It was in this project that he was led into his most original thought.

Understanding the law involves understanding such things as rights and duties. In the empiricist tradition, to which Bentham was loosely attached, understanding is provided by perception. Locke and, following him, Hume made a distinction between simple and complex ideas, which allowed them to understand things, which were not directly perceived. Complex ideas, such as that of a golden mountain, can be understood because they can be analyzed into their simple constituents, of which we have experience. However, this technique does not work for the terms, which Bentham wished to analyze, such as obligation or right. So here, he was forced into a wholly new technique, which he called 'periphrasis'.

This technique anticipates twentieth-century methods of analysis, as does Bentham's related claim that the primary unit of significance is a sentence rather than a word. His idea in paraphrases is not to translate the problematic word into other words. Rather, 'some whole sentence of which it forms a part is translated into another sentence'. So in the analysis of what Bentham called 'fictional entities (such as right, duty, property, obligation, immunity, privilege—the whole language of the law), he uses his technique of paraphrases to place these terms in sentences for which he then gives substitute sentences *to containing the offending term*. For example, sentences about rights are explained by Bentham in terms of sentences about duties. A particular right is for him the benefit which is conferred on someone by the imposition of duties on others. With duties we will still, of course, have fictional entities. But these, in turn, can be placed in sentences, which are translated into sentences about the threat of punishment. Punishment is, for Bentham, the threat of the imposition of pain. So here, at last, we reach what Bentham calls real entities. We reach clear, simple ideas, which can be directly understood by perception. As Bentham says in the *Fragment on Government*, 'pain and pleasure at least are words which a man has no need, we may hope, to go to a lawyer to know the meaning of'. With them, the law can be clarified; for lawyer is ultimate clarifier of what the law actually is.

These projects are projects for change: current conditions are criticized. However, although Bentham's goals were the same as many of the contemporary movements for change, his foundations were not. Bentham was on the side of the struggle for reform of the franchise in England but also of the American and French Revolutions. The central contemporary justification for these revolutions was in terms of natural rights. However, Bentham was consistently opposed to the use of natural rights and he therefore criticized the rhetorical justification of both of these revolutions.

Bentham thinks that a natural right is a 'contradiction in terms'. He thinks that they are nonsense, factious entities. However, Bentham produced a new of analysis in his technique of paraphrases precisely to make sense of fictitious entities. So it might be thought that he could make sense in the same way of natural rights. However, comparing a natural right with a legal right exposes the difference. Both can be analyzed in terms of corresponding duties. However, as seen, Bentham analyses a legal duty in terms of the law or threat of punishment which creates it. There is no corresponding law, he holds, with respect to supposed natural duties. Hence he holds that natural rights are just imaginary rights by contrast with the real rights produced by a actually existing systems of law. As he puts it, 'from real law come real rights-from imaginary laws come imaginary ones'. The so-called rights of man are in fact merely 'counterfeit rights'.

Bentham's most famous slogan expressing this view is 'nonsense on stilts'. This comes from his critical analysis of the French Declaration of the Rights of Man and Citizen in a work usually known as *Anarchical Fallacies*. Bentham's claim is that language which looks as if it is describing what rights there actually are is in fact suggesting what rights there ought to be. That is, instead of citing existing rights, the French Declaration is giving reasons why there ought to be rights. As Bentham puts it in *Anarchical Fallacies*, 'a reason for wishing that a certain right were established, is not that right; want is not supply; hunger is not bread'. So to suppose that such rights actually exist is nonsense. Even worse is to suppose that we can be sure that the correct rights have been found for all time. Bentham is a promoter of experimentation. We have to keep seeing what utility is actually produced by particular systems of rights. Hence it is an additional mistake to think that any rights are unalterable indefeasible, and imprescriptible. This mistake was also made by the French. Hence the famous slogan. The complete remark from which it comes is 'a natural right is simply nonsense: natural and imprescriptibly rights, rhetorical nonsense, nonsense upon stilts'.

Natural rights theory was one attempted answer to the question of the source of obedience to the state and the conditions for legitimate revolution. Another attempted answer also popular in Bentham's day was the original, or social contract. This device, founding obedience on agreement, was used by the leading contemporary defender of British law, William Blackstone. Bentham ridicules such a defense in his *Fragment on Government*. For Bentham, justification of obedience to government depends upon utility, that is upon calculation of whether the 'probable mischiefs of obedience are less than the probable mischief's of resistance'.

Bentham striongly rejects the social contract theory: a contract will not work here for Bentham because, just like rights, all real contracts are legal contracts. Hence they are produced by law and government; and cannot therefore be used to provide a foundation for law and government. Even if its force is not supposed to be the force of a proper contract but merely that of a promise, or agreement, this again will not help to provide justification. For whether government or people should keep their agreements, has again, for Bentham to be tested by the calculation of utility. Yet if utility is to be the ultimate justification of promise keeping, it would have been better to have started rather than traversing a tortuous path through contracts, original contracts, and largely fictional agreements. Again, Bentham designates the supposed alternative source of justification to be merely a fiction and, as he puts it in the *Fragment*, 'the indestructible prerogatives of mankind have no need to be supported upon the sandy foundation of a fiction'.

Although all justification comes from utility, this does not mean that Bentham cannot support secondary ends; that is, things, which, if promoted, will normally, tend to increase utility. He lays down four such intermediate ends which should be promoted by the rights system of law and government: subsistence, abundance, security, equality. These form two pairs so that subsistence takes precedence over abundance; and securing people's expectations takes precedence over equality. The utilitarian argument for this depends upon the psychological claim that deprivation of the former member of each pair causes more pain than the later.

Psychological assumptions also lie behind Bentham's promotion of equality. He claims that in general equal increments of a good will not produce equal increments of utility. That is, he claims that there is diminishing marginal utility. Therefore, in general, provision of a particular good will provide more utility for those who already have less than those who already have more; hence a general tendency towards providing goods for the less well-off; or equality.

Bentham's is a consequentialist in ethics. It looks towards actual and possible future states of affairs for justification of right action, not to what happened in the past. For example, punishment is not retribution for past action, but prevention of future harms: obedience to the state is not because of some past promise, but to prevent future harms. This is for Bentham the right, indeed the only possible way of thinking correctly about these matters. It explains his central stance with regard to reform of the law. The law he found was common law, made by judges, based on precedents and customs. It come from history. For this he wanted to substitute statute law, made by democratic parliaments, and founded on reason. These laws would be independent of history and would be in terms of future benefit.

Law

Bentham was fearful of hobgoblins in his childhood. While attending the lectures of Sir William Blackstone at Oxford in 1763, Banthem once again experienced the fear of hobgoblins. This time they were in the form of fallacious fictions contained in the English common law. It would be Bentham's task to exorcise these hobgoblins and establish a new materialist 'science and art of morals and legislation'. It was in the role of legislator that Bentham saw his life's work.

As a legislator, Bentham saw himself not only as a law reformer but as one who would transform the existing legal and moral basis of society. He would be the Newton of morals and legislation. Law, for Bentham, was the means to establish and maintain a rationally ordered society and was therefore the key element in his social and political thought. Bentham, however, was not a utopian social engineer. His view of law as a means for rationally ordering social change was the product of his critique of the existing legal system and of his understanding of the nature of the economic and social changes taking place in late eighteenth century England. Douglas Hay states that Bentham could not understand the 'personal terms' of justice in the practice of the English law in the eighteenth century in contrast to the sense of justice in terms of 'rational bureaucratic decisions made in the common interest. Bentham was aware of how this system of order and deference worked and that his theory was not based solely on the normative principle of utility but upon a subordinate set of principles which would provide a new system of social discipline. Recent commentators on Bentham's vision of social discipline have failed to appreciate the historical significance of his materialist analysis of the changes in the form of the law required for the ordering of the social relations of production necessary for the development of industrial capitalism. The rule of law would not only provide directly for the maintenance of 'liberty', 'equality', and 'property' within the sphere of the circulation of commodities but it would also provide indirectly the social discipline necessary for the sphere of the production of commodities.

Bentham's materialist analysis of the form of law is significant because it recognized the inadequacy of the practice of the common law to maintain social discipline and because it suggested ways in which law could be used indirectly to establish the new social discipline of the labour process in response to the changing composition of the labouringly class in the eighteenth century. It is important to note that for Bentham the rule of law was not just a set of rational commands establishing a system of social control. The rule of law should not be seen in terms of the exercise of direct social control. It represents a legal definition of changing social relations whereby the law can be the mediation of class struggle. Law was not viewed simply as an instrument of hegemony but as a rational mediation of existing class relations. It would provide artificially an identification of interests by the realization of the principle of utility through the establishment of a system of 'direct' and 'indirect' legislation.

Many of the philosophers and radicals of the Enlightenment were practical reformers who sought in the establishment of a materialist psychology on which to form a social science at once theoretical and capable of being transformed into an art. In 1768 Bentham, having read Helvetius and Beccaria, began to construct his 'Elements of a Critical Jurisprudence' based upon the principle of utility which was derived from his materialist psychology. In 1776 Bentham, published *A Fragment on Government*, which was a scathing critique of Blackstone's interpretation of the common law.

Blackstone's view of the natural right basis of civil government was largely influenced by John Locke. It was Locke, the Whig apologist, who stated that 'Government has no end but the preservation of property'. Bentham regarded the notion of natural right as a fallacious and even dangerous fiction. All rights, according to Bentham, were social conventions designed to protect private interests. The political language of natural right theory was dangerous because it could lead to either despotism or anarchy. Important legal fictions like power, right, trust and property needed to be clearly defined. Like Hobbes, Bentham was concerned to analyse scientifically the structure of power existing in the real world. Power, for Bentham, was not a thing but a relationship between persons or things. It was essentially a relationship of control. Power over persons or things can produce pleasure or pain for human persons. The legislator would create an artificial structure of power relation, which would maximize pleasure and minimize pain for the whole of society.

Bentham identified with the critique of the common law influenced by the writing of Adam Smith, Lord Kames, and the judicial decisions of Lord Mansfield. Although there were important developments in commercial law, the reform of the property law seemed impossible. In the late eighteenth century there was a tremendous increase in legislation of capital statutes mostly concerned with the protection of the natural right of property. Despite the influence of Beccaria and the increasing influence of the ideas of law, reform among lawyers, Parliament resisted all attempts at reform. Bentham believed that the members of Parliament were ignorant of the art of legislation.

By 1780, Bentham completed the initial formulation of his 'art and science of morals and legislation'. The science of morals and legislation is a discourse that is architectonic in that it structure the relationship between other forms of discourse. There are also some other important works like 'Of Laws in General', 'Essays on the Influence of Time and Place in Matters of Legislation' and 'Essay on Indirect Legislation', which Bentham completed around 1780. In the 'Essay on the Influence of Time and Place in Matters of Legislation' Bentham dealt with the problem of legal relativism and social change. He recognized that the establishment of a totally reformed rational system of law would not produce a utopian society. He wrote:

> Perfect happiness belongs to the imaginary region of philosophy and must be classified with the universal elixir and the philosopher's stone. Painful labour, daily subjection, a condition nearly allied to indigence will always be the lot of numbers. Among the higher as well as the lower classes, there will always be desires which cannot be satisfied. Reciprocal security can only be established by the forcible renunciation by each one.

The 'Essay on Indirect Legislation' is perhaps one of the most important and also most neglected of his legal essay. It is in this essay that Bentham acknowledges the importance of custom and tradition in the establishment of the art of legislation. Indirect legislation or social therapeutics aimed, therefore, to condition human behaviour as manifested in contemporary society. This process of 'conditioning' would be through social legislation and the creation of social institutions like prisons, poor-houses, schools, etc. Bentham recognized that the reform of the civil and penal laws of his society would also need to be supplemented by the reform of the constitutional laws. Which would produce the social discipline. By 1780, Bentham's vision of 'science and art of morals and legislation' was now clear to him and he was confident of the benefits it would confer upon society.

It was in the 1780s that Bentham began to examine more systematically the nature of the changes that were taking place in English society. It was at this time that Bentham read Adam Smith's *Wealth of Nations* (1776) and became interested in the study of political economy. Bentham saw his 'Essay on Indirect Legislation' as having a clear relationship to his 'science of political economy'. His first economic work, 'The defence of usury', was written in 1787 in the form of letters from Russia where he was assisting his brother Samuel to set up a factory system for the enlightened despot Catherine the Great. In this work he criticized Adam Smith for inconsistency by making the usury laws an exception to his laissez-fair principle. He had accepted Smith's principles and was now going to push them to their logical conclusion. Following Adam Smith only Jeremy Bentham and J.S. Mill among the classical economists would attempt to fully examine the relationships between legislation, political economy, and social and economic policy formation. For Smith the dynamics of economic development would help establish a 'natural' identity of interests in society. Benthm in his writings recognized that 'interests' could only be harmonized by legislative activity and especially by indirect legislation.

Compared to Adam Smith and most of the other classical political economists Bentham's list of governmental activities was much more extensive. The important point, however, is not the question of the extent of government intervention directly in the economy but the significance of the legislative framework necessary for the development of the economy. The legislator would provide this legislative framework through the art of direct and indirect legislation based on the materialist science of morals and legislation.

In his 'Principles of the Civil Code' Bentham argued that although the principle of utility was fundamental it was also an ideal or goal to be realized. He stated that there were four subordinate principles or goals of legislation, which would provide the means for the realization of the principle of utility. These were security, subsistence, abundance and equality. Security was for Bentham the primary immediate goal of legislation. He wrote:

> We have now arrived at the principal object of the laws; the care of security. This inestimable good is the distinctive mark of civilization; it is entirely the work of laws. Without law there is no security; consequently no abundance nor even subsistence. And the only equality which can exist in such a condition is the equal misery. Among the objects of the law, security is the only one which embraces the future; subsistence, abundance, equality may be regarded for a moment only; but security implies extension in point of time with respect to all the benefits to which it is applied.

It is for the maintenance of security that property is instituted by law according to Bentham. Also 'liberty', which is simply 'negative liberty' or freedom from the coercion of the law, is the product of security. Bentham wrote, 'When most of us speak of liberty what we mean is security – and security is the work of law, coercing those who would interfere with or injure those whom it means to favour.' It is clear that without security the other ends of legislation – subsistence, abundance and equality – cannot be realized. The primary goal of the legislative framework of society necessary for capitalist development is the provision of security. The question of the extent of direct governmental intervention in economic activity is therefore related to the provision of security. Bentham accepted that the legislator need not exercise direct power over the economic interests which were exercising economic power for the provision of subsistence and abundance. It was only when that exercise of economic power threatened the security of the society in terms of its aggregate subsistence and abundance that Bentham favoured direct government interference in the economy. The provision of security is the primary goal of legislative activity. This would be brought about through the art of direct and indirect legislation.

The debates in the 1790s about the reform of the Poor Laws and the problem of poverty provide a good example of how Bentham combined his art of legislation with his rather frightening skill as a social engineer. They illustrate how Bentham would provide for the realization of security, subsistence, and abundance within a society under the impact of Industrial Revolution. In the 1790s, the pauper problem become critical and Bentham suggested a complete reform of the old Poor Laws. As a disciple of Adam Smith, he argued that the Poor Laws were against economic liberty and that they provided unnecessary competition to free employment.

The significance of the debate over the Poor Laws following the introduction of the Speen Hamlate System in 1795, Samuel Whitbread's Reform Bill of 1795, and Pitt's Reform Bill 1796 goes beyond the level of moral ideology. It was in the debates concerning poverty that the classical economists first began to consider the implications of the every-increasing subjection of labour to the needs of capital. There was an increased awareness of the relationship between unemployment and the accumulation of capital. For Bentham this debate also involved the question of how the art of legislation could provide for the process of capital accumulation. He recognized that it could provide means also to maintain the subjection of labour to capital in the labour process. Benthm wrote:

> The law which offers to poverty an assistance independent of industry is, so to speak, a law against industry itself, or at least against frugality. The motive to labour and economy

> is the pressure of the present and the fear of the future: Want. The law, which takes away this pressure and this fear, must be an encouragement to idleness and dissipation. This is to reproach which is reasonably brought against the greater number of establishments created for the poor.

In his unpublished 'Essay on the Subject of the Poor Law' of 1796, Bentham established the definition, object, and theory of Poor Law Legislation. In this essay, he made an important distinction between poverty and indigence. He wrote:

> Poverty is the state of everyone who in order to obtain subsistence is forced to have recourse to labour. Indigence is the state of him who being destitute of property, is at the same time either unable to labour or unable even for labour to procure the supply of which he happens thus to be in want.

Labour was therefore the only natural source of subsistence. It was necessary for the market to provide subsistence for the labour market. In 1786, in a fragment entitled 'Poor's Cry', Bentham argued that the government could do nothing for employment except for removing unnecessary burdens upon the labour force. In another essay in 1796, Bentham argued that the decline of wages was an indication of the decrease of capital in proportion to labour.

The Poor Law is an important example of how Bentham applied his 'Essay on Indirect Legislation' to the problem of establishing and maintaining social discipline. His distinction between 'poverty' and 'indigence' led him to the position that poverty was essential to the creation of wealth. He wrote that, 'As labour is the source of wealth so is poverty of labour. Banish poverty, you banish wealth'. In his criticism of Pitt's Reform Bill he argued that the condition of the non-laboring recipient of poor relief must be less eligible than that of the industrious poor otherwise the very incentive to work hard would be removed.

The proposals, which Bentham put forward for pauper management, are actually quite staggering in terms of their scope and detail. It was an application of the 'Panopticon plan', which had been published in 1791 as a model prison, to the problems of pauper management. The central control of the Poor Law administration was to be vested in a joint stock company with a board of directors called the National Charity Company. The board was to build about 150 'Industry Houses' all over the country and each house would contain about 2000 persons. These Industry Houses would be built on the Panopticon principle of central inspection. That is, they would be circular buildings in which the governed could be inspected from the center as structured by an architectural plan. No relief would be granted except upon the terms of the Industry House which would be that of entering into productive industry. Mendicants and vagrants were to be apprehended and brought into the work house and given employment. Children or non-adult paupers were to be received as apprentices. The insane, dumb, deaf, or blind were to be segregated. The use of the inspection principle of the factory system would not only provide for the management of paupers but also through the time and work disciplines of capitalist production transform the paupers into productive labour.

What is interesting about the pauper management proposals are that they combine Bentham's 'technology of power', as observed by Foucault, with Bentham's concern for the maintenance of the labour market. As Bentham began to extend the original purpose of the Industry Houses from the treatment of the temporarily indigent to the control of the permanently indigent, his pauper management system became the model of a micro-social system which would exist within and in some sense compete with society. Influenced by his brother Samuel, he was fascinated with the possibility of using unskilled labour in manufacturing with completely standardized parts. The application of the 'piece-work' system is a most novel feature of the application of factory discipline to the Industry House. Bentham saw child labour as an essential part of his organization of the labour force. The Industry Houses would provide training, medical treatment, and moral discipline. The use of education to instill social discipline is an important feature of his plan. The Industry Houses become for Bentham a laboratory for social discipline for more extravagant than his original 'Panopticon plan.

Some of the other experiments carried on within the Industry Houses would be Registry Offices, Loan Offices, Frugality Banks, Charitable Remittance Offices, Frugality Inns, Dispensaries, Lying-in Hospitals, Midwifery Lecture Schools, Veterinary Lecture Schools, Military Exercise Schools, Marine Schools, etc. This was no utopian vision for Bentham but part of his overall plan to provide security and subsistence through indirect legislation. Humanitarians would find it useful in its provisions for charity while lawmakers and political economists would find its utility in its provision of security, subsistence, and even abundance. Unfortunately, for Bentham by 1811, his proposals for the Panopticon plan and for the Industry Houses were rejected in the committees of Parliament. Bentham, although severely disappointed did not give up his vision of a rational, legally ordered society as he spent his later years on devising various proposals to reform the stature of government.

The emergence of a market in labour provided the necessity of distinguishing poverty and indigence. It was considered necessary to transform the indigent who was not capable of labour into the pauper who was still capable of labour. A basic prerequisite of capital is not only the existence of a mass of free wage labourers but also social discipline over that labour. Pauperism, like certain forms of criminal activity, seemed to threaten that control over the labour market. It has been argued by many scholars that the prison system in the late eighteenth century was an attempt to maintain the labour market by preventing crime as an alternative to wage labour. This thesis can also be applied to the debate about the Poor Laws. The problem was for capital to control the reproduction of the working class. This control over labour would be brought about not only through new 'technologies of power' but also through legally maintained social relations of production.

In order to fully understand Bentham's writings on political economy or proposals like the 'Panopticon plan' or the 'Pauper management plan', it is necessary to see them as part of his materialist science and art of morals and legislation. According to Bentham only through such a science could be changes taking place in the existing structure of power relations be analysed and only through such an art could a rational structure of power relations be maintained. Bentham argued that legislation could directly or indirectly provide not only for the realization of the principle of utility but also for the subordinate ends of legislation, namely security, subsistence, abundance and equality. Bentham's reform of the Poor Law by the principles of indirect legislation would help to maintain the ever increasing subjection of labour to capital. It would maintain labour as a commodity of exchange within the sphere of circulation and within the sphere of production, it would introduce the discipline of the labour process, which by establishing co-operation and the division of labor would turn man into a machine.

Marx has rightly commented that Bentham was aware of the 'antagonistic character of capitalist accumulation.' Bentham believed that through scientific legislation the maintenance of the social relations of production necessary for capitalist development could be provided. While being an advocate of democratic rights, Bentham would use his materialist science of morals and legislation to establish a system of legislation, which would create the 'cerebral archipelago'. In Foucault's words, there would be no hobgoblins allowed in this machine of legally maintained social relations. Bentham could finally sleep peacefully.

Marx further chided Bentham:

> Within whose boundaries the sale and purchase of labour-power goes on, is in fact a very Eden of the innate rights of man. It is the exclusive realm of Freedom, Equality, Property, and Bentham, because both buyer and seller of a commodity, let us say labour-power, are determined only by their own free-will. They contract as free persons, who are equal before the law. Their contract is the result in which their joint will finds a common legal expression. Equality, because each enters into relation with the other, as with a simple owner of commodities and they exchange equivalent for equivalent. Property, because each disposes only what is his own. And Bentham, because each looks only to his own advantage.

Conclusion

Bentham has not yet received the criticism he deserves. Not that he lacks great critics: If Machiavelli is the most maligned political theorist in popular terms, Bentham surely holds the record for being hated by many scholars and philosophers. Goethe called him "that frightfully radical ass." John Maynard Keynes considered his ideas "the worm which has been gnawing at the insides of modern civilization and is responsible for its present moral decay." Emerson called his philosophy a "stinking philosophy"; Joseph Schumpeter judged them to be the "shallowest of the conceivable philosophies of life." Marx called Bentham "the arch-philistine, the insipid, leather-tongued oracle of the commonplace bourgeois intelligence." Nietzsche despised Bentham, and made up a little verse: 'Soul of washrag: face of poker, overwhelming mediocre'. Any thinker who evokes that caliber of enmity and that sort of attention, cannot be all bad. Whatever the flaws of his doctrine, it is emphatically not mediocre. Substituting invective for argument, these great minds easily make sport of the mad genius, yet utilitarianism survives unscathed.

Despite the attractions of a utilitarian approach to moral and political questions, it has encountered a great deal of criticism. These criticisms have been of two broad sorts; the first group center on claims that utilitarianism underestimates moral complexity and the importance of pluralism whilst the second focus on the issue of moral boundaries. We can think about each of these in turn. There are a number of ways in which utilitarianism underestimates the complexity of moral issues. Firstly, there are problems with making the necessary interpersonal comparisons. Is making comparisons of utility between persons really as easy as utilitarianism claims? How do we know that when Lipika claims to be very happy she is feeling the same as when Ayush claims to be similarly happy? We commonly speak of some people having lower pain thresholds than others. Is this because they experience the same pain but handle it differently or because they experience the pain differently? It may be that there is no metric for utility that applies across persons, no simple scale against which different people can reliable compare happiness. Beyond this there is the further problem that when Lipika and Ayush were engaged in the same activity, experience the same kind of pleasure. Is the sort of experience Rabin has when eating his favourite food the same as Kishore has when eating his favourite food let alone the same as Partha has when playing his favourite music?

The basic utilitarian focus on pleasure also comes in for criticism. It might already have occurred to us that some pleasures may be better than others in ways that reflect more than just the quantity or intensity of the experience. Is the pleasure of watching soap operas, eating burgers or drinking large quantities of alcohol every weekend the same sort of pleasure as is derived from viewing great works of art, engaging in philosophy or bringing up happy children? Don't pleasures differ in their quality as well as their quantity and aren't better quality pleasures worth more? Bentham certainly didn't think so and famously claimed that pushpin was as good as poetry. This has seemed implausible to many people, including Mill. He argued that there are higher and lower pleasures, roughly equivalent to intellectual and physical pleasures, and that 'competent judges' that have experienced both consistently prefer the higher sort. This is because people value the exercise of their complex intellectual faculties over the experience of animal pleasures. Mill forcefully insists that it is better to be a human being dissatisfied than a pig satisfied; better to be Socrates dissatisfied than a fool satisfied And if the fool, or the pig, are of a different opinion, it is because they only know their own side of the question.

Whether or not there is a coherent distinction to be drawn between types of pleasure, utilitarians face a strong challenge to the very claim that pleasure is what is important to us and is the 'spring of action', that Bentham describes. Robert Nozick asks us to imagine a machine into which we could be plugged that would directly stimulate the pleasure centers of the brain whilst we float in a tank. Given that we are supposed to be motivated by the pursuit of maximized pleasure we must ask ourselves whether we would sign up to spend our entire lives in such a 'pleasure machine'. Would one choose to live one's life in this way? Do you think many people would? Perhaps it is not pleasure that is of fundamental importance but something else perhaps the experience of the activities from which pleasure is derived? Note that even making this move is a radical departure from Bentham's or Mill's revisionist utilitarianism. But even this move may not help. Perhaps more sophisticated scientists invent an 'experience machine' that could reproduce in one's brain the experience of doing whatever one chooses. This machine could allow one to experience swimming with dolphins, walking on the moon or dating celebrities in ways which are indistinguishable from the experiences and memories of the things one has actually done. Would this make a difference? Would one now choose to spend one's life in such a machine, blissfully happy and with a life more full of wonderful experiences than anyone has ever lived? Perhaps some of us would choose this fife, though it is more likely that some of us might choose it for a holiday from time to time. Either way, it is probable that most people would resist this choice. The utilitarian has to face the problem that it does not seem that pleasure as such is what we regard as most important or valuable. Even more recent attempts to modify the utilitarian understanding of utility in terms of preference satisfaction rather than pleasure may be vulnerable to arguments featuring more sophisticated machines. Just as it became clear when we discussed interpersonal comparisons, people's interests may resist reduction to any single common denominator. They may instead reflect a plurality of concerns that require a more complex approach to moral and political questions. People may just value a whole load of different things and it may not be possible to account for this pluralism under the umbrella of a single value, however utility is defined.

These problems are compounded by our second set of criticisms, those focused on consequentialism and the question of moral boundaries. Though the prime concern of utilitarianism is human welfare, many critics have pointed out that this concern shows itself in strange ways. Utilitarian calculations seem capable of justifying a whole range of actions that strike us as immoral or unjust. Imagine that there is a vicious serial killer on the streets of a major city, bringing terror to the lives of thousands of people and proving difficult to catch. The police may be justified, in utilitarian terms, in picking up an innocent vagrant, rigging a trial and executing him, rather than continuing to fruitlessly pursue the real killer. The pleasure that thousands feel as a result of their belief that they are more secure may outweigh the pain of the vagrant. Likewise, the shortage of organ donors could be met by using the organs of people that no one will mourn. Each childless criminal or unwanted orphan may nobly save the lives of many others. General utility may also be increased in other counter-intuitive ways. Perhaps the happiness of the overwhelming majority could be maintained at a higher level if the minority were viciously exploited as slaves allowing the majority to live a life of luxury or in a state ethnically divided between one 1arge and one small ethnic group, utility may be maximized if the state apparatus is used to systematically discriminate against the minority culture. What makes these examples particularly telling is the way that utilitarianism does not take these decisions with regret but, as they maximize utility, would seem to celebrate the sacrifice of innocents and the persecution of minorities as the morally right and just thing to do in each situation. Utilitarianism faces further problems when we realise how it treats certain sorts of experiences. We would normally disregard as irrelevant to moral judgement the pleasure that a torturer gets when torturing their victim or that the rapist gets from their assault. We normally think of these pleasures as illegitimate preferences. However, the utilitarian is committed to counting them on the positive side of any calculation.

The utilitarian response to these sorts of criticisms has most often been to point out that a rule utilitarian calculation would not give these results. Rule utilitarianism would justify rules against violence, the execution of innocents and the persecution of minorities on the grounds that, if generally performed, these acts would diminish utility. However, we must remember that the justification of the rule itself is the maximization of utility. If for any given action it could be shown that breaking the rule in this case would maximise utility but not endanger the rule's general support then the utilitarian has to acknowledge that the rule should be broken. In fact instead of a rule such as 'always do x,' the utilitarian would support new rule, 'always do *x* except when circumstances are such as to make not doing *x* the better option'. Since Bentham in particular, and consequentialists more generally, define moral terms by reference to the good then conventional morality can place no limitations on the pursuit of that good. If one finds consequentialism attractive one will just have to bite the bullet here.

Utilitarianism is an individualist theory. Individuals experience pleasure and pain undertaking utilitarian calculations and societies are regarded as collections of individuals. As an individual calculates their own utility they weigh one pleasure against another or decide whether to endure a sacrifice now for the benefit of greater future pleasure. This is all very well, we each perform this balancing act between pains and pleasures every day, but utilitarianism seems to treat the community as if it can do likewise, it is as if the community calculates what balance of pains and pleasures is good and acts accordingly.

The central problem here is that utilitarianism appears to license trade-offs, the sacrifice of one person for the benefit of another. Utilitarianism blurs what we ordinarily think of as important moral boundaries between people. In aggregating the interests of everybody, mixing them into one big pot, the fact that they are the interests of different people is forgotten. In this way everybody's interests are taken into account but in the processes of aggregation and maximization individuals are treated not as the originators of interests but as vessels for utility. What matters is not whether decisions are in all our interests but how to maximise the experience of pleasure. If this means sacrificing some for others then so be it. Critics like Rawls and Nozick claim that utilitarian decision-making ignores the 'separateness of persons', 'that there are different individuals with separate lives and that the life of one should not be outweighed by the interests of others. Rights theorists draw attention to what they claim are moral boundaries between people in order to demonstrate that what is wrong with utilitarianism is that it lacks any proper conception of individual rights.

Problems with Rights

Just as we explored an attractive utilitarian position only to find possible flaws so we must look closely for flaws in theories of rights. Firstly, theories of rights, like utilitarianism, face a problem when it comes to identifying the scope of moral concern. Recall that utilitarianism seemed to have too inclusive a scope so that it had trouble capturing the human character of morality. Since pain and pleasure are the only ground of moral concern, and animals suffer in the same way as people, surely animal welfare is on a par with human welfare? Rights theories that regard rights as something we have simply by virtue of our humanity have a similar problem explaining why humans should be singled out for special treatment. Most theories of rights, however, are potentially too exclusive, ruling out people we usually think of as rights bearers. This is because they justify rights in terms of human autonomy or rationality. The potential exclusivity becomes clear when we realise that newborn infants, the senile, people in a coma are not capable of autonomous or rational action, or of exercising reciprocal moral respect. In this way they may slip through the net of moral concern and end up being regarded as a part of the non-human animal kingdom.

Secondly, and more importantly, Bentham acknowledges that there may be legitimate rights but points out that these can only be legal rights, not natural or moral rights. He is clear that law can create rights but also believes that law is the only creator of rights. If there was a state of nature in prehistory then there was 'no government, consequently no rights' since rights are dependent on a judicial system. Any appeal to 'natural rights is simple nonsense... nonsense upon stilts.' Bentham is clear that a lack of government and rights would lead to great unhappiness and that therefore "a reason exists for wishing that there were such things as rights. But reasons for wishing there were such things as rights, are not rights-a reason for wishing that a certain right were established, is not a right - want is not supply-hunger is not bread".

Since all rights are legal rights that depend on law, and this argument aims at any non-legal understanding of rights as moral rights, the only rights we have are those that we are given by the state. This is not to say that utilitarians do not recognise prior moral claims of the form ought to be a right. Utilitarianism can accept that where there is no right there should be one, and that such a right is morally justified. However, the moral reasons that justify the creation of a right are themselves based on considerations of utility. In this way there can be both legal rights and moral reasons explaining why certain legal rights should be created, but not moral rights themselves.

This utilitarian understanding of rights as based on moral claims that derive from utility is open to the objections concerning the way such rights can be legitimately overridden in trade-offs. Because rights are simply instrumentally justified as means of maximsing utility they lack an absolute character. Bernard Williams asks us to imagine that a number of Red Indian villagers are to be shot by a firing squad but, since Jim is an honoured guest, if Jim shoots one Red Indian himself then the others will be released as a mark of respect. If Jim regards as absolute the right of the single Red Indian not to be killed by him, then the other Red Indians will die. We may regrettably accept this outcome if the total number of Red Indians is two or three, agreeing that Jim should not violate rights. However the Williams example has twenty Red Indians involved and what if the numbers are greater? Should Jim refuse to violate the rights of one person even if this results in the death of one hundred, or one thousand, or ten thousand? The utilitarian point is that if rights are absolute then no matter how large the number of deaths that result Jim should never shoot the Red Indian. Surely, utilitarians argue, this is just stubbornness taken to absurd lengths. There must be some number of deaths for which it would be the right thing to do to shoot the Red Indian. If human beings are important then surely our moral theories cannot be this inflexible. The absolute character of rights would result in more violations of the very rights that are supposed to be absolute. Instead, rights must be treated flexibly, enabling us to minimize rights violations by occasionally sanctioning a violation of rights if this is morally justified. Some theories of rights recognise that rights should not always triumph over concerns of utility. Surely if we can avert moral disasters then rights must be violated and rules broken; what, then, is wrong with trade-offs in those circumstances when standing on rights seems unjustifiable? There is no easy answer here. Assuming that we have rights, the question of whether and when they should be violated is a difficult and complex issue.

As well as there perhaps being a problem with trade-off's there may also be reason to think again about the utilitarian treatment of minorities. Recall that utilitarianism was accused of not treating people properly as it might allow the majority's interests to outweigh the minority's, that the interests of one percent might be sacrificed for the benefit of ninety-nine per cent. The utilitarian response would draw attention to the way in which, when rights block consequemialist reasoning, the interests of the majority are sacrificed to the minority. Theories of rights sacrifice the interests of ninety-nine per cent of the population for the benefit of one per cent. How is this justifiable if people's interests are to be taken seriously? Rather than allowing minorities to sabotage the common good, utilitarianism might be seen as the moral equivalent of democracy. Just as in democratic processes, each person's interest/vote is aggregated together, the majority decision carries the day and the minority, who enter the process knowing that they may not get their preferred option, should accept the will of the majority. A vote, like utility, is a common denominator into which people's interests are converted. Each individual is then equally counted as one and only one and so each is shown equal concern and respect. Why then should the outcome of this aggregative process not be generally accepted? Why should some individuals' interests weigh disproportionately heavily so as to block the outcome that meets the interests of most individuals? Surely, so the argument goes, it is utilitarianism and not theories of rights that take the individual seriously.

Utilitarianism and theories of rights understand the relationship between the good and the right in different ways. The utilitarian understanding is consequentialist: the good is prior to the right. Right actions, indeed standards of right and wrong in general, are identified and justified by reference to a predefined understanding of the good. For utilitarians this good is utility, usually understood in terms of pleasure and pain, and the proper consequentialist response to this good is to maximise it. Utilitarian rights are therefore instrumental in the pursuit of maximised good. As such they are always provisional, potentially overridden by consequentialist reasoning depending on circumstances. Rights are recognised and respected only so long as it is advantageous to the whole. Theories of rights reverse this understanding: the right is prior to the good. Rights are not instrumentally justified and are instead defined separately from the good, which itself is usually understood as a plurality of conceptions of the good pursued by different individuals. Rights are understood to frame our individual and communal pursuits of interests and thus to constrain consequentialist reasoning. Theories of rights do not deny that there is a place for consequentialist reasoning in, for example, the formation of government policy where genera! welfare is an important concern. It is just that such policy deliberations have to take as given the rights that individuals legitimately hold and formulate policy that respects rather than violates rights. Theories of rights usually embody a conception of limited government. Recognising that almost all government action is ultimately coercive, rights delimit a sphere of legitimate government action. Government must work within the framework of certain constraining principles. This is, in the opinion of advocates of rights, 'the one feature that distinguishes law from ordered brutality. If the Government does not take rights seriously, then it does not take law seriously either.

For the utilitarian, on the other hand, rights cannot be ultimately considered as limits on legitimate action but only as rules of thumb that tend to coincide with maximizing utility. As such, utilitarianism appears to adopt a conception of unlimited government, where neither right nor law itself can stand in the way of maximising utility. Of course, utilitarians can and do argue in favour of limited government. They might do so on the grounds that governments are, on the whole, far more efficient at preventing pain than they are at producing pleasure, or that pain weighs more heavily than pleasure in utilitarian calculation. This sort of negative utilitarianism concentrates on limiting the ways in which government and people can impact negatively on the general welfare. In principle, however, these limits cannot be absolute; if the consequences for welfare look to be good enough any limit, right or law can be set aside.

Competing understandings of the relationship between the right and the good underpin two competing understandings of concepts such as individualism, equality, and impartiality. These combine into two opposing answers to the question "how do you take people seriously?" People and their interests are conceptualised in competing ways, as is the proper response to their interests. Should we regard all interests in the same way so that taking people's interests seriously involves a process of aggregation? Every individual is treated equally and impartially in this process. Everyone counts as only one and no one's interests have a privileged status. Everybody has the same input into moral decisions and those decisions reflect the status of all individuals as equal objects of moral concern. Alternatively, are there certain things that it is always immoral to do to anyone, ways of treating people that are inconsistent with regarding them as fully human and protection from which should be enshrined in a theory of rights? Rights depend on an understanding of interests at odds with utilitarianism. Instead of all interests being reducible to the same sort of thing, certain interests that we each have should be regarded as fundamental and in need of protection. These are the interests that inform the idea of the 'separateness of persons', interests of security, liberty and the individual's pursuit of his own and distinctive conception of the good. These interests are fundamental to a proper understanding of the importance of individuals and should not be outweighed by any combination of less important concerns.

One of the most widespread criticisms of utilitarianism is that it cannot take rights seriously enough. Generally speaking, rights take precedence over considerations of immediate utility. They limit or restrict direct appeals to welfare maximization. For example, to have a right to free speech means that one is free to speak one's mind even if doing so will fail to maximize happiness because others will dislike hearing what one has to say. The right not to be compelled to incriminate oneself entails that it would be wrong to force a criminal defendant to testify against himself even if the results of doing so would be good. If rights are moral claims that trump straightforward appeals to utility, then utilitarianism, the critics argue, cannot meaningfully respect rights because their theory subordinates them to the promotion of welfare.

However, the criticism that utilitarianism cannot do right to justice ignores the extent to which utilitarianism can accommodate the moral rules, principles, and norms other than welfare maximization that appear to constitute the warp and woof of our moral lives. To be sure, utilitarians look at rights in a different light than do demonic status grounded on non-utilitarian considerations. For utilitarians, it is not rights, but the promotion of welfare, that lies at the heart of large measure because he believed that invoking natural rights was only a way of dressing up appeals to intuition in fancy rhetoric.

They believe that utilitarianism does not deal satisfactorily with rights and that this failure betrays a deep deficiency in the theory. Two such critics are James Fishkin and David Lyons, respected moral theorists whose views on this issue are representative of those of many opponents of utilitarianism. Fishkin and Lyons, however, attack the theory on distinct grounds. Fishkin maintains that utilitarianism cannot adequately underwrite a commitment to basic human rights whereas Lyons argues that utilitarians, including utilitarian officials, will not see themselves as bound to respect those rights that their own theory justifies and whose institutionalization it supports.

Fishkin tells us that utilitarianism is an insecure basis for human rights. His mainline argument for this proposition rests on the contention that if the ultimate basis for institutionalizing one set of rights defining practices rather than another is utilitarian, then those core human rights have a most uncertain basis. Fishkin rejects the utilitarian approach to rights precisely because it is consequentialist and empirical. Hence, there is no a priori guarantee that the rights that utilitarian endorse will be those favored by non-utilitarian "rights advocates" such as Fishkin. However this line of criticism begs the question against utilitarianism. It assumes without argument that the preferences of the so-called rights advocates – preferences that are formed, as Fishkin affirms, independently of an understanding of the empirical implications of acknowledging and enforcing those putative rights do not provide a secure enough basis for human rights, but he provides no alternative theory of rights, implicitly relying only on intuition and people's common moral beliefs.

Lyons contends that utilitarians must violate rights. He grants that utilitarianism readily provides for the establishment of legal and other institutionally embedded rights, and he believes that these rights will be familiar ones protecting individuals from violations of their persons and property. Although he grants that utilitarianism will support and enforce the rights that we cherish, Lyons nevertheless argues that it "ignores" or fails to "accommodate" their moral force. Utilitarianism justifies those rights at the institutional level, but it does not oblige us to obey them, and puts no moral weight on those rights when assessing individual conduct. For this reason, the completely utilitarian approach to rights is "incoherent."

Objections to Utilitarianism

Many philosophers today deny that utilitarianism provides a plausible thing. They believe that its view of right and wrong is profoundly flawed and contend that the theory faces crippling objection. We can scrutinize the most significant and frequently voiced objections to utilitarianism. These can be grouped into four categories: (1) that the theory requires immoral conduct, (2) that it cannot do justice to promises and other special obligations, (3) that it is indifferent to the distribution of welfare, and (4) that it requires too much of moral agents. It has been agued that if utilitarianism is to establish itself as a plausible theory, let alone prove itself more satisfactory than alternative ethical approaches, then it must rebut these criticisms and overcome the reservations of its critics.

Critics of utilitarianism contend that in any array of situations, utilitarianism not only diverges from ordinary morality but also has implications that are ethically repugnant. Many philosophers argue that utilitarianism must be rejected on moral grounds. For instance, A.C. Ewing contends "utilitarian principles, logically carried out, would result in far more cheating, lying and unfair action than any good man would tolerate." Critics of utilitarianism sometimes charge that the theory cannot satisfactorily explain what is wrong with killing. Instead of appealing to well-being, they favor notions like the sanctity of life, or they contend that killing is intrinsically wrong because it transgresses the victim's autonomy, violates his right to life, or fails to respect his as a person. Like utilitarians however, most of these critics do not view killing as categorically wrong, that is, as impermissible always and in every circumstance whatsoever, and they differ among themselves over such controversial issues as war, euthanasia, and capital punishment. Nevertheless, these theorists believe that the normative concept they favor provide a theoretically more acceptable moral basis for denouncing killing than does utilitarianism.

From a utilitarian perspective, the negative consequences of killing are obvious. In addition to whatever pain the victim suffers, killing the person deprives him of the future wellbeing he would have had. For this reason it is ordinarily one of the most serious harms that can befall a person. Killing someone also typically brings sorrow and grief to family and friends, and murder can easily spread fear, worry, and insecurity through society. All societies firmly prohibit killing other people, at least under ordinary circumstances, and there is a fully compelling utilitarian case for there doing so. Without such a prohibition, social existence would barely be possible.

However, its critics argue that utilitarianism does not condemn killing as strongly and unequivocally as it should. Imagine, they say, an old tramp who is miserably depressed and unhappy, whose future will be one of continued misery, and who has no family or friends. If it can be done painlessly and without anyone noticing, and assuming that the killer would enjoy doing it or that he or others would benefit from the tramp's death in some other way, then killing the tramp would appear to be justified on utilitarian grounds. Yet surely, the critic argues, killing him would be foul and immoral, and because utilitarianism condones it, one must repudiate utilitarianism as a normative theory.

An important and more plausible variant of the immoral-conduct argument focuses on lying; with the critics arguing that utilitarians take truthfulness less seriously than they should. Utilitarians, however, rejoin that there are firm and compelling consequentialist grounds for telling the truth. As moralists of all persuasions have recognized, experience teaches that although lying sometimes appears an attractive short-term expedient, all too frequently it leads to unhappiness in the long run. When people learn that they have been deceived, they are made unhappy, trust among human beings is damaged, and the liar is likely to suffer adverse effects. Further, when mendacity becomes widespread, it has debilitating social effects. As Mill remarks, lying weakens "the trustworthiness of human assertion, which is the principal support of all present social well-being." A lack of veracity, he continues, "does more than any one thing that can be named to keep back civilization, virtue and everything on which human happiness on the largest scale depends"

From a utilitarian point of view, breaking a promise is not always wrong. It is wrong only when the results are bad—worse than the result of keeping the promise. Although contingent, the utilitarian case for keeping promises is nevertheless strong. Broken promises generally result in unmet expectations and disappointment – even hurt, anger, and a sense of betrayal. In addition to the good that may come from keeping a particular promise is the good that results from supporting a system or practice in which people make and rely on one another's promises. Nevertheless, utilitarianism's critics frequently insist that it fails to treat promises seriously enough. Not only, in their view does utilitarianism too readily permit promises to be broken but also, because of its consequentialist perspective, the theory misunderstands what promises are and fails to grasp the distinctive character of the obligation they create. The critics further contend that utilitarianism's inadequate treatment of promises is symptomatic of its inability to do justice to the special obligations that given each person's moral duty its specific, individualized character.

We have reviewed the charge that utilitarianism licenses immoral conduct and examined the contention that it ignores the particularity of our obligations and the special moral ties that bind us to others. These criticisms dovetail with the frequently heard complaint that utilitarianism is indifferent to the distribution of welfare. Because the theory recognizes only one fundamental imperative – namely that welfare be promoted as much as possible – it does not matter, in itself, how that welfare is allocated. As a result, the critics argue, utilitarianism too easily permits one person's happiness to be sacrificed for the benefit of others. It ignores considerations of justice and fairness or, at best, subordinates them entirely to the principle of utility.

In the eyes of most philosophers, the concept of equality is closely linked to that of justice, and some critics fault utilitarianism for giving no independent moral weight to equality. Because utilitarians believe that social well-being should be promoted in whatever manner will maximize it overall, it follows that the precise way in which welfare is distributed among individuals – in particular, whether some individuals end up enjoying greater well-being than others – is, in and of itself, unimportant. From a utilitarian perspective, considerations of overall well-being determine "whether and when and in what way and to what extent people ought to be treated equally."

At the end of the day, what matters is how well people live not how they compare to one another.

Many critics of utilitarianism are still troubled by the fact that in the eyes of utilitarian, no principle of just distribution has independent moral weight. Because utilitarianism concerns itself with issues of distribution only insofar as they affect net wellbeing, the critics believe that the theory inevitably leads to unfair results. In the past thirty years, many philosophers have been persuaded by Johan Rawls that the root problem is that utilitarianism ignores "the separateness of persons." So widespread is this contention that it has become a virtual mantra. What does the phrase mean, and does it really identify some irremediably defect of utilitarianism? Rawls concludes that utilitarianism fails to recognize the separateness of persons:

> This view of social co-operation is the consequence of extending to society the principle of choice for one man, and then, to make this extension work, conflating all persons into one through the imaginative acts of the impartial sympathetic spectator. Utilitarianism does not take seriously the distinction between persons.

The 'separateness-of-persons' argument can be interpreted either as the metaphysical objection that utilitarianism does not adequately recognize that people are distinct individuals or as the moral objection that it does not treat people as autonomous individuals, each with a separate life to live. When Rawls mentions the idea of a sympathetic utilitarian spectator viewing the well-being of all in the same way that a rational and prudential person views the stages of his or her own life, this suggests that he has in mind the metaphysical objection that utilitarianism overlooks the boundaries between people, collapsing them into one social organism. In line with this objection, David Gauthier writes that theories like utilitarianism "suppose that mankind is a super-person, whose greatest satisfaction is the objective of moral action." And Thomas Nagel asserts that any such theory "treats the desires, needs, satisfactions, and dissatisfactions of distinct persons as if they were the desires, etc., of a mass person." Based on the premise that people are merely interchangeable components of a larger organism or as derived from a prior belief that society is best seen as an individual entity choosing rationally how best to pursue its interests.

Its advocates see the moral version of the 'separateness of persons' argument as underwriting the charge that, in its indifference to distribution, utilitarianism permits injustice, condoning in the name of the general good things like slavery that it ought not tolerate. But the argument also connects to the opposite charge that utilitarianism requires too much of us, with its critics now asserting, not that utilitarianism is too lax, but that it is too demanding, to be an acceptable moral theory.

The utilitarian criterion states that an action is right if and only if its expected outcome is at least as good as anything else the agent could have done; otherwise it is wrong. This sets a high standard, and critics of utilitarianism have frequently balked at it. At many points in our day, when we are innocently relaxing, talking with friends or simply at work doing our job, we could probably be doing something else instead that would bring more happiness into the world. For example, instead of watching television tonight, we could visit a nursing home to chat and play cards with its elderly residents. Instead of going to the beach with friends, we could work for the old people and give the rest of the money to a charitable cause.

Amartya Sen has recently asked whether we really need these various formulations of 'utility' as exclusive alternatives. What instead we should do, he suggests, is to regard 'utility' as a plural notion, a vector of many different considerations. Suppose some person prefers bitter truth to comforting delusion, but is palmed off with the latter. We feel sorry for him. Then later he learns that it was all a deception. We feel sorrier for him. Why not take our sympathy as an indicator of the person's utilities? Bare desire fulfillment and experienced desire fulfillment are both relevant, and to insist on a choice between them, Sen says, seems 'arbitrary and uncalled for'. Similarly for the other choices, we have been considering for example, the choice between actual and informed desires.

Utilitarianism, in common with other moral theories, starts with everyday, vague, and depressingly elusive notion: that of a person's welfare or well-being, of the quality of his life, of his life's being happy or successful in the broadest sense, but all of those terms, because so vague and elusive, need content put into them by intelligent stipulation. That is a need, which Bentham and Mill never sufficiently recognized, but which now is more felt.

'Utility', one could then say, consists in the fulfillment of the desires that people actually have. Economists have been drawn to this account because one's actual desires are often revealed in one's choices, and 'revealed preferences' are observable and hence a respectable subject for empirical science. The trouble here is that, notoriously, people mistake their own interests, and if, as we want, 'utility is to be close to well-being, then what must matter for 'utility' will be not people's actual desires, but their desires in some way sanitized. But how sanitized? One way would be to say that desires count towards utility only if 'rational' on some definition—for instance, that they survive maximal criticism by logic. This is an account of 'rational' worked out with exemplary rigour by Richard Brandt. But it is hard to get the balance between actual and sanitized desires quite right. Although utility cannot simply be equated with actual desires, it cannot simply by equated with rational desires either. It is doubtless true that if one were acquainted with all facts now obtainable; he should change some of my desires. But if that daunting education were not given to him, yet the objects of my potentially thus sanitized desires were. He might well not be glad to have them; Utility must, it seems, be tied at least to desires that are actual when satisfied or are part of the education that will change desires. One might say that 'utility' should be explained in terms of informed desires', which is meant to cover the sort of complex combination of actual and sanitized desires. But much remains to be done. Brandt's criteria for a sanitized desire perhaps put too much stress on information, as if all that criticism of desires needs, besides logic, is more the forts the better. Yet sometimes desires are defective because we do not have enough, or the right concepts. Theories need developing which will supply new or better concepts, including value concepts. And with information, more is not always better.

Most need accounts blunder by being too rigid, they rank needs above mere desires, regardless of the levels of satisfaction of each, which is implausible. That was the moral of the story of the scholars' choice between liberty extension or exercise equipment. But T M Scanlon has made an important contribution to the debate by proposing an account of welfare retaining the objectivity of the need accounts while avoiding rigidity. It goes like this. We have many concerns, health and learning being two of them. These concerns will be met to varying degrees. Various combinations of these degrees of satisfaction of our concerns constitute different overall levels of welfare.

Utilitarianism, Williams says, 'essentially involves the notion of negative responsibility: that I am as responsible for what I allow as for what myself do. It does, he says, by being consequentialist, by regarding only the states of affairs that actions produce and not who produces them, or why, as relevant to moral right and wrong. But this is to attack 'the value of integrity'. Any fully developed person has 'commitments' or 'ground projects' that he 'takes seriously at the deepest level, as what his life is about', projects which are closely related to his existence and which to a significant degree given meaning to his life'. He cannot abandon such projects just because the reports from the utility network indicate that as chance or the actions of others have stacked things, utility would be maximized by his doing so. That would be to ask him to commit a kind of suicide, to abandon himself.

This too is an old criticism, but Hampshire finds that recent workings of cost-benefit analysis have given it new force. He writes of the 'coarse, quantitative, calculative Benthamism' of Mr. McNamara and his defense advisors' and contends that what in utilitarianism led the United States to war in Vietnam was nothing peripheral to it, but rather something at its heart: its treating all values as commensurable. Others make much the same point.

Although they occur in the course of an attack on utility as a candidate for what an egalitarian should equalize, Dworkin's arguments are worth considering here too, because they hold an important moral about utility. Dworkin provides several ingenious arguments, but his strongest is this. Suppose that 'utility' is best defined as 'satisfaction of desire', and that the proper desires to consult are our broadest ones, ones that embody the overall value that we attach to our lives. But then how should one compare Jack's level of overall desire satisfaction with Jill's?. We might try different ways. One technique would be to ask each of them, How would you compare your present life with the best life you can imagine, with whatever physical and mental powers and material resources and opportunities you could ask for now. Suppose Jack, who thinks that with all that he could ask for he could them go on to solve the riddle of the origin of the universe, replies that his present life is much less valuable than his ideal life would be. But Jill, who, let us suppose is much more down to earth, thinks the riddle insoluble and has no comparably grand dream at hand, and so she replies that her present life is not much below what her ideal life would be. We could then proceed to take what each considers ideal as marking the same level of utility. This would allow us to treat their answers as indicating their present actual level: Jack would be at a much lower level than Jill. But we would not, for a minute, want to see transfers of goods from Jill to Jack, in order to raise Jack somewhat closer to the ideal. Equality of welfare, on that account of utility, provides no attractive goal at all.

Suppose, therefore, that we try another technique. We ask Jack and Jill, as perhaps a better way to get at their utility levels'. How would you compare your present life with a life that seemed to you to have no value at all? Now suppose that Jack is the sort who believes that an everyday life fully immersed in projects is immensely valuable, and that he is leading such a life, and that he replies that his present life is much better than a valueless one. And suppose that Jill, who is much more demanding and regards such life as of little value, replies that her present life is only slightly better than a valueless one. We could now take what they mean by a valueless life as representing the same level of utility and so regard their answers as establishing that Jack is at a far higher level of utility than Jill. But, again, to transfer resources from Jack to Jill in the name of equality would be a thoroughly unattractive move. Equality of utility, once again, has no plausibility as a goal. So Dworkin is right that to get a good indication of real differences in people's lives we need to eliminate false belief, unreal fantasies, unsound philosophical convictions and the like.

Bentham was aware of his own genius and fierce ambition, and was deeply ambivalent about both. Feeling unappreciated in his own land, he remarked that he would "like to live the remaining years of his life, a year at a time at the end of the next six or eight centuries, to see the effect which his writing would by that time have upon the world." He also wrote of having "formed a plan of universal conquest," by which he intended

> To govern all the nations in the habitable globe after my death. With what weapons? With rhetoric? With fine speeches? With prohibitive and irritant clauses? No: but with reasons, with a chain of articulate and connected reasons all depending upon one principle.

Were Bentham to return today, he would surely be pleased at the extent of his triumph, the influence of his inventions, reforms, and vocabulary, the prestige of contemporary utilitarianism and its derivatives: public choice theory, game theory, and cost-benefit analysis. More generally, too, he might find ours to be a Benthamite world: in its substituting of administration for politics, its oscillating between laissez-faire liberalism and the welfare state, its bureaucratization, the many large public and private organizations that manage, regulate, and channel our lives. Indeed, some of Bentham's ideas have become our commonplace vocabularies and assumptions, to the point where one might say that Bentham has triumphed within each of us. This persistent, seemingly insidious power of his ideas is surely part of what so infuriates his famous critics, but their rage does not succeed in silencing the Bentham within us.

13

John Stuart Mill

> But the peculiar evil of silencing the expression of an opinion is, that it is robbing the human race; posterity as well as the existing generation; those who dissent from the opinion, still more than those who hold it. If the opinion is right, they are deprived of the opportunity of exchanging error for truth: if wrong, they lose, what is almost as great a benefit, the clearer perception and livelier impression of truth, produced by its collision with error.

Opinions differ about whether John Stuart Mill (1806-1873) was fortunate to be born the son of the Scottish historian, philosopher and administrator James Mill. A friend and chief disciple of Jeremy Bentham, the great exponent of utilitarian ethics, James Mill was a stern intellectual who claimed all men are equal. Like Leopold Mozart, he undertook to give his first-born son the benefit of his wisdom by educating him himself. The younger Mill was taught at home, learning Greek at the age of three, then arithmetic, history and Latin, and at twelve logic, metaphysics and ethics. But his education was not a matter of rote learning. As he wrote in his *Autobiography*, his father never let anything he learnt degenerate into a mere exercise of memory. He strove to make the understanding not only go along with every step of the teaching, but if possible, precede it. In their walks together younger Mill was taught to dissect a bad argument and to argue both sides of an issue, something he continued to excel at. Indeed his writings often gave his opponents their best arguments against him. What James neglected was the emotional side of his son's education. He undervalued poetry, feeling and imagination. He was ashamed of exhibiting emotion, and he sadly admitted being unable to feel more than loyal devotion to a father who never displayed any tenderness to him.

At the age of twenty-one, after nearly four years' work as his father's subordinate in East India House, and having produced numerous reviews and articles for such organs as the radical Westminster Review, John suffered a mental breakdown. He had made some good friends in India House, though discouraged by his father from doing so, had formed various debating societies to discuss political economy, logic and analytic psychology with other hopeful young radicals, and 'had what might truly be called an object in life: to be a reformer of the world'. Yet for some years, he wrote, the description 'mere reasoning machine'–commonly applied to followers of Bentham–could with accuracy have been applied to him. In the autumn of 1826 he became insipid and indifferent. 'In this frame of mind it occurred to me to put the question directly to myself, "Suppose that all your objects in life were realized; that all the changes in institutions and opinions which you are looking forward to, could be completely effected at this very instant: would this be a great joy and happiness to you?" And an irrepressible self-consciousness distinctly answered, "No!" At this my heart sank within me: the whole foundation on which my life was constructed fell down.' All those whom Mill respected thought that the greatest source of happiness was pleasure in sympathy with other human beings and their well-being. Unfortunately, though he was convinced that this was true, 'to know that a feeling would make me happy if I had it, did not give me the feeling'. Analytic habits, he decided, have a 'tendency to wear away the feelings'. By strengthening the associations between what is logically or causally linked, and weakening associations due merely to emotion, they undermine desire, passion and even virtue. Pleasure in virtue or the general good, in anything eluded him. Ironically, education by utilitarianism had deprived him of any capacity for what utilitarian consider the only good. The first break in his gloom was reading, six months later, his father died and he resolved to replace him. Mill was moved to tears and realized that he could at least feel. Gradually his capacity for pleasure in life returned, with only occasional relapses. Thereafter he cultivated his feelings through poetry and art, though he insisted that to be happy is to concentrate on the happiness of others, or on some external pursuit, and that to ask yourself if you are happy is to cease to be so.

John Stuart Mill was barely out of the cradle when his most famous of educations began at James's hands. By the romantic standards then in fashion, young Mill can hardly be said to have had a childhood at all. James Mill appears to have thought that lack of years was no bar to difficult learning of any kind. Younger Mill first read Bentham when he was fifteen, having been admitted to the great man's conversation at an even earlier age. Mill never played cricket; instead he had to spend his adolescence being precociously clever at utilitarian ethics, classical economics and lots and lots of history. By the age of twenty Mill probably had more book-learning than most men acquire in their whole lives. This has led some to suppose that Mill's was a 'made mind' or at the very least, that Mill's education made his mind overly susceptible to outside influences. When he was twenty, Mill experienced the most famous burst of tears in the history of ideas. It is still hard to be unmoved by his account of it in the *Autobiography*. Whether Mill wept for his lost youth or for the loss of his youthful utilitarianism has never been entirely clear, but after the emotional crisis Mill put the education and cultivation of the feelings on the agenda of "philosophical radicalism" in a heroic attempt to disassociate utilitarianism from the unfeeling rationalism which the public mind tended to associate with the treadmill and the workhouse.

At the age of twenty-three, Mill followed his father into the service of the East India Company, and stayed there until he retired in 1858. His was one of the very few voices raised in England against the treatment of the prisoners after the Indian Mutiny was put down. Mill's intellectual energy alone is enough to make him an eminent Victorian. All the cross-currents of the age-romanticism, positivism, political economy, the suffrage question (including votes for women), birth control, socialism met in Mill's mind. He was an MP for Westminster from 1865 to 1868. *On Liberty* came out in 1859, by which time Mill had established himself as one of the leading social thinkers of the day, and, in a happy phrase, he became the schoolmaster of liberalism.

J. S. Mill was one of the great thinkers of the nineteenth century. Though he is now mainly remembered as a moral and political philosopher, he was celebrated also for his writings in economics, logic and social reform, and as a literary journalist. He has been claimed variously as a liberal, a precursor of British socialism, and an elitist libertarian. Commentators try to render him consistent in different versions of any of these, but part of his greatness lay in embracing important contradictions. He wanted greater freedom for all, while still holding on to his father's utilitarianism –the right action is the action that produces the greatest happiness of the greatest number–but in a way that promoted what would not be called 'quality of life'. After a breakdown, which he considered partly due to the way his education had omitted cultivation of feeling and imagination; he came to value art, poetry, the 'higher pleasures'. He therefore recommended that educated people should be given extra voters so that they could have a greater say in government. He was fearful of the ignorance and especially the selfishness and brutality of the masses, and that 'the uncultivated cannot be competent judges of cultivation'. And he was opposed to too much help and support being given to the poor as it gaffed initiative.

Also in the 1830s, Mill fell desperately in love with Harriet Taylor, an intelligent women who belonged to a radical Unitarian circle-'rational' Christians who, in the spirit of the Enlightenment, denied the divinity of Christ. The problem was that she was already married, with three children. A crisis was reached in 1833; Mill and Harriet stayed in Paris and were evidently considering living together. The scandal would have wrecked Mill's career, and in the event conventional propriety triumphed. Fortunately the husband, John Taylor, was astonishingly noble-minded; he opened his doors to the lovesick philosopher, set up his wife in a country cottage where she and Mill could spend weekend together; and paid for her to take long trips abroad in Mill's company. All of this was done with care so as to avoid scandal. Even more astonishing to twentieth-century readers is the indubitable fact, proved by one of Harriet Taylor's own letters, that there was no sex; the relationship, passionate and intense, was purely Platonic. In 1843 he published his *System* of *Logic*. No work ever cost his so much trouble: it took him thirteen years to write. Then in 1848 he published his *Principles of Political Economy*, having almost shed in off he had begun work on this massive book in the autumn of 1845. These two works provided the basis for Mill's great reputation in the nineteenth century, dominating their respective disciplines for a generation or more; the *Political Economy* went through thirty-two editions before the century ended. In the 1840s he withdrew increasingly from social life; the society of Harriet Taylor was enough. He drifted away from Carlyle, fell out with Comte because the latter insisted that women were inherently inferior to men, and with the Austins because they did not share his enthusiasm for the 1848 revolution in Paris.

In 1849 John Taylor died, and in 1851 Mill and Harriet married. Their happiness was soon alloyed. Mill was suffering from tuberculosis; a year after their marriage, Harriet exhibited symptoms of the disease. Mill's father and his dear friend John Sterling had died of it: it was to kill two of his brothers. By 1854, he and his wife were expecting, with good reason that they would die within a year. Attempting to secure a respite, in 1854-5 Mill toured, often on foot, in Italy, Sicily and Greece; he returned, miraculously on the mend. He wanted to live a little longer, because he believe he had a great task to perform. He sincerely thought that his wife was the truly creative thinker; his mission was to present her ideas to the world. Therefore they set to work to write drafts containing the essence of their thought, as a legacy to posterity. She had already played a part in revising the *Political Economy;* now they drafted the essay *On Liberty* and the *Autobiography,* and essays on nature, *Utilitarianism* and religion. In 1851, Mill had published under his own name an essay on the 'Enfranchisement of Women' calling for votes for women and access to jobs and careers; later he insisted that the essay had been written by his wife.

In 1858, in the aftermath of the Indian Mutiny, the East India Company was wound up, and its functions transferred to the British state. Mill was pensioned off at three-quarters salary £1500 per year. He was free, and at the end of the year he and Harriet set off for southern Europe. She was taken ill and died of TB quite suddenly at Avignon. Mill was devastated: the spring of life is broken. He buried her in the Protestant cemetery on the outskirts of the city, and bought a house, within sight of it, where henceforth he lived for a part of the year: He raised a costly marble tomb, which he visited every day, lovingly tending the garden a round it; as he expressed it, atheist that he was "Her memory is to me a religion'. His stepdaughter Helen Taylor now became his constant and devoted companion; she was as intellectual and as fiercely radical as her mother, and was to him another such prize in the lottery of life.

Mill had published nothing for ten years; after Harriet Mill's death there came a series of important books within Mill's own estimation, brought him a wider celebrity than his massive treatises on logic and political economy had obtained. The essay *On Liberty* which he claimed was a joint work in which all the best thoughts came from his wife, came out immediately in 1859, followed by *Considerations on Representative Government* in 1861 *and Utilitarianism* in 1863.

As well as developing love of poetry, which James Mill considered the expression of barbarous people who 'feel before they can speculate,' Mill grew away from his father in other ways. After a bitter debate in which his beliefs were attacked, he resigned from the Debating Society, and subsequently tended to deny that he was a Benthamite. He formed friendships with anti-utilitarian disciples of Coleridge, with the Communist-resembling Saint Simon, and with Carlyle, who ridiculed utilitarianism as the worship of machinery, and who wrote what James Mill considered 'insane rhapsody'. Mill now espoused Goethe's 'many sidedness' and was considered by his father 'a deserter from his standard'. But although he criticized his father's mentor Bentham, in fact he refined and enhanced the utilitarianism they both promoted.

Utilitarianism

Mill was a rationalist and a utilitarian who believed that it was possible to plan society, political and social arrangements, social changes and institutions on the basis of values and ideals, chiefly but not exclusively utilitarian. Scholars disagree concerning the version of utilitarianism, hedonistic or ideal, act or rule, that colors his theory; and there is now even a questioning as to whether Mill applied his utilitarianism directly or indirectly, as well as concerning the extent to which he compromised his utilitarianism by reference to other values including justice seen as something distinct from utility. The most plausible interpretation is that Mill was a sophisticated ideal-act utilitarian whose values included knowledge, rationalism and true belief and self-development, and not simply pleasure and happiness, but that he was prepared to be an inconsistent utilitarian as required by the realities of social life. Although he believed in the possibility of rationalistic planning, he generally favored a cautious, careful, non-doctrinaire, flexible approach, one given more to compromise and modification on the basis of facts as they are found in the world, than was Bentham's. Consider here his support for a free society and its qualifications, his case for political and full legal equality for women, his more general support for universal franchise, albeit introduced in a cautious, qualified, weighted way, and his insistence that the state plan colonization rather than leave it to be developed by individuals. Increasingly, the problems encountered by utilitarian rationalism in practical morality are being appreciated. Those encountered by political utilitarians are even greater. Yet it was as a rationalistic utilitarian that Mill approached the problems of defining the proper sphere of government and the principles defining the rights to liberty of thought, expression, and discussion and of action, and what are illegitimate invasions of these rights.

A good deal has been made in recent years of Mill's discussion of the 'art of life'. He claims that the principle of utility is the ultimate principle of the whole of the art of life, where morality is seen simply to be one branch, with other branches such as prudence and aesthetics. This raises the problem as to the principles that inform morality over and above the principle of utility, which informs the whole art of living. It also bears on the issue of state concern for and promotion of morals, as Mill clearly did not see it to be proper for the state to seek to make people lead prudent and noble, admirable lives. John Stuart Mill had become a dedicated disciple of Jeremy Bentham:

> The "principle of utility" understood as Bentham understood, and applied in the manner in which he applied fell exactly into its place as the keystone which held together the detached and fragmentary component parts of my knowledge and beliefs. It gave unity to my conceptions of things. I now had opinions; a creed, a doctrine, a philosophy; in one among the best senses of the word, a religion; the inculcation and diffusion of which could be made the principal outward purpose of a life.

While John Stuart Mill's education had exposed him to the fundamental dogma of a particular creed, it also had the inevitable effect of shaping his personality according to the standards implicit in such dogma. Consequently, according to his own description, Mill had become a "reasoning machine." Beginning in 1826 and lasting about five years, Mill suffered through a period of depression and mental torment. During that time, he come to realize that Bentham's mechanistic and universalistic conception of human nature had failed to appreciate the individual's need to develop his emotional and personal facilities. In short, Bentham failed to realize the importance of those individual and unique qualities that combine to form the human personality. An educational program that ignored such features is essentially incapable of producing that happiness which all utilitarian considered to be fundamental.

John Stuart Mill continued to proclaim his allegiance to utilitarian principles. But at the same time he sought to introduce a series of necessary reforms. First, the Benthamite view of humanity had to be enlarged to include an appreciation of such things as the human spirit, the human conscience, and human idealism. Similarly, the utilitarian view of society would have to be expanded so that it could address itself to such issues as society's interest in humanity's self-education and the nation's concern for its own spiritual character. In any case, however, such reforms necessarily presupposed a reconsideration of utilitarianism's most fundamental concept: pleasure.

In an essay entitled *Utilitarianism*, published in 1863, Mill attempted both to defend utilitarianism from its critics and to expand the notion of pleasure to support what he felt were necessary reforms. In his attempt to establish a mathematical calculus, Bentham had implied that pleasure was simply a quantitative concept. As the good, the value of pleasure could not be increased by bringing any other quality to it. More pleasure was better than less simply because of the amount involved. A distinction among types of pleasure, however, presupposed qualitative differences and, therefore, was unacceptable. For Mill, on the other hand, utilitarianism did not require such a limitation. As a utilitarian, he believed that it was possible to make qualitative distinctions and indeed argued for the recognition of a fundamental qualitative difference between intellectual and sensual pleasure:

> It is quite compactable with the principle of utility to recognize the fact that some kinds of pleasure are more desirable and more valuable than others. It would be absurd that while, in estimating all other things, quality is considered as well as quantity, the estimation of pleasures should be supposed to depend on quantity alone. It is better to be a human being dissatisfied than a pig satisfied; better to be Socrates dissatisfied than a fool satisfied.

In creating a scale from the animal to the human and from the foolish to the wise, it is obvious that Mill is suggesting that the value of pleasure is increased by the presence of intellectual activity. It is not simply that intellectual activity increases the amount, permanency, or fecundity of pleasure; for such changes are purely of a quantitative nature. Rather, according to Mill, intellectual pleasure is superior because of the kind of pleasure, which it is.

Although Mill himself was convinced that the recognition of qualitative distinctions among pleasures was consistent with utilitarianism, his arguments are not necessarily persuasive. By admitting that some pleasures are superior in kind to others, Mill is claiming that there is a source of value other than pleasure itself. Inasmuch as the absence or presence of the active intellect adds to or detracts from the value. Something other than mere pleasure is good, and pleasure alone, consequently, cannot be the good simply. Whereas Mill's distinction between Socrates and the fool may appeal to common sense, it is difficult to justify such a distinction on strictly utilitarian grounds.

In differentiating between the sphere of the intellectual and the realm of the physical, Mill reintroduced a fundamental theme of classical political philosophy. Indeed, for the ancient Greeks the central problem of political order was based upon the fact that, as complex beings, humans have both spiritual and physical needs.

Participating in both the transcendent and mundane poles of reality, humanity requires various goods, which are different in kind. Thus it is faced with the constant challenge of creating a harmonious personal and social order. Typically for the Greeks such a harmony was achieved by recognizing a certain rank among humankind's interests and needs and, consequently, subordinating the lower to the higher. Thus, in the classical spirit, Mill proposed a similar solution. The intellectual pleasures are not only different from their physical counterparts but are at the same time, superior in kind to them. The good life, therefore, is the rational life, and the good society is the one which elicits and supports the life of reason among its citizens.

Mill's emphasis upon the relationship of reason to politics has led some commentators to suggest that there is a certain similarity between his thinking and that of Aristotle. Indeed such comparisons find further evidence in the fact that Mill, like Aristotle, argued that existing societies should be directed towards a realization of the "best polity." Thus, unlike many of his contemporaries, Mill drew his model of political order from an understanding of what was required for the "ideal" society. In doing so, he broke from a tradition that can be traced back through such thinkers as Bentham, Hobbes, and Machiavelli. These men had argued that political order must be created according to an understanding of the human being as it appears in actuality rather than as it is potentially. Mill, on the other hand, like the Greeks, sought to govern the lower in light of the higher. Accordingly, from this perspective, an ethical education should be modeled after Socrates rather than after the fool, and a political society should be constructed in view of the rational polity rather than according to them "merely business part of the social arrangements."

Both Mill's concern for the relationship between reason and politics and the "idealism" of his political writings do, indeed, suggest a certain similarity with the Greeks. Yet the basic character of his work becomes clear only if one is aware of what actually distinguishes Mill from the classical tradition. This becomes apparent if one looks at those arguments, which Mill introduced to support his position that the intellectual pleasure are superior in kind.

The classical tradition, on the other hand, based its justification of the rational life on metaphysical grounds. Accordingly people ought to pursue the life of reason because such a pursuit was intended by the very structure of human nature itself. For the Greeks the soul was intended for reason. Thus humanity's obligation to live the rational life was given by nature and, as a consequence, existed regardless of whether individuals factually fulfilled their obligations or not. Mill, on the contrary, does not rely upon such an argument because, unlike the Greeks, he does not believe in the possibility of metaphysical truth. For Mill, reason is empirical not transcendental. And thus when he called for the life of reason or evoked the ideal of the rational polity, he had a radically different intention than did either Plato or Aristotle.

The Mental Crisis of the Young Mill

Properly understood, utilitarianism does not imply that we should become persons fanatically devoted to doing good, nor does it say that as utilitarian we should love the things we do only because and insofar as our doing so promotes the general good. John Stuart Mill's own life illustrates these points. Mill's father James Mill educated

John Stuart at home in an effort to mold his development along utilitarian lines. By all accounts, the Mill household was not a particularly warm and loving one. James Mill deprived the younger Mill of contact with boys of his own age so as not to impede the rigorous, accelerated, and demanding educational program he had designed for him. So successful was this program, in one respect, that as an adolescent Mill was the intellectual peer of writers and thinkers much older than he was. Although Mill had already absorbed implicitly utilitarian values from his father, reading Bentham at age 15, gave his life intellectual coherence and moral purpose. Thereafter, he was an active writer, debator, and organizer in the cause of utilitarian social reform.

At 20, the younger Mill fell into what he called "a crisis in my mental history," the onset of which he described in his *Autobiography:* "All my happiness was to have been found in the continual pursuit of this end. The end had ceased to charm, and how could there ever again be any interest in the means? I seemed to have nothing left to live for." Following this disturbing realization, Mill slumped into a dark period of depression that lasted for several years. Gradually, Mill emerged from his mental misery and began to enjoy life again. Although he remained a utilitarian, and indeed went on to write his classics *Utilitarianism* and *On Liberty* he advocated a subtle and moderate form of utilitarianism. He was no longer the single-minded utilitarian fanatic he had been.

As an adolescent, Mill's life approximated what critics take to be the utilitarian ideal: he had been, Mill said later, "a mere reasoning machine." However, his mental breakdown illustrates both the pragmatic and deeper reasons for rejecting this supposed ideal as a caricature of utilitarianism. Mill himself drew two explicit conclusions from his experiences, both of which are relevant here. One is that happiness is a by-product of things or activities that we pursue for other reasons. If we aim directly at happiness, it is likely to elude us. This is sometimes called the paradox of hedonism. To take an everyday analogy, recreational tennis players know that tennis is only a game, which one plays for fun. Whether one wins or loses is unimportant; indeed, in the larger scheme of one's life it is totally meaningless. However, those Saturday-morning players who pretend that winning is important and take their matches seriously, trying hard to win, usually end up having more fun than do those players who, because they just want to have fun, simply lob the ball back and forth without trying earnestly to score. There is another way in which happiness is best achieved indirectly. This is the idea that people who are exclusively concerned with their own interests tend to have less happy and less satisfying lives than those whose desires extend beyond themselves. Individuals who care only about their own happiness will generally be less happy than those who care about the well being of others.

As a result, Mill began to attach new importance to music, poetry, and the imaginative arts. Personally, Mill found solace in the beauty of nature, long country walks being among his greatest joys. Philosophically, he realized that there is more to human welfare than physical comfort. The development of our emotions and the refinement of our feelings contribute significantly to our well-being. By cultivating roses, we cultivate an appreciation of their beauty and delicacy, and in this way develop aspects of ourselves, of our "internal culture," that enhance our lives and promote our well-being.

The first objection considered by Mill is that in projecting pleasure as the ultimate end of life, utilitarianism puts forward a mean and unworthy goal as the ultimate good for human beings: "To suppose that life has no higher end than pleasure – no better and nobler object of desire and pursuit–they designate as utterly mean and groveling; as a doctrine worthy only of swine." Pleasure is something pursued by swine; human beings surely are capable of a higher, more refined good. The objection presumes, Mill counters, that human beings are capable "of no pleasures except those of which swine are capable". On the contrary, he claims, "Human beings have faculties more elevated than the animal appetites and, when once made conscious of them, do not regard anything as happiness which does not include their gratification". The life of beasts is indeed inferior when compared to the forms of happiness human being are capable of. What are these higher forms of pleasure and happiness? They include and Mill thinks the ancient Epicureans already recognized this fact, "the pleasure of the intellect, of the feelings and imagination, and of the moral sentiments. All of these pleasures are distinguished from "mere sensation".

The ancient Epicureans, although they recognized the higher pleasures, saw their superiority to consist simply in the fact that these pleasures have "greater permanency, safety, worthiness, etc." i.e., are quantitatively greater over the long run than the sensuous pleasures of the moment. In other words, these thinkers operate with a quantitative form of hedonism. For them, pleasures vary in quantity only, and the basis for preferring the human pleasures to the swinish ones is that, when everything is considered, the former surpass the latter in quantity. Mill proposes, on the contrary, that the human pleasures can be distinguished from their beastly counterparts not only in quantity, but in quality as well. "It is quite compatible with the principle of utility to recognize the fact that some kinds of pleasure are more desirable and more valuable than others". Human beings are capable of these more desirable and valuable pleasures. In stressing them, Mill sees himself as moving beyond Bentham's overly narrow conception of human nature. Moral philosophy should not just be interested in demonstrating how public utility and individual interest can coincide but also in promoting a richness of experience and excellence of character. Mill is as interested in the qualities of the "inner life" as he is in legislative arrangements for attaining social goals.

The Test of Superiority

But what makes one pleasure qualitatively superior to another, and what makes the combined quality and quantity of one pleasure superior to the combined quality and quantity of another? Mill addresses this question by asking how we know what pleasures are superior. His answer is this: "Of two pleasures, if there be one to which all or almost all who have experience of both give a decided preference, irrespective of any feeling of moral obligation to prefer it, that is the more desirable pleasure". The preference of competent judges – those who have experience of both kinds of pleasure and attend only to the intrinsic features of the pleasures – is the criterion to be used in distinguishing pleasures in terms of their relative quality.

Mill believes that competent judges will prefer the qualitatively superior pleasure even when it is accompanied by considerable "discontent." Thus pain or unhappiness comes into the picture as well. Presumably, if the quantity of pain is great, we might reach a point where the value of the quality of the pleasure, no matter how exalted, would be overridden by considerations of the quantity of the pain. If a person had to choose between, on the one hand, a clear mind capable of abstract pleasant thought together with extreme pain, and, on the other, relief from the pain but at the expense of the capacity for such thought, which would be preferable. All such questions for Mill are to be placed before competent judges. The preference of qualified judges gives us a general test for the value of hedonic experience.

The Higher Faculties

The higher-quality pleasures are associated, Mill informs us, with the exercise of the higher human faculties. It is the employment of these faculties, and the enjoyment of the pleasures attendant on this employment, which human beings desire above all else. In fact, they would not substitute a human life involving the use of these higher faculties for a lower beastly life even if the latter were filled with beastly pleasures. The swine may be more content than the human being who uses his mind, imagination, and moral faculties, but happiness and contentment is not the same thing. There will be some discontent in the lives of most human beings, whereas many animals live lives of what appears to be perfect contentment. Moreover, many human beings often fail to exercise their higher faculties, being satisfied with the lower pleasures of the senses. But the degree of quantitative pleasure is not the mark of human happiness: "It is better to be a human being dissatisfied than a pig satisfied; better to be Socrates dissatisfied than a fool satisfied. And if the fool, or the pig, is of a different opinion, it is because they only know their own side of the question. The other party to the comparison knows both sides". The quantity of pleasure involved in the life of a Socrates is so superior to that of a fool, and even more so to that of a pig, that the addition of considerable dissatisfaction to this life leaves it still superior in pleasure.

Such an existence, Mill affirms, is open to most people, and the real obstacles to its being attained by all are "the present wretched education, and wretched social arrangements". Another reason is that many people fail to attain it because they care for nobody but themselves. Such an inordinate concern for one's own happiness is the surest way to fail in attaining it. On the contrary, wide and varied interests greatly enhance the prospects for happiness. "A cultivated mind finds sources of inexhaustible interest in all that surrounds it; in the objects of nature, the achievements of art, the imaginations of poetry, the incidents of history, the ways of mankind, past and present, and their prospects in the future". Add to these some "genuine private affections, and a sincere interest in the public good", and everyone born in a civilized society should be capable of attaining a life filled with satisfactions. Mill, the liberal believer in progress, has no hesitation in affirming that "most of the great positive evils of the world are in themselves removable" And that most vicissitudes of fortune and other disappointments in one's worldly circumstances are "principally the effect either of gross imprudence, of ill-regulated desires, or of bad or imperfect social institutions". All of these obstacles to human happiness can be eradicated.

Liberty

Published in 1859, Mill's *On Liberty* was intended to be both a utilitarian and a progressivist tract. In the spirit of utilitarianism, it attempted to examine the necessary conditions of human happiness. Yet, in the spirit of progressivism, its understanding of human happiness was one which presupposed "utility in its largest sense, grounded on the permanent interests of a man as a progressive being." Thus inasmuch as humankind was an evolving rather than a fixed species, all calculations concerning happiness had to take into account the prospect for human improvement. Programs, which promoted the advancement of civilization, were legitimate because they contributed to social excellence. Similarly, once a specific program had achieved its purpose and raised the civilization level of a particular society, that program, thereby, lost its original justifying rationale. Mill, for example, believed that political despotism was a legitimate form of government for those societies, which had not yet evolved beyond the level of cultural barbarism. However, once its citizens had become capable of being improved by free and equal discussion, the despotic regime no longer served a progressive function and, according to Mill, should be replaced by a more liberal form of rule. Similarly, such liberal institutions are practices as constitutionalism and the recognition of political rights were appropriate techniques for securing intellectual progress in the more modern societies of Europe. Yet, as means to an end, their real value depended upon the efficiency with which they performed their function. Thus in those cases where progress demanded additional safeguards, new techniques would have to be developed. This, according to Mill, was the situation in England during his own time.

In Mill's analysis, the traditional concern of liberal political theory had been to restrict the range of state power. Thus Anglo-American liberal theory had succeeded in subordinating the state to society by promoting the doctrine of political rights and encouraging the recognition of constitutionalism. In time, however, the liberal promotion of society over the state evolved in such a way as to create its own particular challenge to progress. Specifically, now that society had succeeded in capturing the government, the numerical majority was placed in the position of exercising a tyrannical power over any given minority. This power was most apparent in the realm of ideas. For Mill, social progress was essentially the result of intellectual development. Such development, in turn, presupposed that individuals would be allowed to question and challenge the most respected elements of public opinion. Thus for Mill, real cultural progress required that the state not only tolerate but actually foster and protect the practice of individual criticism and dissent.

In the realm of ideas such dissent should be unlimited because, by its very nature, dissent served utility. If an orthodox belief were false, dissent promoted utility by serving truth. If an orthodox opinion were correct, dissent served truth by fostering debate and thereby reaffirming one's commitment to the orthodoxy on intellectual grounds. Finally, if both the orthodox belief and the dissenting opinion reflected partial aspects of the whole truth, utility was ultimately served by their mutually corrective effect upon one another. In each case, then, according to Mill, intellectual dissent promoted social progress.

Mill's concern to protect dissent went beyond the realm of pure thought. Indeed, he extended his principle of liberty to include the public expression of private ideas. It is obvious that such public expression moves one toward the realm of action and thereby raises a series of questions. Yet, because Mill believed that the liberty of thought was so closely related to the liberty of speaking and writing, it was inconceivable to him that it was possible to limit one without at the same time limiting the other.

Eventually, the realm of action is fully and finally entered when one attempts to carry out dissident ideas and beliefs. Here, then, Mill admitted that the principle of absolute liberty must be abandoned. Because of their effects, actions cannot be as free as thoughts. Yet here, too, progress demands that society permit as much freedom in action as is possible. Thus Mill wrote:

> That principle is that the sole end which humankind is warranted, individually or collectively, in interfering with the liberty of action of any of their member, is self-protection. That the only purpose for which power can be rightfully exercised over any member of a civilized community, against his will is to prevent harm to others. His own good, either physical or moral, is not a sufficient warrant.

This argument presupposed a distinction between self-regarding and other-regarding actions. Self-regarding actions are those, which directly and in the first instance affected only the individual actors themselves. According to Mill, society has no legitimate interest in monitoring such acts. Other-regarding actions, on the other hand, were those, which directly and immediately affected someone other than the actors themselves. In those cases, Mill acknowledged that society was permitted to act in order to protect its members from harm and, thereby, promote the greatest happiness of the greatest number. In both instances, however, the role of government was strictly limited. For Mill, the classical belief that the state was concerned with the creation of human and social order in both its temporal and spiritual aspects was simply untenable. This was so primarily because of his concern for the preservation of individuality.

Mill's appreciation of individuality obviously implied a specific view of human nature. Seen as individuals, human beings are characterized more by what sets each apart from others than by what each shares with all in common. Given such diversity, there can be no single model for humanity's spiritual development. Thus, for Mill, the human being is essentially self-defined, and, as a consequence, authenticity rather than virtue becomes the preeminent mode of human excellence. This emphasis upon authenticity becomes especially clear if one compares Mill's understanding of reason with that of the classical Greeks. Whereas the classical tradition understood reason as the means by which the person participated in the community of being, Mill, on the contrary, sees it primarily as a means of self-expression:

> There is no reason that all human existence should be constructed on some one or some small number of patterns. If a person possesses any tolerable amount of common sense and experiences, his own mode of laying out his existence is the best, not because it is the best in itself, but because it is his own mode.

Indeed, the traditional argument that there was one pattern for human existence was ultimately based upon the idea of a set human nature. Similarly the traditional attempt to find the best mode for laying out one's existence presupposed that the needs of the nature determined what was desirable and appropriate for it. However, in his advocacy of eccentricity, Mill effectively questioned the validity of both presuppositions. This challenge, in turns, created certain problems for his own thinking. If humanity has neither a set nature nor a specifically appropriate way of life, the question arises as to what ultimately is the end or goal of that pattern of progress, which appears to underlie all of Mill's thought? Humanity cannot be progressing towards a more humane era if humanity, itself, has no standards or limits. Thus the ambiguity implicitly within Mill's individualistic conception of personality is repeated on a larger scale as the ambiguity of history itself.

In a letter to Harriet in 1855, Mill declared that 'nothing seems more to be needed' than to write about liberty, since 'almost all the projects of social reformers of these days are really liberticide – Comte's particular so'. The murder of liberty he feared was less by political oppression than by the social pressure to conform. *On Liberty*, which he began in 1856, gives an urgent warning that society is encroaching too much on the individual, and lays down limits to how far encroachment by state or society should extend. Constantly campaigning for political freedoms, Mill was far-sighted enough to urge concern for civil freedoms also, aware that even with the total enfranchisement of men and women there would be no cause for complacency. Liberty in primitive society meant protection from the tyranny of political rulers, but he warned that just when we seem to have achieved a large measure of this, other forms of unfreedom loom. There needs protection also against the tyranny of the prevailing opinion and feeling against the tendency of society to. fetter the development and if possible prevent the formation of any individuality not in harmony with its ways. Mill was pursuing the English individualist tradition of Locke, who in 1688 had declared in the purpose of political power to secure the individuals 'natural rights'– to life, free speech, free worship and property. Mill agreed with Bentham that talk of natural rights was 'nonsense on stilts', but, like both Locke and Bentham, he was concerned to preserve a private sphere beyond the reach of laws.

Although Mill claimed to be defending the right to the fullest freedom of expression he explicitly allowed that 'even opinions lose their immunity, when the circumstances in which they are expressed are such as to constitute their expression a positive instigation to some mischievous act. The liberty of the individual must thus far be limited; he must not make himself a nuisance to other people'. This statement is commonly interpreted as qualifying free expression by reference to incitement to riot. However, Mill did not confine what he saw as permissible limitations to speech that incited riots. He allowed intolerance of indecent expressions, and, by his acceptance without protests most of his adult life of defamation and libel laws, he seems to have accepted the limitations they impose as also legitimate.

Lovers of liberty of recent times have favored as legitimate a significant range of limitations to free expression – libel and defamation laws, sub judice laws, restrictions by way of wartime censorship for the sake of national security, and, with less general agreement, censorship of pornographic and obscene material. Increasingly liberals have come to favor many more restrictions on free speech. They favor bans on incitement to racial hatred and violence, and in Australia it is presently being urged that it be made a crime even to write as to cause racist attitudes and actions to occur. Advertising that misleads or which simply fosters to an undesired degree harmful self-regarding behavior is increasingly under control or scrutiny, with proposals to limit even true speech by way of extension of the tort of defamation. Further controls for the sake of protection of privacy are widely being demanded by self-professed liberals even though such controls constitute very serious incursions into free speech. Such far-reaching controls are now coming into being would not have been anticipated by J.S. Mill. In assessing his position and the arguments he advances in its support, it is vital to determine whether these restrictions are directed at preventing harm to others and/or protecting the individual from him or herself. The dangers inherent in such far-reaching, all encompassing harm-prevention and paternalistic controls are very considerable, not least to liberty and the free society.

Mill sought to set out what are illegitimate interferences with freedom of action by reference to the anti-paternalist stance and prevention of harm principles. This attempt has resulted in a good deal of critical discussion of the meaningfulness of the latter principle. It is commonly being argued that no or very few and then only relatively trivial actions are purely self-regarding. Reinterpretations of that principle in terms of legitimate interference being restricted to other-regarding actions, which harmfully affect the interests of others have been advanced as devices for making Mill's position less implausible. There seems little to be gained by exploring new, more plausible interpretations of the principles if we are to be faithful to Mill's thought to formulate a coherent, defensible liberalism. This is because Mill himself saw that a tenable liberalism admits of a great deal of interference with a action of kinds not allowed in terms of his principles. Thus Mill allowed significant interferences for the sake of both weak and strong paternalistic protection of the individual against his or her own ignorance, stupidity and weakness, including moral authoritarian interference to make the individual do what is right and be a morally better person, specifically by way of enforcing performance of utilitarian morality, by way of preventing harm and by way of enforcing the carrying out of social obligations based on utilitarian considerations.

Mill's anti-paternalist stance is qualified in a large variety of cases where the individual is either not the best guardian or not the best judge of his own interests. Hence he allowed the legitimacy of coercion to prevent an ignorant person cross an unsafe bridge, coercion of the uneducated, coercion to ensure thoughtfulness about long-term and irrevocable contracts, even though the latter may be what individuals rationally wish to enter and also the coercion of social pressure in respect of divorce. The restrictions Mill entertained on the sale of liquor, the operation of gaming houses and of brothels are similarly paternalistic. Mill concerned that the state protect weak persons where others make it their business to prey on and profit from the weakness of others. His approval of the ban on religious suicides in India is less clear as many such 'suicides' were in fact result of strong pressure by relatives of the deceased.

A vast range of interferences is deemed legitimate by Mill to prevent harm and thereby to impose utilitarian morality. Harm is widely constructed so as to include the causing of suffering to sentient animals, Mill however did not spell out this restriction in any detail in respect of cruel sports nor did he think it in respect of vegetarianism, legally enforced or otherwise. Bans on offensive, indecent conduct come under the prevention of harm characterization, as does the proposal that provided that have no harmful effects means tests be permissible to prevent marriage among the poor who could not support their children, such controls preventing the harm of the mischievous act of having children one cannot support. On the other hand, a good deal of harmful conduct is exempt from interference or control, namely the harm that comes from successful, fair competition in examinations, business, and the like, as well as the harm that comes from one's bad example copied.

Many restrictions on freedom to act as one pleases are specifically noted by Mill as being legitimate, some being tendentiously described as harmful acts of omission. Hence, it is that Mill permits the curtailment of liberty to enforce the carrying out of what he calls 'assignable duties', his example suggesting that these are determinate social, morally based duties such as that of the policeman, of parents to children, and children to aged parents. Coercion to enforce the rendering of specific services to the community, military, jury service; service as a witness, etc is allowed in this way. For Mill, coercive taxation for the sake of welfare services, culture and other valued goods and not simply for the sake of law and order constitutes a further legitimate ground for interfering with freedom of action.

Mill's moral paternalism is evident in his protection of the weak against those who prey on their weakness in respect of drink, gambling, fornication with prostitutes, and in his being prepared to deny the vote to the immoral, among whom he included the idle and intemperate. It is also inherent in his imposition of utilitarianism – as shown in the prevention of cruelty to animals, more generally in respect of so-called harmful acts, and in his acceptance of Sir William Hamilton's philosophy of utilitarian punishment, which is designed morally to reform the criminal. What is notably absent from Mill's discussion is any claim that purely private immorality – which would consist not in homosexuality or the lesbianism but in self-neglect, self-stultifying, self-harming activities such as intemperance and drug taking leading to addiction – should be rendered illegal, However, Mill was not adverse to social pressure operating here. Sympathizers with Mill's liberalism seek to construe such conduct not as immoral but simply as unaesthetic or imprudent on the basis for the comments in the Logic about the art of life.

Various of these interferences allowed by Mill as legitimate would violate religious freedom, for example some bans on cruelty to animals, the enforcement of parental assignable duties, compulsory military service. Mill did not explore the problems for liberalism raised by this fact. Mill's arguments for liberty appeal to the fact that liberty is a means to, condition or ingredient of goods, and perhaps also to the claim that it is an intrinsic good in its own right, where the goods pointed to are true, rational and lively belief, individuality, self-development, happiness, progress. The arguments set out a strong presumptive case for liberty but are not as strong as Mill and his followers suppose them to be.

Mill rightly noted that both freedom of speech and action are necessary for self-development. However he realized that the people to whom he wished to accord the fullest freedom of expression were imperfectly rational, that 'The prospect of the future depends on the degree in which the laboring classes can be made rational beings'. Mill saw freedom of action in particular as a condition and ingredient of individuality and self-development. It was in this context that he stressed the value of what he called experiments in living. And, although the argument that each is the best judge and guardian of his own interests was urged in support of related conclusions rather more than in respect of self-development, it is relevant there also. Of course the so-called experiments in living are not genuine experiments. The conclusions that can legitimately be drawn from them are highly tentative and qualified. Similarly, only tentative conclusions can be drawn in respect of the claim that each is the best judge and guardian of his own interest. His claim that liberty contributes to progress and improvement has always been questionable. Today, given the less optimistic view about the desirability of what is called progress and improvement, it would be more widely questioned.

Mill's approach was that of defining the legitimate limits to the states and society's right to interfere with liberty and then qualifying his principles with unsystematic exceptions, the implications of which are nowhere carefully worked out. Equally important, he failed fully to examine the arguments for the opposed views of such notable exponents as Plato, Aristotle, St Thomas Aquinas, Hobbes and Hegel. This and his total unawareness of the writings of his contemporary Karl Marx greatly colored Mill's limited coverage. There are important argument and deep insights; many valuable lines of inquiry are suggested, but the final result falls short of being a carefully worked out political philosophy. Today Mill's defense of liberty has an air of unreality completely separated as it is from a consideration of other rights which are of current concern, those of life, justice and equality, privacy, respect, and the like. The discussion of democracy is very dated and fails to anticipate the major developments in democracy such as the increasing remoteness from the people of government, the strengthening of political parties and the party system, the growth and vast increase in power of the bureaucracy and the development of powerful organized pressure groups including the trade unions that have so concerned political theorists such as C.B. Macpherson, Schumpeter, Habermas, Rawls, Dahl and others.

Harriet had weaned Mill from free-market economics, but he was aware of the threat of centralization, which he associated as much with the growth of social democracy in America as with the still untried theories of communism. In this proselytizing for civil as well as political liberty, Mill showed himself wiser and more realistic than his European counterparts – apart from de Tocqueville. Here his espousal of empiricist thinking comes into its own. For all his rhetoric about man being born free but being everywhere in chains, Rousseau's elaboration of political freedom involves the suspect and unfleshed-out notion of the general will. This is the joint will of all the members of the state, in which each individual is seen as 'an indivisible part of the whole'. Should an opinion prevail in the people's assembly that an individual dissents from this only means that his opinion was mistaken, and that had his 'false' opinion won the day, he would not have been free. August Comte, more nearly Mill's contemporary, urged that liberty of conscience and opinion were arbitrary, illusory and dangerous, and should be replaced by 'rational submission' to what he had decided were the true laws of progress and historical development. Rousseau's general will, Comte's true liberty, the 'organic community' of Hegel, and

Marx's 'dictatorship of the proletariat,' were all to influence the totalitarianisms of left and right that would crucify our own century. Mill would have none of them. Expressions like 'self-government' and 'the power of the people over themselves', he said, are misleading. The "people" who exercise the power are not always the same people over whom it is exercised; and the "self-government" spoken of is not the government of each by himself, but of each by all the rest.' Giving a large number, of even everyone, a say in government does not ensure freedom: the wedge of coercion can simply be driven in at another specific dilemmas, Mill's liberal rather than utilitarian side is in evidence. Neither citizen nor state would be justified, he says, in prohibiting the eating of pork in a Muslim country, or the marrying of non-Catholic country. And much as he hates the Mormon practice of polygamy, the fact that both Mormon men and women favor it should exempt it from state interference. Poisons should not be banned, since they can be used for innocent purposes, and alcohol, gambling and idleness are each consumer's business, provided they do no harm to others. Utilitarianism wins, however, in his insistence on compulsory education and no one who is unable to afford it being allowed to have children. And when he asserts that it would not be an infringement of someone's liberty forcibly to prevent her crossing an unsafe bridge, since liberty consists in doing what one desires and he did not desire to fall into the river, the argument, however ingenious, seems designed to open the way to other paternalist safeguards and enorocaneuts.

It can be argued that for Mill, the inconsistency between his two principles was dissolved in his belief in progress and 'man as a progressive being'. Given his notion of 'the imperfect degree of moral cultivation which mankind have yet reached', he seems to have thought that for the time being a certain degree of paternalism might be necessary. Children, barbarians, and the colonized peoples should be liable to state interference and exempted from his principle of liberty, as insufficiently mature to use liberty well and benefit from it. The masses too seem to have been included in this category, even though when arguing against abolishing beer-houses, he says that to do so would only be suitable to a state of society in which 'the laboring classes are avowedly treated as children or savages'. No one valuing freedom, he says, could possibly consent to this treatment of laborers 'unless after all efforts have been exhausted to educate them for freedom and govern them as freemen and it has been definitively proved that they can only be governed as children'. Yet the implication seems to be that if the masses' behavior after they have been vouchsafed freedom does not show them to be free in the way he prescribes, then they should be governed as children. But of course he was confident this would not be the case. It is not strong desires that lead to evil, he said, but weak one. Strong impulses are only 'another name for energy,' and 'those who have most natural feeling are always those whose cultivated feeling may be made the strongest'. He couples 'human freedom and advancement' as if the safeguarding of individual liberty and the promotion of universal pleasure should inevitably, given time, dovetail rather than conflict.

Would Mill rethink his ideas in the light of Western societies today? What would Mill make of the welfare state? Does it infringe the liberty of the individual? Or promote the happiness of the greatest number? Are there too many safeguards, such as the forcible introduction of seatbelts, or prohibitions on smoking in public places?

And what about the question of banning boxing? Would he favor censorship, given the extremes of pornographic and racist material, or would he not, given also that it cannot be proved that pornography has harmful effects, and that incitement to racial hatred, unlike incitement to hate corn-dealers, in his example, need not be immediate? He would surely have revised his optimism about human nature, and been weakened in his conviction that encouraging diversification and eccentricity would make human beings 'a noble and beautiful object of contemplation'. His fastidious, highly moral nature would surely have been horrified that sexual freedom has extended to the behavior prosecuted in the Spanner Case. And he would have loathed the vulgarities of the tabloids, widely accessible pornography, soaps and quiz shows on television, slot machines, the National lottery, Pushpin, and worse, triumphs.

Mill could have anticipated the multi-racial society, in which complexities in freedom, and conflicts between freedoms, are magnified. It is no longer merely a matter of protecting each individual's private realm from the encroachments of the state or of a monolithic society. Should 'halal meat' be the prime diet in British schools with a large Muslim intake? Should Muslim girls in France be forbidden to wear veils in school? Is the French right to impose French culture on their immigrants? These are questions of numbers and priorities, and of balancing one type of freedom against another. They raise the kind of complexities and conflicts, which Mill had no time to consider. But however, flawed by limited time then, and changed time since, Mill's *On Liberty* remains a gloriously English marriage of reason with love, Enlightenment rationality with Romantic sentiment and individualism – a classic exposition of democratic liberalism.

Unlike nineteenth-century commentators whose argument with Mill revolved around the specific issue of freedom of expression, studies of *On Liberty* in the second half of the twentieth century have tended to concentrate almost exclusively on debating the validity of the principle of liberty itself. Much literature has recently been granted analyzing the notions of harm and interests, the question of actions as self-regarding and other-regarding, and the compatibility of Mill's defence of liberty with utilitarianism generally. Meanwhile, the arguments of Chapter 2 of *On Liberty* have come to be regarded as 'overstated' but 'generally sufficient to outweigh those who oppose freedom of experience.

On the one hand, philosophers have analysed the principle of liberty to the extent that it is often dismissed as a total chimera. On the other hand, Chapter 2 of *On Liberty* has come to be regarded as a separate entity from the rest of the work, to be understood and interpreted in isolation form the principle of liberty. Even John Rees concedes that 'it is sometimes said that the principle of self-protection might be completely discarded' without affecting the arguments of Chapter 2. Such a move may not be entirely unwelcome - after all, if *On Liberty* defends freedom of thought and discussion on a basis other than the principle of liberty , then if the latter principle proves to be untenable, the classic arguments for freedom of speech can possibly be saved. Yet, when deprived of their context in the wider argument of *On Liberty,* those arguments appear dry and lifeless, not readily serving Mill's broader aim of promoting human happiness and individuality.

The supposed bifurcation in the argument is observed by Gertrude Himmelfarb, who explains it in terms of an 'odd turn' in Mill's line of argument for freedom of thought and expression:

> instead of defending his position on the grounds he was to use elsewhere in *On Liberty* – the importance of preserving individuality against the pressures of social and political conformity – Mill chose to base his case on quite different grounds. It was not for the sake of the individual dissenter that he denied to mankind the right to silence the single dissenting opinion; it was rather for the sake of truth.

Can it really be that he was so confused in his thinking that he did not recognize a division which these commentators can so easily identify? The *Autobiography* makes it clear that every word in the published version of the essay was carefully weighted and re-weighed by both Mill and Harriet in order to weed out ambiguities. Some cast serious doubt on Mill's intellectual ability, lending support to the argument of some philosophers prominent among them–that *On Liberty* is a mass of contradiction and illogical intrigue. Such a conclusion is strange considering the lasting appeal of the work, as well as the fact that among his contemporaries Mill was considered to be 'the most profound thinker England has produced since the seventeenth century.'

Mill readily conceded in *On Liberty* that the expression of an opinion is not a self-regarding act, but he nonetheless maintained that it should be protected by the principle of liberty, claiming that it is impossible in practice to have true freedom of thought without freedom of expression. His argument does not spring from the right of an individual to express opinions. Rather, as Chapter 5 has attempted to demonstrate, his arguments are based on the idea that people must be free to hear what can be said on all sides of a question if they are to develop intellectually and individually. If people are to hear all sides, people must be free to express all sides. To deny people this right, especially in relation to those questions pertaining to 'morals, religion, politics, social relations, and the business of life', is to decide on these issues for others. To do so is to equate one's own certainty with absolute certainty, with regard to both the truth of the issue at hand and the usefulness of holding that particular opinion. And this is tantamount to claiming one's own infallibility. For Mill, silencing the expression of an opinion is 'robbing the human race; posterity as well as the existing generation; those who dissent from the opinion, still more than those who hold it'. Certainly it is robbing them of the possibility of achieving truth. But more importantly it is robbing them of the opportunity to exercise their intellects, to compare and contrast their own views and opinions in relation to the silenced opinion.

Mill's arguments are not focused primarily on the discovery of truth but on the use and development of human faculties and intellect. Silencing any opinion detracts from the individual's development and thus from the diversity which society needs if it is to grow and progress. It is ultimately not for the sake of truth alone but for the sake of individuality in society that freedom of expression must be permitted. *On Liberty* proceeds on the notion that:

> Mankind are not infallible; that their truths, for the most part, are only half-truths; that unity of opinion, unless resulting from the fullest and freest comparison of opposite opinions, is not desirable, and diversity not an evil, but a good, until mankind are much

> more capable than at present of recognizing all sides of the truth, are principles applicable to men's modes of action, not less than to their opinions.

Diversity of opinion is desirable not simply for its own sake but because it is the product of natural diversity among individuals, which in turn provides inspiration for individuality. Unity of opinion is acceptable when it is the result of free and open discussion. After all 'As mankind improve, the number of doctrines which are no longer disputed or doubted will be constantly on the increase'. For Mill, arguing in favour of individuality and development, it is not sufficient that people should know that something is true; they must also understand the reasons which make it true. And complete freedom, to think and express all opinions is necessary in order for individuals, and therefore for society, to progress.

John Skorupski identifies Mill's 'dialogue model' of *On Liberty* concentrating on the importance of the speaker rather than the hearer, and in this manner he identifies a principle of freedom of expression which is separate from Mill's principle of liberty. Skorupski defines dialogue as 'unconstrained discourse between rational people' which aims at the common pursuit of truth: However, Skorupski proceeds to explain that Mill's defence of liberty of expression, in appealing to 'the growth of truth and of rational qualities of mind', makes 'no reference to the liberty principle, or the rights of the individual. Mill defends liberty of expression by a direct appeal to the internal goal of dialogue. Here, truth assumes an importance of greater value than the individual. For Skorupski it is the social importance of dialogue in the discovery of truth that justifies Mill's account of liberty of expression. Skorupski concludes, therefore, that there must be a principle of freedom of expression which is separate from the principle of liberty, the latter emphasizing the individual, the former emphasizing society. This principle of the communal discovery of truth, while the principle of liberty 'permits interference with acts of expression on the basis of foreseeably harmful nondialogue effects'. Thus on Skorupski's account, speech can be restricted, and indeed can be banned altogether if its possible or probable effects are deemed harmful in their 'non-dialogue effects'. Here Mill's insistence on 'absolute freedom of opinion and sentiment on all subjects, practical or speculative, scientific, moral, or theological' appears to be both impotent and misleading. When the role of the hear is emphasised, on the contrary, Mill's theory can be demonstrated as consistent, both with regard to freedom of thought and discussion and to the wider principle of liberty.

Current interpretations of the principle of liberty place much emphasis on the fact that its first formulation is made by reference to preventing harm to others. In calling for absolute freedom of thought and discussion, Mill believed that any offence given by the expression of an opinion did not constitute such harm. So how is the notion of harm to be understood? John Rees's interpretation points out that in the most important passages of *On Liberty*, Mill almost always returns to the notion of harming interests rather than simply 'harming' or 'affecting' others. His reading has gained widespread acceptance and has informed almost all subsequent philosophical debate about the principle of liberty. Rees offers further clarification of his thesis by citing a passage from On Liberty which says the conduct which a society can demand of its citizens 'consists, first, in not injuring the interests of one another; or rather certain interests, which, either by express legal provision or by tacit understanding, ought to be considered as rights'. But it is not immediately clear what exactly constitutes these 'certain interests'.

That confusion prevails about the issue may have prompted McCloskey to suggest that Mill had no clear concept of interests, and that any attempt to interpret *On Liberty* along such lines is therefore bound to be unsuccessful. Mill occasionally seems to be using a general notion of interests, for example when he says that:

> As soon as any part of a person's conduct affects prejudicially the interests of others, society has jurisdiction over it, and the question whether the general welfare will or will not be promoted by interfering with it, becomes open to discussion.

But it is also clear from *On Liberty* that Mill is at times not speaking about interests in general, but of specific interests which ought to be recognized as rights. One of the more influential studies to have built on Rees' work is that by John Gray. Gray views that argument of *On Liberty* in the context of Mill's larger corpus, including Book VI of the *System of Logic*, and the account of justice and moral rights in the final chapter of Utilitarianism. In the latter work, the most vital interests of human beings are identified as those pertaining to security and to 'the moral rules which forbid mankind to hurt one another'.

Interest and Progress

The cryptic use of the concept of interests attributed to Mill in *On Liberty* is also surprising: other writings make clear his awareness of the problems of interpretation attendant on the use of the concept. In 1829, Macaulay had raised the question of how the notion of interests was to be understood in James Mill's *Encylopaedia Britannica* article 'Government'. Marcaulay's criticisms made a deep impression on John Stuart Mill. Later, writing about the 'Benthamite Theory of Government', he asks: 'what can a philosopher make such complex notions as "interest" and "general interest", without breaking them down into the elements of which they are composed?'

These 'permanent interests' of man as a progressive being are interests in mental and moral development. In the rest of his essay Mill argues for the development of generic intellectual and social capabilities and for autonomy and individuality. Chapter 2, 'Of the Liberty of Thought and Discussion', is on one level an eloquent argument for the importance of free discussion and freedom of expression for the development of our intellectual powers. Unless we have an intense desire to seek the truth and reflect critically on important matters, as well as the mental powers obviously presupposed by such a search, we will not continue developing morally. This dynamic process feeds on itself; the more we use our mental powers, the more we develop them and want to use them.

The idea of progress through intellectual development in turn brings us back to the problem of what it is that Mill means in *On Liberty* when he speaks of 'certain interests, which, either by express legal provision or by tacit understanding, ought to be considered as rights'. That he is not here referring to the 'permanent interests of man as a progressive being' should now be evident.

The permanent interests of mankind as progressive beings dictate that people should refrain from acting in a manner which is hurtful to 'certain interests'. What those latter interests are should be evident from the text of *On Liberty* itself: there is little reason to believe that Mill was being deliberate cryptic. The general thrust of *On Liberty* is to urge people to value freedom rather then constraint, individuality rather than social conformity in human affairs. In the long term, Mill argues, these characteristics are in the best interests of adults in societies which have already advanced beyond the 'backward' stage of development. Because each human being is different.

> The only freedom which deserves the name, is that of pursuing our own good in our own way, so long as we do not attempt to deprive others of theirs, or impede their efforts to obtain it. Each is the proper guardian of his own health, whether bodily, or mental or spiritual.

Thus, to pursue one's own good in one's own way without interfering with others who wish to pursue their own good in their own way is evidently to remain within the province of liberty, the realm of self regarding actions. To prevent others from pursuing what they perceive to be their own interests is to prevent them from achieving their individual good. And this is, in fact, to cause them harm.

The 'certain interests' passage appears at the beginning of *On Liberty's* Chapter 4, as part of the response to Mill's question as to what constitutes 'the rightful limit to the sovereignty of the individual over himself.' His reply is that 'To individuality should belong the part of life in which it is chiefly the individual that is interested; to society, the part which chiefly interests society'. Because all enjoy the protection of society, every one 'owes a return for the benefit, and the fact of living in society renders it indispensable that each should be bound to observe a certain line of conduct towards the rest'.

At the outset of *On Liberty*, however, Mill had answered this same question by claiming that 'All that makes existence valuable to any one, depends on the enforcement of restraints upon the actions of other people'. It is not unreasonable, therefore, to claim that when Mill speaks of interests which ought to be considered as rights he is simply speaking of the interests consequent upon developing one's own individuality in one's own way, as opposed to being constricted by that which others or society generally considers to be for one's good. This is the central thesis of *On Liberty* itself, and denies society any right to impede a person's development as an individual. Because each person is different and has different interests and tastes,

> Each is the proper guardian of his own health, whether bodily, or mental or spiritual. Mankind are greater gainers by suffering each other to live as seems good to themselves, then by compelling each to live as seems good to the rest.

In *On Liberty* his utilitarianism to the question of the relationship between the state and the individual, inquiring into the areas in which civil authorities have the right to legislate against forms of behavior. He defines his subject as "the nature and limits of the power which can legitimately be exercised by society over the individual". Mill's position on this issue expresses the stance of the classic liberal. According to this view, the individual should be allowed liberty over a broad range of activities, the only limit to this liberty being those actions that harm the interests of others. In the process of arguing for his position, Mill delivers a paean to individuality, applauding individualistic "experiments in living" and condemning the mediocrity and deadening conformity to public opinion found in most societies. He warns against the "tyranny of the majority" that can suppress individuality in the interests of the accepted modes of behavior in a society. That the sole end for which mankind are warranted, individually or collectively, in interfering with the liberty of action of any of their member, is self-protection. That the only purpose for which power can be rightfully exercised over any member of a civilized community, against his will, is to prevent harm to others. His own good, either physical or moral, is not a sufficient warrant. He cannot rightfully be compelled to do or forbear because it will be better for him to do so, because it will make him happier, because, in the opinions of others, to do so would be wise, or even right. To justify that, the conduct from which it is desired to deter him must be calculated to produce evil to some one else. The only part of the conduct of any one, for which he is amenable to society, is that which concerns others. In the part, which merely governs himself, his independence is, of right, absolute. Over himself, over his own body and mind, the individual is sovereign. Mill makes it clear that he is defending liberty in the above sense only for "human beings in the maturity of their faculties", not for children or even for people who could not be "improved by free and equal discussion".

There is a sphere of action, Mill claims, in which society should have no direct interest, namely "that portion of a person's life and conduct which affects only himself, or if it also affects others, only through their free, voluntary, and undeceived ambition, and associations with other individuals. Thus there should be, in Mill's view, freedom of thought, opinion, and discussion; freedom of what we might call "life style"; and freedom of association. Only when we pass beyond this private sphere into a distinct public realm in which our actions have a harmful effect on others should there be any curtailment of liberty.

Freedom of Thought

Turning first to freedom of thought, Mill begins by making a bold declaration that "If all mankind minus one were of one opinion, and only one person were of the contrary opinion, mankind would be no more justified in silencing that one person, than he if he had the power, would be justified in silencing mankind". His argument is clearly a utilitarian one, pointing to the desirable consequences that follow from allowing freedom of thought and discussion and the harmful ones that are the products of censorship and control.

In the first place, to suppress an opinion because society thinks it wrong is to assume that society knows, with absolute certainty, what the truth is. This is an assumption of infallibility – the impossibility of being in error. Such an assumption should quickly be dismissed; it flies in the face of that, given any socially approved belief, "other ages, countries, sects, churches, classes, and parties have thought, and even now think the exact reverse". This is not to deny that there is any such thing as truth – although some of Mill's critics claimed that his doctrine implies such skepticism – but rather to note that the best, perhaps only way to avoid error is through public discussion and debate. When society claims to have the truth, in the interest of which it proposes to suppress conflicting opinions, it cannot justify this claim without entering into a debate with the holders of the other view. "Complete liberty of contradicting and disproving our opinion is the very condition which justifies us in assuming its truth for purposes of action; and on no other terms can a being with human faculties have any rational assurance of being right". In the first instance, then, liberty of thought and discussion is justified as means of ascertaining the truth, since without them there is no justification for claiming to know the truth. Given the fallible nature of the human mind, freedom of discussion is essential: "in an imperfect state of the human mind the interests of truth require a diversity of opinion".

It may be the case however, that what society believes and propounds is in fact true. Even in this case, Mill argues, freedom of belief and discussion is justified. Beliefs long and widely held, even when true, can come to be dead dogmas, the reasons for their truth being long lost to those who subscribe to them. It refuses to enter into a debate over these beliefs is precisely to avoid the occasions on which the reasons for them are expressed. Thus to be required to put forth arguments for beliefs has great benefit, for it rescues these beliefs from the domain of habit, superstition, and prejudice, making of them once again "living truth." Those people who do not enter into debate over their cherished beliefs "do not, in any proper sense of the word, know the doctrine which they themselves profess". Indeed, it can be said that, without debate, society loses not only the reasons for its beliefs but also the very meaning of them: "Instead of a vivid conception and a living belief there remains only a few phrases retained by rote; only the shell and husk of the meaning is retained, the finer essence being lost". We gain immeasurably from freedom of discussion even if, as it turns out, we possessed the truth all along.

Mill considers an interesting objection to this position, which urges that the usefulness of some beliefs is so great that society is justified in enforcing them and prohibiting any conflicting opinions. The Church, for example, might claim that some parts of its creed are essential for salvation; a modern state might claim that a conviction of its "manifest destiny" is required in order for civilization to advance; a nation might proclaim that support for its war efforts is essential for success on the battlefield. Mill reminds those who propose usefulness as a justification for enforced belief that "the usefulness of an opinion is itself matter of opinion: as disputable, as open to discussion, and requiring discussion as much as the opinion itself".

The Proper Limits to Human Conduct

Having justified freedom of thought, opinion, and discussion, Mill turns to the question of what limits, if any, should be placed on the human actions that may stem from opinions freely held. And here he is willing to draw line and separate off a class of actions which society or government is morally permitted to suppress. There are also actions, which it is permissible for society to require of individuals. Mill defines these two classes of actions in the following way:

> This conduct consists, first, in not injuring the interests of one another; or rather certain interests, which either by express legal provision, or by tacit understanding, ought to be considered as rights; and secondly, in each person's bearing his share of the labors and sacrifices incurred for defending society or its members from injury and molestation.

The limits concentrate on the first class of actions – the actions legitimately suppressed because they involve harm to others or a violation of the rights of others. An alternative way of expressing Mill's position is to see it as marking out the areas over which society has jurisdiction. He is particularly concerned to argue that society does not have jurisdiction over matters of personal good. In other words, society cannot require that a person do certain things as a means of improving that people own quality of life. Society should not have a paternalistic relation to its citizens. Individuals should be left alone to pursue their interest, this because they know best what these interests are and most highly motivated to pursue them. Moreover, individuals must take their own risks and bear responsibility for the consequences of their actions, indeed, responsibility for their own characters. It is only when these actions impinge in a negative way on others that society is warranted in intervening. As Mill puts it, "As soon as any part of a person's conduct affected prejudicially the interests of others, society has jurisdiction over it, and the question whether the general welfare will or will not be promoted by interfering with it, becomes open to discussion". Actions that bring harm to others by damaging their rightful interests may be legislated against.

Mill is aware of what is still today the major objection to his position on liberty: the response that there is no clear line between actions damaging only to the agent himself and actions inflicting harm on others. As he expresses the objection:

> How (it may be asked) can any part of the conduct of a member of society be a matter of indifference to the other members? No person is an entirely isolated being; it is impossible for a person to do anything seriously or permanently hurtful to himself, without mischief at lest to his near connections, and often far beyond them.

Here we have the "no person is an island" objection. The drunkard not only thwarts his own chances of a full and productive life, he also harms the members of his family by providing inadequate support. And he constitutes a bad example for all who encounter his. In a case like this, the distinction between self-regarding actions and other-regarding actions breaks down. Should not society be authorized, then, in legislating against drunkenness? And likewise against all conditions that cause damage to the agent?

Mill answers this objection by distinguishing between prohibiting and punishing the behavior that inflicts harm on others and prohibiting and punishing the cause of that behavior. If the drunkard violates one of his duties to his family, he can rightfully be punished for doing so. Society has the right to set up laws against dereliction of duty to one's family. But the drunkard should not be punished for his drunkenness, the cause of his dereliction. Likewise, "No person ought to be punished simply for being drunk; but a soldier or a policeman should be punished for being drunk on duty." Thus Mill sums up his views on liberty in two maxims:

> The maxims are, first, that the individual is not accountable to society for his actions, in so far as these concern the interests of no person but himself. Advice, instruction, persuasion, and avoidance by other people if thought necessary for their own good, are the only measures by which society can justifiably express its dislike or disapprobation of his conduct. Secondly, that for such actions are prejudicial to the interests of others, the individual is accountable, and may be subjected either to social or to legal punishment, if society is of opinion that the one or the other is requisite for its protection.

Challenges to the Liberty Principle

Since its publication in 1859, *On Liberty* has generated heated political and philosophical controversies. Some theorists reject Mill's principle on the grounds that a person's actions, even when they appear to concern only himself almost always affect other people as well. Mill does not deny this point, and he is far from believing that each person is an island. He maintains rather that there is some individual conduct that has no direct or significant impact on anyone other than the individual himself. If others have an interest in what he does, that interest is only indirect and of negligible weight compared to the individual's own interest. Is Mill denying that individuals have duties to others? When a bachelor gets drunk at home on his day off from work it is his own business, but this is false of a police officer on duty or of a parent with children to look after. Finally, Mill insists that he is not advocating selfish individualism. Not only do we have duties to others, but we should also encourage people to choose what is best for themselves–in particular, to exercise their higher faculties and to eschew worthless or degraded activities. We can advise them, and we can warn them. "But neither one person, nor any number of persons, is warranted in saying to another human creature of ripe years that he shall not do with his life for his own benefit what he chooses to do with it".

Mill anticipated the objection that society has a right to prevent an individual from setting a bad example for others. To this he rejoins that if the conduct does indeed harm the individual, then the example will be a salutary one because it shows the deleterious results of the behavior in question. Mill also reminds us that, when it comes to dissuading individuals from self-regarding conduct that is bad or harmful, society already has almost absolute power over their education and upbringing. In addition, society has conventional opinion on its side as well as the natural penalties or inevitable ill consequences of the conduct itself. Society does not also need the power to prevent adults from engaging in freely chosen self-regarding conduct of which it disapproves.

Still there is the question of what exactly counts as harm to others and of when our conduct can be said to directly or significantly affect their interests. A number of commentators have thought that Mill was vague on this point and that this vagueness threatens to undermine the liberty principle's viability. If your drinking upsets your friends, is this not a harm that you should consider? An apparently self-regarding action can, it seems, affect other in the sense that they dislike it, find it repugnant, or for some other reason are distressed by your doing it. Some people are bothered by knowing that others read pornography, worship Satan, or enjoy having same sex, practicing black magic and parents sometimes lose sleep worrying about how their grown children are living their lives. This seems to make the conduct in question other regarding and hence potentially open to restriction. Mill, however, was adamant that the harm to others must be real and not imaginary or self-imposed. Mill views the supposed distress of those who disapprove of what others do in private as a "merely contingent or constructive injury", and he gives it no weight. The supposed harm done to the distressed person is, in a sense, self-induced because it depends solely on the person's own subjective attitudes and desires. In Mill's view, we do not prejudice people's interests if, without causing them any discernible damage, we ignore there likes and dislikes when choosing how to live our own life.

There is an extensive secondary literature probing this and other aspect of Mill's liberty principle and debating its application to specific situations. Mill devoted most of the final chapter of *On Liberty* to analyzing problematic cases, but certain theoretical puzzles remain, and real life can throw up complicated factual predicaments. For example, behavior that appears self-regarding (my agreeing to work for half the minimum wage) may turn out to damage the important interests of others (whose endeavor to earn a living wage will be undercut if desperate people are permitted to work for peanuts) and thus fall outside the scope of the liberty principle after all. Difficult cases can also arise when a person's decision is not fully voluntary, rests on misinformation, or seems unreasonable or even irrational given the person's own goals and values. However, there is no reason to assume that the liberty principle must provide an immediate and facile solution to every possible question about the proper limits of liberty. We do not need to pursue how best to apply Mill's principle in various borderline cases. Instead, we return to the question of whether, consistent with his utilitarianism, Mill can defend his principle as firmly and unequivocally as he does.

Utilitarianism and the Liberty Principle

The philosophical problem is that Mill's commitment to personal liberty appears virtually absolute, and yet it seems that utilitarianism can at best supply a presumption in favor of personal freedom, not the categorical underwriting of it that Mill urges. Utilitarians recognise the importance of personal liberty for human well-being, but their support for liberty must, it seems, be empirical and contingent, allowing for possible exceptions. Mill implies as much when he writes that the odds are that when society interferes with individual choice, it will make things worse. This suggests that sometimes interference doesn't make things worse. Accordingly, many commentators believe that in endorsing the liberty principle almost unconditionally, Mill goes further than a utilitarian approach warrants, supplementing his argument with an implicit appeal to values other than welfare.

Mill is not against custom or tradition as such; his point is that one needs to interpret and use in one's own way the ideas and experience that tradition and custom represent. As he sees it, individuality entails deliberating and choosing for oneself the direction and content of one's life. It thus requires personal liberty. When people lack liberty, they are guided not by their own character – by their own desires, needs, and choices – but by conformity to what others believe and do. When this is the case, then "there is wanting one of the principal ingredients of human happiness, and quite the chief ingredient of individual and social progress". Why is this?

One might answer that liberty promotes happiness because people like making choices; they enjoy governing themselves and find it fulfilling to direct their own lives. However, it is debatable whether people always prefer to think for themselves and resist having others determine and structure their choices or direct their lives. Certainly, psychologists have noted that people sometimes seem content to follow the crowd and that some individuals seem positively to fear personal choice and responsibility. It is probably for this reason that Mill does not claim simply that liberty makes people happy. Instead, Mill argues that liberty is valuable because without choice, individuals cannot develop any of the qualities, which are the distinctive endowment of a human being. The human faculties of perception, judgment, discriminative feeling, mental activity, and even moral preference are exercised only in making a choice. He who lets the world, or his own portion of it, chooses his plan for himself employing all his faculties.

The point that liberty and choice develop our distinctively human talents might look like a perfectionist argument for liberty, but Mill's remarks suggest two possible links between personal liberty and individual well-being. First, as a rule, developing these capacities makes a person's life go better because they enhance the person's ability to negotiate his way through the world and to promote his own interests, and to satisfy his needs and desires. Second, to realize one's self by developing and exercising these higher-level abilities and capaities can itself be an important source of satisfaction. People tend to enjoy, and to derive a sense of accomplishment from and flourishing using and improving their talents, especially their mental abilities.

For these two reasons, then, the "free development of individuality is one of the leading essentials of well-being". Furthermore, as people begin to develop and exercise their talents through choice, they come more and more to desire to guide their own lives. Personal liberty becomes a necessary ingredient of their happiness. Although it may be false that everyone desires the freedom to direct his or her own life, it does seem, as Mill thought, that under the right circumstances – in particular, as they experience liberty and develop the capacity to choose and think for themselves – people want increasingly to govern themselves and take satisfaction in doing so.

Mill grants that someone who lacked the necessary qualities to choose for himself might nevertheless "be guided in some good path, and kept out of harm's way" by others. But what, he asks, will be the person's "comparative worth as a human being?" What matters, Mill contends, is not merely what we do, but how and why we do it. It is in this connection that he lays such stress on what he calls "character." This is what a person has when his "desires and impulses are his own – are the expression of his own nature, as it has been developed and modified by his own culture". This emphasis on the value of character may sound like an argument for liberty based on the intrinsic value of autonomy or on a perfectionist ideal, rather than on welfare. But Mill is sounding some deep and properly utilitarian themes.

A central one of these is that full and profound human well-being involves activity. Happiness is not a passive thing – a commodity that someone can give us. Even if they protect us from harm and furnish us with the necessities of life for others to choose for us and to guide our lives as adults is compatible with our achieving only rudimentary well being. To realize greater well-being, individuals must determine their own way. Mill believes that human nature is more like a tree than a machine; it "requires to grow and develop itself on all sides, according to the tendency of its inward forces". Because people differ, they require different conditions to develop and be happy. Free choice makes this diversity possible. Without it, "people can neither obtain there fair share of happiness, nor grow up to the mental, moral and aesthetic stature of which their nature is capable". For this reason, a person's "own mode of laying out his existence is the best, not because it is the best in itself, but because it is his own mode". This remark is more radical than the proposition that individuals are the best judges of what is good for them or that activity is essential to human satisfaction. It is more radical because it implies that something cannot be best for a person unless it is rooted in authentic autonomy.

Mill affirms not only that liberty is central to individual happiness, but also that it is "quite the chief ingredient of individual and social progress." In this vein, he argues that the individuality that liberty makes possible is socially beneficial because it stimulates the lives of others, even those who do not desire liberty. Individuality is also a source of creativity, of novel ideas, and of fresh "experiments of living," which are needed to prevent even the best beliefs and practices from degenerating into mechanical dead tradition. By encouraging individuality and, thus, a "plurality of paths" and "many-sided development," respect for personal liberty is the main source of social progress. In line with this, Mill states in his *Autobiography* that *On Liberty* highlights "a single truth," namely, "the importance to man and society, of a large variety in types of character, and of giving full freedom to human nature to expand itself in innumerable and conflicting directions". However, if society hopes to progress by fostering individuality, it cannot channel people's liberty in pre-selected directions. Society can, of course, choose to encourage personal liberty or to stifle it. But if it is to reap the benefits, Mill describes, society cannot grant people freedom and yet permit them to exercise it only in certain favored ways.

This, then, is the last of the utilitarian or welfare-oriented considerations that Mill provides in favor of the liberty principle. He successfully highlights some important links between personal liberty and human well-being, but are these enough to secure the liberty principle? Do they underwrite a basic right to live our lives as we please insofar as our actions do not injure others? Ultimately, these questions must be left for the reader to answer. Mill's utilitarian case for liberty rests on his understanding of human nature and of the sources of well-being, happiness, and satisfaction and, as we saw in Chapter 2, these are matters about which there is no consensus. Philosophers disagree about the meaning of well-being, and psychologists and social scientists are a long way from comprehending all the factors that promote or retard it. Nevertheless, the liberty principle has firm utilitarian basis, that there are cogent grounds for enshrining it as a basic human right, and that a failure to do so spells a significant loss in long-term human welfare for the reasons Mill discusses. Yet, if personal liberty were merely a presumption and not a right, then the door would be open to abuse; in practice unnecessary and counterproductive restrictions on individuals would almost certainly be authorized. However, this defense of selective paternalism is open to criticism, criticism that highlights the strength of Mill position.

First, it is far from obvious that the paternalist's judgment about what is good for motorcyclists is better informed than their own judgment. The paternalist believes that it is foolish not to wear a helmet, but it doesn't follow from this that it is foolish from the point of view of the motorcyclists who choose to run that risk. Second, even if riding helmetless is inadvisable given the motorcyclists' own values and desires, we mustn't forget Mill's point that there is an alternative to paternalistic coercion: we can educate people about the dangers of motorcycling without a helmet and try to convince them that the joys of doing so are not worth the gamble. Third, forcing otherwise rational people to behave a certain way because we cannot persuade them to act as we think best involves a welfare cost. In forcing them to act contrary to their own judgment of what is desirable, we do something they will find disagreeable, we restrict their individuality, and we hinder their development and growth. Moreover, when we rely on coercion, we lessen the need to treat people as adults by trying to persuade them with reason. We take the pressure off society to raise and educate people to be thoughtful and reflective choosers, which in turn makes it more likely that in the future we will have to fall back on coercion to prevent them from making poor choices. Finally, permitting paternalistic interference sets a dangerous precedent. For these reason, Mill insits that we should endorse the liberty principle as a basic right. They should seek to institutionalize this right and strive to inculcate in others, and internalize in themselves, a commitment to it. In some cases it may be difficult to determine precisely what the liberty principle requires, and in other cases it may be possible to square certain weak forms of paternalism with a commitment to it.

The essay *On Liberty* also poses problems of interpretation, and has provoked a torrent of scholarly dispute. The now orthodox view suggests that the only way through the difficulties is to read the essay in the light of Mill's utilitarianism, which is not contradicted by his defense of liberty as an end because, in the first place, liberty is not other than happiness: it is a part of happiness, naturally or chemically associated with pleasure. The human animal takes pleasure in untrammeled action, the free exercise of its faculties and the sense of power. Liberty is also valuable because it is intrinsically bound up with higher, active pleasures. The reader is advised that there is no substitute including those of creation and self-creation. This is the subject of a whole for reading the text itself, which is memorably eloquent: Mill was self-consciously a rhetorician as well as a logician, and he sets out to persuade the reader by conveying a vivid sense of the pleasure and dignity of free self-development, in accordance with one's natural bent and in defiance of mediocre conformity. He goes so far as to reach forward to Nietzsche in advocating 'pagan self-assertion' as well as 'Christian self-denial'.

Such a similarity ought not to surprise us, for Mill, like Nietzsche, draws upon a romantic philosophy of the self-assertion in early nineteenth-century German thought. He acknowledges his debt to Wilhelm von Humboldt and, in the *Autobiography*, to Goethe; he learnt about this strand of German thinking also from Coleridge and Carlyle. He purveys to a British readership the idea and ideal of 'Bildung', of the unfolding and expression of the self's mix of powers and inclinations, through free and many-sided experience, and their combination into a rich, unique and coherent whole. This philosophy helps Mill to mount a challenge to the doctrine, long dominant in Western thought, that there is a single pattern of human excellence to which all should aspire. For Mill and the German theorists of Bildung, excellence can allow for variety.

Mention should also be made of another source of his ideal of liberty, at once classical and English. In his friend Grote's *History of Greece* Mill found an account of the Athenians under Percles, 'the greatest people who have yet appeared on this planet', whose tolerance of individual diversity 'is most closely connected with the wonderful display of individual genius which made Athens illustrious, and with the comparative mediocrity of modern times'. Mill admires the 'liberality and tolerance of Athenian social life', which underlines the point that the interference with liberty that most concerned him, especially in England, was that of public opinion rather than law. Mill goes so far as to praise eccentricity, an aspect of the essay which some Victorian critics thought went too far. But Mill connects eccentricity, and self-formation rather than slavish conformity, with a trait which Victorians greatly admired, namely strength of character. Liberty then is not inconsistent with utility because it produces a host of good consequences, happiness in many forms.

It follows from this in the second place that liberty should often be protected, even when it immediately produces harm, because of the long-term good it promotes. What appears to be contrary to utility at first sight is consonant with it in the longer view. Wiser persons might interfere with people for their own good, to rescue them from self-damaging excesses: but in the long term they will be happier by learning from their own mistakes, attaining independence and strength of character; they will be happier knowing they are self-made, not manufactured by others. Consideration of the long-term interests in this way justifies free speech and 'experiments of living'. Free speech permits the propagation of error, and experiments in living may prove harmful to the experimenter: but an environment of free speech and experimentation is essential to discovery and progress, which in turn are likely to contribute to the diminution of misery and the growth of happiness. If error is proscribed there is always the danger that elements of the truth will be banned too; for no authority can be sure of infallibility. In the third place, actions which detract from happiness, should not always be prevented because they are not always wrong. They are not wrong if they fall into the domains of prudence and aesthetics rather than morality. And they only come into the latter domain if it would be expedient to discourage them by means of sanctions, which once more invoke consideration of longer-term consequences.

Does Mill's defense of liberty go too far in the direction of individualism? Does it encourage people to think too much of themselves and too little of others? By leaving each to find their own good in their own way, does it fail lo enforce standards. Is it a purely negative or neutral political philosophy, which embodies no positive values? Would it in effect leave each individual to sink or swim, to flourish or go to perdition? Would it, by preventing the imposition of moral standards in private life by public opinion, lead to the corruption and disintegration of society? Conservative critics, best represented by the lawyers Fitjames Stephen from the nineteenth century and Lord Devlin from the twentieth, have leveled such charges. Among many good arguments, one may be highlighted, namely Devlin's insistence that a recognized morality is just as important to a nation's survival as a recognized government, and that public morality cannot ignore what happens in private life. What, he asks, if half the population got drunk every night, or gambled, or became gay, or thought adultery perfectly acceptable? Could society survive? What if Britain had been a nation of debauchees in 1940?

Without doubt, there is a gulf between Devlin and Mill, opened up by a profound difference over the scope of morality. Mill thinks that conduct falls within the domain of morality only if it is right to encourage or discourage it by means of sanctions: and such sanctioning is usually appropriate only if the conduct affects the interests of non-consenting others. Therefore, Mill's theoretical position was more radical than that of the Wolfe den Report of 1957, which recommended the legalization of homosexuality and prostitution, and from which Lord Devlin dissented. For Wolfe den recommended that certain immoral, but private acts should be tolerated by law. Ryan feels that Mill's theory implies that drunkenness, gambling, homosexuality, adultery and prostitution are not in themselves moral issues. This is what his theory implies: in practice his judgments are not always consistent with it, and it is faintly anachronistic and out-of-character to suppose him gladly accepting 'licentious* behavior. When discussing the Contagious Diseases Acts he referred to the use of prostitutes as 'illicit indulgence', vicious indulgence', 'questions of simple morality'.

Generally speaking though, Mill's position is radical, Hampsher-Monk judges it extraordinary and Hart, Devlin's liberal opponent, thought Mill 'fantastic'. There has been a rise of paternalism since Mill's day, which to an extent Hart endorses on, the grounds that we are less inclined to think that individuals know their own best interests, and that their choices are generally free. Mill would legalize the possession and the sale of all drugs, if it goes to hell on heroin, one affects nobody's interests but his own, unless he thereby incapacitate himself for the performance of special duties. He would usually forbid censorship, unless a spoken or printed utterance could clearly be demonstrated to be a direct cause of harm to concrete interests. Not only would he condemn Muslim attempts to silence Salman Rushdie. We do not believe that Mill would have favored the prosecution of those who deny the holocaust or who publish racist arguments. But it is not sure he would reject Andrea Dowrkin's and Catherine McKinnon's recent proposals for legislation against pornography. It cannot be proved that pornography causes sexual violence against women, but pornographic images do not express opinions nor address the rational faculty. Mill's case is for freedom of thought and discussion, not for freedom to excite antisocial desires.

The essay *On Liberty* is not merely a negative argument for noninterference: it is based upon a positive conception of the good. Liberty is good, Mill believes, not because it allows people to do just as they like, turn off their minds, relax and float downstream, it is good because it is bracing and invigorating, because it fosters strong characters and sturdy individuality and promotes progress. It is by no means clear that Mill's enthusiasm for liberty would be undimmed if it turned out that it produced weak, apathetic and sensual conformists. Nor does Mill recommend leaving people alone, to vegetate or deteriorate: they should actively be encouraged to develop what is best in them. To be sure, this is to be done by conviction and persuasion, not by compulsion; but Mill thinks that individuals should be more ready to point out one another's follies and backslidings to a lower level of being.

Many find traces of liberalism in the essay. Mill argues for legislation against producing too many children in a state threatened with over-population. In the light of recent developments in China and India, this no longer appears unthinkable: but he also argues for laws forbidding marriage 'unless the parties can show that they have the means of supporting a family'. Anyone who has seen Ken Leach's film Ladybird, ladybird will be worried by this, and it raises an important theoretical issue; throughout the essay, Mill largely ignores the relationship between liberty and the distribution of wealth and opportunity. This criticism of Mill is well put by McCloskey:

> The impoverished, unemployed person who, because he cannot secure work, suffers from malnutrition and disease, who would, if he could, marry the woman he loves, have a family, be creatively active in his chosen career. But who because of his poverty is unable to do any of these things, is a slave compared with the well-paid worker in the modern liberal welfare state.

Mill's essay neglects the possibility that liberty may be enlarged by increasing state activity rather than reducing it, nor is there any sense of the way in which entrenched concentrations of wealth and privilege can limit the liberty of the unprivileged by controlling their thoughts and opinions. Mill is afraid of the 'tyranny of the majority' in democratic societies, but fails to confront the danger that powerful minorities might manipulate and control the mass. He is horrified by the narrow, stifling conformism promoted by newspapers, the so-called organs of public opinion; but he does not ask about the extent to which their proprietors mould opinion. The thinking of the masses 'is done for them by men much like themselves, addressing them or speaking in their name, on the spur of the moment, through the newspapers'. The wording here implicitly rejects the idea that newspapers represent interests distinct from those of the mass, and that they consciously set about the business of forming the minds of their readers.

There is also an intractable difficulty about the legitimate scope of the 'social sanction', the punishment meted out by the disapproval of public opinion and its consequences. Mill is as much concerned to defend liberty against these informal pressures, as he is to limit the formal interference of the state. The difficulty arises like this: think of some actions with which, according to the liberty principle, we may not interfere - the taking of dangerous drugs, compulsive and ruinous gambling, behavior which is grossly ignoble and degrading, such as loutishness, gluttony or personal unseemliness. But if we do not intervene we open ourselves to the charge of being uncaring, indifferent to others and their fate. Mill does not want this. He wants us to encourage others to improve themselves, and to live fully human, happy lives - happy in the higher sense. But how do you draw the line between helping and encouraging (good), and interfering (bad)? When does friendly advice turn into liberty-threatening pressure of public opinion?

Democracy

The importance that history be understood as a process of emancipation and progress is shown once again in John Stuart Mill's *Considerations on Representative Government*, written for the most part in 1860. According to Mill, the quality of a government ultimately depends upon its ability to improve its people. The purpose of government is to promote progress on the basis of order. This is best achieved, however, when the people are allowed to actively exercise their talents and thereby develop new skills, capacities and abilities. Logically then, Mill's emphasis on an active citizenry implied a governmental system which would encourage a large degree of political participation. Whereas despotism with its emphasis upon such passive qualities as obedience may be appropriate for backward nations, Mill believed that civilized societies require that their citizens actively participate in governing so that they may progress even further. A popular government would allow for all people to share in the exercise of sovereign power. Practically, however, Mill believed that such a situation could exist only among the smallest political units—such as a small town. Thus given the fact that modern civilization seems to require the large nation-state, a representative form of government appears to be the best that is possible.

Having argued on behalf of both political participation and representative government, Mill was anxious, nonetheless, to distinguish his ideal regime from the American model of representative democracy. According to Mill, the American model was an example of a false democracy which merely represented the interests of the majority rather then the will of all. Influenced by his reading of Tocqueville's *Democracy in America*, Mill feared that the form of popular democracy practiced in America would eventually undermine the very conditions of progress, which make self-government possible in the first place. Progress, according to Mill, depended upon the intellectual and moral excellence of a few select geniuses. Accordingly, the unique individual who was capable of leading the masses was the key to social emancipation. Yet, in America, popular sovereignty was practiced in such a way as to threaten true individuality. According to Mill, the radically democratic insistence upon political equality and majority rule eventually would result in a fundamentally inegalitarian society. Such a society, in turn, would negate the very conditions of future progress. In short, Mill sought to strike a compromise. On one hand, he continued to share in the Benthamite commitment to popular self-rule. On the other hand, he was convinced by the Saint Simonian argument that the true interest of all the people was best served in a society which was governed by those experts who knew the "true principles" of political science. Inasmuch as a methodologically rigorous political science could achieve valid insights into the requirements for political order, it seemed only sensible that those who possessed such knowledge should be in the position of serving the community as a whole.

Mill's compromise between democracy and elitism was based upon his prior distinction between the act of governing and the act of controlling. Actually governing should be left to the experts. Inasmuch as the executive, administrative, and legislative functions of government presuppose highly trained and skilled practitioners, they are best left to those experts who are protected from the uniformed demands of the general populace. Thus, according to Mill, a true democracy does not require that the power of governing rest with the people. At most, democratic theory demands that the people ultimately retain the sovereign power of controlling those who govern. Accordingly, Mill suggested that a popularly elected representative assembly should be established in order to oversee and control the performance of the governing elite. Such an assembly would not only serve as a forum for ideas and opinion but, at the same time, would watch over and control the professional elite by approving or rejecting their legislative proposals. In effect, then, Mill sought to establish a "skilled democracy" wherein governing power was at least two steps removed from the people at large.

According to Mill's analysis, representative self-government faced two essential challenges. First, there was the problem of sheer governmental incompetence. And, second, there was the possibility that popular legislation which was theoretically intended for the benefit of all would, in fact, become mere class legislation, which favored either the capitalist or working class exclusively. In the hopes of minimizing such possibilities, Mill suggested a number of reforms. First, in order to insure that minorities would be adequately represented in the popular assembly, Mill advocated the practice of proportional representation. By rejecting the arrangement by which the majority alone determined the representatives from a geographical district, Mill's scheme assured that each minority could be represented according to its proportion of the total vote. Second, in order to insure that everyone's interests were represented, Mill favored extending the franchise far beyond the current British practices. He did, however, allow for certain qualifications. Thus a voter had to be able to read and write and should, at the same time, be a taxpayer. Consequently those on relief or aid would not be permitted to vote. Third, inasmuch as class legislation was due, in part, to shortsighted ignorance, Mill advocated a scheme for weighted voting. Although all qualified voters should be heard, Mill did not believe that all should be heard equally. Thus those who were mentally superior should be allowed to cast more than one ballot. Such a program, according to Mill, would give preponderance to reason and intelligence rather than to mere numbers. Finally, in order to promote responsibility among both the representatives and the voters, Mill favored direct rather than indirect elections and open rather than secret voting. In both cases, the intent was to increase public spirit and, thereby, strengthen the role of political intelligence.

In the *Autobiography* Mill informs us that in the late 1840s and 1850s he and Harriet were 'much less democrats than I had been, and that when he entered parliament in 1865 'as I had shown in my political writings that I was aware of the weak points in democratic opinions, some conservatives had not been without hopes of finding me an opponent of democracy'. But as we read on we find him insisting that his doubts about democracy did not add up to a rejection of it. An immediate move to pure democracy would not be desirable; some sections of the working classes were not ready for it and a system must be devised to safeguard against its problems, but he 'unhesitatingly decided in its favor'.

If we turn to the articles written in 1835 and 1840 on 'Tocqueville on Democracy in America' at the height of Mill's alleged conservative period, we find the same. Mill is more pro-democracy than Tocqueville, and does not do full justice to the Frenchman's doubts. Mill thought that he differed from earlier radicals in doubting that democracy was the best system for all peoples at all times, and he had a rich sense of the downside of democracy. Nevertheless, he presents himself and Tocqueville as defenders of democracy, which they both believed inevitable. He distinguishes democratic institutions from democratic society, and his worries are principally about the latter. Democratic society is characteried by equality of conditions, in itself a good thing but having a tendency to promote mediocrity and conformity. Even these evils are the result of modernity, of progress and mass society rather than of equality itself. And democratic institutions may offer a corrective to some of the evils of democratic society.

The French Revolution of 1848 inspired Mill with a high regard for the artisans of Paris: 'the most intelligent and best-conducted laboring class to be found on the earth's surface' and it fanned his enthusiasm for democracy. The first volume of Grote's *History of Greece* had recently appeared, and from it Mill had taken an ideal of liberal, tolerant democracy in Periclean Athens. But the installation in France of the jingoistic dictatorship of Napoleon III on the basis of repeated democratic plebiscites deeply depressed him and caused him to doubt the wisdom of giving votes to illiterate peasants: 'None are so illiberal, none so bigoted in their hostility to improvement, none so superstitiously attached to the stupidest and worst of old forms and usages, as the uneducated'. This is the determining context of his proposals for restraining and controlling democracy in *Representative Government* of 1861, and of *Thoughts on Parliamentary Reform* of 1859, which is the high-water mark of his doubts about universal suffrage. Especially in the 1850s then, Mill feared that democracy would come too quickly. But the American Civil War began in 1861; Mill became impassioned about it as a heroic crusade against slavery. It gave him new faith in American democracy and in those sections of the British working class who supported the North while their 'betters' supported the South, even though the North's blockade of Southern cotton had thrown them out of work. Mill always thought of himself as a democrat, in the sense that democratic institutions, carefully constructed, were his ultimate ideal.

This, however, does not provide a definitive answer to the question, 'was Mill a democrat?' For we might conclude that Mill was simply mistaken, and that the institutions he advocated were not democratic at all. This is a complex and contentious issue; the literature debating the nature and definition of democracy is now enormous. In order to simplify and set a framework for the discussion, four issues may be signaled. First, we might take the essence of democracy to be very simple: all that is required is that everybody has a vote, and that a genuine choice is offered, i.e., not as in some one-party states where there is only one candidate. Second, democracy might be specified as political equality: all have an equal say in determining how they are governed. Third, we must pay attention to the ideas of radical democrats who insist upon direct and frequent participation if a system is to be judged democratic. Fourth, sensitivity to history is required. Mill must not be assessed by 'timeless' standards, if there are any such, but must be thought of in relation to democracy as it was conceived in the nineteenth century.

Like his father and Bentham, Mill thought that a principal argument for democracy was in terms of self-protection: individuals tend to promote their own interests, and in a non-democratic system those who hold political power will advance their own interests at the expense of the powerless. This is the main ground on which Mill demands votes for women: there is no other way in which they can protect themselves against the tyranny of men. But he was vividly aware that people can only be counted upon to use the vote to defend their interests if they have a sound knowledge of them. Some may be too ignorant or shortsighted, and in their case, the self-protection argument for enfranchisement is undermined. Therefore less advanced peoples, such as the majority of the population of the Indian subcontinent, were not ready for democracy. For the same reason, some individuals in advanced civilizations should not be enfranchised. Mill would exclude those who do not have a basic proficiency in reading, writing and arithmetic.

Mill's argument for this exclusion is by no means a bad one. If a person cannot read, then how, in a society where communication of politically relevant information is mainly by the printed word, can he or she know how to use a vote? He did not wish the exclusion to be insuperable or permanent, thinking that the state should compel parents to have their children educated in basic literacy and numeracy, giving them financial assistance where necessary. But if the defining test of a democrat is supporting adult suffrage, then Mill fails that test. His argument for exclusion was better in the mid-nineteenth century than it is now: today television and radio have taken over from newspapers as the main media for communicating politically relevant information.

Mill goes further down this road, arguing that though all who have attained a basic level of education should have a voice, they should not have an equal voice 'until all are equal in worth as human beings'. Votes should be weighed as well as counted, and therefore additional votes should be given to those with higher intellectual attainments, such as a degree or a professional qualification. This provides ammunitions to those who contend that Mill was no democrat. It is true that he insisted there should be no property qualification for political power as in the pre-democratic British political system: but, as critics have pointed out, the higher educational qualifications would tend to correlate with wealth, especially in the nineteenth century. This recommendation contradicts the political equality which some have seen as the essence of democracy. In Mill's defence it should be remembered that 'fancy franchises' of this kind were 'in the air in the 1850s and 1860s and were proposed in several abortive reform bills. In his *Autobiography* he wrote that extra votes would only be feasible after the establishment of a systematic National Education by which the various grades of politically valuable acquirement may be accurately defined and authenticated. Without this it will always remain liable to strong, possibly conclusive, objections; and with this, it would perhaps not be needed.

In 1870 he publicly declared that the poor should be given more education than the '3Rs': 'In education there is no such thing as "too much"'. His advocacy of educational qualifications rests upon the eminently defensible idea that in a democracy political education designed to produce knowledgeable and effective democrats is essential. On the other hand, he thought that it would be bad if a lettered and cultivated class domination unchecked. He was not with Plato as an advocate of' philosopher-kings': no rulers, no matter how well educated, are infallible and the people are not so imbecile as to be incapable of calling their scientific ruler to account'.

There is a less defensible exclusion. In accordance with the principle laid down by his father of preventing power from falling into the hands of a fraction of society whose interest is contrary to that of society as a whole, Mill would give the vote only to those who pay taxes and are sensible of paying them. Non-tax payers would be tempted to raise public spending recklessly, spending other people's money upon themselves. Merely paying indirect taxes on tea, coffee, sugar, tobacco and alcohol would not suffice to check profligacy. Mill proposes a poll tax in order lo make voters aware of the consequences of their spending wishes. And anyone who is receiving public money in relief of poverty, or who has received such relief during the past five years, should temporarily be disfranchised. Mill had already proposed these disqualifications in 1835, in a list which also included those convicted of a criminal offence and anyone seen drunk during the previous year.

It is difficult to see how these exclusions could reasonably be defended, even in the mid-nineteenth century. Those in receipt of poor relief are still obliged to obey laws and may be called upon to fight for their country, to which, Mill asserted earlier, they should be entitled to give or withhold their consent through voting. And a person might be in receipt of public relief through no fault of his or her own, because of involuntary unemployment or chronic illness. It would not do to reply that such persons ought to save or insure against such eventualities; not all wages were high enough to permit saving or the payment of high premiums.

Mill had broader worries about class or sectional legislation in a democracy. This marks him off from his father, who simplistically thought that votes for all men would imply rule in the interests of all. The younger Mill recognized that even with universal suffrage, a majority of whites might oppress a minority of Negroes; a majority of Catholics might oppress a minority of Protestants. A majority of the poor, or of unskilled laborers, ignorant of the truths of political economy, might legislate against the interests of the rich or the skilled, unwittingly harming their own economic interests in the long term. A conformist majority might oppress dissenting minorities or eccentric individuals. A majority of mediocre persons might elect mediocrities. In an electoral system like the British, many might effectively be disfranchised because they stood no chance of electing an MP whose views coincided with their own.

The remedy Mill favored for these problems was proportional representation, as proposed by Thomas Hare in his *Treatise on the Election of Representatives* of 1859. Hare's scheme was excessively complex, but simpler methods could achieve its general aims. The elector would be able to choose from a list of candidates embracing a wide range of opinions. His vote would count, not only in the constituency in which he lived, but nationwide, so that quite small minorities could club there votes together to elect an MP to their taste. Mill thought that under such a system, outstanding individuals and intellectuals with a national reputation would, be elected and would counterbalance the mediocrities from the localities. The majority of MPs representing class interests would be forced to defend their proposals against the arguments of the representatives of intellect and Mill optimistically thought that the better argument would often prevail. Mill also thought that Hare's scheme would immediately work in favor of the working-class elector, and would ultimately make it unnecessary to give extra votes to the more educated.

Still there was a danger that democracy would put too much power into the hands of the mediocre and ill-educated. Therefore Mill thought that a large part of the business of government should be carried out by professional experts, by a permanent civil service selected by competitive examination. Not only should the executive part of government be in their hands. Mill thought that more of the process of legislation should be done by experts. As early as 1834, he declared that laws should be drafted by a legislative commission. In Britain today, government bills are drafted by civil servants. But, in addition, Mill thought that parliament should only have the power to approve or reject their proposals in toto, not to make changes. Detailed meddling by ignorant amateurs representing special interests produced bad laws. To a considerable extent, Mill wished to restrict parliament to a negative and checking function, able to throw out and replace a government, which had abused its trust or lost contact with the sense of the nation.

The spotlight has so far been turned on Mill the elitist and dubious democrat. It is interesting that this side of his political thought is entirely based upon those fundamental principles he shared with his father and Bentham, concerned with protecting interests and securing efficiency. But as Ryan argueses there is a more radical aspect but this is less 'Benthamite', having affinities with the thought of Rousseau with the 'classical republican' idea of virtue embodied in independence and citizenship and the German romantic conception of *Bildung* or personal development. For the merit of a set of political institutions consists also 'of the degree in which they promote the general mental advancement of the community, including under that phrase advancement in intellect, in virtue, and in practical activity and efficiency'. Mill thought that the possession and use of the vote would be a factor in mental and moral improvement. The voter would be impelled to rise out of the rut of petty concerns to think about public issues. 'Wherever the sphere of action of human beings is artificially circumscribed, their sentiments are narrowed and dwarfed in the same proportion. Let a person have nothing to do for his country, and he will not care for it'. The converse of this was that the apathetic have no moral right to vote.

This concern to elevate the mental and moral character of the people through political involvement also finds expression in Mill's repudiation of the secret ballot. By no later than 1853 he had come to think it would be retrograde, and he openly repudiated it in 1859. This put him at odds with radical allies such as Grote, though Mill pointed out that his father in his *History of British India* had thought it necessary only under certain circumstances. For a century or more, the secret ballot has been associated with progress and therefore it is natural to suppose his stance to be at best quirky and at worst reactionary. But this is a mistake. Contemporary radicals may have favored the secret ballot, but usually in the context of universal manhood suffrage. As long as the suffrage was restricted, an open ballot allowed the non-electors to observe and influence the electors. Mill thought that even under universal suffrage, each elector should publicly declare his or her vote. For the vote was not a right, to be used selfishly: it was a trust, to be used in the public interest, and therefore the public was entitled to know how it was being used. The voter should be shamed out of using the vote in a narrowly self-interested fashion. Publicity and criticism would encourage public spirit, and the advantages of this outweighed the dangers of bribery. Furthermore, the secret ballot would encourage lying about the vote, and 'when people have only a few of the moral feelings they ought to have, there is the more danger in weakening those few'.

The obvious criticism is to point to examples from all round the world of the intimidation of voters, by governments and parties having no inhibitions against the use of violence in elections. But Mill justifies the open ballot in the more advanced states of modern Europe on the, grounds that the power of coercing voters has declined and is declining. This is to imply that open balloting, though preferable, is only desirable where the threat of coercion is absent. Mill's stance on this question is not obviously wrong or reactionary. His concern to encourage citizens to use their votes in a responsible, public-spirited way, coupled with his plan to ensure through a system of proportional representation that every voice is heard and taken into account, brings him towards Rousseau's ideal of a general will which represents principled opinions rather than selfish interests, or the contemporary German philosopher Habermas's idea of a public consensus through use of public reason.

There is another way in which his theory of democracy moves in a radical direction. In spite of his disparaging remarks about local government and the mediocrity of the people it attracts, Mill favors the extension of it, with considerable popular participation: as Tocqueville had taught him, local bodies are essential to liberty. He is in large part an opponent of centralization or, rather, he favors as much, local administration as possible, watched, advised and supervised by the more intelligent center. This was the pattern for the New Poor Law: Mill thought that it should be applied to education too. In 1835, we find him writing in favor of provincial assemblies. Local government, local boards and jury service train 'many men of no great ability or reach of thought to be quite capable of discharging important public functions and of watching and controlling their discharge by others'. In addition, it must not be forgotten that Mill looks forward to democratic control of the workplace, as workers' co-operatives become more common. There is a parallel in his attitudes to India. Whereas James Mill thought that Indians should be passive recipients of enlightened British government, John Stuart Mill advocated the involvement of native Indians in administration because this would educate and improve them.

In assessing Mill's credentials as a democrat, we must be sensitive to the differences between then and now. Today, democracy is routine, taken for granted. Questions have become closed which were open in Mill's day. This does not mean that our answers are right; it means that we no longer pose the questions. His answers are not as eccentric as they seem when ripped out of the context of their time; there was considerable common ground between him and the progressive liberals. When Mill wrote, there were few democracies in the world, and limited experience of democracy. It still made sense, even for a democrat to ask whether all should have the vote without exceptions, and whether each person should have just one vote. It was an open question whether the vote was a right or a responsibility, and whether voting should be open or secret. Bearing this in mind, paying attention to both the elitist and radical strands in Mill's writings, and recognizing that democracy is not a Platonic essence but a contested concept, it seems right to accept Mill's boastful claim that he was a democrat.

Socialism

The question whether Mill was a socialist has been hotly debated. Rival interpretations are sketched. Mill sat at Ricardo's feet and began as a defender of free-market capitalism; this was his position in his debates with co-operative socialist followers of Robert Owen (1771-1859) in 1825, when he produced some devastating arguments. He began to move towards socialism in the 1830s under the influence of Saint-Simonism and the communitarian socialism of Fourier (1772-1837). He thought Fourierism is more realistic than Owenism: it did not require the members of its communities to be perfect altruists, and was prepared to give extra rewards to capital, talent and effort. The critical evolution came between 1847 and 1852, as he completed and brought out the first three editions of the *Principles of Political Economy*, progressively moving towards a more favorable evaluation of socialism. Their correspondence proves that Harriet Taylor him infhenced, sometimes persuading him, to be less cautious than he wished: his reluctance to make assertions without proof has frequently been noted in this book and he thought a conclusive decision between socialism and an ideal regime of private property would not be possible until both had been tried. But his admiration for the co-operative experiments in France before and during the 1848 revolution also pushed him in the same direction. In the last four years of his life, he wrote 'Our ideal of ultimate improvement would class us decidedly under the general designation of socialists' and nowhere in the *Autobiography* is this retracted. Some have thought that a retraction is signaled in the posthumously published *Chapters on Socialism*, but the evidently incomplete nature of that work makes any such inference unsound.

So why, if Mill called himself a socialist, has that description been contested? The answer is that 'socialism' is not a timeless Platonic idea but rather a handy term covering several different theories and practical proposals. We need to be clear which of these Mill agreed with. In the first place, Mill's socialism was different from that of Marx. Of course, there were similarities. Like Marx, he had a vivid sense of class conflict in industrial society. His critique of capitalism occasionally exhibited a 'Marxist' ferocity; he thought that the existing capitalist order enslaved the laborers, and recognized that wealth does not flow to those who create it. But, unlike Marx, he was utterly opposed to any total and revolutionary transformation .of society in one go. This would be anarchy, this would be chaos come again out of which no good could arise. Mill was not a man of violence and thought that if the state took a person's property, it should pay full compensation.

Neither was Mill a state socialist of the Fabian or of any other kind. This was made manifest in his arguments against Saint-Simonism whose supporters proposed a society centrally managed by experts. Mill thought this would be an intolerable tyranny; the people at large would not accept it. It would be inefficient too; a central committee could never match the detailed local knowledge of private individuals. In spite of the fact that he was a public servant, Mill had little faith in the honesty and diligence of paid officials unchecked by a representative body. Nor was he a 'welfare socialist'. He had no time for the idea that ordinary people should be paternalistically looked after: they should learn to look after themselves. He expects citizens to buy private education wherever possible and to provide for sickness and old age by means of private insurance. Where this fails, and for the unemployed, Mill remained throughout his life a defender of the principles of the New Poor Law of 1834 - though he came to condemn some of the harsher features of its actual working. In 1848 he thought it impossible to separate the deserving poor from the able-bodied on whom the rigours of the workhouse should fall with full weight: by 1868 he was lamenting that Chadwick's original plan to separate off the sick, the lunatic, the old and the young and to give them better treatment had not been implemented. So Mill was at odds with the forms of socialism, both marxist and social democratic, which prevailed in the century following his death. This largely explains the incredulity of so many commentators towards his declaration of socialist allegiance.

But if he is compared with the Utopian socialists of the 1830s and 1840s, and with the Christian socialists and co-operators of the mid-nineteenth century, his designation as a socialist is less problematic. Utopian socialism repudiated the selfish individualism of 'economic man' as conceived by classical political economy. It was a high moral ideal based on altruism and community, and it was this that appealed to Mill and Harriet Mill. Mill differed from the Owenites in thinking that it would take many generations to educate the mass of the people for unselfishness. Socialism was a long way off. He also differed from most utopians in thinking that competition was beneficial, and that it would be needed for a long time, perhaps indefinitely. Competition was a vital incentive to hard work and efficiency. Mill persisted in defending competitive markets: and to some this is enough to rule him out as a socialist. But perhaps what he most resembles is a late twentieth-century 'market socialist', who advocates a mix of enterprises - owned by the state, by municipalities, by capitalists and by workers' co-operatives - competing in the market place.

Mill was not thinking of Owenite co-operative communities; he had objections on economic grounds and opposed any kind of' communism' because of the threat it posed to liberty. He favored more modest producers' and consumers' co-operatives. He claimed in 1865 to have advocated these five years before the Rockdale pioneers of 1844, whose co-operative store inspired the co-operative movement. In fact, he first recommended producers' co-operatives in 1834. In the second edition of the *Principles of Political Economy*, he introduced the idea that the form of association of the future was not that which can exist between a capitalist as chief, and workpeople without a voice in the management, but the association of the laborers themselves on terms of equality, collectively owning the capital with which they carry on their operations, and working under managers elected and removable by themselves

In the future, only the least improved workers would consent to work for wages. This is the kernel and essence of Mill's socialism, and it is socialism: Mill was emphatic that all who work in a co-operative should be shareholders and that there should be no laborers merely for hire: 'It is not genuine co-operation, where any of the co-operators are excluded from the division of the whole produce. Workers should pool their savings in order to set up co-operatives, and should also borrow on the open market. Mill had no objections to money lent at interest: he thought that the base rate of 3 per cent in his own day would go lower, and 'who can say that this is too much, or that it is unreasonable for the use of capital to be applied for the purposes of labour. This would not he capital hiring labour, but labour hiring capital.

Mill envisages a role for capitalist employers for many years to come. First, co-operation is suited to improved, educated, public-spirited laborers; lazy and vicious workers need a boss. Second, owner management is efficient and enterprising, because the capitalist receives the fruits of success and pays the penalty for failure. Co-operative management might be cautious, routine; democratically accountable managers would be less able to take risks. If private capitalist firms can interest their employees in the success of the enterprise by profit sharing, they will have well-motivated workers and management, and will survive well in competition with co-operatives. Mill's defense of workers' co-ops rests upon ideals of democracy and independence and upon a desire to promote unselfish motivations, as much as or more than on considerations of efficiency.

Mill's prophecy that co-operatives would eventually prevail have not been realized, and there are many reasons for this. The growing and now multinational scale of corporations is no help, nor is the shortage of producers' co-operatives as a model and inspiration. Perhaps a capitalist environment is hostile to co-operative experiments; Mill had reason to know this. In 1865, he sent a donation of £10 to the Wolver Hampton plate lock Makers' Co-operative. It had been founded in 1864, but now the capitalist employers were trying to ruin it by selling plate locks below cost. 'In such a contest', Mill wrote, 'if prolonged, the competitors who have the smallest means, though they may have every other element of success, must necessarily be crushed through no fault of their own'.

No account of Mill's socialism is complete without reference to his views on land. In the *Principles of Political Economy*, he denied any absolute right of private property in land: no man made it and it remained a common heritage of the people. We have seen that he recommended state action to create peasant proprietors in Ireland. As a member of the Land Tenure Reform Association in the 1870s, he was recommending that the state purchase land on the open market in order to create small farms or large co-operative ones. A year before his death he hinted in private at the eventual possibility of the resumption of all land by the state, with compensation to the landholders.

Some related issues now require consideration: distribution, taxation and the scope of state activity. In 1869 came his 'recantation' of the wages fund theory, in the second part of his review of his former India House colleague Thornton's *On Labour and its Claims*. This has puzzled some economists, who have doubted whether Mill really changed his mind. The truth of the matter is that there was no sudden conversion: Mill's position gradually evolved. By 1869, he did not think that there was a fixed wages fund, so that if some workers got more by striking others would inevitably get less. He recognized that although the level of wages was in some ultimate way determined by the relationship between supply and demand in the market - between the number of workers seeking work, and the number of jobs on offer - nevertheless workers would often not get the market rate unless they organized themselves in trade unions and threatened strike action. Because the initiative lay with the employer, who offered work at a certain wage, wages tended to be lower than they would be if workers initiated the bargain. The wage fund was elastic: workers could get more without harming other workers if they compelled their employers to forfeit some of the profits they would have spent on a lavish lifestyle. But this elasticity was limited. The supply of capital was finite and excessive wage rises would harm investment: to this extent, the wages fund theory remained true. Mill therefore accorded a role to trade unions in securing a more equitable distribution of wealth.

Mill's thoughts on taxation were subtle, complex, and evolving throughout his life: only the main lines can be sketched here. He aimed to combine fairness with cheapness of collection, the promotion of economic growth and redistribution in the interests of greater equality. An ideal system would combine direct and indirect taxes. An income tax was justifiable in an emergency, when an exceptionally large sum had to be raised. But it should not be levied on the basic income required to purchase 'what is necessary for healthful existence', by which Mill meant something more generous than just enough to stave off starvation. Above that level, it should be flat rate; higher rates on higher incomes are unjust, because they penalize hard work and thrift. But in normal times he did not favor an income tax, because it is too easy to evade. It is a tax paid by the conscientious and avoided by the unscrupulous: a tax on honesty.

Mill thought that a house tax, a rate, was a better direct tax; if proportioned to the value of the house it tended to correspond to income and could not be evaded. But basic housing should be exempt 'on the universal principle of sparing from all taxation the absolute necessaries of healthful existence'. He also favored a hefty land tax. Riparian theory explained rent as an unearned increment, which increased with economic growth without any effort on the part of the landlord. Mill hoped that this unearned increment 'will be gradually, and in an increasing proportion, diverted from them to the nation as a whole, from whose collective exertions and sacrifices it really proceeds'. This is in embryo the Fabian socialist theory of taxation, as developed in the 1880s.

In the *Principles of Political Economy*, he proposed a further attack on unearned wealth in the form of heavy inheritance taxes, and thought that this 'would pull down all large fortunes in two generations'. He recognized a right of bequest, but severely limited the right of inheritance, thinking that no one has a right to be rich without effort. The fortunes of those who die intestate, if they have no ascending or descending heirs should go to the state. Collaterals should have no right of inheritance. The children of those who die intestate should receive no more than will suffice to complete their education or training for self-sufficiency, or no more than would give them a comfortable existence. They should not receive enough to keep a spouse and children in comfort. Where there is a will, Mill proposes that there should be a limit on what any individual may inherit.

But what exactly is a 'comfortable independence'? This looks like a wealthy leisured class. It is reminiscent of the 'clerisy' proposed by Coleridge and echoed by Mill, a class of persons having the leisure to read, think and write. He would also allow some to inherit more, where it would make economic sense to keep a business intact in the hands of one heir, or where an individual inherits the responsibility for keeping up an ancestral mansion and park or pleasure ground. Some recent commentators have thought that Mill was a radical egalitarian, others that his proposals were only minimally for redistributition. He favored a heavy graduated inheritance tax, which would compel all to work. Here is further evidence of Mill's increasing radicalism in his final years.

Where indirect taxes are concerned, Mill continues to insist on the principle of exempting the poor. The necessities of a healthful existence should pay no tax; indirect taxes should fall on comforts only. Mill was reluctant to single out 'luxuries' for higher taxation: 'I do not think a distinction can be fairly made between comforts and luxuries, or that I am entitled to call my tea and coffee by the one name, and another person's melons and champagne by the other'. But he did want to distinguish comforts and luxuries from mere status goods, such as jewellery or expensive carriages, which were especially suitable for taxation.

Mill's desire to limit the role of the state, forcibly expressed in Book V of his *Principles of Political Economy* and in the essay *On Liberty*, is well known. In the former, he writes that 'Laissez-faire, in short, should be the general practice: every departure from it, unless required by some great good, is a certain evil'. In *On Liberty* he insists that if all large enterprises were branches of government, 'not all the freedom of the press and popular constitution of the legislature would make this or any other country free otherwise than in name'. It is best to leave individuals to manage their own affairs; they will usually do it more efficiently than the state could, and self-management will be good for personal development.

It would however be a mistake to think that Mill was in favor of a minimal state: he thought that Herbert Spencer was far too hostile to government agency. His general assertion of laissez-faire is curiously qualified by a considerable list of instances where state action is appropriate. Those who, like Dicey, thought that Mill's philosophy anticipated twentieth-century collectivism were not entirely wrong. State intervention is appropriate in cases of market failure; he thought that there was nothing which free trade did absolutely well. Where private interests cannot be relied upon to pay for public goods, such as lighthouses or scientific research, government should step in. Education is a similar case of the utmost importance. Most parents have neither, the motivation nor the knowledge to impel them to purchase in the marketplace an education suited to their children's interests and to the needs of society; therefore the state must intervene. But the kind of intervention Mill proposes is significant. The state may compel parents to have their children educated, and may even pay for that education if they are poor; but it should not be the universal provider. Private providers are best, for they allow for diversity and freedom of thought: a state system could become a system of indoctrination in approved values. There should be universal public examinations to ensure that all children attain certain standards whether educated privately or by the state: but 'All attempts by the State to bias the conclusions of its citizens on disputed subjects are evil'. Mill, it is clear, would have detested the national curriculum.

He was not averse to measures of nationalization or municipalization; natural monopolies such as gas and water or railways could appropriately come into public ownership. He did not object to the provision of services by the state, if that was the only or most efficient way of doing it. For example, he favored a state monopoly of the postal services. There could be municipal provision of gardens, theatres, galleries, baths and housing and state ownership of natural beauties and historic monuments. But public ownership need not imply state management; almost always the state would do better to hire a private agency to run a nationalized industry.

A pattern of values underlies Mill's socio-economic vision. He favored liberty, and was not prepared to contemplate any form of socialism which threatened it: but did not think that liberty equaled to the capitalist free market. He favored independence, and consequently was suspicious of paternalistic welfare. He favored self-government to such an extent as to think that master-servant, employer-employee relationships were unsound and to hope for their eventual supersession. He favored equality: 'I look upon inequality as in itself always an evil, but not at the expense of efficiency, nor if it penalized effort and saving." He had no time for unearned, unmerited advantages, and was utterly committed to equality of opportunity. His account of what was needed to secure the latter is inadequate by modern standards, but he thought that primary education should be compulsory for all, and free secondary and higher education provided for the elite of the poor. He unreservedly supported the opening of the civil service to competitive examination, brusquely dismissing the suggestion that a horse-dealer's son was unsuitable, and that gentlemen could not be expected to mix with one.

Imperialism

Mill was no pacifist, but he thought national selfishness as unacceptable as individual. He hoped for a United States of Europe, but judged it would be long in coming. He was not opposed to a British Empire, believing it important for Britain's prestige and the liberty she stood for. He thought that the white settler colonies were an invaluable outlet for surplus population and capital. He inherited from his Benthamite mentors the anti-paternalist maxim that individuals are the best judges of their own interests and that therefore they should enjoy liberty and self-government. But this maxim was meant to apply 'only to human beings in the maturity of their faculties' to adults, not children, to civilized human beings, not barbarians. Consequently, Mill was not opposed to an advanced country paternally ruling a backward one. In all consistency, imperial administrator as he was, he could not think otherwise. But he was no racist; he did not think there were natural racial characteristics, nor that certain peoples were inherently and eternally backward. The imperial relationship was for him primarily a moral one; it was legitimate to rule another people, only if that rule was exercised for their good. Therefore he thought that an imperial power should take steps to improve its subjects, and as they improved they should participate in their own government; eventually they would become largely self-governing, perhaps as dependencies, as had happened to Canada.

In spite of the fact that his working life was spent at East India House, the *Autobiography* makes very little reference to India. His precise opinions on that subject, and how they evolved, are not easy to establish, for the dispatches he wrote on the relationship between the company and the princes, which was his area of responsibility, were collective efforts produced in an interchange of views. But careful reading, aided by letters and other texts, gives some idea of his stance. Zastoupil argues that after Mill's father's death in 1836, the younger Mill adopted a different approach to that of the older. James Mill was a firm westernizing reformer who thought that the company should act as an enlightened despot in India; he paid little regard to Indian cultural traditions and patriotic feelings. He thought that Indians, if well governed, did not care whether their rulers wore turbans or hats. John Stuart Mill also thought that ordinary Indians preferred being ruled by the British. Influenced however not only by German and French historical thinking but also by a group of Indian administrators inspired by Burkean Whiggism, he recognized that reforming ambitions had to be tempered by a sensitivity to the feelings and opinions of the native population. He was appalled by Macaulay's imposition of the English language in Indian education. But his cultural tolerance never went as far as an acceptance of the equal validity of Hindu culture. It might be necessary to proceed cautiously and respectfully, but the goal remained the modernization and enlightenment of India.

He sincerely believed that the East India Company governed in the interests of the Indians, and was 'the protector of the natives of India against the avarice and domineering spirit of rapacious European adventurers'. He was horrified by the atrocities perpetrated by the English in revenge for the Indian Mutiny and he thought that the move to abolish the East India Company stemmed from a perception that it defended the natives and refused to favor white residents. In his last years he sensed that a new and disgraceful imperial spirit was insolent, bullying, contemptuous of 'inferior races'.

Feminism

Mill said it was predictable that Comte, whom he once admired, should have turned totalitarian, given his views on the inferiority of women. He himself had been a fervent supporter of women's rights even before meeting Harriet Taylor. He had published his first piece of feminist argument, an article attacking double standards, in the *Westminster Review* at the age of eighteen. After meeting Harriet, he gave the woman question top priority, calling it the most important of all practical subjects. He and his stepdaughter started the National Women's Suffrage Society, in 1866 he presented a petition for women's suffrage, and he made a celebrated Parliamentary speech to amend Israeli's 1867 Reform Act to read 'person' instead of 'man'. In debate, he used arguments from *The Subjection of Women*, which he wrote four years before entering Parliament, and published a year after leaving it.

In 1830, when he was twenty-four, he began what he called 'the most valuable friendship of my life'. Mrs. Harriet Taylor, then twenty-three, was an intellectual who wrote essays and poetry. Carlyle described her as 'pale and passionate and sad-looking, a living romantic heroine'. Her husband, a businessman, was no match for her either emotionally or intellectually, and her Unitarian minister, William Johnson Fox, offered to provide her with a suitable intellectual companion. Through him, Mill was invited to one of her dinner parties. 'That man,' wrote Carlyle, 'who up to that time had never looked a female creature, even a cow in the face, found himself opposite those great dark eyes, that were flashing unutterable things, while he was discoursing the unutterable concern in all sorts of' high topics.' They began to exchange letters, manuscripts, books, and increasingly frequent and informal visits. They scandalized everyone, even going on holiday together, but Harriet was almost certainly truthful in assuring her husband that their intimacy was purely intellectual. Before they married, Mill drew up a document renouncing all the rights marriage would legally have given him.

For Harriet's sake, both before and after their marriage, Mill dropped most of his close friends, even his family. She seemed to replace his father in the niche for reverence, which had long ago been carved out in his soul. Mill said that she possessed in combination qualities which in all other persons he had known he had been only too happy to find singly – analytic acuteness, eloquence, scorn for superstition, boundless generosity, wit, feeling, charm, beauty. He called her not only 'the inspirer' but also 'in part the author of all that is best in my writings'. Some commentators consider him wildly to have exaggerated Harriet's brilliance and her input, while others, like his principal biographer, Michael Packet, say that he underestimated his debt to her. His *Logic*, which he began soon after meeting her, owed little to her other than the ferment of inspiration, but thereafter they seem to have discussed, plotted and revised his writing together. Changes in the second edition of *Principles of Political Economy* seem entirely hers, and *On Liberty*, his third major work, he described as 'more directly and literally our joint production then anything else which bears my name', and 'likely to survive longer than anything else that I have written. because the conjunction of her mind with mine has rendered it a kind of philosophic text-book of a single truth'. When Harriet died of consumption in 1865, Mill cried that 'the spring of my life is broken'. Succumbing to the superstition he deplored, he built her a fantastically expensive tomb of imported Curare marble, engraved it with extravagant praises, bought a cottage in Avenging to visit it daily, and was finally buried in it with her.

Mill was at least an incipient feminist before he met Harriet Taylor in 1830, and his background had prepared him for it. His father rejected votes for women in his *Essay on Government*, but Bentham favored them. James Mill may have treated his wife as a 'squash', but Mill's sisters studied a tough curriculum alongside their brothers. In the 1820s, Mill knew and respected the Owenton socialist feminist William Thompson. Then, in the early 1830s, feminist influences streamed in on him from Harriet Taylor, from the Unitarian circle around the Monthly Repository to which she belonged, and from Saint-Simonian and Fourier's socialism. His feminism evolved and deepened. In the mid-1820s, we find him, under the influence of the eighteenth-century philosophical historian John Millar, writing in the spirit of the Scottish Enlightenment: savages and barbarians treat women brutally; their good treatment is a mark of high civilization. In the seraglio and in modern Europe they are used 'as trinkets worn for display... shutting them up like jewels in a case'. In the early 1830s, he and Harriet exchanged letters setting out their views of marriage, and Mill's letter mingled the radical with the conventional and sentimental: 'her occupation should rather be to adorn and beautify... that will be her natural task, if task it can be called which will in so great a measure, be accomplished rather by being than by doing'. Harriet's letter is perfectly unsentimental and robust, and Mill largely gave up such sentimentalities in this matter. Harriet was no doubt a good influence who progressively raised his consciousness. In 1832, he wrote in favor of banning women from factory work by law, so as not to take them away from their families. Some Lancashire women objected, and he conceded that 'the interdiction might be confined to married females, and those whose parents are alive and not in the receipt of parish relief. But by the time of the *Principles of Political Economy* of 1848 he was resolutely opposed to paternalistic treatment of women as if they were children. As early as 1834 we find him objecting to the use of masculine terms to refer to all humans, and by the time he came to reprint his essays in 1859 he was systematically replacing 'he' and 'his' with 'they' and 'their'. He opposed sentimental, vulgar and essential zing talk about 'woman' instead of 'women'. In the 1840s and 1850s came the series of articles highlighting men's violence against women, and in 1867 he moved his amendment to the Parliamentary Reform Bill with the aim of giving votes to women on the same terms as men. In 1869 he published his feminist classic, which had been drafted about 1860.

He argued that subordinating one sex to the other is 'now one of the chief hindrances to human improvement'. Resistance to changing this is firmly entrenched because it is not based on reason but on feeling, so that as each objection is uprooted by rational argument, it always seems as if there is 'some deeper ground, which the arguments do not reach', and feeling simply refills gaps of logic. Going against the 'commonsense' argument, Mill says that the present system is merely based on unverified theory, rather than on comparing or trying out different types of social organization to see which is most conducive to wellbeing. Yet this theory is not the result of hypothesis or deliberation, but simply an example of the way laws sanction existing states of affairs. In primitive times, women's greater physical weakness put them in bondage to men, and this enslavement become regularized between masters. But while the slavery of men has been abolished, women's, which is ubiquitous, has merely been softened, and for them the law of the strongest continues. A women's vows at the alter commit her by law to obedience to her husband in everything except breaking the law; legally her property his, and he can legally rape her. The fact that most men do not take advantage of these laws is no argument in favor of them. Whenever a retrograde institution such as slavery or political absolutism is defended, 'we are always expected to judge of it from its best instances; and we are presented with pictures of loving exercise of authority on one side, loving submission to it on the other – superior wisdom ordering all things for the greatest good of the dependents, and surrounded by their smiles and benedictions. Who doubts that there may be great goodness, and great happiness, and great affection, under the absolute government of a good man? Meanwhile, laws and institutions require to be adapted, not to good men, but to bad.'

Mill rejects the argument that women happily consent to being dominated. They are not in the position of other subjugated classes, since they are bound to their oppressors by ties of affection and, often, children. Attraction between the sexes, women's powerlessness, and men's desire to have 'not a forced slave but a willing one', ensure that they are kept in 'a chronic state of bribery and intimidation combined', while morality and convention pre-emotively instill meekness, which has become, for women, 'an essential part of sexual attractiveness'. Surely the large number of women who write or petition for better education, opportunities and the vote were taught to repress their desire for such things as unfeminine. Mill insists that 'fatality of birth' should not exclude women from the education and employment open to men. His pleas that to be born a girl instead of a boy should not determine someone's position in life, any more than being born black instead of white, a commoner instead of a nobleman. Mill challenges the legal restrictions put on the woman to keep them out of many occupations. What women by nature cannot do, it is quite superfluous to forbid them from doing, freedom and competition, says Mill, will soon sort out who can do what.

Mill points out the speciousness of the argument that women are superior, and therefore, above the fray. Women are told they are better than men, he says, 'by those who are totally opposed to treating them as if they were as good'. If people really believed what they said, how odd that they should consider it 'quite natural and suitable, that the better should obey the worse'. As for the argument that women are 'naturally' inferior, 'naturally' suited only for the domestic sphere, Mill at his most passionate asserts that we cannot know what women naturally are at all. 'What is now called the nature of women is an eminently artificial thing – the result of forced repression in some directions, unnatural stimulation in others'. So cramped are they in intellect and creativity, force-fed in sentiment and sympathy, for the benefit of their masters, that it is no more possible to know the true nature of woman than that of a tree of which one half is 'kept in a vapor bath and the other half in the snow'. Giving them the same education and freedoms as men receive surely eliminate 'nearly all the apparent differences' between the sexes. It would benefit men as well, since too much power makes them arrogant and spoiled. And only marriages between equals and kindred spirits can be truly happy and worthwhile. He insists that to deprive women of the freedom, which is 'ennobling' and 'inspiring' to all humans alike, not only lessens their potentiality for happiness and fulfillment, but also halves the quantity of talent available and impoverishes the whole of humankind.

The Subjection of Women is not impeccably consistent. Mill undermines his nurture versus nature argument, for instance, by talking in other parts of the essay as if he does know what women's psychological characteristics naturally are – not least, unfortunately, when he speculates why women have done less well at painting, writing and philosophy than men, or where he declares them more intuitive. But such inconsistencies are common in this subject, and they cannot mitigate the acuteness with which he transfixes his opponents' inconsistencies, or the passion and power of his polemic. Yet this essay was revolutionary. Greeted with intense hostility, and the only one of Mill's books to lose him money, it came into its own at the beginning of the twentieth century, when it was lauded by feminists and acknowledged by many men, including Bertrand Russell as that catalyst who converted them to the women's cause. If many of the demands, which Mill made for women's rights, have since been granted, his theoretical analysis has hardly been bettered. Recent feminist books may have obscured it, but they have not superseded it.

Mill's essay on *The Subjection of Women* divides into four sections. In the first, he reflects on the belief that women should be subordinate to men, exposing it as an unfounded prejudice and explaining why the prejudice is so deeply entrenched. In the second, he examines the unequal laws relating to marriage, in the third, the exclusion of women from various employments, and in the fourth, he sets out the benefits which would flow from according women freedom and equality. The book is a classic repertory of good arguments against gender discrimination.

Mill's piecemeal demolition of the case against women is sustained by four fundamental lines of argument. First, the associations or environmentalist one that apparent differences between the 'nature' of women and the 'nature' of men may not be natural at all, but wholly artificial, generated by environment, conditioning and education. We do not know what women in general are capable of, because they have rarely, been given the chance to show their mettle. No one has expressed this classic feminist argument more eloquently.

A second structural argument of the book relates the subjection of women to a historical grand narrative leading to the conclusion that the emancipation of women is both likely and morally imperative. Primitive social relations were governed by brutality, force, the law of the strongest; as civilization has advanced, brute force has given way to humanity, reason, justice and freedom. Slaves have been emancipated, serfs and burgesses freed from the oppression of feudal lords, nations have shaken off the yoke of absolute monarchs. Relations between men and women are the only area where the law of the strongest prevails, and this is 'the primitive state of slavery lasting on. It has not lost the train of its brutal origin.' 'There remain no legal slaves, except the misfires of every house'. The historical construction is reinforced by a social and psychological one; Mill emphasizes the plight of women who are married to the lowest dregs of the population, to men little better than animals; they may be subjected to beating, marital rape and even murder. The extremity of his language - 'vilest malefactor', 'atrocity', 'mean and savage natures', victim' and 'executioner', 'absolute monsters', 'animalism and selfishness', 'ferocious savages' - demonstrates the depth of his concern. By this rhetorical strategy he who would put women into subjection is associated with the stage which history has left behind, with the savage and the criminal, with social trash and with those whose higher natures have been overwhelmed by their lower and animal ones.

A third major theme is the ideal of companionship in marriage. No doubt, there have always been examples of it, and the ideal in a recognizably modern form goes back to sixteenth-century Puritanism if not earlier. But Mill is right in thinking that the ideal had become more prevalent and influential, as men's lives became more domestic and as they spent their leisure with their wives rather than in 'the rough amusements and convivial excesses which formerly occupied most men in their hours of relaxation'. He is right too when he argues that true friendship in marriage is almost impossible where the partners are very different in tastes and character, completely impossible when their relationship is that of superior to inferior. His sentences glow with enthusiasm for a marriage between two cultivated equals, identical in opinions and purposes. Undoubtedly he has his own union with Harriet Taylor in mind, and, as a dark contrast and warning, the decidedly uncompanionate marriage of his own parents.

Finally, Mill accumulates a series of utilitarian arguments for the emancipation of women, showing that society will benefit. There are never enough able people to do the world's work and excluding women from higher employment halves the pool of talent. Then there are several ways in which the emancipation of women will benefit men. Men's characters are corrupted when society accords them superiority over others, which they have not merited, when every man, no matter how inadequate, can fancy himself superior to every member of the opposite sex. For Mill this is an exact parallel with the unearned status and power of aristocracy, which in his view, corrupts and enervates; he is committed to the invigorating effects of meritocracy, of which female emancipation is a necessary part.

Not only does the subjection of women corrupt men by ascribing them unmerited status and thereby weakening their sense of justice; it also encourages them in habits of tyranny and domination. Furthermore, companionship in marriage produces ill effects when combined with sex inequality. A man who spends his time with an uncultivated, ill-informed woman insensibly adjusts to his company and slowly degenerates; 'If the wife does not push the husband forward, she always holds him back'. Women can have great influence for good; because of their physical weakness, for instance, they discourage violence and promote the humanizing effects of civilization. But if this softening influence is combined with a lack of education, it can do harm. Women engage in works of charity: but if they do not understand the principles of political economy, the money they dole out to the poor may entrench poverty rather than relieving it. Finally, the uneducated wife holds back the fearless radical man who would otherwise stand up for his principles in spite of society's disapproval. She cannot appreciate his courage and commitment to principles because she cannot understand them; all she sees is the loss of social status to herself, and of job and marriage opportunities to her children. Her influence is all in the direction of mediocrity and respectability.

No one today denies the importance of Mill's *The Subjection of Women*, or that he was a noble and inspiring precursor of modern feminism. But the essay has been subjected to feminist criticism. Doubts have, been expressed about the discussion in Chapter 3 of the aptitudes of women and their suitability to various occupations and activities. Mill prefaces his argument with a restatement of his environmentalist credo, and provides a classic explanation of why women have displayed so little in the way of original genius in the sciences and the arts: it has nothing to do with a lack of ability and everything to do with a lack of opportunity and encouragement. A minor criticism here is that he underestimates the extent of female achievement in the arts and fails to recognize the way in which excellence has been defined in terms of what men do.

But then Mill runs the risk of bringing natural difference, and natural inferiority, back in. For he considers the mental differences between men and women as they presently appear, in order to make out a case for the 'peculiar tendencies and aptitudes characteristic of women'. Women have more rapid insight into character; they tend to be better than men at practice as contrasted with theory; they are more down to earth and realistic, and sensitive to the needs of individuals; they think and judge more quickly; they are capable of greater spirit and enthusiasm; their minds are more mobile and flexible. To the critic this sells the pass to the anti-feminist enemy. The oldest trick in the patriarchialist book is to praise women for their special talents, and then to infer that those talents perfectly equip them to complement and serve men and to assume their role in a separate and inferior sphere. For the differences Mill emphasizes resemble the clichéd contrast between male logic and female intuition. He even hazards the suggestion that these perceived differences may be related to differences in brain size and structure. If women's brains are smaller, then they may be better adapted to speed of response and flexibility, to doing several things at once or in quick succession; if men's brains are larger, then perhaps they will bear more heavy work, single-mindedly grinding slowly and steadily away at problems until they are solved.

But if the text is read carefully and sympathetically, the worst that can be said about Mill's argument is that he has chosen an unfortunate rhetorical strategy. He has decided to give his opponent the benefit of the doubt, and to assume for the sake of argument that the differences, which appear between men and women really are essential differences. Mill thus, as it were, goes into the fray with one hand tied behind his back. But, he can now say, even though his opponent has been allowed to choose his own ground, even though he has given up, for the time being, some of his best arguments, nevertheless he can show that the traditionally accepted characteristics of women fit them to take on executive tasks and to be managers and rulers. This may have seemed a clever argument to Mill: but perhaps he made a dangerous concession to his opponent, and one which can all too easily be turned against him.

Putting the best case for Mill, he never concludes that there are essential differences of character, aptitude and ability between men and women: 'I shall presently show, that even the least contestable of the differences which now exist, are such as may very well have been produced merely by circumstances, without any difference of natural capacity'. From writings at different times in his life it is clear that Mill had a persistent and rooted dislike of commonplace and essential distinctions between 'masculinity' and 'femininity'. But in his careful formulations he avoids the opposite position of asserting categorically that there are no essential differences. True to the scientific stance we saw manifested in the *Logic*, he resolutely refuses to draw conclusions beyond what the evidence will bear. In his day, the relevant sciences were not sufficiency developed to provide firm answers; the relationship between the physical structure of the brain and its intellectual powers was a subject of dispute, and the laws of the formation of character the science which Mill called 'ethnology' had been little studied. Finally, in Mill's defense it should be pointed out that present-day feminists are by no means united over whether to insist upon special female/ feminine characteristics whether natural or cultural or not. There has been a reaction against the 'equality feminism' of Wollstonecraft (1759-97) and de Beauhaviour (1908-86), according to which women's minds can and should be just like men's, and there is now a tendency to celebrate difference (Gillian, 1982). 'Difference feminism' might be less inclined to criticize Mill for saying that women were more likely to favor compromise than conflict, that their enfranchisement would strengthen the influences opposed to violence and bloodshed, and that they would be more likely to protect natural beauty. They might welcome Donner's finding of a 'feminist' ethic of caring in Mill's concern for the culture of the feelings.

From a twentieth-century point of view, it is less easy to defend Mill's prescriptions for married women. He thought that gainful employments should be opened up to women in equal competition with men, and women should receive the education necessary to make that competition fair. For this is essential to a woman's dignity, it raises her value in the eyes of her husband. But 'like a man when he chooses a profession, so, when a woman marries, it may in general be understood that she makes choice of the management of a household, and the bringing up of a family, as the first call upon her exertions'. Here, separate spheres are firmly back in place: to a radical feminist, this shows up the limitations of Mill's "liberal feminism' which fails to recognize that the patriarchal household is the prime site of women's oppression. In mitigation it might be remarked that Mill's recommendation is a qualified one: he insists that individual circumstances should be allowed to vary the rule, that for example talented women should not be precluded by marriage from pursuing vocations. He intends also that women should have careers before they have children and after their children have grown up. And it can be said that scarcely any late nineteenth-century feminists envisaged the two-career family and shared parenting. Given the magnitude of the task of running a household, with few lab our-saving devices, this is hardly surprising. Mill often reminds us that the dominant form of feminism in nineteenth-century Europe was a 'relational' feminism, reemphasizing motherhood and companionate, non-hierarchical marriage. To an extent it would be anachronistic to expect Mill to think other than he did.

But only to an extent: for his wife was perfectly capable of adopting and expressing a more 'advanced' stance. In the exchange of letters on marriage in the 1830s, Mill wrote that 'It does not follow that a woman should actually support herself because she should be capable of doing so... it is not desirable to burden the labour market with a double number of competitors'. Harriet floats the idea of abolishing marriage entirely, opening up all occupations to women so that they would no longer have to 'barter person for bread', and making fathers and mothers equally responsible for the economic support of children. In her essay 'The Enfranchisement of Women' of 1851, she rejects the argument that giving all women jobs would overstock the labour market, insisting that every woman must have her own earnings in order to redress the balance of power in the sexual relationship.

Mill has also been criticized for his arguments in the last chapter of the essay defending the emancipation of women because of the benefits it will bring to men. Such criticism is understandable, but inappropriate. Many late twentieth-century women feel insulted by the implication that, when they claim their rights, they need to take the further step of justifying them; after all, men are not required to justify their right to control their property and to compete for employment. But we must remember that Mill was a utilitarian, committed to the belief that all rights require justification. And once again, his argument should be considered as a carefully chosen rhetorical strategy. Mill knows that given the existing distribution of power, men must be, persuaded to change the law, and therefore it is sensible to show men that they have an interest in doing so. We must distinguish between the arguments, which Mill uses to persuade others, and the arguments by which he himself is persuaded. It is plain from the way he concludes the essay that he wants to end the subjection of women for women's sake, not for men's: 'But it would be a grievous understatement of the case to omit the most direct benefit of all, the unspeakable gain in private happiness to the liberated half of the species'.

Mill can finally be criticized for things he does not say. He is rightly appalled about the practice of husbands taking their sexual pleasure whether their wives want it or not, but has little to say in criticism of the construction of sexuality in such a way as to maximize pleasure for men regardless of the pleasures of women - an issue which has been central to feminism since its revival in the 1970s. Some have thought that he despised sexual pleasure, and that this made him to take an unappealing view of marriage as a 'dowdy and ascetic partnership'. He makes no mention of mechanical contraception, so essential if women are to control their own bodies. He does not come out clearly and publicly in favors of divorce, even though he was privately in favor of 'entire freedom on both sides to dissolve this like any other partnership'. In 1850, he had thought that the time was not yet ripe, though in 1851 he did publish the remark that 'equality of freedom is the final destiny of the institution of marriage'. By the time of *The Subjection of Women* he also thought that the issue could not properly be tackled until women had the vote and could play an equal part in deciding it. This was a sound attitude if divorce was not to be a device whereby men could trade in wives for younger models, leaving their former partners destitute. And in 1870 he told the Royal Commission on the Contagious Diseases Acts that a woman should have a right to divorce if her husband gave her a sexually transmitted disease.

Is it anachronistic to expect a respectable Victorian to be outspoken about these issues? In part the answer must be yes; once again some respect should be accorded to Mill's careful choice of political and rhetorical strategy. After all, when after Mill's death Gladstone was told about his youthful propagandizing for mechanical contraception, he withdrew his support for a monument in Westminster Abbey. But we should not assume that it would have been impossible for Mill to discuss women's sexual pleasure and artificial contraception in the 1860s; for the utopian socialists, as Mill knew, had been discussing these matters in the 1820s.

It can also be contended that Mill does not face up to the economic conditions of women's emancipation. He wants to diminish the dependence of women on men, and to this end would open up all or most professions to both sexes. But women with dependent children need help with childcare, and guarantees that periods out of paid work will not adversely affect their careers and earning abilities. Otherwise, they may face a stark choice between poverty and dependence on a man. Mill fails to confront these issues, and makes matters worse by insisting that the primary responsibility for rearing children rests with the wife. It is not unfair to criticize him on this score; once again, the utopian socialists had already recognized these problems and proposed solutions to them. Harriet Taylor Mill hinted at their ideas in 'The Enfranchisement of Women'. One may speculate that Mill's profound commitment to Malthusianism prevented him from considering arrangements designed to make rearing children easier.

Feminist campaigning played an important part in the last few years of Mill's life. As a member of parliament, he presented petitions and moved an amendment for women's suffrage. In 1868, he sponsored the Married Women's Property Bill. It is worth remembering that when he married Harriet Taylor in 1851, he signed a declaration renouncing the rights over her property, which the law gave him. Out of parliament, he was closely involved, through his stepdaughter Helen, in the work of the National Society for Women's Suffrage. Their behavior has recently attracted some criticism; they tried to control the society, sometimes from Avenging, and to subvert those women who disagreed with them. They wanted to keep the agitation in the hands of ladylike rather than vulgar women, and thought it preferable for a speaker to be feminine or to have a pretty face. They wanted the London Committee to break off relations with the one in Manchester, they tried to get women they disapproved or removed from the committee.

The issue was tactics. Mill was convinced that the prime necessity was the vote: once women had that, they could use their political power to tackle other oppressions. He was as opposed to the Contagious Diseases Acts as anyone, and in 1870 testified powerfully against them to the Royal Commission. But he felt that the two issues should be kept separate, for there was a danger that potential allies on the suffrage issue would be put off by so 'indelicate and unfeminine' a subject as the regulation and inspection of prostitutes. From the point of view of modern and especially radical feminism this is reprehensible, typical of the failings of 'liberal' feminism which focuses on political issues rather than on the more fundamental oppression grounded in the sexual use and abuse of women. But there were contemporary women feminists, in addition to Mill's stepdaughter, who shared his opinions on tactics. If Mill and Helen were at once high-handed and underhand, this reflects the passion of their commitment to the cause. It is at least arguable that Mill was right, and that here again is testimony to his sense of politics as the art of the possible. Even if he was wrong, mistakes about tactics do not minimise the sincerity and wholeheartedness of his feminism.

Conclusion

The literature of commentary on John Stuart Mill is now immense. Controversies about the correct interpretation and assessment of him and his books are legion. Mill's reputation was already controversial during his life. Initially this was because utilitarianism itself was controversial: Literary figures such as Coleridge Carlyle and Dickens looking from the standpoint of the romantic imagination castigated utilitarianism as hard, heartless, mechanical, philistine, godless and base. Mill was receptive to these criticisms; his essay on utilitarianism was a brilliant rescue-operation which showed that it could be as noble and inspiring as any other morality. He made it both publicly and academically respectable as at the very least a plausible and discussable theory of morality, a position it has retained ever since. He also redeemed political economy from its reputation as the' dismal science' and in the second half of the nineteenth century his influence on young men in the universities was enormous: T.H. Green, the Oxford idealist philosopher is said to have murmured on his deathbed in 1882, 'Mill was such a good man'. In the last decade of his life, and especially from the time of his parliamentary candidature, controversy about him widened and intensified; the rapturous he received at public meetings on the one hand, and on the other his vilification by the conservative press, testify to this. In addition to the political stances he adopted, his essays *On Liberty* and *The Subjection of Women* provoked both enthusiasm and hostility. His critics found subversive subtexts: they thought that his barely concealed aims were to subvert Christianity and promote divorce, thereby undermining the very foundations of society. Many thought that his doctrine of liberty, licensing individuals within wide limits to think, speak, and act as they liked was forgetful of the need to protect the coherence and identity of society as a community of belief and action. Others thought that his doctrines about women were justly plain wrong: it was obvious to them that women were inferior, mentally as well as physically and that their place was in the home under the authority of their husbands.

Immediately after his death, Mill was the victim of a sharp attack by Abraham Hayward, both in a *Times* obituary and in *Fraser's Magazine*. Hayward was a conservative lawyer and Mill's contemporary; they had crossed swords in the London Debating Society in the late 1820s and Mill, then a callow Benthamite, had uttered unforgivable words. Hayward had his revenge. He averred that Mill was fanatic in the cause of human progress who did an infinity of harm; he advocated the fanciful rights of women and impracticable revolutionary reforms in the laws relating to land; he advanced socialistic opinions under female training. Hayward also retailed the story of Mill in his teens advocating birth control, and more or less accused him of adultery with Harriet Taylor. The subsequent controversy pronpted prime Minister Gladstone, who had dubbed Mill the 'saint of liberalism,' to withdraw his support for a memorial in Westminster Abbey.

The Victorians of the last quarter of the nineteenth century assessed Mill's significance with some ambiguity. A widely received view, proposed by Dicey, has been that the heyday of liberal individualism ended about 1870, to be followed by gradually ascendant collectivism. Some late nineteenth century commentators such as the neo-Hegelian philosophers Bosanquet, Bradley, Ritchie and to an extent Leslie Stephen thought that Mill is a yesterday's man trapped in an individualistic paradigm belonging to the eighteenth-century Enlightenment.

This judgement was at best a caricature, at worst downright false. Dicey himself insisted that Mill's later teachings prepared the minds of the rising generation to accept collectivism and he cited Stephen and the late nineteenth-century philosopher Sidgwick as authorities for the view that Mill was a socialist. Early Fabian socialists immersed in collectivism were happy to claim Mill as a precursor. The balance of individualism and collectivism in Mill's thought remains an issue even to this day.

Gradually it became fashionable to disparage him as second rate, unoriginal as a philosopher and economist, muddy and confused as a thinker. Bradley, writing in 1876 from a neo-Hegelian, anti-individualist standpoint, picked logical holes in Mill's utilitarianism in order to reject it altogether. During the last quarter of the nineteenth century, these criticisms slowly made their way emerging. It is strikingly voiced in G. E. Moore's *Principia Ethica* of 1903, which discusses Mill's *Utilitarianism*. Mill is there accused of all manner of fallacies, including 'naïve and artless' ones; his 'proof of the principle of utility, already savaged by Bradley, came in for particular scorn: Well, the fallacy in this step is so obvious, that it is quite wonderful how Mill failed to see it'.

For the first half of the twentieth century this rather disparaging view was the dominant one. For example, according to his godson Russell in 1951, Mill's *Logic* and *Principles of Political Economy* were conventional and unimportant; Mill never learnt to think in a mathematical way. Plamenatz, writing in 1949, with obvious liking for Mill and conviction that 'the study of his confusions and errors is nearly always profitable', thought that by the time of his essays *On Liberty* and *Utilitarianism*, Mill was exhausted and prematurely aged by illness, unable to keep control of his arguments.

What were the key problems identified by this critical phase of Mill scholarship. Three aspects of the essay on *Utilitarianism* drew most fire. First, it was contended that his 'proof' of the principle of utility contained a crude logical mistake. Second, his argument that only pleasure is desirable for its own sake was thought to be unconvincing and indeed incoherent. Third, it was said that his distinction between higher and lower pleasures effectively subverted utilitarianism, though Mill himself did not realize this. Nor was it only the essay on *Utilitarianism* which was seen to be fraught with problems. His essay *On liberty* has as its cornerstone the principle that individuals should not be prevented from acting, either by law or by public opinion, when their actions are purely self-regarding, affecting only themselves. This central doctrine, the keystone of Mill's liberalism, was held to be incoherent; few if any actions it was argued, affect only the doers and are purely self-regarding. In the first half of this century *Utilitarianism* and *On Liberty* were probably the most widely read of Mill's works standard fare on university syllabuses in Philosophy, Politics and History. It was widely thought that the two were inconsistent. *Utilitarianism* says that we should promote the good that is to say happiness: *On Liberty* insists that where self-regarding acts are concerned we should not interfere with individuals even for their own good. One work makes happiness most important, the other liberty; one work is utilitarian, the other is not.

A variation on this theme is the contention that the contradictions in his thought reflect stages of his mental development, stages which took him in different directions, directions which he never succeeded in reconciling. The origin of his interpretation is his own *Autobiography*. There we learn that he began as an orthodox Benthamite radical, an heir of the eighteenth century Enlightenment, who became disenchanted and turned to romantic poetry, and to the conservative Carlyle. Critics saw this as the source of all his later contradictions; he continued to be torn between Bentham and Coleridge, the Enlightenment and Romanticism, iconoclasm and reverence for history, individualism and organicism, liberty and authority, radicalism and conservatism, the ethic of pleasure and the ethic of free self-expression.

The second half of the twentieth century has seen a revisionist and hermeneutic trend in Mill scholarship. That is to say, instead of reading his texts destructively, awarding ticks and crosses as if marking an exam paper, Mill is read sympathetically, in an attempt fully to understand his arguments and intents. Two important books by Alan Ryan established this trend. The charge of incoherence leveled at Mill's simple principle in *On Liberty*, based on the distinction between self-and other-regarding actions, seemed incontrovertible to late nineteenth-century philosophers such as Bosanquet and Ritchie, because they were neo-Hegelians who believed that all is but part of one stupendous whole. Therefore a free-standing self uninvolved with others was at each and every moment impossible. The eclipse of Hegelianism robbed this charge of its self-evident force. It was seriously damaged in a classic article by John Rees. Alan Ryan constructed a powerful case for the overall coherence of Mill's thought, arguing that *On Liberty* could only be understood if it was read together with the whole of *Utilitarianism*, including the neglected last chapter on justice, and the last part of the *Logic*. John Gray, Fred Berger and John Skorupski, among others, have developed and strengthened this line of argument. The essential continuity of Mill's thought and therefore his consistency, have been defended by Robson, Halliday and Rees.

These articles and books are heavy artillery; now that they have done their work, it does not make sense to defend the view that Mill's mature work contains crude fallacies and glaring inconsistencies, and interwoven with the debate about Mill's stature as a thinker are debates about his ideological stance. Very often the interpretations proffered are themselves ideological, attempts to co-opt Mill for a particular political position or to hold him up as horror to be avoided. Mention has already been made of the common late-nineteenth-century interpretation of him as a socialist. This was an easier view to hold at a time when party boundaries were fluid, when the liberal chancellor of the exchequer Sir William Harcourt could say in 1894, 'we are all socialists now', and when Fabian socialists could think of permeating either liberals or conservatives. But with the emergence of an independent party of labour around the turn of the century , new ideological boundaries emerged. It came to seem necessary to allocate Mill either to liberalism or to socialism, and in the twentieth century the balance of judgement has awarded Mill to be a liberal by Berlin, and Duncan, socialist scholars like Macpherson have written of Mill with respect but have tended to argue that, while his intentions were good, they were vitiated by the liberal individualist framework which he never abandoned. Yet Mill insisted he was a socialist, and now that socialism is redefining itself after the collapse of the command economies of Eastern Europe, the question looks thoroughly open again. The most powerful attempt to play down Mill's socialist credentials is Hollander's two-volume study of his economics; the opposite case has been well argued by Kurer. Hollander's book has clear agenda of a somewhat scholastic kind: he aspires to show that all the great classical and neo-classical economists Adam Smith, Ricardo, Mill, and the 'marginalists' of the late nineteenth century- were in essential agreement in their defence of a free-enterprise system.

Of course, liberals still claim Mill for their own, and find their current concerns reflected in his thought. The reaction against collectivism after experience of European Fascism and Russian Communism brought a revival in his reputation; he became a Cold War hero. Isaiah Berlin presented Mill as an ethical pluralist like himself. According to this view, Mill recognized that there was no static human nature, no final truth in human affairs and no single account of the good. Humans pursue different goods between which there is no way of judging, and which cannot be combined in a single system, capable of being enforced without violating anyone's preferred values. This is the basis of his case for the tolerance of individual diversity. Berlin's pupil Graeme Duncan did not agree: Mill thought there were right answers to moral question. More recently, John Gray has endorsed Berlin's interpretation.

Mill's capacity to irritate conservatives has not diminished with time. In 1963 his doctrine of liberty was subjected to vicious attack by Maurice Cowling. Cowling contended that Mill was a hypocritical liberal; the freedom he believed in was not freedom for everyone but only freedom for elitist people like himself, for left-wing atheistic intellectuals; he was perfectly happy for the state or for society to interfere with those who did not measure up to his own standards. 'Mill was a proselytizer of genius: the ruthless denigrator of existing positions, the systematic propagator of a new moral posture, a man of sneers and smears and pervading certainty'. At about the same time a similar case was made with similar rudeness by Letwin, who depicted Mill as a stage on a downward slope leading from the eighteenth century sanity and conservatism of David Hume to the Fabian socialism and collectivism of Beatrice Webb. Mill went astray by following alien especially German influences, even though he did not properly understand German Romanticism. He represents the evil of rationalism in politics, being an intolerant, elitist puritan perfectionist, a sham liberal who wanted the government to impose what he considers the good life on all his fellows'. Cowling's and Letwin's attacks, hostile and ideologically motivated though they were, gained purchase because there is a real problem of interpretation here, which must be to what extent did Mill qualify his doctrine of liberty with an advocacy of authority and of collective action for the good of the whole?

A very different and to some extent opposed conservative critique was offered in a provocative book by the American scholar Gertrude Himmelfarb. Her stance towards Mill is related to that strand in American conservative thinking which repudiates 'liberalism. To such critics, the 'advanced liberalism' to which Mill explicitly gives allegiance is more akin to anarchic licence than to healthy freedom. It goes hand-in-hand with a superficial, critical rationalism lacking in respect for tradition and authority, and it dreams of an unrealistic and dangerous equality.

Variants of this critique are offered by Joseph Hamburger and Willmore Kendall. Himmelfarb's interpretation attempts to rescue at least a part of Mill's legacy from this critique. She thinks that Mill's 'conservative' phase in the 1830srepresents Mill at his best - the essays on 'The Spirit of the Age' and 'Civilization', on de Tocqueville, Bentham and Coleridge are a marked improvement on the crudities of Benthamite utilitarianism. This 'other' Mill was a conservative liberal who recognized that freedom had to be balanced with discipline, the demands of the individual with the need of the community. But then in the 1840s Mill swung back to the superficialities of his youth-why? Because of Harriet Taylor, an unpleasant, dogmatic and mediocre woman: 'Yet there is no doubt of the enormity of her influence.'

According to Himmelfarb, Harriet forced him against his will down the road of socialism, and away from eclectic tolerance towards radical dogmatism. She inoculated him with her passion for feminism. This was in fact the cause of the extreme and unqualified libertarianism of his essay *On Liberty*. The morality of utility does not necessarily lend support to the feminist cause; some women, perhaps most women, might be happier with traditional feminine roles. But liberty, taken as an absolute, must imply the emancipation of women. After Harriet's death, Mill moved back towards his richer and more broad- minded stance of the 1830s as for example, his essay on *Representative Government* reveals. For Himmelfarb the essay *On Liberty* is an inferior work, its ideas akin to those which motivated the excesses of campus radicalism in the 1960s.

But important issues for discussion are raised here. First, did Mill abandon, or largely transform his Benthamite heritage? Ryan and Thomas thought this greatly exaggerated, and that fundamentally Mill remained a philosophic radical. They say that his apparent distance from Benthamism is apparent only because Benthamism has been caricatured, an activity of which Mill himself was sometimes guilty. Just as crude Marxism has been blamed, not on the master himself but on his disciple Engels, so the more dogmatic form of philosophic radicalism has been attributed not to the great thinkers such as Bentham and Ricardo, but to that hard and narrow man, James Mill. Even this has been contested by Rees and the essential continuity between the thought of father and son defended.

Second, was there a distinct conservative period in Mill's intellectual evolution? Against Himmelfarb, others have argued for an essential continuity; but this is still an issue for discussion; and related to it is an important debate about whether Mill, after his encounters with the Coleridgeans and de Tocqueville, remained a democrat.

Third, how influential was Harriet Taylor Mill, and what was the nature and quality of that influence? Mill, himself insisted that her influence was paramount and all to the good. Others took a quite different view. Carlyle thought she was 'full of unwise intellect, asking and re-asking stupid questions', with her eyes, that were flashing unutterable things while he was discoursing the utterable concerning all sorts of ' high topics'. And according to Alexander Bain, Mill's friend, disciple and biographer, 'The more common way of representing Mrs Mill's ascendancy, is to say that she imbibed all his views, and gave them back in her own form, by which he was flattered and pleased'. Hayek however proved from their correspondence that she did influence parts of his *Principles of Political Economy* and Packe goes so far as to say that her influence was substantial on every major work Mill published. The contrary was argued by Pappe. This debate has acquired new urgency with the revival of the women's movement since the end of the 1960s. So, for example, Harriet Taylor Mill and her influence have been defended by Alice Rossi and Kate Soper; while Okin has agreed with Pappe.

'Mill's writings in support of political, legal and social equality for women read today like a series of truisms'. In these respects 'the world has gone completely as he would have wished'. Such judgements seemed obvious in the 1960s: but they were always wrong. Their 'western' bias is astonishing; over most of the globe Mill's aspirations for women are still unrealized. Even in the West his feminism does not command universal wholehearted acceptance; the odd academic philosopher can still be found ready to suggest that women are naturally inferior to men, are adapted to a subordinate and domestic role.

There is a far more important reason for challenging the 1960s verdict that *The Subjection of Women* is a set of truisms: in the subsequent revival of feminism, Mill's book has again become highly controversial. Of course modern feminists like Okin find words of praise for Mill-'the first major philosopher since Plato to have argued that goodness was the same in a woman as in a man'. But often the praise is faint. It is suggested that he was quite good for a man, but not altogether satisfactory, because he was a liberal, he allowed gender stereotypes back in, or accepted the bourgeois family, or expected women to conform to masculine ideal of excellence-or simply because he was a man. Annas has argued that his essay was weak and contradictory, Mendus says that his ideal of marriage was depressing, and Caine complains that his behavior towards the emerging women movement was patronizing and obstructive.

A picture has developed of a chilly, bloodless man, over-intellectual, under-sexed, uxorious, priggish and humorless. One might explain this by remarking that people do not like those who preach at them, and Mill was certainly both moralistic and evangelical. Alternatively, one might think Mill was right in his complaint that the English are reluctant to credit those who claim to be motivated by anything other than self-interest. More dramatically, Mill has been a victim of psychohistory, most notably at the hands of Bruce Mazlish. His *Autobiography* encourages such attention, with its account of his extraordinary high-pressure education, his closeness to his father and the failure of the final version to mention his mother. According to Classman, his upbringing was 'cruel and dehumanizing', 'few fathers ever have damaged a son so gravely', with the result that he lived an 'epically unhappy life'.

The general outlook of John Stuart Mill's social philosophy, and especially his ethics, was determined perhaps as much by personal experience as by intellectual considerations. From birth he was destined by his father to carry on the crusade of the Philosophical Radicals, and certainly the elder Mill never envisaged the possibility that the objectives of that crusade could change. The younger Mill from an early age was subjected to the most dogmatic indoctrination' and the most extreme educational "forcing" ever suffered by a man who afterward attained intellectual independence. It was not until after his father's death in 1836 that Mill was able to strike out his own line of approach to ethical questions, though by that time he had long been before the public as an editor and as a contributor to the liberal reviews. In the meantime this enforced precocity had induced a period of nervous exhaustion from which he finally escaped, by absorbing himself in the reading of Wordsworth's poetry. Thus Mill's intellectual life became ambivalent. He retained an exaggerated allegiance, enforced by an intense sense of personal loyalty, toward the philosophy which he had learned from his father and from Bentham and of which he had been predestined to be the exponent. At the same time he achieved a considerable degree of sympathy and appreciation, but hardly a critical understanding, for an antithetical philosophy derived from German idealism which he associated with Wordsworth.

Unfortunately Mill's candor and open-mindedness were not matched by the grasp or the originality required to bring about a really coherent synthesis of philosophies so widely divergent. Mill's thought had all the marks of a transitional period in which the problems have outgrown the apparatus for their solution. Without much exaggeration it might be said that his books followed a formula. On nearly every subject he was likely to begin with a general statement of principles which, taken literally and by itself, appeared to be as rigid and as abstract as anything that his father might have written. But having thus declared his allegiance to the ancestral dogmas, Mill proceeded to make concessions and restatements so far-reaching that a critical reader was left in doubt whether the original statement had not been explained away. The theory of motivation and of value in his ethics was still overtly the hedonistic calculus, and his utilitarianism was still in strict logic the egoistic individualism of Bentham. Yet in no case would these statements correspond with the actual meaning of Mill's philosophy. The qualifications and not the theory were what carried his meaning.

The ethical theory which Mill set forth in his *Utilitarianism* illustrates this defect of his philosophy, yet it is also the root of his revision of liberalism. He began by accepting apparently the greatest happiness principle as it had been stated by Bentham. The desire for one's own greatest pleasure is the individual's only motive, and the greatest happiness of everyone is at once the standard of social good and the object of all moral action. Mill united these propositions by an argument so patently fallacious that it became a standard exhibit in textbooks of logic. He then qualified his hedonism by asserting that pleasures can be graded as superior or inferior in moral quality. This put him in the indefensible logical position of demanding a standard for the measurement of a standard, which is a contradiction in terms and also reduced his utilitarianism to complete indefiniteness, since the standard for judging the quality of pleasures was never stated and if stated, could not itself be a pleasure. The root of all this confusion was that Mill was not willing to accept Bentham's greatest happiness principle for what in effect it was, namely, a rough and ready criterion for judging the utility of legislation. Used for this purpose which was the only purpose that had interested Bentham, it was logically independent of Bentham's theory of psychological motives and might be equally applicable to legislation no matter what standards of personal morality individuals might follow. The distinctive characteristic of Mill's utilitarianism, on the other hand, was that he tried to express a conception of moral character consonant with his own personal idealism. From this point of view Bentham's famous pronouncemen that "pushpin is as good as poetry" if it gives one the same pleasure, is simply vulgar nonsense, while Mill's own pronouncement, that it is " better to be Socrates dissatisfied than a fool satisfied", states a normal moral reaction but is certainly not hedonism. Mill's ethics was important for liberalism because in effect it abandoned egoism, assumed that social welfare is a matter of concern to all men of good will, and regarded freedom, integrity, self-respect, and personal distinction as intrinsic goods apart from their contribution to happiness. Moral convictions of this sort underlay Mill's whole conception of a liberal society.

It was therefore natural that his most characteristic and also most lasting contribution to political thought should have been contained in the essay *On Liberty*. This essay struck a definitely new note in utilitarian literature. As Mill himself said in another place, the utilitarlans of his father's generation had desired liberal government not for of liberty but because they thought it would be efficient government, and it was indeed true that Bentham had changed nothing but when he turned from benevolent despotism to liberalism. For the freedom of thought and investigation, freedom of discussion, and freedom of self-controlled moral judgment and action were goods their own right. They aroused in him a warmth and a fervor that appeared in his other writings but which placed the essay *On Liberty* as one of the classical defenses of freedom in the English language. Mill believed as a matter of course that intellectual and political freedom are in general beneficial both to the society that permits them and to the individual that enjoys them, but the effective part of his argument was not utilitarian. When he said that all mankind has no right to silence one dissenter, he was really affirming that freedom of judgment, the right to be convinced rather than coerced, is an inherent quality of a morally mature personality and that a liberal society is one which both acknowledges that right and shapes its institutions in such a way that the right is realized. To permit individuality and private judgment, as if they were tolerated vices, is not enough; a liberal society puts positive value on them as essential to well-being and as marks of a high civilization. This valuation of free personality affected profoundly Mill's valuation of liberal government. He did not defend popular government because it is efficient. He had grave doubts whether it always is, and he had quite lost his father's confidence that the apparatus of liberal government, such as the suffrage, would always be rationally used for beneficial ends. The real argument for political freedom, he thought, is that it produces and gives scope to a high type of moral character. To hear public questions freely 'discussed, to have a share in political decisions, to have moral convictions and to take the responsibility for making them effective are among the ways in which reasonable human beings are produced.

It is a striking characteristic of Mill's argument for liberty, and even of his essay on *Representative Government,* that strictly political questions are no longer in the foreground. His argument was addressed not to the state but to society. The essay *On Liberty* was an appeal not for relief from political oppression or for a change in political organization, but for a public opinion that is genuinely tolerant, that values differences in point of view, that limits the amount of agreement it demands and that welcomes new ideas as sources of creativity and discovery. The threat to liberty which Mill chiefly feared was not government but a majority that is intolerant of the unconventional, that looks with suspicion on divergent minorities, and is willing to use the weight of numbers to repress and regiment them. This was a possibility that had never troubled the older generation of liberals, indeed that they had never thought of as long as their problem had been to take government out of the hand of an intrenched minority. The elder Mill had supposed that the reform of representation and the extension of the suffrage, given a moderate degree of public education, would solve all serious problems of political liberty. By 1859 it was apparent that even after substantial reforms the millennium did not follow, and that the achievement of liberty was more than a problem in the mechanics of political organization. What Mill recognized, and what the older liberalism had never seen, was that behind a liberal government there must be a liberal society.

This recognition that political institutions are part of a larger social context which largely determines the way in which they work was in itself an important discovery and it indicated an important addition to political concepts. Society or the community becomes a third factor, and a preponderating factor, in the relationship between the individual and government and in securing the individual's liberty. Mill's fear of an oppressive and intolerant public opinion was in part a realization that the individualism of early liberal theory was inadequate. At same time it is difficult to say what precisely this phase of Mill's thinking connoted. That it was a note of disillusionment, as compared with the high hopes of his father's generation, is evident. Probably in part it reflected also the shrinking of a sensitive, fastidious, and highly intellectual personality from the contact with mediocrity implied by practical politics. Perhaps it indicated also a half-expressed fear that the democratizing of society might prove to be incompatible with individual distinction. Such a fear was common enough in the mid-nineteenth century.

When Mill went on from his general estimate of the moral worth of freedom to his practical rule for deciding what limitations either society or the state is justified in imposing on it, his essay was at its weakest. What he proposed was that it is possible to distinguish a class of self-regarding action which affects the interests of no persons besides the agent and with which neither society nor the state ought to interfere. Taken literally this would reduce freedom to a triviality, since an act that affects no one but a single person probably will not affect him very much. The fundamental difficulty with Mill's argument was that it never really analyzed the relationship between freedom and responsibility. At times he retained the traditional view derived from Bentham that any compulsion or even any social influence is an abridgement of liberty. Yet he never supposed that there could be any important freedom without law and when he identified liberty with civilization, he did not imagine that there could be civilization without society. What Mill's theory of liberty required was a thoroughgoing consideration of the dependence of personal liberty on social and legal rights and obligations. It was this which T. H. Green tried to add to liberalism. For all practical purposes Mill simply laid aside the dogma of earlier liberalism that the largest amount of freedom coincides with the absence of legislation and accepted the evident fact that there are many forms of coercion other than that exercised by the law. But one of two results must follow: either legislation cannot be judged at all by the liberal purpose of diminishing coercion or liberal theory must be extended to considering the relation of legal coercion to the effective though non-legal coercion that would exist if the state abstained from acting. This was the issue that Green tried later to meet with the theory of positive freedom. Sor far as Mill was concerned, he merely accepted the need for social legislation, probably on humanitarian grounds, with no clear theory of its justifiable limits.

Defenders and supporters of the welfare state, lamented these attitudes as undemocratic. But it would be anachronistic to criticize them on these grounds. Mill has to be seen in the context of his time. Marx himself spoke of the unemployed as a 'passively rotting mass' primed for the role of 'bribed tool' to betray its own members. Similarly, Mill's repugnance for the lower classes was not only compatible with a desire to improve them, but at least in part the cause of this desire. He looked forward to a time when the fruits of labour would be distributed according to an acknowledged principle of justice, and when the rule ordaining that only those who work, eat, would apply not just to the poor, but to everyone. Government by aristocracy, he declared, was 'worth any struggle to get rid of', and he struggled to design, and achieve greater working-class representation in Parliament, as well as campaigning tirelessly for women's suffrage, a cause which at that time was considered lunatic. He was so enthused by the short-lived second French Revolution of 1830 that he went over to Paris to witness it. He hailed Chartism- a working-class movement for extending the franchise-as 'the victory of the vanquished', and diagnosed 'the social problem of the future' as 'how to unite the greatest individual liberty of action, with a common ownership in the raw material of the globe'. He himself said that though some of his beliefs were undemocratic in the short term, his long-term ideals earned him the title of socialist still more than that of democrat.

Mill's liberalism seems to be elitist and socialist, because he wanted to introduce the new and radical without vulgarizing the old and excellent. Bentham's utilitarianism had offered quantity of pleasure and pain as the only criterion of value. Bentham evaluated every action, law and institution in terms of how many units of happiness it contributed to how many people, famously concluding that if pushpin game gave as much pleasure as poetry, then they were both equally good. In *Utilitarianism*, published in 1863, Mill rejected this purely quantitative notion of pleasure in favor of a qualitative one, declaring, 'It is better to be a human being dissatisfied than a pig satisfied; better to be Socrates dissatisfied than a fool satisfied.' He insisted that anyone with experience of several sorts of pleasure would prefer those of cultivated taste to those of mere sensation. But though he graded pleasures, the measures he used for grading were themselves amounts of pleasure. He simply assumed some calculations in advance. He wanted to promote universal happiness without promoting 'collective mediocrity', to reconcile the principle of utility with his principle of liberty, and he invoked both principles in *On Liberty*.

He was similarly determined to keep 'as firm hold of one side of the truth as I took of the other' in the battle then being waged between the values of the last century and his own, which he compared to a mythical battle over white and black that are simply two sides of the same shield. His father and his father's mentor Bentham were mere men of the eighteenth-century Enlightenment, mocked by the Romantic, transcendentalist friends Mill made as a young man. He wished somehow to maintain the measured reason of the eighteenth century while gingerly embracing the exuberant nonconformity of nineteenth-century Romanticism, aware that this threatened to reintroduce the very evils of superstition and feudalism that the Enlightenment had eradicated. In *On Liberty*, he hymns eccentricity and diversification as productive of genius, and excoriates the tendency to see human nature as a custom-made machine. Instead he compares it to a tree, which needs to spread in harmony with the trend of the inward the way 'we call everything instinct which we find in ourselves and for which we cannot trace any rational foundation' as 'the most pernicious of the false worships of the present day.'

J. S. Mill's model of a desirable society was different from Bentham's and James Mill's. The difference can be made more precise. Bentham and James Mill accepted existing capitalist society without reservation; John Stuart Mill did not. The difference is clearly expressed in the younger Mill's position on the desirability of 'the stationary state' which he, like they, thought would be the culmination of capitalism: they regarded it with dismay, but he welcomed it. He put it poetically in 1848:

> I confess I am not charmed with the ideal of life held out by those, who think that the normal state of human beings is that of struggling to get on; that the trampling, crushing, elbowing, and treading on early other's heels, which form the existing type of social life, are the most desirable lot of human kind, or anything but the disagreeable symptoms of one of the phases of industrial progress. It may be a necessary stage in the progress of civilization. But it is not a kind of social perfection which philanthropists to come will feel any very eager desire to assist in realizing. In the meantime, those who do not accept the present very early stage of human improvement as its ultimate type, may be excused for being comparatively indifferent to the kind of economic progress which excites the congratulations of ordinary politicians; the mere increase of production and accumulation.

Society, in Mill's vision need not be, should not be, what Bentham and James Mill assumed it was and always would be. It need not be and should not be a collection of competing, conflicting, self-interested consumers and appropriators. It could and should be a community of exerters and developers of their human capacities. But it was not that now. The problem was to get it to advance to that. The case for democracy was that it gave all the citizens a direct interest in the actions of the government, and an incentive to participate actively, at least to the extent of voting for or against the government, and, it was hoped, also of informing themselves and forming their views in discussions with others. Compared with any oligarchic system, however benevolent, democracy drew the people into the operations of government by giving them all a practical interest, an interest which could be effective because their votes could bring down a government. Democracy would thus make people more active, more energetic; it would advance them 'in intellect, in virtue, and in practical activity and efficiency'.

This is a rather large claim to make for a system of representative government in which the ordinary person's political activity is confined to voting every few years for a member of Parliament, perhaps a little oftener for local councilors, and perhaps actually holding some elective local office. Even so, the claim might be allowed by contrast with any oligarchic system, which positively discourages general interest and involvement. By that contrast, democracy might seem to lead to self-sustaining, even self-increasing, advancement of the citizens in moral, intellectual, and active worth, every bit of participation giving an ability and an appetite for more.

But here Mill came up against a difficulty which turned out to be insuperable. To see what it was we must look at another basic difference between John Stuart Mill and Bentham. Underlying the difference in their moral evaluations of existing society was a difference in their definitions of happiness or pleasure, the thing they both held should be maximized. Bentham had held that in calculating the greatest happiness one need take into account only the amounts of undifferentiated pleasure and pain actually felt by the individuals. There were no qualitative differences between pleasures: pushpin was as good as poetry. And since, he measured pleasure or utility in terms of material wealth, the aggregate greatest happiness of the whole society was to be attained by maximizing productivity. J. S. Mill insisted, on the contrary, that there were qualitative differences in pleasures, and he refused to equate the greatest aggregate happiness with maximum productivity. The greatest aggregate happiness was to be got by permitting and encouraging individuals to develop themselves. That would make them capable of higher pleasures, and so would increase the aggregate pleasure measured in both quantity and quality.

But at the same time—and this was the fundamental difficulty—Mill recognized that the existing distribution of wealth and of economic power made it impossible for most members of the working class to develop themselves at all, or even to live humanly. He denounced as utterly unjust that the produce of labour should be apportioned as we now see it, almost in an inverse ratio to the labour—the largest portions to those who have never worked at all, the next largest to those whose work is almost nominal, and so in a descending scale, the remuneration dwindling as the work grows harder and more disagreeable, until the most fatiguing and exhausting bodily labour cannot count with certainty on being able to earn even the necessaries of life. This, Mill said, was the very opposite of the only 'equitable principle' of property, the principle of 'proportion between remuneration and exertion'. That was the equitable principle because the only justification of the institution of private property was that it guaranteed to individuals 'the fruits of their own labour and abstinence', not 'the fruits of the labour and abstinence of others'.

But Mill is talking about a capitalist exchange economy, where the produce is the result of the combination of current labour with capital provided by someone else, and where the labourer gets as his share only a wage, and the capitalist gets the rest, both shares being determined by market competition. Mill held that this relation was justified also.

The owner of the capital, Mill saw, must have a share of the product, and he held that this was consistent with the equitable principle because capital is simply the product of previous labour and abstinence. This justified the distribution of the product between wage-labourers and owners of capital: given competition between capitalists for labourers, and between labourers for employment, there was a fair division between those who contributed current labour and those who contributed the fruits of past labour and abstinence. Mill acknowledged that the capital was not usually created by the labour and abstinence of the present possessor, but thought he had made a sufficient case for the labour capital distribution by saying that the present possessor of capital much more probably got it by gift or voluntary contract than by wrongful dispossession of those who had created it by their past labour.

The fact that the present possessors may have got some of their capital by gift, i.e. by inheritance, gave Mill some uneasiness: it seemed clearly inconsistent with his equitable principle of property. But he held that the right to dispose of one's property by bequest was an essential part of the right of property. Thus Mill was satisfied that there was no inconsistency between his equitable principle of property—reward in proportion to exertion—and the principle of reward in proportion to the market value of both the capital and the current labour required for capitalist production. Yet, he found the actual prevailing distribution of the produce of labour wholly unjust. He found the explanation of that unjust distribution in an historical accident, not in the capitalist principle itself.

The principle of private property has never yet had a fair trial in any country; and less so, perhaps, in England than in some others. The social arrangements of modern Europe commenced from a distribution of property which was the result, not of just partition, or acquisition by industry, but of conquest and violence; and notwithstanding what industry has been doing for many centuries to modify the work of force, the system still retains many and large traces of its origin. It was this original violent distribution of property, not anything in the principle of private property and capitalist enterprise as such, that had led to the present miserable position of the bulk of the working class, about the injustice of which Mill was so outspoken: 'The generality of labourers in this and most other countries, have as little choice of occupation or freedom of locomotion, are practically as dependent on fixed rules and on the will of others, as they could be on any system short of actual slavery."

In thus putting the blame on the original feudal forcible distribution of property, and the failure of subsequent property law to rectify it, Mill was able to think that the capitalist principle was not in any way responsible for the existing inequitable distributions of wealth, income and power, and even to think that it was gradually reducing them. What he failed to see was that the capitalist market relation enhances or replaces any original inequitable distribution, in that it gives to capital part of the value added by current labour, thus steadily increasing the mass of capital. Had Mill seen this he could not have judged the capitalist principle consistent with his equitable principle. Failing to see this, he found no fundamental inconsistency, and was not troubled by it. John Stuart Mill may be regarded as the first serious liberal-democratic theorist, in that he was the first liberal to take seriously, and to feel sensitively, the claims of the nascent democracy. He had some reservations, indeed, about a fully democratic franchise. He would not give the vote to those who were illiterate, nor to those who paid no direct taxes, but he was willing to have both literacy and direct taxes extended to the poor. And even those who were to have the vote were not all to have equal votes. The better educated, being more capable of political Judgement, were to have more than one vote each. In these respects Mill's democracy was somewhat more qualified than Bentham's.

But in a more fundamental respect Mill must be counted more of a democrat. For he took people not as they were but as he thought them capable of becoming. He revolted against Bentham's material maximizing criterion of the social good. He could not agree that all pleasures were equal, nor that the market distributed them fairly. He held that men were capable of something better than the money-grubbing and starvation-avoiding existence to which Benthamism condemned them. He rejected the maximization of indifferent utilities as the criterion of social good, and put in its place the maximum development and use of human capacities—moral, intellectual, aesthetic, as well as material productive capacities.

This was an act of democratic faith. It was a turn away from the market. It was a refusal to allow that the market should determine the value or worth of a person. It put other values higher than market values. Yet in the end Mill found himself helpless, unable to reconcile his notion of values with the political economy which he still believed in. The world's work had to go on, and he could see no way in which it could be carried on except by competitive private enterprise. He saw clearly that the prevailing relation between wage-labour and capital was condemned by his own criterion of good, and he thought that it would before long became insupportable by the wage-labourers. His only way out was the hope that a network of co-partnerships in industry, or producers' co-operatives, might turn every worker into his own capitalist, and so enable the system of enterprise to operate without the degradation of wage-labour. It is easy to see now that Mill, in spite of his ranking as an outstanding economist, did not grasp the essence of the capitalist market economy. It was his failure to do so that enabled him to reject the market morality. The founding father of liberal-democratic theory was able to rise above the market morality only because he did not understand the market society.

The same must be said of the next outstanding figure in the English liberal-democratic tradition. T. H. Green, a philosopher with no pretensions as an economist, may be more readily forgiven for his economic naivete. Like Mill he despised and rejected the market morality. He did so even more strongly than Mill, perhaps because he did not have Mill's problem of trying to be faithful to the utilitarian philosophy. Yet he held that the free development of individual personality required the right to accumulate unlimited property through the mechanism of the market, and even required the full right of inheritance. Green recognized that the existence of a proletariat was inconsistent with the rationale of private property, which required that everybody should have enough property, over and above a bare subsistence, to enable him to develop and perfect himself. But he had so little insight into the nature of capitalism that he could attribute the existence of a proletariat not to the nature of capitalist enterprise but to the continuing effect of an original forcible seizure of land in feudal times, and subsequent unrestricted landlordism. By putting the blame on feudalism, and on the continuing rights of unproductive landowners, he exempted capitalism from any responsibility for the condition of the bulk of the people. To say the least, this shows rather less grasp of the essentials the capitalist market economy than Mill had. Mill and Green, between them, set the pattern of English liberal-democratic political theory from their time on. It is probably fair to say that there have been since then no new insights sufficient to carry liberal-democratic theory over the anxities and tensions.

14

Thomas Hill Green

> We content ourselves with enacting that no man shall be used by other men as a means against his will but we leave it to be pretty much a Matter of chance whether or not he shall be guttered to fulfill any social function, to contribute anything to the common good, and to do so freely.

Thomas Hill Green (1836-1882) was born in 1836 into a large clerical family; his father, evangelical in his sympathies, was rector of Birkin, Yorkshire. Green was educated at Rugby (1850-55) and Balliol College, Oxford where he studied classics and philosophy with a little modern history. Early in 1860, he was appointed to lecture on ancient and modern history at Balliol, and in the same year, he was elected a fellow of the College to teach mainly in philosophy. Apart from a brief period between 1865 and 1866, traveling parts of England as a commissioner on the school's inquiry commission, Green's working life was spent in Oxford. He was active on the local council, the Oxford School Board, in the liberal party. In 1878 he was appointed to professorship of Moral Philosophy at Oxford. He occupied this post till his death from blood poisoning in 1882. He was forty-five years old. He had married Charlotte Symonds, the sister of Green's under-graduate friend John Addington Symonds, the Victorian literary figure, in 1871. They had no children.

It is generally argued that Green was undoubtedly a man of the Victorian age. His thought and writings show many typical anxieties and preoccupations of the age. There were broad themes in Victorian life and they certainly dominated Green's outlook. Primarily, there was a deep concern about religion. Green's religion grew from an evangelical background and was expressed through the medium of idealist philosophy. In contemporary religious circles, there was a deep-rooted worry about Biblical criticism, specifically the 'higher criticism' emanating from German theological colleges. The careful dissection of the scriptures revealing inner contradictions was profoundly disturbing to many sensitive minds. The growth of the natural sciences also had a major impact. From a religious standpoint, evolution and science generally seemed to show humans to be animals determined by external stimuli. This undermined the idea of humans possessing free will or exercising moral agency. This anxiety about science connects with a third theme, namely, a widespread concern for 'practical religion' or active moral conduct. Green specifically countered the predominance of the scientific perspective by paying close attention to the concept of the human will. In this area the idea of character was of supreme importance. Character, as a moral term, denoted the essence of practical religion and good conduct. A fourth Victorian concern was the attempt to combine an intense belief in industrialism with a responsible concept of the state and the citizen. The solution to this challenge was seen to lie in some form of moralized capitalism, moralized through the development of character in the citizen body, which was essentially the core of Green's ideas on liberalism.

Very few celebrated philosophers have occupied a space in history simply by their sheer impact upon the undergraduate population of a university. But such is the case of Thomas Hill Green. Beginning with him the official philosophy at Oxford for something like fifty years was to be the kind of objective idealism usually associated with the name of Hegel. The movement toward idealism and away from naturalism and empiricism was not confined to Oxford, nor indeed to Great Britain, for a similar development was occurring in France and in the United States. But the movement owed much to Green's personal influence on successive generations of students at Oxford. And his influence was not confined to the teachers of philosophy, but also, more significantly, to students who were to take their place in government, in the church, and in the professions.

Green's writings consist almost entirely of lectures delivered in the regular course of instruction, which were edited for publication after Green's death by two of his former students. *The Lectures on the Principles of Political Obligation* for which Green is chiefly remembered, were delivered in 1879-1880. Clearly, Green's books were made by and for his disciples. Undoubtedly part of Green's influence was due to the fact that he had himself traveled the path along which he was leading his students; namely, the path from evangelical Christianity to philosophical idealism. Green's father was a clergyman, and the young man had intended to follow his father's profession until he found himself deterred by theological doubts. The difficulties which prevented him from taking orders did not, however, seriously alter his fundamental moral and spiritual outlook. Nettleship, who was Green's closest follower, remarks that this position, at which Green had arrived at the age of twenty-four, was essentially the one which Green held throughout his life. Nettleship summarizes Green's life as that of a man to whom reason was faith made articulate, and for whom both faith and reason found their highest expression in good citizenship.

Green's goal as a philosopher is easy to grasp: it is to re-establish a spiritual view of the world and to work out the implications of such a view for morality and politics. But, the intellectual climate of the day, forced Green to take the offensive and to show the weaknesses inherent in the positivist and naturalist philosophies, which were intellectual style then. Green's immediate concern was with the ethical and social implications of evolutionary naturalism. In his judgment, however, the threat to human values did not come from the theory of evolution as such, which he was inclined to support. Rather, he saw the threat as coming from the ruling assumptions of British philosophy which, from the time of Hobbes and Locke, had taken for granted that the only way to understand the world is to dissolve complex wholes into simple elements, to reduce qualitative differences to differences in quantity, and to explain purposive behavior by means of causal laws. This method, which works well in mathematics and in mechanics, leads to insoluble problems when applied to the analysis of experiences itself. In his Introductions to Hume's *Treatises*, and in course lectures on

Mill's *Logic* and on Spencer's *Psychology,* Green pursues his criticism of empiricism and naturalism in minute detail. Green preserves the greatest respect for Hume, for having carried empiricism to its logical conclusion in skepticism. It was Kant, in Green's opinion, who was the true successor of Hume, not Bentham, Mill, and Spencer in Great Britain who tried to carry on in the empiricist tradition. Kant had learned from Hume how bankrupt was the reductionist approach to the problems of mental and moral philosophy, and had taken a new path. Kant's transcendental method led him to the conclusion that knowledge always presupposes a knower that can never be known, a subject that can never be an object. Green expounds, and to some extent develops, Kant's philosophy in lectures on the *Critique of Pure Reason,* and on the *Metaphysics of Ethics.* But Kant's method also underlies Green's criticism of empiricism and naturalism.

Green and German Idealism

There is a considerable debate on the entrance of idealist thought into England and Scotland. Oxford, in Green's student years, was dominated by the classics. The Oxford examination statute of 1850 contains no mention of Kant or Hegel, or J.S. Mill for that matter. It was not until 1875 that the first questions appeared on Kant and Hegel, due primarily to the efforts of Green.

In German thought Green was interested in the philosophies of Kant, Hegel, Fichet. Green saw all the cardinal defects of British empiricist philosophy through Kantian eyes. Kant had delivered the final death blow to empiricism. The most important philosophical question was Kantian, namely, 'how is knowledge possible'?. Kant had shown the futility of a search for knowledge beyond experience and its necessary preconditions. The central precondition, for Green, was the conscious subject. Conscious experience was always experience of an object by a subject. In order for experience to be possible there must not only be categories but also a conscious synthesizing subject relating objects in judgment and not itself part of the experience. Kant wanted to retain the idea of world independent of consciousness, which we do not know in itself. This is the famous doctrine of the thing-in-itself. In Green's eyes, following Hegel, Kant had fallen into an unnecessary dualism. There was no need to postulate a world independent of the determinations of judgment. The thing-in-itself did not exist for Green. There was no objective world, which did not presuppose a conscious subject. Idealism, for Green, could not consistently draw a distinction between the a priori and a posteriori. It recognized no distinction between intuition and conception, the given and what the mind adds. Green therefore, in his own estimation, like Fichte, took the doctrine of the transcendental subject to its logical conclusion.

Paradoxically, it is the Kantian conscious subject, which also plays a crucial role in Green's moral philosophy, and that also forms the starting point for Green's Hegelianism. It not only forms a starting point, but creates one of the central ambiguities of Green's thought and intellectual legacy. The major idea that Green developed from Hegel was that reason, spirit, or the eternal subject, is the unity implicit in the world and human history. The aim of the philosopher is to articulate the reason of the world. Despite the obviously non-Hegelian language of his later work, Green did not abandon this idea. History was the pattern of reason's unfolding.

However, Green was not credulous over Hegel. It is reported that he thought that Hegel's work 'must all be done over again'. Sidgwick had mentioned that Green had stated in a letter to him that Hegel's philosophy was chaos. Green objected to a number of features of Hegel's thought. Hegel, he confidently stated, had not presented the secret of the universe. He only encapsulated an aspect of human thought. Green rejected triadic and dialectical structures of Hegel's thought. Oddly, Green also objected to the identification of thought and reality in Hegel's system. God, in Hegel, is identified with the process of philosophizing itself, which Green describes as an aberration, which the layman 'will rightly refuse to believe.' The conscious subject thus contains a problematic legacy from Kant and Hegel. It forms the basis to Green's reaction to empiricism and also forms a central focus for his views on morals and politics. Yet the logic of this subject in metaphysics leads Green to the immanent eternal subject identified with philosophical thought, which even Green rejects at points.

The History of Virtue

The Victorians were obsessed with the idea of practical religion or practical righteousness. Faith needed to express itself in works. This emphasis on personal conduct is nicely summed up in the concept of character. Samuel Smiles had popularized the term, but thinkers like J.S. Mill and T.H. Green gave it a distinctively philosophical reading. Character involved a positive conception of power in the individual. It presupposed a predominance of a reasoning faculty, which enabled the individual to order and control his life and environment. Individuals with character could endure hardship and still develop themselves. Character was exemplified in the ability to control one's own life and influence others to do likewise. The person with character was the ideal responsible citizen, the ideal father or mother, teacher or social worker. For many Victorians character in the citizen body was constitutive of the maturity of a state. Green's own grasp of the idea of self- development was primarily Hegelian, nonetheless his aims would have been perfectly laudable to the average intelligent Victorian. Institutions which structured the basis of character growth were also idealized, specifically the family. Green and other idealists gave a central role to the family within the general philosophy of society.

Green's own reading of character and moral conduct was presented in the context of a philosophical history of morality or virtue. The present standpoint in Christianity he regarded as the most adequate expression of a movement going back to the Greeks. Morality was both expressive of the particularity of a culture and of the teleology of spirit. Despite Green being not particularly enamoured of Greek thought, he discusses its theories of virtue sympathetically in the *Prolegomena to Ethics*.

(1.) First, virtue is historically determinate, yet history itself is teleological. Green's treatment of Greek virtue is Hegelian. Like Hegel, who differentiated epochs in world history, the oriental, Greek, Roman and Germanic worlds, Green saw the Greek world as part of a speculative pattern. Christianity was the culmination of previous religions. Many of the English and Scottish idealists followed Hegel in this view. Virtue derived from and was intelligible within a particular culture and epoch. Alistair MacIntyre, in presenting his thesis on the diversity of virtues, argues that many elements of

Aristotle's scheme of virtues would not be intelligible to a Christian precisely because they are not virtues in the Christian sense. Virtues for MacIntyre are integral to social structures, practices and institutions. Courage for the Greek is very different from the Christian understanding. The citizen soldier sacrificing himself for his city-state is not the same as the Christian martyr. Each becomes intelligible in the social space, historical context and tradition of discourse in which they are situated. Green was not blind to the differences pointed out by MacIntyre. He commented that the Quaker philanthropist would scarcely recognize the virtue of the Greek citizen soldier. It was for Green 'indeed in one sense a new type of virtue. The Christian qualities of 'self-adjustment, of sympathy with inferiors, of tolerance for the weak and foolish are very different from the pride of self-sufficing strength, which with Aristotle was inseparable from heroic endurance'. Green's emphasis is given to the teleology of history. The Greek virtues are seen as embryonic Christian virtues. Green comments that 'the differences between our standards of virtue and those recognized by the Greek philosophers arise from the greater fullness of conditions which we include in our conception of the perfecting of human life'. Aristotelian virtues like temperance, fortitude and courage have to be filled out by the requirements of the Christian conscience. For Green, the Christian social worker is equivalent to Aristotle's courageous citizen soldier. Aristotle would find it odd to renounce one's own interests for slaves and aliens, but he would formally understand the concept of self-renunciation for a higher end.

(2) Green further tells that the Greeks realized formally the meaning of 'good'. The formal idea remains the same for Green 'whether the cause of the state or the cause of the kingdom of Christ'. The formal idea is that 'every form of real goodness must rest on a will to be good, which has no object but its own fulfillment'. This formulation, recognized in Greek thought, was widened and made more determinate in the Christian doctrine of 'blessed are the pure in heart'. The Greeks were at the mercy of history as to what they could substantively include in the formal idea. Logically it follows that they could not know the full sense of virtue.

(3) The third point is that for Green the Greek philosophers realized, to an extent, that morality and goodness were not invented, but articulated from existing practices. They saw, in good idealist style, that the philosopher 'had not to bring before man an absolutely new object of pursuit, but to bring them to consider what gave its value to an object already pursued'. Green argues that recognizable forms and practices existed in Greek society, which philosophers could interpret. Families, states, the arts, the sciences, the pursuit of truth as a value and the creation of beauty, the endurance of pain for higher ends, temperance and justice, all of these for Green testified to the Greeks grasp of at least some recognizable elements of virtue.

(4) Green, like Hegel, was inclined to admire the integrated life of the Greek city-state. This model of an ethical life, if modified by an awareness of modern industrial society, acted as a useful tool to use against political individualism and utilitarianism. Humans as intrinsically social creatures only achieve virtue in society. The city-state exists to further the moral development of its citizens. Despite these points it would be a serious mistake to think that Green imagined that the Greek ideal could be simply transferred to industrial Britain.

It will thus be appreciated that Green's metaphysical notion of the self-distinguishing eternal subject revealing itself in history is the root of his views on ethics. His rejection of empiricism in knowledge is also part of his rejection of a naturalistic basis to ethics. The essence of Green's moral philosophy is the doctrine of self-realization. The self is identified with latent capacities, potentialities, or excellences. Thus, self-realization is realizing one's own potentialities. The individual can never give an unconditional account of the true good since he cannot know what his unconditional good is until these latent potentialities are fully realized. The basic argument here is that the human is distinguished from other animals by the ability to think about desires. The fact that the desire is considered implies that the self is distinguished from the desires. The conceived desire is a motive. The self posits an object, which will satisfy the conceived desire. In fact a desire could be defined as a tendency to realize an object. The capacity to choose an object is the will. Green admits that character and circumstances play a crucial role in choice, but this does not affect the fact that the individual chooses. In all action, an individual is positing an object, which will satisfy his conceived desire, which he takes to be good. The true good for Green is that object which provides complete satisfaction, which in essence is the full realization of the self. This self has, a rather problematic relation to the eternal subject. Green thinks that this realization cannot be identified with pleasure. Pleasure is a byproduct of moral action. The self could not be identified with discrete sensations of pleasure. This is the basic idea in Green's rejection of the utilitarian account of morality. Certain objects for Green are more conducive to self-realization. These tend to be the mundane objects of social life, like being a good parent, teacher, social worker, or politician. The theory of history arises here, for Green saw institutions and practices embodying a teleological significance.

Positive Freedom

The foregoing account of Green's moral philosophy throws light on his teachings concerning political rights and obligations. Green doctrine of positive freedom constitutes an integral part of his thinking. In addition, it helps the students make the transition from Green's ethical to his social and political theory. In the lectures on the senses of freedom in morality, Green is not directly concerned with social or civil freedom, but only with the freedom a man experiences in the course of his moral development.

The power of self- objectification differentiates man as a moral agent from purely natural creatures which are determined by natural laws. There are, however, limits to man's freedom. Although he can choose which object he will make his own, his genuine options are limited: as a spiritual being he is limited by the laws of spiritual development: as a natural being he is limited by his physical and social environment, as well as by his own character. In an important sense, therefore, human freedom increases or diminishes according to the choices made by the individual or by the group. Green acknowledges that in applying the word freedom and bondage to the inner life of man he is speaking metaphorically. But he points to the tradition, from Plato, the Stoics, and the early Christians down to Kant and Hegel, in which men are said to be in moral bondage when they are governed by their passions and to achieve freedom to the degree that reason or some higher law obtains the mastery.

Green does not propose to discard the juristic sense of freedom as "power to act according to choice or preference." Such freedom is valuable, both as a condition to the realization of inner freedom and on its own account. "The consciousness of it is the first form of self- enjoyment, of the joy of the self-conscious spirit in itself as in the one object of absolute value." But the enjoyment, which a man has in the mere exercise of free choice "consists essentially in the feeling by the subject of a possibility rather than a reality, of what it has it in itself to become, not of what it actually is." For example, a captive when first liberated experiences boundless joy, but this feeling disappears, as he gradually realizes how many of his expectations are not fulfilled in the mere fact of his liberation from the power of other men.

In the lecture "Liberal Legislation and Freedom of Contract," Green is directly concerned with social and political freedom. He observes that many opponents of progressive legislation like factory acts, education acts, and laws relating to public health have based their opposition on the "supposed inherent right of every man to do what he will with his own." Green argues, much as he did when treating of moral freedom, that the mere freedom of being left alone, although essential to the realization of other freedoms, is itself of no great worth:

> We shall probably all agree that freedom, rightly understood, is the greatest of blessings; that its attainment is the true end of all our effort as citizens. But when we thus speak of freedom, we should consider carefully what we mean by it. We do not mean merely freedom from restraint or compulsion. We do not mean merely freedom to do as we like irrespectively of what it is that we like. We do not mean freedom that can be enjoyed by one man or one set of men at the cost of a loss of freedom to others. When we speak of freedom as something to be so highly prized, we mean a positive power or capacity of doing or enjoying something worth doing or enjoying, and that, too, something that we do or enjoy in common with others.

This "positive power or capacity" is something that a man cannot achieve by himself without the help of others. It is part of the common good in choosing which every man finds his own well being in the well being of the community. The wandering savage, though he enjoys freedom from restraint, is not "really free." Green very brilliantly argues that the urge is not the slave of man, but he is the slave of nature. Of compulsion by natural necessity he has plenty of experience, though of restraint by society none at all. Nor can he deliver himself from that compulsion except by submitting to this restraint. So to submit is the first step in true freedom, because the first step towards the full exercise of the faculties with which man is endowed. For this reason, the humblest member of a civilized society is free beyond the dreams of the "noblest savage".

The fullest exercise of mans faculties can never be realized, however, as long as society discriminates between its members, or indeed, as long as any man on the face of the earth is prevented from advancing to full freedom. "There is no clearer ordinance of that supreme reason, often dark to us, which governs the course of man's affairs, than that no body of men should in the long run be able to strengthen itself at the cost of others' weakness". A society based on slavery is, in this regard, inferior to one founded on free industry. Nevertheless, if working and living conditions in a country like England prevent men from realizing their highest capabilities, this society falls short of the ideal of true freedom. Freedom of contracts is a good, but the right of doing what one wills with his property, which was the maxim of defenders of unlimited freedom of contract, can justly be maintained only as long as it is a means to a higher end. A society in which every man actually contributed to the common good would be a society in which every man had won the battle over his own worst impulses and was therefore truly free in the moral sense. But Green does not envisage such a society on earth. The most he aspires to in a society in which laws and institutions will liberate the powers of all equally to a contribution to a common good.

Political Obligation

Green in *The Principles of Political Obligation* elaborates the relation between the state and rights. According to Green the state presupposes rights and rights of individuals. It is a form which society takes in order to maintain them. The institution through which society maintains the rights of its members is law. A state is therefore a community living according to law. Of the relation between rights and the common good, he says: "No one can have a right except as a member of society and of a society in which some common good is recognized by the members of the society as their own ideal good." This connects his idea of rights with the second stage of his ethical theory according to which, personal good rightly understood is part of a wider common or social good. He also connects both his idea of rights and of law to his third stage. Green points out the 'counter-claim of society', which is the correlate of the moral duty of the members to obey the law. 'This is the claim or right of the individual to have certain powers secured to him by society and the counter-claim of society to exercise certain powers over the individual, alike rest upon the fact that these powers are necessary to the fulfillment of man's vocation, to an effectual self-devotion to the work of developing the perfect character in himself and others'.

This is the metaphysical morality of the true good. Green contends that to develop the perfect character in oneself and others is to make the most and best of humanity in one's own person and in the persons of others. The moral justification for the rights which the law of a particular state confers and for the obligations which it imposes, is that they are necessary to enable every member of the community to seek the true good. If in every state the law secures all the rights and only the rights, which are morally justified, the way is open for the realization of the common good of the universal human fellowship. According to Green, this is the true good because 'the only good which is really common, the only good in which there is no competition of interests'. That this is his contention, that for him the moral foundation of the state is the metaphysical morality of the true good, is shown by what he says later when discussing war. 'There is no such thing as an inevitable conflict between states. There is nothing in the nature of the state that, given a multiplicity of states, makes the gain of the one the loss of the other'. To this he adds: 'It is nothing then in the necessary organization of the state but rather some defect in that organization in relation to its proper function of maintaining and reconciling rights, of giving scope to capacities, that leads to a conflict of apparent interest between one state and another'. This presupposes a pre-established social harmony not only within the nation but in the international world and in neither case is there any such thing.

In particular, he has ignored something important in the 'nature of the state'. It is the government's duty as the agent of the state, to protect and promote the national community's interest abroad. This is an interest in conditions abroad which will enable all members of the national community to live as well as possible, not in conditions which will enable all of mankind to do so. Because there is no pre-established international harmony, the two sets of conditions are not the same. This is not to deny that governments have moral obligations to mankind as well as to their own people; for instance, to preserve international peace and to contribute to the relief of human suffering. These obligations set limits to what it is morally permissible government's to do in promoting the interests of their own communities.

Green's proposition that no one can have a right except as a member of society is entailed by his conception of a right. Because to have a right is to be entitled to have a certain power secured to one by society, one must be a member of society to have the entitlement. His second proposition that the society must be one in which some common good is recognized by the members as their own ideal good, must be disconnected from the metaphysical morality of the true good. This can be done by interpreting, 'some common good' as the conditions which it is in a community's interest to secure, i.e. conditions which will enable all its members to live as well as possible. These are conditions in which they all as members, although not necessarily as private persons, have a common interest. For humanistic social ethics, this reduces to the more modest contention that all human beings are fellow human beings and must treat one another as such. No one must ever be treated by anyone merely as a means but always as an end. He is entitled to this minimum standard of treatment from his community, whatever else, as a member, he may be entitled to from it.

It follows that the moral justification for the rights which the law of a particular state confers and for the obligations which it imposes, is that they are necessary to enable every member to live as well as possible, rather than to develop the perfect character in himself and others. It is in a community's interest that such rights and obligations should be legally conferred and imposed. This preserves the connection between the idea of rights and of a common good, although the latter idea is not Green's true good. The change is necessary to make the idea of a common good compatible with the implications of finitude. It also follows that no one can have a right against his community's interest. Green emphatically agrees. 'A right then to act unsociably, a right to act otherwise than as belonging to a society of which each member keeps the exercise of his powers is a contradiction.' This is a contradiction because it would mean that a community was entitling its members to act in a way incompatible with their membership. Green makes the same claim that to have any rights against the state in the sense of a right to act otherwise than as a member of some society, the state being for its members the society of societies, the society in which all our claims upon each other are mutually adjusted.'

As the 'society of societies', the state is the public community and its interest is the public interest. When he speaks of it as the 'society in which all our claims upon each other are mutually adjusted', Green is implicitly acknowledging that if private interests can not conflict the need for their mutual adjustment would not arise. He goes on to acknowledge it openly when speaking about obedience to bad laws. 'As a general rule no doubt even bad laws, laws representing the interests of classes or individuals as opposed to those of the community, should be obeyed.' Although they deny morally justified rights, such laws should be obeyed because: the public interest on which all rights are founded is more concerned in the general obedience to law than in the exercise of powers by individuals or classes which the objectionable laws unfairly withhold'. To say this, is not to deny that it is in the public interest for such laws to be repealed. It is, although at some cost to the self-interest of individuals or classes who unfairly benefit from the bad laws. In acknowledging this, Green is conceding that the common good can require some sacrifice of personal good. He is tacitly abandoning the metaphysical morality of the true good in favor of humanistic social ethics. It is worth adding that he thinks that there can be occasions on which the public interest is best served by disobedience to bad laws.

Conditions which foster good citizenship must be in the public interest in an enlightened state. However according to Green, 'The effectual action of the state, i.e. the community as acting through law for the promotion of habits of true citizenship, seems necessarily to be confined to the removal of obstacles'. This is because the law cannot enforce moral duties. 'They are duties to act and an act can be enforced. But they are duties to act with certain dispositions and from certain motives and these cannot be enforced'.

Discussing the punishment of an individual offender, Green says: 'The justice of the punishment depends upon the justice of the general system of rights, on the question of whether the social organization in which the criminal has lived and acted, is one which has given him a fair chance of not being a criminal'. Discussing the right to private property, he says: 'The rationale of property in short requires that everyone who will conform to the positive condition of possessing it, namely labor and the negative condition, namely respect for it as possessed by others, should so far as social arrangements can make him so, be a possessor of property himself and of such property as will at least enable him to develop a sense of social responsibility, as distinct from mere property in the immediate necessities of life'. The 'removal of obstacles' then requires government measures to eliminate social conditions which foster crime and to establish those which will enable everyone to become a responsible property owner. It also requires measures, which will ensure that everyone is qualified to fulfill social functions. This suggests that Green's idea of the state, is the idea of what today we call the welfare state, i.e. a state in which social services in fields such as education, health and housing, are publicly provided. The welfare state does not presuppose the metaphysical morality of the true good. A case can be made for it on the basis of humanistic social ethics.

Green does not speak the true good in his account of punishment and of property. The substance of what he says remains intact when common good is interpreted in terms of humanistic social ethics. In the case of marriage, he tacitly concedes that moral requirements can conflict with personal self-interest when he insists that personal incompatibility should not be grounds for divorce. A further word however is necessary about his discussion of property. He says of the right to property that: 'its uncontrolled exercise is the condition for the attainment by man of that free morality which is his highest good'. But if it is not 'to be pretty much a matter of chance' whether the individual is to be' qualified to fulfill any social function', can exercise of the right be completely uncontrolled? The question arises whether by 'free morality' is meant the true good or social responsibility in terms of humanistic social ethics. Green did not think out all the implications of 'the removal of obstacles' for the role of government in economic life.

The Individual and Society

British liberalism had long regarded the state as an enemy of liberty, and had jealously guarded against every extension of its power. The history of English liberties, from the time of King John, but more especially from the civil wars, had habituated first the aristocracy and later the middle classes, to view the state as a necessary evil. There was, however, another way of viewing the state, familiar to the citizen of the Greek polis or of the Roman republic. For the ancients, the state was not an enemy of the freedom of its members, but rather the source and guarantor of freedom. Green, the academician, insisted that the high view of the state common among the Greeks and Romans is nearer the truth than the low view of the state long prevalent among the English. The effective rights, even of middle-class Englishmen, are, in fact, dependent on the state; and the crying need of the times is for men of good will to recognize the possibility of extending to the working classes the rights which are necessary to implement their largely unrealized capacities.

There remain, however, certain questions concerning the respective rights and claims of the individual and of the state. First, one must ask how far the state should go in the direction of helping men to realize their moral and spiritual vocation. A state presuppose other forms of community, with the rights that arise out of them, and only exists as sustaining, securing, and completing them. Although the coercive power of the state does not contribute directly to the recognition of rights, enforcement is necessary to give reality to what otherwise is purely ideal. Without force, rights could not exist: "Nothing is more real than a right, yet its existence is purely ideal, if by "ideal" is meant that which is not dependent on anything material but has its being solely in consciousness. It is to these ideal realities that force is subordinate in the creation and development of states."

Green denies that states are constituted by force alone: kings, conquerors, and dictators contribute to the course of historical development only in the degree that their power has been used to extend and consolidate human rights. States are, according to Green, the highest form of human association. Without going to the length of developing a philosophy of history, Green nevertheless appeals to the principle of an end "immanent in nature", drawing an analogy between the state as an "organized community" and "a living body of which the members at once contribute to the function called life, and are made what they are by that function, according to an idea of which there is no consciousness on their part". The "idea of a state" is immanent in history as the end toward which societies must progress. It is sure that families and other associations, through membership in which men have their rights, antedate the state. The state does not supplant these prior societies. The other forms of community, which precede and are independent of the formation of the state, do not continue to exist outside it.

Green, however, reiterates the principle that a man possesses rights only as a member of society, and that "a right against society, in distinction from a right to be treated as a member of society, is a contradiction in terms". As conditions change or new elements of social good are taken into account, society is warranted in imposing further regulation on the individual's liberty to do as he pleases.

Green takes up the question raised by Locke, revived by the American and French revolutions, and kept alive by the abortive European revolutions of 1848 and 1870, as to when the individual is justified in disobeying the law or in raising a rebellion against established authorities. Green is far from complacent with regard to the existing conditions of European states. He advises, however, that where a popular government is in existence so that there are "settled methods of enacting and repealing laws", a man should obey the law while working for its nullification:

The common good must suffer more from resistance to a law or to the ordinance of a legal authority, than from the individual's conformity to a particular law or ordinance that is bad, until its repeal can be obtained. It is thus the social duty of the individual to conform, and he can have no right, as we have seen, that is against his social duty. Where no such recourse exists, there may indeed be not so much a right as a duty to resist unjust laws and unlawful authorities:

> In such a case, there may arise a social duty to resist, and the exercise of men's powers in fulfillment of that duty may be sustained by such a general recognition of its being for the public good, as to become a right; but the resistance may be a duty before a majority of the citizens approve it, and does not necessarily become a duty when a majority of them do approve it. Resistance should be made, indeed, if at all, not because the majority approve it, but because it is for the public good; but account must be taken of the state of mind of the majority in considering whether it is for the public good or no.

Green finds moral justification of revolutionary activity extremely difficult, because a man's motivation is so readily corrupted: moreover, the effects of a revolution are almost always obscure. Hence, "revolutionists do and must to a great extent go it blind". Similarly, we judge a revolutionary outbreak by its results.

The Moral Foundations of Law

It is now possible for us to proceed to the central problem of *The Principles of Political Obligation,* which is "to consider the moral function or object served by law, or by the system of rights and obligations which the state enforces, and in so doing to discover the true ground or justification for obedience to law." If we compare Green's definition of positive law with account of natural rights the ground or justification for obedience to positive law is immediately apparent. Certain powers should be maintained as rights by society in order that all men may have the opportunity to make the most of themselves. The moral ideal, freedom, is the end which rights are designed to serve. The particular system of rights and obligations recognized by a society is justifiable in the degree that it ministers to the moral ideal. Natural law, so-called is a theoretical ideal system, nowhere realized nor even adequately conceived except by God himself.

The ground for obedience to law can be restated in terms of the distinction between the lower morality of interest and the higher morality of goodness. Green maintains in his ethical writings that men enter on the course of moral development by learning to bend their wills to serve a common interest in which they can perceive their own satisfaction as well as the satisfaction of other persons whom they love and respect. It is at this level of morality that the notion of rights and obligations comes into existence. But, Green maintains, the morality of interest carries within it the seeds of a higher morality, according to which men are motivated not by interest but by devotion to moral goodness on its own account. Men who reach the higher stage of morality continue to support the prior morality of interest, but they do so henceforth in a different spirit.

From the standpoint of the higher morality, Green proposes to criticize institutions which ostensibly serve the morality of interest, not indeed, in order to deny the need for such institutions, but with a view to considering what is of permanent moral value in the institutions of civil life, as established in Europe; in what way they have contributed and contribute to the possibility of morality in the higher sense of the term, and are justified or have a moral claim upon our loyal conformity, in consequence.

The essential difference between the morality of interest and the morality of duty is that the motivation of the former is situated to a large extent in the aspect of a man's self that is most completely immersed in his natural existence. Family piety, love of country, pride in tradition, esteem of ones follows are all sentiments that lend support to the individual's sense of obligation. For less virtuous members of the group there is promise of reward and fear of punishment. Such is the milieu in which rights and obligations originate and in which they best thrive. By contrast, reflective morality admits no other motive than the goodness of the act measured by its tendency to promote the moral ideal. The man of higher morality obeys the laws of his society, but he is not strictly speaking, obliged by them, because he does not obey them out of any regard to his own or other men's interests but simply because of finds them good.

Green emphasizes the distinction between duty and obligation, the most important difference being that obligations can be enforced whereas duties cannot. Green argues that the question sometimes put, whether moral duties should be enforced by law, is really an unmeaning one; for they simply cannot be enforced. They are duties to act, it is true, and an act can be enforced: but they are duties to act from certain dispositions and with certain motives, and these cannot be enforced. From this consideration, it follows that nothing but external acts can be made a matter of obligation. Green's restriction of the meaning of obligation has important implications for his whole theory of rights and the role of the state with respect to rights. According to the doctrine traditional to British liberalism, the rights of man are founded in the eternal law of nature, and the first duty of each individual toward his fellow is to observe these natural rights. Common usage in Green's day paired the terms right and duty, as if they were natural correlates. For Green, who denies that individuals have any rights from nature, duty to one's fellow is determined not by reference to rights but by reference to the moral ideal. Rights come into the picture only to the extent that men recognize the importance of securing to each other powers to realize the capacities inherent in man. Society secures these powers by obliging everyone to respect them. Thus, the proper correlate to rights is not duty but obligation.

Green argues that the human personality, and hence individual moral capacity, is only actualized in society. The interests a moral person has in other persons is not in them merely as a means to his own satisfaction, but in them as self-satisfying beings like himself, and thus in their self-satisfaction. Hence, says Green, a man 'cannot contemplate himself as in a better state, or on the way to the best, without contemplating others, not merely as a means to that better state, but as sharing it with him'. Therefore the notion of a common good is essential to any society, for it is a necessary part of human life in company with others beyond a certain level of material existence to conceive and seek a 'permanent well-being in which the permanent well-being of others is included'. The individual's true good must be bound up with the good of those who share in his society and perhaps ultimately with the good of those who share his humanity. The minimum material conditions necessary for persons to begin to exercise their moral capacities may be the objects of competition between individuals and groups. It is a mistake, however, to think of material goods as exhausting moral good.

According to Green, then, the moral function served by law is twofold: (1) it provides some of the conditions which allow individuals to be moral by restraining them from acting merely from inclination, bringing them to appreciate that they have a life in common with others, leading them to accept the true good as the proper motive for their actions, and hence bringing them to the point where they can fulfill their moral nature; and (2) it helps to harmonize the various actions of individuals in a social context, including the ways they seek self-realization, such that any person in that society has the opportunity to fulfill his moral nature, and hence is the condition of there being a truly common good. These functions imply the 'principles of political obligation' as Green uses the term. The law cannot make people have the ideal good as their motive for action, for such a motive cannot be enforced its role must be confined to requiring and prohibiting certain actions according to their effects on the common good. But since the common good will only be attained fully when individuals pursue it from within, so to speak, the law ought not interfere with their attempts to do so unless it is essential 'to the existence of a society Hence the law ought to be used only when conventional morality and individuals' habitual dispositions cannot be relied upon to promote the common good.

There are, then, three specific grounds for the moral evaluation of law, the state, and government. In the first place, the law may contain provisions that are not necessary to secure the common good, because habitual action and conventional morality can bring about the required conduct without the undermining influence of legal coercion. Speech pare Secondly, the law may not contain certain measures, which it ought to contain because habit and conventional morality are incapable of securing the common good unaided. Speech pares thirdly, the law may not allow some individuals to express or develop their capacity for moral action, and thus prevents any person from fulfilling his moral nature. Green's argument, however, contains a further distinction between 'the law' as an institution, a particular way in which individuals are led to an appreciation of the common good, and 'the law' as a set of specific rules and practices requiring or prohibiting this or that action in these or those circumstances.

It becomes an affront to all moral persons in that society a wrong to has done in their persons. Such a denial enforced through the legal system undermines any duty he might otherwise have had to obey any of its prescriptions. Such a state qua state can have no moral claim on his obedience, although it does not follow that he must disobey or that he might not have other moral reasons for doing what the state has commanded. But even though Green allows that the slave state does still have a claim upon the citizen, he does admit that it may be truly urged that this claim must not override that of the slave upon him.

But he still insists that those slave- laws ought to be obeyed if the violation of the law in the interest of the slave were liable to result in general anarchy, not merely in the sense of the dissolution of this or that form of civil combination, but of the disappearance of the conditions under which any civil combination is possible; for such a destruction of the state would mean a general loss of freedom, a general substitution of force for mutual good-will in men's dealings with each other, that would outweigh the evil of any slavery under such limitations and regulations as an organized state imposes on it.

Green's position on obedience of law is very ambilvant. He argues that the slave's claim to have rights acknowledged by law is recognized by 'the public conscience' but is resisted by some class in its own interest and with the ability to prevent any change to the law, violation of law would not cause any danger to 'the law-abiding habits of the people' and hence disobedience would further the common good rather than jeopardize it. On the other hand, if state and society are closely intertwined, through a religious basis to the state, for example, it may not be possible to challenge the authority of the state without also undermining the basis of social living itself, and hence the citizen's duty is to conform to objectionable laws while working for the development of a more explicit awareness of a good common to all but independent of that particular form of government.

Public opinion, however, cannot be the sole criterion of the justifiability of resistance. A 'hopeless minority' may have a duty of resistance even though it cannot expect 'efficient popular support' if 'repeated renewal and repeated failure' are the only way of 'arousing the public spirit' to the point where the government may be brought to serve its proper role. Similarly, public sentiment in favor of resistance to government, even one that is 'monarchic or oligarchy', does not itself justify resistance if that is likely to endanger the common good.

One of the most debated points in the recent literature on obligation and disobedience is whether disobedience to law can be morally justified within a democratic political system. There are two broad positions on the question. On the one hand, the democratic 'conservatives' argue that the rule of law is so central to the maintenance of democracy that justification of disobedience would undermine those procedures for peaceful and orderly change in response to popular will and the imperatives of justice popular expectation. The democratic 'libertarians', on the other hand, welcome 'the incorporation of responsible law-breaking into democratic theory as a beneficial, though rarely used mechanism.

Green seems to align himself with the conservative group. He argues that if an individual has decided that a law is contrary to the common good, in a country like

England with a popular government and settled methods of enacting and repealing laws, the answer of common sense is simple and sufficient. He should do all he can by legal methods to get the command cancelled, but till it is cancelled he should conform to it. The common good must suffer more from resistance to a law or to the ordinance of a legal authority, than from the individual's conformity to a particular law or ordinance that is bad, until its repeal can be obtained. It is thus the social duty of the individual to conform.

This argument is similar to the conservatives' 'contagion' thesis. They suggest that disobedience sets an example of law breaking as a legitimate means of pursuing political goals and thereby encourages others to act similarly, including those who may be less scrupulous in examining the moral justifiability of their actions or who may have dangerous or pernicious principles. It leads to a breakdown in legitimate and peaceful processes or conflict-resolution, and thereby promotes instability. Disobedience thus under mines democratic society, stirs up primitive instincts, leads to mass lawlessness and anarchy, and weakens the fabric of society.

Green's argument may be less extreme than some of these, but its general philosophical position is the same. The weakness of them all, however, is that they rely on causal relationships for which there is little empirical evidence, or for which the evidence is rarely produced. There are simply no grounds for concluding that all disobedience in a democracy is, or causes, a threat to communal life itself, or that it always undermines that system of government. It may do so in some cases, but that is hardly grounds for the total condemnation. Most of those who allow that disobedience in a democracy might be morally justifiable also insist that legitimate methods for securing change be tried first, and to that extent they are on common ground with Green. But they also argue that these procedures cannot be allowed to dominate democratic systems of government to the exclusion of the common good, and that it is therefore wrong to elevate procedure to the point where laws contrary to the common good must always be obeyed even while their repeal is sought.

Green is in no doubt respecting the moral value of democratic government; active democratic citizenship can ensure that the idea of the common good is 'kept alive' and hence that 'the legislative and administrative agencies of society can be kept free from bias by private interests, and true to the idea of the common good', But the categorical imperative must always remain the moral person's overriding duty, and democracy is valuable so long as it continues to serve the common good. The obligation to obey a democracy must always be conditional upon judgments about the contributions to the common good of the institution of law.

The Idealist Revision of Liberalism

This revision of liberal theory was accomplished in the two decades following 1880 by the Oxford idealists of whom Thomas Hill Green was the most important representative, at least in political philosophy. But there was one important difference. The earlier idealism, because it was largely a criticism of industrialism and its social effects, had never been liberal in its political outlook. What Green accomplished, then might be described as twofold levels of position. On the one hand he captured for liberalism a movement of thought which was to dominate Anglo-American philosophy for a full generation at the turn of the century. On the other hand he revised liberalism to meet the valid objection that, as a one-sided statement of class interests, it had stood for a conception of liberty which, in fact if not in intention, amounted to a reckless disregard for social stability and security. To a considerable degree this revision had only to make coherent and explicit the qualifications by which Mill had in effect explained away the individualism and the egoism of Bentham's form of liberalism.

The principal purpose of idealism was to reconstruct a system of philosophy, while the purpose of directing a political movement was incidental. Looked at after the event it is easy to see that its main achievement in philosophy was critical. It released British thought once and for all from what had become a burdensome tradition: the associational psychology and its supposed implications for logic, and in ethics the pleasure- pain theory of motivation and value with its individualist implications for social philosophy. With respect to the latter the idealists developed and made coherent the criticism of individualism that began with Rousseau's theory of the general will, and that they found still further elaborated in Hegel's theory of freedom. The fundamental philosophical problems of idealism, therefore, were the nature of personality, the nature of the social community, and the relationship between the two.

There were special circumstances that make the study of Green's philosophy difficult. He died relatively young and the only book which he completed and published hardly mention any political or concrete social question. His lectures on the *Principles of Political Obligation* was put together and edited after his death from his notes and from those of his students. Moreover, Green's own experience was in the main academic, though he was concerned throughout his life with the improvement of secondary education. He had at first hand almost no acquaintance with the social problems created by industrialization, though he had been able to observe something of its indirect effects on agricultural labor, and his remarks upon them are always a little remote. Green's direct influence, therefore, was measured almost wholly by the effect of his teaching upon his students, and while this was very great it could hardly be inferred from his published writings. At its root lay a strong sense of the moral injustice of a society that withleed from large portions of its members the goods, partly material but chiefly spiritual, which the culture of that society created. As Green once said, the "underfed denizen of a London yard" has hardly more share in the civilization of England than a slave had in that of Athens. In some measure this feeling was like that which actuated Mill's rejection of a competitive economy but it was also different. There was in Green's ethics, and in idealism generally, a religious element that had no counterpart in utilitarianism, and also Green did not think of the deprivation as primarily economic. Abject poverty, he felt, is likely to entail some measure of moral degradation. Full moral participation in a social life was for Green the highest form of self-development, and to create the possibility of such participation was the end of a liberal society. The source of this conviction with Green was not Hegel. It represented on the one hand his understanding of Christian brotherhood and on the other hand a liberalized conception of Greek citizenship, not reserved as in Aristotle for a privileged few but made available to all men. Accordingly for Green, politics was essentially an agency for creating social conditions that make moral development possible.

But as Green said, Bentham's position tacitly assumed that law is the only restriction on liberty, and this is not true unless freedom is arbitrarily identified by definition with the absence of legal restraint. Against this conception, which Green called "negative freedom," he set up a "positive" definition: liberty is "a positive power or capacity of doing or enjoying something worth doing or enjoying." Freedom must therefore imply not merely a legal but an actual possibility, in view of existing circumstances, of developing human capacities, a genuinely increased power on the part of an individual to share in the goods which a society has produced and an enlarged ability to contribute to the common good. Freedom of contract may be a means to this end and, if so, is a good, but it is not an end in itself. It may, for example, in cases where the bargaining power of employer and employee is grossly unequal, merely reduce the general practice in a trade to that of the least scrupulous employers. The freedom of an Irish tenant to contract with the owner of his land becomes a mere formality when eviction means starvation. In such cases the actual coercion which an employer or a landlord can exert under the legal form of a contract is in fact, Green argued, far more oppressive and far more destructive of effective freedom that the legal coercion exerted by the state when it abridges the right of contract to protect the weaker party.

Green's argument in this lecture was an effective analysis, on a limited scale, of liberal purposes in legislation. It brought out the fact that liberal theory in the past had been largely ad hoc, controlled by the purpose of repealing obsolete legislation, and it argued cogently that liberalism could not be placed plermanently on so narrow a foundation. Liberal policies have to be flexible to meet changes of circumstance and if they are genuinely liberal they have always to follow the guidance of moral purposes. They are essentially an effort to open a humane way of living to larger number of persons. Consequently, he inferred, at the center of a liberal philosophy is the idea of a general good or common human well-being which is capable of being shared by everyone and which provides a standard for legislating. This standard can not be individual liberty alone, or the least possible legal restriction of free choice, because free choice has always to be exercised in a situation, and some situations are such that they reduce choice to a mockery. Choice means opportunity, and opportunity means a society that is not coercive beyond need either in its legal and political structure or in its economic and social structure. Freedom is really a social as much as it is an individual conception; it refers at once to a quality of society and a quality of the persons that make up a society. Hence, it is impossible that a government should be liberal merely by standing aside and refraining from legislation, or that a liberal society should come into being merely, so to speak, by political inadvertence. The function of a liberal government is to support the existence of a free society, and while government cannot make people moral by law, it can remore many of the obstacles that may stand in the way of their moral development. Green's ethics and political philosophy were an elaboration and reinforcement of these ideas, which his *Lecture on Liberal Legislation* applied to the specific case in hand.

The central principle of Green's ethics was the mutuality of the relationship between the individual and the social community of which he is member. As he put it, " the self is a social self." By this he meant, much as Aristotle might, that the highest form of community is one in which equal is associated with equal and in which the bond that holds the community together is the loyalty of the members of the group and its purposes. At the same time to be a member of such a group Government, Green said, depends on will and not on force, because the tie that binds a human being to society is the compulsion of his own nature and not the penalties of the law or the calculation of ulterior advantages. The unanswerable argument for a liberal society is that it recognizes this fundamental social impulse in human nature which is at the some time a moral impulse, and tries to give it realization in a form adequate to the full ideal meaning of morality. This ideal requires that the members of a society meet as moral equals, that they treat each other with respect that all are free to think and act for themselves, and that their thought and actions are guided and controlled by full moral responsibility. For this reason coercion ought to be reduced to a minimum, and this is no truer of coercion exerted by the state than of any other form of coercion which has the effect of making persons less than free moral agents. For Green as for Kant a community of persons is a "Kingdom of ends" in which everyone is treated as an end and not merely as a means. Because this is inherently the ideal nature of a community and of a person, the opportunity ought to be open to everyone to realize such a life up to the limit of his capacities. Hence a really liberal society cannot aim at less than to give to all men the right to moral self-determination and to the moral dignity which is at once the condition and the due of personality.

Green developed this conception chiefly in his analysis of right. A right, he argued, has always two elements. It is in the first place a claim to freedom of action, which is in substance the assertion of an individual's impulse to realize his own inner powers and capabilities. A hedonist psychology, he argued, is fundamentally false because human nature is a mass of desires and tendencies to actions, which are directed not toward pleasure in general but toward concrete satisfactions. The claim, however, is never morally justified merely by the desire, but only by rationalized desire, which takes account of the claims of other persons. What justifies it is the fact that the general good itself allows of such freedom of action. It is a claim to participate and contribute. In consequence the second element in a right is a general social recognition that the claim is warranted, that the individual's freedom really does contribute to the general good. A moral community from Green's point of view, therefore is one in which the individual responsibly limits his claims to freedom in the light of general social interests and in which the community itself supports his claims because the general well-being can be realized only through his initiative and freedom. Ideally it is, as Rousseau said, "a form of association which will defend and protect with the whole common force the person and goods of such associate, and in which each, while uniting himself with all, may till obey himself alone". There is, therefore, a general social good or welfare which is the criterion of the individual's rights and duties—what Plato called the "health" of the community—but it is neither distinct from nor opposed to the happiness of the individual, because it is one in which the individual can share and because the participation is itself a significant part of the individual's happiness. The fundamentally liberal element in Green's ethics consisted in his refusal to contemplate a social good which demanded merely self-sacrifice or self-abnegation on the part of the persons who share and support it. The obligation and the right of the community matches the right and the obligation of its members.

This moral freedom, which Green conceived to arise from the metaphysical nature of the self or personality, was for him the foundation of political liberalism. It is meaningless to inquire in general, he argued, why a human being is subject to rules created by social institutions or why as a member of society he has rights. His liberties and his obligations are two sides of the same social relationship which gives him at once the duties of his place in the social structure and provides him with a personality that can be invested with rights. A human being live their personal lives, and their personalities consist largely in the sharing and participation which such membership implies. The part to be played by government in this social complex is that of regulation and control in the light of this ideal of free participation. A liberal government aims at minimizing coercion, but coercion is of many kinds and can depend on many circumstances. In general any situation is coercive when it frustrates the spontaneous self-expression of native capacities and substitutes compulsion for moral self-control. The justification of legal coercion is precisely that it offsets and neutralizes other forms of coercion which are less tolerable. The right to freedom of judgment and action Green extended to all men, without distinctions of rank or wealth, and he believed that all men do rise more or less to this level in so far as they are given the opportunity to share in the moral culture provided by civilization. Hence he regarded education as the most important social function, and he conceived that the chief difference between ancient and modern civilizations lay in the degree in which the modern nation opens to all men goods which in antiquity were reserved to an aristocracy. For the present, Green thought, the nation is probably the largest unit that has the social cohesiveness needed to make the idea of a common good effective but he was convinced that states ought to direct their policy with due regard for the general human welfare. War, he argued, can never occur without moral fault somewhere, and while it may sometimes be unavoidable, it is always a confession of moral failure.

Green's restatement of liberalism did away with the rigid line between economics and politics by which the older liberals had excluded the state from interfering with the operation of a free market. From Green's point of view even a free market was a social institution rather than a natural condition, and quite possibly it might require legislation to keep it free. The political and the economic, instead of being distinct areas, are interlaced institutions which are certainly not independent of one another and which ought ideally both to contribute to the ethical purposes of a liberal society. In political theory this change implied a radical departure from the attitude toward the state and legislation which had been characteristic of liberalism. Liberalism had always looked with suspicion on the state and had kept its activities within narrow limits, whether by a rigid list of constitutional guaranties or by the assumption that legislation is likely to be an undesirable interference with freedom. Green's liberalism, on the contrary, was frank acceptance of the state as a positive agency to be used at any point where legislation could be shown to contribute to "positive freedom," in short, for any purpose that added to the general welfare without creating worse evils than it removed. It is true that Green himself, and indeed the whole generation of liberals to which he belonged, made no sudden shift of attitude to conform with their change of theory. They remained even nervously fearful of paternalism and the undermining of individual responsibility by social legislation.

In the later nineteenth century, liberalism was running out of ideas and steam. The great onslaught on feudal and aristocratic privileges, launched in 1789, had been widely successful. Many of the classic liberal demands, for political and legal equality for freedom of opinion and its expression, had been quite substantially achieved. It hardly seemed appropriate for what had been a movement and a party of reform, if not of revolution, to become a prop of the status quo. Yet the precoccupation of a major liberal politician like Gladstone with the problem of drink, and the disestablishment of the Church in Wales, suggested that liberalism was coming to the end of its original programme. Gladstone himself sensed this. Towards the end of his long life, in 1896, he described himself as a 'dead man.'

What then was to be done next? Increasingly it was the question of 'the condition of the people', rather than the 'freedom of the individual', which was coming to dominate politics. 'The politics of the future are social politics said Joseph Chamberlain in 1883. This was in part the result of the widening of the franchise, to which Liberals had been committed, and the consequent need of the political parties to develop policies, which would attract popular support. The British Liberal Party in the 1880s and 1890s was a party, which was searching for a new role and new objectives, or at the least a broadening and updating of its traditional role and objectives. 'Politicians in search of a cry' was how Chamberlain characterized the Liberals of the 1890s. They were conscious that great issues of principle and philosophy were at stake.

At the heart of the problem lay two connected issues: the nature of freedom, and the role and functions of the state. The nineteenth century had witnessed an uneven, but steady and cumulatively vast expansion of the activities and responsibilities of both the state and local authorities. More and more aspects of economic and social life came under legal regulation and restriction. Much of this legislation had been the work of liberal governments; yet liberals could not avoid feeling uneasy about these developments. They ran counter both to their belief in the minimal state, and to their belief that freedom consisted essentially in the absence of all but a minimum of law, regulation and compulsion.

But the advance of intervention was not accompanied by a corresponding adjustment of liberal theory. Liberals continued to pay lip-service to the principles of non-intervention, free trade and laissez-faire, and acts of intervention were sanctioned only as exceptions to the general rule—as Mill had said. Nineteenth-century liberals attached great importance to the principle of 'voluntarism'. Moral virtue attached only to acts performed voluntarily; there was no virtue in doing what you were compelled, or ordered, to do. Therefore compulsion was inherently undesirable. And such arguments were reinforced by the established liberal individualist belief that the individual is generally the best judge of her or his interests. Thus the whole climate of liberalism was unsympathetic to the growth of legislation and intervention which was actually taking place, and which many people, including some socialists, identified with socialism.

This was the situation in Britain in which a sustained and concerted effort was made to rethink the liberal concept of freedom and the liberal philosophy of the state. Matthew Arnold had pointed in this direction; but it was left to the idealist philosopher T. H. Green to develop these ideas in a systematic and influential manner. Green took from Hegel and the German idealist tradition more positive conceptions of both the state and society than liberalism could provide. He rejected the old liberal ontology according to which individuals were the primary units, and society was either their secondary creation, or else no more than a collection of individuals: 'Without society, no persons; this is as true as that without persons . . . there could be no such society as we know. He rejected the idea that 'the individual brings with him into society certain rights which he does not derive from society'. Rights could not exist apart from society: 'There can be no right without a consciousness of common interest on the part of members of a society. Similarly he suggested that the traditional liberal antithesis between freedom and law was misconceived. 'In one sense no man is so well able to do as he likes as the wandering savage', yet 'he is the slave of nature' and his 'actual powers ... do not admit of comparison with those of the humblest citizen of a law-abiding state.' Laws and the state can confer and enlarge freedom as well as restrict it. This was more than ever possible since the state had by then been effectively democratized, in Green's view, and therefore 'The danger of legislation, either in the interests of a privileged class or for the promotion of particular religious opinions, we may fairly assume to be over. The popular jealousy of law, once justifiable enough, is therefore out of date.

Green was in no doubt that 'freedom, rightly understood, is the greatest, of blessings'; but he was concerned that freedom should not be defined as 'merely freedom from restraint or compulsion', or 'merely freedom to do as we like irrespective of what it is that we like: 'When we speak of freedom as something to be so highly prized, we mean a positive power or capacity of doing or enjoying something worth doing or enjoying, and that, too, something that we do or enjoy in common with others', and he added to this the further statement that the ideal of true freedom is the maximum of power for all members of human society alike to make the best of themselves.

There are three ways in which this conception makes a radical departure from, or at least enlargement of, the traditional liberal idea of freedom. Green turns freedom from a negative conception—the absence of restraint—to a positive one, the actual power or ability to do things: freedom is bound up conceptually with power. Second, there is a moral element in Green's thinking. The things which people ought to have the power as well as the opportunity to do should be things worth doing. Third, there is an explicitly egalitarian element: all alike should have this power 'to make the best of themselves'. It was argued by Green and the New Liberals that it was through state action that the power or capacity of people could be increased, and that although such action might restrict the freedom of some individuals—property owners, for example—this was justified by the egalitarian principle that all alike were entitled to have their real freedom increased.

This was the way, then, in which Green and those who followed after him tried to justify interventionist state in liberal terms, and break down the old liberal hostility to state activity. Green contended that such a position was not incompatible with a commitment to individualism. The fact that people were relieved of responsibility in respect of, for example, obtaining decent housing conditions, meant that they had more opportunity to develop self-reliance in other areas. Green was as concerned as any nineteenth-century liberal with the moral life of the individual, and in some important respects he did not differ from his predecessors in his view of what self-reliance involved. Thus he seems to have shared the view of his pupil Arnold Toynbee that outdoor relief under the Poor Law should be abolished, because it undermined self-reliance. Green was anxious to stress the continuity of the 'New' liberalism with the old. Behind differences over specific policies lay the same old cause of social good against class interests for which, under altered names, liberals are fighting now as they were fifty years ago. This stress on the general good as opposed to sectional and class interests was one way in which the New Liberals sought to distinguish themselves from both Conservatives and Labour, both parties representative primarily of particular class interests, in the liberal view.

The main elements of the justifying theory of Western liberal democracies—can, be stated as two maximizing claims: the claim to maximize individual utilities, and the claim to maximize individual powers. The first claim is familiar to students of political theory in its nineteenth-century Utilitarian form. The second, immediately familiar, is a useful and revealing way of formulating the extra-Utilitarian claims that were built into the liberal theory as soon as it became liberal-democratic, say from John Stuart Mill on. Both claims are made in the name of individual personality. The argument in both cases is that the liberal society provides for the greatest measure of realization of human personality, though in the two cases the essential character of that personality is seen differently, and the different views have different historical roots. Before examining the two claims it may be useful to place them, provisionally at least, in the Western intellectual tradition.

The first claim is that the liberal-democratic society, by instituting a wider freedom of individual choice than does any non-liberal society, maximizes individual satisfactions or utilities. The claim is not only that it maximizes the aggregate of satisfactions, but that it does so equitably: that it maximizes the satisfactions to which, on some concept of equity, each individual is entitled. This claim implies a particular concept of man's essence. To treat the maximization of utilities as the ultimate justification of a society, is to view man as essentially a consumer of utilities. It is only when man is seen as essentially a bundle of appetites demanding satisfaction that the good society is the one which maximizes satisfactions. This view of man, dominant in Benthamism, goes back beyond the classical political economists. It is firmly embedded in the liberal tradition and has remained a considerable part of the case for the liberal-democratic society today.

The second claim is that the liberal-democratic society maximizes men's human powers, that is, their potential for using and developing their uniquely human capacities. This claim is based on a view of man's essence not as a consumer of utilities but as a doer, a creator, an enjoyer of his human attributes. These attributes may be variously listed and assessed: they may be taken to include the capacity for rational understanding, for moral judgement and action, for aesthetic creation or contemplation, for the emotional activities of friendship and love, and, sometimes, for religious experience. Whatever the uniquely human attributes are taken to be, in this view of man their exertion and development are seen as ends in themselves, a satisfaction in themselves, not simply a means to consumer satisfactions. It is better to travel than to arrive. Man is not a bundle of appetites seeking satisfaction but a bundle of conscious energies seeking to be exerted.

This is almost an opposite view of the essence of man from that of the Utilitarians. It came, indeed, as a reaction against the crude Benthamite view of man as consumer. Benthamism provoked in the nineteenth century a variety of reactions, conservative, radical, and middle of the road, ranging from Carlyle and Nietzsche, through John Stuart Mill, to Ruskin and Marx. All these thinkers brought back, in one way or another, the idea of the essence of man as activity rather than consumption. From Aristotle until the seventeenth century it was more usual to see the essence of man as purposeful activity, as exercise of one's energies in accordance with some rational purpose, than as the consumption of satisfactions. It was only with the emergence of the modern market society, in the seventeenth century England, that this concept of man was narrowed and turned into almost its opposite. Man was still held to be essentially a purposive, rational creature, but the essence of rational behaviour was increasingly held to the unlimited individual appropriation, as a means of satisfying unlimited desire for utilities. Man became an infinite appropriator and an infinite consumer; an infinite appropriator because an infinite desirer. From Locke to James Mill this concept of man became increasingly prevalent. The nineteenth-century reaction against it, radical, moderate, and conservative, was an attempt to reclaim and restate the much older tradition. But the utilitarian concept was by then too deeply rooted in the market society to be driven out of the liberal tradition, while too clearly inadequate to be allowed any longer to dominate it. The result can be seen in John Stuart Mill and T. H. Green and the whole subsequent liberal-democratic tradition: an uneasy compromise between the two views of man's essence, and correspondingly, an unsure mixture of the two maximizing claims made for the liberal-democratic society. It is not surprising that the two concepts of man, and the two maximizing claims, were brought together. For the problem which the first liberal-democratic thinkers faced in the nineteenth century, was to find a way of accommodating the pre-democratic liberal tradition of the previous two centuries to the new moral climate of democracy.

Conclusion

The first half of the nineteenth century was a time of unparalleled development in the British economy. Britain was effectively the most advanced industrial nation in the world. Many liberal economists today, like Hayek and Friedman, still look back with nostalgia to the period between 1830 and 1860, as a time of untrammeled creation of wealth. This was bound up in many minds, with the free flow of the market economy without government intervention. It is in fact doubtful whether such a free market ever existed, except in theory. Many thinkers who grew up in this period were duly affected by the ebullient confidence of free-market capitalism and Green was no exception. Like J.S. Mill, he reflected a belief in free enterprise and the value of private property. Following the lead of his hero John Bright, one of the leading figures of the Manchester School of Economics, Green defended free trade, the market economy, the development of industry, the inevitability of unequal wealth and the freedom of unlimited accumulation. Each citizen had the chance to become a small-scale capitalist in his own right. Nonetheless, a close historical study of the conditions of the urban working class as revealed in the royal commissions and government blue books, show us a very different picture. Conditions of unparalleled poverty and social deprivation prevailed, only marginally alleviated by private charity. Green, like many Victorians, although profoundly worried by such poverty, could not always see its connection with capitalism. Some, of course, would still deny such a connection. Green commented that the labor market is constantly thronged with men who are too badly reared and fed to be efficient laborers; who for this reason, and from the competition for employment with each other, have to sell their labor very cheap. It is certain however, that these influences have no necessary connection with the maintenance of the right to individual property and consequent unlimited accumulation of capital.

Green's answer to the cause of poverty is odd. Poverty was partly the result of a deficiency of character, a point characteristic of many nineteenth century social theories. The other main reason Green traced to the original conquest and ownership of large tracts of land by aristocratic families, which prohibited the development of wide scale land ownership and thus created an itinerant poverty stricken class of wage laborers, susceptible to every flux in the economy. But the moot point is how could Green support the advance of free market capitalism, unlimited accumulation and inequality, with all its consequent aggressive individualism, negative views of liberty and competitiveness, and still argue for the ethical view of society as composed of equally self-realizing citizens?

C.B. Macpherson has argued that Green's thought contains contradictory views on human nature and society. On the one hand there is the vision of humans as self-seeking appetitive, acquisitive creatures; on the other is the vision of humans as ethical, moral and creative creatures; seeking a good shared equally with others. The two views are not compatible for the above theorists; now it is true that Green did value the market place, but he was not just admiring uncritically the economic scene of the nineteenth century. There are two points to be made here. First, Green does see the market mentality as reconcilable with the ethical creative view; second, considerable difficulties remain in the formulation of his argument.

On the first point, the market can been seen to function as a stage in the development of the individual. This is a point from Hegel's political thought which can be found in Green. The market creates mutual dependence between individuals and provides diverse roles for the realization of unique capacities. Individuals, in the market, are forced to think about their wants and how to satisfy them. Individuals are thus forced to conceptualize new wants and desires. In this whole process, as Hegel put it, without his being aware, 'man is no longer wrapped up in his particular impulses, on the contrary, he has plunged into the Reason of the actual world'. The individual develops an intelligent ethical concern for his temporal interests and in the process becomes part of a complex chain of social interconnections. Therefore the market creates the conditions for social solidarity, and despite setting out from a possessive individualist premise, the end result is a realization of mutual dependence and service for others. So the market mentality is viewed as a necessary stage in the development of the citizen toward the ethical creative vision. This argument still does not explain a number of problematics. Can an individual retain his livelihood, which, for the sake of argument, depends upon an acquisitive or competitive mentality, and still be an ethical creative citizen? Is the existence of poverty and unemployment under capitalism inimical to the ethical development of individuals? The denizen of the London Yard with gin shops all round is not likely to develop, as Green clearly realized. So despite Green's and Hegel's idea that the market does not have to be a realm of permanent 'otherness' and individualism, considerable difficulties remain.

This particular problem of human nature is reflected in a number of debates on Green. In the sphere of property Green does oppose taxation of unearned increments and interference with unlimited accumulation, but he also recognized the role of property in the development of the human personality. Green's strong sense of the necessity of property for the building up of character led him, however, not so much to exalt the sacredness of property in the hands of the large owner, as to insist on the necessity of such legislation as would tend to the diffusion of property as widely as possible among the masses.

Green's theory of property is pregnant with number of implications. Green can be seen as presenting a case for individual self-reliance. He seemed to place great value on a class of small proprietors and capitalists. Oddly, his defense against interference with the unearned increment, specifically from land, was not based on natural rights, labor or tradition, but on the simple point of the difficulty of pinning down with any precision the boundaries of the earned. Green's account of property is fluid enough to be taken in other directions. Each individual needed property to realize his potentialities. Inequality or accumulation was justifiable as long as they did not interfere with a like power in others. However, if some individuals oversaved or deliberately paid below subsistence wages, causing deprivation, unemployment and depression in the economy, then there were strong grounds for intervention in property rights. Property rights, like other rights for Green were dependent on their furtherance of the common good. The state acting for the common good could thus intervene in certain situations. However, Green's ambivalent attitude on this issue gave many hostages to fortune. Essentially, he desired a moralized capitalism or responsible private enterprise. Society, industry and culture could be transformed only from within the citizen's dispositions.

The problem of education is also pertinent to the issue of property. If the citizen is to develop, to use opportunities, he needs to know how to do things. This implies some kind of degree of education, which was a prime concern for Green. The general details of Green's involvement in educational matters are fairly well known. In 1864 a Royal Commission on school education was set up. Green was offered an assistant commissionership covering Warwickshire and Staffordshire and later Buckingham, Leicester and Northampton. Green was involved in this work between 1865 and 1866. The problem in looking at Green's ideas is to know whether he was concerned to widen education to all classes, or only to broaden the opportunities for the middle classes. The former idea entailed some interference in property rights and structural change for the common good, the latter implied an adjustment of the existing system. Green did desire education to be widened. Universities should not be class-based institutions but open to the poorer members of the community and religious dissenters. Money should be no barrier to education; in fact, Green maintained that education should be the great leveler in society. He thus suggested, in his report to the Royal Commission that a scheme of endowments should be set up. Whether these would be public or private endowments, how far they would extend, how effective they would be in providing education for the poor, Green does not say much.

The problem of human nature has also affected judgments of Green as a liberal, and related questions as to his influence on liberal thought and practice. The most extreme position has been to ignore Green altogether, a feat achieved by G.M. Young in his survey of the Victorian age. Idealism has also been associated with reactionary conservatives and imperialism, although it would seem odd to put Green into this bracket. The more usual interpretation has been to see idealism as contributing in the 1880s to a change in the climate of opinion towards collectivism. This point is never argued but stated. Haley and Censor, for example in their histories of England take this line. It can be argued that Green's idealism actually transformed liberal theory and practice. However even in these latter accounts the arguments are limited in scope. In the last decade a new consensus has grown, reflected in the work of historians like P.F. Clarke, Michael Freedmen and Stefan Collin, that Green was a Victorian liberal at heart.

In fact, critics' offer is a healthy reminder of the individualist, acquisitive premises built into Green's view of human nature. On the other hand, Green's conception of the creative ethical view of human nature has been told many times in theory, but never really adequately in practice. The essay on 'Liberal Legislation' is crucial for the interpretation of Green as a radical liberal. The main body of Green's argument was written primarily to reassure the more traditional elements in the liberal party. Green constructed a historical scenario of liberalism in the nineteenth century. First, liberalism has struggled for political freedom against aristocratic privilege. Second, with Bright and Cobden, it had struggled for economic freedom against protectionism. Green maintains that liberalism was now moving into a third phase, which we might call social freedom. The social legislation constitutes examples of this phase of social freedom. Green argues that we should investigate the theory underlying this new phase, which in sum was the theory of positive freedom defined as 'a positive power or capacity of doing or enjoying something worth doing or enjoying, and that too, something we do or enjoy in common with others'. True freedom is rational, moral action, a reconciliation of the objects of will and the objects of reason. The progress of mankind is measured by the growth of this freedom, which is coincidental with citizenship. There is considerable evidence to the effect that Green's thought did prepare the ground for the new liberals and the formation of the welfare state, although such a claim must be very carefully dealt with.

Green's concern with the ethical development of the citizen is primary. A citizen is not just a legal member of a state, but also a moral and autonomous being. The citizen has internalized the norms of his society, the norms being directed at the self-realization of the citizen body. Institutions like the family are customary practices directed to the cultivation of individuals. The individual assimilates norms by participating in social life. Citizenship also denotes character and thus rationality. This theory is difficult to reconcile with the divisiveness and legitimating problems of society in the nineteenth century, yet citizenship must be grasped against the background of metaphysical claims underpinning Green's political ideas. Law is designed to provide the conditions for the development of human capacities. Civic and legal institutions should be the outward expression of moral imperatives. The individual is obligated if the state seeks the common good. Rights are derived from the claim of the individual to be a moral agent. It is through the exercise of rights that the individual realizes his powers. They are essentially opportunities to realize excellence.

Green's dilemma is the dilemma of all liberal political theorists-how to frame a basis for the regulation of individual activity, which preserves an area of free action sufficient to allow the exercise of personal individuality, and at the same time protect the interests of society. It is a dilemma which although latent in all liberal political thought-was raised in acute form by the social context of industrialized Victorian England. Green's political theory flows from a definition of the state which he believes, combines the strengths and avoids the weaknesses of Austin's identification of the state with sovereign coercive power and Rousseau's identification of the state as an expression of the general will.

The appeal of Green's thought and its influence reflected a need to adapt liberalism to new, or nearly perceived social problems. Its very imprecision about the nature of man and its requirements enhanced its utility as a device for the exposition of liberal manifesto in a period of transition. By using shifting meanings to 'rights', 'freedom', 'recognition', 'society', 'social good' and 'human nature', Green's philosophy stretched the language of liberal discourse and attached it to a new role for government. What it lost in analytic rigor it gained in practical adaptability, for it provided a means by which liberalism could be justified as an instrument of advocacy for positive action by the state, and it enabled reformers at the end of the nineteenth and the beginning of the twentieth century to use liberal language to support activities far beyond those limits by which earlier liberals had restricted the role and were suspicious of an overbearing state of government. Green's great achievement lies in sincere attempt to moralise in a humane way brutish capitalism.

15

Immanuel Kant

> The time will come when the sun will shine only on free men who know no master but their reason. How consoling for the philosopher who laments the errors, the crimes, the injustices–which still pollute the earth and of which he is often the victim, is this view of the human race, emancipated from its shackles, released from the empire of fate and from that of the enemies of progress, advancing with a firm and sure step along the path of truth, virtue and happiness.

Immanuel Kant, (1724-1804) writing the end of the eighteenth century, is still widely considered the thinker who, more than any other, addresses the philosophical concerns of modernity. His attempt to build philosophy on a scientific basis in order to secure for it objective knowledge remains one of the dominant projects of modern philosophy.

Kant was born in Konigsberg then in Prussia but now part of Russia, in 1724 and died there in 1804. The paucity of the accounts of Kant's life tells not much about the manner in which he lived. Kant avoided all external change in his life. In a letter to his friend Herz, he wrote, "All changes make me anxious." This attitude led him to turn down a professorship at Hale, one of the foremost Protestant universities in Germany. Kant started his academic career by discussing a scientific problem, i.e. he sought to vindicate Newtonian science philosophically-an attempt which later gave rise to his critical philosophy. But it was not until 1770 that he was appointed to the chair of logic and metaphysics and at last found economic security. When his fame spread, his stipend was considerably increased. He was Rector of the University on several occasions.

Kant was stimulating and powerful lecturer. His students were struck by the originality and liveliness of his observations, which were seasoned with a dry ironic humour. He was also a prolific writer. His really decisive breakthrough as a philosopher came only in 1781 when he published the *Critique of Pure Reason*. For him, this work initiated a revolution in thought realistically compared by himself to the Copernican revolution in astronomy. In fairly rapid succession, the other important works followed.

The publication of 'Religion within the Limits of Reason Alone' (1793) offended the then King of Prussia, Frederick William II, who did not practice tolerance in religious matters. Frederick William II ordered his obscurantist minister Wilmer to write to Kant to extract a promise that would not write again on religion. Kant reluctantly agreed with their request, which amounted to a Royal command, implicitly qualifying his promise by saying that he would not write again on religious matters as his Majesty's most loyal subject. After the King's death, Kant considered himself to be absolved from this undertaking and explained that his pledge applied only to the life-time of Frederick William II. He explained his attitude fully in the foreface to his *Contest of Faculties*, in which by implication, he attacked Fredrick Willam II who had died the year before.

Kant was obviously not easy in his mind about this decision. In an unpublished note, he explained his conduct: 'Repudiation and denial of one's inner conviction are evil, but silence in a case like the present one is the duty of a subject; and while all that one says must be true, this does not mean that it is one's duty to speak out the whole truth in public.'

Kant gradually retired from the university. His mind slowly declined, his memory gave way, and he had to abandon lecturing. In 1800, his pupil Wasianski had to begin looking after him. Other pupils began to publish his lectures from notes which they had taken down. In 1803, he fell seriously ill for the first time. His mind became more and more clouded. He finally died on 12 February 1804, a few months before the end of his eightieth year.

Kant never married, and it is said that although he contemplated marriage once or twice, he lost the opportunity while reflecting on the matter. Kant's life was ordered according to a rigid schedule that precluded any spontaneity or disruptions. He would rise at five o'clock and work for two or three hours. He held lectures from seven or eight until nine or ten and would continue work until one o'clock. Then he would dine with one or two friends and occasionally with as many as five. Kant would then walk for an hour, spend the rest of the day in reading and meditation, and retire at ten o'clock. This rational control of his life was exemplified in his abhorrence of emotional expressiveness. All emotions of a "soft-hearted kind," as he himself called them, were alien to his nature. Schiller once said of Kant that had he been able to feel love, he would have been one of the greatest phenomena of mankind; but since he could not, there was something defective in his nature. The only emotion that Kant recognized as valid was the ethical emotion, the universal respect for the freedom of the moral person.

Kant lived a celibate life. His sexual abstinence was indicative of his general indifference to the role of pleasure in life. In the *Critique of Judgment*, he wrote that the value of life is "less than nothing" when it is measured according to the sum of pleasure. The asceticism that pervaded Kant's outlook on the world and the conduct of his life reflects the Protestant adherence to monastic discipline in everyday life. Kant was deeply influenced by the Protestantism of the world in which he lived. Although he explicitly rejected elements of his pietist upbringing, the dominant currents of ascetic Protestantism remained decisive for both his life and thought.

Kant's personal history brought him in close contact with the Pietist sect of the Reformation. Pietism was a form of Protestantism that intensified the ascetic tendencies of the Reformation, emerging in Germany as a reaction against the orthodoxy of the Lutheran church. However there was an uneasy tension in German Pietism between both Lutheran and Calvinist elements. Because of the emotional nature of Pietism, its asceticism was perhaps weaker than that made possible by the thoroughly rational nature of Calvinism. But it was certainly more deceptive to ascetic tendencies than was orthodox Lutheranism. Kant's pietist religious and educational training exposed him to both the Lutheran and Calvinist elements of Protestantism. His parents, particularly his mother, were religious people.

Although Kant later rejected many aspects of pietism, he maintained a high respect for certain aspects of it. He wrote, "Even though the religious ideas of that time and the concepts of what they called virtue and piety were anything but clear and adequate, still they really got hold of the basic thing. You can say what you want about pietism—the people who were serious about it were outstanding in a praiseworthy respect. They possess the highest thing men can possess, that calm, that serenity, that inner peace undisturbed by any passion." On entering the university of Konigsberg, Kant began his studies in the philosophy faculty, which included the study of mathematics and science. Konigsberg was one of the Protestant universities of Germany, founded in 1544. Schultz, who was also one of the most influential professors of theology at the university, helped keep pietism alive in this period. Kant himself seemed to have had contradictory feelings about pietist. He was much attraced by the rationalism of Christian Wolff, who sought to establish a complete system of philosophy on the basis of the modern sciences. Wolff's rational approach to theology, in opposition to the subjective religious impulse of pietist, led first to Wolff's expulsion from the pietist university of Hale, but eventually to his rectorship of it. On the other hand, Kant retained certain sympathies with pietism. When he petitioned Schultz for aid in seeking a university post, Schultz asked, "Do you fear God from your heart? And Kant assured him that he did.

In some respects, Kant sought to distance himself from the religious influences of his youth. German pietism attempted to recover Luther's early teaching regarding the importance of faith rather than dogma. Thus pietism led at times to an excess of emotionalism, an obsession with the internal dimensions of religious faith. Kant's criticism of pietism was directed against this emphasis on internal feelings and the conception of piety as based on a personal relation to God.

Despite Kant's rejection of pietist practice, certain fundamental elements of Protestantism remained decisive for his thought. Paulsen regards Kant as the "finisher of what Luther had begun." Luther had revolted against the confusion of religion and science in scholastic philosophy and attempted to free faith from knowledge and faith epitomizes this Protestant position. In the preface to the *Critique of Pure Reason*, Kant writes, "I have therefore found it necessary to deny knowledge, in order to make room for faith." Moreover, Kant's treatment of practical reason, which emphasizes the individual relation to the moral law as opposed to the dominance of church authority, echoes the Protestant turn toward the inner man.

Kant distanced himself from the formal practice of Christianity and toward the end of his life his writings on religion brought him into conflict with the religious enthusiasts in the government. Yet his moral philosophy can be seen as the "translation of this Christianity from the religious language to the language of reflection: in place of God we have pure reason, instead of the Ten Commandments the moral law, and in place of heaven the intelligible world." In Paulsen's view, Kant reflects the "true spirit" of Christianity. He writes, "Its depreciation of the world and its pumps and glories, its insistence on the equality of all men before God—these are all characteristic of Kant's view of life."

Although Kant criticized the ecclesiastical form of religion, his interpretation of religion on the basis of a rational morality stems from Protestant sources. His emphasis on the moral will, as opposed to the external act, echoes Luther's stress on faith versus works. Kant's notion of the autonomy of the moral person, according to which each individual stands in direct relation to the moral law, is reminiscent of the Protestant notion of the priesthood of all believers. In Luther's view, each individual stands in direct relation to God through his faith, unmediated by the dogma and hierarchy of the church. Moreover, Kant's denial of the value of pleasure reflects the ascetic discipline that so strongly characterized Calvinist strains of Protestantism. But his transposition of these religious tenets into a rational morality did not leave these values untouched. Kant's basic disagreement with the pietism of his youth was its unbridled emotionalism and personalism. Insofar as Lutheranism originally led in the direction of an emotional faith, Kant distanced himself from it. But Kant's inner man distinguishes between acting according to inclination and acting according to duty. Obedience to the rational law, not the inner felt emotion, provides the inner bond of Kantian morality. Consequently, it is not the natural endowment of sensibility that forms the basis of original sin in Kant's philosophy of religion. Instead, he attributes the evil in human nature to an impurity of disposition that shows itself in the failure to make the law the only determining ground of the will.

The effect of these religious elements in Kant's thought extends beyond his moral theory into his discussion of knowledge. Paulsen's suggestion that Kant completed the work of Luther by separating faith from reason is misleading if it implies that Kant's treatment of reason is free of ascetic tendencies. Kant's treatment of knowledge cannot be divorced from the practices that shaped his own orientation toward life. His theory of knowledge, morality, and beauty must be examined in the context of this ascetic ideology.

We have traced two contrasting philosophical currents, rationalism and empiricism, from their common inception in the 'cogito' of Descartes, to their final divergence in Leibniz and Hume. In the eighteenth century, the century of Enlightenment, it was between those two philosophies that a thinking person had to choose. It was Kant's principal contribution to show that the choice between empiricism and rationalism is unreal, that each philosophy is equally mistaken, and that the only conceivable metaphysics that could commend itself to reasonable being must be both empiricist and rationalist at once.

His early works (known as the pre-critical' writings) were followed by a period of silence (1770-1781) and then by the first of the three great Critiques-the *Critique of Pure Reason* (1781,). Conversed with a systematic way with the entire field of epistemology and metaphysics; it was followed by the *Critique of Practical Reason* (1788), concerned with ethics, and the *Critique of Judgment* (1790), concerned largely with aesthetics. Among Kant's other works, the most important are the *Prolegomena to any Future Metaphysics* (1783) and *The Foundation of the Metaphysic of Morals* (1785), the first being a popular exposition of his mature metaphysics, the second his writings on logic, jurisprudence and political philosophy have been less influential, although Hegel's political transformation of the *Critique of Practical Reason* has had an incalculable effect on subsequent political thought and practice.

Of diminutive stature and austere habits, Kant was nevertheless a gregarious man, a brilliant talker, and a loved and respected member of social and literary circles. He was a founding spirit of the German Romantic movement, which was to change the consciousness of Europe, and the father of nineteenth- century idealism. He was the greatest philosopher since Aristotle, and his most important book —the *Critique of Pure Reason*—is of an intellectual depth and grandeur that defy description.

Kant's early philosophical inspiration had been the system of Leibniz. But despite this influence, which is everywhere apparent in the *Critique of Pure Reason*—Kant's philosophy is unique, both in its methods and in its aims. In order to understand those aims we must again consider the impact, during the seventeenth and eighteenth centuries, of the rise of science. Science presented itself as a universal discipline, the premises of which were certain, and the methods of which were disputable only by the adoption of a stance of philosophical skepticism. No one could engage in science without accepting both the established results of his predecessors, and the empirical methods that led to their discovery. Science presented a picture of unanimity and objectivity, which no system of metaphysics could rival. Forced by this fact into unnatural self-consciousness, philosophy found itself with no results that it could offer as its own peculiar contribution to the fund of human knowledge. The very possibility of metaphysics was thrown in doubt, and this doubt was only exacerbated by Hume's radical skepticism-a skepticism, which, according to Kant, aroused him from his 'dogmatic slumbers'. All philosophy, then for Kant, must begin from the question 'How is metaphysics possible?

Kant's proof of these contentions begins from the theory of 'synthetic a priori knowledge. According to Kant, scientific knowledge is a posteriori: it arises from, and is based in, actual experience. Science, therefore, deals not with necessary truths but with matters of contingent fact, however, it rests upon certain universal axioms and principles, which because their truth is presupposed at the start of any thoughts which seem both vulnerable to philosophical skepticism and at the same time basic to our conception of ourselves. Once again, Kant considered himself to be responding to the challenge of Hume's skepticism.

Hume formulated the fundamental premises of this skepticism in two succinct but complex thoughts. First, there is no derivation of an 'ought' from an 'is' which is to say that moral judgments, since they do not describe how things are, gain no justification from natural science. Secondly, since the sole motive to action is desire, and reason itself is no motive, the only rational justification that can be offered for any action lies in showing that it contributes to the satisfaction of an agent's wishes. All reasoning is reasoning about means, and has no authority beyond that of the desire, which compels it. There is no innate power of reason to overrule desire, and hence no power of reason to determine action objectively.

The first great insight contained in Kant's moral philosophy was the realization that Hume's first source of skepticism was of no real significance. Suppose that the 'is—ought' problem were solved, so that moral judgments could be determined with the objectivity of a natural science. That would not refute skepticism. For to refute skepticism we must also show how such judgments provide reasons for acting. In other words, Hume's second objection would still be sufficient to refute the objectivity of morals. On the other hand, if we can show that there are objective reasons for acting, then the 'is—ought' problem becomes insignificant. It no longer matters that we can or cannot derive an 'ought' from an 'is' for morality will gain its rational basis independently. It seemed to Kant therefore that the ancient distinction between theoretical and practical reason should be revived, and the foundations of the second explored with the same discipline that he had devoted to the exposition of the first. This reintroduction and elaboration of the concept of practical reason was among one of the most influential of Kant's achievements and provided the grounds not only for his own partial repudiation of the metaphysics of the first *Critique* but also for many of the insights of later German idealists.

Kant and the Enlightenment

The ideological cauldron from which modern European philosophy emerged is commonly called 'the Enlightenment'. This period of intense philosophical exploration and criticism began in England in the mid-seventeenth century, spread to America and France in the mid-eighteenth century, and finally reached Germany, and eastern and southern Europe just before the beginning of the nineteenth century. In its wake it fomented and rationalized several major revolutions and the Napoleonic wars, as well as initiating radical new developments in philosophy and culture. The Enlightenment was a time of lively intellectual debate and enthusiastic scientific discovery. It was also a time of far-reaching personal, political, and philosophical experimentation— Montaigne's delineation of the private self, Owen's and Fourier's socialist communes, Hume and Holbach's radical challenges lo established philosophy. Diderot, the editor of the Encyclopaedia, and the iconoclastic Voltaire were voluptuaries and sexual revolutionaries as well as devastating debaters, and even the Marquis de Sade can be seen as very much a pail of the Enlightenment. In other words, the Enlightenment, especially in France, was first of all an attitude of rejuvenation, a spirited sense of criticism and experimentation, and an enthusiastic endorsement of change and progress. It was not a distinctive set of doctrines but it is still possible to isolate some of its general characteristics, particularly its humanism, rationality, and universalism.

Humanism

Enlightenment secular humanism has often been misunderstood as an attack on Christianity and religion in general, but it is important to insist that the origins of European humanism lie within the Church, dating from the twelfth century, and that several of the leading Enlightenment philosophers—notably Rousseau—were adamant theists. Rousseau recommended the death penalty for non-believers in his *Social Contract*. It is true that the Enlightenment was often at odds with Church authorities, and the religions defended by the philosophers were rarely orthodox, but it would be a mistake to think of Enlightenment humanism as antagonistic to religion as such.

What humanism did mean most of all, was that the world had become a human world, determined and threatened by human aspirations, and delineated no longer by nature but by national boundaries. The world may have been created by God but it was now in the hands—for better or worse—of humanity. The world was a human stage, with human values, emotions, hopes, and fears, and this humanity was defined, in turn, by a universal human nature. 'In all nations and ages,' wrote David Hume, 'human nature remains still the same.' Racial, national, and cultural differences are superficial – our basic ideas, senses, and sentiments are all the same. And so the Enlightenment philosophers insisted on tolerance of differences, and they took it upon themselves to speak for all humanity. It was also a period of intense curiosity and an abstract sense of brotherhood. Nothing human is foreign to me', defined the temperament of the times. Alexander pope's declaration that 'the proper study of mankind is man' became the working definition of the Enlightenment intellect.

Rationality

The key to human nature, for the philosophers and reformers of the Enlightenment, was its inherent rationality, the inborn faculty of reason. Reason enabled us to discover the intricate, abstract truths of mathematics, and to apply these to our understanding of the workings of the universe. Reason allowed us to ask and answer questions of Nature through carefully planned observations and experiments. The Enlightenment emphasis on rationality should not be confused with the rather narrowly defined philosophical orientation called 'rationalism'—which specifies a special confidence in the powers of human reason to recognize necessary non-empirical truths. The rationality of the Enlightenment includes both rationalism and empiricism. Voltaire, never patient with philosophical niceties, continually mixed the two up. Reason was basic to human nature, and with reason, it was possible to guarantee universal agreement on questions about the world as well as about matters of mathematics.

This confidence in reason and rationality, however, was not confined to matters of science and mathematics. Part of Enlightenment humanism was its keen sense of humanity as part of nature, and it was one of the most fervent beliefs of the period that human social life was subject to the organization of reason according to the nature of human nature and the values of humanism—in particular 'the pursuit of happiness'. Thus the leading philosophers of the time developed a range of naturalistic theories of human nature, of man as a machine (Holbach), of the mind as a Newtonian microcosm (Hume), of reason as a system of built-in knowledge, guaranteed by God (Leibniz). On a larger scale, philosophers developed an even wider range of models for the ideal forms of government and society. Optimism about the future of humanity was virtually the religion of the day, with an emphasis not on faith but on planning, and a sense of inevitable human progress. Even religion was subjected to the scrutiny of rational procedures: the attack was not on religion but on superstition, that is, on those religious doctrines that could not be justified by the new confidence in human reason.

Universalism

The belief in the universality of human nature, one aspect of which is universal reason, already entails the transcendental pretence. If all people are basically the same, and if that sameness lies in part in the universal reach of reason, it is not hard to conclude that everyone, everywhere, ought to believe in the same scientific truths, follow the same moral guidelines, endorse the same political structures, and worship the same god or gods. But it should not be thought that this confidence in universality considered itself to be imperialistic or coercive. Since everyone is rational then everyone would, or should, come—on his or her own—to the same conclusions. Thus the belief in universal reason becomes coupled to a confidence in individual autonomy—the ability of every human being to come to the right conclusions, though perhaps only after considerable education and argument. The good news was that human conflict was about to come to an end, since all disagreements could be negotiated through universal reason. The bad news was not yet evident: that not everyone would in fact agree, indeed would not even agree with the ideals of rationality, universality, and autonomy. The result would be some of the most pig-headed disagreements in history, no longer caused by pride, avarice, or religious competition, but by ideology bolstered with confidence in 'self-evident' truths about the nature of 'human nature'.

One philosopher develops these three themes more systematically than any other, and he was neither French, nor English, but Prussian—Immanuel Kant. Though the Enlightenment philosophy culminates in Germany, its presuppositions were operative throughout the Enlightenment. Indeed, it is only when these canonical beliefs start to come under attack that so elaborate a defence as Kant's is required—and this attack came first in Germany. The irony of this is that the wholly successful French and English Enlightenment received its most brilliant defence in Germany, where the Enlightenment never fully took hold.

The attack on the Enlightenment in Germany gave itself a distinctive name—romanticism. It was first of all a reaction—to the Enlightenment and its excessive humanism, its blind confidence in human reason and rationality, and its arrogant universalism. Cosmopolitan philosophers in London or Paris might pretend that they could speak for all humanity, but equally serious thinkers stuck in the small, fragmented, still largely feudal states of Germany could not easily do so. English and French culture ruled, or aspired to rule the world. It was all the defensive Germans could do just to get their language and culture acknowledged in their own lands. Many of the princes of Germany considered themselves enlightened, and spoke mainly in French. The Enlightenment, in other words, was viewed as a threat in Germany. Romanticism, however cosmic its expressions, was first of all an expression of nationalism and provincial self-assertion. But like so much of the Enlightenment, romanticism projected its provincial anxieties on to the universe itself, and in its later stages elevated the transcendental pretence to the level of an absolute. So far as the transcendental pretence was concerned, Enlightenment and romanticism turned out to be more alike than opposed.

It is possible to make too much of the social origins of intellectual currents, but the more usual problem in philosophy is the total neglect of demographic and political concerns, making the Enlightenment appear as a set of abstract claims about the source and justification of knowledge which emerges out of nowhere. Romanticism similarly appears not as a nationalistic reaction but rather as an irresponsible digression from proper philosophy by poets who did not have the patience to study Locke. But it is no historical accident that the central themes of the Enlightenment originated in cosmopolitan London and Paris, or that the romantic reaction emerged most forcefully in the smaller states of Germany, and neither movement can be comprehended in philosophical terms alone. The Enlightenment must be understood in terms of the philosophers' international aspirations, Voltaire's social activism and prejudices against philosophy, and Kant's comfortable position as a university professor in an age of violent revolutions. Romanticism was indeed a rejection of some of the most cherished Enlightenment principles, but it was also a rejection of the political imperialism of the more powerful Enlightenment nations, and a defence of traditional religion against excessive rationalism. It is not unimportant that several of the leading romantics were converted to Catholicism, endorsed mysticism, and extolled the virtues of poetry over philosophy.

Despite their opposition, both the Enlightenment and romanticism had the same social origins as expressions of middle class—or more properly bourgeois ideology. The preconditions of the Enlightenment were the growth of cities, the enlarging of the civil service, improved education, the centralization of power and government, and as both partial cause and consequence, the rapid expansion of the bourgeoisie in France and England. In feudal Germany, the middle-class was less prominent and less powerful, which helps to explain some of the differences in philosophy. But what the middle-class philosophers throughout Europe felt was an adolescent arrogance appropriate to their ascendancy, and this emerged in the transcendental pretence, whether in the unrestricted claims of universal rationality, or in the uninhibited reach of romanticism.

The attack on the Enlightenment, and its ultimate collapse was not however initiated by the romantics. It began with the devastating arguments of Rousseau's friend David Hume (1711-76). Hume was a typical Enlightenment philosopher. He thought that Isaac Newton was the most important intellectual and cultural figure since ancient times, and his ambition was nothing less than to construct a theory of human nature as elegant as Newton's theories of the universe. He believed in reason and the empirical appeal to the senses, and detested blind obedience to authority on such nonsensical matters as metaphysics and theology. Yet, he turned the Enlightenment on its ear. He used a set of devastating arguments to show that the unqualified faith of the Enlightenment in the powers of reason and experience was limited; in fact, reason and experience could not even justify our most basic beliefs about the world such as, for instance, that such a world exists outside of our experience. He denied that we ever actually experience the necessary connections between events that we call 'causes'; so that there is no way that, we can rationally or empirically justify even the most common causal explanations. It was this scepticism this deep doubt about our abilities to know the world, and for that matter ourselves, that would awaken Kant, in his own words, 'from my dogmatic slumbers'. It is Kant, reacting to Hume, who develops the intellectual machinery that will bring the Enlightenment to its peak, and then, in the hands of his romantic successors, turn against it. But if Hume did not have unqualified confidence in reason, he did share with Rousseau a profound confidence in the human sentiments. 'Reason is and ought to be the slave of the passions', he wrote and so expressed a thesis that would have great appeal to the romantics—though few of them had much sympathy with Hume's empiricism, scepticism, or light touch with philosophical issues.

It is the interweaving of Enlightenment and romanticism that provides the main thread of the story of modern European philosophy, even if these terms are not much used after the turn of the nineteenth century. On the Enlightenment side, is the heavy emphasis on science, universal principles, and rationality. On the romantic side are deep doubts about science, and a reliance on intuition and feeling rather than reason. But what they share is as important as their disgreements. They both believe in the personal significance of the individual, and that through the individual it is possible to understand the whole. Thus it is easy to see how it is that Rousseau occupies a pivotal position in both movements. He was a bona fide member of the Enlightenment, dedicated to rational reform, and the improvement and happiness of humanity. But he was also the proponent of a provincial, simple life of sentiment, and his concept of the General Will would have a powerful appeal for later romantic authors who also sought some supra-personal self. Foremost among his followers was Kant, usually considered the most important defender of the Enlightenment in Germany, but in fact the man who set the stage for the most dramatic romantic themes, including the elevation of the self from mere personal identity to an Absolute Self of transcendental proportions.

Enlightenment attempted to expand the principles of toleration and moderation into general principles of individual life and the – life of society and politics and it is no exaggeration to say that all that is best in the Western liberal tradition comes from enlightenment. Enlightenment, it might be said, disappears as a separate identity into what came to be known as civilization in nineteenth-century Europe. Enlightenment believed in institutionalism and in civil liberties; in the abolition of slavery; in gradualism and moderation; in the reform of manners, morals and politics; in peace and internationalism; in social and economic progress with due respect for national and local tradition; in justice and the rule of law; in freedom of opinion and association; in the balancing of the powers of government and the division of political authority between different agencies of government as a weapon against despotic rule by individuals, groups or majorities; in social equality but not to the extent that it threatened liberty, and above all Enlightenment believed in liberty under an enlightened system of law so that liberty would not disturb the orderly processes of government. This list is Isaiah Berlin's, and he points out that, by the middle of the nineteenth century, most of these ideals were, at least in theory, shared by the civilized governments and peoples of Europe.

In his famous essay *What is Enlightenment*? of 1784, Kant offered a celebrated definition of what it was to be enlightened: to be enlightened was 'dare to know'. Kant chose to regard the whole of eighteenth-century thought as a revolt against ignorance and superstition. Knowing was to know the basis of things, how things really worked. Kant's is a very tempting definition of Enlightenment. It readily brings to mind some of the great intellectual battles of the age. Biblical criticism, for example, began to ask seriously what kind of record of the past the Old and New Testaments actually provided. One thinks of the tremendous growth of interest in accounts of other, non-Christian, civilizations like Ancient Egypt, Persia and China, from which the Christian West perhaps had something to learn. Coupled with this concern with other civilizations went a genuine attempt to write 'philosophical' history, what we would now call comparative cultural sociology. This was a vast intellectual enterprise designed to show that all societies left to themselves were necessarily bound to go through the same processes of growth, maturity and decline.

Enlightenment also meant an enquiry into the means of knowing itself: what we call epistemology. The great harbinger was Locke's *Essay Concerning Human Understanding* (1690), which showed that there was nothing particularly mysterious about how the human mind came to know what it did in fact know. Sensory perception was a full and sufficient cause of the minds understanding of the world outside itself, and the senses really did understand the world about which they relayed information to the mind. The world was really there, and what the senses grasped about it was all that there was to know. Not that theology was to disappear, though it is still a matter of dispute how many enlightened thinkers were in fact atheists. Knowledge of God, and God's purpose for the world, was to be found in the world. That was why God made man in his own image by giving him natural reason. God was a rational God who meant men to understand at least pat of His purpose for mankind. Locke's own claims for his epistemology and his natural religion were characteristically modest.

Kant did not, of course, mean that the Age of Enlightenment was an enlightened age. Enlightenment's progressive discoveries had yet to make their way properly in the world. An enlightened age would come about when Enlightenment's rays had illuminated the last dark corner of the world. Nonetheless, the implications of Kant's 'dare to know' are clear enough. A better world would be created if all the discoveries of Enlightenment to date were to be spread far enough. Enlightenment had become a reforming programme at least by 1784. Kant seems to be saying that all now agree about what Enlightenment is, and that from now on we had better get on with the propagandist job of increasing the number of the enlightened. Of course, Enlightenment could know no frontiers, the 'party of humanity', as they liked to be called, was a European fellowship in civilization waiting for that civilization to be fully realized in practice.

Yet Kant's essay,' What is Enlightenment?' should give us pause. Kant assumes that the question: What is Enlightenment? is worth asking, and perhaps he assumes that it needs to be asked urgently. But Kant's own answer is suspiciously formulaic, automatic even. What Kant is doing is summing up for his age what that age already thinks about itself. He is inviting enlightened Europe to admire itself in its own gilded mirror. The essay is not smug. Enlightenment still has a long way to go before it penetrates its own world completely, but the tone of the essay is confident, and it is also intimate. We know what we are talking about. It is almost like a chairman's report about the progress of an enterprise or about the present condition of a club.

Perhaps Kant's definition of Enlightenment is not really a definition at all, but a translation or a synonym. The age is characterised as being in revolt against 'ignorance and superstition', but that formula is very wide- meshed indeed, and it is meant to be.

It is an umbrella incept so wide that as many thinkers as possible can shelter under it. After all, it creates a fine feeling inside to be told that you have disassociated yourself form ignorance and superstition, and it creates an even finer feeling to be told that you are actually in revolt against them. Thinkers from Edinburgh and Stockholm to Madrid and Naples could share in the dare-devilry of being in the forefront of human knowledge.

One of the things enlightened thinkers disagreed about was politics. The date of Kant's essay, 1784, may in itself be revealing. It comes eight years after the American Declaration of Independence and five years before the French Revolution, yet on the face of it Kant's essay is very unpolitical, and what politics it does contain is extremely conservative. Kant was a citizen of a Prussia ruled by Voltaire's favourite enlightened despot, Frederick the Great. Kant draws a very odd moral for intellectual liberty from enlightened despotism. He says that only an enlightened despot with an efficient army at his back would ever dare to allow freedom of thought and discussion to his subjects, because his possession of physical force means that at the end of the day he can be sure of his subjects' obedience. Kant's own political position can be generalized. The traditional reason given for the un-political, or supinely political, position of German bourgeoisie were politically scared, or bought off, by the princes of Germany, or that they were politically without ambition or even hope. The assumption is that because Kant came from that class, he too was un-political, unlike enlightened men elsewhere in Europe.

There is also something dated about Kant's essay. The distinction between the Age of Enlightenment and an enlightened age is meant to tell us that the Age of Enlightenment is complete, that Enlightenment has come of age, that it has really discovered all or nearly all that has to be known. No doubt there were details still to be filled in, but the intellectual programme of Enlightenment is substantially complete. For the enlightened party, the possibilities of its own given intellectual world are already fixed in 1784, eight years after the American and five years before the French Revolution. Enlightenment from then on is simply an exercise in propaganda, spreading the word in more or less recalcitrant world. Revolution came as a bit of a shock to enlightenment, especially when revolution took on a popular tone, and it is easy to see why. The Enlightenment was proud to call itself the Age of Reason but a fundamental belief in the power of reason to change men's lives was perfectly compatible with an effective contempt for the ignorant and irrational. Believing that all men at birth received the gift of reason sat easily with the counter-belief that the world's circumstances prevented most men's reason from working properly. Natural reason might work automatically in a world which was itself perfectly natural, but an important part of Enlightenment consisted of pointing out just how unnatural most of the world's instititutions and practices were. Irrational institutions and practices perverted natural reason, the habits of deference to aristocratic superiors and adherence to Catholic superstition being the chief culprits. There was therefore no contradiction in saying that most men would have to be taught to use their natural reason all over again, and granted the actual state of the world, that was a programme which stretched well into the future.

Enlightenment's view of human nature was thus optimistic and pessimistic at the same time. In substance, it did not differ very much from the old Christian view that human life was lived between the polarities of good and evil, except that Enlightenment offered a very different explanation of how good and evil got there. There was always a tendency to think that what was good about men came from themselves and what was bad about them came from society. It was left to Hume to point out in the second volume of his *Treatise of Human Nature* (1740) that there was no reason in principle, and every reason in practice, to believe that our impressions of good and evil both come from the society which surrounds us. Hume's argument was deadly, because it meant that ideas of goodness which come to us from the socializing agencies of contemporary society cannot then be used as a lever against that society, but Hume's was a lone voice amid a generalized belief that right reason could be used to find out what it was about justice that was independent of the special circumstances of a particular society at particular time and place.

Enlightenment's critics seem to be unanimous that the Enlightenment was deeply subversive. Burke was already saying that in the early 1790s, and it became the commonplace nineteenth-century view. Enlightenment came to be a byword for shallow and pretentious over-intellectualism, naively deductive, geometrical in spirit, indifferent to anything about men except their natural rights implied, without having anything very definite to put in the place of the institutions of authority it so roundly condemned. Yet we have seen that the temper of Enlightenment was reformist rather than revolutionary and even Rousseau, in a sense the most radical of enlightened thinkers, was really rather timid when it came to matters of practical reform. Revolution came to Enlightenment by surprise, and while there can be no doubt that the slogans of revolution were slogans derived from Enlightenment, it still seems surprising that Enlightenment's nineteenth-century critics should have been so insistent that revolution was Enlightenment's fault.

Various accounts of the connection between Enlightenment and revolution are on offer. The least convincing of all is the idea that there is some kind of direct connection between Enlightenment and revolution. What strikes one most about the case of the American Revolution is the extreme reluctance of the Americans to begin the revolution at all. On their own view of it, the Americans were forced into declaring independence by the intransigence of the British government in the face of demands that could be met within the existing constitutional structure of the British Empire. Again, what strikes one about the French Revolution is the subsequent revolutions in the nineteenth and twentieth centuries, many of which were long in the theoretical making and which were made by self-consciously revolutionary groups who had long prepared for the revolutionary moment. Rousseau may have made revolutionary noises, but we look in vain for a revolutionary programme in his writings, let alone revolutionary tactics.

What was it then which made Enlightenment the source of subversion? Partly, the answer lies in Enlightenment's ubiquity, and in its audience. Enlightenment was not populist. Its audience was the literate bourgeoisie and aristocracy, neither of which could be called naturally revolutionary classes. Nonetheless, a century's worth of Enlightened propaganda must have had some effect on them. Rousseau's ideas about the natural goodness of the people, the idea of natural rights, the idea that most established religion was superstition and that no authority was altogether to be trusted, may have made the enlightened public at least the accomplices of subversion. There was certainly nothing in enlightened social and political thought to prepare its eventual victims for the form the French Revolution would actually take. Whatever the Revolution was, it was hardly a feast of Lockean natural reason. Perhaps the basic mistake of Enlightenment was a psychological mistake in believing that reason could control the passions, and that out of this would come a rational system of ethics capable of sustaining the loyalty of all rational men. The idea of reason controlling the passions is at least as old as Plato, but Plato had confined it to an over-trained elite who would not be let loose to rule the world until at an advanced age when most passion was spent anyway. Enlightenment had much more sanguine hopes of reason. Only a fool could fail to reason syllogistically, and only a complete fool could fail to see the truths of ordinary common sense.

Enlightenment's critics were correct when they homed in on its belief in this universality of human nature. This line of criticism was already alive and well by the middle of the eighteenth century, but it took its full force from the events which followed on from 1789, in particular the revolutionary wars. Enlightened political theory dealt in very broad categories, and the broadest of all was 'human nature. If it was true that the French Revolution was made in the name of the rights of man, then it was impossible that the Revolution could be contained within national boundaries. The rights of man existed everywhere, and it was the revolutionaries' duty to make sure that they were respected everywhere. A new kind of war was invented, the war of liberation, in which the object was not conquest of territory but the export of liberty. A universal human nature had a universal message through the French Revolution. All human beings everywhere deserved to live under the same rationally thought-out institutions, which just happened to have come into being in France first. States and societies in the rest of Europe needed to be remodeled, and it was the attempt to do that which mad e the powers of Old Europe see Napoleon as some kind of Jacobin-at-large. The ubiquity of Enlightenment, and the revolutionary wars, taught a whole generation of European statesmen, the most characteristic of whom was the Austrian chancellor, Metternich, that from then on the political dangers facing European governments were all going to be the same. The French Revolution showed that political problems in the future were going to be pan-European problems, a view which was triumphantly vindicated in the European revolutions of 1848.

From Burke onwards, the French Revolution's enemies never had any doubt that the Revolution had been caused by, or made in the name of, a new view of the world. It was the first modern revolution because it was made in the name of an ideology, and there was no doubt that ideology's roots lay in Enlightenment. What became increasingly obvious was that Old Europe had nothing like an equivalent ideology with which to play the revolutionaries at their own game. The ancient regime had never bothered to cover itself with much theory, beyond saying that the world was organized in the way God wanted it to be, a view bolstered by selective scriptural quotation. Enlightenment's alleged godlessness soon put a stop to that, though in most states atheists were thought of by the authorities as potential subversives until well on into the nineteenth century. Those who did not recognize the authority of divine law were unlikely to have much respect for the man-made laws of states. Post-revolutionary conservative political theory was largely concerned with the construction of a counter-revolutionary ideology which was as complete in its own way as the ideology which was supposed to have been the Revolution's inspiration.

Counter-revolutionary thinkers insisted that Enlightenment must have been democratic because the revolutions which followed on from Enlightenment clothed themselves with democratic legitimacy. That this was consequence of political events rather than political theory could not matter to the Enlightenment's critics, who perhaps understood where Enlightenment's was heading better than enlightened thinkers knew themselves. Enlightenment's critique of authority of all kinds, biblical, ecclesiastical, social and political, in the name of the implicit individualism of the rights of man, was bound to have its effect when revolutionary action had destroyed duly constituted authority. Then Rousseau came into his own. If political authority was not to be royal or aristocratic, then it could only be popular because there was nothing else it could be. In the American case, democracy was tempered by complicated constitutional arrangements so that the people's hands were kept as far from the levers of political power as was decently possible in a popular republic. American democracy was to be pluralist from the beginning, because the founding fathers of the constitution of the United States were as afraid of the 'tyranny of the majority', where that majority was poor, as they had been of the tyranny of George III. The American Constitution was designed to produce a political system in which any number of 'factions' would compete with each other so that no single group would be able to dominate the political system the whole time. This was, in its turn, designed to produce 'moderate' governing decisions, because those decisions would be the result of bargaining between various interest groups and between various governing institutions. Revolutionary democracy in France was very different. There, the Revolution was made against the special interest groups, the aristocracies of the sword, the robe and the church. Rousseau-like, French republicanism was to be profoundly suspicious of special interest groups, especially when loyalty to those groups could get in the way of the moral unanimity of the Republic one and indivisible. The Republic was there to be the expression of the popular will; unlike those of America, the Republic's institutions were not there to blunt or refine the popular will, but to make possible that liberty in action, which was the mark of a truly popular republic.

It was this version of the tyranny of the majority which Enlightenment's and the Revolution's critics feared most. The mob had been a semi-official part of English politics in the eighteenth century and Montesquieu had even said that popular unrest was one of the things which helped to preserve English liberty.

The distance between the spirit of Enlightenment and the mob spirit, irrational, fickle, brutal and destructive, hardly needs to be emphasized, but Enlightenment critics hammered home the point that the spirit of the mob was bound to infect the politics of any country in which authority had come under such intellectual attack that it would begin to lose its nerve, and it was the easiest thing in the world to conflate mob politics with democratic politics.

Kant's Ethics

Imperatives, Kant noted, are of two kinds – the *hypothetical* and the *categorical*. The first kind is distinguished by the presence of a conditional antecedent, 'if' which makes reference to some condition of need or desire. If you want a drink, then go into the drawing –room'. The consequent of such an imperative states an adequate means to the satisfaction of the want or desire mentioned in the antecedent. Such imperatives can be justified objectively, without assuming any special function of practical reason. It suffices to show that, as a matter of fact, the means referred to are adequate to the end supposed. But in an important sense hypothetical imperatives neither have nor claim objectivity: for they provide reasons antecedent. Their motivating force depends upon the actual desires of the subject to whom they are addressed, and derives purely from the motivating force of those desires. According to Hume, there is no other practical employment of reason than in the generation of imperatives of this kind, that is, in a specific and limited application of theoretical reason to the calculation of the means to our ends.

But there is another kind of imperative —the *categorical*—which makes no relation to specific desires or needs, and which therefore depends for its validity on no 'empirical conditions' as Kant puts it. Such imperatives contain no 'if,' no concession to the antecedent interests of the subject. They take the form 'Do this!' or 'you ought to do this!.' The presence of the 'ought' indicates that while they may not obtain validity, they certainly claim it. And the claim here is for a genuine objectivity, independent of theoretical reason. It is a claim to bind the subject irrespective of his actual desires, to lay down, as a dictate of reason, an injunction which must be enforced.

But how is such an imperative justified? It is that Kant discerned the distinctive task and structure of practical reason. *Categorical imperatives* are justified by the invocation of certain principles of practical reason, all of which can be shown to be either derivable from or equivalent to a single governing principle. This governing principle he called the *categorical imperative*. He formulated it in several ways, the first of which was this: 'Act only on that maxim which you can at the same time will as a universal law.' This imperative is designed to capture in a pregnant philosophical phrase the persuasive force of the moral question to which all rational beings respond, the question 'What if others were to act likewise?' It was represented by Kant achieving a priori validity. It had the same ultimate status in practical reason that he attributed to the principles of the pure understanding: any further justification of it must be philosophical. It is as much a precondition of practical thought as the law of causation is a presupposition of science.

The categorical imperative was restated in various forms, and Kant claimed that these forms were all equivalent, different formulations of the same philosophical insight. Two that are of particular importance are these: 'Act so as to will the maxim of your action as a universal law in a Kingdom of Ends', and 'Act so as to treat every rational being, whether in yourself or in another, never as means only but always also as an end.' The first of these means, roughly, that in formulating a principle of conduct, a rational being is constrained to postulate an ideal. In this ideal, or 'Kingdom of Ends', what is, and what ought to be, is the same. In positing such a realm, and himself as part of it, the agent sees himself in relation to other rational beings as one among many, of equal importance with them, deserving and giving respect on the basis of reason alone, and not on the basis of those empirical conditions which create distinctions between people.

The second principle implies that a rational being is constrained by reason not to bend others to his own purposes, not to enslave, abuse, degrade, humiliate, or exploit them, but always to recognize that they contain within themselves the justification of their own existence, and a right to their autonomy. The principles between them constitute the vital Kantian idea that the moral law is founded in, and expressive of the 'respect for persons'.

Kant's claim that the three principles given are simply separate versions of a single principle, is difficult to understand: the principles do not seem the same, and indeed involve different terms in their formulation. However, Kant clearly thought that any philosophical justification of the one would be adequate to ground the others too, perhaps because they each involve some fundamental aspect of a single cluster of concepts: rational agency, autonomy, will, end. These concepts could plausibly be considered to provide the basic ideas of practical reason. It is clear that the three principles contain the seeds of a powerful and commonsensical moral point of view. They enjoin respect for others; they forbid slavery, fraud, theft, violence and sexual misuse; they provide a systematic and plausible test against which the pretensions of any particular morality could be measured and tested. Kant's claim, therefore, to have discovered the fundamental presuppositions of morality may not be entirely unfounded.

The objectivity of the categorical imperative consists in three separate properties. First, it makes no reference to individual desires or needs, indeed to nothing except the concept of rationality as such. Hence, it makes no distinctions among rational agents, but applies, if at all, universally to all who can understand reasons for action. Secondly, the rational agent is constrained by reason to accept the categorical imperative: this imperative is as mush a fundamental law of practical reason as the law of non-contradiction is a law of thought. Not to accept it is not to reason practically. Like the law of non- contradiction, therefore, it cannot be rationally rejected. Thirdly, to accept such a principle is to acquire a motive to act- it is to be persuaded to obedience. Since the imperative makes no reference to any desire, but only to the faculty of reasoning as such, it follows that if all those three claims can be upheld, practical reason alone can provide a motive for action. Hence, the ground of Hume's skepticism- which is that reason is inert, and that all practical reasoning is subservient to desire- is cut away. The moral law becomes not just universal, but necessary, for there is no way of thinking practically that will not involve its explicit or implicit affirmation. The categorical imperative has 'objective necessity' and achieves this by abstracting from all needs and desires, all empirical determinations. It represents the agent as bound by his rational nature alone.

Examples of the Categorical Imperative

Imagine that someone is fleeing from a murderer and tells you he is going home to hide. Then the murderer comes along and asks where the first man went. You believe that if you tell the truth, the murderer will find his victim and kill him. What should you do —should you tell the truth or lie?

We might call this 'The case of the Inquiring Murderer'. In this case, most of us would think it is obvious what we should do: we should lie. Of course, we don't think we should go about lying as a general rule, but in these specific circumstances it seems the right thing to do. After all, we might say, which is more important, telling the truth or saving someone's life? Surely, in a case such as this lying is justified.

Kant however, thought we should never lie, even in a case such as this. Almost alone among the great thinkers, Kant believed that morality is a matter of following absolute rules—rules that admit no exceptions, that must be followed come what may. He believed, for example, that lying is never right, no matter what the circumstances are. It is hard to see how such a radical view could be defended, perhaps, one held that such rules are God's unconditional commands. But Kant did not appeal to theological considerations; he relied only on rational arguments, holding that reason requires that we never lie.

Absolute Rules and the Duty Not to Lie

Being a moral agent, then, means guiding one's conduct by "universal laws"—moral rules that hold, without exception, in all circumstances. Kant thought that the rule against lying was one such rule. Of course, this was not the only absolute rule Kant defended—he thought there are many others; morality is full of them. But it will be useful to focus on the rule against lying as a convenient example. Kant devoted considerable space to discussing this rule, and it is clear that he felt especially strongly about it—he said that lying in any circumstances is "the obliteration of one's dignity as a human being."

The Case of the Inquiring Murderer is Kant's own example. In an essay with the charmingly old-fashioned title "On a Supposed Right to Lie from Altruistic Motives," Kant discusses this case and gives a second argument for his view about it. He writes:

> After you have honestly answered the murderer's question as to whether his intended victim is at home, it may be that he has slipped out so that he does not come in the way of the murderer, and thus that the murder may not be committed. But if you had lied and said he was not at home when he had really gone out without your knowing it, and if the murderer had then met him as he went away and murdered him, you might justly be accused as the cause of his death. For if you had told the truth as far as you knew it, perhaps the murderer might have been apprehended by the neighbours while he searched the house and thus the deed might have been prevented. Therefore, whoever tells a lie, however well intentioned he might be, must answer for the consequences, however unforeseeable they were, and pay the penalty for them. To be truthful (honest) in all deliberations, therefore, is a sacred and absolutely commanding decree of reason, limited by no expediency.

We are tempted to make exceptions to the rule against lying because in some cases we think the consequences of truthfulness would be bad and the consequences of lying good. However, we can never be certain about what the consequences of our actions will be; we cannot know that good results will follow. The results of lying might be unexpectedly bad. Therefore, the best policy is always to avoid the known evil —lying and let the consequences come as they will. Even if the consequences are bad, they will not be our fault, for we will have done our duty.

The problems with this argument are obvious enough—so obvious, in fact, that it is surprising a philosopher of Kant's stature and calibre was not more sensitive to them. In the first place, the argument depends on an unreasonably pessimistic view of what we can know. Sometimes we can be quite confident of what the consequences of our actions will be, and justifiably so; in which case we need not hesitate because of uncertainty. Moreover—and this is a more interesting matter from a philosophical point of view —Kant seems to assume that although we would be morally responsible for any bad consequences of lying, we would not be similarly responsible for any bad consequences of telling the truth, the murderer found his victim and killed him. Kant seems to assume that we would be blameless. But can we escape responsibility so easily? After all, we aided the murderer. This Kantian argument is not very convincing.

Conflicts Between Rules

The idea that moral rules are absolute, allowing no exceptions, is implausible in light of such cases as The Case of the Inquiring Murderer, and Kant's arguments for it are unsatisfactory. But are there any convincing arguments against the idea, apart from its being implausible?

The principal argument against absolute moral rules has to do with the possibility of conflict between cases. Suppose it is held to be absolutely wrong to do A in any circumstances and also wrong to do B in any circumstances. Then what about the case in which a person is faced with the choice between doing A and doing B—when he must do something and there are no other alternatives available? This kind of conflict between cases seems to show that it is logically untenable to hold that moral rules are absolute.

Is there any way that this objection can be met? One way would be for the absolutist to deny that such cases ever actually occur. The Case of the Inquiring Murderer is, of course, a fictitious example; but it is not difficult to find real-life examples that make the same point. During the Second World War, Dutch fishermen regularly smuggled Jewish refugees to England in their boats, and the following sort of thing sometimes happened. A Dutch boat, with refugees in the hold, would be stopped by a Nazi patrol boat. The Nazi captain would call out and ask the Dutch captain where he was bound, who was on board, and so forth. The fishermen would lie and be allowed to pass. Now it is clear that the fishermen had only two alternatives, to lie or to allow their passengers and themselves to be taken and shot. No third alternative was available; they could not, for example, remain silent and outrun the Nazis.

Now suppose the two rules "It is wrong to lie" and "It is wrong to permit the murder of innocent people" are both taken to be absolute. The Dutch fishermen would have to do one of these things; therefore a moral view that absolutely prohibits both is incoherent. Of course this difficulty could be avoided if one held that only one of these rules is absolute; that would apparently be Kant's way out. But this dodge cannot work in every such case; so long as there are at least two "absolute rules," whatever they might be, the possibility will always exit that they might come into conflict.

But Kant went one step further and concluded that consistency requires rules that have no exceptions. It is not hard to see how his basic idea pushed him in that direction; but the extra step was not Kant argued that no moral law, and indeed no practical reasoning, is intelligible without the postulate of freedom; he also argued that only a rational being could be free in the sense that morality requires. In what then does freedom consist? Not, as Spinoza, Hume, and many others had adequately proved, in mere randomness, not in freedom from those laws that govern the universe. The free agent, as soon as we examine the question, we see to be distinguished, not by his lack of constraint, but by the peculiar nature of the constraint, which governs him. He is constrained by reason, in its reception of the moral law. Freedom is subjection to the moral law, and is never more vivid than in the recognition of the necessity of that law and its absolute authority over the actions of the moral agent.

To clarify this thought we must distinguish action in accordance with the law from action from the law. A person might act in accordance with the law out of terror or coercion, or in the hope of reward. In these cases, the law is not his motive, and the maxim governing his action, while it may seem to be categorical, is in fact hypothetical. To act from the law is to act out of an acceptance of the categorical imperative itself, and to be motivated by that acceptance. Since this motivation is itself intrinsic to the categorical imperative, it arises from the exercise of reason alone; in acting from the law, therefore, a rational agent at the same time expresses what Kant called 'the autonomy of the will'. His action stems from his own rational reflection, which suffices to generate the motive of his act. His act is, in a deep sense, his own, and the decision from which it springs reflects his whole existence as a rational being, and not the arbitrary empirical determination of this or that desire.

Opposed to this autonomy is the heteronomy of the agent who acts not in obedience to the commands of reason, but out of passion, fear, or the hope of reward. The 'heteronomous' agent is the one who has withdrawn from the exactions of pure morality and taken refuge in slavery. He accts in subjection, either to nature or to some superior force. He may disguise his amorality by religious scruples, which lead him to act in accordance with the moral law out of hope or fear. But in himself, having failed to achieve the autonomy, which alone commands the respect of rational beings, he stands outside the moral order, unfree, subservient, diminished in his very personhood, and in his respect for himself.

Respect for Persons

The great German philosopher Immanuel Kant thought that human beings occupy a special place in creation. Of course, he was not alone in thinking this. It is an old idea: from ancient times, humans have considered themselves to be essentially different from all other creatures—and not just different but better. In fact, humans have traditionally thought themselves to be quite fabulous. Kant certainly did. On his view, human beings have "an intrinsic worth, i. e., dignity" which makes them valuable "above all price." Other animals, by contrast, have value only insofar as they serve human purposes.

Kant requires us to treat human beings as ends, and never only as means. The world 'only' is important. Kant is not saying that we should never use human beings as means at all. Human society would be impossible if people could never make use of one another. Every time I ride on a bus I make use of the driver, every time I read a book, I make use of the author. Examples could be multiplied. Kant's point is that we should not regard people 'simply' as means to our own end. All human beings are ends in themselves, and when the circumstances arise, we should treat them as such. The question is then: What is it to treat some one as an end?

Kant's choice of the term 'end' stands in need of explanation. The word normally indicates something to be brought about, something which we aim at in our actions. To regard people as ends in this sense would presumably be to aim at bringing into existence as many people as possible, and we should then have to take Kant as advocating a life of maximum sexual indulgence. This is not, what he has in mind. The only continuity between Kant's talk of 'persons as ends' and the normal meaning of 'ends' is that in both senses 'ends' are contrasted with 'means'. This however seems to leave us where we started—with the negative injunction that treating people as ends is treating them not merely as means. Perhaps we can best interpret Kant, initially, as saying that to treat people as beings who have ends. I should not treat human beings as mere means to my own end, because I should recognize that themselves have ends of their own. They have ends, because they are free, rational and autonomous agents, they can act in accordance with purposes and principles, they are persons, not things.

We can further elaborate it as the three-step argument: (i) one necessarily regards oneself as a rational being, as an end; (ii) one therefore has to accept that everyone else is justified in regarding himself/herself as a rational being and as an end; (iii) it is therefore an objectively valid principle that everyone should be treated as a rational being and as an end. The move from (i) to (ii) is justified by the notion of universality as the impersonality of reasons. The difficulty resides in the move from (ii) to (iii), for this requires an extension of the idea of universalizability. It requires a shift from 'universality as impersonality of reasons' to 'universality as impartiality' and there are no good grounds for thinking that one can derive the latter from the former. If I treat my self as a person, I may be logically committed to accepting that others have good reason to treat themselves as persons, but I am not logically committed to the principle that I should treat them as persons. A world of self-respecting egoists is not an irrational world.

We do not think that has provided any further arguments, other that the appeal to the ordinary moral consciousness. Nevertheless, the idea of respect for persons, though it lacks sound justification in Kant is an immensely fruitful idea, and we want to bring out some of its implications. We could understand the idea of 'treating persons as ends' to mean 'treating persons as beings who have ends'. Part of what this will require, then is that we should be motivated by other people's ends, as well as by our own. This is asserted by Kant when he says the ends of any subject who is an end in himself ought as for as possible to be my ends also'. This will involve a concern for the interests of others, helping to promote their happiness and to prevent their suffering. Such a conception of morality forms the substance of the utilitarian ethic, and it is by no means distinctive of Kant. There is, however, in Kant's position something much more distinctive. In so far as treating human beings as ends involve helping to promote their ends, this stems from something more basic, an attitude not just towards their interests, but also towards the persons themselves. It is the attitude which Kant tries to capture with the concepts of 'respect' and of 'dignity'.

Kant contrasts 'value' and 'dignity'. Whatever has a value, he says, 'can be replaced by something else which is equivalent'. 'Value' is thus the kind of worth possessed by all the various individual objects of desire, such as material goods, or personal qualities such as skill, or strength. Such things are essentially replaceable. If I buy a new copy of a book and immediately lose it, and if someone then gives me a replacement copy which is exactly the same as the previous one, it will be just as good as the previous one and I will have lost nothing. Moreover, different kinds of things, which have value, can to some extent compensate for one another. If I have a house with a large garden which I value, this may to some extent compensate for the smallness of the rooms, or the damp in the cellar, and I may be prepared to accept the one as the price I have to pay for the other. Likewise, with personal qualities, if I have certain intellectual skills this may to some extent compensate me for my lack of skill as a game player. Now all such things have value, because of the role which they play in the lives of persons. Persons give value to things. Persons themselves, therefore, as the source of value, must have a quite different kind of worth; 'that which constitutes the condition under which alone anything can be an end in itself, this has not merely a relative worth, that is value, but an intrinsic worth, that is, dignity' contrast to things which have value, persons, in so far as they have dignity, are irreplaceable. If I take the lives of ten people, I cannot compensate for this by bringing into existence ten more people.

As possessors of dignity, persons are the proper objects of the attitude of respect. Respect for dignity is something quite distinct from the promotion of value. Respect for other persons may require me to help promote their ends, but what it does, more basically, is to set limits on my own pursuit of my own ends. In pursuing our own ends, we are precluded from employing means, which will violate the sanctity of other persons. Respect is not the same as either inclination in being something, which we freely and voluntarily will, but it is like fear in being something to which we are subject, and which thwarts our pursuit of our own ends. It is one and the same respect, which we feel for persons as rational beings, and for the moral law as the law of reason.

We do not have room to explore here the more concrete moral implications of this idea of respect for persons. We mention only the most basic of them: respect for persons involves respect for their liberty and autonomy. An ethic which was confined to the promotion of ends would incline to paternalism. It would require me to promote the happiness and prevent the suffering of others even at the cost of imposing on them, if necessary the means to their happiness. For the Kantian ethic, on the other hand, the basic requirement is a respect for the other person's own pursuit of his or her own ends through his or her own free action, and I am to help in the promotion or those ends only in ways which are compatible with that basic respect. Accordingly, Kant lays great emphasis on the notion of human rights, as far as these identify basic freedoms, which have to be respected. In his *Lectures on Ethics* he declared:

> There is nothing more sacred in the wide world than the rights of others. They are inviolable. Woe unto him who trespasses upon the right of another and tramples it

> underfoot! His right should be his security; it should be stronger than any shield or fortress. We have a holy ruler and the most sacred of his gifts to us is the rights of man.

Whether human rights can be regarded as literally inviolable is a matter for argument. Certainly there are problems, for example, where rights conflict. If there is a 'rights for life', for instance, what are we to say of case where it may be necessary to kill one person in order to save the life of another? What a Kantian ethic will certainly insist on, however, is that rights cannot be violated simply for the sake of promoting desirable ends, whether for oneself or for others. On the other hand Kant has not provided an adequate justification of the question 'Why should I respect all human beings as persons? It remains unanswered. Kant's failure here is failure to justify the strong version of universalizability as impartiality rather than mere impersonality. Kant then, unlike Plato and Aristotle, undoubtedly furnishes a morality of altruism. Like Hume, however, he presents the opposite problem. Can he, or anyone else, provide any good reason for adhering to an altruistic morality?

Now Kant's conception of human dignity is not easy to grasp; it is, in fact, probably the most difficult notion. We need to find a way to make the idea clearer. In order to do that, we will consider in some detail one of its most important applications—this may be better than a dry, theoretical discussion. Kant believed that if we take the idea of human dignity seriously, we will be able to understand the practice of criminal punishment in a new and revealing way.

Now Kant's two principles do not constitute an argument in favor of punishment or a justification of it. They merely describe limits on what punishment can justly involve: only the guilty may be punished, and the injury done to the person punished must be compatible to the injury he has inflicted on others. We still need an argument to show that the practice of punishment, conceived in this way, would be a morally good thing. Kant regards punishment as a matter of justice—he says that, if the guilty are not punished, justice is not done. This is one argument. But Kant also provides an additional argument, based on his conception of treating people as "ends in themselves." This additional argument is Kant's distinctive contribution to the theory of retributivism.

On the face of it, it seems unlikely that we could describe punishing someone as "respecting him as a person" or as "treating him as an end-in-himself." How could taking away someone's freedom, by sending him to prison, be a way of "respecting" him? Yet that is exactly what Kant suggests. Even more paradoxically, he implies that executing someone may also be away of treating him "as an end." How can this be? Remember that, for Kant, treating someone as an "end-in-himself" means treating him as a rational being. Thus we have to ask, What does it mean to treat someone as a rational being? Now a rational being is someone who is capable of reasoning about his conduct and who freely decides what he will do on the basis of his own rational conception of what is best. Because he has these capacities, a rational being is responsible for his actions. Mere animals, who lack reason, neither are responsible for their actions; nor are people who are mentally sick and not in control of themselves. In such cases it would be absurd to try to "hold them accountable." We could not properly feel gratitude or resentment toward them, for they are they are not responsible for any good or ill they cause.

On the other hand, rational beings are responsible for their behavior and so may properly be "held accountable" for what they do. We may feel gratitude when they behave well and resentment when they behave badly. Reward and punishment are the natural expression of this gratitude and resentment. Thus in punishing people, we are holding them responsible for their action in a way in which we cannot hold mere animals responsible. By associating punishment with the idea of treating people as rational beings, Kant gave the retributive theory a new depth. In fact, Kant himself would have to agree that if they were not responsible agents, it would make no sense to resent their behavior and punish them for it. But to the extent that criminals are regarded as responsible people, without excuse, who simply choose to violate the rights of others for no rationally acceptable motive, Kantian retributivism will continue to have great persuasive power.

Respect, Impartiality and the Moral Law

There are limitations within Kant's fundamentally rationalistic conception of respect and equality. We shall discover that Kant's respect for a person involves an even more attenuated conception of the individual, as respect for the rational self becomes respect for the moral law, which the rational self exemplifies. The moral law is established as the source of all moral worth. Our sense of equality with others becomes an equal subordination before the moral law, even though Kant wants to conceive of the moral law as something which we legislate for ourselves. The sense of respect as hierarchy is made an integral aspect of out sense of respect for others, since it is mediated through our relationship with the moral law. This is only reinforced through Kant's sense that acting out of a sense of duty involves a systematic subordination of our inclinations.

We want to show that if rationality can ensure universality and impartiality, it often does this at the cost of abstracting from social, sexual and cultural characteristics, which could otherwise help us to a fuller sense of our individualities. Often it encourages us to abstract from important aspects of our experience, just as we have already seen that it encourages us to discount our emotions and desires. Kant's rationalism can only establish a sense of human respect and equality through offering us an increasingly attenuated vision of individuality. It is this which makes it difficult for Kant to develop the fuller sense of individual dignity and autonomy, which he sometimes promises us. This remains a deep tension within his moral theory. Kant's reproduces a deep distrust of human nature. As we subordinate ourselves to the moral law, even if this is a law we supposedly legislate for ourselves, we learn to distrust our needs, wants and desires as simple forms of self-love. This not only affects the sense we have of ourselves, it also deeply influences the character of our relations with others. We learn that the respect we owe to others is really a respect for the moral law.

Let us begin with identifying some of the positive aspects of Kant's position, especially as they have become integral aspects of liberal moral culture. When Kant says that 'All respect for a person is only respect for a law', he is implying that we do not have to humble ourselves before others in the respect we feel for them. We can all equally have the same relationship to the moral law, so we do not have to put ourselves down in relation to others. This is what sustains Kant's sense that we are equally capable of living moral lives. This can be seen as an aspect of the democratic strain in Kant's writings. Even if it brings home that we each have to subordinate ourselves to the moral law, at least we all have to subordinate ourselves and no one can escape from this relationship to the moral law.

In this way Kant is confirming the position of the moral law in all our lives, while making us feel that it is quite appropriate for us to subordinate ourselves to the moral law. It is this very vision of people standing alone before the moral law that makes it easier to think of this independence as something that can be guaranteed through 'abstracting' from the social and historical relations people find themselves in, so it is not compromised and brought into question through the structures of power and dependency reproduced through the development of society. The very notion of not 'encroaching upon their rights' seems to presuppose that individuals have their own individual rights which can be thought about completely independently of the situation of other. He wants to think of 'not exalting oneself over others' in these kinds of terms. This becomes something we very much have a choice about since we are assumed to be free to relate to others in any way we choose. The respect Kant discusses is limited to not interfering in the lives of others. It does not mean that we have to 'venerate others' or show 'positive reverence to them'. Rather it means we should allow others the freedom to work out their own individual lives in relation to the moral law, without the interference of others. This is why respect is called a negative duty. It this way it has become fundamental to liberal social and political theory: At a fundamental level, Kant believes that people should be free to pursue their own ends people are assumed to find satisfaction and fulfillment as long as they are left free to pursue goals and ends they have set for themselves.

Obligation and Inequality

Kant insists that love and respect are always joined together in duty, only in such a way that now one duty and now the other is the subject's principle, with the other joined to it as an accessory. Thus we shall recognize an obligation to help a poor man; but since our favor humbles him marking his welfare dependent on our generosity, it is our duty to behave as if our help is either what is merely due to him or but a slight service of love, and so to spare him humiliation and maintain his self-respect.

Kant is aware of the dangers of making someone's 'welfare dependent on our generosity'. He thinks that this threatens a person's 'self-respect' and that it can humiliate someone. So Kant says that it is our duty to act towards someone as if the obligation towards us does not rally exist- 'to behave as if our help is either what is merely due to him or but a slight service of love'. It is not clear whether this is an issue of charity or justice for Kant. This raises issues which are threatening to the very framework Kant has established for himself. It is difficult for Kant to think about the character of the obligation to the poor and oppressed, because he does not want to acknowledge that someone's welfare is dependent on our generosity. To do so would be to compromise the independence of people, which is so crucial to the presupposition that individuals are equally capable of living moral lives. It also threatens the fundamental conception of individual responsibility for morality and justice.

Sometimes it seems as if Kant is calling us to 'ignore' or 'overlook' the ways in which someone's welfare has become 'dependent upon our generosity'. There seems to be little thought that the situation itself should be transformed. It is as if the social relations of inequality and dependency are to remain unquestioned, and so not a proper object of moral assessment. Our duty seems to lie in minimizing the degree of help we are offering someone. At one level, it seems important to develop the sensitivity and understanding of others, so we realize that the ways we treat this situation of inequality and dependency can make a difference to the ways people feel about themselves. It is important to appreciate that this situation gives us the power to humiliate others and make them feel small. Kant is forced to recognize this aspect of the moral dimensions of relations of power and dependency, but he resists a fuller recognition of their moral nature that would challenge some of his deeply held moral assumptions.

At one level Kant is acutely aware that the ways we treat others can affect the ways in which they think and feel about themselves. So, it is important to think about how people are to relate to situations of dependency and inequality. Kant needs to be able to think that people are owed an equal respect of their relationship to the moral law, regardless of the social relations of power and dependency. It can make a real difference how we give to others, if we are fully alive to the recognition that they are human beings like ourselves. It can be difficult to maintain this sense, especially within a competitive and acquisitive society in which we are brought up to affirm ourselves through thinking that we are 'better' or 'superior' to others. Kant reminds us of an important sense in which we remain equal as human beings, whatever be our individual talents and abilities.

Kant did not fully acknowledge this as a social relationship of subordination, but simply as a relationship between two individuals, which very much reflected their qualities as individuals. He did not want to acknowledge a relationship of dependency that extended beyond a particular interaction. This helps explain why it is important for Kant to relate to others 'as if our help is either what is merely due to him or but a slight service of love' since this can mean that, although a poor person is dependent on the generosity of others, this does not have to compromise the independence he or she has as a moral agent. But sometimes this theoretical challenge is avoided only by almost pretending that this dependency has not been produced. This is to avoid the crucially important moral issues that are raised by issues of power, inequality and dependency. Not only do we have to investigate the different forms of this dependency, but we have to learn to think about the implications this has for our understanding of the autonomy of morals, and for our understanding of what it means for someone to be a person in his or her own right.

But the force of Kant's critical notions of autonomy and the need for people to be treated not merely as means but as ends in themselves can be used to criticize the very patriarchal assumptions of Kant's moral discussion of the relations between the sexes. At a deeper level we have to learn to criticize the fragmentation of reason and emotion which Kant's discussion of sexual relations mirrors, particularly when he says that 'the woman should reign and the man govern; for inclination reigns and understanding governs'. Within this it is all important that our rationality sets the ends we have to organize our activities around since this already presupposes the subordination of women.

Kant was to be more deeply challenged in his thinking about the relations between rich and poor. He could not just assume that riches and power die not make it easier for some people to live a moral life. He had to face the reality of the ways a person's dignity and self-respect are compromised by the social relations of power and subordination, even could not face the social relations of power between the sexes. Kant was aware of the ways in which people having needs, which required others to fulfill them challenge the very independence, which he took for granted. It means that we can no longer assume that people are equally capable of living their lives according to their own individual conception of happiness. Kant had to face the ways this conception threatened to become a mystification, where some people have control and power over the lives of others. He was forced to face the realities of human dependency though he never learned to think about this systematically. He barely faces the nature of the assumptions he makes about 'independence', 'moral autonomy' and 'self-sufficiency' even though he is a ware of the ways these very presuppositions seem to be questioned when people are forced to be dependent upon others. Kant acknowledges that the most 'natural' maxim for people to adopt is "every man for himself: God for us all." But he feels the need to question this kind of rampant individualism especially when he thinks about the needs of the poor. He does not help us understand the 'naturalness' of this maxim, but he knows that it has to be questioned even if 'it is not self- evident that any such law is to be found in reason'.

Kant was concerned to show that people shared a human dignity that needed to be affirmed in the face of an indifferent universe. Within an emerging capitalist market economy, all value was being reduced to the single measure of exchange value. Qualitative distinctions were being subverted as different commodities were brought into relation with each other through the medium of money. Everything had its price and this seemed no different when it came to the skills and talents of people. Kant perceived this as a threat to human dignity, but felt unable to challenge the reign of the commodity within the system of nature, which was essentially a realm of determination. Our dignity and moral worth could not be affirmed within the organizations of the social world, but only if we elevate ourselves above this world into an intelligible world of moral values. It was in this sense that we can recognize ourselves as ends in ourselves. We were to be continually drawn back to an awareness of our duties as moral beings. But this is to fragment our experience, as we seem left without moral terms to challenge the prevailing relations of power and subordination. It can seem as if the poor and oppressed have to learn to bear the indignities and humiliations of social life secure in the knowledge that salvation is only to be sought in a spiritual realm.

But Kant's injunction that we should not treat people merely as means but always as ends in themselves seems also to contain a stronger critique of prevailing relationships of power. Certainly, to the extent that this is reminder of how we are to relate to others in our personal relations, it can limit our moral awareness to sensitivity to how we have been treated, especially if we assume that people are always free to relate with equal respect. So for instance, we can find ourselves blaming an insensitive teacher for our miserable experience within the educational system. We think that if the teacher had been prepared to make more of an effort we would have experienced school quite differently. So we are encouraged to personalize institutional relationships of power. Within a Kantian tradition we find it harder to develop a larger framework of analysis in which the issues concern not only the teacher but the inadequacies of an educational system which trains and employs them. Within the common sense of a liberal moral culture inequalities, become individualized as people learn either, to blame their teachers or else blame themselves for not having worked harder at school. The educational system has assumed a critical position in legitimating social inequalities, especially if people are ready to accept that they have enjoyed an equality of opportunity. This means that if a man ends up as an assembly-line worker he only has himself to blame. If he had tried harder or been cleverer, he could have been the managing director. It becomes difficult to think of inequalities in different terms. People turn in on themselves, as their anger no longer seems to have a legitimate external focus. People learn to take out their frustrations on themselves or those close to them.

Social theory often is locked into an arid framework where we think it is either the individual teacher to blame or else it is the social relations of education we have to transform. We are presented with the stark alternative of either individualistic or social explanations. This is echoed in the debate between liberalism and orthodox Marxism as it is between positivism and phenomenology. We feel forced to choose between notions of individual and social responsibility, thinking that either the individual has to be held responsible for the life he or she makes, or else it is society, which is to be blamed. But these are false choices which frustrate our ability to grasp our individual experience within a social and historical network of relationships.

The uncertainties in Kant's later writings show a concern with the inequalities of social life, especially where some have more than they need while others have less than they need. This produces a form of dependency that threatens the idea that people can exist as ends in themselves. Kant seems to admit that people can exist as ends in themselves. He seems to admit that he had attempted to establish the dignity and intrinsic worth of human beings against the idea of their being treated as replaceable commodities, on too narrow a foundation. He had assumed that we could simply abstract from everyday social relations of power and subordination and guarantee our existence as beings that exist in our own right in an independently defined moral realm. But this was to appropriate a limited conception of morality and so make it impossible to explore the moral issues involved in social relations of power and subordination. Paradoxically, it would also leave him unable to explain what it meant to treat others as means. These were issues Kant did not have to face in his earlier writings since he tacitly assumed that people were independent and self-sufficient, at least as moral agents. Liberal theory has tended to sustain this earlier view.

Structured relations of dependency threaten the ability of a person to live an independent life. Kant seems to promise an enriched conception of autonomy when he seems aware of how much he had assumed material conditions of independence and self-sufficiency. Not only do we have to be prepared to consider the moral issues of inequality and dependency, but we can no longer assume that we can abstract ourselves from prevailing relations of power and subordination. Kant could free himself from a concern with the inequalities of the social world because he did not think they produced structured relations of dependency that threatened our equality before the moral law. When it became clear how issues of dependency threatened his sense of moral issues of inequality and dependency he could no longer stand from the moral issues of inequality and dependency. This also meant considering how people can be treated as means, especially if this threatened their autonomy and independence. This is hardly surprising since Kant is concerned to confirm the sovereignty of the individual against feudal and aristocratic relations of dependency. The idea of the individual as choosing his or her own ends and finding fulfillment in achieving these individual ends has to be placed historically. We have to be wary of generalizing to different historical contexts where relation of power and dependency assume a very different form.

In a society in which people can live independent and self-sufficient lives, we can also imagine that people can be free to choose their own ends. But in a capitalist society where the relations between rich and poor have been structured according to the ownership of the means of production, the issue of dependency becomes central. It also becomes more pressing to consider the various ways people are treated as means, rather than as ends in themselves. The assumption that we are free to relate to others with equal respect becomes suspect. We can no longer define our moral concerns as about how we are individually to relate to others. The Kantian definition of morality is centrally concerned with the issue of 'what ought I to do? is itself built upon a material assumption of independence and self-sufficiency. But Kant makes us crucially aware that it is when relations of dependency threaten our autonomy that we are likely to be treated as means to the ends of others who have power over us, especially if it is power over our means of livelihood. This can potentially extend the language of autonomy beyond a critique of class relations of power to include issues of gender and ethnicity.

At the same time as our moral traditions can help articulate and identify crucial aspects in our moral experience, they can also disempower us and weaken our vision. Though Kant can help us value our independence and autonomy he also makes it difficult to identify the process through which we can become ends in ourselves. As a duty-based conception of morality, Kant focuses our attention on what we might want to do assuming that our desires are inherently selfish and self-seeking. But this can make it difficult to define our own ends, especially if we do not live in a society of independent farmers but within relations of class, sexual and ethnic power and dependency. If we are anxious to do the right thing, this can extend beyond morality to different spheres of our lives. Rather than help us develop a strong and independent sense of self, we can become weakened and undermined if we are always doing what is expected of us without a sense of what we want to do for ourselves. Kant has undermined the very trust and confidence we might otherwise have developed in our feelings, desires, needs and intuitions. Rather we have often learnt to despise this part of our nature, having learnt that at some basic level our natures are not to be trusted. This has been an integral part of a Protestant inheritance that has unwittingly weakened the very individuality that it is supposedly championing. We weaken ourselves as we become suspicious of our own natures. We can become fearful of discovering our own desires, lest they leave us in too much conflict with what is expected of us.

Mill was aware of this deeper conflict in the liberal inheritance, though he tended to think it was an issue of excessive Calvinism. Mill shows the influence of a Kantian moral education and the weaknesses of a rationalist tradition that insists upon weakening our connection with our inclinations. People become incapable of any strong wishes or pleasures and generally cease to have 'either opinions or feelings of home growth'. Mill asks us rhetorically whether we think this is a desirable condition of human nature, while at the same time expecting us partly to recognize ourselves in this picture. Even though we may not like to recognize ourselves in this mirror, Mill thinks it is a condition that liberal theory has rarely faced being ready to guarantee a situation in which people are supposedly equally free to choose their own ends.

Within a moral culture in which people assume themselves to be free because they are guaranteed the freedom to choose their own ends, it becomes difficult to discover a reality of unfreedom. We discover, contrary to Kant, that as we have weakened our inclinations, we have also weakened our capacities for independent thought and judgment. Our reason does not have the kind of independent existence that a rationalist moral tradition has assumed. We can no longer take a liberal political theory at face value but need a language in which to investigate the moral realities it helps produce. The Enlightenment tradition had established its claim to human equality on the basis of an independent faculty of reason. It is because we are rational beings that we can be moral beings and so deserving of equal respect. But this tradition carried a central weakness in that it could only affirm our humanity through denigrating and suspecting our natures.

Our 'self- esteem' and 'dignity' is to be drawn solely from our moral disposition not from our needs, wants and desires. In making us experience our 'insignificance' when we think of our needs, desires, wants and feelings, this can work to undermine whatever 'esteem' and dignity' we might be able to draw from these sources. It can so easily reproduce a morality of self-denial as we negate the significance and meaningfulness of our needs and wants, emotions and feelings. We learn that we have to value ourselves by a 'low standard' when we view ourselves 'as a being of the sensible world'.

Within a Kantian tradition, we cannot accept our needs and desires, our emotions and feelings as aspects of our humanity. They exist at a level beneath our humanity, which has independent sources of its own. The fundamental demarcation between the 'natural man' and the 'moral man' can work to undermine our self-esteem in the very ways that it declares as 'unacceptable' the different feelings of anger, resentment, rage, frustration, passion, dislike and fear. It becomes easy to feel that these feelings only prove our animal nature. They simply confirm our low estimation of ourselves. This can make us feel even more unworthy, worthless and inadequate. This will end to fuel a morality in which we are anxious to prove ourselves, be it in relation to the moral law, or in terms of individual ends and achievements. At another level, we are likely to be plagued by these feelings of inadequacy and worthlessness. Because these emotions and feelings are so easily judged as unacceptable, we do our best to negate them. We banish and exile these feelings to our unconscious, barely wanting to become aware of them. This blinds us to the ways they actually continue to influence our behavior and relationships.

Many feminist critics of Kant have argued that Kant is a misogynist. Susan Mendus has portrayed Kant as an honest but narrow-minded bourgeois. Kant wrote a paper, 'Of the Distinction between the Beautiful and the Sublime in the Interrelations of the Two Sexes'. In it, he differentiates sharply between male and female characteristics and abilities. Here is a list of the ways in which Kant describes men, and the sorts of characteristics and capacities that he ascribes to them – noble, deep, sublime, surmounting difficulties, "Seep meditation, sustained reflection, laborious learning, profundity, abstract speculation, fundamental understanding, reason, universal rules, capable of principles. And here is a list of those he thinks applicable to women: delicate, beautiful, modest, sympathy, compassion, fair, charming, finer feeling, pleasant diversions, sense, sensitivity, feelings, benevolence, complaisance, particular judgements, incapable of principles.

There are a number of things which are unclear about Kant's account of women in this paper. First, it is not clear to what extent he is saying that women are unable to reason in ways that men can, and to what extent he is saying that they should not. Sometimes he explicitly picks out what he sees as female disabilities; thus he says that he does not believe the 'fair sex' to be capable of principles. At other times he writes as if he believes that women are capable of intellectual pursuits, but must not distort or pervert their femininity by pursuing them. Thus he suggests that if a woman fills her head full of Greek or mechanics, she might as well have a beard; that is to say, she will be a freak or monstrosity. This ambivalence about whether it is supposed that women are incapable of certain intellectual pursuits or whether it is supposed that they will simply spoil their femininity if they pursue them, is common both in philosophy and elsewhere.

The second thing which is unclear is whether Kant is or is not saying that women are inferior. He would himself have resisted very strongly the suggestion that he believed women to be generally inferior to men. He intended to talk about what he saw as the complementary virtues of each sex, be inferior, thought women's particular virtues', without which the world would be a bleak place. Nowhere is the embarrassment more keenly felt than in reading Kant's views on the nature of women and the role of women as citizens. The problem is not simply that Kant is dismissive about woman's status as a citizen but rather that the explicit claims made in the political philosophy conflict markedly with what Kant emphasizes that the moral principles he proposes must be applicable not simply to men, nor even to human beings, but to rational beings as such. This generates the hope that in the political philosophy women will be accorded equal status with men. Such expectations are, however, quickly disappointed, for when we reach the political philosophy, we find Kant insisting that women may be passive citizens only—never active citizens. Moreover, his reasons for insisting on this are far from clear: sometimes he gestures at reasons, sometimes he merely states baldly that this is so, but nowhere does he spell out explicitly and consistently exactly why women cannot be active citizens. He vacillate suneasily between the philosophic and the homespun, and frequently he simply appears to indulge in an unthinking endorsement of the prejudices of his day and an uncritical acceptance of the dogma of others—notably Rousseau. However, it would be wrong to suggest or imply that it is only in the treatment of women as citizens that the expectations of the moral philosophy are disappointed: many commentators have remarked upon Kant's Janus-faced attitude in his political writings generally. Thus one critic notes that, 'he [Kant] attacked serfdom and defended the exclusion of the unproperted members of society from all essential political rights almost in the same breath, in both cases in the name of reason'.

Kant's Politics

Hein asserted that an intellectual revolution started in German with the publication of Kant's. *Critigue of Pure Reason*. Marx called Kant's philosophy "the German theory of the French Revolution." Both men had perceived the revolutionary content of Kant's thought. His Copernican revolution in philosophy not only took place in the interval between the American and French revolutions, but also expressed their spirit. Indeed, Kant is the philosopher of the American and French revolutions, for he asserted the independence of the individual in the face of authority, and put the problem of human freedom at the core of his philosophy. But if he is the philosophical champion of the ideas of 1776 and 1789, he is guilty of curious discrepancy. His work has as its apex a political philosophy, which sought to justify that ideas of the American and French revolutions, but which also explicitly denied any individual the right to rebel against established authority.

Although Kant's political writings proper were all written after 1776, they were not an accidental by-product of his interest in the events of the American and French revolutions, but arose quite consistently from his critical philosophy. Kant's political philosophy had two main roots, his ethics and his philosophy of history. In his ethics, Kant sought to make explicit those a priori principles of reason, which ought to guide men in their conduct. He held that these principles ought to take the form of universal laws. While his discussions of those minimum moral principles does not in the first place belong to the sphere of politics, the close affinity between ethics and politics is indicated by the final from which Kant gives to the Categorical Imperative in his *Foundations of the Metaphysics of Morals*. He enjoins one to act as if one were a member of the kingdom of ends, which is a systematic union of different rational beings under common laws. This final formulation presents, indeed, only an ideal we ought, however, to act with a view of bringing it about. Kant's political theory like his ethical theory is derived from his idea of freedom and from the autonomy of the free rational being. In detail, Kant's conception of politics, and especially his conception of the state, is based on the necessity to safeguard the individual's external freedom, i.e., his freedom to have external possessions. In his political writings, his aim is to make explicit the a priori principles of right on the basis of which this freedom of the individual can be safeguarded. In politics as in ethics, his object is to establish those principles on which men can agree by the method of rational discussion. He therefore does not want to base his theory of politics on the principle of happiness, which makes it heteronymous, but instead on the principle of duty, which makes it autonomous. He seeks to make explicit the principles by which the political organization of a state ought to be judged and which ought to guide our political actions. This quest leads Kant to define principles, which ought to regulate political relation between the government and the individual members of the state.

Kant is often thought of as a timid philosopher who never dared to defy the political authorities. It is a fact of his career that he apparently meekly submitted to a rebuke from the civil authorities in 1793 and promised never to write on religious matters again. Most of his political works were written in the form of occasional pieces; none was written as a revolutionary manifesto. But scholars argue that Kant's writings on politics were indeed subversive. There was a thread of common vocabulary that tied many of them together. That vocabulary, in Kant's day, was clearly associated with attacks on the contemporary political system. When Marx called Kant the "philosopher of the French Revolution," he did not have in mind the "Jacobin" Kant who continued his enthusiastic support of the Revolution long after his freedom-loving younger contemporaries such as Schiller and Goethe had became disillusioned with its course. Marx's image of Kant is in fact that of the "philosopher of the bourgeoisie" in its struggle for freedom from the constraints of the feudal order. Kant's position on the rightness of revolution and similar acts is not clear. Is he saying that revolution is wrong always, or only sometimes? If the former, is it entailed by his political philosophy, or can it be rejected as an aberration? The subject is complicated by its controversial nature. There is a temptation to suppose that no one, let alone a founding father of liberalism, could possibly think that revolution is never right.

Kant wrote no single systematic and comprehensive treatise on politics, and his published ideas on resistance are scattered, sometimes repetitively, through writings spanning a decade and a half towards the end of his life. Kant's enthusiasm for the French Revolution, the American Revolution, and the Irish efforts to throw off the English yoke is well known. It earned him the unenviable epithet of "the old Jacobin" though he condemned the excesses of the Reign of Terror and the execution of the King and Queen, these events which turned many of his compatriots against the Revolution and all its works did not make Kant modify his adherence to the principles of the Revolution; and even it was believed that he was to go to Paris as advisor to Sieves. In his published works, there is only one halfhearted commendation for revolution and one passage, which excuses, if it does not justify, revolution. Kant speaks of a people's having "at least some excuse for forcibly dethroning a monarch by appealing to the right of necessity which known no law." But otherwise Kant's denial of the right of revolution is as firm and clear as his express sympathy for the French Revolution. The constitution cannot contain any article that would allow for some authority in the state that could resist or restrain the chief magistrate in cases in which he violates the constitutional laws. It is a human understanding that who is supposed to restrain the authority of the state must have more power than the person whom he is supposed to restrain; But then the latter would be the chief magistrate, not the former; and this supposition contradicts itself.

In *Perpetual Peace*, however, there is another criticism of the moral right of revolution, a criticism which is more deeply rooted in Kant's moral philosophy than in his metaphysics of jurisprudence. The previous agrument, as it were, is a legalistic consequence of the categorical impreative in the form which forbids us from acting on maxims which are self-contradictory when universalized. The new argument is derived from the form of the categorical imperative which requires us to treat human beings as ends-in-themselves, and it leads to what Kant calls the "transcendental formula of public law": "All actions relating to the right of other men are unjust if their maxim is not consistent with publicity." "The illegitimacy of rebellion," he infers, "is thus clear from the fact that its maxim, if openly acknowledged, would make its own purpose impossible and self–defeating. Therefore as a matter of political strategy the design of making revolution would have to be kept "secret" in order to be effective, and is therefore illegitimate.

In place of revolution, Kant favors evolution. The evolution of the state of a more just form of administration, Kant believes is inevitable only if there is public enlightenment and freedom of the press. The free press is the palladium of human rights. It permits the reform of the state by apprising the rulers of the dissatisfactions of the subjects, and it is to the interest of the rulers themselves that these dissatisfactions be removed, since an irrational legislation makes for instability in the government and insecurity of the rulers. Reform can be affected only by the sovereign, but it can be undertaken by him with wisdom only if he is made aware of the inequities and inadequacies of his administration.

Until this reform is effected however, the people must obey. For to disobey is to return to the state of nature and to leave it to chance, or Providence, whether the new government yet to be established will be better or worse than the one which is overthrown. Reform means progress, the metamorphosis of the state; revolution means paleness of the state, a new beginning of civil society from the state of nature without profit. That a government may have been established by an act of lawless violence does not impugn its legal authority and validity, nor reduce its claim to allegiance. Kant is willing to believe that all governments began with power, not with contract. But to inquire into the historical origin of a government for the purpose of thereby impugning its authority is itself punishable.

The sovereign or lawgiver of a people derives his rightful authority from the united people under the contract. It is as though he held his legislative authority from the perfect lawgiver, God. But his actual authority is in all probability based upon his power, with only a post facto justification of it by the ideal of the contract. There is no right to sedition, much less a right of revolution, and least of a right to lay hands on or to take the life of the chief of state. The head of the government's commands are not laws but only ordinances and decrees. The citizen is obligated to the sovereign and subject to the laws given by the sovereign. Soveveign's decrees must be obeyed by the subjects, and even if he proceeds contrary to the law, the citizens must not actively resist him except by exercising their freedom to criticize and petition for reform. But the head of the government may be deposed by the sovereign and the sovereign may modify his administration.

Various abortive forms of government arise when the legislative, judicial, and executive functions of government are confused or verged in the same moral or physical person. If the same person both makes and executes the laws-if, that is, the sovereign in himself the head of the government or the supreme judge-the system of checks and balances is not in effect, and the government is despotic. A government may be monarchial in form while republican in spirit if the sovereignty resides in the united people, and the person of the sovereign represents the interests and rights of the people.

The ultimate agency of legitimate reform in the government lies in the person of the sovereign, but there are limits even on his right to change the constitution. The sovereign cannot validly arrange a transformation of one constitution to another from an aristocracy to a democracy, for these are matters only for the collective will of the people to decide. "Even if the sovereign were to decide to transform himself into a democracy, "Kant writes, "he would be doing the people an injustice, because the people themselves might abhor this kind of constitution and might find that one of the other two was more advantageous to them."

When the sovereign allows himself to be represented in a body of deputies of the people, sovereignty reverts to the collective people; the surrender of sovereignty by the person of the monarch has already occurred, and it cannot be regained at the end of some specified time unless it is freely granted by the body of the people. This event, according to Kant, took place on May 5, 1789 when "the sovereignty of the monarch disappeared completely and passed over to the people, to whose legislative will the property of every citizen now became subject. What was not justified was, first, the surrender of his sovereignty by Louis XVI to the Estates General; and second, the execution of the former monarch-an act which "fills the soul, conscious of the ideas of human justice, with horror." But the success of the Revolution, in sprite of the illegitimacy of its beginning and the crimes which marked its effectuation, "binds the subjects to accept the new order of things as good citizens, and they cannot refuse to honor and obey the suzerain who now possesses authority." Kant's forceful denial of the right of revolution, therefore, is historically focused not against the Estates General and the successor government, but upon the efforts at counter – revolution and restoration of the Bourbons. Thus, he specifically denounces the right claimed by other sovereigns to intervene in French affairs to undo the Revolution.

It is quite clear that Kant's formalism-the notion that a legal right to rebel is self-contradictory and a moral right to rebel is unjustifiable-makes him oppose all revolutions while precisely the same formalism permits him to accept all successful revolutions of the past, especially those of 1688, 1776 and 1789. His enthusiasm for these revolutions, especially that of 1789, is made compatible with his denial of the right of revolution. Thus, Kant can distinguish between revolutions towards the better and revolutions towards the worse, though both are to be condemned. Since revolution produces an interregnum, which is equivalent to the state of nature, revolutions probably have a tendency to end in a worse government than the government, which could have been achieved by gradual reform. Political wisdom, therefore, stands on the side of reform to make the constitution better accord with the ideal of law; but "when nature herself produces revolutions," political wisdom will use them "as a call of nature for fundamental reforms to produce a lawful constitution founded upon principles of freedom, for only such a constitution is durable."

Though Kant defends the French Revelation, he never condones of the illegality and immorality of a man who makes a revolution and what might be called his higher morality. Kant will never approve the rebel who through revolutionary activity establishes a better stage of political culture as a basis for further moral development. He does not accept the doing of evil that good may result. We are not to overthrow by violence even a tyrannical government, which blatantly abuses these rights, for to do this, would conflict with a duty of perfect obligation. We are not, therefore, justified in killing a tyrant in order to preserve the lives of thousands or millions of his subjects. The most one can morally do is to expose the abuses of his power and make proposals for his reform and to disobey him if he commands one to do something immoral and to suffer martyrdom if necessary.

Kant's enthusiasm for the French Revolution is based upon his teleological conception of history, which is a forerunner of Hegel's definition of history as "the progress of the consciousness of freedom." That the final purposes of the world is moral, not eudemonistic, makes it possible for Kant to have a moral enthusiasm for the Revolution which his formalistic moral system does not justify. Had Kant's approval of the Revolution been eudemonistic, the inconsistency would have been greater. But some inconsistency remains because Kantian ethics is not adequate to resolve the painful problems of conflicting duties.

Kant's denial of right to rebel at times obscures the basic liberal intent of Kant's political thought, so that even the charge of authoritarianism has been leveled against him. The general tenor of his political thought makes it sufficiently plain, however, that this charge should not be taken seriously. It should be quite clear that these political ideas were revolutionary for his age. Even the excesses of the French revolution did not make him waver in his sympathy for the aims of 1776 and 1789. But on the specific issues of the individual's attitude towards despotic government he is not a satisfactory guide. Since the primary object of his political thought is to sketch the outlines of a republican constitution, there can be, in his view, no place for a right of rebellion, since it runs counter to the need to obey the law, the indispensable element of this constitution. This is even true of a state such as despotism, for instance, which is not governed in accordance with a republican constitution. For Kant there can never be a right of rebellion. It would be self-contradictory, since it would strike a deadly blow at the existence of law itself which alone can guarantee such a right, and thus violate human freedom.

Revolutionary activity is then condemned outright, even if it takes place in a despotic state. For if it is permissible to rebel, some third party would have to decide whether the ruler or the subjects are right and this third party, from the nature of the situation, cannot be found. The desire to possess this right of rebellion shows that the people wish to be a judge in their own case. Kant leaves no doubt of this when he writes:

> All resistance against the supreme legislative power, every kind of instigation to bring the discontent of the subject into active form, every kind of rising which becomes a

> rebellion constitute the highest and most punishable crime in the commonwealth for they destroy its very foundations.

Rebellion ran never be right; and this interdiction is unconditional, although when a rebellion has been successful it must be accepted by the subjects who are not to seek, by another rebellion, to overthrow the new government. There is only one exception to this rule: the former ruler is allowed to rebel to return to power by means of another rebellion. He has a right to do so since an injustice was done to him, but Kant qualifies this exception by saying that an injustice has not been done to a ruler who has violated the contract with his people, but adds that the people have acted illegally by seeking rights in this manner; however, he does not state whether a despotic ruler has a right to seek a return to power by means of rebellion or not.

Kant, however, knew of the role which political power plays in the realm of fact. Force is inevitable; it is part of nature; without it the state could not be founded. The antagonism, which prevails among men, suffices to make them come together under the rule of law. " Man desires concord, but nature knows what is good for the species and she desires discord." That force is instrumental in bringing about the state docs not give any individual a right to rebel against the government and to violate existing legal arrangements. Kant, differing from Rousseau, even maintained that reasoning about the origins of the supreme authority is useless and dangerous since it is liable to create a spirit of rebellion: The origin of the supreme power is practically inscrutable to the people who are placed under its authority. In other words, the subject ought not actively to probe too deeply into its origin as if the obedience, which he owes to the supreme power, was a debatable right. For, should the subject, after having dug down to the ultimate origin of the state, rise in opposition to the present ruling authority, he would expose himself to be punished, destroyed, and outlawed.

The use of force cannot be avoided, for law implies compulsion, but in a state with a republican constitution, compulsion is administered according to the general principles of Right. The right to compel is vested in the sovereign alone. This does not mean—and here Kant was arguing against Hobbes—that the ruler has no duties or that the subjects have no rights against the ruler, but that the rights of the subject cannot be enforced by the process of law. Their principal right is that of being able to criticize the government in public through writing. This right, " the freedom of the pen," is " the sole palladium of the rights of the people" While the people must suffer injustice without resisting it, they have a right to voice their opinion freely, and it is, in the long run, even their duty to do so.

In "What in Enlightenment?" Kant staked a great deal on the power of a free press to bring about enlightenment. However, things got worse for the reading and writing public. Frederick died in 1786, and with his death came a new king, totally opposed to enlightenment. In 1788 Frederick William II asserted in a cabinet order that "press freedom has degenerated into press impudence, and the book censors have fallen completely asleep."

Kant insists that all that rulers have to do is allow philosophers "to speak freely and publicly and they will indeed do so of their own accord if no one forbids their discussions." The rulers do not have to publicly admit to requesting the philosophers' advice; they can simply overhear or read the philosophers' discussions. The reason why the rulers should allow the philosopher to speak publicly is the standard one of the self-interest; the philosophers throw light on their affairs. Kant disparages the tendency of the higher facaulities of law, theology, and medicine to use their worldly power to interfere with philosophy. No danger should be expected from allowing the philosophers to speak freely because they are "by nature incapable of forming seditious factions or clubs.""Publicity" is required by public law for conceptual reasons. Justice, Kant writes, "can only be conceived of as publicly knowable." Since law or right "can only come from justice", law or right must accordingly be publicly knowable. This a "readily applicable criterion which can be discovered a priori within reason itself." Kant uses the principle of publicity to decide contested issues like the right to rebellion, the binding effect of treaties, the justification of preemptive strikes, and the rights of strong countries. In each of these cases he takes a question that had been debated by natural lawyers in other terms and uses the principles he had borrowed from the language of political writers to resolve it. In each case he believes he is elaborating a systematic politics of reason in contrast to the undisciplined compromises of the natural lawyers.

Kant's usage was not merely an uncreative adoption of the usage of the men of letters and journalism of his time. He went beyond them by integrating their vocabulary into his systematic analyses of reason and its rights and giving it the cover of his philosophy. "Public" and "publicity" became such effective weapons for him precisely because he could not use them in such a presumptively innocuous and no controversial way. Although it appeared on the surface that he was writing unobjectionable pieces or elaborating schemes for perpetual peace based on abstract principles, he was actually subtly appropriating and legitimizing the vocabulary of opposition to the ruling princes. The revolutionary Kant wrestled with Kant the reformer. When he militantly insisted that "the rights of man must be held sacred," he could not help but go on to say, "One cannot compromise here and seek the middle course of a pragmatic conditional law between the morally right and the expedient. All politics must bend its knee before the right..." a true maxim whose meaning, he spelled out as "Let justice reign even if all the rascals in the world should perish from it" –was for him "a stout principle of right." But when he thought of abstractions as the motive force of human action, he had his hesitations. "Very few people act from principles, and that is good; the more general the principles are and the more steadfastly a person adheres to them, the more damage is done." More than that, there was on occasion a distinct tone of aversion in his attitude towards "general philanthropy."

Kant's dilemma deepened. There was always a small strain of the Jacobin in him, and one wonders whether he had ever heard the rumor that he had accepted an invitation from Sieve to come to Paris as his advisor. The root of the dilemma was in an uneasy association between the revolutionary category of the perfect and the political imperative of reason. Kant had only contempt for what he thought of as mindless empiricism and practicality. Confronted with the ills and miseries of a defective social order, he put an urgent question: "How can they be remedied as soon as possible?" Reconciliation might have been a duty of man, but he was quick to insist that it not be confused with "the weak toleration of wrongs which renounces stern measures." Yet here, too, a tension recurred in him between passion and prudence, between principle and practice.

One of Kant's friends has recorded that political matters were not to be mentioned in his study, only at table could they be discussed; then from his table, as another friend reported, "a cosmopolitan and free thinking philosopher watched the experiment which was to realize the idea of a perfect constitution demanded by reason with the same pleasure as a scientist has in looking upon an experiment which is to corroborate an important hypothesis." With whatever wisdom he extracted from the lessons of experience he sought to disengage social ideals from utopian chimaeras, to salvage a faith in the perfect from the dismal failures of brave human effort, and to maintain his optimism about progress in the face of the snail's pace of destiny.

Kant, the philosopher of the enlightenment could not bring himself to blame those who had begun to despair of the health of humanity, its progress towards the better, and other Enlightenment ideals. The utopians loved humankind too much, and the revolutionaries loved men too little. Kant tried to resolve his difficulties by revising his utopian longing and reducing his revolutionary commitment. He made a distinction between millennium and utopian. He defended the reasonable dreams of More, Plato, and Harrington, but separated himself from the pious enthusiasm for "a renovated world after this one will have perished in flames." He vindicated the devotion to "distant aims" and, indeed, "the conscious expectation of the future" as the decisive mark of humanity; but he disdained the confounding of man's true hope with an uncultured and instinct-ridden wish for some form of paradise. Thomas More would have understood. Kant made sure to point out that in the achievement of a universal civic order "with the greatest freedom" what would emerge would be a society "in which there is mutual opposition among the members..." more than that, any "complete solution" is impossible, for "from such crooked wood as man is made of, nothing perfectly straight can be built".

True, in the bitterness Kant had come to feel about the costly revolutionary experiment of his own day, he became persuaded that it was "rash" to propose dreams and, indeed, "culpable to abolish what presently exists." He who had confidently announced that "the ultimate destiny of the human race was the greatest moral perfection" now felt that "we must not hope too much from men in their progress towards the better." He was reluctant to face the mockery of politicians who took "the hopes of man as the dreaming of distraught minds." Yet, as he wrote, "it is sweet, however, to imagine constitutions corresponding to the requirements of reason." utopian ideals were not "empty chimaeras"; and he held the perpetual approaches to their consummation not only thinkable but obligatory. What was to remain throughout as his constant personal guide was, in a happy phrase, "the compass of reason."

Kant begins by puzzling over the question: "What have we to expect of the future? Continual progress or continual regress?" He was tempted to see only the farcical aspect of "all the doings on our globe." And even if it came to command human enthusiasm and sympathy, political zeal and even moral greatness, Kant was convinced—both by "reading the signs of the day" and by facing "the mixture of good and evil in man's predisposition" –that mankind's progress in the course of history would proceed "gradually, not by revolution but by evolution." Kant himself once noted the two most maniacal elements that had been gaining ground in a Europe badly befuddled by "loquacious ignorance" and "airy possibilities": namely, faddish French omni science and systematic German fanaticism. He felt that perhaps for the moment "disdainful silence" would be "more appropriate toward such madness.

Kant had evidently clarified his political position in an article which reconsidered "empty ideals and philosophical dreams—in short, that what sounds all right in theory has no value in practice. He felt certain that "after many failures reason will emerge as victorious"; he still counted on "human nature," for he could not and would not believe it to be "so swallowed up in evil that all respect for rights and duties should be quite extinguished in it." Yet the horror of the violent purge remained; and he was later to write:

> No pretended good intention can wipe off the stain of injustice in the means applied. And if it is to argue that the whole earth would still be in a lawless condition if those who introduced laws had shied from using violence, this is still no excuse. Nor is it an excuse for political revolutionaries that when constitutions have degenerated, the people must be allowed to reform them by force and to be unjust once and for all in order to establish justice later more safely.

Could a philosopher, even if he wanted to change the world, to any more under the circumstances than interpret it and criticize it? Kant was under no simple-minded illusions about the delimited intellectual task.

> That kings should philosophies or philosophers become kings is not to be expected. Nor is it to be wished, since the possession of power inevitably corrupts the untrammeled judgment of reason. But kings or king-like peoples, which rule themselves under laws of equality, should not suffer the class of philosophers to disappear or to be silent, but should let them speak openly. This is indispensable to the enlightenment of the business of government.

The lessons of More's caution, Erasmus' fearfulness, and Spinoza's silence were not lost upon Immanuel Kant. His philosophical attempts to "stray beyond the limits" ran similarly afoul of royal Prussian edicts on orthodoxy and censorship. The courageous effort to revise the conventional interpretations of existing doctrine in the light of reason earned only the "great displeasure" of Frederick William who, in 1794, wrote sternly from Berlin. It was an "abuse of philosophy" to distort and debase "certain fundamental doctrines of Holy scripture and Christianity." The King was disappointed: "We should have expected better things form you. You must yourself realize how irresponsible you behave against your duty as a teacher of youth and against our well-known sovereign intentions." The royal admonition was ominously straightforward: "In case of continued insubordination, you must unfailingly expect unpleasant consequences." Indeed, the King was pressing his officials to institute proceedings against Kant, and expressed his dissatisfaction with the mildness and the slowness of the censorship.

Kant responded, as he admitted, "most submissively." He gave promises of "obedience" and of "not becoming guilty again," as a "most faithful subject." He then in his 71st year promised: "I shall in future completely desist from all public lecturers or papers concerning religion, be it natural or revealed." Kant had tried to work out, in the face of so many difficulties in truth-telling, a personal principle of compromise. "The loss of self-respect, which arises from the consciousness of an insincere mind, would be the greatest evil that could ever befall me, but it is quite certain that it will never happen...It is indeed true that I think many things with the clearest conviction and to my great satisfaction, which I never have the courage to say. But I will never say anything which I do not think". And in Kant's unpublished papers there is the following remarks of ultimate explanation:

> To revoke and deny one's inner conviction is vicious and cannot be demanded of any person, but to remain silent in a case like this is a subject's duty, and while everything a person says must be true, it is not his duty to proclaim publicly all that is true.

Critics have not refrained form the contemptuous note. Nietzsche writes that Kant is an old Tartuffe. Others stress Kant's half-hearted courage and the conformity to authority of a careful old man. The old man of seventy might have calmly awaited the "unpleasant consequences" threatened by the order. The Berlin authorities could scarcely have done more than to prohibit his writings and perhaps to withdraw the increase of his salary. Nevertheless, Kant was not of the stuff of which martyrs are made. And he might comfort himself with the thought that he had already said all that was most essential. So he chose what was in accord with his nature, silence and peace. Of course, if he had declared, like the seventy-year-old Socrates in a similar position, that he had a higher mission in the world than the professorship which had been entrusted to him by the Royal Prussian Commission, that to this mission of teaching truth and combating error and lies he would not and could not become untrue, then a page of his life history, and a page of the history of German philosophy, would have been more splendidly distinguished than is now the case. Here then, was a revolutionary and a reformer, a utopian and a gradualist, a militant and yet a moderate, an endlessly critical philosopher who knew the temptations of ideology and who even in the bitterness of its deceptions retained a feeling of fellowship for those who wanted to associate imagination with power, for those who "dreamed the sweet dream."

Kant's standing as a political thinker has been substantially enhanced in the English-speaking world. Since the appearance of John Rawls's book *A Theory of Justice*, more and more scholars are willing to rank him among the leading figures in the history of political thought. John Rawls's important and much discussed treatise is indebted to him, and that has certainly made an impact. The secondary literature on his political thought has grown appreciably, and not only in Germany where research on Kant flourishes as always. Nevertheless, in view of this rowing interest, it is perhaps justifiable not only to rise some new issues but also to elaborate some of the features which are grouped under the following headings: 'the nature of rational discourse in politics'; 'the nature of political judgment'; 'property as the basis of the legal order'; 'morality and politics'; 'the republican constitution: representation and the separation of powers'; 'Kant and the French revolution'; 'Kant's rejection of the right of rebellion'; 'the rejection of the right of rebellion and twentieth-century totalitarianism'; 'the limits of obedience to government'; and 'Kant's argument against world government'.

Kant states that, in all its enterprises, reason must subject itself to criticism. Critical investigation is open to all, and reason's status can impose no restrictions on it. For the very existence of reason is based on freedom and therefore rules out any kind of despotism. The idea of freedom itself, although a transcendental idea belonging to the realm of nominal, is indeed the only one for whose existence we can find evidence in the phenomenal world, namely in our ability to act morally. Consequently, any discussion of conflicting views must take place in an arena where freedom prevails. Since reason must always be open to argument, it must not seek to subject itself needlessly to censorship—that would be folly. Nor ought it be subjected to it—that would be unjust. Reason must be able to carry out its task of seeking to refute all statements incapable of being justified at the bar of the rightful principles of politics.

The court before which disputes ought to be argued and settled is that of reason itself. It is not, however, a court of justice where a judge can hand down a verdict from above, but rather one where arguments are examined and a conclusion is reached by the exercise of thought. Reason must seek to establish the first principles of politics and arrived at by the use of reason, will prevail. Only by way of discussion before the court of reason can we avoid war. By turning away from reason, particularly by the use of force, at best a temporary truce can be achieved; for any peace which results from the victory of one of the contending sides is no real peace at all, but an armistice leading to further endless wars.

By the right use of reason, disputes are settled in a different way. They are resolved by argument in a manner practiced in a court of law. It is a continuous and consistent mode of arguing and seeks to go to the root of the disputes by unearthing there underlying principles. It is 'an open-ended commitment to reasoned debate'. It is, indeed, our moral duty to discover the better argument and, once we are convinced by it, to concede its rightness. Thus, reason is able to establish perpetual peace which, as Kant emphasized, is not a definitive condition ever likely to be attained on this earth, but a goal to be striven after and approximated to ever more closely.

Kant's metaphorical use of the terms 'war' and 'peace' in the *Critique of Pure Reason* foreshadows the thrust of his political thought which he develops more fully in the political writings. It makes clear that, according to the principles of reason, war, or indeed the use of any coercion except a legal order, is an illegitimate instrument of politics. Political problems cannot be settled by force, and the use of force can be sanctioned by law only when the principles according to which coercion is to be exercised by the state have been settled by rational argument. Consequently, the primary principles of politics have to be defined. Otherwise, a dogmatic approach to politics prevails, and this amounts to despotism.

Discussion before the court of reason entails publicity. It must be freely and equally open to all. This implies toleration, which, according to Goethe, was the watchword of the age for the best minds of the day. But Kant's conception of toleration does not spring from contemporary fashion; it is rooted in the very core of his critical philosophy. But communication ought also to be based on an attempt to attain truth and to avoid falsehood. For it is not enough to communicate one's thoughts in public—falsehoods can, after all, be spread widely by shouting them loudly and repeatedly the argument must be open to public criticism of the most rigorous kind. Public communication also means that any pronouncement based on an authority other than reason can be scrutinized and criticized by those who are not subject to that authority. Kant also argues against falsehood, prejudice, zealotry, misguided enthusiasm, superstition, dogmatism, confused thinking and irrationality of any kind; but be does not seek to have irrational or intolerant views suppressed. They must, of course, be rigorously and publicly criticized. On the other hand, the lawful use of reason must be protected.

There must, then, be standards for the proper use of reason. In the *Critique of Judgment* Kant sets out three maxims on which public discussion ought to be based. The first is the maxim of 'unprejudiced thought' or 'reason which is never passive'. It requires one to think for oneself, that is, to use one's reason independently.

The second maxim is that of 'enlarged thought" which requires us to overcome our narrow approach to the understanding of any matter so that we may acquire 'the personal conditions of our judgment, which cramp the mind of so many others, and reflect upon our judgment from a universal point of view which we can do only by adopting the point of view of others'.

The third maxim is that of consistent thought. It is 'the hardest to attain'. Indeed, to attain it we have to combine the first two maxims and observe them so steadfastly that they become second nature to us.

The public use of reason can provide a yardstick by which we can judge whether and to what extent political arrangements are moving towards a just political society. Moreover, it is the only way in which the standards set by reason and determine whether a state is governed in accordance with just principles of politics. It is indeed a moral duty for men to learn to use their reason independently and to refrain from coercing others arbitrarily in so far as they fail to do so, they have not yet achieved maturity and are guilty of lacking the spirit and courage to do what they ought to do. It is wrong, in principle, for anyone, particularly for a ruler, to deny anyone else the right to achieve maturity. Undoubtedly, when Kant writes about the rights of individual he has, like many of his contemporaries, a very narrow conception, from the point of view of our age, of what kind of individuals can be expected to achieve maturity and autonomy of political judgment. To exclude the majority of the population, wage-earners, employees of any kind, convicted criminals, and all women, reveals a regrettably myopic view of human capacities, though it must be conceded that, in principle, Kant believes that everyone should have the opportunity to achieve independence. But nowhere does he suggest that women have this innate, inalienable capacity. That this restriction is unacceptable today need hardly be stressed.

Kant's principal concern in politics was with the individual—and here he expresses the conviction of the Enlightenment that all individuals should have an equal right to live freely and independently. From Rousseau, he had learnt that it was a duty 'to honor mankind' and one could do so only if one sets about restoring the rights of humankind. And that was a duty for everyone. But rights have to be safeguarded, and only the law can safeguard everyone's rights. But law implies coercion. For Kant, the problem of political theory is how to legitimize coercion, and that means discerning how law can be combined with freedom. In order to accept this system as legitimate, citizens must know that all laws are public and can be scrutinized in public by everyone without their incurring the risk of being oppressed, persecuted or even killed by the rulers. On the other hand, we must also realize that, by not obeying the law, we violate everyone's innate and lawful freedom and everyone's fundamental right to live in civil society.

All this also implies that men have inalienable rights. In a state of nature, the war of all against all may prevail, but in state men live under law. Men are free, equal and self-dependent. This statement is derived from the idea of freedom. Each free person must also be self-dependent. The idea of freedom entails the individual's autonomy, for it postulates the individual's power of exercising his independently, uninhibited by improper constraint. Kant thus starts his enquiry into politics from the standpoint of the individual. This view reflects his emphasis on the need of the free individual to make decisions, a view, which he had propounded in his writings on ethics. The political freedom of the individual can be understood only in terms of legal arrangement guaranteeing the freedom of all individuals. But Kant states the political freedom in a negative manner. He does not consider it to be the purpose of politics to make people happy. Happiness is subjective. He thus strongly condemns utilitarianism in politics, just as he objects to utilitarianism in pure ethics. This argument, of course, does not mean that he does not wish people to be happy. It only means that political arrangements should not be organized in such a way as to aim at promoting happiness, but that they should permit men to attain happiness in their own way.

Kant realizes, indeed, that it is necessary for the ruler to give such laws and act in such a manner that the subject will not seek to destroy the state and to overthrow the system of laws. For this purpose, men must be treated as ends and not as means. A genuine paradox, the paradox of political freedom, appears to arise. Man's freedom can be safeguarded only by his submitting to coercion; for law presupposes coercion, and thus an infringement of the individual's freedom. Rousseau saw this paradox clearly when he stated at the very beginning of the *Social Contract* 'Man is born free, and everywhere he is in chains'. He blamed society for this state of affairs. Kant agrees with him in considering this act of coercion to be a result of man's membership of civil society, of his citizenship of the state, but he solves the paradox by seeing it as a necessary condition of civilization. He resorts to the following explanation. We are free only in so far as, in the case of a conflict of interests, we obey the law to which we would have agreed, i.e. we submit only to coercion which is legally exercised, on the basis of public law given by the sovereign authority. The sovereign ought thus to be obliged to respect the laws which he has given. Kant here differs from Hobbes for whom the sovereign is above the law; law is the sovereign's command to the people. Man, according to Kant, preserves his freedom by remaining his own law-giver. In principle, every subject thus participates in all legislation as a fellow legislator, and the ruler when legislating ought to respect this right of his subjects. This solution ensures freedom and security for all. Political freedom, then, is independence from coercion by another will.

The second principal right equality requires that men must be equal before the law; legislation must not make an exception nor must the law be administered to allow for exceptions. Kant attacks the entire heritage of feudal privilege, a foremost contemporary issue. He also rules out in principle slavery or an inferior political status for a citizen. But he thinks of political equality only, and does not at all consider the question of economic equality. He does not, however, ignore economic issues entirely. He asserts the right of man to own property. He even goes further; for he makes economic independence a criterion for participation in political affairs.

The third principal right, independence requires that each citizen must have a right to participate in the government. He ought to do this not directly, but indirectly by the exercise of the vote. Each citizen must have one vote, however, large his estate may be. No one must have more legislative power than has been agreed to by a law concerning the delegation of legislative power. But while every one is free and equal and ought to enjoy the protection of law in these respects, not every one has a right to participate in the making of law. Kant, if judged by modern criteria, here appears to depart from his own enlightened standpoint. Although in many ways he was ahead of his time, he was not so in all respects. He is still, not surprisingly perhaps, profoundly steeped in eighteenth-century traditions. He may be the philosopher of the American and French revolutions, but it should not be forgotten that the former was essential a revolution of landowners and the latter a revolution of the bourgeoisie. So Kant, perhaps understandably, differentiates between men of independence and those who have none. He classes those who are independent as active citizens and those who are dependent as passive citizens. Only active citizens have a right to vote and to legislate. Women are, on principle, disqualified. But any legislation should always be enacted and carried out as if the passive citizens too were participating, for, inherently, they have the same political right as active citizens. The requirements for independence are, for him, economic. A man must not be dependent on any one else economically, as a servant or as an employee, for otherwise he cannot freely and independently take part in politics. No self-dependent citizen untainted by crime or insanity can abdicate the duty of participating in legislation. He cannot relinquish this duty even if he were mistakenly to find the spectacle of politics abhorrent and beneath his dignity. These three rights of freedom, equality and self-dependence show that, in a properly organized state, men can find security and justice. Kant differs from Rousseau, since he believes that the state of nature is not a state of innocence. Thus, man is not corrupted by society. On the contrary, society has civilized him. Kant rather agrees with Hobbes that the state of nature is the state of a war of all against all.

What is therefore needed is a collectively universal will that alone can give security to each and all. Consequently, everyone has to restrict his freedom so as to make possible the establishment of such a supreme power and to avoid collision with the freedom of others. Kant, following the tradition of his age, uses the analogy of the social contract to explain this existence of the state governing a people by a system of civil law. For Kant, however, the social contract must not be considered a historical fact. On this point, he is quite unambiguous. Any such conception would be fraught with peril; for it is likely to encourage disobedience of, or even active rebellion against the prevailing law. The social contract must therefore be seen as a practical idea of reason. It is a practical idea of reason in so far as it can be applied to the world of practical affairs or to experience, i.e., the phenomenal world; for it allows us to say something about the kind of state which ought to exist, i.e., the state which ought to be established in accordance with the principles of right. The social contract is thus a criterion of political judgment, but it should not lead us to go into historical reasons for drawing practical conclusions. The idea that men have made a contract to establish the state means rather that they have been prepared to submit their own personal will in matters external to them to a universal will. This universal or general will is, of course, the will of reason. It is not the united will of all, even if this were to be found so in fact, nor is it the will of the majority. Kant is again close to Rousseau, but again, where Rousseau is ambiguous, he is decisively clear. He transfers the conception of the general will which might be embodied in the government, to an idea of reason which entitles the government to exercise the power of political action, to coerce others according to universal law. He differs cardinally from Hobbes, who ruled out the question as to whether the sovereign could make just or unjust laws for in Hobbes' view, there can be no such moral yardstick to measure existing laws.

According to what principles, then, should a rightful government be organized, even if completely just political arrangements can never be attained? Kant differentiates between the republican form of government, where the executive is separated from the legislature, and the despotic, where it is not. Republican government is impossible in a democracy; for a democracy is necessarily despotic. A power is established where all rule. It means that all take decisions about all and also against any one who decides to differ from the prevailing majority view.

Republican government, however, is rightful government. A republican constitution is established in accordance with the principles of right if powers independent from one another are set up. First, there is the sovereign in the person of the legislator who represents the united or general will of the people, which, in theory, is the will of reason. The ruler, the government or the executive, cannot be the legislator. Finally, neither the legislator nor the ruler can be the judiciary. For interpreting the law and for making individual judgments, an individual justice is required. For this function, a special representative of the people—a court of law or a jury—has to be appointed.

The legislative sovereign power, according to Kant, ought to be vested in the people. He also states that, in practice, it can only be approximated to the ideal. The most that we can hope for is that this power will be exercised indirectly by representatives of the people. It cannot be expected that all should give laws and agree on legislation. All that can be attained is apparently a representative assembly, which will legislate for all. The people as a whole must be expected to agree to this procedure and accept the legislation.

Kant does not specify in detail how the representatives of the people ought to exercise their power, nor does he say according to what principle they should be chosen. He does not advocate the rule of the majority, and certainly not its unfettered power to legislate, which would have appeared to him only another form of the arbitrary will in action. He does, however, state explicitly that all should combine to give laws and that legislation is to spring from the united will of all. But he criticizes the constitutional practice prevailing in eighteenth-century Britain. For British constitutional monarchy appeared to him merely as a device designed to cloak an autocratic rule. He warns that the danger of a monarch becoming a despot is particularly great, because one man is more easily tempted to become a tyrant. But he also states that where the government is in the hands of the smallest number of people and the representation is at its widest, republican rule will be most easily a assured. He even appears to prefer a monarchy to an aristocracy. Yet he appears to be somewhat obscure on this point. The general drift of his argument is clear, however; his use of the term 'republican' shows us that he is basically anti monarchic. And because he knew of the dangers of one man abusing his power, he. like Rousseau, did not believe that the united will of all could well be represented by one man. There can also be no doubt as to his basic plea for separation of powers and his conviction that the sovereign authority should rest in the people or its representatives. And he is equally clear in his demand that the sovereign must not own any private property so that he may be unable either to exercise private power or to be affected by private interest.

The fundamental element of any republican constitution, however, is respect for law. The subjects as well as the ruler and the sovereign must possess this respect. But the subject or citizen must rebel neither against the laws, which the sovereign has made, nor against the regent who carries them out. This attitude is perhaps surprising, especially if we consider Kant's attitude to the French revolution. It follows, however, from Kant's general conception of the supremacy of law, for to rebel against the supreme power would amount to disregarding, or even overturning the law. This is evil. Kant is most outspoken on this point.

The sovereign has the right to dismiss the ruler, but he has no right to punish the dismissed ruler for actions committed as ruler. Judicial action against and punishment of the ruler are worse than the assassination of a tyrant. In fact, the judicial punishment of a ruler, such as the regicide of Charles I or Louis XVI, is the worst crime imaginable. It is a perversion of the idea of the law itself.

Kant's Theory of State

Kant's argument has been the subject of considerable criticism and has been characterized as both paradoxical and weak. Interestingly, Howard Williams has argued recently that Kant had little alternative but to use a weak and paradoxical argument in order to reconcile the spirit of his moral philosophy with the realities of political authority. Like many Kant scholars, Williams regards Kant as the preeminent champion of individual freedom in the liberal tradition. According to him Kant's defense of freedom 'must center on the individual'. Williams understands this to mean that Kantian freedom 'consists of the individual's freedom to choose and to seek to pursue his own ends in a way that his own individual conscience dictates'. Williams believes that 'the use of force contradicts the autonomy of the individuals'. As Williams sees it, the paradox in Kant's argument runs deep. To escape coercion and the threat of coercion in the state of nature, one must institutionalize coercion in the form of the state. He says: 'Freedom from external coercion is the end but, paradoxically, the possibility of external coercion is also the means'. So, the Kantian state, as envisioned by Williams, is a 'necessary evil' required to safeguard individual freedom. The state's necessity should be clear; it is evil, however, because political authority is inconsistent with the notion of autonomy that Kant develops in his moral philosophy.

Patrick Riley, however, is somewhat clearer on the matter. He also seems to think that there is a tension between Kant's notion of individual freedom and his defense of the authoritative use of coercion by the state. Riley argues that Kant intended to resolve the tension by holding that the state is of instrumental worth since it restricts 'what others can do to me by the willful exercise of their wills' in ways that leave me free to perfect myself as a moral agent and to pursue becoming a good will. Riley thinks the reconciliation between morality and politics is achieved, for Kant, by admitting the prudential necessity of the state; it is through the state and its authorized use of coercion that human beings can create for themselves an environment in which a commitment to moral development is possible. Yet Riley's position reduces to something resembling Williams' view of the Kantian state. Both see the state in Kantian thought as a concession to the violent and unruly disposition of humankind and both seem agreed that this generates a tension between Kant's moral and political philosophy. The difference, of course, is that while Williams interprets this vision of the Kantian state as a necessary evil, Riley interprets it terms of instrumental worth.

These interpretations of Kant's political philosophy add additional support to the common view that Kantian morality distances us from political life. The uncompromising autonomous moral agent must become a 'philosophical anarchist' who forsakes all political authority at least in theory if not in practice. The need for political authority must then be regarded as something of an embarrassment to moral beings who must face the weaknesses and the failings associated with their phenomenal existence. Political necessity requires something more than a surrender of some of one's rights, as it does for Hobbes; it requires the partial alienation of oneself through the partial sublimation of one's autonomy.

One wonders, too, how Kant could have regarded the state as a necessary concession to humankind's wayward nature and still have insisted that justice is a 'pure concept' and that the state is a 'necessary idea of reason'. Nevertheless, it does seem that Kant entertained something like the view Williams ascribes to him in the early stages of his critical philosophy. In the *Critique of Pure Reason,* Kant held that, 'as Hobbes maintains, the state of nature is a state of injustice and violence, and we have no option save to abandon it and submit ourselves to the constraint of law, which limits our freedom solely in order that it may be consistent with the freedom of others and with the common good of all'. Here it seems prudential reason counsels in favor of escaping the ugly environment of a state of nature by surrendering at least a portion of our freedom and having recourse to a system of civil laws and civil authority.

Further, Kant says that acceptance of a social contract means that 'all the people give up their external freedom in order to take it back again immediately as members of a commonwealth, that is the people regarded as the state'. He elaborates:

> Accordingly, we cannot say that a man has sacrificed in the state a part of his inborn external freedom for some particular purpose; rather, we must say that he has completely abandoned his wild, lawless freedom in order to find his whole freedom again undiminished in a lawful dependency, that is, in a juridical state of society, since this dependency comes from his own legislative will.

The point here is hardly equivocal; there is no restriction on one's freedom in civil society. There is no trade-off between freedom and some desired good like security. Instead, one retains one's freedom 'whole and undiminished'. One way to understand Kant's meaning here is to suggest that he relied on the voluntary act of consenting to join civil society as the means for reconciling freedom with political authority. One might say that because an individual voluntarily accepts civil society, he has not restricted his freedom. A person who makes a promise, for example, is obligated to keep his word; he is not free to go against his promise. But because the promise is made voluntarily, the promiser's reluctance to go against his promise does not count as a restriction on this freedom. It is true that Kant made much of the role of consent in his theory of external freedom. In *Perpetual Peace*, for example, he actually defined external freedom in terms of consent saying: 'My external and rightful freedom should be defined as a warrant to obey no external laws except those to which I have been able to give my own consent.' We should note that, if Kant's political thought is to square with his moral philosophy, the consenting subject must be considered a Kantian moral agent. Such a subject is bound by the moral law to choose according to the requirements of that law.

So the concept of moral freedom follows from the basic spirit of Kant's moral philosophy and it is the only concept of freedom that fully expresses what it means for a person to be free according to the strictures of Kantian moral thought. It follows that the use of force to compel A to honor B's moral freedom does not interfere with A's moral freedom nor obstruct A's ability to act autonomously. For if A acted autonomously and followed the moral law, he would not interfere with B's moral freedom in the first place. This should no longer seem mysterious and, consequently, Kant's view of the relation between freedom and authority should no longer seem contradictory or paradoxical. There is an ambiguity in Kant's discussion of interference with one's external freedom that deserves some comment. Autonomy can be understood as the ability of the will to be self-determining according to the dictates of reason. As such, autonomy refers to an internal state that can be obstructed only by such things as killing the autonomous subject, hypnosis, or perhaps by some forms of mind control. Putting a person in jail, on the other hand, restricts one's external freedom but does not obstruct one's internal state of autonomy. Nevertheless, it is just this sort of restriction of external freedom that Kant considered inconsistent with individual autonomy. It might seem then that Kant needs an argument to show that restrictions on external freedom actually do obstruct one's autonomy. Because moral freedom is viewed by Kant as an 'innate right'– that is, because the idea of moral freedom establishes the possibility of 'juridical relations' between persons – each must also enjoy the authority to defend this right to freedom. For Kant, the idea of having a right carries with it the authorization to defend this right against the transgressions of others.

Kant accords the state the usual taxing and police powers, and he even permits a degree of state sponsored redistribution of wealth 'in order to support those members of society who are not able to support themselves'. Additionally, he allows the state certain emergency power that are arguably offensive to a Hobbesian sense of freedom. Kant justifies the exercise of such state powers by appeal to the right of supreme proprietorship and the right of preservation. The former establishes the conditions under which private ownership of property is possible. Kant held that unless we conceive of the state as having the right of supreme proprietorship, the state would have no right to support individual claims of private ownership. We must concede this right to the state as 'the chief necessary condition of the possibility of having external things as one's property'. Because we must concede this right to the state, we must also acknowledge the state's right to tax and redistribute those resources over which it has proprietary control. Since Kant did not hold that there is a moral right to hold property independent of political authority, the taxing and redistribution authority of the state is not prohibited by the moral law. Because the exercise of this authority is permitted by the moral law, a rational being does not lose any moral freedom by consenting to an arrangement in which the state exercises this authority.

The right of state preservation can be given a similar construction. To acknowledge the state as a necessary idea of reason is, at the same time, to concede the state has sufficient authority to defend and preserve itself. This authority can be limited only by the demands of moral freedom, for an autonomous being cannot contractually alienate the external freedom required to perform his or her moral duty. Thus, Kant could sketch a vision of the state in which the exercise of a considerable range of taxing and police powers are consonant with moral freedom. While this will likely remain offensive to anyone who thinks of freedom in the moral traditional form of unhindered action, it does entitle Kant to insist that one retains one's moral freedom 'whole and undiminished' under the 'lawful dependency' of state authority. It is worth noting that Kant's argument both justifies political authority and establishes the normative limits of this authority.

Kant's failure to articulate his concept of moral freedom clearly and distinguish it from its Hobbesian counterpart is unfortunate for reasons other than the resultant confusion, however. He seems to have failed to sense – or at least failed to appreciate the radical and important implications of his theory of freedom. The concept of moral freedom erases many of the problems faced by traditional liberal theories of freedom by showing what it means to be free in the presence of others. This in turn serves as a corrective to the popular view that Kant's political thought is largely oblivious to the need for an awareness of others. The idea of moral freedom shows how the presence of other moral agents informs and structures the way in which we must think about our own freedom, and it does so by shifting our thinking about what it means to be free away from a Hobbesian concern for physical action and toward a moral awareness of others. Under a condition of justice, the moral freedom of each coexists harmoniously with the moral freedom of all; the conflict associated with the Hobbesian understanding of freedom is thus eliminated. Consequently, entrance into civil society does not involve a surrender of individual rights or the alienation of freedom; instead, political authority becomes a necessary requirement for the protection and promotion of external freedom.

So for Kant, political authority is a moral requirement for any society that seriously intends to defend the freedom of the individual from the morally impermissible actions of others. The state exists to secure the external freedom of all, or to bring about a condition of peace. Political authority is the precondition for both peace and freedom, and the two unite under the political condition promoted by the state. Thus understood, the Kantian state is neither a 'necessary evil' nor an 'instrumental good'. It is most certainly not a concession to the 'confined generosity of men' or a necessary compromise between the ideals of Kantian moral philosophy and certain unavoidable truths about the nature of human beings or political reality. Instead, the Kantian state is the rationally necessary instrument for constructing a social condition – a condition of justice – corresponding to the dictates of the moral law. So man, as a moral being sharing a common social setting with his fellows, must also be considered a political being; and the dependency of a true politics upon the moral law explains why such a politics 'cannot therefore take a single step without first paying tribute to morality'. Kant's moralized version of the liberal argument thus avoids the traditional liberal tension between individual freedoms on the one hand political authority on the other.

Similarly, Kant's general disapproval of revolution is hard to square with his fulsome praise of the French Revolution as 'a moral cause', and this vacillation between adherence to the status quo and enthusiasm for change is amongst the most perplexing features of his political philosophy and the most difficult to analyze. Commentators have described these tensions variously as tensions between conservatism and radicalism; idealism and pragmatism; rationalism and empiricism; and as an aspect of the phenomena- nominal distinction of the first *Critique*. That the tensions exist, then, is not in doubt; what must be questioned is why they exist and how deep they run. We have seen already that Airs believed Kant to be simply incapable of spotting the inconsistencies of his own arguments. By contrast, Howard Williams interprets the tensions simply as recognition by Kant of the limits of political endeavor; thus, 'at times, he appears to be advocating the most radical of political changes when donning his philosophical hat, and at others, he appears to be advocating the most cautious of conservatism when donning his everyday, realist hat.

For Williams, however, the tensions are simply recognition of the limits of what is practically possible. Kant's radicalism expresses what he believes to be ideal; his conservatism expresses what he believes to be prudent and practical. A further diagnosis is provided by Cohen in his article 'A Critique of Kant's Philosophy of Law'. Cohen suggests that the conflict in Kant's writings may be resolved only by ascribing to reason factors which are merely contingent and variable. Kant assumes,' he says, 'that reason dictates that men can transmit their titles of nobility to their wives but not conversely. This approach to the problem reduces Kant's position to such an absurdity than one may wonder how such a powerful mind could have been led to it even in old age'. This criticism of Kant—that he confuses the dictates of reason with the merely contingent and socially determined –provides a third diagnosis of the difficulty involved in giving a coherent picture of his political philosophy. It must be repeated however, that these are quite general difficulties involved in interpreting the political philosophy and in determining its relation to the moral philosophy.

Kant on Peace

Kant was probably the most powerful and consistent exponent and champion of the doctrine of human freedom that has ever lived; and during the last twenty years of his life, he became more and more interested in the prevention of war. In a little treatise entitled *Perpetual Peace* published in 1795—the year in which the Peace of Basel had close the first stage of the wars following the French revolution—he has drawn up a scheme with this end in view. This little work is not the first place, nor the only one where he has expressed views upon war and peace and their importance and value for the history of mankind. Scattered through some of his other works are remarks and passages on the subject; for instance, in the *Idea for a Universal History from a Cosmopolitan Standpoint,* in *The Critique of judgment,* in on the *Radical Evil in Human Nature,* and in the *Metaphysical Principles of Law* published respectively in 1784, 1790, 1792, and 1797. But the treatise on *Perpetual Peace* contains the fullest, most independent, and most systematic presentation of his views. The work is not perhaps widely known, and may acquire an increased interest at this time when once again Europe is rent with hatred and destruction, and once again voices are heard, more insistently perhaps than ever, urging the necessity of a new order.

But there are two preliminary points with which it will be well to deal first. In the first place, Kant is no visionary or daydreaming Utopian. His thought is eminently sober and practical. He makes no claim to offer a programmed, cut-and-dried and complete, for the abolition of war at once, or in a lifetime, or in a century. He even makes it clear that the state of perpetual peace is an ideal which we probably cannot expect ever to see completely realized – he writes of "an approximation advancing ad infinitum." He describes the inclination to war as one "which seems to be implanted in human nature." Yet he holds that this approximation to permanent peace by the removal of the causes of war is an "immediate duty".

The second point is the question whether Kant not merely urged the progressive elimination of war as a duty, but further held that no positive moral value at all attached to it. He did not think it inevitable; did he think it in any sense desirable? Kant insisted that war is "the scourge of the human race" which "makes more bad men than it takes away." Again, "reason, from her throne of the supreme law-giving moral power absolutely condemns war as a morally unawful proceeding, and makes a state of peace, on the other hand, an immediate duty." And this, despite the elements of moral values accidentally awakened by war in its course, Kant makes the further important point that no question of right or wrong is ever decided in war; war is a mere trial of strength, and "victory" the favorable result for one side, providing doubtless who was stronger, but not who was right. It seems then that we must conclude that for Kant war is not only not necessary but also not in itself desirable.

Kant teaches that if our actions are to have moral value they must conform to, and be done for the sake of a fundamental law or command. This law he formulates in two ways. The first is: "Act only on that maxim whereby thou can at the same time will that it should become a universal law." And the second: "So act as to treat humanity, whether in the own person or in that of any other, in every case as an end never as means only." These two are but different facets of a single principle based on the conviction that "rational human nature exists as an end it itself." As humans, we all share in a common, universal, rational human nature.

We can now pass to the still more urgent and more difficult problem of the moral attitude of one state towards another. Kant here goes direct to the root of the matter. As far as individuals are concerned, he had sided with Hobbes as against Rousseau, that men in the "state of nature" are hostile to one another—a view which for him no doubt followed from his doctrine of the evil principle innate in every man. He now applies this to the case of individual states considered as independent, which are, he holds in a state of nature towards one another: "nations, as states, may be judged like individuals who, living in the natural state of society—that is to say, uncontrolled by external law—injure one another through their very proximity." He realizes clearly that between independent sovereign states, so long as they remain independent and sovereign, no peace of any lasting kind can be expected. The relations between individual states are here not analogous to those between individuals within a state. For whereas individual citizens are restricted in respect of their independence and freedom within certain limits and by certain rules which they recognize and observe because they themselves have ultimately initiated them, individual states are not so restricted: "states, as such, are under no common external authority; and there is no instance of a state having ever been moved by argument to desist from its purpose." There is no system of checks and balances regulating inter-state relations corresponding to that of constitutional and civil law, which regulates relations between citizens of a state. In the last resort, however subtly the rulers of states may try to cloak their aims and intentions with an air of moral sanctity, they do in fact put into practice the advice of Machiavelli: "a prudent prince ought not to keep faith when by doing so it would be against his interest and when the reasons which made him bind himself no longer exist." Self-interest is, and cannot but is the ultimate maxim for any state that is sovereign and independent; other considerations, if they arise, must take a second place.

The remedy for this proposed by Kant is that states must cease to be entirely independent, for otherwise "the method by which states prosecute their rights can never be by process of law as it is where there is an external tribunal—but only by war." There must be brought into existence a federation of states, which can serve as the basis for an international law that shall be something more than nebulous tissues of courtesies to be disregarded as interest dictates. This, after the demand for a republican civil constitution, is the second positive, definitive condition of permanent peace between nations: "the law of nations shall be founded on a federation of free states." Again: "there can be no question of an international law, except on the assumption of somekind of a law-governed state of things, the externals condition under which any right can belong to man. For the very idea of international law, as public right, implies the publication of a universal will determining the rights and properties of each individual nation; and this status judicious must spring out of a contract of some sort, which may not, like the contract to which the state owes its origin, be founded upon compulsory laws, but may be at the most, the agreement of a permanent free association such as the federation of the different states, to which we have alluded above."

Before this ideal federation of free republican states can be brought to pass, there are certain "preliminary conditions" which must, Kant holds, be first satisfied, and through which the attitude of human beings in different nations towards one another would undergo a gradual regeneration. Kant calls these the "preliminary conditions of perpetual peace between nations." They are:

1. No treaty of peace to be regarded as valid if made with the secret reservation of material for a future war.
2. No independently existing state to be acquired by another through inheritance, exchange, purchase or gift.
3. Standing armies to be gradually abolished as being a perpetual means to peace.
4. No state to interfere violently in the internal constitution of another.
5. No belligerent state to employ modes of hostility, which tend to jeopardize mutual confidence in the subsequent state of peace.

It remains now to inquire what kind of a federation it is which Kant here envisages. How does he think it will come about? What will be the nature of supreme federal authority and of the laws, which will regulate the interrelations of the members of the federative union? This, too, is of some topical interest, for we are hearing today of a movement to establish a "federal union" between nations.

Conclusion

Kant's reputation as a philosopher, despite some fluctuations, is as established and as high as that of any major philosopher. It is not the same with his reputation as a political philosopher in the English-speaking world at least. On the one hand, his writings on politics, law, and history have often been dismissed as confused and wrong-headed, a mixture of inconsistency and servile, illiberal, and undemocratic ideas. His *Metaphysical Elements of Justice*, in particular, has been written off as a tragic lapse explicable only in terms of aging and failing intellect. On the other hand, Kant has sometimes been hailed as a great liberal and constitutionalist a friend of freedom and peace, and ranked with the foremost political philosophers. This is a useful corrective, because most standard textbooks on the history of political thought hold versions of the former position. Many such books ignore Kant. Other textbooks include Kant, but deal with him quickly and roughly. Dunning, for instance, depicts him as both unoriginal and rather pitiable confused, taking logically incompatible ideas from Rousseau and Montesquieu and trying to blend them.

Kant, at least in English speaking countries, is not generally considered to be a great political philosopher. Indeed histories of political thought do not give him pride of place, but generally mention him only incidentally, if at all. Historians of political thought ignore him, however, at their peril. Only too frequently, he is merely seen as a forerunner of Hegel. The reasons for this neglect and misunderstanding are not hard to discover. Historians of philosophy, even Kant scholars, have neglected his political writings because the philosophy of his three *Critiques* has absorbed attention almost entirely. And historians of political thought have paid little attention to him, because he did not write a masterpiece in that field. *The Metaphysical Elements of Right* has interested legal historians rather than historians of political theory.

Furthermore, the very fact that Kant's great works of critical philosophy are so formidable makes his less exacting political writings appear very much less weighty. It also encourages the belief that they are not central to his thought. This assumption, however, is greatly mistaken. While it would be going too far to see in them the ultimate end of his thought, they are not an accidental byproduct. Indeed, they grow organically out of his critical philosophy. In fact, Kant has rightly been called the philosopher of the French Revolution. There is, indeed, an analogy between the spirit of Kant's philosophy and the ideas of the French and American revolutions; for Kant asserted the independence of the individual in face of authority, and the problem of human freedom was at the very core of his thought. Similarly, the revolutionaries of 1776 and 1789 believed that they were attempting to realise the rights of man. Besides, the events of the American and of the French Revolution greatly excited and preoccupied him and he sympathized with the aims of the revolutionaries. He did so although he was a man of conservative disposition who refused to countenance revolution in politics as a legitimate principle of action, and certainly did not advocate revolution in his native country, Prussia. But his approach to politics was already shaped well before 1789, as his essays of 1784 reveal. It is possible that the French Revolution may have stimulated him to continue writing on the subject. But the example and influence of Rousseau must not be underrated. Rousseau had taught him to respect the common man; he was for him the Newton of the moral realm. Rousseau's portrait was the only adornment permitted in his house, and when reading *Emile* he even forgot to take his customary afternoon walk, allegedly the only deviation ever to occur from a daily custom followed with clock-like regularity. Kant's views are also, in many ways, close to the aspirations of the French revolutionaries, but in his demand for perpetual peace he goes further.

There is a link between Kant's philosophy and the ideas of the two major eighteenth-century revolutions, for the American and French revolutions constituted an open break with the political past. An appeal was made to a secular natural order and to the political rights of individuals for the purpose of initiating large-scale political action. The revolutions, of course, arose from the political, social and economic situation in America and France, but the beliefs of the revolutionaries were not intended as a smoke-screen designed to mislead the public. They depended on a political philosophy in which a belief in the right of the individual would be guaranteed. This attitude was new. In earlier revolutions, even in the English civil war and in 1688, Christian theology had still played an important part in shaping revolutionary thinking in the West. The realities of a revolutionary situation are, of course, always complex. It usually presents a pattern of ideology and political practice which is difficult, if not impossible, to disentangle. Kant did not set out to provide a blueprint for revolutionaries or a theory of revolution. On the contrary, he wanted to arrive at philosophical principles on which a just and lasting internal order and world peace could be based, He wanted to provide a philosophical vindication of representative constitutional government, a vindication which would guarantee respect for the political rights of all individuals.

The American and French revolutions had, to some extent, been prepared for by the ideas of the Enlightenment, the intellectual movement which dominated so much of eighteenth-century thought. Incontestably, the revolutionaries largely used the vocabulary of the Enlightenment, which had created a climate of opinion in many ways favourable to revolutionary action. In Kant, many of the intellectual strands of the Enlightenment converge. He presents a culmination of this intellectual movement, but he is also one of its most thoroughgoing critics. Kant himself characterised the Enlightenment as a dynamic process. It was not a static condition, but a continuous process leading to further self-emancipation. The age was not yet enlightened, but still in the process of becoming so. It meant liberation from prejudice and superstition. It also meant the growing ability to think for oneself. This observation echoes Lessing's famous dictum that what mattered most was not to possess the truth, but to pursue it. In Kant's view, man was to become his own master. In his special function as officer, clergyman, civil-servant etc., he should not reason, but obey the authority but as a man, citizen and scholar, he should have 'the courage to use his own intelligence'.

It is worth considering why a low estimation of Kant's political philosophy has been so frequent, because this may help to identify certain obstacles to understanding Kant. Many of his moral and political writings were soon translated into English. Kant's essays and treatises on moral, political and various philosophical subjects appeared in two volumes in 1798-9, and contained a fuller selection of such pieces than has ever been made since. However, Kant's political philosophy was accessible: yet it does not seem to have been taken up, except by a very few, such as de Quincy. Why this lack of interest? An obvious explanation is the hold of Utilitarian ideas over social and political thinking in Britain. Possibly, the Kantian and Utilitarian philosophies were too opposed at too many fundamental points in epistemology and ethics; for the first were to make much impression, the second already had a grip. We do not know whether Bentham ever wrote about Kant: Mill speaks with respect of Kant's moral philosophy, but finds it useless. John Austin damns faint praise, casting aside its most Kantian features.

Nor, perhaps surprisingly, were Kant's fortunes greatly improved when Utilitarianism receded somewhat before the flood of imported Hegelian ides later in the nineteenth century. The British idealists went back to Kant from the first but they went back to him from Hegel. That is, they turned to Kant not for his own sake but for the light to be thrown on Hegel and his development. Consequently, they usually echoed Hegel's assessment that Kant was badly wrong at several points. Moreover, Hegel seems to have a lower opinion of Kant's political philosophy than of any other part of his philosophy. He frequently acknowledges the importance of Kant's ideas, and the great part they played in his own thought. He gives credit for Kant's epistemology, even as he reveals it limitations. He acknowledges agreement with Kant on many basic points in moral philosophy; so much so that many call him 'a Kantian in ethics. This is debatable, for Hegel also condemns Kant's ethics as 'subjective and as formal chill duty is the final undigested lump left within the stomach in product of 'abstract understanding.' Although Hegel pictures Kant as working in the dark, he does generally show that sometimes Kant stumbled on the truth even if he did not always realize it. But when it comes to political philosophy, Kant is almost totally ignored or submerged.

Kant's ideas have thus been a significant political force. But they have also been attacked and modified, sometimes beyond recognition. In any case, they are ideas that look ahead into the future. But more than that Kant's theory of politics philosophically justifies man's right to political freedom, the view that he should no longer be considered to be under tutelage. Man's growing political and intellectual maturity must be recognized. According to Kant, man is in the process of becoming enlightened. Man has both the opportunity and the responsibility to make use of his mind in the spirit of criticism. Such is the temper and the message of the Enlightenment as understood by Kant. Kant's standing and influence as a political philosopher would indubitably have been greater if he had left a more highly or organized comprehensive work on politics. His style did not increase his popularity.

Immanuel Kant read and admired Rousseau; he practically worshipped Isaac Newton. From his perch on the Baltic Sea he surveyed the panorama of the world, and identified himself as the representative of humanity. As such he saw his mission in philosophy to be the defence of science, morality, and the rationality of religion. This was no easy task, for science and religion in particular had been at war for centuries. Kant was living in a transitional age. Science had won a long and hard fought battle against the authority of religion, but though this was all well and good from a scientific point of view, it was a disaster from the point of view of morality and religion. Kant may have worshipped Newton, but he was also a devout Lutheran, and though Newton himself had struggled to reconcile his theories of the universe with his own Christian beliefs, the conflict had not yet been satisfactorily resolved. To be sure, it was a good thing that science had won its autonomy and freedom from the dogmatic interference of religion, but if this meant that all religious and other unscientific beliefs were unjustifiable, and as such irrational, then the victory of science from a religious and humanist point of view was a disaster. Kant's mission, then, was not just to provide foundations; he had to redefine what it meant to be a rational human being. Consequently, he announced his plan to 'deny knowledge, in order to make room for faith'.

Kant's philosophy is consummated in three magnificent volumes that he called 'critiques'. These were critical in the spirit of the Enlightenment, but also idealistic and speculative, with a spirit hardly known among the French philosophers—except in Rousseau. German idealism—often called Kantian idealism—is idealistic in the familiar sense of defending abstract ideals. In philosophy, however, it also has a technical sense the world is constituted out of ideas. It is 'idealistic' too in its assurance that such a world is real and good, an assurance that had been shaken by Hume, who raised serious questions about the foundations of both knowledge and morals. Our knowledge, he had argued, is based only on habit, and morality is based on sentiment, not reason.

The first Critique, *The Critique of Pure Reason,* tackles the problem of knowledge and Hume's scepticism. At the heart of that formidable book, and the dramatic shift in Western thinking that begins with it, is an enormous expansion in the concept of the self, its scope, power, and richness. The primary change is a shift from the passive to the active mode, a rejection of the traditional idea of the human mind as a receptacle or receiver, to the insistence that the mind imposes its order on nature, an order which is fixed and immutable in all of us. 'The understanding does not derive its laws from, but prescribes them to nature. The second, *The Critique of Practical Reason,* is an attempt to analyse and justify the concept of morality, to free it from the unpredictability of sentiment and social fashion, and to defend it as a product of pure practical reason which is, as such, valid for all people at all times and under all conditions. The third Critique, *The Critique of Judgement,* has been considered the least consequential of the three, and is often neglected in English Kantian scholarship; but this is certainly not true on the Continent, where Kant's influence was based at least as much on this work as upon the other two. Goethe confessed that he could not read the first two *Critiques,* but he admired the third, as did Schiller, who reinterpreted the first two in its light, attempting a grand synthesis of Kant's version of the international Enlightenment and the uniquely German romantic reaction to it. On a superficial reading the third *Critique* might seem to be an unwieldy conglomeration of theses about the nature of art and beauty, the role of 'teleology' (purposive explanations) in science, and edifying remarks on the ultimate meaning of life and the universe. But what Kant has in mind in his discussion of beauty is not the protected domain of aesthetics and 'art for art's sake' but something much grander, the beauty of human life and morality, of nature, and of the universe as a whole as an expression of God's beneficence and human destiny. So understood, we can more readily appreciate how the third *Critique* was intended as the synthesis and culmination of the other two, and how it was the third *Critique* that so heavily influenced the German idealists and romantics who followed Kant.

Although the problems that drove Kant to philosophy were deeply felt, it was not in his nature to write, as had his hero Rousseau, an elegant popular treatise or a semi-fictional novel, much less a revealing *Confessions.* His ideas had to be couched objectively and impersonally, for while Rousseau projected outward from his peculiar, personal self to the whole of humanity, Kant began with the view that human reason was universal and objective. One's personal autobiography had little relevance to the important truth about the self that Rousseau had discovered. For Rousseau, that special of self was something to be experienced first of all; for Kant, it was a profound metaphysical thesis to be demonstrated through the cold calculations of deductive logic. But what those deductions revealed—what Kant called his 'Copernican Revolution'—was nothing less than a revision of our view of the self in the world.

The first Copernican revolution had denied the obvious—that the sun revolved while the earth stood still. What Kant denied seemed even more obvious, that the world was 'out there' and independent of our experience of it. The whole history of metaphysics depends upon the belief in the presence of a reality independent of us, from Thales' precocious insights and Plato's brilliant defence of a world of Being beyond our own world of change and becoming, to Descartes's systematic doubts about our knowledge of the external world and the scepticism of Hume. The problem with metaphysics was that no one seemed to have the slightest hold on the true nature of reality, or as Kant put it metaphysics has rather to be regarded as a battle ground quite peculiarly suited for those who desire to exercise themselves in mock combats, and in which no participant has ever yet succeeded in gaining even so much as an inch of territory, not at least in such a manner as to secure him in its permanent possession.

But while Hume's conclusion was that "all such metaphysical efforts should henceforth be committed to the flames as nothing more than sophistry and illusion", Kant insists that metaphysics is inescapable. In particular, there are three metaphysical questions, which the human mind finds unavoidable. Kant summarizes these as God, Freedom, and Immortality'. *The Critique of Pure Reason* has a single central thesis: knowledge of the world is possible because the self—the transcendental self or ego—determines the structure of our every experience.

Kant's arguments and Hume's too, for the leading question of Kant's epistemology are how is it possible for our consciousness to know the world? So long as the world lies outside the realm of our experience, scepticism is inescapable, but to Kant it is also intolerable. The world is the world of our experience, not something outside of it. We are not just acted upon by a world we never know directly; we act upon the world to give it its basic forms.

In an important sense, the German Enlightenment developed in a vacuum. In France and earlier in England, Enlightenment theories were blueprints for reform or revolution, but in Germany the political situation was such that reform was all but unthinkable. The middle class was powerless. Germany was fragmented into hundreds of tiny states and principalities, and apart from Prussia, which was ruled by the iron-fisted but 'enlightened' Frederick the Great, there was no central government as in Paris or London. The tone of the Enlightenment in Germany was somewhat different from that prevailing in Britain and France. On the whole, considerably less emphasis was laid on empiricism than in Britain. The German thinkers were more erudite, but also more abstract and professorial than their English and French counterparts; and they were frequently more heavy-handed. The absence of a metropolitan culture militated against certainty of style, while the parochial politics of the many petty principalities and comparatively small free imperial cities were not conducive to the rise of lively political discussion and debates. Unlike Britain, Germany offered virtually no opportunities for the intellectuals to take part in politics. Frederick the Great was, of course, an intellectual, but an absolute monarch anyhow presents a special case.

It is characteristic of this political stagnation that the political event which most affected eighteenth-century Germany took place in France: the French Revolution aroused German political thought from its somnolence. Nonetheless, modern political thought in Germany virtually began with the impact of 1789. Many thinkers, in Germany as elsewhere, welcomed the revolution at first and believed it to be the dawn of a new age. But disillusion began to set in with the outbreak of the Terror. The revolution in practice spread only to those territories occupied by the French revolutionary armies. Revolutionary sentiment in Germany was a tender plant capable of blossoming forth only under the stimulus of force.

Kant and Goethe, the two leading German minds of the age, assessed the political situation correctly. Both recognised that while in France the revolution had answered a great political need, the political situation in Germany was not at all ripe for revolutionary activity. In Germany as in England and France, the rise of the bourgeoisie was noticeable, but the German bourgeoisie had not become emancipated from the dominance of the princes and the aristocracy. It did not possess the self-confidence of its French and English counterparts. Germany was a much poorer country than either Britain or France, and a rising self-confident class which is prevented from giving free expression to its political ambitions, is much more likely to take revolutionary action than a weak and unsure one. There was little scope for political freedom in Germany. Even in the Prussia of Frederick the Great, freedom of speech, meant only the ability freely to criticise religion, but not the government. In addition, the small size of most German principalities permitted a much closer supervision of the subjects by rulers than in larger countries. The growth of bureaucratic control also impeded economic development and was another operative factor in sapping the self-confidence of the impotent German bourgeoisie.

Given these political, social and economic conditions, it is not surprising that the Enlightenment in Germany was different from other Western countries. German philosophy, unlike British philosophy for instance, continued in many ways to resist the impact of empirical aspects of science. Rationalism dominated the outlook of German and French universities, but the style of German philosophical writing was, on the whole, much less urbane than that of its French counterpart.

In 1789 Immanuel Kant wished the French revolutionaries well, but with no thought that a similar revolution might or should be staged in Prussia. Heine may have compared Kant to Robespierre for the bold radicalism of his thinking, but their revolutions were not on a par. The Enlightenment in England and France fostered a hardheaded, visionary realism. In Germany, it had to settle for an abstract idealism, and enlightenment of the spirit only or as Marx would write in *The German Ideology:*

> While the French bourgeoisie, by means of the most colossal revolution that history has ever known, was achieving domination and conquering the Continent of Europe, while the already emancipated English bourgeoisie was revolutionizing industry and subjugating India politically and all the rest of the world commercially, the impotent German burghers did not get any farther than 'good will'. Kant's good will fully corresponds to the impotence, depression and wretchedness of the German burghers, whose petty interests were never capable of developing into the common interests of a class but had their counterpart in their cosmopolitan swollen-headedness.

16

Hegel

> The significance of that 'absolute' commandment, know thyself—whether we look at it in itself or under the historical circumstances of its first utterance—is not to promote mere self-knowledge in respect of the particular capacities, character, propensities, and foibles of the single self. The knowledge it commands means that ultimately true and real—of spirit is the true and essential being.

Hegel (1770-1831) led a very unexciting life for a thinker who was such an inspiration to his contemporaries and successors. Nineteenth-and twentieth-century social and political thought are unthinkable without Hegel, yet Hegel's own life did not come into much contact with the great events he lived through and commented on. The one exception is the famous occasion when Hegel saw Napoleon-the world soul on horseback at Jena in 1806. Prussia's defeat at the battle of Jena established French hegemony in Germany. That hegemony only lasted a few years. Nevertheless, it was Jena and its aftermath that made Germany one of the key players in world history in Hegel's sense.

Nearly all of Hegel's life was spent as a teacher and a scholar. He was brought up a Protestant in the relatively liberal south German atmosphere of Wurttemberg, and he was a student at Tubingen (1788-93) when the Bastille fell. From then on, Hegel's own life can be seen as a paradigm of the responses and reactions to the French Revolution the initial enthusiasm for Reason and Liberty; the doubts beginning with the establishment of the French republic and then quickening with the execution of the king and queen; the hostility to the wars of conquest, and then the full nationalist reaction when Napoleon conquered nearly the whole of Europe.

While all this was going on, Hegel was quietly climbing the academic ladder. He spent some years as a tutor, then was appointed at the University of Jena (1801) where he completed *The Phenomenology of Mind* (1807), thus setting the agenda for the study of the history of culture for a very long time to come. After that he spent eight years as a rector of a Gymnasium (1808-16) at Nuremberg; he got married and finished his great work on *Logic*. There followed a chair of philosophy at Heidelberg and later (1818-31) at Berlin. We are told that as a lecturer he mumbled, which is odd, considering that some of his works were put together posthumously from lecture notes taken by high-minded students who were members of the Prussian officer corps. His great work, *The Philosophy of Right*, appeared in1821.

Hegel's Christianity was always eccentric, and it is hard to pin down. Some argue that Hegel's theology is the way into his politics, while others argue the reverse.

Hegel was taken in his own day to be a conservative and it is true that he was appainted to his chair in Berlin University to combat dangerously liberal tendencies among its teachers and students. Hegel has the reputation of being a 'difficult' thinker in the English-speaking world, and it is easy to see why. Hegel speaks the language of German idealist philosophy, which is at the same time technical and slippery in translation. Nobody denies the influence of Hegelianism on the development of Marxism, though there are disputes about the extent to which Hegelianism can still be detected in Marxism as a finished product. This question of how influential Hegel was on Marx has had the unfortunate tendency, happily now beginning to be reversed, of making people think that Hegel is only interesting to the extent that he influenced Marxism. Hegel's political theory, it is sometimes said, was seen and seen through by Marx in his *Critique of Hegel's Philosophy of Right,* and this in its turn has led to the view that Hegel on his own isn't up to much. Hegel is in fact a much tougher thinker than this view would have us suppose.

Human Consciousness

As a philosopher, Hegel was interested in how the thinking mind actually views the world. Philosophy is about mind, Hegel calls 'the thinking view of things', and so he is interested in the history of human consciousness. The mind is there for understanding the world outside the self, while that self is still part of the world which the mind seeks to understand. Hegel thinks the mind really does try to grasp the world outside the self. Mind is active. It does not wait for sense impressions queuing up at the fingers' ends or at the eyeball to ask politely for admission to the mind. The mind reaches out to make the world coherent. And Hegel means the world as a whole. Hegel is an idealist; he thinks that an idea of the world presents itself to mind, or created by mind as a whole. Thinking mind are full of impressions from the outside, and the more a mind is a thinking mind the more it will go after those impressions, but mind's real job is to organise these impressions into a coherent whole. In a sense, we have a view of the whole before we have a view of the parts of the world because the mind which reaches out to understand the world is a whole mind already.

Hegel thinks it is a mistake to suppose that we build up a view of the world bit by bit, as if we were mapping a landscape. We may pretend we do that, but we do not. As a theorist of knowledge, Hegel is poles apart from the English empiricist tradition following Locke which holds that we build up a picture of the world gradually as the senses provide more and more sense experience, so that the more experienced adult, 'having seen more of the world', has a fuller picture of the world 'out there' than is possible for the relatively inexperienced child. Children can't know the world as adults know it, and advanced civilizations know the world better than primitive peoples. The triumph of the Lockian scheme is science, which patiently builds up knowledge of the world and organises it into a body of tested and reliable theory. This science contains all the sciences as we know them: natural science, social science, the science of history and political and economic science. Hegel does not think that we look at the world like that.

Writing a quarter of a century after the publication of Kant's revolutionary first *Critique,* whose ideas were now as established as the slogans of the great political revolution in France,. Hegel without Kant's timidity, pursued to the limits the ideas of transcendental idealism, and the significance of the insight that it is we who give structure to our own experience. From Fichte he borrowed the now transformed notion of 'the Absolute', the rejection of the world 'in itself, and the idea that there might be alternative sets of categories—alternative 'forms of consciousness' and forms of life. From Schelling he borrowed the idea of dialectic of such forms, developing through time and history with ourselves as the authors, and becoming increasingly more adequate and encompassing. According to Hegel, every form of consciousness has its truth, in a certain context and from a certain perspective. But a larger context and broader perspective will show that some forms are more satisfactory, more complete, more 'true' than others. The notion of dialectic was the ideal mean between Kant's too-dogmatic 'deduction' of a single set of categories, and the romantics' free-wheeling 'creative idealism' which made it seem as if any pronouncements at face value, interpreting the theological language of the Trinity and the Incarnation quite literally. In terms of structure Hegel's works do tend to culminate in religion and wrote his first essays on religion in general and Christianity in particular. The significance of Hegel's unabashedly theological language is by no means obvious, however, and when he explains that, what the incarnation really means is that every one of us is Spirit, and Jesus is just a representation it is clear that this is no orthodox defence of Christianity. Hegel treats religion not just towards the end of the dialectic but throughout, one of his treatments occurring at an early stage in the guise of 'the Unhappy Consciousness', a rather damning description of religion as schizoid, slavish, and miserable. Such a religion is a battle of oneself against oneself, not a spiritual endeavour but a particularly destructive form of inward self-consciousness.

With the exception of the *Logic,* Hegel's works are all concerned with the necessity of a social conception of humanity. This seems obvious until one glances back at the history of philosophy. Of course philosophers treat people as social creatures when they are discussing politics but when they are discussing the nature of knowledge, consciousness, the self, or religion, they almost always treat the matter as a relationship between the individual and reason, or God. The idea that what we know, think, feel, and worship is circumscribed by, much less is a product of, our relations with other people is treated with disdain as popular superstition, as 'heteronomy'. The Enlightenment since Descartes honoured autonomy above all else, and romanticism valued inward feelings and intuitions just because these were untainted by social conditioning and corruption. Rousseau more than anyone else celebrated this sense of the isolated individual in touch with himself and nature, and out of touch with society. True, he developed the most persuasive theory of the social contract, but he did so against a background of a state of nature in which individuals were 'born free and happy' and were 'indifferent' to one another. The idea that there are no individuals in nature, that knowledge, self, and everything else human is a product not of nature but of culture, is an idea that comes quite new to philosophy and it comes mainly with Hegel.

Hegel's ethical theory is too often seen as subservient to his political views—though the latter are more often understood through their unforeseen consequences in modern German history than through Hegel's own rather moderate opinions. But ethics is, in an important sense, the heart of Hegel's philosophy. His early work on religion tries—following Kant—to understand religious belief and ritual wholly within the secular framework of an ethical theory, to see religion as a vehicle of morality. The *Phenomenology* has as its largest part a series of explorations of various ethical systems and models.

The master-slave section initiates what is to become an elaborate dialectical progression of such diverse ethical theories and ways of life as hedonism, romantic sensibility, the pious life, the success-motivated life of a businessman or scholar, a life defined wholly by one's family, and possibly in conflict with the larger 'civil society' the sophisticated but hypocritical life of the courtier, life in a revolution and the theory of ethics formulated by Kant concerning morality as Practical Reason. The point of the dialectic is, as always, to provide the broadest possible view of ethics and its possibilities, while at the same time making clear what is most essential to morality and the good life.

Hegel does not accept the Kantian conception of morality. In his early essays, despite the Kantian flavour and his devotion to Kant's philosophy of religion, he had attacked Kant's view of morality—as did Schiller—as overly abstract, cold, and alienating. He argued that the formality of Kant's categorical imperative made it very difficult to apply it to any concrete ethical situation, at least without sneaking in personal evaluations, which it was the very point of the moral law to preclude. He particularly objected to the exclusion of feeling and all inclination from moral consideration, recognizing with imagined world might be as real as any other. The dialectic is not so much a method as it is the central idea of Hegel's philosophy, and its purpose, in each of his works, is to demonstrate the ultimate necessity of an all-encompassing acceptance of the self as absolute — which Hegel calls 'Spirit'.

Hegel is the apotheosis of German idealism, and he has been called 'the Aristotle of our post-Renaissance world'. Viewed in itself, outside the historical context and the philosophical tradition in which it was written, Hegel's system appears extravagant, extreme, and almost incomprehensible, but viewed as a vision of history and as the culmination of the whole philosophical tradition, it becomes clear that Hegel's ideas were not wild 'speculations' but rather that they formed a careful synthesis of the current internationalism of history and the subjective movement in philosophy that had started with Descartes and Rousseau. Hegel saw the absurdity of scepticism, and the possibility of profound doubt is simply rejected from his system. 'Perhaps', he writes at the beginning of his first great book, 'the fear of error is itself the greatest error.' He accepted the general move of Kant's first *Critique*, regarding objects as being constituted by consciousness, but he also saw the manifest absurdity of making this an individual matter, as if each of us creates his or her own world; it is consciousness in general that does this, collectively and not individually, through the shared aspects of a culture, a society, and above all through a shared language. But this implies that, though we all strive for mutual agreement our shared concepts are not in fact universal but quite particular and provincial, aspects of the truth but not the whole truth, forms of consciousness rather than—as we would like to think—human consciousness as such. But since Hegel also rejects the idea of a world 'in itself' there can be no 'truth' for human consciousness apart from its own agreement with itself taking into account not only its many voices and Perspectives but also its rich history and multitude of experiences. This explains the complexity of the Hegelian system: it is not merely an argument for the absolute truth but rather an attempt to actually *create* that truth, by moving us all through the history that a good person often acts from impulse rather than from reason, and that someone who acts on the basis of 'duty' may well, even while doing right and exhibiting Kantian 'moral worth', prove to be a wretched character. Most of all he objected to Kant's account of ethics because it lacked any social dimension; it was strictly a relationship between the individual, practical reason, and the moral law. The basis of ethics, Hegel insisted, was not this at all, but rather one's belonging to a particular community of people. Ethics was not a matter of autonomy but heteronomy of being influenced by other people. Nor was it primarily a matter of rational principle, but part of a life of shared values, feelings, and customs—Hegel had argued for the importance of custom before he began the *Phenomenology,* and he still accepts it as the basis for all ethics in his book on politics, *The Philosophy of Right.* The emphasis on shared customs turns Kant topsy-turvy; the reason why morality is so important is not because it applies rationality downward from the heavens to particular earthly situations, but because it is a development up from those basic circumstances in which we come to value certain actions and feelings in the first place. It also places the locus of morals not in the universal and necessary laws of reason, but in the particular rules and dictates of the family. This tends to make Hegel's ethical philosophy rather conservative, for unlike those more 'liberal' thinkers who map out a grand rational scheme about the way things 'ought' to be, and try to impose it on existing society, Hegel begins with ingrained habits and expectations, and argues a kind of sanctity for them. But Hegel does not think that the dialectic stops there; Kant's overly rational view of morality ultimately deserves a place in a fully adequate ethical framework just as surely as the role of the family and the community.

One of the dialectical devices Hegel uses to show how such a movement takes place is to interpose the story of Antigone between his account of custom and his discussion of the ethical norms of civil society. He takes Antigone to represent the divine law of the family, of mutual affection and loyalty. When her brother is killed in an abortive attempt at a coup Antigone's duty is to bury him in accordance with religious law. But as a traitor her brother is denied burial by the king he sought to depose, and she faces a fatal conflict between her divine family duty and the human law of society. She opts for her duty, and is killed by the State in return, but the point of the play for Hegel is nothing less than the nature of the dialectic as such. Life, history and philosophy are defined by such crisis points. For the individual who is caught in the crisis there may well be no 'happy ending', but it is on the basis of such tragedies and sacrifices that the dialectic and human history moves forward. So understood, Kant's view of morality is an extremely sophisticated version of that forward-reaching tendency, but because it is also too narrow and limited it must be moved beyond as well.

Where does the dialectic go from here? In the *Phenomenology,* it moves to the dialectic of religion, which Hegel sees not as the superimposition of Christianity on morals but rather as the reintegration of custom and more abstract conceptions of morality and society. In *The Philosophy of Right* and the *Lectures on the Philosophy of History* it moves to a new and enlarged sense of internationalism, a vision of the Self, or Spirit that embraces us all, finally recognizing itself in all of us, and ending the conflicts that drive us apart. It is not only the culmination of the transcendental pretence; it is 'the end of history', according to Hegel. But this hyperinflation of the self marks the beginning of a new era of European history, a reaction in which the premises and basic ideals of the Enlightenment will come under fire.

Hegel's Dialectic

Lenin wrote, "The quickest way of getting a headache", when he studied Hegel's *Science of Logic,* where the dialectic appears in its fullest form. This difficulty is partly a result of the legendary complexity of Hegel's language. Hegel may have wished to "teach philosophy to speak German", but Germany was not able to listen. The Spirit spoke in mysterious words, because, after Napoleon's defeat, the words that could be understood were no longer permitted. Philosophy had ceased to speak German, Marx said, because German had ceased to be the language of thought.

Hegel's idealism also partly ensured that his thought was genuinely mysterious. The Spirit was a substitute for a class that was incapable of making its own revolution. This mystical substitute was then projected back into history as its moving force. But Hegel is also difficult for reasons that are not the result of character and circumstance. His theories use terms and concepts that are unfamiliar, because they go beyond the understanding of which everyday thought is capable. Ordinary language assumes that things and ideas are stable, that they are either "this" or "that" and, within strict limits, these are perfectly reasonable assumptions. Yet the fundamental discovery of Hegel's dialectic was that things and ideas do change—empires rise and fall, likewise religions and schools of philosophy. And they change because they embody conflicts, which make them unstable. As Hegel explained: that is, they are, but it is equally true that they are not".

It is to this end that Hegel deliberately chooses words that can embody dynamic processes: "The double usage of language, which gives to the same word a positive and a negative meaning, is not an accident, and gives no ground for reproaching language as a cause of confusion. For instance, Hegel uses the term "moment" to indicate that aspect of reality which is both a temporary point of stability and part of a dynamic process. Similarly, "sublate" is used to indicate that process which both produces something new and at the same time preserves, in an altered form, the old elements from which it emerged.

Hegel summarizes some of the key characteristics of the dialectic in his preface to the *Phenomenology*. The first task of the *Phenomenology* is to examine the contradictions in various ways of seeing the world. It goes on to show that these contradictions can only be resolved by adopting the dialectical approach defended by Hegel. Hegel's way of criticizing other philosophical approaches is itself dialectical. He does not wish to show that they are simply wrong but rather that they are one-sided. The partial truth that they contain can then be sublated within his own system.

The more conventional opinion gets fixated on the antithesis of truth and falsity, the more it tends to expect a given philosophical opinion to be either accepted or rejected. It does not comprehend the diversity of the philosophical systems as the progressive unfolding of the truth, but rather sees in it simple disagreements. Indeed, it is this process of criticism and absorption that is Hegel's dialectic. He goes on to give a striking metaphor for this progressive jubilation of other systems, demonstrating the way in which he regards this process as giving access to the truth:

The bud disappears in the bursting forth of the blossom, and one might say that the former is refuted by the latter; similarly, when the fruit appears, the blossom is shown in its turn as a false manifestation of the plant, and the fruit now emerges as the truth of its instead. These forms are not jut distinguished from one another; they also supplant one another as mutually incompatible. Yet at the same time their fluid nature makes them moments of an organic unity in which not only do they not conflict, but in which each is as necessary as the other, and this mutual necessity alone constitutes the life of the whole.

The great principles of Hegel's dialectic are clearly displayed in this passage. "The truth is the whole", not any separate part. But the whole is not just the end result, the whole is the process of development through which the parts come to constitute the whole Moreover, this process of development through which the parts come to constitute the whole and, in doing so, become different than they were in their preexisting form. Moreover, this process of development is not the result of some external cause, but of the inherent, "mutually incompatible" structure of the organism itself. Only in this way can "truth be its own self-movement" rather than a "mode of cognition that remains external to its material".

Hegel is insistent that no real knowledge can emerge from a system that makes a sharp separation between its method and the object that the method is supposed to analyze. "To consider a thing rationally means not to bring reason to bear on the object from the outside and so to tamper with it, but to find that the object is rational on its own account". It followed that "this dialectic is not an activity of subjective thinking applied to some matter externally, but is rather the matter's very soul putting forth its branches and fruit organically".

This notion puts Hegel at odds with Kant's assumption that we must know the instrument of thought before we can know what the instrument can, or cannot tell us about reality. The disagreement is very neatly summarized by Hegel in the shorter *Logic*. "We ought, says Kant, to become acquainted with the instrument, before we undertake the work for which it is to be employed; for if the instrument be insufficient, all our trouble will be spent in vain". Hegel objects to this approach partly because it turns thought "back upon itself". But, more fundamentally, Hegel thinks that Kant's approach is self-contradictory, because knowledge, unlike other tools, cannot be understood "in advance" but only through use. Hegel did not reject the demand that our method of analysis should be open to scrutiny, he merely insisted that such work could only take place in the course of investigation of substantive objects and not as a preliminary to such investigation.

One consequence of this approach is that, if the object develops historically, as a process unfolding over time, the method used by the philosopher must be capable of expressing this dimension of reality. Kant is again at fault in not being able to handle this dimension of reality. Kant makes time a function of human consciousness and attributes to the thing in itself only the mere fact of existence. But, argues Hegel, "the main point is not, that [objects] are, but what they are. It does no good to things to say merely that they have being. What has being, will also cease to be when time creep over it." Those approaches, which reject the dialectic, remain mired in static. They cannot account for how things come into being and pass out of being over time. Hegel describes these approaches as "monochromatic formalism", because they have no way of "coping with that sheer unrest of life". They simply content themselves with categorizing the "paralyzed form" of reality.

"Impatience", says Hegel, "demands the impossible, to wit, the attainment of the end without the means. But the length of the path has to be endured, because each moment is necessary". And each moment contributes to the definition of the totality that emerges at the end of this process; equally it is only the totality that gives meaning to the parts of which it is composed. Thus, for knowledge to become science "it must travel a long way and work it passage".

Even the dialectic, the "triadic form" as Hegel calls it, can be "reduced to a lifeless schema, a mere shadow when scientific organization is degraded into a table of contents". This was Kant's error. "Kant rediscovered this triadic form by instinct, but in his work it was still lifeless and un comprehended". This, in Hegel's view, it is bound to be that fate of any method, including those of both Kant and Fichte, which treats consciousness and reality, subject and object, as separate.

The Science of Logic was Hegel's attempt to bring together all the different ways that we look at the world—empirical thrugh art, religion, natural science—and to show how they are connected. *The Science of Logic* was itself, therefore, another example of one of Hegel's key concepts—totality. Hegel showed how each concept is connected to every other concept. This process continues until the final concept the Absolute Idea is shown to be the summation of all the previous ideas. One concept gives birth to the next by a process of contradiction. Science, like history, is dialectical.

The Science of Logic begins with the most abstract of all human ideas, Being. This is the bare notion of existence shorn of any color, size, shape, taste, or smell. This first concept is also, in its way, a totality. Although Being reveals no characteristic or distinguishing marks, it does, nevertheless, include everything. After all, everything must exist before it can take on any particular characteristics. Being is therefore a quality that is shared by everything that exists; it is the most common of human ideas. Every time we say, "This is—", even before we say what it is, we acknowledge the idea of pure Being. Being is, therefore, only an "immediate" totality. But being also contains its opposite, nothing. The reason is that Being has no qualities and no features that define it. If we try to say what Being is, we are forced to the opposite conclusion, Being equals Nothing.

But even Nothing is more than it seems. If we are asked to define Nothing, we are forced to admit that it has at least one property—the lack or absence of any qualities. This may be only a negative definition, nevertheless, it is a definition. This presents us with a strange dilemma: Being is nothing, and yet nothing is something. Hegel, however, is not so stupid as to think that there is no difference between Being and

Nothing, even though this is what our logical enquiry seems to suggest. All that this contradiction means is that we must search for a new term that which can explain how Being and Nothing can be both equal and separate. This is in Hegel's jargon, an "identity of opposites". Hegel's solution is the concept of Becoming. In German, Becoming means both "coming to be" and "ceasing to be". By replacing two static concepts with one dynamic concept, by seeing a process of change instead of stable definitions, Hegel superseded the ideas of Being and Nothing with a third term that contained both these ideas and at the same time surpassed them. This third term, this new concrete totality which both contains and surpasses the previous two, Hegel calls 'the negation of the negation.'

This process reveals the characteristic stages in the Hegelian dialectic. Lenin seized the key point about all this in his notes on the *Science of Logic*. "Shrewd and clever! Hegel analyses concepts that usually appear dead and shows there is movement in them". Contradictions produce movement—this is the decisive advance that is contained in Hegel's dialectic. Hegel's method not only sees the world as a totality in which each part is connected to all the other parts, it also sees that the relationships between the parts are contradictory. It is the search to resolve these contradictions that pushes thought past commonsense definitions, which see only separate, stable entities.

Some of the most unambiguous passages in the *Science of Logic* insist on the vital role that the idea of contradiction plays in Hegel's system. "Everything is inherently contradictory", he writes, "in the sense that this law in contrast to the others expresses rather the truth and essential nature of things". And again, "contradiction is the root of all movement and vitality; it is only in so far as something has a contradiction within it that it moves, has an urge and activity".

Anything that is defined simply by reference to itself can have no possibility of movement, unless it is struck by an external force. But external force can only ever be a partial explanation because, if we asks where this external force came from, we have to admit that self-movement produced by internal contradiction is a feature of the system at some level. As Hegel puts it:

> Internal self-movement proper is nothing else but the fact that something is, in one and the same respect, self-contained and deficient, the negative of itself. Something is therefore only alive is so far as it contains contradiction wherein it, and moreover, is this power to hold and endure the contradiction within it.

The role that contradiction plays in Hegel's can also be seen in this criticism of a notion that many take to be a definition of the dialectic—reciprocal relations. Reciprocal relations, the idea that two factors mutually influence each other, may be an advance on linear notions of cause and effect, but it falls short. Thought takes refuge in the idea of reciprocity "when the conviction grows that things can no longer be studied satisfactorily from a causal point of view, on account of the infinite progress already spoken of". Hegel then gives an example:

> Thus in historical research the question may be raised in the first form, where the character and manners of a nation are the cause of its constitution and laws, or if they are not rather the effect. Then, as a second step, the character and manners on one side

and the constitution and laws on the other are conceived on the principle of reciprocity: and in that the case the cause will at the same time be an effect, and vice versa.

Master-Slave Dialectic

There is widely held view that Marx was profoundly influenced by the master-slave dialectic in Hegel's *Phenomenology of Spirit*. This view was first popularized by Jean-Paul Sartre, who refers in his *Being and Nothingness* (1943) to 'the famous master-slave relation, which so profoundly influenced Marx'. Probably this remark reflects the influence of Alexander Kojeve's lectures on Hegel in the 1930s. Kojeve presents a reading of the *Phenomenology*, which centralizes the place of the master- slave dialectic in it, in a quasi-Marxist interpretation. Three years after Sartre we find Jean Hyppolite again saying that the dialectic of domination and servitude is the best-known section of the *Phenomenology* because of 'the influence it has had on the political and social philosophy of Hegel's successors, especially Marx'.

The influence of Hegel's *Phenomenology* on Marx can be examined by a study of Marx *Manuscripts* of 1844,in which he introduces his theory of alienation, and then devotes considerable space to a penetrating critique of the *Phenomenology*. In this latter section, Marx praises Hegel for having grasped man as the result of his own labour. Nearly all commentators, innocently assuming that there is indeed a fascinating discussion in the master –slave section of the significance of material labour; in and through this the slave finds himself. Herbert Marcuse was probably the first to do so; 'In1844, Marx sharpened the basic concepts of his own theory through a critical analysis of *Hegel's Phenomenology of Mind*. He described the alienation of labour in the terms of Hegel's discussion of master and slave".

The 'Master-Slave' section occurs early in the *Phenomenology* at the point where consciousness is to turn into self-consciousness. Hegel believes that the self can become conscious of itself only in and through the mediation of another self-consciousness. The first stable relationship that emerges in Hegel's dialectical development of this topic is that of 'Lordship and Bondage'. Satisfaction of his desires through goods and services is provided by the servant's labour. The dialectic moves forward precisely through the servant, however, because 'through work the bondsman becomes conscious of what he truly is'. Work forms and shapes the thing and through this formative activity the consciousness for the servant now, in the work outside it, acquires 'an element of permanence', for it comes to see in the independent being of the object ' its own independence'. The shape does not become something other than himself though being made external to him,' says Hegel, 'for it is precisely this shape that is his pure being –for –self.' He concludes: Though this rediscovery of himself by himself, the bondsman realizes that it is precisely in his work wherein he seemed to live only the life of a stranger that he acquires a sense of him self.

Both Hegel and Marx see work not merely in its utilitarian aspect but as a vehicle of self-realization; thus, they see the servant rather than the master as the locus of a more developed human existence. However, fundamental difference between Marx and Hegel surfaces when we notice that, whereas Marx holds that only a change in the mode of production recovers for the worker his sense of self and its fulfillment, Hegel thinks that the educative effect of work, even within an exploitative relation of production, is sufficient for the worker to manifest to himself his own 'meaning' in his product. Furthermore, at this stage in the phenomenological dialectic, the condition of 'fear and service' is stipulated as necessary to this end.

Hegel defines work as 'desire held in check': it involves putting a distance between the immediate impulses of self-will and formative activity grounded in objective principles. It is really the master who is a slave because his object is the 'unalloyed feeling of self-satisfaction; that is to say, he is a slave to his appetites, but his satisfaction are 'only fleeting', lacking the permanence of objectivity. The servant on the other hand, in the work he creates, achieves mastery of his craft; it is he who rises to the level of universal human reason. However, Hegel introduces the notion that 'fear and service' are necessary to induce the check to desire and to ensure that consciousness rises above self-centered goals to the freedom that comes from a consciousness of the universal power of human creative activity.

In discussion of the *Phenomenology*, Marx praises Hegel for grasping the importance of labour. 'The great thing in Hegel's *Phenomenology* and its final result—the dialectic of negativity as the moving and producing principle—is that Hegel conceives the self creation of man as a process, objectification as loss of object as alienation and as jubilation of this alienation, that therefore grasps the nature of labour and conceives objective man as the result of his own labour. The realization of himself is only possible if man employs all his species –powers, and treats them as objects, which is first only possible in the form of estrangement.

The first thing that should give us pause is that immediately after this praise Marx qualifies it by complaining that the only labour Hegel knows and recognizes is abstract mental labour. The 'abstract mental labour' to which Marx refers is the labour of spirit. *The Phenomenology* is a spiritual odyssey, in which spirit discovers that the objective shapes given to it in consciousness and self-consciousness is nothing but its own self-determination. Spirit comes to know itself through producing itself, in the first instance as something, which stands over against itself. In the final chapter, Marx notes that the world of estrangement thus brought to life is overcome, or negated, in a peculiar way in that—as Hegel puts it—'self consciousness has negated this alienation –objectivity so that it is at home with itself in its otherness as such'. Within this framework spheres of estrangement such as religion, the state, civil society, and so forth, are grasped as spirit's own work. Hegel emphasizes that spirit can come to itself only through setting up opposition and then negating it.

While Marx was impressed by Hegel's phenomenological description of estrangement, what really excited him was the 'metaphysical' aspect of the *Phenomenology*—spirit mediating itself in alienation. This is the process of 'absolute negativity' and it is to this Marx refers when he says that, albeit in mystified form, Hegel grasps man as the product of his own labour, through alienation and the overcoming of alienation. Nevertheless, Marx holds that Hegel's discussion of the problematic of alienation is embedded in speculative illusions, and because of this is a 'merely apparent criticism', shading over into 'uncritical positivism.'

Why does Marx qualify his praise of Hegel in this way? Firstly, despite the wealth of content in the *Phenomenology*, everything is treated under the form of consciousness or self-consciousness. This means that a change in consciousness abolishes estrangement because estrangement itself is understood only as an attitude adopted by consciousness. This 'abolition' leaves everything in reality as it is. Thus the critical apparatus issued in 'uncritical positivism'. Thus, consciousness has no content.

Secondly, since the 'subject' of the movement is 'spirit', Hegel cannot conceive of objectification except as resulting in estrangement—hence he substitutes for the category of objectification that of alienation which, like objectification has the connotation of positing as objective but which also implies the relinquishment of what is manifested, constituting therefore an alienation. Nonetheless, Hegel sees something positive in this process because in this alienation spirit becomes objective to itself. It is an essential moment in spirit's self-actualization and self-awareness. Hegel is not, then, opposed to objectification, on the grounds that it leads to estrangement. He certainly thinks that it does lead to estrangement, but this does not mean that he thinks spirit should rest content in itself and avoid the misfortune of alienation from itself. However, instead of a real historical solution we are provided with a displacement of the problem into general philosophical reflection issuing in a solution used exclusively within philosophy, which preserves estrangement as a moment in the absolute. This is, as Marx says 'merely apparent criticism'. In truth, Hegel's equation of objectification and alienation makes him uncritical of the estrangement brought to life in spirit's self-actualization. That is to say, Hegel, in common with modern political economy, grasps labour as the essence of human development but not as alienated from itself in capitalist society because, if one is unable to posit a genuine historical negation of the negation, the existing conditions become the horizon which blocks off the possibility of a critical standpoint. In fact, these conditions which twist and distort the objectification of man in and trough labour are endorsed as the necessary groundwork within which the coming-to –be of man for himself must occur. The world of estrangement is presented as labour's absolute self- expression.

It is quite illuminating to have a close look at what Hegel has to say concerning fear of death. For this consciousness has been fearful, not of this or that particular thing or just at odd moments, but its whole being has been seized with dread. In that experience, it has been quite unmanned, has trembled in every fiber of its being, and everything solid and stable has been shaken to its foundation. But this pure universal movement, the absolute melting-away of everything stable, is the simple, essential nature of self-consciousness, absolute negativity, pure being for self, self is also explicit for the bondsman, for in the lord it exists for him as his object. Hegel's argument is that the fear of death, which appears to make everything stable and solid, is not to be so. In situations of dire emergency, when our life is at stake, we are wiling to abandon any of our settled habits and actions; and similarly, we know that whole civilizations will suddenly in circumstances of war find, certain technological achievements possible which under less threatening circumstances appeared impossible.

Hegel contends that this fear is structured, stabilized, and given objective form in the person and presence of the master. With the institution of slavery, the slave becomes fixed in his dependence on the master for his life. Only the master's desire for recognition, and later his greed or mercy or insecurity, requires him to let his slaves survive. The master/slave relation is the phenomenological first fully social form of human dependence; the character of this dependence marks this relation may take on social, economic, religious and political forms; it may exist between individual persons, groups of persons, classes of nations. It requires the repression of given desires, and the substitution of the desires of another. It is initially in this substitution that the sociality of desire becomes established, thus allowing human work to begin.

Slavery and Freedom

In seeking to explain and transcend the subordination of working class in advanced industrial societies, Hegel's *Phenomenology* is arguably the most significant text, offering a rich harvest of concepts for Marxist theory. Its analysis of the dynamics of domination and subordination in the master-slave dialectic raises issues, which lie at the heart of the Marxist critique of capitalism. In so far as, he construes the move from slavery to freedom in terms of a movement away from nature or biological constraints, towards self-consciousness. Consciousness and labour as the preconditions of the transformation of oppressive social relationships play a central role in Hegel's political thought. He also sheds light on the power of ideologies by pointing to the extent to which the slave may accept his or her slavery.

Hegel postulates a distinction between two modes of consciousness: 'the one is independent, and its essential nature is to be for itself; the other is dependent, and its essence is life or existence for another. The former is the Master, or Lord, the latter the Bondsman'. For Hegel, self-consciousness exists only to the extent that it is acknowledged or recognized by another, but he emphasizes that the master's recognition is dependent upon the consciousness of the bondman: 'for, just where the master has effectively achieved lordship, he really finds that something has come about quite different from an independent consciousness. It is not an independent, but rather a dependent consciousness that he has achieved. The master relying on the slave becomes dependent, while the slave, in working for the master, achieves independence through the acquisition of knowledge in productive labour. For Hegel, the master represents a purely transient stage in the history of spirit while the significant movement in human development springs from the consciousness of the slave because the slave meets the two preconditions of freedom, namely fear and service. Fear of the master is significant insofar as it imposes discipline and thus constitutes 'the beginning of wisdom'. Without this initial fear of the master, freedom is impossible.

The slave has the possibility of confronting freedom through fear and service, while the master's relation to the world is mediated by, and contained in, the desire for the object, but this satisfaction of desire is seen by Hegel as evanescent. The master remains trapped within his own egotism: experiencing neither fear nor labour, he perceives in the slave only his immediate will and receives from him the formal recognition of an unfreed consciousness. But for the slave, the experience of fear according to Hegel is the first movement of freedom. Fear, combined with service or labour, constitutes the necessary precondition for the development of self-consciousness: 'Without the formative activity shaping the thing, fear remains inward the mute, and consciousness does not become objective for itself'. In serving the master, the slave loses his 'individual self-will' and goes beyond the immediacy of appetite. His divestment of self and fear of the lord mark, for Hegel, the beginning of knowledge and the movement to universal self-consciousness. Freedom is attained 'solely by risking life' when consciousness, which has 'tottered and shaken', is combined with struggle. The fear and service of slavery contain, for Hegel, the possibility of freedom beyond subjectivity. Self-consciousness passes through the slave rather than the master, dependent on the slave for recognition and trapped by desires, which lack substance and objectivity.

The importance of work for Hegel is that in labour the worker moves beyond immediate instinctual life, flees the darkness of nature and becomes truly human. Hegel does not idealise the labour-process – but rather acknowledges the drudgery of mechanistic labour. However, he does characterize the labour-process as a means of enhancing self-consciousness and says that in working upon an object the worker externalizes his self-consciousness and makes it permanent: 'precisely in labour where there seemed to be merely some outsider's mind and ideas involved, the slave becomes aware through this rediscovery of himself by himself, of having and being a "mind of his own".

The slave's proximity to freedom thus rests on his engagement in purposive rational labour. While the master's desire is ephemeral, the slave's labour fosters the development of self-consciousness. His desires embrace those of the master as well as his own, forcing him to move beyond the immediacy of his own will. For Hegel, the feeling of the worthlessness of egotism and the 'habit of obedience' of the slave is a necessary stage in the growth of self-consciousness. In satisfying the needs of others, the slave moves beyond nature towards a genuinely human existence, as he enters into relations with others and becomes part of the division of labour. It is precisely this dimension of slavery as potential consciousness which eats away at the heart of the master-slave relation and the system of slavery arising from it, ultimately leading to its destruction. But in stressing potential rather than actual consciousness, Hegel attributes a degree of responsibility for slavery to the slave rather than the master; Unless the slave struggles to win his freedom, he deserves his servitude, since slavery demands its own negation. A slave is subject to an ethical imperative to free himself. There is no 'absolute injustice' in slaves remaining slaves, argues Hegel, for if they do not risk their lives to gain freedom, their slavery is deserved: 'he who has not the courage to risk his life to win freedom, that man deserves to be a slave'. Slavery, as a system of social relationship, cannot survive unless the slave accepts and is at home in his slavery.

A further justification of slavery for Hegel lies in the fact that slavery may be appropriate to a particular phase of social development and in that sense 'just'. 'Slavery and tyranny', he says, 'are, therefore, in the history of nations a necessary stage and hence relatively justified'. Referring to the slaves' hostility to the efforts of English reformers to abolish slavery, he argues that slavery is accepted as natural by the slaves. While slavery is seen as an absolute injustice by Western reformers, it is the typical legal relationship of a society in which a low value is placed on human life and this evaluation of human life is internalized by the slaves themselves. It is entirely consistent, for Hegel, with the state of nature characteristic of primitive societies. If a man can sell his wife, parents and children into slavery, this demonstrates a contempt for life in general as well as his own and signifies an absence of morality. Taking a broader historical perspective, Hegel sees slavery as part of the transition from the state of nature to a genuinely ethical existence. It arises in a world where 'a wrong is still right', where wrong has some validity and constitutes a necessary moment in the progression towards a higher stage of development. Only when a society reaches maturity may it realize its freedom and eliminate slavery. Where a society is undeveloped, we should expect to find slavery, says Hegel. Even in Greece this 'relative injustice' may be found, since in that culture freedom was not based on the idea of a rational self-consciousness. Only if self-consciousness apprehends itself through thought, human does free itself from contingency and move into the realm of morality and ethical life. Rational reflection is what distinguishes the slave's unfreedom from freedom, and thus it was the Greek slaves resisting their slavery, and not the citizens, who grasped this and sought to attain their 'eternal human rights'.

If we consider the implications of Hegel's analysis of slavery for an understanding of social change, his standpoint may seem at first sight to be rather pessimistic. He attributes responsibility for slavery to the slave and seems to suggest that the slave enjoys his slavery. He also treats slavery as appropriate to particular forms of life, as a necessary stage in social development and therefore inevitable. Hegel's account of slavery is an historical account, which presupposes the potentiality for changes in relationships of domination and subordination, given certain changes in the way of life in which these relationships are grounded.

Hegel's acknowledgement of the slave's identification with his slavery is combined with an awareness of the tensions inherent in any relation of oppression. The dominance of the master over the slave and the slave's acquiescence are neither stable nor eternal. Rather, the relation is one of constant struggle in which the master's authority, from the beginning, may be negated. This may be illustrated by Hegel's observations on slavery in certain African cultures in his *Lectures* on the philosophy of world history. A system of despotism based on force, patriarchal authority and an arbitrary will is inherently weak, says Hegel, for the despot is always in danger of being challenged by his subjects: 'thus even such despotism as this is not completely blind; the peoples of Africa are not just slaves but assert their own will too'. Slavery, as a system of social relations, can never be secure for 'the sword really hangs above the despot's head day and night' and, like his subjects, the despot is vulnerable to the lack of respect for human life.

The movement towards self-consciousness is built into the master-salve relation and incorporates the possibility of freedom for the master as well as the slave. The emancipation of the slave furthers the interest of the master since, as Hegel notes in the *Phenomenology*, only when the slave realizes his freedom does the master move beyond immediacy. This idea is applied to colonial relations in the *Philosophy of Right* where he points out that 'Colonial independence proves to be of the greatest advantage to the mother country, just as the emancipation of the slave turns out to the greatest advantage of the owners'.

Although the master receives recognition from the slave he can, within the existing power relationship, never be sure that the recognition is genuine. It is for this reason that Hegel sees the liberation of the slave as furthering the interests of the master. Camus rightly observes that the master, to his determent, is recognized in his autonomy by a consciousness, which he himself does not recognize as autonomous. Therefore, he cannot be satisfied and his autonomy is only negative. Mastery is a blind alley. Since, moreover, he cannot renounce mastery and become a slave again, the eternal destiny of masters is to live unsatisfied or to be killed.

Furthermore, Hegel is optimistic that when the slaves begin to resist, the system of slavery will perish: 'if a nation does not merely imagine that it wants to be free but actually has the energy to will its freedom,' he says in the *Phenonerology of Mind*, 'then no human power can hold it back in the servitude of a merely passive obedience to authority'. Because freedom constitutes the human essence for Hegel, he emphasizes that the slave has an absolute right to freedom himself and essential to this transition to freedom is rational self-consciousness. While attributing slavery to the will of the slave, Hegel nonetheless envisages a complete reversal of the master-slave relation given the will for change and consciousness of the potential for freedom:

> It is only as thinking intelligence that the will is genuinely a will and free. The slave does not know his essence, his infinity, his freedom; he does not know himself as human in essence; and he lacks this knowledge of himself because he does not think himself. This self-consciousness which apprehends itself through thinking is essentially human, and thereby frees itself from the contingent and the false, is the principle of right, morality and all ethical life.

He contrasts this reflective self-consciousness with appeals to 'feeling, enthusiasm, the heart and the breast', which are absorbed in 'instinctive desire' and 'particularity'. For freedom to be obtained, the slave has to move beyond his own individuality, as well as that of the master, to grasp 'the absolutely rational in its universality which is independent of the particularity of the subjects'. Hegel's identification of the freedom of the slave with reflective self-consciousness, and of the need to move beyond feelings to reason, points clearly to the importance of rational reflection for workers as a means of transforming their position.

Moreover, while Hegel gives an historical analysis of slavery, this does not commit him to a total relativism, which would rule out criticism of particular forms of life. While attracted to the liberal ideas of the French Revolution, for example, Hegel recognized the limitations of the emerging bourgeois society as well as the shortcomings of the liberal theories used to understand and justify the new order. Like Marx and Engels he was well aware that the progressive aspects of liberal capitalism were accompanied by greed, egotism and self-interest, which would lead to the 'creation of a rabble of paupers'. He notes that 'At the same time, this brings with it, at the other end of the social scale, conditions which greatly facilitate the concentration of disproportionate wealth in a few hands'. Hegel did not allow his acknowledgement of the progressive aspects of liberal capitalism to become an apologia for that society. Rather, he saw poverty and class conflict as inevitable features of that mode of production. Hegel draws attention to the pathological effects of a social structure governed by the pursuit of self-interest. Although Hegel did not develop his understanding of the labour-process into an extensive critique of the division of labour of the kind Marx and Engels subsequently elaborated, nonetheless such a critique is implicit in his teleology. The connections he drew between freedom and necessity, consciousness and labour, constituted a significant advance on earlier theories and provided a firm foundation on which to construct an investigation into the development of the division of labour and ways of transcending it.

By showing how slavery is natura or appropriate to particular stages of development, for example, Hegel points to the necessity of a fundamental change in social relationships if slavery is to be eliminated. What is needed is a transformation of the social structure, which generates inequalities and leads to their privatization. Nor will these inequalities be removed by an appeal to moral principles since their subordination is linked to the needs of capital for a reserve army and its own reproduction. Hegel's comments on the 'relative justification' of slavery anticipated Marx's argument in the *Critique of the Gotha Programme* that 'Right can never be higher than the economic structure of society and the cultural development conditioned by it.' Marx's observations on justice have led some commentators to argue that the extraction of surplus value cannot be seen as unjust since it is an essential feature of capitalism and the worker freely exchanges his labour-power for wages. Exploitation is thus a 'natural' feature of capitalist society appropriate to that stage of development and should not be seen in moral terms. It follows form this that it is mistaken to see Marxism as a moral theory aimed at removing injustice: the 'injustice' it analyses are a necessary part of that mode of production and will not be dissolved by a moral critique but only by a radical change in the economic and social structure.

Kant's dualism and Hegel's absolute idealism had both been inadequate to this task. Marx and Engel's marked a new era because they pictured the evolution of consciousness as part of the natural world, as a historic conquest of humankind emerging as a distinct part of nature. They thus provided a natural, material basis on which it was possible to analyze subject and object as a unity of opposites. Only on this basis could they supercede both Kant's dualism and Hegel's vision of a unity predicated on assimilating the natural world to the world of consciousness. They superceded Kant by providing a natural basis on which the unity of knowing and being could be predicated. And they superceded Hegel by developing a dialectic that did not frustrate its own purpose by explaining the real interaction between consciousness and its material basis.

Ethical Life and Overcoming of Alienation

While an outline of Hegel's political philosophy is given in the *Phenomenology of Mind*, in his account of the ethical and social development of spirit, an extended and more developed account is given in his *Philosophy of Right*. This is perhaps Hegel's best-known work, and is a central text in modern political thought. However, it is a work that like many of Hegel's other writings is open to divergent interpretations, and the meaning and significance of Hegel's political philosophy has remained the focus of agitated and heated debate. Immediately after Hegel's death in 1831 there emerged two schools, known as the Young or Left Hegelians and the Old or Right Hegelians, who offered radically different readings of the *Philosophy of Right* and of Hegel's thought as a whole. The Left Hegelians like Marx, Feuerbach and Engels saw in Hegel a utopian view of freedom, community and the triumph of the human spirit, a vision that they tried in their own work to complete; while the Right Hegelians saw in Hegel a theocratic defense of the Prussian state and support for the status quo of absolute monarchy. Since then, almost every shade of political opinion has had protagonists offering what they consider to be a legitimate interpretation of Hegelianism. Even today, Hegel's influence on both left and right wing thinkers continues. If one looks carefully at this puzzling list of followers, interpreters and critics, however, one central feature of Hegel's political philosophy emerges as the focus of interest for both the left and the right: namely, Hegel's searching critique of what he calls "civil society", and by which he means something like liberal commercial society that constitutes the basis of the modern state. It is this critique that has led some like Karl Popper to accuse him of totalitarianism and authoritarianism, while his supporters on both the left and the right have used Hegelian ideas to challenge the fundamental presuppositions of liberalism and modern capitalist societies.

In trying to understand Hegel's political philosophy and his critique of civil society, it is important to remember that it is part of his philosophical project as a whole, which aimed to develop a more unified world-view by revolutionizing our fundamental concepts and ways of thought. Only when this re-thinking of our social categories has been achieved, Hegel suggests, will a better-integrated and less atomistic community be realized. Moreover, he argues that the dialectic of universal and particular is unresolved within civil society, and that the synthesis of these aspects can only be achieved in a higher form of community, which Hegel calls the State.

It is in the *Philosophy of Right* that we discover Hegel's moral and ethical theory. Here Hegel traces the dialectical advance of the normative ideas that shape our thinking about our practical lives. We see how the notion of wrongness develops out of prior ideas, specifically out of the notions of private property and contract. The notion of wrongness in turn leads to the idea of morality, which for Hegel is still an abstract and inadequate concept. The rational political life does not come to a conclusion in the moral life but rather in something beyond it. Hegel insists that what is beyond morality is the ethical life. The ethical life is what overcomes the separation between the individual and society; it is also the life in which true human freedom is finally made manifest.

Creating a Self

The task of the practical, normative life is one of creating or determining a self. At first, we find ourselves in the world as merely natural creatures: our "immediate" impression of ourselves is one of our bodies and their physical environments. Such a creature does not yet have a personality and does not see himself as a distinct person. The transition to the personal self begins when we become aware of ourselves as conscious creatures, as something more than and indeed distinct from our physical bodies Self-consciousness involves an awareness of the self as consciousness. In discovering ourselves as selves aware of our bodies and their environments, we encounter consciousness itself. We also encounter will, since we become aware that we conscious subjects can make changes in the physical domain. When we define ourselves as consciousness and will, we begin to view ourselves as distinct from the natural world: we are not those physical external objects. We comprehend matter and manipulate the external objects. Self-consciousness reveals the self "at a distance" from the physical domain, indeed even from the body. We are separate from all such objects, even from our natural desires and drives.

In being aware of myself as something other than the physical objects I achieve, Hegel claims, a sense of my freedom. It is a purely abstract freedom, however, the freedom of being something more than a physical body shaped by external and internal factors. As abstract, it is inadequate, but it nevertheless provides us with a one-sided insight into our essential nature. What is needed is to give substance to this freedom, to make it concrete and individualized. The personality of the self-conscious, self-identical person is the ground and justification of the abstract concept of right. Personality essentially involves the capacity for rights. It gives rise to the imperative "Be a person and respect others as persons," which Hegel calls the imperative of right. The command of right goes no further than to say, "Do not infringe personality and what personality entails". We are here in the realm of abstract right of personality—rules out slavery as a permissible practice.

The process of creating a self must go beyond this initial abstract stage. It can do this in several ways. First, it may identify itself with the desires it has as a natural, immediate things. It determines itself as the self with these desires, interests, needs. Second, in acting in these desires, it determines itself even further: it is the agent who does this and that the one who shapes the world in specific ways and thereby lends specificity to its own self.

Private Property

In tracing the effort of the abstract personality-as-self-consciousness to give itself concrete substance and to claim the external world as its own, Hegel focuses on the notion of private property. As the personality engages with the world, it grasps, takes possession of, and uses objects in it, claiming them as its own. In this way, there arises the notion of private property. One's sense of personal freedom is manifested in his possession of things. The abstractness and indeterminacy of this freedom is overcome through the possession of concrete things in the world. He is the free possessor of this property, this house, this car, and so on. And in retaining these things and in having continuing privileged access to them he achieves personal freedom. One of the thing he possesses is body, so that he is no longer merely the passive recipient of it. Indeed, the more one's possessions, the greater the extent and degree of his freedom. Private property thus becomes the way in which individual freedom is manifested and made concrete.

Property, in order to continue to be truly one's own, must be used. The best proof of one's ownership of something is that he can sell it to someone else or give it away. One can alienate oneself from it, but one can do this only because the thing is initially his. The ability to separate oneself from one's property also demonstrates that one is not identical with these external objective possessions. Hence this ability to sell property confirms itself as the ability of a conscious, willful person who is free from the immersion in the external world of property.

It is also in the realm of property that we become aware of another person or other people as free, self-relating individuals. One of the ways in which we can alienate ourselves from our private property is to give it to someone else; another way is to exchange it for something another person owns. Such interactions Hegel refers to as contracts. Reason, Hegel tells us, "makes it jus as necessary for men to enter into contractual relationships—gift, exchange, trade, etc.—as to possess property". Exchanging items of property by means of a contract, however, gives rise to the notion of a "common will". "The sphere of contract is made up of this mediation where holding property not merely by means of a thing and my subjective will, but by means of another person's will and so holding it in virtue of my participation in a common will". Hegel insists, however, that the notion of contract does not encompass the area of marriage or the relationship between the individual and the state; it is restricted to the exchange of private property, whereas marriage and citizenship belong to a "sphere of a quite different and higher nature".

Morality

It is in the arena of morality that a person becomes a subject. Prior to the level of morality, an individual may achieve a sense of independence and personality, but this personality is identified only in terms of individual desires and abstract right—the right that flows from ownership of property. Possession of property and contracts themselves rest on individual, subjective and contingent preferences. There is no universal law of conduct to which the individual may appeal and with which he may identify at this earlier stage. Insofar as any universal law is a law of reason, and in as much as reason constitutes the essential nature of human beings, at the stage prior to morality the individual has not been able to identify fully with his essence. At the earlier stage, universal principles are only implicit in the person. These principles become explicit at the level of morality, so that the person comes to actualize his essence to a greater degree. Mere abstract subjectivity at the level of abstract right changes into concrete, actualized subjectivity as the individual identifies with the universal laws of reason, the laws of morality. In attaining such subjectivity, the person becomes a subject.

The universal laws of morality indicate how human beings ought to act and ought to be, not how they actually behave at any moment. Hence, in recognizing moral demands the self has not yet achieved identity with universal law, and to this extent the moral subject still remains abstract and incomplete, not yet fully real. The incompleteness of self in light of the demands imposed by moral law gives rise to the notion of an aim or purpose. The self seeks to become the embodiment of moral law. It recognizes it own rationality in this moral law, but at this stage the law appears as an "ought." In its aim or purpose, the self attempts to become, to be, it attempts to convert "ought" into "is"—to become the actual, objective embodiment of what ought to be. Moral action, according to Hegel, has a special content. This content is welfare, not simply my welfare but the welfare of others as well.

Welfare and Conscience

The moral will has welfare as its content, but because this will is also universal will, it is the welfare of all-individual agents. But what is the content of this welfare? Does it consist of the ends that people actually have—what they actually want? Actual ends do not have the normativity of "the right," and so we cannot define the general welfare in terms of these actual, particular ends: "an intention to secure my welfare or that of others cannot justify an action which is wrong". Being a person of good heart—seeking the welfare, but the good. Welfare is not the good. The good must subsume both right and welfare. The moral will, therefore, must make the good its aim and realize it completely. But how are we to determine what is good?

Here we begin to encounter the problems that Hegel has with the philosophy of Kant. Kant believed that reason alone could determine what is right and good. Hegel grants that a subject has right to listen to reason, but he maintains that reason at the stage of morality is merely "formal." He contrasts this formal reason with objective reason, suggesting among other things, that the former speaks only to the form as one of rational consistency. Kant believed this formal requirement could distinguish actions that are moral from those that are not, but Hegel disagrees. At this point in his argument, however, Hegel is content to point out that formal reason can be correct or incorrect in its judgments. Thus the "right of insight" taken alone would justify a person in acting on the basis of beliefs about the good which turn out to be mistaken. According to this "right," we should listen to our conscience and do what it tells us, even if, as a matter of fact, it misinforms us of what is objectively right or good.

The right of insight leads us to follow our conscience, but the right of objectivity demands that we do what is right and good. Conscience, at the level of the moral will, has no way of determining what is right and good. Its instrument, abstract reason, distinguishes only what is consistent from what is inconsistent, and this, as we have just seen, is insufficient to give content to the pronouncements of conscience. Ideal conscience, true conscience, as Hegel calls it, "is the disposition to will what is absolutely good." The problem we face, however, is that of knowing whether an individual's actual conscience is ideal, true conscience. "Conscience – an individual's actual conscience – is therefore subject to the judgment of its truth or falsity, and when it appeals only to itself for a decision, it is directly at variance with what it wishes to be, namely a rule for a mode of conduct which is rational, absolutely valid, the universal."

In this predicament, conscience runs the risk of mistaking the predilections and biases, the impulses and desires, of the individual agent for absolutely valid, absolutely universal principles. For this reason, "it has become potentially evil". Morality arises out of conscience, but so does evil. Evil are not just a mater of acting from natural inclinations but rather a matter of a self-conscious, reflective agent taking these inclinations and deliberately willing them as the embodiment of right and good. The role of conscience in the moral life at the same time opens up the possibility of evil.

Hegel's assessment of the moral life definitely has its negative aspects. At this stage, self-consciousness is aware of the notion of universal laws and is aware that these laws are the manifestation of reason, the inner nature of self-consciousness. But moral consciousness or the moral will is unable to give any concrete content to these laws and the duties they entail. Moreover, because it understands the will as self-determining, as deriving from its own nature the moral laws it is to follow, moral consciousness appeals to the inner voice of conscience. But it has now way to distinguish false from true conscience, and this opens up possibilities of evil and hypocrisy. So the moral point of view is hardly ideal. As best, it is one stage, one moment, in the effort of consciousness to achieve an adequate sense of self, a concrete, free identity, but all is not negative in Hegel's treatment of morality. We have left behind the merely natural self, with its accidental and incidental features, and we have left behind the stage of contract, where rights are merely negative and reflect at most the arbitrary desires of the participants. The moral self perceives a higher level of existence, one in which its actions are founded on general principles and principles that are rationally valid.

Hegel has high praise for the ethical life what he famously calls *Sittlichkeit*. It is the realization of true freedom; it is the "good become alive" through self-conscious action; and it is the end that drives self-consciousness forward. Unlike the moral order it has "a stable content independently necessary and subsistent in exaltation above subjective opinion and caprice". This content is to be found in the "absolutely valid laws and institutions" of our social existence—in the family, civil society, and the state. Ethical powers regulate the lives of the individuals who participate in these social realms.

The ethical order has both the objectivity that self-consciousness has been seeking and the subjectivity that is the essence of the self. In other words, the subject finds in the ethical order a set of laws—and hence rights, duties and responsibilities—which are objective and which at the same time reflect the real nature of the subject. In following these laws, the subject is following mandates that it gives itself, rules that flow from its own inner being as a rational creature. Thus, the subject is free, not because he does what he contingently and capriciously wants to do, but because he follows the laws of his own real essence. "As substantive in character," Hegel tells us, "these laws and institutions are duties binding on the will of the individual". These duties will appear restrictive only from the standpoint of abstract freedom, the standpoint of unformed or indeterminate subjectivity or arbitrary morality. In fact, just the opposite is really the case:

> The truth is, however, that in duty the individual finds his liberation; first, liberation from dependence on mere natural impulse and from the depression which as a particular subject he cannot escape in his moral reflections on what ought to be and what might be; secondly, liberation from the indeterminate subjectivity which, never reaching reality or the objective determinacy of action, remains self-enclosed and devoid of actuality. In duty the individual acquires his substantive freedom.

The problem we faced in morality, the difficulty of being able to determine on the basis of abstract or formal reason what our duties are, disappears at the ethical level. In an ethical community, it is easy to say what a man must do, what are the duties he has to fulfill in order to be virtuous: he has simply to follow the well-known and explicit rules of his own situation. Participating in an ethical community means assuming certain social roles—for instance, those of husband, father, wife mother, son, daughter, citizen—and thereby taking on the duties and responsibilities inherent in these roles. These obligations are not abstract and indeterminate but are, on the contrary, exceedingly concrete and specific. No longer does a person have to depend on subjective conscience or abstract reasoning to know what he ought to do. We can put too much emphasis on the notion of duties in the ethical sphere. The concept of duty can make the ethical sphere appear more constraining than it really is. Only the person who does not fully participate in his community will sense constraint.

The requirements of our station and our duties are experienced by us as "second nature". In our own minds, they identify us as who we are. Individual willfulness and private conscience vanish and are replaced by "the universal" which "is disclosed in its specific dederminations as rationality actualized". A sense of dignity and a sense of stability arise from participation in this universal. And a sense of deep and genuine freedom also arises: "The right of individuals to be subjectively destined to freedom is fulfilled when they belong to an actual ethical order, because their conviction of their freedom finds its truth in such an objective order, and it is in an ethical order that they are actually in possession of their own essence or their own inner universality". Here we have not just negative freedom, freedom from interference by others, but positive freedom, freedom to be who we essentially are. We enjoy this freedom as particular individuals, for it is particular individuals who make up the ethical order. And we enjoy our rights no less than we recognize our duties. When there is an identity of "the universal will" (the ethical order) with the particular will (the individual person), "right and duty coalesce" –"by being in the ethical order a man has rights in so far as he has duties, and duties in so far as he has rights". Ethical life, far from being coercive, is in fact liberating.

There are three moments or stages in the development of ethical life. The first—the natural or immediate phase—is the family; the second is civil society – "an association of members as self-subsistent individuals...brought about their needs, by the legal system and by an external organization for attaining their particular and common interests;" the third is the state, in which the individuals and their needs and interests are unified. We shall look briefly at each of these stages.

The Family

One enters ethical life through the family. The family is an embodiment of mind and is characterized by love, "which is mind's feeling of its own unity." In the family, we enter into a social organization in which there is both multiplicity and unity. "Hence in a family, one's frame of mind is to have self-consciousness of one's individuality within this unity as the absolute essence of oneself, with the result that one is not in it as an independent person but as a member". One essentially is a member of a particular family, and one's individuality is expressed through the family and one's role in it.

Marriage itself takes "the natural sexual union" and changes it into "a union on the level of mind, into selfconscious love". Hegel acknowledges that a marriage may subjectively arise from the natural inclinations of the two parties, but the objective source of marriage—even in the case of arranged marriages—is "the free consent of the persons, especially in their consent to make themselves one person, to renounce their natural and individual personality to this unity of the one with the other". It is our ethical duty, Hegel affirms, to enter the married state, for in doing so we enter the ethical level of life and transcend accidental passions. Marriage may allow for the satisfaction of physical passion, but its primary aim is to attain a "spiritual bond of union" and to rise above "the contingency of passion and the transience of particular caprice". Marriage contains "the sensuous moment, the one proper to physical life," but the ethical bond at the heart of marriage can "subsist exclusively in reciprocal love and support". The physical moment is subordinated to the ethical character of the marriage relation and to the recognition, by the partners, that marriage is an ethical bond.

Monogamy is an ethical requirement imposed by marriage. In entering the marriage state, individual personality is surrendered to the marital tie, whole-hearted surrender of this personality. "Marriage, and especially monogamy," Hegel tells us, "is one of the absolute principles on which the ethical life of a community depends". But marriage should not be seen as compulsory, from either the point of view of entering it or staying in it. Once the dispositions and actions of the spouses become "hostile and contrary" and estrangement is total, an objective third party—a civil authority capable of seeing beyond any passing whims and moods on the part of the two parties, may grant a divorce.

The inward tie linking husband and wife is given external embodiment in the family's property and capital. The children of the marriage are also the externalization of this internal unity. "It is only in the children that the unity itself exists externally, objectively, and explicitly as a unity, because the parents love and children as their love, as the embodiment of their own substance". The children have the right to maintenance and education by their love, as the embodiment of their own substance". The children have the right to maintenance and education by their parents, and the parents in turn have a right to the service of their offspring. The punishment inevitably involved in the rearing of children has a moral aim: "to deter them from exercising a freedom still in the toils of nature and to lift the universal into their consciousness and will". Children, Hegel warns, "are not things and cannot be the property either of their parents or others." Indeed, in the children there lies the future dissolution of the familay, for when these children come of age "they come recognized as persons in the eyes of the law and as capable of holding free property of their own and founding families of their own."

Civil Society

Hegel's conception of civil society is that of a social and economic organization or system of "complete interdependence, wherein the livelihood, happiness, and legal status of one man is interwoven with the livelihood, happiness, and right of all". The actualization and security of each person's well being depend on his her working within this system, his her desires and needs being held in check by the universal laws governing all of its members. Such members of civil society – "burghers," Hegel calls them—exist as private persons and pursue their own personal interests. Indeed, the laws of the society are a means to the fulfillment of personal interests. At the same time, the laws are such as to link up the well-being of the various citizens and to ensure that in working for one's own interest one is at the same time serving the interests of others. These rational system of laws thus enables the satisfaction of all of the interests in society.

The system of supply and demand operating in civil society involves a process that conceives of needs and work in the abstract and develops a division of labour to serve these needs and to allocate to individuals the role and functions needed to do so. It also creates class division—in particular, the agricultural class, the business class, and the class of civil servants—and the social distinctions that go with them, the individual person who becomes a member of one or the other of these classes thus becomes "something definite, i.e., something specifically particularized". This class status or social position—one's station—provides concrete identity along with concrete duties and rights.

All members of civil society, however, regardless of their social position, equally count as persons in the eyes in the judicial system: "A man counts as a man in virtue of his manhood alone, not because he is a Jew, Catholic, Protestant, German, Italian, etc." In civil society, "the right becomes positive law," law backed up by the sanctions administered by the judicial system. For the first time, Hegel tells us, universal rights acquire "true determinacy", so that the abstractions and controversies of the moral sphere are left behind. The concrete content of positive law relates to matters of contract to the complexity of social, agricultural, and business ties, to family matters, and to the administration of justice.

We are thus lifted by these considerations to a higher level of self-understanding. We begin to discern how the institutions of civil society constitute the forms through which we achieve identity and how reconciliation to the imperatives of this institutional matrix is essential to maintaining and perfecting that identity. Civil society consists roughly of the individual, the executive and enforcement branches of government, the family, the corporation and the market. It is these entities in their institutional interactions and modes of consciousness. It is the state experienced as an external entity, understood to act upon the self, but not yet understood to enter internally into the very constitution of the self and the ethical life which hold the totality together.

Hegel is very much impressed with civil society, calling it 'the achievement of the modern world.' For the market, the conjunction with the other institutions, provides both rooms within which the principle of modern individuality can flourish and the combination by means of which it can be kept under lock and key. When each pursues private ends as an entrepreneur, banker, worker or farmer, he experiences himself to be an agent with rights, interests, conscience, responsibility and freedom. The activities tend to concentrate each participant on its particular interest or concern, drawing attention away from the whole, which enables these interests to be pursued together. But civil society, through its principle of coordination through organized competition, implicates the individual unwittingly in the life of the whole. In it may interests can only be attained through exchange with others, and so out of self-interest one produces or trades with others, and they do so as well: 'The particular person is essentially so related to other particular persons that each establishes himself and finds satisfaction by means of the others.' Civil society, with the entrepreneur and the market as its core, introduces subjectivity into the world and harnesses it for the common good.

But civil society, by itself, is constantly on the verge of going too far, of destroying itself in the clash among particular interests, desires, and principles. It does contain two mediating institutions which help to instill the principles of ethical life into its members and into institutional relations. The family, whose interior form finds its rational basis in the different physical characteristics of the two sexes,' educates its members into ethical life. The wife is determined naturally to concentrate on the internal quality of family life, while the husband represents the family in public life. The recognition of each of the unity they establish out of difference, and the importance that child-rearing carries for the future of the order, constitute the micro-experience out of which implication in the larger ethical life can develop. Because of the substantial interest the whole has in the health of the family as an institution, divorce must not be based on the whim or desire of the parties alone; it must be determined by a representatives of the state whether marriage can be restored or not. The corporation similarly mediates between the particularities of civil society and the ethical life. But even with the family and the corporation, civil society is not self-subsistent. Two of its limitations are particularly important, for they strike at the heart of subjectivity and universality as Hegel understands them. The first flows from the tendency of entrepreneurs, in the competitive pursuit of profit, to squeeze as much out of the workforce as possible. The increase in wealth which results benefits the entire order. But that is only 'one side of the picture.' The other side is the subdivision and restriction of particular jobs. This results in the dependence and distress of the class tied to work of that sort, and these again entail inability to feel and enjoy the broader freedoms and especially the intellectual benefits of civil society.

Hegel argued in the *Phenomenology* that though work is fundamental to the achievement of agency and self-consciousness, alienation this tendency of civil society is self-destructive. It alienates an entire portion of the populace from the common life, pushing it outside the reach of ethical life and making it susceptible to coordination only through force and coercion. The second self-destruction tendency of civil society, again flowing from the very competitive system which enables subjectivity to the and regulates it excesses, is to drive the income of those at the lowest level below subsistence – below the level needed for one to function effectively as a 'member of the society.' This class of paupers becomes a 'rabble,' unjustly treated in itself, resentful of the ethical life it is called upon to follow, and destructive of the larger life through its resistance and the orientation toward it instilled in the public. This tendency must be reversed, but the state confronts a dilemma when it tries to do so. It must adopt welfare programs to lift paupers to a subsistence level; it might call upon private charity to maintain them; or it might give them public employment. But the first two responses violate 'the principle of civil society and the feeling of individual independence and self-respect in its individual member,' and the third exacerbates the evil which produced unemployment: 'an excess of production and the lack of a proportionate number of consumers who are themselves also producers.

As a result and this is Hegel's third claim, civil society is one-sided and abstract. Hegel argues that modern society, based on market mechanisms and abstract rights, uproots individuals from their communities, depriving their lives of the weight given to them by traditional roles and values. Human relations become matters of contract, and there is nothing to be respected for itself. We treat our fellow citizens as abstract persons, but do not have any deeper feeling for them: we respect their freedoms, but do not feel any underlying identity with them. This erosion of the community in modern times means that traditional values and meanings have been lost, and with them the sense of belonging to any particular groups. Instead, we feel contingently aligned with particular class within the market, but have lost the more concrete unity to be found in more traditional societies. We treat each other as means to our ends, but do not feel that we are related by anything other than an external conjunction of interests: we have lost the sense of community.

State

Despite his recognition of achievements the ofcirel society therefore, Hegel stands as a formidable critic of modern liberal society, and it is this that has endeared him to both the Left and the Right: thinkers on the Left have endorsed his criticism of the market as dehumanizing and exploitative, and of the hollowness of liberal freedoms, while thinkers on the Right have echoed his worries about the erosion of community and public sentiment in modern society. Given these limitations of civil society, therefore, Hegel argues that there must be a form of association over and above that of the market place, and this is Hegel's state. Hegelian state was supposed to act as a form of association beyond that of civil society, in which the purely abstract freedom, individualism and community of the latter would be transcended.

First of all, in the state the abstract freedom of civil society is transcended because in the state one does not act as a purely self-interested individual driven by egoistic desires and needs, but rather as a citizen, who recognizes that one has certain duties and social responsibilities. Hegel argues that this is only superficially a limitation of one's abstract freedom, and only appears as such due to a one-sided emphasis on individuality: in fact, the truly rational agent, who adopts a more universal outlook, comes to see that his or her duties are the expression of the rational will, and so are rather expressions of a higher freedom. In the state, Hegel argues, one does not feel a tension between one's individual will and the universal laws: rather, they coincide.

Secondly, in the state the abstract individuality of civil society is transcended, in so far as the individual is not acknowledged to be more than a mere person by society, and is treated as a concrete individual, someone with a determinate place within the social whole. This comes about because as political, not merely economic agents within the state, individuals no longer view themselves as atomistic units, but see themselves as engaged in a wider project, as parts of an overarching social whole.

Thus, thirdly, the state embodies a more concrete notion of community than that found in civil society. Hegel argues that the self-interested motivations of the market place give way to the general interests of the state, as individuals come to feel themselves to constitute one society, with a shared culture and ethical life at stake.

Hegel's theory of the modern state is designed to show how freedom comes to fruition in modernity. The modern state is the one entity capable of encompassing the principles of subjectivity and expressive unity in one diverse and harmonious whole; and freedom cannot be lifted to its highest level until these two domains of realization are drawn together in the same life. The essence of the state is implicitly on the verge of realization in modern life, according to Hegel, but one more ingredient is required to bring it to its fulfillment:

> When the implicit rationality of the state is rendered explicit, not only will its appearance change but its real structure will shift too. For now the members will recognize more

> fully the freedom which is theirs, the limitations they must accept to protect this freedom, and the ethical life they must endorse to enable the state to achieve its highest level of existence. And this recognition will infuse the life of the individual, the family, corporate associations, the market, the civil service and the relations all these entities bear to the state.

Each of the simple levels of consciousness is brought through awareness of its internal insufficiency to a higher and more encompassing level of understanding. Thus, at the first level, Locke is right and is the simple consciousness he represents: property is an essential right of human beings. But this formulation also misleads. It is not merely good to a personality, which is already formed, and demanding it; it is not merely the right of a natural person. The institutionalization of property helps to form the self as a person or agent. The key distinction here is between mere possession and property. Property is the social recognition that something belongs to me. For that recognition to be realized a whole system of laws, rules of contract and exchange, standards of responsibility, understandings of freedom, definitions of crime and punishment have to come into being. These norms, given institutional form by civil society, constitute the self as a person with rights; they introduce first personhood and then subjectivity into the self. Hegel distinguishes person from subject; the first is a bearer of rights and the second advances freedom into the entire realm of morality.

Thus, 'contract presupposes that the parties entering into it recognize each other as persons and property owners.' A similar relation is implied with respect to crime. For there is no institution of property and contract unless it is a crime to break a contract or steal another's property. In a hunting and gathering society, for instance, the self is not recognized as a bearer of rights, the contractual form does not define much of the common life, and responsibility is likely to be diffused among individuals, groups and the gods. So, through the institutional recognition of property, contract and exchange, I am seen and see myself to be an agent, capable of owning, acting according to private will, entering into contract, establishing my own career, accountable legally and morally for stealing from others, and worthy of being held responsible individually for the successes and failures in my life.

The institution of property, embodied in a reciprocal web of recognition, endows the self with the sort of recognition the two parties sought implicitly in the relationship of Lordship and Bondage. They could not achieve it because its institutional preconditions were lacking. The self-consciousness of heroes had not advanced out of its primitive simplicity either to reflection on the distinction between act and action or between the external event and knowledge of the circumstances. On the contrary they accepted responsibility for the whole compass of the deed. Socrates and Christ, later, could project the idea of subjectivity, but it could not become installed fully and securely as a way of life until property and civil society unfolded together.

The state is the only self-subsistent entity. It draws the other essential elements into an inclusive totality, which can sustain itself; and it enables each of the elements to maintain its difference from others while harmonizing with them in a self-subsistent whole. The primary institutions of the state are its constitutional law, an executive branch, a legislative branch, a monarch who is the sovereign power, and a class of civil servants who have their eye on the universal interest or the interests of the state as such.

We cannot explore its institutional structure in detail. But the essence of the state is that through its public and written laws, its sovereign power to resolve the most fundamental conflicts, and its personification of sovereignty in the hereditary monarch, it transcends the sphere of unconscious regulation. It articulates or brings to self-consciousness principles and understandings which govern the land; it is the sphere of self-conscious action in support of the common good; and it nurtures and protects a customary ethic which infuses the inward life of the well-ordered subject, family, church, corporation and civil society. The state is the locus of Spirit, and Spirit comes to its highest and most differentiated political expression in the state.

Bureaucracy

While Hegel allows room for contingency in the modern state, its most fundamental institutions are held to embody rational necessity: each plays an essential role in maintaining the integrity of the state. This conviction, expressive of the view that Spirit installs itself more fully in actuality as history progresses, compels Hegel to endow actuality with rationality wherever it is indispensable to the state. Hegel's philosophy of intrinsic purpose; each bearer of difference is incomplete until completed through union with the other in a family; and the family helps to lift its embers to participation in the higher unity of the state. Hegel finds in the executive rather than in the legislative branch a group of people who are to look after the objective interests of all groups in the society, disregarding the subjective consciousness of those affected by their decisions. Hegel turns here to the civil bureaucracy and the ministers of government. This is the only group that identifies its interest directly with that of the state. These people are uniquely suited to this task by virtue of their background and training. Their identification with the public good is secured through their receiving a salary from the state and through the countervailing pressures exerted by the monarchy, the corporations, and public opinion, which prevent the civil service from ossifying into a class with its own interests. This is the group that most stringently embodies the principle of meritocracy. Individuals are not appointed to office on account of their birth or native personal gifts. The objective factor in their appointment is knowledge and proof of ability. Such proof guarantees that the state will get what it requires; and since it is the sole condition of appointment, it also guarantees to every citizen the chance of joining the class of civil servants.

Although both the civil servant class of the state and the public authority of civil society deal with the activities of the commercial class, the former is differentiated from the latter because its task is the execution of the general laws of the state rather than the regulation of particular conflicts arising from civil society. Although it tends to the interests of the business class, the bureaucracy is insulted from the immediate pressures of civil society. To this end, appointments to public office are not to be contracts that must be periodically renewed but appointments conditional for their perpetuation only on the fulfillment of the duties involved. The executive branch is organized into various departments, whose heads are in direct contract with the monarch. All the institutions of the Hegelian state are in some sense to converge toward the monarch. The entire analysis of Hegel's political philosophy developed in this study leads to an interpretation of the Hegelian state that holds that the more important of the three branches of the state are legislature and the crown and that minimizes the importance of the executive branch in the Hegelian state.

This is not to say that the material well-being and the economic activities of the citizens are disregarded in the Hegelian state. On the contrary, these aspects of life are the chief concern of the entire sphere of civil society and of the bureaucracy within the state proper. But it is to say that when Hegel posits the political state as a sphere higher than civil society, he is indicating that these materialistic concerns are secondary to the more important question of the political consciousness and identity of the citizens in the modern political world. For Hegel, the bureaucracy is without a doubt the most important authority for the realization of political autonomy against social interests and interest groups. George Sabine has rightly expressed the traditional view when he wrote: "The key to Hegel's constitutionalism was the high importance that he attached to an official governing class, the 'universal class' as he called it. It represents the general will and the reason of society. In comparison with the part assigned to officialdom, both representative institutions and the monarchy played a minor role in Hegel's theory of constitutionalism, in spite of the mystical reverence that he gave to the monarchy".

Monarchy

The structure of the state is said by Hegel to follow from the philosophical concept of the free, rational will alone. The state must be treated as a great architectonic structure, as a hieroglyph of the reason which reveals itself in actuality. Everything to do with mere utility, externality, and so forth, must be eliminated from the philosophical treatment of the subject.

The constitution of the state articulates a structure that must be understood as one totality. The three branches of the state are not to be thought of as competing powers, on the "balance of power" model of much of U.S. constitutional law theory, for example. Competing power centers produce no real political sovereignty, no focus for state authority with which the citizens can identify. This focus in the Hegelian state is the constitutional monarchy. It is only through the reference of all public authority back to the final decision-making will of the monarch that, for Hegel, the state can be said to exercise legitimate sovereignty and not just mere power. Sovereignty requires that all the autonomous power centers of the society converge toward a single point of public authority. In the Hegelian system, the office of the crown is deduced from the concept of political sovereignty.

Hegel contends that in feudal times, the monarch was not sovereign at all, but the state itself was not sovereign either. For one thing, the particular functions and powers of the state and civil society were arranged into independent corporations and societies, so that the state as a whole was rather an aggregate than an organism; and, for another thing, office was the private property of individuals and hence what they were to do in their public capacity was left to their own opinion and caprice.

One need only compare this with Hegel's schematization of the "three substantive divisions" of his idea of the state to see that the monarchy has taken the place of the judiciary in the standard scheme of things. The divisions of the Hegelian state are the legislature the executive and the Crown.

The substitution of the crown for the judiciary follows from the Hegelian distinction between civil society and the state. On the standard liberal model, the judiciary is of course part of the state apparatus. However, because it deals with the harmonization of individual, material interests and not with the determination of universal principles related to the political identity of the citizens, for Hegel the judiciary is part of civil society. This leaves a gap in the structure of the state, for three is still a need to connect the particular (executive) and the universal (legislative) branches. But a way must be found to do this that is consonant with the level of universality and subjectivity reached by the state that does not represent a regression back to the level of society. This unifying moment must be established as an institution independent of the other branches, so that "all determinations of the Idea receive their due". Hegel finds all this in the final "I will" of the monarch. His reading of the historical development of political consciousness tells him that in all ages people have looked for a final, unconditional sign of decision as the ultimate basis of political right, but only in the modern period has this aspect of consciousness come into its own within the political system. Previously, one could witness people deriving the last word on great events and important affairs of state from oracles, a 'divine sign', the entrails of animals, the feeding and flight of birds, etc. It was when men had not yet plumbed the depths of self-consciousness or risen out of their undifferentiated unity of substance to their independence that they lacked strength to look within their own being for the final word.

For Hegel, then, it is a sign of the maturation of Spirit that this "final word" is now understood as uttered by the human will rather than sought in nature or religion. It is the triumph of the Spirit that this apotheosized will has now been symbolically internalized into the political system as its apex. This marks the autonomy of politics from nature, religion, or tradition—an autonomy strenuously achieved through the course of human history. Although this will must be situated within the political system, it must also be insulated from the shifting pressures and contingencies of that system, because it could not otherwise provide the necessary substantiality and permanency. Monarchy must therefore be not elective but hereditary.

Foreign Relations

The sovereignty of the state vis-à-vis other states is the complement to the sovereignty of the vis-à-vis its own citizens. The monarch is the pivot between these two sides of constitutional law. Hegel discusses international relations in the context of constitutional law, because the major thrust of Hegel's analysis of international relations is to deny that relations between sovereign states can be brought under any obligatory, enforceable law. In an argument specifically aimed against the Kantian idea of international law expressed in Kant's essay "Perpetual Peace", Hegel insists that because "every state is sovereign and autonomous against its neighbours", it and its neighbours are "in a state of nature in relation of each other". There is no universal court of appeal among states representing a higher authority to which they can appeal to resolve disputes. Consequently, though states may sign treaties to which Hegel affirms they are morally bound, in the final analysis it remains a state's prerogative to interpret the clause of any treaty and abrogate its obligations. The relation between states is a relation between autonomous entities which make mutual stipulations but which at the same time are superior to these stipulations.

Despite the fact that the principles of national sovereignty preclude the establishment of any international legal system, there is nonetheless a system of less formal international relations among nations. Each nation recognizes the integrity and autonomy of other nations. On Hegel's analysis, each nation's internal sovereignty as logically prior to this recognition among nations does not establish sovereignty, it does solidify it. The logical priority of internal over external sovereignty is Hegel's most systematic way of expressing ideas we have come across earlier—the idea that a constitution cannot be imposed on a people externally but must grow out of the historical experiences of that people and the idea that a political system presupposes an economic system on whose integrating mechanisms it can build.

The monarch is more than just a diplomat. The main reason for the conduct of foreign affairs falls to the monarch for internal rather than external considerations, because the complexity of international relations must not be allowed to shatter the internal unity of the state. Every state must speak with only one voice to other states, not primarily to avoid chaos in international affairs but to cement unity at home. The causal priority of domestic over foreign political considerations throughout Hegel's analysis of international relations follows from this concept of the sovereignty of the modern state. This does not mean, however, that there is no feedback mechanism by which the conduct of foreign affairs and the recognition of the sovereignty of the state by other states can enter into the consciousness of the citizens. Rather, it is precisely here that the monarchy as the transition from internal to external sovereignty has a key role to play. In a sense, the monarch is the only world-historical individual in the modern era, because there are no further new fundamental principles to be announced by any world-changing figures in the modern age.

War

Hegel's account of of war in the modern state contains the same lessons. For while Hegel treats the state as a self-subsistent whole, its self-subsistence does not consist simply in its internal composition and the inward identifications of its members. The centrifugal forces of civil society are too powerful for that. The internal dynamic of civil society presses each individual and corporate interest to concentrate exclusively on itself and to forget its dependence upon the whole. But the threat of external enemies dose so for the state as a whole what the risk of death did for the self in the relationship of Lordship and Bondage. It draws particular interest together in awareness of their membership in the state, and it teaches each that sacrifices for the whole is a condition of both membership and individuality. War is not, then, a contingent feature of the modern state, nor is it an evil always to be avoided. It is a necessity expressing a higher purpose.

War is the state of affairs, which deals in earnest with the vanity of temporal goods and concerns. War has the higher significance that by its agency, 'the ethical health of people is preserved in their indifference to the stabilization of finite institutions; just as the blowing of the winds preserves the sea from the foulness which would be the result of a prolonged calm, so also corruption in nations would be the product of prolonged, let along perpetual peace.'

Here, Hegel invests in war a necessity of a modern state system with spiritual significance. Because war inevitably emerges between sovereign states without a common authority, it reveals Spirit at work fulfilling an inner need. Without periodic war, the modern state cannot keep the principle of subjectivity in rein: it must either lose it capacity to maintain the health of the whole in which subjectivity is set or it must maintain its internal structure in a coercive way. Either response corrupts the life of the state, so war must arise periodically to crystallize the minds and identifications of its members. War disciplines subjectivity while allowing the principle itself to remain intact in civil society.

But the later-modern possibility of nuclear holocaust throws this entire identity between system necessity and its fulfillment into disarray. Today war means the risk of extinction, either of civilization or humanity. If it is a need, it is one that must not be fulfilled. Perhaps the late-modern state needs war to maintain itself internally but must resist it to defer the risk of total destruction. That contradiction places the internal structure of the state and the Hegelian ontology of Spirit under the same critical lens. It does not give much comfort, ether to those theories of the modern state which have not peered so deeply as Hegel has into the internal dynamic of subjectivity, civil society and commonality in modernity. For these criticisms cast doubt upon the spiritual unity of the system of interdependencies Hegel examined; they do not show that the system can avoid internal contradictions without Spirit.

Pauperism and Politics

Marx, in his early writings, sought to reveal contradictions in the Hegelian model of the state, to replace it with a more equal and less mediated idea of community, and to sustain the idea of community without drawing upon the 'idealist' philosophy of Spirit in which Hegel situated the state. It is as though in a world without Spirit the perfection of human collective constitutes the only hope. Marx can imagine to bring the excesses of modern subjectivity under control.

In an early essay on pauperism in Germany and England, Marx outlines an anti-Hegelian reading of the state in civil society. Hegel had construed pauperism to be an effect of civil society which the state must eliminate if its inward unity was not to be destroyed through disaffection, conflict and the extension of coercive measures. But while exposing contradictions in policies devised at the level of civil society, Hegel failed to delineate a viable response available to the realized state. Marx picks 'a Prussian' - who in the wake of a local uprising of workers had called for a political response to pauperism – to be the immediate target of his critique. But Hegel hovers in the background both as a source of key concepts deployed and the spiritual object of Marx's wrath.

Hegel explained German misrepresentation of the sources of pauperism by the fact that Germany was undeveloped politically. Marx disputes this explanation and the remedy it implies. If it is admitted that England is the most political country in Europe, with organized interests, contested elections, and competing parties, it will also be granted that England is the country of pauperism, for even the word itself is of English origin... In England the misery of labor is not partial but universal; not confined to the factory districts but extends to the rural districts. And movements against pauperism have a longer history in England than in Germany. In England, each of the contending parties has a solution to pauperism, and each blames the other for not resolving the problem.

Each party selects as cause something that the other could remedy if only it had the will to act. In this way both parties converge in defining the problem of pauperism to reflect a failure of will. One party blames the problem on 'defects in the administration' of the poor laws, laws designed to provide charity for the poor. But the perfection of these instruments seems merely to expand the number of poor coming for aid. The other party blames 'the evil disposition of the poor', endorsing the Malthusian view that 'charity is folly' and that the state must 'leave the poor to their fate.' So the first calls for reform of the laws and the second calls upon the state to control the poor through punitive measures. Each call for action refers to policies available to the state, and each party is therefore able to blame pauperism on the failure of will of the other: 'Where there are political parties, each finds the cause of every evil in the fact that its opponent instead of itself is at the helm of the state.'

The state cannot detect the source of the problem in the basic organization of the civil society over which it presides. For it represents civil society; all of the pressures applied to it flow from civil society; and its ability to act is confined by the necessity to protect the operation of civil society. Hegel could not devise a remedy for pauperism nor, by extension, for alienation in work, because the state he celebrates expresses the contradictions in civil society that would have to be resolved. Hegel, like the Prussian, has too much faith in the independent power of politics to resolve fundamental issues. He has unfounded faith in the healing and unifying drive of Spirit as it expresses itself within the politics he celebrates. But the issues are so fundamental that they can be resolved only by more revolutionary action designed to replace civil society itself by a higher form. When civil society is fraught with contradictions, politics becomes one of the modes by which they are concealed from participants.

Hegel could not resolve pauperism because every political answer he imagined defeated itself without the support of a fictive Spirit. In the absence of Spirit, civil society spawns competing and inadequate responses to pauperism. Some responses make the state too punitive; others separate recipients of charity form the principles of self- reliance and self-respect central to civil society; others draw the poor into forms of organization and control which contradict the same principle of civil society from another direction. The issue is left hanging, because only a revolution which transforms the structure of civil society could solve it. And Hegel insisted that the French Revolution was the last revolution modernity needed. Marx, in his early writings, seeks a form of community which transcends civil society and the 'abstract' state which accompanies it. The community envisaged will resolve pauperism, but it echoes the ideal which Rousseau had already explored and Hegel had already criticized:

> Human emancipation will only be complete when the real individual has absorbed into himself the abstract citizen; when in his every day life, in his work, and his relationship

he has become a specie being, and when he has recognized his own powers, so that he no longer separates his social abilities form himself.

In criticizing the structure and effects of modern civil society, Marx first denies the ontology of Spirit which gives Hegel faith in the curative and unifying power of the state and then tries to discern another way to regulate the principle of subjectivity which flourishes in civil society. His answer is to eliminate civil society itself and to fold individuality into communal life. This idealism becomes more attenuated and cautious as Marx matures, but the initial impulse never changes its direction. It appears that the debate between Hegel and Marx moves within the same sort of circle Marx discerned in the debate between Whigs and Tories. Each party, in opposing its adversary, first blames observed difficulties on practices or principles celebrated by the adversary and then responds by inflating a principle deflated by the opponent. Hegel celebrates bourgeois life, but contains it in Spirit; Marx denies Spirit but insists all the more that bourgeois individuality must be contained within community. One gives room to civil society; the other thinks it must be eliminated if modernity is to realize itself. One incorporates otherness with a complex totality, which emphasizes differentiation and inequality; the other dissolves alienation in a social form, which supports more equality and commonality. One thinks nature itself will become intelligible as Spirit is realized within it; the other thinks that nature becomes intelligible through human mastery of it. One believes that reconciliation to a particular role in a complex whole is they key to freedom; the other thinks revolutionary achievement of a communal whole unlocks freedom. one thinks foreknowledge of death is essential to the historical dialectic of self-consciousness; the other ignores the relation of life to death while extending the possibility of self-consciousness to all members of the realized community. There are certainly broad and fundamental differences between these two thinkers.

It is interesting to note that though Hegel talks of modern society, 'society' is not a standard Hegelian term. Hegel uses it only occasionally most frequently in the context of civil or bourgeois society, normally he uses the word 'nation' (volk) or 'the state' to refer to the social context of individual action and therefore freedom. Society in the modern usage is more of a structural than a cultural concept, focusing on a pattern of concrete empirical relations father than on the more elusive realm of values and ideas. Hegel believes that the social entities with which men realize their freedom are historically formed communities, having distinct cultures and traditions and owing their survival and development to the possession of sufficient political power to exist as sovereign and independent states. Hence in the *Philosophy of Right*, Hegel's most comprehensive and systematic work on political philosophy, it is the state which is described as 'the actuality of freedom'. It must be stressed that Hegel does not mean by 'the state' the coercive organization of a nation or a society or its external constitutional framework; he uses the term more widely as a synonym for an ethical and cultural community, which is also a sovereign political entity.

Rousseau's ideal republic, based on 'the general will', was such a politico-ethical community. As a spiritual community Hegel's state clearly has more in common with Fiche's nation than with Kant's state or the modern liberal conception of it. Outside the German political tradition, Burke by contrasting society as a realm of rather mundane relations with the state as a 'partnership in every virtue and in all perfection', clearly anticipates the Hegelian usage of the state. The argument of Hegel's is that it is in the modern state, the most fully developed and highly organized form of political community, that individual freedom reaches perfection and the most complete realization. The structure of the modern state actualizes expresses, articulates or promotes that comprehensive rational view of freedom which it has taken Western civilization several centuries to develop, and which Hegel thinks emerged with stark clarity after the turmoil of the French Revolution. This is the sense in which 'the modern state is the actuality of the ethical Idea' or an embodiment of 'concrete freedom'. It combines the existence of necessary ethical and civil laws as objective freedom with men's consciousness of themselves as free subjective freedom.

A fundamental feature of the modern state, which vitally affects the issue of freedom, is the distinction between civil society and the state in the political sense 'the strictly political state and its constitution'. Both of these actualize freedom in different ways. Civil society is an area of independent individual and group activity in which desires, needs and interests particular to the individuals concerned are pursued within a structure of social relations such as the market, production, division of labour and the class system and in which there are institutions and agencies, legal codes, courts of law, regulatory authorities and corporations ensuring the satisfaction of particular interests. Civil society is therefore the realm of 'subjectivity' or arbitrary choice, and particularity or self-interest, where government intervention is at a minimum and where, when it occurs, it purpose is to maximize individual welfare. Civil freedom is the self-determination of individuals pursuing particular interests and subjective choices, their private ends. Hegel calls civil society 'the external state, the state based on need, the state as the understanding envisages it'. In such a highly developed modern society, with a complex system of labour, needs are satisfied more fully than ever before in history. Man ceases to be largely at the mercy of nature and lives a civilized and hence freer life. Hegel contends that it is a fundamental mistake as Rousseau did that man was freest in a simple, primitive, 'natural' society in which needs were met without work and social ties were few or non-existent. The freedom found in civil society involves a complex division of labour, a high level of production and varied civil institutions and agencies.

The political state is the sphere where 'universality' rather than 'particularity' reigns, and political freedom is the self-determination of individuals pursuing public ends. Those who participate in the political arena are not there to further primarily their particular interests. They are called upon to promote the universal or general ends of the national community – the common interests, shared values and jointly held ideals. Political participants, whether they are ordinary citizens, voters, civil servants, members of parliament, government ministers or monarchs, are the guardians of the community's ethical life and the self-conscious bearers of the national spirit. On the issue of the proper extent of participation, Hegel walks a middle path between Plato and Rousseau–the two political thinkers who probably influenced him most–by neither confining this guardianship to a narrow intellectual elite, nor involving the whole community in the political process. The constitution of the supreme public authority in the Hegelian rational modern state expresses his concern that in the public arena the 'universal' should necessarily prevail over the 'particular' and that the political participants should conduct themselves not as private individuals but as public actors who are trustees of the community.

Hegel's remarks about patriotism are relevant in this context. Patriotism is the cultural factor, which, together with various structural factors, ensures that the political participants fulfill their civic duties when required. It is 'political sense' or 'state sense', which, together with the working of the institutions, ensures that community values are not sacrificed to particular interests. In the political state men voluntarily transcend the individualistic viewpoint which the civil society fosters and achieve self-realization as self-conscious members of the national community. This 'destiny' is fulfilled by individuals' participation in the public arena of the state. Where political freedom exists, as it does in the rational modern state, the definition of the common good and its practical promotion are the prerogative of a broad stratum of citizens. This synthesis of universality and particularity and objectivity and subjectivity, achieved in the modern state by the presence of rational civil and political institutions, Hegel calls 'the actuality of concrete freedom'.

The political sphere differs from the civil sphere of the modern state by its end, which is not the welfare of single individuals, families and associations but the general welfare of the community, especially its ethical well-being. Hence, the citizens' primary moral relation to the state is one of duty rather than of right. But the opposition of the two terms is misleading. In the context of the modern state ethical duty includes a particular and subjective element, which was absent in earlier civilizations. The rationale of political liberty is that it enables citizens to consider the claims made in the name of the common good by the government. They must have a chance to perceive the justice of the claims, the connection between general welfare and their particular welfare, etc and to give free intellectual assent to the claims.

The scope for assent is somewhat limited in the Hegelian rational modern state. He acknowledges, somewhat obscurely, that to assent to laws and taxes is a function of the representative assembly, but he rules out any form of popular assent to the political system as a whole. The citizens, in his view, have no general right to determine the character of the constitution, which must depend on objective circumstances and needs of the ethical community at the actual stage of its development, and not on subjective ideas or particular interests. Republicanism and any other form of popular sovereignty would, in Hegel's view, open the floodgates to subjective particularity within the public authority, instead of securing for them a proper but limited scope. The rational constitution of the modern state, according to Hegel, is a limited but politically active monarchy, with an executive appointed by and responsible to the king, a civil service recruited on merit and open to all qualified citizens, a representative assembly based largely on indirect, functional representation of social interest through states and corporate and a public opinion free within wide limits.

While all these institutions are parts of the rational structure of the modern state, the representative assembly is the major embodiment of subjective freedom within the political realm. It is the channel of the citizens' wishes, complaints and private views on public affairs and is a mediating organ between particular and universal interests.

The granting of taxes rather than the provision of direct services to the state in kind Hegel regards as an important form of subjective freedom. The specific political rights which Hegel mentions as elements of political freedom are the right of hereditary peers to sit in the upper chamber of the legislature, the right of the members of corporations and other associations and local communities to elect deputies to the Estates, the publicity of parliamentary proceedings, and the right to free speech and free press, subject to laws against sedition and libel. Hegel like Kant argues that the fundamental, and therefore, universal political right is the right of public opinion; other forms of political participation are graduated according to social status and the 'managerial and political sense' developed in civil society.

While Hegel never accepts the necessity of universal suffrage or the responsibility of the executive to the legislature, it is fair to say that in some of his other writings he visualizes the possibility of rather greater involvement of citizens in the modern state than he does in the *Philosophy of Right.* Perhaps a clue to his considered opinion on the matter lies in the remarks that the constitution is the character and development of a nation's self-consciousness and that every nations has the constitution appropriate to it and suitable for it.

These remarks suggest that there are no fixed principles about the extent of political participation; as circumstances change and people's conception of liberty develops, their political rights may do so too. A fully democratic constitution with universal suffrage and popular control over the government might therefore be possible in the fullness of time, although not in the Germany of Hegel's day. Hegel lived in a country where most citizens were simply "subjects" without participation in the work of government, and where, therefore, a political life and tradition like the English was almost wholly lacking. His political theory was an attempt to educate Germans beyond "civil" to "political" life'. Hegel's conception of the nature and scope of civil liberty does not differ significantly from that of the classical liberal political theorists, but his conception of political liberty seems somewhat restricted and anachronistic. It bears more resemblance to Locke's idea of government as a 'trustee' of the people than. Mill's conception of genuinely representative government.

Freedom

It will not be any exaggeration to say that Hegel's conception of freedom is the richest in the history of political philosophy. It is not suggested that it is the most original, the truest or the clearest, only that it is the most comprehensive and complex, that it identifies and incorporates more elements, aspects or dimensions of freedom than any other conception of it in Western political theory. There are three main dimensions of the Hegelian conception of freedom; the metaphysical, the world-historical and socio-political. To begin with the first Hegel divides reality into natural (or material) and spiritual (or mental) and assigns the concept of freedom exclusively to the later sphere. Freedom is for him the distinguishing property, character or essence of spirit or mind. The nature of spirit can best be understood if we contrast it with its direct opposite, which is matter. Just as gravity is the substance of matter, so also can it be said that freedom is the substance of spirit. While gravity impels natural objects towards an external center, spirit has a center within itself and strives towards it; it is therefore self-centered, self-sufficient, self-dependent. The idea that freedom is self-dependence Hegel probably derived from Spinoza, whose philosophy he knew well. Spinoza defines a free being as follows: 'that thing is called free which exists from the necessity of its nature alone and is determined to action by itself alone'. However, Spinoza did not make the sharp distinction between nature and spirit that Hegel makes.

Freedom, in this basic, metaphysical sense, is not in Hegel's view the opposite of necessity. Both material and spiritual reality are governed by necessity since they possess a peculiar, definite structure of existence and this structure is determined by the necessary laws of their being. But spiritual – unlike material – beings can recognize the necessary structure of their being, and this recognition liberates them from the unconscious, helpless dependence on their nature which characterizes merely natural beings or material objects. Moreover, spirit is fundamentally active while matter is passive. Material beings just exist or are there. They sometimes change in accordance with the laws of their being, but this change is no way their independent activity; they have been so to speak programmed in a certain way and change follow from it automatically. Spiritual beings, on the other hand, are active in the sense that their development is the result of their own activity. In a real sense they make themselves what they are; they are self-created as well as self-moved.

The business of spirit is to produce itself, to make itself its own object, and to gain knowledge of itself; in this way, it exits for itself. Natural objects do not exist for themselves; for this reason, they are not free. We may restate the idea of the spirit's independence, self-centeredness or self-sufficiency in terms of self-determination. While the universe of nature is determined by external necessity, the realm of spirit, in all manifestations, is determined by itself, ultimately according to its own perceived essence. This essence is the object of rational knowledge, and by acquiring such knowledge spiritual beings become self-conscious as well as self-determined.

Although nature and spirit radically differ in essence, they are also interdependent parts of a wider reality. They do not exist in watertight compartments. Spirit interacts with nature in the course of its development; it progresses by encountering the resistance of nature and overcoming it, and in this way discovers its own powers; it masters nature theoretically by discovering its properties and laws and practically by using it, to satisfy human needs. The developments in man's control over nature since Hegel's death would have amazed and gratified him were he alive today. The capacity of mankind to destroy life on earth and commit collective suicide has especially confirmed, in a way which he could not foresee, the overwhelming power of spirit over nature. The spirit's power to dominate nature was not, however, absolute in Hegel's view. There are circumstances when nature proves resistant to spirit's influence and in a sense triumphs over spirit. 'Man uses nature for his own ends; but where nature is too powerful, it does not allow itself to be used as means the frost which grips the inhabitants of Lapland and the fiery heat of Africa are forces of too powerful a nature for man to resist, or for the spirit to achieve free movement and to reach that degree of richness which is the precondition and source of a fully developed mastery of reality. The idea that man, through work and social relations, conquers and transforms nature into his servant is more commonly associated with Marx than with Hegel.

Hegel recognizes the first kind of man's mastery over nature, and regards it as an essential element in the spirit's progress towards freedom. This process, which Hegel most frequently refers to as freedom, should not be thought in the Kantian or Fichtian terms of a reason sternly repressing man's natural inclinations. For Hegel these inclinations are the very stuff of man's personality. They provide the driving force behind human action and, transformed by a process of ethical education, become essential elements of man's character.

The two aspects of the process of spiritual mastery of man over nature can be illustrated by two examples. One of them is property. Hegel differs from other thinkers by grounding the institution of property not in the satisfaction of needs, but in the realization of human personality, i.e., man's capacity for rights. Possessing things and controlling nature is of course a means of satisfying wants, but this is not, in his view, property's main rationale. The rationale lies rather in property being an essential stage in the progress from subjectivity to personality. Another sphere in which spirit interacts with nature in order to develop and maximize its freedom is that of ethical conduct. The training of moral character, for example, involves imposing discipline on one's natural inclination, impulses and desires creating a structure of conduct first by external pressure, even coercion, to overcome the force of internal urges, but gradually replacing external control by self-control.

The concept of ethical life (Sittlichkeit) is crucial to Hegel's conception of freedom. Ethical life is the structure of rules, obligations and normative principles which men internalize by living and being brought up in a particular ethical community. Only in the ethical environment does freedom as Hegel understands it emerge and become conceptually meaningful and practically possible.

Freedom and History

Hegel did not originate the idea that freedom had a historical dimension that history was a process in and through which humankind progressed towards freedom – that freedom was the goal of history. The view was implicit in Rousseau's social theory. Kant sketched out a world-historical drama in three acts: the state of nature with freedom as arbitrariness was followed by a state of civilized society where rational law and government secured civil and political liberty, to be succeeded in indefinite future by a 'kingdom of ends', a state of pure altruistic morality and rational autonomy without the need for conventional ethics or positive legislation. Fichte, a great scheme-monger, produced a number of different world-historical scenarios with a fluctuating role of the state but with the firm idea that rational freedom was the goal of both community and history. All three thinkers were utopian in the sense that the goal of history could not be guaranteed within the terms of their theory. Hegel believed that the goal of history could be reached, if not in his own time and place, then at least in his epoch and culture. He made it a realizable task at any rate for that part of humankind which lived in Central and Western Europe and North America, and enjoyed the benefits of Christianity, Enlightenment, market society and modern state institutions. He produced the most comprehensive and consistent theory of progress towards freedom in political theory before Marx.

Hegel discusses the general outline of the historical process in the introduction to the philosophy of world history. Freedom first emerges where stable social and political institutions exist and where at least a minimal form of ethical life is firmly entrenched. Hegel breaks completely with the modern tradition initiated by Hobbes, which considered the paradigm of freedom to be a state of natural independence within a state of nature, which was pre-political and largely pre-social and pre-ethical. He argues that Hobbes correctly demonstrated the intolerable character of the state of nature, which men had to leave at any price, and he is fond of quoting Spinoza's phrase. Freedom comes only in a civilized condition: the state of nature is a state of barbarism while freedom is a creation of culture, society and history; freedom is not something natural, immediately given, found in a ready-made fashion, it is a product of long development and struggle, the result of man's effort, the victory of spirit over nature. The idea that the natural freedom of the state of nature, in which men's instinctual forces have unchecked sway, is a meaningful kind of freedom is therefore strongly denied by Hegel.

Hegel very forcefully declares that the state of nature is rather a state of injustice, or violence, of uncontrolled natural impulses, and of inhuman deeds and emotions. To regard freedom in a purely formal and subjective sense abstracted from its absolutely essential objects and aims, is a perennial misunderstanding; for it means that impulses, desires and passions – which pertain by their nature exclusively to the particular individual – and arbitrariness and random inclinations are identified with freedom, and that any restrictions imposed upon these are seen as restrictions on freedom itself.

The first historical instances of a successful exist from the state of nature were the civilizations of the great Oriental empires of the past and their fossilized contemporary survivals, such as China. These rather undifferentiated social wholes, highly traditional and repressive, and needing a despotic or patriarchal monarch to hold them together. Only he had a privileged status and enjoyed a kind of arbitrary freedom; the rest of society was subject to his or his servants' arbitrariness. The Orientals do not know that the spirit as such is free in themselves because they do not know this, they are not themselves free. They only know that 'One' is free; but for this very reason, such freedom is mere arbitrariness, savagery, and brutal passion, or a milder and tamer version of this which is itself only an accident of nature, and equally arbitrary. This One is therefore merely a despot, not a free man and a human being. The consciousness of freedom first awoke among the Greeks, and they were accordingly free – but, like the Romans, they only knew that 'Some', and not all men as such, are free. Plato and Aristotle did not know this either – thus the Greeks not only had slaves, on which their life and the continued existence of their estimable freedom depended, but their very freedom itself was on the one hand only a fortuitous, undeveloped, transient, and limited efflorescence, and on the other, a harsh servitude of all. The Germanic nations, with the rise of Christianity, were the first to realize that man is by nature free, and that freedom of the spirit is his very essence. This consciousness first dawned in religion, in the innermost region of the spirit; but to incorporate the same principle into secular existence was a further problem, whose solution and application require long and arduous cultural exertions.

Hegel believes that freedom in a recognizable form first emerged in the city states of ancient Greece, especially in Athens. Ethos – the customary law and morality of the polis – replaced the ponderous political controls of the Oriental world. Although the welfare of the social whole was equally paramount in Greece, individuals identified themselves with it without compulsion and, in the service of the community, found the fulfillment of their individual nature. The substantial or objective freedom of the polis Hegel sometimes calls 'beautiful' and the polis itself an ethical work. Individual freedom in ancient Greece and to some extent in republican Rome took the form of political participation by a class of privileged freeman. Not only were they a minority of the inhabitants, but the community ethos militated against the pursuit of private interests of the criticism of established religion, mores or laws. The fate of Socrates is a striking illustration of this communal intolerance. In the later imperial period of Roman history, political freedom disappeared altogether and was replaced by a new kind of despotism but, as it if to compensate people for the loss of public life, a system of wide-range private legal rights developed to safeguard purely personal interests. Christianity brought with it a conception of human dignity and of the equal worth of men as children of God, as well as a critical attitude towards earthly reality – the germs of subjective freedom. The history of European civilization since then has been a process of applying this idea of subjective freedom to all spheres of culture and society. In the course of the historical development, however, there emerge, not just new systems of government or structures of rights, but also new intellectual and moral principles underlying ethical, legal and political structures.

Hegel is fond of making the point that slavery is not a matter of force or tradition but the result of the slaves' own lack of consciousness. This apparently callous remark may be used to illustrate his fundamental thesis. What kept Greek slaves in the conditions of slavery throughout Greek civilization was a set of dominant Greek values and beliefs. It was argued that some men were slaves 'by nature', underpinned by a metaphysical view of nature as a hierarchy of beings. The slaves could not change their fate as long as they participated in Greek culture and accepted its central values and beliefs; they had no alternative world-view to oppose the dominant one and to justify their rebellion. The situation in Rome was much the same. In Hegel's view, it was Christianity, which cut the roots of slavery in the modern world, although much time was to elapse before social and legal realty caught up with the fundamental Christian message. As long as Christianity or its secularized equivalent, the Enlightenment enjoyed a central position in Western civilization, Hegel believed that personal freedom would be safe in the modern world.

The French Revolution was possible because the modern European man possessed a body of ideas, which justified the wholesale rejection of traditional institutions and laws for the sake of more rational arrangements. It was in this sense a culmination of subjective freedom. Hegel gave us a brilliant analysis of this experiment in constructing a free social and political system on new philosophical foundations. The grand experiment in 'holistic social engineering' failed because the conception of freedom behind the French Revolution was one-side and false. Although the Revolution rightly equalized and universalized civil rights, it conceived political rights far too widely.

More crucially, it overemphasized the value of freedom of the particular individual will and ignored the need for a viable ethical and realistic institutional context of freedom. Nevertheless it marked a fundamental turning point in humankind's emancipation from the intellectual shackles of the past, represented by mere tradition or the religious idea of divine right of kings.

The second part of Hegel's implicit answer to the question of how praxis of freedom might be possible lies in the idea of a piecemeal, gradual reformist way of proceeding. It is to argue that Hegel offers a philosophical defense of the status quo, he really championed the rationalization of traditional institutions and a critical revision of traditional attitudes. He believed that the dominant philosophical and rational ideas, together with the experience of the French Revolution and the Napoleonic periods, had provided the ingredients of a clear and coherent public philosophy of freedom which his own was the most adequate. The shape of a rational social and political system – the rational modern state – could be clearly discerned among the debris of the traditional and partially discredited institutions, as could be the necessity of such a state for the actualization of freedom. He expected the contemporary intellectual and political elites to take the lead in applying this public philosophy in practice and to educate the masses to the necessity and rationality of reforms. Although vested interests of privileged groups and traditional prejudices might obstruct and slow down this process, they could not, Hegel thought, stop it altogether.

World-History and Freedom

The world-historical process which Hegel discusses in his philosophy of history clearly results in the extension of freedom to more and more individuals, and in their acquisition of more and more adequate forms of freedom. But is individual freedom really the subject matter of world history? It has been argued by his critics – from the early Marx and other Left Hegelians and radical nineteenth-century humanists to contemporary liberal individualists – that Hegel is not primarily concerned with spirit as it manifests itself in the consciousness and action of individual human beings. The spirit which on this view really interests Hegel is spirit in the sense of a superhuman, metaphysical entity which makes use of men, nations and cultures. That Hegel postulated the existence of such an entity, which Charles Taylor has aptly called 'cosmic Geist', is undeniable; such a metaphysical being was an essential part – a vital underpinning of the Hegelian philosophical system. But it would be wrong to deduce from this that individual freedom – the freedom of finite spirits – was therefore, a matter of indifference to Hegel. Hegel explicitly denies such a conclusion. The ends of the world spirit and of finite spirits are interdependent and inseparable. The development of the former creates a necessary context for the development of the latter, while it is only through the latter that the former becomes self-conscious and actual. This is the goal of world history: the spirit must create for itself a nature and a social world to conform with its nature. The end of the world spirit is realized in substance through the freedom of each individual. The young Marx was therefore less than just to Hegel when he accused him of ignoring men as concrete human beings and grounding his philosophy of the state and of history in a supra-human, metaphysical entity indifferent to the fate of ordinary mortals.

Freedom as Membership of Rational State

Hegel is unequivocal in his thought that the locus of man's present and future freedom is the state. It is here that Hegel's political thought can be tricky for those brought up in the Anglo-Saxon tradition to believe that the state is the locus of constraint and that society is the locus of freedom. In the Lockean tradition, men are members of society and of the state. As members of society men are spontaneously and naturally free to pursue their self-chosen ends, and as members of the state men are obliged to obey those laws which exist so that citizens do not pursue their ends by such illegal means as theft, assault or murder. Society is the locus of freedom and the state is the locus of constraint, and liberalism is a set of arguments about just how much constraint is necessary for men to pursue their self-chosen ends without causing actual harm to others. Freedom and law are two jealous antagonists, as Bentham said, and it is no good pretending otherwise. For the utilitarians, as for Locke, all the state may do is to constrain, and liberals will watch the state as a constraining mechanism every inch of the way.

Hegel does not look at the state like that. Though he knows the liberal position and even has some sympathy with it, Hegel is one of the first thinkers to begin to think beyond liberalism almost before liberalism itself had become a recognised and complete political, social and economic doctrine.

He accepts that the French Revolution was what Marxists were later to call a bourgeois revolution, which means a revolution in the name of Lockean natural rights, and therefore a revolution in the name of liberal, free society coming out of the remnants of a feudal past. Hegel also accepts that the French Revolution has had an irreversible effect on Germany. Not to accept that would be to fly in the face of all reason; the dismantling of the ancien regime is now far advanced even in backward Germany. Men now live in what Hegel calls civil society, a form of society in which men may choose to live any life they please, provided only that they can. Civil society is feudal society's opposite. In feudal societies, men are supposed to live the same lives their fathers led: serfs passed on their serfdom as an inheritance to their children. Hegel is too good a historian to believe that feudalism lasted unchanged till the storming of the Bastille and then disappeared in a moment, but he does think that the French Revolution signals that the old order is definitively over, and that the future belongs to bourgeois society, which means factories and parliaments.

The Lockiean liberty of civil society is the liberty of buyers and sellers, and one of the commodities which will be on sale will be labour. It was his observations of what happens to sellers of labour that made Hegel look at civil society with a slightly jaundiced eye. Bourgeois society was the sphere of what Hegel calls rights, not Right. The freedom of bourgeois society he describes as 'unimpeded activity', and he claims that civil society is concentrated on the 'particular', not the Universal. In the unimpeded activity of buyers and sellers in bourgeois society, Hegel noticed that the sellers of labour often do particularly badly. There is a tendency for a 'rabble of paupers', what was to become the famous 'industrial reserve army' of Chartists and Marxists, to accumulate at the bottom of civil society. What could the freedom of civil society mean to them? Hegel accepts that civil society is freer than the society of the ancient regime, but it is plain to him that civil society cannot universalise freedom. Membership of the rabble of paupers may change, as men go into and out of it as they find and lose buyers for their labour, but the group itself remains, what in the modern idiom could almost be called an underclass.

Why does that matter to Hegel? It matters because of the connection which Hegel insists upon between freedom and rationality. For Hegel, freedom is not a condition which you can be in whether you realise it or not. Part of the mind's progress since men began to think was the progress of the consciousness of freedom, which meant that more men were becoming free and could understand what being free meant. How could this mean anything to a class intensely concerned with where its next meal was coming from? Freedom moves from particularity to generality, until it stumbles over the Hegelian underclass. In the ancient despotisms, only the despot was free, so that the only way for a subject to dream of freedom would be to dream of becoming despot himself. Slaves in ancient cities might have dreamt of becoming free men and owning slaves themselves, but slaves there would always be. The modern worlds claim to modernity, according to Hegel, is that it holds out the hope that all men can he free, but how can this be with a rabble of paupers at the bottom of the social heap?

Hegel's way out of the difficulty comes when he begins to ask himself what it was about previous epochs of world history which meant that in them freedom could not universalise itself. His answer always comes down to the fact that in previous epochs there was no separation between state and society. In the ancient cities, the citizens were the rulers, and part of rule was keeping down the slaves. Freedom was the cause of an intense competition between slaves and free men which free men were meant always to win. In the of bourgeois society there is spanation between stak and society. There are no longer any constraints of the state on what kind of life a citizen might live. All liberalism rests finally on that distinction. Hegel thought though, that men at the bottom of the pile did badly out of the separation between state and society. What was to be done about them?

The answer was obvious: if civil society could not universalise freedom, then it can be redesad in the state. The state, then, must be the locus of true freedom in so far as true freedom can be realized at any particular time. Only the state is capable of concerning itself with the Universal, not the particular. The state has to rise above the selfish striving of civil society, and to be able to do that it must be as separate from civil society as it can possibly be because the State must be able to take a very high-minded view of civil society.

What does the rather grandiose phrase 'separation of the state from civil society' actually meal? It is really an attack on amateurism in government. Mixing society and the state means that rulers come out of society because of their position in it. Local government in England in Hegel's day is an obvious example. Those who were socially at the top of the pile were chose to exercise the function of rule in that society. In this sense, all pre-modern forms of rule were of rule were amateur, especially rule in feudal societies where the functions of boss and ruler met in the feudal lord, so that it was impossible to distinguish between the two roles of economic and social, and political superiors. Adam Smith had argued some sixty year before Hegel's *Philosophy of Right* was published, that in modern commercial society with its increasing divisions of labour and increasing business efficiency, rule too should be professionalised. The militia had had its day; from now on the very model of a modern state was to be the Prussia of Frederick the Great. That position is fully worked out in Hegel's *'Philosophy of Right,* with its plea for rule by a scholarly and socially objective bureaucracy serving a constitutional monarch advised by estates of the realm. Being separate from society, the bureaucracy can take a very long view, and the king, being king by hereditary right and constitutional legitimacy, need fear no competitors for his crown, so that he too is above the selfish competition of civil society.

Hegel thinks that the present does not abolish the past but completes it. Modern constitutional monarchy is not the abolition of medieval or divine right monarchy, but its completion. What Hegel seems to be saying is that constitutional monarchy is monarchy thought out by rational men for whom hereditary succession alone is not enough to make a man king. Constitutional monarchy re-founds an old institution on a rational basis. The same is true for other social institutions and customs. These are not abolished but thought out again. Families do not cease to be families because men have thought out what family life actually means, and customs are not abolished when they are transformed into rationally thought-out law. The modern world in Hegel's language becomes more 'self-conscious'. Mind is its own age reflected in thought, but modern men have history to help them. By reflecting on what has gone before, the modern mind can become more conscious of itself by knowing what it is different from. Mind docs not abolish the past but builds on it. In a sense, men had always known that: even Plato realised that the world of the Homeric poems was over, and that in the future the Homeric hierachy of kings, heroes, ordinary men and slaves would have to be re-argued from scratch.

It can still be objected against Hegel that he has shown how the state is rational, but failed to convince us that, in being rational, it has universalised freedom. It is a notorious problem in Hegel that he can say on the one hand that the state is rational to the extent that it realises freedom, and on the other hand that the state as an end has supreme right over the individual whose supreme duty is to be a member of the state. Whatever that sounds like, it docs not sound to liberal ears like freedom at all. Hegel has been accused of being a 'cock crowing on the dunghill of servility', and it has to be said that on freedom he is hard to pin down.

Perhaps the best approach to Hegel on freedom is to regard his theory of freedom as a philosophical commentary on the epoch of the French Revolution and its aftermath, particularly in Germany. Before 1789, Germany was little more than a geographical expression. There were over three hundred German states, duchies, free towns, seigneuries, towns ruled by bishops, as well as the larger states like Prussia, Bavaria, Saxony and Austria. The effect of the French Revolution was to rationalise the German state system as the smaller states were incorporated into the larger. Hegel was enthusiastic about the French Revolution, which broke out when he was a student at Tubingen, but, as with many other intellectuals, what began as enthusiasm ended in disillusionment. But Hegel never lost the initial inspiration that the Revolution was made in the name of reason and liberty. After the Restoration in 1815, Hegel found himself in a quandary, caught between the sentimental reactionaries, who wanted a return to what was life of Germany's feudal past, and the romantics who thought that the Revolution signaled the end of all restraint whatsoever. Hegel wants to steer a middle course between the two: on the one hand he wants to argue that there is a case for the state, but on the other hand he wants to argue that there is a case only for a certain kind of state.

In the Introduction to *The Philosophy of Right*, Hegel takes up the problem of how we can be free while recognising restraints in his theory of the 'moments of the will'. Hegel says that there are three moments of the will which desires to be free. The first moment Hegel calls 'abstraction', the moment when the will wants to free itself completely from the world's constraints. This, Hegel thinks, is only a single aspect of will, though it is easy to mistake it for the whole will. Examples of the will as 'pure abstraction' would be Hindu mystical asceticism, where the will truly seems independent of the world which surrounds it, or Jacobinism in which the whole of previous history is discarded in favour of a virginal re-beginning. In the first moment of the will the Understanding is not, properly speaking, active in history, for it is by definition indeterminate, not tied down, 'pure mind'.

The second moment of the will is a moment of 'determinacy'. This represents the moment when the will recognises that pure abstraction is an absurdity because it prevents the man whose will it is from taking part in history by existing empirically as a fact, taking part in events, and institutions. Indeterminacy was a denial of the whole world of objects, of the world outside the self. Determinacy is the desire of the self-conscious individual to act in the world. How does the thinking in the service of reason,' the moment of determinacy consists of more than the desire for biological survival and more than just accepting the world as it is. The original negation of the world is replaced by a desire to be 'of the world', what Hegel calls the 'negation of the negation', or echoing Fichte, the 'finite or particularisation of the ego'. It implies that the original negation of the world by 'pure understanding' is itself negated by a desire to re-enter the world of human existence.

How is this to be done? Hegel says through 'singularity', the merging of the two moments of the will. Will, he says, makes itself 'objective' by seeking to repossess what had once seemed to be an alien world, which in simpler language means working to possess object, or simpler still, property. Men seek to negate the separate existence of the world of object by possession, and possession is coercive in the sense that possessors need the protection of the state's law to confirm them in the possession of that without which they would not be part of the world at all. Possessions bind us to the world of other men, and work allows us to make our impression on the world.

It is easy to see here what Hegel does not mean by freedom. He sets his face against any idea of freedom, which means mere caprice. Of course, he seems to be saying that the world of objects impinges on human consciousness, the Hindu ascetic in his cave possibly excepted, but free will docs not consist of being able to do uncaused or unpredictable action. Freedom in the sense of unpredictability would be called madness or eccentricity or negation of the self. Freedom is not the expression of that which is different in each of us, which is not that different anyway, but on the contrary the expression of that which in us is universal. At best, freedom as eccentricity or caprice is to be found in civil society, not the state.

It is through the rationally pondered law of the state that men become free because they recognise in the state their own aspirations writ large, in this sense, the state is 'objective will', will freed of all selfishness and egocentricity. Law as compulsion is therefore freedom realised, as far from the hotch-potch of conflicting selfish wills which go to make up civil society as it could possibly be. Of course, this acceptance of the state entails an acceptance of the state's own limitations at any particular moment in the state's development. What the state is really the maximum amount of freedom which is possible at any given time, and to expect more is to expect the state to jump over the Colossus of Rhodes. Hence the Hegelian aphorism that 'freedom is the recognition of necessity'.

Conclusion

The political intentions and implications of Hegel's political thought have been the subject of an acrimonious debate and bitter controversy that has lasted more than a century. Some commentators have argued that Hegel's aims were fundamentally conservative, indeed reactionary. They regard Hegel as the spokesman for the Restoration in Prussia, as the defender of the reactionary policies of the government of Friedrich Wilhelm III. Hegel's philosophy of history was, in their view, no less reactionary than his philosophy of the state. They argue that it was Hegel's purpose, in giving such importance to history, to defend the value of established institutions and traditions against those radicals who would model all of society according to abstract principles. Nowhere are Hegel's reactionary views more apparent, they contend, than in his making the present Prussian state into the apotheosis of world history. Other commentators, however, especially the Left-wing Hegelian school, have acknowledged Hegel's philosophy of history as the inspiration for their own radical doctrines. They stress the revolutionary implications, if not intentions of his dialectic. In saying that history is a process of dialectical development, of ceaseless conflict, destruction and regeneration, Hegel allegedly passed the death sentence upon any status quo.

If we carefully examine all the passages from Hegel's writings in which he draws some political point from history, we find that neither of these interpretations is correct. The truth lies somewhere in between. Hegel appealed to history to justify the middle path of reform, to criticize both radicals and reactionaries alike. In his view, both the radicals and reactionaries had failed to understand history. The radicals could not see that their ideals have to be adapted to the history of a nation, while the reactionaries were blind to the fact that history undergoes ceaseless changes. If history made it impossible to create a totally new society according to some abstract plan, it also prohibited attempts to return to the past.

In the spectrum of political belief in Germany after the French Revolution, Hegel reveals himself to be a progressive moderate. Unlike the reactionaries, he approved of the fundamental ideals of the French Revolution, such as equality of opportunity, constitutional government, individual liberty, and representative assemblies; and he insisted that it was impossible to return to the older institutions of the ancient regime. Unlike the radicals, however, Hegel did not believe that these ideals could be achieved through popular agitation, still less through sweeping away all the historical traditions and institutions of Germany. The ideals of the Revolution would have to be established through piecemeal reform from above, through gradually adapting them to the historical conditions prevalent in Germany.

There can be no doubt that there is a conservative side to Hegel's historicism. In many of his writings Hegel appealed to history to criticize the attempts by radicals to remodel all of society according to their abstract ideals. The lesson to be drawn from the failure of the Revolution in France, in Hegel's view, was that it is not possible to change the constitution and institutions of a society in complete abstraction from its history, from such given circumstances as its religion, economy, traditions and national character. When the French radicals discovered that their ideals could not be easily imposed upon these circumstances, Hegel maintains, they engaged in a "fury of destruction," destroying all the historical institutions and traditions of France. The result was that there was nothing for them to build upon, so that the country lapsed into anarchy and terror. They imposed a Reign of Terror.

The conservative element of Hegel's historicism largely lay in his naturalism, his belief that the constitution and institutions of a nation are the product of its environment, and in particular its climate, geography, economy, religion, and traditions. Hegel acquired this doctrine from Montesquieu in his youth, and he adhered to it all his life. No less than his illustrious predecessor, he drew a conservative conclusion from it: that the constitution and institutions of a nation are adapted to its circumstances and are therefore appropriate to them. As Hegel put the point succinctly in his *Philosophy of Right*: "Every nation has the constitution appropriate to it and suitable for it". It was largely for this reason that Hegel sharply attacked utopian and radical reformers. In prescribing how the state ought to be, they failed to take into account its natural causes, the circumstances that make it of necessity as it is. The state cannot be created according to an arbitrary plan, but arises from historical causes, from the force of environment acting upon it.

It is no less clear, however, that there is a progressive side to Hegel's historicism. In seeing the end of history as the self-awareness of freedom, as the recognition that all are free, Hegel made the ideals of liberty and equality of the French Revolution into the very end of history itself. He thus bestowed the iron law of necessity upon these ideals. They were goals that people not only ought to strive for but must strive for through the inherent laws of history itself. Since these ideals were inherent in the natural development of history, Hegel argued that it was impossible in the post-revolutionary era to return to the old status quo of the ancient regime. This would be to fail to recognize the fate of the modern world, the fundamental spirit of modern life since the French Revolution. This was the principle of subjectivity, the idea that nothing could be accepted as valid until it accorded with the reason of the individual.

This progressive side of Hegel's historicism becomes especially evident from two of his political articles, his 1799 "On the German Constitution" and his 1814 "Proceedings of the Estates of Wurttemberg." Although they were written on separate occasions and for different reasons, these articles shared a common critical orientation. Both attacked those jurists and aristocrats who were bent on returning to the political structure of the ancient regime. The jurists continued to write as if the Holy Roman Empire still existed and as if nothing had changed since Charlemagne, while the aristocrats insisted upon the return of all their old privileges and powers as if Napoleon had never revamped the entire structure of Germany. The trend of history since the Revolution, Hegel argued, had been against restoring the old feudal constitution of the Holy Roman Empire, which had not been able to adapt to the new situation in Europe. If the princes' attempt to restore this constitution, ignoring all recent history, then they would revive only "empty forms without a substance." The spirit of the times demands, Hegel insisted, the creation of a completely new constitution for German providing for a strong central government, representative institutions, the role of law, and popular influence on legislation.

The progressive and conservative sides of Hegel's historicism are succinctly captured by his famous dictum in the preface to the *Philosophy of Right*: "What is rational is actual, and what is actual is rational". The first phrase expresses Hegel's progressive views on liberty and equality, which have been sanctioned by reason. The second phrase states Hegel's more conservative convictions. Here he means that the present constitution and institutions of a nation are rational in the sense that they arise of necessity from their environment, and are therefore appropriate to it. These two phrases appear to conflict with one another, however, for what if the present constitution violates, or at least does not recognize the principles of liberty and equality? Hegel's reply to this question is that each constitution is appropriate not only to its circumstances but also to its stage in the world-historical development of freedom and equality. The cunning of reason means that even if a nation does not recognize these ideals, it is still a necessary stage in their dialectical development.

What allows Hegel to unite the progressive and conservative sides of his historicism – to reconcile the ideals of the Revolution with the demand of historical continuity – is his belief that these ideals were already present within, and central to the Middle Ages. They do not involve a complete break with feudalism, he believes, but they are simply the final coming to self-consciousness of its underlying spirit. In his essay on the German constitution, for example, Hegel ridicules those who think that the modern principle of representative government arose only with the French Revolution. This principle was in fact basic to government during the feudal period, vassal should have a direct personal share in the shaping of common policy. The representation of the individual in the government was territory in the assemblies. The fundamental challenge to government in the modern age, Hegel maintains, is to unite the medieval ideal of participation in government with the need for a strong central authority. The modern state has simply grown too large and complex for direct participation. If, under these condition, the principle of direct participation is not relinquished, as in the Holy Roman Empire, then the state will simply dissolve into anarchy, a jumble of separate territories.

Both the radicals and reactionaries, Hegel believed, had failed to see that there is reason in history, that the realization of freedom and equality is the inherent law of its development since the Middle Ages. The radicals recognized the authority of reason, to be sure, but they did not understand that it is the law of history itself. It was for this reason that they mistakenly believed that they had to impose reason upon history and to break with the past. On the other hand, the reactionaries fully recognized the value of historical continuity and development, but they did not comprehend that it has an underlying end or reason, the realization of freedom and equality. In considering the politics of Hegel's historicism, it is illuminating to compare Hegel with Burke. Both stressed the value of historical continuity and tradition. Both appealed to history to undermine the claims of French radicals to change all of society according to some abstract plan. Nevertheless, Hegel, unlike Burke, saw history as an argument for rather than against a new constitution based upon reason. Burke argues against the attempt to create a new constitution on the grounds that it is incompatible with historical development. Hegel, however, argues in favor of such a constitution on the grounds that it is necessary to historical development. In general, Hegel affirmed the fundamental legal principle of the Revolution, that laws are legitimate only if they accord with a critical reason. He criticized traditionalists like Burke on the grounds that historical precedent by itself could never be the source of law. Turning the principle of positive law against the traditionalists, he argueds that if the basis of law is history, then law must change with history.

Hegel argues that the world is still not conscious of its condition; the end is to bring this about. This is the aim of world historical human beings, and in this they find their satisfaction. They are conscious of the powerlessness of what is present, of what still coasts along but only appears to be actuality. Spirit, having cultivated itself inwardly, has outgrown its world and is about to pass beyond it; spirit's self-consciousness no longer finds satisfaction in this world, but this kind of dissatisfaction has not yet found what it wills – for this is not as yet affirmatively at hand – and so it stands on the negative side. It is the world historical individuals who have then told people what it is that they will.

World historical individuals serve a cause – that of "the higher universal" - but they do not serve this cause consciously, intentionally, or with knowledge of so doing. Their knowledge of the higher universal or new principle of spirit is not knowledge of "the Idea as such"; it is not rational comprehension of the movement of history. It is only a practical insight into what must be done next in order to further their own personal ends – ends that just happen to coincide with the larger ends of spirit. "Since these individuals are the living expressions of the substantial deed of the world spirit and are thus immediately identical with it, they cannot themselves perceive it and it is not their object and end". Hegel distinguishes the immediate insight of the world historical individual from a reflective or rational knowledge of the idea, which is the prerogative of the philosophical historian who comes along later and comprehends what they have achieved.

World historical individuals help to actualize the freedom of spirit by bringing to birth a new order of things. That puts them among humanity's greatest benefactors. Their conscious intentions, however, are by no means philanthropic. On the contrary, world historical individuals are men of affairs, statesmen, and military commanders, such as Alexander Julius Caesar, Charlemagne, or Napoleon Bonaparte. Along with their practical insight into the higher universal to be actualized, they usually have a sense of their own historical destiny, but they are motivated less by the needs of the human race than by their own personal ambition and glory. Their insight into the needs of the time thus typically takes the form of a knowledge of the way to enhance or protect their own power.

Hegel says that Caesar's crossing the Rubicon, for example, was done only with the intention of preserving himself, protecting his command against those laws and commands of the Roman Republic because he saw that it had become a "lie," "that this hollow structure had to be replaced by a new one and that the structure he himself created was the necessary one". Nor are world historical individuals fastidious in the means they use to achieve their ends. They are often ruthless and unprincipled, "treating other intrinsically admirable interests and sacred rights in a carefree, cursory, hasty and heedless manner. A mighty figure must trample many an innocent flower underfoot, and destroy much that lies in its path".

We have seen that for Hegel a "hero" is someone who creatively brings to birth something new, and that this is incompatible with displaying the rectitude characteristic of a member of a rational social order. World historical individuals are "heroes" in something like this sense. yet because they emerge in periods of decadence and transition, not in the first blossoming of a new order but at the end of an old and decadent one, Hegel does not see them as characterized by "virtue". However, he does not represent world historical individuals as selfish or egoistically motivated in the sense that they seek their own personal happiness. They are driven by what Hegel calls "passion": the concentration of the whole individuality on a single goal. Nor, in Hegel's view, are world historical individuals empty husks. They may have undergone great difficulties in order to accomplish their end, but as soon as they have done so, they die early like Alexander, are murdered like Caesar, or deported like Napoleon. This is what Hegel calls the "cunning of reason" in history, "that it sets passions to work in its service, so that the agents by which it gives itself existence must pay the penalty and suffer the loss".

Judged by moral or ethical standards, world historical individuals are typically bad men. They benefit humanity, but they receive no honor and no gratitude, either in their own time or in subsequent ages. All they receive from posterity is undying fame as "formal subjectivities". Hegel does not dispute this judgment of posterity, or claim that its ingratitude does them any injustice. Nor does he try to disguise or mitigate the wickedness of world historical individuals. On the contrary, the morally good and ethically virtuous are those who oppose the world historical individual, resisting the progressive course of spirit: "Those who, with an ethical vocation and a noble disposition, have resisted what the progress of the idea of spirit has made necessary, stand higher in moral worth than those whose crimes have been transformed into means to higher order".

In Hegel's view this is how it must be, since the interests of spirit represented by world historical individuals are precisely those that require the destruction of the existing ethical life, overriding all moral or ethical claims in favor of the higher right of the world spirit: if it is the task of world historical individuals to help bring a new ethical order to birth by destroying the old one, it is hardly to be expected that their deed will exhibit ethical virtue. World historical individuals share their time's cynical insight into the hollowness of the existing ethical order, which they therefore treat with contempt. Their passions can achieve the destruction of the dying ethical world precisely because "they do not heed any of the restraints which right and morality seek to impose upon them". Passion is the force that brings the new ethical order to birth, because it is the only force powerful enough to break the bonds of the ethical.

There is nothing new in Hegel's idea that some of humanity's greatest benefactors have been criminals and evildoers. This idea stands squarely in the tradition of Mandeville's 'private vices, public benefits," Adam Smith's invisible hand," Turget's views about the role of war and ambition in human progress, and Kant's theory that our rational capacities are developed only through social competition and the drive for unjust ascendancy over others. What perhaps makes Hegel's view more scandalous than its precursors is the further idea that these wicked individuals are absolutely justified in their unethical conduct. When they violate abstract right, morality, and ethics, they "have the absolute right on their side, but a right of a wholly peculiar kind".

Hegel Considers the sphere of world history to be higher than that of the ethical. From its higher standpoint, ethical right and wrong do not cease to exist, but they no longer matter. It is to the sphere of "conscious actuality"– of practical life lived in the present – that such things as "justice and virtue, wrongdoing, violence and vice, guilt and innocence" have their "determinate significance"; it is in this sphere alone that "talents, passions, the splendor, independence, happiness or unhappiness of individuals and states" are to find judgment and justice. But "world history falls outside these points of view". Philosophical historians should not make moral or ethical judgments, not because their discipline is "value free" but because its standpoint on human freedom–the ultimate value–is higher than the ethical standpoint.

From the world-historical standpoint the deeds of the great men who are the individuals of world history, appear justified not only in the inner significance of which those individuals were unconscious, but also form a worldly standpoint. From this point of view, no claims must be raised against world-historical deeds and their perpetrators by moral circles, to which they do not belong. The litany of private virtue–modesty, humility, charity, and temperance–must not be raised against them. World history could wholly dispense with the circle in which falls morality, and the often mistakenly discussed dichotomy between morals and politics. Hegel is particularly interested in attacking those moralists who see in great men and their deeds only wicked passions and vices, and treat the study of history chiefly as a gymnasium in which to exercise our capacity for moral indignation.

Fascism and Hegelianism

According to one dominant interpretation, the intellectual affinities of fascism and national socialism were with philosophic irrationalism. This conclusion makes it necessary to consider their relation to Hegelian nationalism and the Hegelian theory of the state. The relation was in fact somewhat complicated. Hegel's philosophy had been regarded throughout the nineteenth century as the logical antithesis of Schopenhauer's irrationalism. Yet the version of fascist philosophy that Mussolini adopted after he decided that fascism needed a philosophy was obviously borrowed from Italian Hegelianism. It utilized to the full, in its attack on liberalism and parliamentarism, the Hegelian critique of individualism, though this had long been taken into account by the later English theorists of liberalism. On the other hand, German philosophers of national socialism usually ignored Hegel or, explicitly rejected him. Moreover, German critics of national socialism usually regarded it as incompatible with most of what the Hegelian theory of the state had concretely meant in German politics during the nineteenth century. The clues to this apparent discrepancy are to be found partly in the opportunist nature of the philosophy professed by Mussolini and partly in internal differences between Italy and Germany and in the position of the two movements on their respective countries.

That Hegel's system, in intention at least, was the very opposite of irrationalism is too obvious to require elaboration. The center of the system was logic, and its several parts were all supposed to be bound together by a dialectical argument that was rigidly rational. It is true that Hegel's conception of reason was largely "romanticized" and that his dialectic lacked the precision which he claimed for it and which would be needed to make it a reliable method of scientific investigation. But this does not affect his intention, nor does it affect his view of social change. This, according to Hegel, is strictly necessary and logical. It offers little scope to the heroic great minds, since Hegel was notoriously skeptical of the influence of great men in history. Both in Italy and in Germany at the close of World War I it was necessary to argue that the national will, by a sheer act of affirmation or assertion, could rise superior to a lack of material resources and create its economic opportunity by political means. The superiority of political to economic forces was an article of faith for both fascism and national socialism. Both movements were, in fact and by profession, revolutionary, or more truly counter-revolutionary. But the revolutionary possibilities of Hegelianism had long since been exploited by the Marxists, and while Hitler undoubtedly admired and imitated the rabble-rousing tactics of Marxian agitators, he was quite aware that national socialism could not borrow the philosophy of Marxian theorists.

Hegel's political philosophy and the political philosophy of fascism and national socialism agreed in being nationalist and anti-liberal. This agreement, however, implied less unity in philosophical outlook than has often been supposed. Hegel's nationalism had been logically the weakest part of his system. He never gave any sound reason why the nation, rather than any one of a dozen other possible social groups, should be endowed with the moral pre-eminence that he assigned to it. Moreover, Hegel's nationalism, though it included a moral glorification of war, had not been for imperialism. It is incompatible with any genuine moral respect for nationality as a cultural value. On the other hand, long before World War I, nationalism had ceased to depend in any definite way on Hegel. Nationalists everywhere tended to be anti-liberal and anti-parliamentarian—in contrast with the nationalists of the period after the French Revolution—on the ground that representative institutions and popular government are incompatible with a strong national policy. Everywhere they tended to be militarist and to exalt the alleged spiritual value of the warlike virtues. Everywhere they availed themselves of Hegelian argument against the value of individual liberty and equality, but this implied no knowledge of Hegel's philosophy. Hegelianism in its day may well have played its part in imbedding such ideas in the European political tradition, but if so, its work had since been done.

When Mussolini decided that fascism needed a philosophy, he apparently entrusted the task to Giovanni Gentile who, like Benedetto Croce, had long been identified with an Italian school of Hegelian philosophy. Gentile had at hand the Hegelian theory of the state and not having much time he used it. Mussolini took what Gentile offered him, and in consequence the theory of Italian fascism was a theory of "the state" and of its supremacy and sanctity and all-inclusiveness. Its motto became everything for the state; nothing outside the state. Since Mussolini was already in control, it was easy to equate the power of the state with the power of his government. Since the state is the embodiment of an "ethical idea," fascism could be presented as a form of lofty political idealism, in contrast with the self-proclaimed materialism of the Marxists, and as a moral or religious conception of society, in contrast both with the class struggle and with political revivalism, which was described as merely selfish and anti-social inedividualism.

There is no doubt that fascist leaders used a good deal of Hegelian language but there need be very little genuine Hegelianism. Gentile's fascist theory of the state was in truth hardly more than a caricature of Hegelianism. Benedetto Croce, the most distinguished of Italian Hegelians, was also the most important opponent of fascism among Italian philosophers. Long before the rise of fascism he had pointed out that even Gentile's metaphysics contained elements of irrationalism derived from Nietzsche and was doubtfully Hegelian.

It is common knowledge that the *Philosophy of Right* is full of "horrors". Here are some samples: the State is God on earth; society is subordinate to the State; our moral existence is less valuable than our political existence; the perfect form of the constitution is the monarchy; the people must obey the government; loyalty toward the State is man's highest duty, indeed he must be a citizen; an elected legislature is a bad system. Critics omit the rest so as to get to the most horrific of them all, the famous line from the preface, so blasphemous that it has made all right-thinking men and women from every point along the political spectrum tremble with rage for more than a century: "What is rational is real, and what is real is rational". What other reaction can there be to this thought except to say that it is a slap in the face of basic common sense, the final unforgivable insult, an outrage so shocking that most critics—at least this is the impression one gets from their works—find themselves unable to go any further, if not in their reading, at least in their understanding of the *Philosophy of Right*?

Given these orientations, Nietzsche's thought from the beginning was set on a collision course with Hegel's teachings, an antagonism that partially was bequeathed to him by Schopenhauer. Largely under the latter's influence, his early writings were sharply dismissive of Hegel's work, castigating it primarily for its supposed "historical optimism" and its shallow support of prevailing historical tendencies and developments. By linking the rational and the real or reason and actual life-experience, Hegel was said to encourage an uncritical acceptance of external "necessity" and the oblivion of the agonies of concrete human decision.

From this Hegel derived the conclusion that world history and every story "must have an aim" and that "we demand stories only with aims." But, Nietzsche countered,

> We do not at all demand stories about the world process, for we consider it a swindle to talk about it. That my life has no aim is evident even from the accidental nature of its origin; that I can posit an aim for myself is another matter. State? What is that? Well then, open your ears to me, for now I shall speak to you about the death of peoples. State is the name of the coldest of all cold monsters. Coldly it tells lies too; and this lie crawls out of its mouth: 'I, the state, am the people.' That is a lie.

In Popper's *The Open Society and Its Enemies*, Hegel shares the limelight with other suspect thinkers of the past, particularly with Plato and Marx. Bracketing the pronounced differences between these authors—differences underscored by Hegel and later by Marx—the study proceeds to attack all three for their presumed enmity to democratic openness, which in turn derives from their attachment to a speculative historicism and their dismissal of individual freedom in favor of holistic-totalitarian structures. In Popper's portrayal, Hegel—the "source of all contemporary historicism"—was the direct heir and follower of a long line of metaphysical speculation deriving from Heraclitus, Plato, and Aristotle. Together with these predecessors Hegel was ignorant of empirical science and scientific method. Instead of engaging in empirical research, the German thinker relied entirely on speculative insight and dialectical logic with "miraculous" result: "A master logician, it was child's play for his powerful dialectical methods to draw real physical rabbits out of purely metaphysical silk-hats." One reason why Hegelian philosophy was taken very seriously in his time was the general backwardness of German natural science in those days. On the whole, Hegel's following—then and later—was made up of people who preferred "a quick initiation into the deeper secrets of this world to the laborious technicalities of a science which, after all, may only disappoint them by its lack of power to unveil all mysteries." Concentrating on Hegel's philosophy of nature, Popper found the Hegelian opus guilty of mystification and in fact of deliberate deception: "The question arises whether Hegel deceived himself, hypnotized by his own inspiring jargon, or whether he boldly set out to deceive and bewitch others. I am satisfied that the latter was the case."

In the political arena, a similar mystification prevailed, namely, the denigration of individual judgment in favor of overarching authoritarian structures. In Popper's account, Hegel's philosophy was basically a handmaiden of the reactionary, anti-constitutional policies of the Prussian state. Popper narrates that the fight for the open society began only with the ideas of 1789; and the feudal monarchies soon experienced the seriousness of this danger. When in 1815 the reactionary party began to resume its power in Prussia, it found itself in dire need of an ideology. Hegel was appointed to meet this demand, and he did so by reviving the ideas of the first great enemies of the open society-Heraclitus, Plato, and Aristotle. Just as the French Revolution rediscovered the perennial ideas of the great generation and of Christianity—freedom, equality, and the brotherhood of all men—so Hegel rediscovered the Platonic ideas which lie behind the perennial revolt against freedom and reason. Hegelianism is the renaissance of tribalism.

In supporting the Prussian state with its militaristic bent, Popper claimed, Hegel's thought promoted the upsurge not only of tribalism but of a chauvinistic nationalism or collectivism, which, in turn, was the pacemaker of contemporary totalitarian regimes. Popper saw a tight chain of intellectual filiations linking classical teachings with recent modes of political repression. In fact, Hegel's historical significance resided, Popper argued precisely in "that he represents the missing link, as it were, between Plato and the modern form of totalitarianism." Together with Plato, Hegel completely rejected or despised individual rights and constitutional safeguards, indulging instead in a "patronizing worship of the state". Inspired by classical ideals of public unity and homogeneity, Hegelians—both direct disciples and latter-day followers—have all been taught "to worship the state, history, and the nation." Summed up in a nutshell, the political doctrine of Hegelianism was that "the state is everything and the individual nothing," in the sense that the individual "owes everything to the state, his physical as well as his spiritual existence."

As in the case of Plato and later of Marx, Hegel's totalitarian proclivities were buttressed by his historicism, that is, the assumption of a liner historical evolution. For Plato, the realm of ideas or essences existed before or outside the world of phenomena, and the trend of development was a "movement away from the perfection of the ideas" and hence a movement of decay. While maintaining the distinction between essences and appearances, Hegel reserved the telos of evolution by postulating a general trend "towards the idea" and thus an evolutionary scheme of progress. For Hegel, however, this flux is "not decay" and his historicism is basically "optimistic" by pointing to the steady self-realization or actualization of spirit. In Hegel's political philosophy, it was crucially the "spirit of the nation" that determines its "hidden historical destiny," and in order to actualize this spirit a nation had to assert its individuality by "fighting other nations" in a near-permanent condition of warfare. The dangers of this teleology were clearly evident in the concluding section "World History" in the *Philosophy of Right* where Hegel depicted the evolution of Western civilization in the direction of a "Germanic realm," which Popper quickly identifies with the Prussian monarchy and its still more militant and ethnocentric successors. In light of these explicit or implicit forms of intellectual complicity, the verdict on Hegelianism was bound to be severe. In Popper's words, there is a solidarity between the proponents of post-structuralism and deconstruction unite in their attachment to Nietzsche combined with a vehement anti-Hegelianism. There is no possible compromise between Hegel and Nietzsche. Nietzsche's philosophy has a great polemical range; it forms an absolute anti-dialectics and sets out to expose all the mystifications that find a final refuge in the dialectic.

Viewed against this background, historical contests are not struggles for mutual recognition but clashes between separate and incommensurable forces; while constituting a place of confrontation, history is not a "closed field offering the spectacle of a struggle among equals." Far from revealing an ascent of spirit, development simply involves the endlessly repeated play of dominations. Historical combat and struggle for domination are not merely observable occurrences but infiltrate human understanding itself. In fact, reason and truth are themselves implicated in the will to power: "Nothing in man—not even his body—is sufficiently stable to serve as the basis for self-recognition or for understanding other men.' Unable to yield universal insight or genuine synthesis, reason is a partisan accessory of power. Escaping Hegel is a less urgent motive in Derridas writings, but it is present nonetheless. Together with Foucault, Derrida tends to foreground discontinuity over dialectics, dispersal over unity, and difference over sameness.

The question that must be faced, then, by the student of Hegel today is this: What can be retained of his progressivist philosophy of history once it has been submitted to the skeptical attacks of the 'masters of suspicion'? We would like to suggest in conclusion that Hegel's views on the state and political community remain his most enduring influence on the liberal legacy. Typically, liberals in the past have shied away from these concepts, treating them as a sort of monolith inimical to freedom. Hegel's emphasis on authority, order, sovereignty, and law has seemed to many to conceal a conservative, if not a reactionary intent. Hegel's chief accomplishment has been to show that the state and community are not just a precondition for, but a dimension of freedom. The state is not simply an instrument of force and coercion but a locus of shared understandings. A state is more than an instrument for ensuring civil peace; it is a wider network of shared ethical ideas and beliefs. A state is ultimately a meeting of minds, since it depends on a common cultural history and sense of civic identity. The state, then, is charged with the business of articulating some notion of the common good, which traditional forms of liberalism seem unable to do. That the state is not just a broker between competing interest groups but has the positive function of promoting a way of life, some substantive conception of human flourishing. For Hegel, human beings are not just Benthamite utility maximizers but are defined by a range of powers, skills, and capacities that can only be developed in association with others in the state.

Underlying Hegel's argument, then, is a claim not just about the state but about the kinds of persons that inhabit the state. One aspect of liberalism, especially in its Kantian forms, has been tendency to attach priority to the self over all communal ends and purposes. The detached, free-floating, or "unencumbered" self of liberal theory achieves completion in a political setup that is purportedly neutral to questions of the human good and recognizes only the right of people to pursue their own conceptions of the good within that framework. Politics and ethical life are, for Hegel, deeply embedded in the stories, myths, and forms of consciousness which tell us about ourselves. Human character, as both Hegel and Aristotle understood, is not simply a product of our own making but is in large part the result of the upbringing and cultural context to which we have been habituated. This is Hegel's point in saying that while a morality may require choice, it is not itself the product of choice. A choice can only be made within the context of a meaningful way of life, and a moral choice can only be made within the context of morality. This is the rationale behind Hegel's distinction between *Moralitat* and *Sittlichkeit*.

Like the libertarians of our own day, Hegel also celebrated the separation of civil society from the state and welcomed the separation as one of the great accomplishments of modernity. Civil society brought with it an unprecedented growth in freedom, understood here as sheer indeterminacy. But even as he delights in the liberation of individual self-interest from an oppressive politics of the common good, Hegel is also highly critical of those commercial societies, notably England, where everything is judged in terms of exchange value alone. Market liberalism characteristically sees human beings as egoistic calculators of pleasures and pains who regard political activity as a necessary evil to be endured for the ultimate ends of safety, security, peace, and comfort.

It is precisely because Hegel does not wholeheartedly applaud the emancipatory interests at work within civil society that many have complained of his reactionary politics. But this is to misunderstand Hegel. He was a liberal, but a 'pre' and perhaps even a post-market liberal, or a corporate liberal, who regards the existing corporations, voluntary associations, and other institutions of civil life as a means of checking the power of a centralizing, rationalizing bureaucratic state, on the one hand, and the development of rootless, deracinated, anomic populaces on the other. These intermediary associations, we must recall, are forms of ethical life and therefore play an important tutelary function in shaping the individual's capacities for shared moral experience and civic involvement. Only by membership in one of the publicly authorized corporations can a person avoid the corrosive effects of the kind of apolitical individualism unleashed by a commodity-producing society. These lesser groups are important, because they help to prepare men and women for active citizenship. They appear here, as in the work of later pluralist writers, as a training ground for virtue, where various modes of cooperation and competition are inculcated.

One of the best known chapters of any of Hegel's books is devoted to showing that this is so. It is called 'Master and Slave', and occupies an early mid-section of the *Phenomenology.* It is presented without a clear context or purpose, and without any references to other philosophers, or current problems and controversies. He simply tells us the story of two wholly undescribed 'self-consciousnesses' who meet, and almost immediately enter into a fight to the death. Each tries to 'cancel the other because his consciousness threatens the other's view of himself as free and independent. But each one is also trying to 'prove' himself, and recognizes that the actual death of the other would eliminate the only witness to that proof. So the winner lets the loser live and becomes the master, the loser the slave. The master becomes 'a consciousness existing on its own account which is mediated with itself through another consciousness'. In the process both of them learn that there is more to life than survival, and that selfhood is a complex of independence and dependency which mere individual existence cannot account for.

The story is presented wholly in the abstract. Hegel is giving us a parable, which represents not a particular situation but rather the prototype of all human confrontations. It is set, as in Hobbes and Rousseau, in a fictitious 'state of nature', an imaginary reconstruction of what human life might be like in the absence of everything we call 'social', but unlike Hobbes, Hegel does not think that life in such a circumstance would reduce to pure selfishness: pride, vanity, and a sense of status already enter into pre-social conflict. And unlike Rousseau, he does not think that the state of nature produces individuals who are happy, free, and indifferent to one another, much less 'noble savages'. What he suggests is that in the state of nature people are already pre-social and defined by the traits that Rousseau too readily blames on the corrupting influence of society. Human existence is primordially a matter of mutual recognition, and it is only through mutual recognition that we are self-aware and strive for the social meanings in our lives.

The parable develops a fascinating twist, for the master becomes dependent on the slave, not only for his food and comforts but also for his self-image. He is only master in so far as the slave truly regards him as such, but the infuriating residual independence of other people's consciousness is notorious, and it is even more infuriating when the other in question does not openly 'rebel but seems to be going through the motions of absolute obedience. One cannot obtain self-confirmation from a 'yes-man'. As the master becomes increasingly dependent on the slave, and as both of them recognize that this is the case, the power in the relationship shifts until the slave becomes the 'self-existent', and the master the dependent one. As a parable of the origins of society, Hegel here lays the groundwork both for his philosophy of history and for his general theory of society and ethics, in which some less confrontational and more stable social arrangement must replace the master-slave relationship. But in this parable too Karl Marx will find exactly the model he needs to explain the conflict between the economic master and servile classes, and its 'inevitable' resolution.

In Hegel's political philosophy, we have an expression of hope: a hope that out of the self-interested, atomistic narrow individualism of civil society, which is based on the individual rights, a more concrete community will emerge, a community in which we acknowledge our civic duties, our responsibilities for others, our shared culture and our social unity. Hegel did not wish to impose these duties or this community upon us, and in this sense he cannot be called authoritarian: rather, he believed that we would come to feel the emptiness, inadequacy and absurdity of life merely within civil society, and ourselves construct a higher form of community within the State, and bring about the unity of individuality and universality within the social sphere.

However, it is fair to stress that Hegel underestimated the difficulties of bringing about this reconciliation. In particular that the Left critique of Hegel insisted that the state can arise by incorporating the market and market rationality, but may have to abolish it. Nor is it clear as thinkers on the Right have observed that the state will be viable without recourse to anti-democratic political structures: Hegel himself argued for a constitutional monarchy. Hegel is a significant political thinker, then, not because he provided answers, but because he raised important questions, questions that plague liberal orthodoxy even now: namely, notwithstanding the evident achievement of modern, liberal, capitalist states, are they the final word? Must we be content with the alienation, anomie, exploitation, mechanization, abstract freedom and collapse of community that accompanies modern civil society? Or can we hope that history and the development of human culture will evolve one further, final social norms, in which the benefits of liberalism can be retained without these drawbacks? Hegel, and those whom he has influenced on both the Left and the Right, argue that we can, while the defenders of modern liberalism hold that this hope is misguided, and that in seeking to go beyond the freedoms of civil society, and passing into the state, we may gain in some respects, but we risk losing what Hegel admitted was the greatest achievement of modernity so far: individual freedom itself.

In the political realm, therefore, Hegel's attempt to reconcile individuality and universality, freedom and community, has fallen short, and the tension between these social categories remains. Indeed, the same might be said of Hegel's philosophical project as a whole: to his critical successors such as Marx, Feuerbach, Kierkegaard and Adorno the dichotomies Hegel spoke of, and which he tried so hard to transcend, were not successfully resolved in his system, and fundamental antitheses remained. The dissolution of the Hegelian synthesis, and the failure of his project of reconcilement, is the background against which subsequent European thought developed, and it is this failure which forced continental philosophy to face once again the very contradictions and crises that Hegel had tried so hard to overcome.

17

Karl Marx

> In the social production of their life, men enter into definite relations that are indispensable and independent of their will, relations of production which correspond to a definite stage of development of their material productive forces. The sum total of these relations of prduction constitutes the economic structure of sociery, the real foundation, on which rises a legal and political superstructure and to which correspond definite forms of social consciousness. The mode of production of material life conditions the social, political and intellectual life process in general. It is not the consciousness of men that determines their being but on the contrary their social being that determines their consciousness. At a certain stage of their development, the material productive forces of society come into conflict with the existing relations of production, or what is but a legal expression for the same thing-with the property relations within which they have been at work hitherto. From forms of development of the productive forces these relations turn into their fetters. Then begins an epoch of social revolution. With the change of the economic foundation the entire immense superstructure is more or less rapidly transformed.

Karl Marx (1818-1883) was born into a Jewish family, in the Rhineland town of Trier in 1818. The beginning of the nineteenth century was a difficult time for the German Jews. Though there was a measure of civil equality, there was still considerable discrimination against Jews in the professions. Marx's father was obliged to undergo a nominal conversion to Protestant Christianity in order to retain his position as a legal official. It is unclear to what extent Jewish customs were practiced in the household Marx grew up in and how much influence either the rabbinical tradition of his family or the experience of discrimination had on the young Marx. Certainly anti-Semitic jibes were often flung at him by opponents in later controversies. And since Marx himself was not above using the rhetoric of anti-Semitism when it suited his polemic purposes-'What is the secular cult of the Jew? Haggling. What is his secular god? Money'. There is at least some evidence for the suggestion that he suffered from the pathological Jewish self-hate typical of many of the victims of that prejudice.

In the testimony about Marx philosophy aims and behaviour, from a variety of sources it is notable how often the word 'dictator' crops up. Annenkov called him 'the personification of a democratic dictator'. An unusually intelligent Prussian police agent who reported on him in London noted: 'The dominating trait of his character is an unlimited ambition and love of power he is the absolute ruler of his party; he does everything on his own and he gives orders on his own responsibility and will endure no contradiction." Techow who once managed to get Marx drunk and to pour forth his soul gives a brilliant pen-portrait of him. He was 'a man of outstanding personality' with a rare intellectual superiority' and if his heart had matched his intellect and he had possessed as much love as hate, I would have gone through fire for him.' But 'he is lacking in nobility of soul. I am convinced that a most dangerous personal ambition has eaten away all the good in him the acquisition of personal power is the aim of all his endeavours.' Bakunin's final judgment on Marx struck the same note: 'Marx does not believe in God but he believes much in himself and makes everyone serve himself. His heart is not full of love but of bitterness and he has very little sympathy for the human race."

Marx's habitual anger, his dictatorial habits and his bitterness reflected no doubt his justified consciousness of great powers and his intense frustration at his inability to exercise them more effectively. As a young man he led a bohemian, often idle and dissolute life; in early middle age he still found it difficult to work sensibly and systematically, often sitting up all night talking, then lying half-asleep on the sofa for most of the day. In late middle age he kept more regular hours but he never became self-disciplined about work. Yet he resented the smallest criticism. It was one of the characteristics he shared with Rousseau that he tended to quarrel with friends and benefactors, especially if they gave him good advice. When his devoted colleague Dr Ludwig Kugelmann suggested in 1874 that he would find no difficulty in finishing *Capital* if only he would organize his life a little better, Marx broke with him for good and subjected him to relentless abuse.

His angry egoism had physical as well as psychological roots. He led a peculiarly unhealthy life, took very little exercise, ate highly spiced food, often in large quantities, smoked heavily, drank a lot, especially strong bear and as a result had constant trouble with his liver. He rarely took baths or washed much at all. This, plus his unsuitable diet, may explain the veritable plague of boils from which he suffered for a quarter of a century. They increased his natural irritability and seem to have been at their worst while he was writing *Capital.* 'Whatever happens he wrote grimly to Engels, 'I hope the bourgeoisie as long as they exist, will have cause to remember my carbuncles." The boils varied in numbers, size and intensity but at one time or another they appeared on all parts of his body, including his cheeks, the bridge of his nose, his bottom, and his penis. In 1873 they brought on a nervous collapse marked by trembling and huge bursts of rage.

Still more central to his anger and frustration, and lying perhaps at the very roots of his hatred for the capitalist system, was his grotesque incompetence in handling money. As a young man it drove him into the hands of moneylenders at high rates of interest, and a passionate hatred of usury was the real emotional dynamic of his whole moral philosophy. It explains why he devoted so much time and space to the subject, why his entire theory of class is rooted in anti-Semitism, and why he included in *Capital* a long and violent passage denouncing usury which he culled from one of Luther's anti-Semitic diatribes.

Marx's money troubles began at university and lasted his entire life. They arose from an essentially childish attitude. Marx borrowed money heedlessly, spent it, then was invariably astounded and angry when the heavily discounted bills, plus interest, became due. He saw the charging of interest, essential as it is to any system based on capital, as a crime against humanity, and at the root of the exploitation of man by man which his entire system was designed to eliminate. That was in general terms. But in the particular context of his own case he responded to his difficulties by himself exploiting anyone within reach and in the first place his own family. Money dominates his family correspondence. The last letter from his father, written in February 1838 when he was already dying, reiterates his complaint that Marx was indifferent to his family except for the purpose of getting their help. Three months later he was dead. Marx did not trouble to attend his funeral. Instead he started putting pressure on his mother. He had already adopted a pattern of living off loans from friends and demanding periodic sums from the family. He argued that the family was quite rich and had a duty to support him in his important work. Apart from his intermittent journalism, the purpose of which was political rather than to earn money, Marx never seriously attempted to get a job, though he once in London applied for a post as a railway clerk, being turned down on the grounds that his handwriting was too poor. Marx's unwillingness to pursue a career seems to have been the main reason why his family was unsympathetic to his pleas for handouts. His mother not only refused to pay his debts, believing he would then simply contract more, but eventually cut him off completely. Thereafter their relations were minimal. She is credited with the bitter wish that 'Karl would accumulate capital instead of just writing about it.'

By this time, of course, Engels was the new subject of exploitation. From the mid-1840s, when they first came together, until Marx's death, Engels was the main source of income for the Marx family. He probably handed over more than half of what he received himself. The relationship was exploitative on Marx's side and unequal altogether since he was always the dominant and sometimes the domineering partner. Yet in a curious way each needed the other, like a pair of stage comedians in a double act, unable to perform separately, frequently grumbling but always in the end sticking together. The partnership almost broke down in 1863 when Engels felt Marx's insensitive cadging had gone too far. Engels seems to have decided, about this time, that Marx would never be able to get a job or support his family or indeed get his affairs into any kind of order. The only thing to do was to pay him a regular dole. So in 1869 Engels sold out of the business, securing for himself an income of rather more than £800 a year. Of this £350 went to Marx. For the last fifteen years of his life, therefore, Marx was the pensioner of a rentier, and enjoyed a certain security.

In other respects Marx's upbringing was that of the privileged son of an educated bourgeois family. He read for a degree in law first at the University of Bonn, then at Berlin, and it was at Berlin that he came under the influence of the Hegelian philosophy. The effect of that influence cannot be neglected. Though from an early statge Marx defined haw own thought in conscious opposition to the detail of Hegelian social theory, he remained transfixed by Hegel's overall project of charting history as the development, transformation and resolution of humankind into an organic whole, self-consciously in control of a world of its own making. Throughout the 1830s, Marx involved himself in the regular discussions of a group of Hegel's followers in Berlin-the gegelian movement was largely on the question of how religion was to be understood in the development of the human spirit. Not content with the conservative reading of Hegel that regarded the mere existence of organized religion as a guarantee of its rationality, many of the Young Hegelians viewed religion in secular and critical terms, attacking it as a transitory, inadequate and obsolescent product of human consciousness. That in turn led to political criticism. It was a critique of the conditions that generated religious belief, and of the legal and political structures by which Christianity was sustained. Prominent among Marx's Young Hegelian friends was Bruno Bauer, a university lecturer in theology. Bauer collaborated with Marx on a number of projects in the early 1840s, mostly attempts to demonstrate the mythic character of Christianity, to excoriate readings of Hegel that purported to lend philosophical credibility to those myths, and to attack the Prussian ideology of a Christian state.

However, as the distinctively materialist and socialist sides of Marx's thought developed, he began to distance himself increasingly from his Young Hegelian colleagues. At Bauer's suggestion he started writing for a progressive Rhineland newspaper and later became its editor. He wrote on political matters and increasingly on social and economic questions in a way that led in 1843 to the suppression of the paper. But though his own articles had this effect, Marx was often critical of what he took to be the politically naive and irresponsible behavior of the Berlin members of the Young Hegelian circle. The social criticism of this group was, he believed, an immoderate and ungrounded form of intellectual elitism, out of touch with the concerns of the mass of the people and the social realities that might lend some credibility to political criticism.

At the same time as he was pressing for a more realistic and practical politics of radicalism, Marx was developing an account of the relation between politics and society that would lead eventually to his repudiation of Hegel's political philosophy. His experience as a journalist in the early 1840s covering, first the deliberations of the Rhineland Parliament on property laws, and second, the impoverishment of Mosel winegrowers convinced him that law and politics could not be regarded as autonomous activities but should be seen as something determined and conditioned by relations in the social and economic sphere.

He also published another piece in the journal, 'Towards a Critique of Hegel's Philosophy of Right: An Introduction'. Hegel, too, had been skeptical about the rights of man as an expression of true human freedom. He regarded them as empty, abstract and fanatical, reducing 'the union of individuals in the state to a contract and therefore to something based on their arbitrary wills, their opinion, and their capriciously given express consent'. Now though Marx agreed with Hegel in taking the individual in isolation as the guiding thread of theories of natural rights, he did not erupt the view that what was needed to remedy this individualism was great participation in ethical life. What was needed, he said, was something which turned the Hegelian philosophy upside down-greater involvement with the messy business of man's natural life of labour, production, interaction with nature, industry and material consumption. Human emancipation was retarded not by lack of ethics, but by poverty and exploitation. The essay on Hegel introduced for the first time into Marx's writing the idea of the revolutionary overthrow of the existing order by the proletariat and this was the direction that all Marx's subsequent political writing took.

Marx by this time was working closely with Friedrich Engels, heir to a bourgeois manufacturing fortune, and the two of them marked the extent of their break with the rump of the Young Hegelians in the publication of works like *The Holy Family,* which was an onslaught on rather a caricature of the ideas of the Bauer brothers, and later *The German Ideology,* which articulated their materialist view of history and, in Engels's words, 'settled accounts with our former philosophical views'.

Early in 1845, the French government responding to Prussian pressure expelled Marx and other German radicals from Paris, and Marx and Engels left for Brussels. There they founded an International Communist Party and drafted *The Communist Manifesto.* That work spoke of 'a spectre haunting Europe' the spectre of proletarian uprising. It contained an analysis of history, a characterization of the contradictions, of bourgeois society, a vilification of other communist movementes, and a call for universal suffrage to enable workers to gain power and implement a programme based on the abolition of landed and industrial property.

The year of failed revolution in Europe, 1848-9, saw Marx in Paris once more, expelled from Brussels, and then in Cologne and London. He took a deep interest in the revolutionary movements that convulsed Europe during his life, in 1848 and in 1871. In this the point of reference for him, as for all contemporary thinkers, was of course the French Revolution of 1789. Marx returned to that theme many times, but though he celebrated the fall of the ancien regime, he never characterized it as anything other than a bourgeois revolution. Historically its task was the unchaining and setting up modern bourgeois society and breaking down the feudal impediments to capitalist industry and national unity. In that the bourgeoisie succeeded: 'The Revolution was a 'failure' only for the mass whose real conditions for emancipation were substantially different from the conditions within which the bourgeoisie could emancipate itself and society'. Subsequent upheavals in France were even less significant: mere coups d'etat, on Marx's account: but 'the next attempt of the French Revolution will be no longer, as before, to transfer the bureaucratic military machine from one hand to another, but to smash it, and this is the preliminary condition for every real people's revolution on the Continent'.

Marx was working all this time towards his greatest achievement: a systematic account in economic terms of the rise of modern capitalism, the nature of capitalist production, the laws of commodity exchange, the determination of wages and the length of the working day, the effects of mechanization, and the shape and likely results of the successive crises that he believed would eventually wreck the capitalist economic order. Marx's economics was embodied above all in *Capital*, written in London, the first volume of which was published in 1867. The nature and scale of this economic project represent in many ways a break with Marx's philosophical and cultural endeacours in earlier years. Some commentators have suggested that there is a decisive rupture between the concerns of the author of *Capital* and the later works and those of the early Marx. On this account, the early Marx was concerned with humanistic themes—, exploitation, and so on while the later Marx was concerned more with the natural history of social structures and with human individuals only to the extent that they could be regarded as bearers of social relations defined independently of them. But the rupture itself is probably exaggerated. *The Capital* project required an enormous concentration of effort on just a few of the themes that had been developed in the early writings. But very few of other early themes disappear altogether from view. Though there is apparently less explicit discussion in Marx's later work about human emancipation and the nature of alienation in the modern world, and though the terms 'freedom' and 'alienation' are not used so often, it is arguable that the effect of much of the marxian economics is to give serious and sustained substance to those ideas rather than to abandon them.

Though Marx anticipated the end of capitalism, he never wrote much about the shape or structure of the socialist society he expected to take its place. Some of his later writings on events in the 1870s have been treated by commentators as though they contained an implicit theory of politics. In *The Civil War in France,* his enthusiastic discussion of the Commune of 1871 is taken to indicate a belief that its 'pyramidal' democratic structure of revocable delegates prefigured the political structures Marx believed would exist under socialism.

There seem to have been two reasons for this reticence. On the one hand, Marx claimed to repudiate all forms of Utopian speculation as unscientific. He believed that socialist organization was inevitable, on social and economic grounds, and saw no point in, as he put it, 'writing recipes for the cookshops of the future.' The other reason is more complicated. Marx seems to have believed that under socialism the need for state forms and politics as we know it would gradually disappear. The state, as Engels put it, would 'wither away' and the government of men would be replaced by the administration of things. This belief develops one of the main themes of *On the Jewish Question* the denial of the intrinsic importance of politics, considered as a sphere apart from material life. In his later works Marx seens to suggest that politics and the state were necessitated by class conflict, either as a direct coercive agency of the dominant class or as a power standing apart from the classes which prevented class conflict from becoming internecine. Once the capitalist state was overthrown, residual class conflict would persist for a while, and there would be a need for 'a dictatorship of the proletariat'. But that would be a transitional period, for the proletariat distinguished itself from other ruling classes by representing all the oppressed and not rising in the basis of the oppression of any other group. Gradually, then the need for its political dominance of other segments of society would diminish, while at the same time the prosperity that socialist production involved would increasingly free humanity from the need to rely on coercive mechanisms of distribution. Marx's silence on issue of political organization, then, from the publication of 'On the Jewish Question' in 1844 to his death in London nearly forty years later, is not difficult to explain. But it has left a very significant lacuna in modern socialist thought, a tradition which is still largely dominated by the marxian legacy.

Hegel and Marx

Marx's relation to Hegel has been a matter of acrimonious debate and controversy. Marx actually rests his central arguments on a priori claims.

Consequently, the most appropriate criticisms to level against him are philosophical ones. Such criticisms do not prove that Marx's substantive theses are false, but they do establish that such theses are no better than empirical hypotheses and have no further extra-empirical grounding. This is not an irrelevant point to establish, as our concluding chapter spells out the limitations of Marx's purely empirical hypotheses. So, contrary to popular beliefs about Marx's system, 'It was not...' as Robert C. Tucker remarks, 'primarily through the study of economics that Marx was led to his economic interpretation of history; he came to it by the philosophical path'. And that philosophical path originally followed in the footsteps of Hegel. Hence, if one is to understand Marx, it is necessary to understand his relation to Hegel. This is also the case if one is to understand his mistakes.

Marx's thought shows the influence of Hegel's dialectical philosophy in many ways. He first became acquainted with it during his student days in Berlin, adopting in the first place a republican interpretation of Hegel's philosophy of history. Like Hegel, Marx interprets world history as a dialectical progression, but following Feuerbach's materialist reinterpretation of Hegel, Marx comprehends 'material labour as the essence, as the self-validating essence, of humanity'. Marx's critical reformulation of Hegel's philosophy of his for consists in the elimination of the fictitious subject of world history, the so called 'world spirit and in the prolongation of the dialectical process of historical development into the future That realm of freedom which Hegel asserted be fully realized here and now, lies for Marx in the future as a real possibility of the present. The dialectic of productive forces and productive relations which effects historical progress offers in contrast to Hegel's dialectic of world spirit no guarantee that the realm of freedom will be realized; it presents only the objective possibility of such a development.

In place of the constitutional bourgeois state, which for Hegel constituted the end point of historical development, Marx puts forward the concept of the free association of producers'. This is a social order, which dispenses with any. In Marx's work on the 'critique of political economy', a second influence of Hegel makes itself felt. The comprehension of this influence is particularly essential for an adequate under standing of Marx's main work, *Capital,* for it concerns the method which underlies his analysis of the capitalist mode of production. Here Marx makes use of Hegel's dialectical' method, which he claims to have put back on its feet, in order to present the internal dynamic and systematic structure of capitalist production. The capitalist system of production relations constitutes a totality, that is to say, an all inclusive unity which for this very reason must be examined and presented as an interconnected whole. However, empirical research and the processing of specific empirical data must precede the presentation of the totality. The dialectical self-movement of the at once subjective and objective categories, value, money and capital, must be a feature of the object under investigation, not the result of an externally imposed methodological scheme. Marx stresses the difference between his way of handling empirical relationships and facts and that of Hegel who, as Marx maintained develops a scheme of categories first in his *Logic*—and then presents social institutions such as the family, civil society, the state and their internal structures in abstract conformity with his scheme. According to Marx the only adequate dialectical exposition of an object of investigation is one which is sensitive to the dynamic and structural individuality of the object. The self-moving 'subject' of the capitalist refolded of production, that for the sake of which capitalist production takes place at all, is capital itself, which is, however, not something independently real, but rather something which arises out of the unconscious interaction and collaboration of individuals and classes, and which will therefore disappear once capitalist society has been transcended. It is not a real subject of production but a 'pseudo-subject. For this reason it is at best misleading to assert that Marx's category of 'capital' plays the same role in his thought, as does the category of 'spirit in Hegel's thought and system. Whereas the world spirit according to Hegel's idealist philosophy actually produces history, capital is only the seemingly real subject of the capitalist mode of production. The actual 'subject lessens' of this mode of production (Althusser) is by no means only a methodological achievement of Marx; the idea that capital on the one hand objectively appears as the independently real subject of production yet on the other is not 'really real', is not really an independent subject at all, contains an implicit criticism of the mode of production which constitutes it. The free association of producers, according to Marx, is destined to take the place of capitalism, a social order which ruthlessly and short-sighted exploits nature, in which individuals and classes are determined by the structural laws of the mode of production to serve the 'pseudo-subject', capital. The free association of producers, so Marx maintains, will regulate the metabolic interchange between society and nature rationally and, in contrast to capitalist society—where production is subservient and responsive only to the interests of capital—its production will be directed towards satisfying the producers' material requirements and their needs for (social) activity, social life and individual development. It will, as the real subject of production, take the place of the 'pseudo-subject', capital, the mere objectively existing appearance' of a subject of production. Only in this not yet realized subject will the Hegelian World Spirit find its empirical embodiment.

The relationship between Marx and Hegel is not, however, unproblematic Questions concerning this relationship have contributed to the formation of different philosophical trends within Marxism. For Hegelian Marxists, the early writings of Marx inform his whole system of thought. And those writings are permeated throughout by the unmistakably influence of Hegel. Indeed, Hegel is the subject of much of Marx's discussion during the period of his own theoretical development. But even here, Marx's attitude to Hegel is not one of mere uncritical acceptance. In fact, employing Feuerbach's method of transformational criticism in order to turn Hegel right-side up, Marx sought to criticize Hegel's idealist standpoint so as to uncover what he deemed to be of seminal importance when situated in a materialist setting. Instead of focusing on an idealist Spirit, as Hegel does, the early Marx focuses upon humanity and its productive capacities. In the words of Tucker, 'Marx's first system is a phenomenology of man constructed on the model of Hegel's phenomenology of spirit'.

The term dialectical materialism, frequently used to designate Marx's theory, was not used by Marx or Engels, but was introduced by a Russian Marxist,

Plekhanov (1857-1918). The term is, however, a useful one to remind us that Marx stands with Hegel, over and against eighteenth-century rationalists and nineteenth-century positivists, in his understanding of science and in his philosophy of history. Although Marx maintained that there are economic laws, he denied that economic laws are universal, as are the laws of physics and chemistry, maintaining that they are pertinent only to a particular epoch, and that, even within a given epoch, they may vary over a period of time. In the Afterward to the second edition of Capital, Marx explains the place of dialectic in his system. After mentioning his own youthful criticism of "the mystifying side of Hegelian dialectic", he insists, in opposition to classical economists and bourgeois scientists, that there is a "rational kernal within the mystical shell" which must be preserved.

In Hegel's system, Spirit alienates from itself an objective world of its own creation. Through the course of history, it is able to reappropriate that world and achieve knowledge. In Marx's early system, it is man who is alienated through creative activity—through his own form of production, through his own labour. The process of history concerns man's alienation and then ultimate recovery of his labour and, with this being his essential quality, his humanity. Only in communist society is this alienation overcome. History is man's slow progress towards wholeness, towards communism. However, it still remains to be seen how man will be able to transform alienated society into a communist one. But the Marxists of the French structuralist tradition, dismiss Marx's early period as a flirtation with Hegel. According to Louis Althusser, at this time Marx was only at a 'humanist' stage prior to an 'epistemological break' which would bring in the true Marxist phase. After the break, Marx is no longer a humanist and has rejected the Hegelian elements, save one or two subconscious survivals from the past which fit incongruously into the new system.

The controversial relation of Marx to Hegel needs to be erealively intspreted and periodically reassessed. This relation is often misunderstood for doctrinal reasons concerning the supposed difference in kind between Marx's position and preceding philosophy, and because those interested in Marx often have little interest in of Hegel. Engels's influence on marxism hinders a correct understanding of Marx's relation to Hegel. He consistently treats Hegel as if the letter's philosophy were pre-scientific nonsense. In his little book on Feuerbach, in a discussion of the transition from the Hegelian school to "the materialist standpoint," Engels remarks: "It was decided relentlessly to sacrifice every idealist fancy which could not be brought into harmony with the facts conceived in their own and not in a fantastic connection. And materialism means nothing more than this. If "materialism" means going beyond philosophical nonsense, then philosophy is nonsense. Elsewhere he suggests that Marx's contribution lay in extracting the true idea from its Hegelian formulation. "Marx was and is,' he wrote, the only one who could undertake the work of extracting from the Hegelian logic the kernel which comprised Hegel's real discoveries in this sphere in the simple shape in which it becomes the only true form of development of thought." The two views are incompatible. The first one suggests a distinction in kind, hence a "break." between Hegel and Marx; the second one suggests that Marx remains a Hegelian. The first view is expressed more frequently, more forcefully, and remains more influential. Yet if one holds, not that Hegel's ideas are false, but rather that they can be further developed, then the latter view is closer to an accurate description of how Marx relates to his predecessor.

The political figures who determined the course of marxism were not often interested in, or competent to judge such philosophical nuances. Lenin, who refers far more frequently to Engels than to Marx, was severely critical of Hegel in his early work on *Materialism and Empiriocriticism*. He later took a more nuanced position in his *Philosophical Notebooks* where he studied Hegel's *Science of Logic* in some detail, forming a more positive impression of Hegel, whom he came to regard as indispensable to understanding Marx.

Unlike Lenin's later, more clement view of Hegel, later marxists tend to follow Engels's more schematic, negative view of the great idealist philosopher as someone needing merely to be overcome. The Soviet primer on marxism claims to present the form of Marx's and Engels's views as updated by Lenin. In fact it relies on Lenin's earlier, more negative assessment of Hegel.

Marx is in part responsible for a persistent devaluation of the importance of his relation to Hegel. In a famous remark in the afterword to the second German edition of *Capital*, he obscurely suggests that his own position results from the inversion of Hegel's. Since Engels, generations of marxists have approached Marx's position as the inversion of Hegel's. Anglo-American analytical philosophy, which arose out of the revolt against British idealism, and has traditionally been skeptical about Hegel, usually approaches Marx without adequate consideration of Hegel. Even Lukacs, whose very nuanced treatment of Hegel is the main source of what is called Hegelian marxism, continues to insist on a difference in kind between marxism and Hegel.

A series of reasons suggest the importance of Marx's relation to Hegel for understanding his own theories. First great philosophers like Kant or Hegel alter the debate in durable ways. Hegel is unquestionably a great philosopher, clearly one of the small handful of the greatest of all philosophical minds. When Marx began to write, Hegel could not be overlooked. If he did not provide all the solutions, he at least offered much of the intellectual framework, much of the vocabulary, and useful hints to which Marx reacts in his effort to resolve the outstanding problems.

A second reason is Marx's close relation to the young Hegelians. Hegelianism did not die, although it was quickly transformed when Hegel died suddenly during a cholera epidemic in 1831. Shortly after his death, his school shattered into three main fragments: the center Hegelians, or so-called old Hegelians, and those of the Right and the Left, the so-called young Hegelians.

All the representatives of these diverse tendencies were attached to Hegel's theories. All were persuaded that in his system Hegel had brought philosophy to a high point and to an end. Heinrich Heine, the great German poet, a student of Hegel and a friend of Marx, spoke for all the Hegelians in claiming that our philosophical revolution is concluded; Hegel has closed the great circle. Yet as could be expected, the representatives of the different Hegelian tendencies drew widely differing conclusions from Hegel's system. The shattering of the Hegelian school was precipitated by a theological conflict. David F. Strauss, the author of an influential work, *The Life of Jesus Critically Examined,* inferred from his reading of Hegel that the incarnation did not take place in a single person but in the entire human race. In the controversy surrounding the appearance of his book, Strauss designated its participants as members of the center, right, and left wings of the Hegelian school.

The old Hegelians, who were philosophical centrists, attempted, not without difficulty, to defend the system as Hegel left it. Yet they were caught short by events which prevented them from realizing their intention, including the controversy loosed by Strauss, The right and the left Hegelians were separated by their relation to Hegel as well as by further academic, political, and religious factors. Then, as now religion was associated with political power and resistance to change. The right-wing Hegelians, who emphasized the religious element in Hegel's thought, all had positions in the university. With the exception of Eduard Gans, a professor of law, the left-wing Hegelians, who de-emphasized the religious element in Hegel's thought, were all located outside the university. The right-wing Hegelians tended to stress the religious element in Hegel's thought, which the left wing Hegelians tended to eliminate.

Religion and politics have long been related. Although the shattering of the Hegelian school occurred for theological reasons, the differences between the right and left Hegelians were often political. In simplifying, we can situate the rupture between these two tendencies in the interpretation of Hegel's brilliant aphorism, in the preface to the *Philosophy of Right:* "What is actual is rational, and what is rational is actual." Right-wing Hegelians even today often tend to accept the situation that obtains, which is regarded as rational, whereas left-wing Hegelians, such as Marx, underline in general the imperfections of the real world that is not quite rational enough and must be rendered still more rational. Those on the right content themselves with the real world as it is and frequently worship the past; those on the left refuse the world as it is in favor of a better, future world, denying the preeminence of the past. The former find the situation already reasonable, good even the best of all possible worlds; the latter, who regard the situation as unreasonable, desire to transform it.

The contribution of the left-wing Hegelians, often designated, in opposition to the right-wing Hegelians, as the young Hegelians, consisted in spreading democratic ideas and in awakening the intellectual consciousness of Germany. Prior to Marx, who was also a young Hegelian, they were, however, unsuccessful in transforming their philosophical ideas into a political movement. Among the young Hegelians, besides Strauss, the Bauer brothers Bruno and Edgar, Feuerbach, who strongly influenced Marx, Arnold Ruge, with whom he collaborated, Moses Hess, and Cieszkowski should be mentioned. Ruge helped to consolidate Hegelianism as a political movement. Cieszkowski, a Polish count, studied in Berlin with Michelet. He refused the standard interpretation of Hegel's idea that philosophy concerns only the past in favor of a view of philosophy turned resolutely toward the future. In stripping away the contemplative dimension of philosophy, he helped to transform into a form of action. This tendency was further reinforced by Hess who, following Hegel, foresaw a social revolution resulting from the growing contradiction between wealth and poverty.

A third reason is that although Marx was deeply immersed in Hegel's writings, this relation, which is at least mentioned by everyone who discusses Marx, is rarely studied in detail. Marx, who intended to address the relation, never did so. In a letter to Engels when he was at work on the project that culminated in *Capital*, he suggested he would eventually like to write a short book on what remained of Hegel's method; but the book was never written. Engels who did study Marx's relation to Hegel, did so badly. His short account of the relation of his and Marx's theories to Hegelianism in his study of Feuerbach is philosophically too weak to be more than an indication of what he thought the relation to be.

Finally, no one denies that Marx's thought shows the influence of Hegel's in many different ways and on many different levels, including explicit discussion of Hegel's writings, further development of such Hegelian themes as alienation and objectification, utilization of Hegelian categories like the distinction between appearance and reality or essence, the adaptation of the ideas of negation and contradiction to history, and so on. From beginning to end, his writings reflect an interest in Hegel as well as Hegel's influence on his own thought,

Marx's interest in Hegel began very early, before he began to write, and remained a constant throughout his writings. It is a main theme in the famous letter to his father, written in 1837, after two years of study at the university. Here Marx, still a teenager insists on the unavoidable importance of philosophy, reports that he has already read Hegel from end to end, mentions the need to escape from the conceptual folds of Hegel's theory, a task which would occupy him over the remainder of his life, and reports that he has already tried to work out a philosophy of right, or law the very topic of Hegel's *Philosophy of Right*.

Marx began to write for publication in the early 1840s. His initial writings include two texts directly devoted to criticizing Hegel's *Philosophy of Right*. He continued to address aspects of Hegel's philosophy both directly and indirectly in later writings all the way through *Capital*. The *Paris Manuscripts* contain extensive commentary on Hegel's *Phenomenology*. *The Grundrisse* provides important remarks on method, where Marx adopts a modified Hegelian approach. It is well known that *Capital* reflects the influence of the categorical framework developed in Hegel's *Logic*.

Nevertheless, even this interpretation of Marx cannot, in all honesty, fail to notice the many features of his mature system, which derive from Hegel, particularly The Philosophy of History. In these lectures delivered at Berlin, Hegel produces a 'Philosophical History' of the World. Such a history is not presupposition less: it assumes that reason is at work in the world 'The history of the world presents us with a rational process'. Marx also seems to have regarded history as a rational process driven by an underlying mechanism—the 'dialectic of negativity'. Moreover, for Hegel, 'in the history of the world, the individuals we have to do with are Peoples; Totalities that are States'. Similarly, for Marx, the objects of historical analysis are 'totalities': classes, economic structures and social formations.

Hegel considers the history of the world to embody the development of Spirit. But he makes the further claim that the development of Spirit is accompanied by the growth of freedom. Spirit involves the development of freedom through time:

The Orientals have not attained the knowledge that Spirit—Man as such—is free; and because they do not know this, they are not free. They only know that one is free. The consciousness of freedom first arose among the Greeks, and therefore they were free. But they, and the Romans likewise, know only that some are free not man as such. The German nations, under the influence of Christianity, were the first to attain the consciousness, that man, as man, is free: that it is the freedom of Spirit, which constitutes its essence.

Marx, too, adopts an epochal periodization of history but, as a materialist, he bases each historical division on material factors. Whereas Hegel concentrates on the cultural and the political, Marx takes as his central concern the material production from which human beings create their world. Marx considers the history of the world to embody the development of the forces of production in short, technological development. Stressing the relations of production, which have divided humanity, Marx sees different methods of production as lying at the heart of each historical epoch. For Marx, the type of society studied in any historical period is defined in terms of the mode of production. But the historically developing modes of production have involved an increasing productive capability. As Marx sees the satisfaction of need to be a central feature of freedom the development of productivity provides the foundation for the growth of freedom through history. Hence, Marx can be seen to follow Hegel closely, except that freedom can now be understood in material terms, and only a revolution in the relations of production can turn bourgeois formal freedom based on rights into the genuinely productive freedom of communism, where humanity as a whole has control over nature.

Feuerbach and Marx

Ludwig Feuerbach (1804-72) was already a well-known writer in 1841. He had studied at Berlin under Hegel and Schleiermacher, but abandoned Hegelian idealism and Christianity at an early stage. In *Thoughts on Death and Immortality* (1830) he criticized theories of eternal life, and in a *History of Modern Philosophy from Bacon to Spinoza* (1833) and studies of Bayle and Leibniz he manifested his sympathy with the free thinking tradition. He opposed independent reason to all forms of dogmatism, called for the philosophical rehabilitation of nature, and criticized Hegelianism on the ground that, as it began with the spirit, it was bound to confine itself to the spirit and to define nature as a secondary manifestation of the latter. But he first became celebrated with *The Essence of Christianity* (1841), a naturalistic critique of religion expressed in Hegelian language. Feuerbach did not care for the term 'materialism' because of its unfavourable moral associations, but on the basic issue he adopted a materialistic standpoint. He argued that 'the secret of theology is anthropology', i.e., that everything men have said about God is an expression in 'mystified' terms of their knowledge about themselves. The real truth of religion is atheism, or simply the positive affirmation of humanity. In general, everything that man can apprehend in thought is the object of his own essence. 'Man becomes self-conscious in the object: consciousness of the object is man's self-knowledge.... the object is the manifest essences of man, his true, objective self. And this applies not only to spiritual objects but also to those of sense. even the objects that are furthest from man, in so far as they are objects to him, are a manifestation of his essence'. This of course does not mean that things owe their being to human consciousness, but only that the definitions whereby we apprehend them are definitions of ourselves projected on to the object, so that things are always perceived in human terms and are a projection and image of our self-consciousness. On the other hand, 'man is nothing without an object': it is only in objectivity that he recognizes himself. This idea of the mutual dependence of subject and object (the subject constituting itself in self-knowledge through the object, the object constituting itself in the projection of self-knowledge) is not further analyzed by Feurerbach; in general, he expresses it in the formula that man belongs to the essence of nature and nature to the essence of man.

But Feuerbach was interested above all in the particular kind of objectification that occurs in religious alienation. When men relate to the object in an essential and necessary manner, when they affirm in it the fullness and perfection of their species-essence, that object is God. God is thus the imaginative projection of man's species-essence, the totality of his powers and attributes raised to the level of infinity. Every species-essence is 'infinite', i.e., as an essence; it is full of perfection and is a model or standard for individual beings. Man's knowledge of God is an attempt to perceive himself in the mirror of exteriority; man exteriorize his own essence before he recognizes it in himself, and the opposition between God and man is a 'mystified' version of the opposition between the species and the individual. God cannot in principle have any other predicates than those, which men have abstracted from themselves; he is real in so far as these predicates are real. Religion, however, inverts the relationship between subject and predicates, giving human predicates—in the shape of Deity—the primacy over what is real, human, and concrete. Religion is a self-dichotomy of man, his reason, and feelings, the transference of his intellectual and affective qualities on to an imaginary divine being which asserts its own independence and begins to tyrannize over its creator.

Religious alienation, the 'dream of the spirit', is not only an error but an impoverishment of man, since it takes away all his best qualities and faculties and bestows them on the Deity. The more religion enriches the essence of God, the more it devitalizes man; the nature of religion is most clearly symbolized in the ritual of blood-sacrifice. Humanity must be humiliated, degraded and stripped of its dignity in order that the Deity may be revealed in majesty. 'Man asserts in God what he denies in himself.' Moreover, religion paralyses men's ability to live together in concord, for it diverts the energy of love on to the divinity and rejects the real fellowship of man into an imaginary heaven. It destroys the feeling of solidarity and mutual love, encourages egoism, depreciates all the values of earthly life, and makes social equality and harmony impossible. To overthrow religion is to realize the true values of religion, which are those of humanity. When people come to themselves, and realize that the personifications of religion are the fruit of their own childish imagination, they will be able to form genuinely humanistic societies. The cult of fictitious otherworldly beings will give place to the cult of life and love.

The Essence of Christianity was an attempt to apply the Hegelian category of alienation to the formulation of a purely naturalistic and anthropocentric viewpoint. Unlike Hegel, Feuerbach regarded alienation as an altogether negative phenomenon. In Hegel's view, Being realizes its essence by first excluding and then reabsorbing it in a process of self-enrichment; what it potentially contains must be made external before it can be actualized. The Absolute Idea attains to self-consciousness through its own alienated manifestations; it is not pure act, like the God of the Scholastics, but come to fulfillment only through history and the successive phases of alienation. Feuerbach, on the other hand, considers alienation as purely evil and erroneous and possesses no positive value. Religious mystification divides man from his species and opposes the individual to himself; it wastes human energy in the cult of unreal beings and distracts it from the one true value, that of man in and for himself.

Feuerbach's later writing display an ever-widening rift with Hegelianism and a more and more explicit materialism of the eighteenth-century kind. In the preface to the second edition of *The Essence of Christianity* (1843) he rejects the theory that subject and object condition each other, declaring that our apprehension of things is primarily sensual and passive, and only secondarily active and conceptual. In *Lecturers on the Essence of Religion* he repeats his view and also emphasizes that religious imaginations result from man's feeling of dependence on nature, whereas he had previously treated them as an objectification of the 'essence of humanity'. Originally he envisaged that the overthrow of religion would put an end to human egoism; now he asserted that egoism is a natural and inevitable human trait, present in even the most altruistic of actions, he reverted to the Enlightenment stereotype of 'natural egoism'. In his earlier work, he had described the process of God-creating projection but had not explained its causes. He now tried to fill the gap, but did not go further than stating that the source of religious imagination is generally ignorance and man's inability to interpret correctly his own situation in nature. Realizing his dependence on nature, which is eternal and inescapable, man fails to comprehend this dependence in rational categories; instead he devises anthropomorphic fancies to express his fear of Nature's incalculable caprices and the positive feelings of gratitude of hope that she arouses in him. Religion is an ersatz satisfaction of human need that cannot be met in any other way: man seeks to compel nature to obey them by using magic or appealing to divine goodness i.e. they try to achieve by imagination what they cannot have in reality. As knowledge increases, religion, which is an infantile state of mind, gradually yields to a rational world-view, and men are able, by the arts of civilization and technology, to control forces that were previously untameable. At the same time Feuerbach draws attention to the sources of religious imagination that lie in the very nature of the cognitive processes, especially that of abstraction. Since we can only think or express ourselves in terms of abstracts, we are apt to credit them with an independent existence vis-à-vis individual, which are in fact the only reality. In the same way, God and other religious figments, personifying human ideas, feelings, and abilities, are illegitimate autonomizations of the legitimate instruments of cognition. The idea or generic concept of God in the metaphysical sense is based on the same necessity and the same foundations, as is the concept of things or of fruit. The gods of polytheists are nothing but names and collective or generic concepts imagined as actual beings'; but 'in order to understand the meaning of general concepts it is not necessary to deify them and turn them into independent beings that differ from individual essences.

In *Lectures on the Essence of Religion* there is no longer any trace of Feuerbach's Hegelian upbringing. Religion is explained in simple Enlightenment terms as the result of fear and ignorance, and Feuerbach also takes over the Enlightenment theory of perception as merely sensual and empirical. *The Lectures* were a novelty in German philosophy, dominated as it was by the categories of Kant and Hegel, but to the rest of Europe they were merely a repetition of well-known theories. The essential feature was that Feuerbach consistently saw religion as the root of all social evil. He believed that when religious mystification was done away with there would be an end of the sources of social inequality, exploitation, egoism, and slavery. Religion was the source and epitome of all the evil in history; and he expected that public enlightenment, sweeping away religious prejudice, would at the same time eradicate social servitude. This was one of the main points, though not the only one, on which Marx soon took up a sharply critical attitude towards Feuerbach's philosophy.

By the end of the 1840s, Feuerbach had completely rejected Hegelianism, regarding it, like all other forms of idealism, as nothing but a continuation of religious fiction. All the creations of classic German philosophy, such as Hegel's Idea, Fichte's Ego, or Schilling's Absolute, appeared to him to imply as substitutes for the Deity, reduced to a more abstract form by philosophical imagination. Interpreting humanity in purely zoological categories, he saw the social community as a form of natural co-operation within the species, distorted or depraved by religious prejudice, while in moral speculation he did not advance beyond the eudemonistic schema of the Enlightenment. The sweep of his rhetoric, with its humanistic and free thinking ideas, won him many adherents. *The Essence of Christianity* had immense influence in Germany and played a large part in transforming the Young Hegelian camp by radicalizing its anti-religious orientation. To Marx in particular, Feuerbach's philosophy was not only a point of repulsion but also one of the main stimuli that enabled him to reject Hegelian categories in his own thinking. He also owed much to Feuerbach as regards knowledge of the history of philosophy, especially in the sixteenth and seventeenth centuries. He adopted the critique of Hegelianism as a philosophy that 'put the predicate where the subject should be' and gave human creations priority over man himself, and made use of it in his analysis of Hegel's philosophy of law.

It might be thought that after Marx's criticisms the philosophy of Feuerbach was completely outdated, especially in view of his rather dull and repetitive style. Yet it continues to excite interest among seekers after a universal humanistic formula, and even among theologians. The radical anthropocentrism which is its chief feature may be summed up as follows. Firstly, man is the only value; all others are instrumental and subordinate. Secondly, man is always a live, finite, concrete entity. Thirdly, there are permanent features of human nature, which make it possible for men to live in a harmonious community based on mutual love and respect for life.

Fourthly, the abolition of religion in the dogmatic and mystical forms in which it has hitherto been known will open the way to a new, authentic religion of humanity, enabling men to attain what has been their true object in all religious, namely the satisfaction of their need of happiness, solidarity, equality and freedom.

The philosophy of the *Manuscripts* is confirmed and completed by Marx's *Theses on Feuerbach,* written in the spring of 1845. Published by Engels in 1888, after Marx's death, they were regarded as an epitome of the new world-view and are among the most frequently quoted of the author's works. They contain the most trenchant formulation of Marx's objections to Feuerbachian materialism, especially his opposition of a purely contemplative theory of knowledge to a practical one and the different meaning he ascribed to religious alienation. The reproach that Marx leveled against Feuerbach and all previous materialism was that they envisaged objects merely in a contemplative way and not as 'sensuous, practical, human activity, not subjectively', with the result that it was left to idealism to develop the active side—'but only abstractly, since of course idealism does not know real, actual, sensuous activity as such'. This objection repeats the thought expounded in more detail in the *Manuscripts*: perception is itself a component of man's practical relationship to the world, so that its object is not simply 'given' by indifferent nature but is a humanized object, conditioned by human needs and efforts. The same practical standpoint appears in Marx's refusal to enter into a speculative dispute on the conformity of thought with its object. 'In practice man must prove the truth, that is, the reality and power, the thissidedness of his thinking. The dispute over the reality or non-reality of thinking which is isolated from practice is a purely scholastic question.' As might be expected, and *The German Ideology* later confirms, the cognitive function of practice does not merely signify that the success of an activity confirms the accuracy of our knowledge, nor that practical life expresses the range and purpose of human interests; it means also that veracity is itself the 'reality and power' of thought i.e. that those ideas are true in which man confirms himself as a 'species-being'. On this ground Marx dismisses as 'scholastic' the Cartesian question as to the conformity between a pure act of thought and reality. The epistemology question is not a real question, because the pure act of perception or thought which it premises is a mere speculative fiction. Since the mind, having achieved self-understanding, apprehends itself as a coefficient of practical behavior, it follows that the questions that may legitimately be put to it as to the meaning of its acts are also questions as to its effectiveness from the point of view of human society.

Marx also repeats in *the Theses* his criticism of Feuerbach's theory of religion, viz. that it reduces the world of religion to its secular basis but does n to explain the duality in terms of the internal disharmony of man's situation in the world, and is therefore unable to offer an effective cure; the mind can only be freed from mystification if the negativities of social life from which it arises are removed by practical action.

Further, Marx criticizes Feuerbach's conception of the essence of man as 'an abstraction inherent in a particular individual', whereas it is in fact 'the totality of social relationships'. The effect of Feuerbach's conception is that he takes as his point of departure the individual in his species-characteristics, and reduces the tie between human beings to a natural tie. The same thought appears in the *Tenth Thesis,* having previously been expressed in Marx's essay *On The Jewish Question:* 'The standpoint of the old materialism is civil society; the standpoint of the new is human society, or socialized humanity.' This correspondences to Marx's previous contention that civil society must coincide with political society, so that both of them cease to exist in the old form: no longer will the first be a mass of conflicting egoisms, the second an abstract, unreal community; man, himself a true community, will absorb his own species-nature and realize his personality as a social one.

In the important *Third Thesis* Marx expounds his opposition to the doctrines of utopian socialism based on eighteenth century materialism. It is not sufficient to say that human begins are the product of conditions and upbringing, since conditions and upbringing are also the work of human beings. To assret only the former proposition amounts to 'dividing society' into two parts, of which one is superior to society. The coincidence of the changing circumstances and of human activity can be conceived and rationally understood only as revolutionary praxis.' This statement means that society cannot be changed by reformers who understand its needs, but only by the basic mass whose particular interest is identical with that of society as a whole. In the revolutionary praxis of the proletariat the 'educator' and 'educated' are the same: the development of mind is at the same time the historical process by which the world is transformed, and there is no longer any question of priority between the mind and external conditions or vice versa. In this situation of revolutionary praxis the working class is the agent of a historical initiative and is not merely resisting or reacting to the pressure of the possessing classes.

The same 'practical' viewpoint is dominant in Marx's conception of the cognitive functions of the mind and its role in the historical process; 'practical' is always regarded as implying 'social'', and 'social life is practical by its very essence'. So is the task of philosophy as defined in the *Eleventh Thesis,* in what are perhaps Marx's most-quoted words: 'The philosophers have only interpreted the world in various ways; the point, however, is to change it'. It would be a caricature of Marx's thought to read this as meaning that it was not important to observe or analyse society and that only direct revolutionary action mattered. The whole context shows that it is a formula expressing in a nutshell the viewpoint of 'practical philosophy' as opposed to the 'contemplative attitude of Hegel or Feuerbach—the viewpoint which Hess, and through him Ciezskowski, suggested to Marx and which became the philosophical nucleus of Marxism. To understand the world does not mean considering it from outside, judging it morally or explaining it scientifically; it means society understanding itself, an act in which the subject changes the object by the very fact of understanding it. This can only came about when the subject and object coincide, when the difference between educator and educated disappears, and when thought itself becomes a revolutionary act, the self-recognition of human existence.

Feuerbach provided a new philosophy particularly for the young radical intellectuals of the 1840s, arguing one another through the contradictions of the 'German misery' and neo-Hegelian philosophy. Why the 1840s? Because they were the testing years of this philosophy. In 1840, the Young Hegelians, who believed there was a goal to history – the realm of reason and liberty – looked to the heir to the throne for the realization of their hopes – the end of the autocratic and feudal Prussian order, the abolition of censorship, in short, the installation of a regime of political, intellectual and religious liberty. But hardly had he reached the throne than this so-called 'liberal' heir, now Frederick William IV, returned to despotism. This confirmation and reaffirmation of tyranny was a terrible blow to the theory, which was the basis and sum of all their hopes. In principle, history should be reason and liberty; in fact, it was merely unreason and slavery. The facts had provided a lesson to be learnt: this very contradiction. But how could it be grasped? At this point *The Essence of Philosophy*. The texts may not have liberated humanity, but they did release the Young Hegelians from their theoretical impasse. Precisely at the moment of their greatest disarray, Feuerbach gave them an exact answer to the dramatic question they were asking each other about man and history the echo of this relief and enthusiasm can be seen forty years later in Engels. Feuerbach was precisely the 'New Philosophy' that made all speculative philosophy, that put the world which philosophy had made to walk on its head back on to its feet again, that denounced every alienation and every illusion but also gave reasons for them, and made the unreason of history thinkable and criticizable in the name of reason itself that at least reconciled idea and fact, and made the necessity of a world's contradiction and the necessity of its liberation comprehensible. This is why the neo-Hegelians, as the old Engels had to admit, 'all become at once Feuerbachians'. This is why they received his books as manifestoes announcing the paths of the future.

Feuerbach's writings were particularly interesting. First of all, they are of historical interstate. Simply because they were the most famous and the most lasting but also and primarily because they belong to a historical moment and had a historical role. Feuerbach was both witness to and actor in the crisis in the theoretical development of the Young Hegelian movement. It is essential to read Feuerbach to understand the writings of the Young Hegelians between 1840 and 1845. In particular, this reveals the extent to which Marx's early works are impregnated with Feuerbach's thought. Not only is Marx's terminology from 1842 and 1845 Feuerbachian (alienation, species being, total being, 'inversion' of subject and predicate, etc.) but, what is probably more important, so is the basic philosophical problematic. Articles like *On the Jewish Question or the Critique of Hegel's Philosophy of the State* cannot be understood outside the context of the Feuerbachian problematic. Naturally, Marx's themes go beyond Feuerbach's immediate preoccupations, but the theoretical schemata and problematic are the same. To use his expression, Marx did not really 'settle accounts' with this problematic until 1845. *The German Ideology* is the first work indicating a conscious and definitive rupture with Feuerbach's philosophy and his influence.

A comparative study of Feuerbach's writings and Marx's early works makes possible a historical reading of Marx's writings, and a better understanding of his development. Once Feuerbach's writings in the years from 1830 to 1845 have been read it is impossible to make any mistakes as to the derivation of the majority of the concepts traditionally used to justify 'ethical interpretations of Marx. Such famous expressions as 'philosophy's world-to-be', 'the inversion of subject and predicate', 'for man the root is man himself', 'the political State is the species-life of man', the 'suppression and realization of philosophy', 'philosophy is the head of human emancipation and the proletariat is its heart', etc., etc., are expressions directly borrowed from Feuerbach, or directly inspired by him. All the expressions of Marx's idealist 'humanism' are Feuerbachian. Admittedly, Marx did not merely quote or repeat Feuerbach, who was always thinking about politics, but hardly ever talked about it. His whole concern was with the criticism of religion, of theology, and with that secular disguise for theology known as speculative philosophy. The young Marx, on the contrary, was haunted first by politics and then by that for which politics is merely the 'heaven': the concrete life of alienated men. But in *On the Jewish Question, Hegel's Philosophy of the State,* etc., and even usually in *The Holy Family,* he is no more than an avant-grade Feuerbachian applying an ethical problematic to the understanding of human history. In other words, we can say that at this time Marx was merely applying the theory of alienation, that is, Feuerbach's theory of 'human nature', to politics and the concrete activity of man, before extending it to political economy in the *Manuscripts.* It is important that the real origin of these Feuerbachian concepts should be recognized, not so as to assess everything according to a standard of attribution but so as to avoid attributing to Marx the invention of concepts and a problematic he had only borrowed. It is even more important that it be recognized that these borrowed concepts were not borrowed one by one, in isolation, but en bloc, as a set: this set being precisely Feuerbach's problematic. This is the essential point. For borrowing a concept in isolation may only be of accidental and secondary significance. Borrowing a concept in isolation does not bind the borrower vis-à-vis the context from which he extracted it (for example, the borrowings from Smith, Ricardo and Hegel in *Capital*). But borrowing a systematically interrelated set of concepts, borrowing a real problematic, cannot be accidental, it binds the borrower. Marx literally espoused Feuerbach's problematic, that he profoundly identified himself with it, and that to understand the meaning of most of his statements during this period, even where these bear on the material of later studies (for example, politics, social life, the proletariat, revolution etc.) and might therefore seem fully Marxist, it is essential to situate oneself at the very heart of this identification, and to explore all its theoretical consequences and inferences.

It is true that Marx espoused a whole problematic, his rupture with Feuerbach, his famous 'settling of accounts with our erstwhile philosophical conscience', implied the adoption of a new problematic even if it did integrate a certain number of the old concepts, did so into a whole which confers on them a radically new significance.

At this point, knowledge of Feuerbach's problematic and of why Marx broke with Feuerbach can come to our aid. For through Feuerbach we have an indirect access to Marx's new problematic. We can find out what was the problematic that Marx broke with, and we can discover the theoretical horizon 'opened up' by this rupture. If it is true that we can learn as much about a man by what he rejects as by what he adheres to, then a thinker as exacting as Marx should be illuminated by his break with Feuerbach occurred at the decisive point in the constitution of Marx's definitive theoretical position, a knowledge of Feuerbach thereby becomes an irreplaceable means of access to Marx's philosophical position, rich in theoretical implications.

In the same way, it makes possible a better understanding of the relation between Marx and Hegel. If there was this rupture between Marx and Feuerbach, the critique of Hegel to be found in most of the former's early works must, at least as far as is ultimate philosophical presuppositions are concerned, be regarded as inadequate, or even incorrect, to the extent that it was a critique from a Feuerbachian viewpoint, that is, a viewpoint that Marx later rejected. Now, usually for reasons of convenience, there is a constant and innocent tendency to believe that, even though Marx later modified his viewpoint, the critique of Hegel to be found in the early works is none the less justifiable and can therefore be 'retained'. But to do so is to neglect the basic fact that Marx set himself apart from Feuerbach when he realized that the Feuerbachian critique of Hegel was a critique 'from within Hegelian philosophy itself', that Feuerbach was still a 'philosopher', who had, indeed, 'inverted' the body of the Hegelian edifice, but had retained its ultimate structure and bases, that is, its theoretical presuppositions. In Marx's eyes, Feuerbach had stopped within Hegelian territory, he was as much a prisoner of it as its critic since he had merely turned Hegel's own principles against Hegel himself. He had not changed 'elements'. The truly Marxist critique of Hegel depends precisely on this change of elements, that is, on the abandonment of the philosophical problematic whose recalcitrant prisoner Feurerbach remained. Marx's theoretical position has broken with the traditional philosophical problematic whose last theoretician was Hegel and from which Feuerbach tried desperately but in vain to free himself.

The Theory of Capitalism

Marx concisely lays out many of these themes in the famous work. *The Communist Manifesto*, co-authored with Engle's in 1847. This pamphlet was written when movements for democracy were challenging the rule of monarchs. From Chartist demands for universal manhood suffrage in Britain to demands for Polish national independence, the European continent was in turmoil. Marx and Engels wrote for a small, obscure group known as the Communist League.

Marx and Engles explain the logic whereby capitalism arises and will destroy itself. The key to this process lies in class struggles between the proletariat and the bourgeoisie, whose conflicts can only be resolved with the victory of the working class and the establishment of socialism. They begin the essay by stating that all history is the history of class struggle. From the earliest form of civilization, a ruling class has controlled production and politics, ensuring that it maintains economic control over an oppressed stratum. As social conditions change, new classes come into prominence. Marx and Engels briefly trace the history of capitalism, trying it to the destruction of feudalism and the rise of the bourgeoisie, who incessantly search for markets. In their words, "The East-Indian and Chinese markets, the colonization of America, trade with the colonies, the increase in the means of exchange and in commodities generally, gave to commerce, to navigation, to industry, an impulse never before known."

Marx and Engels appear to praise the bourgeoisie. They write that "the bourgeoisie, historically, has played a most revolutionary role." The rise of the bourgeoisie establishes a worldwide market system, encouraging the development of industry, commerce, and communications. It creates massive industries and unprecedented wealth, subjecting nature to machinery and technology. The bourgeoisie demolishes the superstitions of feudalism, putting "an end to all feudal, patriarchal, idyllic relations. It produces a more cosmopolitan and urban world, destroying, in one of Marx and Engels most unforgettable phrases, "the idiocy of rural life." With the rise of the bourgeoisie, "natural one-sidedness and narrow-mindedness become more and more impossible."

But this progress comes at quite a cost. Bourgeois rule "has left remaining no other nexus between man and man than naked self-interest, than callous 'cash payment." All seemingly natural relations between ruler and ruled, all mutual rights and obligations, are severed by capitalism. The bourgeoisie upsets all social relations, throwing them into anarchy, as it scours the world for new markets, uproots communities by moving production to new, cheaper locations, and revolutionizing the workplace by introducing new technologies and laying off workers. Moreover, the rule of the bourgeoisie translates into the dominion of money over all society. As Marx and Engels write, capitalism promotes the dizzying pace of modern life, and "all that is solid melts into air, all that is holy is profaned." Not only do social conditions continually change, but everything has a price under capitalism. Every thing has become a commodity. There is nothing outside of the market, nothing sacred or holy that cannot be bought or sold.

Most property becomes private property under capitalism, owned by private individuals rather than by the state or the community. Ownership of industry replaces ownership of land as the major source of wealth. Capitalism is an internally contradictory economic system and production and consumption are often not in equilibrium. This results in crises of production, when too many commodities are produced and cannot be consumed. The bourgeoisie either lays off workers when crises occur looks for new markets to conquer, or tries to exploit existing markets more efficiently. Because capitalism is a worldwide system, crises quickly become international. All nations are drawn into the capitalist system and share in its problems.

The conflict between the bourgeoisie and the proletariat is the major contradiction of capitalism. Workers are brought together in factories and workshop to produce goods, yet the commodities they produce belong to the capitalist, a private individual. In their search for profits capitalists closely monitor and discipline workers. Marx and Engels use military metaphors such as describing workers as an "industrial army" to capture the experience of the workplace. Labor lose all joy, mass production reigns, and the worker "becomes an appendage of the machine, and it is only the most simple, most monotonous, and most easily acquired knack that required of him." There is constant pressure on wages to decline, as the capitalist attempts to cut wages in order to increase profits.

Yet, the proletariat is growing ever larger as capitalism develops. Workers under capitalism can more easily recognize their oppression, for they have few ties, outside of economic ones, to the ruling class. More and more people are forced to leave farms and enter wage labor, and mass production makes conditions of work increasingly similar. As the bourgeoisie extends throughout the world it creates its own gravediggers in the proletariat, for it needs new workers to exploit. The proletariat will become conscious of its differences from the bourgeoisie, as workers are forced into unions to represent and defend their interests. Workers will demand that the state regulate the labor process, and class struggles will become politicized. The victory of the proletariat will be unique in history, for the proletariat represents the great masses of people. Marx and Engels write: "All previous historical movements were movements of minorities, or in the interests of minorities. The proletarian movement is the self-conscious, independent movement of the immense majority, in the interests of the immense majority."

Such a struggle for power on the part of the proletariat will not be easy, however. This is in part because, in another famous phrase, "the ruling ideas of any age have ever been the ideas of its ruling class." Marx designates such ruling ideas as ideologies, which are distorted, fragmentary representations of reality that justify the hegemony of the ruling class. Ideologies idealize existing conditions theorizing the existing society as the best of all possible worlds. Any ruling class, which comes to power, tries to parade its interests as the interests of all classes in society. Rulers appeal to universal ideas, whether they be religious, nationalistic, or political. The bourgeoisie inaugurates the ideal of the universal rights of man, such as freedom of speech, freedom of assembly, freedom of religion, etc. these are ideologies because they supposedly allow everyone equal freedom, when in reality freedom is dictated by economic power. It is empty and meaningless in substance. Those who control the material means of production control intellectual production. The owner of a large newspaper has much more of an ability to practice freedom of speech, and gets his ideas heard by millions than the average worker. Those with wealth control schools, the media, and other sources of information. The economically powerless have difficulty publicizing their views. Thus, the dominant ideas of the age are the ideas of the ruling class.

Under capitalism the rule of the bourgeoisie is reinforced by the power of the state, which is "the executive committee of the bourgeoisie," in Marx's terms. The state, through police and the military, enforces existing property relations, and laws are set up to protect the wealthy. From Marx's perspective it would not be surprising that 95 percent of the people in US prisons are from poverty back grounds. They have little access to political and legal power, and crimes against property are punished harshly. Marx and Engels discuss how communism will change this situation. Communism will abolish the rule of private wealth over workers, so that workers do not produce more capital for capitalists but can enjoy the fruits of their labors. They argue that ridding society of capitalism and instituting socialism will change all social relations, such as gender relations, in a more egalitarian direction.

Marx contends that capitalism is an essentially exploitative system, which he explains in his labor theory of value. He states that a commodity's exchange value, or price, is directly measured by the amount of labor embodied in it. As it takes a greater amount of work and more sophisticated labor to make cars rather than pins, cars cost more than pins. Yet, making pins and making cars involve very different types of labor. To compare them, the concrete differences between types of work must be erased and defined in regard to abstract labor, whose value can then be calculated in terms of wages. Abstract labor allows the computation of socially necessary labor time, i.e., the average amount of time required to produce a commodity in a given industry. Commodities exchange at their values, or the amount of socially necessary labor time that it takes to make them.

The exploitation of labor can be understood through the concept of socially necessary labor time. The worker is paid his full value as a commodity, for he receives a sufficient wage to reproduce himself as a laborer. Yet the laborer produces more wealth than is necessary for the cost of subsistence, for only a proportion of the working day is necessary to reproduce the worker's life. The rest of the working day the proletariat produces profits for the capitalist. Exploitation occurs entirely within the sphere of production, as the worker creates revenue for the capitalist and does not receive his just share of resources.

Marx traces the rise of capitalism through several stages. In medieval times, guild production predominated, when each worker produced independently for trade in the home. Marx argues that simple cooperation arises with the beginnings of capitalism. Workers come together in a single workplace and rising capitalists supply the capital equipment and raw material for production. Workers increase their productivity in this setting, for they can produce items more quickly than when working completely independently of one another. At this stage, workers still perform their work at their own pace. The capitalist pays these artisans a wage and markets their products for a profit.

The capitalist soon realizes that he can increase profits and efficiency by extending the division of labor in the workplace. Marx names this phase of capitalism manufacture. Workers lose control over production, as each laborer specializes in a single, simple operation. The striving for capitalist profits dominates the organization of the workplace. Under manufacture, the capitalist becomes an essential part of the production process, for he supplies the capital necessary for production, while workers supply the labor.

This is not in any sense a "natural" process. In *Capital Marx* demonstrates that in early nineteenth-century Britain farmers were forced off the land through various enclosure laws and poor people were compelled to work or face jail time through the poor laws. The state, through its coercive and oppressive powers and legal and police forces, supported the rise of capitalism, not only in Britain but throughout the world. We can see the same sorts of things happening now, as many governments in the Third World aid corporate production efforts in their countries. The market disrupts existing ways of life and forces production for the market upon the people.

The final stage of capitalism that Marx documents is modern industry. Capitalists utilize machinery to increase profits through lowering costs, increase the specialized division of labor in large factories, and deprive workers of any control over the production process. Modern industry displays a major contradiction of capitalism, for production is planned and socialized within the workplace, which is highly rationalized. Exchange, the consumption of products, is not planned, but dependent on market forces. Thus, many firms fail when they cannot sell their products, and recessions and sometimes depressions occur. Firms attempt to overcome these problems by becoming larger so they can control more of the market and centralize production. But monopolies cannot stop the crises of capitalism.

The accumulation of capital, the constant increase of capital, is a major dynamic within capitalism. Capitalism is dependent on sustained economic growth, requiring continual reinvestment and the search for new markets. Capitalists wish to increase profits, which means cutting costs, especially labor. The wages of labor are kept low because of what Marx characterizes "the reserve army of workers," the unemployed, who compete for jobs. Capitalists also reduce costs by replacing workers with new technology, or attempting to increase the productivity of workers. This process is at the heart of the crisis-ridden nature of capitalism. As capitalists accumulate they require more labor, wages rise as unemployment drops, rising wages eat into profits, capitalists curtail investment as their profits decline, workers are laid off, wages decline, the reserve army rises, and the whole process keeps repeating itself, in cycles of recession, growth, recession, etc. replacing workers with machines or increasing the productivity of labor temporarily mitigate this process, but they cannot halt the fundamental dynamic of capitalism.

These cycles were particularly prominent in nineteenth-century capitalism, though the Great Depression of the 1930s was the most dramatic demonstration of the crisis-ridden nature of capitalism. Today the West still experiences economic crises, but not the massive depressions that shook capitalism in the 1930s. In the wake of the Great Depression, the welfare state arose, creating social programs such as unemployment insurance and social security, which gave workers some degree of security. The welfare state was based on industrial trade unions fighting for higher wages and state action favoring labor. Yet, since the 1970s, the welfare state has been in the crisis and capitalists have searched for new ways to make profits. From a Marxist perspective the current fascination with globalization is based on a search for new sources of profit. Corporations decrease their cost of production through employing inexpensive labor in Third World countries and importing cheap foreign goods, while states cut social programs such as welfare to make available more cheap labor for the workforce.

Marx argues that the nature of capitalism follows contradictory laws, which promote constant crises. He also demonstrates that the nature of capitalism is determined by particular historical contexts, and its specific shape depends on the strength of the state, the power of the working class, and other social factors. Markets require a host of social and legal institutions in order to develop: they are in no sense outgrowths of "natural" human desires. Particularly, markets require coercive social mechanisms to maintain the power of capitalists. Government and social policies, in the absence of a strong labor movement, will be favorable to corporations.

Marx shows that the rise of capitalism was not a peaceful process, but involves new sources of power and exploitation compared to previous epochs in history.

The distinctiveness of capitalism lies in its worldwide search for markets, new types of class struggle, and the pervasiveness of commodity production in all forms of social life.

Asiatic Mode of Production

In Marx's discussion of colonialism, his Eurocentric views are most pronounced. They are inseparable from his theory of capitalism. Marx believes that capitalism is the first mode of production, which expends throughout the world because of its own internal dynamics based on the pursuit of profit, rather than through military plunder so that leaders can expand their riches. Accordingly, Marx develops a theory of imperialism, the expansion of Western capitalist countries into the non-Western world. But Marx has deficient theory of imperialism and colonialism. He simimplistically transfers his sophisticated analysis of Europe to non-European societies. Marx terms this non-Western social formation the "Asiatic mode of production" and he sees it as an unchanging, static, non-dialectical area of the globe. According to Marx, non-Western peoples lack a history. In his words, "Indian society has no history at all, at least no known history. What we call its history, is but the history of the successive intruders who founded their empires on the passive basis of that unresisting and unchanging society." Marx's statement regarding French peasants' inability to form a strong, cohesive class is true of his view of non-Westerns: "They cannot represent themselves, they must be represented." In the case of the colonized, this means that the colonizer has the power to depict their history as he sees fit.

Not only does Marx deny non-Western peoples their own cultural and historical integrity, but he sometimes falls into stereotypes of European superiority and non-Western inferiority. This result in Marx's endorsement of European colonial expansion as a necessary steps in the progress of the world and its advance toward socialism. The oppressive Asiatic mode of production needs an external agent to overthrow it, which appears with European colonialism. As edward Said points out, Marx used documents supplied by the colonialists to develop his theory for imperialism, having no real knowledge of the history of native peoples. Said also states that Marx was writing for a European and North American audience, which he took for, granted.

Marx's Eurocentric biases are demonstrated in many of his comments about non-Western peoples and religions. He explores an inferior "Oriental mind" behind many non-Westerners' attitudes. Opinions and biases, he refers to the "fanaticism of Islam," collapsing its adherents into a mob. He calls nineteenth-century China "a living fossil" destined to be overthrown by western progress. Consequently, Chinese opposition to Western imperialism is simply a defensive reaction against modernization.

Marx's comments on British imperialism in India are very interesting in this context. For Marx, the political unity of India and its modern means of transport are the result of British rule. Marx recognizes that British imperialism destroyed Indian culture, separating India "from all its ancient traditions, and from the whole of its past history." Indian agriculture is also disrupted by European invaders. But in "blowing up [the] economic basis of the Oriental mode of production." European imperialism "produced the greatest, and, to speak the truth, the only social revolution ever heard of in Asia." Marx writes that "whatever may have been t he crimes of England she was the unconscious tool of history in bringing about that revolution." Avineri states. "Marx's sole criteria for judging the social revolution imposed on Asia are those of European, bourgeois society itself."

These outrageous Eurocentric comments are crucial, if not damning, criticisms of Marx's theory. Though it is not easy to dismiss these criticisms, a close reading of Marx reveals that his theories are more complex than this interpretation. Marx criticizes European imperialists for their brutal treatment of native peoples, sometimes coming close to advocating wars of national liberation against colonialism, especially in the case of Ireland. In his discussion of British imperialism in India. Marx seems at times to have a sense of the autonomy and integrity of native industry. Finally, Marx states on at least one occasion that his theory applies to Western Europe only and that there may be different roads that countries will travel to modernity.

Marx ruthlessly criticizes the bourgeoisie for its monetary gluttony, brutality, and destruction of native industry. Marx indicts British colonialism in India, stating that it was based on plunder and murder as hideous as the slave trade. The British exploited the Indians both financially and physically. As Marx states, the British taxed Indians so that it crushed "the mass of the Indian people to the dust, and ... its exaction necessitates a resort to such infamies as torture." Imperialism brutalized Europeans and natives. When many Indians took up arms against the British in 1857. European newspapers accused the Indians of murderous atrocities against Europeans. Marx would have none of this. Indian violence was only the "reflex" of British violence against them, for torture was an important part of British rule. British elites defined their atrocities as examples of military prowess, and applauded "atrocities" when committed by natives against their French rivals, or by the bourgeoisie against workers in European countries.

The European bourgeoisie will stop at nothing to gain profits. Marx accuses the Europeans of introducing opium into China, selling and spreading it in order to make money. Marx called this a "free trade in poison." The British destroyed local Indian agriculture, forcing farmers to cultivate poppies for opium. British industry then sold it in China, maintaining a monopoly on the opium trade. The British government was a complicit partner in this trade, all the while hypocritically denouncing the drug trade. The costs of British imperialism actually outweighed the benefits. Only a few elite groups benefited from it, including East Indian bond holders and various branches of British administration. Marx is especially harsh in his criticisms of British aristocrats, who he thinks would rather plunder foreign peoples than engage in skilled work in Britain. In sum, the costs of British imperialism essentially resulted in a tax on the working classes of Britain and India.

European imperialism destroyed internal native industry, often not replacing it with anything else. Marx states that India had been "the great workshop of cotton manufactures, since immemorial times," but that Britain demolished it, in part through imports. British landlords in India "had it in their power to undermine, and thus forcibly convert part of the Hindoo self-sustaining communities into mere farms, producing opium, cotton, indigo, hemp, and other raw materials in exchange for British stuffs". Marx also at times seems to recognize that Indians have a very rich culture, in many ways superior to that of Europe. He writes of the Indians "whose country has been the source of our ancient languages, our religions, and who represent the type of the ancient German in the Jat and the type the ancient Greek in the Brahmin." In such a context expulsion of foreigners is just. Marx states: "dispassionate and thoughtful men may perhaps be led to ask whether a people are not justified in attempting to expel foreign conquerors who have so abused their subjects." Indians will not enjoy the fruits of their own labor until a socialist revolution occurs in Britain, or "the Hindoos themselves shall have grown strong enough to throw off the English yoke altogether.

Despite Marx's comments about the "Oriental mind" he attributed their seeming static history to a structural principle. These nations lacked extensive private property, so that the expansion of wage labor and the concomitant bourgeois—proletariat social relation integral to capitalism could not develop. This lack of private property was compounded by a strong central government, which financed public works, faced by small villages, which formed a self-enclosed world. Marx states: "The village isolation produced the absence of roads in India, and the absence of roads perpetuated the village isolation." Such a society was not very dynamic. The over-centralization of these governments resulted in part from the necessity of artificially fertilizing the soil through irrigation.

While Marx's many comments seem to indicate that he thought he had derived a universal theory of history and society, at other times he is more circumspect. In a letter to the editor of a Russian journal, Marx writes that his model of economic history is only applicable to Western Europe. He argues, in reference to Russia, that this nation is trying to emulate the capitalist countries of Western Europe. If Russia desires to go down this path its peasants must be converted into wage laborers, and then it "will experience its [capitalism's] pitiless law like any other profane people." But Marx argues that he is absolutely not positing this process as an inevitable law, for any good theory of a people must explore "the historical circumstances in which it finds itself." He points to his example in ancient Rome, where proletarians did not become wage laborers in the modern sense, but sided with Roman elites and contributed to the promotion of slavery, much as poor whites did in the US. Marx says that in these cases "there developed a mode of production which was capitalist but based on slavery." Thus, the existence of a proletariat does not necessarily produce capitalism, and "events strikingly analogous but taking place in different historical surroundings led to totally different results." Marx calls for an attention to historical circumstances and an avoidance of "a general historic-philosophical theory, the supreme virtue of which consists in being super-historical.

Marx thinks that if conditions warrant it certain countries might not follow the classic European line of capitalist development. Thus, even though China is an agrarian country, Marx notes that "among the rebelling plebes there have emerged people who point to the poverty of some and the richness of others, who demanded and demand a redistribution of property, even the total abolition of private property." Marx also argues that the village community of Tsarist-dominated Russia, a "form of the primeval common ownership of land," could lead to Russian communism if Russia and the West had simultaneous revolutions.

The Issue of Ireland

The complexity of Marx's views on colonialism becomes even more pronounced when he discusses Ireland. Dominated as a colony by England, the Irish were often regarded by the English as an inferior "race," akin to the British racist views of other subject peoples. Marx does not view the Irish in this way. Rather than viewing colonialism as a secondary phenomenon in the struggle for socialism, he sees the Irish demands for national liberation as a key element in any British proletarian revolution. British workers will not cut their ties to the ruling class until Irish independence forced them to rethink their social relations.

Colonialism allows English and Irish proletariat to be split into two hostile camps, as they see one another as competitors. The British worker views his Irish counterpart as lowering his standard of living. He also derives a sense of superior satisfaction and privilege from his relation to Irish workers, which ties the British proletariat to the ruling class. This antagonism is the major reason why the English working class has not revolted, although the material conditions for revolution existed in England. Indeed, for English workers "the national emancipation of Ireland is not a question of abstract justice or humanitarian sentiment, but the first condition of their own social emancipation.

Thus, Marx calls for the British working class, and the English more generally, to own up to "the great crime which it has committed against Ireland over many centuries." Often applauding the "Irish people," he advocates Irish self-government and independence from England, along with an agrarian revolution, which would redistribute wealth in Ireland. Irish r evolution is "not only a simple economic question but at the same time a national question." Marx attributes this to the fact that English landlords controlled much of Ireland's land and were hated as oppressors. Ridding Ireland of English landlords and redistributing land is "a question of life and death for the majority of the Irish people," and agrarian revolution is inseparable from national independence.

Marx castigates English elites for ruling Ireland "by the most atrocious reign of terror and the most damnable corruption." The English bourgeoisie and aristocracy desire to turn Ireland into a massive pasture in order "to supply the English market with meat and wool at the cheapest possible prices." They also wish to eliminate as much of the native population as possible "by eviction and forcible emigration" so that English capital can do what it will in a context of "security."Marx thus views the Irish conflict as the result of a legitimate struggle for independence on the part of the Irish people. He recognizes that nationhood and identity are intertwined in the Irish case, and that colonial peoples must struggle to establish their own distinctiveness apart from the colonizer.

Alienation

The concept of alienation, regarded today as one of the central concepts of marxism, and widely used by both marxists and non-marxists, entered the dictionaries of philosophy only in the second half of the twentieth century. Thus conceived, alienation is always self-alienation, i.e., the alienation of man (of his self) from himself (from his human possibilities) through himself (through his own activity). And self-alienation is not just one among the forms of alienation, but the very essence and basic structure of alienation. On the other hand, self-alienation is not merely a descriptive concept; it is also a normative concept-a call for a revolutionary change of the world – de-alienation.

However, before it was recognized as an important philosophical term it was widely used outside philosophy: it everyday life, in the sense of turning or keeping away from former friends or associates; in economy and law, as a term for the transfer of property from one person to another; in medicine and psychiatry, as a name for deviation from normality, insanity. And before it was developed as a philosophical concept in Marx, it was developed as a philosophical concept by Hegel and Feuerbach. In his elaboration of alienation, Hegel in turn had a number of precursors. Some of them used the term without coming close to its Hegelian idea without using the term. The Christian doctrine of original sin and redemption has been regarded by many as one of the first versions of the story of man's alienation and de-alienation. Some have insisted that the concept of alienation found its first expression in Western thought in the Old Testament concept of idolatry. And some have maintained that the source of Hegel's view of nature as a self-alienated form of the Absolute Spirit can be found in Plato's view of the natural world as an imperfect picture of the noble world of Ideas. In modern times the terminology and problematic of alienation can be found especially in the social theorists. Thus, Hugo Grotius used alienation as a name for transfer of sovereign authority over oneself to another person. But regardless of whether they use the term like Grotius or not like Hobbes and Locke, the very idea of the social contract can be interpreted as an attempt at making progress in de-alienation through a deliberate partial alienation. This list of precursors could easily be enlarged. But probably no thinker before Hegel could be read and understood in terms of alienation and de-alienation better than Rousseau. Rousseau draws contract between the natural man, which could be compared with the contrast between the non-alienated and self-alienated man; and his project of overcoming the contradiction could be regarded as a programmer for abolishing self-alienation. However, despite all precursors, including Rousseau, the true philosophical history of alienation begins with Hegel.

Although the idea of alienation appears in the early writings of Hegel, its explicit elaboration as a philosophical term begins with his *Phenomenology of Mind*. And although the discussion of alienation is most direct and concentrated in the section entitled 'Mind alienated from itself; Culture', it is really the central concept and the leading idea of the whole book. In the same way, although there is no explicit discussion of alienation in his later works, the whole philosophical system of Hegel was contrasted with the help of ideas of alienation and de-alienation.

In one basic sense, the concept of self-alienation is applied in Hegel to the Absolute. The absolute idea mind, which is the only reality for Hegel, is a dynamic self engaged in a circular process of alienation and de-alienation. It becomes alienated from itself in nature and returns from its self-alienation in the finite mind, man. Self-alienation and de-alienation are in this way the form of Being of the Absolute.

In another basic sense, self-alienation can be applied to the finite mind, or man. In so far as he is a natural being, man is a self-alienated spirit. But in so far as he is a historical being, able to achieve an adequate knowledge of the Absolute, he is able to become a de-alienated being, the finite mind fulfilling its vacation to accomplish the construction of the Absolute. Thus, the basic structure of mind can also be described as self-alienation and de-alienation.

There is a further sense in which alienation can be attributed to man. It is an essential characteristic of finite mind to produce things, to express itself in objects, to objectify itself in physical things, social institutions and cultural products; and every objectification is of necessity an instance of alienation: the produced objects become alien to the producer. Alienation in this sense can be overcome only in the sense of being adequately known.

A number of further senses of alienation have been discovered in Hegel, for example by Scratch who has concluded that Hegel uses the term in two quite different senses: 'alienation,' which means 'a separation or discordant relation, such as might obtain between the individual and the social substance, or as "self-alienation" between one's actual condition and essential nature', and 'alienation, which means 'a surrender or sacrifice of particularity and willfulness, in connection with the overcoming of alienation, and the restatement of unity'.

In his *Contribution to the Critique of Hegel's Philosophy,* and in The *Essence of Christianity,* Feuerbach criticized Hegel's view that nature is a self-alienated form of Absolute mind in the process of de-alienation. For Feuerbach man is not a self-alienated God, but God is self-alienated man–he is merely man's essence abstracted. Thus, man is alienated from himself, an imagined alien higher being and bows before him as a slave. The de-alienation of man consists in the abolition of that estranged picture of man, which is God.

Feuerbach concept of alienation was first criticized and extended by Moses Hess, but a criticism along the same lines was carried out more fully and deeply by Marx in the *Economic and Philosophical Manuscripts.* Marx praised Hegel for having grasped 'the self-creation of man as a process, objectification as loss of the object, as alienation and transcendence of this alienation. But he criticized Hegel for having identified objectification with alienation, and for having regarded man as self-consciousness, and the alienation of man as the alienation of his consciousness.

Marx was greatly influenced by Feuerbach's criticism of religious alienation, but he contended that religious alienation is only the among the many forms of human self-alienation. Man not only alienates a part of himself in the form of God; he also alienates other products of his spiritual activity in the form of philosophy, common sense, art, morals; he alienates products of his economic activity in the form of the commodity, money, capital; he alienates products of his social activity in the form of the state, law, social institutions. There are many forms in which man alienates the products of his activity from himself and makes of them a separate, independent and powerful world of objects to which he is related as a slave, powerless and dependent. All these kinds of alienation are in the last analysis one; they are different aspects of forms of man's self-alienation, different forms of the alienation of man from his human 'essence' or 'nature', from his humanity.

Since alienated labour: (1) alienates nature from man, and (2) alienates man from himself, from his own active function, his life activity; so it alienates him from the species.(3) It alienates from man his own body, external nature, his mental life and his human life. (4) A direct consequence of the alienation of man from the product of his labour, from his life activity and form his species life is that man is alienated from other men. In general, the statement, that man is alienated from others and that each of the others is likewise alienated from human life.

The criticism unmasking of alienation was not an end in itself for Marx. His aim was to pave the way for a radical revolution and for the realization of communism understood as 'the re-integration of man, his return to himself, the suppression of man's self-alienation'. Although the terms alienation and de-alienation are not very much used in Marx's later writings, all of them, including *Capital,* present a criticism of the existing alienated man and society and a call for de-alienation. And there is at least one great work of the later Marx, *the Grundrisse,* in which the terminology of alienation is widely used.

The *Economic and Philosophical Manuscripts* were first published in 1932, and the *Grundrisse* first published in 1939 became assessable in practice only after their re-publication in 1953. There may have been many reasons for the neglect of the concepts of alienation and de-alienation in all interpretations of Marx in the nineteenth century and in the first decades of the twentieth. Some important aspects of alienation were discussed for the first time in Lukacs's *History and Class Consciousness* under the term 'reification', but there is no general and explicit discussion of alienation in the book. Thus the discussion only began after the publication of the *Economic and Philosophical Manuscripts in* 1932. Marcuse (1932) was among the first to stress the importance of the *Manuscripts* and to draw attention to the concept of alienation in them. Cornu (1934) was one of the first to study the 'young Marx' more carefully, and Lefebvre (1939) was perhaps the first who tried to introduce the concept of alienation into the then established interpretation of marxism.

A more widespread and intense discussion of alienation began after the Second World War. Those who have taken part in it include not only marxists but also existentialists and not only philosophers but also psychoanalysts, sociologists, literary critics, writers. Among non-marxists it was especially Heidegger who gave an important impulse to the discussion of alienation. In *Being and Time* (1967) he used alienation to describe one of the basic traits of the inauthentic mode of man's Being. Further important impulses came from Sartre, who used 'alienation' in both his existentialist and his marxist phase. Tallish, in whose combination of Protestant theology, existential philosophy and marxism the concept of alienation plays a prominent role. Kojeve interpreted Hegel with the help of insights from the young Marx. Hyppolite discussed alienation and especially relationship between alienation and objectification in Hegel and Marx.

Among the marxists, Lukacs studied alienation in Hegel and Marx, and tried to specify his own concept of alienation and its relationship to reification; Bloch, who used the concept without a special insistence on it, tried to draw a clear distinction between *Entfremdung* and *Verfremdung*; and Fromm not only carefully studied the concept of alienation in Marx, but made it a key tool of analysis in his sociological, psychological and philosophical studies.

Those marxists who tried to revive and develop Marx's theory of alienation in the 1950s and 1960s have been heavily criticized for idealism and Hegelianism, on one side by the representatives of the established Stalinist interpretation of Marx, and on the other by the so called structuralit marxists like Althusser. Althusser sought to impugn the pre-eminent status accorded by many to these early writings, arguing that whatever the superficial similarities between them and Marx's mature work, there were two radically distinct modes of thought. The problematic of each – that is, the theoretical framework was fundamentally different: in the young Marx, an ideological drama of human alienation and self-realization, which humanity the author of its unfolding destiny much in the manner of the world spirit according to Hegel; thereafter, however, a science, historical materialism, theory of social formations and their history; and its concepts of structural explanation: the forces and relations of production, determination by the economy, superstructure, state, ideology. The two systems of thought were separated by an 'epistemological break' in which a new science emerges from its ideological pre-history. Such opponents of the theory of alienation have insisted that what was called alienation in the early Marx was much more adequately described in later works by scientific terms such as private property, class domination, exploitation, division of labour, etc. But it has been argued in reply that the concepts of alienation and de-alienation cannot be fully reduced to any of the concepts which have been offered as replacements, and that for a truly revolutionary interpretation of Marx the concept of alienation is indispensable. As a result of these debates the number of marxists who still oppose any use of alienation has considerably declined.

Many who were ready to accept Marx's concept of alienation did not accept that of self-alienation, which seemed to them unhistorical, because it implied that there is a fixed and unchangeable human essence or nature. Against such a view it has been argued that alienation from oneself should be not understood as alienation from a factual or ideal or normative human nature, but as alienation from historically created human possibilities, especially from the human capacity for freedom and creativity. Thus, instead of supporting a static or unhistorical essentialist view of man, the idea of self-alienation is a call for a constant renewal and progressive development of human beings.

A further controversial point is whether alienation applied in the first place to individuals, or to society as a whole. According to some of those who see it as applying in the first place to individuals, the non-adjustment of the individual to the society in which he lives is a sign of his alienation. Others have argued that a society can also be sick or alienated, so that an individual who is not adapted to the existing society is not himself necessarily alienated. Many of those who regarded alienation as applicable only to individuals make it even narrower by conceiving of it as a purely psychological concept referring to a state of mind. Thus according to Eric From alienation is 'an individual feeling or state of dissociation from self, from others, and form the world at large'. Others have insisted that alienation is not simply a feeling, but in the first place an objective fact, a way of being. Most of the theorists of alienation have made a distinction between different forms of alienation . Schaff finds two basic forms: objective alienation and subjective alienation; others have identifyied four types of dienation: alienation of men from nature, from their fellow men, from the work of their products, from themselves.

A question, which has been particularly widely discussed, is whether self-alienation is an essential, imperishable property of man as man, or is characteristic only of one historical stage in human development. Some existentialist philosophers have maintained that alienation is a permanent structural moment of human existence. It is a permanent human predicament besides his authentic existence, man also leads a non-authentic one, and it is illusory to expect that he will one day live only authentically. The opposed view is that the originally non-self-alienated human being, in the course of development, alienated himself from himself, but will in the future return to himself. This view is to be found in Engels and in many present-day marxists; Marx himself seems to have thought that man had always been self-alienated thus far, but that he nonetheless could and should come into his own.

Many are of the view of communism as de-alienation and someone skeptical about the possibilities, limits and forms of de-alienation. Thus according to one answer, an absolute de-alienation is possible; all alienation – social and individual – can be once and for all abolished. The most radical representatives of such an optimistic viewpoint have even maintained that all self-alienation has already been eliminated in principle in socialist countries; that it exists there only in the form of individual insanity or as an insignificant 'remnant of capitalism'. It is not difficult to see the problems with such a view. Absolute de-alienation would be possible only if humanity were something given once and for all, and unchangeable. And from a factual standpoint, it is easy to see that in what is called 'socialism' many 'new' forms of alienation exist. Thus against the advocates of absolute de-alienation it has been maintained that only a relative de-alienation is possible. According to this view it is not possible to eliminate all alienation, but it is possible to create a basically non-alienated society that would stimulate the development of non-self-alienated, really human individuals.

Depending on the view of the essence of self-alienation, the means recommended for overcoming alienation have also differed. Those who regard self-alienation as a psychological fact dispute the importance or even relevance of any external change in circumstances and suggest that the individual's more effort, 'a revolution within the self', is the only cure. And those who regard self-alienation as a neurotic phenomenon are quite consistent in offering a psychoanalytical treatment for it. At the other pole stand those philosophers and sociologists who accept economic determinism, regard individuals as passive products of social and especially economic organization. For such marxists the problem of de-alienation is reduced to the problem of social transformation, problem of the abolition of private property.

As against both the views a third conception has been proposed according to which de-alienation of society and of individuals are closely connected, so that neither can be carried out without the other, nor can one be reduced to the other. It is possible to create a social system that would be favorable to the development of de-alienated individuals, but it is not possible to organize a society which would automatically produce such individuals. An individual can become a non-alienated, free and creative being only through his own activity.

Equally, the problem of de-alienation of economic life cannot be solved by the mere abolition of private property. The transformation of private property into state property does not introduce an essential change in the situation of the worker, or the producer. The de-alienation of economic life also requires the abolition of state property, its transformation into real social property, and this cannot be achieved without organizing the whole of social life on the basis of the self-management of the immediate producers. But the self-management of producers is not of itself a sufficient condition. It does not solve automatically the problem of de-alienation in distribution and consumption, and it is not by itself sufficient even for the de-alienation of production. Some forms of alienation in production have their roots in the nature of present-day means of production, so that they cannot be eliminated by a mere change in the form of managing production.

Commodity Fetishism

Marx's analysis of commodity fetishism is more or less confined to *Capital* I (ch. 1, sect. 4). Having established that commodity production constitutes a social relationship between producers, a relationship that brings different types, skills and quantities of labour into equivalence with each other as values Marx enquires how this relationship appears to the producers or more generally to society. For the producers, it is presented to them as a social relation, existing not between themselves, but between the products of their labour'. The social relationship between tailor and carpenter appears as a relationship between coat and table in terms of the ratio at which those things exchange with each other rather than in terms of the labours embodied in them. But Marx is quick to point our that this appearance of commodity relations as a relationship between things is not false. It exists, but conceals the relationship between the producers: 'the relations connecting the labour one individual with that of the rest appear not as direct social relations between individuals it work, but as what they really are, material relations between persons and social relations between things.

Marx's theory of commodity fetishism is never taken up again explicitly and at length, in *Capital* or elsewhere. Nevertheless, its influence can clearly be discerned in his criticisms of classical political economy. Commodity fetishism is the simplest and most universal example of the way in which the economic forms of capitalism conceal underlying social relations. The simplicity of commodity fetishism makes it a starting point and example for analysing non-economic relations. It establishes a dichotomy between appearance and concealed reality. It discusses social relations conducted as and in the form of relations between commodities or things and this has application to the theory of reification and alienation.

Historical Materialism

Historical materialism refers to that central body of doctrine, frequently known as the materialist conception of history, which constitutes the social-scientific core of marxist theory. According to Engels historical materialism designates that view of the course of history which seeks the ultimate cause and the great moving power of all important historic events in the economic development of society, in the changes in the modes of production and exchange, in the consequent division of society into distinct classes, and in the struggle of these classes against one another. Engels credited Marx with being the originator of historical materialism. In accord with the theory itself, they stressed the historical and material preconditions of its formulation.

Although scholars disagree about the degree of continuity of various themes between Marx's early and later writings, few would deny the materialist view of history, which Marx and Engels began to hammer out at the time of *German Ideology*. At this time, however, they began quite self-consciously to utilize historical materialism as, in Marx's words, the 'guiding thread' of all their subsequent studies. Historical materialism is not, strictly speaking, a philosophy; rather it is best interpreted as an empirical theory. Thus Marx and Engels frequently emphasizes the scientific character of their enterprise, and *German Ideology* claims that its approach rests not on philosophically derived abstractions or dogmas, but rather on observation and an accurate depiction of real conditions. These claims receive their most memorable statement in a very compact passage from *Marx's Preface to A Contribution to the Critique of Political Economy*. Marx refers to it at least twice in *Capital* as a guide to his materialist perspective.

Throughout the mature Marx's economic works the idea that a contradiction between force and relations of production underlies the dynamic of the capitalist mode of production is present. More generally, such a contradiction accounts for history existing as succession of modes of production, since it leads to the necessary collapse of one mode and its suppression by another. And the couple, forces/ relations of production, in any mode of production underlies the whole of society's processes, not just the economic ones. The connection between them and the social structure was stated in some of Marx's most succinet sentences:

> In the social production of their life men enter into definite relations that are indispensable and independent of their will, relations of production which correspond to a definite state of development of their material productive forces. The sum total of these relations of production constitutes the economic structure, the real basis on which rises a legal and political superstructure.

The power of the contradiction between relations and forces to act as the motor of history is also stated in the same place: at a certain stage of their development, the material productive forces of society come in conflict with the existing relations of production within which they have been at work hitherto; and 'from forms of development of the productive forces these relations turn into their fetters' there by initiating social revolution. The productive forces were conceived by Marx as including means of production and labour power. Their development, therefore, encompasses such historical phenomena as the development of machinery, changes in the small labour process, the opening up of new sources of energy, and the education of the proletariat. There remain, however, several elements whose definition is disputed. Some writers have included science itself as a productive force and Cohen even includes geographical space as a force.

The manner in which the development of the forces and relations of productions occurs, and the effects of this development, has been the subject of one of the main controversies in marxist thought. The familiar interpretation of the celebrated passage from the *Preface* is this: within a mode of production there lies a correspondence both between forces and relations, and as a result of this, between the relations of production and legal, ideological and other social relations. The correspondence appears to be one where the forces of production are primary, the relations of production are determined by the forces, and they themselves determine the superstructure. These respective positions of the three elements in the chain of causation acquire significance from their implications for historical development. Thus, the development of the forces of production leads to a contradiction between them and the relations of production which 'turn in to their fellers and the intensification of this contradiction leads to the breakdown of the existing made of production and its superstrecture. One problem with this interpretation is whether it is valid to conceive of the forces of production as the prime movers?

In the revival of marxist theory in the third quarter of this century, this particular interpretation of Marx's thesis has been contested. An important consideration for some was that the thesis appeared to carry a political implication which was rejected: it was argued that Stalin's policy of rapid industrialization with its forced collectivization and political repression stemmed from his conception of the primacy of the forces of production, so that if the productive forces in the Soviet Union could become those of modern industry, socialist relations of production would have their proper basis. Moreover, Marx's own writings appeared to be ambiguous on the primacy of the productive forces, and in places, he writes as though the relations of production dominate and generate changes in the forces. In *Capital* I, for example, especially in the discussion of the development of the real subsumption of labour to capital, Marx writes as though the capitalist relations of production revolutionize the instruments of production and the labour process.

The themes of the 'Preface' echoes throughout the marxian corpus and must, of course, be interpreted in the light of the elaboration they receive elsewhere. In the 'Preface' Marx contends that the economic structure of society, constituted by its relations of production, is the real foundation of society. It is the basis 'on which rises a legal and political superstructure and to which correspond definite forms of social consciousness'. On the other hand, society's relations of production, themselves 'correspond to a definite stage of development of society's material productive forces'. In this manner, the mode of production of material life conditions the social, political and intellectual life process in general.

As the society's productive forces develop, they clash with existing production relations, which now fetter their growth. Then begins an epoch of social revolution as this contradiction divides society and as people become, in more or less ideological forms, 'conscious of this conflict and fight it out. The conflict is resolved in favour of the productive forces, and new, higher relations of production, whose material preconditions have 'matured in the womb of the old society', emerge which better accommodate the continued growth of society's productive capacity. The bourgeois mode of production represents the most recent of several progressive epochs in the economic formation of society, but it is the last antagonistic form of production. With its demise, the prehistory of humanity will come to a close.

We can argue that the core thesis of historical materialism is that the different socio-economic organizations of production which have characterized human history arise or fall as they enable or impede the expansion of society's productive capacity. The growth of the productive forces thus explains the general course of human history. The productive forces, however, include not just the means of production tools, machines, factories and so on, but labour power – the skills, knowledge, experience, and other human faculties used in work. The productive forces represent the powers society has at its command in material production.

The relations of production, which are said to correspond to society's productive level, link productive forces and human beings in the process of production. These relations are of two broad types: on the one hand those technical relations that are necessary for the actual production process to proceed; on the other the said relations that govern access to the forces and products of production. The contrast is between the material work relations and their socio-economic integument, and Marx pointedly criticizes those who confound the two. Types of economic structure are differentiated by their dominant social production relations.

The related concept mode of production is similarly equivocal. Sometimes Marx uses it in the restricted sense of the technical nature or manner of producing, as when capitalism is said to introduce 'constant daily revolutions in the mode of production'. More frequently, Marx employs the concept in a second sense, namely that of the social system of producing, which is carried on within, and as a result of a certain set of ownership relations. Thus, capitalist relations of production define a specific connection between people and productive forces, while the capitalist mode of production involves the production of commodities, a certain manner of obtaining surplus, labour time determination of value, and so on. In addition, Marx sometimes used 'mode of production' to encompass both the technical and social properties of the way production may subsist within any actual social formation.

The expansion of the productive forces determines the relations and mode of production, which obtain because, as Marx wrote to Annenkov, 'men never relinquish what they have won'. In order to retain 'the fruits of civilization' they will change their way of producing – either their material or social relations of production or both – to accommodate the acquired productive forces and facilitate their continued advance. The resulting economic structure in turn shapes the legal and political superstructure. The relations of production can influence the momentum and qualitative direction of the development of the productive forces. Capitalism in particular is distinguished by its tendency to raise society to a productive level undreamt of before. This is in line with historical materialism, however, since Marx's thesis is that the relation of production which emerge do so precisely because they have the ability to promote the development of society's productive capacity.

Some present-day marxists deny the dominant role of the productive forces in favour of the idea that relations and forces are mutually determining. But while Marx certainly allows for the interaction and indeed describes specific instances of the relations of production influencing the productive forces, in all his general theoretical moments he gives privacy to productive forces. Because historical materialism sees the productive forces as enjoying explanatory primacy, it is able to give an answer to the question of why in general different socio-economic formations arise when they do.

The legal and political institutions of society are clearly superstructural for Marx: their fundamental character is determined by the nature of the existing economic structure. Which other social institutions are properly part of the superstructure is a matter of debate. Certainly Marx thought that the various spheres and realms of society reflect the dominant mode of production and that the general consciousness of an epoch is shaped by the nature of its production. The marxist theory of ideology contends, in part, that certain ideas originate or are widespread because they sanction existing social relations or promote particular class interests. The economy's determination of legal and political structure though, will tend to be relatively direct, while its influence over other social realms, culture, and consciousness generally is more attenuated and nuanced. Historical materialism perceives a general hierarchy among the realms of social life, but these relations must be elaborated, not just for society in general, but also for each specific type of socio-economic organization. In line with this, an important footnote in *Capital* I suggests that the mode of production of an era determines the relative importance of the various shapers of the social world of that period. The nature and strength of the mechanisms theorized by the base-superstructure metaphor, however, are among the most vexed and controversial questions of historical materialism. Marx's theory does not view the superstructure as an epiphenomenon of the economic base, nor overlook the necessity of legal and political institutions. It is precisely because a superstructure is needed to stabilize society that the economic structure brings about those institutions that are best suited to it. Nor are 'superstructure' and 'base' related like a statue and plinth; that superstructures affect or react back on the base is one of the fundamental tenets of historical materialism.

Law, in particular, is necessary to 'sanction the existing order' and grant it 'independence from mere chance and arbitrariness'. This function itself gives the legal realm some autonomy since the existing relations of production are represented and legitimated in an abstract, codified form, which in turn fosters the ideological illusion that the law is entirely autonomous with respect to the economic structure. In addition, under capitalism the fictio, juris of a contract' between free agents obscures the real nature of production, in particular, the 'invisible threads' which bind the wage-laborer to capital. In precapitalist societies, for example in feudalism, tradition and custom perform a similar stabilizing function and may also win a degree of autonomy. There, the true nature of the social relations of production is obscured by entanglement with the relations of personal domination, which characterize the other spheres of feudal life.

Marx's stress on class analysis, surprisingly absent from the 'Preface', connects with the above themes of historical materialism in several significant ways. In the social organization of production, people stand in different relations to the forces and products of production. The individual's economic position as that is understood in terms of the existing social production relations establishes certain material interests in common with others and determines class membership. Hence, follow the familiar definitions of the bourgeoisie and proletariat by reference to the purchase and sale of labour power and the underlying ownership or non-ownership of the means of production. A central thesis of historical materialism is that class position, so defined, determines the characteristic consciousness or worldview of its members. Marx's discussion in *18th Brumaire* emphasizes that on the basis of its socio-economic position each class creates 'an entire superstructure of distinct and peculiarly formed sentiments, illusions, modes of thought and views of life'. The differing material interests of classes divide them and lead to their struggle.

The ultimate success or failure of a class is determined by its relation to the advanc of the productive forces. In the words of *German Ideology*, 'the conditions under which definite productive forces can be applied are the conditions of the rule of a definite class of society'. The class which has the capacity and the incentive to introduce or preserve the relations of production required to accommodate the advance of the productive forces has its hegemony ensured. Thus Marx thought that the eventual success of the proletarian cause, like the earlier rise of the bourgeoisie, was guaranteed by the fundamental currents of history while, for example, the heroic slave revolts of the ancient world were doomed to failure. Historical materialism views class rule, hitherto, as both inevitable and necessary to force the productivity of the direct producers beyond the subsistence level. 'No antagonism, no progress', states *The Poverty of Philosophy*. This has been the law that civilization has followed and the productive forces have been developed by virtue of this system of class antagonism. The productive progress brought by capitalism, however, eliminates the historical justification for, class rule. Since the state is primarily the vehicle by which a class secures its rule, it will wither away in post-class society.

Historical materialism contends that class conflict and the basic trajectory of human history can be explained by the advance of the productive forces. Their advance, however, must be understood in terms of a theoretical model that reveals the character of the specific modes of production involved. Such a theory will be very abstract with regard to any particular society. Thus, for example, Marx presents the evolution of capitalism in abstraction from the specific physiognomy of any particular capitalist nation-state. *Capital* underwrites the claim that socialism is 'inevitable', but it does not empower one to predict the arrival of socialism at any particular time or place – only to affirm that the 'tendency' of capitalist development is such as to bring it about. Nor does the specific course of each society simply repeat same universal dialectic of forces and relations of production. Societies are rarely isolated, untouched and uninfluenced by productive advances outside them. Accordingly, every social group of the globe is not fated to pass through the same stage of economic development, nor is the evolution of any particular social formation solely a matter of internal productive events. Although historical materialism permits countries to lag behind or even skip steps, their course must still be explained within the over-arching pattern of socio-economic evolution, and that development is due to the productive forces.

The 'Preface' offers an historical schema the Asiatic, ancient, feudal, and modern bourgeois modes of production as the major epochs in humanity's advance, but these mark the general stages of socio-economic evolution as a whole – not the steps which history obliges every nation, without exception, to climb. In a famous letter of November 1877, Marx characteristically denied propounding 'any historic-philosophical theory imposed by fate upon every people'; but this oft-quoted remark does not amount to a rejection of historical determinism. Marx could consistently believe in a necessary, productive force-determined evolution of history without holding that every social group is preordained to follow the same course. It seems likely, in fact that Marx would have been willing to revise his particular tabulation of historical periods, since he did not analyse in detail humanity's early modes of production. Modification of Marx's historical schema as well as of his analysis of capitalism is in principle compatible with the basic tenets of historical materialism. It should be borne in mind that historical materialism does not pretend to explain every last detail of history. From its broad purview, many historical events, and certainly the specific forms they take, are accidental. Nor does the theory seek to explain scientifically individual behavior, though it attempts to situate that behavior within its historical confines. In so far as there are ineluctable tendencies in history, these results from, and the choices of individuals. The explanatory ambitions of historical materialism as a social-scientific theory do not commit it to philosophical determinism.

Because historical materialism is so central to marxism, diverse political and intellectual currents in marxism have surfaced by their differing interpretations of that theory. One standard interpretation has been presented above, but controversy rages over the basic concepts and theorems of the theory, and the relative importance of its various components. The task of rendering historical materialism as an empirically plausible theory without reducing it to a collection of truisms has proved very formidable. Given the far-ranging claims of the theory and the lack of an interpretative consensus, an accurate assessment of its viability is exceedingly difficult.

The idea that the productive forces are primary, despite the problems it presents, has been vigorously defended by Cohen. He demonstrates the coherence of the thesis in its own terms and argues that it does have a valid, logical centrality in Marx's own writing. The basic difficulty in understanding the connection between forces and relations of production is that whereas the two are seen as necessarily compatible with each other within a mode of production, one of them has to develop in such a way that a contradiction or incompatibility matures; their progress, therefore, has an element of asymmetry unevenness and it has to be a systematic rather than accidental asymmetry. Thus, compatibility cannot mean mutual and even determination. It could mean that the relations develop, causing development of the forces, which then react back on the relations but in such a way that the effect of relations on forces is multiplied while that of forces on relations of production would be primary but the maturation of the forces would run up against the 'fetters', which characterize the contradiction. Cohen, however, does not adopt this interpretation. Instead, he argues that the development of the forces is primary because it results from a factor which is, in a sense, exogenous, there is a motive force which lies outside the forces and relations of production and acts first upon the former Cohen asserts that this motive force is human rationality, a rational and ever-present impulse of human beings to try to better their situation and over come scarcity by developing the productive forces.

Cohen's emphasis upon human beings' rational pursuit of their interest in overcoming material want is intellectually a fascinating and courageous in his defence of Marx's view on the primacy of the forces of production. As Levine and Wright argue, even if the action of human interests is seen in the context of class interests, thereby avoiding a non-n Marxist individualism, it neglects the question of class capacities. The interests of a class do not guarantee its effective it in shaping history. Levine and Wright define class capacities "as those organizational, ideolpqical and materical rcsources arailafle to classes in class shruggle" and argue that the 'transformation of interests into practices is the central problem for any adequate theory of history'. This become a particularly acute issue when the theory of the forces and relations of production confronts the problem of the type of contradiction that will lead to the collapse of the capitalist mode of production and the installation of socialism. Writers who argue for the importance of class capacity as well as class interests in carrying through such a transformation see themselves as postulating the significance of class struggle in contrast to the economic determinism of an inexorable law working out of the contradictory development of forces and relations in response to some basic human inferests.

Popper has criticized Marx's theory of historical materialism on ground of historicism. For Popper, Hegel and Marx are guilty of the misguided and noxious view that history has a pattern and a meaning that, if grasped, can be used in the present to predict and fashion the future. The conflation of metaphysics and history involved in Popper's version of historicism may have been present in Hegel but it is not characteristic of the main thrust of Marx's work. It was Marx's view that history itself had no meaning beyond that which men in their varying stages of development assigned to it. Equally, the question of whether Marx's own thought is to be judged historicist is bound up with the question of its scientific character, with his critique of utopianism, and with the status of his predictions.

The second current sense of the term is found in the historical relativism of the 'return to Hegel' in the works of the young Lukacs, Korsch, and to some extent,

Gramsci. Korsch, referring explicitly to Hegel, claimed that 'we must try to understand every change, development and version of marxist theory, since its original emergence from the philosophy of German idealism, as a necessary product of its epoch'. In the same sense, Gramsci, in his critique of Bukharian could refer to marxism as absolute historicism'. The main critic of this vision of marxism is Althusser who in the fifth chapter of *Reading 'Capital'* makes historicism, together with humanism, the main object of his attack. Principally this debate involved once again, with the nature of Marx's science and also the complex question of the relationship of Marx to Hegel.

Marx forcefully insists that it is man, real, living man who does all that, who possesses and fights; history is not, as it were, a person apart using man as a means to achieve its own aims; history is nothing bu*t* the activity of man pursuing his aims. Although Marx sees communism as the "goal of history," he is referring to a historically created potential that requires human intervention to be actualized. Marx sharply rejects every school of thought which would subject history to some lawfulness *or* purposiveness external and alien to the content of activities of concrete historical individuals.

Such tensions in Marx's work can be resolved in a number of ways; the differences in interpretation of Marx, such as we find between Plekhanov and Lukacs, result from the ambiguities and inconsistencies in his texts. There is therefore no "authentic" Marx, but a careful reading will avoid simple and dogmatic positions of any kind and bring out the tensions and changes in his work. The problem with relying on Marx's methodological reflections is that they often grossly oversimplify and misrepresent the complexity of his actual analyses. Perhaps the most fundamental tension in Marx's work is the discrepancy between what he says in his theoretical summaries and what he does in his concrete studies. Here a key problem relates to the issue of whether or not Marx was a technological determinist, whether he privileged forces of production (technology, knowledge, work relations) over relations of production (social classes) as the fundamental causal dynamic of history. The crucial interpretative problems in the "Preface" concern the strength of the causal force behind the "determining" operation of the economic base, the meaning of the "correspondence" between forces and relations of production, and what elements constitute the economic base of society and its mode of production. Deterministic readings of Marx in large part emerge from different answers to these questions.

On the economic determinist reading, the base comprises both the forces and relations of production, both technology and economic classes, and it "determines" the superstructure in the strong sense of a one way, mechanical causal force that prevents any reciprocal interaction between the base and superstructure. While many of Marx's critics still hold to this reading, orthodox marxists such as Kautsky and Plekhanov rejected it and emphasized the reciprocal interaction between base and superstructure. Yet they and many others adopt a technological determinist reading of Marx. Like economic determinism, the technological determinist reading holds that the base determines the superstructure, but it adds that the most important factor determining the base itself is technological. In other words, a more fundamental rung is added to the causal hierarchy of society: the growth of technology determines the nature of economic entirety relations, which in turn determine the superstructure of social life.

On the technological determinist reading, Marx holds that the ultimate driving force in history is technological and that class relations are to be explained according to their function in promoting or retarding this growth. This thesis need not argue for a one-way causal determination of forces over relations of production; it need only maintain that the productive forces ultimately determine the relations of production, that relations of production are ultimately to be explained by the development of the forces of production. Thus, although "analytic marxists Cohen and Shaw criticize a nondialectical version of technological determinism that recognizes only one-way causality between forces and relations of production, and claim that Marx saw reciprocal influence on both sides, they remain technological determinists insofar as they functionally subordinate the relations to the forces of production and assert the main role of social relations is to develop technology. Cohen attempts to support his "primacy of the productive forces thesis" with the "developmental thesis" that human beings, fundamentally rational in nature and living in constant conditions of scarcity, seek to acquire ever greater control over nature and therefore strive constantly to develop the forces of production. The relations of production that best develop the forces of production become the ruling social classes and survive as long as they serve the role of advancing technological growth.

For all their analytic sophistication, the major flaw of Cohen's and Shaw's interpretations is their failure to emphasize the distinctly political character of Marx's historical explanations and the complex political-economic dialectic he develops— a problem that stems from their false separation of productive forces and work relation. They transform a revolutionary political vision intended for the working class into an academic theory of history designed for historians. It is precisely this functionalist subordination of the relations to the forces production that prompts other theorists to decry determinism and to insist on the primacy of the relations of production. As early as 1933, theorists such as Sidney Hook had begun to argue against the technological determinist claims made by Kautsky and Plekhanov and to champion the primacy of the relations of production. This argument was most ambitiously developed by Hindess and Hirst who reject .the primacy of the productive forces, however qualified or reciprocal in nature, as a "techneicism," as a functionalist subordination of consciousness, politics, and class struggle to technology. For Hindess and Hirst, the primacy of the forces of production thesis "renders inexplicable any operation of the relations of production which has the effect of not [merely] distributing the conditions of production so as to reproduce the forces."

Hindess and Hirst claim that for Marx, "it is the relations of production which are the crucial element in any concept of the economic level." Unlike Cohen and Shaw, they privilege class struggle as the fundamental motor of history: "It is the forms of class struggle and the outcomes which determine the specific forms of production." To support their reading, they point to quotes ignored by Cohen and

Shaw where Marx defines class relations as "the specific economic form in which unpaid surplus labor is pumped out of the direct producers," which suggests that the relations of production determine the forces of production.

The opposing claims of these theorists each provide only a partially correct and one-sided reading of Marx. The technological determinist reading rightly emphasizes that Marx grants fundamental importance to the role of technology in human life. For Marx, "Technology discloses man's mode of dealing with nature, the process of production by which he sustains his life, and thereby also lays bare the mode of formation of his social relations, and of the mental conceptions that flow from them." Marx does indeed claim that technology and the productive forces are key to explaining social change: "In acquiring new forces of production men change their mode of production; and in changing their mode of production, in changing the way of earning their living, they change all their social relations. The handmill gives you society with the feudal lord; the steam-mill, society with the industrial capitalist." He also argues elsewhere that "The economic relations and consequently the social, moral, and political state of nations changes with the change in the material powers of production." These emphases are conveniently glossed over in Hindess and Hirst's interpretation of Marx and they wrongly deny the forces of production any significant determining power in history. But they correctly point to counteremphases on the role of class struggle in history as an independent causal force that cannot be adequately captured by technological determinism. Neither position grasps the tensions and ambiguities in Marx's analyses. The one-sidedness of the readings of Cohen and Shaw and Hindess and Hirst need to be rejected in favor of a more nuanced, contextualist approach.

In his book *Analyzing Marx*, Richard Miller criticizes both economic and technological determinist readings of Marx, while also trying to preserve Marx's unique emphasis on the importance of economic relations and technology in structuring society. Miller develops forceful arguments against every major aspect of the technological determinist interpretation of Marx: "Economic structures do not endure because they provide maximum productivity. Productive forces do not develop autonomously. Change in productive forces, in the narrowly technological sense that excludes work relations, is not the basic sources of change in society at large."

Like technological determinists, Miller claims that Marx always rooted social change within the dynamics of a given mode of production, but Miller argues for a broader and nonreductionist understanding of the causal forces comprising a mode of production. This argument makes the important claim that elements within a mode of production are inseparable and so it is impossible to isolate forces or relations as primacy. Miller makes two key moves in granting a broader context of causal factors in Marx's work. First, he argues that Marx included work relations, or "modes of cooperation," among forces of production, thereby denying causal priority to technological factors as many way autonomous from social relations. This crucial move was blocked by Cohen and Shaw with a nondialectical logic that forces a categorical separation between social and material logics that is entirely foreign to Marx's method. If we undo this dichotomy to claim, with Marx himself, that work relations are integral aspects of the forces of production, then technological determinism becomes untenable.

Second, Miller claims that Marx believed social change frequently came about due to internal contradictions within a given economic structure, independent of its relation with forces of production. On Miller's interpretation, Marx holds that social change can be stimulated as much by economic relations as by technological development; economic structures can select productive forces as much as productive forces can select economic structures. Miller rejects Cohen and Shaw's functionalist subordinatioh of relations to forces of production as well as Hindess and Hirst's voluntarism to argue in favor of a "*zig-zag* dialectic" between forces and relations, "with priority on neither side." Miller therefore adopts a symmetrical thesis is as much to be explained as due to structure and the processes to which they give rise as the nature of changes in structures is due to forces. Forces and relations of production, in other words are too interdependent to raise any causal priority claim. Miller also rejects the schizophrenic reading that Marx is a technological determinist in his general statements but not in his concrete analyses; the possibility for symmetrical causation is left open by Marx's general theory and realized in his specific explanations. Marx's general statement that relations correspond to forces is only "a synopsis of a specific scenario for change in structure and not an assessment of the balance of ultimate causal influences." Rather than subscribing to a monolithic model privileging forces or relations of production, Marx treats primacy as relative to the questions being asked." In our own terms, Marx is a contextualist who privileges different causal factors in different contexts.

If we open the pages of the *Capital,* it is hard to resist the conclusion that in his most important and definitive work, Marx privileges relations over forces of production. In a sustained analysis he describes the shift from feudalism to capitalism as a shift from a mode of production based on handicrafts to one initially based on manufacturing. Capitalism develops by appropriating and extending the cooperative form of labor employed in handicrafts within a new context of manufacturing whose aim is the maximization of surplus value. The "starting point" of capitalism involves assembling in one place and one labor process a number of workers under the control of a capitalist. Formerly independent and specialized crafts workers engaged in a variety of tasks now occupy positions within a more complex division of labor that is indifferent to needs and creative abilities, appropriating human beings as sheer labor power. In the transition from feudal handicrafts to capitalist manufacturing, before the era of large-scale industry, there is no basic change in the technical basis of production since "handicraft skill is the foundation of manufacturing." Rather, the change leading to a new mode of production occurs at the level of work and ownership relations through a political struggle between classes. The productive forces of feudal society are put to new use in a different social context. Newly established capitalist work relations and production relations, in turn, condition subsequent technological developments in the form of machine production and large-scale industry.

It is clear, however, that Marx believes that capitalism does not arise through a technological revolution, but rather through "the revolution in the relations of production." In fact, for Marx, it is the relations of production that are most crucial in explaining the transition to capitalism. The incredible unleashing and development of the productive forces characteristic of capitalism can only occur after a revolution in relations of production. Before the technological basis of industrial capitalism could be developed, the proletariat first had to be formed as a class. The mass of newly created proletarians thrown onto the labor market resulted from the dissolution of bands of feudal retainers and the forced expropriation of peasants from the land. The motivation behind this was economic: through a rapid expansion in wool manufacturing and a rise in the price of wool, the new nobility found it most profitable to drive the peasantry off the land in order to raise sheep. The desire here was to acquire money, not to develop technology.

Marx says that "the revolution in property relations on the land were accompanied, not determined by improved methods of cultivation, greater co-operation, a higher concentration of the means of production and so on." Newly emerging bourgeois property relations also led to the destruction of subsidiary trades in the countryside and to the creation of a home market. Hence, Marx speaks of "the productive forces resulting from co-operation and the division of labour. He states that the expansion of industries carried on by means of machinery and the invasion of fresh branches of production by machinery were dependent upon the growth of a class of workers who, owing to the semi-artistic nature of their employment, would increase their numbers only gradually, and not by leaps and bounds."

Of course, as Hindess and Hirst fail to see, the productive forces have their own influence and effect the nature of work and ownership relations. In Chapter 15 of *Capital,* Marx shows how the machinery employed in large-scale industry had great consequences on further developments in technology and on the social mode of production as a whole. It forced a mechanization of all aspects of production, transforming workshops, domestic industry, and agriculture. Initially machinery increased the demand for workers, intensively exploiting women, children, and all forms of unskilled labor. Subsequently, however, it displaced manual labor, allowed greater capitalist domination over the working class, and heightened class struggle. The impact of large-scale industry was most pronounced in agriculture, where machines displaced a multitude of workers, overturned the economic foundation of the old familial system, and substituted the wage-laborer for the peasant. Yet the development of machinery cannot be understood apart from a legal and political context. Marx analyzes how the implementation of the Factory Acts, beginning in 1835, transformed the character of technical, work, and capital composition.

Thus, we find a dialectic of influence between forces and relations of production, base and superstructure. His qualifications concerning his use of abstractions and his warnings against their dangers and misuse is dramatically evident in a key correspondence regarding the application of historical materialism to non-Western countries. Railing against a critic who misinterpreted his views concerning the question of what path of development Russia should pursue, Marx takes pains to emphasize Russia as a unique social and historical formation that cannot fit unqualifiedly into the context of his theory. Referring to his chapter on primitive accumulation in *Capital,* Marx claims that his intention is only to chart the emergence in Western Europe of the evolution of capitalism feudal society. Thus, he says, the critic wrongly "insists on transforming my historical sketch of the genesis of capitalism in Western Europe into an historic-philosophic theory of the general path of development prescribed by fate to all nations, whatever the historical circumstances in which they find themselves, in order that they may ultimately arrive at the economic system which ensures, together with the greatest expansion of the productive powers of social labour, the most complete development of man". Marx then offers a comparison between subjugation of labor and "big money capital" in Roman and modern times and concludes: "Thus events strikingly analogous but taking place in different historical surroundings led to totally different results. By studying each of these forms of evolution separately and then comparing them one can easily find the clue to this phenomenon, but one will never arrive there by using as one's master key a, general historical philosophical theory, the supreme virtue of which consists in being supra-historical."

We see that Marx struggles against a Eurocentric, universal history that reduces all historical cultures and dynamics to that of the modern West. Against critics like Leff, Marx does not unqualifiedly treat his own categories "as timeless, of universal application to all social phenomena." While in the most general and abstract sense, all societies are organized around production, Marx insists that the forms such production take are very different and that the categories applied to modern bourgeois society cannot be applied unqualifiably to precapitalist societies.

Yet, there are profound ahistorical, Eurocentric, and totalizing dimensions to Marx's analyses. For many critics, Marx's qualifications represent the logical self-destruction of his theory and reveal an inherent reductionist drive to totalize beyond and despite perceived limitations on its historical range. Initiating his categorical rejection of Marxism, Baudrillard asks, "What does it mean to say valid for all epochs but fully applicable only for some'?" Similarly, Balbus asks: "How can the category of production be both historically specific and transhistorical?" and he concludes, "Marx clearly wants to have it both ways: the concept of a mode of production both is and is not a transhistorical category. How is it possible, in other words, that Marx's historically specific categories provide the means to grasp the fundamental dynamics of societies? And does this mean that historical materialism itself is only "fully valid" in capitalist society and only partially valid in all preceding epochs. What sense does it make to say that such a theory is both a general theory of history and of partial applicability to all but a small fraction of that history?

Marx's inconsistencies or contradictions, his qualifying distinctions between different forms of labor, exchange, production, and so on, provide the conceptual and historical basis of his critique of political economy. They allow him to demystify the ideology of political economy that universalizes throughout history categories that apply only to capitalist society, where "labour in reality has here become the means of creating wealth in general and has ceased to be organically linked with particular individuals in any form." It is this "indifference" toward particular kinds of labour that Marx so forcefully exposes, criticizes, and negates in his own work.

It is a virtue of Marx's approach that he historicizes not only the categories of political economy, but those of his own method.

When Marx states, therefore, that the categories of historical materialism are valid for all epochs, but only "fully valid" for some, he is speaking the dialectical language of continuity/discontinuity where the "full validity" of the categories of exchange, labor, and production is realized because capitalist society has abstracted production from a socionatural context and has rid itself of all elements that would hinder the reified goals of exchange value and production for private profit. Consequently, "production" is an abstraction that applies to every social epoch, but only through a "rational" analysis that identifies the specific features of each mode of production. The thrust of Marx's qualifying remarks, therefore, do not logically undermine historical materialism as a methodology, they only oppose dogmatic, a *priori* applications of the theory in abstraction from specific historical contexts.

The problem that arises with Marx's theory is not that his qualifying remarks ensnare him in irresolvable logical antinomies, but that (1) they may be so serious and extensive as to undermine the explanatory power of historical materialism as a general theory of history, as opposed to a theory that applies only or mainly to modern capitalist society, and that (2) "production" is nevertheless coded as the fundamental logic of history. Recent critical work suggests that the "partial validity" of historical materialism vis-a-vis precapitalist societies may be even more partial than Marx thought. Sahlins provides intriguing evidence" that the notion of transhistorical scarcity is a myth and that many early cultures spent the bulk of their time in ritual festival and play. Sahlins also claims that culture and kinship relation are for more important in these societies than Marx allowed. Both Sahlins and Baudrillard argue that Marx imposes a utilitarian means-end logic on precapitalist societies in which exchange is primarily symbolic in character the potlatch or the gift exchange as described by Marcel Mauss. Baudrillard effectively shows that Marx takes use value to be an unproblematic given, relating to innate human needs, when in fact it is a historical construction of societies that have rationalized both subjects and objects.

Giddens argues that materialist categories do not have the structural primacy Marx granted them and he draws a distinction between "class-divided societies" and "class societies." The former category refers to precapitalist societies where classes indeed exist, but "class analysis does not serve as a basis for identifying the basic structural principle of organization of that society." "Class society," in contrast, refers to capitalist society where classes are of fundamental importance in the structuring of society. Habermas argues that Marx conflates material production with symbolic interaction and subsequently misses the fundamental importance of language, communication, and moral development as determinants of historical change. Perry Anderson claims that the forces of production in Asiatic societies were more developed and dynamic than Marx allowed and that Marx's remarks about "peoples with history" suggest an Eurocentric ideology. Bookchin convincingly argues that domination and hierarchy ultimately stem from institutionalized differences of age and sex rather than surplus production and economic classes. Bookchin also claims that Marx has internalized the Western view of nature as stingy inert matter and reproduces the myth of scarcity that requires an antiecological outlook and justifies domination as necessary for social development.

All of these critiques point to the same underlying problem: Marx has falsely universalized categories specific to modern society. Despite his seemingly cautious use of rational abstractions, Marx's theory has reductive and bourgeois dimensions. While Marx analyzes the specificity of different forms of labor and production, he reduces all forms of human interaction and practice to the model of work. Though he is right that all human societies produce the means of their subsistence, he wrongly foists an econometric logic on precapitalist social forms by subsuming a diversity of cultural practices and logics under the concept "mode of production" which *a priori* assigns a primacy to economic values and relationships. His privileging of production over other forms of action and interaction is arbitrary. If, as Lukacs argues, precapitalist societies are an organic whole where "economic elements are inextricably joined to political and religious factors" and "economic and legal categories are objectively and substantively so interwoven as to be inseparable, then it is impossible to justify the claim that material production is primary, "the first historical act" and that the economic is "ultimately" or in "the last instance" the most decisive factor in history. Echoing Lukacs' point, Seidman states that "economic laboring practices always are embedded in a sociocultural and political context that involves normative and legal regulation and structures of institutional and political authority as well as gendered identities and relations." Hence, to privilege economic activity as the "first premise of as human history," as Marx and Engels do, is to succumb to ethnocentric and androcentric prejudices.

Class Struggle and Revolution

The concept of class occupies a central place in marxist theory, though neither Marx nor Engels ever expounded it in a systematic form. In one sense it was the starting point of Marx's whole theory; for his discovery of the proletariat as the idea in the real itself, a new political force engaged in a struggle for emancipation, led him directly to an analysis of the economic structure of modern societies and its process of development. During this period, Engels, from the perspective of political economy, was making the same discovery which he developed in *The Condition of the Working Class in England.* Thus it was the class structure of early capitalism, and the class struggles in this form of society, which constituted the main reference point for Marxist theory of history. Subsequently, the idea of class struggle as the driving force of history was forcefully asserted in the *Communist Manifesto* in a famous phrase, that "the history of monkind is the history of class struggles" but at the same time Marx and Engels recognized that class was a uniquely prominent feature of capitalist societies- even suggesting in the *German Ideology* that 'class itself is a product of the bourgeoisie; and they did not undertake any sustained analysis off the principal classes and class relations in other forms of society. Kautsky, in his discussion of class, occupation and status, had argued that many of the class struggles mentioned in the *Communist Manifesto* were in fact conflicts between status groups and that Marx and Engels were quite aware of this fact since in the same text they observed that in the earlier epochs of history, we find almost everywhere a complicated arrangement of society into various orders, a manifold gradation of social rank', and contrasted this situation with the 'distinctive feature' of the bourgeois epoch, when 'society as whole is more and more splitting up into two great hostile camps, into two great classes directly facing each other-bourgeoisie and proletariat'. Marx argues in general terms that it is always the direct relation between the owners of the conditions of production and the direct producers, which reveals the innermost secret, the hidden foundation, of the entire social edifice.

Most later marxists have followed Marx and Enlgels in concentrating their attention on the class structure of capitalist societies, and they have had to deal with two main questions. The first concerns precisely the complications of social ranking or stratification in relation to the basic classes. In the fragment on 'the three great classes of modern society' which Engels published as the final chapter of *Capital III,* Marx observes that even in England, where the economic structure is most highly and classically developed, intermediate and transitional strata obscure the class boundaries. Elsewhere in the *Theories of Surplus Value* he refers explicitly to the growth of the middle class as a phenomenon of the development of capitalism: 'What [Ricardo] forgets to emphasize is the continual increase in numbers of the middle classes ... situated midway between the workers on one side and the capitalists and landowners on the other". Further on he says again, with respect to Malthus, 'his greatest hope ...is that the middle class will increase in size and the working proletariat will wake up a constantly diminishing proportion of the total population (even if it grows in absolute numbers). That is in fact, the tendency of bourgeois society'. The observations do not fit easily with the idea of an increasing polarization of bourgeois society between 'two great classes'; and since the middle class has continued to grow, marxist social scientists, form Bernstein to Poulantzas, have been obliged repeatedly to examine the political significance of this phenomenon, especially in relation to the socialist movement.

The second question concerns the situation and development of the two principal classes in capitalist society, bourgeoisie and proletariat. In the *18th Brumaire* Marx gave this negative definition of a fully constituted class: 'In so far as millions of families live under economic conditions of existence that separate their mode of life, their interests, and their culture from those of the other classes, and put them in hostile opposition to the latter, they form a class. In so far as there is merely a local interconnection among these small-holding peasants, and the identity of their interests begets no community, no national bond and no political organization among them, they do not form a class.' In *the Poverty of Philosophy* describing the emergence of the working class, Marx expressed the same idea in positive terms: Economic conditions had in the first place transformed the mass of the people into workers. The domination of capital created the common situation and common interests of this class. Thus this mass is already a class in relation to capital, but not yet a class for itself only in the struggle, this mass unites and forms itself into a class for itself. The interests which it defends become class interests. Among later marxists, Poulantzas has rejected this distinction between 'class-in-itself 'and 'class-for-itself', arguing as though classes sprang into existence fully equipped with class consciousness and a political organization, in specific opposition to the view expounded by Lukacs which attributed crucial importance to the development of class consciousness, conceived as being brought to the proletariat from outside by a revolutionary party.

Most marxists, in fact, have recognized that in the case of the working class the development of a 'socialist' or 'revolutionary' consciousness poses problems which require more careful and thorough study. Class interest itself is no longer conceived as an objective and unambiguous social fact but rather as having a sense which is constructed through interaction and discussion out of the experiences of everyday life and the interpretations of those experiences in political doctrines, hence as something which may assume diverse forms, as is indicated in one way by the historical divisions in the working class movement. At one extreme, some marxists have suggested that a distinctive class interest and class-consciousness of the working class is virtually extinct as a consequence of its more or less complete assimilation into advanced industrial society; while others have question fundamentally the view that political action is determined mainly by class relation or have rejected the conception of ruling class interests in an era of comprehensives state regulation of social life. In a less extreme way the socialist movement in advanced capitalist societies has been seen as depending only partly upon the working class, and increasingly upon an alliance of various groups; a position which gains plausibility or the prominence in recent years of new social movements which are not class-based, among them the women's movement, the green movement place movement and diverse ethnic and national movements.

Such questions are, if anything, even more germane to the study of class structure in non-capitalist societies. In the Asiatic society, as Marx defined it, the development of classes, as the principal agents of social change, seems to be excluded by the absences of private property, and the dominant group in this type of society may be seen as comprising not the owners of the means of production but the controllers of the state apparatus. In ancient slave society the lines of actual social conflict is far from clear-though the distinction between master and slave obviously is-and Marx himself referred sometimes to the class struggles between creditors and debtors. There are also difficulties in identifying the social conflicts which led to the decline of feudalism, and marxists have been in substantial disagreement about the part played by class struggles between lords and serfs, and on the other hand, the significance of the emergence of a new class-the town burgesses-and the conflict, which Marx emphasized, between town and a more general issue is that of the place of the peasantry in the class structure and its political role in different types of society. Marx did not regard the peasants of nineteenth-century France as a class in the full sense, still less a revolutionary class; but the socialist revolutions of the twentieth century have taken place mainly in peasant societies, and sections of the peasantry have played an important part in revolutionary movements, as they still do in many Third World countries, although they may often bleed by urban based parties or urban intellectuals.

An issue of a different kind, which has confronted the marxist of the present generation, concerns the emergence of a new class structure in the state socialist societies. In broad terms, two alternative approaches can be distinguished. The first asserts that a new dominant class, stratum or elite has established itself in power. Thus Trotsky, while denying that a new class had appeared in the USSR, regarded the bureaucracy as the ruling group in a degenerated workers' state. The second approach is best exemplified by the transformation of the class structure in Poland in which there has been a gradual disappearance of class differences as a result of the declining importance of the relationship of individuals to the means of production, and that this is accompanied by a diminution in secondary differences related to the nature of work and to attributes of social position such as income, education and access to cultural goods.

The overthrow of the communist dictatorships in Eastern Europe in1989 was accomplished, however, by broad popular coalition rather than by a particular class, and these even indicate that the principal division in the state socialist societies was one between ruling elite of a distinctive type, and the mass of the population which was subordinated to it. This was, therefore, a kind of stratification sui generic, not wholly comparable with other forms of stratification and class structure, though sharing some features with them. The eventual outcome of these revolutions is not yet clear, but in so far as capitalist economies are reintroduced, a class system similar to that in Western Europe will also reemerge, and in some cases has already appeared, along with its political concomitants.

Marxist studies since the end of the nineteenth century have made it abundantly clear that class structure is a much more complex and ambiguous phenomenon than appears from most of the writing it of Marx and Engels, who were greatly influenced in the views by the undoubted salience of class relations in early capitalism, and above all by the irruption into political life of the workingclass movement here-among them the transformations of class structure in capitalist and socialist societies and their political implications, the constitution and role of classes in the Third World, the relation of classes and class struggles to other social groups, including nations, and to other forms of social conflict –remain as a challenge to more profound and rigorous investigations.

In the words of the *Communist Manisfesto:* 'The history of all hitherto existing society is the history of class struggles.' But this thesis has been qualified in various ways since it was first formulated. Engels modified it to refer to written history in order to take account of the early communal societies in which class divisions had not yet emerged. Subsequently Kautsky argued that some of the class struggle mentioned in the *Communist Manifesto* were in fact conflicts between status groups, and that this view conformed with Marx's and Engels's own observation in the same text that pre-capitalist societies were all characterized by 'a manifold gradation of social rank'. In the case of feudal society, for example, there has been disagreement among marxist historians about the nature and significance of class conflict, some complexity of class affiliations and divisions and this came to be the general marxist view-that major classes are most clearly differentiated, class consciousness most fully developed, and class conflict most acute in capitalist society, which constitutes in these respects a culminating point in the historical evolution of class- divided forms of society. Form this perspective modern class struggles have a central importance in Marxist theory, because their outcome is conceived as a transition to socialism; that is, to a classless society.

It is understandable, therefore, that subsequent marxist research and debate should have concentrated to a very great extent upon the development of class conflict in modern times, from the emergence of working-class movements in the nineteenth century to the present day. The crucial issue is whether, over this period, there has in fact been an intensification of class conflict. Within marxism the first to question this idea explicitly-though Marx and Engels had already suggested some doubts in their references to the labour aristocracy and to a more general embargo easement to the working class, at least in Britain-was Bernstein who contended that it was evident by the end of the nineteenth century that a polarization of classes and an intensification of class conflict were not occurring. Among the factors he adduced to explain this changing situation were the growth of the middle class, the growing complexity of the class structure, and rising levels of living; these themes have figured prominently in all subsequent discussions. Recent historical studies have also drawn attention to other features: thus Foster in a study of the labour movement in three nineteenth-century English towns examines in detail the development and decline of a revolutionary class consciousness in the second quarter of the century and explains the decline a result of changes associated with liberalization (extension of the suffrage, growth of mass parties, legal recognition of trade unions) which made possible a predisposition of capitalist authority. Clearly, this is process, which has been repeated, in different forms in later historical periods. A particular problem has always been posed by the development of American society, where neither a mass socialist party nor political class struggles on an extensive scale have ever emerged; and American exceptionalism' has been the object of much sociological analysis, marxist and others since the early years of this century. This situation has led some marxists and other radical thinkers in the USA to make very sweeping revision of marxist theory: for example C. Wright Mills dismissal of the conception of a fundamental class conflict and of the working class as the primary agent of social change as a 'labour metaphysics 'or Marcuse's broadly similar argument about the 'incorporation' of the working class in advanced capitalist society.

Another kind of issue is posed by the conflicts in the socialist countries of Eastern Europe, where it is a matter of deciding whether movements of opposition and rebellions, such as those of 1956 (Hungary), 1989 (Czechoslovakia), or 1981 (Poland), and the upheavals of 1989 were class conflicts, or if not, what social forces they represented. Here the interpretation depends upon a prior judgment about whether there was new ruling class. It is also evident that in some of these societies national struggles have acquired considerable importance and this phenomenon has a much wider significance, for in the western capitalist countries too, in the past few decades, social conflicts have involved not only, or even mainly, classes, but national, ethnic or religious groups, as well as a number of broad social movements-feminist, ecological, anti-nuclear. In the event, the overthrow of the Communist dictatorships in Eastern Europe at the end of 1989 was largely the outcome of a conflict between a ruling elite of a distinctive type and a broad democratice movement, rather than a conflict between classes. Since then, however, new divisions and conflicts have emerged in the post communist societies, to some extent in the form of class conflict as a capitalist economy is re-established, and most dramatically in the growth of increasingly strident nationalist movements.

The task of present-day marxist analysis is to comprehend these diverse struggles in the framework of a consistent theory, and to determine empirically the specific importance of class conflicts in diverse structural and historical conditions. This also involves-as a number of recent marxist studies demonstrate-reexamining class conflict in the late twentieth century, not simply in terms of a confrontation between bourgeoisie and proletariat, but more in terms of alliances between various social groups which on one side dominate and direct economic and social life and on the other side are subordinated and directed.

Class and the Proletariat

In 1852 Marx wrote "No credit is due to me for discovering the existence of classes in modern society nor yet the struggle between them. Long before me bourgeois historians had described the historical development of this class struggle and bourgeois economists the economic anatomy of the classes." What was distinctive to Marx's work on class was its emphasis on the early nineteenth-century socialist idea that one particular class, the proletariat, was a potential agency for the socialist revolution. What Marx did new that was to prove: (1) that the existence of classes is only bound up with particular, historic phases in the development of production; (2) that the class struggles necessarily leads to the dictatorship of the proletariat; (3) that this dictatorship itself only constitutes the transition to the abolition of all classes and to a classless society.

The term proletariat, which can be traced back to ancient Rome and which was revived in the eighteenth and nineteenth-century historical discussions of the Roman Empire, was given a new meaning by Marx. For the Romans, it meant the propertyless people who lacked resources and skills and who could serve their states only by the procreation and rearing of children. Politically, it meant people whose property was insufficient to make them independent of the will of others and who, therefore, were debarred from citizenship rights. The term referred to the unemployed and unemployable for which the state provided bread. Marx first displayed an interest in the proletariat, in his writings of 1843, for precisely the reason that had made previous political thinkers uneasy. Proletarians, though dependent upon their state, lived on its margins and were not integrated into it. By turning to the proletariat, therefore, Marx and other nineteenth-century socialists gave notice that they were proposing previously undreamed of revolutionary changes that could appeal only to people who had nothing to lose.

Marx originally used the term proletariat, in his writings of 1843 and 1844, to refer to the most suffering and the most alienated members of society, the people who were most separated from an independent and cultured existence. But his use of the term became more complex and ambiguous when in the *Communist Manifesto* he used it to refer not to the unemployed and the outcasts, but to the increasing numbers of industrial workers. One reason why Marx emphasized this new proletariat was that he came to see it as the productive class, which made possible the economic and other achievements of capitalism.

Class Struggle and Class Consciousness

'The history of all hitherto existing society is the history of class struggles'—so Marx and Engels confidently assert at the beginning of *The Communist Manifesto*. Unfortunately, Marx does not present us with any detailed discussion of his conception of 'class'. Volume III of *Capital* breaks off just at the point where Marx was to discuss this concept after outlining some of the difficulties involved.

We shall begin with what appear to be certain ambiguities in Marx's conception of 'class'. One problem which confronts anyone attempting to understand what Marx says concerning class is that Marx appears to use the term 'class' both loosely and more technically, the latter when the term is employed specifically in the context of his theory of history. With regard to this, the delimitation of the class of the bourgeoisie does seem clear. The bourgeoisie consists of those who own sufficient capital to live off it, and therefore directly or otherwise, off the surplus-labour of another class. But what are the defining characteristics of the proletariat? There are several possible answers. The proletariat might be that class which does not own sufficient means of production to hire workers and this would accommodate all of the population in the capitalist mode under both its terms; or, on the other hand, the proletariat might be that class which sells its labour.

The difficulty is further compounded by the possibility of an even larger third class arising if the proletariat were to be restricted to those who sell their labour and produce surplus- value. This conception of the proletariat would entail placing all those who sell their labour but do not produce surplus-value (e.g. state school teachers, cashiers, etc.) in a class distinct from both the bourgeoisie and the proletariat.

Now, *The Communist Manifesto* can be seen to bypass these difficulties when it states: 'Our epoch, the epoch of the bourgeoisie, possesses this distinctive feature: it has simplified the class antagonisms. Society as a whole is more and more splitting up into two great hostile camps, into two great classes directly facing each other: Bourgeoisie and Proletariat.' It is clear that, at this time, Marx considered capitalist society to be dividing into the owners of the means of production, and the producers of surplus-product. This does not overcome the theoretical problem of the actual specificity of each class, but it overcomes any practical problem concerning class struggle. Moreover, the various criteria which might be employed to determine one's class would, in this case, make no real difference. The same people would be regarded as proletarian on purely economic and on more sociological grounds.

Unfortunately, there is, if anything, empirical evidence to the contrary of what Marx asserts in this famous passage if a non-binary conception of 'class' is employed. Not only can there be seen to be a decline in the size of the proletariat and a rise in the number of those occupying a third class, but this middle class provides, to a large extent, an area of gradations between those who dominate economically, politically and ideologically, and those who are correspondingly dominated. What is important is that Marx himself, later in his life in *Theories of Surplus Value,* acknowledged the existence of an expanding middle class.

We are not merely confronting Marx with a development which he could not foresee; we are concerned with a development of which he was aware and which needed to be accommodated within his theory. One thing is clear: Marx cannot be employing a binary conception of 'class'. In the *Capital,* where Marx refers to three great classes ('wage-labourers, capitalists and landowners), two of these 'classes', the capitalists and the landowners, might be considered factions of one class, the bourgeoisie. But it is difficult to regard the middle class as a faction of another class when Marx, in *Theories of Surplus Value,* locates it between capitalists and workers. This problem of a growing middle class does not seem to have confronted Marx at the time of writing *The Communist Manifesto*. Consequently, the failure to delimit the proletariat was not important at that time. But with the growth of a middle class acknowledged in later writings, a failure on Marx's part to theorize the middle class and distinguish it accurately from the proletariat constitutes a serious silence.

Hal Draper offers the following definition of 'class' to be understood in the context of Marx's theory of history, rather than as an everyday descriptive term. Classes define themselves not simply in terms of the process of production: they must be defined in relation to surplus production, and specifically in relation to control over the appropriation of the surplus product.

But if we are not careful, this definition readily lends itself to the interpreting of classes in capitalist society in terms of surplus value. Now, it is generally held in Marxist circles that the ruling class is in control of the means of production. John E. Roemer, however, has rebutted the claim that the labour theory of exploitation gives the result that those who benefit by the extraction of surplus value correspond in all relevant cases to those who own the means of production. What is of immense interest in this theory of exploitation and class is that it generates classes of exploiters and exploited for not only feudal and capitalist societies, but socialist ones as well; thus Roemer makes a tremendous advance over earlier marxist approaches to the question of class by appearing to bring within the purview of marxist theory the exploitation which occurs in contemporary socialist societies. Marx's labour theory of value and its correlative theory of exploitation did not provide the conceptual tools to make sense of exploitation in post-capitalist social formations.

Repressive state apparatuses function predominantly through by violence. It distinguishes them from ideological state apparatuses, which function 'by ideology'. But what, here, is 'ideology?' Althusser proposes two theses: first, 'ideology represents the imaginary relationship of individuals to their real conditions of existence' and second, 'ideology has a material existence' because 'an ideology always exists in an apparatus, and its practice, or practices'. As practices are material, to the extent that ideology is located in those practices, ideology is material. The ideological apparatuses, Althusser mentions, are the Church, the media, and the educational institutions: the schools and universities, trode unions and political parties.

But ideology might not just serve to reproduce an inegalitarian economic system; real inequality might be generated by and within ideological institutions. For example, confession is an activity situated within Catholic Church. This institution is located, not at the economic, nor at the political, but at the ideological level. Yet the power to hear confession, like the power of excommunication, gave the Church considerable political power. Moreover, for payment, the clergy could reduce the time an individual would ostensibly have to spend in purgatory. This ability to extract payment contributed to the wealth of the Church. And real inequality could arise within the Church because bishops could, for example, add to their private wealth by selling ecclesiastical preferment.

What, one might ask, has any of this to do with our conception of 'class'? Well, it is our thesis that because ideology has institutional manifestations, inequality is often not confined to the economic sphere alone, but is often located in the ideological one as well. The relations within ideological institutions must be given adequate weighting when one seeks to theorize the reproduction of social inequalities. The same can be said for the relations within political institutions. This means that Poulantzas's is correct to utilize ideological and political criteria, as well as economic, to determine the class which has the potential to engage in revolutionary activity. Poulantzas notion of 'class' is that, classes are situated in class struggle: 'Social classes coincide with class practices, i.e, the class struggle, and are only defined in their mutual opposition". Poulantzas's basic conclusion is that only manual, non- supervisory workers who produce surplus value directly (productive labour) is the proletariat. Other categories of wage-labourers (unproductive employers, mental labour, supervisory labour) must be placed in a separate class either the 'new' petty bourgeoisie, or in the case of managers, the bourgeoisie itself.

In *What is to be Done*? Lenin argues that the working class, left to itself, is so immersed an capitalist life that the form of struggle which it can take is restricted to wage demands. Left by itself, it is only capable of achieving a 'trade union consciousness' and cannot see the situation as a whole. It cannot step outside of its relations with the bourgeoisie in order to conceive of the possibility of transcending capitalist society. Lenin calls the revolutionary perspective which can conceive of transcending capitalism: 'social democratic consciousness'. But where can this consciousness come from? Genuine revolutionary thought comes not out of the proletarian, but out of the bourgeois intellectuals who side with the working class. Lenin goes so far as to quote Kautsky approvingly: 'Modern socialist consciousness can arise only on the basis of profound scientific knowledge. The vehicle of science is not the proletariat, but the bourgeois intelligentsia'. The intellectuals who attain a position of theoretical eminence in the revolutionary party are the source of revolutionary ideas and strategy.

The party serves the function of organizing the revolutionary struggle of the proletariat. Lenin maintains that the party is to be led by 'professional' revolutionaries: '...the organizations of revolutionaries must consist first, foremost and mainly of people who make revolutionary activity their profession'. These revolutionaries are to be maintained by the party, a body which does not produce a surplus-product nor, as a consequence, surplus-value. Clearly, they live on the surplus- labour of the proletariat.

Moreover, the most obvious role taken by the party leaders is that of supervising the revolutionary activity of the working class. Lenin was of the opinion that the proletariat is locked in an economic struggle with the bourgeoisie, and will tend, as a result, to see the solution of its problems within the context of the present economic order—higher wages, etc. Lenin thus considers the workers incapable, on their own, of achieving anything other than a 'trade union consciousness'. As a result, action instigated by the masses themselves will not be of a consciously revolutionary form. The spontaneous upsurge of the workers must, therefore, be opposed and replaced by revolutionary activity directed by the party. Lenin's whole approach rests on an elitist attitude towards the proletariat, which he felt needed the non-proletarian intelligentsia to lead it. And the 'iron discipline' which he advocated in the party leaves no room for doubt what 'leadership' means here.

Clearly, the question of class consciousness cannot be divorced from epistemological issues. Lukacs faces up to this squarely, and develops his theory from a specific epistemological standpoint. True to Marx, Lukacs is of the view that conceptions of the world are related to class position. Each class position will, according to the theory, generate its own worldview and, corelatively, its own knowledge. This presents us with sociology of knowledge, which appears at first glance to leave us with a relativist account of truth. However, Lukacs wishes to establish that the 'truths' of the proletariat are in some way superior to those of the bourgeoisie.

What might enable the dichotomy to be overcome is the experimenting activity of the subject as a result of which it comes to ascertain its objective nature. Here, in praxis, lies Lukacs' final attempt to demonstrate the superiority of proletarian knowledge. However, the bourgeoisie is also capable of such activity. Only when one overrates the nature of the proletariat as an object of the historical process does its subjective praxis seem to overcome the subject/object distinction in a way, which is unavailable to the bourgeoisie. Thus, proletarian knowledge is superior because it is not merely reflective, but based on historical activity in the world, and in tune with the process of change within the historical totality. Theory and action are united in revolutionary praxis. It is, however, difficult not to notice that, despite its supposed unique epistemological position, no significant revolutionary theory has arisen amongst the proletariat.

We have also seen that Marxist/Leninist conceptions of revolutionary organization maintain political and ideological domination by retaining supervisory roles and notions of privileged access to knowledge. We have further seen that the term 'class consciousness' is employed to facilitate such domination over the workers. It is not what the workers think, but what the party leaders think they ought to think that constitutes the revolutionary consciousness 'imputed' to the workers. This expose of political and ideological domination enables us to explain why the former Soviet Union had a class system in the past. It is due not to any Stalinist deviation, but to the class structure in Leninist revolutionary praxis, which is carried forward to post-revolutionary institutions.

The Dictatorship of the Proletariat

The collisions between individual workers and individual bourgeoisie take more and more the character of collisions between two classes. Thereupon the workers begin to form trade unions against the bourgeois; they club together in order to keep up the rate of wages; they found permanent associations in order to make provision beforehand for these occasional revolts.

At this stage, the struggle always goes against the workers; but each new struggle has the effect of drawing together workers in various industries and in different localities, until the focus of organization is no longer the trade union but instead the Communist Party. As a political party, workers compel recognition of their interest, for example, in limiting the length of the working day. Ultimately, however, they cannot be satisfied with such half-measures. Eventually, "the more or less veiled civil war, raging within existing society...breaks out into open revolution, and....the violent overthrow of the bourgeoisie lays the foundation for the sway of the proletariat". The final defeat of the bourgeoisie is called by Marx "winning the battle of democracy" for democracy is the rule of the people, and the proletariat is the people.

All previous historical movements were movements of minorities, or in the interest of minorities. The proletarian movement is the self-conscious, independent movement of the immense majority, in the interests of the immense majority. We have seen above that the first step in the revolution by the working class is to raise the proletariat to the position of ruling class, to win the battle of democracy. The proletariat will use its political supremacy to wrest, by degrees, all capital from the bourgeoisie, to centralize all instruments of production in the hands of the state, i.e., of the proletariat organized as the ruling class, and to increase the total productive forces as rapidly as possible. According to Marx, political power is inherently an expression of class supremacy. When the proletariat wins political control, it must use the power of the state against the minority which has previously used it against the majority. Nor dare it hesitate to act, and act decisively. In effect, it must set up a dictatorship to rule until the old order has been destroyed and conditions have been prepared for the establishment of a truly socialistic society. For this reason, Marx approved the slogan of the Paris revolutionaries of 1848, "Overthrow of the bourgeoisie! Dictatorship of the working class".

Justice

Until quite recently there was little overt or extended theoretical reflection about: the place that principles of justice occupy within marxist thought. Two conflicting attitudes as often as not in tension under the same pen—have been common in the tradition: on the one hand, explicit, sometimes fervent, disavowals of any reliance on considerations of justice, as being irrelevant to the case for socialism and against capitalism; on the other hand, a widespread use in practice of arguments precisely from justice, unreflectively or unknowingly yet time and again resorted to in Marxist social criticism.

From the early 1970s, however, an intensive interest among philosophers in the concept of distributive-justice began to leave its imprint on the discussion of Marx's ideas, generating considerable exegetical literature, itself polarized in accordance with the two traditionally conflicting attitudes. Principles of distributive justice concern the proper division of benefits and burdens within a society or other collectivity. Did Marx condemn capitalism in the light of any such principles?

Many say that he did not. They cite: (1) his insistence in the *Capital* that the wage relation, as an exchange of equivalent values (labour power for the wage), involves no injustice to the worker; (2) Marx's polemic in *Critique of the Gotha Programme,* against socialist appeals to notions of 'fair distribution or 'right'; (3) his view that standards of right and justice are infernal to specific modes of production and, as such, historically relative; and (4) his characterization of morality in general as ideological, part of a dependent, changing superstructure.

Proponents of this viewpoint argue further: (5) that to impute to Marx a care for justice bends his meaning towards a narrow concern with reforming the sphere of distribution in come differentials, wage levels and the like wherein fact his aim was more fundamental and revolutionary, the transformation of production and property relations; (6) that the imputation denatures, also, his effort to identify the real historical forces leading to the overthrow of capitalism, substituting a project of ethical enlightenment he would himself have dubbed idealist; (7) that, as a juridical principle, justice could not anyway be implemented in a com monist society, which Marx conceived as having no juridical apparatuses of state and law; and (8) that his vision of communism excluded those circumstances (of scarcity and conflict) which render norms of justice necessary, anticipating instead a distributive standard (To each according to their needs') which lay beyond justice. (9) If Marx did condemn 'capitalism, finally, he did so, on this interpretation, in the light of values other than justice: primarily, freedom and self-realization.

Other commentators believe Marx did criticize capitalism as unjust. They argue: (1) that his description of the wage relation as an exchange of equivalents was merely provisional, applying to the sphere of circulation—and followed by a characterization of the production process in which he displayed that relationship as in truth exploitative: not a genuine exchange at all but appropriation by the capitalist of unpaid surplus labour; (2) that notwithstanding his own polemics against moralistic criticism, he presented exploitation as wrongful or unfair, calling it 'robbery' and theft; (3) that by ranking, in *Critique of the Gotha Programme* the principle of distribution according to need above the principle of distribution according to work and this in turn above the distributional norms of capitalism, Marx proffered, implicitly, trans historical, non-relative criteria of moral ordering, a sort of hierarchy of standards of distributive justice; and (4) that his apparent statements of moral relativism expressed, in fact, a moral realism, specifying the material conditions necessary for achieving 'higher' standards of fairness, rather than denying that such historically transcendent ethical judgements could be made.

In addition, these commentators contend, (5) a concern with distribution is not intrinsically reformist, since, broadly conceived, distribution covers the most general division of social goods and beds, including the ownership of productive resources a revolutionary preoccupation indeed. (6) Equally, while Marx did not think that moral criticism by itself was sufficient, still, as a complement to materialist historical analysis of the potential agencies of change, it had a place in his thought. (7) Categorizing principles of justice as juridical is too narrow; they can be envisaged also, independently of any instruments of coercion, as simply ethical principles for evaluating and determining the allocation of social benefits and burdens. (8) To each according to their needs' is such a principle, a norm of distributive justice, its aim an equal right to self-realization; even though viewed by Marx as to be achieved with the disappearance of coercive state apparatuses. (9) The distinction made in the opposing interpretation, finally, between his views of justice and of freedom, is exegetically arbitrary: so far as Marx did sometimes belittle ethical criticism or characterize moral norms as being historically limited or relative, freedom and other values figured alongside justice amongst his targets.

Partly because he was no moral philosopher, and indeed impatient with ethical advocacy and analysis, partly because of his play with 'dialectical' contradictions in expounding the nature of the wage relation, it is not possible to render all of Marx's ideas in this area consistent with one another. A resolution of the controversy requires some effort of intellectual reconstruction, an attempt to make the best sense that can be made of his various viewpoints. The most cogent such reconstruction broadly vindicates those who say Marx did think capitalism unjust.

Some sense can be made of the apparent evidence to the contrary; whereas no satisfactory answer has been given to the questions, which trouble the opposing interpretation. For, first, there is no persuasive account of why Marx should have described exploitation as 'robbery' if he did not see it as a wrong. Second, that he condemned the unfreedoms rather than the injustices of capitalism poses a spurious alternative: concerned, as he was, with the distribution of freedom, his criticism in this matter was itself a critique of injustice. Third, though obscured by some of what Marx himself says, the principle 'to each according to their needs' is both a principle of moral equality and if we construe the notion of communist abundance in any realistic fashion— a norm of distributive justice.

On the other hand, Marx's express refusal to offer criticism in terms of justice is explicable as being due to the narrow conception of this value which he overtly entertained: a conception associating justice with internal to a given social norms, moreover, covering most limited sense: distribution of consumption goods. But these two conceptual associations are not obligatory. Marx thought capitalism injust. Implicitly, his critique was a critique of social injustice.

State

The concept of state is an important category in marxist thought, for marxists regards the state as the institution whose function is to maintain and defend class domination and exploitation. The classical marxist view is expressed in the famous formulation of Marx and Engels in the *Communist Manifesto*: 'The executive of the modern state is but a committee for managing the common affairs of the whole bourgeoisie.' This is a more complex statement than it appears at first sight; it does represent the core proposition of marxism on the subject of the state.

Marx himself never attempted a systematic analysis of the state. But his first lengthy piece of writing after his doctoral dissertation, namely *Critique of Hegel's*

Philosophy of Right is in large part concerned with the state; and the subject occupies an important place in many of his works, notably in his historical writings, for instance in *Class Struggles, in France*(1985), *18th Burmaire* (1852) and *Civil War in France* (1871). Engels too deals at length with the state in many of his wirings, for instance in *Anti-Duhring* (1878) and in *Origin of the Family Private Property and the State* (1894).

One of Lenin's most famous pamphlets, *State and Revolution*, written on the eve of the Bolshevik revolution, was intended as a restatement of the marxist theory of the state against the Second International 'revisionism'; and others in the marxist tradition have been concerned with the state, most notably, Gramsci. But it is only since the 1960s that the state has become a major field of investigation and debate within marxism. This relative neglect may be attributed in part to the general impoverishment of marxist thought produced by the predominance of Stalinism from the later 1920s, to the late 1950s; and also to an overeconomist' bias which tended to allocate a mainly 'derivative' and 'superstructural' role to the state, and to see it, unproblematically, as the mere servant of dominant economic classes. Much of the recent work on the state has, on the contrary, been concerned to explore and explain its 'relative autonomy' and the complexities, which attend its relationship to society.

The classical Marxist definitions of politics and the state appear to place their main emphasis on the centrality of coercion. Tucker expresses a widely held view when he says that 'the state is seen in classical marxism as fundamentally a repressive force'. Miliband's presentation of politics in *The Communist Manifesto* as the 'organised power of one class for oppressing another' stands as Marx's 'primary view' and there can be little doubt that comments of this kind abound in the classical writings, whether we think of *Civil War in France* where the state is depicted as 'a public force for social enslavement.. an engine of class despotism'. Marx's jottings on Bakunin refer to the need for the proletariat to employ 'coercive' measures, or Engels's pithy definition of the state as 'a special repressive face'. Engels also tells Bebel even under socialism, the state is only necessary 'to hold down one's adversaries by force'. A social movement becomes political, comments Marx, when it assumes a form 'possessing general, socially coercive force'. In an exhaustive account of Marx's views on politics and bureaucracy, Draper locates the essence of the state in 'institutionalized forcible coercion'. Jessop argues that Lenin is guilty of one-sided emphasis on the repressive role of the state. It is a problem for the whole classical marxist tradition.

The question is rather more complicated. If there is widespread agreement that an emphasis on politics-as-coercion is a prominent and even predominant strand in classical marxism, the argument is also advanced that Marx embraced another and quite different view of the state. The most frequently cited sources of this claim are Plamenatz and Sanderson who found alongside Marx's view of the state as organized coercion, a theory of the state 'as a parasite on the whole of society' and it is this 'other' theory, it is argued, which should caution us against discussing the marxian state purely in terms of class oppression. Miliband gave this argument a qualified endorsement and Richard Hunt has clamed that the two rival concepts, the parasite state and the class state, can be found side by side within individual passages in Marx and Engels's political writings. In Tucker, we encounter the problem of an unresolved tension, if not outright contradiction, between the state as alienated social power and the state as organ of class rule. Maguire has even argued for three concepts of the state in Marx : a 'servile' state; a 'dominant' state and a 'pretentious' state in which servility aspires to domination.

Now this line of argument clearly implies that Marx's view of politics is not nearly as narrow as it might at first appear. It hints at a wider conception of the state which Jessop, echoing the formulations of Poulantzas, characterizes as the factor of social cohesion in the social formation and it is a point which has an important bearing on the problem of consent. If the state in Marx and Engels is conceived both as a 'social power' and 'a factor of social cohesion' and an organ of class coercion, then 'space' is provided for precisely those ideological and cultural dimensions apparently absent from the coercive definitions. In so far as Marx and Engels suggest that the state has a role to play as a socially necessary institution, they anticipate, argues Jessop, Gramsci's subsequent analysis of 'hegemony' : the exercise of moral and intellectual leadership aiming at winning the 'active consent' of the dominated. This broad hint makes it possible to break with what Poulantzas has called the 'ideologically contaminated' schema of the state 'as the tool or instrument of the dominant classes', since the other theory of politics, the state as a cohesive factor with economic, ideological and political functions, lays the basis for an end to 'reductionism' and the development of the conception of the 'relative autonomy' of the capitalist state.

While Western marxists in the Althusserian/Poulantzian tradition locate the broader view in Marx's later writings, and particular emphasis is placed upon the analysis of Bonapartism in the *Eighteenth Brumaire,* whereas 'exegetists' like Richard Hunt and Maguire find a 'dominant/parasite' state in Marx's earliest writings, both sets of commentators are agreed on the absence of a 'homogeneous marxism' on the presence of 'discontinuities and disjunctions, incompleteness and indeterminacy' in Marx's theory of the state.

The young Marx was steeped in the traditions of the French Revolution and the Enlightenment. He consciously identified his standpoint with what he called the 'ever new philosophy of reason' as a philosophy which extended back to Heraclitus and Aristotle, embracing in the sweep of its development, Machiavelli and Campanella, Hobbes, Spinoza and Grotius, Rousseau, Fichte and, of course, Hegel. This philosophy, particularly in its recent form, looks upon the state, declared Marx grandly, 'as the great organism, in which legal, moral and political freedom must be realised, and in which the individual citizen in obeying the laws of the state only obeys the natural laws of his own reason, of human reason'. At the heart of this 'great organism' lies consent. The individual, in obeying the state, obeys his own reason.

Like Arnold Ruge and the other Hegelian radicals of his day, the young Marx held the view that Hegel's defence of monarchy, bureaucracy and the principle of representation by estates gravely compromised his own ideals. Hence in the pages of the news papers he briefly edited, he attacked censorship and anti-peasant legislation as practices perverting the community-based ideal of the rational state. What has happened, Marx protests, is that a mere part of the state, the 'government', has usurped the wider role of the state and, in the case of laws preventing peasants from collecting firewood, government has degraded the structure of the state into 'an instrument of the forest owner'. Every citizen becomes the victim of 'vexatious bullying' and in permitting forest owners even to levy their own fines, the government is prepared to allow a 'material problem' to be handled in a 'non-political way' i.e. without any connection with 'the whole of the reason and morality of the state'.

These passages are of great interest because they indicate that the young Marx does not merely have an ethical view of the state as an expression of 'universality', a general will, but that, alongside this view, there stands a coercive, instrumentalist conception of politics. It is true that this coercive instrumentalism is in conflict with what Marx sees as the concept of the modern state a perversion of its rational ideal. Richard Hunt, noting the passage cited above in which Marx speaks of the degradation of the state to an instrument of private interest, criticizes the 'rash inference' of those who see in this kind of sentiment the inception of Marx's theory of government as an 'organ of class domination'. It is certainly true that for the time being, partisan coercion does contradict Marx's 'ideal' state in which the coercive activities of ruling, judging, taxing and administering are seen as 'free creations of the spirit' and 'dissolved at every moment in the unity of the whole'. Nevertheless Marx's reference to the state as 'a servant of the forest owner' does establish the existence of a coercive instrumentalism, which, although presented as the perversion of an ideal, clearly anticipates his later position.

Indeed, when Marx comes to write his *Critique of Hegel's Philosophy of Right*, there is a significant shift in his view of politics. Whereas previously he had spoken of the illegitimate acts of government as 'non-political', contrary to the spirit of politics as the interests of the community as a whole, now the term 'politics' tends to be used in a pejorative way. Thus Hegel is criticized for confusing the state 'as the whole of the existence of the people' with the 'political state' which, Marx tells us, merely represents 'the nature of the modern State as it is' and is unacceptable because it presupposes a fixed 'antithesis' between state and civil society. Private property predominates and the police, judiciary and administration act not as the deputies of civil society itself, 'in and through whom it administers its own general interest', but rather as the 'representatives of the state for the administration of the state over and against civil society'. The 'political state', declares Marx, 'rules without really ruling' and in a 'true democracy', it will necessarily be 'annihilated'.

In the *Jewish Question* the distinction between a 'true state' and a 'political state' completely falls away. The term 'political' is employed pejoratively throughout so that while Marx sees political emancipaiton as 'a big step forward' it is not 'real, practical emancipation'. Human emancipation is only accomplished when social power no longer stands outside the individual as political power and the 'abstract citizen' is reabsorbed into the real man. All states are now theological notions. This is especially true of the democratic state and there is therefore no further reference to a 'true democracy' which avoids the religiosity of the 'political state'. Since, as Marx puts it, 'the existence of religion is the existence of a defect, the source of this defect can only be sought in the nature of the state itself, even if this 'theological' nature only stands revealed when the political state exists 'in its completely developed form'. Whereas in the *Critique* the 'true state' had been identified as an 'actual political society' now Marx argues that the 'political character of civil society' has been 'abolished' as the political spirit is withdrawn from society and is gathered up and established as 'the sphere of the community, the general concern of the nation, ideally independent of those particular elements of civil life'. The democratic state perfects this process of separating the general from the particular so that to the idealism of the state with its 'abstract, artificial man', there corresponds the materialism of civil society with its man of egoism.

These passages are of remarkable importance. On the one hand, politics is conceived of as an instrument of financial power and yet, on the other, it is presented as 'an illusory sovereignty' – an abstract community as 'spiritual' in relation to civil society as heaven is to earth. It is precisely at this point in the development of Marx's political thought that we can see what has happened to those 'broader', universalistic conceptions of his 'youth'. They have not simply been rejected : they have been absorbed so that they invest the partisan, 'instrumental' character of the state with an apparent or illusory communality.

Marx and Engels do not present the state simply as the servant of private interests. The state stands as the servant of the private in the name of the public. It is an instrument of the 'particular', given the fact that the slavery of civil society provides the natural foundation on which the modern state rests. But it is more than this. It is the instrument of the particular expressed as the general, the servant of individual interests presenting themselves in universal terms. The cause of equality among men is defended, so that the cause of inequality among them can be acknowledged as fundamental and absolute. Everything is upside down. The state as a class instrument coexists uneasily with the state as social power that, for Marx, is a consequence not of theoretical inconsistency, but of the nature of politics itself.

The two sides, partisan instrumentality and universal pretension, ideology and force, coercion and consent are indissolubly fused together in 'the self-conceit of the political sphere'. Thus when Marx speaks in 1844 of the state as 'the active, conscious and official expression' of the present structure of society – a comment echoed in the polemic against Proudhon – it is clear that particular class interests can only be served if they are projected in this 'active, conscious and official' universalistic way. Marx, in *The Holy Family*, speaks of the ruling bourgeoisie acknowledging the state as 'the official expression of its own exclusive power and the political recognition of its own special interests. Every class aiming at domination, Marx comments, 'must first conquer political power in order to represent its interest in turn as the general interest.' A class unable to present its particular interests in general terms, would be unable to rule : it would be unable to convert its social power into a power which could be properly called political.

The Special Instrument of Coercion

It should be clear therefore that Marx does not merely view politics as coercion. 'Mixed up' with this coercion is consent, a sense of community, a belief in brotherhood, a universal citizenship. In other words, when we examine the way in which Marx did develop a coercive concept of politics, what transpires is the fact that this is a coercion of a most peculiar kind. It is a coercion which is concentrated in the hands of the state, generalized in its scope and presented ideologically as a force for the 'common good'. It is public and official, organized and legitimate. It claims to act in the interests of society as a whole.

From this it must follow that political coercion cannot be reduced to mere 'physical force'. Politics involves a physical force with an ideological character, a coercion that commands consent and this is a point, which commentators sympathetic to a coercion-oriented view of politics often miss. Draper, for example, is somewhat taken aback that Engels, after describing the state as a body of armed men, prisons and coercive institutions of all kinds, should also comment that 'the state presents itself to us as the first ideological power over man'. This is why Marx and Engels invariably speak of the state as an 'organized' coercion, a 'public' force, an 'official' expression of class rule: a 'negative' coercion which receives its 'positive' endorsement from society at large. A state, which, as Draper says, 'maintains itself exclusively by the naked application of forcible suppression' is not only 'precarious and expensive': it cannot serve the general interests of a ruling class. Bereft of even an illusory commonality, it would be unable to functin as an instrument of class domination. Marx not only has a broad view of politics, he also has a synthetic one. But it might be thought that while Marx's broad view of politics as coercion fused with consent is relevant to the modern liberal democratic state, it cannot apply to explicitly authoritarian political systems and that where parliamentary procedures, civil liberties, competing political parties and a free suffrage are absent, the concept of the state as pure coercion still stands.

It is of course a highly abnormal situation when, as Marx says of the French bourgeoisie after 1851, 'its own interests dictate that it should be delivered from the danger of its own rule' – that in order to preserve 'its social power intact, its political power must be broken'. Logically, Marx argues, bourgeois interests find their 'pure political expression' in the parliamentary regime. Why then does the bourgeoisie itself demand that its own 'bourgeois parliament must, first of all, be laid to rest' ? That, in order to continue exploiting other classes, it too must be condemned to 'similar political nullity'. The answer to this Bonapartist paradox cannot be found unless the relationship between the 'normal' parliamentary form and the 'exceptional', authoritarian state is properly understood. If the liberal democratic republic is, for Marx and Engels, 'the logical form of bourgeois rule', it is also a potentially dangerous one. The desire to be freed from the logical form of its own rule arises in situations where, as in the case of the first Napoleon, the bourgeoisie are too strong. But the movement from one state-form to the other is only possible because in both sets of circumstances, the state acts as the generalized expression, an ideologically charged instrument of bourgeois class rule.

The State as a Class Instrument

The idea of the state as a class instrument is most notably stated in Marx and Engels' comment in the *Communist Manifesto* that 'the executive of the modern state is but a committee for managing the common affairs of the whole bourgeoisie'. Here the state is regarded as a direct representative of the economically dominant class. In particular, the state is regarded as an instrument of coercion and administration that backs up the exploitation of labour by capital with coercion and control in the political sphere. Marx talks of 'the instrument of that class rule – the state, the centralized and organized government power'.

One well-known instrumentalist interpretation of Marx is Ralph Miliband's *The State in Capitalist Society*, which argues:

> In the Marxist scheme, the 'ruling class' of capitalist society is that class which owns and controls the means of production and which is able, by virtue of the economic power thus conferred upon it, to use the state as its instrument for the domination of society.

In particular, the instrumentalist view stresses the fact that the state is a coercive instrument that can be used as a tool by the ruling class to gain political acceptance of its economic power. The criticism of this view is that by stressing coercion it leaves little room for a sophisticated account of how consent is achieved through more subtle means. A theory of consent would also recognize that a diverse range of interests needs to be appealed to, whereas the instrumentalist view tends to assume that the two main classes are fairly cohesive and that they act on clear interests. In Miliband this instrumentalist view of the state is combined with elite theory, which is used to show how the ruling class can rely on the selection of a reliable state personnel who will serve their interests.

Miliband argues that Marx and Engels 'never departed from the view that the state was above all the coercive instrument of a ruling class'. However, this view might be questioned by some of Marx's historical studies. Marx's writings on the regime of Louis Bonaparte suggest that, because of rival factions within the ruling class, the French state rose above these differences and assumed a more autonomous nature under the authoritarian control of a single dictator. Indeed, Miliband himself draws parallels between this situation and that of fascist Germany, where promised to defend its economic interests, but over which it had no genuine control. However, the instrumentalist view of the state might also be questioned by events at the other end of the class spectrum. These were the events surrounding the Paris Commune of 1870 when the workers of Paris rose up and established their own regime. The aim of the Commune was to abolish private property and establish a socialized system of production under the control of a democratically elected government. However, the economic ruling class eventually managed to bloodily suppress the Commune and re-establish its own dictatorship.

Although Marx's study of these events contains many instrumentalist metaphors, *The Civil War in France* contains the important statement explaining the failure of the Commune that 'the working class cannot simply lay hold of the ready-made state machinery, and wield it for its own purposes'. This indicates that although sections of the capitalist class may seek to use the state as their own instrument, it cannot be used by just any social group. The working class cannot, therefore, use the existing state as an instrument for its own rulership. Rather, it must smash the existing state and establish a new one that is better suited to defending a system of common ownership what becomes known as the dictatorship of the proletariat. This suggests that the state is more than just an instrument of the dominant group or class but has a more deeply inscribed character based on its relation to the economic system. In other words, the capitalist state is capitalist not simply because it is under the control of the bourgeois class but because of its intrinsic relationship to the capitalist system. This explains why it is possible for groups like the fascists, Bonapartists, Islamic populists and other sections of the petite bourgeoisie to come to power without threatening the overall class character of the state which remains capitalist. This view of the state has a functional rather than an instrumental emphasis based on its relation to the mode of production.

The State as a Guarantor of Social Cohesion

This third position sees the state as a guarantor of social cohesion. In particular, it recognizes that cohesion within society is not guaranteed by economic developments, but that the state must act as a mediator between the economic and political spheres. The state becomes historically necessary once society moves beyond a basic subsistence level of production. Its development may well be linked to the rise of class society; however, it might be also argued that, regardless of this fact, the state also has a socially necessary function in relation to such factors as the distribution of surplus product, the regulation of different interests and the mediation of different conflicts. It argues that the state must function in the best interests of the economic mode of production – that is, under capitalism, the state must act in accordance with the demands of private property and the market economy.

This can be seen in Marx's study of France in *the Eighteenth Brumaire of Louis Bonaparte.* Here capitalism was raven by different factional interests which in turn had different political representatives – for example the financial bourgeoisie was represented by the Orleanist monarchy. Marx argues that under Louis Philippe and the parliamentary republic the state was the instrument of the ruling class, but under Louis Bonaparte it seemed to attain an autonomous position. He then goes on to add that Bonaparte does in fact represent a social class as well, but this class is that of the small peasant and not the ruling class. This clearly goes against the view that the state is simply the instrument of the economically dominant class. In fact, Marx argues that the ruling class had lost its vocation to rule. Into this void steps the figure of Bonaparte, causing Marx to remark that 'France therefore seems to have escaped the despotism of a class only to fall back beneath the authority of an individual'.

The conclusion to be drawn from this study is that the Bonapartist state was necessary in order to hold things together when class and factional conflicts could not be resolved. So power fell into the hands of the state executive, which assumed an autonomous or parasitic character. However, although the state arose above the different factions of the ruling class, it was still required to respond to the overall needs to capitalist development. Although the case of Louis Bonaparte is an exceptional one, this view of the state as a factor of social cohesion can be applied more generally to describe the process whereby the state seeks to resolve or contain the conflicts between different groups and interests in order to protect the general needs of the economic system – to resolve class conflicts in order to further capitalist interests. Such a view, can be found in the work of Nicos Poulantzas, who draws on Gramsci's notion of 'hegemony' to show how the state attempts to hold the social order together – to resolve social conflicts and secure consent. This indicates that the functioning of the capitalist economy is not guaranteed but has to be socially secured and that it is the state that attempts to perform this necessary function.

This is the clearest case of a political or state-centred rather than economic process of social cohesion to be drawn from Marx's work. Nevertheless, Perry Anderson has argued that Marx's work still suffers from being too narrowly focused on a peculiar dictatorial state and that he failed to analyse the British parliamentary state under which he lived. Marx tends to generalize Bonapartism as a typical rather than exceptional form of state. The result is that Marx never produced any coherent or comparative account of the political structures of bourgeois class power at all. This lack of sufficient material on the political structures of bourgeois class power means it is necessary to supplement Marx's views on the state with a more developed position on the operation of bourgeois democracy and the institutional complexity and durability of the modern state. Anderson and Poulantzas both turn to Gramsci in order to develop this position.

Finally, Engels' book *The Origin of the Family, Private Property and the State* has also been influential in historically situating the rise of the state and linking it to the growth of class society and the development of the family. Engels argues that the state has not existed from all eternity and that there have been early societies that did without state power. However, 'at a certain stage of economic development, which necessarily involved the split of society into classes, the state became a necessary because of this split'. This occurs once human labour is able to produce more than is necessary for the maintenance of the producers, so the state is linked to the production, protection and distribution of this surplus. Most generally, the state is an organization of the possessing class for its protection against the non-possessing class, the means by which the most powerful economic class becomes the politically dominant class. Thus the ancient state was, above all, the state of the slave-owners for holding down the slaves, just as the feudal state was the organ of the nobility for holding down the peasant serfs and bondsmen, and the modern representative state is an instrument for exploiting wage labour by capital.

Most interesting is the link Engels makes to the institution of the family, an aspect of society neglected by Marx. He argues that the emergence of private property requires a monogamous nuclear family, which is capable of organizing the inheritance of private property by producing children of undisputed parentage and guaranteeing the supremacy of the male line. With this comes the increased exploitation of women since household management now becomes a private affair and the wife becomes the chief servant of the household. While the man becomes the main wage-labourer, the woman of the family is confined to domestic slavery.

Thus, Engels shows how the division of labour within society is more than just a class issue but is also linked to a system of patriarchal relations. If classical marxism is strong on questions of class conflict, it is often weak on other issies of social division such as those based on gender and race. More recently, some feminist scholars have attempted to develop aspects of Engels' analysis and move marxism away from a simple class-based analysis to gender - based analysis in order to examine other forms of social division and conflict and other structures of domination such as the patriarchal one.

Relative Autonomy of the State

Many sholars have argued that the notion of 'relative autonomy' of the state acting 'on behalf of' the bourgeoisie rather than 'at its behest' is central to Marx's political theory, even in the case of the liberal state-form. Hence the celebrated formula of the *Communist Manifesto*, so often characterized as narrowly instrumentalist, is much more broadly ideological than is often assumed, for consider the implications of asserting that "the executive of the modern state is but a committee for managing the common affairs of the whole bourgeoisie'. Politics is clearly a separate sphere, which embodies the general interests of the bourgeoisie because, as individual members of their class, they are divided among themselves. A general form has to be given to average interests. While the individual law injures the capitalist, 'the whole fabric protects his interests and hence this is the crucial point that the bourgeoisie needs a state because, as individuals, they cannot directly rule themselves. Nor do they really want to. Buying and selling, investing and accumulating are economic activities which have seemingly been withdrawn from the state's sphere of operaion. The bourgeoisie, says Engels, 'turns the power of government against the proletariat and keeps out of its way as far as possible' and this makes it entirely understandable that a division of labour should be involved between a class and its political representatives.

This division of labour is not just a characteristic of the exceptional form of the state where the 'extra-parliamentary mass of the bourgeoisie' turn to adventures like Bonaparte: it is a general feature of political rule. Even the gulf between parliamentary representatives and the class they represent is real: a situation in which according to their education and their individual position the two may be separated as widely 'as heaven from earth'. When Engels comments that normally the state of 'the most powerful, economically dominnat class' is also 'the politically dominant class as well', this should not be taken to mean that the capitalists 'hold political office while accumulating profits in a way which gives them a decisive veto power. Wealth employs its power indirectly, says Engels. There can be no automatic translation of class power into state power since the very directness of the bourgeoisie's involvement in the economy yields particularistic interests, which undermine a capacity to act disinterestedly on behalf of the class as a whole.

In short, the *Manifesto's* 'instrumentalist' formula presumes something which its critics invariably overlook – the irreducibly specific character of the political sphere. This is not something which Marx discovers after 1848–9; it is a view of the state which Marx inherits from the Enlightenment and takes for granted in all his political writings. Just as Rousseau in the *Social Contract* distinguishes between the particular interest and the general interest, between the 'will of all' as a mere collectivity of particular interests and the 'general will' which makes each individual 'an indivisible part of the whole', so Marx, in presenting the state as 'a great organism', naturally assumes that the whole is irreducible to its parts. The 'idealism of the state' necessarily transcends its materialistic particulars. Marx rejects a 'simple reductionism' because even where the state serves the bourgeoisie as 'the political idealism of its daily practice', this still presumes a gulf between the two.

Under Bonaparte, Marx tells us, the bourgeoisie, by rebelling out of enthusiasm for its purse against its own politicians, now 'submits to the superior command of an alien will'. But although the state would seem to have made itself completely independent, Bonaparte's mission is stil to safeguard 'bourgeois order' and he is therefore the representaive of a class whose political power 'he has broken' and 'daily breaks it anew'. None of this contradicts Marx's view of the state as a special instrument of coercion : on the contrary, what it demonstrates is why this coercion, in exceptional circumstances, should appear so special, for what Bonaparte does is to underline, in a dramatic way, its generalized character. A coercion implemented through the bourgeoisie's 'natural' representatives – parliamentarians, newspaper editors, and party politicians – normally sensitive to capitalist pressures, yields to the coercion of an adventurer who mobilizes the peasantry, priests, army and lumpen proletariat in order to ensure that the political community remains an illusory one and thus arrests the slide from liberal into socialist rule. Even without their normal representatives, the bourgeoisie still rule. Napoleon I might despotically suppress 'the liberalism of bourgeois society' but French businessmen are able to shake Napoleon's power by an artificially created famine which delays the opening of his Russian campaign. Napoleon III has his autonomy constrained by the fact that he protects the material power of the bourgeoisie whose interests dictate that it should be delivered from the danger of its own rule. Of course, adventurers like Bonaparte are tempted by the heavenly aspirations of a political idealism to go beyond the materialist needs of the bourgeoisie, as in 1859, when, according to Marx, he alienates the business and financial community and rules 'henceforth by the sword alone'. But this is an exceptional situation, which proves the rule for Bonaparte can only survive for another decade by placating bourgeois interests. It was, after all, the bourgeoisie who 'invited Bonaparte to suppress and annihilate its speaking and writing section' in order to pursue its private affairs with 'full confidence' and this business confidence acts as a formidable constraint on state autonomy.

In *The Philosophy of Right,* Hegel had sought to present the state as the embodiment of society's general interest, as standing above particular interests, and as being therefore able to overcome the division between civil society and the state and the split between the individual as private person and as citizen. Marx rejects these claims in his *Critique* on the ground that the state, in real life, does not stand for the general interest but defend the class interest. But he soon moved to the view that 'political emancipation' is not human emancipation. This required a much more thorough reorganization of society, of which the main feature was the abolition of private property. The view of the state as the instrument of a ruling class, so privileged by virtue of its ownership and control of the means of production, remained fundamental throughout for Marx and Engels. The state, Engels said, is 'as a rule, the state of the most powerful, economically dominant class, becomes also the politically dominant class, and thus acquires new means of holding down and exploiting the oppressed class'. This, however, leaves open the question why and how the state, as an institution separate from the economically dominant class, plays this role; and the question is particularly relevant in capitalist society, where the distance between the state and economic forces is usually quite marked.

Two different approaches have in recent years, been advanced to provide an answer to this question. The first approach relies on the instrumental role of the state by offering a number of ideological and political factors: for instance, the pressures which economically dominant classes are able to exercise upon the state. The second approach emphasizes the structural constraints to which the state is subject in a capitalist society, and the fact that, irrespective of the ideological and political dispositions of those who are in charge of the state, its policies must ensure the accumulation and reproduction of capital. In the first approach, the state is the state of the capitalists; in the second, it is the state of capital. However, the two approaches are not exclusive but complementary.

Notwithstanding the differences between them, both approaches accept in common a view of the state as subordinate to and constrained by forces and pressures external to itself: the state, in these perspectives, is indeed an agent or instrument, whose dynamic and impulse is supplied from outside. This leaves out of account of a very large part of the marxist view of the state, as conceived by Marx and Engels. For they attributed to the state a considerable degree of autonomy. This is particularly clear in relation to the phenomenon to which both Marx and Engels gave particular attention, namely dictatorial regimes such as the Bonapartist regime in France after Louis Napoleon Bonaparte's coup of 1852. In the *18th Brumaire,* Marx said that France seemed as a result of the coup d'etat 'to have escaped the despotism of a class only to fall back beneath the despotism of an individual, and indeed beneath the authority of an individual without authority'. 'The struggle', he argued seems to have reached the compromise that all classes fall on their knees, equally mute and equally impotent, before the rifle butt'. Bonapartism, Marx also said in *The Civil War in France* nearly twenty years later, 'was the only form of government possible at a time when the bourgeoisie had already lost, and the working class had not yet acquired the faculty of ruling the nation' and Engels also noted in *Origin of the Family* that, 'by way of exception', 'periods occurs in which the warring classes balance each other so nearly that the state power, as ostensible mediator, acquires, for the moment, a certain degree of independence of both'. The absolute monarchies of the seventeenth and eighteenth centuries, and the regimes of Napoleon I and Napoleon III, were examples of such periods, as was the rule of Bismarck in Germany: 'here', says Engels, 'capitalists and workers are balanced against each other and equally cheated for the benefit of the impoverished Prussian cabbage Junkers'.

These formulations come very close to suggesting not only that the state enjoys a 'relative autonomy', but that it has made itself altogether independent of society.

An early case in point is that of 'Oriental despotism', to which Marx and Engels devoted much attention in the 1850s and 1860s; but it applies more generally. In fact, the marxist theory of the state, far from turning the state into an agency or instrument subordinate to external forces, sees it much more as an institution in its own right, with its own interests and purposes. In the *18th Brumaire,* Marx also speaks as an 'immense bureaucratic and military organization, an ingenious and broadly based state machinery, and an army of half a million officials alongside the actual army, which numbers a further half million'; and he goes on to describe this force as a 'frightful parasitic body, which surrounds the body of French society like a caul and stops up all its pores'. Such'state machinery' must be taken to have interests and purposes of its own.

This historical narrative does not deny the role of the state as concerned to serve the purposes and interests of the dominant class: what is involved, in effect, is a partnership between those who control the state, and those who own and control the means of economic activity. This is the notion, which must be taken to underlie the concept of state monopoly capitalism, which is the description of present-day advanced capitalism used by 'official' communist writers. The description is vulnerable, in so far as it suggests a merger of the political and economic realms, whereas the real position is one of partnership, in which the political and economic realms retain a separate identity, and in which the state is able to act with considerable independence in maintaining and defending the social order of which the economically dominant class is the main beneficiary. This independence is implied even in the formulation of the *Communist Manifesto* and which seems to turn the state into such a subordinate institution. For Marx and Engels speak here of 'the common affairs of the whole bourgeoisie': this clearly implies that the bourgeoisie is made up of different and particular elements; that it has many separate and specific interests as well as common ones; and that it is the state which must manage its common affairs. It cannot do so without a considerable measure of autonomy. A major function of the state in its partnership with the economically dominant class is to regulate class conflict and to ensure the stability of the social order. The class rule, which the state sanctions and defends, assumes many different forms, from the democratic republic to dictatorship; the form which class rule assumes is a matter of great importance to the working class. In a context a private ownership and appropriation, however, it remains class rule, whatever its form.

Poulantzas-Miliband Debate

So Marx and Engels do not really have an explicit theory of cohesion and consent in the way, for example, that Gramsci does. But their work does provide a crucial starting point for theorists who do seek to make this aspect more prominent. That they can do so is because Marx and Engels' work has an implicit account of cohesion and consent, and aspects that we have covered–the cohesive function of capitalist production, the mystifying ideology that it produces, the commodification of social life – provide a good basis for developing a more explicit theory. Most of all, it is the idea of the state as a factor of social cohesion that presents the greatest opportunities, but again, as this theory is in need of more explicit elaboration, the work of Nicos Poulantzas, offers the possibilities present in Marx's work.

Marx's account of the situation in France shows that the bourgeoisie was prepared to lose its control of the state apparatus, because the strong executive under the control of Louis Bonaparte was better able to guarantee its continued domination and social power. Poulantzas uses Marx's analysis of France to argue that the state, rather than being the instrument of any one class, is "relatively autonomous" and that this autonomy allows it to play the role of organizing the different classes and class factions, intervening to arrange compromises among the dominating classes and between these and the dominated classes. The state has a general function in managing class contradictions. In this way, it secures social cohesion and maintains the necessary conditions for the reproduction of the mode of production.

The state must secure the cohesion of a class-divided society. This is a necessary social function that is not reducible to the narrow interests of any one particular group. That the state is able to act as a factor of social cohesion is due to its autonomy from the economic sphere. Poulantzas makes much of Marx's point about capitalism separating the worker from the means of production and this provides the basis for the autonomy of the political sphere. Unlike previous modes of production, under capitalism it is no longer necessary to secure exploitation by political means and the state is not directly implicated in organizing economic production. This "relative autonomy" in fact allows the state to present itself as the representative of the 'general interest' in the way suggested by Marx and Engels. It is able to stand above competing and divergent economic interests, or, if necessary, to present these interests as the popular will. This is important ideologically as 'the state assumes a specific autonomy vis-à-vis these socio-economic relations, in putting itself forward as the representative of the unity of the people/nation'.

The autonomy of the state apparatus from the economic class struggle is also important because it means that the economically dominant class does not have to correspond to the politically dominant class. Political domination does not flow automatically from the economic situation. Rather, it has to be achieved, leaving this process open to hegemony. The concept of hegemony implies that domination and leadership have to be achieved, and the state becomes crucial as a site where this hegemony is established and negotiated. The state must act as the cohesive factor in the unity of a social formation, but how this is achieved is a political rather than merely an economic matter. Hence 'the capitalist state, characterized by hegemonic class leadership, does not directly represent the dominant classes' political power center, as the organizing agent of their political struggle.

It can be seen from the use of the pluralism that there is no one unified ruling class, but rather a plurality of class factions, each with different interests. This goes against the view in the *Communist Manifesto* that society is more and more splitting up into two great classes. In fact it is the classes themselves that are splitting up, with factions formed on the basis of different interests, powers and relations within classes, determined by economic, political and ideological factors. Given these divisions, social cohesion becomes all the more important. The state becomes the site of the construction of what Poulantzas calls a 'power bloc'. He argues that the capitalist state and the specific characteristics of the class struggle in a capitalist formation make it possible for a 'power bloc', composed of several politically dominant classes or factions to function. Amongst these dominant classes or factions one of them holds a particular dominant role, which can be characterized as a hegemonic role. State power corresponds to the interests of the power bloc. However, this power bloc is not straightforwardly reducible to class interests but is a product of the complex process by which hegemony is constructed. The state's role is to act as the factor of political unity of the power bloc under the protection of the hegemonic group.

The unity of the capitalist state stems from the fact that it represents the political unity of the people-nation and that it constitutes the political unity of the power bloc under the protection of the hegemonic class or faction. That state is able to play this role of organizing and unifying the bourgeoisie and representing its long-term interest in so far as it has relative autonomy from particular factions and interests. This is possible because the state is separated from the means of production. Once the cohesion of the dominant class factions has been achieved, the consent of the broader masses must be mobilized. The capitalist state is described as an institutional ensemble with the function of organizing hegemony within the power bloc and mobilizing active consent to this. Gramsci describes this process as an 'unstable equilibrium of compromise'. Poulantzas goes on to divide these state apparatuses into two types. The repressive state apparatuses include the police, army, prisons, judiciary, civil service, etc., while the ideological state apparatuses include educational, religious, cultural, informational, trade unions, political parfies, family and other bodies that contribute to the reproduction of social relations. Such an approach suggests that the state comes to play an increasingly important role in everyday life, utilizing a diverse array of apparatuses to secure cohesion and consensus within society.

In fact Poulantzas's later work tends to emphasize, perhaps overemphasize, the tendency towards interventionist and exceptional forms of state. Implicitly rejecting Marx's distinction between political society and civil society, he argues that the state now cuts across all forms of life and that state institutions and apparatuses are embodiments of class relations and practices. He argues that this period of what he calls monopoly capitalism, requires an interventionist state with strong or authoritarian character. These 'exceptional' states are marked by their increased control over social and the economic life and the rise of bureaucracy and administrative apparatuses. Like the writers of the Frankfurt School, Poulantzas argues that the increasingly dominant role of the state accompanies the economic domination of monopoly capital. There is a change in the role of state apparatuses and political parties and a breakdown of the boundaries between public and private spheres. Poulantzas shifts from a structuralist position to a relational view of the state. In other words, the fact that the state is divided by class contradictions leads to the view that the state is not a thing, but a set of relations. The state is not an intrinsic entity, a thing, an instrument or a subject; 'it is rather a relationship of forces, or more precisely the material condensation of such a relationship among classes, factions'. The fact that the state is a social relation means that class struggle are inscribed into the state. The state no longer stand above class relations; these are inscribed into its very nature.

However, it is the institutions that comprise the state Miliband lists the government, the administration, the military and the police, the judicial branch, sub-central government and parliamentary assemblies in which "state power" lies, and it is through them that this power is wielded in its different manifestations by the people who occupy the leading positions in each of these institutions. What Miliband claims is that most of those who occupy the leading positions in the state institutions in present-day capitalist society are of the same class origins as those who wield economic power. It is hardly surprising, therefore, that with the same class origins and, as is thus likely, the same class affiliations, the leaders of the state represent the interests of capital.

This would be unproblematic when the property qualification prevailed, but what about the case where suffrage is universal. Not every individual who occupies a leading position in the state is from a bourgeois background. What of those who rise to leading positions from a lower-class origin? Why should such individuals represent the interests of capital? Miliband replies that it is undoubtedly true that a process of social dilution has occurred in the state service, and has brought people born in the working classes, and even more commonly in the lower-middle classes, into elite positions inside the state system. But to speak of 'democratization' in this connection is somewhat misleading. What is involved here is rather a process of 'bourgeoisification' of the most able and thrusting recruits from the subordinate classes. As these recruits rise in the state hierarchy, so do they become part, in every significant sense, of the social classes to which their position, income and status gives them access.

Miliband's analysis of capitalist society suggests that the common class affiliation of the owners of capital and the leaders of the state institutions is what dictates an immediate concern with the protection of the interests of the bourgeoisie. This has led to a famous debate between Miliband and Poulantzas, who takes issue with Miliband for two reasons: (1) because he sees the state as being such that it would protect the interest of the dominant economic class even if a class identity between the owners of capital and the leaders of the state did not obtain; and (2) because the state adopts policies which are not in the immediate interest of dominant economic class, there is greater degree of relative autonomy of the state.

In contrast to Miliband's approach, Poulantzas focuses not open the social actors, but upon the location of the political instance within the social formation as a total structure. For Poulantzas,

> the relation between the bourgeois class and the state is an objective relation. This means that if the function of the state in a determinate social formation and the interests of the dominant class in this formation coincide, it is by reason of the system itself: the direct participation of members of the ruling class in the state apparatus is not the cause but the effect, and moreover a chance and contingent one, of this objective coincidence.

When it is perceived that the state serves to preserve the interests of the dominant economic class as a matter of course, then the actual class origins of the wielders of state power are irrelevant. In fact, Poulantzas goes so far as to argue, the interests of the dominant economic class can occasionally be even better served when the leaders of the state institutions are not from the same class background. But a possible counter-example to the marxist claim that the state always represents an economic class is the autonomy of the Bonapartist state. Marx himself appears at first to consider the Bonapartist state as representing, not a class, but one man—Louis Bonaparte.

Here, the state appears to experience a genuine autonomy vis- a-vis the economy, and this would appear to rest on its coercive nature. However, Marx writes: 'Only under the second Bonaparte does the state seem to have attined a completely autonomous position." He continues: 'But the state power does not hover in mid-air. Bonaparte represents a class, indeed he represents the most numerous class of French society, the small peasant proprietors".

This brings us to the question of the exact nature of the 'relative autonomy' of the state. Marx argues that the Bonapartist state, instead of serving the interests of the peasants, actually served the interests of the bourgeoisie, who were not capable of managing the state themselves. That Bonaparte was able to serve the interests of an economic class other than the one he represented, suggests that the state can, at least in certain circumstances, behave independently of its ostensible class base. Moreover, why should Bonaparte serve the interests of the bourgeoisie if they did not put him into power? A satisfactory answer to this question would surely suggest that Bonaparte's power did not in fact rest on the peasantry.

Marx's argument seems to rely on an equivocation involving the word 'represents'. One sense of the word suggests that the way in which Bonaparte represented the peasants was by presenting their case; and we might possibly assume that this gave him power since by doing so he was backed by the peasants. The other sense suggests that the representation was merely nominal, and no sunstantive support from the peasants can be assumed to follow. But, as Miliband remarks 'represents' is here a confusing word. In the context, the only meaning that may be attached to it is that the small holding peasants hoped to have their interests represented by Louis Bonaparte. But this does not turn Louis Bonaparte or the state into the mere instrument of their will; at the most, it may limit the executive's freedom of action somewhat.

This seems to allow Marx the best of the both worlds. Bonaparte can rely on the support of the peasants, but he does not have to pursue their interests. Such an interpretation of what Marx meant by 'Bonaparte represents a class...the small-peasant proprietors' appears to explain how it is that Bonaparte held power (the peasants, hoping to have their interests represented, backed him up), yet did not actually serve the interests of the peasants. And as Bonaparte thus 'represents' the most numerous economic class the peasantry—his power looks to be assured.

However, Marx does observe that the state has grown to significant proportions and has done so across major social transformations. The task of the first French revolution was to destroy all separate local, territorial, urban and provincial powers in order to create the civil unity of the nation. It had to carry further the centralization that the absolute monarchy had begun, but at same time it had to develop the extent, the attributes and the number of underlings of the governmental power. Napoleon perfected this state machinery.

But if one recalls Miliband's claim that the state is a system of institutions, and his warning against identifying the state with one of those institutions, namely the government, questions immediately arise concerning what it is that must be smashed. Since Marx insists that central administrative functions will remain after the revolution, one might suspect that Marx has reduced the problem of the state to that of the government. The machine which he observes previous revolutions to have perfected, rather than having smashed, is the form of government which is taken to be the promoter of bourgeois interests. This identification may lead one to overlook certain difficulties concerning any 'transitional' state which may be thought a requisite following the next major social transformation.

It may also allow some sense to be made of those who argue that the state must be smashed and yet a transitional state is required by the revolution. For, as Miliband comments on Marx's remark about smashing the state, the obvious and crucial question which this raises is what kind of post-revolutionary state is to succeed the smashed bourgeois state. For it is of course one of the basic tenets of marxism, and one of its basic differences with anarchism, that while the proletarian revolution must smash the old state, it does not abolish the state itself: a state remains in being, and even endures for a long time to come, even though it begins immediately to 'wither away'. In one sense of 'state' understood in terms of a form of government serving the interests of the bourgeoisie, the state is smashed. In another sense, the state is employed temporarily in aid of the revolution.

Moreover, is the state bound to reproduce a social formation? Even though Poulantzas is critical of 'functionalist' social theory, it would seem that he in fact offers such a functionalist analysis. The state may well be thought to exist in order to reproduce a social formation, but why must it do so? What is it about the structure of society as a whole, which ensures that the state will carry out this function assigned to it? Without a satisfactory answer to these questions, Miliband is right to accuse Poulantzas of 'super determinism'. He argues that Poulantzas goes much too far in dismissing the nature of the state elite as of altogether no account. For what his exclusive stress on 'objective relations' suggests is that what the state does is in every particular and at all time wholly determined by these 'objective relations': in other words, that the structural constraints of the system are so absolutely compelling as to turn those who run the state into the merest functionaries and executants of policies imposed upon them by the system.

Nevertheless, Poulantzas insists that 'inside the structure of several levels dislocated by uneven development, the state has the particular function of consisting the factor of cohesion between the levels of a social formation'. He adds that it operates as a factor of "order" or "organizational principle" of a formation in the sense of the cohesion of the ensemble of the levels of a complex unity, and as the regulating factor of its global equilibrium as a system. Poulantzas regards one ramification of this view to be that the political sphere is that area where 'contradictions' in the formation are condensed. This enables Poulantzas to argue that the specificity of political practice depends on its having state power as its objective. The political sphere, being the point of cohesion, is crucial for transformations of the social formation.

Before the First World War, Lenin, like Marx and Engels before him, had made a distinction between different forms of regime, to the point of referring to the United States and Britain, in contrast to Tsarist Russia, as countries 'where complete political liberty exists'. With the First World War, Lenin no longer took such distinctions to be significant. In *State and Revolution*, he said that the 'monstrous oppression of the working people by the state, which is merging more and more with the all powerful capitalist associations, is becoming increasingly monstrous. The advanced capitalist countries are becoming military convict prisons for the workers'. In the pamphlet itself, he insisted that, with the war, 'both Britain and America, the biggest and last representatives – in the whole world – of Anglo-Saxon "liberty", in the sense that they had no military cliques and bureaucracy, have completely sunk into the all-European filthy, bloody morass of bureaucratic-military institutions which subordinate everything to themselves and suppress everything'. Given the immense authority which Lenin's pronouncements came to enjoy in the world of marxism as a result of the Bolshevik revolution, his virtual equation of 'bourgeois democracy' with other forms of capitalist rule for instance fascism may well have contributed to the baneful marxist neglect of such distinctions in subsequent years.

Lenin's concern, in *State and Revolution* and elsewhere, was to combat the 'revisionist' notion that the bourgeois state might be reformed; he insisted it must be 'smashed'. This was the point which Marx himself had made in the *18th Brumaire*: 'all revolutions perfected this machine instead of smashing it and which he reiterated at the time of the Paris Commune 'the next attempt of the French Revolution will be no longer, as before, to transfer the bureaucratic-military machine from one hand to another, but to smash it, and this is the preliminary condition for every real people's revolution on the Continent'. The state would then be replaced by the "dictatorship of the proletariat", in which there would occur what Lenin called 'a gigantic replacement of certain institutions by other institutions of a fundamentally different type instead of the special institution of a privileged minority, the majority itself can directly fulfill all these functions, and the more the functions of state power are performed by the people as a whole, the less need there is for the existence of this power. "This echoes faithfully the basic propositions of classical marxism on the subject. In a famous passage of *Anti-Duhring* Engels had said: 'The first act by virtue of which the state really constitutes itself the representative of the whole of society – the taking possession of the means of production in the name of society – this is, at the same time, its last independent act as a state. State interference in social relations becomes, in one domain after another, superfluous, and then withers away of itself; the government of persons is replaced by the administration of things, and by the conduct of processes of production. The state is not abolished. It withers away." This, and many other references to the state in the writings of Marx and Engels, show the affinities of classical marxism to anarchism: the main difference between them, at least in regard to the state, is that classical marxism rejected the anarchist notion that the state could be done away with on the very morning of the revolution.

Classical Marxism and Lennism always stressed the coercive role of the state, almost to the exclusion of all else: the state is essentially the institution whereby a dominant and exploiting class imposes and defends it's power and privileges against the class which it dominates and exploits. One of Gramscis major contributions to marxist thought is his exploration of the fact that the domination of the ruling class is not only achieved by coercion but is also elicited by consent: and Gramsci also insisted that the state played a major role in the cultural and ideological fields and in the organization of consent. This process of legitimation, in which both the state and many other institutions in society are engaged, has attracted considerable attention from marxists in contemporary period. A question which has in this connection preoccupied a number of theorists in recent years is how far the state in capitalist-democratic regime is able to cope with the task of eliciting consent in circumstances of crisis and contraction. On the one hand, the state in these regimes is required to meet a variety of popular expectations. On the other, it is also required to meet the needs and demands of capital. Habermas has rightly argued that the growing incompatibility of these requirements produces a 'crisis of legitimation' which is not readily resolved within the framework of capitalist-democratic regimes.

The establishment of the Soviet state offered a major conceptual challenge to the marxist theory of the state; for here was a society in which the means of production had come under public ownership, and whose regime proclaimed its allegiance to marxism. This raised the question of the nature of the state, which had been brought into being. Any discussion of that question was, however, over-shadowed by the experience of Stalinism and, as was to be expected, Stalinist thought on the state insisted on its paramount and enduring importance: far from 'withering away', the state must be reinforced as the prime motor in the construction of socialism, and also in order to deal with its many enemies at home and abroad. The 'revolution from above' so Stalin spoke, was made on the initiative of the state. This state, Stalin also claimed, was a 'state of a new type', which represented the interests of the workers, the peasants and the intelligentsia–in other words, of the whole Soviet population. It was, in this sense, no longer a class state, seeking to maintain the power and privileges of a ruling class to the detriment of the vast majority; it was rather, a 'state of the whole people'.

This claim has been strongly contested by marxist critics of the Soviet regime. Their own view of the Soviet state and of the state in all Soviet type regimes has been greatly influenced by their judgment of the nature of Soviet-type societies. Those critics who viewed them as class societies also took the state in them to be the instrument of a 'new class', and, as such not significantly different, in conceptual terms, from the state in other class societies. State did not become the dictatorship of the proletariat; rather it became the distatorship *over* the proletarict. Those critics, on the other hand, who viewed Soviet type societies as 'transitional' between capitalism and socialism, and who rejected the notion of a 'new class', spoke of the state in these societies as a 'deformed workers' state', under the control of a 'bureaucracy' avid for power and privilege, and which a workers' revolution would eventually dislodge. This debate still proceeds; but there is at any rate no disagreement among its protagonists as to the immense power wielded by the state in these societies. Nor is this affected by the fact that the state itself is controlled by the party leaders.

Marxists concerned with the state in capitalist societies are also confronted by many different questions and problems: what is the precise nature and role of the state in advanced capitalist societies today? How does its class character manifest itself? How far can it be transformed into the instrument of the subordinate classes? How can it be prevented, in a future socialist society, from appropriating an undue measure of power; or, Marx put it in the *Critique of the Gotha Programme*, how can the state in such a society be converted from an organ superimposed upon society into one completely subordinated to it?' These and many other unresolved questions about the state are certain to give it a major place in marxist discussion and discourses for many years to come.

Socialism

Marx is hopeful that the dictatorship will be short-lived. In a letter to Joseph Weydemeyer, 1852, Marx disclaims credit for discovering the existence of classes and of class struggle, but he claims credit for having a clear understanding of the line of march, which the struggle must follow.

While the proletariat is still engaged in the task of abolishing private property and the class distinctions to which property gives rise, the state serves the purposes of the working class. But once property has been abolished and brought under state ownership, class distinctions will disappear; then the state also will disappear, because, being part of the superstructure of society, it will have no material foundation for its existence:

When, in the course of development, class distinctions have disappeared and all production has been concentrated in the hands of a vast association of the whole nation, the public power will lose its political character. Political power properly so called, is merely the organized power of one class for oppressing another. If the proletariat during its contest with the bourgeoisie is compelled, by the force of circumstances, to organize itself as a class, if, by means of a revolution, it makes itself the ruling class and, as such, sweeps away by force the old conditions of production, then it will, along with these conditions, have swept away the conditions for the existence of class antagonisms and of classes generally, and will thereby have abolished its own supremacy as a class.

Unlike most of their predecessors Owen, Fourier and St. Simon Marx and Engels saw socialism not as an ideal for which an attractive blueprint could be drawn up, bur as the product of the laws of development of capitalism which the classical economists had been the first to discover and try to analyse. The form or forms which socialism might take could therefore only be revealed by an historical process which was still unfolding. Given this perspective, Marx and Engels quite logically refrained from any attempt to provide a detailed description, or even a definition, of socialism. To them it was first and foremost a negation of capitalism which would develop its own positive identity (communism) through a long revolutionary process in which the proletariat would remake society and in so doing remake itself.

The modern socialist movement started the publication in 1848 of *The Communist Manifesto* by Marx and Engels. Its roots go back at least two hundred years to the period of the English Civil war (1642—52), which produced radical Diggers with a brilliant spokesman - Gerard Win Stanley whose ideas correctly correspond, in important respects, to the principles of socialism, as we know them today. Upstanding forerunners were Conspiracy of the Equals during the Revolution, the great English Utopians (Owen, Fourier, St. Simon;) of the early nineteenth, and the English Chartists of the 1830s and 40s who first incorporated socialist democracy, equality, and collectivism rescale working-class movement.

This most important text on the subject is critique of the *Gotha Programme* (1875) was directed against the programmes by the congress at which the two parties which of German workers' movement united to form the Workers Party, later renamed the Democratic Party of Germany. In this Marx distinguishes between two communist societies. The 'first phase' is the form of society which will immediately succeed capitalism. This phase will bear the marks of its origin: the workers as the new ruling class will need their own state (the Dictatorship of the Proletariat) to protect them against their enemies; people's mental and spiritual horizons will be colored by bourgeois ideas and values; income, though no longer derived from the ownership of property, will have to be calculated according to work done rather than according to need. Nevertheless society's productive forces will develop rapidly under this new order, and in the course of time the limits imposed by the capitalist past will be transcended. Society will then enter what Marx called the higher stage of communist society under which the state while wither away, a totally different attitude to work will prevail, and society will be able to inscribe on its banner the motto 'from each according to his ability, to each according to his need'.

Communism—as a form of society—was discussed by Marx on various occasions, in both early and late texts, though only in very general terms since he disclaimed any intention of "writing recipes for the cook shops of the future". In the *Economic and Philosophical Manuscripts* he wrote that 'Communism is the positive abolition of private property, of human self-alienation, and thus the real appropriation of human nature, through and for man. It is therefore the return of man himself as a social, that is, really human being; a complete and conscious return which assimilates all the wealth of previous development.' Later he and Engels gave this conception a more precise sociological meaning by specifying the abolition of classes and of the division of labour as preconditions for a communist society: thus, in the *German Ideology* Marx argued that in order to achieve such a society it would be necessary for individuals to reestablish their control over these material powers and abolish the division of labour. This is not possible without a community. The illusory community which, up to the present, individuals have coimbinned, always acquired an independent existe since apart from them, and since it was a union of one class against another it represented to the dominated class not only a completely community but also a new shackle an genuine community individuals gaine their in and through their association freedom. It was this sense too that Marx and Engels referred to early tribal societies—without private property class divisions, or an extensive division or labour—as primitive communism. In subsequent works Marx emphasized the economic character of the future communist society as a 'society of associated producers', arguing in *Capital III (ch.* 48) that freedom in the economic sphere could consist only in 'the fact that socialized humanity, the associated producers, regulate their interchange with nature rationally, bring it under their common control, instead of being ruled by it as by some blind power'.

Only in the *Critique of the Gotha Programme* Marx distinguished between two stages of communist society: an early phase, when it has just emerged from capitalist society, in which the individual is paid for his labour and buys consumer goods and a higher phase in which each person contributes to society according to his ability and draws from the common stock according to his needs. It was Lenin, in *State and Revolution,* w ho gave currency to a description of these two stages as 'socialism' and 'communism' and the terminology then became part of Leninist orthodoxy. But although official pronouncements in the USSR and other countries of Eastern Europe until recently still referred to these two stages, this is not the focal point of present-day discussions among marxists, which have to do mainly with two issues that arise from the actual experiences of existing socialist countries. One concerns the role of the market in a socialist system, or rather, as market relations are increasingly introduced, the effective operation of socialist market economy, which is seen as bringing both greater economic efficiency through a more rational allocation of resources in production and distribution, and a substantial decentralization of decision-making to 'self-managed' public enterprises of all kinds as well as to small-scale privately owned businesses. This should, however, be viewed in the context of the continuing allocation of a large part of the gross national product by non-market mechanisms in the form or extensive social services, though this is now also a feature of the developed capitalist societies.

The second issue concerns Marx's view of human needs and the organization of human labour to satisfy those needs in communist society which has formed a vague background to marxist conceptions of the future social order but has been little studied in an explicit way until recent years, again in relation to the practical problem of socialism. One important study by Heller points to some inconsistencies in Marx's own conception. In the *Grundrisse* the alienation of labour is overcome and it also becomes a vital need, since all labour becomes essentially intellectual labour, the field for the self-realization of the human personality'; but *Capital* while alienation cease, labour does not become attractive for "the sphere of material production remains a realm of necessity, and 'the true realm of freedom' begins only beyond it, in leisure time. Hence, there remains an obligation to work in the society of associated producers. A solution of the problem within Marx's own work is to be found, Heller argues, in the idea that in this type of society a new 'structure of needs' will emerge, and everyday life will not be but around productive labour and material cons umption but around those activities and human relationships which are ends in themselves and become the primary needs. But she recognizes, on one side, the immense difficulties that remain in determining what are true social needs in the realm of production and of ensuring that everyone has a voice in deciding how productive capacity should be allocated and on the other, that Marx's ideas on the new system of needs are

Utopian—but fruitful in as much as they establish a norm against which to measure the quality of present-day life. In a similar way Stojanovic who sees the main prospects for essential innovations in marxism in its critical confrontation with socialist society as it now exists, argues that the construction of a developed socialist society is possible only if approached from the standpoint o nature communism.

In recent Marxist discussions of a future classless society the distinction between socialism and communism as 'lower' and 'higher' stages has lost much of its importance, and seems indeed simplistic. The movement towards such a society may pass through many stages, at present quite unforeseeable, and it may also experience interruptions and regressions. What now seems important to most participants in the debate is the need for a more profound empirical and critical study of existing social institutions, practices, and norms, in both capitalist and socialist countries, from the point of view of their inherent potentialities for development towards Marx's ideal, together with a more rigorous elaboration of the moral norms of a socialist society. Wellmer's argument which rejects the notion of 'an economically grounded mechanism of emancipation' and claim that it is 'necessary to include socialist democracy, socialist justice, socialist ethics and socialist consciousness among the components of a socialist society to be incubated within the womb of a capitalist order, can as well be applied to the existing socialist countries, with due regard to their specific characteristics and problems.

Utopianism

One utopian feature of Marx's thought was the belief that economic scarcity could be overcome. He believed that people would learn to moderate their greed for possessions and material pleasures, and would use modern industry and technology to produce more goods and services than the demand for them. A second utopian feature was the belief that people would work and co-operate without any material incentive. Economic activity would require no other motive than moral commitment. A third utopian feature was the belief that not only would economic abundance bring to an end conflicts over the distribution of economic resources, but it would end all other permanent conflicts. The proposal to transcend or go beyond the state, partly in the sense of abolishing armies, police forces and permanent bureaucracies, assumes that, in a socialist society, a combination of individual restraint, social restraint and industrial growth will enable the problems of psychological differences, personal rivalries, power struggles, territorial disputes, religious controversies and disputes about social ends and means to be solved by discussion and agreement. This is the anarchist part of Marx's thought: the belief that socialism will eventually end all permanently divisive social conflicts and dispense with a need for laws backed by force.

Needless to say, Marx denied that he was a utopian; he regarded his revolutionary projects as realistic, and he denounced the utopianism he attributed to others. It should be noted, however, that though Marx and Engels polemicised against the utopianism of Robert Owen, Charles Fourier and Saint-Simon, and though they claimed to have replaced utopian with scientific socialism, it was the means and not the ends of the utopian socialists that were the targets of their criticism. In common with the utopians and the anarchists, Marx believed that society could be reconstituted on the assumption that once private property and the state were abolished, people would act fraternally and morally. His objection to the utopians and the anarchists was not that their assumptions were unsound but that their means were unrealistic. They were accused of neglecting the objective historical trends and forces which promoted their ends for a reliance on social blueprints that rested on nothing but their subjective wishes and powers of persuasion. Marx claimed that, in contrast to the utopians who set themselves against history, the social ends he favored were built into history and expressed themselves in objective trends and forces.

We can also note some further utopian features of Marx's revolutionary theory, features sometimes described as Promethean and romantic. Prometheus was the Greek god, frequently referred to by Marx in glowing terms, who stole fire from heaven to give to humankind and who championed woman beings against Zeus. The Prometheus theme in Marx's revolutionary thought is the desire to replace the Judaic and Christian acceptance of the sovereignty of a revealed God with the secular political undertaking of building a heaven on earth in accordance with human wishes. The romantic themes are the beliefs that (1) societies can be created which will be inhabited by noble, autonomous and unique individuals and that (2) these societies will also be natural and organic communities. These utopian and quasi-religious features of Marx's revolutionary theory help to explain its enduring attraction. But what is more exciting, certainly for devotees, is Marx's insistence that by means of a proper understanding of history, science, and economics he had turned apparently utopian hopes into realistic aspirations.

It is difficult, Marx suggests, for us to imagine what life holds for those who will live in the classless society. Men whose minds have been formed in a class society attach great significance to notions such as justice and equality, which, however, are ideological in content. As he looks to the future, Marx disassociates himself from these socialists who speak of "equal right" and of "fair distribution of the proceeds of labour". In his opinion, notions of this sort are relevant only within the framework of a class society. In the society of the future, where class distinctions no longer exist, no man will ask whether someone else is getting more than his share, for men will recognize that "the free development of each is the condition for the free development of all."

In a higher phase of communist society, after the enslaving subordination of the individual to the division of labour, and therewith also the antithesis between mental and physical labour, has vanished; after labor has become not only a means of life but life's prime want; after the productive forces have also increased with the all-round development of the individual, and all the springs of cooperative wealth flow more abundantly only then can the narrow horizon of bourgeois right be crossed in its entirety and society inscribe on its banners: "From each according to his ability, to each according to his needs!"

Conclusion

Hundred Twenty Five Years after Marx's death, the ideas which he launched upon the world, have come to constitute one of the most lively and influential currents of modern thought, acquaintance with which is indispensable to all who work in the social sciences or are engaged in political movements. Yet it is equally clear that these ideas have acquired none of the fixity of a closed and completed system, but are still actively evolving; and in the course of this century they have assumed a great variety of forms. This has occurred not only by extension into new fields of enquiry, but also through an internal differentiation, in response on one side to critical judgements and new intellectual movements, and on the other to changing social and political circumstances.

In the period since Marx's death, his ideas have perhaps been more diversely interpreted and more widely challenged than at any time since the great controversies of the early part of the century.There has been deconstruction and reconstruction of the Marxist theory of history, the post-war development of capitalism, the problems that have beset socialist societies, and in particular such contentious issues as economic planning and market socialism.

Karl Marx has had more impact on actual events, as well as on the minds of men and women, than any other intellectual in modern times. The reason for this is not primarily the attraction of his concepts and methodology, though both have a strong appeal to unrigorous minds, but the fact that his philosophy has been institutionalized in two of the world's largest countries, Russia and China, and their many satellites. In this sense he resembles St Augustine, whose writings were most widely read among church leaders from the fifth to the thirteenth century and therefore played a predominant role in the shaping of medieval Christendom. But the influence of Marx has been even more direct, since his theory was actually carried into effect, with incalculable consequences for mankind by his three most important followers, Lenin, Stalin and Mao Tse-tung, all of whom, in this respect, were faithful marxists.

Marx was a child of his time, the mid-nineteenth century, and marxism was characteristic nineteenth-century philosophy in that it claimed to be scientific. 'Scientific' was Marx's strongest expression of appraval, which he habitually used to distinguish himself from his many enemies. He and his work were 'scientific'; they were not. He felt he had found a scientific explanation of human behaviour in history akin to Darwin's theory of evolution. The notion that marxism is a science, in a way that no other philosophy ever has been or could be, is implanted in the public doctrine of the states his followers founded, so that it colours the teaching of all subject in their schools and universities. This has spilled over into the non-marxist world, for intellectuals, especially academics, are fascinated by power, and the identification of marxism with massive physical authority has tempted many teachers to admit marxist 'science' to their own disciplines, especially such inexact or quasi-exact subjects as economics, sociology, history and geography. No doubt if Hitler, rather than Stalin, had won the struggle for Central and Eastern Europe in 1945, and so imposed his will on a great part of the world, Nazi doctrines which also claimed to be scientific, such as its race-theory, would have been given an academic gloss and penetrated universities throughout the world. But military victory ensured that marxist, rather than Nazi, science would prevail.

The first thing we must ask about Marx, therefore, is: in what sense, if any, was he a scientist? That is, to what extent was he engaged in the pursuit of objective knowledge by the careful search for and evaluation of evidence? On the face of it, Marx's biography reveals him as primarily a scholar. He was descended on both sides from lines of Talmudic scholars. He never received any Jewish education or attempted to acquire any, or showed any interest in Jewish causes. But it must be said that he developed traits characteristic of a certain type of scholar, especially Talmudic ones: a tendency to accumulate immense masses of half-assimilated materials and to plan encyclopedic works which were never completed; a withering contempt for all non-scholars; and extreme assertiveness and irascibility in dealing with other scholars. Virtually all his work, indeed, has the hallmark of Talmudic study: it is essentially a commentary on, a critique of the work of others in his field.

Marx, then, was unwilling either to investigate working conditions in industry himself or to learn from intelligent working men who had experienced them. Why should he? In all essentials, using the Hegelian dialectic, he had reached his conclusions about the fate of humanity by the late 1840s. All that remained was to find the facts to substantiate these could be earnered from newspaper reports, government blue books and evidence collected by earlier writers; and all this material could be found in libraries. Why look further? The problem, as it appeared to Marx, was to find the right kind of facts: the facts that fitted. The philosopher Karl Jaspers summerising Marx's method has commented that the that style of Marx's writings is not that of the investigator; he does not quote examples or adduce facts which run counter to his own theory but only those which clearly support or confirm that which he considers the ultimate truth. The whole approach is one of vindication, not investigation, but it is a vindication of something proclaimed as the perfect truth with the conviction not of the scientist but of the believer.

Marx made brilliant use of epigrams and aphorisms. Many of these were not his invention. Marat produced the phrases "the workers have no country' and the proletarians have nothing to lose but their chains" 'Religion is the opium of the people" came from Heine. Luis Blanc provided 'From each according to his abilities, to each according to his needs.' From Karl Schapper came 'Workers of all countries unite" and from Blanqui 'the dictatorship of the proletariat'. But Marx was capable of producing his own: 'In politics the Germans have thought what other nations have done.' 'Religion is only the illusory sun around which man revolves, until he begins to revolve around himself.' 'Bourgeois marriage is the community of wives." The revolutionary daring which hurls at its adversaries the defiant words: "am nothing and I must be everything." The ruling ideas of each age have been the ideas of its ruling class.' Moreover he had a rare gift for pointing up the sayings of others and using them at exactly the right stage in the argument, and in deadly combination. No political writer has ever excelled the last three sentences of the *Manifesto:* "The workers have nothing to lose but their chains. They have a world to gain. Workers of the world unite." It was Marx's journalistic eye for the short, pithy sentence which, more than anything else, saved his entire philosophy from oblivion in the last quarter of the nineteenth century.

But if poetry supplied the vision and journalistic aphorism the highlights of Marx's work, its ballast was academic jargon. Marx was an academic; or rather, and worse, he was a failed academic. An embittered, would-be don, he wanted to astonish the world by founding a new philosophical school, which was also a plan of action designed to give him power. Hence his ambivalent attitude to Hegel. Marx says in his preface to the second German edition of *Capital:* 'I frankly proclaimed myself a disciple of that great thinker' and 'toyed with the use of Hegelian terminology when discussing the theory of value' in *Capital.* But he says, his own 'dialectical method' is in 'direct opposition' to Hegel's. For Hegel, the thought-process is the creator of the real, whereas 'in my view, on the other hand, the ideal is nothing more than the material when it has been transposed and translated inside the human head.' Hence, he argues, 'in Hegel's writings, dialectic stands on its head. You must turn it the right way up again if you want to discover the rational kernel that is hidden away within the wrappings of mystification."

Marx, then, sought academic fame by what he saw as his sensational discovery of the fatal flaw in Hegel's method, which enabled him to replace the entire Hegelian system with a new philosophy; indeed, a super-philosophy which would make all existing philosophies outmoded. But he continued to accept that Hegel's dialectic was 'the key to human understanding', and he not only used it but remained its prisoner till the end of his life. For the dialectic and its contradictions explained the culminating universal crisis which was his original poetic vision as a teenager. As he wrote towards the end of his life 14 January 1873, business cycles express 'the contradictions inherent capitalist society and will produce the culminating point of these cycles, a universal crisis'. This will 'drum dialectics' into the heads even of the upstarts of the new German empire'.

Thus far Marx's explanation of what was wrong with the world was a combination of student-cafe anti-Semitism and Rousseau. He broadened it into his mature philosophy over the next three years, 1844 – 46, during which he decided that the evil element in society, the agents of the usurious money-power from which he revolted, were not just the Jews but the bourgeois class as a whole. To do this he made elaborate use of Hegel's dialectic. On the one hand there was the money-power, wealth, capital, the instrument of the bourgeois class. On the other, there was the new redemptive force, the proletariat. The argument is expressed in strict Hegelian terms, using all the considerable resources of German philosophical jargon at its academic worst, though the underlying impulse is clearly moral and the apocalyptic crisis is still poetic. Thus: the revolution is coming, which in Germany will be philosophic: A sphere which cannot emancipate itself without emancipating itself from all the other spheres, which is in short a total loss of humanity capable of redeeming itself only by a total redemption of humanity. This dissolution of society, as a particular class, is the proletariat. What Marx seems to be saying is that the proletariat, the class which is not a class, the dissolvent of class and classes, is a redemptive force which has no history, is not subject to historical laws and ultimately ends history in itself, curiously enough, a very Jewish concept, the proletariat being the Messiah or redeemer. The revolution consists of two elements: 'the head of the emancipation, is *philosophy,* its heart is the *proletariat.* Thus the intellectuals would form the elite, the generals, the workers the foot-soldiers.

Having defined wealth as Jewish money-power expanded into the bourgeois class as a whole, and having defined the proletariat in his new philosophical sense, Marx then proceeds, using Hegelian dialectic, to the heart of his philosophy, the events leading up to the great crisis. Marx had thus succeeded in defining the cataclysmic event he had first seen as a poetic vision. But the definition is in German academic terms. It does not actually mean anything in terms of the real world beyond the university lecture room.

Marx's does not develop a complex theory of the psyche, or of indentification processes that might make for a more complex understanding of power relations. Further, Marx's discussion of imperialism raises fundamental questions about his social theory. For the most part, Marx sees European societies as superior to those that they were colonizing, not only technologically but also as having a higher level of civilization. His shows that inherent problems of evolutionary approaches to society which structure them in a hierarchical way, so that some societies are superior and more advanced than others. Such a perspective undercuts the integrity of other cultures. Marx demonstrates how a theory of knowledge tied to progress can exclude many views of the world as either irrelevant or just wrong. Thus, the histories and beliefs of entire cultures, particularly outside of the West, were not extensively studied by Marx.

Marx creates a historical salvation narrative, with the proletariat as the embodiment of good that he disguises as scientific. Notwithstanding Marx's claim that he is developing a materialist, economically based theory of society, he produce a normative framework which allows him to evaluate different cultures in a hierarchical manner, as he especially compares the "rational" West with the "irrational" non-West. In the wake of anthropological investigations of non-modern cultures, it is apparent that almost of all people can give good reasons for their conduct, for what is considered rational is tied very closely to cultural and social contexts, and varies from society to society. These considerations certainly mean that any philosophy of history based on a nation of inevitable rational progress must be rejected.

Marx's concentration on labor and economics inhibits him from analyzing others factors in structuring social life, from gender and race to administrative surveillance and culture more generally. Marx often investigates societies as self-contained wholes. While this allows him to make connections between phenomena as disparate as class and religion, it also raises some problems. Marx tends to compare entire societies with one another (the English with Indians, for example), and he sometimes argues that one is superior to the other. If Marx had seen cultures and societies as more permeable, open to reciprocal influences, he might not have made such hierarchical judgments. The task for a social science now is to study social differences without essentialzing and positioning them as inferior or subordinate.

Marx's analysis of democracy also has difficulties. Marx has a limited view of the relationship of civil society to democracy. Many theorists now argue that civil society is much more than a market economy, as it is the realm where voluntary organizations, from unions to church groups, can arise. Such groups need a space to develop mutual ideas and solidarity. If civil society is eliminated, so is the arena for the generation of sauces of solidarity and mutuality. Communist dissidents such as Vaclav Havel remind us that this is exactly what happened under communist and other authoritarian regimes, as the free, public spaces, which allowed people to develop common ideas, and beliefs were thwarted by these governments.

These are strong criticisms of Marx's perspective. Yet Marx's view of colonialism also raises some interesting issues that should be retained in present day social theory. Marx refuses to romanticize non-Western cultures; he recognizes that they too suffered such internal oppression, from inter-tribal warfare to class, gender, and racial domination, and a simple minded cultural relativism can blind Westerners to the injustices that exist in the non-Western societies. Marx's rethinking of the lord-bondsman dialectic, if applied to colonialism, also opens up some interesting ways of thinking, as it combines changing types of historically determined economic and cultural oppression in a sensitive and sophisticated manner. Marx does not always heed his own call to explore cultures in their particular historical context, but that does not mean that this invitation should be rejected. Too often, contemporary sociology is satisfied with general statements about cultures and societies, and cultural critic are quick to criticize the West without exploring the complex internal dynamics and concrete historical circumstances of the countries and cultures they are discussing.

Our present concern with gender, sexual orientation, and race as sources of identity and social stratification can blind us to the continued importance of class, not only in shaping our economic life chances, but in subtly influencing the very ways that we act in the world and view our society. Marx shows that class denotes a certain experiential reality. Many recent studies have documented this fact, discussing a distinctive working class culture that is different from middle-class or bourgeois culture. For example, Pierre Bourdieu analyzes the social advantages of a person being born into the middle and upper classes. He states that such a person is endowed with a certain "cultural capital", which is inscribed in his or her very type of personality, ways of bearing, subtly accrue to those born in the upper classes. Much of Bourdieu's work shows how cultural capital is not evenly distributed among different classes, and the ways in which cultural capital helps reproduce the class structures of modern societies. Class mobility is difficult not only because of the lack of material resources, but also because of the difficulties faced by individuals in the working and poorer classes in assimilating the cultural capital associated with the upper classes. Accordingly, Bourdieu argues that sports are one of the few means of upward mobility for people in working and poorer classes. Sports represent for boys and increasingly for girls what beauty has always represented for girls, a market of cultural capital based on physical capital.

From a marxist view, the obsession with difference whether it is based on gender, race, or sexual orientation that we now see among groups reflects the competition of civil society and does little to critique capitalism. In a perverse way, seemingly radical demands for minority emancipation reflect the logic of a competitive market place and make solidarity harder to achieve. It also leads people away from the problems created by capitalism. The philosopher Richard Rorty writes that many contemporary US leftists "specialize in the 'politics of difference' or 'of identity' or 'recognition'. This cultural left thinks more about stigma than about money, more about deep and hidden psycho sexual motivations than about shallow and evident greed. Rorty is certainly sympathetic to these cultural critics of the left, as he is a major figure in the postmodern turn of much recent philosophy. Moreover, these cultural issues can be glimpsed in Marx's work. But Rorty, like Marx, fears that a focus on ideas and beliefs can blind us to the important economic practices that are profoundly influencing us.

In several ways, Marx can help us understand our contemporary world. His idea that theory is closely related to practice, and that intellectual and social power cannot be separated from class, remains convincing to us. Marx views economics as the root cause, the true reality of many of our actions and beliefs. He is often right, as it makes sense, for example, to understand political discussion about policies in terms of which class they will benefit. Yet, this view means discarding entire realms of phenomena as unimportant, or derivative. Rather than seeing the economy, or any other one factor, as the sole source of our actions, another strategy might be to pluralize and conceptualize this type of explanation. For example, Marx's theory of ideology exemplifies the idea that a more fundamental economic reality is responsible for the "superstructure" of surface appearances, as we saw in his analysis of religion. It seems tous that this profound source of spiritual meaning which is not fading away. Yet religion also does sometimes hide a deeper reality and camouflage economic interests, as in the US Christian Right's justification of the accumulation of wealth and the free market through its interpretation of scripture. Religion or any other social institution should be studied as complex, contradictory phenomenon embedded in particular historical circumstances.

Marx's ideas about alienation still resonate with much contemporary experience. So many jobs are dull and repetitive. People feel most fulfilled when they can be challenged by their wok and participate in the workplace, and have their ideas heard and respected. The quality of an individual's life is tied to the quality not only of the job he does, but to the community in which he lives. Many communities lack the resources and economic power to control their own fate. Alienation is still a major problem of capitalism. Overcoming it requires a radical restructuring of many aspects of the contemporary workplace, and revamping communities as well, perhaps through the redistribution of wealth from richer to poorer locales. Marx's approach to alienation can provide insights into contemporary mass media and mass culture. Thinkers such as Marx Horkheimer and Theodor Adorno of the Frankfurt School, writing in the marxist tradition, argue that mass culture follows the same logic as mass production. The fashioning of cultural products is similar to factory-made items-both are commodities, made to be bought and sold for a profit, and so take on standardized and uniform characteristics. Most television shows and films following a logic of predictability and calculability, where sequels and new shoes/movies use the same formulas to attract and keep audiences. Jut, as in other realms of production, the culture industry is not controlled by the workers. This culture industry creates mass-produced concepts, which do not encourage people to think critically about their lives, or conceptualize alternatives to capitalist society.

Marx also demonstrates some distinctive features of our modern life. While one must be sensitive to hierarchical judgments when comparing the present and the past, it is important to keep in mind the distinguishing characteristic of our social world. Modern society is distinctive because of the rise of capitalism and industrialism, its rapidly increased scope and pace of change relative to other historical eras, and the emergence of new types of institutions, such as business corporations and a state concerned with social welfare, which use rational knowledge such as social statistics and econometric models of forecasting to understand the social world and ensure their continued existence. In our global world, Marx alerts us especially to the role of capitalism in structuring our lives. While other factors influence globalization, dominance by global corporations must be a central factor in understanding it by its consequences. Contemporary capitalist globalization is defined by a search for markets, low wages, and profits. Marx warns us that it is not a benign process that will automatically benefit everyone, but will profit the rich much more than the poor, and will create new struggles over social wealth and power.

Many scholars have presented marxism as a "historical movement," that indeed it is. But it is a movement in the sense in which Christianity is a movement; one in which there are important disagreements as to what the message of the founder really was. The comparison is certainly apt—in more than one respect, some would say. Writing on marxism nowadays is a frustrating business. It is scarcely possible to put forward any interpretation of Marx, of even any ascription to marxism of any fundamental tenet that will not be loudly and abusively disputed by some who claim to be marxists.

For Marx almost never employs the language of 'ought' and he energetically denounces the practice of characterizing capitalism as "unjust." All such language, he held, is moralistic claptrap—"ideological nonsense about right and other trash so common among the democrats and French socialists." By and large, Marx instead argues that a transition from capitalism to socialism is "inevitable." He does not hold that there ought to be a revolution but that there will be. This would seem to make Marx's central claim a kind of open-ended prediction; and of course, so viewed, his work invites, and has certainly received, criticism on such embarrassing questions as why, one hundred years and more later, the revolution has not in fact taken place in the countries that one would have supposed were most distinctively eligible for it and just what the proposed time-modulus of the prediction was supposed to be.

Many people who think marxism in error think, along the following lines: Marx had an ingenious theoretical structure that led to certain general predictions about capitalism, and time has simply shown those predictions to be erroneous. And many marxists think, that although it is surprising and worrisome that things haven't gone just the way one might have expected on the basis of Marx's writings, nevertheless his criticisms are fundamentally sound; and eventually history will afterall prove him to have been right even if it is not entirely obvious so far. Many critics argue that Marx was wrong all along: not just in his predictions, but in his theoretical structure.

Marx argued from certain general features of capitalism that both he and his bourgeois opponents agreed about. Marx believed that those very features necessarily led to the demise of capitalism and to the necessity and desirability of a change to socialism. In does not matter whether he or anyone thinks that this change must or ought to be violent; for their argument is that his analysis is fundamentally faulty, to the extent that it does not in fact give us good reason either for expecting or desiring the change at all peaceful or otherwise. Marx was wrong, not in detail and not in incidentals, nor in excusable failure to see what the future held in store. He was wrong, at the core—wrong in principle.

The core doctrines of marxism are two, closely related but distinguishable. They are: (I) that capitalism necessarily involves the "exploitation" of labor, in a sense of 'exploitation' that grounds a fundamental criticism of the system; and (2) that capitalism is a system that generates and reinforces class conflict, in particular between owners and nonowners of the "means of production," the conflict being due to a fundamental conflict of interest between those classes. In the absence of doctrine (1), doctrine (2)would either make no sense or at least be reduced to a doctrine with no distinctive marxian interest. The class conflict in question is due, fundamentally, to the exploitation asserted in (1). And, in the absence of (2), a socialist revolution—the essence of which is that it eliminates private ownership of the means of production, that is, the existence of a distinct capitalist class—would make no sense. Moreover, Marx's apocalyptic view that capitalism would ultimately destroy itself due to its internal "contradictions" is based on the exploitative "relations of production" that define capitalism.

But mainly, of course, socialists have leaned on Marx's apocalyptic assessment of capitalism, and in particular his belief that capitalism will necessarily lead to a growing "mass of misery, oppression, slavery, degradation, exploitation.' Insofar as that prediction is based on the simple theory of exploitation, it is as we have seen, utterly unsupported. William Leon McBryde remarks that he finds the claim above "intuitively highly plausible when applied to the most advanced industrial societies of Marx's day, but by the same token far less plausible when applied to most advanced contemporary societies." Hostility implies conflict of interests. But are the "classes" in capitalist society in conflict? Are their interests as classes opposed? That there is nothing in the basic features of capitalism that imply this. Marx, of course, must hold that this conflict was absolutely fundamental. We should expect a class interest to be something that unifies its members, something that gives them reason to identify with one another and perhaps even to make some sacrifices on its behalf. A feeling that we all stand or fall together arises.

Second, the new kinds of classes Marx envisages do not behave in the same way as the old ones exemplified by the Ancient Regime. The old–style classes were fixed subsets of the populace; mobility from one to the other was extremely rare The members of those classes did not have to do anything to be members: all you had to do was have the right parents. Since the membership in such classes was fixed, there was no problem identifying one's fellow members; and moreover, once a member, always a member. No problem about people sneaking across the lines.

Finally, let us bear in mind that Marx's argument is supposed to be purely economic. The idea is not that by some kind of ill-understood chemistry, capitalists get together and so do proletarians. The interests of these classes are to arise directly from their "relationship to the means of production," namely, in that the capitalists own those means while the proletarians do not and have nothing to sell but the sweat of their bodies.

The issue before us, then is whether the "relations of production" in question do in fact yield a class interest or interests of the kind in question. In particular, of course, it is whether they yield an interest on the part of the working classes in eliminating the other class.

What makes someone a capitalist, a member of the "bourgeoisie," is that he owns capital. And that is all. "How much?" It has nothing, as such, to do with who your parents were—though there is a decent chance that, if they did well, then you would inherit some capital and hence find you have become a capitalist. Nor are there any laws saying that you, and you are forever barred from membership. Anyone can play, in one way or another; or, at any rate, anyone who is not literally earning at subsistence level. In a purely market society, the laws protect people and their property: any kind of property, any person's property, so long as it was legitimately acquired. And, in fact, the membership of the capitalist class is unstable. It is also, of course, vague. Moreover, we have to bear in mind that, as things are, all sorts of noncapitalists make greater incomes than most capitalists. Nor, were things all that different in Marx's day. The real wages of workers were of course, much lower than now, but the substantial spread from low to high, with income derived from earnings on capital, wages or a mix of both, was already there. This would make it a bit difficult for the aspiring member in good standing of the bourgeoisie to know who his friends were, and likewise a bit difficult for the workers to know who the enemy was. Engels himself, for instance, was probably on the bourgeois side of the line, if anything —luckily for Marx, who survived for many years on frequent doles from the faithful Engels. The marxian class antagonisms, alas, do not have clearly separate and identifiable antagonists.

Let us give Marx the proposition that the interests of owners and workers within any particular enterprise are opposed, at least in the short run. Marx's capitalists operate in an economy characterized by considerable competition—perhaps "perfect" competition. And Marx is clear that even if the individual owner happened to be a benevolent fellow and would have preferred to pay his employees more, the forces of the market will deprive him of this luxury. Competition provides the motivation also for technological progress, which increases the productivity of labor. And large capitalism, with the nineteenth-century version of high technology, is what Marx has in mind. These features of the situation make for a general pressure toward lower wages.

There is a further uncomfortable point concerning the class "solidarity" of the capitalists; viz.; that insofar as they are capitalists. The people with whom they are most evidently in conflict are, in fact, the other members of his class. Far from expecting the members of this group to cleave together and support each other, we in fact find that they are always on the lookout for ways to obtain a competitive advantage. This too is a very unsatisfactory basis for "class" interest. why would members of a class so constituted want to make sacrifices for one another's welfare? Would they have any reason to do this that would not be an even better reason for supporting the welfare of noncapitalists—say, contributing to unemployment insurance and welfare funds?

Critics point out that history has shown Marx to be wrong in his main claims. For example, during the very decades that he labored away to "prove" that the proletariat must, under capitalism, sink deeper and deeper into misery, the real income of the English working class rose steadily. The error is not happenstance. It is in the central logic of the theory. Marx may have made some contributions to economics. But his foundational ideas, the ones that form the main basis of his call for revolution, can only by fallacy lead in the direction. One critic has argued that the core of marxism turns out to be like the core of the onion rather than of the avocado: instead of the rich juicy pit of solid theory, the last peel leaves us with nothing.

The status of marxism as a science regularly troubled the Western marxists. Basic texts of the Second International and Soviet Marxism championed marxism as a universal science of history and nature, these definitions to be reduction of a social theory to a natural science; and a positivist approach undermined the critical categories of subjectivity and class-consciousness, which were foreign to pure nature. All the Western marxists agreed that marxism required a theory of culture and consciousness; and in order to accentuate these dimensions they confined marxism to social and historical reality. Marxism, for them, was not a general science but a theory of society. In their efforts to rescue marxism from positivism and crude materialism the Western marxists argued that Marx did not simply offer an improved theory of political economy. Marxism was primarily a critique. In his most utopian formulations Lukacs viewed marxism as committed to the abolition of political economy or to emancipation from the rule of the economy. The categories of political economy themselves expressed an economic domination that marxism sought to subvert.

Korsch recalled that Marx subtitled all his major works 'critique'. Marxism was not exhausted by the discovery of new laws of social development; critique also required an intellectual engagement with bourgeois consciousness and culture. Vulgar marxists mistakenly believed that marxism meant the death of philosophy, but according to the Western marxists, it preserved the truths of philosophy until their revolutionary transformation into reality. Marx outlined the essential role of philosophy in '*Contribution to the Critique of Hegel's Philosophy of Right* where he asserted that the proletariat was the heart of emancipation, but philosophy was its head. Both were essential: 'Philosophy cannot realize itself without the transcendence of the proletariat, and the proletariat cannot transcend itself without the realization of philosophy.' Marx's early writings—his encounters with Hegel, the Young Hegelians and Feuerbach—revealed the philosophical core of marxism, and they breathed a utopian and libertarian spirit that was more subdued in his later writings. In this sense Western marxism is almost synonymous with a return to the early Marx.

The texts of the young Marx offered a correction to the widespread presentation of marxism as an anti-philosophical materialism. Marxism was materialist, but it was clear from Marx's criticism of Feuerbach, which turned exactly on this point, that he did not advocate a simple or passive materialism. Feuerbach had failed to incorporate the philosophical truths of German idealism into his outlook, and since he was unable to conceptualize the critical role of thought and philosophy, quietism pervaded his materialism. Marx hardly provided an apology for philosophy; he forcefully reiterated that the point was to transform, not simply understand the world. Yet he did validate the philosophical enterprise. Over a century later, Adorno in the first sentence of his *Negative Dialectics* alluded to Marx's critique of Feuerbach as justifying philosophy: 'Philosophy, which once seemed obsolete, lives on because the moment to realize it was missed'.

The Western marxists undertook a wide variety of cultural studies, which ranged over literature, music and art they also, increasingly, subjected to scrutiny popular, mass and commercial culture; since in their view mass culture constituted bourgeois society as much as did the labour process—perhaps more so. Some of them, especially the Frankfurt School, turned to psychoanalytic theory for similar reasons; it was not only a cutting edge of bourgeois culture, but also promised to illuminate how the individual imbibed culture.

The philosophical and theoretical formulations of Western marxism merged into political formulations that challenged Leninism. The philosophical concepts of subjectivity, consciousness and self activity could be translated into such political organizations as workers or factory councils, which seemed more faithful political expressions of the Western marxist commitments than did the vanguard party. They became the object of a sustained interest and qualified defense, which had affinities with the Marxism of the *Praxis* group of Yugoslav philosophers and sociologists.

Critics have argued that Western marxism constitutes an abandonment of classical marxism by its neglect of political economy and its departure from materialism and they discover in the texts of the Western marxists idealism and a remoteness from the prosaic realities of party life. Yet it must not be forgotten that Marx to was often distant from daily politics. Moreover, the Stalinization of the working class movement, and fascism, which forced many Western marxists into exile, were hardly conducive to practical politics by unidiomatic marxists. In any event, the Western marxists produced a compelling literature, often in fields ignored by others; and this literature was provoked by the weaknesses of the classical tradition they are sometimes accused of deserting.

Marxism is anything but simple, in fact it is highly complex, controversial, and, in virtue of its protean nature, difficult to describe briefly. The views of marxism depend on the authority cited. According to Perry Anderson, marxism is important because of sheer intellectual scope, as a theory of historical development, and as a political call to arms. Yet all three reasons are suspect. First, there are other wide-ranging theories that one might decline to endorse. Second, in on important sense, marxism, which features a reflection theory of knowledge, is anti-historical. And. third, there are numerous political calls lo arms one might reasonably decline to answer.

It would be an obvious mistake simply to condemn marxism, which has been politically powerful, sometimes enlightened, but also politically harmful in many ways, sometimes intellectually creative but very often intellectually stultifying or worse. But if the concern is Marx's philosophy the situation is somewhat different. We believe marxism tends to obscure, even to hide Marx's philosophical contribution for a number of reasons. These include the marxist insistence on the continuity between Marx and marxism; the marxist view that taken together they constitute a single unified world view; the marxist emphasis on marxism and even on Marx's position as science; the marxist idea of the division of labor between Marx and Engels who is often described as the philosopher of marxism, and so on.

The term "marxism, " which was not used in Marx's lifetime, has been routinely employed since then to refer to a view, or set of views, allegedly common to Marx and his following. This term seems to have been first used by Plekhanov the Russian marxist philosopher, shortly after Marx's death to describe a position allegedly common to Marx and his epigones. Plekhanov's student, Lenin the central figure of the Russian Revolution, politically and perhaps even theoretically the most influential marxist of the twentieth century, defines marxism as the system of the views and teachings of Karl Marx. This canonical definition suggests a complex relation between Marx and marxism, in which the latter is continuous with, hence authorised as, the "official" source of Marx's views. It is a little like saying: if you want to know what Marx's theory is about, you will need to study the marxists instead of Marx; they will tell you what you need to know. This implication was not lost on later marxists. Stalin, Lenin's political successor, noting the difference in the periods in which Marx and Lenin were active, contends that "Leninism" is the further development of Marxism under the specific conditions obtaining in the era of imperialism and of the proletarian revolution in general, the theory and tactics of the dictatorship of the proletariat in particular.

There are many difficulties in untangling Marx from Marxism. One is the multiform, varied, persistent, omnipresent extension of the influence of the former through the latter in a bewildering series of intellectual domains. Understood as an intellectual movement, marxism includes the extension of Marx's ideas to an increasingly wider range of social phenomena virtually across the board. An incomplete list would include in no particular order: literature, literary theory, political economy, sociology, history, historiography, political theory, religion, ethics, philosophy of science, psychology, ethnology, and so on, a simply staggering list of fields. Understood, on the contrary, not as an intellectual approach to one or more fields but as a political tendency, "marxism" refers to the complex political movement following from the concern to work out an acceptable view of political goals and political action.

Marxism divides roughly into official marxism that, during the Soviet period, ended with the demise of the Soviet Union, was constantly concerned with political orthodoxy, hence little inclined inward conceptual innovation, and unofficial marxism that, since it was never concerned with political orthodoxy, has always been far more lively. "Official" marxism, especially "official" presentations of marxist philosophy, have often been rather dull statements of a politically sanctioned point of view, lacking any real philosophical bite, devoid of more than the most distant philosophical interest. Unofficial marxist theory has often proven much more lively in applying and developing insights from Marx in interesting, often insightful and occasionally fascinating ways.

Marx theories are important, indeed a decisive source of insight into modern society and ourselves. Our discussion would be poorer without Marx. It would be unfortunate if, in the rapid disintegration of political marxism, Marx's ideas were to disappear. After Hegel and certainly after marxism, Marx's theories remain and will contain to remain relevant for as long as money is in short supply, and as long as problems intrinsic to modern industrial world such as poverty, differences in real opportunity between the rich and the poor, and similar economic difficulties continue to endure.

Interpretation of Marx's theories has often suffered from a broadly marxist approach which counterposes Marx to philosophy, thereby preventing an interpretation of Marx within classical German philosophy. In insisting on a distinction in kind between idealism and materialism, marxism since Engels implies the need for a similar distinction between Marx and the philosophical tradition. This distinction is often understood as one between non-science and science, where marxism claims for itself the status of science as understood in the spirit of modern natural science. 'This suggests an approach to Marx and marxism based on a distinction in kind between Marx and marxism as science and all forms of philosophy. This approach reaches a high point in the attempt of Louis Althusser the French orthodox marxist, to produce a "scientific" reading of *Capital* as if prior readings were somehow unscientific, unworthy of the name, hence false. The so-called "scientific" reading of Marx's texts advanced by Althusser suggests the possibility of going beyond mere interpretation in order to grasp Marx's writings on a deeper, immanent level. This approach is a variation on the idea, familiar from new criticism to strict legal constructionism, according to which interpretation need not, indeed should not refer to the context in which texts arise.

In interpreting Marx, it will be useful to consider his relation to the German idealist tradition for two main reasons. First, as a contextualist Marx insists on the relation of thought to context. To read his thought other than through its relation to the context in which it emerged is to read it against its own grain. It seems better to respect rather than to violate the criteria advanced by the position in its own interpretation. Second, Marx's theories are formulated in reaction to other theories, which were under discussion at the time he was active, and which can usefully be taken into account to grasp his intentions. There is no alternative to understanding Marx as best we can in his time and place from the perspective afforded by our time and place. Any reading of Marx must occur from the present vantage point. It is never possible to do more than that, and it must be conceded that other readings of his theories are possible. The politically motivated idea that there is one and only one correct reading, only one way to understand his position, which is the justification of Althusser's supposedly "scientific" reading of Marx, is simply indefensible.

It has become fashionable in some circles to decry marxism. In one way this is odd. We do not speak in the same tones of Platonism or Kantianism though studies of Kant and Plato abound. Interpretive commentary on the work of major thinkers is a common and legitimate scholarly enterprise, and not always a merely scholastic one. In the social sciences, at least, explicit reflection on established paradigms is a normal, and perfectly proper way in which problems are clarified and disciplines advance, particularly in times of theoretical crisis. Because the pioneering work of a Durkheim or a Keynes does constitute a paradigm, in Kuhn's sense, the form which theoretical debate takes is often that of a questioning return to, and reinterpretation of, the writings of an acknowledged past master. The context of such discussion is often a growing awareness of empirical anomalies which the relevant paradigms have difficulties encompassing. Every generation reappropriates its intellectual heritage in accord with its needs and priorities.

But there is, none the less, a particular problem with interpreting and understanding Marx. This problem is a moral as much as an intellectual one. No other modern social thinker has .influenced social and political movements as much as he. Some one-third of the world's population now live under governments which claim Marx's imprimatur for their policies and indeed legitimate their very existence in terms of his supposed theory of history. Marxist parties, of varying size and strength, claim to speak for the people everywhere they are permitted. This is not the case with a Kant or a Weber, and greatly raises the stakes of intellectual debate. Questions of what Marx meant by this or that have an inescapably political as well as a scholarly context, and may sometimes have very practical implications. In many cases the claim that Marx held such and such a view is itself absurd as this may be considered sufficient to confer authority upon that view. Nobody has yet been incarcerated or killed for their heretical interpretation of Kant, Plato or Weber is therefore a merely academic pursuit. However disinterested one's scholarly motives, conclusions often become part of other people's politics. The study of Marx can be a coded form of social criticism, it can be snivelling apologetics, but it can hardly be politically innocent. It is, of course, this political context of Marx scholarship-the association of marxist theory with what is claimed to be socialist practice-which gives marxism its rhetorical force. The accusation of 'scholasticism', 'academic' marxism, is a convenient moral bludgeon with which to beat 'bourgeois' intellectuals into shamefaced conformity, or marginalize the political pertinence of their researches.

It is very often just those-they frequently turn out to inhabit universities-who believe themselves to possess, in their own pet version of Marx, the truth incarnate, the revealed secret of history, who are the first to denounce serious Marx scholarship as marxology. In this environment the study of what Marx actually said not merely to be an academically defensible but a politically virtuous enterprise. If intellectuals are to be of any service to humanity, they must first of all serve the truth. The political context of Marxist debate, in short, makes it more, rather than less important to respect the constraints of academic scholarship when trying to expound his ideas. That is not to say definitive or a disinterested interpretation of Marx's thought to be either possible or desirable. Marx wrote an enormous amount over a period of many years. His legacy is very varied. Texts like *Capital* I, finished for the press, and revised through several editions, form the smaller part of the corpus that has come down to us. Unpublished drafts like *The German Ideology,* the *Grundrisse,* or the remaining volumes of *Capital,* all now treated as major works are part of our inheritance in ways they were often not for earlier generations. Apart from his 'economics', Marx penned political tracts like the *Manifesto,* an inordinate amount of penny-a-line journalism and even poetry. He left a voluminous private correspondence. There are obvious problems as to what weight to give to these different kinds of texts, dating from different periods of his life. Not all that Marx wrote was clear, unambiguous or even consistent. It would be exceedingly surprising if it were. But beyond this, why should we in any case seek to be definitive? It seems perfectly reasonable to read Marx in different ways at different times and for different purposes. It is a testimony to his greatness that we can do so, notwithstanding all attempts to freeze his ideas into formulaic and dogmatic moulds. Marx's thought lives in so far as it is interpreted anew by others, in the light of their changing needs. It is no more eternal than the nineteenth century that produced it. Definitiveness, then, a chimerical grail. Indeed its assertion to be profoundly authoritarian and coercive, indicative of an approach to theory which is the opposite of emancipatory.

This is not, however, to argue for an interpretive free-for-all. As Max Weber once remarked, Marx is not a taxicab one can drive where one will. It is often possible to demonstrate that Marx did not adhere to positions commonly ascribed to him. There is for us both a scholarly and a political point in engaging in such debate, scholastic and marxist as it might frequently appear. Precisely because Marx's name is so often invoked to authorize and legitimate contemporary doctrines and practices, to know what he did and did not say, and what can and cannot fairly be said in his name, becomes important and urgent.

This is, then, Marx must be read, interpreted, reinterpreted and deconstructed not in order to establish some new, impeccably accredited orthodoxy but rather to challenge the authority claims of the old. We hope thereby to suggest the possibility of reading Marx differently, of seeing him as pioneering an approach to the understanding of society and history which offers more empirical purchase than that normally identified with his name. '*Capital* is not the Holy Bible, and provenance no criterion of truth. That Marx said something does not make it right, and he was frequently, and demonstrably, wrong. Textual commentary is the necessary currency of a study such as this. But the test of an adequate analytic framework is its capacity to make sense of the world, not its conformity with Marx's or anybody else's texts.

The fundamental concepts of Marx's have been comprehensively misunderstood, indeed fetishized within mainstream marxism, and that the 'theory of history' which historical materialism is normally taken as offering rests on these fetishized foundations. Misunderstandings among marxists of what these concepts denote, and how they may legitimately be used, testify to a failure to comprehend their anchorage in Marx's distinctive methodology: the analytic practice. These misunderstandings have done enormous violence to what is most innovative and emancipatory in Marx's social thought. Rather more importantly, they eventuate in a form of historical materialism which does equal violence to real history - both that history people have made in the past, and that they might seek to make in the present. Marx's own praxis offers an alternative, and an analytically superior version of historical materialism.

Karl Marx lived and wrote during what he understood to be the most momentous social transformation in the history of humanity—the emergence of capitalist modernity. Marx was one of the first social theorists to analyze systematically the capitalist mode of production and to see it as constituting a modern world radically different from all previous social forms. Marx noted that although capitalism produced a massive rupture in the fabric of history, knowledge of the origins and nature of the new social system transforming the entire globe was occluded. This was the result of the sheer novelty and complexity of the wage and market system, of the oppressiveness of its effects on human beings, and of an ideology that obscures underlying social relations, presenting the movement of commodities and the hegemony of exchange value as if governed by natural laws.

The underlying motivations of Marx's work were to understand thoroughly the nature of the capitalist mode of production, to analyze it as a radically new form of society, and to lay bare its fundamental mechanisms of operation. These analytic aims were subordinated to the political goals of exposing these operations as mechanisms of domination, of tearing off the veils that clouded the political vision of the working class, of organizing the working class into a unified international body, and of abolishing capitalism as a system based on exploitation, dehumanization, and class antagonism. In order to accomplish these tasks, Marx required immense historical knowledge, a historical method that treats all social and cultural phenomena as socially constituted, a social theory informed by this assumption, and a theory of history that grasps the basic outlines and mechanisms of historical change. Such modes of understanding allowed Marx to contextualize capitalism and understand its origins, trajectories, and seemingly impending demise.

Marx's critical outlook was developed by assimilating numerous theoretical and political influences. Most importantly, these included French Utopian socialism, English political economy, and German idealism. Marx shared many political sentiments with the Utopian socialists, but he condemned their lack of theoretical rigor and developed a scientific socialism based on empirical analysis rather than moralizing rhetoric. Through a scientific account of human activity, Marx sought to grasp the dynamics of social and historical change, to uncover the constituting forces of the present, and to predict the probability of future events.

Although Marx uncritically embraced the positivist attitude that elevated scientific knowledge, and method over all other forms of knowledge he rejected the positivist search for ahistorical "laws" of development and its pretension to value neutrality. For Marx, the whole point of science was to help the working class overthrow forces of oppression. In *Capital,* Marx alternated passages of dense empirical analysis of capitalism with stinging attacks on its "vampire-like" thirst for the blood of living labor. Marx's scientific attitude was informed by a strong moral sense, by a "categorical imperative to overthrow all those conditions in which man is an abased, enslaved, abandoned, contemptible being." But Marx saw no contradiction between the scientific and moral-political character of his theory. Most theorists simply interpreted the world, but Marx maintained that the time had come to change it, by merging science and critique, theory and practice. Marx thus sought a theory of history and society that was both endowed "with the precision of natural science" and also was "in its very essence critical and revolutionary."

Marx believed that dialectics grants this revolutionary character to social and historical analysis. Marx's version of science was radically different from what later emerged as "scientific marxism," and the differences stemmed principally from Marx's more supple appropriation of Hegelian dialectics. Against the ahistorical methods of Western philosophy, Hegel developed a dialectical vision of reality that treats all phenomena as historically and socially produced, and sees conflict and contradiction as the driving forces behind historical change. The dialectical method made it possible for Marx to overcome the reifying approach of positivist science that sees social reality as static and given. Marx's emphasis on the historical constitution of all things was evident in his critique of Feuerbach's materialism. According to Marx, Feuerbach grasped the reality of the sensuous empirical world, but failed to see that it was "not a thing given direct from all eternity, remaining ever the same, but the product of industry and of the state of society ... an historical product."

Hegel's dialectical method had revolutionary implications because, according to Marx, it helped to overcome fatalistic resignation to the way things are, and shifted focus to how they have been constituted and can be changed. In Marx's hands, dialectical method revealed the changing forms of conflict and crisis that operate in society, undermine its stability, and create new social dynamics. Dialectics also enabled Marx to move beyond the positivist method of treating phenomena as external and separate from one another by grasping the movement of things in their interrelationship, as different aspects of the same structure or system, as "opposites" united in the same relation. This allowed Marx, for example, to see gross wealth and poverty as inseparable effects of the capitalist market.

Of course, Marx argued that Hegel, by emphasizing the causal primacy of consciousness over social activity and relationships, understood dialectics in a mystified, inverted manner; consequently, Marx redefined dialectics in a materialist context. For Marx, the contradictions that propel history forward are not, as for Hegel, logical contradictions among opposing ideas, but conflicting material forces rooted within a particular social system. Marx shared Hegel's view that human beings transform themselves and their societies through the activity of production, but Marx saw this activity as the work of human beings rather than "Spirit." In his call for a "real history" of human beings in their changing forms of productive labor, Marx developed the "materialist interpretation of history" and was one of the first modern social theorists to interpret history as the product of human beings in their concrete, productive activity. For Marx, the primary forces of history were not ideas, political machinations, or war, but rather production, commerce, and industry: "In the whole conception of history up to the present this real basis of history has either been totally neglected or else considered as a minor matter quite irrelevant to the course of history."

On Marx's conception, dialectics is neither an immanent historical force, nor a totalizing worldview that subsumes all differences into an undifferentiated whole; rather, it is a supple empirical method, "a way of thinking that brings into focus the full range of changes and interactions that occur in the world." Theorists such as Lenin, Trotsky, Gramsci, and Lukacs rightly emphasized dialectics as the heart of Marx's methodology, but dialectics must also be understood as a theoretical and political vision that projects future emancipatory possibilities based on the analysis of existing society and past history. Where dialectical method relates to analysis of the present and past, dialectical vision is future oriented and grounds the norm of human emancipation in actual historical possibilities disclosed by dialectical method, while seeking to overcome debilitating oppositions in social and personal life.

In order to carry out a materialist analysis of modern capitalism, Marx, beginning in 1844, immersed himself in the study of political economy. While he drew from Ricardo, Smith, Mill, and others, Marx developed a sharp critique of political economy and shifted its analytic and political perspective. He showed that political economy was not a science, but rather an ideology that analyzed rent, profit, and other categories apart from the exploitation of the working class. Where political economy operated from the hidden point of view of capital, Marx analyzed social and economic phenomena from the perspective of the working class and its struggles for autonomy from capitalist exploitation.

Marx was decisively influenced by the Enlightenment movement and was very much a modernist in his basic temperament. He personified the Enlightenment emphasis on critique and its demand for rational social reconstruction and universal values. Early in his life, he called for a "ruthless criticism of everything existing" and carried through sharp but fragmentary attacks on religion, philosophy, property, law, money, the state, and Hegel. It is no accident that Marx entitled a later work, in the spirit of Kant, *Critique of Political Economy.* "Critique" for Marx, however, did not involve an analysis of autonomous forms of knowledge and their limits, but rather of the socio-historical conditions underlying knowledge and the crisis tendencies that threaten the stability of capitalist society. Marx also embraced the modernist celebration of change and innovation as liberating forces. Far from advocating a return to simple communal life, Marx's historical vision was oriented toward the future. He emphasized the limitations of static, isolated social forms and praised the dynamic qualities of capitalism that overturned tradition and provincial boundaries to unleash new social forces and establish new universal human relations. Marx praised the "revolutionary" bourgeoisie for accomplishing "wonders far surpassing Egyptian pyramids, Roman aqueducts, and Gothic cathedrals" for liberating the productive forces that "slumbered in the lap of social labour" for creating new wants, international interdependency, and the urban environment; and for rescuing much of the population from the "idiocy of rural life."

Despite its empirical and scientific character, Marx's theory belongs to the "philosophy of history" tradition. While rejecting the theological interpretation of history, Marx nevertheless retained the narrative codes of salvation within the secular context of progress. With Condorcet, Comte, and other Enlightenment thinkers, Marx developed a metanarrative that linked advances in science, technology, and rationality with advances in freedom and progress. Marx thus accepted the Enlightenment view that history, in however a tortured or indirect way, represents a progressive development toward a rational society and free individuality. But unlike apologists for the modern world, Marx was acutely aware of the negative side of modernity, and he condemned capitalism as a system of exploitation that thwarts the very possibilities for progress and emancipation that it calls into being. Moroever, unlike Habermas, Marx did not accept the rationalist faith in the power of reason and lofty moral principles to dissolve social conflict and self-interest. Marx believed instead that those who abuse power can only be removed through force, and he derided all liberal attempts to reconcile antagonisms without changing their fundamental sources rooted in class domination. Marx was rationalist enough, however, to believe that the proletariat would break its capitalist chains once it attained a rational understanding of the material conditions of its oppression.

While Marx analyzed the emergence of a universal history, he saw this as the result of real historical developments, of an increasingly global form of capitalism, rather than as a manifest destiny or the autonomous march of reason. The idea of a universal history, of a common social goal and international form of association, was fundamental to Marx's vision of history and concept of human liberation. From the beginning to the end of his career, Marx was decisively influenced by the Hegelian-Romantic vision of a social and individual being no longer divided against itself, of a harmonious and unlamented mode of human existence that overcomes the forms of antagonism and fragmentation created by the historical process. Marx's vision of emancipation foresaw the possibility of a future communist society where the conflicts among human beings and between humanity and nature can be overcome, where the human species can join in a rational and democratic association that reconciles particular and general interests, where national differences are eliminated in an international social order, and where the contradiction between human essence and human existence is abolished so that human beings develop rather than mutilate themselves in their activity.

Following Hegel, Marx interpreted history as a process of differentiation, driven by conflicts and contradictions. In its historical development, an original unity, be it a concept or a communal clan, is sundered apart, alienated from itself, differentiated into various aspects, and eventually returns to itself in a climactic moment that signals the end of history, at least as hitherto known. For Marx, history involves the alienation of a subject—not Reason, but humanity—from its creative powers. But the movement of history allows for an eventual recuperation of these powers in a higher, more developed form. Marx's theory of history traced the historical process of domination and alienation, but it analyzed the tendencies whereby this same process ultimately can lead to human liberation.

Marx's historical vision is a materialist translation of Hegel's notion of a "concrete identity," of a differentiated unity that can become whole again after protracted alienation through historical movement. Since Marx's unity, unlike Hegel's, is not guaranteed by history, but has to be produced out of tendencies and possibilities within the present, his emancipatory norm requires a political vision of how the working class can collectively transform present possibilities of freedom into a social reality and thereby win the emancipation of all humanity. Throughout his life, Marx sought a viable theory and practice that would empower workers all over the globe to seize the reins of history. Once this was accomplished, he believed, the movement of communism would bring the end of one history, the hitherto existing history of human alienation, and inaugurate the beginning of a new history of human freedom. This vision of a future communist society is an apocalyptic vision of a rupture in history as great as capitalism, yet which also builds on the achievements of the entire historical past.

Against all readings that essentialize Marx as a particular kind of theorist, such as a humanist or a positivist, or that claim he developed a crudely reductionist method, Marx should be read as a supple and complex, but not always consistent theorist of historical change and revolution. As Adamson forcefully demonstrated, we cannot speak of the marxist theory of history since Marx developed various models and visions, and frequently changed his mind on fundamental issues. Although Marx advances a forceful, monoperspectival interpretation of history as determined by the dynamics of production and class struggle, he employs, within this context, various theoretical and political models to examine social reality from numerous standpoints. Throughout all of his works, Marx advances a Hegelian vision of history as a continuous evolutionary process driven by the dynamic of objectification. In their interaction with nature through productive activity, human beings concretize and embody their personality and creative powers in their objects. As they shape and change their world, they simultaneously shape and change themselves. The development of the individual follows the evolution of its social forms of interaction, which themselves are determined by the dynamics of production.

This evolutionary view emphasizes lines of continuity from tribal to communist society. Marx employs three different continuity models in different stages of his work: (1) the humanist model, which interprets history as both the alienation and realization of the human essence; (2) the productive forces model, which interprets history as the progressive augmentation of the productive forces, a movement governed by the contradiction between the forces and, relations of production; and (3) the class struggle model, which interprets historical change as resulting from the struggles between contending classes. While these are logically distinct models, Marx frequently combines them in his concrete historical analyses.

The humanist model is developed mainly in the early stage of Marx's work, but remnants of it turn up frequently in his later works. Following Hegel, Marx sees history as the progressive development of human freedom throughout various stages of history. But this is a double movement where freedom emerges only through the advance of alienation. For Hegel, alienation involves the separation of Reason from itself in the process of its objectification in history. Marx, in contrast, understands alienation: as the separation of human producers from the "objective conditions of production," the communal context of their labor, and their own "species-being" and "human essence." These later two phases derive from Feuerbach and designate sociality, historicity, and creative activity as fundamental attributes of a distinctly human, rather than merely animal nature.

Like Hegel's Spirit, Marx's human essence unfolds in the process of historical development and is realized in a final stage of history. Marx views history as a continuous movement of a two-sided process: the humanization of nature and the naturalization of humanity. The humanization of nature is the process whereby human beings progressively enlarge the field of their objectification and gain increasing control over nature; the naturalization of humanity involves the evolution of the human being from a limited to a universal being and the consequent realization of its sensuous, natural powers in a free social context. Both aspects of the historical process result from the human interaction with nature through productive activity.

Marx grasps the totality of history not only as the alienation of the laboring subject from the process and products of production, but also as the reintegration or return of man into himself – a movement that culminates in communism. While presented as the "negation of the negation," communism is nonetheless defined as a positive movement, insofar as it appropriates the whole wealth of history, both human wealth and technological-economic wealth. The early Marx sees communism as "the positive supersession of private property, as human self-estrangement, and hence the true appropriation of the human essence through and for man; it is the complete restoration of man to himself as a social, i.e., human being, a restoration which has become conscious and which takes place within the entire wealth of previous periods of development."

Usurping the place of spirit in Marx's materialist rewriting of the Hegelian narrative, communism is the practical movement that overcomes the conflicts, contradictions, and disunities produced in history. Communism reunites individuals with the material conditions of their existence, with nature, with one another, and with their own human essence: "it is the genuine resolution of the conflict between man and nature, and between man and man, the true resolution of the conflict between existence and being, between objectification and self-affirmation, between freedom and necessity, between individual and species. It is the solution to the riddle of history and knows itself to be the solution". The riddle of history is that freedom is contained in alienation and cannot be attained without the entire process of social differentiation: "Liberation is a historical and not a mental act, and it is brought about by historical conditions, the development of industry, commerce, agric culture, and the conditions of intercourse." Marx believes the movement of history, the dynamic of differentiation/recuperation, leads toward the emergence of communism. The "very difficult and protracted process" of communism is "the goal of historical movement."

Thus, Marx's initial vision of history is thoroughly inspired by Hegel and Feuerbach. It deploys a metaphysical concept of a human essence whose inner nature is realized in the process of history. History is the single, localizable story of the realization and universalization of human freedom. The self-actualization of humanity unfolds through a teleology. Like Hegel, Marx sees nature as completing itself through human freedom and self-awareness.

The productive forces model first appears in *The German Ideology*. Just one year after completing the *Economic and Philosophic Manuscripts*, influenced by Engels' work on political economy, Marx attained a much more detailed and empirical understanding of the material forces behind historical change. He abandoned Feuerbach's terminology and much of his Hegelian baggage. The essentialist view of the *Economic and Philosophic Manuscripts* whereby a historical subject expresses its nature is relinquished in favor of a "pragmatological" view that stresses the active role of human beings in shaping their history. This view posits a dialectic between needs and productive activity, where the existence of needs requires production and production creates new needs. In place of a nondifferentiated account of the universal meaning of history, Marx with Engels, now divides history into a series of "modes of production"—tribal, ancient, feudal, capitalist, and communist—each of which represents a different form of social interaction with nature and creates different modes of life. Once again, we find a single, universal narrative of history, this time interpreted as the evolution of human activity through successive historical generations.

Despite a periodization scheme in which both capitalism and communism are represented as historical ruptures, Marx and Engels underline the fundamental continuity in history across successive modes of production. From this standpoint, continuity is understood not in terms of the realization of the human essence, but rather the cumulative development of the productive forces themselves: "at each stage of history there is found a material result: a sum of productive forces, a historically created relation of individuals to nature and to one another, which is handed down to each generation from its predecessor; a mass of productive forces, capital funds and conditions." Each historical product is "the result of the activity of a whole succession of generations, each standing on the shoulders of the preceding one, developing its [i.e., the former's] industry and its intercourse, modifying its social system according to the changed needs of the new system."

This and other statements made by Marx in subsequent works points to the following dynamic of historical change: the technical basis of a given society calls into being certain relations of production that serve optimally to promote the continued development of the productive forces. Relations of production "correspond to" forces when they further the growth of the productive forces, and they become a conservative "fetter" to this growth when a particular social class tries to retain its social power rather than promote technological development that threatens this power. At this stage there is a "contradiction" rather than a 'correspondence' between the forces and relations of production; a new set of relations and hence a new economic base and a new superstructure will emerge in order to better promote technological advance. The relations of production are subordinate to forces of production insofar as their function merely is to promote technological development. The contradiction between forces and relations is described as the fundamental "motor" of historical change. Thus, on this model, the development of the productive forces is the main impetus behind the ever-expanding division of labor and the process of social differentiation.

The third continuity model, the class struggle model, is anticipated both in *The Holy Family* and *The German Ideology,* but makes its first explicit appearance with the publication of *The Communist Manifesto.* It also turns up in the 1859 Preface to *A Contribution to the Critique of Political Economy,* and is the privileged model of *Capital.* On this perspective, the unity of all written history is interpreted from the standpoint of class struggle: "Freeman and slave, patrician and plebian, lord and serf, guild-master and journeyman, in a word, oppressor and oppressed, stood in constant opposition to one another, carried on an uninterrupted, now hidden, now open fight, a fight that each time ended, either in a revolutionary re-constitution of society at large, or in the common ruin of the contending classes." Although capitalism is again represented as a break in history, it is also seen as "the product of a long course of development, of a series of revolutions in the modes of production and of exchange." As a form of class society, capitalism stands in continuity with all past societies; it is the last antagonistic form of the social process of production and prepares to bring "the prehistory of human society" to a close. Communism inaugurates both the end of alienated history and the beginning of nonalienated, free history.

Thus, one can identify various continuity models that Marx develops in different stages of his thought. Rather than seeing these models as incompatible, or as discontinuous formulations divided by an "epistemological break" they stand as different perspectives on history, each articulating a different yet related aspect of continuity, and that Marx employs all of them together in his later work. There are also fundamental lines of coherence that link these models together in a multiperspectival vision of history. While after 1844 Marx abandoned the metaphysical concept of human essence, along with the anthropological model of history, the problematic of alienation is integral to later writings (e.g., the *Grundrisse, Capital,* and *Theories of Surplus Value*) where terms such as "alienation" and "objectification" still appear frequently. The humanist model is presupposed in both the productive forces and class struggle model insofar as the development of productive forces involves a progressive separation of labor from the process and products of production, and alienation is a motivating force of class struggle. There is a direct link, moreover, between the productive forces model, and the class struggle model since Marx sometimes interprets class struggle as the active political expression of the contradiction between the forces and relations production. This contradiction "necessarily on each occasion burst out in revolution" and the "collisions of various classes." On the technological determinist model, this involves a struggle between ascending and descending classes, between those classes that advance the development of the productive forces and those that impede it.

Underlying all three continuity models are the constant themes of the mutual transformation of human beings and nature through production; economics, technology, and class struggle as the decisive causal forces of social change; the evolution of individuals and society by means of the evolution of the productive forces and the division of labor; and the progressive advance of history toward communism and human emancipation.

Under these conditions, the social nature of the human being appears as something accidental or extraneous; it is degraded into a mere means for the realization of private, egoistic ends. To recover the true social nature and integrity of human beings, Marx calls for the overthrow of private interests, the recuperation of species-being, and the return of the individual to itself as a coherent totality: "Only when real, individual man resumes the abstract citizen into himself and as an individual man has become a *species-being* in his empirical life, his individual work and his individual relationships, only when man has recognized and organized his forces prepress as social forces so that social-force is no longer separated from him in the form of political force, only then will human emancipation be completed."

Although there are deterministic and teleological tendencies in Marx's work, these occur mainly in the abstract summaries or presentations of his method. The thrust of his concrete analyses, in contrast, points in nondeterministic and nonteleological directions. From his texts, it is clear that Marx does not posit a linear development of modes of production leading from tribal to communist society, does not see history as a seamless narrative of progress, does not believe in an immanent law of motion leading inevitably toward communism, and does not embrace an economic or technological determinist account of social change. Rather, he sees discontinuities between Western and non-Western social forms and, within Western history, between precapitalist and capitalist societies; he holds that human beings shape, and are shaped by, their social and natural environment; he claims that history is a human product; and he believes that the "unfolding" of the contradictions of capitalism guarantee nothing but what conscious political subjects can make of them.

It would be wrong to argue that the dominant view of Marx is a facile reductionist and totalizer. Although he treats all social practices as derivative of labor and is too economistic in his analysis of precapitalist societies, Marx is opposed to any universal method that attempts to substitute deduction of historical laws for concrete analysis of specific social situations. Within the framework of historical materialism, Marx adopts a rich, complex, and multicausal analysis of social change. Diachronically, he analyzes continuities and discontinuities; synchronically, he analyzes social change from the standpoints of economics, politics, technology, work relations, war, and other factors. The methodology of *Capital* is "irreducibly pluralistic" in its "variety of different forms of analysis and descriptive matter." These include economic, historical, political, and sociological arguments and modes of description, along with moral critiques of exploitation and alienation. The variety displayed in these different elements in Marx's analysis in *Capital* shows that his treatment of capitalism does not take the form of a unified deductive system from which all relevant particulars can be deduced. Instead, Marx's account is a family of related explanatory arguments, bits of analysis, historical comments, and descriptive efforts loosely organized by a common perspective. No general theory akin to atomic theory permits Marx to unify all his material into a single deductive system.

The fact that Marx adopts a pluralist, multicausal mode of analysis does not mean that he is an eclectic who vacuously believes everything determines everything else. As Althusser insisted the logic of overdetermination Marx employs rejects both economistic monism and the theoretical void of epistemological pluralism, which asserts that all perspectives and explanatory frameworks are equally valid and which fails to specify ultimately determining causes in society. Marx believes that only a materialist analysis can represent real social dynamics, and yet within this framework he specifies numerous factors of determination as they interrelate within a "structure in dominance." Despite the different models, standpoints, and tensions in Marx's works, there is also a good deal of coherence and consistency. Marx always tries to account for change in terms of dynamic developments within a society that lead to internal contradictions, but he does not limit this to a simple contradiction between forces and relations of production. He consistently roots the basic factors of social change in the mode of production of social life, appealing to technology, economics, work relations, and political forces.

One such line of continuity and coherence is the Hegelian vision of history as a dialectic of alienation and freedom, differentiation and unification, loss and recuperation. On this vision, human emancipation, just like the freedom of Spirit, cannot be achieved in pure, abstract, and unmediated form; rather, freedom is a historical product that requires a process of differentiation and alienation. Against Rousseau, Marx does not believe that humanity is born free and then placed in chains. It is only when there is established a complex social division of labor, an advanced development of technology, a creation of universal forms of human association, and the evolution of individuals beyond "sheep-like or tribal consciousness" into beings rich in abilities and needs that the historical preconditions of human freedom exist. But since differentiation unfolds as alienation, the process reaches a point where the divisions and antagonisms that dynamically drive history forward are no longer needed and become an impediment to further progress; emancipation can be attained only through the abolition of conflicts, contradictions, and oppositions.

For Marx, this stage in history is reached in nineteenth-century capitalist society. Marx praises capitalism for its powerful development of the productive forces, for establishing universal social relations, and for producing complex individuals, but he condemns it for organizing these dynamics around the imperatives of production for private profit and there by blocking the historical movement of democracy, equality, and freedom. Only through the abolition of capitalism and the creation of communism can the historically accumulated powers of humanity be realized in conditions of freedom.

Through analysis of actual historical possibilities, Marx foresees the end of human need and greed and envisages a transition from the realm of necessity to the realm of freedom. "Freedom can only consist in socialized man, the associated producers, rationally regulating their interchange with Nature, bringing it under their common control, instead of being ruled by it as by the blind forces of Nature." In Marx's vision, the task of communism is to overturn all forces of alienation in order to allow human beings to gain control over the conditions of their practical existence, to appropriate the objective and subjective wealth of history, and to overcome all debilitating oppositions. This requires the abolition of the capitalist state, private property, religion, money, and all other alienating forces that mediate the direct relationship among freely interacting human beings and between each individual and its own nature.

By abolishing all false mediations and oppositions, Marx believes that communism can resolve the most fundamental contradiction, that between human essence and existence, between potentiality and actuality, such that objectification is no longer alienation but self-actualization. By abolishing the division of labor in the form of the "fixation of social activity," communism is the movement of human beings developing their multifaceted abilities in various ways without being restricted to any one mode of activity. "Only at this stage of history does self-activity coincide with material life, which corresponds to the development of individuals into complete individuals." The ultimate goal of communism is to return to the individual the most important possession he or she can have, the free time needed to develop one's personality and creative abilities. Communism is defined therefore as a "fresh confirmation of human powers and a fresh enrichment of human nature." It is designed to render it "impossible that anything should exist independently of individuals" as an alien power.

Human progress from now on is to be measured in terms of the degree of the all-around development of human individuals themselves; the social imperative shifts from development of objective to subjective forces. The social whole that Marx envisages is not an abstract or homogenous whole that erases all distinctions and levels individuality, but rather a concrete or mediated unity that allows for the genuine flourishing of differences in an unantagonistic way. Where precapitalist societies produced sociality without sufficient individuality, and capitalism produced individuality without sufficient sociality, Marx sees the goal of communism to be the overcoming of this opposition through the creation of the social individual, of free and creative individuals interacting harmoniously in solidarity with one another. To borrow Adorno's phrase, Marx's vision of history is informed by a "negative dialectics" that eschews oppressive homogeneity without abandoning the norm of unity and community.

There were only eleven mourners at Karl Marx's funeral on 17 March 1883. 'His name and work will endure through the ages,' Fredrich Engels predicted in a graveside oration at Highgate cemetery. It seemed an unlikely boast, but he was right. The history of the twentieth century is Marx's legacy. Stalin, Mao, Che, Castro - the icons and monsters of the modern age have all presented themselves as his heirs. Whether he would recognise them as such is quite another matter. Even in his lifetime, the antics of self-styled disciples often drove him to despair. On hearing that a new French party claimed to be Marxist, he replied that in that case 'I, at least, am not a Marxist'. Nevertheless, within one hundred years of his death half the world's population was ruled by governments that professed Marxism to be their guiding faith. His ideas have transformed the study of economics, history, geography, sociology and literature. Not since Jesus Christ has an obscure pauper inspired such global devotion or been so calamitously misinterpreted.

It is time to strip away the mythology and try to rediscover Karl Marx the man. There have been thousands of books about Marxism, but almost all have been written by academics and zealots for whom it is a near-blasphemy to treat him as a figure of flesh and blood - a Prussian emigre who became a middle-class English gentleman; an angry agitator who spent much of his adult life in the scholarly silence of the British Museum Reading Room; a gregarious and convivial host who fell out with almost all his friends; a devoted family man who impregnated his housemaid; and a deeply earnest philosopher who loved drink, cigars and jokes.

For the West, during the Cold War, he was the demonic begetter of all evil, the founder of an awesomely sinister cult, the man whose baleful influence must be suppressed. In the Soviet Union of the 1950s he assumed the status of a secular God, with Lenin as John the Baptist and, of course, Stalin himself as the redeeming Messiah. This alone has been quite enough to convict Marx as an accomplice in the massacres and purges: But why? Marx himself certainly never asked to be included in the Holy Trinity, and would have been appalled by the crimes committed in his name. The bastard creeds espoused by Stalin, Mao or Kim Il Sung treated his work rather as modern Christians use the Old Testament: much of it simply ignored or discarded, while a few resonant slogans ('opium of the people', 'dictatorship of the proletariat') are wrenched out of context, turned upside down and then cited as apparently divine justification for the most brutal inhumanities.

Only a fool could hold Marx responsible for the Gulag; but there is, alas, a ready supply of fools. 'In one way or another, the most important facts of our time lead back to one man Karl Marx,' Leopold Schwarzschild wrote in 1947, in the preface to his splenetic biography *The Red Prussian.* 'It will hardly be disputed that it is he who is manifested in the very existence of Soviet Russia, and particularly in the Soviet methods.' The resemblance between Marx's methods and those of Stalin was apparently so indisputable that Schwarzschild did not bother to adduce any evidence for his preposterous assertion, contenting himself with the observation that the tree is known by its fruit which, like so many proverbs, is rather less axiomatic than it sounds. Should philosophers be blamed for any and every subsequent mutilation of their ideas?

Just as half-witted or power-hungry followers deified Marx, so his critics have often succumbed to the equal and opposite error of imagining him as an agent of Satan. There were times when Marx seemed to be possessed by demons, writes a modern biographer, Robert Papyri. 'He had the devil's view of the world, and the devil's malignity. Sometimes he seemed to know that he was accomplishing works of evil.' This school of thought more of a borstal, really reaches its absurd conclusion in *Was Karl Marx a Satanist*?, a bizarre book published in 1976 by a famous American hot-gospeller, the Reverend Richard Wurmbrand.

After the end of the Cold War and the apparent triumph of God over Satan, countless wiseacres declared that we had reached what Francis Fukuyama smugly called the 'End of History'. Communism was as dead as Marx himself, and the blood-curdling threat with which he concluded the *Communist Manifesto,* the most influential political pamphlet of all time, now seemed no more than a quaint historical relic: 'Let the ruling classes tremble at a communistic revolution. The proletarians have nothing to lose but their chains. They have a world to win. *Working men of all countries, unite*!' The only fetters binding the working class today are mock-Rolex watches, but these latter-day proletarians have much else which they hate to lose microwave ovens, holiday timeshares and satellite dishes. They have bought their council houses and their shares in privatised utilities; they made a nice little windfall when their building society turned into a bank. In short, we are all bourgeois now. Even the British Labour Party has gone Thatcherite.

Why, they wondered, would anyone wish to write about still less read about such a discredited, outmoded, irrelevant figure? The more we studied Marx, the more astoundingly topical he seemed to be. Today's pundits and politicians who fancy themselves as modern thinkers like to mention the buzz-word 'globalisation' at every opportunity without realising that Marx was, already on the case in 1848. The globe-straddling dominance of McDonald's and MTV would not have surprised him in the least. The shift in financial power from the Atlantic to the Pacific-thanks to the Asian Tiger economics and the silicon boom towns of west-coast America was predicted by Marx more than a century before Bill Gates was born.

There is, however, one development which neither Marx nor we had foreseen: that in the late 1990s, long after he had been written off even by fashionable liberals and post-modernist lefties, he suddenly be hailed as a genius by the wicked old bourgeois capitalists themselves. The first sign of this bizarre reassessment appeared in October 1997, when a special issue of the *New Yorker* billed Karl Marx as 'the next big thinker', a man with much to teach us about political corruption, monopolisation, alienation, inequality and global markets. 'The longer I spend on Wall Street, the more convinced I am that Marx was right,' a wealthy investment banker told the magazine. 'I am absolutely convinced that Marx's approach is the best way to look at capitalism.' Since then, right-wing economists and journalists have been queuing up to pay similar homage. Ignore all that communist nonsense, they say: Marx was really 'a student of capitalism'.

Even this intended compliment serves only to diminish him. Karl Marx was a philosopher, a historian, an economist, a linguist, a literary critic and a revolutionist. Although he may not have had a 'job' as such, he was a prodigious worker: his collected writings, few of which were published in his lifetime, fill fifty volumes. What neither his enemies nor his disciples are willing to acknowledge is the most obvious yet startling of all his qualities: that this mythical ogre and saint was a human being. The McCarthyite witch-hunt of the 1950s, the wars in Vietnam and Korea, the Cuban Missile Crisis, the invasions of Czechoslovakia and Hungary, the massacre of students in Tiananmen Square all these bloody blemishes on the history of the twentieth century were justified in the name of Marxism or anti-Marxism. No mean feat for a man who spent much of his adult life in poverty, plagued by carbuncles and liver pains, and was once pursued through the streets of London by the Metropolitan Police after a rather over exuberant pub brawl.

Marx has been read as revolutionary, a scientist, a philosopher, an economist, and no doubt as other persona. But we must read him something of a politician. Marx's interventions into left-liberal and left-socialist politics are precisely relevant to the free market/mixed economy debates that are crucial to the future everywhere. Postmodernism is used here as a way of reconstructing our relationship to the past in order to render it more relevant to present-day politics. In effect, Marx is rescued from the marxist grand narrative and opened up to reinterpretation within a new cultural paradigm. There are now 'multiple Marxes' to contend with instead one. Re-assessments are periodically in order, and the new interpretative methodologies of postmodernism provide an intellectual reason for doing this. The new political situation globally provides another more pressing political one. Re-reading Marx is itself an important way of moving on intellectually and politically. Derrida has attempted to rescue Marx from the clutches of the marxist grand narrative and to argue for 'multiple Marxes' who can be applied to a changing socio-political context in a creative fashion:

> Upon re-reading the *Manifesto* and a few other great works of Marx, I said to myself that I know of few texts in the philosophical tradition, perhaps none, whose lesson seemed more urgent today. It will always be a fault not to read and reread and discuss Marx-which is to say also a few others and to go beyond scholarly 'reading' or 'discussion'. It will be more and more a fault, a failing of theoretical, philosophical, political responsibility. When the dogma machine and the 'Marxist' ideological apparatuses. (States, parties, cells, unions, and other places of doctrinal production) are in the process of disappearing, we no longer have any excuse, only alibis, for turning away from this responsibility. There will be no future without this, not without Marx, no future without Marx, without the memory and the inheritance of Marx: in any case of a certain Marx, of his genius, of at least one of his spirits. For this will be our hypothesis or rather our bias: there is more than one of them, there must be more than one of them.

Surveying the contemporary geopolitical situation after the collapse of the Soviet empire and the end of the Cold War, Derrida finds a world desperately in need of marxist radicalism, but not of marxist dogmatism:

> For it must be cried out, at a time when some have the audacity to neo-evangelize in the name of the ideal of liberal democracy that has finally realized itself as the ideal of human history: never have violence, inequality, exclusion, famine, and thus economic oppression affected as many human beings in the history of the earth and of humanity. Instead of singing the advent of the ideal of liberal democracy and of the capitalist market in the euphoria of the end of history, instead of celebrating the 'end of ideologies' and the end of the great emancipatory discourses, let us never neglect this obvious macroscopic fact, made up of innumerable singular sites of suffering: no degree of progress allows one to ignore that never before, in absolute figures, never have so many men, women, and children been subjugated, starved, or exterminated on the earth.

If this is a true picture of our current world, then it has been failed by marxism in its traditional guise, and the argument for a more open-ended postmodern marxism gains considerable momentum in consequence. The socio-political problems Marx identified are still with us, but not the same consciousness; the new consciousness requires a fundamental revision of attitude towards the grand narratives of the post-marxism included. In a prototypically postmodern move, pragmatism replaces dogmatism. Yet again, however, we have to recognise that any 'transformation' of Marx's basic theses would be anathema to the classical orthadox marxist constituency. What is dogma to Derrida is to the latter the key to humankind's socio-political salvation. It is hard to see how any compromise can be brokered between such fundamentally divergent viewpoints.

The topic of marxism remains a site where some of the most bitter exchanges have taken place about the value of postmodernism as a cultural ethos. Marxism may have its faults, but for many those faults pale beside those of which postmodernism is guilty:

> Without memory of morning or hope of night, without lost paradises or imminent collapses, antagonistic classes go on fighting, most disorderly and unpredictable struggle. Now we see what Marxism so fears in postmodernism and poststructuralism and why in its fear it has been unable to distinguish between its friends and its adversaries. It fears itself, or rather its own practice, whose image it cannot bear to contemplate. Marxist theory has confronted its inadequacy to its own practice and thus its own unequal development, its own contradictions.

Thereby requiring new interventions *ad infinitum.* On a field of conflicting forces whose balance of power shifts endlessly, we have no fixed reference points, nothing to guide us but the knowledge of our own errors. One such error, the knowledge of which ought by now to have emerged clearly enough, is the very concept of postmodernism itself. In its totalizing, transcendental pretensions, this concept precisely forecloses progress in thought by denying the possibility that the fissures, disjunctions, breaks in contemporary social reality are symptoms of an impending crisis. For the signal feature of postmodernism most inimical to historical materialism is its claim to be the end of all crises, the end of all narratives, the end of resistance and revolutionary transformation. The debate on postmodernism will prove to have been productive to the extent that it awakens in us the consciousness of its own limits, which are not the limits of history itself but rather the boundaries of that territory where Marxist theory has always intervened most effectively: the present conjuncture. The only truly irremediable error would be to believe that this present will endure forever.

Epilogue

> No universal history leads from savagery to humanitarianism, but there is one that leads from the slingshot to the megaton bomb.
>
> **—Adorno**

The modern thought is under attack by the postmodern discourses. Most of the cherished ideals and ideas of the modern thought have been subjected to assault by Foucault, Lyotard, Baudrillard, Dervida Rorty, and others. The connection between postmodern discourse and history is direct insofar as the very identity of the postmodern is premised on a historical break with preceding modern thought. The sharp historical consciousness of postmodern theory informs its methodological attack on universalist, foundationalist, and essentialist theories that abstract from changing sociohistorical conditions to ground theory in a timeless norm or standpoint.

The prefix "post" is ambiguous to the extent that it has temporal and philosophical meanings, signifying both a movement after and rejection of modern movements in theory and the arts. We also need to distinguish among "postmodernism," a critical movement within theory and the arts; "postmodern, theory," a theoretical development within philosophy and theory that breaks from core tenets of modern theory; and "postmodernity," a term that implies a larger, more systematic claim that we are in a new historical era. The argument of Jameson that we are in a new postmodern culture but not a new postmodernity that allegedly has superseded the main dynamics of "modernity" demonstrates that these claims are independent. Yet the accumulation of so many postmodern discourses in fields ranging from architecture and anthropology to philosophy and social theory leads one to wonder if indeed we are not in a new "post-culture" a "post-modern period" or a "postmodernity" where the hallmarks of the modern world—humanism, rationalism, progressivist theories of history, discrete nation states, and so on—are historically obsolete or philosophically bankrupt.

Still, it is important to realize that postmodern tenets are not wholly new or original. Indeed, new theoretical developments always have important anticipations in earlier times. The "new science" of the seventeenth century, for example, was not a total break with the past but a continuation of twelfth-century Greco-Arabic natural science and of some fertile ideas of fourteenth-century European medievalism. Similarly, many postmodern moves replay long-standing dissatisfaction with Enlightenment concepts and values. Long before Foucault and

Lyotard, Burke and other conservatives attacked the Enlightenment for its alleged superficial rationalism, naive optimism, and reckless utopianism, and some of these critiques were first voiced within the philosophical community itself. Voltaire, Condillac, Hume, Kant, Comte, and Spencer assailed rationalist faith in the unlimited powers of "pure reason" to know the world, Critical quarters of modern social theory and art issued further challenges to the universalism, foundationalism, and realism, as Nietzsche did in the nineteenth century and Dewey, Heidegger, Rorty, and others have done in the twentieth century. Nearly every major tenet of postmodernism, such as the embrace of diversity over uniformity and desire over thought, was powerfully prefigured by existentialism and Romanticism. In fact, one could find anticipations of postmodern theory with the first appearance of relativism and skepticism in the arguments of the sophists or Pyrrhonists, or with the Heraclitean critique of the static Parmenidean ontology.

Thus, postmodern theory should be understood not as an absolute rupture or break with modern theory, but rather as a continuation of the critical aspects of modern thought itself and the skeptical, relativist, pluralist, and pragmatist underground tradition of Western philosophy. As a prefix, "post" has more meaning as a philosophical than a temporal designator, pointing to an attitude skeptical of the powers of reason that appears throughout both Western and Eastern history. Thus, the postmodern belief that nothing is new and everything has been done can be applied to postmodernism itself. Advocates of the postmodern tend to exaggerate the novelty of their theories and to dehistoricize their work in relation to preceding traditions of thought. In social theory and historiography, we can point to the critique of totalizing, universal histories by Von Ranke, Herder, arid Weber; the denunciation of radical and utopian schemes of change by Burke; the rejection of foundationalism and timeless truths in favor of relativism by Montesquieu, Herzen, and Dilthey; the attack on the notion of a fixed human nature by Vico, Rousseau, and Marx; the abandonment of metaphysical theories of history by Dilthey; the disavowal of grand-narrative schemes as illusory or dangerous in favor of a strict empiricism by Hume and Popper; the celebration of incommensurable cultural differences by Machiavelli, Vico, Montesquieu, Montaigne, and Herder; the adoption of a ultracasual mode that analyzes a complex interrelationship of numerous social forces by Montesquieu and Marx; and the emphasis on the literary nature of historiography by Trevelyan. The list is hardly exhaustive.

In the fields of social theory, philosophy, and historiography, postmodern theorists break with any attempt to situate reason outside of history. Many modern theorists seek to ground epistemological and normative claims in timeless, universal foundations rooted in clear and distinct ideas, a priori categories of the mind, purified structures of consciousness, human nature, or the laws of history or nature. Postmodern theorists deny that such foundations exist and seek to complete the break with premodern essentialism and foundationalism that many modern theorists failed to accomplish. The "quest for certainty" such foundationalism validates is overturned in the certainty that such a quest is groundless. Rejecting all static, historical conceptions of phenomena, postmodern theorists—following Hegel, Marx, Weber, Dewey, and others—adopt historicizing, contextualizing approaches to culture, literature, philosophy, and other "texts," reading them as artifacts produced within specific social, historical, and linguistic conditions. For postmodern theorists, everything is historically constituted, even desire and the body, dimensions of human life that typically have been considered pregiven and invariable. In particular, postmodern theorists abandon essentialist and idealist analyses of the subject as a unified consciousness that projects its intentions into the field of social action. They reject not only simplistic Entightenment models of a rationally motivated subject, but also the more general ideal of a conscious, autonomous self. By extension, they break with the notion of humanity as evolving, unified macro – subject. There is no collective agent of history in the form of Hegel's Spirit or Marx's Proletariat, only different historical groups and individuals.

This detotalizing move informs the postmodern critique of evolutionism and the philosophy of history. Postmodern theorists argue that history is not a continuous, linear path of development that encompasses all cultures within one great, movement and culminates in universal harmony at the impetus of teleological laws. Rather, history is a discontinuous, fractured plurality of micronarratives governed by an indeterminant play of contingent forces devoid of purposes, immanent logic, or coherent direction. The deconstruction of history follows the same movement as the dismantling of the subject, author, and text. Rather than seeking a universal history that subsumes disparate peoples into the abstraction of "humanity," postmodern theorists acknowledge temporal discontinuity and celebrate cultural diversity. Lyotard's declaration of war against totalizing met a narratives that reduce difference to uniformity is the battle cry of the postmodern movement that seeks to liberate the full plurality of historical and cultural voices. Thus, following the lead of Rousseau, Herder, Weber, and other modern dissenters from Eurocentric progressivism, postmodern theorists reject the devaluation of premodern cultures, sometimes—as is true of the early work of Baudrillard and Foucault —going so far is to evince nostalgia for past eras uncorrupted by instrumental reason. The core political vision of postmodern theorists is that of the liberation of difference and plurality from the oppressive and homogenizing effects of modern theory.

Postmodern theorists abandon the modern sociological belief in society as an ordered whole that can be grasped through systemic theory. They believe society is too dispersed, fragmented, differentiated, and complex to be adequately represented or mapped in a coherent theory, and they therefore produce partial and fragmented accounts of the world. They reject Marxian dialectics as a totalizing device and instead, with Hume, tend to see things as entirely loose and separate. Like Toynbee, they tend to see history as merely "one damn thing after another." Ironically, while they reject modern foundationalism, they retain modern individualism, both epistemologically (the isolated knowing self) and politically (the desiring monad). For Perry Anderson the postmodern emphasis on discontinuity, indeterminacy, and contingency results in "the randomization of history." Postmodern theorists, he claims, fail to grasp important continuities, developmental trajectories, and underlying causal mechanisms behind historical change—such as Marx and Habermas both attempt to theorize.

Postmodern theorists also deny the modern norms of truth and objectivity and claim that knowledge is unavoidably subjective and partial. Embracing a skeptical, ironic, and relativist viewpoint, they see all interpretations as equally good or bad, relevant or irrelevant, and they reduce historical facts to fictional constructions. Some postmodern theorists speak as though historical events have no independent status beyond the linguistic fictions of writers. Influenced by the Nietzschean-Foucauldian critique of the modern will to truth, postmodernists regard the real significance of truth and objectivity as their political function of legitimating scientific and political authority. Where many modern theorists have championed science and Enlightenment rationality as emancipatory, postmodern theorists attack these forces as repressive, pointing to the disastrous consequences of the rationalization the social world, such as the production of new modes of destruction, violence, and social control.

Thus, the modern linkage between reason and freedom comes undone in the postmodern description of rationalized domination. Rather than rethinking this relationship, as do critical modern theorists, many postmodern theorists reject the ideals of both reason and freedom and find nothing but the seeds of a totalitarian order in modern Utopian schemes of a rational transformation of society and humanity. The realization of the ideals of the French slogan "Liberty, Equality, Fraternity!" in the Reigh of Terror and Napoleanic invasions, or the catastrophic outcome of the Bolshevik revolution are precisely the kind of examples postmodern theorists have in mind when they refuse modern activist programs based on abstract, Utopian, global, or elitist visions of change. Accordingly, Lyotard finds the main characteristic of the "postmodern condition" to be "incredulity toward metanarratives. For Lyotard, a "metanarrative" is similar to the narratives produced by the philosophy of history tradition. It is a modernist vision of history as progress, as a linear, teleological movement of events toward the confluence of reason and freedom, grounded in foundationalist principles. For Lyotard and others, the metanarratives articulated by Leibniz, Kant, Turgot, Condorcet, St. Simon, Comte, Hegel, Marx, and Habermas are no longer credible in the wake of the deformation of reason in history and the philosophical critique of assumptions concerning the unity of history, the perfectibility of humankind, and the teleology of reason and freedom.

While they may reject metanarratives and lack positive normative conceptions of freedom, many postmodern theorists nevertheless use historical analyses to historicize modernity and promote political resistance to domination. Thus, Deleuze and Guattari and Lyotard in his early work analyze how capitalism tries to colonize desire and the libido, and they seek ways of escaping psychological and bodily repression. The early work of Baudrillard studies modern rationalization processes, which he thinks reduce the individual and forms of communication and exchange to crude utilitarian functions. Foucault's genealogies seek to expose how our identities have been constituted by normalizing powers so that they recreated in less coercive forms. Postmodern feminists attack essentialist theories of gender identity in order to free subjects for new social roles and psychological identities.

It is also instructive to compare different theories of the subject. Postmodern theories reject the essentialist view of the subject that is employed by the some modern theories. The continuist narratives of modern theory often depend on a theory of human nature, a conscious subject, or an evolving macro subject, a unified humanity. In his archaeological works, Foucault defines his task as purging history of all anthropological influences and eliminating the category of the subject. In his early and middle works, Foucault did not so much solve the problem of the subject as dissolve it by merely rejecting it as an active, substantive agency. His structuralist dismissal of the subject reduces it to an empty category and essentializes it as a pure nothingness, a product of discourse and power. Instead of developing an account of ways in which subjects can influence the course of events through knowledge and conscious intervention, Foucault reifies history as a pregiven result that occurs entirely behind the backs of subjects. Rather than analyzing a dialectic of intended and unintended consequences, Foucault sees no consequences to action at all because there are no agents of action. In his later works he abandons this view to acknowledge agency and the potential for autonomy, and thereby moves closer to the kind of modern account of the subject given by Marx and Habermas. But Foucault's later account moves toward the individualist-voluntarist side; at no time does he adequately balance the two perspectives of structure and agency. Ultimately, he never grants the full importance of social relations for subjective freedom, and tends to define individuality and sociality in opposition to one another.

From this perspective, the postmodern call for a radically free individuality is impossible given its negation of social relations and community. Postmodern theorists tend to see only the coercive aspects of subjectification that implode individuals into a normalised mass, and not the emancipatory aspects that differentiate the individuals from others and allow for the rich aesthetic-expressive attitude postmodernists celebrate. Postmodern theorists fail to grasp progressive tendencies in history toward greater forms of freedom and individuation. Foucault has a nondialectical discontinuous vision of a new subject entirely different than the moderr subject, a "total innovation." His belated acknowledgement of the positive aspects of modern subjectivity is severed froth a theory that connects historical-critical attitudes from an institutional framework and a larger appreciation of the historical development of subjectivity.

We see that postmodern theories are predicated on a rejection of the cardinal features of the modern traditions of history, philosophy, and social and political theory. Modern theory in various forms has come under attack for the allegiance to narratives of historical progress, the embrace of science, determinism, and objective laws of history, the search ' for necessary and universal foundations for theory, the humanist belief in free, creative agency, the ahistorical appeal to human nature, the equation of freedom and rationality, totalizing forms of theorizing and global and elitist models of social change. In place of such claims and tenets, postmodern visions of history typically see no progress or directional tendencies in history, deny the authority of science and validity of facts and causal and objective analysis, reject foundationalism and universal values, decenter the subject to determining social or linguistic forces, link rationalization to domination, reject global, utopian, systemic forms of theorizing and politics, and abandon normative language and epistemology.

Today, the core concerns of the modern era-rationality, freedom, progress, individualism, truth, and objectivity—are being challenged by postmodern theorists. Amidst the bloody turmoil of the Middle East and Bosnia-Herzagovina, the resurfacing of global tensions in areas such as North and South Korea, and the spectacle of suffering in places such as Rwanda, Kant's and Condorcet's visions of a future marked by universal reason, peace, and happiness seem hopelessly naïve and irritating. There is no doubt that modern values have received problematic philosophical formulation and political embodiment, and therefore that postmodern critiques can—as they have—contribute toward the revaluation and reinvigoration of modern values and theory. Yet, all too often, the aim of postmodern critiques has been to destroy the modern intellectual and political traditions, with the result that they have failed to redeem its important creative resources and have offered little or no positive alternatives to modern theory and politics. Rather, postmodern theories have done much to disarm effective social critique, while contributing to a climate of pessimism, skepticism, relativism, and a loss of faith in human potential to organize social and individual existence on a free, rational, and peaceful basis. The postmodern counter–vision sees modern history as the bearer of a new dark age, rather than the harbinger of progress and enlightenment. In postmodern culture, the modern sense of change, novelty, dynamism, and unrealized possibilities of the future gives way to a gloomy pronouncement of stasis and exhaustion of historical energies. The end of history thereby signifies the end of liberatory visions and struggles or, voiced differently, the eternity of capitalism.

In the shadows of the Enlightenment, can the notions of progress, freedom, rationality, selfhood, truth, and objectivity be reconstructed and salvaged in a politically progressive rather than conservative orientation, or are we truly moving toward the dystopian visions of Orwell, Huxley, and the cyber punks? The contrasting theories and politics we find represented by Marx, Foucault, and Habermas point to competing responses to the secular forces of science, technology, individualism, and Enlightenment that define the modern world. At least since the French Revolution, battle lines have been drawn between enemies and champions of the revolutionary forces of modernity and the crucial issues that rose there are still hotly debated and far from resolved. Marx and Habermas represent quite different positions on the side of those who wish to advance liberatory aspects of modernity, while Foucault represents a postmodern approach that seeks to construct theoretical and political alternatives to modernity and modern theory. Yet, these lines of distinction cannot be drawn so simply. Marx and Habermas represent competing positions within the modern framework and Foucault, in addition to offering postmodern alternatives to both Marx and Habermas, also draws from many of the same modern elements that inform their work. He straddles the borderline between modern and postmodern theory, rather than taking the leap of unfaith into the extreme postmodernism of Baudrillard, Lyotard, and others.

The question, therefore, is not what we can create ex nibilo in our allegedly new postmodern epoch in order to produce wholly new models of theory and politics, but which resources remain within the modern tradition that are useful for conceptualizing our historical present and creating an alternative future, and which elements are obsolete or problematic, and can be improved on by the postmodern critiques. This is precisely what is at stake in the modern postmodern debates, and critical theory promises to yield valuable in sights into the important theoretical and political issues and conditions that confront us today.

At the most general level, however, the differences separating modernity and post modernly are best characterized according to two major competing tendencies within modern thought: the Hegelian and the Nietzschean visions of history, the former opening the philosophical horizons of modern thought and the latter closing them. Marx and Habermas advance Hegelian visions of history that emphasize historical continuities, progressive tendencies of social development, emerging forms of rationality and subjectivity, the role of the individual within society, freedom as a social construction and relationship, and the reconciliation of conflicts and opposites. Foucault, in contrast, propounds a Nietzschean vision of history as a random succession of modes of violence and power that leaves antagonisms intact strives to create differences without unity, defines freedom as an individual accomplishment, attacks Enlightenment rationality, and finds no progressive movement in history. With Hegel, against Nietzsche, we must continue to be guided by the vision of reconciliation of objective and subjective worlds of reason and freedom, of rational laws that promote both community and individual freedom. In its deconstructive impulses, however, the Nietzschean vision helps to detranscendentalize the Hegelian vision of history, to curb its metaphysical proclivities, and to maintain the tension between opposing values. Neither Marx nor Habermas in any case accept Hegel's belief that the owl of Minerva flies too late, that philosophy can only interpret the world retrospectively, once events have transpired and it is too late to change them. But the Nietzschean vision is still useful in its focus on the future, on the need for a revaluation of values, and on maintaining an optimistic outlook, a joyful wisdom, that is lacking in postmodern theory except as textual play divorced from life concerns.

In this context we read postmodern theory less as an absolute rupture with modern theory, irreconcilably opposed to it, than as a critical response to the problems with and failures of modern theory that can be appropriated in a positive way. The concept of postmodern theory is valid not in the sense of something new and radical that comes after modern theory, since almost all of its key ideas were anticipated or developed already in the counter-Enlightenment, critical quarters of modern theory, and in avant-garde art; it is valid also in the sense of being against modern theory or, more precisely, certain features of modern theory and the Western philosophical tradition. As against the modern, it represents the coalescence of previous skeptical and antirationahst currents of thought in a focused and dramatic way that seems to allow for at least a provisional use of the term "postmodern."

Modern thought challenged the dogmatic and metaphysical basis of premodern worldviews and initiated a rationalizing, secularizing movement in theory. But the modern revolution was incomplete and retained a number of metaphysical beliefs, such as in a teleology of history, natural law or rights, or an unchanging human nature. Some versions of modern theory—those of Weber, Marx, Dewey, and others—challenged foundationalism, ahistoricism, essentialism, and other problems, but did not fully overcome them, as Marx did not overcome scientism or Eurocentrism and Habermas remained mired in teleology and transcendentalism. In large part, the exuberant optimism, simplifications, and naiveté of much modern theory must be understood against the background of stupendous advances in science, rationality, technology, and medicine, in addition to the desire to overcome the hegemony of medieval forms of ignorance, superstition, hierarchy, and religious intolerance. This crucial historical context is ignored in most postmodern critiques of Enlightenment and modern theory. In many ways, the modern rationalist tradition overcompensated for previous deficits in rationality, just as postmodern theorists frequently overcompensate for the problems in modern positions and jettison important theoretical and political advances. In Nietzsche's framework, the nihilism of postmodern theory represents the failure of the highest ideals of humanity as embodied in Enlightenment values.

Yet in his undialecncal negation of postmodern theory, Habermas fails to grasp the ways in which postmodern theory itself represents an advance in a cognitive learning process. In this case, that learning involves a realization that core claims of modern philosophy and social theory are philosophically untenable and politically problematic. Postmodern theory is a radicalization of the historicizing, detranscendentalizing impulse of Enlightenment rationality. Postmodern theory represents a critical, anti-metaphysical attitude—one that begins within modern theory itself—that seeks a more sophisticated and complex understanding of social and historical reality than that provided by-crude modern accounts such as are epitomized by Comte arid Spencer. We can therefore read postmodern theory as continuing the revolution modern theory began by criticizing the metaphysical residues modern theory and by pushing further some of its key critical themes. Hostmodern theories are effective for historicizing, localizing, concretizing^ and differentiating ahistorical and overly abstract aspects of modern theory, and thus for reconstructing modern theory in more satisfactory form.

Thus, while we see modern emphases on developmental and progressive tendencies in history, systemic interrelatedness, macroanalysis, and normative criticism on; behalf of emancipatory change to be principles worth preserving, find important value in postmodern critiques. Specifically there are things to be learned from the postmodern -critiques of linear and Eurocentric models of progress and emancipation; the emphasis on the dangers of science, technology, and rationality; the focus on historical difference, heterogeneity, and discontinuity over identity, unity, universality, and linear continuity; the substitution of contingency and indeterminacy for rigid law, determinism, and teleological guarantees; the insistence on the interpretive and constructed nature of historical narratives; the sensitivity toward the relation between power and knowledge and hence the dangers of replicating domination within critical discourses themselves; the emphasis on theory with practical and moral dimensions over esoteric abstractions; and the subsequent rejection of the universal intellectual in favor of the specific intellectual engaged in concrete struggles.

Yet we cannot understand the transition from the modern to the postmodern as itself representing a linear, unambiguous path of progress. For while postmodern theory has often advanced beyond modern theory in its critique of dogmatic assumptions and metaphysical residue clinging to secular theories, it also regresses behind the best aspects of modern theory by frequently adopting irrationalist, individualist, nondialectical, and cynical position that militate against appropriating existing possibilities for social change and progress. While postmodern theories effectively deconstruct the contradictions and metaphysical tenets in modern theory, they tend toward an undialectical negation of modern theory; and canner reconstruct the contributions of modern historiography and social theory. On the rare occasions that a postmodernist attempts to develop positive ethical or political positions, he or she does not, and cannot, avoid substantive reference to the concepts and values of the modern tradition.

Foucault vituperated against the "enlightenment blackmail" that forces one to take a stand either for or against rationality without adopting a critical attitude. We must also acknowledge the postmodern blackmail that tries to force a choice between one extreme position or another, between humanism or structuralism, objectivism or relativism, determinism or indeterminism, linear progress or aleatory movement, universalism or localism, rationalism or irrationalism. In succumbing to the black or white fallacy that denies important options to extreme positions, postmodern theorists reject as metaphysical what can be reconstructed as rational-concepts such .is agency, normative foundations, or historical progress.

At the turn of the century, pragmatists like James and Dewey were already engaged in the project of seeking a middle road between allegedly opposing theories such as idealism and empiricism. This project needs to be reinvigorated today, especially with regards to the opposition between modern and postmodern theory. To the extent that theory is useful for criticism and practical change, we need new theories that combine aspects of both modern and postmodern theories and that have political relevance for the contemporary era. Important linkages and mediations still need to be made between explanation and interpretation, structure and agency, macro- and microanalysis, absolutism, and relativism, voluntarism and determinism, universalism and communalism, community and individuality, global and local politics, capitalism and disciplinary power, class policies and new social movements, naive optimism and cynical pessimism. As we move into the next century, we need general theories that are sensitive to differences, that are aware of the limits of abstraction, and that are grounded in specific empirical analyses, while being critical, hermeneutic, and normative in content and vision.

Rather than seeing postmodern theory in general as a new paradigm of critical theory to be appropriated in a wholesale manner, we should see it as providing important tools for the reconstruction of modern theory. The very nature of any "post" theoretical discourse militates-against a balanced and critical dialogue between older and newer work. Rather than abandoning every fundamental aspect of modern thought and social theory, as postmodernists propose, it is better to salvage and critically reconstruct modern theories in light of valuable postmodern critiques. After Voltaire, after Marx, after Foucault, after Derrida, and after

Habermas, the projects of enlightenment and democracy remain incomplete and worth struggling for on the basis the alternative intellectual strategy as offered by Kant.

The *Critique of Pure Reason,* Kant noted in his preface, arose in response to a "call to reason to undertake anew the most difficult of all its tasks, namely that of self-knowledge, and to institute a tribunal which will assure to reason its lawful claims and dismiss all groundless pretensions." In his transcendental philosophy the assurance of reason's lawful claims took the form of an analytic of truth and the dismissal of groundless pretensions the form of a critique of dialectical illusions. Two centuries later Foucault noted the continuity of his post-Nietzschean genealogy with the classical critique of reason: "I think that the central issue of philosophy and critical thought since the eighteenth century has been, still is, and will, I hope, remain the question: What is this reason that we use? What are its historical effects? What are its limits, and what are its dangers?" But he stressed the discontinuity as well: "If the Kantian question was that of knowing what limits knowledge has to renounce transgressing, it seems to me that the critical question today is in what is given to us as universal, necessary, obligating, what place is occupied by whatever is singular, contingent, and the product of arbitrary constraints?" Thus Foucault's practical critique of reason looked not for formal structures with universal value but for transformable singularities it was interested not in necessary limitations but in the "possibility of no longer being, doing, or thinking, what we are, do, or think. Though he occasionally acknowledged the possibility of pursuing an analytic of truth in general, his own work centered on the genealogical deconstruction of rationalistic pretensions.

Notwithstanding the highly original form in which he cast them, the basic changes one finds in Foucault's notion of a critique of reason are not peculiar to him. They stem rather from the relentless detranscendentalization of reason and decentering of the rational subject by Marx and Darwin, Nietzsche and Freud, historicism and pragmatism to signal only a few of the many deflationary currents of nineteenth-and twentieth-century thought. The intrinsic impurity of reason, its embeddedness in culture and society, and the embodied and engaged nature of its bearers, are now widely acknowledged. Thus, even critical theorists less radically deconstructionist than Foucault share his view that the basic structures of thought are not accessible to the sorts of introspective survey of the contents of consciousness favored by the classical critique of reason. They agree that examining the "nature, scope, and limits" of reason calls for modes of socio–historical inquiry that go beyond the traditional bounds of philosophical analysis. And they also agree that the critique of impure reason has practical import. Once we have turned our attention from consciousness to culture and society, it becomes evident that there are normative and evaluative presuppositions and consequences attaching to any social practice. Rational practices-including epistemic practices like theorizing-have to be viewed in their sociocultural contexts if they are to be properly understood. In this sense, the critique of impure reason is part of the study of culture and society. As a critical endeavor, it aims to enhance and transform our self-understanding in ways that affect how we live.

This sort of practically significant socio-historical critique of impure reason has been a live option for postmetaphysical thinking at least since the time of the Left-Hegelians. A variant of it dominated the philosophical scene in the United States during the heyday of American Pragmatism. The point of departure of the remarks that follow is the program for critical social theory advanced by Max Horkheimer and his colleagues at the Institute for Social Research in the early 1930s. On the reading offered here, that approach has the virtue of developing by transforming both aspects of Kant's critique of reason, the assurance of reason's lawful claims as well as the dismissal of groundless pretensions. In contrast to exclusively deconstructionist approaches, it allows for a critical reconstruction of Enlightenment conceptions of reason and the rational subject, a kind of "determinate negation" through which they are given socio–cultural forms rather than simply dismantled. It is in this spirit that Horkheimer, in his inaugural lecture as Director of the Institute, characterized critical theory as an "ongoing dialectical interpenetration" of philosophy and empirical research, a form of "philosophically oriented social inquiry."

Early in the 1930s Max Horkheimer found himself in an intellectual milieu similar to ours in one respect: it was marked by a sharp swing away from previously dominant forms of neo-Kantianism and toward pronounced forms of antirationalism. In his 1934 discussion of "The Rationalism Debate in Contemporary Philosophy," Horkheimer endorsed without reservation the historicist view that "there is no final picture of either the essence or the appearance of reality. The very idea of a supernatural subject who could comprehend it is madness. It is the human being who thinks, not the Ego or Reason. And that is not something abstract, such as the human essence, but always human beings living in a particular historical epoch. It is just this embeddedness in historical life that rationalists ignored when they projected worldview untainted by "any trace of the societal beings that produced them, rather as if they were pure mirrors of an eternal order." On the other hand, Horkheimer warned none of this warranted a swing to the opposite, antirationalist extremes represented in his day by existentialism. To hypostatize Existence was not to escape metaphysical thinking, but only to turn in the old set of fundamental categories for a new one. Critical theory required more than the simple invocation of concrete-sounding, but no less essentialistic determinations of this sort. It called for a materialist account of its nature, conditions, and limits. If the subject of knowledge and action could no longer be viewed as solitary, disengaged, and disembodied and if the structures of reason could not longer be viewed as timeless necessary and unconditioned, then the transformation called for the critique of reason in the direction of socio-historical inquiry.

At the same time, Horkheimer repeatedly urged that this project not be viewed reductionistically. In particular, he was careful to distinguish it from the increasingly influential sociology of knowledge being developed at the time by Karl Mannheim. And with good reason: his critical social theory shared with Mannheim's sociology of knowledge a recognition of the socially conditioned character of human thought. He wished, however, to hold fast to a strong distinction between true and false consciousness and thus to avoid the relativistic implications of Mannheim's approach. Even though traditional philosophy's radical dichotomy between the ideal and the real could no longer be upheld it was not necessary to retreat to a relativism of socially conditioned perspectives. What was needed was a new concept of truth which, while renouncing any God's-eye view, retained the dichotomy between the true and the false, albeit in a more suitably human form.

Thus, in his 1930 review of Mannheim's *Ideology and Utopia,* Horkheimer argued that the historically conditioned character of thought is not per se incompatible with truth. Only against the background of traditional, ontological-theological conceptions of eternal, unchanging truth did that seem to be the case. But there was no need of an absolute guarantee to distinguish meaningfully between truth and error. Rather, what was required was a concept of truth consistent with our finitude, with our historicity, with the dependence of thought on changing social conditions. On such a concept, failure to measure up to absolute, unconditioned standards was irrelevant. To regard this failure as leading directly to relativism was just another version of the "God is dead, everything is permitted" fallacy of disappointed expectations. As Horkheimer put it: "That all our thoughts, true and false, depend on conditions that can change ... in no way affects the validity of science. It is not clear to me why the fact of being historically conditioned should affect the truth of a judgement." In the first instance, the challenge was to deontologize and detranscendentalize the notion of truth.

In his 1935 essay "On the Problem of Truth," Horkheimer attempted to do just that. He argued against the equation of fallibility with relativity. To grant that there is no final and conclusive theory of reality of which we are capable, is not at all to abandon the distinction between truth and error. We make that distinction in relation to the "available means of knowledge." The claim that a belief is true must stand the test of experience and practice in the present. Knowing that we are fallible, that what stands the test today may well fail to do so tomorrow or in the next century, does not prevent us, or even exempt us, from making and defending claims to truth here and now. The abstract recognition that all our beliefs are open to correction does not make a rationally warranted belief any less warranted, any less rational.

A few years later, in 1939, having emigrated to New York, Horkheimer published in the journal of the transplanted Institute for Social Research an essay on "The Social Function of Philosophy." He stressed the ways in which philosophy did not fit neatly into the system of specialized sciences. From the time of Socrates, he wrote, it has taken on "the unpleasant task of throwing the light of consciousness upon even those human relations and modes of response which have become so deeply rooted that they seem natural, immutable, and eternal." Given this interest in questioning what is normally taken for granted, in probing behind established modes of thought and action, it is no wonder, Horkheimer went on, that philosophical discussions are so much more radical and unconciliatory than discussions in the sciences. Unlike other pursuits philosophy does have a field of action marked out for it within the given. Rather, its function is to keep us from losing ourselves in those ideas and activities which the existing order of society instills into its members, to help us to understand what we are doing in the interest of enabling us consciously to shape our lives. In short, philosophy is critical enlightenment, an ongoing attempt to bring reason into the world. On the other hand, Horkheimer was fully aware that this sort of radical, practically oriented reflection on reason and its realizations could no longer be carried out in the manner of classical philosophy. There is, he argued, no way of comprehending the structures of reason that does not involve socio-historical inquiry. And if the actualization of reason is to be more than a pious wish, philosophical utopias will have to be replaced by empirically based accounts of concrete relations and tendencies that can lead to an improvement of human life. For that purpose too the mission of philosophy had to be continued in the medium of social research.

From this standpoint, Horkheimer judged Mannheim's sociology of knowledge to be practically, no less than theoretically, wrong-headed. Treating styles, methods and systems of thought merely as the expression of specific social situations promoted a skeptical deflation of philosophical notions of reason rather than their refraction in the denser medium of empirical research. The attitude taken to philosophical ideas does not comprise objective testing and practical application, but a more or less complicated correlation to a social group. It is not calculated to explain the social function of philosophy, but rather to perform one itself-namely, to discourage thought from its practical tendency of pointing to the future. This had been a major theme of Horkheimer's earlier essays as well. In "On the Problem of Truth", for instance, he had written: "Since the recognition of the truth of particular ideas disappears behind the display of conditions, the coordination with historical unities, this impartial relativism reveals itself as the friend of what exists at any given time. What is coming into being needs conscious decision in its struggle, while the limitation to mere understanding and contemplation serves what is already in existence."

Thus, while Horkheimer joined with the then dominant forms of anti-rationalism in calling for an investigation of the real conditions of thought, he distanced himself from them in refusing to celebrate the newly minted hypostatizations of History, Society, Life, and Existence. What the critics of rationalism failed to appreciate is that the turn to the psychological, social, and historical roots of thought did not herald the end of reason; it was the latest and most radical phase in its ongoing self-critique. The detachment they announced from the subject-centered categories "originally absolutes by bourgeois liberal thought" usually went hand-in-hand with a methodological indifference to questions of validity. In certain varieties of historicism for instance, this took the form of an aestheticized tour of the past, with the aim of understanding everything rather than taking sides. The claims to validity of past systems of thought were not taken seriously and rationally evaluated. Instead, critique was replaced by "reverential empathy and description." What concerned Horkheimer about the methodological replacement of critical examination, with detached contemplation, was the skepticism it generated with respect to the basic normative ideas of truth, justice, freedom, responsibility and the like. While the hegemonic forms of these ideas were all too often distorted, the aim of the materialist critique of reason was not to discard them altogether but to unmask their specific distortions so as to render them unserviceable for the justification of injustice and oppression: "Whenever in history nations or classes have secured their continued existence not only with cold steel but with moral, metaphysical, and religious ideas, these ideas were in the end exposed to attack from those being dominated. A struggle against the cultural supports of social conditions usually introduces and accompanies political rebellion. For this reason, devaluation of the specific ideas through which a despised state of affairs is grounded, supported, and transfigured is as old as these struggles themselves." Of course, at that time Horkheimer had particular reason to worry about the abstract negation of the conceptual repertoire of rationalist individualism in favor of its binary opposites history and tradition, community and culture. This sort of simple inversion, combined with skepticism about any strong claims to validity, fostered and justified passivity in the midst of an increasingly irrational and dangerous world. The individual was pictured as thoroughly submerged in the social whole, and the historical movement of the whole as governed by sub- or supra-personal forces beyond the reach of reason. The idea of rationally influencing the shape of social life by attempting to put the insights of historical, social, and cultural studies into effect appeared ridiculously naive, overcome, deposes. As Horkheimer pointed out, the peculiar reflexivity of thought about individual and social life is such that thinking something is so can help make it so. The kind of insight into the depths of existence and the shallowness of Enlightenment at which German philosophy excelled was only too effective in nourishing cynical and accommodative attitudes toward a world in the process of going mad.

Traditional and Critical Theory

In the context of contemporary critical theory, left-Hegelian formulae of "realizing reason" and promoting "a rational organization of society" have a disagreeably totalizing ring to them. And there is much in the early Horkheimer that bears criticism on this score: his tendency to conceptualize society as at least potentially a unified subject with a unified will and, hence, to marginalize considerations of social, cultural, and political pluralism; his over-reliance on Marxian political economy, particularly class analysis, in identifying the causes and conditions of injustice in existing social orders; his subscription to a philosophy of history or "grand meta narrative" that underplayed the roles of contingency, locality, and identity in struggles against oppression. In fact, given the currently widespread opposition to general accounts of reason and rationalization of any sort, it may be well to begin by asking why Horkheimer's approach deserves to be taken seriously at all.

The grand "either or" structuring much of postmodernist rhetoric sets the particular against the universal: either one is for the totality, necessity, authority, and homogeneity of the universal, or one rejects it in the name of the fragmentary, contingent, spontaneous, and heterogeneous particular. But that opposition simply ignores the dialectical relation between the general and the particular. More specifically, no generalizing approach to the critique of reason can serve as the closed framework or unimpeachable "tribunal" that Kant thought it to be. If the end of foundalionalism means anything, it signifies at least the permanent openness of any proposed universal frame to deconstructive and reconstructive impulses what Adorno called the non-identical. On the other hand, it is implausible to suppose that social and cultural studies can get along without general conceptions of reason and rationalization. The interpretive and evaluative frameworks that invariably, albeit often tacitly, inform the ways in which socio-cultural phenomena are selected, described, ordered, analyzed, appraised, explained, and so forth, typically include categories and assumptions tailored to grasping the "rationalization" of modern society. And these are usually of philosophical provenance, for the simple reason that modern philosophy has centered around the critique of reason. This is obvious in the work of classical social theorists like Marx, Durkheim, and Weber no less than in that of contemporary deconstructionist critics like Foucault, Derrida, and Rorty. Accordingly, the assumption underlying the remarks that follow is that some general, philosophical level of analysis of ideas of reason, rationality, truth, objectivity, subjectivity, autonomy, and so forth, is still of fundamental importance for critical social and cultural inquiry. This is, of course, not to say that it is the only significant mode of inquiry, or that it could replace more contextually specific modes, or that it is itself unaffected by the results of the latter. The hope is that many of the objectionable features of the classical critique of reason can be overcome by deabsolutizing ideas of reason through stressing their relations to social practice and building deconstructive concerns into reconstructive endeavors from the start.

With this in mind, let us turn to Horkheimer's programmatic contrast between "Traditional and Critical Theory" and situate his approach in relation to views now current among critical theorists. The axis on which the contrast turns is the reflexivity in both its primary senses of social inquiry. Horkheimer repeatedly insisted both upon the fact that social researchers are themselves engaged in socially situated forms of social action and upon the importance of their bringing this to conscious awareness and thinking through its implications, The social sciences, in modeling themselves after the natural sciences, were attempting to position themselves centrally in an industrial society increasingly dependent on monitoring and managing key socio-economic variables. By promoting a positivistic image of themselves as just "telling it like it is," they could claim to offer a "view from nowhere" with all of its rights and privileges; other approaches thereby became marginalized as prescientific, ideological, self-interested, or the like. One of the first tasks of critical theory was to challenge the privileged "non-position" of social-scientific knowledge by analyzing the modes of its production, the roles it played in society, the interests it served, and the historical processes through which it came to power.

Leaving aside the details of Horkheimer's analysis, which reflects in key respects the Marxian political-economic framework he took over, it is important for present purposes to note that he did not regard the deconstruct ion of allegedly disembodied social knowledge as entailing the delegitimation of empirical social research as such. On the contrary, processing and deploying vast bodies of "factual" knowledge useful for social reproduction within an established social framework is a requirement of any developed society. The problem arises from its absolutization, "as though it were grounded in the nature of knowledge as such or justified in some other ahistorical way." And the solution is to recognize the sorts of interests that such knowledge serves in the present society, as well as the place it might occupy in a better society, and by thus "locating" it to leave ample space for other interests and other types of knowledge.

Unlike "traditional" theory, then, critical social theory takes as topics of investigation the reflexivity of social research, the division of labor - including scientific and scholarly labor - in which it is carried on, and its social functions; that is, it studies "what theory means in human life." It reflects, in particular, on the contexts of its own genesis and application, that is, on its own embeddedness in the social matrix out of which it arises and within which it will find its uses. Unlike contemporary deconstructionists, however, Horkheimer does not understand this as prohibiting all but "local" knowledge. Rather, he seeks to locate both traditional and critical research within a broad account of contemporary society which, he wants to claim, is more adequate than any of its competitors.

While the goals and directions of research in the natural sciences are less and less a purely intrascientific matter, in the social sciences the events, structures, and processes that influence the agenda of research also belong to the subject matter of research. More generally, social inquiry is a moment of the very process of social reproduction it aims to comprehend. The social world is produced and reproduced in and through the social actions of social actors, including the activities of agents engaged in analyzing it. This peculiar reflexivity has a number of implications. For one thing, it suggests a social constructionist view of social reality, which positivism completely misses with its passive, perceptual models of subject-object relations. For another, it means that social subjects of knowledge are shaped by the same sorts of historical forces that shape their objects of knowledge: for them to understand something of the latter is also to understand something of themselves. Finally, it means that in some sense the topics and resources of social inquiry are the same: the social world is itself constructed in part via the very ideas that researchers employ to understand it. This is true, in particular, of the types of social research carried on within established social structures, for example, in studying business and administration. The domain of objects investigated is in some measure reproduced by activities according to the very notions used to comprehend it. Thus, what C. Wright Mills would later call "bureaucratic" social science could largely restrict itself to processing data with conceptual resources that were themselves operative in the very production of the phenomena being studied.

Critical social theory breaks with that type of approach by, among other things, taking the reflexivity of social inquiry explicitly into account. This entails a challenge to the traditional dichotomies between genesis and justification, justification and application, fact and norm and so forth, which were used to rope off a "neutral" field for social research. Critical theory is concerned precisely with the historical and social genesis of the facts it examines and with the social contexts in which its results will have their effects. It stresses that social research is itself a form of social interaction in which the objects of knowledge are potentially subjects of the very same knowledge, and thus that it is willy-nilly a potential factor in changing social relations. Consciously taking up this reflexive relation to social practice, critical social theory expressly aims at becoming a factor in social change by becoming part of the self-consciousness of oppressed social groups. It does not consider the purposes it serves to be external to the context of inquiry.

Through a social-practical reformulation of certain Kantian ideas, Horkheimer could argue that the moral-political orientation of critical social inquiry was not arbitrary but inherently rational. In the framework of the philosophy of consciousness, Kant had argued that reason was at bottom a capacity not for speculation but for freedom. Once we turn our attention from consciousness to culture and society, the privileged status that Western philosophy has generally accorded to knowledge and representation becomes even less plausible. In fact, if knowledge itself is understood to be a social product, the traditional oppositions between theory and practice, fact and value, and the like break down, for there are practical dimensions to any social activity, theorizing included. Translated into social-theoretical terms, the primacy of practical reason means, according to Horkheimer, that an interest in "reasonable conditions of life" is intrinsic to the exercise of our rational capacities. At present it is important to note that this practical concern enters into the very construction of a critical theory and is at work in the research processes informed by the theory. It is, in fact, what lends consistency and coherency to a tradition of thought that accepts the ongoing necessity of adapting its concepts, theories, techniques, and the like to an ever-changing reality. The transmission of critical theory in as rigorous a fashion as possible is a condition of its historical success. That transmission does not, however, take place via established practices and fixed procedures but via an interest in social change. This interest is aroused ever anew by prevailing injustices, but it must be shaped and guided by the theory and in turn react back upon it."

One can, and Horkheimer sometimes does, formulate the practical interest that guides and shapes critical theory in "pragmatic" terms of striving to reduce suffering and promote happiness. In this formulation, the moral-political ideas that give expression to that interest function only regulative, not constitutive by, that is, they serve to guide and evaluate thought and action and not to represent realized or realizable states of affairs. But too often Horkheimer formulates that interest in terms of the holistic representations with which the Marxist tradition abounds. Thus he readily translates "reasonable conditions of life" into a "rational organization of society" in which an "all embracing subject" does away with "the opposition between the individual's purposefulness, spontaneity, and rationality, and the processes and relations of social labor on which society is built." The idealist conception of freedom as self-conscious self-determination is thereby projected onto a unified macro subject of which individuals are harmonious moments. It is against just such "totalizing" representations that postmodernist thinkers have launched their most telling attacks. However, there is no need to construe the sociocultural embodiment of practical reason in those terms. Habermas, who pursues a similar line of thought, rejects that construal as a residue of the "philosophy of consciousness" and focuses instead on the conditions and procedures of democratic pluralism.

Sociocultural critique is best thought of as a polymorphic, multi-layered, and multidimensional enterprise. Not all critical work need be or can be done in the same way or at the same level of specificity or generality. Moreover, determining for what purposes and in what contexts different groups occupy the same or different "positions" inevitably involves pragmatic considerations. There is no objective reason why, for certain purposes and in certain contexts, a more universal we should not be appropriate. It could be useful, for instance, in attacking the cultural supports of a general order of domination from which numerous groups suffer, or in analyzing the expanding global networks of symbolic and material interchange. Critics who appeal to one notion or another of encapsulated forms of life to deny that in important respects we are all in the same situation are simply living in the past. We do not have first to create a global space; that is already being done, and at breakneck speed. To better understand this process, we have to go beyond local cultural studies and try to comprehend the internationalization of politics and economics, science and technology, information and communication that now affects the inside of every local culture.

Cultural criticism is not the self-sufficient, self-enclosed undertaking its more textualistically inclined practitioners sometimes make it appear to be. For obvious reasons, critics located in the humanities tend to foreground the sorts of phenomena they have been trained to identify and analyze and to background everything else. We can use only the tools we have at our disposal. But that need not prevent us from recognizing that such phenomena are embedded in a broader social matrix and from acknowledging the interdependence of "textual" studies with social and cultural studies of various other sorts. One of the broadest goals of a genuinely multidisciplinary research practice would be a "critical theory of the present," that is, a general view of contemporary society, its problems, and its prospects. That is what Horkheimer referred to as a "comprehensive existential judgement," which he delivered in classical Marxist terms. Writing in the midst of profound socioeconomic changes, however, he added an important qualifier: owing to the continuous transformation of its object, this is a judgement with an in eliminable historical dimension. Thus critical theory had to be understood as an ongoing attempt to "reflect a living totality" an ever-renewed effort to comprehend contemporary society from a practically interested point of view. "It is not a metaphysics of history but rather a changing picture of the world that develops in connection with practical efforts to improve it... [and that] offers no clear prognosis for historical development." To be sure, Horkheimer was himself convinced that this object would remain essentially the same so long as capitalism was the dominant social formation, and thus that the "essential content" of Marxist political economy would remain valid through all the necessary adaptations and adjustments. But one need not hold this position to see the value of situating local cultural practices within a larger field of relationships. It is, in fact, not difficult to show that antichloristic critics usually rely on some general view of contemporary society, its tensions, and its tendencies, in conceiving and carrying out their specific interventions. Because these big pictures are seldom openly avowed, they do not get properly scrutinized and thus function largely as sets of unexamined assumptions. To many, this is preferable; it seems, to running the risks of totalizing thought. But again, those are not the only alternatives. Critical theorists can develop and deploy practically interested, theoretically informed, general accounts in a fallibilistic and open manner, that is, without claiming closure. The point is to view big pictures and grand narratives as ongoing accomplishments. They are never finished, but have to be constructed, deconstructed, and reconstructed in ever-changing circumstances.

Locating particular practices in a larger field is one way of gaining distance from them, of not leaving the final say about their significance to participants and their traditions. Critical theorists of very different stripes agree in seeing a need for some such "outsider's" perspective to get beyond shared meanings and their hermeneutic retrieval. Foucault's way of creating distance from the practices we live in, for instance, is to display their "lowly origins" in contingent historical circumstances, to dispel their appearance of self-evident given ness by treating them as the outcome of multiple relations of force. The Frankfurt School approach is also based on a rejection of what Marx characterized as the specific "German ideology" of understanding ideas solely in terms of other ideas. Its guiding principle is that the full significance of ideas can be grasped only by viewing them in context of the social practices in which they figure, and by studying the genesis, structures, and functions of those practices. And its underlying intention is to transform our self-understanding in ways that affect how we live. Gaining a critical perspective on what is normally taken for granted for instance, by showing that the genesis of what has heretofore seemed universal and necessary involves contingent relations of force and an arbitrary closing off of alternatives, or that what parades as fair and impartial actually helps to maintain unjustifiable imbalances in social benefits and burdens-can affect the way we act. Ideas and beliefs, values and norms, standards and procedures formerly accepted as purely and simply rational may come to be seen as in the service of particular interests and this may undermine the authority that derives from their presumed rationality. Whether or not this is so, and the extent to which it is so, are not matters of conceptual necessity or theoretical inference but of contingent historical conditions. The practical significance of critical insight varies with the circumstances.

While critical social theory does not take participants' views of their practices as the last word in interpreting and assessing them, it differs from exclusively deconstructionist approaches in taking them seriously, in seeking to engage them in the very process of gaining distance from them. In a word, it treats them dialectically: the dialectical critique of reason does not abstractly negate ideas of reason but seeks critically to appropriate them and to enlist them in the struggle for a better world. Thus, in an essay entitled "Philosophy and Critical Theory" Herbert Marcuse stressed that idealist and individualist conceptions of reason and rational practice were not mere ideology, for they established reason as a critical instance: "The individual was to examine and judge everything given," and this meant that "the concept of reason contained the concept of freedom as well. For such examination and judgement would be meaningless if human beings were not free to act in accordance with their insights." From his perspective, it was precisely the situation-transcending import of ideas of reason a red flag to deconstructionists that was their saving grace. Critical theory "opposes making reality into a criterion...

When truth cannot be realized within the established order, it always appears to the latter as mere Utopia. This transcendence speaks not against, but for, its truth. This interest in the "truth content" of ideas, Marcuse went on, distinguished critical theory from the type of strictly conceptualist approach of the sociology of knowledge. Research that considers only "the dependent and limited nature of consciousness" betrays critical theory's "interest in the liberation of human beings." That interest "binds it to certain ancient truths universal propositions whose progressive impetus derives precisely from their universality ... for they claim that everyone should be rational, free, and happy." In a society that gives the lie to all these universals adherence to universality is more important than its philosophical destruction. The area of tension between an established social order and the ideas of reason it relies on is just where dialectical critique drives its wedge.

In the same spirit, Horkheimer urged critical theorists not to surrender such ideas to the regressive forces who used them to justify their privileged positions and betrayed them whenever it was in their interest to do so. They should, instead, critically reappropriate them for progressive purposes: "The battle cries of the Enlightenment and of the French Revolution are valid now more than ever. The dialectical critique of the world borne along by them consists precisely in showing that they have retained rather than lost their actuality. Politics should not abandon those demands, but realize them not, however, by clinging in utopian fashion to historically conditioned definitions of them, but in accordance with their meaning: be content of these ideas is not eternal but subject to historical change because the human impulses that demand something better take [historically] different forms.

The context-transcendence of ideas of reason harbors not only a Utopian but also a subversive potential, for claims to unconditional validity are permanently exposed to criticism from all sides. Understood in this way, they point in the opposite direction from those metaphysical representations that occupy deconstructionist critics, namely toward an ongoing critique of dogmatism, bias, and self-deception in their many forms. The tension between the real and the ideal that their context-transcending import builds into the constructions of social life marks a normative surplus of meaning that critical theorists can draw upon in seeking to transcend and transform the limits of their situations.

One can even question whether the latter option is really available, for we are always and inescapably participants in social life before, during, and after any critical studies in which we might engage. There is no extramundane standpoint from which we can set our social world as a whole at a distance. It is thus not surprising that would-be total critics of Western "logo centrism" invariably rely on the same idealizing presuppositions regarding meaning, reference, truth, logic, and the like that they seek to undercut, and that radical critics of modern rationalism continually draw on assumptions specific to the modern worldview, such as the disenchantment of the world and the possibility of reflectively questioning inherited beliefs and values, gaining critical distance from traditional roles and norms, and challenging ascribed individual and group identities. Nor is it surprising that the values which underlie their criticisms typically include a host of distinctively modern orientations toward pluralism, diversity, tolerance, human dignity, equal respect, and the like.

There must then, be a reconstructive as well as a deconstructive side to any critique of reason, for it will be important to identify and analyze those presuppositions to which participants in the discourse of modernity either have no alternative at all, or none they would want to defend.

The Aufhebung of Philosophy

In "Philosophy and Critical Theory" Marcuse developed variations upon the familiar theme of continuing-through-transforming the critique of reason. "Reason," he wrote, "is the fundamental category of philosophical thought," the category by which "it has bound itself to human destiny." In classical philosophy it "represents the highest human potential. In the modern period, it comes to be represented as self-conscious self-determination, that is, as the freedom to act on one's own insight and judgement". With this concept of freedom as reason," Marcuse wrote, echoing Marx, "philosophy seems to reach its limit. What remains outstanding to the realization of reason is not a philosophical task". Any direct leap to political practice, however, would be a potentially dangerous short circuit, for there was a theoretical dimension of the outstanding task. The philosophical concept of free rational action was seriously inadequate, and not merely by way of accidental deficiencies. Rather, its inadequacies bore the character of systematic distortions that had to be understood and explained. And because the distortions in question were linked to the role that conceptions of reason and freedom played in the reproduction of the social order, understanding and explaining them required some form of critical social inquiry.

Marcuse did not mean by this simply to reduce individualistic and idealistic conceptions of reason and freedom to ideology. They were more than that; they had a truth content that critique had to preserve even while transforming. "In the bourgeois epoch the reality of reason became the task that the free individual was to fulfill... The material conditions of life, however, allotted freedom to reason only in pure thought and will... If reason means shaping life according to people's free decisions on the basis of their knowledge, then the demand for reason henceforth means the creation of a social organization in which individuals can collectively regulate their lives in accordance with their needs." With this insight, philosophy's interest in pure reason becomes the interest of critical social theory in historically embodied reason. This interest can be pursued in several different but interrelated ways: by critically deconstructing distorted concepts of reason and freedom that serve as cultural supports of orders of unfreedom, injustice, unhappiness; by preserving the truth content of traditional ideas through reconstructing them in social-practical terms; and, of course, by using both critical and constructive ideas in the struggle against inhuman conditions of existence. And this is an interest intrinsic to reason, for practical reason is by its nature oriented toward free rational action and against what contradicts it. Thus the concept of ideology is not only a theoretical but also a practical-political concept: it is internally related to an interest in changing social conditions in which people are not free to live their lives in the light of their own experience and judgement and in accordance with their own perception of their needs. In this sense, critical social theory gives a "human form" to philosophical ideals and "incorporates" them into the struggle for a better world.

The fact that such ideals are not actually realized and appear to be merely Utopian does not speak against them, in Marcuse's view: "The Utopian element was long the only progressive element in philosophy" To be sure, critical theory is not interested in merely Utopian ideals, but in ones which, however unrealizable in the present order of things, represent actual potentials of social development. This interest in identifying potentials in the present for a more reasonable form of life in the future is built into the categories of critical social theory: they present not a view from nowhere but from the standpoint of practical reason. And this, Marcuse explains, is what distinguishes critical theory from the sociology of knowledge: it does not reduce philosophical ideas to social conditions. It does, to be sure, analyze "the specific social conditions at the root of philosophy's inability to pose the problem of reason in a more comprehensive way." It does so, however, not in the interest of skeptically debunking all claims to truth, but in that of preserving through reconstructing truths that past generations struggled to attain:

That man is a rational being, that this being requires freedom, and that happiness is his highest good are all universal propositions whose progressive impetus derives precisely from their universality. Universality gives them an almost revolutionary character, for they claim that all, and not merely this or that particular person should be rational, free, and happy. In a society whose reality gives the lie to all these universals, philosophy cannot make them concrete. Under such conditions, adherence to universality is more important than its philosophical destruction.

In a "Postscript" to Marcuse's essay, Horkheimer endorsed the idea that critical social theory could be understood as inheriting philosophy's concern with the life of reason. Its defining insight, he agreed, is that the possibility of giving reasonable form to individual existence depends upon the possibility of instituting reasonable conditions of social life, and thus that philosophy's concern with the life of reason has to be continued at the level of social theory. Like Marcuse, Horkheimer characterized the object of the practical interest guiding critical social inquiry as a "free, self-determining society," which he went on to specify in terms of "real agreement" in a "real democracy," whose overriding aim is "the happiness of all individuals" in a "world that satisfies the needs and powers of human beings. Or, as he also put it, "concern for the abolition of injustice ... is the materialist content of the idealist concept of reason. This general strategy of linking a deindividualized conception of practical reason to the theory of justice is familiar today in the versions of nee Kantianism developed by Rawls, Habermas, and others. A bridge from the 1930s discussion to the contemporary discussions can conveniently be constructed from elements of Horkheimer's critique of Kantian ethics in a 1933 essay entitled "Materialism and Morality."

Horkheimer stresses that morality and moral theory in their current senses are historical phenomena that have to be understood in historical terms. On his account, their characteristic opposition between duty and interest, the universal and the particular, is an expression of the very real tension in capitalist society between the possessive individualism required to thrive in a market economy and a concern for the general welfare which, invisible-hand notions notwithstanding, is ill-served by market mechanisms. Against the background of the inequitable distribution of misery and happiness, burdens and pleasures, poverty and wealth that resulted from capitalist development, the move from traditional ethics to rationalist moralities of the Kantian type can be seen as shifting the burden of deep-seated social tensions to the site of the individual conscience. It is the isolated moral subject who must struggle to overcome the opposition between self-interest and the general interest, precisely by renouncing the former in the name of the latter. The spiritualized universalism that commands in the moral domain is just the other face of the narrow egoism that reigns in the market-place. It is, Horkheimer argues, just this transposition of social-tructural problems into the inner lives of individuals that is the ideological function of morality. For there is no possibility of reducing the tension between individual goods and the common good through the moral intentions of individual agents acting within the given institutional framework. A social-structural problem requires a social-structural response, which Horkheimer characterizes generally as the effective incorporation of individuals into collective decision-making processes.

Horkheincer does not completely reject Kantian ethics. He argues that if modern moral theory in its paradigmatic Kantian form is a contingent historical construction that has to be understood genealogically, it is not to say that it is merely ideology or false consciousness and should therefore be dismantled without remainder. It possesses a truth content as well, which it is the task of his dialectical critique to free from its ideological trappings, transform, and retain in a more adequate conception of the relation between the universal and the particular. The idea of their reconciliation that Kant elaborated under the title of "the highest good" could not, as he evidently saw, be even approximately realized within the existing order of society. In projecting its realization into the nominal beyond, he gave distorted expression to the truth that morality impels us to transcend the social order which gave birth to it, an order in tension with the very idea of practical reason to which it appeals for justification. It is precisely the Utopian element in Kant's idea of a perfected order in which the conflict between self-interest and the general interest are overcome that dialectical critique takes as the point of transition to its reconstructive movement.

Horkheimer never discussed at any length the institutions and procedures that might effectively allow individuals to have a say in the collective decision-making processes that were to replace the blind operation of market forces. He was much more concerned with re-centering the eudemonistic element of ethics that had been marginalized in moral theory. But he repeatedly insisted that the ideals of freedom, justice, and equality not be surrendered to the regressive forces that had expropriated them to justify unnecessary suffering. Rather, they were to be reclaimed and deployed in the struggle against the causes of human misery. "Dialectical critique is borne along by them. They are nothing but the isolated traits of a rational society as anticipated in morality. Politics should not abandon these demands but realize them." But first they had to be freed from their moralistic confines by shifting theoretical attention away from private efforts by isolated individuals to subdue unruly inclinations and toward collective efforts by social groups to transform unjust relations. Though guided by universal ideals, the public politics that was thus to reclaim center stage from private morality could not cling to unchanging formulations of them. Their content was "not eternal but subject to historical change," they took different forms in different historical circumstances. That is, the concrete meaning or content of abstract ideas and principles had to be continuously rein scribed into ever changing contexts. This general commitment to political and social ideals that are universal in import but require ongoing recontextualization is common to most critical social theorists. But another element in Horkheimer's *Aufhebung* of Kantian morality distinguishes his position strongly from the one later elaborated by Habermas: he replaces Kant's "fact of pure reason" with an "ungrounded feeling" of compassion for suffering humankind.

Morality, he wrote, "admits of no grounding, either through intuition or through argument. Rather, it represents a frame of mind. To describe the latter, to make comprehensible its personal conditions and the mechanisms for transmitting it from generation to generation is the business of psychology. At its center, Horkheimer ventured, is a moral sentiment or feeling directed toward all persons as potential members of a happy human race, to their needs and capacities, to the alleviation of their suffering and the development of their powers. To this moral sentiment "it appears that all living beings have a claim to happiness, for which it asks no justification or grounds. The specific form this sentiment takes in our day, "when the poverty of humanity cries out in such contradiction to its potential wealth," is sympathy or compassion. It expresses itself in a "solidarity" with the wretched of the earth that motivates the critical theorist to pursue a politics aimed at realizing-while-transforming the universal ideals mentioned above.

Notwithstanding the attractions of this way of avoiding problems of "grounding," Horkheimer's account creates as many problems as it solves. Granted that feelings of indignation, compassion, love, solidarity, and the like neither need nor admit of philosophical grounding in pure practical reason, the issue remains whether they are susceptible to rational criticism and justification in any sense. The fact that questions of the sorts: Sympathy with whom? Solidarity with which side? Indignation at what? can be, are, and should be repeatedly raised and critically considered suggests that the sharp split between irrational feelings and rational discourse is another untenable opposition that has to be broken down. To drop the idea of pure rational motivation is not *ipso facto* to deny that motives can be elaborated, criticized, defended, and shaped by reasons, particularly when these are presented in the context of communicative exchanges with other agents moved by similar or different motives. Moreover, as Horkheimer himself is at pains to insist, psychic dispositions have to be viewed in relation to established social and cultural patterns. It is in this vein, for instance, that he explains the consciousness of a pure rational ought, the feeling of being bound by absolute commands, as a sublime form of internalized social compulsion. Thus, he cannot treat the psychic disposition he calls moral feeling as an independent variable prior to and unaffected by social relations. Why should we accord such special status to a feeling for the feelings of all other human beings or an interest in the generalizability of interests? Are they and the corresponding universalistic ideals any more than mere curiosities of particular historical cultures?

One source of these problems is Horkheimer's jump from the absence of pure rational-that is, non-empirical-motivations for morality to tire absence of any rational justification of its basic commands. A related source is the tendency he has to equate rational justification with ultimate grounding of some sort. As we cannot have the latter, we must do without the former as well. If, however, Horkheimer had introduced into his discussion of morality the non-foundationalist sense of rational justification he appealed to in his discussion of truth, this equation could not have been sustained.

Adopting a more pragmatic approach to moral justification would also have fit quite well with Horkheimer's historical account, in connection with his analysis of modern ideologies, of how the appeal to generally acceptable reasons comes to play an ever greater role in legitimating social orders. With the disappearance of value-imbued cosmologies, the privatization of religion, and the growing disenchantment of the world, it is increasingly the only form of justification available. As a result, it becomes more and more difficult to convince exploited and oppressed groups that they deserve their suffering and that their tormentors deserve whatever degrees of power, privilege, and wealth they happen to enjoy. The early modern ideologies that once accomplished this improbable task have been and continue to be relentlessly shredded with the sharp tools of criticism. This increasingly leaves contemporary societies with very little else to appeal to in legitimating their laws, institutions, and policies than the free and reasoned agreement of their members. But is this state of affairs anything more than an arbitrary outcome of contingent historical processes? What, in particular, does it have to do with practical reason?

Once we get beyond the Cartesian-Hobbesian paradigm of the solitary subject as the proper framework for analyzing the structures of thought and action, once we acknowledge their intrinsically social character, agreements freely arrived at on the basis of considering reasons pro and con come to be central to rationality in theory and in practice. This has been argued in respect to truth claims from Pierce to Putnam and Habermas and in respect to justice claims from Mead to Rawls and Habermas. Whatever problems there may be with specific proposals, it is becoming increasingly difficult to think of plausible alternatives to one form or another of communicative rationality. If some such approach to practical reason could be sustained, then the gap that Horkheimer saw between unreadable feelings of compassion and rational justification of universal ideals would not be as unbridgeable as it seemed. One could then argue both in a neo-Kantian vein that democratic forms of decision-making test accord with the communicative structure of practical reason and in a neo-Aristotelian or neo-Hegelian vein that the dispositions of character and motivation needed to sustain democratic institutions and practices can be reliably reproduced only in certain types of socio-cultural settings. It is just this sort of dual-track program that we must attempt to develop in our critical social theory.

Bibliography

Ackrill, J.L. (1975): *Aristotle the Philosopher*. Oxford, Oxford. University Press.

Adamson, Walter (1985): *Marx and the Disillusionment of Marxism*. Berkeley, University of California Press.

Adorno, Theodor W. (1973): *Negative Dialectics*. London, Routledge.

Allan, D.J. (1970): *The Philosophy of Aristotle*. Oxford, Oxford University Press.

Allen, J.W. (1967): *A History of Political Thought in the Sixteenth Centry*. London, Methuen.

Althusser, Louis. (1969) *For Marx*. London, Allen Lane.

Anderson P (1976): *Considerations on Western Marxism*. London, New Left.

— (1984): *In the Tracks of Historical Materialism*. London, Verso Books.

Andrews, A. (1967): *The Greek Society*. Harmondsworth, Penguins.

Anglo, Sydney (1969): *Machiavelli: A Dissection*. New York, Harcourt.

Annas, J. (1977): 'Mill and the Subjection of Women.' *Philosophy*, 52, pp. 174-194.

— (1981): *An Introduction to Plato's Republic*. Oxford, Oxford University Press.

Arblaster, A.(1984): *The Rise and Decline of Western Liberalism*. Oxford, Blackwell.

Aristotle (1962): *The Nicomachean Ethics*. W.D. Ross (Ed.), Oxford, Clarendon Press.

— (1979) ; *The Politics*. E. Barker (Trans.) Oxford, Oxford University Press.

Arnhart, Larry (1981): *Aristotle on Political Reasoning: A Commentary on the "Rhetoric."* Dekalb, Northern Illinois University Press.

Ashcraft, R. (1971): 'Hobbes' Natural Man', *Journal of Politics*, 33, pp.1077-1091.

—(1978) : 'Ideology and Class in Hobbes. Political Theory *Political Theory*, 6, pp. 27-62.

—(1986): *Revolutionary Politics and Locke's Two Treatises of Government*. London, Allen & Unwin.

—(1987):*Locke's Two Treatises of Government*. London, Unwin & Hyman.

—(Ed.) (1991): *John Locke: Critical Assessments*,. 4 vols. London, Routledge.

—(1968.) *The Social and Political thought of Karl Marx*. London, Cambridge University Press.

Avineri, S. (1972): *Hegel's Theory of the State*. Cambridge, Cambridge University Press.

Balbus, Isaac D. (1982): *Marxism and Domination*. Princeton, Princeton University Press.

Ball, T. (1984): 'The Picaresque Prince: Reflections on Machiavelli and Moral Change,' *Political Theory*, 12, pp 521-536.

Bambrough, R. (1965): *New Essays on Plato*. Oxford, Oxford University Press. (Ed.) (1967): *Plato, Popper and Politics*. London, Cambridge University Press.

Barker, Ernest. (1959): *The Political Thought of Plato and Aristotle*. New York, Dover Publications.

Barnes, J. (Ed.) (1992): *The Cambrdge Campanion to Aristotle*. Cambridge, Cambridge University Press.

Bathory, Peter Dennis. (1981): *The Political Theory as Public Confession: The Social* and *Political Thought of St. Augustine of Hippo*. New Brunswick, N.J. Transaction Books.

Baudrillard, Jean (1975): *The Mirror of Production.* St. Louis, Telos Press.

Baumgold, D.(1988) *Hobbes' Political Theory.* Cambrdge, Cambridge University Press.

Beiser, F. (Ed.) (1991): *The Cambridge Companion to Hegel.* Cambridge, Cambridge University Press.

Bellamy, R. (Ed.) (1990): *Victorian Liberalism: Nineteenth Century Political Thought and Practice.* Cambridge, Polity Press.

Berlin, I (1959): *John Stuart Mill and the Ends of Life.* London, Edgar G. Dunstan & Co.

—(1964): 'Hobbes, Locke and Professor Macpherson' *Political Quarterly,* October-December, pp. 444-468.

Bentham, J. (1962): *An Introduction to the Principles of Morals and Legislation.* New York, Russell & Russell.

— (1965): *Anarchical Fallacies.* Baltimore, John Hopkins University Press. (1977): *A Fragment of Government.* J.H. Burns and H.L.A. Hart (Eds.) London, Athlone Press.

Berki, R.N. (1977): *The History of Political Thought: A Short Introduction.* London, Dent.

Bloom, A. (1968): *The Republic of Plato.* New York, Basic Books.

Bluhm, T. (1978.) *Theories of the Political System: Classical of Political Thought and Modern Political Analysis.* Englewood Cliffs, N.J.: Prentice Hall.

Booth , William James. (1986): *Interpreting the World: Kant's Philosophy of History and Politics.* Toronto.

Bookckin, Murray (1986): *Post-Scarcity Anarchism.* Montreal, Black Rose Book.

Bottomore, T. (1973) *Karl Marx.* Oxford, Basil Blackwell.

—(1981): *Modern Interpretations of Marx.* Oxford, Oxford University Press.

—(1991): *A Dictionary of Marxist Thought.* Oxford, Blackwell.

Brinton, C, (1933): *English Political Thought in the Nineteenth Century.* London, Allen Lane.

Britton, Karl. (1969): *John Stuart Mill: Life and Philosophy.* New York, Dover Publications.

Broome, J.H. (1963): *Rousseau: A Study of His Thought.* Oxford, Oxford University Press.

Brown, K.C. (Ed.) (1965): *Hobbes' Studies.* Cambridge, Harvard University Press.

Brown, Peter (1967): *Augustine of Hippo: A Biography.* Berkeley, University of California Press.

Burke E. (1969): *Reflections on the Revolution in France.* C.C. O'Brien (Ed.), Harmondsworth, Penguins.

Burnham, J.(1943): *The Machiavellians.* New York, Double Day.

Butterfield, H. (1962): *The Statecraft of Machiavelli.* New York, Collier.

Canavan, F.P. (1960): *The Political Reason of Edmund Burke.* Durham, Duke University Press.

Carnoy, M. (1984): *State and Political Theory.* Princeton, Princeton University Press.

Charvet, J. (1974): *The Social Problem in the Philosophy of Rousseau.* London, Dent.

Cassirer, Ernst. (1963): *The Question of Jean-Jacques Rousseau.* Bloomington, Indiana University Press.

Caver, T. (1983): *Marx and Engels: The Intellectual Relationship.* Brighton, Harvester.

—(Ed.) (1990): *The Cambridge Companion to Marx.* Cambridge, Cambridge University Press.

Chabod, F. (1958): *Machiavelli and the Renaissance.* New York, Harper & Row.

Chapell, V. (Ed.) (1994): *The Cambridge Companion to Locke.* Cambridge, Cambridge University Press.

Chapman, J.W. (1956): *Rousseau- Totalitarian or Liberal?* New York, Columbia University Press.

Cleaver, Harry (1979): *Readubg Capital Politically*. Austin, University of Texas Press.

Cobban, A. (1960): *Edmund Burke and the Revolt against the Eighteenth Century*. London, Allen & Unwin.

—(1964): *Rousseau and the Modern State*. London, Unwin.

Cohen, G.A.1978: *Karl Marx's Theory of History: A Defense*. Princeton, Princeton University Press.

Colletti, L, (1969): *From Rousseau to Lenin*. New Delhi, Oxford University Press.

Compleston, Frederick. (1955): *Thomas Aquinas*. London, Search Press.

Condren, Conal (1985): *The Status and Appraisal of Classic Text*. Princeton, Princeton University Press.

Cone, Carl. B.(1964): *Bruke and the Nature of Politics*. Kentucky, Kentucky University Press.

Conniff, J. (1977): 'Burke, Bristol and the Concept of Representation. *Western Political Quarterly*, 30, pp. 329-341.

Connolly, William E.(1993): *The Augustinian Imperative: A Reflection on the Politics of Morality*. Newbury Park, Calif. Sage Publications.

Cook, I.(1998): *Reading Mill: Studies in Political Theory*. London, Macmillan.

Cornforth, M. (1968): *The Open Philosophy and the Open Society*. London, Lawrence and Wishart.

Cowling, Maurice.(1963): *Mill and Liberalism*. London, Cambridge University Press.

Cranston, Maurice.(1957): *John Locke: A Biography*. New York, Macmillan.

Crespigny, A. de and Minogue, K. (ed) (1975): *Cotemporary Political Thinkers*. London, Methuen.

Croce, B. (1969): *What is Living and What is Dead in the Philosophy of Hegel*? New York, Russell & Russell.

Crossman. R. (1939): *Plato Today*. London, Allen & Unwin.

Davidson, W.L. (1957): *Political Thought in England: The Utilitarians from Bentham to Mill*. Oxford, Oxford University Press.

de Garzia Sebastian. (1989): *Machiavelli in Hell*. Princeton, Princeton University Press.

Deane, Herbert A. (1963.) *The Political and Social Ideas of St. Augustine*. New York, Columbia University Press.

Derrida, Jacques. (1994): *Specters of Marx*. New York, Routtedge.

Draper, H. (1977): *Karl Marx's Theory of Revolution: State and Bureaucracy*. New York, Monthly Review Press.

Dunn, J. (1968a): *The Political Thought of John Locke*. Cambridge, Cambridge, University Press.

— (1979): *Western Political Theory in the Face of the Future*. Cambridge, Cambridge University Press.

—(1984): *Locke*. Oxford, Oxford University Press.

Durant, W (1953): *The Story of Philosophy*. New York, Pocket Books.

Ebenstein, W. (1969): *Great Political Thinkers*. New Delhi, Oxford University Press.

Elshtain, Jean Bethke. (1981.) *Public Man, Private Woman*. Princeton, Princeton University Press.

Elster, Jon. (1985): *Making Sense of Marx*. New York, Cambridge University Press.

Evans, J. (1986): *Feminism and Political Theory*. New York, Alfred A. Knopf.

Findlay, J.N. (1958): *Hegel: A Re-examination*. London, Allen & Unwin.

Finley, M. I. (1963): *The Ancient Greeks*. Harmondsworth, Penguins.

Finnis, John (1998): *Aquinas*. Oxford, Oxford University Press.

Fleischer, Helmut (1973): *Marxism and History*. London, Allen Lane.

Foster, M.B.(1975): *Masters of Political Thought: Plato to Machiavelli.* Calcutta, Oxford University Press.

Foucault, Michel (1980): *Power/ Knowledge*. New York, Pantheon.

—(1984): "What is Enlightenment?" In Paul Rabinow (ed.), T*he Foucault Reader*, pp. 32-50. New York, Pantheon.

Foucault, Michel (1991): *Remarks on Marx*. New York, Semiotext (e).

Freeman, M. (1980): *Edmund Burke and the Critique of Political Radicalism.* Oxford, Blackwell.

Fromm, Erich (1955): *The Sane Society*. New York, Henry Holt.

Fukuyama, Francis (1992): *The End of History and the Last Man*. New York, The Free Press.

Gadamer, H. (1986): *The Idea of Good in Platonic-Aristotelian Philosophy*. New Haven, Yale University Press.

Gallie, W. B. (1979): 'Kant's View of Reason in Politics, *Philosophy,* LIV.

Gatens, M. (1991): *Feminism and Philosophy: Perspectives on Difference and Equality.* Cambridge, Polity Press.

Gauthier, D.P. (1969): *The Logic of Leviathan*. Oxford, Clarendon Press.

Gay, P. (1952): *The Dilemma of Democratic Socialism. Eduard Bernstein's Challenge to Marx.* New York, Columbia University Press.

— (1970): *The Enlightenment: An Interpretation*, 2 vols. London, Wildwood House.

Germino, Dante. (1972): *Modern Western Political Thought: Machiavelli to Marx.* Chicago, Rand McNally.

Giddens, A. (1995): *A Contemporary Critique of Historical Materialism*. London, Macmillan.

Gilbert, Alan (1981): *Marx's Politics: Communists and Citizens*. New Brunswick, Rutgers University Press.

Gilbert, Felix.(1965): *Machiavelli and Guicciardini: Political and History in Sixteenth Century Florence*. Princeton, Princeton University Press.

Gilby, Thomas, (1958): *The Political Thought of Thomas Aquinas*. Chicago, University of Chicago Press.

Gilson, Etienne, (1960): *The Christian Philosophy of Saint Augustine*. New York, Random House.

Goldsmith, M.M. (1966): *Hobbes' Science of Politics*. New York, Columbia University Press.

Gough, J. W. (1950): *John Locke's Political Philosophy.* Oxford, Blackwell.

Gouldner, A.W.(1980): *The Two Marxisms: Contradictions and Anomalies in the Development of Theory.* New York, Oxford University Press.

Gouldner, Alvin W. (1965): *Enter Plato: Classical Greece and the Origins of Social Theory*. New York: Basic Books.

Grabmann, Martin, (1963): *Thomas Aquinas: His Personality and Thought*. New York, Russell and Russell.

Gramsci, A.(1971): *Prison Notebooks*. London, Lawence & Wishart.

Grant, Ruth W. (1987) *John Locke's Liberalism*. Chicago, University of Chicago Press.

Gray, J. (1983a): *Mill on Feminism*. London, Routledge.

—(1983b): *Mill on Liberty: A Defense*. London, Routledge.

—(1989): *Liberalism: Essaya in Political Philosophy*. London, Routledge.

Grene, Marjorie. (1963): *A Portrait of Aristotle*. Chicago, University of Chicago Press.

Green, T. H. (1924): *Lectures on the Principles of Political Obligation*. London, Longmons.

Grimsley, R. (1973): *The Philosophy of Rousseau*. Oxford, Oxford University Press.

Guyer, Paul (Ed) (1994): *The Cambridge Companion to Kant*. Cambridge, Camcridge University Press.

Habermas, Jurgen (1971): *Knowledge and Human Interests*. Boston, Beacon Press.

— (1973): *Theory and Practice*. Boston, Beacon Press.

— (1975): *Legitimation Crisis*. Boston, Beacon Press.

— (1984): *Theory of Communicative Action*, Vol. 1. Boston, Beacon Press.

—(1987): *Lectures on The Philosophical Discourse of Modernity*. Cambridge, MIT Press.

Hacker, A (1961): *Political Theory: Philosophy, Ideology, Science*. New York, Macmillan.

Haffman, S (1977): *Marx and Theory of Praxis*. London, Oxford University Press.

Hale, J.R. (1960): *Machiavelli and Renaissance Italy*. New York, Macmillan.

Halevy, E (1928): *Growth of Phisosophical Radcalism*. M. Morris (Trans.). London, Faber & Faber.

Hall, J.C. (1973): *Rousseau: An Introduction to His Political Philosophy*. Cambridge, Harvard University Press.

Hallowell, J.H. (1960): *Main Currents in Modern Political Thought*. New York, Holt.

Hamburger, Joseph. (1965) *Intellectuals in Politics: John Stuart Mill and the Philosophic Radicals*. New Haven, Yale University Press.

Hampsher-Monk, I.W. (1987): *The Political Philosophy of Edmund Burke*. London, (1992): *Modern Political Thought from Hobbes to Marx*. Oxford, Basil Blackwell.

Hampton, J. (1986): *Hobbes and the Social Contract Tradition*. Cambridge, Cambridge University Press.

Harrison, R. (1983): *Bentham*. London, Routledge.

Hart, H.L.A. (1982): *Essays on Bentham, Jurisprudenve and Political Theory*. Oxford, Oxford University Press.

Hearnshaw, F.J.C. (Ed.) (1931): *The Social and Political Ideas of Some Representtive Thinkers of the Revoutionary Era*. London, George Harrap.

Hegel, G.W.F.(1969): *Philosophy of Right*, T.M. Knox (Trans.) Oxford, Oxford University Press.

Heilbroner, R. (1980): *Marxism: For and Against*. New York, Oxford University Press.

Heller, Agnes (1982): "Habermas and Marxism." In Thompson and Held (1982) (Ed) *Habermas: Critical Dcbates*. Cambridge, MIT Press pp. 21-41.

Himmelfarb, Gertrfarb. (1974): *On Liberty and Libcralism: The Case of John Stuart Mill*. New York, Knopf.

Hindess, Barry, and Hirst, Paul (1977): *Modes of Production and Social Formation*. London, Macmillan.

Hirst, Paul (1985): *Marxism and Historical Writing*. London, Routledge.

Hobbes, T. (1991): *Leviathan*. R. Tuck (Ed.), Cambridge, Cambridge University Press.

Honneth, Axel (1991): *The Critique of Power: Reflective Stages in a Critical Social Theory*. Cambridge, MIT Press.

Hook, S (1962): *From Hegel to Marx: Studies in the Intellectual Development of Karl Marx*. New York, University of Michigan Press.

Howard, Dick (1980-81): 'Kant's Political Theory'. *Review of Metaphysis*, XXXIV.

Hulling, M. (1983): *Citizen Machiavelli*. Princeton, NJ, Princeton University Press.

Hunt, C. (1957): *The Theory and Practice of Communism*. London, Geoffrey Bees.

Hunt, R.N. (1975): *The Political Ideas of Marx and Engels*. London, Macmillan.

Jameson, Fredric (1991): *Postmodernism, or the Cultural Logic of Late-Capitalism*. Durham, Duke University Press.

Johnston, David (1986): *The Rhetoric of Levathan: Thomas Hobbes and the Politics of Cultural Transformation.* Princeton, Princeton University Press.

Johnson, Oliver. (1977): 'Autonomy in Kant and Rawls'. *Ethics*, LXXXVII.

Jowett, B. (1905): *Aristotle's Politics*. Oxford, Clarendon Press.

—(1953): *The Republic of Plato*. Oxford, Oxford University Press.

Kant, E. (1965): *The Metaphysical Elements of Rights*. New York.

Kaufman, W. (1965): *Hegel's Political Philosophy*. New York, Atherton.

Kellner, Douglas (1983): "Science and Method in Marx's Capital." *Radical Science Journal*, # 139, 54.

— (1984): *Herbert Marcuse and the Crisis of Marxism*. Berkeley, University of California Press.

Kelly, George Armsling (1968): 'Rousseau, Kant and History'. *Journal of History of Ideas*, XXIX.

Kendall, Willmore (1941): *John Locke and the Doctrine of Majority-Rule*. Urbana, University of Illinois Press.

Kennedy, E. and Mendus, S. (1987): *Women in Western Political Philosophy.* Brighton, Harvester.

Kirk, R. (1960): *The Conservative Mind: From Burke to Eliot.* New York, Garden City.

Kitto, H.D.F. (1951): *The Greeks*. Harmindsworth, Penguins.

Klosko, George. (1986): *The Development of Plato's Political Theory*. New York, Methuen.

—1995 *History of Political Theory: An Introduction. 2 Vols*. New York Holt, Rinehart and Winston.

Kolakowski, L. (1981): *Main Currents of Marxism*, 3 vols. Oxford, Oxford University Press.

Krammick, I (1977): *The Rage of Edmund Burke: Portrait of an Ambivalent Conservative.* New York, Basic Books.

Kraut, R. (Ed.) (1993): *The Cambridge Companion to Plato*. Cambridge, Cambridge University Press.

Kymlicka, W. (1990): *Contemporary Political Philosophy: An Introduction.* Oxford, Clarendon Press.

Laclau, Ernesto, and Mouffe, Chantal (1985): *Hegemony and Socialist Strategy: Toward a Radical Democratic Politics*. London, Verso.

Lamprecht, S.P. (1918): *The Moral and Political Phislosophy of John Locke.* New York, Columbia University Press.

Larrain, Jorge (1986): *A Reconstruction of Historical Materialism*. London, Allen and Unwin.

Laski, H.J. (1920): *Political Thought from Locke to Bentham*. Oxford, Oxford University Press.

—(1936): *Rise of European Liberalism*. London, Unwin Books.

Laslett, Peter. 1963 "Introduction." In John Locke, *Two Treatises of Government*. New York: Cambridge University Press.

Leff, Gordon (1969): *Histoty and Social Theory*. New York, Anchor.

Lerner, M. (1950): *Niccolo Machiavelli's The Prince and the Discourses: An Introduction.* New York, Random House.

Lessnoff, M. (1986): *Social Contract*. London, Macmillan.

Levinson, Ronald B. (1953): *In Defense of Plato*. Cambridge Mass, Harvard University Press.

Lichtheim, George (1964): *Maxism: Historical and Critical Study*. New York, Praeger.

—(1971): *From Marx to Hegel and Other Essays*. London, Orbach & Chambers.

Little, Daniel (1986): *The Scientific Marx*. Minneapolis, University of Minnesota Press.

Locke, J. (1960): *Two Treatises of Civil Government*, P. Laslett (Ed.). Cambridge, Cambridge University Press.

Lord, Carnes (1982) *Education and Culture in the Political Thought of Aristotle*. Ithaca, Cornell University Press.

Lukacs, Georg (1971): *History and Class Consciousness*. Cambridge, MIT Press.

Lyotard, Jean-Francois (1984): *The Postmodern Condition*. Minneapolis, University of Minnesota Press.

Machiavelli. N. (1950): *The Prince and the Discourse*. M. Lerner(Ed.) New York, Random House.

MacIntyre, Alasdair. 1988. *Whose Justice? Which Rationality*? Notre Dame, University of Notre Dame Press.

—(1972): *Hegel: A Collection of Essays*. New York, Anchor.

Mack, MP (1962): *Jeremy Bentham: An Odyssey of Ideas*. New York, Columbia University Press.

Mackie, J.L. (1994): *Problems from Locke*. Oxford. Oxford University Press.

McMurtry, John (1978): *The Structure of Marx's World-View*. Princeton, Princeton University Press.

Macpherson, C.B.

—(1964) *The Political Theory of Possessive Individualism: Hobbes to Locke*. Oxford, Oxford University Press.

—(1980): *Burke*. Oxford, Oxfoed University Press.

—(1973): *Democratic Theory*. Oxford, Oxford University Press.

—(1977): *The Life and Times of Liberal Democracy*. Oxford, Oxford University Press.

Mansfeld, H.C.(1979): *Machiavelli's New Modes and Orders*. Ithaca, Cornell University Press.

— (1989): *Taming the Prince: The Ambivalence of Modern Executive Power*. New York, Free Press.

Marcuse, H. (1954): *Reason and Revolution: Hegel and the Rise of Social Theory*. London, Routledge & Kegan Paul.

Marshall, J. (1994): *Locke: Resistance, Revolution and Responsibility*. Cambridge, Cambridge University Press.

Marx, K. (1975): *The Communist Manifesto*. Moscow, Progress Publishers.

—(1977a): *Selected Works*, I. Moscow, Progress Publishers.

—(1977b): *Selected Works, II*. Moscow, Progress Publishers.

—(1977): *Selected Works, III*. Moscow, Progress Publishers.

Masters, R.D. (1968): *Political Philosophy of Rousseau*. Princeton, Princeton University Press.

Maxey, C.C. (1948): *Political Philosophies*. New York, Macmillan.

Mazlish, Bruce. (1975): *James and John Stuart Mill: Father and Son in the Nineteenth Century*, New York, Basic Books.

McCloskey, H.J.(1971): *John Stuart Mill: A Critical Study*. London, Macmillan.

McIntosh, D. (1984): 'The Modernity of Machiavelli'. *Political Theory*, 12, PP. 184-203.

McLellan, D. (1969): *The Young Hegelians and Karl Marx*. London, Macmillan.

McNeilly, N. (1968): *The Anatomy of Leviathan*. London, Macmillan.

Megill, Allan (1985): *Prophets of Extremity*. Berkeley, University of California Press.

Mehta, Uday Singh, (1992) *The Anxiety of Freedom: Imagination and Individduality in Looke's Political Thought*. Ithaca, Cornell University Press.

Meinecke, F. (1957): *Machiavellianism: The Doctrine of Raison d'Etat and its Place in History*. D. Scott (Trans.) London, Routledge & Kegan Paul.

Melzer, Arthur M. (1990): *The Natural Goodness of Man: On the System of Rousscau's Thought*. Chicago, University of Chicago Press.

Meszaros, Istvan, (1970): *Marx's Theory of Alienation*. New York, Harper and Row.

Miller, James (1984) *Rousseau: Dreamer of Democracy*. New Haven, Yale University Press.

Miller, Richard W. (1984): *Anlyzing Marx*. Princetion, Princeton University Press.

Miliband, R. (1977): *Marxism and Politics*. Oxford, Oxford University Press.

Mill, J.S. (1924): *Autobiography*. New York, Random house.

—(1950): *Bentham and Coleridge*. London , Fontana.

—(1976): *Utiltarianism: On Liberty and Considerations on Representative Government*. London, Fontana.

—(1985): *The Subjection of Women*. M. Warnock (Ed.), London, Dent.

Minogue, K.R. (1973): *Hobbes' Leviathan*. New York, Everyman's Library.

Morrall, J.B. (1979): *Aristotle*. London, Hutchinson.

Mulgan, R.G. (1977): *Aristotle's Political Theory*. Oxford, Clarendon Press.

O Gorman, F. (1973): *Edmund Burke: His Political Philosophy*. London, Allen & Unwin.

Oakeshott, Michael. (1975.) *Hobbes On Civil Association*. Oxford, Basil Blackwell.

O'Brien, C.C. (Ed.) (1968): *Burke's Reflections on the Revolution in France*. Harmondsworth, Penguins.

Okin, Susan Moller. (1979): *Women in Western Political Thought*. Princeton, Princeton University Press.

Ollman, Bertell (1976): *Alienation*. Cambridge, Cambridge University Press.

Olschki, L. (1976): *Machiavelli the Scientist*. Berkeley, University of California Press.

Osborn, A.M. (1940): *Rousseau and Burke*. New York, Simon & Schuster.

Packe, Michael (1954): *The Life of John Stuart Mill*. New York, Macmillan.

Parekh, B. (Ed.) (1974): *Jeremy Bentham: Ten Critical Essays*. London, Croom Helm.

—(1982): *Contemporary Political Thinkers*. Oxford,Oxford University Press.

Parkin, C.W. (1969): 'Burke and the Conservative Tradition', in *Political Ideas*. D. Thomson (Ed.), Harmondsworth, Penguins.

Parry, G. (1978): *John Locke*. London, Allen & Unwin.

Pateman, C. (1988): *The Sexual Contract*. Oxford, Polity.

Pelczynski, Z.A. (Ed.) (1984): *State and Civil Society: Studies in Hegel's Political Philosophy*. London, Athlone Press.

Pitkin, Hanna Fenichel (1984): *Fortune Is a Woman: Gender and Politics in the Thought of Niccolo Nachiavelli*. Berkeley, University of California Press.

Plamentaz, J. (1963): *Man and Society, 2 vols*. London, Longman.

—(1966): *The English Utilitarians*. Oxford, Basil Blackwell.

—(1969): *German Marxism and Russian Communism*. London, Longman.

Plant, R. (1983): *Hegel*. Oxford, Basil Blackwell.

—(1991): *Modern Political Thought*. Oxford, Basil Blackwell.

Plato (1955): *The Republic*. Harmndsworth, Penguins.

Pocock, J.G.A. (1975): *The Maciavellian Moment: Florentine Political Thought and the Atlantic Republican Tradition*. Princeton, Princeton University Press.

Polin, R. (1953): *Political Philosophy of Thomas Hobbes*. Paris,

Popper, K.R. (1945): *The Open Society and its Enemies, 2 vols.* London, Routledge & Kegan Paul.

Poulanzas, N. (1973): *Political Power and Social Classes*. London, New Left.

Raab, F. (1964): *The English Face of Machiavelli: A Changing Interpretation*-1500-1700. London, Routledge.

Rader, Melvin (1979): *Marx's Interpretation of History*. New York,Oxford University Press.

Radhakrishnan, S. (1974): *Eastern Religions and Western Thought*. New Delhi, Oxford University Press.

Rayan, Michael (1982): *Marxism and Deconstruction*. Baltimore, Johns Hopkins University Press.

Ray, B.N. (2006): Political Theory, New Delhi, Authors Press.

Rawls, J. (1971): *A Theory of Justice.* Oxford, Oxford University Press.

Rees, J. (1956): *Mill and his Early Critics*. London, University of Leicester Press.

Rees, John C. (1985): *Jon Stuart Mill's On Liberty.* New York, Oxford University Press.

Reis, Hans. (1991): *Kant-Political Writings*. Cambridge, Cambridge University Press.

Riley, P. (1986): *The General Will Before Rousseau: The Transformation of the Divine into the Civic*. Princeton , Princeton University Press.

Ring, J. (1985): *Mill's Feminism.* New York, Harvester Wheatsheaf.

Robson, John M. (1968): *The Improvemeint of Mankind: The Scoal and Politica Thought of John Stuart Mill*. London, Routledge.

Rockmore, Tom (1989): *Habermas on Historical Materialism*. Bloomington, Indiana University Press.

Rogow, Arnold A. (1986): *Thomas Hobbes: Radical in the Sevrivec of Reaction.* New York, Norton.

Rorty, Richard (1989): *Contingency, Irony, and Solidarity*. Cambridge, Cambridge University Press.

Rosdolsky, R. (1977): *The Making of Marx's Capital.* London, Pluto.

Rosen, F. (1983): *Jeremy Bentham and Representative Democracy*. Oxford, Oxford University Press.

Rosenblum, N.L.(1978): *Bentham's Theory of the State*. Cambridge, Harvard University Press.

Rousseau J. (1958): *Social Contract and Discourses*. G. D.H. Cole (Trans). London, Dent.

Rowe, M.W. (2007): "Wittgenstein, Plato and the Historical Socrates" *Philosophy*, 82, pp. 45-85.

Russell, B. (1961): *History of Western Philosophy*. London, Allen & Unwin.

Ryan, A. (1965): 'Locke and the Dictatorship of the Bourgeoisie.,' *Political Studies,* 13, PP. 219-230.

— (1970): *The Philosophy of John Stuart Mill.* London, Macmillan.

—(1984): *Property and Political Theory*. Oxford, Blackwell.

Salkever, Stephen G. (1990): *Finding the Mean: Theory and Practice in Aristotelian Political Philosophy*. Princeton, Princeton University Press.

Schaff, Adam (1970): *Marxism and the Human Individual.* New York: McGraw-Hill.

Shaw, William H. (1978): *Marx's Theory of History.* Stanford, Stanford University Press.

Scruton, Roger (1982): *Kant*. Oxford, Oxford University Press.

Seidler, Victor J. (1986): *Kant: Respect and Injustice—The Limits of Liberal Moral Theary.* London, Routtedge.

Seligar, M. (1968): *The Liberal Politics of John of Locke.* London, Allen & Unwin.

Semple, J. (1992): *Bentham's Prison: A Study of the Panoptical Penitentiary.* Oxford, Clarendon Press.

Shklar, Judith N. (1969): *Men and Citizens: A Study of Rousseau's Social Theory.* London, Cambridge University Press.

Shumer, S.M. (1979): "Machiavelli: Republican Politics and its Corruption," *Political Theory*, 7, pp. 5-34.

Sibley, M.Q. (1981): *Political Ideas and Ideologies.* New Delhi, Surjeet Publications.

Singer, (1980): *Marx.* Oxford, Oxford University Press.

—(1983), *Hegel.* Oxford, Oxford University Press.

Skinner, Q. (1981): *Machiavelli.* Oxford, Oxford University Press.

—(1990): *The Fundations of Modern Political Thought, 2 vols.* Cambridge, Cambridge University Press.

— (1998): *Liberty Before Liberalism.* Cambridge, Cambridge University Press.

Skorupski, J. (1998): *The Cambridge Companion to Mill.* Cambridge, Cambridge University Press.

Smith, S.B. (1989): *Hegel's Critique of Liberalism.* Chicago, University of Chicago Press.

Sorell, T. (1986): *Hobbes.* London Routledge.

Spragens, Thomas A., Jr. (1973): *The Politics of Motion.* Lexington, University of Kentucky Press.

Starobinski, J. (1988): *Jean-Jacques Rousseau: Transparency and Obstruction.* Paris, Plon.

Stephen, L. (1961): *Hobbes.* Ann Arbor, University of Michigan Press.

Strauss, Leo (1952): *The Political Philosophy of Hobbes: Its Basis and Its Genesis.* Chicago, University of Chicago Press.

—(1958): *Thoughts on Machiavelli.* Glencoe Ill., Free Press.

Swanson, Judith A. (1992): *The Public and the Private in Aristotle's Political Philosophy.* Ithaca, Cornell University Press.

Talmon, Jacob L. (1952): *The Rise of Totalitarian Democracy.* Boston, Beacon Press.

Taylor, C. (1979): *Hegel and Modern Society.* Cambridge, Cambridge University Press.

Ten, C.L. (1980): *Mill on Liberty.* Oxford, Clarendon Press.

Thomas, W. (1985): *Mill.* Oxford, Oxford University Press.

Thompson, Dennis, F. (1976): *John Stuart Mill and Representative Government.* Princeton, Princeton University Press.

Thorson, T.L. (1963): *Plato: Totalitarian or Democrat?* New Jersey, Prentice Hall.

Tocqueville, A. de. (1968): *Democracy in America, 2 vols.*, London, Fontana.

Tuck, R. (1989): *Hobbes.* Oxford, Oxford University Press.

Tucker, Robert. (1972): *Philosophy and Myth in Karl Marx.* Cambridge, Cambridge University Press.

Tulloch, G (1989): *Mill and Sexual Equality.* London, Blackwell.

Tully, J. (1980): *A Discourse on Property: John Locke and His Adversaries.* Cambridge, Cambridge University press.

—(1993): *An Approach to Political Philosophy: Locke in Contexts.* Cambridge, Cambridge University Press.

Viroli, M. (1998): *Machiavelli.* Oxford, Oxford University Press.

Vlastos, G (Ed.) (1971): *Plato: A Collection of Critical Essays.* Noter Dame.

Volpe, G. Della (1978): *Rousseau and Marx*. London, Lawrence and Wishart.

Von Leyden, W. (1982): *Hobbes and Locke: The Politics of Freedom and Obligation*. London, Macmillan.

Warrender, Howard (1957): *The Political Philosophy of Hobbes: His Theory of Obligation*. Oxford, Oxford University Press.

Watkin, J.W.N. (1973): *Hobbes' Stystem of Ideas*. London, Hutchinson.

Wellmer, Albreacht (1971): *Critical Theory of Society*. New York, Continuum.

White, Hayden (1973): *Metahistory: The Historical Imagination in Nineteenth-Centruy Europe*. Baltimore, Johns Hopkins University Press.

White, S.K. (1994): *Edmund Burke: Modernity, Politics and Aesthetics*. Thousand Oaks, Sage.

Whitefield, J.M. (1947): *Machiavelli*. Oxford, Oxford University Press.

Wilkins, B.T. (1967): *The Problem of Burke's Political Philosophy*. Oxfoed. Blackwell.

Willford, M. (1975): "Bentham on the Rights of Woman," *Journal of the History of Ideas*, pp.167-176.

Wolfe, B. (1996): *Marxism: One Hundred Years in the Life of a Doctrine*. New York, Avon.

Wolin, Sheldon S. (1960): *Politics and Vision: Continuity and Innovation in Western Political Thought*. Little Brown.

Wood, Ellen Mieksins, and Neal Wood (1978): *Class Ideology and Ancient Political Theory: Socrates, Plato, and Aristotle in Social Context*. Oxford, Blackwell.

Wood, N. (1984): *John Locke and Agrarian Capitalism*. Berkeley, University of California Press.

Yack, Bernard (1993): *The Problems of a Political Animal: Community, Justice, and Conflict in Aristotelian Political Thought*. Berkeley, University of California Press.

Yolton, J. (1956): *John Locke and the Way of Ideas*. Oxford, Clarendon Press.

—(Ed.) (1977): *The Locke Reader*. Cambridge, Cambridge University Press.

Zeller, E. (1955): *Outlines of the History of Greek Philosophy*. New York, Meridian.

Index

□□□